BARNES & NOBLE

German Dictionary

English-Deutsch
German-Englisch

Stephen Jones

BARNES
&NOBLE
B O O K S
NEW YORK

Copyright © 1982 by Laurence Urdang Associates
Glossary of menu terms and special American usage entries
copyright © 1983 by Hippocrene Books
All rights reserved.

This edition published by Marboro Books Corp.,
a division of Barnes & Noble, Inc.,
by arrangement with Hippocrene books.

1992 Barnes & Noble Books

ISBN 0-88029-936-3

Printed and bound in the United States of America

M 9 8 7 6 5 4 3 2 1

Abbreviations/Abkürzungen

acc accusative, Akkusativ
adj adjective, Adjektiv
adv adverb, Adverb
anat anatomy, Anatomie
arch architecture, Architektur
art article, Artikel
astrol astrology, Astrologie
astron astronomy, Astronomie
biol biology, Biologie
bot botany, Botanik
chem chemistry, Chemie
coll colloquial,
    umgangssprachlich
comm commerce, Kommerz
dat dative, Dativ
derog derogatory, geringschätzig
elec electricity, Elektrizität
f feminine, Femininum
fig figurative, figürlich
gen genitive, Genetiv
geog geography, Erdkunde
gramm grammar, Grammatik
impol impolite, unhöflich
interj interjection, Ausruf
Jur Jura, Rechtswesen, law
Komm Kommerz, commerce
m masculine, Maskulinum
math mathematics, Mathematik
mech mechanics, machine,
    Mechanik
med medicine, Medizin

mil military, militärisch
mot motoring, Kraftfahrzeuge
n noun, Hauptwort, Substantiv
naut nautical, Schiffahrt
neut neuter, Neutrum
phone telephone, Telefon
phot photography, Photographie
pl plural, Plural
pol politics, Politik
poss possessive, possessiv
prep preposition, Präposition
pron pronoun, Pronomen,
    Fürwort
psychol psychology, Psychologie
rail railways, Eisenbahn
rel religion, Religion
Schiff Schiffahrt, nautical
sing singular, Singular, Einzahl
tech technical, Technik
Telef Telefon, telephone
TV television, Fernsehen
umg. umgangssprachlich,
    colloquial
univ university, Universität
unz. unzählbar, mass noun
US American, Amerikanisch
v verb, Verbum, Zeitwort
V vide (see, siehe)
Wissensch Naturwissenschaft,
    science
zool zoology, Zoologie

German pronunciation

a bald [balt]
a: sagen ['za:gən]
e Telefon [tele'fo:n]
e: nehmen ['ne:mən]
ɛ Geld [gɛlt]
ɛ: Bär [bɛ:r]
i Idee [i'de:]
i: bieten ['bi:tən]
ɔ Holz [hɔlts]
o Rosette [ro'zetə]
o: Mohn [mo:n]
u bunt [bunt]
u: Schnur [ʃnu:r]
y fünf [fynf]
y: kühl [ky:l]
ə Butter ['butər]
œ böse ['bœzə]
œ: Möbel ['mœbəl]
ai bei [bai]
au Haus [haus]
ɔy Freund [frɔynt]
ã Chance ['ʃã:sə]
ɛ̃ Terrain [tɛ'rɛ̃:]
õ Champignon ['ʃampinjõ]

b Bad [ba:t]
d Dank [daŋk]
f Frau [frau]
g gut [gu:t]
h halb [halp]
j ja [ja:]
k Kind [kint]
l Lied [li:t]
m Mensch [mɛnʃ]
n neu [nɔy]
p Person [pɛr'zo:n]
r Rad [ra:t]
s falls [fals]
t Gerät [gə're:t]
v Wein [vain]
z Reise ['raizə]
ç ich [iç]
x Buch [bu:x]
ʃ Schuh [ʃu:]
ʒ Garage [ga'ra:ʒə]
ŋ lang [laŋ]

The sign ' precedes a syllable having primary stress.

Aussprache auf Englisch

a hat [hat]
e bell [bel]
i big [big]
o dot [dot]
ʌ bun [bʌn]
u book [buk]
ə alone [ə'loun]
a: card [ka:d]
ə: word [wə:d]
i: team [ti:m]
o: torn [to:n]
u: spoon [spu:n]
ai die [dai]
ei ray [rei]
oi toy [toi]
au how [hau]
ou road [roud]
eə lair [leə]
iə fear [fiə]
uə poor [puə]

b back [bak]
d dull [dʌl]
f find [faind]
g gaze [geiz]
h hop [hop]
j yell [jel]
k cat [kat]
l life [laif]
m mouse [maus]
n night [nait]
p pick [pik]
r rose [rouz]
s sit [sit]
t toe [tou]
v vest [vest]
w week [wi:k]
z zoo [zu:]
θ think [θiŋk]
ð those [ðouz]
ʃ shoe [ʃu:]
ʒ treasure ['treʒə]
tʃ chalk [tʃo:k]
dʒ jump [dʒʌmp]
ŋ sing [siŋ]

Das Zeichen ' steht vor einer Silbe mit Hauptbetonung.
Das Zeichen , steht vor einer Silbe mit Nebenbetonung.

Guide to the dictionary

English irregular plural forms are shown at the headword and in the text. The following categories of plurals forms are considered regular:

cat	cats
glass	glasses
fly	flies
half	halves
wife	wives

German plurals are shown for most words (for example, **Gemälde**) but not for many compounds (for example, **Wandgemälde**). The label *pl -* indicates that the plural does not vary.

Where no gender is shown for a German noun, it may be masculine or feminine, for example **Abgeordnete(r)**. Adjectival nouns are shown by -(r) or -(s), the final letter being used according to the article, for example: **der Abgeordnete, ein Abgeordneter, die Abgeordnete, eine Abgeordnete, Abgeordnete** (*pl*).

Under a German headword, a sub-entry may be shown preceded by a dash. The full form may be obtained by adding the sub-entry to the nearest preceding full word, less that part after the vertical strokes, if any. Thus, **außerhalb** is shown as follows:

> **außer‖dem** *adv* besides. **-halb** *adv, prep* outside.

Irregular verbs listed in the verb tables are marked with an asterisk in the body of the dictionary.

Many English adverbs are not shown in the dictionary if they are regularly formed, that is, by the addition of -(*al*)*ly* to the adjective.

Leitfaden für das Wörterbuch

Englische unregelmäßige Plurale sind bei dem Stichwort und im Text gezeigt. Die folgenden Kategorien von Pluralformen sind als regelmäßig anzusehen:

cat	cats
glass	glasses
fly	flies
half	halves
wife	wives

Deutsche Plurale sind für die meisten Wörter angeführt (z.B. **Gemälde**), aber nicht für viele zusammengesetzte Wörter (z.B. **Wandgemälde**). Das Zeichen *pl* - deutet an, daß der Plural mit dem Singular identisch ist.

Wo kein Geschlecht für ein deutsches Hauptwort angegeben ist, kann es sowohl männlich als auch weiblich sein, z.B. **Abgeordnete(r)**. Hauptworte, die aus Adjektiven gebildet sind, sind folgendermaßen gekennzeichnet -(r) oder -(s), wobei der letzte Buchstabe von dem Artikel abhängt, z.B. **der Abgeordnete, ein Abgeordneter, die Abgeordnete, eine Abgeordnete, Abgeordnete** (*pl*).

Hinter einem deutschen Stichwort, findet man öfter eine weitere Eintragung hinter einem Strich. Das komplette Wort erhält man durch Hinzufügen dieses Wortes an das vorherige Wort ohne den Teil hinter die Vertikalen, wenn nötig. So ist z.B. **außerhalb** wie folgt gezeigt:

außer‖dem *adv* besides. **-halb** *adv*, *prep* outside.

Unregelmäßige Verben, die in der separaten Liste aufgeführt sind, sind mit einem Sternchen (*) bei den Stichwörtern angezeigt.

Viele englische Adverbien sind in dem Wörterbuch nicht aufgeführt, wenn sie aus den Adjektiven regelmäßig durch die Nachsilbe -(*al*)*ly* gebildet sind.

German irregular verbs

Infinitive	Preterite	Past Participle
backen	backte (buk)	gebacken
bedingen	bedang (bedingte)	bedungen
befehlen	befahl	befohlen
beginnen	begann	begonnen
beißen	biß	gebissen
bergen	barg	geborgen
bersten	barst	geborsten
bewegen	bewog	bewogen
biegen	bog	gebogen
bieten	bot	geboten
binden	band	gebunden
bitten	bat	gebeten
blasen	blies	geblasen
bleiben	blieb	geblieben
bleichen	blich	geblichen
braten	briet	gebraten
brauchen	brauchte	gebraucht (brauchen)
brechen	brach	gebrochen
brennen	brannte	gebrannt
bringen	brachte	gebracht
denken	dachte	gedacht
dreschen	drosch	gedroschen
dringen	drang	gedrungen
dürfen	durfte	gedurft
empfehlen	empfahl	empfohlen
erkiesen	erkor	erkoren
erlöschen	erlosch	erloschen
erschrecken	erschrak	erschrocken
essen	aß	gegessen
fahren	fuhr	gefahren
fallen	fiel	gefallen
fangen	fing	gefangen
fechten	focht	gefochten
finden	fand	gefunden
flechten	flocht	geflochten
fliegen	flog	geflogen

Infinitive	Preterite	Past Participle
fliehen	floh	geflohen
fließen	floß	geflossen
fressen	fraß	gefressen
frieren	fror	gefroren
gären	gor	gegoren
gebären	gebar	geboren
geben	gab	gegeben
gedeihen	gedieh	gediehen
gehen	ging	gegangen
gelingen	gelang	gelungen
gelten	galt	gegolten
genesen	genas	genesen
genießen	genoß	genossen
geschehen	geschah	geschehen
gewinnen	gewann	gewonnen
gießen	goß	gegossen
gleichen	glich	geglichen
gleiten	glitt	geglitten
glimmen	glomm	geglommen
graben	grub	gegraben
greifen	griff	gegriffen
haben	hatte	gehabt
halten	hielt	gehalten
hängen	hing	gehangen
hauen	haute (hieb)	gehauen
heben	hob	gehoben
heißen	hieß	geheißen
helfen	half	geholfen
kennen	kannte	gekannt
klimmen	klomm	geklommen
klingen	klang	geklungen
kneifen	kniff	gekniffen
kommen	kam	gekommen
können	konnte	gekonnt
kriechen	kroch	gekrochen
laden	lud	geladen
lassen	ließ	gelassen (lassen)
laufen	lief	gelaufen

Infinitive	Preterite	Past Participle
leiden	litt	gelitten
leihen	lieh	geliehen
lesen	las	gelesen
liegen	lag	gelegen
lügen	log	gelogen
mahlen	mahlte	gemahlen
meiden	mied	gemieden
melken	melkte (molk)	gemolken (gemelkt)
messen	maß	gemessen
mißlingen	mißlang	mißlungen
mögen	mochte	gemocht
müssen	mußte	gemußt
nehmen	nahm	genommen
nennen	nannte	genannt
pfeifen	pfiff	gepfiffen
preisen	pries	gepriesen
quellen	quoll	gequollen
raten	riet	geraten
reiben	rieb	gerieben
reißen	riß	gerissen
reiten	ritt	geritten
rennen	rannte	gerannt
riechen	roch	gerochen
ringen	rang	gerungen
rinnen	rann	geronnen
rufen	rief	gerufen
salzen	salzte	gesalzen (gesalzt)
saufen	soff	gesoffen
saugen	sog	gesogen
schaffen	schuf	geschaffen
schallen	schallte (scholl)	geschallt
scheiden	schied	geschieden
scheinen	schien	geschienen
sheißen	schiß	geschissen
schelten	schalt	gescholten
scheren	schor	geschoren
schieben	schob	geschoben
scheißen	schoß	geschossen
schinden	schund	geschunden

Infinitive	Preterite	Past Participle
schlafen	schlief	geschlafen
schlagen	schlug	geschlagen
schleichen	schlich	geschlichen
schleifen	schliff	geschliffen
schleißen	schliß	geschlissen
schließen	schloß	geschlossen
schlingen	schlang	geschlungen
schmeißen	schmiß	geschmissen
schmelzen	schmolz	geschmolzen
schnauben	schnob	geschnoben
schneiden	schnitt	geschnitten
schreiben	schrieb	geschrieben
schreien	schrie	geschrie(e)n
schreiten	schritt	geschritten
schweigen	schwieg	geschwiegen
schwellen	schwoll	geschwollen
schwimmen	schwamm	geschwommen
schwinden	schwand	geschwunden
schwingen	schwang	geschwungen
schwören	schwor	geschworen
sehen	sah	gesehen
sein	war	gewesen
senden	sandte	gesandt
sieden	sott	gesotten
singen	sang	gesungen
sinken	sank	gesunken
sinnen	sann	gesonnen
sitzen	saß	gesessen
sollen	sollte	gesollt (sollen)
spalten	spaltete	gespalten (gespaltet)
speien	spie	gespie(e)n
spinnen	spann	gesponnen
sprechen	sprach	gesprochen
sprießen	sproß	gesprossen
springen	sprang	gesprungen
stechen	stach	gestochen
stecken	steckte (stak)	gesteckt
stehen	stand	gestanden
stehlen	stahl	gestohlen

Infinitive	Preterite	Past Participle
steigen	stieg	gestiegen
sterben	starb	gestorben
stieben	stob	gestoben
stinken	stank	gestunken
stoßen	stieß	gestoßen
streichen	strich	gestrichen
streiten	stritt	gestritten
tragen	trug	getragen
treffen	traf	getroffen
treiben	trieb	getrieben
treten	trat	getreten
triefen	triefte (troff)	getrieft
trinken	trank	getrunken
trügen	trog	getrogen
tun	tat	getan
verderben	verdarb	verdorben
verdrießen	verdroß	verdrossen
vergessen	vergaß	vergessen
verlieren	verlor	verloren
verschleißen	verschliß	verschlissen
verzeihen	verzieh	verziehen
wachsen	wuchs	gewachsen
wägen	wog (wägte)	gewogen (gewägt)
waschen	wusch	gewaschen
weben	wob	gewoben
weichen	wich	gewichen
weisen	wies	gewiesen
wenden	wandte	gewandt
werben	warb	geworben
werden	wurde	geworden (worden)
werfen	warf	geworfen
wiegen	wog	gewogen
winden	wand	gewunden
wissen	wußte	gewußt
wollen	wollte	gewollt (wollen)
wringen	wrang	gewrungen
zeihen	zieh	geziehen
ziehen	zog	gezogen
zwingen	zwang	gezwungen

Unregelmäßige Verben

Infinitive	Präteritum	Partizip Perfekt
abide	abode	abode
arise	arose	arisen
awake	awoke	awoke
be	was	been
bear	bore	borne *or* born
beat	beat	beaten
become	became	become
begin	began	begun
bend	bent	bent
bet	bet	bet
beware		
bid	bid	bidden *or* bid
bind	bound	bound
bite	bit	bitten
bleed	bled	bled
blow	blew	blown
break	broke	broken
breed	bred	bred
bring	brought	brought
build	built	built
burn	burnt *or* burned	burnt *or* burned
burst	burst	burst
buy	bought	bought
can	could	
cast	cast	cast
catch	caught	caught
choose	chose	chosen
cling	clung	clung
come	came	come
cost	cost	cost
creep	crept	crept
cut	cut	cut
deal	dealt	dealt
dig	dug	dug
do	did	done
draw	drew	drawn
dream	dreamed *or* dreamt	dreamed *or* dreamt

Infinitive	Präteritum	Partizip Perfekt
drink	drank	drunk
drive	drove	driven
dwell	dwelt	dwelt
eat	ate	eaten
fall	fell	fallen
feed	fed	fed
feel	felt	felt
fight	fought	fought
find	found	found
flee	fled	fled
fling	flung	flung
fly	flew	flown
forbid	forbade	forbidden
forget	forgot	forgotten
forgive	forgave	forgiven
forsake	forsook	forsaken
freeze	froze	frozen
get	got	got
give	gave	given
go	went	gone
grind	ground	ground
grow	grew	grown
hang	hung *or* hanged	hung *or* hanged
have	had	had
hear	heard	heard
hide	hid	hidden
hit	hit	hit
hold	held	held
hurt	hurt	hurt
keep	kept	kept
kneel	knelt	knelt
knit	knitted *or* knit	knitted *or* knit
know	knew	known
lay	laid	laid
lead	led	led
lean	leant *or* leaned	leant *or* leaned
leap	leapt *or* leaped	leapt *or* leaped
learn	learnt *or* learned	learnt *or* learned
leave	left	left

Infinitive	Präteritum	Partizip Perfekt
lend	lent	lent
let	let	let
lie	lay	lain
light	lit *or* lighted	lit *or* lighted
lose	lost	lost
make	made	made
may	might	
mean	meant	meant
meet	met	met
mow	mowed	mown
must		
ought		
pay	paid	paid
put	put	put
quit	quitted *or* quit	quitted *or* quit
read	read	read
rid	rid	rid
ride	rode	ridden
ring	rang	rung
rise	rose	risen
run	ran	run
saw	sawed	sawn *or* sawed
say	said	said
see	saw	seen
seek	sought	sought
sell	sold	sold
send	sent	sent
set	set	set
sew	sewed	sewn *or* sewed
shake	shook	shaken
shear	sheared	sheared *or* shorn
shed	shed	shed
shine	shone	shone
shoe	shod	shod
shoot	shot	shot
show	showed	shown
shrink	shrank	shrunk
shut	shut	shut
sing	sang	sung

Infinitive	Präteritum	Partizip Perfekt
sink	sank	sunk
sit	sat	sat
sleep	slept	slept
slide	slid	slid
sling	slung	slung
slink	slunk	slunk
slit	slit	slit
smell	smelt *or* smelled	smelt *or* smelled
sow	sowed	sown *or* sowed
speak	spoke	spoken
speed	sped *or* speeded	sped *or* speeded
spell	spelt *or* spelled	spelt *or* spelled
spend	spent	spent
spill	spilt *or* spilled	spilt *or* spilled
spin	spun	spun
spit	spat	spat
split	split	split
spread	spread	spread
spring	sprang	sprung
stand	stood	stood
steal	stole	stolen
stick	stuck	stuck
sting	stung	stung
stink	stank *or* stunk	stunk
stride	strode	stridden
strike	struck	struck
string	strung	strung
strive	strove	striven
swear	swore	sworn
sweep	swept	swept
swell	swelled	swollen *or* swelled
swim	swam	swum
swing	swung	swung
take	took	taken
teach	taught	taught
tear	tore	torn
tell	told	told
think	thought	thought

Infinitive	Preterite	Past Participle
throw	threw	thrown
thrust	thrust	thrust
tread	trod	trodden
wake	woke	woken
wear	wore	worn
weave	wove	woven
weep	wept	wept
win	won	won
wind	wound	wound
wring	wrung	wrung
write	wrote	written

Glossary of menu terms

There is lots to eat in German-speaking countries: five meals a day are about standard, and there's plenty of scope for snacks — especially nice when traveling with children. **Frühstück** (breakfast) is usually light, perhaps coffee or chocolate and bread; **Zweites Frühstück** (second breakfast) is more serious and will probably feature food that seems like a U.S.-style light lunch. But in the middle of the day comes **Mittagessen** (lunch) which is usually the main meal of the day. In late afternoon, there is **Kaffee mit Kuchen** (coffee and cake and a lot more), and finally **Abendbrot** (supper).

German cuisine is based on the foods the countries produce. Expect to eat simple, hearty food quite fresh from the farm. In Austria, the influence of Hungarian cooking provides some diversion, and in German Switzerland, the French and Italian neighbors have left a pleasing mark. Game is often featured; it is certainly worth trying.

There are many designations in German for establishments which serve food. In large towns, most common is **Restaurant** (the German word is **Gaststätte**); in the country, you will find **Gasthaus** or **Gasthof**. A **Bierstube** or **Weinstube** will serve some food as well as beer or wine, rather like an English pub. Restaurants usually offer full meals, but the menu may not be broken into courses or types of food (appetizers, first courses, meat dishes, fish, etc.). Most restaurants offer one or more **Gedeck** (fixed-priced meal), usually including soup, entrée with one or more vegetable, and a light dessert, no substitutions or additions permitted. These meals are often excellent values. Be sure to tell the waiter that you are having the set meal before you order.

Hotel dining rooms generally offer good **Kaffee mit Kuchen**, but if you are away from your hotel, try a **Café** or **Konditorei**. These places are also good for a light breakfast or a snack at almost any time.

By law, German eating places must list all charges, including service, on the menu in the price of each item. It is still customary, however, to leave a small tip, perhaps 5%, on the table.

Vorspeisen (Hors d'Oeuvre)

Beefsteak Tartar raw ground beef served with raw egg and onion

Bismarckhering pickled herring with onion and spices

Eiersalat egg salad

Froschschenkel frogs' legs

Gänseleber goose liver

Käsebrot open-faced cheese sandwich

Kaviar caviar

Lachsbrot open-faced salmon sandwich

Lachsalm slices of smoked salmon

Ochsenzungesalat salad of sliced tongue

Rollmops bits of smoked herring with mustard, onion, and pickle

Westfälischer Schinken raw cured ham from Westphalia

Würste (Sausages)

Blutwurst blood sausage

Bratwurst grilled pork sausage (spiced)

Knackwurst (or **Knockwurst**) sausage of pork or beef, rather like our hot dog

Leberwurst liver sausage

Wienerwurst Vienna sausage, on the order of small hot dogs

Weisswurst white veal sausage flavored with herbs (a specialty of Munich)

Eierspeisen (Egg Dishes)

Omelette omelette, served plain (**natur**) or with various stuffings (**gefüllt**), e.g.: **mit Champignons** with mushrooms; **mit Fines Herbes** with herbs, as parsley, tarragon, chives; **mit Geflügelleber**

with chicken livers; **mit Schinken** with ham; **Spanisches** with tomato and onion sauce

Pfannkuchen a sort of egg pancake, also served plain (**natur**) or stuffed (**gefüllt**) with **Käse** with cheese; **mit Schinken** with ham; **mit Speck** with bacon

Pochierte Eier poached eggs

Rührei scrambled eggs

Spiegeleier (or **Setzeier**) fried eggs

Weichgekochte Eier soft-cooked eggs

Wachsweiche Eier medium-cooked eggs

Fischgerichte (Seafood)

Aal eel

Austern oysters

Dorsch codfish

Forellen trout

Hecht pike

Heilbutt halibut

Hummer lobster

Jacobsmuscheln scallops, coquilles

Krabben shrimp; for the larger shrimp, Germans usually use the Italian word **scampi**

Schellfisch haddock

Seezunge sole; prepared in many different ways in Germany: fried, baked, in various sauces, etc.

Suppen (Soups)

Bauernsuppe "peasant soup": mixed vegetable soup

Biersuppe soup of beer with spices

Bohnensuppe bean soup

Brühe broth: **Fleischbrühe,** meat broth; **Geflügelbrühe,** chicken broth; **Fischbrühe,** fish broth

Champignonrahmsuppe cream of mushroom soup

Kartoffelsuppe potato soup

Leberknödelsuppe dumplings of chopped liver, onion, and spices, in broth

Linsensuppe lentil soup

Nudelsuppe mit Huhn chicken noodle soup

Tomatensuppe tomato soup

Zwiebelsuppe onion soup

Hauptgerichte (Main meat Dishes

Bauernschmaus "the peasant's delight"; platter of bacon, sausages, sauerkraut, mashed potatoes, and dumplings

Burgunderschinken ham cooked in wine sauce with vegetables

Cordon Bleu slices of veal with ham and cheese dipped in batter and fried

Deutsches Beefsteak fried ground beef, with onion rings and potatoes (Note: the term "steak" on German menus often denotes what an American would call Salisbury steak, or hamburger; for something more like the American idea of steak, see **Lendensteak**)

Eisbein pickled ham hocks with sauerkraut and mashed potatoes

Filet Goulasch "Beef Stroganoff": strips of beef cooked in sour cream with onions and mushrooms

Frikadellen fried meat balls

Gulyas (Austria) goulash; spicy stew

Hackrahmsteak ground meat patty in browned cream gravy

Hammelkeule roast leg of lamb

Hammelkotelette lamb chop, grilled

Hasenpfeffer stew of pieces of hare, marinated in wine and spices, then cooked in the marinade with onions and mushrooms

Kalbsbrust Gefüllte mit Geflügelleber breast of veal, rolled and stuffed with chicken livers, ham, etc.

Kalbshirn mit Rührei calf brains with scrambled eggs

Kalbskotelette veal chop, grilled

Kalbsleber mit Zwiebeln calf liver with onions

Kalbsmilch sweetbreads

Kalbsschnitzel veal cutlet; see also **Wienerschnitzel**

Königsberger Klops large meat balls served in a sour cream sauce with capers

Lendensteak tenderloin steak (usually offered with a variety of sauces; if you prefer plain, ask for **"natur"**

Pfeffersteak steak coated with ground

peppercorns and grilled

Rehbraten roast venison; **Rehrücken** saddle of venison

Rostbraten roast beef (Germany); minute steak (Austria)

Roulades thin slices of veal rolled and stuffed with a variety of stuffings and garnishes

Sauerbraten roast beef marinated with wine and spices and vinegar, then potroasted with vegetables

Schmorbraten pot roast

Schnitzel usually a thin-sliced pan-fried veal cutlet; but sometimes pork (**Schweineschnitzel**) or other meat; prepared in a number of different ways, associated with different areas, as **Holsteinerschnitzel** (topped with a fried egg), **Schwäbischeschnitzel** (with sour cream sauce), and, the most famous, **Wienerschnitzel** (breaded, with a lemon slice and various other garnishes)

Schweinefüsse pigs' feet

Schweinekotelette pork chop: **natur** (plain) or with a variety of sauces

Schweinslendchen pork tenderloin

Ungarischer Gulasch chunks of meat cooked with paprika, onions, and other vegetables

Wiener Rostbraten beef loin fried in butter with onions

Geflügel und Wild (Fowl and Game)

Backhuhn or **Brathuhn** fried chicken

Damwildkeule roast leg of venison

Fasan im Topf pheasant roasted in casserole

Förstertopf mit Pilzen casserole of venison with mushrooms

Frikassee vom Huhn fricasséed chicken

Gansbraten roast goose

Geflügelleber chicken livers

Geflügelragout chicken stew

Kapaun capon

Puterbraten roast turkey

Rebhuhn partridge

Rehbraten roast venison

Rehrücken saddle of venison

Supreme vom Masthuhn boned breast of chicken

Wiener Backhuhn chicken Vienna style: breaded and deep fried with parsley.

Wildschweinbraten roast of wild boar

Gemüse und Beilagen (Vegetables and Side dishes)

Apfelrotkohl or **-kraut** red cabbage cooked with apples

Artischockenhertzen artichoke hearts

Aubergine eggplant

Beete beets

Blumenkohl cauliflower

Dicke Bohnen broad beans (fava)

Erbsen peas

Grüne Bohnen green beans

Gurkensalat cucumber salad

Karotten carrots

Kartoffeln potatoes, the most common accompaniment to the meat dish in Germany; some of the more common ways they are listed on the menu: **Bratkartoffeln** potatoes boiled, sliced and pan-fried; **Gebackene Kartoffeln** baked potatoes; **Herzoginkartoffeln** "dutchess" potatoes: mashed, shaped and browned in oven; **Kartoffelknödel** potato dumplings; **Kartoffelpuffer** potato pancakes; **Pommes Frites** French-fried potatoes; **Würfelkartoffeln** fried diced potatoes

Kartoffelsalat German potato salad, served either hot (**heiss**), sautéed onions and bacon poured over sliced boiled potatoes with vinegar dressing; or cold (**kalt**), with vinegar dressing poured over sliced potatoes and chopped onions

Kohl cabbage

Krautsalat coleslaw

Lattich lettuce

Möhren carrots

Nudeln noodles

Obstsalat fruit salad

Pilzen mushrooms

Rosenkohl Brussel sprouts

Salatplatte salad; may indicate anything from a simple green salad to more elaborate affairs including vegetables, meats, and a variety of dressings

Spätzle short thick noodles often served with meat dishes; preparation varies from area to area

Spinat spinach

Steckrübe turnips

Succini zucchini

Zwiebeln onions

Süssspeisen (Desserts)

Apfelstrudel mixture of apples and spices rolled in very thin pastry and baked

Apfelsinen oranges

Arme Ritter a sort of French toast; bread dipped in batter and fried

Auflauf souffle; the German version may be heavier than the French

Eierschaum whipped custard of egg yolks and sugar, flavored with wine, similar to Italian zabaione

Eis or **Eiskrem** ice cream; may be served in a bowl (**Eisbecher**) with various syrups or fruit toppings; in German Switzerland, **Glace**

Eistorte ice cream cake

Englischer Kuchen pound cake

Erdbeeren strawberries

Haselnussrahm hazelnut cream

Himbeeren raspberries

Käsetorte cheesecake

Königskuchen "King's cake": rum-flavored layer cake with almonds, currants, and raisins

Mohrenkopf "Moor's head": dome-shaped cake filled with custard or whipped cream and topped with chocolate

Pfirsichen peaches

Schokoladencremetorte chocolate layer cake filled with a rich chocolate cream

Getränke (Beverages)

Apfelsinesaft orange juice

Bier beer; **Oktoberbier** is the dark beer enjoyed at the *Oktoberfest*

Himbeersaft raspberry juice; very popular with children

Kaffee coffee; in Austria often served **mit Schlag** or in Germany, **mit Schlagsahne** (whipped cream)

Kirsch brandy distilled from cherries

Kümmel caraway-seed-flavored liqueur

Milch milk

Mineralwasser mineral water

Schnapps brandy

Schokolade chocolate, usually served hot

Tee tea

Wasser water; **Eiswasser** ice water

English−Deutsch

A

a, an [ə, ən] *art* ein *m*, eine *f*, ein *neut*. *once a year* einmal im Jahr. *50 kilometres an hour* 50 Kilometer pro Stunde.

aback [ə'bak] *adv* **taken aback** verblüfft, überrascht.

abandon [ə'bandən] *v* (*leave*) verlassen; (*give up*) aufgeben. *n* **with abandon** ungezwungen. **abandoned** *adj* verfallen.

abashed [ə'baʃt] *adj* verlegen.

abate [ə'beit] *v* abnehmen.

abattoir ['abətwɑ:] *n* Schlachthaus *neut*.

abbey ['abi] *n* Abtei *f*. **abbess** *n* Äbtissin *f*. **abbot** *n* Abt *m*.

abbreviate [ə'bri:vieit] *v* (ab)kürzen. **abbreviation** *n* Abkürzung *f*.

abdicate ['abdikeit] *v* abdanken. **abdication** *n* Abdankung *f*.

abdomen ['abdəmən] *n* Bauch *m*, Unterleib *m*. **abdominal** *adj* Leib-, abdominal.

abduct [əb'dʌkt] *v* entführen. **abduction** *n* Entführung *f*.

aberration [abə'reiʃən] *n* Abweichung *f*, (*optics, astron*) Aberration *f*. **mental aberration** Geistesverirrung *f*.

abet [ə'bet] *v* begünstigen, Vorschub leisten. (+*dat*).

abeyance [ə'beiəns] *n* **in abeyance** in der Schwebe.

abhor [əb'ho:] *v* hassen, verabscheuen. **abhorrence** *n* Abscheu (vor) *m*. **abhorrent** *adj* abscheulich.

*****abide** [ə'baid] *v* bleiben, verweilen; (*tolerate*) ausstehen. **abide by** festhalten an.

ability [ə'biləti] *n* Fähigkeit *f*, (*skill*) Geschicklichkeit *f*. **to the best of one's ability** nach besten Kräften.

abject [,abdʒekt] *adj* (*wretched*) elend; (*contemptible*) verächtlich, gemein.

ablaze [ə'bleiz] *adj*, *adv* brennend, in Flammen. **set ablaze** entflammen.

able ['eibl] *adj* fähig; (*talented*) geschickt, begabt. **be able** können, fähig sein; (*be in a position to*) in der Lage sein. **ably** *adv* geschickt.

abnormal [ab'nɔ:ml] *adj* anormal, abnorm; (*unusual*) ungewöhnlich; (*malformed*) mißgestaltet. **abnormality** *n* Abnormität *f*, Mißbildung *f*.

aboard [ə'bɔ:d] *adj*, *adv* (*ship*) an Bord. **go aboard** an Bord gehen, einsteigen.

abode [ə'boud] *V* **abide**. *n* Wohnsitz *m*.

abolish [ə'boliʃ] *v* abschaffen, beseitigen.

abominable [ə'bominəbl] *adj* scheußlich. **abominate** *v* verabscheuen. **abomination** *n* Abscheu *m*.

aborigine [abə'ridʒini] *n* Ureinwohner *m*. **aboriginal** *adj* Ur-, ursprünglich.

abortion [ə'bɔ:ʃən] *n* (*miscarriage*) Fehlgeburt *f*; (*termination of pregnancy*) Abtreibung *f*. **abortive** *adj* mißlungen.

abound [ə'baund] *v* im Überfluß vorhanden sein. **abound in** reich sein an.

about [ə'baut] *adv* (*approximately*) ungefähr, etwa; (*nearby*) in der Nähe. *prep* (*concerning*) über; (*around*) um ... herum. **be about to** do something eben etwas tun wollen. **walk about** hin- und herlaufen.

above [ə'bʌv] *prep* über. *adv* oben. **above-mentioned** oben erwähnt, obig. **above board** offen, ehrlich.

abrasion [ə'breiʒən] *n* Abschleifen *neut*. Abrieb *m*; (*wound*) Abschürfung *f*. **abrasive** *adj* abschleifend.

abreast [ə'brest] *adv* **keep abreast of** Schritt halten mit.

abridge [ə'bridʒ] *v* (ab)kürzen. **abridgement** *n* Abkürzung *f*.

abroad [ə'brɔ:d] *adv* (*go*) ins Ausland. (*be*) im Ausland.

abrupt [ə'brʌpt] *adj* (*sudden*) plötzlich; (*brusque*) kurz, unhöflich.

abscess ['abses] *n* Abszeß *m*.

abscond [əb'skɒnd] *v* flüchten.

absent ['absənt] *adj* abwesend. **absent-minded** geistesabwesend. **absentee** *n* Abwesende(r). **absence** *n* Abwesenheit *f*; (*lack*) Mangel *m*.

absolute ['absəluːt] *adj* völlig, vollkommen, absolut; (*unconditional*) bedingungslos; (*pure*) rein. **absolutely** *adv* völlig; (*interj*) gewiß! **absolutism** *n* Absolutismus *m*.

absolve [əb'zɒlv] *v* entbinden, freisprechen.

absorb [əb'zɔːb] *v* aufsaugen, absorbieren. **absorbed in thought** in Gedanken vertieft. **absorbent** *adj* absorbierend. **absorbent cotton** Watte *f*. **absorbing** *adj* fesselnd.

abstain [əb'stein] *v* (*voting*) seine Stimme enthalten. **abstain from** verzichten auf. **abstinence** *n* Enthaltsamkeit *f*.

abstemious [əb'stiːmiəs] *adj* mäßig, enthaltsam.

abstract ['abstrakt] *adj* abstrakt, theoretisch. **abstraction** *n* Abstraktion *f*.

absurd [əb'sɔːd] *adj* unsinnig, lächerlich. **absurdity** *n* Unsinn *m*.

abundance [ə'bʌndəns] *n* Überfluß *m*, Reichtum *m*. **abundant** *adj* reichlich. **abundant in** reich an.

abuse [ə'bjuːz; *n* ə'bjuːs] *v* mißbrauchen; (*insult*) beleidigen; *n* Mißbrauch *m*, Beschimpfung *f*. **abusive** *adj* beleidigend.

abyss [ə'bis] *n* Abgrund *m*. **abysmal** *adj* abgrundtief; (*fig*) grenzenlos.

academy [ə'kadəmi] *n* Akademie *f*; (*private school*) Internat *m*. **academic** *adj* akademisch.

accede [ak'siːd] *v* (*agree*) zustimmen (+*dat*). (*join*) beitreten (+*dat*); (*throne*) besteigen.

accelerate [ak'seləreit] *v* (*mot*) gasgeben; (*make quicker*) beschleunigen; (*go faster*) schneller werden. **acceleration** *n* Beschleunigung *f*. **accelerator** *n* Gaspedal *neut*.

accent ['aksənt] *n* Akzent *m*. **accentuate** *v* betonen.

accept [ak'sept] *v* akzeptieren, annehmen; (*agree*) zusagen (+*dat*). **acceptable** *adj* annehmbar. **acceptance** *n* Annahme *f*.

access ['akses] *n* Zutritt *m*, Zugang *m*. **accessible** *adj* erreichbar.

accessory [ak'sesəri] *n* (*mot*) Zubehörteil *m*; (*law*) Mitschuldige(r).

accident ['aksidənt] *n* (*mishap*) Unfall *m*; (*chance*) Zufall *m*. **accidental** *adj* zufällig.

acclaim [ə'kleim] *v* zujubeln (+*dat*). *n* (*also* **acclamation**) Beifall *m*, Lob *neut*.

acclimatize [ə'klaimətaiz] *v* angewöhnen, akklimatisieren.

accolade ['akəleid] *n* Auszeichnung *f*.

accommodate [ə'kɒmədeit] *v* (*put up*) unterbringen; (*help*) aushelfen. **accommodating** *adj* hilfreich. **accommodation** *n* Unterkunft *f*.

accompany [ə'kʌmpəni] *v* begleiten. **accompaniment** *n* Begleitung *f*. **accompanist** *n* Begleiter(in).

accomplice [ə'kʌmplis] *n* Mittäter *m*.

accomplish [ə'kʌmpliʃ] *v* vollbringen, vollenden. **accomplished** *adj* gebildet, gewandt. **accomplishment** *n* Durchführung, Vollendung *f*.

accord [ə'kɔːd] *v* übereinstimmen. *n* Übereinstimmung *f*, Einklang *m*. **of one's own accord** freiwillig. **in accordance with** gemäß (+*dat*): *in accordance with the rules* den Regeln gemäß. **accordingly** *adv* dementsprechend, deswegen. **according to** laut (+*gen*).

accordion [ə'kɔːdiən] *n* Akkordeon *neut*.

accost [ə'kɒst] *v* ansprechen.

account [ə'kaunt] *n* (*bill*) Rechnung *f*; (*bank*, *etc*) Konto *neut*; (*report*) Bericht *m*. **accounts** *pl n* Bücher *pl*. **current account** Scheckkonto *neut*. **savings account** Sparkonto *neut*. **on account** auf Konto. **on account of** wegen (+*gen*), auf Grund (+*gen*). **on no account** auf keinen Fall. **take into account** berücksichtigen. *v* **account for** erklären. **accountable** *adj* verantwortlich. **accountant** *n* Buchhalter *m*.

accrue [ə'kruː] *v* auflaufen.

accumulate [ə'kjuːmjuleit] *v* anhäufen, sich häufen. **accumulation** *n* Anhäufung *f*.

accurate ['akjurət] *adj* genau, exakt; (*correct*) richtig. **accuracy** *n* Genauigkeit *f*.

accuse [ə'kjuːz] *v* anklagen. **the accused** der/die Angeklagte(r). **accusation** *n* Anklage *f*. **accusative** *n* Akkusativ *m*.

accustom [ə'kʌstəm] *v* become accustomed to sich gewöhnen an. **accustomed** *adj* gewöhnlich, üblich.

ace [eis] *n* (*cards*) As *neut*. *adj* (*coll*) erstklassig.

ache [eik] n Schmerz m. v schmerzen, weh tun.

achieve [ə'tʃiːv] v durchführen, vollbringen; (reach) erlangen. **achievement** n Vollendung f, (success) Erfolg m.

acid ['asid] n Säure f. adj sauer.

acknowledge [ək'nolidʒ] v anerkennen; (admit) zugeben. **acknowledge receipt** Empfang bestätigen. **acknowledgment** n Anerkennung f.

acne ['akni] n Pickel m, Akne f.

acorn ['eikoːn] n Eichel f.

acoustic [ə'kuːstik] adj akustisch. **acoustics** pl n Akustik f sing.

acquaint [ə'kweint] v bekannt machen. **be acquainted with** kennen (+acc). **get acquainted with** kennenlernen (+acc). **acquaintance** n Bekannte(r).

acquiesce [akwi'es] v sich fügen. **acquiescence** n Ergebung f. **acquiescent** adj fügsam.

acquire [ə'kwaiə] v erwerben, bekommen. **acquisition** n Erwerb m. **acquisitive** habsüchtig, gierig.

acquit [ə'kwit] v (law) freisprechen. **acquittal** n Freisprechung f.

acrid ['akrid] adj scharf, beißend.

acrimony ['akriməni] n Bitterkeit f. **acrimonious** adj bitter, beißend.

acrobat ['akrəbat] n Akrobat m. **acrobatic** adj akrobatisch. **acrobatics** pl n Akrobatik f sing.

across [ə'kros] adv hinüber, herüber. prep (quer) über (+acc), jenseits (+gen), auf der anderen Seite.

act [akt] v handeln, tun; (behave) sich verhalten; (theatre) (eine Rolle) spielen. **act on** wirken auf. n Handlung, Tat f; (law) Gesetz neut; (theatre) Aufzug m. **acting** adj amtierend; n (theatre) Spielen neut. **actor** n Schauspieler m. **actress** n Schauspielerin f.

action ['akʃən] n Handlung f; (deed) Tat f; (effect) Wirkung f; (law) Klage f; (battle) Gefecht neut.

active ['aktiv] adj tätig, aktiv. **activate** v aktivieren. **activist** n Aktivist m. **activity** n Tätigkeit f. **activities** pl n Unternehmungen pl.

actual ['aktʃuəl] adj wirklich, eigentlich, tatsächlich. **actually** adv wirklich, tatsächlich. interj allerdings.

actuate ['aktjueit] v in Gang bringen.

acupuncture ['akjupʌŋktʃə] n Akupunktur f.

acute [ə'kjuːt] adj scharf, heftig; (angle) spitz; (person) scharfsinnig; (med) akut.

adamant ['adəmənt] adj unnachgiebig.

Adam's apple [adəm'zapl] n Adamsapfel m.

adapt [ə'dapt] v anpassen; verändern. **adapted to** geeignet für. **adaptable** adj anpassungsfähig. **adaptation** n (theatre) Bearbeitung f. **adaptor** n (for plug) Zwischenstecker m.

add [ad] v (figures) addieren; (word, sentence) hinzufügen. **add up** addieren. **addition** n (math) Addition f; (something added) Zugabe f, Zutat m. **in addition** außerdem. **in addition to** zusätzlich zu. **additional** adj zusätzlich, weiter. **additive** n Zusatz m.

addendum [ə'dendəm] n Zusatz m.

adder ['adə] n (snake) Natter m.

addict ['adikt; v ə'dikt] n Süchtige(r); (coll) Fanatiker m. **drug addict** Rauschgiftsüchtige(r). **addicted** süchtig. **addiction** n Sucht f.

address [ə'dres] v (letter) addressieren; (person) anreden. n Adresse f, Anschrift f; (speech) Anrede f. **address book** Adreßbuch neut. **addressee** n Empfänger m.

adenoids ['adənoidz] pl n Polypen pl.

adept [ə'dept] adj geschickt, erfahren.

adequate ['adikwət] adj (quantity) ausreichend, genügend; (quality) annehmbar.

adhere [əd'hiə] v **adhere to** haften or kleben an (+dat); (belief, etc.) festhalten an (+dat). **adhesive** adj klebrig, haftend. **adhesive tape** Klebeband neut. **adherent** n Anhänger m.

adjacent [ə'dʒeisənt] adj angrenzend.

adjective ['adʒiktiv] n Adjektiv neut, Eigenschaftswort neut.

adjoin [ə'dʒoin] v angrenzen (an). **adjoining** adj angrenzend, anliegend.

adjourn [ə'dʒəːn] v vertagen. **adjournment** n Vertagung f.

adjudicate [ə'dʒuːdikeit] v Recht sprechen, entscheiden. **adjudicator** n Schiedsrichter m.

adjust [ə'dʒʌst] v anpassen; berichtigen; (tech) einstellen. **adjust to** sich anpassen an. **adjustable** adj einstellbar. **adjustment** n Anpassung, Einstellung f.

ad-lib ['ad'lib] adv frei. v improvisieren.

administer [əd'ministə] v verwalten.
administer justice Recht sprechen.
administration n Verwaltung f. **administrative** adj Verwaltungs-. **administrator** n Verwalter m.

admiral ['admərəl] n Admiral m.

admire [əd'maiə] v bewundern, hochschätzen. **admirable** adj bewundernswert. **admiration** n Bewunderung f.

admission [əd'miʃən] n Eintritt m; (acknowledgment) Zugeständnis neut.

admit [əd'mit] v (let in) hereinlassen, zulassen; (concede) zugeben. **admittance** n Zutritt, Eintritt m. **no admittance** Zutritt verboten.

adolescence [adə'lesns] Jugend f. **adolescent** adj jugendlich. n Jugendliche(r).

adopt [ə'dopt] v (child) adoptieren; (idea) annehmen, übernehmen. **adoption** n Adoption f; Übernahme f.

adore [ə'doɪ] v lieben; (rel) verehren. **adorable** adj entzückend. **adoration** n Verehrung f.

adorn [ə'doɪn] v schmücken. **adornment** n Schmuck m.

adrenaline [ə'drenəlin] n Adrenalin neut.

adrift [ə'drift] adj, adv (naut) treibend; (fig) hilflos.

adroit [ə'droit] adj gewandt, geschickt.

adulation [adju'leiʃən] n Lobhudelei f.

adult ['adʌlt] n Erwachsene(r). adj erwachsen; (animal, plant) ausgewachsen.

adulterate [ə'dʌltəreit] v verfälschen. **adulteration** n Verfälschung f.

adultery [ə'dʌltəri] n Ehebruch m. **adulterer** n Ehebrecher(in).

advance [əd'vaɪns] v vorwärts gehen, vorrücken; (make progress) Fortschritte machen; (cash) vorschießen; (cause) fördern; (tech) vorstellen. n Vorrücken neut, Fortschritt m; Vorschuß m. **in advance** im voraus. **advancement** n Beförderung f.

advantage [əd'vaɪntidʒ] n Vorteil m. **take advantage of** ausnutzen (+acc). **advantageous** adj vorteilhaft.

advent ['advənt] n Ankunft f; (rel) Advent m.

adventure [əd'ventʃə] n Abenteuer m. **adventurer** n Abenteurer m. **adventurous** adj gewagt.

adverb ['advəɪb] n Adverb neut, Umstandswort neut.

adversary ['advəsəri] n Gegner m.

adverse ['advəɪs] adj widrig, ungünstig. **adversity** n Mißgeschick neut, Not f.

advertise ['advətaiz] v anzeigen. **advertisement** n Anzeige f. **advertising** n Reklame, Werbung f.

advise [əd'vaiz] v (be)raten, empfehlen; (comm) benachrichtigen. **advisable** adj ratsam. **adviser** n Berater m. **advice** n Rat m, Ratschlag m; (comm) Avis neut.

advocate ['advəkeit] v befürworten.

aerial ['eəriəl] n Antenne f. adj Luft-.

aerodynamics [eərədai'namiks] n Aerodynamik f.

aeronautics [eərə'nottiks] n Aeronautik f, Flugwesen neut.

aeroplane ['eərəplein] n Flugzeug neut.

aerosol ['eərəsol] n Sprühdose f, Spray neut.

aesthetic [its'θetik] adj ästhetisch.

affair [ə'feə] n Angelegenheit f, Sache f; (love affair) (Liebes) Affäre f.

affect[1] [ə'fekt] v (influence) (ein)wirken auf, beeinflussen. **affected** adj (moved) bewegt.

affect[2] [ə'fekt] v (pretend) vorgeben. **affectation** n Affektation f. **affected** adj geziert.

affection [ə'fekʃən] n Zuneigung f, Liebe f. **affectionate** adj liebevoll.

affiliated [ə'filieitid] adj angeschlossen. **affiliated company** Tochtergesellschaft f. **affiliation** n Verbindung f, Mitgliedschaft f.

affinity [ə'finəti] n Zuneigung f; (chem) Affinität f.

affirm [ə'fəɪm] v behaupten. **affirmation** n Behauptung f. **affirmative** adj bestätigend.

affix [ə'fiks] v befestigen, ankleben (an).

afflict [ə'flikt] v betrüben. **affliction** n Leiden neut.

affluent ['afluənt] adj wohlhabend, reich. **affluence** n Wohlstand m.

afford [ə'foɪd] v sich leisten (können); (allow) gewähren.

affront [ə'frʌnt] v beleidigen. n Beleidigung f.

afloat [ə'flout] adj, adv schwimmend; (boat) auf dem Meere.

afoot [ə'fut] adv im Gang.

aforesaid [ə'foɪsed] adj vorher erwähnt.

afraid [ə'freid] adj ängstlich, erschrocken, bange. **be afraid of** Angst haben vor. **be afraid to** sich scheuen. **I am afraid I must ...** ich muß leider ...

afresh [ə'freʃ] *adv* von neuem, noch einmal.

Africa ['afrikə] *n* Afrika *neut.* **African** *n* Afrikaner(in). *adj* afrikanisch.

aft [aːft] *adj* Achter-. *adv* achtern.

after ['aːftə] *conj* nachdem. *prep* nach, hinter. *adv* später, nachher. *adj (naut)* Achter-. **after all** schließlich. **shortly after** kurz danach.

after-effect *n* Nachwirkung *f.*

afterlife ['aːftəlaif] *n* Leben nach dem Tode *neut.*

aftermath ['aːftəmaθ] *n* Auswirkung *f.*

afternoon [aːftə'nuːn] *n* Nachmittag *m.* **good afternoon!** guten Tag!

aftershave ['aːftəʃeiv] *n* Rasierwasser *neut.*

after-taste *n* Nachgeschmack *m.*

afterthought ['aːftəθɔːt] *n* nachträglicher Einfall *m.*

afterwards ['aːftəwədz] *adv* nachher, später, danach.

again [ə'gen] *adv* wieder, noch einmal, nochmals; *(moreover)* ferner. **again and again** immer wieder.

against [ə'genst] *prep* gegen. **as against** im Vergleich zu.

age [eidʒ] *n (person)* Alter *neut*; *(era)* Zeitalter *neut.* **age group** Altersgruppe *f.* **at the age of . . .** im Alter von . . . of age volljährig. **old age** (hohes) Alter *neut. v* alt werden. **aged** *adj (elderly)* betagt. **aged five years** fünf Jahre alt. **under age** minderjährig.

agency ['eidʒənsi] *n* Agentur *f.*

agenda [ə'dʒendə] *n* Tagesordnung *f.*

agent ['eidʒənt] *n* Agent *m*, Vermittler *m*; *(chem)* Wirkstoff *m.*

aggravate ['agrəveit] *v* verschlimmern; *(coll)* ärgern. **aggravation** *n* Verschlimmerung *f*; Ärger *m.*

aggregate ['agrigət] *adj* gesamt, ganz. *n* Summe *f.*

aggression [ə'greʃən] *n* Angriff *m*, Aggression *f.* **aggressive** *adj* aggresiv. **aggressor** *n* Angreifer *m.*

aghast [ə'gaːst] *adj* entsetzt.

agile ['adʒail] *adj* agil, flink. **agility** *f* Flinkheit *f.*

agitate ['adʒiteit] *v* schütteln. **agitated** *adj* beunruhigt. **agitation** *n* Beunruhigung *f.*

agnostic [ag'nostik] *n* Agnostiker *m.* **agnosticism** *n* Agnostizismus *n.*

ago [ə'gou] *adv* vor: *a year ago* vor einem Jahr. **a moment ago** soeben. **a long time ago** schon lange her. **a short time ago** vor kurzem.

agog [ə'gog] *adj* gespannt.

agony ['agəni] *n* Qual *f*, Agonie *f.* **agonize over** sich quälen über.

agree [ə'griː] *v (concur)* übereinstimmen, einverstanden sein; *(date, etc.)* vereinbaren; *(consent)* zustimmen; *(be in agreement)* einig sein. *eggs do not agree with me* ich kann Eier nicht vertragen. **agreed!** einverstanden! **agreeable** *adj* angenehm. **agreement** *n* Übereinstimmung *f (written)* Abkommen *neut.*

agriculture ['agrikʌltʃə] *n* Landwirtschaft *f.* **agricultural** *adj* landwirtschaftlich.

aground [ə'graund] *adv* **run aground** stranden.

ahead [ə'hed] *adv* vorwärts. **straight ahead** gerade aus. **go ahead** fortfahren.

aid [eid] *n* Hilfe *f. v* helfen (+ *dat*).

aim [eim] *v (gun)* richten; *(intend)* zielen. *n* Ziel *neut.* **aimless** *adj* ziellos.

air [eə] *n* Luft *f*; *(appearance)* Aussehen *neut*; *(music)* Lied *neut. v (laundry)* trocknen; *(views)* bekanntmachen. **go by air** fliegen. **airy** *adj* luftig.

airbed ['eəbed] *n* Luftmatratze *f.*

airborne ['eəbɔːn] *adj* in der Luft; Luft-.

air-conditioned *adj* klimatisiert. **air-conditioning** *n* Klimaanlage *f.*

air-cooled *adj (mech)* luftgekühlt.

aircraft ['eəkraːft] *n* Flugzeug *neut.*

airfield ['eəfiːld] *n* Flugplatz *m.*

air force *n* Luftwaffe *f.*

air lift *n* Luftbrücke *f.*

airline ['eəlain] *n* Luftverkehrsgesellschaft *f.* **airline passenger** *n* Fluggast *m.*

airmail ['eəmeil] *n* Luftpost *f.* **by airmail** mit Luftpost.

airport ['eəpɔːt] *n* Flughafen *m.*

air-raid *n* Luftangriff *m.*

air steward *n* Steward *m.* **air stewardess** *n* Stewardeß *f.*

airtight ['eətait] *adj* luftdicht.

aisle [ail] *n* Gang *m.*

ajar [ə'dʒaː] *adj* halboffen.

akin [ə'kin] *adj* **akin to** ähnlich (+ *dat*).

alabaster ['aləbaːstə] *n* Alabaster *m.*

à la carte [alaː'kaːt] *adv* nach der Speisekarte, à la carte.

alarm [ə'laːm] *n* Alarm *m*; *(unrest)* Beunruhigung *f. v* beunruhigen. **alarm clock** Wecker *m.*

alas [ə'las] *interj* leider! o weh!

albatross ['albətros] *n* Albatros *m*.

albino [al'bi:nou] *n* Albino *m*.

album ['albəm] *n* Album *neut*.

alchemy ['alkəmi] *n* Alchimie *f*. **alchemist** *n* Alchimist *m*.

alcohol ['alkəhol] *n* Alkohol *m*. **alcoholic** *adj* alkoholisch. *n* Alkoholiker *m*. **alcoholism** *n* Alkoholismus *m*. **non-alcoholic** *adj* alkoholfrei.

alcove ['alkouv] *n* Nische *f*.

alderman ['ɔːldəmən] *n* Ratsherr *m*.

ale [eil] *n* Bier *neut*.

alert [ə'ləːt] *adj* wachsam, munter. *v* warnen. **on the alert** auf der Hut.

algebra ['aldʒibrə] *n* Algebra *f*.

alias ['eiliəs] *adv* sonst . . . genannt, alias. *n* Deckname *m*.

alibi ['alibai] *n* Alibi *neut*.

alien ['eiliən] *n* Fremde(r), Ausländer *m*. *adj* fremd. **alienate** *v* entfremden. **alienation** *n* Entfremdung *f*.

alight¹ [ə'lait] *v* (*from bus*) aussteigen.

alight² [ə'lait] *adj*, *adv* brennend, in Flammen. **set alight** entflammen.

align [ə'lain] *v* ausrichten. **alignment** *n* Ausrichtung *f*.

alike [ə'laik] *adj*, *adv* gleich.

alimentary canal [ali'mentəri] *m* Nährungskanal *m*.

alimony ['aliməni] *n* Unterhalt *m*, Alimente *pl*.

alive [ə'laiv] *adj* lebend, am Leben. **alive with** wimmelnd von.

alkali ['alkəlai] *n* Alkali *neut*. **alkaline** *adj* alkalisch.

all [ɔːl] *adj* alle, sämtliche *pl*. *pron* alles, das Ganze. *adv* ganz. **all over** vorbei. **all gone** alle, weg. **above all** vor allem. **all at once** auf einmal. **at all** überhaupt. **all day** den ganzen Tag. **all right** in Ordnung, okay.

allay [ə'lei] *v* beruhigen.

allege [ə'ledʒ] *v* angeben, behaupten. **alleged** *adj* angeblich. **allegation** *n* Behauptung *f*.

allegiance [ə'liːdʒəns] *n* Treue *f*.

allegory ['aligəri] *n* Allegorie *f*. **allegorical** *adj* allegorisch.

allergy ['alədʒi] *n* Allergie *f*. **allergic** *adj* allergisch (gegen).

alleviate [ə'liːvieit] *v* erleichtern.

alley ['ali] *n* Gasse *f*. **bowling alley** Kegelbahn *f*.

alliance [ə'laiəns] *n* (*pol*) Bündnis *neut*. **form an alliance** ein Bündnis schließen.

allied ['alaid] *adj* verbündet, alliiert.

alligator ['aligeitə] *n* Alligator *m*.

alliteration [əlitə'reiʃən] *n* Alliteration *f*. **alliterative** *adj* alliterierend.

allocate ['aləkeit] *v* zuteilen.

allot [ə'lot] *v* (*distribute*) zuteilen; (*assign*) bestimmen. **allotment** *n* Zuteilung *f*; (*garden patch*) Schrebergarten *m*.

allow [ə'lau] *v* erlauben, gestatten. **allow for** berücksichtigen. **will you allow me (to)?** darf ich? **allowance** *n* Erlaubnis *f*; (*money*) Rente *f*.

alloy ['aloi; *v* ə'loi] *n* Legierung *f*. *v* legieren.

allude [ə'luːd] *v* **allude to** anspielen auf (+*acc*). **allusion** *n* Anspielung *f*.

allure [ə'ljuə] *n* Reiz *m*. *v* verlocken. **alluring** *adj* verlockend.

ally ['alai; *v* ə'lai] *n* Verbündete(r); (*pol*) Alliierte(r). *v* **ally oneself with** sich verbünden mit. **the Allies** die Alliierten.

almanac ['ɔːlmənak] *n* Jahrbuch *neut*, Almanach *m*.

almighty [ɔːl'maiti] *adj* allmächtig; (*coll*) gewaltig. **the Almighty** der Allmächtige.

almond ['aːmənd] *n* Mandel *f*.

almost ['ɔːlmoust] *adv* fast, beinahe.

alms [aːmz] *pl n* Almosen *neut sing*.

aloft [ə'loft] *adv* (*be*) oben; (*go*) nach oben.

alone [ə'loun] *adj*, *adv* allein. **leave alone** bleiben lassen. **leave me alone!** laß mich in Ruhe!

along [ə'loŋ] *prep* entlang (+*acc*): *along the coast* die Küste entlang. *adv* vorwärts, weiter; mit: *come along* mitkommen. **along with** zusammen mit. **get along with someone** mit jemandem gut auskommen. **alongside** *prep* neben (+*acc or dat*); (*ship*) längseits (+*gen*).

aloof [ə'luːf] *adj* zurückhaltend.

aloud [ə'laud] *adv* laut. **read aloud** vorlesen.

alphabet ['alfəbit] *n* Alphabet *neut*. **alphabetical** *adj* alphabetisch.

Alps [alps] *pl n* Alpen *pl*. **alpine** *adj* Alpen-.

already [ɔːl'redi] *adv* schon, bereits.

Alsatian [al'seiʃən] *n* (*dog*) Schäferhund *m*. *adj* elsässisch.

also ['ɔːlsou] *adv* auch, ebenfalls; (*moreover*) ferner.

altar ['ɔːltə] n Altar m.

alter ['ɔːltə] v (modify) (ab-, ver)ändern; (become changed) sich (ver)ändern. **alteration** n (Ab-, Ver)Änderung f; (building) Umbau m.

alternate [ɔɪl'təɪnət; v 'ɔɪltəneit] adj abwechselnd. v abwechseln.

alternative [ɔɪl'təɪnətiv] adj ander. n Alternative f. **there is no alternative** es gibt keine andere Möglichkeit.

although [ɔːl'ðou] conj obwohl, obgleich, wenn auch.

altitude ['altitjuːd] n Höhe f.

alto ['altou] n Alt m, Altstimme f.

altogether [ɔːltə'geðə] adv insgesamt, im ganzen; völlig.

altruistic [altru'istik] adj altruistisch.

aluminium [aljuˈminiəm] n Aluminium neut.

always ['ɔːlweiz] adv immer, stets; schon immer.

am [am] V be.

amalgamate [ə'malgəmeit] v (tech) amalgamieren; (fig) vereinigen.

amass [ə'mas] v aufhäufen.

amateur ['amətə] n Amateur m. adj Amateur-.

amaze [ə'meiz] v erstaunen, verblüffen. **amazed** er erstaunt über. **amazement** n Erstaunen neut. **amazing** adj erstaunlich; (coll) sagenhaft.

ambassador [am'basədə] n Botschafter m.

amber ['ambə] n Bernstein m. adj bernsteinfarb, gelb.

ambidextrous [ambi'dekstrəs] adj beidhändig.

ambiguous [am'bigjuəs] adj zweideutig; unklar.

ambition [am'biʃən] n Ehrgeiz m, Ambition f. **ambitious** adj ehrgeizig, ambitiös.

ambivalence [am'bivələns] n Ambivalenz f. **ambivalent** adj ambivalent.

amble ['ambl] v schlendern.

ambulance ['ambjuləns] n Krankenwagen m.

ambush ['ambuʃ] n Hinterhalt m. v aus dem Hinterhalt überfallen.

ameliorate [ə'miːliəreit] v (make better) verbessern; (get better) besser werden. **amelioration** n Verbesserung f.

amenable [ə'miːnəbl] adj zugänglich; (accountable) verantwortlich.

amend [ə'mend] v (ab)ändern; ergänzen, richtigstellen. **make amends for**

wiedergutmachen. **amendment** n (to a motion) Ergänzung f.

amenities [ə'miːnətiz] pl n Vorzüge pl, moderne Einrichtungen pl.

America [ə'merikə] n Amerika neut. **American** n Amerikaner(in); adj amerikanisch.

amethyst ['aməθist] n Amethyst m.

amiable ['eimiəbl] adj freundlich, liebenswürdig.

amicable [ə'mikəbl] adj freundschaftlich, friedlich.

amid [ə'mid] prep mitten unter (+dat).

amiss [ə'mis] adj verkehrt, nicht richtig. **take amiss** übelnehmen.

ammonia [ə'mouniə] n Ammoniak neut.

ammunition [amju'niʃən] n Munition f.

amnesia [am'niːziə] n Gedächtnisverlust m.

amnesty ['amnəsti] n Amnestie f.

amoeba [ə'miːbə] n Amöbe f.

among [ə'mʌŋ] prep unter, zwischen (+dat); bei (+dat). **among other things** unter anderem. **among ourselves/yourselves/themselves** miteinander, untereinander.

amoral [ei'morəl] adj amoralisch.

amorous ['amərəs] adj verliebt; liebevoll.

amorphous [ə'mɔːfəs] adj (chem) amorph; formlos.

amount [ə'maunt] n (of money) Betrag m, Summe f; (quantity) Menge f. **amount to** betragen. **it amounts to the same** es läuft auf das gleiche hinaus.

ampere ['ampeə] n Ampere neut.

amphibian [am'fibiən] n Amphibie f. **amphibious** adj amphibisch; (vehicle) Amphibien-.

amphitheatre ['amfiθiətə] n Amphitheater neut; (lecture room) Hörsaal m.

ample ['ampl] adj ausreichend, reichlich.

amplify ['amplifai] v verstärken. **amplification** n Verstärkung f. **amplifier** n Verstärker m.

amputate ['ampjuteit] v amputieren. **amputation** n Amputation f.

amuse [ə'mjuːz] v belustigen, amüsieren; (entertain) unterhalten. **be amused by or about** lustig finden. **amusing** adj lustig, unterhaltend. **amusement** n Unterhaltung f.

anachronism [ə'nakrənizəm] n Anachronismus m. **anachronistic** adj anachronistisch.

anaemia [ə'niːmiə] n Anämie, Blutarmut f. anaemic adj anämisch, blutarm.

anaesthetic [anəs'θetik] n Betäubungsmittel neut. under anaesthetic unter Narkose. anaesthetize v betäuben.

anagram ['anəgram] n Anagramm neut.

analogy [ə'nalədʒi] n Ähnlichkeit f, Analogie f. analogous adj analog, ähnlich.

analysis [ən'aləsis] n Analyse f. analyse v analysieren. analytical adj analytisch.

anarchy ['anəki] n Anarchie f. anarchist Anarchist m.

anathema [ə'naθəmə] n (rel) Kirchenbann m. that is anathema to me das ist mir ein Greuel.

anatomy [ə'natəmi] n Anatomie f. anatomical adj anatomisch.

ancestor [ansestə] n Vorfahr m, Ahn m.

anchor ['aŋkə] n Anker m. v befestigen. ride at anchor vor Anker liegen. weigh anchor den Anker lichten.

anchovy [antʃəvi] n Anschovis f.

ancient ['einʃənt] adj alt, uralt; aus alter Zeit, antik.

ancillary [an'siləri] adj zusätzlich, Hilfs-.

and [and] conj und.

anecdote ['anikdout] n Anekdote f.

anemone [ə'nemoni] n Anemone f.

anew [ə'njuː] adv von neuem, wieder.

angel ['eindʒəl] n Engel m. angelic adj engelhaft.

angelica [an'dʒelikə] n Angelika f.

anger ['aŋgə] n Zorn m, Ärger m. v ärgern. in anger im Zorn. angry adj ärgerlich, zornig. be angry sich ärgern, böse sein.

angina [an'dʒainə] n Angina f.

angle[1] ['aŋgl] n Winkel m, Ecke f; (coll) Gesichtspunkt m. be at an angle to einen Winkel bilden mit.

angle[2] ['aŋgl] v angeln (nach). angler n Angler m. angling n Angeln neut.

anguish ['aŋgwiʃ] n Qual f.

angular ['aŋgjulə] adj winkelig, eckig.

animal ['animəl] n Tier neut. adj tierisch, animalisch. animal fat Tierfett neut. animal kingdom Tierreich neut.

animate ['animeit] v beleben; begeistern. animated adj lebhaft. animated cartoon Zeichentrickfilm m.

animosity [ani'mosəti] n Feindseligkeit f.

aniseed ['anisiːd] n Anis m.

anisette [ani'zet] n Anisett m.

ankle ['aŋkl] n (Fuß)Knöchel m.

annals ['anlz] pl n Annalen pl.

annex [ə'neks; n 'aneks] n (to building) Anbau m. v (country) annektieren. annexation n Annexion f.

annihilate [ə'naiəleit] v vernichten. annihilation n Vernichtung f.

anniversary [ani'vəisəri] n Jahrestag m. wedding anniversary Hochzeitstag m.

annotate ['anəteit] v kommentieren. annotation n Anmerkung f.

announce [ə'nauns] v ankündigen, ansagen, anzeigen. announcement n Ankündigung f, Ansage f; (radio) Durchsage f. announcer n (radio) Ansager m.

annoy [ə'noi] v belästigen, ärgern. be annoyed at or with sich ärgern über (+acc). annoyance n Belästigung f.

annual ['anjuəl] adj jährlich; Jahres-. n (book) Jahrbuch neut; (plant) einjährige Pflanze f.

annul [ə'nʌl] v annullieren. annulment n Annullierung f.

anode ['anoud] n Anode f.

anomaly [ə'noməli] n Anomalie f.

anonymous [ə'noniməs] adj anonym, ungenannt.

anorak ['anərak] n Anorak m.

another [ə'nʌðə] pron, adj (a different) ein anderer; (an additional) noch ein. one another einander, sich.

answer ['ansə] n Antwort f; (solution) Lösung f. v antworten, erwidern. answer back unverschämt antworten. answer for verantwortlich sein für. answerable adj verantwortlich.

ant [ant] n Ameise f.

antagonize [an'tagənaiz] v reizen, entfremden. antagonist n Gegner m, Feind m. antagonistic adj feindselig.

antecedent [anti'siːdənt] adj früher.

antelope ['antəloup] n Antilope f.

antenatal [anti'neitl] adj vor der Geburt. antenatal care Schwangerschaftsvorsorge f.

antenna [an'tenə] m (insect) Fühler m; (radio) Antenne f.

anthem ['anθəm] n Hymne f. national anthem Nationalhymne f.

anthology [an'θolədʒi] n Anthologie f.

anthropology [anθrə'polədʒi] n Anthropologie f. anthropological adj anthropologisch.

anti-aircraft [anti'eəkraɪft] adj Fliegerabwehr-. anti-aircraft gun Fliegerabwehrkanone f.

antibiotic [antibai'otik] *n* Antibiotikum *neut. adj* antibiotisch.

antibody ['anti,bodi] *n* Antikörper *m*.

anticipate [an'tisipeit] *v* (*expect*) erwarten; (*foresee*) voraussehen. **anticipation** *n* Erwartung *f*. **in anticipation** of in Erwartung (+*gen*).

anticlimax [anti'klaimaks] *n* Enttäuschung *f*.

anticlockwise [anti'klokwaiz] *adj, adv* dem Uhrzeigersinn entgegen.

antics ['antiks] *pl n* Possen *pl*.

anticyclone [anti'saikloun] *n* Hochdruckgebiet *neut*.

antidote ['antidout] *n* Gegenmittel (gegen) *neut*.

antifreeze ['antifriz] *n* Frostschutzmittel *neut*.

antipathy [an'tipəθi] *n* Antipathie *f*, Abneigung *f*.

antique [an'tiik] *adj* antik, altertümlich. *n* Antiquität *f*. **antiquated** *adj* veraltet. **antiquity** *n* Altertum *neut*.

anti-Semitic [antisə'mitik] *adj* antisemitisch.

antiseptic [anti'septik] *n* Antiseptikum *neut. adj* antiseptisch.

antisocial [anti'souʃəl] *adj* gesellschaftsfeindlich; (*person*) unfreundlich.

antithesis [an'tiθəsis] *n* Gegensatz *m*.

antler ['antlə] *n* Geweihsprosse *f*.

antonym ['antənim] *n* Antonym *neut*.

anus ['einəs] *n* After *m*.

anvil ['anvil] *n* Amboß *m*.

anxious ['aŋkʃəs] *adj* (*worried*) beunruhigt, besorgt; (*desirous*) begierig (nach). **be anxious to do something** gespannt sein, etwas zu tun. **anxiety** *n* Angst *f*, Besorgnis *f*.

any ['eni] *pron* irgendein, welche. *adv* etwas. *any faster* schneller, etwas schneller. *any more?* noch mehr? *do you want any?* wollen sie welche? *I haven't any money* ich habe kein Geld. *I can't do it any longer* ich kann es nicht mehr machen. **anybody** *pron* (irgend) jemand; (*everybody*) jeder. **anyhow** *adv* jedenfalls. **anyone** *pron see* **anybody**. **anything** *pron* (irgend) etwas; (*everything*) alles. **anytime** *adv* jederzeit. **anyway** *adv* jedenfalls, sowieso. **anywhere** *adv* irgendwo(hin); (*everywhere*) überall.

apart [ə'paɪt] *adv* auseinander, getrennt. **apart from** abgesehen von.

apartheid [ə'paɪteit] *n* Apartheid *f*.

apartment [ə'paɪtmənt] *n* Wohnung *f*.

apathy ['apəθi] *n* Apathie *f*. **apathetic** *adj* apathisch.

ape [eip] *n* Affe *m*. *v* nachäffen.

aperitive [ə'perətiv] *n* Aperitif *m*.

aperture ['apətjuə] *n* Öffnung *f*; (*phot*) Blende *f*.

apex ['eipeks] *n* Spitze *f*.

aphid ['eifid] *n* Blattlaus *f*.

aphrodisiac [afrə'diziak] *n* Aphrodisiakum *neut*.

apiece [ə'piis] *adv* (*per person*) pro Person; (*for each article*) pro Stück.

apology [ə'polədʒi] *n* Entschuldigung *f*. **apologetic** *adj* entschuldigend. **apologize** sich entschuldigen.

apoplexy ['apəpleksi] *n* Schlaganfall *m*.

apostle [ə'posl] *n* Apostel *m*.

apostrophe [ə'postrəfi] *n* Apostroph *m*, Auslassungszeichen *neut*.

appal [ə'poil] *v* entsetzen. **appalling** *adj* entsetzlich.

apparatus [apə'reitəs] *n* Apparat *m*, Gerät *neut*.

apparent [ə'parənt] *adj* (*obvious*) offenbar; (*seeming*) scheinbar. **apparently** adv dem Anschein nach.

apparition [apə'riʃən] *n* Erscheinung *f*, Geist *m*.

appeal [ə'piil] *n* Appell *m*, dringende Bitte *f*; (*charm*) Anziehungskraft *f*; (*law*) Berufung *f*. *v* appeal against (*law*) Berufung einlegen gegen. **appeal for** dringend bitten um. **appeal to** (*turn to*) appellieren, sich wenden an; (*please*) gefallen (+*dat*). **appealing** *adj* reizvoll.

appear [ə'piə] *v* (*seem*) scheinen; (*become visible, present itself*) erscheinen; (*crop up*) auftauchen. **appearance** *n* Erscheinung *neut*; (*look*) Anschein *m*.

appease [ə'piiz] *v* beruhigen; (*hunger*) stillen. **appeasement** *n* Beruhigung *f*.

appendix [ə'pendiks] *n* (*in book*) Anhang *m*; (*anat*) Blinddarm *m*. **appendicitis** *n* Blinddarmentzündung *f*.

appetite ['apitait] *n* Appetit *m*. **appetizer** *n* Appetitshappen *m*. **appetizing** *adj* appetitlich.

applaud [ə'ploid] *v* Beifall klatschen (+*dat*); applaudieren (+*dat*); (*fig*) loben.

apple ['apl] *n* Apfel *m*. **apple juice** Apfelsaft *m*. **apple tree** Apfelbaum *m*. **apple sauce** Apfelmus *neut*.

appliance [ə'plaɪəns] n Gerät neut.
applicable [ə'plɪkəbl] adj zutreffend.
applicant ['æplɪkənt] n Kandidat m.
apply [ə'plaɪ] v anwenden; (be valid) gelten. **apply for** (job) sich bewerben um. **apply to** sich wenden an. **apply oneself** to sich bemühen um. **application** n Anwendung f; (job) Bewerbung f. **applied** adj angewandt.
appoint [ə'pɔɪnt] v anstellen, ernennen. **appointed** adj vereinbart. **well appointed** gut ausgestattet. **appointment** n Anstellung f; (meeting) Verabredung f.
apportion [ə'pɔːʃən] v zuteilen.
appraisal [ə'preɪzl] n Schätzung f.
appreciable [ə'priːʃəbl] adj merkbar.
appreciate [ə'priːʃieit] v schätzen; (understand) verstehen; (be grateful for) dankbar sein für; (increase in value) im Wert steigen. **appreciation** n (gratitude) Anerkennung f; (in value) Wertzuwachs m. **appreciative** adj anerkennend.
apprehend [æpri'hend] v (understand) begreifen; (seize) verhaften. **apprehensive** adj angstvoll.
apprentice [ə'prentis] n Lehrling m. **apprenticeship** n Lehre f.
approach [ə'prəutʃ] v (come near) sich nähern; (a place) nähern; (someone) sich wenden an. n Herankommen neut; (attitude) Einstellung f; (access) Zugang m. **approachable** adj zugänglich.
appropriate [ə'prəupriət; v ə'prəuprieit] adj geeignet (+ dat). v sich aneignen.
approve [ə'pruːv] v (agree) zustimmen; (pass, endorse) billigen, genehmigen. **approve of** billigen. **approved** adj bewährt. **approval** n Billigung f; Genehmigung f. **on approval** auf Probe.
approximate [ə'prɒksɪmət] adj ungefähr. **approximately** adv ungefähr, etwa.
apricot ['eɪprɪkɒt] n Aprikose f.
April ['eɪprəl] n April m.
apron ['eɪprən] n Schürze f.
apt [æpt] adj (remark) passend. **apt at** geschickt in. **be apt to do something** geneigt sein, etwas zu tun. **aptitude** n (gift) Begabung f.
aqualung ['ækwəlʌŋ] n Unterwasseratmungsgerät neut.
aquarium [ə'kwɛərɪəm] n Aquarium neut.
Aquarius [ə'kwɛərɪəs] n Wassermann m.
aquatic [ə'kwætɪk] n Wasser-.
aqueduct ['ækwɪdʌkt] n Aquädukt m.
Arab ['ærəb] n Araber m. adj or **Arabian**,

Arabic arabisch. **Arabic** n arabische Sprache f.
arable ['ærəbl] adj **arable land** Ackerland neut.
arbitrary ['ɑːbɪtrəri] adj willkürlich.
arbitrate ['ɑːbɪtreit] v entscheiden. **arbitration** n Schiedspruch m. **arbitrator** n Schiedsrichter m.
arc [ɑːk] n Bogen m.
arcade [ɑː'keɪd] n Arkade f.
arch [ɑːtʃ] n (architecture) Bogen m. v (sich) wölben. adj Erz-. **archway** n Bogengang m.
archaeology [ɑːki'ɒlədʒi] n Archäologie f. **archaeological** adj archäologisch. **archaeologist** n Archäologe m.
archaic [ɑː'keiik] adj altertümlich.
archbishop [ɑːtʃ'bɪʃəp] n Erzbischof m.
archduke [ɑːtʃ'djuːk] n Erzherzog m.
archer ['ɑːtʃə] n Bogenschütze m. **archery** n Bogenschießen neut.
archetype ['ɑːkitaip] n Vorbild neut; (psychol) Archetyp m.
archipelago [ɑːki'peləgou] n Archipel m.
architect ['ɑːkitekt] n Architekt m. **architecture** n Architektur f.
archives ['ɑːkaivz] pl n Archiv neut sing.
ardent ['ɑːdənt] adj eifrig, begeistert.
ardour ['ɑːdə] n Eifer m.
arduous ['ɑːdjuəs] adj mühsam, anstrengend.
are [ɑː] V be.
area ['ɛərɪə] n (measurement) Fläche f; (region) Gebiet neut. Zone f.
arena [ə'riːnə] n Arena neut.
argue ['ɑːgjuː] v streiten; (case) diskutieren; (maintain) behaupten. **argument** n Streit m; (reasoning) Argument neut. **argumentative** adj streitlustig.
arid ['ærɪd] adj trocken, dürr.
Aries ['ɛəriːz] n Widder m.
***arise** [ə'raiz] v (come into being) entstehen; (get up) aufstehen.
arisen [ə'rɪzn] V arise.
aristocracy [æri'stɒkrəsi] n Adel m, Aristokratie f. **aristocrat** n Aristokrat m. **aristocratic** adj aristokratisch.
arithmetic [ə'rɪθmətɪk] n Arithmetik f. **arithmetical** adj arithmetisch.
arm¹ [ɑːm] n Arm m. (of chair) Seitenlehne f. **arm in arm** Arm in Arm. **with open arms** mit offenen Armen.
arm² [ɑːm] n (weapon) Waffe f. v bewaffnen. **arms race** Wettrüsten neut.

coat of arms Wappen *neut*. **armed forces** Streitkräfte *pl*.

armament ['aɪməmənt] *n* Kriegsausrüstung *f*.

armchair ['aɪmtʃeə] *n* Sessel, Lehnstuhl *m*.

armistice ['aɪmistis] *n* Waffenstillstand *m*.

armour ['aɪmə] *n* (*suit of*) Rüstung *f*; (*of ship, tank*) Panzerung *f*. **armoured** *adj* gepanzert.

armpit ['aɪmpit] *n* Achselhöhle *f*.

army ['aɪmi] *n* Armee *f*, Heer *neut*. **join the army** zum Militär gehen.

aroma [ə'roumə] *n* Aroma *neut*, Duft *m*.

arose [ə'rouz] *V* arise.

around [ə'raund] *adv* ringsherum, rundherum; auf allen Seiten; (*nearby*) in der Nähe. *prep* um ... herum, rings um; (*approximately*) ungefähr. **look around** (*for*) sich umsehen (nach). **turn around** sich umdrehen.

arouse [ə'rauz] *v* wecken; (*suspicion*) erregen.

arrange [ə'reindʒ] *v* (*put in order*) anordnen; (*meeting*) verabreden; (*holidays*) festsetzen. (*see to it*) arrangieren, einrichten; (*music*) bearbeiten. **arrangement** *n* Anordnung *f*, (*agreement*) Vereinbarung *f*; (*music*) Bearbeitung *f*. **make arrangements** Vorbereitungen treffen.

array [ə'rei] *n* Aufstellung *f*.

arrears [ə'riəz] *pl n* Rückstände *pl*. **in arrears** im Rückstand *m*.

arrest [ə'rest] *v* (*thief*) verhaften; (*halt*) anhalten; *n* Verhaftung *f*. **under arrest** in Haft, verhaftet. **arresting** *adj* fesselnd.

arrive [ə'raiv] *v* ankommen; (*fig*) gelangen. **arrival** *n* Ankunft *f*. **late arrival** Spätankömmling *m*.

arrogance ['ærəgəns] *n* Hochmut *m*. **arrogant** *adj* hochmütig, eingebildet.

arrow ['ærou] *n* Pfeil *m*.

arse [aɪs] *n* (*vulgar*) Arsch *m*.

arsenal ['aɪsənl] *n* Arsenal *neut*.

arsenic ['aɪsnik] *n* Arsenik *neut*.

arson ['aɪsn] *n* Brandstiftung *f*. **arsonist** *n* Brandstifter *m*.

art [aɪt] *n* Kunst *f*. **arts** *pl* Geisteswissenschaften *pl*. **arts and crafts** Kunstgewerbe *neut sing*. **art gallery** Kunstgalerie *f*. **art school** Kunstschule *f*. **work of art** Kunstwerk *neut*.

artefact ['aɪtifækt] *n* Artefakt *neut*.

artery ['aɪtəri] *n* Arterie *f*.

arthritis [aɪ'θraitis] *n* Arthritis *f*.

artichoke ['aɪtitʃouk] *n* Artischocke *f*.

article ['aɪtikl] *n* Artikel *m*; (*newspaper*) Zeitungsartikel *m*, Bericht *m*. **article of clothing** Bekleidungstück *neut*.

articulate [aɪ'tikjulət] *adj*. **to be articulate** sich gut ausdrücken.

articulated lorry [aɪtikjuleitid] *n* Sattelschlepper *m*.

artifice ['aɪtifis] *n* Trick *m*.

artificial [aɪti'fiʃəl] *adj* (*manmade*) künstlich, Kunst-; (*affected*) affektiert. **artificial respiration** künstliche Atmung *f*.

artillery [aɪ'tiləri] *n* Artillerie *f*.

artisan [aɪti'zan] *n* Handwerker *m*.

artist ['aɪtist] *n* Künstler *m*; (*painter*) Maler *m*. **artiste** *n* Artist(in). **artistic** *adj* künstlerisch.

as [æz] *conj, prep* (*while*) als, während; (*in the way that*) wie, sowie; (*since*) da, weil; (*in role of*) als. **as ... as** (eben)so ... wie. **as far as** soweit. **as if** als ob. **as long as** solange **as soon as** sobald. **as it were** sozusagen. **as well** auch.

asbestos [æz'bestos] *n* Asbest *m*.

ascend [ə'send] *v* aufsteigen. **ascendant** *adj* vorherrschend. **ascent** *n* Aufstieg *m*. **Ascension** *n* Himmelfahrt *f*.

ascertain [æsə'tein] *v* feststellen.

ascetic [ə'setik] *adj* askethisch. *n* Asket *m*.

ash[1] [æʃ] *n* (*cinder*) Asche *f*. **ashtray** *n* Aschenbecher *neut*.

ash[2] [æʃ] *n* (*tree*) Esche *f*.

ashamed [ə'feimd] *adj* **be ashamed** sich schämen.

ashore [ə'ʃɔɪ] *adv* am Ufer. **go ashore** an Land gehen.

Ash Wednesday *n* Aschermittwoch *m*.

Asia ['eiʃə] *n* Asien *neut*. **Asian** *n* Asiat *m*; *adj* asiatisch.

aside [ə'said] *adv* beiseite. **aside from** außer. **step aside** zur Seite treten. **turn aside from** sich wegwenden von.

ask [aɪsk] *v* (*to question*) fragen; (*request*) bitten. **ask a question** eine Frage stellen.

askew [ə'skju] *adv* verschoben, schief.

asleep [ə'sliɪp] *adj, adv* **be asleep** schlafen. **fall asleep** einschlafen.

asparagus [ə'spærəgəs] *n* Spargel *m*.

aspect ['aspekt] *n* (*appearance*) Aussehen *neut*; (*of a problem*) Aspekt *m*.

asphalt ['asfalt] *n* Asphalt *m*.

asphyxiate [əs'fiksieit] *v* ersticken. **asphyxiation** *n* Erstickung *f*.

aspic ['aspik] n Aspik m.

aspire [ə'spaiə] v **aspire** to streben nach. **aspiring** adj hochstrebend.

aspirin ['asprin] n Aspirin neut.

ass [as] n Esel m.

assail [ə'seil] v angreifen. **assailant** n Angreifer m.

assassin [ə'sasin] n Attentäter m, Mörder m. **assassinate** v ermorden. **assassination** n Ermordung f.

assault [ə'soːlt] v angreifen, überfallen. n Angriff m. **indecent assault** Sittlichkeitsverbrechen neut.

assemble [ə'sembl] v (congregate) sich versammeln; (put together) montieren, zusammenbauen; (bring together) versammeln. **assembly** n (people) Versammlung f; (tech) Montage f. **assembly hall** Aula f. **assembly line** Fließband.

assent [ə'sent] v zustimmen (+ dat). n Zustimmung f.

assert [ə'səːt] v (insist on) bestehen auf; (declare) erklären. **assertion** n Behauptung f. **assertive** adj selbstsicher.

assess [ə'ses] v (for tax) bewerten; (estimate) schätzen. **assessment** n Bewertung f.

asset ['aset] n Vorteil m. **assets** pl Vermögen neut sing.

assiduous [ə'sidjuəs] adj fleißig.

assign [ə'sain] v zuteilen, bestimmen. **assignment** n Aufgabe f.

assimilate [ə'simileit] v aufnehmen. **assimilation** n Aufnahme f.

assist [ə'sist] v helfen (+ dat). **assistance** n Hilfe f. **assistant** n Helfer m. **sales assistant** n Verkäufer m.

associate [ə'souzieit; n ə'souziət] v verbinden. n Kollege m, Mitarbeiter m; (comm) Partner m. **association** n (club) Verein m, Verband m; (link) Verbindung f.

assorted [ə'soːtid] adj verschiedenartig, gemischt. **assortment** n Sortiment neut.

assume [ə'sjuːm] v (suppose) annehmen; (take over) übernehmen.

assure [ə'ʃuə] v (convince) versichern (+ dat), versprechen; (ensure) sicherstellen. **assurance** n (assertion) Versicherung f; (confidence) Selbstsicherheit f. **life assurance** Lebensversicherung f.

asterisk ['astərisk] n Sternchen neut.

asthma ['asmə] n Asthma neut.

astonish [ə'stoniʃ] v erstaunen, verblüffen.

be **astonished (at)** erstaunt sein (über), sich wundern (über). **astonishing** adj erstaunlich. **astonishment** n Erstaunen neut.

astound [ə'staund] v bestürzen, erstaunen.

astray [ə'strei] adv **go astray** in die Irre gehen. **lead astray** vom rechten Weg abführen.

astride [ə'straid] adv rittlings. prep rittlings auf (+ dat).

astringent [ə'strindʒənt] adj zusammenziehend.

astrology [ə'strolədʒi] n Astrologie f. **astrologer** n Astrologe m. **astrological** adj astrologisch.

astronaut ['astronoːt] n Astronaut m.

astronomy [ə'stronəmi] n Astronomie f. **astronomer** n Astronom m. **astronomical** adj astronomisch.

astute [ə'stjuːt] adj scharfsinnig.

asunder [ə'sʌndə] adv auseinander.

asylum [ə'sailəm] n Asyl neut. **lunatic asylum** Irrenanstalt f. **political asylum** politisches Asyl neut.

at [at] prep (place) in, zu, bei, an, auf; (time) um, zu, in; (age, speed) mit; (price) zu. **at school** in der Schule. **at four o'clock** um vier Uhr. **at my house** bei mir. **at home** zuhause. **at (age) 65** mit 65. **at Christmas** zu Weihnachten. **at peace** in Frieden.

ate [et] V eat.

atheist ['eiθiist] n Atheist m.

Athens ['aθinz] n Athen neut.

athlete ['aθliːt] n Athlet m. **athletic** adj athletisch. **athletics** n (Leicht)Athletik f.

Atlantic [ət'lantik] n Atlantik m.

atlas ['atləs] n Atlas m.

atmosphere ['atməsfiə] n Atmosphäre f. **atmospheric** adj atmosphärisch, Luft-.

atom ['atəm] n Atom neut. **atomic** adj Atom-. **atomic bomb** Atombombe f. **atomic power** Atomkraft f. **atomic reactor** Atomreaktor m.

atone [ə'toun] v **atone for** büßen, wiedergutmachen. **atonement** n Buße f.

atrocious [ə'trouʃəs] adj grausam, brutal; (coll) scheußlich. **atrocity** n Greueltat f.

attach [ə'tatʃ] v (affix) befestigen, anhängen; (connect) anschließen; (to a letter) beifügen. be **attached to** mögen, lieb haben. **attach oneself to** sich anschließen an. **attachment** n (liking) Anhänglichkeit f; (fixture) Anschluß m.

attaché [ə'taʃei] n Attaché. **attaché case** Aktentasche f.

attack [ə'tak] v angreifen; (criticize) tadeln, kritisieren. n Angriff m. **heart attack** Herzanfall m.

attain [ə'tein] v erreichen, gelangen zu. **attainable** adj erreichbar.

attempt [ə'tempt] v versuchen, wagen. n Versuch m.

attend [ə'tend] v (school) besuchen; (meeting) beiwohnen (+ dat); (lecture) hören. **attend to** sich kümmern um. **attendance** n Anwesenheit f. **good attendance** gute Teilnahme f. **attendant** n Wächter(in).

attention [ə'tenʃən] n Aufmerksamkeit f; (care) Pflege f; (machine) Wartung f. **pay attention to** aufpassen auf. **stand at attention** Haltung annehmen.

attic ['atik] n Dachkammer f.

attire [ə'taiə] n Kleidung f. v kleiden.

attitude ['atitjuːd] n Einstellung f, Verhalten neut.

attorney [ə'təːni] n (lawyer) Rechtsanwalt m. **power of attorney** Vollmacht f.

attract [ə'trakt] v anziehen; (attention) erregen. **attraction** n Anziehung f; (charm) Reiz m, Anziehungskraft f. **attractive** adj attraktiv.

attribute [ə'tribjuːt; n 'atribjuːt] v zuschreiben (+ dat). n Eigenschaft f. **attributable** adj zuzuschreiben (+ dat).

attrition [ə'triʃən] n Abnutzung f. **war of attrition** Zermürbungskrieg m.

aubergine ['oubəʒiːn] n Aubergine f.

auburn ['oːbən] adj kastanienbraun.

auction ['oːkʃən] n Auktion f, Versteigerung f. v versteigern. **auctioneer** n Versteigerer m.

audacious [oː'deiʃəs] adj kühn. **audacity** n (boldness) Wagemut m; (cheek) Frechheit f.

audible ['oːdəbl] adj hörbar.

audience ['oːdjəns] n (people) Publikum neut, Zuhörer pl; (interview) Audienz f.

audiovisual [oːdiou'viʒuəl] adj audiovisuell.

audit ['oːdit] v (Rechnungen) prüfen. n Rechnungsprüfung f. **auditor** n Rechnungsprüfer m.

audition [oː'diʃən] n (theatre) Sprech-, Hörprobe f. v eine Hörprobe abnehmen.

auditorium [oːdi'toːriəm] n Hörsaal m.

augment [oːg'ment] v vermehren; (grow) zunehmen.

August ['oːgəst] n August m.

aunt [aːnt] n Tante f.

au pair [ou 'peə] n Au-pair-Mädchen neut.

aura ['oːrə] n Aura f; (med) Vorgefühl neut.

auspicious [oː'spiʃəs] adj günstig.

austere [oː'stiə] adj (person) streng; (surroundings) nüchtern. **austerity** n Strenge f.

Australia [o'streiljə] n Australien neut. **Australian** n Australier(in); adj australisch.

Austria ['ostriə] n Österreich neut. **Austrian** n Österreicher(in); adj österreichisch.

authentic [oː'θentik] adj echt, authentisch. **authenticity** n Echtheit f.

author ['oːθə] n (writer) Schriftsteller m, Autor m; (of a particular item) Verfasser m.

authority [oː'θorəti] n Autorität f; (expert) Fachmann m. **on good authority** aus guter Quelle. **the authorities** die Behörden pl. **authoritarian** adj autoritär.

authorize ['oːθəraiz] v genehmigen, bevollmächtigen. **authorization** n Genehmigung f.

autobiography [oːtoubai'ogrəfi] n Autobiographie f.

autocratic [oːtou'kratik] adj autokratisch.

autograph ['oːtəgraːf] n Autogramm neut. v unterschreiben.

automatic [oːtə'matik] adj automatisch, selbsttätig. **automatic transmission** Automatik f.

automobile ['oːtəməbiːl] n Wagen m, Auto neut.

autonomous [oː'tonəməs] adj autonom, unabhängig. **autonomy** n Autonomie f.

autopsy ['oːtopsi] n Autopsie f.

autumn ['oːtəm] n Herbst m. **autumnal** adj herbstlich, Herbst-.

auxiliary [oːg'ziljəri] adj Hilfs-, Zusatz-, zusätzlich. n Hilfskraft f.

avail [ə'veil] n **to no avail** nutzlos. v **avail oneself of** Gebrauch machen von, sich bedienen (+ gen).

available [ə'veiləbl] adj (obtainable) erhältlich; (usable) verfügbar. **be available** zur Verfügung stehen. **availability** n Erhältlichkeit f.

avalanche ['avəlɑːnʃ] n Lawine f.

avant-garde [avã'gaːd] adj avantgardistisch. n Avantgarde f.

avarice ['avəris] n Geiz m. **avaricious** adj geizig.

avenge [ə'vendʒ] v rächen. **avenge oneself on** sich rächen an.

avenue ['avinjuː] n Allee f.

average ['avəridʒ] n Durchschnitt m. adj durchschnittlich, Durchschnitts-. **on average** im Durchschnitt.

averse [ə'vəis] adj abgeneigt. **aversion** n Abneigung f.

avert [ə'vəit] v (gaze) abwenden; (danger) verhindern.

aviary ['eiviəri] n Vogelhaus neut.

aviation [eivi'eifən] n Luftfahrt f. **aviator** n Flieger m.

avid ['avid] adj gierig (auf). **avidity** n Begierde f.

avocado [avə'kaːdou] n Avocado(birne) f.

avoid [ə'void] v vermeiden; (person) aus dem Wege gehen (+dat). **avoidable** adj vermeidbar.

await [ə'weit] v erwarten.

***awake** [ə'weik] v (wake up) aufwachen; (rouse) wecken; (arouse) erwecken. **be awake** wach sein. **wide awake** munter. **awaken** v erwecken.

award [ə'woid] v verleihen. n Preis m.

aware [ə'weə] adj bewußt (+gen). **awareness** n Bewußtsein neut.

away [ə'wei] adv weg, fort. adj (absent) abwesend. **she is away** sie ist verreist.

awe [oi] n Ehrfurcht f. **awesome** adj (impressive) imponierend; (frightening) erschreckend.

awful ['oiful] adj furchtbar.

awhile [ə'wail] adv eine Weile, eine Zeitlang.

awkward ['oikwəd] adj (clumsy) ungeschickt, linkisch; (embarrassing) peinlich; (contrary) widerspenstig.

awning ['oinin] n Markise f.

awoke [ə'wouk] V awake.

awoken [ə'woukn] V awake.

axe or US **ax** [aks] n Axt f.

axiom ['aksiəm] n Axiom neut.

axis ['aksis] n Achse f.

axle ['aksl] n Achse f.

B

babble ['babl] v plappern; (water) plätschern.

baboon [bə'buin] n Pavian m.

baby ['beibi] n Baby neut, Säugling m. **baby carriage** Kinderwagen m. **babyish** adj kindisch. **babysit** v babysitten. **babysitter** n Babysitter m.

bachelor ['batʃələ] n Junggeselle m.

back [bak] n (anat) Rücken m; (rear) Rückseite f; (football) Verteidiger m. adj hinter, Hinter-. adv zurück. v (bet on) wetten auf; (support) unterstützen; (reverse) rückwärts fahren. **back out** v sich zurückziehen.

backache ['bakeik] n Rückenschmerz m.

backbone ['bakboun] n Rückgrat neut, Wirbelsäule f.

backdate [,bak'deit] v zurückdatieren.

backer ['bakə] n Förderer m.

backfire [,bak'faiə] v (car) fehlzünden; (plan) fehlschlagen.

background ['bakgraund] n Hintergrund m.

backhand ['bakhand] n (sport) Rückhandschlag m.

backlash ['baklaʃ] n (politische) Reaktion f.

backlog ['baklog] n Rückstand m.

backside ['baksaid] n Hinterteil neut, Hintern m.

backstage ['baksteidʒ] adj, adv hinter den Kulissen.

backstroke ['bakstrouk] n Rückenschwimmen neut.

backward ['bakwəd] adj zurückgeblieben.

backwards ['bakwədz] adv zurück, rückwärts.

backwater ['bakwoitə] n Stauwasser neut.

backyard [bak'jaid] n Hinterhof m.

bacon ['beikən] n (Schinken)Speck m.

bacteria [bak'tiəriə] pl n Bakterien pl.

bad [bad] adj schlecht, schlimm; (naughty) böse; (food) faul, verfault. **bad-tempered** mißgelaunt.

bade [bad] V bid.

badge [badʒ] n Abzeichen neut.

badger ['badʒə] n Dachs m. v plagen.

badminton ['badmintən] n Federballspiel neut.

baffle ['bafl] v verblüffen.

bag [bag] n Beutel m, Sack m; (paper) Tüte f; (handbag) Tasche f. **baggage** n Gepäck neut. **baggy** adj bauschig. **bagpipes** pl n Dudelsack m sing.

barren

bail¹ [beil] n (security) Kaution f. v gegen Kaution freilassen.

bail² or **bale** [beil] v **bail out** (boat) ausschöpfen; (from aeroplane) abspringen; (help) aushelfen.

bailiff ['beilif] n Gerichtsvollzieher m.

bait [beit] n Köder m. v ködern; (tease) quälen.

bake [beik] v backen. **baker** n Bäcker m. **bakery** Bäckerei f.

balance ['baləns] n Gleichgewicht neut; (scales) Waage f; (of account) Saldo m; (amount left) Rest m. v ausgleichen. **balance sheet** Bilanz f.

balcony ['balkəni] n Balkon m.

bald [boild] adj kahl.

bale¹ [beil] n Ballen m.

bale² [beil] V **bail²**.

ball¹ [boil] n (sport) Ball m; (sphere) Kugel f.

ball² [boil] n (dance) Ball m.

ballad ['baləd] n Ballade f.

ballast ['baləst] n Ballast neut.

ball bearing n Kugellager neut.

ballet ['balei] n Ballett neut. **ballet dancer** Ballettänzer(in).

ballistic [bə'listik] adj ballistisch.

balloon [bə'luːn] n Ballon m; (toy) Luftballon m.

ballot ['balət] n Abstimmung f.

ball-point pen n Kugelschreiber m.

ballroom ['boilrum] n Tanzsaal m.

balmy ['baimi] adj sanft, lindernd.

bamboo [bam'buː] n Bambus m.

ban [ban] v verbieten. n Verbot neut.

banal [bə'naɪl] adj banal.

banana [bə'naɪnə] n Banane f.

band¹ [band] n Gruppe f; (music) Band f, Kapelle f; (criminals) Bande f. v **band together** sich vereinen.

band² [band] n (strip) Band neut, Binde f.

bandage ['bandidʒ] n Bandage f, Binde f. v bandagieren.

bandit ['bandit] n Bandit m.

bandy ['bandi] adj krummbeinig. v **bandy words** streiten.

bang [baŋ] n Knall m. v (sound) knallen; (strike) schlagen; (door) zuknallen.

bangle ['baŋgl] n (Arm)Spange f.

banish ['baniʃ] v verbannen.

banister ['banistə] n Treppengeländer neut.

banjo ['bandʒou] n Banjo neut.

bank¹ [baŋk] n (river) Ufer neut; (sand) Bank f.

bank² [baŋk] n (comm) Bank f. v (money) auf die Bank bringen. **bank on** sich verlassen auf. **bank account** n Bankkonto neut. **banker** n Bankier m. **banker's card** Scheckkarte f. **bank holiday** n Feiertag m. **banknote** n Banknote f.

bankrupt ['baŋkrʌpt] adj bankrott. n Bankrotteur m. go **bankrupt** Bankrott machen. **bankruptcy** Bankrott m.

banner ['banə] n Banner neut.

banquet ['baŋkwit] n Bankett neut.

banter ['bantə] v necken. n Neckerei f.

baptism ['baptizəm] n Taufe f. **baptize** v taufen.

bar [baɪ] n (drink) Bar f; (rod) Stange f, Barre f; (chocolate) Tafel f. v (door) verriegeln; (ban) verbieten.

barbarian [baɪ'beəriən] n Barbar m. **barbaric** adj barbarisch.

barbecue ['baɪbikjuː] n Barbecue neut. v am Spieß braten.

barbed wire [baɪbd] n Stacheldraht m.

barber ['baɪbə] n Barbier m, Friseur m.

barbiturate [baɪ'bitjurət] n Barbitursäure f.

bare [beə] adj nackt; (trees) kahl; (empty) leer; (mere) bloß. v entblößen. **barefoot** adj barfuß. **bare-headed** adj mit bloßem Kopf. **barely** adv kaum.

bargain ['baɪgin] n (good buy) Gelegenheitskauf m. (deal) Geschäft neut. v feilschen. **collective bargaining** tarifverhandlungen pl. **into the bargain** obendrein.

barge [baɪdʒ] n Lastkahn m. v **barge in** hereinstürzen.

baritone ['baritoun] n Bariton m.

bark¹ [baɪk] v (dog) bellen. n Bellen neut.

bark² [baɪk] n (tree) Rinde f.

barley ['baɪli] n (crop) Gerste f; (in soup) Graupen pl.

barmaid ['baɪmeid] n Barmädchen neut.

barman ['baɪmən] n Barmann m.

barn [baɪn] n Scheune f.

barometer [bə'rɔmitə] n Barometer neut.

baron ['barən] n Baron m.

baronet ['barənit] n Baronet m.

baroque [bə'rɔk] adj barock.

barracks ['barəks] n Kaserne f.

barrage ['baraːʒ] n (dam) Damm m; (mil) Sperrfeuer neut; (of questions) Flut f.

barrel ['barəl] n Faß neut.

barren ['barən] adj unfruchtbar; (desolate) wüst.

barricade [bari'keid] n Barrikade f. v verbarrikadieren.

barrier ['baria] n Schranke f.

barrister ['barista] n Rechtsanwalt m.

barrow ['barou] n Schubkarren m.

bartender ['baitendə] n Barmann m.

barter ['baitə] n Tauschhandel m. v tauschen; (haggle) feilschen.

base¹ [beis] n (bottom) Fuß m, Boden m; (basis) Basis f; (mil) Stützpunkt m; (chem) Base f. v gründen. **be based on** basieren auf (+dat).

base² [beis] adj (vile) gemein.

baseball ['beisbɔːl] n Baseball m.

basement ['beismant] n Kellergeschoß neut.

bash [baʃ] v (heftig) schlagen. **have a bash!** versuch's mal!

bashful ['baʃful] adj schüchtern.

basic ['beisik] adj grundsätzlich, Grund-. **basically** adv im Grunde.

basil ['bazl] n Basilienkraut neut.

basin ['beisin] n (washbasin, river basin) Becken neut; (dish) Schale f.

basis ['beisis] n Basis f, Grundlage f.

bask [bask] v sich sonnen.

basket ['baiskit] n Korb m. **basketball** n Basketball m.

bass¹ [beis] n (music) Baß m. **bass guitar** Baßgitarre f. **double bass** Kontrabaß m.

bass² [bas] n Seebarsch m.

bassoon [bə'suːn] n Fagott neut.

bastard ['baistəd] n Bastard m; (derog) Schweinehund m.

baste [beist] v (meat) mit Fett begießen.

bastion ['bastjən] n Bollwerk neut.

bat¹ [bat] n (sport) Schlagholz neut. v without batting an eyelid ohne mit der Wimper zu zucken.

bat² [bat] n (zool) Fledermaus f.

batch [batʃ] n Stoß m.

bath [baːθ] n Bad neut. v baden. **have or take a bath** ein Bad nehmen. **bathroom** n Badezimmer neut. **bathtub** n Badewanne f. **baths** pl n Schwimmbad neut sing.

baton ['batn] n (music) Taktstock m.

battalion [bə'taljən] n Bataillon neut.

batter¹ ['batə] v (strike) verprügeln.

batter² ['batə] n (cookery) Schlagteig m.

battery ['batəri] n Batterie f.

battle ['batl] n Schlacht f; (fig) Kampf m. v kämpfen. **battlefield** n Schlachtfeld neut. **battleship** n Schlachtschiff neut.

bawl [bɔːl] v brüllen, heulen.

bay¹ [bei] n (coast) Bai f, Bucht f.

bay² [bei] n **keep at bay** abwehren.

bay³ [bei] n (tree) Lorbeer m. **bay leaf** Lorbeerblatt neut.

bayonet ['beiənit] n Bajonett neut. v bajonettieren.

bay window n Erkerfenster neut.

bazaar [bə'zaː] n Basar m.

*be [biː] v sein; (be situated) liegen, stehen. v aux (in passive) werden. **There is/are es gibt.** the book is on the table das Buch liegt auf dem Tisch. I want to be an engineer ich will Ingenieur werden. how much is that car? wieviel kostet der Wagen

beach [biːtʃ] n Strand m. v (boat) auf den Strand setzen.

beacon ['biːkən] n Leuchtfeuer neut.

bead [biːd] n Perle f.

beak [biːk] n Schnabel m.

beaker ['biːkə] n Becher m.

beam [biːm] n (wood) Balken m; (light) Strahl m. v strahlen.

bean [biːn] n Bohne f.

*bear¹ [beə] v (carry, yield) tragen, (tolerate) ertragen, leiden; (child) gebären. **bring pressure to bear on** Druck ausüben auf. **bear right** sich nach rechts halten.

bear² [beə] n (zool) Bär m.

beard [biəd] n Bart m.

bearing ['beəriŋ] n (posture) Haltung f; (relation) Beziehung f; (tech) Lager neut. **bearings** pl n Orientierung f sing.

beast [biːst] n Tier neut; (cattle) Vieh neut; (person) Bestie f. **beastly** adj (coll) scheußlich.

*beat [biːt] v schlagen. n (stroke) Schlag m; (music) Rhythmus m; (policeman's) Revier neut.

beaten ['biːtn] V beat.

beautiful ['bjuːtəful] adj schön. **beautifully** adv ausgezeichnet. **beauty** n Schönheit f.

beaver ['biːvə] n Biber m.

became [bi'keim] V become.

because [bi'kɔz] conj weil. **because of** wegen (+gen).

*become [bi'kʌm] v werden. **becoming** adj passend.

bed [bed] n Bett neut; (garden) Beet neut. **river bed** Flußbett neut. **seabed** n Meeresboden m. **bedclothes** pl n Bettwäsche f sing. **bedridden** adj bettlägerig. **bedroom** n Schlafzimmer neut. **bedsitter** n Einzimmerwohnung f. **bedspread** n Bettdecke f. **bedtime** n Schlafenzeit f.

bee [biː] n Biene f.

beech [biːtʃ] n Buche f.

beef [biːf] n Rindfleisch neut.

beehive ['biːhaiv] n Bienenstock m.

been [biːn] V be.

beer [biə] n Bier neut.

beetle ['biːtl] n Käfer m.

beetroot ['biːtruːt] n. rote Bete f.

before [bi'foː] conj bevor, ehe; prep vor; adv (time) zuvor, früher; (ahead) voran. **beforehand** adv im voraus.

befriend [bi'frend] v befreunden.

beg [beg] v (for money) betteln; (beseech) bitten. **beggar** n Bettler m.

began [bi'gan] V begin.

***begin** [bi'gin] v beginnen, anfangen. **beginner** n Anfänger m. **beginning** n Anfang m, Beginn m.

begrudge [bi'grʌdʒ] v mißgönnen.

begun [bi'gʌn] V begin.

behalf [bi'haːf] n **on behalf of** im Namen von. **on my behalf** um meinetwillen.

behave [bi'heiv] v sich verhalten, sich betragen. **behave well)** sich gut benehmen. **behave yourself!** benimm dich! **behaviour** n Benehmen neut, Verhalten neut.

behind [bi'haind] prep hinter. adv (in the rear) hinten; (back) zurück; (behind schedule) im Rückstand. n (coll) Hinterteil neut. **behindhand** adv im Rückstand.

***behold** [bi'hould] v sehen, betrachten. **beholder** m Betrachter m.

beige [beiʒ] adj beige.

being [biːiŋ] n (existence) (Da)Sein neut; (creature) Wesen neut, Geschöpf neut. **for the time being** einstweilen. **come into being** entstehen. **human being** Mensch m.

belated [bi'leitid] adj verspätet.

belch [beltʃ] v rülpsen; (fumes) ausspeien. n Rülpsen neut.

belfry ['belfri] n Glockenturm m.

Belgium ['beldʒəm] n Belgien neut. **Belgian** n Belgier(in). adj belgisch.

belief [bi'liːf] n Glaube m; (conviction) Überzeugung f. **believe** v glauben (+dat). **believe in** glauben an (+acc). **believable** adj glaublich. **believer** n Gläubige(r).

bell [bel] n Glocke f; (on door) Klingel f.

belligerent [bi'lidʒərənt] adj (country) kriegsführend; (person) aggressiv.

bellow ['belou] v brüllen. n Gebrüll neut.

bellows ['belouz] n Blasebalg m.

belly ['beli] n Bauch m.

belong [bi'loŋ] v gehören (+dat); (be a member) angehören (+dat). **belongings** pl n Eigentum neut sing; Sachen pl.

beloved [bi'lʌvid] adj geliebt. n Geliebte(r).

below [bi'lou] prep unter. adv unten.

belt [belt] n Gürtel m. v (coll) verprügeln. **belt up!** halt die Klappe!

bemused [bi'mjuːzd] adj verwirrt.

bench [bentʃ] n Bank f; (work table) Arbeitstisch m.

***bend** [bend] v biegen; (be bent) sich beugen. n Kurve f.

beneath [bi'niːθ] prep unter.

benefactor ['benəfaktə] n Wohltäter m. **benefactress** n Wohltäterin f.

beneficent [bi'nefisənt] adj wohltätig.

beneficial [benə'fiʃəl] adj vorteilhaft, nützlich.

benefit ['benəfit] n Nutzen m, Gewinn m. v nützen. **benefit from** Nutzen ziehen aus.

benevolence [bi'nevələns] n Wohltätigkeit f. **benevolent** adj wohltätig.

benign [bi'nain] adj gütig; (tumour) gutartig.

bent [bent] V bend. adj krumm, verbogen; (dishonest) unehrlich. **be bent on** versessen sein auf (+acc).

bequeath [bi'kwiːð] v vermachen.

beret ['berei] n Baskenmütze f.

berry ['beri] n Beere f.

berserk [bə'səik] adj **go berserk** wild werden, toben.

berth [bəːθ] n (mooring) Liegeplatz m; (bunk) Koje f. **give a wide berth to** einen weiten Bogen machen um (+acc).

beside [bi'said] prep neben. **be beside oneself with** außer sich sein vor (+dat). **besides** prep außer. adv außerdem.

besiege [bi'siːdʒ] v belagern.

best [best] adj best. adv am besten, bestens. n das Beste. **do one's best** sein Bestes tun. **at best** höchstens. **best man** Trauzeuge m.

bestial ['bestjəl] adj bestialisch.

bestow [bi'stou] v **bestow upon** schenken (+dat).

bestseller [best'selə] n Bestseller m.

bet [bet] v wetten. n Wette f.

betray [bi'trei] v verraten. **betrayal** n Verrat m.

better ['betə] adj, adv besser. n das Bessere. v verbessern. **get the better of** übertreffen. **better oneself** sich verbessern.

between [bi'twiin] prep zwischen. adv dazwischen. **between you and me** unter uns.

beverage ['bevəridʒ] n Getränk neut.

*****beware** [bi'weə] v sich hüten vor (+ dat). **beware the dog** Vorsicht Vorsicht–bissiger Hund!

bewilder [bi'wildə] v verwirren, verblüffen.

beyond [bi'jond] prep uber ... hinaus, jenseits (+ gen); mehr als. adv jenseits, darüber hinaus. **beyond compare** unvergleichlich. **he is beyond help** ihm ist nicht mehr zu helfen.

bias ['baiəs] n Neigung f. **biased** adj voreingenommen.

bib [bib] n Latz m.

Bible ['baibl] n Bibel f.

bibliography [bibli'ogrəfi] n Bibliographie f.

biceps ['baiseps] n Bizeps m.

bicker ['bikə] v zanken.

bicycle ['baisikl] n Fahrrad neut.

*****bid** [bid] v (offer) bieten; (cards) reizen. n (offer) Angebot neut; (attempt) Versuch m. **bid someone welcome** jemanden willkommen heißen. **bidder** n Bieter m.

bidden ['bidn] V bid.

bidet ['bidei] n Bidet neut.

biennial [bai'eniəl] adj zweijährig.

big [big] adj groß. **big-headed** adj eingebildet. **big-hearted** adj großherzig.

bigamy ['bigəmi] n Bigamie f.

bigot ['bigət] n Frömmler m. **bigoted** adj bigott. **bigotry** n Bigotterie f.

bikini [bi'kiini] n Bikini m.

bilateral [bai'latərəl] adj bilateral.

bilingual [bai'lingwəl] adj zweisprachig.

bill¹ [bil] n (in restaurant) Rechnung f; Banknote f; (comm) Wechsel m; (pol) Gesetzentwurf m; (poster) Plakat neut. v fakturieren. **billboard** n Plakattafel f.

bill² [bil] n (beak) Schnabel m.

billiards ['biljədz] n Billard neut.

billion ['biljən] n Billion f; (US) Milliarde f.

bin [bin] n Kiste f; (dustbin) Mülleimer m.

binary ['bainəri] adj binär.

*****bind** [baind] v (tie) binden; (oblige) verpflichten. **binding** adj bindend. n (book) Einband m.

binoculars [bi'nokjuləz] pl n Feldstecher m.

biography [bai'ogrəfi] n Biographie f. **biographer** n Biograph m. **biographical** adj biographisch.

biology [bai'olədʒi] n Biologie f. **biological** adj biologisch. **biologist** n Biologe m.

birch [bəitʃ] n Birke f; (rod) Birkenrute f.

bird [bəid] n Vogel m.

birth [bəiθ] n Geburt f. **date of birth** Geburtsdatum neut. **birth certificate** Geburtsurkunde f. **birth control** Geburtenregelung f. **birthday** Geburtstag m. **birthmark** Muttermal neut.

biscuit ['biskit] n Biskuit m, Keks m.

bisexual [bai'seksuəl] adj bisexuell.

bishop ['biʃəp] n Bischof m.

bison ['baisən] n Bison m.

bit¹ [bit] V bite. n (morsel) Bißchen, Stückchen neut: a bit of bread ein Stückchen Brot. a bit frightened ein bißchen ängstlich.

bit² [bit] n (harness) Gebiß neut; (drill) Bohreisen neut.

bitch [bitʃ] n Hündin f; (woman) Weibsstück neut.

*****bite** [bait] v beißen. n (mouthful) Bissen m; (wound) Biß m. **bite to eat** Imbiß m.

bitten ['bitn] V bite.

bitter ['bitə] v bitter; (weather) scharf. **to the bitter end** bis zum bitteren Ende. **bitterness** n Bitterkeit f.

bizarre [bi'zai] adj bizarr, seltsam.

black ['blak] adj schwarz. n (colour) Schwarz neut; (person) Schwarze(r). **blackberry** ['blakbəri] n Brombeere f. **blackbird** ['blakbəid] n Amsel f. **blackboard** ['blakbəid] n Wandtafel f. **blackcurrant** [,blak'kʌrənt] n schwarze Johannisbeere f. **blacken** ['blakn] v schwarz machen. **black eye** n blaues Auge neut. **blackhead** ['blakhed] n Mitesser m. **blackleg** ['blakleg] n Streikbrecher m. **blackmail** ['blakmeil] n Erpressung f. **blackmailer** n Erpresser m. **black market** n schwarzer Markt m. **black marketeer** Schwarzhändler m. **black out** (darken) verdunkeln; (faint) ohnmächtig werden. **black-out** n Verdunkelung f; Ohnmachtsanfall m; (elec) Stromausfall m.

black pudding n Blutwurst f.
blacksmith ['blaksmiθ] n Schmied m.
bladder ['bladə] n Blase f.
blade [bleid] n (razor, knife) Klinge f; (grass) Halm m; (tech) Blatt neut; (propellor) Flügel m.
blame [bleim] v tadeln, die Schuld geben (+dat). n Schuld f, Tadel m. I am to blame for this ich bin daran schuld. **blameless** adj untadelig.
blancmange [blə'mɒnʒ] n Pudding m.
bland [bland] adj sanft, mild.
blank [blaŋk] adj leer, unausgefüllt. n (form) Formular neut; (cartridge) Platzpatrone f. **blank cheque** Blankoscheck m.
blanket ['blaŋkit] n Decke f. adj Gesamt-, allgemein.
blare [bleə] v schmettern. n Schmettern neut.
blaspheme [blas'fiːm] v lästern. **blasphemy** n Gotteslästerung f.
blast [blɑːst] n Explosion f; (of wind) (heftiger) Windstoß m. v sprengen.
blatant ['bleitənt] adj offenkundig.
blaze [bleiz] n Brand m, Feuer neut. v lodern.
blazer ['bleizə] n Blazer m.
bleach [bliːtʃ] v bleichen. n Bleichmittel neut.
bleak [bliːk] adj kahl; (fig) trostlos.
bleat [bliːt] v (sheep) blöken; (goat) meckern. n Blöken neut, Meckern neut.
bled [bled] V **bleed**.
*bleed [bliːd] v bluten; (brakes, radiators) entlüften. **bleeding** adj blutend.
blemish ['blemiʃ] n Makel m.
blend [blend] v mischen. n Mischung f.
bless [bles] v segnen. **blessing** n Segen m.
blew [bluː] V **blow**[1].
blind [blaind] adj blind; (corner) unübersichtlich. n (window) Rouleau neut. v blenden; (fig) verblenden. **blind alley** Sackgasse f. **blindfold** v die Augen verbinden (+dat). adv mit verbundenen Augen.
blink [bliŋk] v blinzeln.
bliss [blis] n Wonne f. **blissful** glückselig.
blister ['blistə] n Blase f.
blizzard ['blizəd] n Schneesturm m.
blob [blob] n Tropfen m.
bloc [blok] n Block m.
block [blok] n (wood) Klotz m; (stone) Block m; (US) Häuserblock m; (in pipe) Verstopfung f; (barrier) Sperre f. v

blockieren; verstopfen. **writing block** Schreibblock m. **blockade** n Blockade f. **blockage** n Verstopfung f.
bloke [blouk] n Kerl m.
blond [blond] adj blond. **blonde** n Blondine f.
blood [blʌd] n Blut neut. **in cold blood** kaltblütig. **blood clot** Blutgerinnsel neut. **blood pressure** Blutdruck m. **blood test** Blutuntersuchung f. **bloodthirsty** adj blutdurstig. **blood transfusion** Blutübertragung f. **blood vessel** Blutgefäß neut. **bloody** adj blutig; (coll) verdammt.
bloom [bluːm] v blühen. n Blüte f.
blossom ['blosəm] n Blüte f. v blühen.
blot [blot] n Fleck m; (of ink) Tintenklecks m. v (make dirty) beschmieren. **blot out** auslöschen.
blotch [blotʃ] n Fleck m; Klecks m.
blotting paper n Löschpapier neut.
blouse [blauz] n Bluse f.
*blow[1] [blou] v blasen; (of wind) wehen; (fuse) durchbrennen. **blow over** vorbeigehen. **blow up** (explode) sprengen. **blow the horn** (mot) hupen. **blow one's nose** sich die Nase putzen.
blow[2] [blou] n Schlag m; (misfortune) Unglück neut.
blowlamp ['bloulamp] n Lötlampe f.
blown [bloun] V **blow**[1].
blowout ['blouaut] n (mot) geplatzter Reifen m, Reifenpanne f.
blubber ['blʌbə] n Walfischspeck m.
blue [bluː] adj blau; (depressed) niedergeschlagen. n Blau neut. **bluebell** n Glockenblume f. **blueberry** n Heidelberee f. **bluebottle** n Schmeißfliege f. **the blues** Blues m sing.
bluff [blʌf] v bluffen. n Bluff m.
blunder ['blʌndə] n (dummer) Fehler m, Schnitzer m. v (stumble) stolpern; (make mistake) einen Schnitzer machen.
blunt [blʌnt] adj stumpf. v stumpf machen; (enthusiasm) abstumpfen.
blur [bləː] v verwischen, verschmieren. **blurred** adj verschwommen.
blush [blʌʃ] v erröten. n Erröten neut.
boar [boː] n Eber m. **wild boar** Wildschwein m.
board [boːd] n (wooden) Brett neut; (comm) Aufsichtsrat m. v (train) einsteigen in (+acc). **board and lodging** Unterkunft und Verpflegung f. **boarding house** Pension f. **boarding school** Internat neut.

boast [boust] v prahlen, angeben. n
Prahlerei f. **boaster** n Prahler m.

boat [bout] n Boot neut. **in the same boat**
in der gleichen Lage.

bob [bob] v sich auf- und abbewegen;
(hair) kurz schneiden.

bobbin ['bobin] n Spule f.

bobsleigh ['bobslei] n Bobsleigh m.

bodice ['bodis] n Mieder neut.

body ['bodi] n Körper, Leib m; (corpse)
Leiche f; (of people) Gruppe f; (car)
Karosserie f. **bodily** adj körperlich.

bog [bog] n Sumpf m. v **get bogged down**
steckenbleiben. **boggy** adj sumpfig.

bogus ['bougas] adj falsch, unecht.

bohemian [bə'hiːmiən] adj (fig)
zigeunerhaft, ungebunden. n (fig)
Bohemien m.

boil[1] [boil] v kochen. **boiler** n Kessel m.
boiling adj kochend.

boil[2] [boil] n (sore) Furunkel m.

boisterous ['boistərəs] adj ungestüm, laut.

bold [bould] adj kühn, tapfer; (cheeky)
frech. **boldness** n Kühnheit f.

bolster ['boulstə] n Kissen neut. **bolster
up** (fig) unterstützen.

bolt [boult] n (door) Riegel m; (screw)
Bolzen m; (lightning) Blitzstrahl m;
(cloth) Rolle f. v (door) verriegeln; (attach
with bolts) anbolzen; (food)
hinunterschlingen; (dash) (hastig)
fliehen.

bomb [bom] n Bombe f. v bombardieren.
go down a bomb einen Bombenerfolg
haben. **bombard** v bombardieren. **bombardment** n Beschießung f. **bomber** n
(aeroplane) Bombenflugzeug neut. **bombing** n Bombenangriff m.

bond [bond] n (tie) Bindung f; (comm)
Schuldschein m.

bone [boun] n Knochen m, Bein neut;
(fish) Gräte f. v (meat) die Knochen entfernen aus; (fish) entgräten.

bonfire ['bonfaiə] n Gartenfeuer neut.

bonnet ['bonit] n Haube f; (mot)
Motorhaube f.

bonus ['bounəs] n Bonus m.

bony ['bouni] adj knochig.

book [buk] n Buch neut; (notebook) Heft
neut. v (record) buchen; (reserve)
reservieren. **bookcase** n Bücherschrank
m. **booking office** Fahrkartenschalter m.
bookkeeping n Buchhaltung f. **bookmaker** n Buchmacher m. **bookshop** n Buch-
handlung f.

boom [buːm] n (sound) Dröhnen neut;
(econ) Konjunktur f; (naut) Baum m. v
dröhnen.

boost [buːst] v Auftrieb geben (+dat),
(tech) verstärken. n Auftrieb m.

boot [buːt] n Stiefel m; (mot) Kofferraum
m.

booth [buːð] n Bude f. **telephone booth**
Telephonzelle f.

booze [buːz] (coll) v saufen. n
alkoholisches Getränk neut. **boozer** n
Säufer m.

border ['boːdə] n (of country) Grenze f;
(edge) Rand m. v grenzen. **borderline** n
Grenze f. **borderline case** Grenzfall m.

bore[1] [boː] V bear[1].

bore[2] [boː] v (drill) bohren; (a hole) aus-
bohren; (cylinder) ausschleifen. n
Kaliber neut.

bore[3] [boː] v (weary) langweilen. n
langweiliger Mensch m. **be bored** sich
langweilen. **boredom** n Langeweile f. **boring** adj langweilig.

born [boːn] adj geboren. **she was born
blind** sie ist von der Geburt blind.

borne [boːn] V bear[1].

borough ['bʌrə] n Stadtbezirk m.

borrow ['borou] v borgen, entleihen. **borrower** n Entleiher m.

bosom ['buzəm] n Busen m. **bosom friend**
Busenfreund m.

boss [bos] n Boß, Chef m. v **boss around**
herumkommandieren. **bossy** adj herrisch.

botany ['botəni] n Botanik f. **botanical** adj
botanisch. **botanical gardens** botanischer
Garten m. **botanist** n Botaniker m.

both [bouθ] adj, pron beide(s). **both** (of
the) **dogs** beide Hunde. **both ... and**
sowohl ... als or wie auch.

bother ['boðə] v (disturb) belästigen, stör-
en; (take trouble) sich Mühe geben. n
Belästigung f. **bothersome** adj lästig.

bottle ['botl] n Flasche f. v in Flaschen
füllen. **bottled** adj in Flaschen, Flaschen-.
bottleneck n (fig) Engpaß m. **bottle
opener** n Flaschenöffner m.

bottom ['botəm] n Boden m; (coll: anat)
Hintern m. adj **bottom gear** erster Gang
m.

bough [bau] n Ast m.

boulder ['bouldə] n Felsbrocken m.

bounce [bauns] v (of ball) hochspringen;
(of cheque) platzen. **bounce around**
herumhüpfen. **bouncer** n (coll) Rausch-
meißer m.

bought [boːt] V buy.
bound¹ [baund] V bind.
bound² [baund] n (leap) Sprung m, Satz m. v springen.
bound³ [baund] n (limit) Grenze f. out of bounds betreten verboten!
bound⁴ [baund] adj bound for unterwegs nach. outward/homeward bound auf der Ausreise/Heimreise.
bound⁵ [baund] adj (obliged) verpflichtet. He is bound to win er wird bestimmt gewinnen.
boundary ['baundəri] n Grenze f.
bouquet [buːkei] n (flowers) Blumenstrauß m; (of wine) Blume f.
bourgeois ['buəʒwaː] adj bourgeois. n Bourgeois m. **bourgeoisie** n Bourgeoisie f.
bout [baut] n (of illness) Anfall m; (fight) Kampf m.
bow¹ [bau] v (lower head) sich verbeugen. n Verbeugung f.
bow² [bou] n (music, archery) Bogen m; (ribbon) Schleife f.
bow³ [bau] n (naut) Bug m.
bowels ['bauəlz] pl n Darm m sing; Eingeweide pl. open or move one's bowels sich entleeren.
bowl¹ [boul] n (basin) Schüssel f, Schale f.
bowl² [boul] v (ball) werfen. n Holzkugel f. bowls n Kegelspiel neut. play bowls kegeln.
box¹ [boks] n (container) Schachtel f, Kasten m; (theatre) Loge f; (court) Stand m.
box² [boks] v (sport) boxen. box someone's ears jemanden ohrfeigen. **boxer** n Boxer m. **boxing** n Boxen neut.
Boxing Day n zweiter Weihnachtsfeiertag m.
box office n (theatre) Kasse f.
boy [boi] n Junge m, Knabe m. **boyfriend** n Freund m. **boyhood** n Jugend f. **boyish** n knabenhaft.
boycott ['boikot] n Boykott m. v boykottieren.
bra [braː] n Büstenhalter m, BH m.
brace [breis] n Paar neut; (tech) Stütze f. v stützen. **braces** pl n Hosenträger pl.
bracelet ['breislit] n Armband neut.
bracing ['breisiŋ] adj erfrischend.
bracken ['brakən] n Farnkraut neut.
bracket ['brakit] n (parenthesis) Klammer f; (support) Träger m.

brag [brag] v prahlen, angeben. **braggart** n Prahler m.
braille [breil] n Blindenschrift f.
brain [brein] n Gehirn neut; Verstand m; Intelligenz f. **brainwashing** n Gehirnwäsche f. **brainwave** n Geistesblitz m. **brainy** adj klug.
braise [breiz] v schmoren.
brake [breik] n Bremse f. v bremsen. **brake pedal** Bremspedal neut.
bramble ['brambl] n (bush) Brombeerstrauch m; (berry) Brombeere f.
bran [bran] n (Weizen)Kleie f.
branch [braintʃ] n Zweig m; (of bank) Zweigstelle f; (department) Abteilung f. v branch off abzweigen.
brand [brand] n (of goods) Marke f; (cattle) Brandzeichen neut. v (name) brandmarken. **brand-new** adj nagelneu. **brand name** Markenname m.
brandish ['brandiʃ] v schwingen.
brandy ['brandi] n Weinbrand m.
brass [braːs] n Messing neut; (music) Blasinstrumente pl. adj Messing-.
brassiere ['brasiə] n Büstenhalter m.
brave [breiv] adj mutig, tapfer. v trotzen. **bravery** n Mut m, Tapferkeit f.
brawl [broːl] n Rauferei f. v raufen.
brawn [broːn] n Muskelkraft f; (cookery) Sülze f.
brazen ['breizn] adj (fig) unverschämt.
breach [briːtʃ] n Bruch m; (mil) Bresche f. v durchbrechen; (law) übertreten. **breach of contract** Vertragsbruch m. **breach of the peace** Friedensbruch m.
bread [bred] n Brot neut. v (cookery) panieren. **bread and butter** Butterbrot neut. **breadwinner** n Brotverdiener m.
breadth [bredθ] n Breite f, Weite f.
*break [breik] v brechen; (coll) kaputt machen; (law) übertreten; (promise) nicht halten; (day) anbrechen. n Bruch m; (gap) Lücke f; (rest) Pause f; (opportunity) Chance f. **break away** sich losreißen. **break down** (mot) eine Panne haben; (person) zusammenbrechen. **break in** (burgle) einbrechen; (animal) abrichten. **break out** ausbrechen. **break up** zerbrechen; (school) in die Ferien gehen.
breakable ['breikəbl] adj zerbrechlich.
breakage ['breikidʒ] n Bruchschaden m.
breakdown ['breikdaun] n (mot) Panne f. **nervous breakdown** Nervenzusammenbruch m.

breakfast ['brekfəst] n Frühstück neut. v frühstücken.

breakthrough ['breikθruː] n Durchbruch m.

breast [brest] n Brust f. Busen m. **breastbone** n Brustbein neut. **breast-stroke** n Brustschwimmen neut.

breath [breθ] n Atem m. **out of breath** außer Atem.

breathe [briːð] v atmen. **breathe in** einatmen. **breathe out** ausatmen.

bred [bred] V **breed**.

*breed [briːd] v (increase) sich vermehren; (animals) züchten; (fig) erzeugen. n (of dog) Rasse f. **breeding** n Zucht f; (education) Erziehung f.

breeze [briːz] n Brise f.

brew [bruː] v brauen. n Bräu neut. **brewery** n Brauerei f.

bribe [braib] v bestechen. n Bestechungsgeld neut. **bribery** n Bestechung f.

brick [brik] n Ziegelstein m. **bricklayer** n Maurer m.

bride [braid] n Braut f. **bridal** adj bräutlich, hochzeitlich. **bridegroom** n Bräutigam m. **bridesmaid** n Brautjungfer f.

bridge[1] [bridʒ] n Brücke f; (violin) Steg m. v überbrücken.

bridge[2] [bridʒ] n (card game) Bridge neut.

bridle ['braidl] n Zaum m.

brief [briːf] adj kurz. v instruieren. **briefcase** n Aktentasche f. **briefing** n Anweisung f. **briefly** adv kurz. **briefs** pl n Slip m sing.

brigade [bri'geid] n Brigade f. **brigadier** n Brigadegeneral m.

bright [brait] adj hell, leuchtend; (clever) klug. **brighten** v aufheitern. **brightness** n Glanz m (tech) Beleuchtungsstärke f.

brilliance ['briljəns] n Glanz m, Brillanz f. **brilliant** adj glänzend, brillant; (clever) scharfsinnig.

brim [brim] n Rand m; (hat) Krempe f.

brine [brain] n Salzwasser neut. **in brine** eingepökelt, Salz-.

*bring [briŋ] v bringen. **bring about** veranlassen. **bring along** mitbringen. **bring down** herunterbringen; (prices) herabsetzen. **bring up** (child) erziehen; (vomit) erbrechen.

brink [briŋk] n Rand m.

briquette [bri'ket] n Brikett m.

brisk [brisk] adj schnell, lebhaft.

bristle ['brisl] n Borste f.

Britain ['britn] n (Great Britain) Großbritannien neut. **British** adj britisch. **the British** die Briten. **Briton** Brite m, Britin f.

brittle ['britl] adj spröde.

broad [brɔːd] adj breit. **broadly** adv im allgemeinen.

broadcast ['brɔːdkɑːst] v übertragen. n Sendung f. **broadcasting** n Rundfunk m. **broadcasting corporation** n Rundfunkgesellschaft f.

brochure ['brəuʃuə] n Broschüre f.

broke [brəuk] V **break**. adj (coll) pleite.

broken ['brəukn] V **break**.

broker ['brəukə] n Makler m.

bronchitis [broŋ'kaitis] n Bronchitis f.

bronze [bronz] n Bronze f. adj aus Bronze, Bronze-; (colour) bronzefarben.

brooch [brəutʃ] n Brosche f.

brood [bruːd] n Brut f. v brüten. **broody** adj brütig.

brook [bruk] n Bach m.

broom [bruːm] n Besen m; (bot) Ginster m. **broomstick** n Besenstiehl m.

broth [broθ] n Brühe f.

brothel ['broθl] n Bordell neut.

brother ['brʌðə] n Bruder m. **Smith Bros.** Gebrüder Smith. **brothers and sisters** Geschwister pl. **brotherhood** n Bruderschaft f. **brother-in-law** n Schwager m. **brotherly** adj brüderlich.

brought [brɔːt] V **bring**.

brow [brau] n (forehead) Stirn f; (eyebrow) Augenbraue f; (of hill) Bergkuppe f.

brown [braun] adj braun. n Braun neut. v bräunen.

browse [brauz] v weiden; (in book) durchblättern.

bruise [bruːz] n blaue Flecke f, Quetschung f. v quetschen.

brunette [bruː'net] adj brünett. n Brünette f.

brush [brʌʃ] n Bürste f; (paintbrush) Pinsel m; (undergrowth) Unterholz neut. v bürsten. **brush past** vorbeistreichen.

brusque [brusk] adj brüsk.

Brussels ['brʌsəlz] n Brüssel neut. **Brussels sprouts** Rosenkohl m.

brute [bruːt] n Tier neut; (person) brutaler Mensch m. **brutal** adj brutal. **brutality** n Brutalität f.

bubble ['bʌbl] n Blase f. v sprudeln. **bubbly** adj sprudelnd.

buck¹ [bʌk] n Bock m; (US coll) Dollar m.

buck² [bʌk] v bocken. **buck up** (hurry) sich beeilen; (cheer up) munter werden.

bucket ['bʌkit] n Eimer m. **bucketful** n Eimervoll m.

buckle ['bʌkl] n Schnalle f. v anschnallen.

bud [bʌd] n Knospe f. v knospen. **nip in the bud** im Keim ersticken. **budding** adj angehend.

buddy ['bʌdi] n (coll) Kumpel m.

budge [bʌdʒ] v (sich) bewegen.

budgerigar ['bʌdʒərigaɪ] n Wellensittich m.

budget ['bʌdʒit] n Budget neut. v budgetieren.

buffalo ['bʌfəlou] n Büffel m; (bison) Bison m.

buffer ['bʌfə] n Puffer m.

buffet¹ ['bʌfit] n (blow) Schlag m. v stoßen.

buffet² ['bufei] n (meal) Büffett neut.

bug [bʌg] n Wanze f. v (coll) ärgern.

bugle ['bjuːgl] n Signalhorn neut.

*build [bild] v bauen. n Körperbau m. **build up** aufbauen. **builder** n Baumeister m. **building** n Gebäude neut, Haus neut. **built-in** adj eingebaut.

built [bilt] V build.

bulb [bʌlb] n (flower) Zwiebel f; (lamp) Glühbirne f. **bulbous** adj zwiebelförmig.

Bulgaria [bʌl'geəriə] n Bulgarien neut. **Bulgarian** adj bulgarisch. n Bulgare m. Bulgarin f.

bulge [bʌldʒ] v anschwellen. n Schwellung f. Ausbauchung f.

bulk [bʌlk] n Masse f; (greater part) Hauptteil m. **bulky** adj umfangreich.

bull [bul] n (cattle) Stier m; (animal) Bulle f; (coll: nonsense) Quatsch m. **bulldog** n Bulldogge m. **bulldozer** n Bulldozer m. **bullfight** n Stierkampf m.

bullet ['bulit] n (Gewehr)Kugel f.

bulletin ['bulatin] n Bulletin neut.

bullion ['buljən] n Gold-, Silberbarren pl.

bully ['buli] v einschüchtern. n Tyrann m.

bum [bʌm] n (tramp) Bummler m, Landstreicher m.

bump [bʌmp] v stoßen (gegen). n Stoß m; (on the head) Beule f. **bumper** n (of car) Stoßstange f. adj **bumper crop** Rekordernte f.

bun [bʌn] n (hair) Haarknoten m; (cake) Kuchen m; (bread roll) Brötchen neut.

bunch [bʌntʃ] n Bündel neut. **bunch of flowers** Blumenstrauß m. **bunch of grapes** Weintraube f. **bunch of keys** Schlüsselbund m.

bundle ['bʌndl] n Bündel neut. v zusammenbündeln.

bungalow ['bʌŋgəlou] n Bungalow m.

bungle ['bʌŋgl] v verpfuschen. **bungler** n Pfuscher.

bunion ['bʌnjən] n entzündeter Fußballen m.

bunk [bʌŋk] n Koje f.

bunker ['bʌŋkə] n Bunker m; (golf) Sandgrube f.

buoy [boi] n Boje f.

burden ['bəːdn] n Last f. v belasten.

bureau ['bjuərou] n Büro neut; (desk) Schreibtisch m.

bureaucracy [bju'rokrəsi] n Bürokratie f. **bureaucrat** n Bürokrat m. **bureaucratic** adj bürokratisch.

burglar ['bəːglə] n Einbrecher m. **burglary** n Einbruchsdiebstahl m.

burial ['beriəl] n Beerdigung f, Begräbnis neut.

*burn [bəːn] v brennen; (set alight) verbrennen. n Brandwunde f. **burn oneself** (or one's fingers) sich (die Finger) verbrennen.

burnt [bəːnt] V burn. adj (food) angebrannt.

burrow ['bʌrou] n (of rabbit) Bau m. v graben.

*burst [bəːst] v platzen. n (of shooting) Feuerstoß m; (of speed) Spurt m. **burst out laughing/crying** in Lachen/Tränen ausbrechen. **burst tyre** geplatzter Reifen m.

bury ['beri] v begraben; (one's hands, face) vergraben.

bus [bʌs] n Bus m, Autobus m. **bus driver** Busfahrer m. **bus conductor** Busschaffner m. **bus stop** Bushaltestelle f.

bush [buʃ] n Busch m. **bushy** adj buschig.

business ['biznis] n Geschäft neut. **that's none of your business** das geht dich nichts an. **businessman** n Geschäftsmann m. **businesswoman** n Geschäftsfrau f.

bust¹ [bʌst] n (breasts) Busen m; (sculpture) Büste f.

bust² [bʌst] (coll) adj (bankrupt) pleite; (broken) kaputt. v zerbrechen, kaputt machen.

bustle ['bʌsl] n Aufregung f. v **bustle about** herumsausen.

busy ['bizi] n (*occupied*) beschäftigt; (*hardworking*) fleißig; (*telephone*) besetzt. v **busy oneself with** sich beschäftigen mit.

but [bʌt] *conj* aber. *prep* außer. *adv* (*merely*) nur. **not only ... but also** nicht nur ... sondern auch. **nothing but** nichts als. **but for** ohne.

butane ['bjuːtein] n Butan *neut*.

butcher [butʃə] n Fleischer m, Metzger m. **butcher's shop** Metzgerei f, Fleischerei f.

butler ['bʌtlə] n Butler m.

butt[1] [bʌt] n (*thick end*) dickes Ende *neut*; (*of cigarette*) Stummel m.

butt[2] [bʌt] n (*of jokes*) Zielscheibe f.

butt[3] [bʌt] v (*with the head*) mit dem Kopf stoßen. n Kopfstoß.

butter ['bʌtə] n Butter f. v mit Butter bestreichen.

buttercup ['bʌtəkʌp] n Butterblume f.

butterfly ['bʌtəflai] n Schmetterling m.

buttocks ['bʌtəks] pl n Gesäß *neut sing*.

button ['bʌtn] n Knopf m. v (zu)knöpfen. **buttonhole** n Knopfloch *neut*.

buttress ['bʌtris] n Strebepfeiler m.

*buy [bai] v kaufen. **buy in** einkaufen. **buyer** n Käufer(in).

buzz [bʌz] v summen. n Summen *neut*. **buzzer** n Summer m.

by [bai] *prep* (*close to*) bei, neben; (*via*) über; (*past*) an ... vorbei; (*before*) bis; (*written by*) von. *adv* vorbei. **by day** bei tage. **by bus** mit dem Bus. **by that** (*mean, understand*) damit. **by and by** nach und nach. **by-election** Nachwahl f. **bypass** n Umgehungsstraße f. **by-product** n Nebenprodukt *neut*. **bystander** n Zuschauer m.

address Telegrammanschrift f. **cable railway** Drahtseilbahn f.

cackle ['kakl] v gackern. n Gegacker *neut*.

cactus ['kaktəs] n Kaktus m.

caddie ['kadi] n Golfjunge m.

cadence ['keidəns] n (*music*) Kadenz f. **cadenza** n Kadenz f.

cadet [kə'det] n Kadett m.

café ['kafei] n Café *neut*.

cafeteria [kafə'tiəriə] n Selbstbedienungsrestaurant *neut*.

caffeine ['kafiːn] n Koffein *neut*.

cage [keidʒ] n Käfig m. v in einen Käfig sperren.

cake [keik] n Kuchen m; (*soap*) Tafel f. v **be caked with mud** vor Schmutz starren.

calamine ['kaləmain] n Galmei m.

calamity [kə'laməti] n Unheil *neut*, Katastrophe f.

calcium ['kalsiəm] n Kalzium *neut*.

calculate ['kalkjuleit] v kalkulieren, berechnen. **calculating** *adj* berechnend. **calculation** n Berechnung f. **calculator** n (*mech*) Rechner m.

calendar ['kaləndə] n Kalender m.

calf[1] [kaːf] n (*young cow*) Kalb *neut*. **calfskin** n Kalbleder *neut*.

calf[2] [kaːf] n (*anat*) Wade f. **calf muscle** Wadenmuskel m.

calibre ['kalibə] n Kaliber *neut*.

call [koːl] v rufen; anrufen; (*a doctor*) holen; (*regard as*) halten für. n Ruf m; (*phone*) Anruf m; (*demand*) Aufforderung f. **call for** verlangen. **call off** (*cancel*) absagen. **callbox** n Telefonzelle f. **caller** n (*visitor*) Besucher m; (*phone*) Anrufer m. **calling** n Berufung f. **call-up** n Einberufung f.

callous ['kaləs] *adj* gefühllos, herzlos.

calm [kaːm] *adj* ruhig. n Ruhe, Stille f; (*naut*) Windstille f. v or **calm down** (sich) or beruhigen.

calorie ['kaləri] n Kalorie f.

came [keim] V come.

camel ['kaməl] n Kamel *neut*. **camelhair** n Kamelhaar m.

camera ['kamərə] n Kamera f, Fotoapparat m. **cameraman** n Kameramann m.

camouflage ['kaməflaːʒ] n Tarnung f; (*zool*) Schutzfärbung f. v tarnen.

camp [kamp] n Lager *neut*. v lagern; (*go camping*) campen, zelten. **camp bed** n Feldbett *neut*. **camper** n Camper m. **camping** n Camping *neut*. **camp site** n Campingplatz m.

C

cab [kab] n (*taxi*) Taxi *neut*; (*horse-drawn*) Droschke f; (*in truck*) Fahrerhaus *neut*.

cabaret ['kabərei] n Kabarett *neut*.

cabbage ['kabidʒ] n Kohl *neut*, Kraut *neut*.

cabin ['kabin] n Hütte f; (*naut*) Kabine f.

cabinet ['kabinit] n Schrank m; (*pol*) Kabinett *neut*. **cabinet-maker** n Möbeltischler m.

cable ['keibl] n (*elec, telegram*) Kabel *neut*; (*rope*) Tau *neut*, Seil *neut*. **cable**

campaign [kam'pein] n (mil, pol) Feldzug m; Kampagne f. v **campaign for** (fig) werben um, kämpfen für.

campus ['kampəs] n Universitätsgelände neut.

camshaft ['kamʃaɪft] n Nockenwelle f.

***can¹** [kan] v (be able) können; (be allowed, may) dürfen.

can² [kan] n (tin) Dose f, Büchse f. v konservieren.

Canada ['kanədə] n Kanada neut. **Canadian** adj kanadisch; n Kanadier(in).

canal [kə'nal] n Kanal m.

canary [kə'neəri] n Kanarienvogel m.

cancel ['kansəl] v (meeting) absagen; (arrangement) aufheben; (stamp) entwerten; (cross out) durchstreichen. **cancellation** n Absage f; Aufhebung f.

cancer ['kansə] n (med) Krebs m. **Cancer** (astrol) Krebs m. **breast cancer** Brustenkrebs m. **lung cancer** Lungenkrebs m.

candid ['kandid] adj offen, ehrlich.

candidate ['kandidət] n Kandidat m.

candle ['kandl] n Kerze f. **candle light** n Kerzenlicht neut. **candlestick** Leuchter m.

candour ['kandə] n Offenheit f; Ehrlichkeit f.

candy ['kandi] n Kandiszucker m; (US: sweet) Bonbon neut.

cane [kein] n (walking stick) Spazierstock m. **sugar cane** Zuckerrohr m. **cane sugar** Rohrzucker m.

canine ['keinain] adj Hunde-, Hunds-. **canine tooth** Eckzahn m.

canister ['kanistə] n Kanister m.

cannabis ['kanəbis] n Haschisch neut.

cannibal ['kanibəl] n Kannibale m.

cannon ['kanən] n Kanone f.

canoe [kə'nuː] n Kanu neut. v Kanu fahren.

canon ['kanən] n Domherr m; (rule) Kanon m.

can opener n Büchsenöffner m.

canopy ['kanəpi] n Baldachin m.

canteen [kan'tiːn] n (restaurant) Kantine f.

canter ['kantə] n Handgalopp m. v Handgalopp reiten.

canton ['kantən] n Kanton m.

canvas ['kanvəs] n Segeltuch neut; (artist's) Leinwand f.

canvass ['kanvəs] v werben.

canyon ['kanjən] n Cañon m, Schlucht f.

cap [kap] n (hat) Kappe f, Mütze f, (lid) Kappe f. v (fig) übertreffen.

capable ['keipəbl] adj (able to do something) fähig (zu); (skilled) begabt. **capability** n Fähigkeit f.

capacity [kə'pasəti] n (volume) Inhalt m; (of ship) Laderaum m; (talent) Talent m. **in the capacity of** als. **filled to capacity** voll (besetzt).

cape¹ [keip] n (cloak) Cape neut, Umhang m.

cape² [keip] n (geog) Kap neut.

caper¹ ['keipə] n Kapriole f. v kapriolen.

caper² ['keipə] n (cookery) Kaper f.

capital ['kapitl] n (city) Hauptstadt f; (comm) Kapital neut. adj (main) Haupt-; (comm) Kapital-; (splendid) großartig. **capitalism** n Kapitalismus m. **capitalist** n Kapitalist m. adj kapitalistisch. **capital punishment** Todesstrafe n.

capitulate [kə'pitjuleit] v kapitulieren (vor).

capricious [kə'priʃəs] adj launenhaft.

Capricorn ['kaprikoɪn] n Steinbock m.

capsize [kap'saiz] v kentern.

capsule ['kapsjuːl] n Kapsel f.

captain ['kaptin] n (mil) Hauptmann m; (naut) Kapitän m; (sport) Mannschaftsführer m. v (sport) führen.

caption ['kapʃən] n (picture) Erklärung f; (heading) Überschrift f.

captive ['kaptiv] n Gefangene(r). adj gefangen. **captivity** n Gefangenschaft f. **captor** n Fänger m.

capture ['kaptʃə] v gefangennehmen; (animal) einfangen. n Genangennahme f.

car [kaɪ] n (mot) Wagen m, Auto neut; (rail) Wagen m. **by car** mit dem Auto.

caramel ['karəmel] n Karamel m.

carat ['karət] n Karat neut.

caravan ['karəvan] n (mot) Wohnwagen m; (oriental) Karawane f.

caraway ['karəwei] n Kümmel m.

carbohydrate [kaɪbə'haidreit] n Kohlehydrat neut.

carbon ['kaɪbən] n Kohlenstoff m. **carbon copy** Durchschlag m. **carbon dioxide** Kohlendioxid neut; (in drinks) Kohlensäure f. **carbon paper** Kohlepapier neut.

carburettor ['kaɪbjuretə] **carburetor** n Vergaser m.

carcass ['kaɪkəs] n Kadaver m.

card [kaɪd] n Karte f. **cardboard** n Pappe f. **cardboard box** Pappschachtel f. **card**

game Kartenspiel *neut.* **card index** Kartei *f.*

cardiac ['kɑɪdiæk] *adj* Herz-.

cardigan ['kɑɪdigən] *n* Wolljacke *f.*

cardinal ['kɑɪdənl] *n* Kardinal *m. adj* grundsätzlich.

care [keə] *n (carefulness)* Sorgfalt *f; (looking after)* Pflege *f; (worry)* Sorge *f.* **take care** sich hüten; achtgeben. **take care of** *(look after)* pflegen; *(see to)* erledigen. **v care about** sich kümmern um. **care for** *(look after)* pflegen; *(see to)* sorgen für; *(like)* mögen. **carefree** *adj* sorgenfrei. **careful** *adj* sorgfältig; *(cautious)* vorsichtig. **carefulness** *n* Sorgfalt *f;* Vorsicht *f.* **careless** *adj* unachtsam, nachlässig. **carelessness** *n* Nachlässigkeit *f.*

career [kə'riə] *n* Laufbahn *f,* Karriere *f.*

caress [kə'res] *v* liebkosen. *n* Liebkosung *f;* Kuß *m.*

cargo ['kɑɪgou] *n* Fracht *f.* **cargo plane** Transportflugzeug *neut.* **cargo ship** Frachtschiff *neut.*

caricature ['kærikətjuə] *n* Karikatur *f. v* karikieren.

carnal ['kɑɪnl] *adj* fleischlich.

carnation [kɑɪ'neiʃən] *n* Nelke *f.*

carnival ['kɑɪnivəl] *n* Karneval *m,* Fasching *m.*

carnivorous [kɑɪ'nivərəs] *adj* fleischfressend.

carol ['kærəl] *n* Weihnachtslied *neut.*

carpenter ['kɑɪpəntə] *n* Zimmermann *m,* Tischler *m.* **carpentry** *n* Zimmerhandwerk *neut.*

carpet ['kɑɪpit] *n* Teppich *m. v* mit einem Teppich belegen.

carriage ['kæridʒ] *n (rail)* (Eisenbahn) Wagen *m; (transport)* Transport *f; (posture)* Haltung *f.* **carriageway** Fahrbahn *f.*

carrier ['kæriə] *n* Träger *m; (med)* Keimträger *m; (comm)* Spediteur *m.* **carrier bag** Tragebeutel *m.*

carrot ['kærət] *n* Mohrrübe *f,* Möhre *f.*

carry ['kæri] *v* tragen; *(transport)* befördern. **carry out** ausführen. **carry cot** Tragbettchen *neut.*

cart [kɑɪt] *n* Karren *m.*

cartilage ['kɑɪtilidʒ] *n* Knorpel *m.*

cartography [kɑɪ'tɒgrəfi] *n* Kartographie *f.*

carton ['kɑɪtən] *n* Karton *m.*

cartoon [kɑɪ'tuɪn] *n* Karikatur *f; (film)* Trickfilm *m.* **cartoonist** *n* Karikaturenzeichner *m.*

cartridge ['kɑɪtridʒ] *n* Patrone *f.* **cartridge paper** Zeichenpapier *neut.*

carve [kɑɪv] *v (in wood)* schnitzen; *(in stone)* meißeln; *(meat)* vorschneiden. **carving** *n* Schnitzerei *f.*

cascade [kas'keid] *n* Kaskade *f.*

case¹ [keis] *n (affair, instance)* Fall *m; (law)* Sache *f.* **in case** falls. **in case of** im Falle (+*gen*). **in any case** auf jeden Fall.

case² [keis] *n (suitcase)* Koffer *m; (for cigarettes, camera)* Etui *neut; (tech)* Gehäuse *neut.*

cash [kaʃ] *n* Bargeld *neut. v* einlösen. **cash on delivery** per Nachnahme. **pay cash** bar zahlen. **cash desk** Kasse *f.*

cashier [ka'ʃiə] *n* Kassierer(in).

cashmere [kaʃ'miə] *n* Kaschmir *m.*

casing ['keisiŋ] *n* Gehäuse *neut.*

casino [kə'siɪnou] *n* Kasino *neut.*

casket ['kɑɪskit] *n* Kästchen *neut; (coffin)* Sarg *m.*

casserole ['kæsəroul] *n (vessel)* Kasserolle *f; (meal)* Schmorbraten *m. v* schmoren.

cassette [kə'set] *n* Kassette *f.* **cassette recorder** Kassettenrecorder *m.*

cassock ['kæsək] *n* Soutane *f.*

*cast [kɑɪst] *v* werfen; *(metal)* gießen; *(theatre)* besetzen. *n (theatre)* Besetzung *f.*

caste [kɑɪst] *n* Kaste *f.*

castle ['kɑɪsl] *n* Burg *f,* Schloß *neut; (chess)* Turm *m. v (chess)* rochieren.

castor oil ['kɑɪstə] *n* Rizinusöl *neut.*

castrate [kə'streit] *v* kastrieren. **castration** *n* Kastration *f.*

casual ['kaʒuəl] *adj* beiläufig; *(careless)* nachlässig; *(informal)* leger. **casual labour** Gelegenheitsarbeit *f.*

casualty ['kaʒuəlti] *n* Verletzte(r). **casualties** *pl n (mil)* Ausfälle *pl.* **casualty department** Unfallstation *f.*

cat [kat] *n* Katze *f.* **tom cat** Kater *m.*

catalogue ['katəlɒg] *n* Katalog *m.*

catalyst ['katəlist] *n* Katalysator *m.*

catamaran [katəmə'ran] *n* Katamaran *neut.*

catapult ['katəpʌlt] *n* Katapult *neut.*

cataract ['katərakt] *n (med)* grauer Star *m;* Wasserfall *m.*

catarrh [kə'tɑɪ] *n* Katarrh *m.*

catastrophe [kə'tastrəfi] *n* Katastrophe *f.* **catastrophic** *adj* katastrophal.

*catch [katʃ] v fangen; (bus, train) nehmen, erreichen; (surprise) ertappen; (illness) sich zuziehen. n Fang m.

category ['katəgəri] n Kategorie f. **categorical** adj kategorisch.

cater ['keitə] v **cater for** versorgen. **catering** n Bewirtung f.

caterpillar ['katəpilə] n Raupe f. **caterpillar track** Gleiskette f.

cathedral [kə'θiːdrəl] n Dom m, Kathedrale f.

cathode ['kaθoud] n Kathode f.

catholic ['kaθəlik] adj (rel) katholisch; universal. n Katholik(in). **Roman Catholic** römisch-katholisch.

catkin ['katkin] n Kätzchen neut.

cattle ['katl] pl n Vieh neut sing, Rindvieh neut sing. **cattle shed** Viehstall m.

catty ['kati] adj (coll) gehässig.

caught [kɔːt] V catch.

cauliflower ['kɔliflauə] n Blumenkohl m.

cause [kɔːz] n Ursache f; (reason) Grund m; (interests) Sache f. v verursachen, veranlassen.

causeway ['kɔːzwei] n Damm m.

caustic ['kɔːstik] adj ätzend; (fig) beißend.

caution ['kɔːʃən] n Vorsicht f. v warnen (vor). **cautious** adj vorsichtig.

cavalry ['kavəlri] n Kavallerie f.

cave [keiv] n Höhle f. v **cave in** einstürzen. **cavern** n Höhle f.

caviar ['kaviaː] n Kaviar m.

cavity ['kavəti] n Hohlraum m; (in tooth) Loch neut.

cease [siːs] v aufhören; (fire) einstellen. **ceasefire** n Feuereinstellung f. **ceaseless** adj unaufhörlich.

cedar ['siːdə] n Zeder f.

ceiling ['siːliŋ] n Decke f; (fig) Höchstgrenze f.

celebrate ['seləbreit] v feiern. **celebrated** adj berühmt. **celebration** n Feier f. **celebrity** n Berühmtheit f.

celery ['seləri] n Sellerie m or f.

celestial [sə'lestiəl] adj himmlisch.

celibacy ['selibəsi] n Zölibat neut or m, Ehelosigkeit f. **celibate** adj ehelos.

cell [sel] n Zelle f.

cellar ['selə] n Keller m.

cello ['tʃelou] n Cello neut.

cellophane ['seləfein] n Zellophan neut.

cellular ['seljulə] adj zellular.

cement [sə'ment] n Zement m. v zementieren; (fig) binden.

cemetery ['semətri] n Friedhof m.

cenotaph ['senətaːf] n Ehrenmal m.

censor ['sensə] n Zensor m. v zensieren. **censorship** n Zensur f.

censure ['senʃə] n Tadel m. v tadeln.

census ['sensəs] n Volkszählung f.

cent [sent] n Cent m. **per cent** Prozent neut.

centenary [sen'tiːnəri] n Hundertjahrfeier f.

centigrade ['sentigreid] adv Celsius.

centimetre ['sentimiːtə] n Zentimeter neut.

centipede ['sentipiːd] n Tausendfuß m.

centre ['sentə] n Zentrum neut, Mittelpunkt m. adj Zentral-. v **centre around** sich drehen um. **centre on** sich konzentrieren auf. **centre forward** (sport) Mittelstürmer m. **centre half** Mittelläufer m. **centre of gravity** Schwerpunkt m. **centrepiece** n Tafelaufsatz m. **central** adj zentral, Zentral-. **Central America** Mittelamerika neut. **central heating** Zentralheizung f. **central station** Hauptbahnhof m.

centrifugal [sen'trifjugəl] adj zentrifugal. **centrifugal force** Zentrifugalkraft f.

century ['sentʃuri] n Jahrhundert neut.

ceramic [sə'ramik] adj keramisch. **ceramics** n Keramik f.

cereal ['siəriəl] n Getreide neut. **breakfast cereal** Getreideflocken pl.

ceremony ['serəməni] n Zeremonie f. **ceremonial** adj zeremoniell. **ceremonious** adj zeremoniös.

certain ['sɔːtn] adj bestimmt, gewiß; (sure) sicher. **for certain** bestimmt. **certainly** adv sicherlich, gewiß. **certainty** n Sicherheit f.

certificate [sə'tifikət] n Bescheinigung f. **certification** n Bescheinigung f. **certify** v bestätigen.

cervix ['sɔːviks] n (anat) Gebärmutterhals m.

cesspool ['sespuːl] n Senkgrube f.

chafe [tʃeif] v reiben.

chaffinch ['tʃafintʃ] n Buchfink m.

chain [tʃein] n Kette f. v anketten. **chain reaction** Kettenreaktion f. **chain smoker** Kettenraucher m. **chainstore** n Kettenladen m.

chair [tʃeə] n Stuhl m; (armchair) Sessel m; (at meeting) Vorsitz m. v (meeting) den Vorsitz führen. **chairlift** n Sesselbahn f. **chairman** Vorsitzende(r).

chalet ['ʃalei] n Chalet neut.

chalk [tʃɔːk] n Kreide f. v mit Kreide schreiben.

challenge ['tʃalindʒ] n Aufforderung f; (objection) Einwand m. v auffordern; (question) bestreiten. **challenger** n Herausforderer m.

chamber ['tʃeimbə] n Kammer f. **chamber music** Kammermusik f. **chamber pot** Nachttopf m.

chameleon [kəmiːliən] n Chamäleon m.

chamois ['ʃamwɑː] n Gemse f; (leather) Sämischleder neut.

champagne [ʃamˈpein] n Champagner m.

champion ['tʃampiən] n (sport) Meister m, Sieger m; (defender) Verfechter m. v (cause) verfechten. **championship** n Meisterschaft f.

chance [tʃɑːns] n Zufall m; (opportunity) Gelegenheit f; (possibility) Chance f, Möglichkeit f. v riskieren. **by chance** zufällig. **stand a chance** Chancen haben. **take a chance** sein Glück versuchen. **no chance!** keine Spur!

chancellor [tʃɑːnsələ] n Kanzler m.

chandelier [ʃandəˈliə] n Kronleuchter m.

change [tʃeindʒ] v (modify) (ab-, ver)ändern; (exchange) (aus)tauschen; (become changed) sich (ver)ändern; (trains) umsteigen; (clothes) sich umziehen; (money) wechseln. **change gear** schalten. **change into** (sich) verwandeln in. **change over to** übergehen zu. n (Ab-, Ver)Änderung f; (Ver)Wandlung f; (small change) Kleingeld neut. **change of life** Wechseljahre pl. **for a change** zur Abwechselung.

changeable adj veränderlich. **changeless** adj unveränderlich.

channel [tʃanl] n Kanal m; (fig) Weg m. v lenken. **through official channels** durch die Instanzen. **English Channel** der Ärmelkanal.

chant [tʃɑːnt] v intonieren. n Gesang m.

chaos ['keiɔs] n Chaos neut; (mess) Durcheinander neut.

chap¹ [tʃap] v (skin) rissig machen; (become chapped) aufspringen.

chap² [tʃap] n (coll) Kerl m.

chapel ['tʃapəl] n Kapelle f.

chaperon ['ʃapəroun] n Anstandsdame f. v begleiten.

chaplain ['tʃaplin] n Kaplan m.

chapter ['tʃaptə] n Kapitel neut; (branch) Ortsgruppe f.

char¹ [tʃɑː] v (burn) verkohlen.

char² [tʃɑː] n (cleaning lady) Putzfrau f.

character ['karəktə] n Charakter m; (personality) Persönlichkeit f; (theatre) Person f; (reputation) Ruf m; (letter) Buchstabe m. **characteristic** n Kennzeichen neut; adj charakteristisch. **characterize** v charakterisieren.

charcoal ['tʃɑːkoul] n Holzkohle f; (for drawing) Reißkohle f.

charge [tʃɑːdʒ] n (cost) Preis m; (firearm) Ladung f; (mil) Angriff m; (law) Anklage f; (elec) Ladung f. v (firearm, battery) laden; (price) verlangen; (attack) angreifen. **be in charge of** verantwortlich sein für. **bring a charge against** anklagen.

chariot ['tʃariət] n Streitwagen m.

charity ['tʃarəti] n Nächstenliebe f, Wohltätigkeit f; (organization) Wohlfahrtseinrichtung f. **charitable** adj wohltätig.

charm [tʃɑːm] n (personal) Scharm m, Reiz m; (magic word) Zauberwort neut; (trinket) Amulett neut. v entzücken. **charming** entzückend, scharmant.

chart [tʃɑːt] n (naut) Seekarte f; Diagramm neut.

charter ['tʃɑːtə] n Verfassungsurkunde f; (naut, aero) Charter m. v chartern. adj Charter-.

chase [tʃeis] v verfolgen, jagen. n Verfolgung f, Jagd f.

chasm ['kazm] n Abgrund m.

chassis ['ʃasi] n Fahrgestell neut.

chaste [tʃeist] adj keusch. **chastity** n Keuschheit f.

chastise [tʃasˈtaiz] v strafen.

chat [tʃat] v plaudern, sich unterhalten. n Plauderei f.

chatter ['tʃatə] v schnattern; (teeth) klappern. n Geschnatter neut; (teeth) Klappern neut.

chauffeur ['ʃoufə] n Chauffeur m.

chauvinism ['ʃouvinizəm] n Chauvinismus m. **chauvinist** n Chauvinist m.

cheap [tʃiːp] adj billig, preiswert; (base) gemein.

cheat [tʃiːt] v betrügen. n Betrüger m, Schwindler m.

check [tʃek] v (inspect) prüfen, kontrollieren; (hinder) (ver)hindern; (look up) nachsehen; (tick) abhaken. **check in** sich anmelden. **check out** (hotel) abreisen. n Kontrolle f; (bill) Rechnung f; (check) Scheck m; (chess) Schach m; (pattern) Karo neut. **checklist** n Kontrolliste f.

checkmate n Schachmatt neut. **checkpoint** Kontrollpunkt m. **check-up** n (med) ärztliche Untersuchung f.

cheek [tʃiːk] n (anat) Wange f. Backe f; (impudence) Frechheit f. **cheeky** adj frech.

cheer [tʃiə] v jubeln; (applaud) zujubeln (+ dat); (encourage) aufmuntern. **cheer up** aufmuntern. n Beifallsruf m, Hurra neut. **cheers!** interj prost! **cheerful** adj fröhlich. **cheerlo!** interj tschüs!

cheese [tʃiːz] n Käse f. **cheesecake** n Käsekuchen m; **cheesecloth** n Musselin m.

cheetah ['tʃiːtə] n Gepard m.

chef [ʃef] n Küchenchef m.

chemical ['kemikl] adj chemisch. **chemicals** pl n Chemikalien pl.

chemist ['kemist] n Chemiker m; (dispensing chemist) Apotheker m. **chemist's shop** Apotheke f.

chemistry ['kemistri] n Chemie f.

cheque [tʃek] n Scheck m. **chequebook** n Scheckbuch neut. **cheque card** Scheckkarte f.

cherish ['tʃeriʃ] v (feeling) hegen; (person) lieb haben.

cherry ['tʃeri] n Kirsche f; (tree) Kirschbaum m.

chess [tʃes] n Schach neut. **chessboard** n Schachbrett neut. **chessman** n Schachfigur f.

chest [tʃest] n (anat) Brust f; (container) Kiste f; (trunk) Truhe f. that's a weight off my chest da fällt mir ein Stein vom Herzen.

chestnut ['tʃesnʌt] n (sweet chestnut) (Eß)Kastanie f; (horse chestnut) (Roß)Kastanie f; (tree) Kastanienbaum m; (brown horse) Braune(r) m.

chew [tʃuː] v kauen. **chewing gum** Kaugummi m.

chick [tʃik] n Küken neut. **chicken** n Huhn neut; (for eating) Hähnchen neut. adj (coll) feige. **chicken soup** Hühnerbrühe f.

chicory ['tʃikəri] n Zichorie f; (salad plant) Chicorée f.

chief [tʃiːf] n (pl -s) Chef m, Leiter m; (of tribe) Häuptling m. adj Haupt-, erster. **chieftain** m Häuptling m.

chilblain ['tʃilblein] n Frostbeule f.

child [tʃaild] n (pl -ren) Kind neut. **with child** schwanger. **childbirth** n Entbindung

f. **childhood** n Kindheit f. **childish** adj kindisch. **childlike** adj kindlich.

Chile ['tʃili] n Chile neut. **Chilean** adj chilenisch. n Chilene m, Chilenin f.

chill [tʃil] n Kältegefühl neut; (fever) Schüttelfrost m. **chilled** adj (drink) gekühlt. **chilly** adj fröstelnd.

chilli ['tʃili] n Cayennepfeffer m.

chime [tʃaim] v (bell) läuten. n Geläut neut.

chimney ['tʃimni] n Schornstein m. **chimney sweep** Schornsteinfeger m.

chimpanzee [tʃimpən'ziː] n Schimpanse m.

chin [tʃin] n Kinn neut.

china ['tʃainə] n Porzellan neut. adj Porzellan-. **china clay** Kaolin neut.

China ['tʃainə] n China neut. **Chinese** adj chinesisch; n Chinese m, Chinesin f.

chink¹ [tʃink] n (fissure) Ritze f, Spalt m.

chink² [tʃink] n (sound) klirren. n Klirren neut.

chip [tʃip] n Splitter m. **chips** pl Pommes frites pl; (crisps) Chips pl. **chipped** adj (china) angestoßen.

chiropodist [ki'rɔpədist] n Fußpfleger(in). **chiropody** n Fußpflege f.

chirp [tʃəːp] v zirpen. n Gezirp neut. **chirpy** adj munter.

chisel ['tʃizl] n Meißel m. v meißeln.

chivalrous ['ʃivəlrəs] adj ritterlich. **chivalry** n Ritterlichkeit f.

chives [tʃaivz] pl n Schnittlauch m sing.

chlorine ['klɔːriːn] n Chlor neut. **chlorinate** v chlorieren.

chlorophyll ['klɔrəfil] n Chlorophyll neut.

chocolate ['tʃɔkələt] n Schokolade f. adj (colour) schokoladenbraun.

choice [tʃois] n Wahl f; (selection) Auswahl f. adj auserlesen.

choir ['kwaiə] n Chor m. **choirboy** Chorknabe m.

choke [tʃouk] v ersticken, würgen; (throttle) erwürgen. n (mot) Starterklappe f.

cholera ['kɔlərə] n Cholera f.

cholesterol [kə'lestərol] n Cholesterin neut.

choose [tʃuːz] v wählen; (select) auswählen; (prefer) vorziehen. **choosy** adj wählerisch.

chop¹ [tʃop] v (food) zerhacken; (wood) spalten. n Kotelett neut.

chop² [tʃop] v **chop and change** schwanken, wechseln.

chopsticks ['tʃopstiks] pl n Eßstäbchen pl.

chord [koːd] n (music) Akkord m.

chore [tʃoː] n lästige Pflicht f.

choreographer [kɔriˈɔgrəfə] n Choreograph m. **choreography** n Choreographie f.

chorus ['koːrəs] n Chor m; (of song) Refrain m.

chose [tʃouz] V choose.

chosen ['tʃouzn] V choose.

Christ [kraist] n Christus m.

christen ['krisn] v taufen. **christening** n Taufe f.

Christian ['kristʃən] adj christlich. n Christ m, Christin f. **Christian name** Vorname m. **Christianity** n Christentum neut.

Christmas ['krisməs] n Weihnachten pl. **Christmas card** Weihnachtskarte f. **Christmas present** Weihnachtsgeschenk neut. **Christmas tree** Weihnachtsbaum m.

chrome [kroum] n (plating) Verchromung f. adj (yellow) chromgelb. **chrome-plated** adj verchromt.

chromium ['kroumiəm] n Chrom neut.

chronic ['kronik] adj (med) chronisch.

chronicle ['kronikl] n Chronik f.

chronological [krɔnəˈlodʒikəl] adj chronologisch.

chrysalis ['krisəlis] n Puppe f.

chrysanthemum [kriˈsanθəməm] n Chrysantheme f.

chubby ['tʃʌbi] adj pausbäckig.

chuck [tʃʌk] v (coll) werfen.

chuckle ['tʃʌkl] v glucksen, kichern. n Kichern neut.

chunk [tʃʌŋk] n Klumpen m, Stück neut.

church [tʃəːtʃ] n Kirche f. **church-goer** n Kirchgänger m. **churchyard** n Kirchhof m.

churn [tʃəːn] n (butter) Butterfaß neut; (milk) Milchkanne f. v (fig) aufwühlen.

chute [ʃuːt] n Rutsche f.

cider ['saidə] n Apfelwein m.

cigar [siˈgaː] n Zigarre f.

cigarette [sigəˈret] n Zigarette f. **cigarette end** Zigarettenstümmel m. **cigarette lighter** n Feuerzeug neut.

cinder ['sində] n Zinder m.

cine camera ['sini] n Filmkamera f.

cinema ['sinəmə] n Kino neut.

cinnamon ['sinəmən] n Zimt m.

circle ['səːkl] n Kreis m; (theatre) Rang m. v umkreisen. **circular** adj kreisförmig,

rund. **circulate** v zirkulieren, umlaufen; (send round) in Umlauf setzen. **circulation** n Umlauf m; (blood) Kreislauf m.

circuit ['səːkit] n Umlauf m; (elec) Stromkreis m.

circumcise ['səːkəmsaiz] n beschneiden. **circumcision** n Beschneidung f.

circumference [səˈkʌmfərəns] n Umfang m.

circumscribe ['səːkəmskraib] v umschreiben.

circumstance ['səːkəmstans] n Umstand m. **under the circumstances** unter diesen Umständen. **under no circumstances** auf keinen Fall.

circus ['səːkəs] n Zirkus m.

cistern ['sistən] n Zisterne f.

cite [sait] v zitieren.

citizen ['sitizn] n Bürger(in); (of country) Staatsangehörige(r). **citizenship** n Staatsangehörigkeit f.

citrus ['sitrəs] adj **citrus fruit** Zitrusfrucht f.

city ['siti] n Stadt f.

civic ['sivik] n städtisch.

civil ['sivl] adj (polite) höflich, freundlich; (not military) Zivil-. **civility** n Höflichkeit f. **civil engineer** Bauingenieur m. **civil rights** Bürgerrechte pl.

civilian [səˈviljən] adj Zivil-. n Zivilist m.

civilization [ˌsivilaiˈzeiʃən] n Zivilisation f. **civilize** v zivilisieren. **civilized** adj zivilisiert.

clad [klad] adj bekleidet; (tech) umkleidet.

claim [kleim] v verlangen, Anspruch erheben auf. n Anspruch m; (right) Anrecht neut. **claimant** n Antragsteller m.

clairvoyant [kleəˈvoiənt] n Hellseher(in).

clam [klam] n Muschel f.

clamber ['klambə] v klettern.

clammy ['klami] adj feucht, klebrig.

clamour ['klamə] n Geschrei neut. v **clamour for** rufen nach.

clamp [klamp] n Klammer f, Krampe f. v verklammern. **clamp down on** unterdrücken.

clan [klan] n Sippe f.

clandestine [klanˈdestin] adj heimlich.

clang [klaŋ] n Schall m, Klirren neut. v schallen, klirren.

clank [klaŋk] n Gerassel neut; Klappern neut. v rasseln, klappern.

clap [klap] v (*applaud*) klatschen, Beifall spenden (+ dat); (*hit*) schlagen, klapsen. n (*tap*) Klaps m. **clapper** n (*bell*) Klöppel m. **clapping** n Klatschen neut.

claret ['klarət] n Rotwein m, Bordeaux m.

clarify ['klarəfai] v klären. **clarification** n Klärung f.

clarinet [klarə'net] n Klarinette f. **clarinettist** n Klarinettist m.

clash [klaʃ] v kollidieren, zusammenprallen; (*argue*) sich streiten; (*colours*) nicht zusammenpassen. n Knall m; (*conflict*) Konflikt m.

clasp [klaːsp] v umklammern; n Haspe f, Klammer f.

class [klaːs] n Klasse f; (*lesson*) Stunde f. v klassieren. **class-conscious** adj klassenbewußt. **classroom** n Klassenzimmer f. **classy** adj (*coll*) klasse, erstklassig.

classic ['klasik] adj klassisch. **classics** pl n die alten Sprachen pl. **classical** adj klassisch. **classicism** n Klassik f.

classify ['klasifai] v klassifizieren. **classification** n Klassifizierung f.

clatter ['klatə] v klappern. n Klappern neut.

clause [klɔːz] n (in *document*) Klausel f.

claustrophobia [klɔːstrə'foubiə] n Platzangst f.

claw [klɔː] n Kralle f, Klaue f. v zerkratzen.

clay [klei] n Lehm m, Ton m.

clean [kliːn] adj rein, sauber; (*paper*) weiß. adv ganz. v reinigen, putzen, saubermachen. **clean up** aufräumen. **come clean** gestehen. **cleaner** n (*woman*) Putzfrau f. **cleaning** n Reinigen neut. **cleanness** n Sauberkeit f. **cleanly** adj reinlich. **clean-shaven** adj glattrasiert.

cleanse [klenz] v reinigen.

clear [kliə] adj klar; (*sound, meaning*) deutlich, klar; (*road, way*) frei; (*glass*) durchsichtig. v räumen; (*table*) abräumen; (*road*) freimachen; (*forest*) roden; (*authorize*) freigeben. **clearance** n Räumung f; (*authorization*) Freigabe f; (*tech*) Spielraum m. **clearcut** adj (*fig*) eindeutig. **clearing** n Lichtung f. **clearly** adv offensichtlich.

clef [klef] n Notenschlüssel m.

clench [klentʃ] v (*fist*) zusammenballen.

clergy ['klɔːdʒi] n Klerus m. **clergyman** n Geistliche(r) m; Kleriker m.

clerical ['klerikəl] adj geistlich. **clerical work** Büroarbeit f.

clerk [klaːk] n Büroangestellte(r); (*sales clerk*) Verkäufer(in).

clever ['klevə] adj klug, gescheit; (*crafty*) raffiniert. **cleverness** n Klugheit f.

cliché ['kliːʃei] n Klischee neut.

click [klik] n Klicken neut. v klicken.

client ['klaiənt] n Kunde m, Kundin f. **clientele** n Kundschaft f.

cliff [klif] n Klippe f.

climate ['klaimət] n Klima neut.

climax ['klaimaks] n Höhepunkt m.

climb [klaim] v klettern; (*ascend*) steigen; (*mountain*) besteigen. n Aufstieg m. **climb up** hinaufklettern auf. **climb down** hinabsteigen. **climber** n (*mountaineer*) Bergsteiger m. **climbing** n (*mountaineering*) Bergsteigen neut.

***cling** [kliŋ] v sich klammern (an); (*fig*) hängen (an).

clinic ['klinik] n Klinik f. **clinical** adj klinisch.

clink [kliŋk] n Klirren neut. v klirren.

clip¹ [klip] v (*hair*) schneiden; (*dog*) scheren; (*ticket*) knipsen. **clipping** n (*newspaper*) Zeitungsausschnitt m.

clip² [klip] n (*fastener*) Klammer f, Klemme f. v **clip together** zusammenklammern.

clitoris ['klitəris] n Kitzler m, Klitoris f.

cloak [klouk] n Umhang m. **cloakroom** n Garderobe f; (*WC*) Toilette f.

clock [klok] n Uhr f. **clockwise** adj, adv im Uhrzeigersinn. **clockwork** n Uhrwerk neut.

clog [klog] n Holzschuh m. v verstopfen.

cloister ['klɔistə] n Kreuzgang m.

close¹ [klouz] v zumachen, schließen. n Ende neut; Schluß m. **close down** eingehen. **closed** adj (*shop*) geschlossen; (*road*) gesperrt.

close² [klous] adj nahe; (*intimate*) vertraut; (*careful*) genau; (*weather*) schwül. adv knapp. **close to** in der Nähe (+ gen or von). **close together** dicht zusammen. *that was close!* das war knapp! **closely** adv genau, gründlich. **close-up** n Nahaufnahme f.

closet ['klozit] n Schrank m.

clot [klot] n Klümpchen neut; (*of blood*) Blutgerinnsel neut. v gerinnen.

cloth [kloθ] n (*material*) Stoff m, Tuch neut; (*for wiping*) Lappen m.

clothe [klouð] v (be)kleiden. **clothes** pl n Kleider pl. **clothes brush** Kleiderbürste f.

clothes line Wäscheleine f. **clothes peg** Wäscheklammer f. **clothing** n Kleidung f.

cloud [klaud] n Wolke f. **cloud over** sich bewölken.

clove[1] [klouv] n (spice) Gewürznelke f.

clove[2] [klouv] n **clove of garlic** Knoblauchzehe f.

clover ['klouvə] n Klee m.

clown [klaun] n Clown m.

club [klʌb] n (association) Klub m, Verein m; (weapon) Keule f; (golf) Golfschläger m. **clubfoot** n Klumpfuß m.

clue [kluː] n Spur f, Anhaltspunkt m. **I haven't a clue** ich habe keine Ahnung f.

clump [klʌmp] n Klumpen neut; (of bushes) Gebüsch neut.

clumsy ['klʌmzi] adj unbeholfen, linkisch.

clung [klʌŋ] V cling.

cluster ['klʌstə] n Traube f. v **cluster around** schwärmen um.

clutch [klʌtʃ] n (fester) Griff m; (mot) Kupplung f. v sich festklammern an. **clutch at** greifen nach.

clutter ['klʌtə] n Unordnung f, Durcheinander neut. v vollstopfen.

coach [koutʃ] n Kutsche f; (rail) Wagen m; (sport) Trainer m. v eintrainieren.

coagulate [kou'agjuleit] v gerinnen.

coal [koul] n Kohle f. **coal-mine** n Kohlenbergwerk neut.

coalition [kouə'liʃən] n (pol) Koalition f.

coarse [koːs] adj grob; (vulgar) ordinär.

coast [koust] n Küste f. **coastal** adj Küsten-. **coastline** n Küstenlinie f.

coat [kout] n Mantel m; (of animal) Fell neut, Pelz m; (of paint) Anstrich m. v bestreichen. **coated** adj überzogen. **coathanger** n Kleiderbügel m. **coating** n Überzug m.

coax [kouks] v beschwatzen.

cobbler ['koblə] n Schuster m.

cobra ['koubrə] n Kobra neut.

cobweb ['kobweb] n Spinngewebe neut.

cocaine [kə'kein] n Kokain neut.

cock[1] [kok] n (male chicken) Hahn m; (male bird) (Vogel)Männchen neut.

cock[2] [kok] v (gun) spannen; (ears) spitzen.

cockle ['kokl] n (shellfish) Herzmuschel f.

cockpit ['kokpit] n Kanzel f, Kabine f.

cockroach ['kokroutʃ] n Küchenschabe f.

cocktail ['kokteil] n Cocktail neut.

cocoa ['koukou] n Kakao m.

coconut ['koukənʌt] n Kokosnuß f.

cocoon [kə'kuːn] n Kokon m, Puppe f.

cod [kod] n Kabeljau m.

code [koud] n Kode m.

codeine ['koudiːn] n Kodein neut.

coeducation [kouedju'keiʃən] n Gemeinschaftserziehung f.

coerce [kou'əːs] v zwingen. **coercion** n Zwang m.

coexist [kouig'zist] v koexistieren. **coexistence** n Koexistenz f.

coffee ['kofi] n Kaffee m. **coffee bar** Café neut.

coffin ['kofin] n Sarg m.

cog [kog] n Radzahn neut. **cogwheel** Zahnrad neut.

cognac ['konjak] n Kognak m.

cohabit [kou'habit] v (ehelich) zusammenwohnen.

coherent [kou'hiərənt] adj zusammenhängend.

coil [koil] n Rolle f; v aufwickeln.

coin [koin] n Münze f. v prägen. **coinbox** n (phone) Münzfernsprecher m.

coincide [kouin'said] v zusammenfallen; (agree) übereinstimmen. **coincidence** n Zufall m. **coincidental** zufällig.

colander ['koləndə] n Durchschlag m.

cold [kould] adj kalt. **I am/feel cold** mir ist kalt. n Kälte f; (med) Erkältung f. **catch cold** sich erkälten. **in cold blood** kaltblütig. **coldly** adv (fig) gefühllos, unfreundlich. **cold store** Kühlhaus neut.

coleslaw ['koulsloː] n Krautsalat m.

colic ['kolik] n Kolik f.

collaborate [kə'labəreit] v zusammenarbeiten. **collaboration** n zusammenarbeit f. **collaborator** n Mitarbeiter m; (in war) Kollaborateur m.

collapse [kə'laps] v einstürzen; (person) zusammenbrechen. n Einsturz m; (fig, med) Zusammenbruch m. **collapsible** adj zusammenklappbar.

collar ['kolə] n Kragen m; (for dog) Halsband m. **collarbone** n Schlüsselbein neut.

colleague ['koliːg] n Kollege m, Kollegin f.

collect [kə'lekt] v sammeln; (fetch) abholen; (taxes) eignnehmen; (come together) zusammenkommen. **collect call** (phone) R-Gespräch neut. **collected** adj (calm) gefaßt. **collection** n Sammlung f; (rel) Kollekte f; (mail) Leerung f. **collective** adj kollektiv. **collective bargaining** Tarifverhandlungen pl. **collector** n Sammler m; (of taxes) Einnehmer m.

college ['kɔlidʒ] n Hochschule f; (at Oxford, etc.) College neut. **technical college** Realschule f.

collide [kə'laid] v kollidieren, zusammenprallen.

colloquial [kə'loukwiəl] adj umgangssprachlich.

Cologne [kə'loun] n Köln neut. **eau de Cologne** Kölnischwasser neut.

colon ['koulən] n (anat) Dickdarm m; (gram) Doppelpunkt m.

colonel ['kə:nl] n Oberst m.

colony ['kɔləni] n Kolonie f. **colonial** adj Kolonial-. **colonialism** Kolonialismus m. **colonize** v kolonisieren.

colossal [kə'lɔsəl] adj kolossal, riesig.

colour ['kʌlə] n Farbe f; (fig) Ton m, Charakter m. **colours** pl Fahne f sing. v färben (also fig), kolorieren. **colour bar** Rassenschranke f. **colour-blind** adj farbenblind. **coloured** adj farbig. **coloured man/woman** Farbige(r). **colour film** Farbfilm m. **colourful** adj farbig, bunt. **colour television** Farbfernsehen neut.

colt [koult] n Fohlen neut.

column ['kɔləm] n Säule f; (in newspaper) Spalte f; (mil) Kolonne f. **columnist** n Kolumnist m.

coma ['koumə] n Koma f.

comb [koum] n Kamm m. v kämmen; (fig) durchkämmen.

combat ['kɔmbat] v bekämpfen. n Kampf m, Gefecht neut.

combine [kəm'bain] v (join) n 'kɔmbain] v vereinigen, verbinden; (come together) sich vereinigen. n Konzern m. **combine harvester** Mähdrescher m.

combustion [kəm'bʌstʃən] n Verbrennung f. **combustible** adj brennbar.

*come [kʌm] v kommen. **come about** geschehen. **come across** stoßen auf. **come back** zurückkommen. **come from** herkommen von stammen aus. **come near** sich nähern. **come on** weiterkommen; (make progress) fortschreiten. **come on!** los!; weiter! **come out** herauskommen. **come through** durchkommen. **come to** (arrive at) ankommen an, gelangen an; (amount to) sich belaufen auf; (regain consciousness) zu sich kommen. **comeback** n Comeback neut.

comedy ['kɔmədi] n Komödie f. **comedian** n Komiker m.

comet ['kɔmit] n Komet m.

comfort ['kʌmfət] n Bequemlichkeit f. Komfort m; (solace) Trost m. v trösten. **comfortable** adj bequem; (room, etc.) komfortabel.

comic ['kɔmik] adj komisch, lustig; (theatre) Komödien-. n (person) Komiker m; (paper) Comic neut. **comical** adj komisch.

comma ['kɔmə] n Komma neut.

command [kə'maind] n (order) Befehl m; (mil) Oberbefehl m; (mastery) Beherrschung f. v (instruct) befehlen; (be in charge of) kommandieren. **commander** n Befehlshaber m; (mil) Kommandant m. **commandment** n Gebot neut. **commando** n Kommando neut.

commemorate [kə'meməreit] v gedenken (+gen), feiern. **commemoration** n Gedächtnisfeier f.

commence [kə'mens] v beginnen, anfangen. **commencement** n Beginn m, Anfang m.

commend [kə'mend] v (praise) loben; (entrust) anvertrauen. **commendable** adj lobenswert.

comment ['kɔment] n (remark) Bemerkung f; (annotation) Anmerkung f. v kommentieren, Bemerkungen machen. **commentary** n Reportage f. **commentator** n Kommentator m.

commerce ['kɔmə:s] n Handel m, Kommerz m. **commercial** adj kommerziell, geschäftlich, Handels-. **commercialize** v kommerzialisieren.

commiserate [kə'mizəreit] v **commiserate with** bemitleiden.

commission [kə'miʃən] n Auftrag m; (committee) Kommission f; (fee) Provision f; (mil) Offizierspatent neut. v (person) beauftragen; (thing) bestellen. **commissioner** n Bevollmächtigte(r).

commit [kə'mit] v (offence) begehen. **commit oneself** sich verpflichten. **commitment** n Verpflichtung f.

committee [kə'miti] n Ausschuß m, Kommission f.

commodity [kə'mɔditi] n Ware f. **commodities** pl Grundstoffe pl.

common ['kɔmən] adj gemein, gemeinsam; (abundant) weit verbreitet; (vulgar) gemein, ordinär. **Common Market** Gemeinsamer Markt m. **commonplace** adj alltäglich. **commonsense** n gesunder Menschenverstand m.

commotion [kə'mouʃən] *n* Erregung *f*, Aufruhr *m*.

commune ['kɔmjuːn] *n* Kommune *f*, Gemeinschaft *f*.

communicate [kə'mjuːnikeit] *v* mitteilen; (*illness*) übertragen. **communicative** *adj* gesprächig. **communication** *n* Kommunikation *f*; (*message*) Mitteilung *f*. **communications** *pl n* Verkehrswege *pl*.

communism ['kɔmjunizəm] *n* Kommunismus *m*. **communist** *adj* kommunistisch. *n* Kommunist(in).

community [kə'mjuːnəti] *n* Gemeinschaft *f*.

commute [kə'mjuːt] *v* (*travel*) pendeln; (*a sentence*) herabsetzen. **commuter** *n* Pendler *m*.

compact[1] [kəm'pakt] *adj* kompakt, dicht.

compact[2] ['kɔmpakt] *n* (*agreement*) Vertrag *m*, Pakt *m*.

companion [kəm'panjən] *n* Begleiter(in); Genosse *m*, Genossin *f*. **companionable** *adj* gesellig. **companionship** *n* Gesellschaft *f*.

company ['kʌmpəni] *n* Gesellschaft *f*; (*firm*) Gesellschaft *f*, Firma *f*; (*theatre*) Truppe *f*; (*mil*) Kompanie *f*.

compare [kəm'peə] *v* vergleichen; (*match up to*) sich vergleichen lassen. **comparable** *adj* vergleichbar. **comparative** *adj* relativ; (*gram*) steigernd. **comparatively** *adv* verhältnismäßig. **comparison** *n* Vergleich *m*. **in comparison with** im Vergleich zu.

compartment [kəm'paːtmənt] *n* Abteilung *f*.

compass ['kʌmpəs] *n* Kompaß *m*. **pair of compasses** Zirkel *m*.

compassion [kəm'paʃən] *n* Mitleid *neut*. **compassionate** *adj* mitleidig.

compatible [kəm'patəbl] *adj* vereinbar.

compel [kəm'pel] *v* zwingen.

compensate ['kɔmpənseit] *v* (*money*) entschädigen; (*balance out*) ausgleichen. **compensation** *n* Entschädigung *f*; Ausgleich *m*.

compete [kəm'piːt] *v* konkurrieren, sich bewerben; (*take part*) teilnehmen. **competition** *n* Wettbewerb *m*; (*comm*) Konkurrenz *f*. **competitive** *adj* konkurrenzfähig. **competitor** *n* (*sport*) Teilnehmer(in); (*comm*) Konkurrent(in).

compile [kəm'pail] *v* kompilieren.

complacent [kəm'pleisnt] *adj* selbstzufrieden.

complain [kəm'plein] *v* klagen. **complain about/to** sich beschweren über/bei. **complaint** *n* Klage *f*, Beschwerde *f*.

complement ['kɔmpləmənt] *n* Ergänzung *f*. *v* ergänzen; (*go together*) zusammenpassen. **complementary** *adj* komplementär.

complete [kəm'pliːt] *v* vollenden, vervollständigen; (*form*) ausfüllen. *adj* vollständig, vollendet. **completely** *adv* völlig, vollständig, ganz und gar. **completion** *n* Vollendung *f*.

complex ['kɔmpleks] *adj* kompliziert. *n* (*psychol*) Komplex *m*.

complexion [kəm'plekʃən] *n* Teint *m*.

complicate ['kɔmplikeit] *v* verwickeln, komplizieren. **complicated** *adj* kompliziert. **complication** *n* Komplikation *f*, Schwierigkeit *f*.

compliment ['kɔmpləmənt] *n* Kompliment *neut*. *v* komplimentieren. **complimentary** *adj* höflich, artig. **complimentary ticket** Freikarte *f*.

comply [kəm'plai] *v* sich fügen. **comply with** (*rules*) sich halten an; (*request*) erfüllen.

component [kəm'pounənt] *n* Bestandteil *m*.

compose [kəm'pouz] *v* komponieren. **composed** *adj* gefaßt. **be composed of** bestehen aus. **composer** *n* Komponist *m*. **composite** *adj* zusammengesetzt. **composition** *n* Komposition *f*; (*piece of music*) (Musik)Stück *neut*.

compost ['kɔmpost] *n* Kompost *m*.

composure [kəm'pouʒə] *n* Gefaßtheit *f*.

compound [kəm'paund] *n* Zusammensetzung *f*; (*chem*) Verbindung *f*; *adj* zusammengesetzt, gemischt.

comprehend [kɔmpri'hend] *v* verstehen, begreifen. **comprehensible** *adj* verständlich. **comprehension** *n* Verständnis.

comprehensive [ˌkɔmpri'hensiv] *adj* umfassend. **comprehensive school** *n* Gesamtschule *f*.

compress [kəm'pres; *n* 'kɔmpres] *v* verdichten, zusammendrücken. *n* (*med*) Kompresse *f*. **compressed** *adj* zusammengedrückt. **compressed air** Preßluft *f*. **compression** *n* Verdichtung *f*. **compressor** *n* Verdichter *m*.

comprise [kəm'praiz] *v* bestehen aus.

compromise ['kɔmprəmaiz] *n* Kompromiß *m or neut*. *v* einen Kompromiß schließen; (*expose*) kompromittieren.

compulsion [kəmˈpʌlʃən] n Zwang m. **compulsive** adj Zwangs-. **compulsory** adj Zwangs-.

compunction [kəmˈpʌŋkʃən] n Gewissensbisse pl, Reue f.

computer [kəmˈpjuːtə] n Computer m.

comrade [ˈkɒmrid] n Genosse m, Genossin f; Kamerad(in). **comradeship** n Kameradschaft f.

concave [kɒnˈkeiv] adj konkav, Hohl-.

conceal [kənˈsiːl] v verbergen, verstecken; (fact, etc.) verschweigen.

concede [kənˈsiːd] v zugeben, einräumen; (right) bewilligen.

conceit [kənˈsiːt] n Einbildung f, Eitelkeit f. **conceited** adj eingebildet.

conceive [kənˈsiːv] v (plan) erdenken; (child) empfangen; (thoughts) fassen. **conceive of** sich vorstellen (+acc). **conceivable** adj denkbar, vorstellbar.

concentrate [ˈkɒnsəntreit] v konzentrieren. **concentrate on** sich konzentrieren auf. **concentrated** adj konzentriert. **concentration** n Konzentration f.

concentric [kənˈsentrik] adj konzentrisch.

concept [ˈkɒnsept] n Begriff m, Idee f. **conception** n Vorstellung f; (of child) Empfängnis f.

concern [kənˈsəːn] v betreffen, angehen; (worry) beunruhigen. n (worry) Besorgnis f, Sorge f; (interest) Interesse neut; (comm) Betrieb m. **concern oneself with** sich befassen mit. **as far as I am concerned** von mir aus. **that's not your concern!** das geht Sie nichts an! **concerning** adj betreffend.

concert [ˈkɒnsət] n Konzert neut.

concerted [kənˈsəːtid] adj konzertiert.

concerto [kənˈtʃəːtou] n Konzert neut.

concession [kənˈseʃən] n Konzession f. **concessionaire** n Konzessionär m.

conciliate [kənˈsilieit] v versöhnen. **conciliation** n Versöhnung f. **conciliatory** adj versöhnlich.

concise [kənˈsais] adj kurz, knapp.

conclude [kənˈkluːd] v schließen. **conclude that** den Schluß ziehen, daß. **conclusive** adj (evidence) schlüssig.

concoct [kənˈkɒkt] v zusammenbrauen.

concrete [ˈkɒŋkriːt] adj konkret; (made of concrete) Beton-. n Beton m.

concussion [kənˈkʌʃən] n (med) Gehirnerschütterung f.

condemn [kənˈdem] v verurteilen. **condemnation** n Verurteilung f.

condense [kənˈdens] v kondensieren. **condensation** n Kondensation f. **condensed milk** Kondensmilch f.

condescend [kɒndiˈsend] v sich herablassen. **condescending** adj herablassend. **condescension** n Herablassung f.

condition [kənˈdiʃən] n (state) Zustand m; (requirement) Bedingung f, Voraussetzung f. **conditions** pl. on condition that unter der Bedingung, daß. **out of condition** (sport) in schlechter Form. **conditional** adj bedingt.

condolence [kənˈdouləns] n Beileid neut.

condom [ˈkɒndom] n Kondom neut.

condone [kənˈdoun] v verzeihen.

conducive [kənˈdjuːsiv] adj förderlich.

conduct [kənˈdʌkt; n ˈkɒndʌkt] v führen; (orchestra) dirigieren; (elec) leiten. **conduct oneself** sich verhalten. n Führung f; (behaviour) Verhalten neut.

conductor [kənˈdʌktə] n (music) Dirigent m; (bus) Schaffner(in).

cone [koun] n (shape) Kegel m; (ice cream) Waffeltüte f; (bot) Zapfen m.

confectioner [kənˈfekʃənə] n Süßwarenhändler m. **confectionery** n Süßwaren pl.

confederation [kənˌfedəˈreiʃən] n Bund m.

confer [kənˈfəː] v (bestow) verleihen; (discuss) konferieren. **conference** n Konferenz f.

confess [kənˈfes] v bekennen, gestehen; (rel) beichten. **confession** n Geständnis neut; (rel) Beichte f. **confessional** n Beichtstuhl m.

confetti [kənˈfeti] n Konfetti pl.

confide [kənˈfaid] v anvertrauen. **confide in** vertrauen (+dat). **confidence** n Vertrauen neut; (in oneself) Selbstvertrauen neut. **confident** adj zuversichtlich; selbstsicher. **confidential** adj vertraulich.

confine [kənˈfain] v (limit) beschränken; (lock up) einsperren. **confinement** n (in prison) Haft f; (childbirth) Niederkunft f.

confirm [kənˈfəːm] v bestätigen; (rel) konfirmieren. **confirmation** n Bestätigung f; Konfirmation f.

confiscate [ˈkɒnfiskeit] v beschlagnahmen. **confiscation** n Beschlagnahme f.

conflict [ˈkɒnflikt; v kənˈflikt] n Konflikt m, Streit m. v widerstreiten (+dat). **conflict of interests** Interessenkonflikt m. **conflicting** adj widerstreitend.

conform [kən'fo:m] v (tally) übereinstimmen (mit); (to rules) sich fügen (+ dat). **conformist** n Konformist.

confound [kən'faund] v (surprise) erstaunen; (mix up) verwechseln. **confound it!** verdammt!

confront [kən'frʌnt] v konfrontieren; (enemy) entgegentreten (+ dat). **confrontation** n Konfrontation f.

confuse [kən'fju:z] v (mix up) verwechseln (mit); (perplex) verwirren. **confused** adj (person) verwirrt; (situation) verworren. **confusion** n Verwirrung f.

congeal [kən'dʒi:l] v gerinnen.

congenial [kən'dʒi:niəl] adj freundlich, gemütlich.

congenital [kən'dʒenitl] adj angeboren.

congested [kən'dʒestid] adj überfüllt. **congestion** n Stauung f; (traffic) Verkehrsstauung f.

conglomeration [kən,gloməˈreiʃən] n Anhäufung f, Konglomerat neut.

congratulate [kən'gratjuleit] v beglückwünschen. **congratulations** pl n Glückwünsche pl.

congregate ['kongrigeit] v sich versammeln. **congregation** n Versammlung f.

congress ['kongres] n Kongreß m. **congressman/woman** n Abgeordnete(r).

conifer ['konifə] n Nadelbaum m. **coniferous** adj Nadel-.

conjecture [kən'dʒektʃə] n Vermutung f.

conjugal ['kondʒugəl] adj ehelich.

conjugate ['kondʒugeit] v (gramm) konjugieren.

conjunction [kən'dʒʌŋkʃən] n Vereinigung f; (gramm, astrol) Konjunktion f.

conjunctivitis [kən,dʒʌŋkti'vaitis] n Bindehautentzündung f.

conjure ['kʌndʒə] v **conjure up** heraufbeschwören. **conjurer** n Zauberkünstler m. **conjuring trick** Zauberkunststück neut.

connect [kə'nekt] v verbinden; (phone, etc.) anschließen. **connection** n Verbindung f; (phone, rail) Anschluß m. **in connection with** im Zusammenhang mit.

connoisseur [konə'sə:] n Kenner m.

connotation [konə'teiʃən] n Nebenbedeutung f.

conquer ['konkə] v erobern, besiegen; (fig) überwinden, beherrschen. **conqueror** n Eroberer m. **conquest** n Eroberung f.

conscience ['konʃəns] n Gewissen neut.

conscientious [konʃi'enʃəs] adj pflichtbewußt.

conscious ['konʃəs] adj bewußt. **consciousness** n Bewußtsein neut.

conscript ['konskript] v einziehen. n Wehrpflichtige(r). **conscription** n Wehrpflicht f.

consecrate ['konsikreit] v weihen.

consecutive [kən'sekjutiv] adj aufeinanderfolgend.

consensus [kən'sensəs] n Übereinstimmung f.

consent [kən'sent] v zustimmen (+ dat). n Zustimmung f.

consequence ['konsikwəns] n Folge f, Konsequenz f. **of no consequence** unbedeutend. **consequently** adv folglich.

conserve [kən'sə:v] v erhalten; (energy) sparen. **conservation** n Schutz m, Erhaltung f. **conservative** adj konservativ; n Konservative(r). **conservatory** n Treibhaus neut; (music) Musikhochschule f.

consider [kən'sidə] n (think about) überlegen; (regard as) halten für. **considerate** adj rücksichtsvoll. **consideration** n (thought) Überlegung f; (thoughtfulness) Rücksicht f. **considering** prep in Anbetracht (+ gen).

consign [kən'sain] v versenden. **consignee** n Empfänger m. **consignment** n Sendung f. **consignor** n Absender m.

consist [kən'sist] v **consist of** bestehen aus. **consistency** n (of substance) Dichte f. **consistent** adj konsequent. **consistent with** vereinbar mit.

console [kən'soul] v trösten. **consolation** n Trost m. **consolation prize** Trostpreis m.

consolidate [kən'solideit] v stärken; (comm) konsolidieren. **consolidation** n Stärkung f.

consommé [kən'somei] n Fleischbrühe f.

consonant ['konsənənt] n Konsonant m.

conspicuous [kən'spikjuəs] adj (visible) sichtbar; (striking) auffallend.

conspire [kən'spaiə] v sich verschwören. **conspiracy** n Verschwörung f. **conspirator** n Verschwörer m.

constable ['kʌnstəbl] n Polizist m.

constant ['konstənt] adj beständig, konstant; (continual) dauernd. **constantly** adv ständig.

constellation [konstə'leiʃən] n Sternbild neut.

constipation [konsti'peiʃən] n (Darm)Verstopfung f.

constituency [kən'stitjuənsi] n Wahlkreis m. **constituent** n Wähler m.

constitute ['konstitjuːt] v bilden, darstellen. **constitution** n (pol) Grundgesetz m, Verfassung f; (of person) Konstitution f.

constrain [kən'strein] v zwingen. **constraint** n Zwang m, Druck m.

constrict [kən'strikt] v zusammendrücken, einengen.

construct [kən'strʌkt] v bauen, konstruieren; (argument) aufstellen. **construction** n Bau m, Konstruktion f. **constructive** adj konstruktiv.

consul ['konsəl] n Konsul m. **consulate** n Konsulat neut.

consult [kən'sʌlt] v zu Rate ziehen, konsultieren; (book) nachsehen in. **consultant** n Berater m. **consultation** n Konsultation f. **consulting room** Sprechzimmer neut.

consume [kən'sjuːm] v verzehren; (money, time) verbrauchen. **consumer** n Verbraucher m.

contact ['kontakt] n Verbindung f, Kontakt m. v sich in Verbindung setzen mit. **be in contact with** in Verbindung stehen mit.

contagious [kən'teidʒəs] adj ansteckend.

contain [kən'tein] v enthalten; (feelings) beherrschen. **contain oneself** sich beherrschen. **container** n Behälter m; (for goods transport) Container m. **container ship** Containerschiff m.

contaminate [kən'taməneit] v verseuchen. **contamination** n Verseuchung f.

contemplate ['kontəmpleit] v (observe) nachdenklich betrachten; (think about) nachdenken über; (doing something) vorhaben. **contemplation** n Betrachtung f; Nachdenken neut.

contemporary [kən'tempərəri] adj zeitgenössisch; (modern) modern. n Zeitgenosse m.

contempt [kən'tempt] n Verachtung f. **contemptible** adj verächtlich. **contemptuous** adj voller Verachtung f.

contend [kən'tend] v kämpfen; (assert) behaupten.

content¹ ['kontent] n Inhalt m. **contents** pl Inhalt m sing. **table of contents** Inhaltsverzeichnis neut.

content² [kən'tent] adj zufrieden. **contentment** n Zufriedenheit f.

contention [kən'tenʃən] n Streit m; (assertion) Behauptung f.

contest ['kontest; v kən'test] n Wettkampf m. v bestreiten. **contestant** n Bewerber(in).

context ['kontekst] n Zusammenhang m.

continent ['kontinənt] n Festland neut, Kontinent m. **continental** adj Kontinental-.

contingency [kən'tindʒənsi] n Eventualität f.

continue [kən'tinjuː] v fortfahren, weitermachen; (something) fortsetzen; (go further) weitergehen. **continual** adj wiederholt. **continually** adv immer wieder. **continuation** n Fortsetzung f. **continuous** adj beständig.

contort [kən'toːt] v verdrehen. **contortion** n Verdrehung f. **contortionist** n Schlangenmensch m.

contour ['kontuə] n Umrißlinie f.

contraband ['kontrəband] n Schmuggelware f.

contraception [kontrə'sepʃən] n Empfängnisverhütung f. **contraceptive** adj empfängnisverhütend. n empfängnisverhütendes Mittel neut.

contract ['kontrakt; v kən'trakt] n Vertrag m. v (become smaller) sich zusammenziehen; (illness) sich zuziehen. **contraction** n Zusammenziehung f. **contractor** n (building) Bauunternehmer m.

contradict [kontrə'dikt] v widersprechen. **contradiction** n Widerspruch m. **contradictory** adj sich widersprechend.

contralto [kən'traltou] n (voice) Alt m; (singer) Altistin f.

contraption [kən'trapʃən] n komisches Ding neut.

contrary [kən'treəri; (opposite) 'kontrəri] adj (person) widerspenstig; (opposite) entgegengesetzt. n Gegenteil m. **on the contrary** im Gegenteil.

contrast ['kontraːst; v kən'traːst] v (compare) vergleichen. **contrast with** kontrastieren mit. n Kontrast m. **in contrast to** im Gegensatz zu.

contravene [kontrə'viːn] v verstoßen gegen. **contravention** n Verstoß m.

contribute [kən'tribjuːt] v beitragen; (money) spenden. **contribution** n Beitrag m. **contributor** n Beitragende(r); (to newspaper, etc.) Mitarbeiter m.

contrive [kən'traiv] v (plan) ausdenken. I contrived to meet him es gelang mir, ihn zu treffen.

control [kən'troul] v (curb) zügeln; (machine) steuern. n Leitung f. **controls** pl n Steuerung f. **under/out of control** unter/außer Kontrolle.

controversial [kɔntrə'vɜ:ʃəl] adj umstritten. **controversy** n Streitfrage f, Kontroverse f.

convalesce [kɔnvə'les] v genesen, gesund werden. **convalescence** n Genesungszeit f.

convection [kən'vekʃən] n Konvektion f.

convenience [kən'vi:njəns] n Bequemlichkeit f; (advantage) Vorteil m. **public convenience** Bedürfnisanstalt f. **convenient** adj (suitable) passend; (time) gelegen; (advantageous) vorteilhaft.

convent ['kɔnvənt] n Kloster neut; (school) Klosterschule f.

convention [kən'venʃən] n (meeting) Tagung f; (agreement) Konvention f; (custom) Brauch m, Konvention f. **conventional** adj konventionell.

converge [kən'vɜ:dʒ] v konvergieren.

converse [kən'vɜ:s] v sich unterhalten, sprechen. **conversation** n Unterhaltung f, Gespräch neut.

convert [kən'vɜ:t; n 'kɔnvɜ:t] v umwandeln; (rel) bekehren. n Bekehrte(r). **conversion** n Umwandlung f; (rel) Bekehrung f.

convertible [kən'vɜ:təbl] adj um-, verwandelbar. n (mot) Kabrio(lett) neut.

convex ['kɔnveks] adj konvex.

convey [kən'vei] v (goods) befördern; (news) übermitteln. **conveyance** n (law) Übertragung f; (vehicle) Fahrzeug neut.

convict [kən'vikt; n 'kɔnvikt] v verurteilen. n Verurteilte(r). **conviction** n (belief) Überzeugung f; (law) Verurteilung f.

convince [kən'vins] v überzeugen. **convincing** adj überzeugend.

convivial [kən'viviəl] adj fröhlich, heiter.

convoy ['kɔnvoi] n (mil) Konvoi m.

convulsion [kən'vʌlʃən] n Zuckung f.

cook [kuk] v kochen; (a meal) zubereiten. n Koch m, Köchin f. **cooker** n Herd m. **cookery** n Küche f. **cookery book** Kochbuch neut. **cooking** n Küche f.

cool [ku:l] adj kühl. v abkühlen. **cooled** adj gekühlt. **coolness** n Kühle f.

coop [ku:p] n Hühnerkäfig m. v **coop up** einsperren.

cooperate [kou'ɔpəreit] v zusammenarbeiten. **cooperation** n Zusammenarbeit f, Kooperation f. **cooperative** adj (helpful) hilfsbereit; kooperativ. n Genossenschaft f, Kooperative f.

coordinate [kou'ɔ:dineit] v koordinieren. n (math) Koordinate f. **coordination** n Koordination f.

cope [koup] v **cope with** fertigwerden mit.

copious ['koupiəs] adj reichlich.

copper¹ ['kɔpə] n (metal) Kupfer neut. adj kupfern; (colour) kupferfarben.

copper² ['kɔpə] n (coll) Polyp m.

copulate ['kɔpjuleit] v sich paaren. **copulation** n Paarung f.

copy ['kɔpi] n Kopie f; (book) Exemplar neut; (newspaper) Nummer f. v kopieren. **copyright** n Copyright neut.

coral ['kɔrəl] n Koralle f.

cord [kɔ:d] n Schnur f.

cordial ['kɔ:diəl] adj herzlich.

cordon ['kɔ:dn] n Absperrkette f. v **cordon off** absperren.

corduroy ['kɔ:dərɔi] n Kord m.

core [kɔ:] n (apple) Kernhaus neut. v entkernen. **to the core** durch und durch.

cork [kɔ:k] n (material) Kork m; (for bottle) Korken m, Pfropfen m. adj korken. **corkscrew** n Korkenzieher m.

corn¹ [kɔ:n] n Korn neut, Getreide neut; (maize) Mais m; (wheat) Weizen m.

corn² [kɔ:n] n (on foot) Hühnerauge neut.

corner ['kɔ:nə] n Ecke f, Winkel m; (mot) Kurve f; (sport) Eckball m. v in die Enge treiben.

cornet ['kɔ:nit] n (music) Kornett neut; (ice cream) Eistüte f.

coronary ['kɔrənəri] adj koronar. **coronary thrombosis** Koronarthrombose f.

coronation [kɔrə'neiʃən] n Krönung f.

coroner ['kɔrənə] n Leichenbeschauer m.

corporal¹ ['kɔ:pərəl] adj körperlich. **corporal punishment** Prügelstrafe f.

corporal² ['kɔ:pərəl] n (mil) Obergefreite(r) m.

corporation [kɔ:pə'reiʃən] n Körperschaft f; (city authorities) Gemeinderat m.

corps [kɔ:] n Korps neut.

corpse [kɔ:ps] n Leiche f.

correct [kə'rekt] adj richtig; (proper) korrekt. v korrigieren. **correction** n Korrektur f.

correlation [korə'leifən] n Wechselbeziehung f.

correspond [korə'spond] v entsprechen (+dat); (write) korrespondieren. **correspondence** n Entsprechung f; Korrespondenz f. **corresponding** adj entsprechend.

corridor ['kɔridɔt] n Gang m.

corrode [kə'roud] v zerfressen; (become corroded) rosten. **corrosion** n Korrosion f.

corrupt [kə'rʌpt] v bestechen. adj bestechlich, korrupt. **corruption** n Bestechung f, Korruption f.

corset ['kɔrset] n Korsett neut.

cosmetic [koz'metik] adj kosmetisch. **cosmetic surgery** chirurgische Kosmetik f. **cosmetics** pl n Schönheitsmittel pl.

cosmic ['kozmik] adj kosmisch.

cosmopolitan [kozmə'politən] adj kosmopolitisch.

cost [kost] v kosten. n Preis m, Kosten pl. **costs** pl n Unkosten pl. **cost of living** Lebenshaltungskosten pl.

costume ['kostjuːm] n Kostüm neut.

cosy ['kouzi] adj gemütlich.

cot [kot] n Kinderbett neut.

cottage ['kɔtidʒ] n Hütte f, Häuschen neut. **cottage cheese** Hüttenkäse m.

cotton ['kotn] n Baumwolle f. adj Baumwoll-. **cotton wool** Watte f.

couch [kautʃ] n Couch f.

cough [kof] n Husten m. v husten.

could [kud] V can.

council ['kaunsəl] n Rat m. **councillor** m Rat m.

counsel ['kaunsəl] v beraten. n Rat m.

count¹ [kaunt] v zählen; (be valid) gelten. n (number) (Gesamt)Zahl f. **count on** rechnen mit.

count² [kaunt] n (noble) Graf m.

counter¹ ['kauntə] n (shop) Ladentisch m, Theke f; (bank) Schalter m; (game) Spielmarke f.

counter² ['kauntə] adv entgegen. adj entgegengesetzt. v entgegnen.

counteract [kauntə'rakt] v entgegenwirken (+dat).

counterattack ['kauntərə,tak] n Gegenangriff m.

counter-clockwise adj, adv dem Uhrzeigersinn entgegen.

counterfeit ['kauntəfit] adj gefälscht. v fälschen.

counterfoil ['kauntə,foil] n Kontrollabschnitt m.

counterpart ['kauntə,part] n Gegenstück neut.

countess ['kauntis] n Gräfin f.

country ['kʌntri] n Land neut; (homeland) Heimat f; (pol) Land neut, Staat m. adj Land-. **in the country** auf dem Lande. **country house** Landhaus neut. **countryman** n Landmann m. **fellow countryman** Landsmann m. **countryside** Landschaft f.

county ['kaunti] n Grafschaft f.

coup [kuː] n Coup m; (pol) Staatsstreich m. **coup de grâce** Gnadenstoß m.

couple ['kʌpl] n Paar neut; (married couple) Ehepaar neut. **a couple of** ein paar.

coupon ['kuːpon] n Coupon m, Gutschein m.

courage ['kʌridʒ] n Mut m, Tapferkeit f. **courageous** adj mutig, tapfer.

courier ['kuriə] n Kurier m; (tour guide) Reiseleiter(in).

course [kɔːs] n Lauf m; (study) Kurs(us) m; (race) Bahn f; (of action) Richtung m. v laufen. **of course** natürlich, selbstverständlich. **in the course of** im Laufe (+gen).

court [kɔːt] n (royal) Hof m; (law) Gericht neut. v (lover) werben um. **court martial** Kriegsgericht neut. **court-martial** v vor ein Kriegsgericht stellen. **courtroom** n Gerichtssaal m. **courtyard** n Hof m.

courtesy ['kəːtəsi] n Höflichkeit f. **courteous** adj höflich.

cousin ['kʌzn] n Cousin m, Vetter m; Kusine f, Base f.

cove [kouv] n Bucht f.

cover ['kʌvə] v (be)decken; (extend over) sich erstrecken über; (include) einschließen. n (lid) Deckel m; (of book) (Schutz)Umschlag m. **covering** n (Be)Deckung f.

cow [kau] n Kuh f. v einschüchtern. **cowshed** n Kuhstall m.

coward ['kauəd] n Feigling m. **cowardice** n Feigheit f. **cowardly** adj feige.

cower ['kauə] v kauern.

coy [koi] adj spröde.

crab [krab] n Krebs m.

crack [krak] n (slit) Spalt m, Riß m; (sound) Krach m. v krachen; (break) brechen; (nut) knacken; (egg) aufschlagen; (joke) reißen. **crack up** (coll) zusammenbrechen. **cracker** n (firework)

Knallfrosch m; (Christmas) Knallbonbon m; (biscuit) Keks m.

crackle ['krakl] v knistern. n Knistern neut.

cradle ['kreidl] n Wiege f. v wiegen.

craft [kraft] n (trade) Handwerk neut, Gewerbe neut; (skill) Kunstfertigkeit f; (ship) Schiff neut. **craftsman** n Handwerker m, Künstler m. **crafty** adj schlau, listig.

cram [kram] v hineinstopfen; (study) pauken.

cramp [kramp] n (med) Krampf m; (clamp) Krampe f. v hemmen.

cranberry ['kranbəri] n Preiselbeere f.

crane [krein] n Kran m; (bird) Kranich m.

crank [krank] n Kurbel f; (odd person) Kauz m. v ankurbeln. **crankshaft** n Kurbelwelle f.

crap [krap] n (vulgar) Scheiße f.

crash [kraʃ] n (sound) Krach m; (mot) Zusammenstoß m; (aero) Absturz m. v stürzen (gegen); (sound) krachen. **crash helmet** Sturzhelm m.

crate [kreit] n Kiste f.

crater ['kreitə] n Krater m.

cravat [krə'vat] n Halstuch neut, Krawatte f.

crave [kreiv] v erbitten. **crave for** sehnen nach. **craving** n Sehnsucht f.

crawl [kroːl] v kriechen. n Kriechen neut; (swimming) Kraulstil m.

crayfish ['kreifiʃ] n Flußkrebs m.

crayon ['kreiən] n Farbstift m.

craze [kreiz] n (coll) Manie f. **crazy** adj verrückt.

creak [kriːk] v knarren. n Knarren neut.

cream [kriːm] n Sahne f, Rahm m; (skin) Creme f. **cream-coloured** adj cremefarben. **creamy** adj sahnig.

crease [kriːs] n Falte f, Kniff m. v falten.

create [kri'eit] v erschaffen; (cause) verursachen. **creation** n Schöpfung f; (product) Werk neut. **creative** adj schöpferisch. **creator** n Schöpfer m. **creature** n Lebewesen neut, Geschöpf neut.

credentials [kri'denʃəlz] pl n (identity papers) Ausweispapiere pl.

credible ['kredəbl] adj glaubhaft, glaubwürdig.

credit ['kredit] n (comm) Guthaben neut, Kredit m. v Glauben schenken (+dat). **on credit** auf Kredit. **take the credit for**

sich als Verdienst anrechnen. **creditable** adj rühmlich. **credit card** Kreditkarte f. **creditor** n Gläubiger m.

credulous ['kredjuləs] adj leichtgläubig.

creed [kriːd] n Bekenntnis neut, Kredo neut.

*****creep** [kriːp] v kriechen, schleichen. n Kriechen neut.

cremate [kri'meit] v einäschern. **cremation** n Einäscherung f. **crematorium** n Krematorium neut.

crept [krept] V creep.

crescent ['kresnt] n Mondsichel f.

cress [kres] n Kresse f.

crest [krest] n (of mountain) Bergkamm m; (of wave) Wellenkamm m; (coat of arms) Wappen neut.

crevice ['krevis] n Spalte f, Sprung m.

crew [kruː] n Besatzung f, Mannschaft f.

crib [krib] n Kinderbett neut.

cricket[1] ['krikit] n (insect) Grille f.

cricket[2] ['krikit] n Kricket neut.

crime [kraim] n Verbrechen neut. **criminal** adj verbrecherisch, kriminell. n Verbrecher(in).

crimson ['krimzn] n Karmesinrot neut.

cringe [krindʒ] v sich ducken.

crinkle ['krinkl] v kraus machen. n Kräuselung f. **crinkly** adj kraus.

cripple ['kripl] n Krüppel m. v lähmen.

crisis ['kraisis] n (pl -ses) Krise f.

crisp [krisp] adj knusprig. **crisps** pl n Chips pl. **crispy** adj knusprig.

criterion [krai'tiəriən] n (pl -a) Kriterium neut.

critic ['kritik] n Kritiker m. **critical** adj kritisch. **criticism** n Kritik f. **criticize** v kritisieren.

croak [krouk] v (person, crow) krächzen; (frog) quaken. n Krächzen neut; Quaken neut.

crochet ['krouʃei] v häkeln. **crochet hook** Häkelnadel f. **crochet work** Häkelarbeit f.

crockery ['krokəri] n Geschirr neut.

crocodile ['krokədail] n Krokodil neut.

crocus ['kroukəs] n Krokus m.

crook [kruk] n (shepherd's) Hirtenstab m; (villain) Gauner m. **crooked** adj gekrümmt; (dishonest) krumm.

crop [krop] n (harvest) Ernte f; (whip) Reitpeitsche f. v (cut) stutzen. **crop up** auftauchen.

croquet ['kroukei] n Krocket neut.

cross [krɔs] n Kreuz neut; (crossbreed) Kreuzung f. adj Quer-; (annoyed) böse, ärgerlich. v kreuzen, überqueren. **cross over** hinübergehen. **cross one's mind** einfallen (+dat). **crossbow** n Armbrust f. **crossbreed** n Kreuzung f. **cross-country** adj Gelände-. **cross-examination** n Kreuzverhör m. **cross-eyed** adj schielend. **crossing** n Kreuzung f; (rail) Bahnübergang m; (border) Überfahrt f. **crosslegged** adj mit überschlagenen Beinen. **cross-reference** n Kreuzverweisung f. **crossroads** n Straßenkreuzung f; (fig) Scheideweg m. **cross-section** n Querschnitt m. **crosswind** n Seitenwind m. **crossword** n Kreuzworträtsel neut.

crotchet ['krɔtʃit] n (music) Viertelnote f.

crouch [krautʃ] v sich ducken.

crow [krou] n Krähe f. v krähen. **crow's feet** Krähenfüße pl. **crow's nest** (naut) Mastkorb m.

crowd [kraud] n Menge. v **crowd around** sich drängen um. **crowded** adj gedrängt.

crown [kraun] n Krone f. v krönen.

crucial ['kruːʃəl] adj kritisch, entscheidend.

crucifixion [ˌkruːsiˈfikʃən] n Kreuzigung f. **crucify** v kreuzigen.

crude [kruːd] adj roh; (person) grob. **crude oil** Rohöl neut. **crudeness** n Roheit f.

cruel ['kruːəl] adj grausam. **cruelty** n Grausamkeit f.

cruise [kruːz] v (boat) kreuzen; (aircraft) fliegen. n Kreuzfahrt f. **cruiser** n (naut) Kreuzer m.

crumb [krʌm] n Krume f; (coll) Brocken m.

crumble ['krʌmbl] v zerkrümeln. **crumbly** adj krümelig.

crumple ['krʌmpl] v zerknittern.

crunch [krʌntʃ] v knirschen. n Knirschen neut. **crunchy** adj knusprig.

crusade [kruːˈseid] n Kreuzzug m. **crusader** n Kreuzfahrer m.

crush [krʌʃ] v zerdrücken; unterdrücken. n Gedränge neut. **crushing** adj überwältigend.

crust [krʌst] n Kruste f.

crustacean [krʌˈsteiʃən] n Krustentier neut.

crutch [krʌtʃ] n Krücke f.

cry [krai] v (shout) schreien; (weep) weinen. n Schrei m, Ruf m. **cry out** auf-schreien. **a far cry from** ein weiter Weg von.

crypt [kript] n Krypta f.

crystal ['kristl] n Kristall m.

cub [kʌb] n Junge(s) neut; (fox, wolf) Welpe m; (scout) Wölfling m.

cube [kjuːb] n Würfel m; (math) Kubikzahl f. **cubic** adj würfelförmig. **cubic centimetre** Kubikzentimeter neut. **cubic capacity** (mot) Hubraum m.

cubicle ['kjuːbikl] n Kabine f.

cuckoo ['kukuː] n Kuckuck m.

cucumber [kjuːˈkʌmbə] n Gurke f.

cuddle ['kʌdl] v herzen, liebkosen.

cue[1] [kjuː] n (theatre) Stichwort neut.

cue[2] [kjuː] n (billiards) Billardstock m.

cuff[1] [kʌf] n (shirt) Manschette f; (trousers) Aufschlag m. **cufflink** n Manschettenknopf m.

cuff[2] [kʌf] n Ohrfeige f, Klaps m. v klapsen.

culinary ['kʌlinəri] adj kulinarisch, Küchen-.

culminate ['kʌlmiˌneit] v kulminieren. **culmination** n Höhepunkt m.

culprit ['kʌlprit] n Täter m.

cult [kʌlt] n Kult m.

cultivate ['kʌltiˌveit] v bebauen, kultivieren; (fig) pflegen. **cultivation** n Kultur f.

culture ['kʌltʃə] n Kultur f. **cultural** adj kulturell.

cumbersome ['kʌmbəsəm] adj sperrig, schwer zu handhaben.

cunning ['kʌniŋ] adj schlau, listig. n List f.

cup [kʌp] n Tasse f; (trophy) Pokal m. **cup final** Pokalendspiel neut. **cup tie** Pokalspiel neut.

cupboard ['kʌbəd] n Schrank m.

curate ['kjuərət] n Unterpfarrer m.

curator [kjuəˈreitə] n Konservator m.

curb [kəːb] v zügeln. n Zaum m; (kerb) Bordstein m.

curdle ['kəːdl] v gerinnen.

cure [kjuə] v (illness) heilen; (smoke) räuchern; (salt) einsalzen. n Heilmittel neut.

curfew ['kəːfjuː] n Ausgehverbot m.

curious ['kjuəriəs] adj (inquisitive) neugierig; (odd) seltsam. **curiosity** n Neugier f.

curl [kəːl] n Locke f, Kräuselung f. v (sich) kräuseln. **curly** adj lockig, kraus.

currant ['kʌrənt] n Korinthe f.

currency ['kʌrənsi] *n* (*money*) Währung *f*.
current ['kʌrənt] *adj* (*present*) gegenwärtig; (*common*) gebräuchlich, üblich. *n* Strom *m*. **current account** Scheckkonto *neut*. **current events** Zeitgeschehen *neut*.
currently *adv* zur Zeit.
curry ['kʌri] *n* Curry *neut*. **curry powder** Curry(pulver) *neut*. **curry sauce** Currysoße *f*.
curse [kəːs] *v* verfluchen; (*swear*) fluchen. *n* Fluch *m*.
curt [kəːt] *adj* knapp, barsch.
curtail [kəːˈteil] *v* abkürzen. **curtailment** *n* Abkürzung *f*; Einschränkung *f*.
curtain ['kəːtn] *n* Gardine *f*; (*theatre*) Vorhang *m*.
curtsy ['kəːtsi] *n* Knicks *m*. *v* knicksen.
curve [kəːv] *n* Kurve *f*. *v* sich biegen. **curved** *adj* bogenförmig, gekrümmt.
cushion ['kuʃən] *n* Kissen *neut*. *v* polstern.
custard ['kʌstəd] *n* Vanillesoße *f*.
custody ['kʌstədi] *n* Aufsicht *f*; (*arrest*) Haft *f*.
custom ['kʌstəm] *n* (*habit*) Gewohnheit *f*; (*tradition*) Brauch *m*. (*customers*) Kundschaft *f*. **customary** *adj* gewöhnlich. **customer** *n* Kunde *m*, Kundin *f*. **customs** *n* Zoll *m*. **customs duty** Zoll *m*. **customs official** Zollbeamte(r) *m*.
*cut [kʌt] *n* Schnitt *m*; (*wound*) Schnittwunde *f*; (*in wages*) Kürzung *f*; (*coll: share*) Anteil *m*. *v* schneiden; (*prices*) herabsetzen; (*wages*) kürzen. **cut off** (*phone*) trennen.
cute [kjuːt] *adj* (*coll*) niedlich.
cuticle ['kjuːtikl] *n* Oberhaut *f*; (*on nail*) Nagelhaut *f*.
cutlery ['kʌtləri] *n* Besteck *neut*.
cutlet ['kʌtlit] *n* Kotelett *neut*.
cycle ['saikl] *n* Zyklus *m*; (*bicycle*) Fahrrad *neut*. *v* radfahren. **cycling** *n* Radsport *m*. **cyclist** *n* Radfahrer(in).
cyclone ['saikloun] *n* Zyklon *m*.
cylinder ['silində] *n* Zylinder *m*. **cylinder block** Motorblock *m*. **cylinder capacity** Hubraum *m*. **cylinder head** Zylinderkopf *m*.
cymbals ['simbəlz] *pl n* Becken *neut sing*.
cynic ['sinik] *n* Zyniker(in). **cynical** *adj* zynisch. **cynicism** *n* Zynismus *m*.
cypress ['saiprəs] *n* Zypresse *f*.
Cyprus ['saiprəs] *n* Zypern *neut*. **Cypriot** *n* Zypriot(in). *adj* zypriotisch.
cyst [sist] *n* Zyste *f*.

Czechoslovakia [ˌtʃekəsləˈvakiə] *n* die Tschechoslowakei *f*. **Czechoslovakian** *n* Tschechoslowake *m*, Tschechoslowakin *f*. *adj* tschechoslowakisch.

D

dab [dab] *v* betupfen. *n* Tupfen *m*.
dabble ['dabl] *v* plätschern. **he dabbles in art** er beschäftigt sich nebenbei mit Kunst. **dabbler** *n* Dilettant *m*.
dad [dad] *n* Vati *m*, Papa *m*.
daffodil ['dafədil] *n* Narzisse *f*.
daft [daːft] *adj* (*coll*) blöd(e), doof.
dagger ['dagə] *n* Dolch *m*.
daily ['deili] *adj*, *adv* täglich. **daily paper** Tageszeitung *f*.
dainty ['deinti] *adj* (*person*) niedlich; (*food*) lecker.
dairy ['deəri] *n* Molkerei *f*. **dairy produce** Milchprodukte *pl*.
daisy ['deizi] *n* Gänseblümchen *neut*.
dam [dam] *n* Damm *m*. *v* eindämmen.
damage ['damidʒ] *v* beschädigen; verletzen. *n* Schaden *m*. **damages** *pl n* (*compensation*) Schadenersatz *m sing*.
damn [dam] *v* verdammen. *interj* verdammt!
damp [damp] *adj* feucht. *n* Feuchtigkeit *f*. **dampen** *v* befeuchten.
damson ['damzən] *n* Pflaume *f*.
dance [daːns] *n* Tanz *m*. *v* tanzen. **dancer** *n* Tänzer(in). **dance hall** Tanzsaal *m*. **dancing** *n* Tanz *m*; Tanzen *neut*.
dandelion ['dandiˌlaiən] *n* Löwenzahn *m*.
dandruff ['dandrəf] *n* Schuppen *pl*.
Dane [dein] *n* Däne *m*, Dänin *f*. **Danish** *adj* dänisch.
danger ['deindʒə] *n* Gefahr *f*. **in** (*or* **out of**) **danger** in/außer Gefahr. **dangerous** *adj* gefährlich.
dangle ['dangl] *v* baumeln; baumeln lassen.
dare [deə] *v* wagen, riskieren; (*challenge*) herausfordern. **daring** *adj* wagemutig; (*risky*) gewagt. *n* Mut *m*.
dark [daːk] *adj* finster; (*esp colour*) dunkel. *n* Dunkelheit *f*. **in the dark** im Dunkeln; (*fig*) nicht im Bilde. **darken** *v* (sich) verdunkeln. **darkness** *n* Dunkelheit

f. Finsternis *f*. **darkroom** *n* Dunkelkammer *f*.

darling ['dɑːlɪŋ] *n* Liebling *m*. *adj* lieb.

darn [dɑːn] *v* stopfen. **darning** *n* Stopfen *neut*.

dart [dɑːt] *v* schießen, sausen; *n* Pfeil *m*. **darts** *pl n* (game) (Pfeilwerfen) *neut sing*.

dash [daʃ] *v* (smash) zerschlagen; (rush) stürzen. *n* (punctuation) Gedankenstrich *m*; (rush) Stürzen *neut*; (addition) Schuß *m*. **dashboard** *n* Armaturenbrett *neut*. **dashing** *adj* schneidig.

data ['deitə] *pl n* Daten *pl*. **data processing** Datenverarbeitung *f*.

date[1] [deit] *n* Datum *neut*; (appointed day) Termin *m*; (with someone) Verabredung *f*. *v* (letter) datieren. **dated** *adj* altmodisch.

date[2] [deit] *n* (fruit) Dattel *f*.

dative ['deitiv] *n* Dativ *m*.

daughter ['dɔːtə] *n* Tochter *f*. **daughter-in-law** *n* Schwiegertochter *f*.

daunt [dɔːnt] *v* entmutigen.

dawdle [dɔːdl] *v* trödeln.

dawn [dɔːn] *n* Tagesanbruch *m*; (Morgen)Dämmerung *f*; (fig) Anfang *m*. *v* dämmern (also fig).

day [dei] *n* Tag *m*. **daylight** Tageslicht *neut*.

daze [deiz] *v* betäuben. **dazed** *adj* benommen.

dazzle ['dazl] *v* blenden.

dead [ded] *adj* tot. **dead man/woman** Tote(r). **the dead** die Toten *pl*. **deaden** *v* dämpfen. **dead certain** todsicher. **dead end** Sackgasse *f*; (fig) totes Geleise *neut*. **deadline** *n* Termin *m*.

deaf [def] *adj* taub. **deaf aid** Hörgerät *neut*. **deaf mute** Taubstumme(r). **deafen** *v* taub machen.

***deal** [diːl] *n* Geschäft *neut*. *v* handeln; (cards) austeilen. **deal with** (attend to) sich befassen mit; (resolve) erledigen. **a great/good deal of** viel. **dealer** *n* Händler *m*; (cards) Kartengeber *m*. **dealings** *pl n* Beziehungen *pl*.

dealt [delt] *V* deal.

dean [diːn] *n* Dekan *m*.

dear [diə] *adj* (beloved) lieb; (expensive) teuer. (in letters) Dear Mr. Smith Lieber Herr Smith, Sehr geehrter Herr Smith. *n* Liebling *m*. **dearly** *adv* herzlich.

death [deθ] *n* Tod *m*; (case of death) Todesfall *m*. **deathbed** *n* Sterbebett *neut*. **death penalty** Todesstrafe *f*.

debase [di'beis] *v* entwerten.

debate [di'beit] *n* Debatte *f*. *v* debattieren, diskutieren.

debit ['debit] *n* Soll *neut*; Lastscrift *f*. *v* belasten.

debris ['debriː] *n* Schutt *m*, Trümmer *pl*.

debt [det] *n* Schuld *f*. **in debt** verschuldet. **debtor** *n* Schuldner *m*.

decade ['dekeid] *n* Jahrzehnt *neut*

decadence ['dekədəns] *n* Dekadenz *f*. **decadent** *adj* dekadent.

decanter [di'kantə] *n* Karaffe *f*.

decapitate [di'kapiteit] *v* enthaupten. **decapitation** *n* Enthauptung *f*.

decay [di'kei] *v* verfallen. *n* Verfall *m*. **tooth decay** Karies *f*.

deceased [di'siːst] *adj* verstorben. **the deceased** der/die Verstorbene.

deceit [di'siːt] *n* Täuschung, Betrug *m*. **deceitful** *adj* betrügerisch.

deceive [di'siːv] *v* täuschen.

December [di'sembə] *n* Dezember *m*.

decent ['diːsənt] *adj* (respectable) anständig; (kind) freundlich. **decency** *n* Anstand *m*.

deceptive [di'septiv] *adj* täuschend.

decibel ['desibel] *n* Dezibel *neut*.

decide [di'said] *v* entscheiden; (make up one's mind) sich entscheiden. **decided** *adj* entschieden. **decision** *n* Entscheidung *f*; (of committee) Beschluß *m*. **make a decision** eine Entscheidung treffen. **decisive** *adj* entscheidend.

deciduous [di'sidjuəs] *adj* (trees) Laub-.

decimal ['desiməl] *adj* Dezimal-.

decipher [di'saifə] *v* entziffern.

deck [dek] *n* Deck *neut*; (of cards) Pack *neut*. **deckchair** *n* Liegestuhl *m*.

declare [di'kleə] *v* erklären. **declaration** *n* Erklärung *f*.

decline [di'klain] *v* ablehnen; (gram) deklinieren.

decompose [,diːkəm'pouz] *v* zerfallen.

decor ['deikɔː] *n* Ausstattung *f*.

decorate ['dekəreit] *v* schmücken; (room) tapezieren; (mil) auszeichnen. **decoration** *n* Verzierung *f*; (of room) Dekoration *f*; (mil) Orden *m*.

decoy ['diːkɔi] *n* Lockvogel *m*.

decrease [di'kriːs] *v* (make less) vermindern; (become less) abnehmen. *n* Abnahme *f*.

decree [di'kriː] *n* Erlaß *m*.

decrepit [di'krepit] adj hinfällig.
dedicate ['dedi,keit] v widmen; (rel) weihen. dedication n (book) Widmung f; (to duty, etc.) Hingabe f; (rel) Einweihung f.
deduce [di'djuts] v schließen (aus).
deduct [di'dʌkt] v abziehen. deduction n Abzug m.
deed [diid] n Tat f; (document) Urkunde f.
deep [diip] adj tief. deep freeze Tiefkühlschrank m. deep-frozen adj tiefgekühlt, Tiefkühl-.
deer [dia] n Hirsch m.
deface [di'feis] v entstellen.
default [di'fɔlt] n Unterlassung f. v (with payments) in Verzug kommen.
defeat [di'fiit] v schlagen, besiegen. n Niederlage f.
defect [di'fekt; v di'fekt] n Fehler m, Defekt m. v (pol) überlaufen. defective adj fehlerhaft, defektiv.
defence [di'fens] n Verteidigung f. defenceless adj schutzlos.
defend [di'fend] v verteidigen. defendant n Angeklagte(r). defender n Verteidiger m. defensive adj defensiv, Verteidigungs-.
defer [di'fə:] v (postpone) verschieben. defer to (yield to) nachgeben (+dat). deferment n Verschiebung f.
defiance [di'faians] n Trotz m. defiant adj trotzig, unnachgiebig.
deficiency [di'fiʃansi] n Unzulänglichkeit f, Mangel m. deficient adj (defective) defektiv, mangelhaft; (inadequate) unzulänglich.
deficit ['defisit] n Defizit neut, Fehlbetrag m.
define [di'fain] v definieren, genau erklären. well defined adj deutlich. definite adj klar, deutlich. definitely adv bestimmt. definition n Erklärung f, Definition f; (phot) Schärfe f.
deflate [di'fleit] v die Luft ablassen aus. deflation (pol) Deflation f.
deform [di'fɔːm] v deformieren, entstellen. deformed adj deformiert, verformt. deformity n Mißbildung f.
defraud [di'frɔːd] v betrügen.
defrost [di'frɔst] v abtauen.
deft [deft] adj flink.
defunct [di'fʌŋkt] adj verstorben; (fig) nicht mehr bestehend.
defy [di'fai] v (resist) trotzen; (challenge) herausfordern.

degenerate [di'dʒenəreit; adj di'dʒenərit] v degenerieren. adj degeneriert.
degrade [di'greid] v erniedrigen, entehren. degradation n Erniedrigung f. degrading adj erniedrigend.
degree [di'gri] n Grad m. to a high degree in hohem Maße.
dehydrate [di'haidreit] v trocknen. dehydrated adj getrocknet, Trocken-.
deign [dein] v sich herablassen.
dejected [di'dʒektid] adj niedergeschlagen.
delay [di'lei] v (postpone) aufschieben. n Verzögerung f, Aufschub m. to be delayed (train, etc.) Verspätung haben. without delay unverzüglich.
delegate ['deləgeit; 'deləgit] v delegieren. n Delegierte(r). delegation m Delegation f.
delete [di'liit] v tilgen, streichen.
deliberate [di'librət; v di'librəit] adj (intentional) absichtlich. v nachdenken. deliberately adv absichtlich. deliberation n Überlegung f.
delicate ['delikət] adj (fragile) zart; (fine) fein; (situation) heikel. delicacy n Zartheit f; (food) Delikatesse f.
delicious [di'liʃəs] adj köstlich.
delight [di'lait] n Freude f, Vergnügen neut. v erfreuen. delighted adj erfreut, entzückt. delightful adj entzückend.
delinquency [di'liŋkwənsi] n Straffälligkeit f. delinquent adj delinquent. n Delinquent m.
delirious [di'liriəs] adj in Delirium. delirium n Delirium neut, Fieberwahn m.
deliver [di'livə] v (goods) (aus)liefern; (rescue) befreien; (a woman in childbirth) entbinden. deliverance n Befreiung f. delivery n (Aus)Lieferung f; Entbindung f.
delta ['deltə] n Delta neut.
delude [di'luud] v täuschen. delusion n Täuschung f.
deluge ['deljuudʒ] n Flut f.
delve [delv] v delve into erforschen.
demand [di'maind] v verlangen. n Verlangen neut; (for a commodity, etc.) Nachfrage f. on demand auf Verlangen. demanding adj anspruchsvoll.
demented [di'mentid] adj wahnsinnig.
democracy [di'mokrəsi] n Demokratie f. democrat n Demokrat m. democratic adj demokratisch.

demolish [di'mɔliʃ] v abbrechen. **demolition** n Abbruch m.

demon ['diːmən] n Teufel m.

demonstrate ['demənstreit] v demonstrieren. **demonstration** n Demonstration f.

demoralize [di'morəlaiz] v demoralisieren. **demoralization** n Demoralisation f.

demure [di'mjuə] adj bescheiden.

den [den] n Höhle f; (room) Bude f.

denial [di'naiəl] n Leugnung f.

denim ['denim] adj Denim-. **denims** pl n Jeans pl.

Denmark ['denmaːk] n Dänemark neut.

denomination [di,nomi'neiʃən] n (rel) Bekenntnis neut; (of banknote) Nennwert m. **denominator** n Nenner m. **common denominator** gemeinsamer Nenner m.

denote [di'nout] v bezeichnen.

denounce [di'nauns] v brandmarken.

dense [dens] adj dicht, dick. **density** n Dichte f.

dent [dent] n Beule f. v einbeulen.

dental ['dentl] adj Zahn-.

dentist ['dentist] n Zahnarzt m. **dentistry** n Zahnheilkunde f.

denture ['dentʃə] n (künstliches) Gebiß neut.

denude [di'njuːd] v entblößen.

denunciation [dinʌnsi'eiʃən] n Denunziation f.

deny [di'nai] v leugnen; (responsibility) ablehnen; (allegation) dementieren. **deny oneself** sich versagen.

deodorant [diː'oudərənt] n Desodorans neut.

depart [di'paːt] v abfahren; (fig) abweichen. **departure** n (person) Weggehen neut; (train) Abfahrt f; (aeroplane) Abflug m.

department [di'paːtmənt] n Abteilung f; (pol) Ministerium neut. **department store** Warenhaus neut.

depend [di'pend] v **depend on** abhängen von; (rely on) sich verlassen auf. **it (all) depends** es kommt darauf an. **dependable** adj zuverlässig. **dependant** n Familienangehörige(r). **dependent** adj abhängig (+von).

depict [di'pikt] v schildern.

deplete [di'pliːt] v erschöpfen. **depletion** n Erschöpfung f.

deplore [di'plɔː] v bedauern. **deplorable** adj bedauernswert.

deport [di'pɔːt] v deportieren. **deport oneself** sich verhalten. **deportation** n Deportation f. **deportment** n Haltung f.

depose [di'pouz] v absetzen.

deposit [di'pozit] v deponieren. n (surety) Kaution f; (down payment) Anzahlung f; (sediment) Niederschlag m. **deposit account** Sparkonto neut.

depot ['depou] n Depot neut.

depraved [di'preivd] adj lasterhaft, verworfen.

depreciate [di'priːʃieit] v an Wert verlieren. **depreciation** n Wertminderung f.

depress [di'pres] v niederdrücken, deprimieren. **depressed** adj deprimiert. **depressing** adj deprimierend. **depression** n Depression f.

deprive [di'praiv] v berauben.

depth [depθ] n Tiefe f. **in depth** gründlich.

deputy ['depjuti] n Stellvertreter m. adj stellvertretend.

derail [di'reil] v entgleisen. **derailment** n Entgleisen neut.

derelict ['derilikt] adj (building) baufällig.

deride [di'raid] v verspotten. **derision** n Spott m. **derisory** adj spöttisch.

derive [di'raiv] v ableiten; (originate) stammen; (gain) gewinnen. **derivation** n Herkunft f.

derogatory [di'rogətəri] adj geringschätzig.

descend [di'send] v hinabsteigen; (from train) aussteigen. **be descended from** abstammen von. **descendant** n Nachkomme m. **descent** n Abstieg m; Abstammung f.

describe [di'skraib] v beschreiben. **description** n Beschreibung f.

desert[1] ['dezət] n Wüste f.

desert[2] [di'zəːt] n (something deserved) Verdienst neut. **deserts** pl n Lohn m sing.

desert[3] [di'zəːt] v verlassen; (mil) desertieren. **deserter** n Deserteur m. **desertion** n Verlassen neut; (mil) Desertion f.

deserve [di'zəːv] v verdienen.

design [di'zain] n Entwurf m; (drawing) Zeichnung f; (pattern) Muster neut. v entwerfen, planen.

designate ['dezigneit] v bezeichnen. **designation** n Bezeichnung f.

desire [di'zaiə] v wünschen, begehren; (ask for) wollen. n Wunsch m; (sexual) Begierde f. **desirous of** begierig nach.

desk [desk] *n* Schreibtisch *m*.

desolate ['desələt] *v* wüst, öde; *(person)* trostlos.

despair [di'speə] *v* verzweifeln. *n* Verzweiflung *f*.

desperate ['despərət] *adj* verzweifelt; *(situation)* hoffnungslos.

despicable [di'spikəbl] *adj* verächtlich.

despise [di'spaiz] *v* verachten.

despite [di'spait] *prep* trotz (+ *gen*).

despondent [di'spondənt] *adj* mutlos.

despot ['despot] *n* Gewaltherrscher *m*, Despot *m*. **despotism** *n* Despotismus *m*.

dessert [di'zət] *n* Nachtisch *m*. **dessert spoon** Dessertlöffel *m*.

destiny ['destəni] *n* Schicksal *neut*. **destined** *adj* ausersehen, bestimmt. **destination** *n* *(post)* Bestimmungsort *m*; *(travel)* Reiseziel *neut*.

destitute ['destitjut] *adj* notleidend, bedürftig.

destroy [di'stroi] *v* zerstören, vernichten. **destroyer** *n* Zerstörer *m*. **destruction** *n* Zerstörung *f*. **destructive** *adj* zerstörerisch.

detach [di'tatʃ] *v* losmachen, abtrennen. **detached** *adj* *(house)* Einzel-; *(fig)* objektiv. **detachment** *n* Objektivität *f*; *(mil)* Abteilung *f*.

detail ['diːteil] *n* Einzelheit *f*, Detail *neut*. **further details** Näheres *neut*; nähere Angaben *pl*. *v* detaillieren. **detailed** *adj* eingehend.

detain [di'tein] *v* aufhalten; *(arrest)* verhaften.

detect [di'tekt] *v* entdecken. **detection** *n* Aufdeckung *f*. **detective** *n* Detektiv *m*. **detective story** Kriminalroman *m*.

détente [dei'tãnt] *n* Entspannung *f*.

detention [di'tenʃən] *n* *(law)* Haft *m*; *(school)* Nachsitzen *neut*.

deter [di'təː] *v* abschrecken.

detergent [di'təːdʒənt] *n* Reinigungsmittel *neut*.

deteriorate [di'tiəriəˌreit] *v* sich verschlechtern. **deterioration** *n* Verschlechterung *f*.

determine [di'təːmin] *v* bestimmen; *(decide)* sich entschließen. **determined** *adj* entschlossen. **determination** *n* Entschlossenheit *f*.

detest [di'test] *v* hassen, verabscheuen. **detestable** *adj* abscheulich.

detonate ['detəˌneit] *v* detonieren.

detour ['dituə] *n* Umweg *m*.

detract [di'trakt] *v* **detract from** beeinträchtigen.

detriment ['detrimənt] *n* Schaden *m*, Nachteil *m*. **detrimental (to)** *adj* schädlich (für).

devalue [di'valjuː] *v* abwerten. **devaluation** *n* Abwertung *f*.

devastate ['devəˌsteit] *v* verwüsten. **devastating** *adj* vernichtend. **devastation** *n* Verwüstung *f*.

develop [di'veləp] *v* (sich) entwickeln. **developer** *n* Entwickler *m*. **developing** *n* Entwicklungs-. **development** *n* Entwicklung *f*.

deviate ['diːviˌeit] *v* abweichen. **deviation** *n* Abweichung *f*.

device [di'vais] *n* Gerät *neut*, Vorrichtung *f*; *(trick)* Trick *m*.

devil ['devl] *n* Teufel *m*. **talk of the devil** den Teufel an die Wand malen. **devilish** *adj* teuflisch.

devious ['diːviəs] *adj* weitschweifig; *(dishonest)* krumm, unaufrichtig.

devise [di'vaiz] *v* ausdenken, erfinden.

devoid [di'void] *adj* **devoid of** ohne, frei von.

devolution [ˌdiːvə'luːʃən] *n* Dezentralisation *f*.

devote [di'vout] *v* widmen, hingeben. **devoted** *adj* ergeben. **be devoted to someone** sehr an jemandem hängen. **devotee** *n* Anhänger(in). **devotion** *n* Ergebenheit *f*.

devour [di'vauə] *v* verschlingen.

devout [di'vaut] *adj* fromm, andächtig.

dew [djuː] *n* Tau *m*.

dexterous ['dekstrəs] *adj* gewandt, flink. **dexterity** *n* Gewandtheit *f*.

diabetes [ˌdiaə'biːtiz] *n* Zuckerkrankheit *f*. **diabetic** *adj* zuckerkrank. *n* Diabetiker *m*.

diagnose [ˌdiaəg'nouz] *v* diagnostizieren, erkennen. **diagnosis** *n* Diagnose *f*. **diagnostic** *adj* diagnostisch.

diagonal [dai'agənəl] *adj* diagonal. *n* Diagonale *f*.

diagram ['daiəˌgram] *n* Diagramm *neut*, Schaubild *neut*.

dial ['daiəl] *n* *(phone)* Wählscheibe *f*. *v* wählen. **dialling tone** Amtszeichen *neut*.

dialect ['daiəlekt] *n* Dialekt *m*.

dialogue ['daiəlog] *n* Dialog *m*.

diameter [dai'amitə] *n* Durchmesser *m*.

diamond ['daiəmənd] *n* Diamant *m*; *(cards)* Karo *neut*; *(sport)* Spielfeld *neut*. *adj* diamanten.

diaper ['daɪəpə] n Windel f.
diaphragm ['daɪəˌfram] n (anat) Zwerchfell neut; (contraceptive) (Okklusiv)Pessar neut.
diarrhoea [ˌdaɪə'rɪə] n Durchfall m.
diary ['daɪərɪ] n Tagebuch neut.
dice [daɪs] pl n Würfel pl. v (cookery) in Würfel schneiden.
dictate [dɪk'teɪt] n diktieren. **dictating machine** Diktiergerät neut. **dictation** n Diktat neut. **dictator** n Diktator m. **dictatorial** adj diktatorisch. **dictatorship** n.
dictionary ['dɪkʃənərɪ] n Wörterbuch neut.
did [dɪd] V do.
die [daɪ] v sterben. **die away** schwächer werden. **die out** aussterben.
diesel ['diːzəl] adj Diesel-. **diesel engine** Dieselmotor m.
diet [daɪət] n Kost f, Nahrung f; (for weight loss) Abmagerungskur f; (for convalescence, etc.) Diät f, Schonkost f. v eine Abmagerungskur machen.
differ ['dɪfə] v sich unterscheiden; (think differently) anderer Meinung sein. **difference** n Unterschied m. **different** adj verschieden, unterschiedlich; (another) anderer. **differential** adj unterschiedlich. n (mot) Differentialgetriebe neut.
difficult ['dɪfɪkəlt] adj schwer, schwierig. **difficulty** n Schwierigkeit f.
*****dig** [dɪg] V graben. **dig up** ausgraben.
digest [daɪ'dʒest; n 'daɪdʒest] v verdauen. n Auslese f. **digestible** adj verdaulich. **digestion** n Verdauung f.
digit ['dɪdʒɪt] n (figure) Ziffer f; (finger) Finger m; (toe) Zehe f.
dignified ['dɪgnɪˌfaɪd] adj würdevoll.
dignity ['dɪgnɪtɪ] n Würde f.
digress [daɪ'gres] v abschweifen. **digression** n Abschweifung f.
digs [dɪgz] pl n (coll) Bude f sing.
dilapidated [dɪ'lapɪˌdeɪtɪd] adj baufällig.
dilate [daɪ'leɪt] v (sich) weiten.
dilemma [dɪ'lemə] n Dilemma neut. **be in a dilemma** in der Klemme sitzen.
diligence ['dɪlɪdʒəns] n Fleiß m. **diligent** adj fleißig, gewissenhaft.
dilute [daɪ'luːt] v (with water) verwässern; verdünnen. adj (also diluted) verwässert.
dim [dɪm] adj trübe; (light, vision) schwach; (coll: stupid) dumm. v verdunkeln.
dimension [dɪ'menʃən] n Dimension f. **dimensions** pl Ausmaße pl.

diminish [dɪ'mɪnɪʃ] v (sich) vermindern. **diminishing** adj abnehmend.
diminutive [dɪ'mɪnjutɪv] adj winzig.
dimple ['dɪmpl] n Grübchen neut.
din [dɪn] n Lärm m, Getöse neut.
dine [daɪn] v speisen, essen. **diner** n (person) Tischgast m; (rail) Speisewagen m; (restaurant) Speiselokal neut. **dining car** Speisewagen m. **dining room** Eßzimmer neut. **dining table** Eßtisch m.
dinghy ['dɪŋgɪ] n Dingi neut, Beiboot neut. **rubber dinghy** Schlauchboot neut.
dingy ['dɪndʒɪ] adj trübe.
dinner ['dɪnə] n Abendessen neut; (at midday) Mittagessen neut; (public) Festessen neut. **dinner jacket** Smoking m. **dinner party** Diner neut.
dinosaur ['daɪnəˌsoʊ] n Dinosaurier m.
dip [dɪp] v (ein)tauchen; (slope down) sich senken. **dip one's lights** (mot) abblenden. n Senkung f; (bathe) Bad neut. **dip switch** Abblendschalter m.
diploma [dɪ'plouma] n Diplom neut.
diplomacy [dɪ'ploumasɪ] n Diplomatie f. **diplomat** n Diplomat m. **diplomatic** adj diplomatisch.
dipstick ['dɪpstɪk] n (mot) Ölmeßstab m.
dire [daɪə] adj schrecklich; (urgent) dringend.
direct [dɪ'rekt] adj direkt. v dirigieren, leiten; (aim) richten; (give directions) den Weg zeigen (+dat); (order) anweisen. **direction** n Richtung f; Leitung f; **directions** pl (for use) Gebrauchsanweisung f sing; (instructions) Anweisungen pl. **directly** adv (immediately) unmittelbar; (straight towards) direkt, gerade. **director** n Direktor m, Leiter m; (theatre, film) Regisseur m. **(telephone) directory** n Telefonbuch neut.
dirt [dɜːt] n Schmutz m, Dreck m. **dirt cheap** spottbillig. **dirty** adj schmutzig, dreckig.
disability [dɪsə'bɪlətɪ] n Körperbehinderung f. **disability pension** Invalidenrente f.
disadvantage [dɪsəd'vɑːntɪdʒ] n Nachteil m. **disadvantageous** adj ungünstig, unvorteilhaft.
disagree [dɪsə'griː] v nicht übereinstimmen; (argue) sich streiten. **disagreeable** adj unangenehm. **disagreement** n Meinungsverschiedenheit f.

disappear [ˌdɪsəˈpɪə] v verschwinden. **disappearance** n Verschwinden neut.

disappoint [ˌdɪsəˈpɔɪnt] v enttäuschen. **disappointed** adj enttäuscht. **disappointing** adj enttäuschend. **disappointment** n Enttäuschung f.

disapprove [ˌdɪsəˈpruːv] v **disapprove of** mißbilligen. **disapproval** n Mißbilligung f.

disarm [dɪsˈɑːm] v entwaffnen; (pol) abrüsten. **disarmament** n Abrüstung f. **disarming** adj entwaffnend.

disaster [dɪˈzɑːstə] n Katastrophe f, Unglück neut. **disastrous** adj katastrophal.

disband [dɪsˈband] v (sich) auflösen.

disc or US **disk** [dɪsk] n Scheibe f; (record) Schallplatte f.

discard [dɪsˈkɑːd] v ablegen.

disc brake n Scheibenbremse f. **disc jockey** n Disk-Jockey m.

discern [dɪˈsəːn] v (perceive) wahrnehmen; (differentiate) unterscheiden. **discernible** adj wahrnehmbar. **discerning** adj einsichtig.

discharge [dɪsˈtʃɑːdʒ] v (dismiss) entlassen; (gun) abschießen; (duty) erfüllen; (ship) entladen; (of wound) eitern. n (med) Ausfluß m.

disciple [dɪˈsaɪpl] n Jünger m.

discipline [ˈdɪsɪplɪn] n Disziplin f. v disziplinieren; (train) schulen.

disclaim [dɪsˈkleɪm] v ablehnen. **disclaimer** n Dementi neut.

disclose [dɪsˈklouz] v enthüllen. **disclosure** n Bekanntmachung f.

discolour [dɪsˈkʌlə] v (sich) verfärben. **discoloration** n Verfärbung f.

discomfort [dɪsˈkʌmfət] n Unbehagen neut.

disconcert [dɪskənˈsəːt] v aus der Fassung bringen.

disconnect [dɪskəˈnekt] v trennen; (elec) abschalten.

disconsolate [dɪsˈkɒnsələt] adj trostlos.

discontinue [dɪskənˈtɪnjuː] v aufhören; (something) einstellen.

discord [ˈdɪskɔːd] n (disagreement) Zwietracht f; (music) Diskordanz f. **discordant** adj diskordant.

discotheque [ˈdɪskətek] n Diskothek f.

discount [ˈdɪskaunt] v (ignore) außer Acht lassen. n Rabatt m.

discourage [dɪsˈkʌrɪdʒ] v entmutigen; (dissuade) abraten. **discouraging** adj entmutigend.

discover [dɪsˈkʌvə] v entdecken. **discoverer** n Entdecker m. **discovery** n Entdeckung f.

discredit [dɪsˈkredɪt] v in Verruf bringen.

discreet [dɪsˈkriːt] adj diskret, verschwiegen.

discrepancy [dɪsˈkrepənsi] n Widerspruch m, Diskrepanz f.

discretion [dɪsˈkreʃən] n Diskretion f, Takt m. **at your discretion** nach Ihrem Gutdünken.

discriminate [dɪsˈkrimiˌneɪt] v unterscheiden. **discriminate** (against) diskriminieren. **discriminating** adj anspruchsvoll. **discrimination** n (racial, etc.) Diskriminierung f.

discus [ˈdɪskəs] n Diskus m.

discuss [dɪsˈkʌs] v besprechen, diskutieren; (in writing) behandeln. **discussion** n Besprechung f, Diskussion f.

disease [dɪˈziːz] n Krankheit f. **diseased** adj krank.

disembark [dɪsɪmˈbɑːk] v an Land gehen.

disengage [dɪsɪnˈgeɪdʒ] v sich losmachen. **disengage the clutch** auskuppeln.

disfigure [dɪsˈfɪgə] v entstellen. **disfigurement** n Entstellung f.

disgrace [dɪsˈgreɪs] n Schande f. v Schande bringen über. **disgraceful** adj schändlich.

disgruntled [dɪsˈgrʌntld] adj mürrisch.

disguise [dɪsˈgaɪz] v verkleiden; (voice) verstellen. n Verkleidung f. **in disguise** verkleidet.

disgust [dɪsˈgʌst] n Ekel m (vor). v anekeln. **disgusting** adj ekelhaft, widerlich.

dish [dɪʃ] n Schüssel f, Schale f; (meal) Gericht neut. **dishes** pl Geschirr neut sing. **wash the dishes** abspülen. **dishcloth** n (for drying) Geschirrtuch neut; (for mopping) Lappen m.

dishearten [dɪsˈhɑːtn] v entmutigen.

dishevelled [dɪˈʃevəld] adj in Unordnung; (hair) zerzaust.

dishonest [dɪsˈonist] adj unehrlich, unaufrichtig. **dishonesty** n Unehrlichkeit f. **dishonour** n Unehre f, Schande f. v schänden. **dishonourable** adj unehrenhaft.

dishwasher [ˈdɪʃwoʃə] n Geschirrspülmaschine f.

disillusion [disi'luːʒən] v ernüchtern, desillusionieren. **be disillusioned about** die Illusion verloren haben über.

disinfect [disin'fekt] v desinfizieren. **disinfectant** n Desinfektionsmittel neut.

disinherit [disin'herit] v enterben.

disintegrate [dis'inti‚greit] v (sich) auflösen, (sich) zersetzen. **disintegration** n Auflösung f.

disinterested [dis'intristid] adj unparteiisch.

disjointed [dis'dʒointid] adj unzusammenhängend.

disk V disc.

dislike [dis'laik] v nicht mögen. n Abneigung f (gegen).

dislocate [ˈdisləˌkeit] v verrenken. **dislocation** n Verrenkung f.

dislodge [dis'lodʒ] v verschieben.

disloyal [dis'loiəl] adj untreu. **disloyalty** n Untreue f.

dismal [ˈdizməl] adj trübe, niederdrückend.

dismantle [dis'mantl] v abmontieren.

dismay [dis'mei] v bestürzen. n Bestürzung f, Angst f.

dismiss [dis'mis] v wegschicken; (employee) entlassen; (idea) ablehnen. **dismissal** n Entlassung f.

dismount [dis'maunt] v absteigen.

disobey [disə'bei] v nicht gehorchen (+dat). **disobedience** n Ungehorsam m. **disobedient** adj ungehorsam.

disorder [dis'oidə] n Unordnung f; (med) Störung f.

disorganized [dis'oiɡənaizd] adj unordentlich.

disown [dis'oun] v ableugnen; (child) verstoßen.

disparage [di'sparidʒ] v herabsetzen. **disparaging** v geringschätzig.

disparity [di'pariti] n Unterschied m.

dispassionate [dis'paʃənit] adj unparteiisch.

dispatch [dis'patʃ] v absenden; (person) entsenden. n Versand m, Abfertigung f; (report) Meldung f.

dispel [dis'pel] v vertreiben.

dispense [di'spens] v ausgeben. **dispense with** verzichten auf. **dispenser** n Verteiler m. **dispensing chemist** Apotheker(in).

disperse [di'spəis] v zerstreuen.

displace [dis'pleis] v versetzen; (replace) ersetzen; (water) verdrängen. **displacement** n (naut) Wasserverdrängung f.

display [di'splei] v zeigen; (goods, etc.) auslegen. n (goods) Auslage f; (feelings) Zurschaustellung f; (parade) Entfaltung f.

displease [dis'pliːz] v mißfallen (+dat). **displeased** adj ärgerlich. **displeasure** n Mißfallen neut.

dispose [di'spouz] v dispose of (get rid of) beseitigen, wegwerfen; (have at disposal) verfügen über. **disposed** adj geneigt. **disposable** adj zum Wegwerfen; Einweg-. **disposal** n Beseitigung f. **have at one's disposal** zur Verfügung haben. **be at someone's disposal** jemandem zur Verfügung stehen. **disposition** n Natur f, Art f.

disproportion [disprə'poiʃən] n Mißverhältnis neut. **disproportionate** adj unverhältnismäßig.

disprove [dis'pruːv] v widerlegen.

dispute [di'spjuːt] v (contest) bestreiten; (argue) disputieren. n Streit m. **trade dispute** Arbeitsstreitigkeit f.

disqualify [dis'kwoliˌfai] v disqualifizieren, ausschließen. **disqualification** n Disqualifikation f.

disregard [disrə'gaid] v nicht beachten.

disrepute [disrə'pjuit] v Verruf m. **bring into disrepute** in Verruf bringen. **disreputable** adj (notorious) verrufen.

disrespect [disrə'spekt] n Respektlosigkeit f. **disrespectful** adj respektlos.

disrupt [dis'rʌpt] v stören, unterbrechen. **disruption** n Störung f.

dissatisfied [dis'satisˌfaid] adj unzufrieden.

dissect [di'sekt] v sezieren.

dissent [di'sent] n abweichende Meinung f. v anderer Meinung sein.

dissident [ˈdisidənt] n Dissident m.

dissimilar [di'similə] v unähnlich.

dissociate [di'sousieit] v **dissociate oneself from** sich lossagen von.

dissolve [di'zolv] v (sich) auflösen; (meeting) aufheben.

dissuade [di'sweid] v abraten (+dat).

distance [ˈdistəns] n Ferne f, Entfernung f; (gap) Abstand m. **in the distance** in der Ferne. **keep one's distance** Abstand halten. **distant** adj fern, entfernt.

distaste [dis'teist] n Abneigung f. **distasteful** adj unangenehm.

distended [di'stendid] adj ausgedehnt.

distil [di'stil] v destillieren. **distillery** n Brennerei f.

distinct [di'stiŋkt] *adj* (*different*) verschieden; (*clear*) deutlich, ausgeprägt.
distinction *n* (*difference*) Unterschied *m*; (*merit*) Würde *f*. **of distinction** von Rang. **gain a distinction** sich auszeichnen. **distinctive** *adj* kennzeichnend.
distinguish [di'stiŋgwiʃ] *v* unterscheiden; (*perceive*) erkennen. **distinguish oneself** sich auszeichnen. **distinguishable** *adj* erkennbar. **distinguished** *adj* hervorragend.
distort [di'stoːt] *v* verdrehen; (*truth*) entstellen. **distortion** *n* Verdrehung *f*.
distract [di'strakt] *v* ablenken. **distracted** *adj* verwirrt, außer sich. **distraction** *n* Ablenkung *f*; (*amusement*) Unterhaltung *f*; (*madness*) Wahnsinn *m*.
distraught [di'strɔːt] *adj* verwirrt, bestürzt.
distress [di'stres] *n* Not *f*; (*suffering*) Leid *neut*, Qual *f*. *v* betrüben, quälen. **distress signal** Notsignal *m*.
distribute [di'stribjut] *v* verteilen. **distribution** *n* Verteilung *f*. **distributor** *n* Verteiler *m*.
district ['distrikt] *n* Gebiet *neut*, Gegend *f*; (*of town*) Viertel *neut*; (*administrative*) Bezirk *m*. *adj* Bezirks-. **district attorney** Staatsanwalt *m*.
distrust [di'trast] *v* mißtrauen (+ *dat*). *n* Mißtrauen *neut*.
disturb [di'stəːb] *v* stören; (*worry*) beunruhigen. **disturbance** *n* Störung *f*. **disturbances** *pl* (*pol*) Unruhen *pl*. **disturbing** *adj* beunruhigend.
disused [dis'juːzd] *adj* außer Gebrauch.
ditch [ditʃ] *n* Wassergraben *m*. *v* (*coll*) im Stich lassen.
ditto ['ditou] *adv* ebenfalls, dito. **ditto mark** Wiederholungszeichen *neut*.
divan [di'van] *n* Divan *m*, Sofa *neut*.
dive [daiv] *v* tauchen; (*from board*) einen Kopfsprung machen; (*aero*) stürzen. *n* Tauchen *neut*; Kopfsprung *m*; (*aero*) Sturzflug *m*. **diver** *n* Taucher *m*.
diverge [dai'vəːdʒ] *v* auseinandergehen.
diverse [dai'vəːs] *adj* verschieden.
divert [dai'vəːt] *v* ableiten; (*traffic*) umleiten. **diversion** *n* Ablenkung *f*; (*mot*) Umleitung *f*. **diversity** *n* Verschiedenheit *f*.
divide [di'vaid] *v* (sich) teilen.
dividend ['dividend] *n* Dividende *f*.
divine [di'vain] *adj* göttlich. *v* erraten.

division [di'viʒən] *n* Teilung *f*; (*math, mil*) Division *f*; (*comm*) Abteilung *f*.
divorce [di'vɔːs] *v* (Ehe)Scheidung *f*. *v* scheiden. **divorced** *adj* geschieden. **get divorced** sich scheiden lassen. **divorcee** *n* Geschiedene(r).
divulge [dai'valdʒ] *v* preisgeben.
dizzy ['dizi] *adj* schwindlig. **dizziness** *n* Schwindel *m*.
***do** [duː] *v* tun, machen. **that will do!** (*that's enough*) das genügt! **that won't do** (*that's no good*) das geht nicht! **How do you do?** Guten Tag! *I could do with the money* ich könnte das Geld gut gebrauchen. **do away with** abschaffen. **do in** (*coll*) umbringen. **do up** (*coll*) überholen. **do without** verzichten auf.
docile ['dousail] *adj* fügsam.
dock[1] [dok] *n* Dock *neut*. **docks** *pl* Hafenanlagen *pl*. *v* (*ship*) docken.
dock[2] [dok] *n* (*law*) **in the dock** auf der Anklagebank *f*.
dock[3] [dok] *v* (*cut*) stutzen; (*pay*) kürzen.
doctor ['doktə] *n* (*of medicine*) Arzt *m*, Ärztin *f*; (*as title*) Doktor *m*.
doctrine ['doktrin] *n* Lehre *f*.
document ['dokjumənt] *n* Urkunde *f*, Dokument *neut*. **documents** *pl* Papiere *pl*. *v* urkundlich belegen. **documentary** *adj* urkundlich. *n* Lehrfilm *m*.
dodge [dodʒ] *v* beiseitespringen; (*avoid*) ausweichen. *n* Kniff *m*.
dog [dog] *n* Hund *m*. **dog-eared** *adj* mit Eselsohren. **dogged** *adj* hartnäckig. **dog kennel** Hundehütte *f*.
dogma ['dogmə] *n* Dogma *neut*. **dogmatic** *adj* dogmatisch.
do-it-yourself [ˌduːitjɔːˈself] *adj* zum Selbermachen; Bastler-.
dole [doul] *n* Stempelgeld *neut*. **go on the dole** stempeln gehen. *v* **dole out** verteilen.
doll [dol] *n* Puppe *f*.
dollar ['dolə] *n* Dollar *m*.
dolphin ['dolfin] *n* Delphin *m*.
domain [də'mein] *n* Bereich *neut*.
dome [doum] *n* Kuppel *f*.
domestic [də'mestik] *adj* häuslich, Haus-; (*national*) inländisch, Innen-. **domestic animal** Haustier *neut*. **domesticate** *v* (*tame*) zähmen.
dominate ['domiˌneit] *v* beherrschen. **dominant** *adj* (vor)herrschend; (*music, biol*) dominant. **domination** *n* Herrschaft *f*.
domineering [domi'niəriŋ] *adj* herrisch.

dominion [dəˈminjən] n Herrschaft f; (country) Dominion neut.

domino [ˈdominou] n Dominostein m. **dominoes** pl Dominospiel neut sing.

don [don] v (clothes) anziehen; (hat) aufsetzen.

donate [dəˈneit] v stiften, spenden. **donation** n Spende f, Stiftung f. **donor** n Spender m.

done [dʌn] V do.

donkey [ˈdoŋki] n Esel m.

doom [duːm] n Verhängnis neut. **doomed** adj verloren.

door [doː] n Tür f. **out of doors** draußen. **doorbell** Türklingel f. **doorhandle** n Türgriff m. **doorway** n Türöffnung f; Torweg m.

dope [doup] n (coll) Rauschgift neut. v (sport) dopen.

dormant [ˈdoːmənt] adj schlafend.

dormitory [ˈdoːmitəri] n Schlafsaal m. (US: student house) Wohnheim m.

dormouse [ˈdoːmaus] n Haselmaus f.

dose [dous] n Dosis f. v dosieren.

dot [dot] n Punkt m.

dote [dout] v **dote on** vernarrt sein in. **dotted** [ˈdotid] adj übersät (mit). **dotted line** punktierte Linie f.

double [ˈdʌbl] adj doppelt, Doppel-. adv doppelt, zweimal. n das Doppelte; (film) Double neut. **doubles** n (sport) Doppelspiel neut. v verdoppeln; (fold) falten. **double-barrelled** adj doppelläufig. **double-bass** Kontrabaß m. **double-cross** v betrügen. **double-decker** Doppeldecker m. **double meaning** Zweideutigkeit f.

doubt [daut] n Zweifel m. v bezweifeln. **doubt whether** zweifeln, ob. **doubtful** adj zweifelhaft. **doubtless** adv ohne Zweifel, zweifellos.

dough [dou] n Teig m. **doughnut** n Krapfen m.

dove [dʌv] n Taube f.

dowdy [ˈdaudi] adj schäbig, schlampig.

down¹ [daun] adv hinab, herab; hinunter, herunter; unten. I went down the road ich ging die Straße hinunter. **up and down** auf und ab.

down² [daun] n (feathers) Daunen pl.

downcast [ˈdaunˌkaist] adj niedergeschlagen.

downfall [ˈdaunˌfoːl] n Sturz m.

downhearted [ˌdaunˈhaitid] adj mutlos.

downhill [ˈdaunˈhil] adv bergab.

downpour [ˈdaunˌpoː] n Wolkenbruch m.

downright [ˈdaunˌrait] adv völlig, höchst.

downstairs [ˌdaunˈsteəz] adv unten. she came downstairs sie kam nach unten.

downstream [ˌdaunˈstriːm] adv stromabwärts.

downtrodden [ˈdaunˌtrodn] adj unterworfen.

downward [ˈdaunwəd] adj Abwärts-, sinkend.

downwards [ˈdaunwədz] adv abwärts.

dowry [ˈdauəri] n Mitgift f.

doze [douz] v dösen. n Schläfchen neut.

drab [drab] adj eintönig, farblos.

draft [draift] n (plan) Konzept neut, Entwurf m; (comm) Tratte f; (mil) Aushebung f. v entwerfen; (mil) ausheben.

drag [drag] v schleppen, schleifen. n **drag on** sich in die Länge ziehen.

dragon [ˈdragən] n Drache m. **dragonfly** n Libelle f.

drain [drein] n Abfluß m; (fig) Belastung f. v ablassen; (water) ableiten; (fig) erschöpfen. **drainage** n Entwässerung f. **drainpipe** n Abflußrohr neut.

drama [ˈdraimə] n Drama neut. **dramatic** adj dramatisch. **dramatize** v dramatisieren.

drank [draŋk] V drink.

drape [dreip] v drapieren. n (curtain) Vorhang m. **draper** n Tuchhändler m.

drastic [ˈdrastik] adj drastisch.

draught or US **draft** [draift] n Zug m; (naut) Tiefgang m. **draughts** n Damespiel neut. **draught beer** Bier vom Faß. **draughtsman** n Zeichner m. **draughty** adj zugig.

*draw [droː] v ziehen; (curtain) zuziehen; (picture) zeichnen; (money) abheben; (public) anziehen; (water) schöpfen; (sport) unentschieden spielen. n (lottery) Ziehung f; (sport) Unentschieden neut. **draw near** sich nähern. **draw up** (document) ausstellen. **drawback** n Nachteil m. **drawbridge** n Zugbrücke f. **drawer** n Schublade f. **drawing** n Zeichnung f. **drawing pin** n Heftzwecke f. **drawing room** Salon m.

drawl [droːl] v schleppend sprechen.

drawn [droːn] V draw.

dread [dred] n Furcht f, Angst f. v Angst haben vor. **dreadful** adj furchtbar.

*dream [driːm] n Traum m. v träumen.
dreamer n Träumer n **dreamy** adj
träumerisch.

dreamt [dremt] V dream.

dreary ['driəri] adj trübe, düster.

dredge [dredʒ] v (river) ausbaggern.
dredger n Bagger m.

dregs [dregz] pl n Bodensatz m sing; (fig)
Abschaum m sing.

drench [drentʃ] v durchnässen.

dress [dres] v (sich) anziehen; (wound)
verbinden; (clothes) Kleidung f; (woman's)
Kleid neut. **dress designer**
Modezeichner m. **dresser** n (furniture)
Küchenschrank m. **dressing** n (salad)
Soße f; (med) Verband m. **dressing gown**
Morgenrock m. **dressing room** (theatre)
Garderobe f. **dressing table** Toiletten-
tisch m. **dressmaker** n Damenschneider-
ei f. **dress suit** Gesellschaftsanzug m.

drew [druː] V draw.

dribble ['dribl] v tröpfeln; (football) drib-
beln. n Tröpfeln neut.

drier ['draiə] n Trockner m.

drift [drift] v treiben; (coll) sich treiben
lassen; (snow) Verwehung f; (tendency)
Tendenz f. **drifter** n (person) Vagabund
m.

drill [dril] n Bohrmaschine f; (training)
Drill m. v (holes) bohren; (train) trainier-
en, drillen.

*drink [driŋk] v trinken; (animal, coll)
saufen. n Getränk neut; (cocktail, etc.)
Drink m. **drinker** n Trinker m (coll)
Säufer m.

drip [drip] v tropfen, triefen. n Tropfen m.
drip-dry adj bügelfrei. **dripping** adj
triefend. n Schmalz neut.

*drive [draiv] v treiben; (vehicle) fahren.
n Fahrt f; (tech) Antrieb m; (mil)
Kampagne f. **drive mad** verrückt
machen. **drive-in** (cinema) Autokino
neut.

drivel ['drivl] v sabbern, geifern. n
Quatsch m.

driver ['draivə] n Fahrer m, Chauffeur m.
driver's license Führerschein m.

driving ['draiviŋ] adj Treib-; (mot) Fahr-;
(rain) heftig. n Fahren neut. **driving lessons** Fahrunterricht m. **driving licence**
Führerschein m. **driving school** Fahr-
schule f. **driving test** Fahrprüfung f.

drizzle ['drizl] n Sprühregen m. v nieseln.

drone [droun] v summen. n Drohne f.

droop [druːp] v (schlaff) herunterhängen;
(flower) welken.

drop [drop] n (of water) Tropfen m; (fall)
Fall, Sturz m. v (fall) fallen; (let fall)
fallen lassen; (passenger) absetzen;
(bomb) abwerfen. **drop in** vorbeikommen.
drop off (to sleep) einschlafen. **drop-out** n
Dropout m.

drought [draut] n Dürre f.

drove [drouv] V drive.

drown [draun] v ertrinken. **drown out**
übertönen.

drowsy ['drauzi] adj schläfrig.

drudge [drʌdʒ] n Packesel m. **drudgery** n
Plackerei f.

drug [drʌg] n (medicinal) Droge f; (narcotic) Rauschgift neut. v betäuben. **drug
addict** Rauschgiftsüchtige(r).

drum [drʌm] n Trommel f. v trommeln.
drummer n Trommler m. **drumstick** n
Trommelstock m.

drunk [drʌŋk] V drink. adj betrunken;
(coll) besoffen. n Betrunkene(r). **get
drunk** sich betrinken; (coll) besoffen werden. **drunken** adj betrunken. **drunkard** n
Trinker m; (coll) Säufer m. **drunkenness** n
Betrunkenheit f.

dry [drai] adj trocken; (wine) herb. v
trocknen. **dry up** austrocknen; (dishes)
abtrocknen. **dry-clean** chemisch reinigen.
dry cleaner chemische Reinigung f. **dry
dock** Trockendock neut. **dry land** fester
Boden m.

dual ['djuəl] adj doppelt. **dual-purpose** adj
Mehrzweck-.

dubbed ['dʌbd] adj (film) synchronisiert.

dubious ['djuːbiəs] adj zweifelhaft, dubi-
ös.

duchess ['dʌtʃis] n Herzogin f.

duck[1] [dʌk] n Ente f.

duck[2] [dʌk] v sich ducken; (under water)
untertauchen.

duct [dʌkt] n Kanal m.

dud [dʌd] adj wertlos. n Niete f, Versager
m.

due [djuː] adj (suitable) gebührend; (payment) fällig. the train is due at 7 o'clock
der Zug soll (planmäßig) um 7 Uhr
ankommen. adv **due east** genau nach
Osten. **due to** infolge (+gen). **in due
course** zur rechten Zeit. I am due to ich
muß.

duel ['djuəl] n Duell neut.

duet [djuˈet] n Duett neut.

dug [dʌg] *V* **dig.**

duke [djuːk] *n* Herzog *m*.

dull [dʌl] *adj* (*colour*) matt, düster; (*pain*) dumpf; (*boring*) langweilig, uninteressant; (*stupid*) dumm. **dullness** *n* Düsterkeit *f*, Trübe *f*. *v* abstumpfen.

duly [ˈdjuːli] *adv* gebührend, ordnungsgemäß.

dumb [dʌm] *adj* stumm; (*coll: stupid*) doof. **deaf and dumb** taubstumm. **dumbfound** *v* verblüffen.

dummy [ˈdʌmi] *n* (*baby's*) Schnuller *m*; (*tailor's*) Schneiderpuppe *f*; (*imitation*) Attrappe *f*.

dump [dʌmp] *n* Müllhaufen *m*, Müllkippe *f*. *v* abladen.

dumpling [ˈdʌmpliŋ] *n* Knödel *m*, *Kloß m*.

dunce [dʌns] *n* Dummkopf *m*.

dune [djuːn] *n* Düne *f*.

dung [dʌŋ] *n* Mist *m*.

dungeon [ˈdʌndʒən] *n* Kerker *m*.

duplicate [ˈdjuːplikət; *v* ˈdjuːplikeit] *n* Duplikat *neut*. *v* verdoppeln; (*make copies*) vervielfältigen, kopieren. *adj* doppelt. **duplication** *n* Verdoppelung *f*. **duplicator** *n* Vervielfältigungsmaschine *f*.

durable [ˈdjuərəbl] *adj* dauerhaft.

duration [djuˈreiʃən] *n* Dauer *f*.

during [ˈdjuəriŋ] *prep* während (+*gen*).

dusk [dʌsk] *n* (Abend)Dämmerung *f*. **dusky** *adj* düster.

dust [dʌst] *n* Staub *m*. *v* abstauben. **dustbin** *n* Mülleimer *m*. **dustcart** *n* Müllwagen *m*. **duster** *n* Staubtuch *neut*. **dustman** *n* Müllabfuhrmann *m*. **dusty** *adj* staubig.

duty [ˈdjuːti] *n* Pflicht *f*; (*task*) Aufgabe *f*; (*tax*) Zoll *m*, Abgabe *f*. **off/on duty** außer/im Dienst. **duty-free** *adj* zollfrei. **dutiful** *adj* pflichtbewußt.

Dutch [dʌtʃ] *adj* holländisch. **Dutchman** *n* Holländer *m*. **Dutchwoman** *n* Holländerin *f*.

duvet [ˈduːvei] *n* Federbett *neut*.

dwarf [dwoːf] *n* Zwerg *m*. *adj* zwergenhaft.

*dwell [dwel] *n* wohnen. **dwell on** bleiben bei. **dwelling** *n* Wohnung *f*.

dwelt [dwelt] *V* **dwell.**

dwindle [ˈdwindl] *v* abnehmen.

dye [dai] *n* Farbstoff *m*. *v* färben.

dyke [daik] *n* Deich *m*, Damm *m*.

dynamic [daiˈnamik] *adj* dynamisch. **dynamics** *n* Dynamik *f*.

dynamite [ˈdainəmait] *n* Dynamit *neut*.

dynamo [ˈdainəmou] *n* Dynamo *m*.

dynasty [ˈdinəsti] *n* Dynastie *f*.

dysentery [ˈdisəntri] *n* Ruhr *f*.

dyslexia [disˈleksiə] *n* Legasthenie *f*, Wortblindheit *f*.

dyspepsia [disˈpepsiə] *n* Verdauungsstörung *f*.

E

each [iːtʃ] *adj, pron* jeder, jede, jedes. *adv* je. **each other** einander, sich.

eager [ˈiːgə] *adj* eifrig. **eagerness** Eifer *m*.

eagle [ˈiːgl] *n* Adler *m*.

ear¹ [iə] *n* (*anat*) Ohr *neut*; (*hearing*) Gehör *neut*. **earache** *n* Ohrenschmerzen *pl*. **eardrum** *n* Trommelfell *neut*. **earlobe** *n* Ohrläppchen *neut*. **earring** *n* Ohrring *m*. **earshot** *n* within/out of earshot in/außer Hörweite.

ear² [iə] *n* (*of corn*) Ähre *f*.

earl [əːl] *n* Graf *m*.

early [ˈəːli] *adj, adv* früh; (*soon*) bald.

earn [əːn] *v* verdienen. **earnings** *pl n* Einkommen *neut sing*.

earnest [ˈəːnist] *adj* ernsthaft. *n* **in earnest** im Ernst.

earth [əːθ] *n* Erde *f*. *v* (*elec*) erden. **earthly** *adj* irdisch. **earthenware** *n* Steingut *neut*. **earthquake** *n* Erdbeben *neut*. **earthworm** *n* Regenwurm *m*.

earwig [ˈiəwig] *n* Ohrwurm *m*.

ease [iːz] *n* Leichtigkeit *f*; (*comfort*) Behagen *neut*. *v* erleichtern. **at ease** behaglich. **with ease** ohne Mühe.

easel [ˈiːzl] *n* Staffelei *f*.

east [iːst] *n* Osten *m*. *adj also* **easterly** östlich, Ost-. *adv also* **eastwards** nach Osten; ostwärts. **eastern** *adj* östlich; orientalisch.

Easter [ˈiːstə] *n* Ostern *neut*.

easy [ˈiːzi] *adj* leicht. **easily** *adv* leicht, mühelos; (*by far*) bei weitem. **easy-going** *adj* ungezwungen.

*eat [iːt] *v* essen; (*of animals*) fressen.

eaten [iːtn] *V* **eat.**

eavesdrop [ˈiːvzdrop] *v* lauschen.

ebb [eb] *n* Ebbe *f*; (*fig*) Tiefstand *m*. *v* verebben.

ebony ['ebəni] n Ebenholz neut.

eccentric [ik'sentrik] adj exzentrisch. n Sonderling m.

ecclesiastical [iklizi'æstikl] adj kirchlich.

echo ['ekou] n Echo neut. v widerhallen.

eclipse [i'klips] n Finsternis f. v verfinstern; (fig) in den Schatten stellen.

ecology [i'kolədʒi] n Ökologie f. ecological adj ökologisch.

economy [i'konəmi] n Wirtschaft f; (thrift) Sparsamkeit f. economic adj ökonomisch, wirtschaftlich, Wirtschafts-. economical adj sparsam, wirtschaftlich. economics n Volkswirtschaft f. economist n Volkswirtschaftler m. economize v sparen (an).

ecstasy ['ekstəsi] n Ekstase f. ecstatic adj ekstatisch.

eczema ['eksimə] n Ekzem neut.

edge [edʒ] n Rand m. on edge nervös.

edible ['edəbl] adj eßbar.

edit ['edit] v redigieren. edition n Ausgabe f. editor n Redakteur m.

editorial [,edi'toːriəl] adj Redaktions-. n Leitartikel m.

educate ['edju,keit] n erziehen, ausbilden. education n Bildung f, Erziehung f; (system) Schulwesen neut. educational adj pädagogisch.

eel [iːl] n Aal m.

eerie ['iəri] adj unheimlich.

effect [i'fekt] n Wirkung f; (impression) Eindruck m. have an effect on wirken auf. in effect in Wirklichkeit. effective adj wirksam. effectiveness n Wirksamkeit f.

effeminate [i'feminət] adj weibisch.

effervesce [efə'ves] v sprudeln. effervescent adj sprudelnd.

efficiency [i'fiʃənsi] n Leistungsfähigkeit f. efficient adj (person) tüchtig; (effective) wirksam; (machine) leistungsfähig.

effigy ['efidʒi] n Abbild neut.

effort ['efət] n Anstrengung f. Mühe f. make an effort sich anstrengen. make every effort sich alle Mühe geben. effortless adj mühelos.

egg [eg] n Ei neut. v egg on reizen. boiled egg gekochtes Ei neut. fried egg Spiegelei neut. scrambled egg Rührei neut. egg cup Eierbecher m. eggshell n Eierschale f.

ego ['iːgou] pron Ich neut. egoism n Egoismus m. egoist n Egoist m.

Egypt ['iːdʒipt] n Ägypten neut. Egyptian adj ägyptisch; n Ägypter(in).

eiderdown ['aidədaun] n Federbett neut.

eight [eit] adj acht. n Acht f. eighth adj acht; n Achtel neut.

eighteen [ei'tiːn] adj achtzehn. eighteenth adj achtzehnt.

eighty ['eiti] adj achtzig. eightieth adj achtzigst.

either ['aiðə] pron einer (eine, eines) von den. on either side auf beiden Seiten. either ... or ... entweder ... oder ...

ejaculate [i'dʒakjuleit] v (utter) ausstoßen; ejakulieren.

eject [i'dʒekt] v ausstoßen.

eke [iːk] v eke out (add to) ergänzen.

elaborate [i'labərət] adj ausführlich, genau ausgearbeitet. v elaborate on eingehend erörtern. elaboration n Ausarbeitung f.

elapse [i'laps] v vergehen.

elastic [i'lastik] adj elastisch. elastic band Gummiband neut.

elated [i'leitid] adj begeistert, froh.

elbow ['elbou] n Ellbogen m.

elder¹ ['eldə] adj älter. n Ältere(r).

elder² ['eldə] n (tree) Holunder m.

elderly ['eldəli] adj älter.

eldest ['eldist] adj ältest. n Älteste(r).

elect [i'lekt] v wählen. election n Wahl f. elector n Wähler m. electorate n Wählerschaft f.

electric [ə'lektrik] adj also electrical elektrisch. electrical engineering Elektrotechnik f. electric blanket Heizdecke f. electric chair elektrischer Stuhl m. electric cooker Elektroherd neut. electrician n Elektriker m. electricity n Strom m, Elektrizität f.

electrify [ə'lektrifai] v elektrifizieren. electrifying adj (fig) elektrisierend.

electronic [elak'tronik] n elektronisch. electronics n Elektronik f sing.

elegant ['eligənt] adj elegant.

element ['eləmənt] n Element neut. elementary adj elementar.

elephant ['elifənt] n Elefant m.

elevate ['eliveit] v heben; (promote) erheben. elevation n Hochheben neut; (promotion) Erhebung f. elevator n Aufzug m.

eleven [i'levn] adj elf. eleventh adj elft.

eligible ['elidʒəbl] adj wählbar. be eligible in Frage kommen. be eligible for berechtigt sein zu. eligibility n Eignung f.

eliminate [i'limineit] v beseitigen; (sport) ausscheiden. **elimination** n Beseitigung f; Ausscheidung f.

élite [ei'liːt] n Elite f.

ellipse [i'lips] n Ellipse f. **elliptical** adj elliptisch.

elm [elm] n Ulme f.

elocution [elə'kjuːʃən] n Sprechkunde f.

elope [i'loup] v entlaufen. **elopement** n Entlaufen neut.

eloquent ['eləkwənt] adj (person) redegewandt. **eloquence** n Redegewandtheit f.

else [els] adv sonst. **anyone else?** sonst noch jemand? **someone else** jemand anders. **nothing else** nichts weiter. **elsewhere** adv anderswo, woanders.

elucidate [i'luːsideit] v aufklären. **elucidation** n Aufklärung f.

elude [i'luːd] v entgehen (dat).

emaciated [i'meisieitid] adj abgemagert.

emanate ['eməneit] v ausströmen (aus); (fig) herstammen (von).

emancipate [i'mansipeit] v befreien, emanzipieren. **emancipated** adj emanzipiert. **emancipation** n Befreiung f.

embalm [im'baːm] v einbalsamieren.

embankment [im'baŋkmənt] n Damm m; (road) Uferstraße f.

embargo [im'baːgou] n Handelssperre f.

embark [im'baːk] v sich einschiffen (nach); (fig) sich einlassen (in).

embarrass [im'barəs] v in Verlegenheit bringen. **be embarrassed** verlegen sein. **embarrassment** n Verlegenheit f.

embassy ['embəsi] n Botschaft f.

embellish [im'beliʃ] v verzieren.

embers 'embəz] pl n Glut f sing.

embezzle [im'bezl] v unterschlagen. **embezzlement** n Unterschlagung f.

embitter [im'bitə] v verbittern.

emblem ['embləm] n Sinnbild neut.

embody [im'bodi] v verkörpern. **embodiment** n Verkörperung f.

embossed [im'bost] adj erhaben.

embrace [im'breis] v umarmen; (include) umfassen. n Umarmung f.

embroider [im'broidə] v (be)sticken; (story) ausschmücken. **embroidery** n Stickerei f.

embryo ['embriou] n Embryo m.

emerald ['emərəld] n Smaragd m. **emerald green** smaragdgrün.

emerge [i'məːdʒ] v (from water) auftauchen; (appear) hervorkommen. **emergence** n Auftauchen neut.

emergency [i'məːdʒənsi] n Notfall m. adj Not-. **emergency exit** Notausgang m.

emigrate ['emigreit] v auswandern. **emigration** n Auswanderung f. **emigrant** n Auswanderer m.

eminent ['eminənt] adj hervorragend, erhaben. **eminence** n Erhöhung f.

emit [i'mit] v von sich geben. **emission** n Ausstrahlung f.

emotion [i'mouʃən] n Gefühl neut. **emotional** adj Gefühls-; (excitable) erregbar; (full of feeling) gefühlvoll.

empathy ['empəθi] n Einfühlung f.

emperor ['empərə] n Kaiser m.

emphasis ['emfəsis] n (pl -ses) Nachdruck m. **emphasize** v betonen, unterstreichen. **emphatic** adj nachdrücklich.

empire ['empaiə] n Reich neut.

empirical [im'pirikl] adj empirisch.

employ [im'ploi] v (use) verwenden; (appoint) anstellen. **be employed** beschäftigt or tätig sein. **employee** n Angestellte(r); (as opposed to employer) Arbeitnehmer m. **employer** n Arbeitgeber m. **employment** n Arbeit f, Beschäftigung f.

empower [im'pauə] v ermächtigen.

empress ['empris] n Kaiserin f.

empty ['empti] adj leer. v leeren. **emptiness** n Leere f.

emulate ['emjuleit] v nacheifern (dat).

emulsion [i'mʌlʃən] n Emulsion f. **emulsify** v emulgieren.

enable [i'neibl] v ermöglichen.

enact [i'nakt] v verordnen; (law) erlassen.

enamel [i'naməl] n Emaille f; (teeth) Zahnschmelz m. v emaillieren.

enamour [i'namə] v **be enamoured of** verliebt sein in.

encase [in'keis] v umschließen.

enchant [in'tʃaːnt] v entzücken. **enchanting** adj entzückend. **enchantment** n Zauber m, Entzücken neut.

encircle [in'səːkl] v umringen.

enclose [in'klouz] v einschließen; (in letter) beifügen. **enclosed** adj (in letter) beigefügt. **enclosure** n Einzäunung f; (in letter) Anlage f.

encore ['oŋkoɪ] interj noch einmal! n Zugabe f.

encounter [in'kauntə] v treffen; (difficulties) stoßen auf. n Begegnung f; (mil) Gefecht neut.

encourage [in'kʌridʒ] v ermutigen; (promote) fördern. **encouragement** n Ermutigung f.

encroach [in'krəutʃ] v eindringen (in). **encroachment** n Eingriff m.

encyclopedia [insaiklə'piːdiə] n Enzyklopädie f.

end [end] n Ende neut; (finish) Schluß m; (purpose) Zweck m. v beend(ig)en; (come to an end) zu Ende gehen. **ending** n Ende neut. **endless** adj unendlich.

endanger [in'deindʒə] v gefährden.

endeavour [in'devə] v sich anstrengen, versuchen. n Versuch m, Bestrebung f.

endemic [en'demik] adj endemisch.

endive ['endiv] n Endivie f.

endorse [in'dɔːs] v indossieren; (approve of) billigen. **endorsement** n Vermerk m; Billigung f.

endow [in'dau] v stiften. **endowed with** begabt mit. **endowment** n Ausstattung f, Stiftung f.

endure [in'djuə] v ertragen. **enduring** adj beständig.

enemy ['enəmi] n Feind m. adj Feind-.

energy ['enədʒi] n Energie f. **energetic** adj energisch.

enforce [in'fɔːs] v durchsetzen. **enforcement** n Durchsetzung f.

engage [in'geidʒ] v (employ) anstellen; (tech) einschalten; (enemy) angreifen. **engaged** adj (to be married) verlobt; (occupied) besetzt. **get engaged** sich verloben. **engagement** n (to marry) Verlobung f; (appointment) Verabredung f.

engine ['endʒin] n Motor m; (rail) Lokomotive f. **engine driver** Lokomotivführer m.

engineer [endʒi'niə] n Ingenieur m. v (fig) organisieren. **engineering** n Technik f.

England ['iŋglənd] n England neut.

English ['iŋgliʃ] adj englisch. **(the) English (language)** (das) Englisch(e), die englische Sprache. **I am English** ich bin Engländer(in). **English Channel** Ärmelkanal m. **Englishman** n Engländer m. **Englishwoman** n Engländerin f.

engrave [in'greiv] v gravieren. **engraving** n Stich m.

engrossed [in'grəust] adj vertieft.

engulf [in'gʌlf] v (overcome) überwältigen.

enhance [in'hɑːns] v verstärken.

enigma [i'nigmə] n Rätsel neut. **enigmatic** adj rätselhaft.

enjoy [in'dʒɔi] v genießen, Freude haben an. **enjoy oneself** sich (gut) unterhalten.

enjoyment n Freude f. **enjoy yourself!** viel spaß/Vergnügen!

enlarge [in'lɑːdʒ] v (sich) vergrößern. **enlargement** n Vergrößerung f.

enlighten [in'laitn] v aufklären. **enlightened** adj aufgeklärt. **enlightenment** n Aufklärung f.

enlist [in'list] v (help) in Anspruch nehmen; (in army) sich melden.

enmity ['enməti] n Feindseligkeit f.

enormous [i'nɔːməs] adj riesig, ungeheuer.

enough [i'nʌf] adv genug. **be enough** genügen. **have enough of something (be tired of)** etwas satt haben.

enquire [in'kwaiə] adv sich erkundigen, fragen. **enquiry** n Nachfrage f.

enrage [in'reidʒ] v wütend machen. **enraged** adj wütend.

enrich [in'ritʃ] v bereichern.

enrol [in'rəul] v einschreiben; (in club) als Mitglied aufnehmen; (oneself) beitreten (dat). **enrolment** n Aufnahme f.

ensign [in'sain] n (naut) (Schiffs)Flagge f.

enslave [in'sleiv] v versklaven.

ensue [in'sjuː] v (darauf) folgen. **ensuing** adj darauffolgend.

ensure [in'ʃuə] v gewährleisten, sichern.

entail [in'teil] v mit sich bringen.

entangle [in'taŋgl] v verstricken. **entangled** adj verstrickt.

enter ['entə] v (go in) eintreten; (a room) hineintreten in; (in book) einschreiben; (sport) sich anmelden.

enterprise ['entə,praiz] n (concern) Unternehmen neut; (initiative) Initiative f. **private enterprise** freie Wirtschaft f. **enterprising** adj unternehmungslustig.

entertain [entə'tein] v (amuse) unterhalten; (feelings) hegen; (as guests) gastlich bewirten. **entertaining** adj unterhaltsam. **entertainment** n Unterhaltung f.

enthral [in'θrɔːl] v entzücken. **enthralling** adj entzückend.

enthusiasm [in'θuːziˌazəm] n Begeisterung f. **Enthusiasmus** m. **enthusiastic** adj begeistert, enthusiastisch.

entice [in'tais] v verlocken. **enticement** n Anreiz m. **enticing** adj verlockend.

entire [in'taiə] adj ganz. **entirely** adv ganz, völlig, durchaus. **entirety** n Gesamtheit f.

entitle [in'taitl] v berechtigen (zu).

entity ['entəti] n Wesen neut.

entrails ['entreilz] *pl n* Eingeweide *pl.*

entrance¹ ['entrəns] *n (going in, fee)* Eintritt *m; (way in)* Eingang *m.*

entrance² [in'trans] *v* entzücken.

entrant ['entrənt] *n (sport)* Teilnehmer(in); *(for exam)* Kandidat *m.*

entreat [in'tri:t] *v* ernstlich bitten. **entreaty** *n* Bitte *f.*

entrenched [in'trentʃt] *v* **become entrenched** sich festsetzen.

entrepreneur [,ontrəprə'nəi] *n* Unternehmer *m.*

entrust [in'trʌst] *v (thing)* anvertrauen *(dat); (person)* betrauen (mit).

entry ['entri] *n* Eintritt *m; (into country)* Einreise *f; (comm)* Posten *m; (theatre)* Auftritt *m.* **no entry** Eintritt verboten.

entwine [in'twain] *v* umwinden.

enunciate [i'nʌnsi,eit] *v* aussagen; *(state)* ausdrücken.

envelop [in'veləp] *v* einwickeln; *(fig)* umhüllen.

envelope ['envə,ləup] *n* Umschlag *m.*

enviable ['enviəbl] *adj* beneidenswert.

envious ['enviəs] *adj* neidisch *(of auf).* **be envious of** beneiden.

environment [in'vaiərənmənt] *n* Umgebung *f.* **the environment** Umwelt *f.* **environmental** *adj* Umwelt-.

envisage [in'vizidʒ] *v* sich vorstellen.

envoy ['envoi] *n* Bote *m.*

envy ['envi] *v* beneiden. *n* Neid *m.*

enzyme ['enzaim] *n* Enzym *neut.*

epaulet ['epələt] *n* Epaulette *f.*

ephemeral [i'femərəl] *adj* vergänglich.

epic ['epik] *adj (poetry)* episch; heldenhaft. *n* Heldengedicht *neut.*

epicure ['epikjuə] *n* Feinschmecker *m.*

epidemic [epi'demik] *n* Epidemie *f. adj* epidemisch.

epilepsy ['epilepsi] *n* Epilepsie *f.* **epileptic** *adj* epileptisch; *n* Epileptiker(in).

epilogue ['epilog] *n* Epilog *m.*

Epiphany [i'pifəni] *n* Epiphanias *neut.*

episcopal [i'piskəpəl] *adj* bischöflich.

episode ['episoud] *n* Episode *f.*

epitaph ['epi,tɑːf] *n* Grabschrift *f.*

epitome [i'pitəmi] *n* Inbegriff *m.*

epoch ['iːpɔk] *n* Epoche *f.*

equable ['ekwəbl] *adj (person)* gelassen.

equal ['iːkwəl] *adj* gleich (+ *dat).* **be equal to** gleichen (+ *dat); (be able)* gewachsen sein (+ *dat). equal in size* von gleicher Größe. *n* Gleichgestellte(r). *v* gleichen (+ *dat),* gleich sein (+ *dat).* **equality** *n*

Gleichheit *f; (pol)* Gleichberechtigung *f.* **equalize** *v* gleichmachen. **equally** *adv* ebenso, in gleichem Maße.

equanimity [ekwə'nimət] *n* Gleichmut *m.*

equate [i'kweit] *v* gleichstellen. **equation** *n* Gleichung *f.*

equator [i'kweitə] *n* Äquator *m.* **equatorial** *adj* äquatorial.

equestrian [i'kwestriən] *adj* Reit-, Reiter-.

equilateral [,iːkwi'lætərəl] *adj* gleichseitig.

equilibrium [,iːkwi'libriəm] *n* Gleichgewicht *neut.*

equinox ['ekwinoks] *n* Tagundnachtgleiche *f.*

equip [i'kwip] *v* ausrüsten, ausstatten. **equipment** *n* Ausrüstung *f,* Einrichtung *f.*

equity ['ekwəti] *n* Billigkeit *f; (law)* Billigkeitsrecht *f.*

equivalent [i'kwivələnt] *adj* gleichwertig. **be equivalent to** gleichkommen *(dat). n* Gegenstück *neut.*

era ['iərə] *n* Epoche *f,* Ära *f.*

eradicate [i'radi,keit] *v* ausrotten. **eradication** *n* Ausrottung *f.*

erase [i'reiz] *v* ausradieren, tilgen. **eraser** *n* Radiergummi *m.*

erect [i'rekt] *v* errichten. *adj* aufrecht. **erection** *n* Errichtung *f; (anat)* Erektion *f.*

ermine ['əːmin] *n* Hermelin *m.*

erode [i'roud] *v* zerfressen. **erosion** *n* Zerfressung *f.*

erotic [i'rotik] *adj* erotisch. **eroticism** *n* Erotik *f.*

err [əi] *v* sich irren.

errand ['erənd] *n (Boten)Gang m.*

erratic [i'ratik] *adj* unberechenbar.

error ['erə] *n* Fehler *m,* Irrtum *m; (of compass)* Abweichung *f; (oversight)* Versehen *neut.* **erroneous** *adj* irrtümlich.

erudite ['erudait] *adj* gelehrt.

erupt [i'rupt] *v (volcano)* ausbrechen. **eruption** *n* Ausbruch *m; (skin)* Hautausschlag *m.*

escalate ['eskə,leit] *v (a war)* steigern, eskalieren. **escalation** *n* Eskalation *f.* **escalator** *n* Rolltreppe *f.*

escalope ['eskə,lop] *n* Schnitzel *neut.*

escape [is'keip] *v* entkommen (+ *dat); (fig)* entgehen (+ *dat). (of liquid)* Ausfluß *m.* **have a narrow escape** mit knapper Not entkommen.

escort [i'skoːt] *n* 'eskoːt] *v* begleiten. *n (mil)* Eskorte *f.*

esoteric [esɔˈterik] *adj* esoterisch.

especial [iˈspeʃəl] *adj* besonder, speziell. **especially** *adv* besonders.

espionage [ˈespiəˌnɑːʒ] *n* Spionage *f*.

esplanade [ˌespləˈneid] *n* Esplanade *f*.

essay [ˈesei] *n* (*school*) Aufsatz *m*; (*literary*) Essay *m*.

essence [ˈesns] *n* Wesen *neut*; (*extract*) Essenz *f*.

essential [iˈsenʃəl] *adj* wesentlich; (*indispensable*) unentbehrlich, unbedingt notwendig. **essentially** *adv* im wesentlichen.

establish [iˈstabliʃ] *v* einrichten, aufstellen; (*a fact*) feststellen; (*found*) gründen. **establishment** *n* Gründung *f*; (*comm*) Unternehmen *neut*.

estate [iˈsteit] *n* (*of deceased*) Nachlaß *m*; (*of noble*) Landsitz *m*. **housing estate** Siedlung *f*. **real estate** Immobilien *pl*. **estate agent** Grundstücksmakler *m*. **estate car** Kombiwagen *m*.

esteem [iˈstiːm] *n* Achtung *f*. *v* hochschätzen.

estimate [ˈestiˌmeit; *n* ˈestimət] *v* schätzen (auf). *n* (Ab)Schätzung. **estimation** *n* Ansicht (*opinion*) *f*.

estuary [ˈestjuəri] *n* (Fluß)Mündung *f*.

eternal [iˈtəːnl] *adj* ewig. **eternity** *n* Ewigkeit *f*.

ether [ˈiːθə] *n* Äther *m*. **ethereal** *adj* ätherisch.

ethical [ˈeθikl] *adj* ethisch, sittlich. **ethics** *n* Ethik *f*.

ethnic [ˈeθnik] *adj* ethnisch, Volks-.

etiquette [ˈetiket] *n* Etikette *f*.

etymology [ˌetiˈmolədʒi] *n* Etymologie *f*.

Eucharist [ˈjuːkərist] *n* heilige Messe *f*.

eunuch [ˈjuːnək] *n* Eunuch *m*, Verschnittene(r) *m*.

euphemism [ˈjuːfəˌmizəm] *n* Euphemismus *m*. **euphemistic** *adj* beschönigend.

euphoria [juˈfɔːriə] *n* Wohlbefinden *neut*, Euphorie *f*.

Europe [ˈjuərəp] *n* Europa *neut*. **European** *adj* europäisch; *n* Europäer(in). **European Economic Community (EEC)** Europäische Wirtschaftsgemeinschaft (EWG) *f*. **European Community** Europäische Gemeinschaften (EG) *pl*.

euthanasia [ˌjuːθəˈneiziə] *n* Euthanasie *f*, Gnadentod *m*.

evacuate [iˈvakjuˌeit] *v* (*depart*) aussiedeln; (*empty*) entleeren; (*people*) evakuieren. **evacuation** *n* Evakuierung *f*.

evade [iˈveid] *v* ausweichen, entgehen (+ *dat*); (*tax*) hinterziehen.

evaluate [iˈvaljuˌeit] *v* abschätzen. **evaluation** *n* Abschätzung *f*.

evangelical [ˌiːvanˈdʒelikəl] *adj* evangelisch. **evangelism** *n* Evangelismus *m*. **evangelist** *n* Evangelist *m*.

evaporate [iˈvapəˌreit] *v* verdampfen. **evaporated milk** Kondensmilch *f*. **evaporation** *n* Verdampfung *f*.

evasion [iˈveiʒən] *n* Ausweichen *neut*. **tax evasion** Steuerhinterziehung *f*. **evasive** *adj* ausweichend. **evasive action** Ausweichmanöver *neut*.

eve [iːv] *n* Vorabend *m*. **Christmas Eve** Heiliger Abend *m*. **New Year's Eve** Sylvesterabend *m*.

even [ˈiːvən] *adj* eben, gerade. *adv* sogar. *even bigger* noch größer. *even more* noch mehr. **not even** nicht einmal. *even if* wenn auch. **even-handed** *adj* unparteiisch.

evening [ˈiːvniŋ] *n* Abend *m*. **in the evening** abends, am Abend. **this evening** heute abend. **evening dress** Gesellschaftsanzug *m*. **evening meal** Abendessen *neut*.

event [iˈvent] *n* Ereignis *neut*; (*sport*) Disziplin *f*. **in the event of** im Falle (+ *gen*). **eventful** *adj* ereignisvoll.

ever [ˈevə] *adv* je(mals); (*always*) immer. *have you ever been to Berlin?* sind Sie schon einmal in Berlin gewesen? **ever so** sehr. **for ever** für immer. **evergreen** *adj* immergrün. **everlasting** *adj* ewig.

every [ˈevri] *adj* jede; alle *pl*. **every day** jeden Tag. **every one** jeder einzelne. **every other day** jeden zweiten Tag. **every so often** hin und wieder. **everybody/everyone** *pron* jeder. **everything** *pron* alles. **everywhere** *adv* überall.

evict [iˈvikt] *n* exmittieren. **eviction** *n* Exmission *f*.

evidence [ˈevidəns] *v* Zeugnis *neut*; Beweis *m*. **give evidence** Zeugnis ablegen. *v* beweisen.

evil [ˈiːvl] *adj* übel, böse. *n* Übel *neut*, Böse *neut*.

evoke [iˈvouk] *v* hervorrufen.

evolve [iˈvolv] *v* (sich) entwickeln. **evolution** *n* Entwicklung *f*; (*biol*) Evolution *f*.

ewe [juː] *n* Mutterschaf *neut*.

exacerbate [igˈzasəˌbeit] *v* verschlimmern.

exact [ig'zakt] *adj* genau, exakt. *v* verlangen; *(payment)* eintreiben. **exacting** *adj* anspruchsvoll. **exactly** *adv* genau.

exaggerate [ig'zadʒəˌreit] *v* übertreiben. **exaggerated** *adj* übertrieben. **exaggeration** *n* Übertreibung *f*.

exalt [ig'zɔlt] *v* erheben; *(praise)* preisen. **exaltation** *n (joy)* Wonne *f*. **exalted** *adj* erhaben; *(excited)* aufgeregt.

examine [ig'zamin] *v* untersuchen, prüfen; *(law)* verhören. **examination** *n* Prüfung *f*; *(inspection)* Untersuchung *f*. **medical examination** ärztliche Untersuchung *f*.

example [ig'zɑːmpl] *n* Beispiel *neut*. **for example** zum Beispiel. **set an example** ein Beispiel geben.

exasperate [ig'zɑːspəˌreit] *v* zum Verzweifeln bringen. **exasperation** *n* Verzweiflung *f*.

excavate ['ekskəˌveit] *v* ausgraben. **excavation** *n* Ausgrabung *f*. **excavator** *n (mech)* Bagger *m*.

exceed [ik'siːd] *v* überschreiten. **exceedingly** *adv* höchst.

excel [ik'sel] *v* sich auszeichnen. **excellence** *n* Vorzüglichkeit *f*. **Excellency** *n* Exzellenz *f*. **excellent** *adj* ausgezeichnet, vorzüglich.

except [ik'sept] *prep* außer. **except for** abgesehen von. *v* ausschließen. **exception** *n* Ausnahme *f*. **take exception to** übelnehmen.

excerpt ['eksəːpt] *n* Auszug *m*.

excess [ik'ses] *n* Übermaß *neut*, Überfluß *m* (an). *adj* Über-. **excess fare** Zuschlag *m*. **excessive** *adj* übermäßig.

exchange [iks'tʃeindʒ] *v* (aus-, um)tauschen; *(money)* wechseln. *n* Austausch *m*; *(phone)* Zentrale *f*. **foreign exchange** Devisen *pl*. **exchange rate** Wechselkurs *m*.

exchequer [iks'tʃekə] *n* Schatzamt *neut*.

excise ['eksaiz] *v (cut out)* herausschneiden. **excise duty** indirekter Steuer *m*.

excite [ik'sait] *v* erregen, aufregen. **get excited** sich aufregen. **excitement** *n* Aufregung *f*.

exclaim [ik'skleim] *v* ausrufen. **exclamation** *n* Ausruf *m*. **exclamation mark** Ausrufungszeichen *neut*.

exclude [ik'skluːd] *v* ausschließen. **exclusive** *adj* ausschließlich; *(fashionable)* exklusiv. **exclusive of** *also* **excluding** ausschließlich. **exclusion** *n* Ausschluß *m*.

excommunicate [ekskə'mjuːniˌkeit] *v* exkommunizieren. **excommunication** *n* Exkommunikation *f*.

excrement ['ekskrəmənt] *n* Exkrement *neut*, Kot *m*.

excrete [ik'skriːt] *v* ausscheiden. **excretion** *n* Ausscheidung *f*.

excruciating [ik'skruːʃieitiŋ] *adj* peinigend.

excursion [ik'skəːʃən] *n* Ausflug *m*.

excuse [ik'skjuːz] *n* Ausrede *f*. *v* entschuldigen, verzeihen. **excuse me!** Verzeihung!

execute ['eksiˌkjuːt] *v (carry out)* ausführen; *(person)* hinrichten. **execution** *n* Ausführung *f*; Hinrichtung *f*. **executioner** *n* Henker *m*. **executor** *n* Testamentvollstrecker *m*.

executive [ig'zekjutiv] *adj* vollziehend. *n (comm)* Geschäftsführer *m*.

exemplify [ig'zempliˌfai] *v* als Beispiel dienen für.

exempt [ig'zempt] *v* befreien (von). *adj* **exempt from** frei von.

exercise ['eksəˌsaiz] *n* Übung *f*; *(of duty)* Ausübung *f*. *v* üben; *(wield)* ausüben. **physical exercise** Leibesübung *f*. **exercise book** Schulheft *neut*.

exert [ig'zəːt] *v* ausüben. **exert oneself** sich anstrengen. **exertion** *n* Anstrengung *f*.

exhale [eks'heil] *v* ausatmen.

exhaust [ig'zɔːst] *v* erschöpfen. **exhausted** *adj* erschöpft. **exhausting** *adj* anstrengend. **exhaustion** *n* Erschöpfung *f*. *n* exhaust *(gases)* Abgase *pl*. **exhaust pipe** Auspuffrohr *neut*.

exhibit [ig'zibit] *v* zeigen; *(goods)* ausstellen. **exhibition** *n* Ausstellung *f*. **exhibitor** *n* Aussteller *m*.

exhilarate [ig'ziləˌreit] *v* erheitern. **exhilarated** *adj* angeregt, heiter. **exhilarating** erheiternd. **exhilaration** *n* Erheiterung *f*.

exile ['eksail] *n* Verbannung *f*; *(person)* Verbannte(r). *v* verbannen.

exist [ig'zist] *v* existieren, sein. **existence** *n* Dasein *neut*, Existenz *f*. **existing** bestehend.

exit ['egzit] *n* Ausgang. *v* abtreten.

exodus ['eksədəs] *n* Auswanderung *f*; *(coll)* allgemeiner Ausbruch *m*.

exonerate [ig'zonəˌreit] *v* freisprechen (von).

exorbitant [ig'zɔːbitənt] *adj* übermäßig.
exorcize [ˈeksɔːsaiz] *v* austreiben.
exotic [igˈzɔtik] *adj* exotisch, fremdartig.
expand [ikˈspænd] *v* (sich) ausdehnen; (*develop*) entwickeln, erweitern. **expanse** *n* Weite *f*, weite Fläche *f*. **expansion** *n* Ausdehnung *f*; (*of firm*) Erweiterung *f*; (*pol*) Expansion *f*.
expatriate [eksˈpeitrieit] *vv* ausbürgern. *n* im Ausland Lebende(r).
expect [ikˈspekt] *v* erwarten; (*support*) annehmen. *She is expecting* sie ist in anderen Umständen. **expectation** *n* Erwartung *f*.
expedient [ikˈspiːdiənt] *adj* zweckdienlich. *n* Notbehelf *m*.
expedition [ˌekspiˈdiʃən] *n* Expedition *f*.
expel [ikˈspel] *v* ausstoßen; (*from school*) ausschließen.
expenditure [ikˈspenditʃə] *n* Ausgabe *f*.
expense [ikˈspens] *n* (Geld)Ausgabe *f*. **expenses** *pl* Unkosten *pl*. *at my expense* auf meine Kosten. *at the expense of* zum Schaden von. **expensive** *adj* teuer, kostspielig.
experience [ikˈspiəriəns] *n* Erfahrung *f*; (*event*) Erlebnis *neut*. *v* erfahren, erleben. **experienced** *adj* erfahren.
experiment [ikˈsperimənt] *m* Experiment *neut*, Probe *f*. *v* experimentieren. **experimental** *adj* Experimental-.
expert [ˈekspəːt] *n* Fachmann *m*, Sachkundige(r). *adj* geschickt, gewandt. **expertise** *n* Sachkenntnis *f*.
expire [ikˈspaiə] *v* (*breathe out*) ausatmen; (*lapse*) verfallen; (*die*) sterben. **expiry** *n* also **expiration** Ablauf *m*.
explain [ikˈsplein] *v* erklären. **explanation** *n* Erklärung *f*. **explanatory** *adj* erklärend. *be self-explanatory* sich von selbst verstehen.
explicit [ikˈsplisit] *adj* deutlich, ausdrücklich.
explode [ikˈsploud] *v* explodieren. **explosion** *n* Explosion *f*.
exploit[1] [ˈeksploit] *n* Heldentat *f*, Abenteuer *m*.
exploit[2] [ikˈsploit] *v* ausbeuten. **exploitation** *n* Ausbeutung *f*.
explore [ikˈsplɔː] *v* erforschen. **explorer** *n* (Er)Forscher *m*. **exploration** *n* Erforschung *f*. **exploratory** *adj* forschend, Forschungs-.
exponent [ikˈspounənt] *n* (*person*) Verfechter *m*.

export [ikˈspɔːt; *n* ˈekspɔːt] *v* exportieren. *n* Export *m*. **exportation** *n* Ausfuhr *f*. **exporter** *n* Exporteur *m*. **export trade** *n* Exporthandel *m*.
expose [ikˈspouz] *v* aussetzen; (*phot*) belichten; (*impostor*) aufdecken. **exposed** *adj* (*unprotected*) ungeschützt. *be exposed to* ausgesetzt sein (+ *dat*). **exposure** *n* (*phot*) Belichtung *f* (*med*) Unterkühlung *f*.
express [ikˈspres] *v* ausdrücken. *adj* Eil-, Schnell-. **express letter** Eilbrief *m*. **express train** D-zug *m*. **expression** *n* Ausdruck *m*. **expressionism** *n* Expressionismus *m*. **expressionless** *adj* ausdruckslos. **expressive** *adj* ausdrucksvoll. **expressly** *adv* ausdrücklich.
expulsion [ikˈspʌlʃən] *n* Ausweisung *f*.
exquisite [ˈekswizit] *adj* ausgezeichnet; (*pain*) heftig.
extend [ikˈstend] *v* ausdehnen; (*develop*) erweitern; (*hand*) ausstrecken; (*cover area*) sich erstrecken. **extension** *n* Erweiterung *f*; (*comm*) Verlängerung *f*; (*phone*) Nebenanschluß *m*; (*building*) Anbau *m*. **extensive** *adj* ausgedehnt. **extent** *n* Umfang *m*. *to a certain extent* bis zu einem gewissen Grade.
exterior [ikˈstiəriə] *adj* äußer, Außen-. *n* das Äußere; (*appearance*) äußeres Ansehen *neut*.
exterminate [ikˈstəːmiˌneit] *v* ausrotten. **extermination** *n* Ausrottung *f*.
external [ikˈstəːnl] *adj* äußer, äußerlich, Außen-.
extinct [ikˈstiŋkt] *adj* ausgestorben; (*volcano*) ausgebrannt. *become extinct* aussterben. **extinction** *n* Aussterben *neut*.
extinguish [ikˈstiŋgwiʃ] *v* (aus)löschen. **(fire) extinguisher** Feuerlöscher *m*.
extort [ikˈstɔːt] *v* erpressen. **extortion** *n* Erpressung *f*. **extortionate** *adj* erpresserisch. **extortionate price** Wucherpreis *m*.
extra [ˈekstrə] *adj* zusätzlich, Extra-. *adv* besonders. **extras** *pl* *n* (*expenses*) Sonderausgaben *pl*; (*accessories*) Sonderzubehörteile *pl*.
extract [ikˈstrakt; *n* ˈekstrakt] *v* ausziehen; (*tooth*) ziehen; (*numerals*) gewinnen. *n* Auszug *m*. **extraction** *n* Ausziehen *neut*; (*tooth, minerals*) Extraktion *f*.
extradite [ˈekstrədait] *v* ausliefern. **extradition** *n* Auslieferung *f*.

extramural [‚ekstrə'mjuərəl] *adj* außerplanmäßig.

extraordinary [ik'strɔːdənəri] *adj* außerordentlich, seltsam.

extravagant [ik'strævəgənt] *adj* verschwenderisch; (*exaggerated*) übertrieben.

extreme [ik'striːm] *adj* höchst, letzt; (*fig*) extrem; *n* Extrem *m*, äußerste Grenze *f*. **extremism** Extremismus *m*. **extremist** *n* Extremist *m*.

extricate ['ekstri‚keit] *v* herauswickeln.

extrovert ['ekstrəvɔːt] *adj* (*psychol*) extravertiert. *n* Extravertierte(r).

exuberance [ig'zjuːbərəns] *n* Übermut *m*. **exuberant** *adj* übermütig.

exude [ig'zjuːd] *v* ausschlagen; ausstrahlen.

exultation [‚egzʌl'teiʃən] *n* Jubel *m*.

eye [ai] *n* Auge *neut*; (*of needle*) Öse *f*. *v* anschauen.

eyeball ['aibɔːl] *n* Augapfel *m*.

eyebrow ['aibrau] *n* Augenbraue *f*.

eye-catching ['aikætʃiŋ] *adj* auffallend.

eyelash ['ailaʃ] *n* Wimper *f*.

eyelid ['ailid] *n* Augenlid *neut*.

eye shadow *n* Lidschatten *m*.

eyesight ['aisait] *m* Sehkraft *f*.

eyewitness ['ai‚witnis] *n* Augenzeuge *m*.

F

fable ['feibl] *n* Fabel *f*.

fabric ['fabrik] *n* Stoff *m*, Gewebe *neut*. **fabricate** *v* herstellen; (*fig*) erfinden.

fabulous ['fabjuləs] *adj* fabelhaft, sagenhaft.

façade [fə'saːd] *n* Fassade *f*.

face [feis] *n* Gesicht *neut*; (*of clock*) Zifferblatt *neut*; (*surface*) Oberfläche *f*; (*cheek*) Stirn *f*. **pull faces** Fratzen schneiden; *v* gegenüberstehen; (*fig*) entgegentreten; (*of house, etc.*) liegen nach.

facet ['fasit] *n* Facette *f*; (*fig*) Aspekt *m*.

facetious [fə'siːʃəs] *adj* scherzhaft.

facial ['feiʃəl] *adj* Gesichts-.

facile ['fasail] *adj* (*easy*) leicht; (*superficial*) oberflächlich. **facilitate** *v* erleichtern.

facility *n* Leichtigkeit *f*. **facilities** *pl n* Einrichtungen *pl*.

facing ['feisiŋ] *prep* gegenüber. *n* Verkleidung *f*.

facsimile [fak'simili] *n* Faksimile *neut*.

fact [fakt] *n* Tatsache *f*; (*reality*) Wirklichkeit *f*. **in fact** in der Tat, tatsächlich.

faction ['fakʃən] *n* Faktion *f*.

factor ['faktə] *n* Faktor *m*; (*comm*) Agent *m*.

factory ['faktəri] *n* Fabrik *f*. **factory worker** Fabrikarbeiter(in).

fad [fad] *n* Mode *f*.

fade [feid] *v* verschießen, verblassen; (*flower*) verwelken; (*sound*) schwinden. **faded** *adj* verschossen.

fag [fag] *n* (*coll: tiresome job*) Plackerei *f*. **fagged** *adj* erschöpft.

fail [feil] *v* fehlschlagen, scheitern; (*to do something*) unterlassen; (*in exam*) durchfallen; (*let down*) im Stich lassen. *n* **without fail** unbedingt.

faint [feint] *adj* (*colour*) blaß; (*sound*) leise; (*memory*) schwach. *v* ohnmächtig werden. *n* Ohnmacht *f*.

fair¹ [feə] *adj* (*hair*) hell, blond; (*beautiful*) schön; (*just*) gerecht, fair. **fair chance** aussichtsreiche Chance *f*. **play fair** fair spielen. **fair and square** offen und ehrlich. **fairly** *adv* (*quite*) ziemlich.

fair² [feə] *n* Messe *f*; (*funfair*) Jahrmarkt *m*. **fairground** Messegelände *neut*; Rummelplatz *m*.

fairy ['feəri] *n* Fee *f*. *adj* feenhaft, Feen-. **fairy tale** Märchen *neut*.

faith [feiθ] *n* Vertrauen *neut*; (*belief*) Glaube *m*. **faithful** *adj* treu; (*accurate*) getreu. **yours faithfully** hochachtungsvoll.

fake [feik] *v* fälschen; *n* Fälschung *f*; (*person*) Schwindler. *adj* vorgetäuscht.

falcon ['fɔːlkən] *n* Falke *m*.

*fall [fɔːl] *n* Sturz *m*, Fall *m*; (*fig*) Untergang *m*. *v* fallen; (*prices*) abnehmen; (*curtain*) niedergehen; (*fortress*) genommen werden. **fall asleep** einschlafen. **fall back** sich zurückziehen. **fall down** (*person*) hinfallen; (*building*) einstürzen. **fall in love with** sich verlieben in. **fall into** geraten in. **fall out with** zanken mit. **fall through** durchfallen.

fallacy ['faləsi] *n* Trugschluß *m*.

fallen ['fɔːlən] *V* **fall**.

fallible ['faləbl] *adj* fehlbar.

fall-out ['fɔːlaut] *n* Niederschlag *m*.

fallow ['falou] *adj* fahl.

false [fɔːls] *adj* falsch; (*person*) untreu; (*thing*) gefälscht. **false alarm** blinder Alarm *m.* **false start** Fehlstart *m.* **falsehood** *n* Lüge *f.* **falsify** fälschen.

falter ['fɔːltə] *v* stolpern; (*hesitate*) zögern; (*courage*) versagen.

fame [feim] *n* Ruhm *m.*, Berühmtheit *f.*

familiar [fə'miljə] *adj* bekannt; (*informal*) ungezwungen. **familiarity** *n* Vertrautheit *f.*

family ['faməli] *n* Familie *f*; (*bot, zool*) Gattung *f. adj* Familien-.

famine ['famin] *n* Hungersnot *f.*

famished ['famiʃt] *be* **famished** großen Hunger haben.

famous ['feiməs] *adj* berühmt. **famously** *adv* (*coll*) glänzend.

fan¹ [fan] *n* (*hand*) Fächer *m*; (*mot, elec*) Ventilator *m.* **fan belt** *n* Keilriemen *m.*

fan² [fan] *n* (*admirer*) Fan *m.*

fanatic [fə'natik] *n* Fanatiker(in). **fanatical** *adj* fanatisch.

fancy ['fansi] *n* Neigung *f* (zu); (*fantasy*) Phantasie *f.* **take a fancy to** eingenommen sein für. *v* gern haben *adj* schick. **fancy dress** Maskenkostüm *m.*

fanfare ['fanfeə] *n* Fanfare *f.*

fang [faŋ] *n* Fangzahn *m*; (*of snake*) Giftzahn *m.*

fantastic [fan'tastik] *adj* phantastisch; (*coll*) sagenhaft, toll.

fantasy ['fantəsi] *n* Phantasie *f.*

far [faː] *adj* fern, entfernt. *adv* fern, weit. **as far as** bis (nach). **by far** bei weitem. **far and near** nahe und fern. **far better** viel besser. **far off** weit weg. **on the far side** auf der anderen Seite.

farce [faːs] *n* Posse *f*; (*fig*) Farce *f.*

fare [feə] *n* Fahrpreis *m*; (*food*) Kost *f. v* ergehen.

farewell [feə'wel] *interj* lebe wohl! *n* Lebewohl *neut. adj* Abschieds-. **bid farewell to** Abschied nehmen von.

far-fetched [ˌfaːfetʃt] *adj* weit hergeholt.

farm [faːm] *n* Bauernhof *m.* **dairy farm** Meierei *f.* **poultry farm** Geflügelfarm *f. v* Landwirtschaft betreiben; (*land*) bebauen. **farm out** (*work*) weitergeben. **farmer** *n* Landwirt *m*, Bauer *m.* **farmhouse** *n* Bauernhaus *neut.* **farming** *n* Landwirtschaft *f.* **farmworker** Landarbeiter(in).

far-sighted [ˌfaː'saitid] *adj* weitsichtig.

fart [faːt] *n* (*vulgar*) Furz *m. v* furzen.

farther ['faːðə] *adj, adv* weiter, ferner.

farthest ['faːðist] *adj* fernst, weitest. *adv* am weitesten.

fascinate ['fasiˌneit] *v* faszinieren. **fascinating** *adj* fesselnd. faszinierend. **fascination** *n* Bezauberung *f.*, Faszination *f.*

fascism ['faʃizəm] *n* Faschismus *m.* **fascist** *adj* faschistisch. *n* Faschist *m.*

fashion ['faʃən] *n* Mode *f*; (*manner*) Art (und Weise) *f.* **in fashion** modisch. **out of fashion** unmodisch. *v* bilden, gestalten. **fashionable** *adj* modisch. **fashion show** Modeschau *f.*

fast¹ [faːst] *adj, adv* (*quick*) schnell, rasch; (*firm*) fest; (*colour*) echt. *my watch is fast* meine Uhr geht vor.

fast² [faːst] *v* fasten. *n* Fasten *neut.*

fasten ['faːsn] *v* befestigen, festbinden; (*door*) verriegeln. **fastener** *n* Verschluß *m.*

fastidious [fa'stidiəs] *adj* wählerisch, anspruchsvoll.

fat [fat] *adj* (*person*) dick, fett; (*greasy*) fett, fettig. *n* Fett *neut.*

fatal ['feitl] *adj* tödlich. **fatalistic** *adj* fatalistisch. **fatality** *n* Todesfall *m.*

fate [feit] *n* Schicksal *neut.* **fateful** *adj* verhängnisvoll.

father ['faːðə] *n* Vater *m. v* zeugen. **Father Christmas** der Weihnachtsmann. **father-in-law** *n* Schwiegervater *m.* **fatherland** *n* Vaterland *neut.*

fathom ['faðəm] *n* Faden *m. v* sondieren; (*fig*) eindringen in.

fatigue [fə'tiːg] *n* Ermüdung *f. v* ermüden. **fatiguing** *adj* mühsam, ermüdend.

fatuous ['fatjuəs] *adj* albern.

fault [fɔːlt] *n* Fehler *m*; (*tech*) Störung *f.*; (*blame*) Schuld *f. It's my fault* es ist meine Schuld. *Whose fault is this?* wer ist daran schuld? **at fault** im Unrecht. **find fault (with)** tadeln.

fauna ['fɔːnə] *n* Fauna *f.*

favour ['feivə] *n* Gunst *f*; (*kindness*) Gefallen *m.* **in favour of** zugunsten von (*or* + *gen*). **be in favour of** einverstanden sein mit. **in his favour** zu seinen Gunsten. **find favour with** Gunst finden bei. *Do me a favour and . . .* Tun sie nur den Gefallen und . . . . **favourable** *adj* günstig. **favourite** *adj* Lieblings-; *n* Liebling *m*; (*sport*) Favorit *m.*

fawn [fɔːn] *n* Rehkalb *neut. adj* rehfarbig.

fear [fiə] *n* Furcht *f.*, Angst *f.* **fears** *pl n* Befürchtungen *pl. v* sich fürchten (vor), Angst haben (vor). **fearful** *adj* (*person*) ängstlich; *(thing)* furchtbar. **fearless** *adj* furchtlos. **fearsome** *adj* schrecklich.

feasible ['fiːzəbl] *adj* möglich. **feasibility** *n* Möglichkeit *f*.

feast [fiːst] *n* Fest *neut*; *(meal)* Festessen *neut*. *v* sich ergötzen (von).

feat [fiːt] *n* Kunststück *neut*.

feather ['feðə] *n* Feder *f*. **featherweight** *n* Federgewicht *neut*.

feature ['fiːtʃə] *n (of face)* Gesichtszug *m*; *(characteristic)* Eigenschaft *f*, Kennzeichen *neut*; *(newspaper)* Feature *neut*. *v* darstellen. **feature film** Spielfilm *m*.

February ['februəri] *n* Februar *m*.

fed [fed] *V* feed.

federal ['fedərəl] *adj* Bundes-; *(Swiss)* eidgenössisch. **Federal Republic of Germany** Bundesrepublik Deutschland. **federalism** *n* Föderalismus *m*. **federalist** *n* Föderalist *m*. **federation** *n* Bundesstaat *m*; *(organization)* Verband *m*.

fee [fiː] *n* Gebühr *f*. **school fees** Schulgeld *neut sing*.

feeble ['fiːbl] *adj* schwach, kraftlos. **feeble-minded** *adj* schwachsinnig. **feebleness** *n* Schwachheit *f*.

*feed [fiːd] *v* essen; *(of animals)* fressen; *(cattle)* füttern; *(person)* zu essen geben; *(tech)* zuführen. *n* Futter *neut*; *(tech)* Zufuhr *f*. **be fed up with** *(coll)* satt haben, die Nase voll haben. **feedback** *n* Rückkopplung; *(fig)* Rückwirkung. **feeding** *n* Nahrung *f*; *(animals)* Fütterung *f*.

*feel [fiːl] *v* (sich) fühlen; *(detect, sense)* empfinden; *(pulse)* betasten. **I feel cold** mir is kalt. **I feel better** es geht mir besser. **It feels hard** es fühlt sich hart an. **I don't feel like working** ich habe keine Lust zur Arbeit. *n (atmosphere)* Stimmung *f*. **feeler** *n* Fühler *m*. **feeling** *n* Gefühl *neut*. **hurt someone's feelings** jemanden verletzen.

feet [fiːt] *V* foot.

feign [fein] *v* simulieren.

feline ['fiːlain] *adj* Katzen-.

fell¹ [fel] *V* fall.

fell² [fel] *v (tree)* fällen.

fellow ['felou] *n* Genosse *m*, Genossin *f*; *(coll)* Kerl *m*. **fellow-countryman** *n* Landsmann *m*. **fellow men** Mitmenschen *pl*. **fellowship** *n* Kameradschaft *f*; Gesellschaft *f*.

felony ['feləni] *n* Schwerverbrechen *neut*. **felon** *n* Schwerverbrecher *m*.

felt¹ [felt] *V* feel.

felt² [felt] *n* Filz *m*.

female ['fiːmeil] *adj* weiblich. *n* Weib *neut*; *(of animals)* Weibchen *neut*.

feminine ['feminin] *adj* weiblich. *n (gramm)* Femininum *neut*. **femininity** *n* Weiblichkeit *f*.

feminism ['feminizəm] *n* Frauenrechtlertum *neut*. **feminist** *n* Frauenrechtler(in), Feminist(in).

fence [fens] *n* Zaun *m*. *v (sport)* fechten. **fence in** *or* **off** einzäunen.

fend [fend] *v* **fend off** abwehren. **fend for oneself** sich allein durchschlagen.

fender ['fendə] *n (US)* Kotflügel *m*. *(fireguard)* Kaminvorsetzer *m*;\

fennel ['fenl] *n* Fenchel *m*.

ferment [fə'ment; *n* 'fɜːment] *v* gären (lassen). *n (fig)* Unruhe *f*. **fermentation** *n* Gärung *f*.

fern [fɜːn] *n* Farn *m*.

ferocious [fə'rouʃəs] *adj* wild, grausam; *(dog)* bissig. **ferocity** *n* Wildheit *f*.

ferret ['ferit] *n* Frettchen *neut*. *v* **ferret out** ausforschen. **ferret about** herumsuchen.

ferry ['feri] *n* Fähre *f*. *v* übersetzen.

fertile ['fɜːtail] *adj* fruchtbar. **fertility** *n* Fruchtbarkeit *f*. **fertilization** *n* Befruchtung *f*; *(of land)* Düngung *f*. **fertilize** *v* befruchten; *(land)* düngen. **fertilizer** *n* Düngemittel *neut*.

fervent ['fɜːvənt] *adj* glühend, eifrig.

fester ['festə] *v* verfaulen; *(wound)* eitern.

festival ['festəvl] *n* Fest *neut*.

festive ['festiv] *adj* festlich. **festivity** *n* Fröhlichkeit *f*.

fetch [fetʃ] *v* holen; *(collect)* abholen; *(price)* erzielen. **fetching** *adj* reizend.

fête [feit] *n* Gartenfest *neut*.

fetid ['fiːtid] *adj* übelriechend.

fetish ['fetiʃ] *n* Fetisch *m*.

fetter ['fetə] *v* fesseln. **fetters** *pl n* Fessel *f sing*.

feud [fjuːd] *n* Fehde *f*. *v* sich befehden.

feudal ['fjuːdl] *adj* feudal, Lehns-. **feudalism** *n* Feudalismus *m*.

fever ['fiːvə] *n* Fieber *neut*. **feverish** *adj* fiebrig; *(activity)* fieberhaft.

few [fjuː] *adj, pron* wenige. **a few** einige, ein paar.

fiancé [fi'onsei] *n* Verlobte(r) *m*. **fiancée** *n* Verlobte *f*.

fiasco [fi'askou] *n* Fiasko *neut*, Mißerfolg *m*.

fib [fib] *n* Flunkerei *f*. *v* flunkern. **fibber** *n* Flunkerer *m*.

fibre ['faibə] *n* Faser *f*. **fibreglass** *n* Glasfiber *f*.

fickle ['fikl] *adj* unbeständig. **fickleness** *n* Unbeständigkeit *f*.

fiction ['fikʃən] *n* Erdichtung *f*; *(as genre)* Erzählungsliteratur *f*. **work of fiction** Roman *m*. **fictitious** *adj* fiktiv. **fictitious character** erfundene Person *f*.

fiddle ['fidl] *v* tändeln, spielen. *n* Schwindel *m*; *(violin)* Fiedel *f*. **fiddler** *n* *(violinist)* Fiedler *m*.

fidelity [fi'delati] *n* Treue *f*.

fidget ['fidʒit] *v* zappeln. **fidgety** *adj* zappelig.

field [fiːld] *n* Feld *neut*; *(mining)* Flöz *neut*; *(fig: sphere)* Bereich *m*. **field glasses** Feldstecher *m*. **fieldwork** *n* Feldforschung *f*.

fiend [fiːnd] *n* Teufel *m*; *(evil person)* Unhold *m*. **fiendish** *adj* teuflisch.

fierce [fiəs] *adj* wild, grausam. **fierceness** *n* Wildheit *f*.

fiery ['faiəri] *adj* feurig.

fifteen [fif'tiːn] *adj* fünfzehn. **fifteenth** *adj* fünfzehnt.

fifth [fifθ] *adj* fünft. *n* Fünftel *neut*.

fifty ['fifti] *adj* fünfzig. **fiftieth** *adj* fünfzigst. **fifty-fifty** *adv* halb und halb.

fig [fig] *n* Feige *f*; *(tree)* Feigenbaum *m*.

*****fight** [fait] *v* kämpfen; *(fig)* bekämpfen. **have a fight** sich streiten. *n* Kampf *m*; *(quarrel)* Streit *m*; *(brawl)* Schlägerei *f*.

figment ['figmənt] *n* Erzeugnis der Phantasie *neut*.

figure ['figə] *n* *(number)* Ziffer *f*; *(of person)* Figur *f*; *(diagram)* Zeichnung *f*, Diagramm *neut*. **figure of speech** Redewendung *f*. *v* *(appear)* auftreten; *(coll: reckon)* meinen. **figure out** ausrechnen.

filament ['filəmənt] *n* *(elec)* Glühfaden *m*.

file¹ [fail] *n* *(documents)* Akte *f*; *(folder)* Mappe *f*; *(row)* Reihe *f*. *v* *(letters)* ablegen; *(suit)* vorlegen; *(mil)* defilieren. **filing cabinet** Aktenschrank *m*. **filing clerk** Registrator *m*.

file² [fail] *n* *(tool)* Feile *f*. *v* feilen.

filial ['filiəl] *adj* Kindes-.

fill [fil] *v* *(an)*füllen; *(with objects)* vollstopfen; *(tooth)* plombieren; *(hole)* zustopfen; *(become full)* sich füllen. **fill up** auffüllen; *(mot)* auftanken.

fillet ['filit] *n* Filet *neut*.

film [film] *n* Film *m*. *v* filmen. **make a film** einen Film drehen.

filter ['filtə] *n* Filter *m* or *neut*. *v* filtrieren. **filter-tip** *n* Filtermundstück *neut*.

filth [filθ] *n* Dreck *m*, Schmutz *m*. **filthy** *adj* dreckig, schmutzig; *(indecent)* unflätig; *(weather)* scheußlich.

fin [fin] *n* Flosse *f*.

final ['fainl] *adj* letzt, End-; *(definitive)* endgültig. *n* *(sport)* Endspiel *neut*. **finals** *pl n* *(exams)* Abschlußprüfung *f* *sing*. **finale** *n* Finale *neut*. **finalist** *n* Endspielteilnehmer(in). **finalize** *v* abschließen. **finally** *adv* schließlich, zum Schluß.

finance [fai'nans] *n* Finanzwesen *neut*. *v* finanzieren. **finances** *pl n* Finanzen *pl*. **financial** *adj* finanziell, Finanz-.

finch [fintʃ] *n* Fink *m*.

*****find** [faind] *v* finden. **find guilty** für schuldig erklären. **find oneself** sich befinden. **find out** herausfinden; *(a person)* ertappen. *n* Fund *m*. **findings** *pl n* Beschluß *m sing*.

fine¹ [fain] *adj* fein; *(weather)* schön; *(splendid)* gut, herrlich; *(hair)* dünn; *(point)* spitz; *(clothes)* elegant.

fine² [fain] *n* Geldstrafe *f*. *v* mit einer Geldstrafe belegen.

finesse [fi'nes] *n* Feinheit *f*; *(cards)* Schneiden *neut*.

finger ['fiŋgə] *n* Finger *m*. *v* betasten. **fingernail** *n* Fingernagel *m*. **fingerprint** *n* Fingerabdruck *m*.

finish ['finiʃ] *v* aufhören, zu Ende gehen; beenden; *(complete)* vollenden; *(food)* aufessen; *(drink)* austrinken. *n* Ende *neut*; Schluß *m*. **finished** *adj* fertig.

finite ['fainait] *adj* endlich.

Finland ['finlənd] *n* Finnland *neut*. **Finn** *n* Finne *m*, Finnin *f*. **Finnish** *adj* finnisch.

fir [fəː] *n* Tannenbaum *m*.

fire [faiə] *n* Feuer *neut*; Brand *m*. **catch fire** Feuer fangen. **set fire to** in Brand stecken. *v* *(a gun)* abfeuern; *(with a gun)* schießen; *(mot)* zünden.

fire alarm *n* Feueralarm *m*; *(device)* Feuermelder *m*.

firearms ['faiəraːmz] *pl n* Schußwaffen *pl*.

fire brigade *n* Feuerwehr *f*.

fire drill *n* Feueralarmübung *f*.

fire engine *n* Feuerwehrauto *neut*.

fire escape *n* Nottreppe *f*.

fire extinguisher n Feuerlöscher m.

fire-guard n Kaminvorsetzer m.

fireman ['faiəmən] n Feuerwehrmann m.

fireplace ['faiəpleis] n Kamin m.

fireproof ['faiəpruːf] adj feuerfest.

fireside ['faiəsaid] n Kamin m. adj häuslich.

fire station n Feuerwache f.

firewood ['faiəwud] n Brennholz m.

firework ['faiəwəːk] n Feuerwerkskörper m. **fireworks** pl n Feuerwerk neut sing.

firing squad n Exekutionskommando neut.

firm¹ [fəːm] adj fest, hart; (resolute) entschlossen. **firm friends** enge Freunde pl.

firm² [fəːm] n Firma f.

first [fəːst] adj erst. **first name** Vorname m. adv or firstly erstens, zuerst, zunächst. **at first** zuerst. **come first** (sport) gewinnen. **first aid** erste Hilfe. **first-class** adj erstklassig.

fiscal ['fiskəl] adj fiskalisch. **fiscal year** Finanzjahr neut.

fish [fiʃ] n Fisch m; v fischen; (in river) angeln. **fishbone** n Gräte f. **fisherman** n Fischer. **fishhook** n Angelhaken m. **fishing** n Fischen neut, Angeln neut. **fishing boat** Fischerboot neut. **fishing rod** Angelrute f. **fishmonger** n Fischhändler m. **fishy** n (coll: suspicious) verdächtig.

fission ['fiʃən] n Spaltung f.

fissure ['fiʃə] n Spalt m.

fist [fist] n Faust f.

fit¹ [fit] adj (suitable) geeignet, angemessen; (healthy) gesund; (sport) fit, in guter Form. n (clothes) Sitz m. v (clothes) sitzen; (insert) einsetzen. **fit in** sich einfügen. **fit into** sich hineinpassen in. **fitness** n Gesundheit f; (sport) Fitneß f. **fitter** n (mech) Monteur m. **fitting** adj passend. **fittings** pl n Zubehör neut sing.

fit² [fit] n (med) Anfall m.

five [faiv] adj fünf.

fix [fiks] v befestigen (an); (arrange) bestimmen; (eyes) richten (auf); (repair) reparieren. n (coll) Klemme f. **fix** (drugs) Fix m.

fizz [fiz] v zischen, sprudeln. **fizzy** adj sprudelnd, sprudel-.

flabbergast ['flæbəgaːst] v verblüffen.

flabby ['flæbi] adj schlaff.

flag¹ [flæg] n Fahne f; (naut) Flagge f. **flag down** stoppen.

flag² [flæg] v (wane) nachlassen.

flagrant ['fleigrənt] adj offenkundig.

flair [fleə] n natürliche Begabung f, feine Nase f.

flake [fleik] n (snow, cereals) Flocke f; (thin piece) Schuppe f. v **flake off** sich abschuppen.

flamboyant [flæmˈbɔiənt] adj auffallend.

flame [fleim] n Flamme f. **burst into flames** in Flammen aufgehen. **old flame** alte Flamme f.

flamingo [fləˈmingou] n Flamingo m.

flan [flæn] n Torte f.

flank [flæŋk] n Flanke f. v flankieren.

flannel ['flænl] n (material) Flanell m; (facecloth) Waschlappen m.

flap [flæp] n Klappe f; (of skin, etc.) Lappen m. v flattern.

flare [fleə] v flackern; (dress) sich bauschen. **flare up** aufflackern. n (naut) Lichtsignal neut; (of dress) Ausbauchung f.

flash [flæʃ] Blitz m; (phot) Blitzlicht neut. **news flash** Kurznachricht f. v aufblitzen; (fig) sich blitzartig bewegen. **flashback** n Rückblende f. **flashbulb** n Blitzlichtlampe f. **flasher** n (mot) Blinker m. **flashlight** n Taschenlampe f. **flashy** adj auffällig.

flask [flaːsk] n Flasche f; (laboratory) Glaskolben m. **vacuum flask** Warmflasche f.

flat¹ [flæt] adj platt, flach; (level) eben; (refusal) glatt. **fall flat** ein glatter Versager sein.

flat² [flæt] n Wohnung f.

flatter ['flætə] v schmeicheln. **flattering** adj schmeichelnd. **flattery** n Schmeichelei f.

flatulence ['flætjuləns] n Blähsucht f.

flaunt [flɔːnt] v paradieren mit, prunken mit.

flautist ['flɔːtist] n Flötist(in).

flavour ['fleivə] n Geschmack m. v würzen. **flavouring** n Würze f.

flaw [flɔː] n (crack) Sprung m; (defect) Makel m. **flawless** adj tadellos.

flax [flæks] n Flachs m.

flea [fliː] n Floh m.

fleck [flek] n Flecken neut. v tüpfeln.

fled [fled] V flee.

*flee [fliː] v fliehen.

fleece [fliːs] n Vlies neut. v (coll) rupfen. **fleecy** adj flockig.

fleet [fliːt] n Flotte f.

fleeting ['fliːtiŋ] adj flüchtig.

Flemish ['flemiʃ] adj flämisch.

flesh [fleʃ] n Fleisch neut. **flesh-coloured** adj fleischfarben. **fleshly** adj fleischlich. **fleshy** adj fleischig.

flew [flu:] V fly¹.

flex [fleks] n Schnur f. v biegen; (muscles) zusammenziehen. **flexibility** n Biegsamkeit f. **flexible** adj biegsam, flexibel.

flick [flik] v schnellen, schnippen. n Schnippchen neut.

flicker ['flikə] v flackern. n Flackern neut.

flight¹ [flait] n (flying) Flug m. **flight of stairs** Treppe f. **flighty** adj launisch.

flight² [flait] n (fleeing) Flucht f.

flimsy ['flimzi] adj dünn, schwach.

flinch [flintʃ] v zurückschrecken (vor).

*****fling** [fliŋ] v schleudern, werfen. **fling away** wegwerfen. **fling open** aufreißen.

flint [flint] n Feuerstein m.

flip [flip] v klapsen, schnellen. n Klaps m.

flippant ['flipənt] adj leichtfertig, keck.

flirt [flə:t] v flirten. **flirtatious** adj kokett.

flit [flit] v flitzen.

float [flout] v schwimmen, treiben; (boat) flott sein. n (angling) Kokschwimmer m. **floating** adj schwimmend.

flock [flok] n (sheep) Herde f; (birds) Flug m. v sich scharen.

flog [flog] v peitschen, prügeln. **flogging** adj Prügelstrafe f.

flood [flʌd] n Flut f. v fluten.

floor [flo:] n (Fuß)Boden m; (storey) Stock m. v (coll) verblüten.

flop [flop] v plumpsen; (fail) versagen. n (failure) Niete f, Versager m.

flora ['flo:rə] n Flora f. **floral** adj Blumen-.

florist ['florist] n Blumenhändler m.

flounder ['flaundə] v herumplatschen, stolpern.

flour ['flauə] n Mehl neut. **flour mill** n Mühle f. **floury** adj mehlig.

flourish ['flʌriʃ] v (thrive) gedeihen. n Schnörkel m.

flout [flaut] v verspotten.

flow [flou] v fließen, strömen. n Fluß m; (fig) Strom m.

flower ['flauə] n (plant) Blume f; (bloom) Blüte f. v blüten. **flowerbed** n Blumenbeet neut. **flowerpot** n Blumentopf m. **flower-seller** n Blumenverkäufer(in). **flowery** adj blumenreich.

flown [floun] V fly¹.

flu [flu:] n Grippe f.

fluctuate ['flʌktjueit] v schwanken. **fluctuation** n Schwankung f.

flue [flu:] n Abzugsrohr neut.

fluent ['fluənt] adj fließend.

fluff [flʌf] n Flaum m, Federflocke f. v (coll) verpfuschen. **fluffy** adj flaumig, flockig.

fluid ['fluid] n Flüssigkeit f. adj flüssig.

fluke [flu:k] n (coll) Dusel m.

flung [flʌŋ] V fling.

fluorescent [fluə'resnt] adj fluoreszierend. **fluorescent light** Leuchtstofflampe f.

fluoride ['fluəraid] n Fluorid neut.

flush¹ [flʌʃ] v (blush) erröten; (WC) spülen. **flush out** ausspülen. n Erröten neut. **flushed** adj erregt.

flush² [flʌʃ] adj (level) glatt. **be flush** (coll) bei Kasse sein.

fluster ['flʌstə] v nervös machen, verwirren. **in a fluster** ganz verwirrt.

flute [flu:t] n Flöte f. **flute-player** n Flötenspieler(in).

flutter ['flʌtə] v flattern. n Flattern neut.

flux [flʌks] n Fluß m; (tech) Schmelzmittel neut. **in flux** im Fluß.

*****fly¹** [flai] fliegen; (time) entfliehen; (flee) fliehen; (goods) im Flugzeug befördern. n (in trousers) Hosenschlitz m. **flyer** n (aero) Flieger m. **flying** adj fliegend. **flying visit** Stippvisite f. **flyover** n Überführung f. **flywheel** n Schwungrad neut.

fly² [flai] n (insect) Fliege f.

foal [foul] n Fohlen neut.

foam [foum] n Schaum m. v schäumen. **foam rubber** Schaumgummi m. **foaming** adj schäumend.

focal ['foukəl] adj fokal. **focal point** Brennpunkt m.

fodder ['fodə] n Futter neut.

foe [fou] n Feind m.

fog [fog] n Nebel m. **foggy** adj neblig. **foghorn** n Nebelhorn m. **foglamp** n Nebelscheinwerfer m.

foible ['foibl] n Schwäche f.

foil¹ [foil] v vereiteln, verhindern.

foil² [foil] n (metal) Folie f.

foist [foist] v foist something on someone jemandem etwas andrehen.

fold¹ [fould] v (sich) falten; (paper) kniffen; (arms) kreuzen; (business) eingehen. n Falte f; Kniff m. **folder** n (for papers) Mappe f.

fold² [fould] n (for sheep) Pferch m.
foliage ['fouliidʒ] n Laub neut.
folk [fouk] n Leute pl. **folks** pl n (relations) Verwandte pl. **folk-dance** n Volkstanz m. **folklore** n Folklore f. **folk-song** n Volkslied neut.
follow ['folou] v folgen (+dat); (instructions) sich halten an; (profession) ausüben. **as follows** folgendermaßen. **follow from** sich ergeben aus. **follow up** verfolgen.
folly ['foli] n Narrheit f.
fond [fond] adj zärtlich; (hopes) kühn. **be fond of** gern or lieb haben. **fondness** n Vorliebe f.
fondle ['fondl] v streicheln.
font [font] n Taufbecken m.
food [fuid] n Lebensmittel pl, Essen neut. **food and drink** Essen und Trinken neut. **foodstuff** n Nahrungsmittel pl.
fool [fuil] n Narr m, Närrin f, Tor m. v zum Narren halten; betrügen. **fool around** herumalbern. **foolish** adj albern, dumm. **foolishness** n Torheit f.
foot [fut] n (pl feet) Fuß m; (of bed, page) Fußende neut. **on foot** zu Fuß. **football** n (game) Fußballspiel neut; (ball) Fußball m. **foothills** pl n Vorgebirge neut sing. **foothold** n Halt m. **gain a foothold** Fuß fassen. **footnote** n Anmerkung f. **footpath** n Fußweg m. **footprint** n (Fuß)Spur f. **footstep** n Schritt m. **footwear** n Schuhzeug neut.
for [fox] prep für. conj denn. **leave for London** nach London abreisen. **for fun** aus Spaß. **for joy** vor Freude. **stay for three weeks** drei Wochen bleiben. **what for?** wozu?
forage ['foridʒ] n Furage f. v furagieren.
forbade [fox'bad] V forbid.
***forbear** [fox'beə] v sich enthalten (+gen).
***forbid** [fox'bid] v verbieten. **forbidden** adj verboten. **forbidding** adj bedrohlich.
forbidden [fox'bidn] V forbid.
force [fois] n Kraft f; (violence) Gewalt f. v (compel) zwingen; (a door) aufbrechen. **by force** gewaltsam. **in force** (current) in Kraft. **armed forces** Streitkräfte pl. **police force** Polizei f. **forced** adj gekünstelt. **forceful** adj eindringlich. **forcible** adj gewaltsam. **forcibly** adv zwangsweise.
forceps ['foiseps] pl n Zange f sing.
ford [foid] n Furt f. v durchwaten.

fore [foi] adj Vorder-. **come to the fore** hervortreten.
forearm ['foiraim] n Unterarm m.
forebear ['foibə] n Vorfahr m.
foreboding [foi'boudin] n Vorahnung f.
***forecast** ['foikaist] v voraussagen. n Voraussage f. **weather forecast** Wettervorhersage f.
forecourt ['foikoit] n Vorhof m.
forefather ['foifaiðə] n Vorfahr m.
forefinger ['foifingə] n Zeigefinger m.
forefront ['foifrʌnt] n **in the forefront** im Vordergrund.
foreground ['foigraund] n Vordergrund m.
forehand ['foihand] n (sport) Vorhandschlag m.
forehead ['forid] n Stirn f.
foreign ['forən] adj fremd, ausländisch, Auslands-. **foreign body** Fremdkörper m. **foreign language** Fremdsprache f. **foreign minister** Außenminister m. **foreign policy** Außenpolitik f. **foreigner** n Fremde(r), Ausländer(in).
foreleg ['foileg] n Vorderbein neut.
foreman ['foimən] n Vorarbeiter m, Aufseher m; (jury) Sprecher m.
foremost ['foimoust] adj vorderst. **first and foremost** zu allererst.
forename ['foineim] n Vorname m.
forensic [fə'rensik] adj forensich.
forerunner ['foirʌnə] n Vorgänger m.
***foresee** [foi'sii] v voraussagen.
foresight ['foisait] n Vorsorge f.
foreskin ['foiskin] n Vorhaut m.
forest ['forist] n Forst m, Wald m. **forest fire** Waldbrand m.
forestall [foi'stoil] v zuvorkommen (+dat).
foretaste ['foiteist] n Vorgeschmack m.
***foretell** [foi'tel] v vorhersagen.
forethought ['foiθoit] n Vorbedacht m.
forever [fə'evə] adv immer, ständig.
foreword ['foiwəid] n Vorwort neut.
forfeit ['foifit] v verwirken. n Verwirkung f. adj verwirkt.
forgave [fə'geiv] V forgive.
forge [foidʒ] v (metal) schmieden; (plan) ersinnen; (document) fälschen. n Schmiede f. **forgery** n Fälschung f.
***forget** [fə'get] v vergessen. **forgetful** adj vergeßlich.
***forgive** [fə'giv] v verzeihen, vergeben. **forgiveness** n Verzeihung f. **forgiving** adj versöhnlich.

forgiven [fə'givn] V forgive.

*forgo [for'gou] v verzichten auf.

forgot [fə'got] V forget.

forgotten [fə'gotn] V forget.

fork [fotk] n Gabel f; (in road) Gabelung f. v **fork out** (coll: pay) blechen.

forlorn [fə'lotn] adj verlassen, hilflos.

form [fotm] n Gestalt f, Form f; (to fill out) Formular neut. **on form** in Form. v bilden.

formal ['fotməl] adj formell.

format ['fotmat] n Format neut.

formation [fot'meifən] n Bildung f; (geol, mil) Formation f.

former ['fotmə] adj vorig; (one-time) ehemalig; (of two) jene(r). **formerly** adv früher.

formidable ['fotmidəbl] adj furchtbar.

formula ['fotmjulə] n (pl -ae) Formel f; (med) Rezept neut. **formulate** v formulieren. **formulation** n Formulierung f.

*forsake [fə'seik] v (person) verlassen.

forsaken [fə'seikn] V forsake.

forsook [fə'suk] V forsake.

fort [fott] n Festung f.

forte [fott] adv (music) laut. n Stärke f.

forth [fotθ] adv (place) hervor; (time) fort. **and so forth** und so weiter or fort. **back and forth** hin und her.

fortify ['fotti,fai] v (mil) befestigen; (hearten) ermutigen; (food) anreichern. **fortification** n Befestigung f; (fortress) Festung f.

fortitude ['fotti,tjutd] n Mut m.

fortnight ['fottnait] n vierzehn Tage. **fortnightly** adj vierzehntägig. adv alle vierzehn Tage.

fortress ['fottris] n Festung f.

fortuitous [fot'juitəs] adj zufällig.

fortune ['fottʃən] n Glück neut; (fate) Schicksal neut; (wealth) Vermögen neut. **fortunate** adj glücklich. **fortunately** adv glücklicherweise.

forty ['fotti] adj vierzig.

forum ['fotrəm] n Forum neut.

forward ['fotwəd] adj vorder, Vorder-; (impudent) vorlaut. adv vorwärts. v (goods) spedieren; (letter) nachschicken. n (sport) Stürmer m.

fossil ['fosl] n Fossil neut.

foster ['fostə] v pflegen; (feelings) Legen. adj Pflege-.

fought [fott] V fight.

foul [faul] adj (dirty) schmutzig; (disgust-

ing) widerlich; (weather) schlecht. v verschmutzen. n (sport) Regelverstoß m.

found¹ [faund] V find.

found² [faund] v gründen. **be founded on** beruhen auf. **foundation** n (of building) Grundmauer f; (of institute, firm, etc.) Gründung f; (basis) Grundlage f; (institute) Stiftung f. **founder** n Gründer m.

foundry ['faundri] n Gießerei f.

fountain ['fauntin] n Springbrunnen m. **fountain pen** Füllfeder f.

four [fot] adj vier. **fourth** adj viert; n Viertel neut.

fourteen [fot'titn] adj vierzehn.

fowl [faul] n Haushuhn neut.

fox [foks] n Fuchs m. v (coll) täuschen.

foyer ['foiei] n Foyer m.

fraction [frakʃən] n Bruchteil m; (math) Bruch m.

fracture ['fraktʃə] n (med) Knochenbruch m. v zerbrechen.

fragile ['fradʒail] adj zerbrechlich.

fragment ['fragmənt] n Bruchstück neut, Brocken m.

fragrance ['freigrəns] n Duft m, Aroma neut. **fragrant** adj duftig, wohlriechend.

frail [freil] adj schwach, gebrechlich. **frailty** n Schwäche f.

frame [freim] n Rahmen m. v einrahmen. **spectacle frame** Brillengestell neut.

France [frans] n Frankreich neut.

franchise ['frantʃaiz] n (pol) Wahlrecht neut; (comm) Konzession f.

frank [frank] adj offen, freimütig. **frankly** adv frei, offen. **frankness** n Freimut m.

frantic ['frantik] adj wild, rasend.

fraternal [frə'tətnl] adj brüderlich.

fraud [frotd] n Betrug m, Unterschlagung f; (person) Schwindler(in). **fraudulent** adj betrügerisch.

fraught [frott] adj voll. **fraught with danger** gefahrvoll.

fray¹ [frei] v (sich) ausfransen.

fray² [frei] n Rauferei f.

freak [fritk] n (of nature) Mißbildung f; (event, storm) Ausnahmeerscheinung f. adj anormal.

freckle ['frekl] n Sommersprosse f.

free [frit] adj frei; kostenlos. v befreien, freimachen. **free and easy** ungezwungen. **free speech** Redefreiheit f. **free will** freier Wille m. **freedom** n Freiheit. **freely** adv reichlich.

freelance ['fritlains] n freier Schriftsteller m. adj freiberuflich tätig.

freemason ['friːmeɪsn] n Freimaurer m.

***freeze** [friːz] v (water) frieren; (food) tiefkühlen. **freeze to death** erfrieren. *I'm freezing* ich friere. n (comm) Stopp m. **freezer** n Tiefkühltruhe f. **freezing point** Gefrierpunkt m.

freight [freit] n Fracht f; (freight costs) Frachtgebühr f.

French [frentʃ] adj französisch. **Frenchman** n Franzose m. **Frenchwoman** n Französin f. **French horn** Waldhorn neut. **french fries** n pl Pommes frites pl.

frenzy ['frenzi] n Raserei f.

frequency ['friːkwənsi] n Frequenz f. **frequent** adj häufig, frequent; v häufig besuchen. **frequently** adv öfters, häufig.

fresco ['freskou] n Fresko neut.

fresh [freʃ] adj frisch; (water) süß; (air) erfrischend; (cheeky) frech. **fresh water** Süßwasser neut. **freshen** v auffrischen. **freshness** n Frische f.

fret [fret] v sich Sorgen machen.

friar ['fraiə] n Mönch m.

friction ['frikʃən] n Reibung f.

Friday ['fraidei] n Freitag m. **Good Friday** Karfreitag m.

fridge [fridʒ] n Kühlschrank m.

fried [fraid] adj gebraten. **fried egg** Spiegelei neut. **fried potatoes** Bratkartoffeln.

friend [frend] n Freund(in). **make friends with** sich befreunden mit. **friendly** adj freundlich, freundschaftlich. **friendship** n Freundschaft f.

frieze [friːz] n Fries m.

frigate ['frigit] n Fregatte f.

fright [frait] n Schreck m. **frighten** v erschrecken. **frightening** adj erschreckend. **frightened** adj erschrocken. **be frightened of** Angst haben vor. **frightful** adj schrecklich.

frigid ['fridʒid] adj frigid. **frigidity** n Frigidität f.

frill [fril] n Rüsche, Krause f. **frilly** adj gekräuselt.

fringe [frindʒ] n Franse f; (edge) Randzone f; (hair) Pony neut. **fringe benefits** Nebenbezüge pl.

frisk [frisk] v herumlüpfen; (search) absuchen. **frisky** adj munter, lebhaft.

fritter ['fritə] v **fritter away** verzetteln.

frivolity [fri'vɒliti] n Leichtfertigkeit f. **frivolous** adj (person) leichtfertig; (worthless) nichtig.

frizz [friz] v (sich) kräuseln. **frizzy** adj kraus.

fro [frou] adv **to and fro** auf und ab, hin und her.

frock [frok] n Kleid neut.

frog [frog] n Frosch m.

frolic ['frolik] n Spaß m, Posse f. **frolicsome** adj lustig, ausgelassen.

from [from] prep von; (place) aus, von; (to judge from) nach. *Where are you from?* wo kommen Sie her?

front [frʌnt] n Vorderseite f, vorderer Teil m; (mil, pol) Front f; (fa,cade) Fassade f. adj Vor-, Vorder-. **front door** Haustür f. **front room** Vorderzimmer neut. **in front of** vor.

frontier ['frʌntiə] n Grenze f.

frost [frost] n Frost m. v (cookery) glasieren. **frostbite** n Erfrieren neut; (wound) Frostbeule f. **frostbitten** adj erfroren. **frosty** adj frostig.

froth [froθ] n Schaum m. **frothy** adj schäumig.

frown [fraun] n Stirnrunzeln neut. v die Stirn runzeln. **frown on** mißbilligen.

froze [frouz] V freeze.

frozen ['frouzn] V freeze. adj gefroren. (comm) eingefroren; (food) tiefgekühlt. **frozen over** zugefroren.

frugal ['fruːgəl] adj sparsam.

fruit [fruːt] n Obst neut, Früchte pl; (result, yield) Frucht f. **fruitful** adj fruchtbar. **fruition** n Erfüllung f. **fruitless** adj fruchtlos. **fruit machine** Spielautomat neut. **fruit salad** Obstsalat m. **fruit tree** Obstbaum m. **fruity** adj würzig.

frustrate [frʌ'streit] v vereiteln, frustrieren. **frustrated** adj vereitelt, frustriert. **frustration** n Vereitelung f, Frustration f.

fry [frai] v (in der Pfanne) braten. **frying-pan** n Bratpfanne f.

fuchsia ['fjuːʃə] n Fuchsia f.

fudge [fʌdʒ] n Karamelle f.

fuel ['fjuəl] n Brennstoff; (for engines) Treibstoff m; (mot) Benzin neut. v tanken. **fuel gauge** Treibstoffmesser m. **fuel oil** Brennöl neut.

fugitive ['fjuːdʒitiv] adj flüchtig. n Flüchtling m.

fulcrum ['fulkrəm] n Drehpunkt m.

fulfil [ful'fil] v erfüllen. **fulfilment** n Erfüllung f; (satisfaction) Befriedigung f.

full [ful] adj voll; (after meal) satt. adv direkt, gerade. **pay in full** voll bezahlen. **write out in full** ausschreiben. **full-grown**

adj ausgewachsen. **full moon** Vollmond *m*. **fullness** *n* Fülle *f*. **full stop** Punkt *m*. **full-time** *adj* ganztägig. **fully** *adv* voll, völlig.

fumble ['fʌmbl] *v* umhertasten. **fumble with** herumfummeln an.

fume [fjuːm] *v* dampfen; (*coll*) wütend sein. *n* Dunst *m*, Dampf *m*. **fumigate** *v* ausräuchern.

fun [fʌn] *n* Spaß *m*. **it's fun** es macht Spaß. **for fun** aus Spaß. **in fun** zum Scherz. **have fun** sich amüsieren. **have fun!** viel Spaß/vergnügen! **make fun of** sich lustig machen über.

function ['fʌŋkʃən] *n* Funktion *f*; (*task*) Aufgabe *f*; (*gathering*) Veranstaltung *f*. *v* (*tech*) funktionieren; tätig sein. **functional** *adj* funktionell, zweckmäßig. **functionary** *n* Beamte(r).

fund [fʌnd] *n* Fonds *m*; (*fig*) Vorrat *m*. *v* fundieren.

fundamental [fʌndə'mentl] *adj* grundlegend, grundsätzlich.

funeral ['fjuːnərəl] *n* Begräbnis *neut*.

fungus ['fʌŋgəs] *n* (*pl* -i) Pilz *m*.

funnel ['fʌnl] *n* Trichter *m*; (*ship*) Schornstein *m*.

funny ['fʌni] *adj* (*amusing*) komisch, lustig, spaßhaft; (*strange*) komisch, seltsam. **funny-bone** *n* Musikantenknochen *m*.

fur [fəː] *n* Pelz *m*; (*on tongue*) Belag *m*; (*in boiler*) Kesselstein *m*. **fur coat** Pelzmantel *m*. **furry** *adj* pelzartig, Pelz-; belegt.

furious ['fjuəriəs] *adj* wütend.

furnace ['fəːnis] *n* (Brenn)Ofen *m*.

furnish ['fəːniʃ] *v* (*a room*) möblieren; (*supply*) versehen, ausstatten. **furnishings** *pl n* Möbel *pl*.

furniture ['fəːnitʃə] *n* Möbel *pl*.

furrow ['fʌrou] *n* Furche *f*.

further ['fəːðə] *adj*, *adv* weiter. **until further notice** bis auf weiteres. *v* fördern. **furthermore** *adv* ferner, überdies. **furthest** *adj* weitest; *adv* am weitesten.

furtive ['fəːtiv] *adj* (*person*) hinterlistig; (*action*) verstohlen.

fury ['fjuəri] *n* Wut *f*.

fuse [fjuːz] *n* (*elec*) Sicherung *f*; (*explosives*) Zünder *m*. *v* (*join*, *melt*) (ver)schmelzen; (*elec*) sichern; (*elec*: *blow a fuse*) durchbrennen. **fuse box** Sicherungskasten *m*.

fuselage ['fjuːzə,lɑːʒ] *n* Rumpf *m*.

fusion ['fjuːʒən] *n* Verschmelzung *f*.

fuss [fʌs] *n* Getue, Theater *neut*. **make a fuss** viel Wesens machen (um). **fussy** *adj* kleinlich.

futile ['fjuːtail] *adj* zwecklos, wertlos. **futility** *n* Zwecklosigkeit *f*.

future ['fjuːtʃə] *n* Zukunft *f*. *adj* künftig. **in future** in Zukunft. **futures** *pl n* (*comm*) Termingeschäfte *pl*. **futuristic** *adj* futuristisch.

fuzz [fʌz] *n* Fussel *f*. **fuzzy** *adj* (*hair*) kraus; (*vision*) verschwommen.

G

gabble ['gabl] *v* schwätzen.

gable ['geibl] *n* Giebel *m*. **gabled** *adj* gegiebelt.

gadget ['gadʒit] *n* Apparat *m*, Gerät *neut*.

gag¹ [gag] *v* knebeln. *n* Knebel *m*.

gag² [gag] *n* (*coll*: *joke*) *n* Witz *m*. *v* einen Witz reißen.

gaiety ['geiəti] *n* Heiterkeit *f*.

gain [gein] *n* Gewinn *m*. *v* gewinnen; (*of clock*) vorgehen. **gain on** einholen. **gains** *pl* (*comm*) Profit *m*.

gait [geit] *n* Gang *m*.

gala ['gɑːlə] *n* Festlichkeit *f*.

galaxy ['galəksi] *n* Sternsystem *neut*; (*ours*) Milchstraße *f*.

gale [geil] *n* heftiger Wind *m*, Sturmwind *m*.

gallant ['galənt] *adj* tapfer; (*courteous*) ritterlich. **gallantry** *n* Tapferkeit *f*; Ritterlichkeit *f*.

gall bladder [goːl] *n* Gallenblase *f*.

galleon ['galiən] *n* Galeone *f*.

gallery ['galəri] *n* Galerie *f*.

galley ['gali] *n* Galeere *f*; (*kitchen*) Schiffsküche *f*.

gallon ['galən] *n* Gallone *f*.

gallop ['galəp] *n* Galopp *m*. *v* galoppieren.

gallows ['galouz] *n* Galgen *m*.

gallstone ['goːlstoun] *n* Gallenstein *m*.

galore [gə'loː] *adv* in Hülle und Fülle.

galvanize ['galvənaiz] *v* galvanisieren, verzinken; (*fig*: *stimulate*) anspornen (zu).

gamble ['gambl] *v* um Geld spielen. **gamble on** wetten auf. **gamble with** aufs Spiel setzen. **gambler** n Spieler m. **gambling** n Spielen (um Geld) neut. n Wagnis neut.

game [geim] n Spiel neut. (hunting) Wild neut. **give the game away** den Plan verraten. adj (leg) lahm. **be game for** bereit sein zu. **gamekeeper** n Wildhüter m.

gammon ['gamən] n (geräucherter) Schinken m.

gang [gaŋ] n (criminals) Bande f. (workers) Kolonne f. v **gang up** sich zusammenrotten. **gangster** n Gangster m.

gangrene ['gaŋgriːn] n Brand m.

gangway ['gaŋwei] n (theatre) Gang m. (naut) Laufplanke f.

gaol [dʒeil] V jail.

gap [gap] n Lücke f.

gape [geip] v klaffen. (person) gähnen.

garage ['garaːdʒ] n Garage f. (mot: workshop) Autowerkstatt f. v in eine Garage einstellen or unterbringen.

garbage ['gaːbidʒ] n Müll m. **garbage can** Mülleimer m.

garble ['gaːbl] v verstümmeln.

garden ['gaːdn] n Garten m. v im Garten arbeiten. **gardening** n Gartenbau m. **garden party** Gartenfest neut.

gargle ['gaːgl] v gurgeln. n Mundwasser neut.

gargoyle ['gaːgoil] n (arch) Wasserspeier m.

garland ['gaːlənd] n Girlande f, Blumengewinde neut. v bekränzen.

garlic ['gaːlik] n Knoblauch m.

garment ['gaːmənt] n Kleidungsstück neut.

garnish ['gaːniʃ] v (cookery) garnieren. n Garnierung f.

garrison ['garisn] n Garnison f. v (town) besetzen. (troops) in Garnison legen.

garter ['gaːtə] n Strumpfband neut.

gas [gas] n Gas neut. (US: petrol) Benzin neut. **step on the gas** Gas geben. v (poison) vergasen. (slang: chatter) schwätzen. **gasbag** n (coll) Windbeutel m. **gas cooker** Gasherd m. **gas fire** Gasheizung f.

gash [gaʃ] v aufschneiden. n klaffende Wunde f.

gasket ['gaskit] n Dichtung f.

gas main n Gasleitung f.

gas meter n Gasmesser m.

gasoline ['gasəliːn] n (US) Benzin neut.

gasp [gaːsp] v keuchen. n **Keuchen** neut.

gas station n Tankstelle f.

gastric ['gastrik] adj gastrisch, Magen-.

gate [geit] n Tor neut.

gâteau ['gatou] n Torte f.

gateway ['geitwei] n Torweg m.

gather ['gaðə] v sammeln. (people) (sich) versammeln. (flowers, etc.) lesen. (dress) raffen. (deduce) schließen (aus). **gathering** n Versammlung f.

gaudy ['goːdi] adj (colours) grell, bunt.

gauge [geidʒ] v abmessen. (judge) schätzen. n Normalmaß neut. (rail) Spurweite f. **pressure gauge** Druckmesser m.

gaunt [goːnt] adj mager.

gauze [goːz] n Gaze f.

gave [geiv] V give.

gay [gei] adj (colours) bunt. (person) heiter, lustig. (slang: homosexual) warm.

gaze [geiz] v starren (auf). n (starrer) Blick neut.

gazelle [gəˈzel] n Gazelle f.

gazetteer [gazəˈtiə] n Namensverzeichnis neut.

gear [giə] n (mot) Gang m. (gear wheel) Zahnrad neut. (equipment) Gerät neut, Ausrüstung f. **in gear** eingeschaltet. **change gear** (up or down) Gang herauf or herab setzen. **gearbox** n Getriebe(gehäuse) neut.

geese [giːs] V goose.

gelatine ['dʒeləˌtiːn] n Gelatine f. (explosive) Sprenggelatine f.

gelignite ['dʒelignait] n Gelatinedynamit neut.

gem [dʒem] n Edelstein m, Gemme f.

Gemini ['dʒeminiː] n Zwillinge pl.

gender ['dʒendə] n Geschlecht neut. (gramm) Genus f.

gene [dʒiːn] n Gen neut, Erbeinheit f.

genealogy [dʒiːniˈalədʒi] n Genealogie f. **genealogist** n Genealoge m.

general ['dʒenərəl] adj allgemein. n General m. **in general** im Allgemeinen. **General Assembly** n Generalversammlung f. **general election** allgemeine Wahlen pl. **generate** ['dʒenəreit] v erzeugen, verursachen. **generator** n Generator m, Stromerzeuger m. **generation** n Generation f, Zeitalter m. (production) Erzeugung f.

generic [dʒiˈnerik] adj allgemein, generell.

generous ['dʒenərəs] adj großzügig, freigebig. **generosity** n Großzügigkeit f.

genetic [dʒiˈnetik] adj genetisch, Entstehungs-. **genetics** n Genetik f.

Geneva [dʒi'ni:və] *n* Genf *neut.* **Lake Geneva** der Genfer See *m.*

genial ['dʒi:niəl] *adj* freundlich, herzlich. **geniality** *n* Freundlichkeit *f.*

genital ['dʒenitl] *adj* Geschlechts-. **genitals** *pl n* Geschlechtsteile *pl.*

genitive ['dʒenitiv] *n* Genitiv *m.*

genius ['dʒi:njəs] *n* Genie *neut*; (*talent*) Begabung *f.*

genocide ['dʒenəsaid] *n* Völkermord *m.*

genteel [dʒen'ti:l] *adj* wohlerzogen, vornehm.

gentle ['dʒentl] *adj* sanft, mild. **gentleman** *n* Herr *m.* **gentleness** *n* Mildheit *f.*

gentry ['dʒentri] *n* Landadel *m.*

gents [dʒents] *n* (*sign*) Herren *pl.*

genuine ['dʒenjuin] *adj* echt, wahr. **genuineness** *n* Wahrheit *f.*, Echtheit *f.*

genus ['dʒi:nəs] *n* Gattung *f.*, Sorte *f.*

geography [dʒi'ogrəfi] *n* Erdkunde *f.*, Geographie *f.* **geographical** *adj* geographisch. **geographer** *n* Geograph(in).

geology [dʒi'olədʒi] *n* Geologie *f.* **geologist** *n* Geologe *m.*

geometry [dʒi'omətri] *n* Geometrie *f.* **geometric** *adj* geometrisch.

geranium [dʒə'reiniəm] *n* Geranie *f.*

geriatric [dʒeri'atrik] *adj* geriatrisch. **geriatrics** *n* Geriatrie *f.*

germ [dʒə:m] *n* Keim *m.*, Bakterie *f.*

German measles *n* Röteln *pl.*

Germany ['dʒə:məni] *n* Deutschland *neut.* **German** *adj* deutsch; *n* Deutsche(r); (*language*) Deutsch *neut.* **Federal Republic of Germany** *n* Bundesrepublik Deutschland (BRD) *f.* **German Democratic Republic** *n* Deutsche Demokratische Republik (DDR) *f.*

germinate ['dʒə:mineit] *v* Keimen. **germination** *n* Keimen *neut.*

gesticulate [dʒe'stikju,leit] *v* wilde Gesten machen.

gesture ['dʒestʃə] *n* Geste *f.* *v* eine Geste machen.

***get** [get] *v* (*obtain*) bekommen, erhalten; (*become*) werden. **get hold of** bekommen. **get in** einsteigen. **get married** sich verheiraten. **get off** aussteigen. **get ready** vorbereiten.

geyser ['gi:zə] *n* Geiser *m.*

ghastly ['gɑ:stli] *adj* schrecklich, furchtbar.

gherkin ['gə:kin] *n* Essiggurke *f.*

ghetto ['getou] *n* Getto *neut.*

ghost [goust] *n* Gespenst *neut*, Geist *m.* **ghostly** *adj* gespenstisch.

giant ['dʒaiant] *n* Riese *m.* *adj* riesenhaft.

gibberish ['dʒibəriʃ] *n* Quatsch *m.*

gibe [dʒaib] *v* spotten (über). *n* Spott *m.*

giblets ['dʒiblits] *pl n* Hühnerklein *neut.*

giddy ['gidi] *adj* schwind(e)lig. **giddiness** *n* Schwindel *m.*

gift [gift] *n* Geschenk *neut*; (*talent*) Begabung *f.* **gifted** *adj* begabt.

gigantic [dʒai'gantik] *adj* riesenhaft, gigantisch.

giggle ['gigl] *v* kichern. *n* Gekicher *neut.*

gill [gil] *n* (*fish*) Kieme *f.*

gilt [gilt] *adj* vergoldet. *n* Vergoldung *f.*

gimmick ['gimik] *n* Trick *m.*

gin [dʒin] *n* Gin *m.*, Wacholderschnapps *m.*

ginger ['dʒindʒə] *n* Ingwer *m.* **gingerbread** *n* Pfefferkuchen *m.* **ginger-haired** *adj* rothaarig.

gingerly ['dʒindʒəli] *adv* vorsichtig.

gipsy ['dʒipsi] *n* Zigeuner(in). *adj* Zigeuner.

giraffe [dʒi'rɑ:f] *n* Giraffe *f.*

***gird** [gə:d] *v* umgürten, umlegen.

girder ['gə:də] *n* Träger *m.*, Tragbalken *m.*

girdle ['gə:dl] *n* Gurt *m.* *v* umgürten.

girl [gə:l] *n* Mädchen *neut.* **girl friend** Freundin *f.* **girlhood** *n* Mädchenjahre *pl.* **girlish** *adj* mädchenhaft.

girt [gə:t] *V* **gird.**

girth [gə:θ] *n* Umfang *m*; (*horse*) Gurt *m.*

gist [dʒist] *n* Wesentliche *neut*, Hauptpunkt *m.*

***give** [giv] *v* geben; (*gift*) schenken (*hand over*) überreichen. *n* Elastizität *f.* **give away** (*betray*) verraten. **give back** zurückgeben. **give in** nachgeben. **give up** aufgeben.

given ['givn] *V* **give.** *adj* (an)gegeben.

glacier ['glasiə] *n* Gletscher *m.*

glad [glad] *adj* froh, fröhlich, glücklich. **gladness** *n* Fröhlichkeit *f.*, Glücklichkeit *f.*

glamour ['glamə] *n* bezaubernde Schönheit *f.* **glamorous** *adj* bezaubernd.

glance [glɑ:ns] *v* (*flüchtig*) blicken, einen Blick werfen. *n* flüchtiger Blick *m.*

gland [gland] *n* Drüse *f.* **glandular** *adj* drüsig, Drüsen-. **glandular fever** *n* Drüsenfieber *m.*

glare [gleə] *v* grell leuchten; (*stare*) starren. **glare at** anstarren. *n* blendendes Licht *neut.*

glass [glɑːs] n Glas neut. **glasses** pl Brille f sing. **glassfibre** n Glaswolle f.

glaze [gleiz] n Glasur f. v verglasen; (windows) mit Glasscheiben versehen. **glazier** n Glaser m.

gleam [gliːm] n Schimmer m. v schimmern.

glean [gliːn] v (nach)lesen.

glee [gliː] n Fröhlichkeit f. **gleeful** adj fröhlich.

glib [glib] adj zungenfertig.

glide [glaid] v gleiten. **glider** n Segelflugzeug neut.

glimmer ['glimə] n Schimmer m. v schimmern.

glimpse [glimps] n flüchtiger Blick. v erspähen.

glint [glint] n Glitzern neut. v glitzern.

glisten ['glisn] n Glanz m. v glänzen.

glitter ['glitə] n Funkeln neut. v funkeln.

gloat [glout] v sich hämisch freuen über. **gloating** n Schadenfreude f.

globe [gloub] n (Erd)Kugel f. **global** adj global. **globular** adj kugelförmig.

gloom [gluːm] n Düsternis f, Dunkelheit f; (mood) Trübsinn m. **gloomy** adj düster.

glory ['glɔːri] n Ruhm m, Ehre f. v sich freuen. **glorify** v verherrlichen. **glorious** adj glorreich, herrlich.

gloss [glɔs] n Glanz m. v polieren. **gloss paint** Ölfarbe f. **gloss over** vertuschen.

glossary ['glɔsəri] n Glossar neut, (spezielles) Wortverzeichnis neut.

glove [glʌv] n Handschuh m. **fit like a glove** passen wie angegossen.

glow [glou] n Glühen neut. v glühen.

glucose ['gluːkous] n Traubenzucker m.

glue [gluː] n Klebstoff neut. v kleben.

glum [glʌm] adj mürrisch.

glut [glʌt] n Überfluß m; (comm) Überangebot neut. v sättigen.

glutton ['glʌtən] n Vielfraß m. **gluttonous** adj gefräßig. **gluttony** n Gefräßigkeit f.

gnarled [naːld] adj knorrig.

gnash [naʃ] v knirschen.

gnat [nat] n Mücke f.

gnaw [nɔː] v nagen an (+dat).

gnome [noum] n Zwerg m, Gnom m.

*****go** [gou] v gehen; (travel) fahren, reisen; (machine) funktionieren, in Betrieb sein; (time) vergehen; (coll: become) werden. **go ahead** fortfahren. **go away** weggehen; (travel) verreisen. **go down** hinuntergehen; (price) fallen. **go out** hinausgehen; (fire) erlöschen. **go up** hinaufgehen; (prices) steigen. **have a go at** einen Versuch machen mit. **it's no go!** es geht nicht!

goad [goud] n Stachelstock m. v antreiben.

goal [goul] n Ziel neut; (sport) Tor m. **goalkeeper** n Torwart m.

goat [gout] n Ziege f.

gobble ['gobl] v **gobble (down)** (food) hinunterschlingen. **gobble up** verschlingen.

goblin ['goblin] n Kobold m.

god [god] n Gott m. **thank God!** Gott sei dank! **godchild** n Patenkind neut. **goddaughter** n Patentochter f. **goddess** n Göttin f. **godfather** n Pate m. **godmother** n Patin f. **godsend** n Glücksfall m. **godson** n Patensohn m.

goggles ['goglz] pl n Schutzbrille f sing.

gold [gould] n Gold neut. **golden** adj golden. **goldfish** n Goldfisch m. **gold leaf** n Blattgold neut. **gold mine** Goldgrube f. **gold-plated** adj vergoldet. **goldsmith** n Goldschmied.

golf [golf] n Golf(spiel) neut. **golfclub** n Golfschläger m. **golf course** Golfplatz m. **golfer** n Golfspieler m.

gondola ['gondələ] n Gondel f.

gone [gon] V go.

gong [gon] n Gong m.

gonorrhoea [gonə'riə] n (med) Gonorrhöe f.

good [gud] adj gut; (pleasant) angenehm; (child) brav. n Gute neut, Wohl neut. **good afternoon** guten Tag. **goodbye** interj auf Wiedersehen. **good evening** guten Abend. **good for nothing** nichts Wert. **good-for-nothing** n Taugenichts m. **good-looking** adj gut aussehend. **good morning** guten Morgen. **good night** gute Nacht. **do (someone) good** (jemanden) wohltun. **it's no good** es nützt nichts. **goodness** n Güte f. **goods** pl n Güter pl.

Good Friday n Karfreitag m.

goose [guːs] n (pl geese) Gans f.

gooseberry ['guzbəri] n Stachelbeere f. **play gooseberry** Anstandswauwau spielen.

gore [gɔ] n Blut neut. v aufspießen.

gorge [gɔːdʒ] n (geog) Schlucht f. v **gorge oneself** (coll) sich vollessen.

gorgeous ['gɔːdʒəs] adj wunderschön, prachtvoll.

gorilla [gə'rilə] n Gorilla m.

gorse [gɔːs] n Stechginster m.

gory [gɔːri] adj blutig.

gospel ['gɔspəl] n Evangelium neut.

gossip ['gɔsip] n Geschwätz neut; (person) Klatschbase f. v schwätzen.

got [gɔt] V get.

Gothic ['gɔθik] adj gotisch.

gotten ['gɔtn] V get.

gouge [gaudʒ] v aushöhlen. n Hohleisen neut.

goulash ['guːlaʃ] n Gulasch neut.

gourd [guəd] n Kürbis m.

gourmet ['guəmei] n Feinschmecker m.

gout [gaut] n Gicht f. **gouty** gichtkrank, gichtisch.

govern ['gʌvən] v (country) regieren; (determine) bestimmen; (tech) regeln. **governess** n Gouvernante f. **government** n Regierung f. **governmental** adj Regierungs-. **governor** n Gouverneur m.

gown [gaun] n Kleid neut.

grab [grab] v ergreifen, (an)packen. n (plötzlicher) Griff m.

grace [greis] n Gnade f. Güte f; (prayer) Tischgebet neut. *14 days' grace* 14 Tage Aufschub. *Your Grace* Eure Hoheit. **graceful** adj anmutig. **gracious** adj angenehm, gnädig.

grade [greid] n Grad m, Stufe f; (comm) Qualität f; (US) (Schul)Klasse f; (slope) Gefälle neut. v sortieren, einordnen.

gradient ['greidiənt] n Gefälle neut.

gradual ['gradjuəl] adj stufenweise, allmählich.

graduate ['gradjuət; v 'gradjueit] n Graduierte(r); (high school) Absolvent(in). v abstufen; (university) promovieren. **graduation** n Promovierung f; (high school) Absolvieren neut.

graffiti [grə'fiːti] pl n Graffiti neut sing.

graft[1] [graːft] n (bot) Pfropfreis neut; (med) Transplantat neut. v pfropfen; transplantieren.

graft[2] [graːft] n Korruption f.

grain [grein] n Getreide neut, Korn neut; (sand, etc.) Körnchen neut; (wood) n Maserung f. **grainy** adj körnig.

gram [gram] n Gramm neut.

grammar ['gramə] n Grammatik f. **grammatical** adj grammatisch. **grammar school** Gymnasium neut.

gramophone ['graməfoun] n Platten-

spieler m. **gramophone record** (Schall)Platte f.

granary ['granəri] n Kornkammer f.

grand [grand] adj groß, großartig. **grand piano** Flügel m. **grandeur** n Erhabenheit f.

grand-dad n also **grandpa** (coll) Opa m.

grand-daughter n Enkelin f.

grandfather ['gran,faːðə] n Großvater m.

grandma ['granmaː] n also **granny** (coll) Oma f.

grandmother ['gran,mʌðə] n Großmutter f.

grandparents ['gran,peərənts] pl n Großeltern pl.

grandson ['gransʌn] n Enkel m.

grandstand ['granstand] n Haupttribüne f.

grand total n Gesamtbetrag m.

granite ['granit] n Granit m.

grant [graːnt] v gewähren; (admit) zugestehen. n (student) Stipendium neut; (subsidy) Subvention f, Zuschuß m.

granule ['granjuːl] n Körnchen neut. **granular** adj körnig, granuliert.

grape [greip] n (Wein)Traube f. **grapevine** n Rebstock m.

grapefruit ['greipfruːt] n Grapefruit neut, Pampelmuse f.

graph [graf] n graphische Darstellung f, Schaubild neut.

grapple ['grapl] v sich auseinandersetzen (mit), ringen (mit).

grasp [graːsp] v greifen, packen; (understand) begreifen. n Griff m, Griff m habgierig. **grasping** adj habgierig.

grass [graːs] n Gras neut; (lawn) Rasen m. v (coll) pfeifen.

grate[1] [greit] n (Feuer)Rost m, Gitter neut.

grate[2] [greit] v (cookery) reiben; (teeth) knirschen. **grate on one's nerves** auf die Nerven gehen.

grateful ['greitful] adj dankbar.

gratify ['gratifai] v befriedigen. **gratification** n Befriedigung f. **gratitude** n Dankbarkeit f.

gratuity [grə'tjuəti] n Trinkgeld neut.

grave[1] [greiv] n Grab neut. **gravedigger** n Totengräber m. **gravestone** n Grabstein m. **graveyard** n Friedhof f.

grave[2] [greiv] adj ernsthaft, schwerwiegend.

gravel ['gravəl] n Kies m. **gravelpit** n Kiesgrube f.

gravity ['grævəti] *n* Schwerkraft *f*; (*seriousness*) Ernsthaftigkeit *f*, Ernst *m*.

gravy ['greivi] *n* (Braten)Soße *f*.

graze¹ [greiz] *n* (*med*) Abschürfung *f*. *v* abschürfen; (*touch*) leicht berühren.

graze² [greiz] *v* (*animal*) (ab)weiden. **grazing** *n* Weide *f*.

grease [griːs] *n* Fett *neut*, Schmalz *neut*; (*tech, mot*) Schmiere *f*. *v* schmieren.

great [greit] *adj* groß; (*important*) bedeutend; (*coll*) großartig, toll. **greatly** *adv* in hohem Maße. **great-grandparents** *pl* Urgroßeltern *pl*. **greatness** *n* Größe *f*.

Great Britain *n* Großbritannien *neut*.

Greece [griːs] *n* Griechenland *neut*. **Greek** *adj* griechisch; *n* Grieche *m*, Griechin *f*.

greed [griːd] *n* Gier *f* (nach). **greedy** *adj* gierig.

green [griːn] *adj* grün. *n* Grün *neut*. **greenfly** *n* grüne Blattlaus *f*. **greengage** *n* Reineclaude *f*. **greengrocer's** *n* Obst- und Gemüseladen *m*. **greenhouse** *n* Treibhaus *neut*. **greens** *pl n* (*cookery*) Grünzeug *neut*.

Greenland ['griːnlənd] *n* Grönland *neut*. **Greenlander** *n* Grönländer *m*.

greet [griːt] *v* grüßen, begrüßen. **greeting** *n* Gruß *m*, Begrüßung *f*.

gregarious [gri'gɛəriəs] *adj* gesellig.

grenade [grə'neid] *n* Granate *f*.

grew [gruː] *V* grow.

grey [grei] *adj* grau; (*gloomy*) trübe. *n* Grau *neut*. **greyhound** *n* Windhund *m*.

grid [grid] *n* Gitter *neut*; (*network*) Netz *neut*.

grief [griːf] *n* Trauer *f*. **grievance** *n* Beschwerde *f*. **grieve** *v* trauern.

grill [gril] *v* grillen; (*question*) einem strengen Verhör unterziehen. *n* Bratrost *m*, Grill *m*.

grille [gril] *n* Gitter *neut*.

grim [grim] *adj* (*person*) grimmig, verbissen; (*prospect*) schlimm, hoffnungslos.

grimace [gri'meis] *n* Grimasse *f*. *v* Grimassen schneiden.

grime [graim] *n* Schmutz *m*, Ruß *m*.

grin [grin] *n* Lächeln *neut*, Grinsen *neut*. *v* lächeln, grinsen.

*grind [graind] *v* mahlen; (*knife*) schleifen; (*teeth*) knirschen. *n* (*coll*) Plackerei *f*. **grinder** *n* (*coffee, etc.*) Mühle *f*.

grip [grip] *v* (an)packen, festhalten. *n* Griff *m*.

gripe [graip] *v* zwicken. *n* Kolik *f*; Bauchschmerzen *pl*.

grisly ['grizli] *adj* gräßlich.

gristle ['grisl] *n* Knorpel *m*. **gristly** *adj* knorpelig.

grit [grit] *n* Splitt *m*; (*coll*) Mut *m*, Entschlossenheit *f*. **grit one's teeth** die Zähne zusammenbeißen.

groan [groun] *n* Stöhnen *neut*. *v* stöhnen.

grocer ['grousə] *n* Lebensmittelhändler *m*. **grocer's shop** Lebensmittelgeschäft *neut*. **groceries** *pl n* Lebensmittel *pl*.

groin [groin] *n* (*anat*) Leistengegend *f*.

groom [grum] *n* (*of bride*) Bräutigam *m*; (*for horse*) (Pferde)Knecht *m*. *v* pflegen. **well groomed** gepflegt.

groove [gruːv] *n* Rinne *f*, Furche *f*.

grope [group] *v* tasten (nach). **gropingly** *adv* tastend, vorsichtig.

gross [grous] *adj* grob; (*comm*) Brutto-; (*fat*) dick. *n* Gros *neut*. **Gross National Product** (GNP) Bruttosozialprodukt *neut*. **gross weight** Bruttogewicht *n*.

grotesque [grə'tesk] *adj* grotesk.

grotto ['grotou] *n* Grotte *f*.

ground¹ [graund] *V* grind.

ground² [graund] *n* Boden *m*, Erde *f*. *v* (*aero*) still legen. **ground floor** Erdgeschoß *neut*. **grounds** *pl* (*of house*) Anlagen *pl*; (*coffee*) Bodensatz *m*; (*reason*) Grund *m*.

group [grup] *n* Gruppe *f*. *v* gruppieren.

grouse¹ [graus] *n* Birkhuhn *neut*.

grouse² [graus] *v* (*coll*: *grumble*) meckern. *n* Beschwerde *f*.

grove [grouv] *n* Hain *m*.

grovel ['grovl] *v* kriechen (vor). **grovelling** *adj* kriecherisch.

*grow [grou] *v* wachsen; (*become*) werden; (*plants*) züchten. **grow better** sich bessern. **grow old** alt werden. **grow out of** (*clothes*) herauswachsen aus; (*habit*) entwachsen (+*dat*); (*arise from*) entstehen aus. **grow up** heranwachsen. **grower** *n* Züchter. **growing** *adj* wachsend. **growth** *n* Wachstum *neut*; (*increase*) Zunahme *f*; (*med*) Gewächs *neut*.

grown [groun] *V* grow. *adj* erwachsen. **grown-up** Erwachsene(r).

grub [grʌb] *n* Made *f*; (*slang*: *food*) Futter *neut*. **grubby** *adj* schmutzig, dreckig.

grudge [grʌdʒ] *v* mißgönnen. *n* Mißgunst *f*.

gruelling ['gruəliŋ] *adj* mörderisch.

gruesome ['gruːsəm] *adj* grausam.

gruff [grʌf] *adj* barsch.

grumble ['grʌmbl] *v* schimpfen, murren. *n* Murren *neut.*

grumpy ['grʌmpi] *adj* mürrisch.

grunt [grʌnt] *n* Grunzen *neut. v* grunzen.

guarantee [garən'tiː] *n* Garantie *f,* Gewährleistung *f. v* garantieren, gewährleisten. **guarantor** *n* Gewährsmann *m.*

guard [gaːd] *n* Wächter *m,* Wache *f. v* (be)schützen, bewachen. **guard against** sich hüten vor. **on one's guard** auf der Hut. **guard of honour** Ehrenwache *f.*

guerrilla [gə'rilə] *n* Guerillakämpfer *m.* **guerilla warfare** Guerillakrieg *m.*

guess [ges] *n* Schätzung *f,* Vermutung *f. v* schätzen, vermuten. **guesswork** *n* Mutmaßung *f.*

guest [gest] *n* Gast *m.* **guest house** Pension *f.* **guestroom** Fremdenzimmer *neut.*

guide [gaid] *n* Führer *m;* (*book*) Handbuch *neut. v* führen, leiten. **guide book** Reiseführer *m.*

guild [gild] *n* Gilde *f,* Vereinigung *f.*

guillotine ['gilətiːn] *n* Guillotine *f;* (*for paper*) Papierschneidemaschine *f. v* guillotinieren.

guilt [gilt] *n* Schuld *f;* (*feeling of*) Schuldgefühl *neut.* **guilty** *adj* schuldig. **guilty conscience** schlechtes Gewissen *neut.* **find guilty** für schuldig erklären.

guinea pig ['gini] *n* Guinee *f,* **guinea pig** Meerschweinchen *neut;* (*fig: in experiment*) Versuchskaninchen *neut.*

guitar [gi'taː] *n* Gitarre *f.* **guitar player** Gitarrenspieler(in) *m.*

gulf [gʌlf] *n* Golf *m.*

gull [gʌl] *n* Möwe *f.*

gullet ['gʌlit] *n* Schlund *m.*

gullible ['gʌləbl] *adj* naiv, leichtgläubig. **gullibility** *n* Leichtgläubigkeit *f.*

gully ['gʌli] *n* Rinne *f.*

gulp [gʌlp] *v* hinunterschlucken. *n* Schluck *m.*

gum[1] [gʌm] *n* (*glue*) Klebstoff *m;* (*from tree*) Gummi *neut;* (*sweet*) Gummibonbon *neut.* **chewing gum** Kaugummi *neut. v* kleben.

gum[2] [gʌm] *n* (*in mouth*) Zahnfleisch *neut.*

gun [gʌn] *n* Gewehr *neut;* (*hand gun*) Pistole *f;* (*large*) Kanone *f.* **stick to one's guns** nicht nachgeben. *v* **gun down** erschießen.

gurgle ['gɔːgl] *n* Gurgeln *neut. v* gurgeln.

gush [gʌʃ] *v* hervorquellen, entströmen. *n* Strom *m,* Guß *m.* **gushing** *adj* überschwenglich.

gust [gʌst] *n* Bö *neut. v* blasen.

gusto ['gʌstou] *n* Schwung *m.* **with gusto** eifrig.

gut [gʌt] *n* Darm *m.* **guts** *pl* Eingeweide *pl;* (*coll*) Mut *m.*

gutter ['gʌtə] *n* (*roof*) Dachrinne; (*street*) Gosse *f.* **gutter press** Schmutzpresse *f.*

guy[1] [gai] (*coll*) *n* Kerl *m.*

guy[2] [gai] *n* Halteseil *neut.* **guy-rope** *n* Spannschnur *f.*

gymnasium [dʒim'neiziəm] *n* Turnhalle *f.* **gymnast** *n* Turner(in). **gymnastic** *adj* gymnastisch. **gymnastics** *n* Gymnastik *f.*

gynaecology [gainə'kolədʒi] *n* Frauenheilkunde *f,* Gynäkologie *f.* **gynaecologist** *n* Frauenarzt *m,* Gynäkologe *m.* **gynaecological** *adj* gynäkologisch.

gypsum ['dʒipsəm] *n* Gips *m.*

gyrate [ˌdʒai'reit] *v* wirbeln.

gyroscope ['dʒairəˌskoup] *n* Giroskop *neut.*

H

haberdasher ['habədaʃə] *n* Kurzwarenhändler *m.* **haberdashery** *n* Kurzwaren *pl.*

habit ['habit] *n* Gewohnheit *f.* **be in the habit of** gewöhnt sein. **habitual** *adj* gewohnt, üblich.

habitable ['habitəbl] *adj* bewohnbar. **habitat** *n* Heimat *f.* **habitation** *n* Wohnung *f.* **unfit for human habitation** für Wohnzwecke ungeeignet.

hack[1] [hak] *v* (zer)hacken. **hacksaw** *n* Metallsäge *f.*

hack[2] [hak] *n* (*horse*) Mietpferd *neut,* Gaul *m;* (*writer*) Lohnschreiber *m.*

hackneyed ['haknid] *adj* abgedroschen, banal.

had [had] *V* have.

haddock ['hadək] *n* Schellfisch *m.*

haemorrhage ['heməridʒ] *n* Blutung *f,* Blutsturz *m. v* bluten.

haemorrhoids ['heməroidz] *pl n* Hämorrhoiden *pl.*

haggard ['hægəd] *adj* hager, verstört.
haggle ['hægl] *v* feilschen.
Hague [heig] *n* Den Haag *m*.
hail[1] [heil] *n* Hagel *m*. *v* hageln. **hailstone** *n* Hagelkorn *neut.* **hailstorm** *n* Hagelschauer *m*.
hail[2] [heil] *v* (*greet*) begrüßen; (*call up*) zurufen. **hail from** herkommen von.
hair [heə] *n* (*single*) Haar *neut*; (*person's*) Haar *neut*, Haare *pl*. **hairy** *adj* behaart, haarig.
hairbrush ['heəbrʌʃ] *n* Haarbürste *f*.
haircut ['heəkʌt] *n* Haarschnitt *m*. **have a haircut** sich die Haare schneiden lassen.
hair-do *n* Frisur *f*.
hairdresser ['heə,dresə] *n* Friseur *m*, Friseuse *f*.
hair-dryer ['heə,draiə] *n* Haartrockner *m*.
hair-net *n* Haarnetz *neut*.
hairpin ['heəpin] *n* Haarnadel *f*.
hair-raising ['heə,reiziŋ] *adj* aufregend.
hake [heik] *n* Seehecht *m*.
half [haːf] *n* Hälfte *f*. *adj* halb. *adv* halb, zur Hälfte; (*almost*) beinahe. **at half price** zum halben Preis.
half-and-half *adv* halb-und-halb.
half-back ['haːfbak] *n* Läufer *m*.
half-baked [,haːf'beikt] *adj* (*idea*) halbfertig, nicht durchgedacht.
half-breed ['haːfbriːd] *n* Mischling *m*.
half-brother ['haːfbrʌðə] *n* Halbbruder *m*.
half-hearted [,haːf'haːtid] *adj* gleichgültig, lustlos.
half-hour [haːf'auə] *n* halbe Stunde *f*. **half-hourly** *adv* jede halbe Stunde.
half-mast [,haːf'maːst] *n* **at half-mast** halbmast.
half-sister ['haːfsistə] *n* Halbschwester *f*.
half-term [,haːf'təːm] *n* Semesterhalbzeit *f*.
half-time [,haːf'taim] *n* Halbzeit *f*.
halfway [,haːf'wei] *adv* in der Mitte, halbwegs.
halfwit ['haːfwit] *n* Schwachkopf *m*. **halfwitted** *adj* dumm, blöd.
halibut ['halibət] *n* Heilbutt *m*.
hall [hoːl] *n* Halle *f*, Saal *m*; (*entrance*) Diele *f*, Flur *m*. **hall of residence** Studentenheim *neut*. **hall porter** Hotelportier *m*.
hallmark ['hoːlmaːk] *n* Feingehaltsstempel *m*; (*characteristic*) Kennzeichen *neut*.
hallowed ['haloud] *adj* verehrt.
Hallowe'en [halou'iːn] *n* Abend vor Allerheiligen *m*.

hallucinate [hə'luːsineit] *v* halluzinieren. **hallucination** *n* Halluzination *f*.
halo ['heilou] *n* Glorienschein *m*.
halt [hoːlt] *n* Halt *m*, Pause *f*; (*railway*) Haltestelle *f*. *v* Pause machen; (*put a stop to*) halten lassen.
halter ['hoːltə] *n* Halfter *f*.
halve [haːv] *v* halbieren; (*reduce*) auf die Hälfte reduzieren.
ham [ham] *n* Schinken *m*. (**radio**) **ham** Radio-amateur *m*.
hamburger ['hambəːgə] *n* Frikadelle *f*.
hamlet 'hamlit] *n* Dörfchen *neut*.
hammer ['hamə] *n* Hammer *m*. *v* hämmern. **hammer and tongs** (*coll*) mit aller Kraft.
hammock ['hamək] *n* Hängematte *f*.
hamper[1] ['hampə] *v* behindern, hemmen.
hamper[2] ['hampə] *n* Packkorb *m*, Eßkorb *m*.
hamster ['hamstə] *n* Hamster *m*.
hamstring ['hamstriŋ] *n* Knieflechse *f*. *v* (*coll*) lähmen.
hand [hand] *n* Hand *f*; (*of clock*) Zeiger *m*. *v* (*give*) geben. **at** *or* **to hand** zur Hand. **hand in** einreichen. **hand out** austeilen. **hand over** übergeben. **in hand** im Gange. **on the one hand ... on the other hand ...** einerseits ... anderseits ....
handbag ['handbag] *n* Handtasche *f*.
handbook ['handbuk] *n* Handbuch *neut*; (*travel*) Reiseführer *m*.
handbrake ['handbreik] *n* Handbremse *f*.
handcream ['handkriːm] *n* Handcreme *f*.
handcuff ['handkʌf] *v* Handschellen anlegen (+*dat*). **handcuffs** *pl n* Handschellen *pl*.
handful ['handful] *n* Handvoll *f*.
handicap ['handikap] *n* Behinderung *f*; (*sport*) Handikap *neut*. *v* (*horse*) extra belasten; (*person*) hemmen. **handicapped** *adj* (*med, etc.*) behindert.
handicraft ['handikraːft] *n* Handwerk *neut*.
handiwork ['handiwəːk] *n* Handarbeit *f*.
handkerchief ['haŋkətʃif] *n* Taschentuch *neut*.
handle ['handl] *n* Griff *m*; (*door*) (Tür)Klinke *f*. *v* anfassen, handhaben; (*deal with*) behandeln, sich befassen mit. **handlebar** *n* Lenkstange *f*. **handling** *n* Behandlung *f*.
handmade [,hand'meid] *adj* mit der Hand gemacht.

hand-out ['handaut] n Almosen neut; (leaflet) Prospekt m, Werbezettel m.
hand-pick [hand'pik] v (sorgfältig) auswählen.
handrail ['handreil] n Geländer neut.
handshake ['handʃeik] n Händedruck m.
handsome ['hansəm] adj schön, stattlich.
handstand ['hand,stand] n Handstand m.
hand-towel n Handtuch neut.
handwriting ['hand,raitiŋ] n (Hand)Schrift f.
handy ['handi] adj greifbar, zur Hand; (adroit) geschickt, gewandt.
***hang** [haŋ] v hängen; (person) erhängen. n (of a dress) Sitz m. **to get the hang of** beherrschen, begreifen. **hang on** (phone) am Apparat bleiben. **hang up** (phone) auflegen; (picture, coat) aufhängen.
hangar ['haŋə] n Flugzeughalle f.
hanger ['haŋə] n (for clothes) Kleiderbügel m.
hangover ['haŋouvə] n (coll) Kater m.
hanker ['haŋkə] v sich sehnen (nach). **hankering** n Verlangen neut.
haphazard [,hap'hazəd] adj zufällig.
happen ['hapən] v geschehen, vorkommen. **happen upon** finden. **happen along** erscheinen. **happening** n Ereignis neut.
happy ['hapi:] adj glücklich, zufrieden. **happy-go-lucky** adj sorglos. **happiness** n Glück neut, Glückseligkeit f.
harass ['harəs] v quälen, aufreiben.
harbour ['haibə] n Hafen m. v (protect) beherbergen.
hard [haid] adj hart; (difficult) schwer, schwierig; (callous) gefühllos. **hard-boiled** adj hartgekocht; (coll) hartnäckig. **hard-pressed** adj in schwerer Bedrängnis. **hard up** (coll) schlecht bei Kasse. **hard-of-hearing** adj schwerhörig.
harden ['haidn] v härten, hart machen; (become hard) hart werden.
hardly ['haidli] adj kaum. **hardly ever** fast nie.
hardware ['haidweə] n Eisenwaren pl; (computers) Hardware f.
hardy ['haidi] adj kräftig, abgehärtet; (plant) winterfest.
hare [heə] n Hase m.
haricot ['harikou] n weiße Bohne f.
hark [haik] v horchen. interj hör mal!
harm [haim] v schaden (+ dat), verletzen. n Schaden m, Leid neut. **harmful** adj schädlich. **harmfulness** n Schädlichkeit f.

harmless adj harmlos. **harmlessness** n Harmlosigkeit f.
harmonic [hai'monik] adj harmonisch.
harmonica [hai'monikə] n Mundharmonika f.
harmonious [hai'mouniəs] adj harmonisch, wohlklingend.
harmonize ['haimənaiz] v harmonisieren. **harmonization** n Harmonisierung f.
harmony ['haiməni] n Harmonie f; (agreement) Einklang m, Übereinstimmung f.
harness ['hainis] n (Pferde)Geschirr neut. v spannen; (fig) nutzbar machen.
harp [haip] n Harfe f. v **harp on** (coll) dauernd reden von.
harpoon [hai'puin] n Harpune f. v harpunieren.
harpsichord ['haipsi,koid] n Cembalo neut.
harrowing ['harouiŋ] adj qualvoll, schrecklich.
harsh [haiʃ] adj hart; (voice) rauh; (strict) streng. **harshness** n Strenge f, Härte f.
harvest ['haivist] n Ernte f. (time) Erntezeit f. v ernten, einbringen. **harvester** n (mech) Mähdrescher f. **Harvest Festival** Erntedankfest neut.
hash [haʃ] n Haschee neut. **make a hash of** (coll) verpfuschen.
hashish ['haʃi:ʃ] n Haschisch neut.
haste [heist] n Eile f. **make haste** sich beeilen. **hasten** v sich beeilen; beschleunigen. **hasty** adj eilig; (rushed) übereilt. **hastiness** n Voreiligkeit f.
hat [hat] n Hut m. **eat one's hat** einen Besen fressen. **keep under one's hat** für sich halten.
hatch¹ ['hatʃ] v ausbrüten. **hatch a plot** ein Komplott schmieden.
hatch² [hatʃ] n (naut) Luke f; (serving) Servierfenster neut.
hatchet ['hatʃit] n Beil neut. **bury the hatchet** das Kriegsbeil begraben.
hate [heit] v hassen, verabscheuen. n also **hatred** Haß m, Abscheu m. **hateful** adj hassenswert.
haughty ['hoiti] adj hochmütig. **haughtiness** n Hochmut m.
haul [hoil] v ziehen, schleppen. n (coll: booty) Fang m. **haulage** n Transport m, Spedition f. **haulier** n Transportunternehmer m, Spediteur m.
haunch [hointʃ] n Hüfte f; (of animal) Keule f, Lende f.

haunt [hɔɪnt] v (ghost) spuken in. **haunted** adj gespenstig.

*****have** [hav] v haben. I have to go ich muß gehen. I will have it repaired ich werde es reparieren lassen I have got a car ich habe ein Auto. he's had it es ist aus mit ihm. **be had** (be cheated) reingelegt sein. **have a tooth out** sich einen Zahn ziehen lassen. **have it out with** sich auseinandersetzen mit.

haven [heivn] n Hafen m; (fig) Asyl neut.

havoc [havək] n Verheerung f. **play havoc with** verheeren.

hawk [hɔːk] n Habicht m, Falke m.

hawthorn [ˈhɔːθɔːn] n Hagedorn m.

hay [hei] n Heu neut. **make hay** Heu machen, heuen. **hay fever** Heuschnupfen m. **haystack** n Heuschober m.

haywire [ˈheiwaiə] adj (coll) kaputt. **go haywire** kaputtgehen.

hazard [ˈhazəd] n (danger) Gefahr f; (risk) Risiko neut; (chance) Zufall m; (golf) Hindernis neut. v aufs Spiel setzen, wagen. **hazardous** adj gefährlich, riskant.

haze [heiz] n Dunst m, leichter Nebel m; (fig) Verschwommenheit f. **hazy** adj dunstig; verschwommen.

hazel [ˈheizl] n Haselstrauch m. adj (colour) nußbraun. **hazelnut** n Haselnuß f.

he [hiː] pron er.

head [hed] n Kopf m; (leader) Leiter m; (top) Spitze f. v leiten, führen. **head for** zugehen nach. **head off** umlenken. **per head** pro Kopf. **by a head** um eine Kopflänge f.

headache [ˈhedeik] n Kopfweh neut, Kopfschmerzen pl.

headfirst [ˌhedˈfɜːst] adj kopfüber.

heading [ˈhedin] n Titel m, Überschrift f.

headlamp [ˈhedlamp] n Scheinwerfer m.

headland [ˈhedlənd] n Landzunge f, Landspitze f.

headline [ˈhedlain] n Schlagzeile f.

headlong [ˈhedlɒn] adv kopfüber; ungestüm, blindlings.

headmaster [ˌhedˈmɑːstə] n (Schul)Direktor m. **headmistress** n Direktorin f, Vorsteherin f.

head office n Hauptsitz m.

headphones [ˈhedfounz] pl n Kopfhörer m sing.

headquarters [ˌhedˈkwɔːtəz] n (mil) Hauptquartier neut; (comm) Hauptsitz m.

headrest [ˈhedrest] n Kopfstütze f.

headscarf [ˈhedskɑːf] n Kopftuch neut.

headstrong [ˈhedstrɒn] adj eigensinnig.

head waiter n Ober(kellner) m.

headway [ˈhedwei] n Fortschritte pl. **make headway** vorankommen, Fortschritte machen.

heal [hiːl] v heilen. **healer** n Heiler m. **healing** n Heilung f. adj heilend, heilsam.

health [helθ] n Gesundheit f. **your health!** zum Wohl! **health insurance** Krankenversicherung f. **health resort** Kurort m. **healthy** adj gesund.

heap [hiːp] n Haufe(n) m. v häufen. **heaps better** (coll) viel besser. **heap up** anhäufen.

*****hear** [hiə] v hören; (listen) zuhören. **hearing** n Gehör neut; (law) Verhör neut. **hearing aid** Hörgerät neut. **hearsay** n Hörensagen neut. **preliminary hearing** Voruntersuchung f.

heard [hɜːd] V hear.

hearse [hɜːs] n Leichenwagen m.

heart [hɑːt] n Herz neut. **change of heart** Gesinnungswechsel m.

heart attack n Herzanfall m.

heartbeat [ˈhɑːtbiːt] n Herzschlag m.

heart-breaking [ˈhɑːtbreikiŋ] adj herzzerbrechend. **heart-broken** adj untröstlich.

heartburn [ˈhɑːtbɜːn] n Sodbrennen neut.

heart failure n Herzschlag m.

heartfelt [ˈhɑːtfelt] adj tiefempfunden.

hearth [hɑːθ] n Kamin m.

hearty [ˈhɑːti] adj herzlich. **heartily** adv herzlich, von Herzen.

heat [hiːt] n Hitze f, Wärme f; (sport) Vorlauf m. **in the heat of passion** (law) im Affekt. v hitzen. **heated** adj (fig) erregt. **heating** n Heizung f. **heatproof** adj hitzebeständig. **heat-stroke** n Hitzschlag m. **heatwave** n Hitzewelle f.

heath [hiːθ] n Heide f.

heathen [ˈhiːðn] n Heide m. adj heidnisch, unzivilisiert.

heather [ˈheðə] n Heidekraut neut.

heave [hiːv] v hieven; hochheben; (sigh) ausstoßen; (anchor) lichten. n Heben neut.

heaven [hevn] n Himmel m. **go to heaven** in den Himmel kommen. **to move heaven and earth** (fig) Himmel und Erde in Bewegung setzen. **for heaven's sake** um Himmels Willen. **heavenly** adj himmlisch. **heavenly body** Himmelskörper m.

heavy ['hevi] adj schwer, schwerwiegend; (mood) träge; (book) langweilig. **heaviness** n Schwere f; (mood) Schwerfälligkeit f. **heavy-duty** adj Hochleistungs-. **heavyweight** n (sport) Schwergewichtler m.

Hebrew ['hiːbruː] n Hebräer m. adj hebräisch.

heckle ['hekl] v durch Fragen belästigen. **heckler** n Zwischenrufer m.

hectare ['hekteə] n Hektar neut.

hectic ['hektik] adj hektisch.

hedge [hedʒ] n Hecke f, Heckenzaun m. **hedgerow** n Hecke f.

hedgehog ['hedʒhog] n Igel m.

heed [hiːd] v achtgeben auf. n Beachtung. **heedful** adj achtsam. **heedless** adj achtlos.

heel [hiːl] n Ferse f; (of shoe) Absatz m. v (shoes) mit Absätzen versehen. **take to one's heels** die Beine in die Hand nehmen. **down-at-heel** (fig) schäbig. **well-heeled** adj wohlhabend.

hefty ['hefti] adj kräftig.

heifer ['hefə] n Färse f.

height [hait] n Höhe f; (person) Größe f; (fig) Höhepunkt m. **heighten** v verstärken.

heir [eə] n Erbe m. **heiress** n Erbin f. **heirloom** n Erbstück neut.

held [held] V **hold**¹

helicopter ['helikoptə] n Hubschrauber m.

hell [hel] n Hölle f. interj zum Teufel! **to hell with** zum Teufel mit. **hellish** adj höllisch.

hello [həˈlou] interj Guten Tag; (on telephone) hallo!

helm [helm] n Steuer neut, Ruder neut. **helmsman** n Steuermann m.

helmet ['helmit] n Helm m.

help [help] v helfen (+ dat). n Hilfe f. I can't help it ich kann nichts dafür, ich kann nicht anders. **help yourself** bedienen Sie Sich! **helper** n Helfer(in). **helpful** adj hilfreich. **helping** n Portion f. **helpless** adj hilflos.

hem [hem] n Saum m. v säumen. **hem in** einengen.

hemisphere ['hemiˌsfiə] n Halbkugel f, Hemisphäre f.

hemp [hemp] n Hanf m.

hen [hen] n Huhn neut.

hence [hens] adv von hier; (therefore) deshalb, daher. **a week hence** in einer Woche. **henceforth** fortan, von jetzt an.

henna ['henə] n Henna f.

henpecked ['henpekt] adj **henpecked husband** Pantoffelheld m.

her [həː] pron (acc) sie; (dat) ihr. poss adj ihr.

herald ['herəld] n Herold m. v (fig) einleiten. **heraldic** adj heraldisch, Wappen-. **heraldry** n Heraldik f, Wappenkunde f.

herb [həːb] n Kraut n. **herbal** adj Kräuter-. **herbalist** n Kräuterkenner(in).

herd [həːd] n Herde f. v hüten, zusammentreiben.

here [hiə] adv hier; (to here) hierher. **hereafter** adv in Zukunft. **herewith** adv hiermit.

hereditary [hiˈredətəri] adj erblich. **heredity** n Vererbung f, Erblichkeit f.

heresy ['herəsi] n Ketzerei f. **heretic** n Ketzer(in). **heretical** adj Ketzerisch.

heritage ['heritidʒ] n Erbe neut, Erbgut neut.

hermit ['həːmit] n Eremit m. **hermitage** n Klause f.

hernia ['həːniə] n Bruch m.

hero ['hiərou] n Held m. **heroine** n Heldin f. **heroic** adj heroisch, heldenmutig. **heroism** n Heldentum neut.

heron ['herən] n Reiher m.

herring ['heriŋ] n Hering m. **herringbone** n (pattern) Fischgrätenmuster neut. **pickled herring** Rollmops m.

hers [həːz] poss pron ihrer m, ihre f, ihres neut. **herself** pron (reflexive) sich; selbst. **by herself** allein.

hesitate ['heziteit] v zögern. **hesitant** adj zögernd. **hesitation** n Zögern neut, Bedenken neut.

heterosexual [hetərəˈseksuəl] adj heterosexuell.

***hew** [hjuː] v hauen.

hewn [hjuːn] V **hew**.

hexagon ['heksəgən] n Sechseck neut.

heyday ['heidei] n Höhepunkt m, Blütezeit f.

hiatus [haiˈeitəs] n Lücke f.

hibernate ['haibəneit] v Winterschlafhalten. **hibernation** n Winterschlaf m.

hiccup ['hikʌp] n Schluckauf m, Schlucken m. v den Schluckauf haben.

hid [hid] V **hide**¹.

hidden ['hidn] V hide¹.

***hide¹** [haid] v (conceal) verstecken, verbergen; (keep secret) verheimlichen.

hide² [haid] n (skin) Fell neut, Haut f.

hideous ['hidiəs] adj abscheulich, schrecklich.

hiding¹ ['haidiŋ] n Versteck neut. **be in hiding** sich versteckt halten.

hiding² ['haidiŋ] n (thrashing) Prügel neut.

hierarchy ['haiəraiki] n Hierarchie f, Rangordnung f. **hierarchical** adj hierarchisch.

high [hai] adj hoch; (wind) stark.

highbrow ['haibrau] adj intellektuell. n Intellektuelle(r).

hi-fi ['haifai] adj hi-fi. n Hi-Fi.

high frequency n Hochfrequenz f.

high jump n Hochsprung m.

highland ['hailənd] n Bergland neut.

highlight ['hailait] n Höhepunkt m.

highly ['haili] adv höchst, in hohem Grad, stark. **highly strung** überempfindlich.

highness ['hainis] n Höhe f. **Your Highness** Eure Hoheit.

highpitched [,hai'pitʃt] adj hoch.

high point n Höhepunkt m.

high-rise building n Hochhaus neut.

high-spirited adj lebhaft, temperamentvoll.

high street n Hauptstraße f.

high tide n Hochwasser neut.

highway ['haiwei] n Landstraße f.

hijack ['haidʒak] v (aeroplane) entführen. n Entführung f. **hijacker** n Entführer m, Hijacker m.

hike [haik] v wandern. n Wanderung f. **hiker** n Wanderer m.

hilarious [hi'leəriəs] adj lustig. **hilarity** n Lustigkeit f.

hill [hil] n Hügel m, Berg m. **hillside** n Hang m. **hilltop** n Bergspitze f.

him [him] pron (acc) ihn; (dat) ihm. **himself** pron (reflexive) sich; selbst. **by himself** allein.

hind [haind] adj hinter, Hinter-. **hindsight** n with hindsight im Rückblick.

hinder ['hində] v (ver)hindern. **hindrance** n Hindernis neut, Hinderung f.

Hindu [hin'du:] n Hindu m. adj Hindu-.

hinge [hindʒ] n Scharnier neut, Gelenk neut. **to hinge on** abhängen (von).

hint [hint] n Wink m. v andeuten.

hip [hip] n Hüfte f. **hip-bone** n Hüftbein neut. **hip-joint** n Hüftgelenk neut.

hippopotamus [hipə'potəməs] n Nilpferd neut.

hire [haiə] v (ver)mieten; (staff) anstellen. n Miete f. **hire-car** n Mietwagen m. **hire purchase** Ratenkauf m, **hire-purchase agreement** Teilzahlungsvertrag m.

his [hiz] poss adj sein. poss pron seiner m, seine f, seines neut.

hiss [his] v zischen. n Zischen neut.

history ['histəri] n Geschichte f. **history book** Geschichtsbuch neut. **historian** n Historiker(in). **historic** adj historisch. **historical** adj historisch, geschichtlich.

***hit** [hit] v schlagen, stoßen. n Schlag m, Stoß m; (record) Schlager m. **make a hit** (fig) Erfolg haben. **hard hit** schwer getroffen. **hit upon** zufällig finden.

hitch [hitʃ] v befestigen; (horse) anspannen. n (problem) Haken m. **hitchhike** v per Anhalter fahren.

hitherto [,hiðə'tu:] adv bisher.

hive [haiv] n Bienenkorb m. v **hive off** abzweigen.

hoard [hoid] n Schatz m, Hort m. v sammeln, hamstern.

hoarding ['hoidiŋ] n Reklamewand f.

hoarse [hois] adj rauh, heiser.

hoax [houks] n Falschmeldung f. v zum Besten haben.

hobble ['hobl] v hinken, hoppeln; (horse) fesseln.

hobby ['hobi] n Hobby neut. **hobby horse** n Steckenpferd neut.

hock¹ [hok] n (joint) Sprunggelenk neut.

hock² [hok] n (wine) Rheinwein m.

hockey ['hoki] n Hockey neut.

hoe [hou] n Hacke f. v hacken.

hog [hog] n (Schlacht)Schwein neut; (coll) Vielfraß m. **go the whole hog** aufs Ganze gehen.

hoist [hoist] v hochziehen. n Aufzug m, Kran m.

***hold¹** [hould] v halten; (contain) enthalten. n Halt m, Griff m; (fig) Einfluß m. **hold back** zurückhalten. **hold down** (job) behalten. **hold up** (delay) aufhalten; (rob) überfallen. **hold-up** n (traffic) Stockung f; (robbery) Überfall m.

hold² [hould] n (naut) Frachtraum m, Schiffsraum m.

holder ['houldə] n (owner) Inhaber m.

holding ['houldiŋ] n (land) Grundbesitz m, Guthaben neut. **holding company** Dachgesellschaft f.

hole [houl] n Loch neut.

holiday ['holədi] n Feiertag m, Ruhetag m. **holidays** pl Ferien pl, Urlaub m sing. go on holiday verreisen, in die Ferien gehen, auf Urlaub gehen. **holidaymaker** n Feriengast m, Urlauber(in).

Holland ['holənd] n Holland neut, die Niederlände pl.

hollow ['holou] n Höhle f, Loch neut. adj hohl, leer. v (aus)höhlen. **hollowness** n Hohlheit f, Leerheit f.

holly ['holi] n Stechpalme f.

holster ['houlstə] n Pistolenhalfter f.

holy ['houli] adj heilig.

homage ['homidʒ] n Huldigung f. do or pay homage huldigen.

home [houm] n Heim neut, Haus neut, Zuhause neut; (institution) Heim neut. at home zu Hause. at home with vertraut mit. make yourself at home mach dich bequem. go home nach Hause gehen. hammer home (nail) fest einschlagen. adj häuslich; (national) inner, Innen-. home affairs innere Angelegenheiten pl. home market Binnenmarkt m. **homecoming** n Heimkehr f, Heimat f, Vaterland neut. **homeless** adj obdachlos. **homely** adj heimisch, gemütlich. be **homesick** Heimweh haben. **homesickness** n Heimweh neut. **homeward** adj Heim-; adv heimwärts. **homework** n Hausaufgaben pl.

homicide ['homisaid] n Mord m; (person) Mörder m.

homogeneous [homə'dʒiniəs] adj gleichartig, homogen.

homosexual [homə'seksuəl] adj homosexuell. n Homosexuelle(r). **homosexuality** n Homosexualität f.

honest ['onist] adj ehrlich, aufrecht. **honesty** n Ehrlichkeit f, Aufrichtigkeit f.

honey ['hʌni] n Honig m; (darling) Liebling m, Schatz m. **honey-bee** n Honigbiene f. **honeycomb** n Honigwabe f. **honeymoon** n Hochzeitsreise f.

honeysuckle ['hʌnisʌkl] n Geißblatt neut.

honour ['onə] n Ehre f; (reputation) guter Ruf m. **honours** pl Auszeichnungen pl. v (ver)ehren; (cheque) einlösen. **honourable** adj ehrenvoll; (in titles) ehrenwert.

hood [hud] n Kapuze f; (US: on car) Motorhaube f; (coll) Gangster m. **hoodwink** v täuschen.

hoof [huːf] n Huf m.

hook [huk] n Haken m. v haken. **hook up** (coll) anschließen.

hooligan ['huːligən] n Rowdy m. **hooliganism** n Rowdytum neut.

hoop [huːp] n Reif(en) m.

hoot [huːt] v hupen. n Hupen neut.

hop[1] [hop] v hüpfen. n Sprung m.

hop[2] [hop] n (bot) Hopfen m.

hope [houp] v hoffen (auf). n Hoffnung f. **hopeful** adj hoffnungsvoll; (promising) vielversprechend. **hopefully** adv hoffentlich. **hopeless** adj hoffnungslos. **hopelessness** n Hoffnungslosigkeit f.

horde [hoːd] n Horde f.

horizon [hə'raizn] n Horizont m. **horizontal** adj waagerecht, horizontal.

hormone ['hoːmoun] n Hormon neut.

horn [hoːn] n Horn neut; (mot) Hupe f. **horned** adj gehörnt. **horn-rimmed spectacles** Hornbrille f. **horny** adj (hands) schwielig.

hornet ['hoːnit] n Hornisse f.

horoscope ['horəskoup] n Horoskop neut.

horrible ['horibl] adj schrecklich, fürchterlich.

horrid ['horid] adj scheußlich, abscheulich.

horrify ['horifai] v erschrecken, entsetzen. **horrifying** adj entsetzlich.

horror ['horə] n Entsetzen neut, Grausen neut. **horror-stricken** adj von Grausen gepackt.

hors d'oeuvre [oː'dəːvr] n Vorspeise f.

horse [hoːs] n Pferd neut, Roß neut. on **horseback** zu Pferd. **horse chestnut** Roßkastanie f. **horseman** n Reiter m. **horsepower** (hp) n Pferdestärke (PS) f. **horse race** n Pferderennen neut. **horseradish** n Meerrettich m.

horticulture ['hoːtikʌltʃə] n Gartenbau m.

hose [houz] n (stockings) Strümpfe pl; (tech, mot) Schlauch m; (in garden) Gartenschlauch m.

hosiery ['houziəri] pl n Strumpfwaren pl.

hospitable [ho'spitəbl] adj gastfreundlich.

hospital ['hospitl] n Krankenhaus neut, Klinik f.

hospitality [hospi'taliti] n Gastfreundschaft f.

host[1] [houst] n Gastgeber m, Wirt m.

host[2] [houst] n (large number) Masse f, Menge f.

hostage ['hostidʒ] n Geisel m, f.

hostel ['hostl] n Herberge f. **student hostel** Studentenheim neut. **youth hostel**

Jugendherberge f. **hostelry** n Wirtshaus neut.

hostess ['houstis] n Gastgeberin f, Wirtin f; (air hostess) Stewardeß f.

hostile ['hostail] adj feindlich, feindselig (gegen). **hostility** n Feindseligkeit f, Feindschaft f.

hot [hot] adj heiß; (food, drink) warm. **hotdog** n (heißes) Würstchen. **hot meal** warme Mahlzeit. **hot-water bottle** Wärmflasche f.

hotel [hou'tel] n Hotel neut, Gasthof m. **hotel register** n Fremdenbuch neut. **hotelier** n Hotelier m.

hound [haund] n Jagdhund m. v jagen, verfolgen.

hour ['auə] n Stunde f. **after hours** nach Geschäftsschluß. **for hours** stundenlang. **hourglass** n Sanduhr f. **hourly** adj, adv stündlich. **hourly wage** Stundenlohn m.

house [haus; v hauz] n Haus neut; (theatre) Publikum neut. **House of Commons** Unterhaus neut. **House of Lords** Oberhaus neut. **House of Representatives** Abgeordnetenhaus neut. v unterbringen.

houseboat ['hausbout] n Hausboot neut.

household ['haushould] n Haushalt m.

housekeeper ['haus‚kiːpə] n Haushälterin f. **housekeeping** n Haushaltung f. **housekeeping money** Haushaltsgeld neut.

housemaid ['hausmeid] n Dienstmädchen neut. **housemaid's knee** (med) Kniescheibenentzündung f.

house-warming ['haus‚wɔːmiŋ] n Einzugsfest neut.

housewife ['hauswaif] n Hausfrau f.

housework ['hauswəːk] n Hausarbeit f.

housing ['hauziŋ] n Unterbringung f, Wohnung f; (tech) Gehäuse neut. **housing estate** Siedlung f.

hovel ['hovəl] n Schuppen m.

hover ['hovə] v schweben. **hovercraft** n Luftkissenfahrzeug neut.

how [hau] adv wie. **how do you do?** guten Tag. **how are you?** wie geht es Ihnen? **how much** or **how many** wieviel. **however** adv aber, jedoch; (in whatever way) wie auch immer.

howl [haul] v heulen. n Heulen neut.

hub [hʌb] n Nabe f; (fig) Mittelpunkt m. **hub cap** Radkappe f.

huddle ['hʌdl] v sich zusammendrängen. **huddled** adj kauernd.

hue [hjuː] n Farbe f, Färbung f.

huff [hʌf] n **in a huff** gekränkt, beleidigt.

hug [hʌg] v umarmen. n Umarmung f.

huge [hjuːdʒ] adj riesig, riesengroß.

hulk [hʌlk] n (naut) Hulk m.

hull [hʌl] n (naut) Rumpf m; (of seed, etc.) Hülse f, Schale f. v enthülsen.

hum [hʌm] v summen, brummen. n Summen neut, Brummen neut.

human ['hjuːmən] adj menschlich. **human being** Mensch m. **human nature** Menschheit f, menschliche Natur f. **humane** adj human. **humanist** n Humanist(in). **humanitarian** adj menschenfreundlich. **humanity** n Menschheit f.

humble ['hʌmbl] adj demütig, bescheiden; (lowly) niedrig. **humiliate** v demütigen. **humiliating** adj demütigend. **humility** n Demut f, Bescheidenheit f.

humdrum ['hʌmdrʌm] adj langweilig, alltäglich.

humid ['hjuːmid] adj feucht. **humidity** n Feuchtigkeit f.

humour ['hjuːmə] n Humor m; (mood) Stimmung f, Laune f. v (person) nachgeben (+dat). **sense of humour** Humor m. **humorous** adj lustig, humorvoll.

hump [hʌmp] n Buckel m. v (coll: carry) schleppen. **humpback** n Bucklige(r). **humpbacked** adj bucklig.

hunch [hʌntʃ] n (coll) Vorahnung f.

hundred ['hʌndrəd] adj hundert. n Hundert neut. **hundredth** adj hundertst; n Hundertstel neut. **hundredweight** Zentner m.

hung [hʌŋ] V hang.

Hungary ['hʌŋgəri] n Ungarn neut. **Hungarian** adj ungarisch; n Ungar(in).

hunger ['hʌŋgə] n Hunger m. v hungern. **hunger for** sehnen nach. **hungry** adj hungrig. **be hungry** Hunger haben.

hunt [hʌnt] n Jagd f, Jagen neut; (for person) Verfolgung f. v jagen; verfolgen. **hunter** n Jäger m; (horse) Jagdpferd neut. **hunting** n Jagd f.

hurdle ['həːdl] n Hürde f; (fig) Hindernis neut.

hurl [həːl] v werfen.

hurricane ['hʌrikən] n Orkan m. **hurricane lamp** Sturmlaterne f.

hurry ['hʌri] v eilen, sich beeilen; (something) beschleunigen. n Eile f, Hast f. **hurry up** mach schnell! **hurried** adj eilig, übereilt.

*hurt [həːt] v (*injure*) verletzen; (*ache*) schmerzen, weh tun; (*offend*) kränken, verletzen. n Verletzung f; Schmerzen neut. **hurtful** adj schädlich.

hurtle ['həːtl] v stürzen, sausen.

husband ['hʌzbənd] n (Ehe)Mann m. v (*resources*) sparsam umgehen mit. **husbandry** n Landwirtschaft f.

hush [hʌʃ] n Stille f, Ruhe f. v beruhigen.

husk [hʌsk] n Hülse f. v enthülsen.

husky ['hʌski] adj (*voice*) rauh, heiser.

hussar [həˈzaː] n Husar m.

hustle ['hʌsl] v drängen. **hustle and bustle** Gedränge neut.

hut [hʌt] n Hütte f.

hutch [hʌtʃ] n Stall m.

hyacinth ['haiəsinθ] n Hyazinthe f.

hybrid ['haibrid] n Kreuzung f, Mischling m. adj Misch-.

hydraulic [haiˈdrɔːlik] adj hydraulisch.

hydrocarbon [ˌhaidrouˈkaːbən] n Kohlenwasserstoff m.

hydro-electric [ˌhaidrouiˈlektrik] adj hydroelektrisch.

hydrogen ['haidrədʒən] n Wasserstoff m. **hydrogen bomb** Wasserstoffbombe f. **hydrogen peroxide** Wasserstoffsuperoxyd neut.

hyena [haiˈiːnə] n Hyäne f.

hygiene ['haidʒiːn] n Hygiene f, Gesundheitspflege f. **hygienic** adj hygienisch.

hymn [him] n Kirchenlied neut, Hymne f. **hymnbook** n Gesangbuch neut.

hypersensitive [haipəˈsensətiv] adj überempfindlich.

hyphen ['haifən] n Bindestrich m.

hypnosis [hipˈnousis] n Hypnose f. **hypnotic** adj hypnotisch. **hypnotist** n Hypnotiseur m. **hypnotize** v hypnotisieren.

hypochondria [haipəˈkondriə] n Hypochondrie f. **hypochondriac** adj hypochondrisch. n Hypochonder m.

hypocrisy [hiˈpokrəsi] n Heuchelei f. **hypocrite** n Heuchler(in). **hypocritical** adj heuchlerisch.

hypodermic [haipəˈdəːmik] adj subkutan. **hypodermic syringe** Spritze f.

hypothesis [haiˈpoθəsis] n (pl **-ses**) Hypothese f. **hypothetical** adj hypothetisch.

hysterectomy [histəˈrektəmi] n Hysterektomie f.

hysteria [hisˈtiəriə] n Hysterie f. **hysterical** adj hysterisch; (*coll: funny*) zum Schreien komisch.

I

I [ai] pron ich.

ice [ais] n Eis neut. v (*cookery*) mit Zuckerguß überziehen. **icing** n Zuckerguß m. **ice age** n Eiszeit f. **iceberg** n Eisberg m. **icebox** n Kühlschrank m. **ice cream** n Eis neut. **ice cube** n Eiswürfel m. **icy** adj eisig.

Iceland ['aislənd] n Island neut. **Icelandic** adj isländisch. **Icelander** n Isländer(in).

icicle ['aisikl] n Eiszapfen m.

icon ['aikon] n Ikone f.

idea [aiˈdiə] n Idee f; (*concept*) Begriff m. *I've no idea* ich habe keine Ahnung.

ideal [aiˈdiəl] n Ideal neut. adj ideal. **idealism** n Idealismus neut. **idealist** n Idealist m. **idealistic** adj idealistisch. **ideally** adv idealerweise.

identical [aiˈdentikəl] adj identisch.

identify [aiˈdentifai] v identifizieren; (*recognize*) erkennen. **identification** n Identifizierung f; (*pass*) Ausweis m.

identity [aiˈdentiti] n Identität f. **identity card** Personalausweis m. **identity papers** Ausweispapiere pl.

ideology [aidiˈolədʒi] n Ideologie f. **ideological** adj ideologisch. **ideologist** n Ideologe m, Ideologin f.

idiom ['idiəm] n Mundart f, Idiom neut. **idiomatic** adj idiomatisch.

idiosyncrasy [ˌidiəˈsiŋkrəsi] n Eigenart f. **idiosyncratic** adj eigenartig.

idiot ['idiət] n (*coll*) Idiot m, Dummkopf m; (*med*) Blödsinnige(r). **idiocy** n Blödsinn m.

idle ['aidl] adj (*person*) faul, untätig; (*words, etc.*) eitel, unnütz. **idleness** n Faulheit f. **idler** n Faulenzer m.

idol ['aidl] n Idol neut. **idolize** v vergöttern.

idyllic [iˈdilik] adj idyllisch.

if [if] conj wenn, falls; (*whether*) ob. **even if** selbst wenn. **if only** wenn ... nur. **if not** falls nicht. **if so** in dem Fall.

ignite [igˈnait] v (ent)zünden.

ignition [ig'niʃən] n Zündung f. **ignition key** Zündschlüssel m.

ignorant ['ignərənt] adj unwissend; (uneducated) ungebildet. **be ignorant of** nicht wissen or kennen. **ignorance** n Unkenntnis f.

ignore [ig'noɪ] v ignorieren, unbeachtet lassen.

ill [il] adj (sick) krank; (bad) schlimm, böse. **fall ill** krank werden. **ill-at-ease** adj unbehaglich. **ill-bred** schlecht erzogen. **ill-disposed** adj bösartig. **ill-fated** adj unselig. **ill-natured** adj boshaft. **illness** n Krankheit f. **ill-treat** v mißhandeln.

illegal [i'liɪgəl] adj illegal, gesetzwidrig. **illegality** n Ungesetzlichkeit f.

illegible [i'ledʒəbl] adj unleserlich. **illegibility** n Unleserlichkeit f.

illegitimate [ˌili'dʒitimit] adj (child) unehelich; (unlawful) ungesetzlich.

illicit [i'lisit] adj unzulässig, gesetzwidrig.

illiterate [i'litərit] adj analphabetisch, ungebildet. n Analphabet(in).

illogical [i'lodʒikəl] adj unlogisch.

illuminate [i'luɪmiˌneit] v erleuchten. **illuminated** adj beleuchtet. **illumination** n Beleuchtung f.

illusion [i'luːʒən] n Illusion f. **illusory** adj illusorisch.

illustrate ['iləstreit] v (book) illustrieren; (idea) erklären. **illustration** n Illustration f, Bild n.

illustrious [i'lʌstriəs] adj berühmt.

image ['imidʒ] n Bild neut, (idea) Vorstellung f; (public) Image neut. **imagery** n Symbolik f.

imagine [i'madʒin] v sich vorstellen or denken. **imaginable** adj denkbar. **imaginary** adj eingebildet, Schein-. **imagination** n Phantasie f. **imaginative** adj phantasiereich.

imbalance [im'baləns] n Unausgeglichenheit f.

imbecile ['imbəˌsiːl] n Schwachsinnige(r). adj schwachsinnig.

imitate ['imiˌteit] v nachahmen, imitieren. **imitation** n Nachahmung f; adj künstlich, Kunst-.

immaculate [i'makjulit] adj makellos.

immaterial [ˌimə'tiəriəl] adj belanglos.

immature [ˌimə'tjuə] adj unreif, unentwickelt. **immaturity** n Unreife f.

immediate [i'miːdiət] adj unmittelbar, direkt. **immediately** adv sofort.

immense [i'mens] adj riesig, ungeheuer.

immerse [i'məɪs] v versenken, tauchen. **immersion** n Versunkenheit f, Immersion f. **immersion heater** Tauchsieder m.

immigrate ['imiˌgreit] v einwandern. **immigrant** n Einwanderer m, Einwanderin f. **immigration** n Einwanderung f.

imminent ['iminənt] adj drohend.

immobile [i'moubail] adj bewegungslos, unbeweglich. **immobility** n Unbeweglichkeit f. **immobilize** v unbeweglich machen.

immodest [i'modist] adj schamlos.

immoral [i'morəl] adj unsittlich, unmoralisch. **immorality** n Sittenlosigkeit f.

immortal [i'moɪtl] adj unsterblich, ewig. **immortality** n Unsterblichkeit f.

immovable [i'muɪvəbl] adj unbeweglich.

immune [i'mjuɪn] adj immun (gegen). **immunity** n Immunität f. **immunization** n Impfung f.

imp [imp] v Kobold m.

impact ['impakt] n Anprall m, Stoß m; (effect) Wirkung f, Einfluß m.

impair [im'peə] v beeinträchtigen. **impairment** n Beeinträchtigung f.

impart [im'paɪt] v geben, erteilen.

impartial [im'paɪʃəl] adj unparteiisch. **impartiality** n Unparteilichkeit f.

impassable [im'paɪsəbl] adj ungangbar, unpassierbar.

impasse [am'paɪs] n Sackgasse f.

impassive [im'paisiv] adj ungerührt.

impatient [im'peiʃənt] adj ungeduldig. **impatience** n Ungeduld f.

impeach [im'piɪtʃ] v anklagen. **impeachment** n Anklage f.

impeccable [im'pekəbl] adj tadellos. **impeccability** n Tadellosigkeit f.

impede [im'piːd] v (be)hindern. **impediment** n Verhinderung f. **speech impediment** Sprachfehler m.

impel [im'pel] v (an)treiben. **impelled** adj gezwungen.

impending [im'pendiŋ] adj bevorstehend, drohend.

imperative [im'perətiv] adj dringend notwendig. n (gramm) Imperativ m.

imperfect [im'pəɪfikt] adj unvollkommen, fehlerhaft. **imperfection** n (blemish) Fehler m.

imperial [im'piəriəl] adj kaiserlich. **imperialism** n Imperialismus m. **imperialist** adj imperialistisch.

imperil [im'peril] v gefährden.
impermanent [im'pəːmənənt] *adj* unbeständig.
impersonal [im'pəːsnl] *adj* unpersönlich. **impersonality** *n* Unpersönlichkeit *f*.
impersonate [im'pəːsə,neit] v sich ausgeben als.
impertinent [im'pəːtinənt] *adj* frech, unverschämt. **impertinence** *n* Frechheit *f*, Unverschämtheit *f*.
impervious [im'pəːviəs] *adj* undurchdringlich.
impetuous [im'petjuəs] *adj* ungestüm, impulsiv. **impetuosity** *n* Ungestüm *neut*.
impetus ['impətəs] *n* Antrieb *m*, Schwung *m*.
impinge [im'pindʒ] v eingreifen (in), stoßen (an).
implement ['implimənt; v 'impliment] *n* Werkzeug *neut*, Gerät *neut*. v durchführen.
implicate ['implikeit] v hineinziehen. **implication** *n* Bedeutung *f*, Konsequenz *f*.
implicit [im'plisit] *adj* (*tacit*) unausgesprochen; (*unquestioning*) absolut. **implicitly** *adv* unbedingt.
implore [im'plɔː] v dringend bitten. **imploring** *adj* flehentlich.
imply [im'plai] v bedeuten.
impolite [impə'lait] *adj* unhöflich. **impoliteness** *n* Unhöflichkeit *f*.
import [im'pɔːt] v einführen, importieren. *n* Einfuhr *f*, Import *m*. **importer** *n* Importeur *m*, Einfuhrhändler *m*. **imports** *pl n* Importwaren *pl*.
importance [im'pɔːtəns] *n* Wichtigkeit *f*, Bedeutung *f*. **important** *adj* wichtig.
impose [im'pouz] v auferlegen. **impose upon** mißbrauchen. **imposing** *adj* imponierend. **imposition** *n* Auferlegung *f*; (*unreasonable demand*) Zumutung *f*.
impossible [im'posəbl] *adj* unmöglich. **impossibility** *n* Unmöglichkeit *f*.
impostor [im'postə] *n* Betrüger(in).
impotent ['impətənt] *adj* impotent. **impotence** *n* Impotenz *f*.
impound [im'paund] v beschlagnahmen.
impoverish [im'povəriʃ] v arm machen. **impoverished** *adj* verarmt.
impregnate ['impreg,neit] v befruchten, schwanger machen; (*fabric, wood, etc.*) imprägnieren. **impregnable** *adj* uneinnehmbar.
impress [im'pres] v beeindrucken. **impres-**

sion *n* Eindruck *m*; (*book*) Auflage *f*.
impressionism *n* (*painting*) Impressionismus *m*.
imprint [im'print; *n* 'imprint] v aufdrücken (auf); (*fig*) einprägen in. *n* Stempel *m*; (*fig*) Eindruck *m*.
imprison [im'prizn] v einsperren. **imprisonment** *n* Haft *f*, Gefangenschaft *f*.
improbable [im'probəbl] *adj* unwahrscheinlich. **improbability** *n* Unwahrscheinlichkeit *f*.
impromptu [im'promptjuː] *adj* improvisiert.
improper [im'propə] *adj* unpassend, unsittlich.
improve [im'pruːv] v verbessern; (*become better*) sich verbessern, besser werden. **improvement** *n* Verbesserung *f*.
improvise ['imprəvaiz] v improvisieren. **improvisation** *n* Improvisierung *f*.
impudent ['impjudənt] *adj* frech, unverschämt. **impudence** *n* Unverschämtheit *f*.
impulse ['impʌls] *n* Antrieb *m*, Drang *m*. **impulsive** *adj* impulsiv.
impure [im'pjuə] *adj* unrein. **impurity** *n* Unreinheit *f*; (*extraneous substance*) fremde Bestandteile *pl*.
in [in] *prep* (*place*) in, an, auf; (*time*) in, während, (*into*) in . . . hinein *or* herein. **in the street** auf der Straße. **in the evening** abends. **in bad weather** bei schlechtem Wetter. **in three days' time** nach drei Tagen. **in that** insofern als. **be in** (*at home*) zu Hause sein.
inability [,inə'biləti] *n* Unfähigkeit *f*. **inability to pay** Zahlungsunfähigkeit *f*.
inaccessible [,inak'sesəbl] *adj* unzugänglich, unerreichbar. **inaccessibility** *n* Unzugänglichkeit *f*.
inaccurate [in'akjurit] *adj* ungenau; (*incorrect*) falsch. **inaccuracy** *n* Ungenauigkeit *f*, Fehler *m*.
inactive [in'aktiv] *adj* untätig. **inactivity** *n* Untätigkeit *f*.
inadequate [in'adikwit] *adj* ungenügend, mangelhaft. **inadequacy** *n* Unzulänglichkeit *f*, Mangelhaftigkeit *f*.
inadvertent [,inəd'vəːtənt] *adj* unabsichtlich, versehentlich.
inane [in'ein] *adj* leer, albern.
inanimate [in'animit] *adj* leblos.
inarticulate [,inaː'tikjulit] *adj* undeutlich. **be inarticulate** sich nicht gut ausdrücken können.

inasmuch [ˌinəzˈmʌtʃ] *conj* **inasmuch as** da.

inaudible [inˈɔːdəbl] *adj* unhörbar.

inaugurate [iˈnɔːgjuˌreit] *v* (feierlich) eröffnen. **inauguration** *n* (feierliche) Eröffnung *f*. **inaugural** *adj* Einführungs-.

inborn [inˈbɔːn] *adj* angeboren.

incapable [inˈkeipəbl] *adj* unfähig. **incapacity** *n* Unfähigkeit *f*.

incendiary [inˈsendiəri] *adj* Brand-. **incendiary bomb** Brandbombe *f*.

incense[1] [ˈinsens] *n* Weihrauch *m*.

incense[2] [inˈsens] *v* wütend machen.

incentive [inˈsentiv] *n* Ansporn *m*; (*bonus*) Leistungsanreiz *m*.

incessant [inˈsesənt] *adj* ständig, unaufhörlich.

incest [ˈinsest] *n* Blutschande *f*. **incestuous** *adj* blutschänderisch.

inch [intʃ] *n* Zoll *m*.

incident [ˈinsidənt] *n* Vorfall *m*, Ereignis *neut*.

incinerator [inˈsinəˌreitə] *n* Verbrennungsofen *m*. **incinerate** *v* verbrennen. **incineration** *n* Verbrennung *f*.

incite [inˈsait] *v* anregen. **incitement** *n* Anregung *f*, Aufreizung *f*.

incline [inˈklain] *v* neigen; (*slope*) abfallen. **inclination** *n* Neigung *f*. **inclined** *adj* geneigt.

include [inˈkluːd] *v* einschließen. **included** *adj* (*in price*) inbegriffen. **inclusive** *adj* einschließlich. **inclusive of** *also* **including** einschließlich. **inclusion** *n* Einbeziehung *f*.

incognito [ˌinkogˈniːtou] *adv* inkognito.

incoherent [ˌinkəˈhiərənt] *adj* inkonsequent; (*speech*) unklar.

income [ˈinkʌm] *n* Einkommen *neut*, Einkünfte *pl*. **income tax** Einkommensteuer *f*. **income tax return** Einkommensteuererklärung *f*.

incompatible [ˌinkəmˈpatəbl] *adj* unvereinbar. **incompatibility** *n* Unvereinbarkeit *f*.

incompetent [inˈkompitənt] *adj* unfähig. **incompetence** *n* Unfähigkeit *f*.

incomplete [ˌinkəmˈpliːt] *adj* unvollständig.

incomprehensible [inˌkompriˈhensəbl] *adj* unbegreiflich.

inconceivable [ˌinkənˈsiːvəbl] *adj* unfaßbar. **inconceivability** *n* Unfaßbarkeit *f*.

inconclusive [ˌinkənˈkluːsiv] *adj* ohne Beweiskraft.

incongruous [inˈkongruəs] *adj* unangemessen.

inconsiderate [ˌinkənˈsidərit] *adj* rücksichtslos, besinnungslos.

inconsistent [ˌinkənˈsistənt] *adj* inkonsequent; (*person*) unbeständig. **inconsistency** *n* Widerspruch *m*.

inconspicuous [ˌinkənˈspikjuəs] *adj* unauffällig.

incontinence [inˈkontinəns] *n* (*med*) Inkontinenz *f*.

inconvenient [ˌinkənˈviːniənt] *adj* ungelegen. **inconvenience** *n* Ungelegenheit *f*. *v* stören, lästig sein (+ *dat*).

incorporate [inˈkorpəˌreit] *v* (*combine*) vereinigen; (*comm*) inkorporieren; (*contain, include*) enthalten. **incorporation** *n* (*comm*) Gründung *f*.

incorrect [ˌinkəˈrekt] *adj* unrichtig; (*inexact*) ungenau.

increase [inˈkriːs] *v* zunehmen; (*in number*) sich vermehren; (*prices*) steigen. *n* Vermehrung *f*, Zunahme *f*; Steigerung *f*; (*wages*) Lohnerhöhung *f*. **increasingly** *adv* immer mehr.

incredible [inˈkredəbl] *adj* unglaublich. **incredibility** *n* Unglaublichkeit *f*. **incredibly** *adv* unglaublicherweise; (*coll*: *extremely*) unglaublich.

incredulous [inˈkredjuləs] *adj* skeptisch, ungläubig. **incredulity** *n* Skepsis *f*.

increment [ˈinkrəmənt] *n* Zunahme *f*.

incriminate [inˈkrimineit] *v* beschuldigen. **incrimination** *n* Beschuldigung *f*.

incubate [ˈinkjuˌbeit] *v* ausbrüten. **incubation** *n* Ausbrütung *f*. **incubator** *n* (*for babies*) Brutkasten *m*.

incur [inˈkəː] *v* sich zuziehen. **incur debts** Schulden machen. **incur losses** Verluste erleiden.

incurable [inˈkjuərəbl] *adj* unheilbar.

indebted [inˈdetid] *adj* verschuldet.

indecent [inˈdiːsnt] *adj* unanständig. **indecency** *n* Unanständigkeit *f*.

indeed [inˈdiːd] *adv* tatsächlich, wirklich.

indefinite [inˈdefinit] *adj* unbestimmt. **indefinitely** *adv* auf unbestimmte Zeit.

indelible [inˈdeləbl] *adj* unauslöschlich; (*ink*) wasserfest.

indemnify [inˈdemnifai] *v* entschädigen. **indemnity** *n* Entschädigung *f*.

indent [in'dent] v (type) einrücken. **indentation** n Einrückung f.

independence [indi'pendəns] n Unabhängigkeit f, Selbstständigkeit f. **independent** adj unabhängig, selbstständig; (pol) parteilos; n (pol) Unabhängige(r).

indescribable [indi'skraibəbl] adj unbeschreiblich.

indestructible [indi'strʌktəbl] adj unzerstörbar.

index [indeks] n (in book) Register neut; (file) Kartei f; (cost of living) Index m. **index finger** Zeigefinger m.

India ['indjə] n Indien neut. **Indian** adj indisch; (American) indianisch; n Inder(in); (American) Indianer(in). **India ink** chinesische Tusche f. **Indian summer** Nachsommer m.

indicate ['indikeit] v anzeigen; (hint) andeuten. **indication** n Anzeichen neut; (idea) Andeutung f; (information) Angabe; (med) Indikation f. **indicative** adj anzeigend. **indicator** n (sign) Zeichen neut; (mot) Richtungsanzeiger m, Blinker m

indict [in'dait] v anklagen (wegen). **indictment** n Anklageschrift f.

indifferent [in'difrənt] adj gleichgültig; (poor quality) mittelmäßig. **indifference** n Gleichgültigkeit f; Mittelmäßigkeit f.

indigenous [in'didʒinəs] adj einheimisch.

indigestion [indi'dʒestʃən] n Verdauungsstörung f. **indigestible** adj unverdaulich.

indignant [in'dignənt] adj empört. **indignation** n Empörung f.

indignity [in'dignəti] n Demütigung f.

indirect [indi'rekt] adj indirekt.

indiscreet [indi'skriːt] adj indiskret, taktlos. **indiscretion** n Vertrauensbruch m, Indiskretion f.

indiscriminate [indi'skriminit] adj rücksichtslos. **indiscriminately** adv ohne Unterschied.

indispensable [indi'spensəbl] adj unerläßlich, unentbehrlich. **indispensability** n Unerläßlichkeit f, Unentbehrlichkeit f.

indisposed [indi'spouzd] adj indisponiert, unpäßlich.

indisputable [indi'spjuːtəbl] adj unbestreitbar.

indistinct [indi'stiŋkt] adj unklar.

individual [indi'vidjuəl] n Individuum neut, Person f. adj einzeln, persönlich, individuell. **individualist** n Individualist(in). **individuality** n Individualität f, Eigenart f. **individually** adv einzeln.

indoctrinate [in'doktri,neit] v unterweisen. **indoctrination** n Unterweisung f.

indolent ['indələnt] adj lässig. **indolence** n Lässigkeit f.

indoor ['indɔː] adj Haus-, Zimmer-. **indoor swimming pool** Hallenbad neut. **indoors** adv im Haus; (go) ins Haus.

induce [in'djuːs] v (cause) verursachen; (persuade) überreden. **inducement** n Anreiz m.

indulge [in'dʌldʒ] v (a person) nachgeben (+ dat); (oneself) verwöhnen. **indulgence** n Nachsicht f; Verwöhnung f. **indulgent** adj nachsichtig.

industry ['indəstri] n Industrie f. **industrial** adj industriell. **industrialist** n Industrielle(r). **industrious** adj fleißig.

inebriated [i'niːbrieitid] adj betrunken.

inedible [in'edibl] adj nicht eßbar.

inefficient [ini'fiʃnt] adj unfähig; (thing) unwirksam. **inefficiency** n Leistungsunfähigkeit f.

inept [i'nept] adj albern. **ineptitude** n Albernheit f.

inequality [ini'kwoləti] n Ungleichheit f.

inert [i'nəːt] adj inaktiv; (person) schlaff. **inertia** n Trägheit f.

inevitable [in'evitəbl] adj unvermeidlich. **inevitability** n Unvermeidlichkeit f.

inexpensive [inik'spensiv] adj billig, preiswert.

inexperienced [inik'spiəriənst] adj unerfahren.

infallible [in'faləbl] adj unfehlbar. **infallibility** n Unfehlbarkeit f.

infamous ['infəməs] adj schändlich. **infamy** n Schande f.

infancy ['infənsi] n frühe Kindheit f. **be still in its infancy** noch in den Kinderschuhen stecken. **infant** (baby) Säugling m; (small child) Kleinkind neut. **infantile** adj kindisch.

infantry ['infəntri] n Infanterie f. **infantryman** n Infanterist m.

infatuated [in'fatjueitid] adj vernarrt (in). **infatuation** n Vernarrtheit f.

infect [in'fekt] v infizieren, anstecken. **infection** n Infizierung f, Ansteckung f. **infectious** adj ansteckend.

infer [in'fət] v folgern. **inference** n (conclusion) Schlußfolgerung f.

inferior [in'fiəriə] adj minderwertig. **inferiority** n Minderwertigkeit f. **inferiority complex** Minderwertigkeitskomplex m.

infernal [in'fətnl] adj höllisch, (coll) verdammt. **inferno** n Inferno neut.

infertile [in'fəttail] adj unfruchtbar. **infertility** n Unfruchtbarkeit f.

infest [in'fest] v heimsuchen, plagen. **infestation** n Plage f.

infidelity [infi'deliti] n Untreue f.

infiltrate [in'filtreit] v einsickern in; (pol) unterwandern. **infiltration** n Einsickern neut; Unterwanderung f. **infiltrator** n Unterwanderer m.

infinite ['infinit] adj unendlich. **infinity** n Unendlichkeit f. **infinitesimal** adj winzig. **infinitive** [in'finitiv] n (gramm) Infinitiv m, Nennform f.

infirm [in'fətm] adj schwach. **infirmary** n Krankenhaus neut. **infirmity** n Krankheit f.

inflame [in'fleim] v entzünden; (fig) erregen. **inflamed** (med) entzündet. **inflammable** adj brennbar. **inflammation** n Entzündung f. **inflammatory** adj (fig) aufrührerisch.

inflate [in'fleit] v aufblasen; (price) übermäßig steigern. **inflatable** adj aufblasbar. **inflated** adj aufgebläht; (fig) aufgeblasen; (price) überhöht. **inflation** n Aufgeblasenheit; (comm) Inflation f. **inflationary** adj inflationistisch.

inflection [in'flekʃən] n Biegung f; (of voice) Modulation f.

inflict [in'flikt] v (blow) versetzen; (pain) zufügen; (burden) aufbürden. **infliction** n Zufügung f; (burden) Last f.

influence ['influəns] n Einfluß m; (power) Macht f. v beeinflussen, Einfluß ausüben auf. **influential** adj einflußreich.

influenza [influ'enzə] n Grippe f.

influx ['inflʌks] n Zustrom m.

inform [in'fɔtm] v benachrichtigen, unterrichten. **inform against** anzeigen.

informal [in'fɔtml] adj informell. **informality** n Ungezwungenheit f.

information [infə'meiʃən] n Auskunft f, Information f, Nachricht f; (data) Angaben pl. **information bureau** Auskunftsbüro neut. **informative** adj lehrreich. **informed** adj informiert. **informer** n Angeber(in).

infra-red [infrə'red] adj infrarot.

infringe [in'frindʒ] v verstoßen gegen; (rights) verletzen. **infringement** n Verletzung f.

infuriate [in'fjuərieit] v wütend machen. **infuriated** adj wütend.

ingenious [in'dʒitnjəs] adj (person) erfinderisch; (device) raffiniert. **ingenuity** n Erfindungsgabe f.

ingot ['iŋgət] n Barren m.

ingrained [in'greind] adj tief eingewurzelt.

ingredient [in'gritdjənt] n Zutat f.

inhabit [in'habit] v bewohnen. **inhabitable** adj bewohnbar. **inhabitant** n Einwohner(in).

inhale [in'heil] v einatmen. **inhalation** n Einatmung f.

inherent [in'hiərənt] adj angeboren.

inherit [in'herit] v erben. **inheritance** n Erbe neut. **inherited** adj ererbt. **inheritor** n Erbe m, Erbin f.

inhibit [in'hibit] v hemmen; (prevent) hindern. **inhibition** n Hemmung f.

inhospitable [inhə'spitəbl] adj ungastlich.

inhuman [in'hjutmən] adj unmenschlich. **inhumanity** n Unmenschlichkeit f.

iniquitous [i'nikwətəs] adj (unjust) ungerecht; (sinful) frevelhaft. **iniquity** n Ungerechtigkeit f, (sin) Sünde f.

initial [i'niʃl] adj anfänglich, Anfangs-. n Anfangsbuchstabe m. **initials** pl n Monogramm neut. **initially** adv am Anfang.

initiate [i'niʃieit] v einführen (in); (start) beginnen. n Eingeweihte(r). **initiation** n Einweihung.

initiative [i'niʃiətiv] n Initiative f. **take the initiative** die Initiative ergreifen. **initiator** n Anstifter m.

inject [in'dʒekt] v einspritzen. **injection** n give/have an injection eine Spritze geben/bekommen.

injure ['indʒə] v verletzen. **injured party** Geschädigte(r). **injurious** adj schädlich. **injury** n Verletzung f, Wunde f.

injustice [in'dʒʌstis] n Unrecht neut, Ungerechtigkeit f.

ink [iŋk] n Tinte f, Tusche f. **inkblot** n Tintenklecks m. **inkwell** n Tintenfaß neut.

inkling ['iŋkliŋ] n Ahnung f.

inland ['inlənd] adj Binnen-. **Inland Revenue** Steuerbehörde f.

in-laws ['inlɔts] pl n angeheiratete Verwandte pl. **daughter-in-law** Schwiegertochter f. **father-in-law**

Schwiegervater *m.* **mother-in-law** Schwiegermutter *f.* **son-in-law** Schwiegersohn *m.*

*inlay ['inlei] *v* einlegen. *n* eingelegte Arbeit *f.*; *(dentistry)* Plombe *f.*

inlet ['inlet] *n* Meeresarm *m.*

inmate ['inmeit] *n* Insasse *m.*, Insassin *f.*

inn [in] *n* Gasthof *m.*, Wirtshaus *neut.* **innkeeper** *n* Gastwirt(in).

innate [,i'neit] *adj* angeboren. **innately** *adv* von Natur.

inner ['inə] *adj* inner, Innen-. **innermost** *adj* innerst.

innocent ['inəsnt] *adj* unschuldig, schuldlos. **innocence** *n* Unschuld *f.*, Schuldlosigkeit *f.*

innocuous [i'nokjuəs] *adj* harmlos, unschädlich.

innovation [inə'veifən] *n* Neuerung *f.* **innovator** *n* Neuerer *m.*

innuendo [,inju'endou] *n* Stichelei *f.*

innumerable [i'njuːmərəbl] *adj* zahllos, unzählig.

inoculate [i'nokjuleit] *v* (ein)impfen. **inoculation** *n* Impfung *f.*

inorganic [,inoɪ'ganik] *adj* unorganisch.

input ['input] *n* Eingabe *f.*, Input *m.*

inquest ['inkwest] *n* gerichtliche Untersuchung *f.*

inquire [in'kwaiə] *v* sich erkundigen (nach). **inquiry** *n* Anfrage *f.*; *(examination)* Untersuchung *f.*, Prüfung *f.* **inquiry office** Auskunftsbüro *neut.*

inquisition [,inkwi'zifən] *n* Untersuchung *f.*; *(rel)* Ketzergericht *neut.*

inquisitive [in'kwizitiv] *adj* neugierig.

insane [in'sein] *adj* geisteskrank; *(coll)* verrückt. **insanity** *n* Geisteskrankheit *f.*

insatiable [in'seifəbl] *adj* unersättlich. **insatiability** *n* Unersättlichkeit *f.*

inscribe [in'skraib] *v* (auf)schreiben. **inscription** *n* Beschriftung *f.*; *(in book)* Widmung *f.*

insect ['insekt] *n* Insekt *neut.* **insecticide** *n* Insektizid *neut.*

insecure [,insi'kjuə] *adj* unsicher. **insecurity** *n* Unsicherheit *f.*

inseminate [in'semineit] *v* befruchten. **insemination** *n* Befruchtung *f.*

insensible [in'sensəbl] *adj* gefühllos; *(unconscious)* bewußtlos.

insensitive [in'sensətiv] *adj* unempfindlich. **insensitivity** *n* Unempfindlichkeit *f.*

inseparable [in'sepərəbl] *adj* untrennbar.

insert [in'sɔːt; *n* 'insəːt] *v* einfügen, einsetzen. *n* Beilage *f.* **insertion** *n* Einsatz *m.*

inshore [,in'fɔɪ] *adj* Küsten-. *adv* zur Küste hin.

inside [,in'said] *adj* inner, Innen-. *adv (be)* drinnen; *(go)* nach innen. *prep* in, innerhalb; *(into)* in ... hinein. *n* Innenseite *f.*, Innere *neut.* **insides** *(intestines)* Eingeweide *pl.*

insidious [in'sidiəs] *adj* heimtückisch.

insight [insait] *n* Einblick *m.*; *(understanding)* Verständnis *neut.*

insignificant [,insig'nifikənt] *adj* unbedeutend, unwichtig. **insignificance** *n* Bedeutungslosigkeit *f.*

insincere [,insin'siə] *adj* unaufrichtig. **insincerity** *n* Unaufrichtigkeit *f.*

insinuate [in'sinjueit] *v* zu verstehen geben, andeuten. **insinuation** *n* Andeutung *f.*

insipid [in'sipid] *adj* fade.

insist [in'sist] *v* bestehen (auf). **insistence** *n* Bestehen *neut.* **insistent** *adj* beharrlich.

insolent ['insələnt] *adj* unverschämt, frech. **insolence** *n* Unverschämtheit *f.*, Frechheit *f.*

insoluble [in'soljubl] *adj* unauflöslich; *(problem)* unlösbar.

insolvent [in'solvənt] *adj* zahlungsunfähig.

insomnia [in'somniə] *n* Schlaflosigkeit *f.*

inspect [in'spekt] *v* untersuchen, besichtigen. **inspection** *n* Untersuchung *f.*, Besichtigung *f.* **inspector** *n* Inspektor *m.*

inspire [in'spaiə] *v* inspirieren, begeistern; *(give rise to)* anregen. **inspiration** *n* Inspiration *f.*, Anregung *f.* **inspiring** *adj* anregend.

instability [,instə'biləti] *n* Unbeständigkeit *f.*

install [in'stoɪl] *v* einsetzen, einrichten. **installation** *n* Einrichtung *f.*

instalment [in'stoɪlmənt] *n* Rate *f.* **instalment plan** Teilzahlungssystem *neut.*

instance ['instəns] *n (case)* Fall *f.*; *(example)* Beispiel *neut.* **for instance** zum Beispiel (z.B.).

instant ['instənt] *n* Augenblick *m.* *adj* sofortig. **instant coffee** Pulverkaffee *m.* **instantaneous** *adj* augenblicklich. **instantly** *adv* sofort.

instead [in'sted] *adv* statt dessen. **instead of** (an)statt (+ *gen*).

instep ['instep] n Rist m, Spann m.

instigate ['instigeit] v anstiften. **instigation** n Anstiftung f. **instigator** n Anstifter(in).

instil [in'stil] v (teach) beibringen (+ dat).

instinct ['instiŋkt] n (Natur)Trieb m, Instinkt m. **instinctive** adj instinktiv; (automatic) unwillkürlich.

institute ['institjuːt] n Institut neut. v einführen; (found) gründen. **institution** n Institut neut; (home) Anstalt f; (foundation) Stiftung f.

instruct [in'strʌkt] v unterweisen; (teach) unterrichten. **instruction** n Vorschrift f; (teaching) Unterrichtung f. **instructive** adj lehrreich. **instructor** n Lehrer(in). **instructions for use** Gebrauchsanweisung f.

instrument ['instrəmənt] n Instrument neut; (tool) Werkzeug neut; (means) Mittel neut. **instrumental** adj (helpful) förderlich. **be instrumental in** durchsetzen.

insubordinate [ˌinsə'boːdənət] adj widersetzlich. **insubordination** n Widersetzlichkeit f.

insufficient [ˌinsə'fiʃənt] adj unzureichend. **insufficiency** n Unzulänglichkeit f.

insular ['insjulə] adj insular. **insularity** n Beschränktheit f.

insulate ['insjuleit] v isolieren. **insulation** n Isolierung f. **insulating tape** Isolierband neut.

insulin ['insjulin] n Insulin neut.

insult [in'sʌlt; n 'insʌlt] v beleidigen, beschimpfen. n Beleidigung f. **insulting** adj beleidigend.

insure [in'ʃuə] v versichern. **insurance** n Versicherung f. **insurance broker** Versicherungsmakler m. **insurance policy** Versicherungspolice f. **insurance premium** Versicherungsprämie f.

insurmountable [ˌinsə'mauntəbl] adj unüberwindlich.

insurrection [ˌinsə'rekʃən] n Aufstand m.

intact [in'takt] adj unberührt.

intake ['inteik] n Aufnahme f, Einlaß m.

intangible [in'tandʒəbl] adj unfaßbar.

integral ['intigrəl] adj wesentlich. n (math) Integral-.

integrate ['intigreit] v integrieren; (people) eingliedern. **integration** n Integration f; Eingliederung f. **integrity** n Integrität f; (completeness) Vollständigkeit f.

intellect ['intilekt] n Intellekt m. **intellectual** adj intellektuell; n Intellektuelle(r).

intelligent [in'telidʒənt] adj intelligent. **intelligence** n Intelligenz f; (information) Information f; (secret service) Geheimdienst m.

intelligible [in'telidʒəbl] adj verständlich, klar.

intend [in'tend] v beabsichtigen, die Absicht haben.

intense [in'tens] adj stark, intensiv; (colour) tief; (person) ernsthaft. **intensely** adj (highly) äußerst. **intensify** v verstärken. **intensity** n Stärke f. **intensive** adj intensiv.

intent[1] [in'tent] n Absicht f, Vorsatz m. **to all intents and purposes** im Grunde.

intent[2] [in'tent] adj **intent on** versessen auf.

intention [in'tenʃən] n Absicht f; (plan) Vorhaben neut; (aim) Ziel neut; (meaning) Sinn m. **intentional** adj absichtlich.

inter [in'təː] v beerdigen. **interment** n Beerdigung f.

interact [ˌintər'akt] v aufeinander wirken. **interaction** n Wechselwirkung f.

intercede [ˌintə'siːd] v ... verwenden (bei). **intercession** n Fürsprache f.

intercept [ˌintə'sept] v abfangen. **interception** n Abfangen neut.

interchange [ˌintə'tʃeindʒ] n Austausch m; (roads) (Autobahn) Kreuz/Dreieck neut. v austauschen.

intercom [intə'kom] n Sprechanlage f.

intercourse ['intəkoːs] n Verkehr m, Umgang m. **sexual intercourse** Geschlechtsverkehr m.

interest ['intrist] n Interesse neut; (comm) Zinsen pl; (advantage) Vorteil m. **interested** adj interessiert; (biased) beteiligt.

interfere [ˌintə'fiə] v (person) sich einmischen; (adversely affect) stören. **interference** n Einmischung f; Störung f. **interfering** adj lästig, störend.

interim ['intərim] n Zwischenzeit f. adj vorläufig.

interior [in'tiəriə] n Innere neut. adj inner, Binnen-.

interjection [ˌintə'dʒekʃən] n Ausruf m; (gramm) Interjektion f.

interlock [ˌintə'lok] v ineinandergreifen. **interlocking** adj verzahnt.

interlude ['intəluːd] n (interval) Pause f.

intermediate [ˌintə'miːdiət] adj Zwischen-. **intermediary** n Vermittler m.

interminable [in'təːminəbl] adj endlos.

intermission [,intə'miʃən] n Pause f.
Unterbrechung f. **without intermission**
pausenlos.

intermittent [,intə'mitənt] adj stoßweise,
periodisch.

intern [in'tə:n] v internieren. n Assistentenarzt m. **internment** n Internierung
f.

internal [in'tə:nl] adj inner; (domestic)
Innen-, Inlands-; (within organization)
intern.

international [,intə'naʃənl] adj international.

interpose [,intə'pouz] v dazwischenstellen.
interposition n Zwischenstellung f.

interpret [in'tə:prit] v dolmetschen;
(explain) auslegen; (theatre, music) interpretieren. **interpreter** n Dolmetscher(in);
Interpret(in). **interpretation** n Dolmetschen neut; Auslegung f; Interpretation
f.

interrogate [in'terəgeit] v verhören. **interrogation** n Verhör neut. **interrogator** n
Fragesteller m.

interrogative [,intə'rogətiv] adj fragend;
(gramm) Frage-. n (gramm) Interrogativ
m.

interrupt [,intə'rʌpt] v unterbrechen.
interruption n Unterbrechung f.

intersect [,intə'sekt] v schneiden. **intersection** n Kreuzungspunkt m; (mot)
Kreuzung f.

intersperse [,intə'spə:s] v verstreuen.

interval ['intəvəl] n Zwischenraum m;
(break) Pause f; (timespan) Abstand m;
(music) Tonabstand m.

intervene [,intə'vi:n] v (interfere) eingreifen; (come between) dazwischentreten. **intervention** n Intervention f, Eingreifen neut.

interview ['intəvju:] n Interview neut. v
interviewen. **interviewee** n Interviewte(r).
interviewer n Interviewer m.

intestine [in'testin] n Darm m. **intestines**
pl Eingeweide pl. **intestinal** adj Darm-.

intimate[1] ['intimət] adj vertraut. **intimacy**
n Vertrautheit f.

intimate[2] ['intimeit] v andeuten. **intimation** n Andeutung f, Wink m.

intimidate [in'timideit] v einschüchtern.
intimidation n Einschüchterung f.

into ['intu] prep in (+acc) hinein/herein.
be into (coll) sich interessieren für. **get
into** (difficulties, etc.) geraten in. **look
into** (investigate) untersuchen.

intolerable [in'tolərəbl] adj unerträglich.
intolerant [in'tolərənt] adj intolerant.
intolerance n Intoleranz f.

intonation [,intə'neiʃən] n Intonation f.
intone v intonieren.

intoxicate [in'toksikeit] v berauschen.
intoxicated adj berauscht; (drunk)
betrunken. **intoxication** n Rausch m.

intransitive [in'transitiv] adj (gramm)
intransitiv.

intravenous [,intrə'vi:nəs] adj intravenös.

intrepid [in'trepid] adj unerschrocken.

intricate ['intriket] adj kompliziert. **intricacy** n Kompliziertheit f.

intrigue ['intri:g; v in'tri:g] n Intrige f. v
faszinieren; (plot) intrigieren. **intriguing**
adj faszinierend.

intrinsic [in'trinsik] adj wesentlich.

introduce [,intrə'dju:s] v einführen; (person) vorstellen. **introduction** n
Einführung f; (in book) Einleitung f,
Vorwort neut; Vorstellung f. **introductory**
adj einleitend. **letter of introduction**
Empfehlungsbrief m.

introspective [,intrə'spektiv] adj selbstprüfend. **introspection** n Selbstprüfung f.

introvert ['intrəvə:t] n introvertierter
Mensch m. **introverted** adj introvertiert.

intrude [in'tru:d] v hineindrängen; (interfere) sich einmischen. **intruder** n Eindringling m. **intrusion** n Eindrängen neut;
Einmischung f. **intrusive** adj zudringlich;
(nuisance) lästig.

intuition [,intjui'iʃən] n Intuition f. **intuitive** adj intuitiv.

inundate ['inʌndeit] v überschwemmen.
inundation n Überschwemmung f; Flut f.

invade [in'veid] v überfallen. **invader** n
Eindringling m. **invasion** n Einfall m,
Invasion f.

invalid[1] [in'vælid] n Kranke(r), Invalide m.

invalid[2] [in'vælid] adj ungültig. **invalidate** v
fürungültig erklären. **invalidation** n
Ungültigkeitserklärung f. **invalidity** n
Ungültigkeit f.

invaluable [in'væljuəbl] adj unschätzbar.

invariable [in'veəriəbl] adj konstant,
unveränderlich. **invariably** adv ausnahmslos.

invective [in'vektiv] n Beschimpfung f.

invent [in'vent] v erfinden. **invention** n
Erfindung f. **inventor** n Erfinder(in).

inventory ['invəntri] n Inventar neut,
Bestandsverzeichnis neut; (stocktaking)
Bestandsaufnahme f.

invert [in'vəɪt] v umkehren. **inversion** n Umkehrung f.

invertebrate [in'vəɪtibrət] adj wirbellos. n wirbelloses Tier neut.

invest [in'vest] v investieren, anlegen. **investment** n Investition f, Anlage f. **investor** n Kapitalanleger m.

investigate [in'vestigeit] v untersuchen. **investigation** n Untersuchung f. **investigator** n Prüfer(in).

invigorating [in'vigəreitiŋ] adj stärkend.

invincible [in'vinsəbl] adj unüberwindlich. **invincibility** n Unüberwindlichkeit f.

invisible [in'vizəbl] adj unsichtbar. **invisibility** n Unsichtbarkeit f.

invite [in'vait] v einladen. **invitation** n Einladung f. **inviting** adj verlockend.

invoice ['invois] n Rechnung f. v in Rechnung stellen.

invoke [in'vouk] v anrufen. **invocation** n Anrufung f.

involuntary [in'vɒləntəri] adj unwillkürlich; (unintentional) unabsichtlich.

involve [in'vɒlv] v (entail) mit sich bringen; (draw into) hineinziehen. **involved** adj verwickelt. **involvement** n Verwicklung f; Rolle f.

inward [in'wəd] adj inner. adv also **inwards** nach innen. **inwardly** adv im Innern.

iodine ['aiədiɪn] n Jod neut.

ion ['aiən] n Ion neut.

irate [ai'reit] adj wütend.

Ireland ['aiələnd] n Irland neut. **Irish** adj irisch. **Irishman/woman** n Irländer(in), Ire m, Irin f.

iris ['aiəris] n (eye) Iris f; (flower) Schwertlilie f.

irk [əɪk] v ärgern. **irksome** adj ärgerlich.

iron ['aiən] n Eisen neut; (ironing) Bügeleisen neut. adj eisern. v bügeln. **Iron Curtain** Eiserner Vorhang m. **ironing board** n Bügelbrett neut. **ironmonger** n Eisenwarenhändler m.

irony ['aiərəni] n Ironie f. **ironic** adj ironisch.

irrational [i'raʃənl] adj unlogisch; (unreasonable) unvernünftig. **irrationality** n Unvernunft f.

irredeemable [iri'diɪməbl] adj untilgbar; (beyond improvement) unverbesserlich.

irregular [i'regjulə] adj unregelmäßig. **irregularity** n Unregelmäßigkeit f.

irrelevant [i'reləvənt] adj belanglos. **irrelevance** n Belanglosigkeit f.

irreparable [i'repərəbl] adj nicht wiedergutzumachen.

irresistible [,iri'zistəbl] adj unwiderstehlich.

irrespective [,iri'spektiv] adj abgesehen (von), ohne Rücksicht (auf).

irresponsible [iri'sponsəbl] adj unverantwortlich, verantwortungslos. **irresponsibility** n Unverantwortlichkeit f, Verantwortungslosigkeit f.

irrevocable [i'revəkəbl] adj unwiderruflich.

irrigate ['irigeit] v bewässern. **irrigation** n Bewässerung f.

irritate ['iriteit] v reizen. **irritable** adj reizbar. **irritant** n Reizmittel neut. **irritation** n Reizung f.

Islam ['izlaɪm] n Islam m. **Islamic** adj islamisch.

island ['ailənd] n Insel f. **islander** n Inselbewohner(in).

isolate ['aisəleit] v isolieren. **isolated** adj abgesondert; (lonely) einsam. **isolated case** Einzelfall m. **isolation** n Isolierung f; Einsamkeit f. **isolationism** n Isolationismus m.

issue ['iʃuɪ] n Frage f; (newspaper) Ausgabe f; (offspring) Nachkommenschaft f. v ausgeben; (orders) erteilen.

isthmus ['isməs] n Landenge f.

it [it] pron (nom, acc) es; (dat) ihm.

italic [i'talik] adj kursiv. **italics** pl n Kursivschrift f sing. **in italics** kursiv gedruckt.

Italy ['itəli] n Italien neut. **Italian** adj italienisch. n Italiener(in).

item ['aitəm] n Gegenstand m; (on agenda) Punkt m; (in newspaper) Artikel m. **itemize** v verzeichnen.

itinerary [ai'tinərəri] n Reiseplan m.

its [its] poss adj sein, ihr. **itself** pron sich; selbst. **by itself** von selbst.

ivory ['aivəri] n Elfenbein neut.

ivy ['aivi] n Efeu m.

J

jab [dʒab] *n* Stoß *m*, Stich *m*; (*coll: injection*) Spritze *f*. *v* Stechen.

jack [dʒak] *n* (*mot*) (Wagen)Heber *m*; (*cards*) Bube *m*. **v jack up** aufbocken.

jackal ['dʒakoɪl] *n* Schakal *m*.

jackdaw ['dʒakdɔɪ] *n* Dohle *f*.

jacket ['dʒakit] *n* Jacke *f*; (*book*) (Schutz)Umschlag *m*.

jack-knife ['dʒaknaif] *n* Klappmesser *neut*.

jackpot ['dʒakpot] *n* Jackpot *m*.

jade [dʒeid] *n* Nephrit *m*, Jade *m*.

jaded ['dʒeidid] *adj* erschöpft, abgemattet.

jagged ['dʒagid] *adj* zackig.

jaguar ['dʒagjuə] *n* Jaguar *m*.

jail [dʒeil] *n* Gefängnis *neut*. *v* ins Gefängnis werfen, einsperren. **jailer** *n* (Gefängnis)Wärter *m*.

jam[1] [dʒam] *v* einklemmen, verstopfen. **jam on the brakes** heftig auf die Bremse treten. **jam-packed** *adj* vollgestopft. *n* Engpaß *m*, Klemme *f*. **traffic jam** (Verkehrs)Stockung *f*.

jam[2] [dʒam] *n* Marmelade *f*.

janitor ['dʒanitə] *n* Hauswart *m*, Pförtner *m*.

January ['dʒanjuəri] *n* Januar *m*.

Japan [dʒə'pan] *n* Japan *neut*. **Japanese** *adj* japanisch; *n* Japaner(in).

jar[1] [dʒaɪ] *n* Glass *neut*.

jar[2] [dʒaɪ] *v* kreischen. **jar on one's nerves** einem auf die Nerven gehen. **jarring** *adj* mißtönend.

jargon ['dʒaɪgən] *n* Jargon *m*, Kauderwelsch *neut*.

jasmine ['dʒazmin] *n* Jasmin *m*.

jaundice ['dʒɔɪndis] *n* Gelbsucht *f*. **jaundiced** *adj* gelbsüchtig; (*fig*) neidisch, voreingenommen.

jaunt [dʒɔɪnt] *n* Ausflug *m*. *v* einen Ausflug machen. **jaunty** *adj* lebhaft, flott.

javelin ['dʒavəlin] *n* Speer *m*.

jaw [dʒɔɪ] *n* Kiefer *m*, Kinnbacken *m*. **jawbone** *n* Kinnbacken *m*.

jazz [dʒaz] *n* Jazz *m*. **jazz band** Jazzkapelle *f*.

jealous ['dʒeləs] *adj* eifersüchtig. **jealousy** *n* Eifersucht *f*.

jeans [dʒiɪnz] *pl n* Jeans *pl*.

jeep [dʒiɪp] *n* Jeep *m*.

jeer [dʒiə] *v* spotten. **jeer at** verspotten. **jeering** *adj* höhnisch.

jelly ['dʒeli] *n* Gelee *neut*. **jellyfish** *n* Qualle *f*.

jeopardize ['dʒepədaiz] *v* gefährden. **jeopardy** *n* Gefahr *f*.

jerk [dʒəɪk] *v* stoßen, rücken. *n* Ruck *m*, Stoß *m*. **jerkily** *adv* stoßweise.

jersey ['dʒəɪzi] *n* Pullover *m*; (*fabric*) Jersey *m*.

Jerusalem [dʒə'ruɪsələm] *n* Jerusalem *neut*.

jest [dʒest] *n* Scherz *m*. *v* scherzen. **jesting** *adj* scherzhaft. **jestingly** *adv* in Spaß.

jet [dʒet] *n* (*liquid*) Strahl *m*; (*tech*) Düse *f*; (*aero*) Düsenflugzeug *neut*. **jet-black** *adj* rabenschwarz. **jet engine** Düsenmotor *m*. **jet-propelled** *adj* mit Düsenantrieb.

jettison ['dʒetisn] *v* abwerfen; (*discard*) wegwerfen.

jetty ['dʒeti] *n* Landungssteg *m*, Mole *f*.

Jew [dʒuɪ] *n* Jude *m*, Judin *f*. **Jewish** *adj* jüdisch.

jewel ['dʒuɪəl] *n* Edelstein *m*, Juwel *neut*; (*fig*) Perle *f*. **jeweller** *n* Juwelier *m*. **jewellery** *n* Schmuck *m*.

jig [dʒig] *n* Gigue *f*. *v* eine Gigue tanzen.

jigsaw ['dʒigsɔɪ] *n* Puzzlespiel *neut*, Geduldspiel *neut*.

jilt [dʒilt] *v* sitzenlassen.

jingle ['dʒingl] *n* (*sound*) Geklingel *neut*; (*radio, etc.*) Werbelied *neut*. *v* klingeln.

jinx [dʒinks] *n* Unheil *neut*. *v* verhexen.

job [dʒob] *n* Arbeit *f*; (*post*) Stelle *f*; (*task*) Aufgabe *f*. **jobless** *adj* arbeitslos.

jockey ['dʒoki] *n* Jockei *m*.

jocular ['dʒokjulə] *adj* scherzhaft.

jodhpurs ['dʒodpəz] *pl n* Reithose *f*.

jog [dʒog] *v* stoßen; (*run*) trotten. *n* Stoß *m*. **jog trot** *n* Trott *m*.

join [dʒoin] *v* verbinden, vereinigen; (*club, etc.*) beitreten (+ *dat*). (**come together**) zusammenkommen. *n* Verbindungsstelle *f*; (*seam*) Naht *f*. **join in** mitmachen. **joiner** *n* Tischler *m*. **joinery** *n* Tischlerarbeit *f*.

joint [dʒoint] *n* (*anat*) Gelenk *neut*; Verbindung *f*; (*cookery*) Braten *m*; (*slang: place*) Lokal *neut*. *adj* Gesamt-. **jointed** *adj* gegliedert. **jointly** *adv* gemeinsam.

joist [dʒoist] *n* Querbalken *m*, Träger *m*.

joke [dʒouk] *n* Witz *m*, Scherz *m*. *v* scherzen. **joker** *n* Spaßvogel *m*; (*cards*) Joker *m*. **jokingly** *adv* im Spaß.

jolly ['dʒoli] *adj* lustig. **jolliness** *n* Lustigkeit *f*.

keep

jolt [dʒoult] n Stoß m. v stoßen.

jostle ['dʒosl] v anstoßen. n Stoß m.

jot [dʒot] n Jota neut. v jot down notieren.

journal ['dʒɜːnl] n Zeitschrift f; (diary) Tagebuch neut. **journalism** n Zeitungswesen neut. **journalist** n Journalist(in).

journey ['dʒɜːni] n Reise f. v (ver)reisen.

jovial ['dʒouviəl] adj lustig, jovial. **joviality** n Lustigkeit f.

joy [dʒɔi] n Freude f, Wonne f. **joyful** adj erfreut. **joyfulness** n Fröhlichkeit f.

jubilant ['dʒuːbilənt] adj jubelnd, frohlockend. **jubilation** n Jubel m, Frohlocken neut.

jubilee ['dʒuːbiliː] n Jubiläum neut; (celebration) Jubelfest neut.

Judaism ['dʒuːdeiˌizəm] n Judentum neut.

judge [dʒʌdʒ] n (law) Richter; (expert) Kenner m. v beurteilen; (value) (ein)schätzen. **judgment** n Beurteilung f; (law) Urteil neut.

judicial [dʒuː'diʃəl] adj gerichtlich. **judiciary** n Gerichtswesen neut.

judicious [dʒuː'diʃəs] adj wohlüberlegt; (reasonable) vernünftig.

judo ['dʒuːdou] n Judo neut.

jug [dʒʌg] n Krug m, Kanne f.

juggernaut ['dʒʌgənɔːt] n Moloch m; (mot) Fernlastwagen m.

juggle ['dʒʌgl] v jonglieren. **juggler** n Jongleur m.

jugular ['dʒʌgjulə] n Drosselader f.

juice [dʒuːs] n Saft m. **juicy** adj saftig.

jukebox ['dʒuːkbɔks] n Jukebox f.

July [dʒuː'lai] n Juli m.

jumble ['dʒʌmbl] n Durcheinander neut. v durcheinander bringen. **jumble sale** Basar m, Ramschverkauf m.

jump [dʒʌmp] n Sprung m. v springen; (be startled) zusammenzucken. **jump at the chance** die Gelegenheit ergreifen. **jumpy** adj nervös.

jumper ['dʒʌmpə] n Pullover m.

junction ['dʒʌŋkʃən] n (road) Kreuzung f; (rail) Knotenpunkt m.

juncture ['dʒʌŋkʃə] n Augenblick m. **at this juncture** an dieser Stelle.

June [dʒuːn] n Juni m.

jungle ['dʒʌŋgl] n Dschungel m.

junior ['dʒuːnjə] adj junior, jünger. **junior school** Grundschule f.

juniper ['dʒuːnipə] n Wacholder m.

junk¹ [dʒʌŋk] n Trödel m. **junk shop** Trödelladen m.

junk² [dʒʌŋk] n (naut) Dschunke f.

junta ['dʒʌntə] n Junta f.

Jupiter ['dʒuːpitə] n Jupiter m.

jurisdiction [dʒuəris'dikʃən] n Gerichtsbarkeit f.

jury ['dʒuəri] n die Geschworene pl; (quiz, etc.) Jury f. **trial by jury** Schwurgerichtsverhandlung f. **juror** n Geschworene(r).

just [dʒʌst] adv (recently) gerade, eben; (only) nur; (exactly) genau. **just about** so ungefähr. **just as good** ebenso gut. **just a little** ein ganz klein wenig. adj gerecht, justly adv mit Recht, gerecht.

justice ['dʒʌstis] n Gerechtigkeit f; (judge) Richter m. **Justice of the Peace** Friedensrichter m.

justify ['dʒʌstifai] v rechtfertigen. **justification** n Rechtfertigung f. **justifiable** adj berechtigt.

jut [dʒʌt] v jut out hervorragen.

jute [dʒuːt] n Jute f.

juvenile ['dʒuːvənail] adj jugendlich. **juvenile court** Jugendgericht neut. **juvenile delinquent** jugendlicher Straftäter m. **juvenile delinquency** Jugendkriminalität f.

juxtapose [dʒʌkstə'pouz] v nebeneinanderstellen.

K

kaleidoscope [kə'laidəskoup] n Kaleidoskop neut.

kangaroo [kaŋgə'ruː] n Känguruh neut.

karate [kə'raːti] n Karate neut.

kebab [ki'bab] n Kebab m.

keel [kiːl] n Kiel m.

keen [kiːn] adj (sharp) scharf; (hearing) fein; (enthusiastic) eifrig. **keenness** n Eifer f.

*keep [kiːp] v halten, behalten; haben; (remain) bleiben; (preserve, store) aufbewahren; (of food) sich halten; (support) versorgen. **keep away** fernhalten. **keep fit** sich gesund erhalten. **keep in mind** im Gedächtnis behalten. **keep on** fortfahren. **keep out!** Eintritt verboten! **keep up with** Schritt halten mit. **keeper** n Wächter m; (animals) Züchter m. **be in keeping with** passen zu. **keepsake** n Andenken neut.

keg [keg] *n* Faß *neut.*

kennel ['kenl] *n* Hundehütte *f.*

kept [kept] *V* keep.

kerb [kəːb] *n* Straßenkante *f.*

kernel ['kəːnl] *n* Kern *m.*

kerosene ['kerəsiːn] *n* Petroleum *neut.*

ketchup ['ketʃəp] *n* Ketchup *m.*

kettle ['ketl] *n* Kessel *m.* **kettledrum** *n* Pauke *f.* **a pretty kettle of fish** eine schöne Bescherung. **a different kettle of fish** was ganz anderes.

key [kiː] *n* Schlüssel *m;* (*piano, typewriter*) Taste *f;* (*music*) Tonart *f.* **keyboard** *n* Tastatur *f.* **keyring** *n* Schlüsselring *m.*

khaki ['kaːki] *adj* khaki.

kick [kik] *v* mit dem Fuß treten *or* stoßen. *n* Fußtritt *m;* (*football*) Schuß *m;* (*fig*) Schwung *m.* **kick-off** *n* Anstoß *m.* **kick off** anstoßen.

kid¹ [kid] *n* (*goat*) Zicklein *neut;* (*leather*) Ziegenleder *neut;* (*child*) Kind *neut.*

kid² [kid] *v* (*coll*) auf den Arm nehmen.

kidnap ['kidnap] *v* entführen. **kidnapper** *n* Entführer *m*, Kidnapper *m.*

kidney ['kidni] *n* Niere *f.* **kidney bean** weiße Bohne *f.* **kidney stone** Nierenstein *m.*

kill [kil] *v* töten, umbringen; (*animals*) schlachten. **kill oneself laughing** sich totlachen. **killer** *n* Mörder *m.* **killing** *n* Tötung *f.* *adj* tötend.

kiln [kiln] *n* Brennofen *m.*

kilo ['kiːlou] *n* Kilo *neut.*

kilogram ['kiləgram] *n* Kilogramm *neut.*

kilometre ['kiləmiːtə] *n* Kilometer *m.*

kin [kin] *n* Verwandte *pl.* **next of kin** nächste(r) Verwandte(r).

kind¹ [kaind] *adj* freundlich, gütig. **kindly** *adj* gütig. **kindness** *n* Güte *f.*

kind² [kaind] *n* Sorte *f*, Art *f;* (*species*) Gattung *f.* **all kinds of** allerlei. **in kind** in Waren.

kindergarten ['kindəgaːtn] *n* Kindergarten *m*, Krippe *f.*

kindle ['kindl] *v* entzünden.

kindred ['kindrid] *n* Verwandtschaft *f.*

kinetic [kin'etik] *adj* kinetisch. **kinetics** *n* Kinetik *f.*

king [kiŋ] *n* König *m.* **kingdom** *n* Königreich *neut.* **animal kingdom** Tierreich *neut.*

kink [kiŋk] *n* Knick *m.* *v* knicken.

kiosk ['kiːosk] *n* Kiosk *m.* **telephone kiosk** Telephonzelle *f.*

kipper ['kipə] *n* Bückling *m*, Räucherhering *m.*

kiss [kis] *n* Kuß *m*, Küßchen *neut.* *v* küssen. **kiss goodbye** einen Abschiedskuß geben (+ *dat*).

kit [kit] *n* Ausrüstung *f;* (*mil*) Gepäck *neut.*

kitchen ['kitʃin] *n* Küche *f.* **kitchenette** *n* Kochnische *f.*

kite [kait] *n* Drachen *m;* (*bird*) Gabelweihe *f.*

kitten ['kitn] *n* Kätzchen *neut.*

kitty ['kiti] *n* Kasse *f.*

kleptomaniac [kleptə'meiniak] *n* Kleptomane *m.*

knack [nak] *n* Kniff *m*, Trick *m.* **get the knack of** den Dreh heraushaben (+ *gen*).

knapsack ['napsak] *n* Rucksack *m.*

knave [neiv] *n* Schurke *m;* (*cards*) Bube *m.*

knead [niːd] *v* kneten.

knee [niː] *n* Knie *neut.* **kneecap** *n* Kniescheibe *f.*

***kneel** [niːl] *v* knien.

knelt [nelt] *V* kneel.

knew [njuː] *V* know.

knickers ['nikəz] *pl n* Schlüpfer *m sing;* Höschen *neut sing.*

knife [naif] *n* Messer *neut.* *v* (er)stechen.

knight [nait] *n* Ritter *m;* (*chess*) Springer *m.* **knighthood** Rittertum *neut.* **knightly** *adj* ritterlich.

***knit** [nit] *v* stricken; (*brow*) runzeln. **knitted** *adj* Strick-. **knitting** *n* Strickzeug *neut.* **knitting needle** Stricknadel *f.* **knitwear** *n* Strickwaren *pl.*

knob [nob] *n* Knopf *m*, Griff *m.*

knobbly ['nobli] *adj* knorrig.

knock [nok] *v* (*strike*) schlagen; (*on door*) klopfen; (*criticize*) heruntermachen. *n* Schlag *m;* Klopfen *neut.* **knock off** (*coll: steal*) klauen; (*work*) Feierabend machen. **knock out** k.o. schlagen.

knot [not] *n* Knoten *m;* (*in wood*) Ast *m.* *v* knoten.

***know** [nou] *v* wissen; (*be acquainted with*) kennen; (*know how to*) können; (*understand*) verstehen. **know-all** Besserwisser *m.* **know-how** *n* Knowhow *neut.* **knowing** *adj* geschickt; (*sly*) schlau. **knowingly** *adv* absichtlich. **be in the know** Bescheid wissen. **known** *adj* bekannt.

knowledge ['nolidʒ] *n* Kenntnis *f.* **knowledgeable** *adj* kenntnisreich.

known [noun] V know.
knuckle ['nʌkl] n Fingerknöchel m.
knuckle down eifrig herangehen. **knuckle under** nachgeben.

L

label ['leibl] n Zettel m; (sticky) Klebezettel neut; (luggage) Anhängezettel neut. v mit einem Zettel versehen; (fig) bezeichnen.
laboratory [lə'borətəri] n Labor neut. **laboratory assistant** Laborant(in).
labour ['leibə] n Arbeit; (work-force) Arbeitskräfte pl; (birth) Wehen pl. v (schwer) arbeiten, sich anstrengen. **laboured** adj schwerfällig; (style) mühsam. **labourer** n (ungelernter) Arbeiter m.
laburnum [lə'bəinəm] n Goldregen m.
labyrinth ['labərinθ] n Labyrinth neut.
lace [leis] n Spitze f; (shoe) Schnur f. v schnüren. **lacy** adj Spitzen-.
lacerate ['lasəreit] v zerreißen. **laceration** n Zerreißung f.
lack [lak] v mangeln (an). n Mangel m. **be lacking** fehlen.
lackadaisical [‚lakə'deizikəl] adj schlapp.
lacquer ['lakə] n Lack m. v lackieren.
lad [lad] n Junge m, Bursche m.
ladder ['ladə] n Leiter f; (stocking) Laufmasche f. **ladder-resistant** adj maschenfest.
laden ['leidn] adj beladen.
ladle ['leidl] n Schöpflöffel m. v ausschöpfen.
lady ['leidi] n Dame f. **Ladies** n (sign) Damen pl. **ladies' man** Frauenheld m. **ladybird** Marienkäfer m. **lady-in-waiting** n Hofdame f. **ladylike** adj damenhaft.
lag[1] ['lag] v **lag behind** zurückbleiben. n Zeitabstand m.
lag[2] [lag] v (cover) verkleiden.
lager ['laɡə] n Lagerbier neut.
lagoon [lə'ɡuun] n Lagune f.
laid [leid] V lay[1].
lain [lein] V lie[1].
lair [leə] n Lager neut.
laity ['leiəti] n Laienstand m.
lake [leik] n (Binnen)See m.
lamb [lam] n Lamm neut; (meat) Lammfleisch neut.

lame [leim] adj lahm, hinkend; (excuse) schwach. v lahm machen. **lameness** n Lahmheit f; Schwäche f.
lament [lə'ment] v (weh)klagen; (regret) bedauern. n Klagelied neut. **lamentable** adj beklagenswert; bedauerlich. **lamentation** n Jammer m.
laminate ['lamineit] v schichten. **laminated** adj beschichtet.
lamp [lamp] n Lampe f; (street) Laterne f. **lamplight** n Lampenlicht neut. **lamppost** n Laternenpfahl m. **lampshade** n Lampenschirm m.
lance [lains] n Lanze f. v (med) mit einer Lanzette eröffnen, aufstechen. **lance corporal** n Hauptgefreite(r) m.
land [land] n Land neut. v an Land gehen; (aircraft) landen; (goods) abladen. **landing** n Landung f; (stairs) Treppenabsatz m. **landing craft** Landungsboot neut. **landing stage** Landesteg m.
landlady ['landleidi] n Wirtin f.
landlord ['landloid] n (Gast-)Wirt m.
landmark ['landmaik] n Wahrzeichen neut; (milestone) Markstein m.
landowner ['landounə] n Grundbesitzer m.
landscape ['landskeip] n Landschaft f. **landscape gardener** Kunstgärtner m. **landscape gardening** Kunstgärtnerei f. **landscape painter** Landschaftsmaler(in)
landslide ['landslaid] n Erdrutsch m. adj (pol) überwältigend.
lane [lein] n (country) (Feld)Weg m, Pfad m; (town) Gasse f; (mot) Spur f. (sport) Rennbahn f.
language ['langwidʒ] n Sprache f; (style) Stil m, Redeweise f. **bad language** Schimpfworte pl. **foreign language** Fremdsprache f.
languish ['langwiʃ] v schmachten.
lanky ['lanki] adj schlaksig.
lantern ['lantən] n Laterne f.
lap[1] [lap] n (anat) Schoß m; (circuit) Runde f.
lap[2] [lap] v (drink) auflecken.
lapel [lə'pel] n Revers m or neut.
lapse [laps] n Versehen neut; (mistake) Irrtum m; (time) Zeitspanne f. v (time) vergehen; (from faith) abfallen.
larceny ['laisəni] n Diebstahl m.
larch [laitʃ] n Lärche f.

lard [laɪd] n Schmalz neut. v spicken. **larding needle** Sticknadel f.

larder [ˈlaɪdə] n Speisekammer f.

large [laɪdʒ] adj groß; (considerable) beträchtlich. **at large** auf freiem Fuß m. **large as life** in Lebensgröße. **large-scale** adj Groß-. **largesse** n Freigiebigkeit f. **largely** adv weitgehend. **largeness** n Größe f.

lark[1] [laɪk] n (bird) Lerche f.

lark[2] [laɪk] n Spaß m. v **lark about** Possen treiben.

larva [ˈlaɪvə] n Larve f. **larval** adj Larven-.

larynx [ˈlarɪŋks] n Kehlkopf m. **laryngitis** n Kehlkopfentzündung f.

laser [ˈleɪzə] n Laser m. **laser beam** Laserstrahl m.

lash [laʃ] v (whip) peitschen; (tie) festbinden. n Peitschenschnur f; (eyelash) Wimper f. **lash out** ausschlagen.

lass [las] n Mädchen neut, Mädel m.

lassitude [ˈlasɪtjuːd] n Mattigkeit f.

lasso [laˈsuː] n Lasso m. v mit einem Lasso fangen.

last [laɪst] adj letzt. **at last** endlich, schließlich. **last but not least** nicht zuletzt. **last year** im vorigen Jahr. adv also **lastly** zuletzt. v (time) dauern; (supply) ausreichen; (be preserved) (gut) halten. **lasting** adj anhaltend, dauernd.

latch [latʃ] n Klinke f. v einklinken. **latch onto** (understand) spitzkriegen.

late [leɪt] adj spät; (tardy) verspätet; (deceased) selig; (former) ehemalig. **be late** Verspätung haben. **lately** adv neuerdings. **lateness** n Verspätung f. **later** adj später. **latest** adj spätest; (newest) neuest. **at the latest** spätestens.

latent [ˈleɪtənt] adj latent.

lateral [ˈlatərəl] adj seitlich. **laterally** adv seitwärts.

lathe [leɪð] n Drehbank f.

lather [ˈlaɪðə] n Seifenschaum m. v schäumen; (beat) verprügeln.

Latin [ˈlatɪn] adj lateinisch. n Latein neut. **Latin America** n Lateinamerika neut. **Latin-American** adj lateinamerikanisch.

latitude [ˈlatɪtjuːd] n Breite f; (fig) Spielraum m. **latitudinal** adj Breiten-.

latrine [ləˈtriːn] n Klosett neut, Latrine f.

latter [ˈlatə] adj letzt. **latterly** adv neuerdings.

lattice [ˈlatɪs] n Gitter neut; (pattern) Gitterwerk neut.

laugh [laɪf] v lachen. **laugh at** sich lustig machen über. **laugh off** mit einem Scherz abtun. **laughable** adj lächerlich. n Lachen neut. **laughter** n Gelächter neut.

launch [lɔːntʃ] n (boat) Barkasse f; (of boat) Stapellauf m; (of rocket) Abschuß m; (start) Start m. v (boat) vom Stapel lassen; (fig) in Gang setzen.

launder [ˈlɔːndə] v waschen. **launderette** n Waschsalon m. **laundry** n Wäscherei f; (washing) Wäsche f.

laurel [ˈlɔrəl] n Lorbeer m.

lava [ˈlaɪvə] n Lava f.

lavatory [ˈlavətəri] n Klosett neut, Toilette f.

lavender [ˈlavɪndə] n Lavendel m. adj (colour) lavendelfarben.

lavish [ˈlavɪʃ] adj verschwenderisch. **lavishness** n Verschwendung f.

law [lɔ] n (single law) Gesetz neut; (system) Recht neut; (study) Jura pl. **lawabiding** adj friedlich. **lawcourt** Gerichtshof m. **lawful** adj rechtmäßig, gesetzlich. **lawless** adj gesetzwidrig. **lawsuit** n Prozeß m. **lawyer** n Rechtsanwalt m.

lawn [lɔn] n Rasen m; (fabric) Batist m. **lawnmower** n Rasenmäher m. **lawn tennis** Tennis neut.

lax [laks] adj locker.

laxative [ˈlaksətiv] n Abführmittel neut.

lay[1] [leɪ] v legen; (put down) setzen, stellen; (table) decken. **lay down** hinlegen; (law) vorschreiben. **lay off** (dismiss) entlassen.

lay[2] [leɪ] adj Laien-. **layman** n Laie m.

lay-by [ˈleɪbaɪ] n Parkstreifen m.

layer [ˈleɪə] n Schicht f.

lazy [ˈleɪzi] adj faul. **laze** v faulenzen. **laziness** n Faulheit f. **lazybones** n Faulpelz m.

lead[1] [liːd] v leiten, führen. **leader** n Führer m, Leiter m; (in newspaper) Leitartikel m. **leadership** n Führerschaft f. **leading** adj führend, Haupt-. n (dog's) Leine f; (theatre) Hauptrolle f; (cable) Schnur f; (hint) Hinweis m.

lead[2] [led] n Blei neut; (in pencil) Bleistiftmine f.

leaf [liːf] n Blatt neut. **leaflet** n (pamphlet) Prospekt m. v **leaf through** durchblättern. **leafy** adj belaubt.

league [liːg] n (association) Bund neut; (sport) Liga f.

leak [liːk] n Leck neut; (pol) Durchsickern neut. v lecken; durchsickern. **leakage** n Lecken neut. **leaky** adj leck.

*lean[1] [liːn] v (sich) lehnen. **lean on** sich stützen auf; (*rely on*) sich verlassen auf. **leaning** n Neigung f.

lean[2] [liːn] adj mager.

leant [lent] V **lean**[1]

*leap [liːp] v hüpfen, springen. n Sprung m. **look before you leap** erst wägen, dann wagen. **by leaps and bounds** sprunghaft. **leap frog** Bockspringen neut. **leapyear** n Schaltjahr neut.

leapt [lept] V **leap**.

*learn [ləːn] v lernen; (*find out*) erfahren. **learned** adj gelehrt. **learner** n Anfänger m; (*driver*) Fahrschüler(in). **learning** n Wissen neut.

learnt [ləːnt] V **learn**.

lease [liːs] n Mietvertrag m, Pachtvertrag m. v (ver)mieten, pachten. **leaseholder** n Pächter(in).

leash [liːʃ] n Leine f.

least [liːst] adj (*smallest*) kleinst; (*slightest*) geringst. **at least** mindestens. **not in the least** nicht im geringsten.

leather ['leðə] n Leder neut. adj ledern. **leathery** adj lederartig.

*leave[1] [liːv] v verlassen, lassen; (*go away*) (ab-, ver)reisen, weggehen. **leave off** aufhören. **leave out** ·auslassen. **left-luggage office** Gepäckaufbewahrung f.

leave[2] [liːv] n (*permission*) Erlaubnis f; (*holiday*) Urlaub m. **take one's leave of** Abschied nehmen von.

lecherous ['letʃərəs] adj wollüstig. **lechery** n Wollust f.

lectern ['lektən] n Lesepult neut.

lecture ['lektʃə] n Vortrag m, Vorlesung f. v einen Vortrag halten. **lecturer** n Dozent m. **lecture hall** Hörsaal m.

led [led] V **lead**[1].

ledge [ledʒ] n Sims m or neut.

ledger ['ledʒə] n Hauptbuch neut.

lee [liː] n (*naut*) Leeseite f.

leech [liːtʃ] n Blutegel m.

leek [liːk] n Porree m.

leer [liə] n anzügliches Grinsen. v anzüglich grinsen.

leeway ['liːwei] n Abtrift f; (*fig*) Spielraum m.

left[1] [left] V **leave**[1].

left[2] [left] adj link. adv (nach) links. **on the left** links. **left-handed** adj linkshändig. **left-wing** adj Links-.

leg [leg] n Bein neut; (*cookery*) Keule f; (*sport*) Lauf m. **be on one's last legs** auf

dem letzten Loch pfeifen. **leggy** adj langbeinig.

legacy ['legəsi] n Legat neut.

legal ['liːgəl] adj gesetzlich, rechtlich. **legality** n Gesetzlichkeit f. **legalize** v legalisieren.

legend ['ledʒənd] n Sage f, Legende f. **legendary** adj sagenhaft, legendär.

legible ['ledʒəbl] adj leserlich. **legibility** n Leserlichkeit f.

legion ['liːdʒən] n Legion f. **legionary** n Legionär m.

legislate ['ledʒisleit] v Gesetze geben. **legislation** n Gesetzgebung f. **legislative** adj gesetzgebend. **legislator** n Gesetzgeber m.

legitimate [lə'dʒitimət] adj rechtmäßig; (*child*) ehelich; (*justified*) berechtigt. **legitimacy** n Rechtmäßigkeit; Ehelichkeit f.

leisure ['leʒə] n Freizeit f. **leisurely** adv ohne Hast.

lemon ['lemən] n Zitrone f. adj zitronengelb. **lemonade** n Zitronenlimonade f. **lemon squeezer** Zitronenpresse f.

*lend [lend] v (ver)leihen. **lend a hand** helfen. **lending library** Leihbibliothek f.

length [leŋθ] n Länge f; (*of cloth*) Stück neut; (*time*) Dauer f. **at length** (*in detail*) ausführlich; (*at last*) schließlich. **lengthen** v (sich) verlängern. **lengthways** adv längs. **lengthy** adj übermäßig lang.

lenient ['liːniənt] adj nachsichtig (gegenüber). **leniency** Nachsicht f.

lens [lenz] n Linse f; (*photographic*) Objektiv neut.

lent [lent] V **lend**.

Lent [lent] n Fastenzeit f.

lentil ['lentil] n Linse f.

Leo ['liːou] n Löwe m. **leonine** adj Löwen-.

leopard ['lepəd] n Leopard m.

leper ['lepə] n Leprakranke(r). **leprosy** n Lepra f.

lesbian ['lezbiən] adj lesbisch. n Lesbierin f.

less [les] adv weniger. adj geringer. prep minus. **lessen** v (sich) vermindern. **lesser** adj kleiner, geringer.

lesson ['lesn] n (*in school*) Stunde f; (*warning*) Warnung f. **lessons** pl Unterricht m sing.

lest [lest] conj damit ... nicht.

*let [let] v lassen; (rooms, etc.) vermieten. let's go gehen wir. let alone (not annoy) in Ruhe lassen; (much less) geschweige denn let down enttäuschen, im Stich lassen. let go gehen lassen. let go of loslassen. let up (coll) nachlassen.

lethal ['liːθəl] adj tödlich.

lethargy ['leθədʒi] n Lethargie f. **lethargic** adj lethargisch.

letter ['letə] n Brief m; (of alphabet) Buchstabe m. **letter box** Briefkasten m.

lettuce ['letis] n Kopfsalat m.

leukaemia [luːˈkiːmiə] n Leukämie f.

level ['levl] adj gerade, eben; (equal) gleich. **level crossing** Bahnübergang m. **level-headed** adj nüchtern. draw level with einholen. v ebnen; (make equal) gleichmachen. n Ebene f, Niveau neut.

lever ['liːvə] n Hebel m.

levy ['levi] n Abgabe f. v erheben.

lewd [luːd] adj lüstern. **lewdness** n Lüsternheit f.

liable ['laiəbl] adj (responsible) verantwortlich. **be liable to** neigen zu. **liability** n Verantwortlichkeit f. **limited liability** (comm) mit beschränkter Haftung. **be liable for** haften für. **liable to prosecution** strafbar.

liaison [liˈeizon] n Verbindung f; (love affair) (Liebes)Verhältnis neut.

liar ['laiə] n Lügner(in).

libel ['laibəl] n Verleumdung f. v (schriftlich) verleumden. **libellous** adj verleumderisch.

liberal ['libərəl] adj liberal; (generous) großzügig. n Liberale(r). **liberalize** v liberalisieren.

liberate ['libəreit] v befreien. **liberation** n Befreiung f. **liberator** n Befreier m.

liberty ['libəti] n Freiheit f. **at liberty** frei.

Libra ['liːbrə] n Waage f.

library ['laibrəri] n Bibliothek f, Bücherei f. **librarian** n Bibliothekar(in).

libretto [liˈbretou] n Libretto neut, Textbuch neut.

lice [lais] V louse.

licence ['laisəns] n Genehmigung f, Lizenz f. **driving licence** Führerschein m. **marriage licence** Eheerlaubnis f. **license** v genehmigen. **licensed** adj konzessioniert.

lichen [laikən] n Flechte f.

lick [lik] v lecken; (coll: defeat) besiegen; (flames) züngeln. n Lecken neut.

lid [lid] n Deckel m; (eyelid) Lid neut.

lie¹ [lai] n Lüge. v lügen.

*lie² [lai] v liegen. **lie down** sich hinlegen. **lie in** (coll) sich ausschlafen.

lieutenant [lefˈtenənt] n Leutnant m.

life [laif] n Leben neut. **lifebelt** n Rettungsgürtel m. **lifeboat** n Rettungsboot neut. **lifeguard** n Bademeister m. **life insurance** Lebensversicherung f. **life jacket** Schwimmweste f. **lifeless** adj leblos. **lifelike** adj naturgetreu. **lifesize** adj lebensgroß. **lifetime** n Lebenszeit f.

lift [lift] n Aufzug m, Fahrstuhl m. v (auf)heben. **give a lift to** (im Auto) mitnehmen.

*light¹ [lait] n Licht neut; (lamp) Lampe f. **a light** (for cigarette) Feuer neut. v anzünden.

light² [lait] adj leicht; (colour) hell.

lighten¹ ['laitn] v (reduce weight) erleichtern, leichter machen.

lighten² ['laitn] v (brighten) sich erhellen, heller werden.

lighter ['laitə] n (cigarette) Feuerzeug neut.

lighthouse ['laithaus] n Leuchtturm m.

lighting ['laitiŋ] n Beleuchtung f.

lightning ['laitniŋ] n Blitz m. **lightning conductor** Blitzableiter m. **flash of lightning** Blitzschlag m.

light ['laitweit]weight adj leicht. n Leichtgewichtler m.

light-year ['laitjiə] n Lichtjahr neut.

like¹ [laik] adj gleich (+dat), ähnlich (+dat). prep wie. **what's it like?** wie ist es? **like-minded** adj gleichgesinnt. **likewise** adv gleichfalls.

like² [laik] v gern haben; mögen. **do you like it?** gefällt es Ihnen? (food) schmeckt es (Ihnen)? **likeable** adj liebenswürdig. **liking** n Zuneigung f; (taste) Geschmack m.

likely ['laikli] adj wahrscheinlich. **likelihood** n Wahrscheinlichkeit f.

lilac ['lailək] n (colour) Lila neut. adj lilafarben.

lily ['lili] n Lilie f.

limb [lim] n Glied neut. **limbs** pl Gliedmaßen pl.

limbo ['limbou] n (rel) Vorhölle f. **in limbo** (fig) in der Schwebe, in Vergessenheit.

lime¹ [laim] n (mineral) Kalk neut.

lime² [laim] n (tree) Linde f, Lindenbaum m; (fruit) Limonelle f.

limit ['limit] n Grenze f, Schranke f. v begrenzen, beschränken. **limited** adj beschränkt; (comm) mit beschränkter Haftung.

limousine ['liməˌziːn] n Limousine f.

limp[1] [limp] v hinken. n Hinken neut.

limp[2] [limp] adj schlaff.

line [lain] n Linie f, Strich m; (row) Reihe f; (of print) Zeile f; (washing) Leine f; (wrinkle) Falte f. v linieren; (coat, etc.) füttern. **lineage** n Abstammung f. **linear** adj Linear-.

linen ['linin] n Leinen neut. **bed linen** Wäsche f.

liner ['lainə] n (ship) Linienschiff m, Überseedampfer m.

linesman ['lainzmən] n Linienrichter m.

linger ['liŋgə] v verweilen. **lingering** adj (illness) schleichend.

lingerie ['lāʒəriː] n (Damen)Unterwäsche f.

linguist ['liŋgwist] n Linguist(in). **linguistic** adj linguistisch. **linguistics** n Linguistik f.

lining ['lainiŋ] n Futter neut, Fütterung f.

link [liŋk] n (of chain) Glied neut; (connection) Verbindung f. v verbinden. **link arms** sich einhaken (bei).

linoleum [li'nouliəm] n Linoleum neut.

linseed ['linˌsiːd] n Leinsamen m. **linseed oil** Leinöl neut.

lint [lint] n Zupfleinen neut.

lion ['laiən] n Löwe m. **lioness** n Löwin f. **lion's share** Löwenanteil m.

lip [lip] n Lippe f; (edge) Rand m; (coll: impudence) Frechheit f. **lip service** Lippendienst m. **lipstick** n Lippenstift m.

liqueur [li'kjuə] n Likör m.

liquid ['likwid] n Flüssigkeit f. adj flüssig. **liquidate** v (comm) liquidieren. **liquidation** n Liquidierung f. **liquidator** n Liquidator m. **liquidity** n Flüssigkeit f.

liquor ['likə] n alkoholisches Getränk neut.

liquorice ['likəris] n Lakritze f.

lisp [lisp] v lispeln. n Lispeln neut.

list[1] [list] n Liste f, Verzeichnis neut. v verzeichnen.

list[2] [list] n (naut) Schlagseite f. v Schlagseite haben.

listen ['lisn] v hören auf, zuhören (+ dat).
listener n Zuhörer m. **listening device** Abhörgerät neut.

listless ['listlis] adj lustlos.

lit [lit] V light[1].

litany ['litəni] n Litanei f.

literacy ['litərəsi] n die Fähigkeit, lesen und schreiben zu können f. **literate** adj gelehrt. **be literate** lesen und schreiben können.

literal ['litərəl] adj buchstäblich.

literary ['litərəri] adj literarisch.

literature ['litrətʃə] n Literatur f.

lithe [laið] adj geschmeidig.

litigation [liti'geiʃən] n Prozeß m.

litre ['liːtə] n Liter neut.

litter ['litə] n (rubbish) Abfall m; (stretcher) Tragbahre f; (animals) Wurf m. **litter bin** Abfallkorb m.

little ['litl] adj klein. adv wenig. **a little** ein bißchen, ein wenig.

liturgy ['litədʒi] n Liturgie f.

live[1] [liv] v leben; (reside) wohnen.

live[2] [laiv] adj (alive) lebend; (radio, etc.) live; (electricity) stromführend. **live broadcast** Livesendung f.

livelihood ['laivlihud] n Lebensunterhalt m.

lively ['laivli] adj lebhaft. **liveliness** n Lebhaftigkeit f.

liver ['livə] n Leber f.

livestock ['laivstok] n Vieh neut.

livid ['livid] adj (coll: angry) wütend.

living ['liviŋ] adj lebendig, am Leben. n Lebensunterhalt m. **make a living** sein Brot verdienen. **living room** Wohnzimmer neut.

lizard ['lizəd] n Eidechse f.

load [loud] n Last f, Belastung f. v (be)laden.

loaf[1] [louf] n Laib m, Brot neut.

loaf[2] [louf] v **loaf around** faulenzen. **loafer** n Bummler m, Faulenzer m.

loan [loun] n Anleihe f; (credit) Darlehen neut. v leihen.

loathe [louð] v hassen, nicht ausstehen können. **loathing** n Abscheu m. **loathsome** adj abscheulich.

lob [lob] n (sport) lobben. n Lob m.

lobby ['lobi] n Vorhalle f; (pol) Interessengruppe f.

lobe [loub] n Lappen m.

lobster ['lobstə] n Hummer m.

local ['loukəl] adj örtlich, Orts-. n Ortsbewohner m. **local government** Gemeindeverwaltung f. **locality** n Ort m. **localize** v lokalisieren.

locate [lə'keit] v ausfindig machen. **location** n Standort m.

lock[1] [lok] n Schloß neut; (canal) Schleuse f. v verschließen. **lock in** einsperren. **lock out** aussperren. **lock up** verschließen.

lock[2] [lok] n (of hair) Locke f.

locker ['lokə] n Schließfach neut.

locket ['lokit] n Medaillon neut.

locomotive [,loukə'moutiv] n Lokomotive f.

locust ['loukəst] n Heuschrecke f.

lodge [lodʒ] v (a person) unterbringen; (complaint) einreichen. n (hunting) Jagdhütte f. **lodger** n Untermieter m. **lodgings** pl Wohnung f sing, Zimmer neut sing.

loft [loft] n (Dach)Boden m. **lofty** adj hoch.

log [log] n Klotz m; (naut) Log neut. v (naut) loggen, ins Logbuch eintragen.

logarithm ['logəriðəm] n Logarithmus m.

loggerheads ['logəhedz] pl n **be at loggerheads with** in den Haaren liegen mit.

logic ['lodʒik] n Logik f. **logical** adj logisch.

loins [loinz] pl n Lenden pl. **loincloth** n Lendentuch neut.

loiter ['loitə] v schlendern. **loiterer** n Schlenderer m.

lollipop ['loli,pop] n Lutscher m.

London ['lʌndən] n London neut.

lonely ['lounli] adj einsam. **loneliness** n Einsamkeit f.

long[1] [loŋ] adj lang.

long[2] [loŋ] v sich sehnen (nach).

long-distance adj Fern-.

longevity [lon'dʒevəti] n Langlebigkeit f.

longing ['loŋiŋ] n Sehnsucht f.

longitude ['londʒitjuːd] n Länge f. **longitudinal** adj Längen-.

long-playing record n Langspielplatte f.

long-term adj langfristig.

long-winded adj langatmig.

loo [luː] n (coll) Klo neut.

look [luk] n (glance) Blick m; (appearance) Aussehen neut; (expression) Miene f. v schauen, blicken, gucken (auf); (appear) aussehen. **look after** aufpassen auf; (care for) sorgen für. **look for** suchen. **look forward to** sich freuen auf. **look into** untersuchen. **look out!** paß auf!

loom[1] [luːm] v **loom up** aufragen.

loom[2] [luːm] n Webstuhl m, Webmaschine f.

loop [luːp] n Schleife f, Schlinge f. v eine Schleife machen.

loophole ['luːphoul] n Lücke f.

loose [luːs] adj schlaff, locker; (free) los.

loosen v lösen, lockern. **loose change** Kleingeld neut. **loose translation** freie Übersetzung f.

loot [luːt] n Beute f. v plündern. **looter** n Plünderer m. **looting** n Plünderung f.

lop [lop] v **lop off** abhacken.

lopsided [,lop'saidid] adj schief.

lord [loːd] n Herr m; (noble) Edelmann m. **House of Lords** Oberhaus neut.

lorry ['lori] n Lastkraftwagen (Lkw) m.

*****lose** [luːz] v verlieren; (clock) nachgehen. **lose one's way** sich verlieren. **loser** n Verlierer(in). **loss** n Verlust m; (decrease) Abnahme f. **dead loss** (coll) Niete f, Versager m.

lost [lost] V lose.

lot [lot] n Los neut; (fate) Schicksal neut; (land) Bauplatz m. **draw lots** Lose ziehen. **a lot of** viel, eine Menge.

lotion ['loufən] n Lotion f.

lottery ['lotəri] n Lotterie f.

lotus ['loutəs] n Lotos m.

loud [laud] adj laut; (colour) schreiend. **loudmouth** n Maulheld m. **loudness** n Lautstärke f. **loudspeaker** n Lautsprecher m.

lounge [laundʒ] n Wohnzimmer neut; (hotel) Foyer neut. v faulenzen.

louse [laus] n (pl lice) Laus f. **lousy** adj (slang) saumäßig.

love [lʌv] n Liebe f; (person) Liebling m; (sport) null. v lieben. **love doing something** etwas gern tun. **love affair** Liebesaffäre f. **loveless** adj lieblos. **love letter** Liebesbrief m. **loveliness** n Schönheit f. **lovely** adj lieblich, schön. **lover** n Liebhaber(in), Geliebte(r). **lovesick** adj liebeskrank. **loving** adj liebevoll.

low [lou] adj niedrig; (deep) tief; (sad) niedergeschlagen; (base) ordinär. **lowly** adj bescheiden. **low tide** Niedrigwasser neut.

lower ['louə] v senken, niederlassen; (fig) erniedrigen.

loyal ['loiəl] adj treu. **loyalty** n Treue f.

lozenge ['lozindʒ] n Pastille f.

lubricate ['luːbrikeit] v schmieren, ölen. **lubricant** n Schmiermittel neut. **lubrication** n Schmierung f.

lucid ['luːsid] adj deutlich, klar.

luck [lʌk] n (happiness, fortune) Glück neut; (fate) Schicksal neut; (chance) Zufall m. **luckily** adv glücklicherweise. **lucky** adj glücklich.

lucrative ['luːkrətiv] *adj* gewinnbringend.

ludicrous ['luːdikrəs] *adj* lächerlich.

lug [lʌg] *v (carry, drag)* schleppen.

luggage ['lʌgidʒ] *n* Gepäck *neut*. **luggage rack** Gepäcknetz *neut*.

lukewarm ['luːkwɔːm] *adj* lauwarm.

lull [lʌl] *n (pause)* Pause *f*; *(calm)* Stille *f*.

lullaby ['lʌləbai] *n* Wiegenlied *neut*.

lumbago [lʌm'beigou] *n* Hexenschuß *m*, Lumbago *f*.

lumber[1] ['lʌmbə] *n (timber)* Bauholz *neut*; *(junk)* Plunder *m*. **lumber room** Rumpelkammer *f*.

lumber[2] ['lʌmbə] *v* schwerfällig gehen.

luminous ['luːminəs] *adj* leuchtend.

lump [lʌmp] *n* Klumpen *m*, Beule *f*. **lump sugar** Würfelzucker *m*. **lump sum** Pauschalsumme *f*. *v* **lump together** zusammenfassen. **lumpy** *adj* klumpig.

lunar ['luːnə] *adj* Mond-.

lunatic ['luːnətik] *n* Wahnsinnige(r). **lunacy** *n* Wahnsinn *m*.

lunch [lʌntʃ] *n* Mittagessen *neut*. *v* zu Mittag essen. **lunchtime** Mittagspause *f*.

lung [lʌŋ] *n* Lunge *f*. **lung cancer** Lungenkrebs *m*.

lunge [lʌndʒ] *v* losstürzen (auf).

lurch[1] [ləːtʃ] *v* taumeln.

lurch[2] [ləːtʃ] *v* **leave in the lurch** im Stich lassen.

lure [luə] *v* (an)locken. *n* Köder *m*.

lurid ['luərid] *adj* grell.

lurk [ləːk] *v* lauern.

luscious ['lʌʃəs] *adj* köstlich, lecker.

lush [lʌʃ] *adj* saftig.

lust [lʌst] *n* Wollust *f*, Begierde *f*. *v* **lust after** begehren. **lustful** *adj* lüstern.

lustre ['lʌstə] *n* Glanz *m*. **lustrous** *adj* strahlend.

lute [luːt] *n* Laute *f*.

Luxembourg ['lʌksəmbəːg] *n* Luxemburg *neut*.

luxury ['lʌkʃəri] *n* Luxus *m*; *(article)* Luxusartikel *m*. **luxuriant** *adj* üppig. **luxurious** *adj* luxuriös.

lynch [lintʃ] *v* lynchen.

lynx [links] *n* Luchs *m*.

lyrical ['lirikəl] *adj* lyrisch.

lyrics ['liriks] *pl n* Lyrik *f sing*, Text *m sing*.

M

mac [mak] *n* Regenmantel *m*.

macabre [mə'kɑːbr] *adj* grausig.

macaroni [makə'rouni] *n* Makkaroni *pl*.

mace[1] [meis] *n* Amtsstab *m*.

mace[2] [meis] *n (cookery)* Muskatblüte *f*.

machine [mə'ʃiːn] *n* Maschine *f*. *v* maschinell herstellen. **machine gun** Maschinengewehr *neut*. **machinery** *n* Maschinerie *f*. **machine tool** Werkzeugmaschine *f*. **machinist** *n* Maschinenarbeiter(in).

mackerel ['makrəl] *n* Makrele *f*.

mackintosh ['makintoʃ] *n* Regenmantel *m*.

mad [mad] *adj* wahnsinnig, verrückt; *(angry)* wütend. **madhouse** *n* Irrenhaus *neut*. **madly** *adv* wie verrückt. **madman** *n* Verrückte(r) *m*. **madness** *n* Wahnsinn *m*.

madam ['madəm] *n* gnädige Frau *f*.

made [meid] *V* **make**.

magazine [magə'ziːn] *n (publication)* Zeitschrift *f*, Illustrierte *f*; *(also warehouse, rifle)* Magazin *neut*.

maggot ['magət] *n* Made *f*. **maggoty** *adj* madig.

magic ['madʒik] *n* Zauberei *f*. *adj also* **magical** Zauber-, zauberhaft. **magician** *n* Zauberer *m*; *(entertainer)* Zauberkünstler *m*.

magistrate ['madʒistreit] *n* Friedensrichter *m*.

magnanimous [mag'naniməs] *adj* großmütig. **magnanimity** *n* Großmut *f*.

magnate ['magneit] *n* Magnat *m*.

magnet ['magnət] *n* Magnet *m*. **magnetic** *adj* magnetisch. **magnetism** *n* Magnetismus *m*; *(fig)* Anziehungskraft *f*. **magnetize** *v* magnetisieren.

magnificent [mag'nifisnt] *adj* prächtig. **magnificence** *n* Pracht *f*.

magnify ['magnifai] *v* vergrößern. **magnifying glass** Lupe *f*. **magnification** *n* Vergrößerung *f*.

magnitude ['magnitjuːd] *n* Größe *f*, Ausmaß *neut*.

magnolia [mag'noulia] *n* Magnolie *f*.

magpie ['magpai] *n* Elster *f*.

mahogany [mə'hogəni] *n (wood)* Mahagoni *neut*. *adj* Mahagoni-.

maid [meid] *n* Mädchen *neut*; *(servant)*

Dienstmädchen *neut.* **old maid** alte Jungfer *f.*

maiden ['meidən] *n* Mädchen *neut.* **maiden name** Mädchenname *m.* **maiden speech** Jungfernrede *f.*

mail [meil] *n* Post *f. v* schicken, absenden. **mailbox** Briefkasten *m.* **mail-order company** Versandhaus *neut.* **mailboat** *n* Paketboot *neut.*

maim [meim] *v* lähmen.

main [mein] *adj* Haupt-, hauptsächlich. **mains** *pl n* (*gas, water*) Hauptleitung *f;* (*elec*) Netz *neut sing.* **mainstay** *n* (*fig*) Hauptstütze *f.* **main street** Hauptstraße *f.*

maintain [mein'tein] *v* erhalten; behaupten. **maintenance** *n* Erhaltung *f;* (*tech, mot*) Wartung *f.*

maisonette [meizə'net] *n* Wohnung *f.*

maize [meiz] *n* Mais *m.*

majesty ['madʒəsti] *n* Majestät *f.* **His/Her/Your Majesty** Seine/Ihre/Eure Majestät. **majestic** *adj* majestätisch.

major ['meidʒə] *n* (*mil*) Major *m;* (*music*) Dur *neut. adj* (*significant*) bedeutend; (*greater*) größer. **majority** *n* Mehrheit *f;* (*law*) Mündigkeit *f.*

***make** [meik] *v* machen; (*produce*) herstellen; (*force*) zwingen; (*build*) bauen; (*reach*) erreichen. *n* (*brand*) Marke *f;* (*type*) Art *f.* **make good** (*succeed*) Erfolg haben. **make out** vergeben. **makeshift** *adj* Behelfs-. **make-up** *n* Schminke *f.*

maladjusted [malə'dʒʌstid] *adj* verhaltensgestört.

malaria [mə'leəriə] *n* Malaria *f.*

male [meil] *n* Mann *m;* (*animals*) Männchen *neut. adj* männlich. **male nurse** Krankenpfleger *m.*

malevolent [mə'levələnt] *adj* mißgünstig. **malevolence** *n* Mißgunst *f.*

malfunction [mal'fʌŋkʃən] *n* Funktionsstörung *f.*

malice ['malis] *n* Böswilligkeit. **malicious** *adj* böswillig.

malignant [mə'lignənt] *adj* böswillig; (*med*) bösartig.

malinger [mə'liŋgə] *v* sich krank stellen, simulieren.

mallet ['malit] *n* Schlegel *m.*

malnutrition [malnju'triʃən] *n* Unterernährung *f.*

malt [moilt] *n* Malz *neut.*

Malta ['moiltə] *n* Malta *neut.* **Maltese** *n* Malteser(in) *adj* maltesisch.

maltreat [mal'triit] *v* mißhandeln, schlecht behandeln. **maltreatment** *n* schlechte Behandlung *f.*

mammal ['maml] *n* Säugetier *neut.*

mammoth ['maməθ] *n* Mammut *neut. adj* riesig.

man [man] *n* (*pl* **men**) Mann *m;* (*human*) Mensch *m. v* bemannen. **manliness** *n* Mannhaftigkeit *f.* **manly** *adj* mannhaft. **manslaughter** *n* Totschlag *m.*

manage ['manidʒ] *v* (*control*) leiten, führen; (*cope*) zurechtkommen, auskommen. **management** *n* Geschäftsleitung *f,* Direktion *f.* **manager** *n* Leiter *m,* Manager *m.*

mandarin ['mandərin] *n* Mandarin *m;* (*fruit*) Mandarine *f.*

mandate ['mandeit] *n* Mandat *neut.* **mandatory** *adj* verbindlich.

mandolin ['mandəlin] *n* Mandoline *f.*

mane [mein] *n* Mähne *f.*

maneuver [mə'nuːvə] *n* (*US*) Manöver *neut. v* manövrieren.

mange [meindʒ] *n* Räude *f.*

mangle[1] ['maŋgl] *n* (Wäsche)Mangel *f. v* mangeln.

mangle[2] ['maŋgl] *v* (*disfigure*) verstümmeln.

manhandle [man'handl] *v* grob behandeln, mißhandeln.

mania ['meiniə] *n* Manie *f.* **maniac** *n* Wahnsinnige(r). **manic** *adj* manisch.

manicure ['manikjuə] *n* Maniküre *f. v* maniküren. **manicurist** *n* Maniküre *f.*

manifest ['manifest] *adj* offenbar. *v* erscheinen. **manifestation** *n* Offenbarung *f;* (*symptom*) Anzeichen *neut.*

manifesto [mani'festou] *n* Manifest *neut.*

manifold ['manifould] *adj* mannigfaltig.

manipulate [mə'nipjuleit] *v* manipulieren. **manipulation** *n* Manipulation *f.*

mankind [man'kaind] *n* Menschheit *f.*

man-made [,man'meid] *adj* künstlich.

manner ['manə] *n* (*way*) Art *f,* Weise *f;* (*behaviour*) Manier *f,* Benehmen *neut.* **mannered** *adj* manieriert. **mannerism** *n* Manierismus *m.*

manoeuvre [mə'nuːvə] *n* Manöver *neut. v* manövrieren.

manor ['manə] *n* Herrensitz *m,* Herrenhaus *neut.*

manpower ['man,pauə] *n* Arbeitskräfte *pl.*

mansion ['manʃən] *n* (herrschaftliches) Wohnhaus *neut.*

mantelpiece ['mantlpiːs] n Kaminsims m or neut.

manual ['manjʊəl] adj manuell, Hand-. n Handbuch neut.

manufacture [manjuˈfaktʃə] v herstellen, erzeugen. n Herstellung f, Erzeugung f. **manufacturer** n Hersteller m, Fabrikant m.

manure [məˈnjuə] n Dünger m, Mist m. v düngen.

manuscript ['manjuskript] n Manuskript neut. adj handschriftlich.

many ['meni] adj viele. **how many?** wieviele? **many times** oft. **a good many** ziemlich viele.

map [map] n (Land)Karte f; (of town) Stadtplan m. v eine karte machen von.

maple ['meipl] n Ahorn m.

mar [maː] v verderben, beeinträchtigen.

marathon ['marəθən] n Marathonlauf m. adj Marathon-.

marble ['maːbl] n Marmor m; (toy) Marmel f.

march [maːtʃ] n Marsch m. v marschieren. **march past** vorbeimarschieren an. **March** [maːtʃ] n März m.

marchioness [maːʃəˈnes] n Marquise f.

mare [meə] n Stute f.

margarine [maːdʒəˈriːn] n Margarine f.

margin ['maːdʒin] n Rand m; (limit) Grenze f; (profit) Gewinnspanne f. **marginal** adj Rand-; (slight) geringfügig.

marguerite [maːgəˈriːt] n Gänseblümchen neut.

marigold ['marigould] n Ringelblume f.

marijuana [mariˈwaːnə] n Marihuana neut.

marina [məˈriːnə] n Yachthafen m.

marinade [mariˈneid] v marinieren. n Marinade f.

marine [məˈriːn] adj See-, Meeres-. n (shipping) Marine f; (mil) Marineinfanterist m. **mariner** n Matrose m.

marital ['maritl] adj ehelich.

maritime ['maritaim] adj See-, Schiffahrts-.

marjoram ['maːdʒərəm] n Majoran m.

mark[1] [maːk] n (currency) Mark f. Zeichen neut; (school) Note f; (stain) Fleck m; (distinguishing feature) Kennzeichen neut. v bezeichnen; (note) notieren, vermerken. **marked** adj markant, ausgeprägt. **markedly** adv ausgesprochen.

mark[2] [maːk] n (currency) Mark f.

market ['maːkit] n Markt m. v auf den Markt bringen. **marketing** n Marketing neut. **market place** Marktplatz m. **market research** Marktforschung f.

marmalade ['maːməleid] n Orangenmarmelade f.

maroon[1] [məˈruːn] adj (colour) rotbraun.

maroon[2] [məˈruːn] v (naut) aussetzen.

marquee [maːˈkiː] n großes Zelt neut.

marquess ['maːkwis] n Marquis m.

marriage ['maridʒ] n Heirat f, Ehe f; (wedding) Hochzeit f; (ceremony) Trauung f. **marriage certificate** Trauschein m.

marrow ['marou] n (of bone) Mark neut; (vegetable) Eierkürbis m. **marrowbone** n Markknochen m.

marry ['mari] v heiraten; (get married) sich verheiraten mit. **married couple** Ehepaar neut.

Mars [maːz] n Mars m. **Martian** adj Mars-; n Marsbewohner m.

marsh [maːʃ] n Sumpf m. **marshy** adj sumpfig.

marshal ['maːʃəl] n Marschall m. v einordnen; (troops) aufstellen.

martial ['maːʃəl] adj militärisch, Kriegs-.

martin ['maːtin] n Mauerschwalbe f.

martyr ['maːtə] n Märtyrer(in). **martyrdom** n Martyrium neut.

marvel ['maːvəl] n Wunder neut. v staunen (über). **marvellous** adj wunderbar.

marzipan [maːziˈpan] n Marzipan neut.

mascara [maˈskaːrə] n Wimperntusche f.

mascot ['maskət] n Maskottchen neut.

masculine ['maskjulin] adj männlich; (manly) mannhaft; (of woman) männisch. n (gramm) Maskulinum m. **masculinity** n Männlichkeit f, Mannhaftigkeit f.

mash [maʃ] v zerquetschen. **mashed potatoes** Kartoffelpüree neut.

mask [maːsk] n Maske f. v maskieren.

masochist ['masəkist] n Masochist m. **masochism** n Masochismus m.

mason ['meisn] n Maurer m. **masonic** adj Freimaurer-. **masonry** n Mauerwerk neut.

masquerade [maskəˈreid] n Maskerade f. v sich ausgeben (als).

mass[1] [mas] n Masse f. v sich ansammeln. adj Massen-. **the masses** die breite Masse. **mass meeting** Massenversammlung f. **mass-produce** v serienmäßig herstellen. **mass production** Massenherstellung f.

mass² [mas] n (rel) Messe f.

massacre ['masəkə] n Massaker neut, Blutbad neut. v massakrieren.

massage ['masaʒ] n Massage f. v massieren. **masseur** n Masseur m. **masseuse** n Masseuse f.

massive ['masiv] adj massiv.

mast [maist] n Mast m.

mastectomy [ma'stektəmi] n Brustamputation f.

master ['maistə] n Herr m; (school) Lehrer m; (artist) Meister m. v meistern. **masterful** adj meisterhaft. **masterpiece** n Meisterwerk neut. **mastery** n Beherrschung f.

masturbate ['mastəbeit] v onanieren. **masturbation** n Onanie f.

mat [mat] n Matte f; (beer) Untersetzer m. **matted** adj mattiert.

match¹ [matʃ] n Streichholz neut.

match² [matʃ] n (equal) Gleiche(r); (sport) Spiel neut. v anpassen. **meet one's match** seinen Meister finden. **matchless** adj unvergleichlich.

mate [meit] n (friend) Kamarad(in); (chess) (Schach)Matt neut; (animal) Männchen neut, Weibchen neut; (naut) Schiffsoffizier m. v sich paaren; (chess) matt setzen.

material [mə'tiəriəl] n Stoff m. adj materiell; (important) wesentlich. **materials pl** Werkstoffe pl. **materialist** n Materialist m. **materialistic** adj materialistisch.

maternal [mə'təinl] adj mütterlich; mütterlicherseits. **maternal grandfather** Großvater. **maternity** n Mutterschaft f. **maternity dress** Umstandskleid neut. **maternity home** Entbindungsheim neut.

mathematics [maθə'matiks] n Mathmatik f. **mathematical** adj mathematisch. **mathematician** n Mathematiker m.

matinee ['matinei] n Matinee f.

matins ['matinz] n Frühgottesdienst m.

matrimony ['matriməni] n Ehestand m, Ehe f. **matrimonial** adj ehelich, Ehe-.

matrix ['meitriks] n Matrix f.

matron ['meitrən] n (school) Hausmutter f; (nurse) Oberin f.

matter ['matə] n Stoff m, Materie f; (affair) Sache f; (pus) Eiter m. v von Bedeutung sein. **what's the matter?** was ist los? **it doesn't matter** es macht nichts. **matter-of-fact** adj sachlich.

mattress ['matris] n Matratze f.

mature [mə'tjuə] adj reif. v reifen. **maturity** n Reife f.

maudlin ['moidlin] adj weinerlich.

maul [moil] v zerreißen.

mausoleum [moisə'liəm] n Mausoleum neut, Grabmal neut.

mauve [mouv] adj malvenfarben.

maxim ['maksim] n Grundsatz m.

maximum ['maksiməm] n Maximum neut. adj Höchst-, Maximal-.

***may** [mei] v mögen, können. **may I?** darf ich? **maybe** adv vielleicht.

May [mei] n Mai m. **mayday** (SOS) Maydaysignal neut.

mayonnaise [,meiə'neiz] n Mayonnaise f.

mayor [meə] n Bürgermeister m. **mayoress** n Bürgermeisterin f.

maze [meiz] n Labyrinth neut, Irrgarten m.

me [mii] pron (acc) mich; (dat) mir.

meadow ['medou] n Wiese f.

meagre ['miigə] adj mager, dürr.

meal¹ [miil] n Mahlzeit f, Essen neut.

meal² [miil] n (flour) Mehl neut.

***mean¹** [miin] v (word, etc.) bedeuten; (person) meinen; (intend) vorhaben, beabsichtigen.

mean² [miin] adj (slight) gering; (base) gemein; (tight-fisted) geizig. **meanness** n Gemeinheit f.

mean³ [miin] n Durchschnitt m. adj mittler, Durchschnitts-.

meander [mi'andə] v sich winden. n Windung f.

meaning ['miinin] n (significance) Bedeutung f; (sense) Sinn m. **meaningful** adj bedeutsam. **meaningless** adj sinnlos.

means [miinz] n Mittel neut. **by means of** durch, mittels. **by no means** auf keinen Fall. **by all means** selbstverständlich.

meant [ment] V **mean¹**.

meanwhile ['miinwail] adv mittlerweile.

measles ['miizlz] n Masern pl. **German measles** Röteln pl.

measure ['meʒə] v messen. n Maß neut. **measurement** n Messung f, Maß neut.

meat [miit] n Fleisch neut. **meatball** n Fleischklößchen. **meaty** adj fleischig.

mechanic [mi'kanik] n Mechaniker m. **mechanical** adj mechanisch. **mechanics** n Mechanik f. **mechanism** n Mechanismus m. **mechanize** v mechanisieren.

medal ['medl] n Medaille f, Orden m. **medallion** n Schaumünze f.

meridian

meddle ['medl] v sich (ein)mischen (in). **meddlesome** adj zudringlich.

media ['miːdiə] pl n Medien pl. **mass media** Massenmedien pl.

mediate ['miːdieit] v vermitteln. **mediation** n Vermittlung f. **mediator** n Vermittler m.

medical ['medikəl] adj medizinisch, ärztlich. **medical certificate** Krankenschein m. **medical student** Medizinstudent m. **medicament** n Arzneimittel neut. **medicinal** adj heilkräftig. **medicine** n Arznei f, Arzneimittel neut; (science) Medizin f.

medieval [medi'iːvl] adj mittelalterlich.

mediocre [miːdi'oukə] adj mittelmäßig. **mediocrity** n Mittelmäßigkeit f.

meditate ['mediteit] v meditieren; (reflect) nachdenken (über). **meditation** n (rel) Meditation f; Nachdenken neut.

Mediterranean [medita'reiniən] n Mittelmeer neut. adj Mittelmeer-.

medium ['miːdiəm] adj mittler, Mittel-. n Mitte f; (spiritualist) Medium neut. **medium-sized** adj mittelgroß.

medley ['medli] n Gemisch neut; (music) Potpourri neut.

meek [miːk] adj mild, sanft. **meekness** n Milde f, Sanftmut f.

***meet** [miːt] v treffen, begegnen (+ dat); (by appointment) sich treffen (mit); (requirements) erfüllen; (call for) abholen. **meeting** n Treffen neut; (session) Versammlung f, Sitzung f.

megaphone ['megəfoun] n Megaphon neut.

melancholy ['melənkəli] n Melancholie f, Trübsinn m. **melancholic** adj melancholisch.

mellow ['melou] adj reif; (person) freundlich, heiter.

melodrama ['melədraːmə] n Melodrama neut. **melodramatic** adj melodramatisch.

melody ['melədi] n Melodie f. **melodious** adj wohlklingend.

melon ['melən] n Melone f.

melt [melt] v schmelzen. **melt away** zergehen. **melting point** Schmelzpunkt m.

member ['membə] n Mitglied m. **membership** n Mitgliedschaft f.

membrane ['membrein] n Membrane f.

memento [mə'mentou] n Andenken neut.

memo ['memou] n (note) Notiz f; (message) Mitteilung f.

memoirs ['memwaːz] pl n Memoiren pl.

memorable ['memərəbl] adj denkwürdig.

memorandum [memə'randəm] n (note) Notiz f; (message) Mitteilung f.

memorial [mi'moːriəl] n Denkmal neut. adj **memorial service** Gedenkgottesdienst m.

memory ['meməri] n (power of) Gedächtnis neut; (of something) Erinnerung f. **memorize** v auswendig lernen.

men [men] V **man**.

menace ['menis] n Drohung f. v bedrohen. **menacing** adj drohend.

menagerie [mi'nadʒəri] n Menagerie f.

mend [mend] v reparieren; (clothes) flicken; (socks, etc.) stopfen. n ausgebesserte Stelle f. **on the mend** (coll) auf dem Wege der Besserung.

menial ['miːniəl] adj niedrig.

menopause ['menəpoːz] n Wechseljahre pl, Menopause f.

menstrual ['menstruəl] adj Menstruations-. **menstruate** v die Regel haben, menstruieren. **menstruation** n Menstruation f, Monatsblutung f.

mental ['mentl] adj geistig, Geistes-; (slang) verrückt. **mental deficiency** Schwachsinn m. **mental hospital** Nervenheilanstalt f. **mental illness** Geisteskrankheit f. **mentality** n Mentalität f, Gesinnung f. **mentally ill** geisteskrank.

menthol ['menθəl] n Menthol neut.

mention ['menʃən] v erwähnen. n Erwähnung f. **don't mention it!** bitte sehr!

menu ['menjuː] n Speisekarte f, Menü neut.

mercantile ['məːkəntail] adj kaufmännisch, Handels-.

mercenary ['məːsinəri] adj gewinnsüchtig, geldgierig. n Söldner m.

merchandise ['məːtʃəndaiz] n Waren pl, Handelsgüter pl. v verkaufen.

merchant ['məːtʃənt] n Kaufmann m; (wholesaler) Großhändler m. **merchant navy** Handelsflotte f.

mercury ['məːkjuri] n Quecksilber neut. **Mercury** n Merkur m.

mercy ['məːsi] n Erbarmen neut, Gnade f. **merciful** adj barmherzig. **merciless** adj erbarmungslos.

mere [miə] adj bloß, rein.

merge [məːdʒ] v verschmelzen; (comm) fusionieren. **merger** n Fusion f.

meridian [mə'ridiən] n Meridian m.

meringue [mə'raŋ] n Meringe f. Baiser neut.

merit ['merit] n Verdienst neut; (value) Wert m. v verdienen.

mermaid ['mətmeid] n Seejungfrau f.

merry ['meri] adj lustig, fröhlich. **make merry** feiern. **merry-go-round** n Karussell neut. **merriment** n Lustigkeit f.

mesh [meʃ] n Masche f. v ineinandergreifen. **meshed** adj maschig.

mesmerize ['mezməraiz] v hypnotisieren; (fig) faszinieren.

mess [mes] n Durcheinander neut, Unordnung f; (mil) Messe f. v beschmutzen. **mess about** herumpfuschen. **mess up** verderben, verpfuschen. **messy** adj unordentlich.

message ['mesidʒ] n Mitteilung f; (news) Nachricht f. **messenger** n Bote m.

met [met] V meet.

metabolism [mi'tabəlizm] n Stoffwechsel m. **metabolic** adj metabolisch.

metal ['metl] n Metall neut. **metallic** adj metallisch. **metallurgy** n Metallurgie f.

metamorphosis [metə'mɔːfəsis] n Metamorphose f, Verwandlung f. **metamorphose** v verwandeln.

metaphor ['metəfə] n Metapher f. **metaphorical** adj metaphorisch.

metaphysics [,metə'fiziks] n Metaphysik f. **metaphysical** adj metaphysisch.

meteor ['miitiə] n Meteor m. **meteoric** adj meteorartig, plötzlich.

meteorology [,miitiə'rolədʒi] n Meteorologie f, Wetterkunde f. **meteorological** adj meteorologisch, Wetter-.

meter ['miitə] n Messer m. **gas meter** Gasuhr f. **parking meter** Parkuhr f.

methane ['miiθein] n Methan neut.

method ['meθəd] n Methode f; (procedure) Verfahren neut. **methodical** adj methodisch.

methylated spirits ['meθileitid] n Brennspiritus m.

meticulous [mi'tikjuləs] adj übergenau, peinlich genau.

metre ['miitə] n Meter m or neut. **metric** adj metrisch.

metronome ['metrənoum] n Metronom neut, Taktmesser m.

metropolis [mə'trɔpəlis] n Metropole f, Hauptstadt f.

mice [mais] V mouse.

microbe ['maikroub] n Mikrobe f.

microfilm ['maikrəfilm] n Mikrofilm m.

microphone ['maikrəfoun] n Mikrophon neut.

microscope ['maikrəskoup] n Mikroscop neut. **microscopic** adj mikroscopisch; (tiny) verschwindend klein.

mid [mid] adj mittler, Mittel-. **in mid air** mitten in der Luft. **midday** n Mittag m.

middle ['midl] n Mitte f. adj mittler, Mittel-. **middle-aged** adj im mittleren Alter. **middle-class** adj bürgerlich, bourgeois. **middle classes** Mittelstand m.

Middle Ages pl n Mittelalter neut.

Middle East n Naher Osten m.

midge [midʒ] n Mücke f.

midget ['midʒit] n Zwerg m.

midnight ['midnait] n Mitternacht f.

midsummer ['mid,sʌmə] n Hochsommer m.

midst [midst] n Mitte f. **in the midst of** mitten unter (+ dat).

midwife ['midwaif] n Hebamme f. **midwifery** n Geburtshilfe f.

might[1] [mait] V may.

might[2] [mait] n Macht f; (force) Gewalt f. **mighty** ['maiti] adj mächtig. adv sehr.

migraine ['miigrein] n Migräne f.

migrate [mai'greit] v abwandern. **migrant** adj Wander-; n Umsiedler m. **migration** n Wanderung f.

mike [maik] n (coll) Mikrophon neut.

mild [maild] adj mild, sanft. **to put it mildly** gelinde gesagt. **mildness** n Sanftheit f.

mildew ['mildjuu] n Mehltau m, Moder m.

mile [mail] n Meile f. **mileage** n Meilenzahl f. **milestone** n (fig) Markstein m.

militant ['militənt] adj militant, kämpferisch. n (pol) Radikale(r).

military ['militəri] adj militärisch, Militär-, Kriegs-.

milk [milk] n Milch f. v melken. **milk tooth** n Milchzahn m. **milky** adj milchig. **Milky Way** Milchstraße f.

mill [mil] n Mühle f; (works) Fabrik f. v mahlen. **run-of-the-mill** adj mittelmäßig. **miller** n Müller m.

millennium [mi'leniəm] n Jahrtausend neut.

milligram ['mili,gram] n Milligramm neut.

millilitre ['mili,liitə] n Milliliter neut.

millimetre ['mili,miitə] n Millimeter neut.

millinery ['milinəri] n Müte pl.

million ['miljən] n Million f. **millionaire** n Millionär n. **millionairess** n Millionärin f.

milometer [mai'lomitə] n Meilenzähler m, Kilometerzähler m.

mime [maim] n (actor) Mime m. v mimen.

mimic ['mimik] v nachäffen. **mimicry** n Nachäffung f.

mince [mins] v zerhacken. n (mincemeat) Hackfleisch neut. **mincer** n Fleischwolf m. **mince about** geziert gehen. **mincing** adj geziert, affektiert. **not mince one's words** kein Blatt vor den Mund nehmen.

mind [maind] n Geist m, Verstand m; (opinion) Meinung f. v etwas dagegen haben; (look after) aufpassen auf. **frame of mind** Gesinnung f, Stimmung f. **make up one's mind** sich entschließen. **mind out!** paß auf! Achtung! **Never mind!** macht nichts! I don't mind ist mir egal.

mine[1] [main] poss pron meiner m, meine f, meines neut; der, die, das meine or meinige. **a friend of mine** ein Freund von mir. **it's mine** es gehört mir.

mine[2] [main] n (coal, etc.) Bergwerk neut; (mil) Mine f. v minieren. **miner** n Bergarbeiter m. **minefield** n Minenfeld. **mining** n Bergbau m. **minesweeper** n Minensuchboot neut.

mineral ['minərəl] n Mineral neut. adj mineralisch. **mineral water** Mineralwasser neut.

mingle ['mingl] v (sich) vermischen.

miniature ['minitʃə] n Miniatur f. adj Klein-.

minimum ['miniməm] n Minimum neut. **minimal** adj Mindest-, Minimal-.

minister ['ministə] n (pol) Minister m; (rel) Pfarrer m. **ministry** n (pol) Ministerium neut.

mink [miŋk] n Nerz m.

minor ['mainə] adj kleiner, geringer; (trivial) geringfügig. n (under age) Minderjährige(r); (music) Moll neut. **minority** n Minderheit f; (under age) Minderjährigkeit f.

minstrel ['minstrəl] n Minnesänger m.

mint[1] [mint] n (cookery) Minze f.

mint[2] [mint] n (money) Münzanstalt f. v münzen.

minuet [minju'et] n Menuett neut.

minus ['mainəs] prep weniger, minus. it's minus 20 degrees wir haben 20 Grad Kälte.

minute[1] ['minit] n Minute f. **just a minute!** Moment mal!

minute[2] [mai'njurt] adj winzig.

miracle ['mirəkl] n Wunder neut, Wundertat f. **miraculous** adj wunderbar. **miraculously** adv durch ein Wunder.

mirage ['mirɑːʒ] n Luftspiegelung f.

mirror ['mirə] n Spiegel m. v widerspiegeln.

mirth [məːθ] n Fröhlichkeit f, Lustigkeit f.

misadventure [misəd'ventʃə] n Unfall m, Unglück neut.

misanthropist [miz'ænθrəpist] n Menschenfeind m. **misanthropic** adj menschenfeindlich.

misapprehension [misæpri'henʃən] n Mißverständnis neut.

misbehave [misbi'heiv] v sich schlecht benehmen. **misbehaviour** n schlechtes Benehmen neut.

miscalculate [mis'kælkjuleit] v sich verrechnen.

miscarriage [mis'kæridʒ] n Fehlgeburt f. **miscarriage of justice** Fehlspruch m, Rechtsbeugung f. **miscarry** v eine Fehlgeburt haben; (go wrong) mißlingen.

miscellaneous [misə'leiniəs] adj vermischt. n Verschiedenes neut. **miscellany** n Gemisch neut.

mischance [mis'tʃɑns] n Unfall m.

mischief ['mistʃif] n Unfug m. **mischievous** adj schelmisch, durchtrieben. **mischief-maker** n Störenfried m.

misconception [miskən'sepʃən] n Mißverständnis neut.

misconduct [mis'kondʌkt] n schlechtes Benehmen neut.

misconstrue [miskən'struː] v mißdeuten.

misdeed [mis'diːd] n Untat f, Verbrechen neut.

misdemeanour [misdi'miːnə] n Vergehen neut.

miser ['maizə] n Geizhals m. **miserly** adj geizig. **miserliness** n Geiz m.

miserable ['mizərəbl] adj (unhappy) unglücklich; (wretched) elend.

misery ['mizəri] n Elend neut, Not f.

misfire [mis'faiə] v versagen; (mot) fehlzünden. n Versager m; Fehlzündung f.

misfit ['misfit] n Einzelgänger m.

misfortune [mis'fortʃən] n Unglück neut.

misgiving [mis'givin] n Zweifel m.

misguided [mis'gaidid] *adj* (*erroneous*) irrig.

mishap ['mishap] *n* Unglück *neut*.

*****mishear** [mis'hiə] *v* sich verhören.

misinterpret [misin'tərprit] *v* mißdeuten.

*****mislay** [mis'lei] *v* verlegen.

*****mislead** [mis'liːd] *v* irreführen. **misleading** *adj* irreführend.

misnomer [mis'noumə] *n* falsche Bezeichnung *f*.

misplace [mis'pleis] *v* verlegen. **misplaced** *adj* (*inappropriate*) unangebracht.

misprint ['misprint] *n* Druckfehler *m*.

miss¹ [mis] *v* (*shot*) verfehlen; (*train, opportunity*) verpassen, versäumen; (*absent friend*) vermissen. *n* Fehlschuß *m*. **missing** *adj* fehlend; (*person*) vermißt.

miss² [mis] *n* (*title*) Fräulein *neut*.

missile [mis'ail] *n* Rakete *f*, Geschoß *neut*. **guided missile** Fernlenkrakete *f*.

mission [mi'ʃən] *n* Mission *f*; (*task*) Auftrag *m*; (*pol*) Gesandtschaft *f*. **missionary** *n* Missionar(in).

mist [mist] *n* (*feuchter*) Dunst *m*, Nebel *m*.

*****mistake** [mis'teik] *n* Fehler *m*, Irrtum *m*. *v* verwechseln. **be mistaken** im Irrtum sein.

mister ['mistə] *n* Herr *m*.

mistletoe [mis'ltou] *n* Mistel *f*.

mistress ['mistris] *n* (*lover*) Mätresse *f*; (*school*) Lehrerin *f*; (*of house or animal*) Herrin *f*.

mistrust [mis'trʌst] *v* mißtrauen. *n* Mißtrauen *neut*, Argwohn *m*. **mistrustful** *adj* mißtrauisch.

*****misunderstand** [misʌndə'stand] *v* mißverstehen. **misunderstanding** *n* Mißverständnis *neut*.

misuse [mis'juːs; *v* mis'juːz] *v* mißbrauchen. *n* Mißbrauch *m*.

mitigate ['mitigeit] *v* mildern. **mitigating circumstances** strafmildernde Umstände *pl*.

mitre ['maitə] *n* Bischofsmütze *f*.

mitten ['mitn] *n* Fausthandschuh *m*.

mix [miks] *v* (ver)mischen. *n* Mischung *f*. **mix up** verwechseln. **mixer** *n* Mixer *m*. **mixture** *n* Mischung *f*; (*med*) Mixtur *f*.

moan [moun] *n* Stöhnen *neut*. *v* stöhnen.

mob [mob] *n* Pöbel *m*, Gesindel *neut*.

mobile ['moubail] *adj* beweglich; (*motorized*) motorisiert. *n* Mobile *neut*. **mobility** *n* Beweglichkeit *f*. **mobilization** *n* Mobilisierung *f*. **mobilize** *v* mobilisieren.

moccasin ['mokəsin] *n* Mokassin *m*.

mock [mok] *v* verhöhnen, verspotten. *adj* Schein-. **mock trial** Scheinprozeß *m*. **mockery** *n* Verhöhnung *f*. (*travesty*) Zerrbild *neut*. **mocking** *adj* spöttisch.

mode [moud] *n* Weise *f*, Methode *f*.

model ['modl] *n* Modell *neut*; (*pattern*) Muster *neut*, Vorbild *neut*; (*fashion*) Mannequin *neut*. *adj* vorbildlich, musterhaft. *v* modellieren; (*clothes*) vorführen.

moderate ['modərət; *v* 'modəreit] *adj* gemäßigt, mäßig. *v* mäßigen. **moderation** *n* Mäßigung *f*. **in moderation** mit Maß.

modern ['modən] *adj* modern. **modernity** *n* Modernität *f*. **modernize** *v* modernisieren. **modernization** *n* Modernisierung *f*.

modest ['modist] *adj* bescheiden; (*reasonable*) vernünftig. **modesty** *n* Bescheidenheit *f*.

modify ['modifai] *v* abändern, modifizieren. **modification** *n* Abänderung *f*, Modifikation *f*.

modulate ['modjuleit] *v* modulieren.

mohair ['mouheə] *n* Mohair *m*.

moist [moist] *adj* feucht. **moisture** *n* Feuchtigkeit *f*.

molar ['moulə] *n* Backenzahn *m*.

molasses [mə'lasiz] *n* Melasse *f*.

mold (*US*) *V* mould.

mole¹ [moul] *n* (*birthmark*) Muttermal *neut*, Leberfleck *m*.

mole² [moul] *n* (*zool*) Maulwurf *m*.

molecule ['molikjuːl] *n* Molekül *neut*. **molecular** *adj* molekular.

molest [mə'lest] *v* belästigen.

mollusc ['moləsk] *n* Weichtier *neut*.

molt (*US*) *V* moult.

molten ['moultən] *adj* geschmolzen, flüssig.

moment ['moumənt] *n* Moment *m*, Augenblick *m*. **momentary** *adj* momentan, augenblicklich.

monarch ['monək] *n* Monarch(in). **monarchy** *n* Monarchie *f*.

monastery ['monəstəri] *n* Kloster *neut*. **monastic** *adj* kloster-.

Monday ['mʌndi] *n* Montag *m*.

money ['mʌni] *n* Geld *neut*. **money box** Sparbüchse *f*. **money order** Zahlungsanweisung *f*. **monetary** *adj* Währungs-.

mongolism ['mongəlizm] *n* Mongolismus *m*.

mongrel ['mʌŋgrəl] n Mischling m, Kreuzung f.

monitor ['monitə] n (TV) Monitor m. v überwachen, kontrollieren.

monk [mʌŋk] n Mönch m. **monkish** adj mönchisch.

monkey ['mʌŋki] n Affe m. v **monkey around** herumalbern.

monogamy [mə'nogəmi] n Monogamie f. **monogamous** adj monogam.

monogram ['monəgram] n Monogramm neut.

monologue ['monəlog] n Monolog m.

monopolize [mə'nopəlaiz] v monopolisieren. **monopoly** n Monopol neut.

monosyllable ['monəsiləbl] n einsilbiges Wort neut.

monotonous [mə'notənəs] adj monoton. **monotony** n Monotonie f.

monsoon [mon'suːn] n Monsun m.

monster ['monstə] n Ungeheuer neut; (malformation) Mißbildung f. **monstrous** adj ungeheuer.

month [mʌnθ] n Monat m. **monthly** adj monatlich; n (magazine) Monatsschrift f.

monument ['monjument] n Denkmal neut. **monumental** adj kolossal.

mood [muːd] n Laune f, Stimmung f. **be in a good/bad mood** guter/schlechter Laune sein. **moody** adj launisch.

moon [muːn] n Mond m. **full moon** Vollmond m. **moonlight** n Mondschein m.

moor[1] [muə] n Heide f, Moor neut.

moor[2] [muə] v (boat) vertäuen. **mooring** n Liegeplatz m.

mop [mop] n Mop m. v aufwischen.

mope [moup] v traurig sein, (coll) Trübsal blasen.

moped ['mouped] n Moped neut.

moral ['morəl] adj moralisch. n (of story) Lehre f. **morals** pl Moral f sing, Sitten pl. **morale** n Morale f. **morality** n Sittlichkeit f. **mores** pl n Sitten pl.

morbid ['moːbid] adj (fig) schauerlich.

more [moː] adj mehr; (in number) weitere, mehr. adv mehr, weiter. **more rapid** schneller. **more and more** immer mehr. **more or less** mehr oder weniger. **once more** noch einmal. **moreover** adv überdies, fernerhin.

morgue [moːg] n Leichenhaus neut.

morning ['moːniŋ] n Morgen m, Vormittag m. **in the mornings** morgens. **this morning** heute früh.

moron ['moːron] n Schwachsinnige(r). **moronic** adj schwachsinnig.

morose [mə'rous] adj mürrisch.

morphine ['moːfiːn] n Morphium neut.

morse code [moːs] n Morsealphabet neut.

morsel ['moːsəl] n Bissen m, Stückchen neut.

mortal ['moːtl] adj sterblich; (wound) tödlich. **mortality** n Sterblichkeit f.

mortar ['moːtə] n (for bricks) Mörtel m; (mil) Granatwerfer m.

mortgage ['moːgidʒ] n Hypothek f.

mortify ['moːtifai] v demütigen. **mortification** n Demütigung f.

mortuary ['moːtjuəri] n Leichenhaus neut.

mosaic [mə'zeiik] n Mosaik neut.

mosque [mosk] n Moschee f.

mosquito [mə'skiːtou] n Moskito m.

moss [mos] n Moos neut. **mossy** adj bemoost.

most [moust] adj die meisten. adv äußerst, höchst; am meisten. n das Meiste. **most people** die meisten Leute. **at most** höchstens. **mostly** adv meistens, größtenteils.

motel [mou'tel] n Motel neut.

moth [moθ] n Motte f. **mothball** n Mottenkugel f.

mother ['mʌðə] n Mutter f. v bemuttern **on one's mother's side** mütterlicherseits. **mother country** Mutterland neut. **motherhood** n Mutterschaft f. **mother-in-law** Schwiegermutter f. **motherless** adj mutterlos. **motherly** adj mütterlich. **mother-of-pearl** n Perlmutt neut.

motion ['mouʃən] n Bewegung f; (pol) Antrag m. v zuwinken. **set in motion** in Gang setzen.

motivate ['moutiveit] v motivieren. **motivation** n Motivierung f.

motif [mou'tiːf] n Motiv m.

motive ['moutiv] n Beweggrund m.

motor ['moutə] n Motor m. **motor accident** Autounfall m. **motorcar** n Wagen m, Auto neut. **motor cycle** n Mottorrad neut. **motorist** n Autofahrer m.

mottled ['motld] adj gefleckt.

motto ['motou] n Motto neut.

mould[1] [mould] or US **mold** n (tech) Form f; (type) Art f. v bilden, formen; (tech) gießen.

mould[2] [mould] or US **mold** n (mildew) Schimmel m. **mouldy** adj schimmelig.

moult [moult] or US **molt** v sich mausern.

mound [maund] n (Erd)Hügel m.

mount[1] [maunt] v (horse) besteigen. n (frame) Gestell neut; (horse) Reittier neut.

mount[2] [maunt] n Berg m, Hügel m.

mountain ['mauntən] n Berg m. **mountaineer** n Bergsteiger m.

mourn [moın] v trauern (um). **mourning** n Trauer f. **go into mourning** Trauer anlegen.

mouse [maus] n (pl **mice**) Maus f. **mousetrap** n Mausefalle f.

mousse [muıs] n Kremeis neut.

moustache [mə'staıʃ] or US **mustache** n Schnurrbart m.

mouth [mauθ] n Mund m; (opening) Öffnung f; (river) Mündung f; (animal) Maul neut. **mouthful** n Mundvoll m. **mouthpiece** n Mundstück neut. **mouthwash** n Mundwasser neut.

move [muıv] v (sich) bewegen; (emotionally) rühren; (house) umziehen. **movable** adj beweglich. **movement** n Bewegung f. **moving** adj rührend. **moving staircase** Rolltreppe f.

movie ['muıvi] n Film m. **go to the movies** ins Kino gehen.

*****mow** [mou] v mähen. **mower** n (Rasen)Mäher m.

mown [moun] V mow.

Mr ['mistə] n Herr m.

Mrs ['misiz] n Frau f.

much [mʌtʃ] adj, adv viel. **how much?** wieviel?

muck [mʌk] n (dung) Mist m; (dirt) Dreck m. **mucky** adj schmutzig, dreckig.

mucus ['mjuıkəs] n Schleim m.

mud [mʌd] n Schlamm m. **muddy** adj schlammig. **mudguard** n Kotflügel m. **mudslinger** n Verleumder(in).

muddle ['mʌdl] n Durcheinander neut, Wirrwarr m. v **muddle through** sich durchwursteln. **muddled** adj konfus.

muff [mʌf] n Muff m.

muffle ['mʌfl] v (noise) dämpfen. **muffler** n Schal m; (mot) Schalldämpfer m.

mug [mʌg] n Krug m, Becher m. v (rob) überfallen. **muggy** adj (weather) schwül.

mulberry ['mʌlbəri] n Maulbeere f.

mule [mjuıl] n Maulesel m. **mulish** adj störrisch.

multicoloured [,mʌlti'kʌləd] adj bunt, vielfarbig.

multiple ['mʌltipl] adj mehrfach, vielfach.

multiply ['mʌltiplai] v (sich) vermehren; (math) multiplizieren. **multiplication** v Vermehrung; (math) Multiplikation f. **multiplicity** n Vielfalt f.

multiracial [,mʌlti'reiʃəl] adj gemischtrassig.

multitude ['mʌltitjuıd] n Menge f. **multitudinous** adj zahlreich.

mumble ['mʌmbl] v murmeln. n Gemurmel neut.

mummy[1] ['mʌmi] n (embalmed) Mumie f.

mummy[2] ['mʌmi] n (coll) Mutti f.

mumps [mʌmps] n Ziegenpeter m.

munch [mʌntʃ] v schmetzend kauen.

mundane [mʌn'dein] adj alltäglich, banal.

municipal [mjuı'nisipəl] adj städtisch, Stadt-. **municipality** n Stadt f, Stadtbezirk m.

mural ['mjuərəl] n Wandgemälde neut.

murder ['məıdə] n Mord m, Ermordung f. v (er)morden. **murderer** n Mörder m. **murderous** adj mörderisch, tödlich.

murmur ['məımə] v murmeln. n Murmeln neut.

muscle ['mʌsl] n Muskel m. **muscular** adj (person) muskulös.

muse [mjuız] n Muse f. v (nach)denken.

museum [mjuı'ziəm] n Museum neut.

mushroom ['mʌʃrum] n Pilz m, Champignon m. v (coll) sich ausbreiten.

music ['mjuızik] n Musik f. **musical** adj musikalisch. **musician** n Musiker m. **music stand** Notenständer m.

musk [mʌsk] n Moschus m.

musket ['mʌskit] n Flinte f, Muskete f. **musketeer** n Musketier m.

Muslim ['mʌzlim] n Mohammedaner(in). adj mohammedanisch.

muslin ['mʌzlin] n Musselin m.

mussel ['mʌsl] n Muschel f.

*****must**[1] [mʌst] v müssen.

must[2] [mʌst] n Most m. **musty** adj muffig, schimmelig.

mustard ['mʌstəd] n Senf m.

muster ['mʌstə] v antreten lassen. **muster one's courage** sich zusammennehmen. **pass muster** Zustimmung finden.

mutation [mjuı'teiʃən] n Veränderung f; (biol) Mutation f.

mute [mjuıt] adj stumm. n Stumme(r); (music) Sordine f.

mutilate ['mjuıtileit] v verstümmeln. **mutilation** n Verstümmelung f.

mutiny ['mjuːtini] n Meuterei f. v meutern. **mutineer** n Meuterer m. **mutinous** adj meuterisch.

mutter ['mʌtə] v murmeln.

mutton ['mʌtn] n Hammelfleisch neut.

mutual ['mjuːtʃuəl] adj gegenseitig.

muzzle ['mʌzl] n Maul neut; (protection) Maulkorb m.

my [mai] poss adj mein, meine, mein. **myself** pron mich (selbst). **by myself** allein.

mystery ['mistəri] n Rätsel neut, Geheimnis neut. **mysterious** adj geheimnisvoll, mysteriös. **mystic** n Mystiker(in). adj mystisch. **mysticism** n Mystizismus m. **mystify** v täuschen, verblüffen.

myth [miθ] n Mythos m. **mythical** adj mythisch. **mythological** adj mythologisch. **mythology** n Mythologie f.

N

nag [nag] v herumnörgeln an. n Gaul m.

nail [neil] n Nagel m. v (an)nageln. **nail down** zunageln. **nailbrush** n Nagelbürste f. **nail-file** n Nagelfeile f. **nail polish** Nagellack m. **nail scissors** Nagelschere f sing.

naïve [naiˈiːv] adj naiv. **naïveté** n Naivität f.

naked ['neikid] adj nackt. **nakedness** n Nacktheit f.

name [neim] n Name m; (reputation) Ruf m. **by name** namentlich. **by the name of** namens. **what's your name?** wie heißen Sie? v nennen; (mention) erwähnen. **namely** adv nämlich.

nanny ['nani] n Kindermädchen neut.

nap [nap] n Nickerchen neut.

napkin ['napkin] n (table) Serviette f.

nappy ['napi] n Windel f.

narcotic [naːˈkotik] n Narkotikum neut. adj narkotisch.

narrate [nəˈreit] v erzählen. **narration** n also narrative Erzählung f. **narrative** adj Erzählungs-. **narrator** n Erzähler(in).

narrow ['narou] adj eng, schmal; (fig) beschränkt. v sich verengen. **narrowly** adv (just) mit Mühe. **narrow-minded** adj engstirnig.

nasal ['neizəl] adj Nasen-; (voice) nasal.

nasturtium [nəˈstəːʃəm] n Kapuzinerkresse f.

nasty ['naːsti] adj ekelhaft, widerlich; (serious) ernst, schlimm; (person) gemein, böse.

nation ['neiʃən] n Nation f, Volk neut. **national** adj national, Volks-. **nationalism** n Nationalismus m. **nationality** n Staatsangehörigkeit f. **nationalization** f Verstaatlichung f. **nationalize** v verstaatlichen. **national anthem** Nationalhymne f. **National Insurance** Sozialversicherung f.

native ['neitiv] adj eingeboren. n Eingeborene(r).

nativity [nəˈtivəti] n Geburt f. **nativity play** Krippenspiel neut.

natural ['natʃərəl] adj natürlich, Natur-. **natural resources** Naturschätze pl. **naturalist** n Naturforscher m. **naturalize** v einbürgen.

nature ['neitʃə] n Natur f.

naughty ['noːti] adj unartig, ungezogen. **naughtiness** n Ungezogenheit f.

nausea ['noːziə] n Übelkeit f, Brechreiz m; (seasickness) Seekrankheit f. **nauseating** adj widerlich.

nautical ['noːtikəl] adj nautisch, Schiffs-. **nautical mile** Seemeile f.

naval ['neivəl] adj Flotten-, See-. **naval battle** Seeschlacht f.

navel ['neivəl] n Nabel m.

navigate ['navigeit] v navigieren. **navigable** adj schiffbar. **navigation** n Navigation f. **navigator** n Navigator m.

navy ['neivi] n Flotte f, Kriegsmarine f. **navy-blue** adj marineblau.

near [niə] adj nahe. adv nahe, in der Nähe. prep in der Nähe (von or +gen), nahe an. **nearby** adv in der Nähe; adj nahe gelegen. **nearly** adv fast, beinahe.

neat [niːt] adj ordentlich; (alcohol) rein, unverdünnt. **neatness** n Ordentlichkeit f.

necessary ['nesisəri] adj nötig, erforderlich. **necessarily** adv notwendigerweise. **necessitate** v erfordern. **necessity** n Notwendigkeit f. **necessities** pl Bedarfsartikel pl.

neck [nek] n Hals m. **neckerchief** n Halstuch neut. **necklace** n Halskette f. **necktie** n Krawatte f.

nectar ['nektə] n Nektar m.

née [nei] *adj* geborene.

need [niːd] *v* Bedürfnis *neut*, Bedarf *m*; *(necessity)* Notwendigkeit *f*. **if need arise** im Notfall. **needful** *adj* nötig. **neediness** Armut *f*. **needless** *adj* unnötig. **needy** *adj* arm.

needle ['niːdl] *n* Nadel *f*; *(indicator)* Zeiger *m*. *v (coll)* reizen. **needlework** *n* Handarbeit *f*.

negate [ni'geit] *v* annullieren, verneinen. **negation** *n* Annullierung, Verneinung *f*. **negative** *adj* negativ; *(answer)* ablehnend. *n (phot)* Negativ *neut*.

neglect [ni'glekt] *v* vernachlässigen. *n* Vernachlässigung *f*.

negligée ['negliʒei] *n* Negligé *neut*.

negligence ['neglidʒəns] *n* Nachlässigkeit *f*. **negligent** *adj* nachlässig. **negligible** *adj* geringfügig.

negotiate [ni'gouʃieit] *v* verhandeln. **negotiation** *n* Verhandlung *f*. **negotiator** *n* Vermittler *m*.

Negro ['niːgrou] *n* Neger *m*. *adj* Neger-. **Negress** *n* Negerin *f*.

neigh [nei] *v* wiehern. *n* Wiehern *neut*.

neighbour ['neibə] *n* Nachbar(in). **neighbourhood** *n* Nachbarschaft *f*. **neighbourly** *adj* freundlich.

neither ['naiðə] *adj, pron* kein (von beiden). **neither ... nor ...** weder ... noch ....

neon ['niːon] *n* Neon *neut*.

nephew ['nefjuː] *n* Neffe *m*.

nepotism ['nepətizəm] *n* Vetternwirtschaft *f*.

nerve [nəːv] *n* Nerv *m*; *(cheek)* Frechheit *f*. **nerves** *pl* Nervosität *f sing*. **nervous** *adj* Nerven-; *(on edge)* nervös. **nervousness** *n* Nervosität *f*. **nervy** *adj* nervös. **nerve-racking** *adj* nervenaufreibend.

nest [nest] *n* Nest *neut*. *v* nisten.

nestle ['nesl] *v* sich anschmiegen.

net¹ [net] *n* Netz *neut*; *(fabric)* Tüll *m*. *v* fangen.

net² [net] *adj (comm)* netto, Netto-. **net amount** Nettobetrag *m*. **net price** Nettopreis *m*. **net profit** Reingewinn *m*.

Netherlands ['neðələndz] *pl n* Niederlände *pl*.

nettle ['netl] *n* Nessel *f*. *v* ärgern. **nettle rash** Nesselausschlag *m*. **grasp the nettle** die Schwierigkeit anpacken.

neurosis [nju'rousis] *n* Neurose *f*. **neurotic** *adj* neurotisch. *n* Neurotiker(in).

neuter ['njuːtə] *adj (gramm)* sächlich. *n* Neutrum *neut*. *v (male)* kastrieren; *(female)* sterilisieren.

neutral ['njuːtrəl] *adj* neutral. *n (mot)* Leerlauf *m*. **neutrality** *n* Neutralität *f*. **neutralize** *v* neutralisieren.

never ['nevə] *adv* nie, niemals. **never-ending** *adj* endlos. **never-failing** *adj* unfehlbar. **nevermore** *adv* nimmermehr. **nevertheless** *adv* nichtsdestoweniger.

new [njuː] *adj* neu; *(strange)* unbekannt. **newborn** *adj* neugeboren. **newcomer** *n* Neuankömmling *m*. **new-fangled** *adj* neumodisch. **newish** *adj* ziemlich neu. **newly** *adv* neulich. **newly-wed** *adj* jungvermählt. **newness** *n* Neuheit *f*. **news** *pl n* Nachrichten *pl*. **newspaper** *n* Zeitung *f*. **newsagent** *n* Zeitungshändler *m*. **news flash** Kurznachricht *f*. **newsstand** *n* Zeitungskiosk *m*. **newsworthy** *adj* aktuell.

newt [njuːt] *n* Wassermolch *m*.

New Testament *n* Neujahr *neut*. **New Year's Day** Neujahr *neut*. **New Year's Eve** Sylvester *neut*.

next [nekst] *adj* nächst, nächstfolgend; *adv* gleich daran, nächstens. *prep* neben, bei. **next door** nebenan.

nib [nib] *n* (Füllfeder)Spitze *f*.

nibble ['nibl] *v* nagen, knabbern (an). *n* Nagen *neut*, Knabbern *neut*; *(morsel)* Happen *m*.

nice [nais] *adj* nett; *(kind)* freundlich. **nicely** *adv* nett. **nicety** *n* Feinheit *f*.

niche [nitʃ] *n* Nische *f*.

nick [nik] *v* einkerben; *(coll: catch)* erwischen. *n* Kerbe *f*; *(coll)* Gefängnis *neut*; Polizeiwache *f*.

nickel ['nikl] *n* Nickel *neut*; *(US)* Fünfcentstück *neut*. *adj* Nickel-. **nickel-plated** *adj* vernickelt.

nickname ['nikneim] *n* Spitzname *m*.

nicotine ['nikətiːn] *n* Nikotin *neut*.

niece [niːs] *n* Nichte *f*.

niggle ['nigl] *v* trödeln.

night [nait] *n* Nacht *f*; *(evening)* Abend *m*. **all night** die ganze Nacht. **goodnight** gute Nacht. **nightclub** *n* Nachtlokal *neut*. **nightdress** *n* Nachthemd *neut*. **nightly** *adj* nächtlich. **nightmare** *n* Alptraum *m*. **nighttime** *n* Nacht *f*.

nightingale ['naitiŋgeil] *n* Nachtigall *f*.

nil [nil] *n* Null *f*.

nimble ['nimbl] *adj* flink. **nimbleness** *n* Gewandtheit *f*.

nine [nain] adj neun. n Neun f. **ninth** adj neunt; n Neuntel neut.

nineteen [nain'tiːn] adj neunzehn. n Neunzehn f. **nineteenth** adj neunzehnt.

ninety ['nainti] adj neunzig. n Neunzig f. **ninetieth** adj neunzigst.

nip [nip] v kneifen, zwicken. **nip in the bud** im Keim ersticken.

nipple ['nipl] n Brustwarze f; (baby's bottle) Lutscher m; (tech) Nippel m.

nit [nit] n Niß f, Nisse f.

nitrogen ['naitrədʒən] n Stickstoff m.

no [nou] adv nein. adj kein. **on no account** auf keinen Fall. **in no way** keineswegs. **no more** nicht mehr. **no smoking** Rauchen verboten. **no-smoking compartment** Nichtraucher m.

noble ['noubl] adj edel, adlig. **nobility** n Adel m, Adelsstand m. **nobleman** n Edelmann m.

nobody ['noubədi] pron niemand, keiner.

nocturnal [nok'təːnəl] adj nächtlich, Nacht-.

nod [nod] v nicken. n Nicken neut. **nod off** einschlafen.

noise [noiz] n Lärm m, Geräusch neut. **noiseless** adj geräuschlos. **noisy** adj laut.

nomad ['noumad] n Nomade m, Nomadin f. **nomadic** adj nomadisch.

nominal ['nominl] adj nominell, Nenn-.

nominate ['nomineit] v ernennen. **nomination** n Ernennung f.

nominative ['nominətiv] n (gramm) Nominativ m.

nonchalant ['nonʃələnt] adj unbekümmert. **nonchalance** n Gleichgültigkeit f.

nondescript ['nondiskript] adj nichtssagend.

none [nʌn] pron kein; (person) niemand. adv keineswegs.

nonentity [non'entəti] n Unding neut; (coll: person) Null f.

nonetheless [ˌnʌnðə'les] adv nichtsdestoweniger.

nonsense ['nonsəns] n Unsinn m. interj Unsinn! Quatsch! **nonsensical** adj sinnlos. **stand no nonsense** sich nichts gefallen lassen.

non-smoker [non'smoukə] n Nichtraucher(in). **non-smoking compartment** Nichtraucher(abteil) m.

non-stop [non'stop] adj pausenlos; (train) durchgehend.

noodles ['nuːdlz] pl n Nudeln pl.

noon [nuːn] n Mittag m. **at noon** zu Mittag.

no-one ['nouʌn] pron keiner, niemand.

noose [nuːs] n Schlinge f.

nor [noː] adj noch. **nor do I** ich auch nicht.

norm [noːm] n Norm f. **normal** adj normal. **normality** n Normalität f. **normalize** v normalisieren. **normally** adv normalerweise.

north [noːθ] n Norden m. adj also **northerly, northern** nördlich, Nord-. adv also **northwards** nach Norden, nordwärts. **North America** Nordamerika neut. **north-east** n Nordosten m. **North Pole** Nordpol m. **north-west** n Nordwesten m.

Norway ['noːwei] n Norwegen neut. **Norwegian** adj norwegisch; n Norweger(in).

nose [nouz] n Nase f. **nosy** adj (coll) neugierig.

nostalgia [no'staldʒə] n Nostalgie f. **nostalgic** adj wehmütig.

nostril ['nostrəl] n Nasenloch neut.

not [not] adv nicht. **not a** kein. **is it not? or isn't it?** nicht wahr?

notch [notʃ] n Kerbe f. v einkerben.

note [nout] n Vermerk m, Notiz f; (letter) Zettel m; (music) Note f; (money) Schein m; (importance) Bedeutung f. v merken. **take notes** Notizen machen.

nothing ['nʌθiŋ] pron nichts. n Nichts neut. **nothing but** nichts als.

notice ['noutis] n Notiz f; (law) Kündigung f. v bemerken. **period of notice** Kündigungsfrist f. **take notice (of)** achtgeben (auf). **give notice** kündigen. **until further notice** bis auf weiteres. **noticeable** adj bemerkenswert. **noticeboard** n Anschlagtafel f.

notify ['noutifai] v melden, benachrichtigen. **notification** n Meldung f; Benachrichtigung f.

notion ['nouʃən] n Begriff m. **have no notion** keine Ahnung haben.

notorious [nou'toːriəs] adj notorisch.

notwithstanding [notwið'standiŋ] prep trotz (+ gen).

nougat ['nuːgaː] n Nugat m.

nought [noːt] n Null f. **come/bring to nought** zunichte kommen/bringen.

noun [naun] n Hauptwort neut.

nourish ['nʌriʃ] v (er)nähren. **nourishing** adj nahrhaft. **nourishment** n Ernährung f.

novel ['nɔvəl] adj neu, neuartig. n Roman m. **novelist** n Romanschriftsteller(in). **novelty** n Neuheit f.

November [nə'vembə] n November m.

novice ['nɔvis] n Anfänger(in); (rel) Novize m, f.

now [nau] adv jetzt, nun; (straightaway) sofort. **now and again** ab und zu, hin und wieder. **nowadays** adv heutzutage.

nowhere ['nouweə] adv nirgends, nirgendwo. **from nowhere** aus dem Nichts.

noxious ['nɔkʃəs] adj schädlich.

nozzle ['nɔzl] n Schnauze f. Ausguß m.

nuance ['njuãs] n Nuance f. Schattierung f.

nuclear ['njuːkliə] adj Kern-. **nuclear energy** Atomkraft f. **nuclear reactor** Kernreaktor m.

nucleus ['njuːkliəs] n Kern m.

nude ['njuːd] adj nackt. **nudist** n Nudist(in). **nudity** n Nacktheit f.

nudge [nʌdʒ] n Rippenstoß m. v leicht anstoßen.

nugget ['nʌgit] n Goldklumpen m.

nuisance ['njuːsns] n Ärgernis neut.

null [nʌl] adj nichtig, ungültig. **null and void** null und nichtig.

numb [nʌm] adj starr, erstarrt. v taub machen.

number ['nʌmbə] n Nummer f; (amount) Anzahl f; (figure) Ziffer f. v numerieren. **number-plate** n Nummernschild neut. **numeral** n Ziffer f. **numerous** adj zahlreich.

nun [nʌn] n Nonne f.

nurse [nəːs] n Krankenschwester f. Krankenpfleger(in). v pflegen; (feed baby) stillen. **nursemaid** n Kindermädchen neut. **nursing** n Krankenpflege f. **nursing home** n Privatklinik f.

nursery ['nəːsəri] n (in house) Kinderzimmer neut; (institution) Krippe f. Kindertagesstätte f; (bot) Gärtnerei f. **nurseryman** n Pflanzenzüchter m. **nursery rhyme** n Kinderlied neut, Kinderreim m. **nursery school** n Kindergarten m.

nurture ['nəːtʃə] v erziehen.

nut [nʌt] n Nuß f; (for bolt) Mutter f. **nutcracker** Nußknacker m. **nuts** adj (coll) verrückt. **nutmeg** n Muskatnuß f.

nutrient ['njuːtriənt] n Nährstoff m. adj nährend. **nutrition** n Ernährung f. **nutritious** adj nahrhaft.

nuzzle ['nʌzl] v sich schmiegen (an).

nylon ['nailon] n Nylon neut. **nylons** pl Strümpfe pl.

nymph [nimf] n Nymphe f.

O

oak [ouk] n Eiche f. (wood) Eichenholz neut. **oaken** adj eichen.

oar [ɔː] n Ruder neut, Riemen m. **oarsman** n Ruderer m.

oasis [ou'eisis] n (pl -ses) Oase f.

oath [ouθ] n Eid m; (swear word) Fluch m.

oats [outs] pl n Hafer m sing. **oatmeal** n Hafermehl neut.

obedient [ə'biːdiənt] adj gehorsam. **obedience** n Gehorsam m.

obese [ə'biːs] adj fettleibig. **obesity** n Fettleibigkeit f.

obey [ə'bei] v gehorchen (+dat); (an order) befolgen.

obituary [ə'bitjuəri] n Todesanzeige f.

object ['ɔbʒikt; v əb'ʒekt] n Gegenstand m; (aim) Ziel neut; (gramm) Objekt neut. **money is no object** Geld spielt keine Rolle. **objective** adj objektiv. v einwenden (gegen). **objection** n Einwand m, Einspruch m. **objectionable** adj unangenehm.

oblige [ə'blaidʒ] v (coerce) zwingen. **be obliged to do something** etwas tun müssen. **much obliged!** besten Dank! **obligation** n Verpflichtung f. **obligatory** adj verbindlich.

oblique [ə'bliːk] adj schräg.

obliterate [ə'blitəreit] v auslöschen, tilgen. **obliteration** n Auslöschung f, Vertilgung f.

oblivion [ə'bliviən] n Vergessenheit f. **oblivious (to)** adj blind (gegen).

oblong ['ɔblɔŋ] n Rechteck neut. adj rechteckig.

obnoxious [əb'nɔkʃəs] adj gehässig.

oboe ['oubou] n Oboe f. **oboist** n Oboist(in).

obscene [əb'siːn] adj obszön. **obscenity** n Obszönität f. Unzüchtigkeit f.

obscure [əb'skjuə] adj (dark) dunkel, düster; (meaning, etc.) obskur, undeutlich.

obscurity n Dunkelheit f; Undeutlichkeit f.

observe [əb'zɜːv] v beobachten; (remark) bemerken. **observer** n Beobachter m. **observation** n Beobachtung f; Bemerkung f.

obsess [əb'ses] v quälen, heimsuchen. **obsessed** adj besessen. **obsession** n Besessenheit f.

obsolescent [obsə'lesnt] adj veraltend. **obsolescence** n Veralten neut.

obsolete ['obsəliːt] adj überholt, veraltet.

obstacle ['obstəkl] n Hindernis neut.

obstetrics [ob'stetriks] n Geburtshilfe f. **obstetrician** n Geburtshelfer(in).

obstinate ['obstinət] adj hartnäckig. **obstinacy** n Hartnäckigkeit f.

obstruct [əb'strʌkt] v versperren, blockieren; (hinder) hemmen. **obstruction** n Versperrung f; Hemmung f; (obstacle) Hindernis neut.

obtain [əb'tein] v erhalten, bekommen. **obtainable** adj erhältlich.

obtrusive [əb'truːsiv] adj aufdringlich.

obtuse [əb'tjuːs] adj stumpf.

obvious ['obviəs] adj offensichtlich.

occasion [ə'keiʒən] n Gelegenheit f; (possibility) Möglichkeit f; (cause) Anlaß m. **occasional** adj gelegentlich.

occult ['okʌlt] adj okkult. **the occult** okkulte Wissenschaften pl.

occupy ['okjupai] v (person) beschäftigen; (house) bewohnen; (mil) besetzen. **occupied** adj (phone booth, etc.) besetzt. **occupant** n Bewohner(in). **occupation** n Beschäftigung f; (profession) Beruf m; (mil) Besatzung f. **occupational** adj beruflich.

occur [ə'kɜː] v vorkommen. **it occurs to me** es fällt mir ein. **occurrence** n Ereignis neut.

ocean ['ouʃən] n Ozean m, Meer neut. **oceanic** adj ozeanisch. **ocean-going** adj Hochsee-.

ochre ['oukə] adj ockerfarbig.

octagon ['oktəgən] n Achteck neut. **octagonal** adj achteckig.

octave ['oktiv] n Oktave f.

October [ok'toubə] n Oktober m.

octopus ['oktəpəs] n Tintenfisch m.

oculist ['okjulist] n Augenarzt m.

odd [od] adj (strange) seltsam; (numbers) ungerade. **oddity** n Seltsamkeit f. **oddly** (enough) seltsamerweise. **oddments** pl n Reste pl. **oddness** n Seltsamkeit f. **odds** pl n (Gewinn)Chancen pl. **at odds with** uneins mit. **odds and ends** Krimskrams m.

ode [oud] n Ode f.

odious ['oudiəs] adj verhaßt.

odour ['oudə] n Geruch m. **odourless** adj geruchlos.

oesophagus [iː'sofəgəs] n Speiseröhre f.

of [ov] prep von or gen.

off [of] prep fort, weg. adv weg, entfernt; ab. adj (food) verdorben, nicht mehr frisch. **go off** weggehen; (food) verderben. **take off** (clothes) ausziehen; (holiday) frei nehmen. **switch off** ausschalten. **off and on** ab und zu. **off duty** dienstfrei.

offal ['ofəl] n Innereien pl.

offend [ə'fend] v kränken, beleidigen. **offender** n Missetäter(in). **offence** n Vergehen neut, Verstoß m. **take offence (at)** Anstoß nehmen (an). **offensive** adj widerwärtig; n (mil) Angriff m.

offer ['ofə] v (an)bieten. n Angebot neut. **offering** n (gift) Spende f.

offhand [of'hand] adj lässig.

office ['ofis] n Büro neut; (official position or department) Amt neut. **officer** n (mil) Offizier. **take office** das Amt antreten. **office staff** Büropersonal neut.

official [ə'fiʃəl] n Beamte(r). adj amtlich; (report, function) offiziell. **officially** adj offiziell.

officious [ə'fiʃəs] adj aufdringlich.

offing ['ofiŋ] n **in the offing** in Sicht, drohend.

off-licence ['oflaisns] n Wein- und Spirituosenhandlung f.

off-peak [of'piːk] adj außerhalb der Hauptverkehrszeit.

off-putting ['of,putiŋ] adj abstoßend.

off-season [of'sizn] n stille Saison f.

offset [of'set; n 'ofset] v ausgleichen. n (printing) Offsetdruck m.

offshore ['ofʃot] adj Küsten-. adv von der Küste entfernt, auf dem Meere.

offside [of'said] adj abseits.

offspring ['ofspriŋ] n Nachkommenschaft f.

offstage ['ofsteidʒ] adv hinter den Kulissen.

often ['ofn] adv oft, häufig.

ogre ['ougə] n Ungeheuer neut, Riese m.

oil [oil] n Öl n; (petroleum) Erdöl neut. v ölen. **oilfield** Ölfeld neut. **oil-paint** n

Ölfarbe f. **oil-painting** n Ölgemalde neut. **oily** adj fettig.

ointment ['ointmənt] n Salbe f.

old [ould] adj alt. **grow old** alt werden. **five years old** fünf Jahre alt. **old age** Alter neut. **old-fashioned** adj altmodisch.

olive ['oliv] n Olive f. **olive-green** adj olivgrün. **olive branch** n Ölzweig m. **olive oil** Olivenöl neut. **olive tree** Ölbaum m.

Olympics [ə'limpiks] pl n Olympische Spiele pl. **Olympiade** f, Olympiade f.

omelette ['omlit] n Omelett neut.

omen ['oumən] n Vorzeichen neut. **ominous** adj verhängnisvoll, drohend.

omit [ou'mit] v auslassen; (to do something) unterlassen. **omission** n Unterlassung f.

omnipotent [om'nipotənt] adj allmächtig. **omnipotence** n Allmacht f.

on [on] prep (position) an, auf; (concerning) über. adv (forward) fort, weiter. **have on** one sich haben. **on fire** in Brand. **on foot** zu Fuß. **on time** pünktlich. **put on** (clothes) anziehen; (manner) affektieren. **switch on** einschalten.

once [wʌns] adv, conj einmal. **at once** sofort. **once and for all** ein für allemal. **all at once** auf einmal, plötzlich.

one [wʌn] adj ein, eine, ein. n Eins f. pron man. **oneself** pron sich (selbst). **by oneself** allein. **one-piece** adj einteilig. **one-way street** Einbahnstraße f.

onion ['ʌnjən] n Zwiebel f.

onlooker ['onlukə] n Zuschauer(in).

only ['ounli] adj einzig. adv nur; (with times) erst. conj jedoch. **only just** gerade. **not only ... but also ...** nicht nur ... sondern auch ....

onset ['onset] n Anfang m.

onslaught ['onslott] n Angriff m.

onus ['ounəs] n Last f, Verpflichtung f.

onward ['onwəd] adv vorwärts, weiter.

ooze [uːz] v (aus)sickern.

opal ['oupəl] n Opal m.

opaque [ə'paik] adj undurchsichtig.

open ['oupən] v öffnen, aufmachen; (book) aufschlagen; (event, shop) eröffnen; (begin) anfangen. adj offen, auf. **open-air** adj Freiluft-. **in the open air** im Freien. **with open arms** herzlich. **open-handed** adj freigiebig. **opening** n Öffnung f, (shop) Eröffnung f. **open-minded** adj aufgeschlossen.

opera ['opərə] n Oper f. **opera house** Oper f. Opernhaus neut. **opera singer** Opernsänger(in). **operatic** adj Opern-.

operate ['opəreit] v funktionieren, laufen; (med, tech, comm) operieren. **operation** n Arbeitsablauf m, Betrieb m; Operation f. **operative** adj tätig, wirksam; n Arbeiter m.

ophthalmic [of'θalmik] adj Augen-. **ophthalmologist** n Augenarzt m. **ophthalmology** n Ophthalmologie f.

opinion [ə'pinjən] n Meinung f, Ansicht f. **in my opinion** meines Erachtens. **opinion poll** Meinungsumfrage f.

opium ['oupiəm] n Opium neut.

opponent [ə'pounənt] n Gegner(in).

opportune [opə'tjuːn] adj rechtzeitig. **opportunist** n Opportunist(in). **opportunity** [opə'tjuːnəti] n Gelegenheit f; (possibility) Möglichkeit f. **take the opportunity** die Gelegenheit ergreifen.

oppose [ə'pouz] v bekämpfen, sich widersetzen (+dat). **opposed** adj feindlich (gegen). **as opposed to** im Vergleich zu. **opposing** adj (ideas) widerstreitend. **opposition** n Widerstand m; (pol) Opposition f.

opposite ['opəzit] adj gegenüberliegend. n Gegenteil neut.

oppress [ə'pres] v unterdrücken. **oppression** n Unterdrückung f. **oppressive** adj bedrückend; (weather) schwül.

opt [opt] v sich entscheiden (für).

optical ['optikl] adj optisch. **optician** n Optiker m. **optics** n Optik f.

optimism ['optimizəm] n Optimismus m. **optimist** n Optimist(in). **optimistic** adj optimistisch.

optimum ['optiməm] n Optimum neut. adj optimal.

option ['opʃən] n Wahl f; (comm) Option f. **have no option (but to)** keine andere Möglichkeit haben (, als zu). **optional** adj wahlfrei.

opulent ['opjulənt] adj opulent, üppig. **opulence** n Opulenz f, Üppigkeit f.

or [oː] conj oder. **or else** sonst.

oracle ['orəkl] n Orakel neut.

oral ['oːrəl] adj mündlich; (med) oral. n mündliche Prüfung f.

orange ['orind3] n Apfelsine f, Orange f. adj orange.

orator ['orətə] n Redner m. **oration** n Rede f. **oratory** n Redekunst f.

orbit ['oːbit] a Umlaufbahn f. v umkreisen.

orchard ['ɔːtʃəd] n Obstgarten m.

orchestra ['ɔːkəstrə] n Orchester neut. **orchestral** adj Orchester-, orchestral.

orchid ['ɔːkid] n Orchidee f.

ordain [ɔː'dein] v ordinieren, weihen; (decree) anordnen.

ordeal [ɔː'diːl] n schwere Prüfung f.

order ['ɔːdə] n Ordnung f; (series) Reihenfolge f; (comm) Bestellung f, Auftrag m; (command) Befehl m; (rel) Orden m. v (comm) bestellen; (command) befehlen. **put in order** ordnen. **in order to ... um ... zu ...** .

orderly ['ɔːdəli] adj ordentlich. n (med) Sanitäter m.

ordinal ['ɔːdinl] adj Ordinal-.

ordinary ['ɔːdənəri] adj gewöhnlich, normal. **out-of-the-ordinary** außerordentlich. **ordinarily** adv normalerweise.

ore [ɔː] n Erz neut.

oregano [ori'gɑːnou] n Origanum neut.

organ ['ɔːgən] n Organ neut.; (music) Orgel f. **organist** n Organist(in).

organic [ɔː'gænik] adj organisch.

organism ['ɔːgənizəm] n Organismus m.

organize ['ɔːgənaiz] v organisieren. **organization** n Organisation f; (association) Verband m. **organizer** n Organisator m.

orgasm ['ɔːgæzəm] n Orgasmus m.

orgy ['ɔːdʒi] n Orgie f.

orient ['ɔːriənt] v orientieren. **the Orient** Morgenland neut, Orient m. **oriental** adj orientalisch. n Orientale m, Orientalin f.

orientate ['ɔːrienteit] v orientieren. **orientation** n Orientierung f.

origin ['ɔːridʒin] n Ursprung m; Herkunft f, Entstehung f. **original** adj ursprünglich; (unusual) originell; n Original neut. **originality** n Originalität f. **originate** v entstehen.

ornament ['ɔːnəmənt] n Ornament neut. v verzieren, schmücken. **ornamental** adj ornamental.

ornate [ɔː'neit] adj reich verziert.

ornithology [ɔːni'θɔlədʒi] n Ornithologie f, Vogelkunde f. **ornithologist** n Ornithologe m, Ornithologin f.

orphan ['ɔːfən] n Waise f, Waisenkind neut. v verwaisen. **orphanage** n Waisenhaus neut.

orthodox ['ɔːθədɔks] adj orthodox.

orthopaedic [ɔːθə'piːdik] adj orthopädisch. **orthopaedics** n Orthopädie f.

oscillate ['osileit] v oszillieren, schwingen. **oscillation** n Schwingung f.

ostensible [o'stensəbl] adj scheinbar.

ostentatious [osten'teiʃəs] adj großtuerisch. **ostentation** n Prahlerei f.

osteopath ['ostiəpæθ] n Osteopath(in).

ostracize ['ostrəsaiz] v verbannen.

ostrich ['ostritʃ] n Strauß m.

other ['ʌðə] adj, pron ander. **other than** anders als. **each other** einander. **somebody or other** irgend jemand. **one after the other** einer/eine/eins nach dem/der andern.

otherwise ['ʌðəwaiz] adv sonst.

otter ['otə] n Otter m.

***ought** [ɔːt] v sollen. **you ought to do it** Sie sollten es tun.

ounce [auns] n Unze f.

our [auə] adj unser. **Our Father** Vaterunser neut. **ours** poss pron unsere. **ourselves** uns (selbst).

oust [aust] v vertreiben.

out [aut] adv aus, hinaus, heraus; (outside) draußen. **come out** herauskommen; (book, etc.) erscheinen. **go out** hinausgehen. **out of the question** ausgeschlossen. **out-of-date** veraltet.

outboard ['autbɔːd] adj Außenbord-. n Außenbordmotor m.

outbreak ['autbreik] n Ausbruch m.

outbuilding ['autbildiŋ] n Nebengebäude neut.

outburst ['autbəːst] n Ausbruch m.

outcast ['autkɑːst] n Ausgestoßene(r).

outcome ['autkʌm] n Ergebnis neut.

outcry ['autkrai] n Aufschrei m.

***outdo** [aut'duː] v übertreffen.

outdoor ['autdɔː] adj Außen-. **outdoor swimming pool** Freibad neut. **outdoors** adv draußen.

outer ['autə] adj äußer, Außen-. **outer garments** Oberkleidung f. **outer space** Weltraum m.

outfit ['autfit] n Ausstattung f; (coll: team) Mannschaft f. **outfitter** n (Herren)Ausstatter m.

outgoing ['autgouiŋ] adj (pol) abtretend; (friendly) gesellig.

***outgrow** [aut'grou] v hinauswachsen über; (clothes) herauswachsen aus.

outhouse ['authaus] n Anbau m, Nebengebäude neut.

outing ['autiŋ] n Ausflug m.

outlandish [aut'landiʃ] adj seltsam, grotesk.

outlaw ['autlɔɪ] n Vogelfreie(r). v ächten.

outlay ['autleɪ] n Auslage f, Ausgabe f.

outlet ['autlɪt] n Auslaß m.

outline ['autlaɪn] n Umriß m. v umreißen.

outlive [aut'lɪv] v überleben.

outlook ['autluk] n Aussicht f; (attitude) Auffassung f.

outlying ['autlaɪɪŋ] adj entlegen.

outnumber [aut'nʌmbə] v (zahlenmäßig) überlegen sein (+dat).

outpatient ['autpeɪʃənt] n ambulanter Patient m.

outpost ['autpoust] n Vorposten m.

output ['autput] n Leistung f, Output m.

outrage ['autreɪdʒ] n Schande f. **outraged** adj beleidigt, schockiert. **outrageous** adj frevelhaft.

outright ['autraɪt; adv aut'raɪt] adj, adv ganz, völlig; (immediately) sogleich, auf der Stelle.

outside [aut'saɪd; adj 'autsaɪd] n Äußere neut; Außenseite f. adj äußer, Außen-. prep außerhalb (+gen). adv (go) hinaus; (be) draußen. **outsider** n Außenseiter(in).

outsize ['autsaɪz] adj übergroß. n Übergröße f.

outskirts ['autskɜːts] pl n Umgebung f sing, Staatrand m sing.

outspoken [aut'spoukən] adj freimütig.

outstanding [aut'standɪŋ] adj hervorragend; (not settled) unerledigt.

outstrip [aut'strɪp] v überholen.

outward ['autwəd] adj äußer. adv also **outwards** nach Außen. **outward-bound** adj auf der Ausreise. **outwardly** adv äußerlich.

outweigh [aut'weɪ] v überwiegen.

outwit [aut'wɪt] v überlisten.

oval ['ouvəl] n Oval neut. adj oval.

ovary ['ouvərɪ] n Eierstock m.

ovation [ou'veɪʃən] n Ovation f, Beifallssturm m.

oven ['ʌvn] n (cookery) Backofen m; (industrial, etc.) Ofen m.

over ['ouvə] adv über, hinüber, herüber; (finished) zu Ende; (during) während; (too much) allzu. prep über; (more than) mehr als. **over and over again** immer wieder. **over there** drüben. **all over England** in ganz England. **it's all over** es ist aus.

overall ['ouvərɔːl] adj gesamt. adv insgesamt. n also **overalls** pl Overall m, Schutzanzug m.

overbalance [ouvə'baləns] v umkippen.

overbearing [ouvə'beəriŋ] adj anmaßend, arrogant.

overboard ['ouvəbɔːd] adv über Bord.

overcast [ouvə'kaːst] adj bedeckt, bewölkt.

overcharge [ouvə'tʃaːdʒ] v zuviel verlangen von.

overcoat ['ouvəkout] n Mantel m.

***overcome** [ouvə'kʌm] v überwinden. adj (with emotion) tief bewegt.

overcrowded [ouvə'kraudid] adj überfüllt.

***overdo** [ouvə'duː] v übertreiben. **overdo it** zu weit gehen. **overdone** adj (cookery) übergar.

overdose ['ouvədous] n Überdosis f.

***overdraw** [ouvə'drɔː] v überziehen. **overdraft** n (Konto)Überziehung f.

overdrive ['ouvədraɪv] n Schongang m.

overdue [ouvə'djuː] adj überfällig; (train) verspätet.

overestimate [ouvə'estimeit] v überschätzen.

overexpose [ouvəik'spouz] v (phot) überbelichten.

overfill [ouvə'fil] v überfüllen.

overflow [ouvə'flou; n 'ouvəflou] v überlaufen. n Überlauf m.

overgrown [ouvə'groun] adj überwachsen.

***overhang** [ouvə'haŋ; n 'ouvəhaŋ] v überhängen. n Überhang m.

overhaul [ouvə'hɔːl] v überholen. n Überholung f.

overhead [ouvə'hed] adj obenliegend. **overheads** pl n allgemeine Unkosten pl.

***overhear** [ouvə'hiə] v (zufällig) hören.

overheat [ouvə'hiːt] v überheizen; (mot) heißlaufen.

overjoyed [ouvə'dʒɔid] adj entzückt, außer sich vor Freude.

overland [ouvə'land] adj Überland-.

overlap [ouvə'lap; n 'ouvəlap] v sich überschneiden (mit). n Überscheiden neut, Übergreifen neut.

***overlay** [ouvə'lei; n 'ouvəlei] v bedecken, belegen. n Auflage f, Bedeckung f.

overleaf [ouvə'liːf] adv umseitig, umstehend.

overload [ouvə'loud; n 'ouvəloud] v überbelasten. n Überbelastung f.

overlook [ouvə'luk] v (room, etc.) überblicken; (let pass) nicht beachten.

overnight [ouvə'nait] adv über Nacht. **stay overnight** übernachten. adj Nacht-. **overnight case** Handkoffer m.

overpower [ouvə'pauə] v überwältigen.

overrate [ouvə'reit] v überschätzen.

overrule [ouvə'ruːl] v zurückweisen; (person) überstimmen.

*****overrun** [ouvə'rʌn] v überschwemmen, überlaufen.

overseas [ouvə'siːz] adv in Übersee. adj überseeisch, Übersee-.

overseer [ouvə'siə] n Vorarbeiter m.

overshadow [ouvə'ʃadou] v überschatten.

*****overshoot** [ouvə'ʃuːt] v hinausschießen über.

oversight [ouvəsait] n Versehen neut.

*****oversleep** [ouvə'sliːp] v sich verschlafen.

overspill ['ouvəspil] n Überschuß m.

overt [ou'vəːt] adj offenkundig.

*****overtake** [ouvə'teik] v überholen.

*****overthrow** [ouvə'θrou; n 'ouvəθrou] v (um)stürzen. n Umsturz m.

overtime ['ouvətaim] n Überstunden pl. work overtime Überstunden machen.

overtone ['ouvətoun] n Nuance f.

overture ['ouvətjuə] n (music) Ouvertüre f.

overturn [ouvə'təːn] v umkippen.

overweight [ouvə'weit] adj (zu) dick, fettleibig.

overwhelm [ouvə'welm] v überwältigen. overwhelming adj überwältigend.

overwork [ouvə'wəːk] v (sich) überanstrengen.

overwrought [ouvə'rɔːt] adj nervös, überreizt.

ovulate ['ovjuleit] v ovulieren. ovulation n Ovulation f. ovum n Ei neut, Eizelle f.

owe [ou] v schulden; (have debts) Schulden haben. owing adj zu zahlen. owing to infolge or wegen (+gen).

owl [aul] n Eule f.

own [oun] adj eigen. v besitzen; (admit) zugeben. own up gestehen. owner n Inhaber(in). ownership n Besitz m.

ox [oks] n (pl oxen) Ochse m, Rind neut. oxtail Ochsenschwanz m.

oxygen ['oksidʒən] n Sauerstoff m.

oyster ['oistə] n Auster f.

P

pace [peis] n (step) Schritt m; (speed)

Geschwindigkeit f. Tempo neut. v schreiten. keep pace with Schritt halten mit. pacemaker n Schrittmacher m.

Pacific [pə'sifik] n Pazifik m.

pacify ['pasifai] v befrieden. pacifier n (for baby) Schnuller m. pacifism n Pazifismus m. pacifist n Pazifist(in).

pack [pak] n Pack m, Packung f; (cards) Spiel neut; (dogs) Meute f. v einpacken; (stuff) vollstopfen. package n Paket neut. packaging n Verpackung f. packet n Packung f, Päckchen neut. packhorse n Lastpferd neut.

pact [pakt] n Pakt m, Vertrag m.

pad¹ [pad] n Polster neut; (paper) Block m; (sport) Schützer m; (ink) Stempelkissen neut. padding n Polsterung f.

pad² [pad] v trotten.

paddle¹ ['padl] n Paddel neut. v paddeln. paddle-steamer n Raddampfer m.

paddle² ['padl] v (wade) planschen, herumpaddeln.

paddock ['padək] n Pferdekoppel f; (on racecourse) Sattelplatz m.

paddyfield ['padifiːld] n Reisfeld neut.

padlock ['padlok] n Vorhängeschloß neut. v (mit einem Vorhängeschloß) verschließen.

paediatric [piːdi'atrik] adj pädiatrisch. paediatrician n Kinderarzt m, Kinderärztin f. paediatrics n Kinderheilkunde f.

pagan ['peigən] adj heidnisch. n Heide m, Heidin f.

page¹ [peidʒ] n (book) Seite f.

page² [peidʒ] n (boy) Page m.

pageant ['padʒənt] n Festzug m. pageantry n Prunk m.

paid [peid] V pay.

pail [peil] n Eimer m.

pain [pein] n Schmerz m, Schmerzen pl; (suffering) Leid neut. v peinigen. take pains sich Mühe geben. on pain of bei Strafe von. painful adj schmerzhaft. painkiller n schmerzstillendes Mittel neut. painless adj schmerzlos. painstaking adj sorgfältig.

paint [peint] n Farbe f, Lack m. v anstreichen; (pictures) malen. paintbrush n Pinsel m. painted adj bemalt. painter n Maler(in). painting n Gemälde neut.

pair [peə] n Paar neut; (animals) Pärchen neut; (married couple) Ehepaar neut. v pair off paarweise anordnen. a pair of trousers eine Hose.

pal [pal] n (coll) Kamerad m, Kumpel m.

palace ['pæləs] n Palast m.

palate ['pælit] n (Vorder)Gaumen m; (taste) Geschmack m. **palatable** adj schmackhaft.

pale [peil] adj blaß, bleich. v blaßwerden. **pale ale** helles Bier neut. **paleness** n Blässe f.

palette ['pælit] n Palette f.

pall[1] [poil] v (become boring) jeden Reiz verlieren.

pall[2] [poil] n (for coffin) Leichentuch neut; (fig) Hülle f. **pall-bearer** n Sargträger m.

palm[1] [paim] n (of hand) Handfläche f. **palmist** n Handwahrsager(in). **palmistry** n Handlesekunst f.

palm[2] [paim] n (tree) Palme f.

palpitate ['pælpiteit] v (heart) unregelmäßigschlagen; (tremble) beben, zittern.

pamper ['pæmpə] v verwöhnen.

pamphlet ['pæmflit] n Broschüre f.

pan [pæn] n Pfanne f.

pancreas ['pæŋkriəs] n Bauchspeicheldrüse f.

panda ['pændə] n Panda m.

pander ['pændə] v nachgeben (+ dat).

pane [pein] n (Fenster)Scheibe f.

panel ['pænl] n Tafel f; (door) Füllung f; (dress) Einsatzstück m; (instrument) Armaturenbrett neut. v täfeln. **panelling** n Täfelung f.

pang [pæŋ] n (of remorse) Gewissensbisse pl.

panic [pænik] n Panik f. v hinreißen (zu). **panic-stricken** adj von panischer Angst erfüllt. **panicky** adj überängstlich.

pannier ['pæniə] n (Trag)Korb m; (motorcycle) Satteltasche f.

panorama [,pænə'rɑimə] n Panorama neut. Rundblick m. **panoramic** adj panoramisch.

pansy ['pænzi] n Stiefmütterchen neut.

pant [pænt] v keuchen, schnaufen.

panther ['pænθə] n Panther m.

panties ['pæntiz] pl n (coll) Schlüpfer m sing, Höschen neut sing.

pantomime ['pæntəmaim] n Pantomime f.

pantry ['pæntri] n Speiseschrank m.

pants [pænts] pl n (trousers) Hose f sing; (underpants) Unterhose f sing. **pantyhose** Strumpfhose f.

papal ['peipl] adj päpstlich.

paper ['peipə] n Papier neut; (newspaper) Zeitung f; (scientific) Abhandlung f. v (a room) tapezieren. **paperback** n Taschenbuch neut. **paper bag** Tüte f. **paperclip** n Büroklammer f. **paper-thin** adj hauchdünn. **paperweight** n Briefbeschwerer m. **paperwork** n Büroarbeit f.

paprika ['pæprikə] n Paprika m.

par [pai] n Nennwert m, (golf) Par neut. **on a par with** gleich (+ dat).

parable ['pærəbl] n Parabel f.

parachute ['pærəʃuit] n Fallschirm m. v mit dem Fallschirm abspringen.

parade [pə'reid] n Parade f. v (march past) vorbeimarschieren. **parade ground** Paradeplatz m.

paradise ['pærədais] n Paradies neut.

paradox ['pærədoks] n Paradox neut. **paradoxical** adj paradox.

paraffin ['pærəfin] n Paraffin neut.

paragraph ['pærəgraif] n Absatz m.

parallel ['pærəlel] n Parallele f. adj parallel. v entsprechen (+ dat).

paralyse ['pærəlaiz] v paralysieren. **paralysed** adj gelähmt. **paralysis** n (pl -ses) Lähmung f, Paralyse f. **paralytic** adj paralytisch; (coll) besoffen.

paramilitary [,pærə'militəri] adj paramilitärisch.

paramount ['pærəmaunt] adj äußerst wichtig, überragend.

paranoia [,pærə'nɔiə] n Paranoia f. **paranoid** adj paranoid.

parapet ['pærəpit] n Brüstung f.

paraphernalia [,pærəfə'neiliə] n Zubehör neut.

paraphrase ['pærəfreiz] n Umschreibung f, Paraphrase f. v umschreiben.

paraplegia [pærə'pliidʒə] n Paraplegie f. **paraplegic** adj paraplegisch.

parasite ['pærəsait] n Parasit m, Schmarotzer m. **parasitic** adj parasitisch.

parasol ['pærəsol] n Sonnenschirm m.

paratrooper ['pærə,truipə] n Fallschirmjäger m.

parcel ['paisl] n Paket neut, Päckchen neut; (of land) Parzelle f. **parcel post** Paketpost f. **parcels office** Gepäckabfertigung f. v **parcel out** austeilen.

parch [paitʃ] v dörren. **parched** adj ausgetrocknet; (coll) sehr durstig.

parchment ['paitʃmənt] n Pergament neut.

pardon ['paidn] n Verzeihung f. v verzeihen (+ dat); (law) begnadigen. **I beg your pardon** or **pardon me** Verzeihung! **pardonable** adj verzeihlich.

pare [peə] v schälen; (prices, costs, etc.) herabsetzen, beschneiden.

parent ['peərənt] n Vater m, Mutter f. **parents** pl Eltern pl. **parentage** n Abkunft f. **parental** adj elterlich.

parenthesis [pə'renθəsis] n (pl -ses) Parenthese f.

parish ['pariʃ] n (Kirchen)gemeinde f. adj Gemeinde-.

parity ['pariti] n Parität f.

park [paɪk] n Park m. v (mot) parken. **car park** Parkplatz m. **no parking** Parken verboten. **parking place** or **lot** Parkplatz m. **parking light** Standlicht neut. **parking meter** Parkuhr f.

parliament ['paɪləmənt] n Parlament neut. **member of parliament** Abgeordnete(r), Parlamentarier m. **parliamentary** adj parlamentarisch, Parlaments-.

parlour ['paɪlə] n Wohnzimmer neut. **Ice-cream parlour** Eisdiele f.

parochial [pə'roukiəl] adj Gemeinde-; (fig) engstirnig.

parody ['parədi] n Parodie f. v parodieren.

parole [pə'roul] n Bewährung f. **release on parole** auf Bewährung entlassen.

paroxysm ['parəksizəm] n Anfall m.

parrot ['parət] n Papagei m.

parsley ['paɪsli] n Petersilie f.

parsnip ['paɪsnip] n Pastinake f.

parson ['paɪsn] n Pfarrer m. **parsonage** n Pfarrhaus neut.

part [paɪt] n Teil m; (theatre) Rolle f. adj Teil-. v trennen; (people) sich trennen; (hair) scheiteln. **for my part** meinerseits. **in part** teilweise. **take part (in)** teilnehmen (an).

*partake [parteik] v partake of (eat) zu sich nehmen.

partial ['paɪʃəl] adj Teil-; (biased) eingenommen. **be partial to** (coll) eine Vorliebe haben für. **partially** adv teilweise.

participate [pa'tisipeit] v teilnehmen (an). **participant** n Teilnehmer(in). **participation** n Teilnahme f.

participle ['paɪtisipl] n Partizip neut.

particle ['paɪtikl] n Teilchen neut.

particular [pə'tikjulə] adj besonder, speziell; (fussy) wählerisch. **particulars** pl n Einzelheiten pl. **particularly** adv besonders.

parting ['paɪtiŋ] n Abschied neut; (hair) Scheitel m.

partisan [paɪti'zan] n Anhänger m.

partition [paɪ'tiʃən] n Aufteilung f, Trennung f; (wall, etc.) Scheidewand f.

partly ['paɪtli] adv zum Teil, teils.

partner ['paɪtnə] n Partner(in). **partnership** n Partnerschaft f.

partridge ['paɪtridʒ] n Rebhuhn neut.

party ['paɪti] n (pol, law) Partei f; (social gathering) Party f. **be a party to** beteiligt sein an.

pass [paɪs] v (go past) vorbeigehen(an); (go beyond) überschreiten, übertreffen; (exam) bestehen; (of time) vergehen; (time) vertreiben; (hand) überreichen; (approve) billigen; (sport) zuspielen. n (travel document) Zeitkarte f. **pass away** sterben. **pass off** (as) ausgeben (als). **pass out** (coll) ohnmächtig werden. **pass up** verzichten auf.

passage ['pasidʒ] n Durchfahrt f, Reise f; (in book) Stelle f, (corridor) Gang m; (of time) Verlauf m.

passenger ['pasindʒə] n Fahrgast m, Reisende(r); (aeroplane) Fluggast m.

passion ['paʃən] n Leidenschaft f; (anger) Zorn m; (rel) Passion f. **passionate** adj leidenschaftlich.

passive ['pasiv] adj passiv. **passivity** n Passivität f.

Passover ['paɪsouvə] n Passahfest neut.

passport ['paɪspoɪt] n (Reise)Paß m.

password ['paɪswəɪd] n Kennwort neut.

past [paɪst] n Vergangenheit f. adj vergangen. prep nach, über; (in front of) an ... vorbei. **ten past six** zehn (Minuten) nach sechs. **half past six** halb sieben. **in the past** früher.

pasta ['pastə] n Teigwaren pl.

paste [peist] n Paste f; (glue) Klebstoff m. v kleben.

pastel ['pastəl] adj pastel **colour** Pastellfarbe f.

pasteurize ['pastʃəraiz] v pasteurisieren.

pastime ['paɪstaim] n Zeitvertreib m.

pastor ['paɪstə] n Pfarrer m, Pastor m. **pastoral** adj (poetry) Hirten-; (rel) pastoral.

pastry ['peistri] n Teig m; (cake) Tortengebäck neut.

pasture ['paɪstʃə] n Weide f, Grasland neut.

pasty¹ ['peisti] adj teigig; (complexion) bleich.

pasty² ['pasti] n Pastete f.

pat [pat] n (leichter) Schlag m. v klopfen, patschen. **pat on the back** (v) beglückwünschen.

patch [patʃ] n Flicken m, Lappen m; (on eye) Augenbinde f. v flicken. **patchwork** n Flickwerk neut. **patchy** adj ungleichmäßig.

pâté ['patei] n Pastete f.

patent ['peitənt] n Patent neut. adj patentiert, Patent-; (obvious) offenkundig. v patentieren.

paternal [pə'tərnl] adj väterlich. **paternal grandfather** Großvater väterlicherseits. **paternity** n Vaterschaft f.

path [paːθ] n Weg m, Pfad m. **pathway** n Weg m, Bahn f.

pathetic [pə'θetik] adj (moving) rührend; (pitiable) kläglich.

pathology [pə'θolədʒi] n Pathologie f. **pathological** adj pathologisch. **pathologist** n Pathologe m, Pathologin f.

patience ['peiʃəns] n Geduld f. **patient** adj geduldig, duldsam. n Patient(in).

patio ['patiou] n Patio m.

patriarchal ['peitriɑːkəl] adj patriarchalisch.

patriot ['patriət] n Patriot(in). **patriotic** adj patriotisch. **patriotism** n Patriotismus m.

patrol [pə'troul] n Patrouille f. v durchstreifen. **patrol car** Streifenwagen m. **patrolman** n Streifenpolizist m.

patron ['peitrən] n Patron m, Gönner m. **patronage** n Gönnerschaft f. **patronize** v (theatre, restaurant) besuchen; (person) gönnerhaft behandeln. **patronizing** adj gönnerhaft.

patter[1] ['patə] n (rain) Prasseln neut. v prasseln.

patter[2] ['patə] n (speech) Geplapper neut, Rotwelsch neut. v plappern.

pattern ['patən] n Muster neut.

paunch [pointʃ] n Wanst m. **paunchy** adj dickbäuchig.

pauper ['poːpə] n Arme(r).

pause [poːz] n Pause f. v anhalten, zögern.

pave [peiv] v pflastern. **pave the way** den Weg bahnen. **pavement** n Bürgersteig m.

pavilion [pə'viljən] n Pavillon m.

paw [poː] n Pfote f, Tatze f. v (ground) stampfen auf.

pawn[1] [poin] n (chess) Bauer m.

pawn[2] [poin] v verpfänden. **pawnbroker** n Pfandleiher m.

pay [pei] n Lohn m, Gehalt neut. v zahlen; (bill) bezahlen; (be worthwhile) sich lohnen; (visit, compliment) machen. **pay attention** achtgeben auf. **pay homage** huldigen (+ dat). **pay for** bezahlen. **payable** adj fällig. **payday** n Zahltag m. **paying guest** zahlender Gast m. **payload** n Nutzlast f. **payment** n (Be)Zahlung f; (cheque) Einlösung f.

pea [piː] n Erbse f.

peace [piːs] n Frieden m; (quiet) Ruhe f. **make one's peace with** sich aussöhnen mit. **leave in peace** in Ruhe lassen. **peace of mind** Seelenruhe f. **peace treaty** Friedensvertrag m. **peaceable** adj friedlich. **peaceful** adj ruhig.

peach [piːtʃ] n Pfirsich m.

peacock ['piːkok] n Pfau m.

peak [piːk] n Spitze f, Gipfel m. adj Höchst-, Spitzen-. **peaked** adj spitz.

peal [piːl] v (bells) läuten. n Geläute neut. **peal of thunder** Donnerschlag m.

peanut ['piːnʌt] n Erdnuß f.

pear [peə] n Birne f. **pear-shaped** adj birnenförmig.

pearl [pəːl] n Perle f. adj Perlen-.

peasant ['peznt] n Bauer m. adj bäuerlich.

peat [piːt] n Torf m.

pebble ['pebl] n Kieselstein m.

peck [pek] v picken, hacken. n Picken neut; (kiss) (flüchtiger) Kuß m. **peckish** adj (coll) hungrig.

peculiar [pi'kjuːljə] adj (strange) seltsam. **peculiar to** eigentümlich (+ dat). **peculiarity** n Eigentümlichkeit f.

pedal ['pedl] n Pedal neut, Fußhebel m. v (a bicycle) fahren.

pedantic [pi'dantik] adj pedantisch.

peddle ['pedl] v hausieren. **peddler** n Hausierer m.

pedestal ['pedistl] n Sockel m. **put on a pedestal** vergöttern.

pedestrian [pi'destriən] n Fußgänger(in). adj Fußgänger-; (humdrum) langweilig, banal. **pedestrian crossing** Fußgängerüberweg m. **pedestrian precinct** Fußgängerzone f.

pedigree ['pedigriː] n Stammbaum m.

pedlar ['pedlə] n Hausierer m.

peel [piːl] n Schale f. v schälen. **peeler** n Schäler m.

peep [piːp] v gucken, verstohlen blicken. n verstohlener Blick m. **peephole** n Guckloch neut.

peer[1] [piə] v (look) spähen, gucken.

peer[2] [piə] n (equal) Ebenbürtige(r); (noble) Peer m. **peerage** n Peerwürde f. **peerless** adj unvergleichlich.

peevish ['piːviʃ] adj verdrießlich.

peg [peg] n Pflock m; (coathook) Haken m; (clothes) Klammer f. v anpflöcken; (prices) festlegen. **off the peg** von der Stange.

pejorative [pə'dʒɒrətiv] adj herabsetzend.

pelican ['pelikən] n Pelikan m.

pellet ['pelit] n Kügelchen neut; (shot) Schrotkorn neut.

pelmet ['pelmit] n Falbel f.

pelt[1] [pelt] v (throw) bewerfen.

pelt[2] [pelt] n (skin) Fell neut, Pelz m.

pelvis ['pelvis] n (anat) Becken neut.

pen[1] [pen] n (writing) (Schreib)Feder f, Federhalter m.

pen[2] [pen] n (animals) Pferch m, Hürde f. v einpferchen.

penal ['piːnl] adj Straf-. **penalize** v bestrafen. **penalty** n (gesetzliche) Strafe f. **penalty kick** Elfmeterstoß m.

penance ['penəns] n Buße f.

pencil ['pensl] n Bleistift m. v (in a date) vorläufig festsetzen. **pencil-sharpener** n Bleistiftspitzer m.

pendant ['pendənt] n Anhänger m.

pending ['pendiŋ] adj (noch) unentschieden. prep bis.

pendulum ['pendjuləm] n Pendel neut.

penetrate ['penitreit] v durchdringen, eindringen (in). **penetrating** adj durchdringend. **penetration** n Durchdringen neut.

penguin ['peŋgwin] n Pinguin m.

penicillin [peni'silin] n Penizillin neut.

peninsula [pə'ninsjulə] n Halbinsel f. **peninsular** adj Halbinsel-.

penis ['piːnis] n Penis m.

penitent ['penitənt] adj bußfertig. n Büßer(in). **penitence** n Buße f.

penknife ['nennaif] n Taschenmesser neut.

pen-name n Pseudonym neut.

pennant ['penənt] n Wimpel m.

penny ['peni] n Penny m, Pfennig m. **penniless** adj mittellos.

pension ['penʃən] n Rente f. **pensioner** n Rentner(in).

pensive ['pensiv] adj gedankenvoll.

pent [pent] adj **pent up** (feelings) angestaut, zurückgehalten.

pentagon ['pentəgən] n Fünfeck neut.

Pentagon (US) Pentagon neut. **pentagonal** adj fünfeckig.

penthouse ['penthaus] n Dachwohnung f.

penultimate [pi'nʌltimit] adj vorletzt.

people ['piːpl] pl n Leute pl, Menschen pl; sing (nation) Volk neut.

pepper ['pepə] n Pfeffer m. **peppercorn** n Pfefferkorn neut. **peppermint** n Pfefferminze f. **peppery** adj pfefferig, scharf.

per [pə] prep pro. **per capita** pro Kopf.

perceive [pə'siːv] v wahrnehmen; (understand) begreifen. **perceptible** adj spürbar. **perception** n Wahrnehmung f. **perceptive** adj (person) scharfsinnig.

per cent adv, n Prozent neut. **sixty per cent** sechzig Prozent. **percentage** n Prozentsatz m.

perch [pəːtʃ] n Sitzstange f; (fish) Barsch m. v sitzen.

percolate ['pəːkəleit] v durchsickern. **percolator** n Kaffeemaschine f.

percussion [pə'kʌʃən] n (music) Schlaginstrumente pl.

perennial [pə'reniəl] adj beständig; (plant) perennierend. n perennierende Pflanze f.

perfect ['pəːfikt; v pə'fekt] adj vollkommen, vollendet, perfekt. v vervollkommnen. **perfection** n Vollkommenheit f. **perfectionist** n Perfektionist(in). **perfectly** adv (coll) ganz, völlig.

perforate ['pəːfəreit] v perforieren. **perforation** n Perforation f.

perform [pə'fɔːm] n machen, ausführen; (music, play) aufführen, spielen. n (work, output) Leistung f; (music, theatre) Aufführung f. **performer** n Artist(in).

perfume ['pəːfjuːm] n (fragrance) Duft m; (woman's) Parfüm neut. v parfümieren.

perhaps [pə'haps] adv vielleicht.

peril ['peril] n Gefahr f. **perilous** adj gefährlich.

perimeter [pə'rimitə] n Umkreis ; (outer area) Peripherie f.

period ['piəriəd] n Periode f, Frist f; (lesson) Stunde f; (menstrual) Regel f, Periode f; (full stop) Punkt m. **periodic** adj periodisch. **periodical** n Zeitschrift f. **periodically** adv periodisch, von Zeit zu Zeit.

peripheral [pə'rifərəl] adj peripherisch, Rand-. **periphery** n Peripherie f.

periscope ['periskoup] n Periskop neut.

perish ['periʃ] v umkommen, sterben;

(materials) verwelken. **perishable** *adj* leicht verderblich.

perjure [ˈpɜːdʒə] *v* **perjure oneself** meineidig werden. **perjurer** *n* Meineidige(r). **perjury** *n* Meineid *m*.

perk¹ [pɜːk] *v* **perk up** munter werden. **perky** *adj* munter.

perk² [pɜːk] *n (coll: of job)* Vorteil *m*, Vergünstigung *f*.

perm [pɜːm] *n* Dauerwelle *f*.

permanent [ˈpɜːmənənt] *adj* dauernd, ständig, permanent. **permanence** *n* Permanenz *f*, Ständigkeit *f*.

permeate [ˈpɜːmieit] *v* durchdringen. **permeable** *adj* durchlässig.

permit [pəˈmit; *n* ˈpɜːmit] *v* erlauben, gestatten; *(officially)* zulassen, genehmigen. *n* Genehmigung *f*; *(certificate)* Zulassungsschein *m*. **permissible** *adj* zulässig. **permission** *n* Erlaubnis *f*, Genehmigung *f*. **permissive** *adj* freizügig.

permutation [ˌpɜːmjuˈteiʃən] *n* Permutation *f*.

pernicious [pəˈniʃəs] *adj* bösartig.

perpendicular [ˌpɜːpənˈdikjulə] *adj* senkrecht. *n* Senkrechte *f*.

perpetrate [ˈpɜːpitreit] *v* begehen. **perpetration** *n* Begehung *f*. **perpetrator** *n* Täter *m*.

perpetual [pəˈpetʃuəl] *adj* beständig, ewig. **perpetuate** [pəˈpetʃueit] *v* verewigen, fortsetzen.

perplex [pəˈpleks] *v* verwirren, verblüffen. **perplexed** *adj* perplex, verwirrt.

persecute [ˈpɜːsikjuːt] *v* verfolgen. **persecution** *n* Verfolgung *f*. **persecutor** *n* Verfolger(in).

persevere [ˌpɜːsiˈviə] *v* beharren, nicht aufgeben. **perseverance** *n* Beharrlichkeit *f*. **persevering** *adj* beharrlich.

persist [pəˈsist] *v (person)* beharren (bei); *(thing)* fortdauern. **persistence** *n* Beharren *n*, Hartnäckigkeit *f*. **persistent** *adj (person)* hartnäckig; *(questions, etc.)* anhaltend.

person [ˈpɜːsn] *n* Person *f*. **personal** *adj* persönlich. **personal matter** Privatsache *f*. **personality** *n* Personalität *f*; *(personage)* Persönlichkeit *f*.

personnel [ˌpɜːsəˈnel] *n* Personal *neut*, Belegschaft *f*. **personnel department** Personalabteilung *f*. **personnel manager** Personalchef *m*.

perspective [pəˈspektiv] *n* Perspektive *f*.

perspire [pəˈspaiə] *v* schwitzen, transpirieren. **perspiration** *n* Schweiß *m*.

persuade [pəˈsweid] *v* überreden; *(convince)* überzeugen. **persuasion** *n* Überredung *f*; Überzeugung *f*. **persuasive** *adj* überredend; überzeugend.

pert [pɜːt] *adj* keck.

pertain [pəˈtein] *v* betreffen. **pertaining to** betreffend. **pertinacious** *adj* hartnäckig. **pertinent** *adj* angemessen.

perturb [pəˈtɜːb] *v* beunruhigen.

peruse [pəˈruːz] *v* durchlesen.

pervade [pəˈveid] *v* erfüllen, durchdringen. **pervasive** *adj* durchdringend.

perverse [pəˈvɜːs] *adj* pervers, widernatürlich. **perversion** *n* Perversion *f*, Verdrehung *f*. **perversion of justice** Rechtsbeugung *f*. **pervert** *v* verdrehen. *n* perverser Mensch *m*.

pest [pest] *n* Schädling *m*; *(coll: person)* lästiger Mensch *m*. **pesticide** *n* Pestizid *neut*.

pester [ˈpestə] *v* quälen, plagen.

pet [pet] *n* Haustier *neut*; *(darling)* Schätzchen *neut*. *adj* Lieblings-, *v* liebkosen. **pet name** Kosename *m*.

petal [ˈpetl] *n* Blumenblatt *neut*.

petition [pəˈtiʃən] *n* Bittschrift *f*.

petrify [ˈpetrifai] *v* versteinen. **petrified** *adj (coll)* starr, bestürzt.

petrol [ˈpetrəl] *n* Benzin *neut*. **petrol station** Tankstelle *f*. **petroleum** *n* Erdöl *neut*.

petticoat [ˈpetikout] *n* Unterrock *m*.

petty [ˈpeti] *adj (unimportant)* unbedeutend; *(mean)* kleinlich. **petty cash** Kleinkasse *f*.

petulant [ˈpetjulənt] *adj* verdrießlich.

pew [pjuː] *n* Kirchensitz *m*.

pewter [ˈpjuːtə] *n* Hartzinn *neut*.

phantom [ˈfantəm] *n* Phantom *neut*, Gespenst *neut*. *adj* Schein-.

pharmacy [ˈfaːməsi] *n* Apotheke *f*. **pharmacist** *n* Apotheker(in).

pharynx [ˈfariŋks] *n* Schlundkopf *m*.

phase [feiz] *n (tech)* Phase *f*; *(stage)* Stadium *neut*, Etappe *f*.

pheasant [ˈfeznt] *n* Fasan *m*.

phenomenon [fəˈnomənən] *n (pl -a)* Phänomen *neut*. **phenomenal** *adj* phänomenal.

phial [ˈfaiəl] *n* Ampulle *f*.

philanthropy [fiˈlanθrəpi] *n* Philanthropie *f*. **philanthropic** *adj* philanthropisch, menschenfreundlich. **philanthropist** *n* Philanthrop, Menschenfreund *m*.

philately [fi'lætəli] *n* Briefmarkensammeln *neut.* **philatelist** *n* Briefmarkensammler(in).

philosophy [fi'lɔsəfi] *n* Philosophie *f.* **philosopher** *n* Philosoph *m.* **philosophical** *adj* philosophisch.

phlegm [flem] *n* Schleim *m*, Phlegma *neut.* **phlegmatic** *adj* phlegmatisch.

phobia ['foubiə] *n* Phobie *f.*

phone [foun] *n* (*coll*) Fernsprecher *m*, *v* anrufen. **phone booth** *or* **box** Telefonzelle *f.*

phonetic [fə'netik] *adj* phonetisch. **phonetics** *n* Phonetik *f.*

phoney ['founi] *adj* (*coll*) falsch, fingiert. *n* Schwindler *m.*

phosphate ['fosfeit] *n* Phosphat *neut.*

phosphorescence [fosfə'resəns] *n* Phosphoreszenz *f.* **phosphorescent** *adj* phosphoreszierend.

phosphorus ['fosfərəs] *n* Phosphor *m.*

photo ['foutou] *n* Foto *neut.*

photocopy ['foutou,kɔpi] *n* Fotokopie *f.* *v* fotokopieren.

photogenic [,foutou'dʒenik] *adj* fotogen.

photograph ['foutəɡra:f] *n* Lichtbild *neut*, Foto *neut.* *v* aufnehmen, fotografieren. **photographer** *n* Fotograf *m.* **photographic** *adj* fotografisch. **photography** *n* Fotografie *f.*

phrase [freiz] *n* (*expression*) Ausdruck *m*, Redewendung *f*; (*music*) Phrase *f.* *v* fassen.

physical ['fizikəl] *adj* physisch, körperlich. **physical education** Leibeserziehung *f.*

physician [fi'ziʃən] *n* Arzt *m*, Ärztin *f.*

physics ['fiziks] *n* Physik *f.* **physicist** *n* Physiker *m.*

physiology [,fizi'olədʒi] *n* Physiologie *f.* **physiological** *adj* physiologisch.

physiotherapy [,fiziou'θerəpi] *n* Physiotherapie *f.*

physique [fi'zi:k] *n* Körperbau *m.*

piano [pi'anou] *n* Klavier *neut.* **pianist** *n* Klavierspieler(in).

pick[1] [pik] *v* (*choose*) auswählen, (*fruit*) pflücken; (*lock*) knacken. *n* **pick of the bunch** (*coll*) das Beste (von allen).

pick[2] [pik] *or* **pickaxe** *n* Spitzhacke *f.*

picket ['pikit] *n* Pfahl *m*; (*strike*) Streikposten *m.* *v* (*factory, etc.*) Streikposten aufstellen vor.

pickle ['pikl] *n* Pökel *m.* *v* einpökeln. **pickled** *adj* gepökelt; (*coll: drunk*) blau. **pickles** *pl n* Eingepökeltes *neut sing.*

picnic ['piknik] *n* Picknick *neut.*

pictorial [pik'tɔ:riəl] *adj* Bilder-.

picture ['piktʃə] *n* Bild *neut*; (*painting*) Gemälde *neut*; (*film*) Film *m.* *v* (*imagine*) sich vorstellen. **pictures** *pl* Kino *neut sing.* **picture book** Bilderbuch *neut.* **picture postcard** Ansichtskarte *f.*

picturesque [,piktʃə'resk] *adj* pittoresk.

pidgin ['pidʒən] *n* Mischsprache *f.*

pie [pai] *n* (*meat*) Pastete *f*; (*fruit*) Torte *f.*

piece [pi:s] *n* Stück *neut*; (*part*) Teil *m*; (*paper*) Blatt *neut.* **piece of advice** Ratschlag *m.* **fall to pieces** in Stücke gehen, zerfallen. **go to pieces** zusammenbrechen. *v* **piece together** zusammenstellen. **piecemeal** *adv* stückweise. **piecework** *n* Akkordarbeit *f.*

pier [piə] *n* Pier *m*, Kai *m.*

pierce [piəs] *v* durchbohren, durchstechen. **piercing** *adj* durchdringend.

piety ['paiəti] *n* Frömmigkeit *f.*

pig [pig] *n* Schwein *m.* **pigheaded** *adj* störrisch. **piglet** *n* Schweinchen *neut.* **pigskin** *n* Schweinsleder *neut.* **pigsty** *n* Schweinestall *m.* **pigtail** *n* Zopf *m.*

pigment ['pigmənt] *n* Pigment *neut*, Farbstoff *m.* **pigmentation** *n* Pigmentation *f.*

pike [paik] *n* (*fish*) Hecht *m*; (*weapon*) Pike *f*, Spieß *m.*

pilchard ['piltʃəd] *n* Sardine *f.*

pile[1] [pail] *n* (*heap*) Haufen *m*, Stapel *m.* *v* (an)häufen, stapeln. **pile-up** *n* (*mot*) (Massen)Karambolage *f.*

pile[2] [pail] *n* (*post*) Pfahl *m*, Joch *neut.*

pile[3] [pail] *n* (*of carpet*) Flor *m.*

piles [pailz] *pl n* Hämorrhoiden *pl.*

pilfer ['pilfə] *v* klauen. **pilferage** *n* Diebereı *f.*

pilgrim ['pilgrim] *n* Pilger(in). **pilgrimage** *n* Pilgerfahrt *f*, Wallfahrt *f.*

pill [pil] *n* Pille *f*, Tablette *f.* **the pill** (*contraceptive*) die Pille.

pillage ['pilidʒ] *v* (aus)plündern. *n* Plünderung *f.*

pillar ['pilə] *n* Pfeiler *m*, Säule *f.* **pillarbox** *n* Briefkasten *m.*

pillion ['piljən] *n* Soziussitz *m.* **ride pillion** auf dem Sozius fahren.

pillow ['pilou] *n* Kopfkissen *neut.* **pillow case** *n* Kissenbezug *m.*

pilot ['pailət] *n* Pilot *m.* *v* steuern, lenken. **pilot light** Zündflamme *f.*

pimento [pi'mentou] n Piment m or neut.

pimp [pimp] n Zuhälter m.

pimple ['pimpl] n Pustel f, Pickel m. **pimply** adj pickelig.

pin [pin] n Stecknadel f. v befestigen. **pin down** festnageln. **pincushion** n Nadelkissen neut.

pinafore ['pinəfɔ:] n Schürze f. **pinafore dress** Kleiderrock m.

pincers ['pinsəz] pl n Zange f sing; (crab's) Krebsschere f sing.

pinch [pintʃ] v zwicken, kneifen; (coll) klauen. n Kneifen neut, Zwicken neut; (salt, etc.) Prise f.

pine[1] [pain] n Kiefer f, Pinie f. **pine cone** n Kiefernzapfen m.

pine[2] [pain] v sich sehnen (nach). **pine away** verschmachten.

pineapple ['painæpl] n Ananas f.

ping-pong ['piŋpɔŋ] n (coll) Tischtennis neut.

pinion ['pinjən] n (tech) Ritzel m. v fesseln.

pink [piŋk] adj rosa, blaßrot. n (flower) Nelke f. v (mot) klopfen. **in the pink** kerngesund.

pinnacle ['pinəkl] n Spitzturm m; (fig) Gipfel m.

pinpoint ['pinpoint] v ins Auge fassen, hervorheben.

pint [paint] n Pinte f.

pioneer [ˌpaiə'niə] n Pionier m, Bahnbrecher m. v den Weg bahnen für. **pioneering** adj bahnbrechend.

pious ['paiəs] adj fromm.

pip[1] [pip] n (fruit) (Obst)Kern m.

pip[2] [pip] n (sound) Ton m; (mil) Stern m; (on card) Auge neut; (on dice) Punkt m.

pipe [paip] n Rohr neut, Röhre f; (tobacco, music) Pfeife f; (sound) Pfeifen neut. v (liquid) durch Röhren leiten; (play pipes, etc.) pfeifen; (cookery) spritzen. **pipedream** n Luftschloß neut. **pipeline** n Rohrleitung f.

piquant ['pi:kənt] adj pikant.

pique [pi:k] n Groll m.

pirate ['paiərət] n Seeräuber m. **piracy** n Seeräuberei f.

pirouette [piru'et] n Pirouette f. v pirouettieren.

Pisces ['paisi:z] n Fische pl.

piss [pis] v (vulgar) pissen. n Pisse f.

pistachio [pi'staːʃiou] n Pistazie f.

pistol ['pistl] n Pistole f.

piston ['pistən] n Kolben m.

pit [pit] n Grube f; (mining) Zeche f, Bergwerk neut. **pitted** adj vernarbt; (corroded) zerfressen.

pitch[1] [pitʃ] v werfen; (tent) aufschlagen. n Wurf m; (sport) Feld neut; (music) Tonhöhe f; (level) Grad m. **pitcher** n Werfer m; (jug) Krug m. **pitchfork** n Mistgabel f.

pitch[2] [pitʃ] n (tar) Pech neut.

pitfall ['pitfɔːl] n Fallgrube f, Falle f.

pith [piθ] n Mark neut. **pithy** adj markig.

pittance ['pitəns] n Hungerlohn m.

pituitary [pi'tjuːitəri] n Hirnanhangdrüse f, Hypophyse f.

pity ['piti] n Mitleid neut. v bemitleiden. **it's a pity** es ist schade, es ist ein Jammer m.

pivot ['pivət] n Drehpunkt m. v sich drehen.

placard ['plækaːd] n Plakat neut.

placate [plə'keit] v beschwichtigen.

place [pleis] n Platz m; (town, locality) Ort m; (spot) Stelle f. **go places** (coll) es weit bringen. **out-of-place** adj (remark) unangebracht. **placename** n Ortsname m. **place of interest** Sehenswürdigkeit f. **take place** stattfinden. v stellen, legen, setzen; (identify) identifizieren, erkennen.

placenta [plə'sentə] n Plazenta f.

placid ['plæsid] adj ruhig, gelassen.

plagiarize ['pleidʒəraiz] v plagiieren. **plagiarism** n Plagiat m.

plague [pleig] n Seuche f, Pest f. v plagen, quälen.

plaice [pleis] n Scholle f.

plain [plein] adj einfach, schlicht; (obvious) klar; (not pretty) unansehnlich. adv einfach. n Ebene f. **plainly** adv offensichtlich. **speak plainly** offen reden.

plaintiff ['pleintif] n Kläger(in).

plaintive ['pleintiv] adj traurig, wehmütig.

plait [plæt] n Zopf m, Flechte f. v flechten.

plan [plæn] n Plan m; (drawing) Entwurf m, Zeichnung f. v planen; (intend) vorhaben. **according to plan** planmäßig.

plane[1] [plein] adj flach, eben. n Ebene f; (aeroplane) Flugzeug neut.

plane[2] [plein] n (tool) Hobel m. v (ab)hobeln.

planet ['plænit] n Planet m.

plank [plæŋk] n Planke f, Diele f.

plankton ['plæŋktən] n Plankton neut.

planning ['planiŋ] n Planung f.
plant [plaint] n Pflanze f; (factory) Betrieb m, Fabrik f. v pflanzen. **plantation** n Pflanzung f.
plaque [plaik] n Gedenktafel f.
plasma ['plazmə] n Plasma neut.
plaster ['plaːstə] n (med) Pflaster neut; (of Paris) Gips m. v bepflastern. **adhesive plaster** Heftpflaster neut. **plaster cast** Gipsabdruck m; (med) Gipsverband m.
plastic ['plastik] n Kunststoff m. adj Kunststoff-.
plate [pleit] n (for food) Teller m; (tech) Platte f, Scheibe f. v (metal) plattieren. **gold-plated** adj vergoldet.
plateau ['platou] n Hochebene f, Plateau neut.
platform ['platform] n (rail) Bahnsteig m; (speaker's) Tribüne f; (fig: pol) Parteiprogramm neut.
platinum ['platinəm] n Platin neut.
platonic [plə'tonik] adj platonisch.
platoon [plə'tuːn] n (mil) Zug m.
plausible ['ploːzəbl] adj glaubhaft.
play [plei] n Spiel neut; (theatre) Schauspiel neut, Stück neut; (tech) Spielraum m. v spielen. **play safe** kein Risiko eingehen. **playboy** n Playboy m. **player** n Spieler(in); (actor) Schauspieler(in). **playful** adj scherzhaft. **playground** n Spielplatz m; (school) Schulhof m. **playing card** Spielkarte f. **playing field** Sportplatz m. **playmate** n Spielkamerad(in). **plaything** n Spielzeug neut. **playwright** n Dramatiker m.
plea [pliː] n dringende Bitte f; (law) Plädoyer neut.
plead [pliːd] v (law) plädieren. **plead for** flehen um.
please [pliːz] v gefallen (+dat), Freude machen (+dat). adv bitte! **pleasant** angenehm; (person) freundlich, nett. **pleased** adj zufrieden. **pleasing** adj angenehm. **pleasurable** adj vergnüglich. **pleasure** n Vernügen neut.
pleat [pliːt] n Falte f. v in Falten legen.
plebiscite ['plebisait] n Volksabstimmung f, Plebiszit neut.
pledge [pledʒ] n Pfand neut; (promise) Versprechen neut. v versprechen.
plenty ['plenti] n Fülle f, Reichtum m. **plenty of** eine Menge, viel.
pleurisy ['pluərisi] n Rippenfellentzündung f.

pliable ['plaiəbl] adj biegsam. **pliability** n Biegsamkeit f.
pliers ['plaiəz] pl n Zange f sing.
plight [plait] n Notlage f.
plimsoll ['plimsəl] n Turnschuh m.
plod [plod] v sich hinschleppen, schwerfällig gehen.
plonk¹ [ploŋk] v **plonk down** hinschmeißen.
plonk² [ploŋk] n (coll) billiger Wein.
plot¹ [plot] n Komplott neut; (in novel) Handlung f. v sich verschwören; (on map) einzeichnen. **plotter** n Verschwörer(in).
plot² [plot] n (land) Parzelle f, Grundstück neut.
plough [plau] n Pflug m; (astron) Großer Bär m. v (um)pflügen. **ploughman** n Pflüger m.
pluck [plʌk] v pflücken; (poultry) rupfen; (music) zupfen. n (courage) Mut m. **plucky** adj mutig. **pluck up courage** Mut fassen.
plug [plʌg] n (elec) Stecker m; (stopper) Stöpsel m. v verstopfen; (coll) befürworten. **plug in** anschließen, einstecken.
plum [plʌm] n Pflaume f, Zwetschge f.
plumage ['pluːmidʒ] n Gefieder neut.
plumb [plʌm] n Senkblei neut. adj senkrecht. v (sound) sondieren. **plumber** n Klempner m. **plumbing** n Klempnerarbeit f; (pipes) Rohrleitungen pl f.
plume [pluːm] n Feder f; (of smoke) Streifen m.
plummet ['plʌmit] v abstürzen.
plump¹ [plʌmp] adj (fat) rundlich, mollig. **plumpness** n Rundlichkeit f.
plump² [plʌmp] v (fall) plumpsen. **plump for** sich entscheiden für.
plunder ['plʌndə] v plündern. n (spoils) Beute f.
plunge [plʌndʒ] v tauchen; (fall) stürzen. n Sturz m.
pluperfect [plur'pəfikt] n (gramm) Vorvergangenheit f.
plural ['pluərəl] adj Plural-. n Plural m, Mehrzahl f.
plus [plʌs] prep plus. adj Plus-. n Plus neut.
plush [plʌʃ] adj (fig) luzuriös.
Pluto ['pluːtou] n Pluto m.
ply¹ [plai] v (trade) ausüben; (travel) verkehren.

ply² [plai] n (of yarn) Strähne f. **plywood** n Sperrholz neut.

pneumatic [nju'mætik] adj pneumatisch. **pneumatic tyre** n Luftreifen m. **pneumatic drill** Preßluftbohrer m.

pneumonia [nju'mouniə] n Lungenentzündung f.

poach¹ [poutʃ] v (cookery) pochieren. **poached egg** verlorenes Ei neut.

poach² [poutʃ] v wildern. **poacher** n Wilddieb m.

pocket ['pokit] n Tasche f. adj Taschen-. v in die Tasche stecken, einstecken. **to be in pocket** gut bei Kasse sein. **pocketknife** n Taschenmesser neut. **pocket-money** Taschengeld neut.

pod [pod] n Schote f.

podgy ['podʒi] adj (coll) mollig, dick.

poem ['pouim] n Gedicht neut. **poet** n Dichter m. **poetess** n Dichterin f. **poetic** adj poetisch, dichterisch. **poetry** n Dichtkunst f; (poems) Gedichte f.

poignant ['poinjənt] adj schmerzlich; (wit) scharf; (grief) bitter.

point [point] n (tip) Spitze f; (place, spot) Punkt m; (in time) Zeitpunkt m; (main thing) Hauptsache f. **be on the point of doing** eben tun wollen. **point of view** Standpunkt m. **points** pl n (rail) Weichen pl. **that's the point!** das ist es ja! **there's no point in** es hat keinen Zweck, zu. v spitzen; (indicate) (mit dem Finger) zeigen. **point out** hinweisen auf. **pointed** adj zugespitzt; (remark) treffend, beißend. **pointless** adj sinnlos.

poise [poiz] n Haltung f; (calmness) Gelassenheit f.

poison ['poizən] n Gift neut. v vergiften. **poisoner** n Giftmörder(in). **poisonous** adj giftig.

poke [pouk] n Stoß m, Puff m. v stoßen; (fire) schüren.

poker¹ ['poukə] n (for fire) Feuerhaken m.

poker² ['poukə] n (gambling) Poker(spiel) neut.

Poland ['poulənd] n Polen neut. **Pole** n Pole m, Polin f. **Polish** adj polnisch.

polar ['poulə] adj polar. **polar bear** Eisbär m.

pole¹ [poul] n (geog) Pol m. **pole star** n Polarstern m.

pole² [poul] n Pfosten m, Pfahl m; (telegraph, etc.) Stange f. **pole-vault** n Stabhochsprung m.

police [pə'liːs] n Polizei f. n (polizeilich) überwachen. adj polizeilich, Polizei-. **police force** Polizei f. **policeman** n Polizist m, Schutzmann m. **police station** Polizeiwache f, Polizeirevier neut.

policy¹ ['poləsi] n Politik f; (personal) Methode f.

policy² ['poləsi] n (insurance) Police f.

polio ['pouliou] n Kinderlähmung f.

polish ['poliʃ] n Politur f; (floors, furniture) Bohnerwachs neut; (shoes) Schuhcreme f. v polieren; (furniture) bohnern; (shoes) wichsen. **polished** adj poliert; (fig) fein, elegant. **polisher** n Polierer m.

polite [pə'lait] adj höflich. **politeness** n Höflichkeit f.

politics ['politiks] n Politik f. **political** adj politisch. **politician** n Politiker m.

polka ['polkə] n Polka f.

poll [poul] n (voting) Abstimmung f; (opinion poll) Meinungsumfrage f.

pollen ['polən] n Pollen m, Blütenstaub m. **pollinate** v befruchten.

pollute [pə'luːt] v verschmutzen, verunreinigen. **pollution** n (environmental) Umweltverschmutzung f.

polo ['poulou] n Polo neut. **polo-neck** n Rollkragen m.

polygamy [pə'ligəmi] n Polygamie f. **polygamous** adj polygam.

polygon ['poligən] n Polygon neut.

polytechnic [,poli'teknik] n Polytechnikum neut.

polythene ['poliθiːn] n Polyäthylen neut. adj **polythene bag** Plastiktüte f.

pomegranate ['pomigranit] n Granatapfel m.

pomp [pomp] n Prunk m, Pracht f. **pomposity** n Bombast m. **pompous** adj bombastisch.

pond [pond] n Teich m.

ponder ['pondə] v nachdenken (über). **ponderous** adj schwer; (movement) schwerfällig.

pony ['pouni] n Pony neut, Pferdchen neut. **pony-tail** Pferdeschwanz m.

poodle ['puːdl] n Pudel m.

poof [puf] n (derog) Schwule(r) m.

pool¹ [puːl] n (pond) Teich m; (blood, etc.) Lache f; (swimming) (Schwimm)Bad neut.

pool² [puːl] n (game) Pool m; (fund) Kasse f. v (resources) vereinigen. **football pools** Fußballtoto m.

poor [puə] *adj* arm, bedürftig; *(earth)* dürr; *(bad)* schlecht. **the poor** die Armen *pl.* **poorly** *adj (coll)* krank, unwohl.

pop¹ [pop] *n* Knall *m*, Puff *m*; *(drink)* Limonade *f.* *v* knallen; *(burst)* platzen. **pop in** schnell vorbeikommen. **pop up** *(appear)* auftauchen.

pop² [pop] *adj* pop music Popmusik *f.* **pop song** Schlager *m.*

pope [poup] *n* Papst *m.*

poplar ['poplə] *n* Pappel *f.*

poppy ['popi] *n* Mohn *m.*

popular ['popjulə] *adj* populär; *(well-liked)* beliebt; *(of the people)* Volks-. **popularity** *n* Popularität *f.*

population [.popju'leifən] *n* Bevölkerung *f.* **populate** *v* bevölkern. **populous** *adj* volkreich.

porcelain ['poslin] *n* Porzellan *neut. adj* Porzellan-.

porch [pottʃ] *n* Vorhalle *neut.*

porcupine ['potkjupain] *n* Stachelschwein *neut.*

pore¹ [pot] *n* Pore *f.*

pore² [pot] *v* pore over eifrig studieren, brüten über.

pork [potk] *n* Schweinefleisch *neut.* **pork butcher** Schweineschlächter *m.* **pork chop** Schweinskotelett *neut.* **roast pork** Schweinebraten *m.*

pornography [pot'nogrəfi] *n* Pornographie *f.* **pornographic** *adj* pornographisch; *(film, book)* Porno-.

porous ['potrəs] *adj* porös.

porpoise ['potpəs] *n* Tümmler *m.*

porridge ['poridʒ] *n* Haferflockenbrei *m.* **porridge oats** Haferflocken *pl.*

port¹ [pott] *n (harbour)* Hafen *m*; *(town)* Hafenstadt *f.*

port² [pott] *n (naut)* Backbord *neut. adj* Backbord-.

port³ [pott] *n (wine)* Portwein *m.*

portly ['pottli] *adj* wohlbeleibt.

portable ['pottəbl] *adj* tragbar. **portable radio** Kofferradio *neut.*

portent ['pottent] *n* Omen *neut*, Vorzeichung *f.* **portentous** *adj* ominös.

porter ['pottə] *n (rail, etc.)* Gepäckträger *m.*

portfolio [pott'fouliou] *n* Mappe *f*; *(pol)* Portefeuille *neut.* **minister without portfolio** Minister ohne Geschäftsbereich *m.*

porthole ['potthoul] *n* Luke *f.*

portion ['potʃən] *n (food)* Portion *f*; *(share)* (An)Teil *m.*

portrait ['pottrət] *n* Porträt *neut.* **portray** *v* malen; *(fig)* schildern. **portrayal** *n* Porträt *neut*, Schilderung *f.*

Portugal ['pottjugəl] *n* Portugal *neut.* **Portuguese** *adj* portugiesisch; *n* Portugiese *m*, Portugiesin *f.*

pose [pouz] *n* Pose *f.* *v* sitzen, posieren; *(problem)* stellen. **pose as** sich ausgeben als. **poseur** *n* Poseur *m.*

posh [poʃ] *adj* vornehm.

position [pə'zifən] *n* Position *f*, Stellung *f*; *(situation)* Lage *f*; *(attitude)* Standpunkt *m*; *(standing)* Rang *m.* *v* stellen.

positive ['pozətiv] *adj* positiv.

possess [pə'zes] *v* besitzen. **possessed** *adj* besessen. **possession** *n* Besitz *m.* **take possession of** in Besitz nehmen. **possessive** *adj (person)* besitzgierig. **possessor** *n* Inhaber(in).

possible ['posəbl] *adj* möglich; *(imaginable)* eventuell. **possibility** *n* Möglichkeit *f.* **possibly** *adv* möglicherweise.

post¹ [poust] *n (pole)* Pfahl *m*, Pfosten *m.* **deaf as a post** stocktaub.

post² [poust] *n (mil)* Posten *m*; *(job)* Stelle *f.* *v* aufstellen.

post³ [poust] *n (mail)* Post *f.* **by post** per Post. **postage stamp** Briefmarke *f.* **postcard** *n* Postkarte *f.* **postman** *n* Briefträger *m.* **post office** Postamt *neut.* *v* zur Post bringen; *(send)* (mit der Post) schicken. **keep someone posted** jemanden auf dem laufenden halten. **postage** *n* Porto *neut*, Postgebühr *f.* **postal** *adj* Post-.

poste restante [poust'testãt] *adv* postlagernd.

poster ['poustə] *n* Plakat *neut.*

posterior [po'stiəriə] *adj* später, hinter. *n* Hintern *m.*

posterity [po'steräti] *n* Nachwelt *f.*

postgraduate [poust'gradjuit] *n* Doktorand(in).

post-haste *adv* schnellstens.

posthumous ['postjuməs] *adj* postum.

post-mortem [poust'mottəm] *n* Autopsie *f.*

post-natal [pous'neitl] *adj* postnatal.

postpone [pous'poun] *v* verschieben. **postponement** *n* Verschiebung *f.*

postscript ['pousskript] *n* Postskriptum *neut.*

postulate ['postjuleit] *v* voraussetzen, annehmen.

posture ['postʃə] n (Körper)Haltung f.

post-war adj Nachkriegs-.

pot [pot] n Topf m; (tea, coffee) Kanne f. v (coll) schießen. **go to pot** vor die Hunde gehen. **pot-bellied** adj dickbauchig.

potassium [pə'tasjəm] n Kalium neut.

potato [pə'teitou] n Kartoffel f. **boiled potatoes** Salzkartoffeln pl. **chipped or french-fried potatoes** Pommes frites pl. **roast or fried potatoes** Bratkartoffeln pl.

potent ['poutənt] adj stark; (sexually) potent. **potency** n Stärke f; Potenz f.

potential [pə'tenʃəl] adj möglich, potential. n Potential neut.

pothole ['pothoul] n Höhle f.

potion ['pouʃən] n Arzneitrank m. **love potion** Liebestrank m.

potluck [pot'lʌk] n **take potluck with** (coll) probieren, es riskieren mit/bei.

potted ['potid] adj (meat) eingemacht; (plant) Topf-; (version) gekürzt.

potter ['potə] v **potter around** herumhantieren, herumbasteln.

pottery ['potəri] n Töpferwaren pl, Steingut neut.

potty ['poti] n Töpfchen neut.

pouch [pautʃ] n Beutel m.

poultice ['poultis] n Breiumschlag m.

poultry ['poultri] n Geflügel neut.

pounce [pauns] v springen, sich stürzen. n Sprung m, Satz m.

pound¹ [paund] v zerstampfen; (hit) hämmern, klopfen.

pound² [paund] n (currency, weight) Pfund neut.

pour [poː] v gießen. **pour out** (a liquid) ausgießen; (drink) einschenken; (come out) herausströmen.

pout [paut] v schmollen, maulen.

poverty ['povəti] n Armut f. **poverty-stricken** adj verarmt.

powder ['paudə] n Pulver neut; (face) Puder m. v (face) pudern. **powder room** Damentoilette f. **powdery** adj pulverig.

power ['pauə] n Macht f; (tech) Kraft f; (elec) Strom m. v betreiben, antreiben. **great power** (pol) Großmacht f. **powerful** adj mächtig. **powerless** adj machtlos. **power station** Kraftwerk neut.

practicable ['praktikəbl] adj durchführbar.

practical ['praktikəl] adj praktisch.

practice ['praktis] n Praxis f; (exercise) Übung f; (custom) Brauch m; (procedure) Verfahren neut. v see **practise**.

practise ['praktis] v üben; (profession) ausüben; (med, law) praktizieren. **practised** adj geübt.

practitioner [prak'tiʃənə] n Praktiker m. **medical practitioner** praktischer Arzt m.

pragmatic [prag'matik] adj pragmatisch. **pragmatism** n Pragmatismus m. **pragmatist** n Pragmatiker m.

Prague [prag] n Prag neut.

prairie ['preəri] n Prärie f.

praise [preiz] v loben. n Lob neut. **praiseworthy** adj lobenswert.

pram [pram] n Kinderwagen m.

prance [prams] v tänzeln.

prank [praŋk] n Streich m, Possen m.

prattle ['pratl] v plappern, schwatzen. n Geplapper neut, Geschwätz neut.

prawn [proːn] n Garnele f.

pray [prei] v beten; (ask) bitten. **prayer** n Gebet neut. **prayerbook** Gebetbuch neut.

preach [priːtʃ] v predigen. **preacher** n Prediger(in). **preaching** n Lehre f.

precarious [pri'keəriəs] adj unsicher, gefährlich.

precaution [pri'kotʃən] n Vorkehrung f. **precautionary** adj vorbeugend.

precede [pri'siːd] v vorhergehen. **precedence** n Vorrang m. **precedent** n Präzedenzfall m. **order of precedence** Rangordnung f. **preceding** adj vorhergehend.

precinct ['priːsiŋkt] n Bezirk m. **precincts** pl Umgebung f.

precious ['preʃəs] adj kostbar, wertvoll; (jewels) edel. adv (coll) äußerst.

precipice ['presipis] n Abgrund m.

precipitate [pri'sipiteit] v (bring about) herbeiführen; (chem) fällen. **precipitation** n (haste) Hast f; (chem) Fällung f; (rain, etc.) Niederschlag m.

précis [preisi] n Zusammenfassung f. v zusammenfassen.

precise [pri'sais] adj präzis, genau. **precisely** adv genau. **precision** n Genauigkeit f; (tech) Präzision f.

preclude [pri'kluːd] v ausschließen; (prevent) vorbeugen.

precocious [pri'kouʃəs] adj frühreif. **precociousness** n Frühreife f.

preconceive [.priːkən'siːv] v vorher ausdenken. **preconception** n Vorurteil neut.

precondition [.priːkən'diʃən] n Voraussetzung f.

precursor [priˈkɔːsə] n Vorläufer(in).
precursory adj vorausgehend.

predatory [ˈpredətəri] adj räuberisch.
predator n Raubtier neut.

predecessor [ˈpriːdisesə] n Vorgänger(in).

predestine [priˈdestin] v prädestinieren.
predestination n Vorbestimmung f.
Prädestination f.

predicament [priˈdikəmənt] n schwierige
Lage f.

predicate [ˈpredikət] n (gramm) Prädikat
neut. v aussagen.

predict [priˈdikt] v voraussagen. **predict-
able** adj voraussagbar. **prediction** n
Voraussage f.

predominate [priˈdomineit] v vorwiegen.
predominance n Vorherrschaft f. **predominant** adj vorwiegend.

pre-eminent [priˈeminənt] adj hervorragend. **pre-eminence** n Überlegenheit f.

preen [priːn] v (sich) putzen.

prefabricate [priˈfabrikeit] v vorfabrizier-
en. **prefabricated** adj Fertig-.

preface [ˈprefis] n Vorwort neut. v
einleiten.

prefect [ˈpriːfekt] n (pol) Präfekt m;
(school) Aufsichtsschüler(in).

prefer [priˈfəː] v vorziehen, lieber haben.
preferable adj vorzuziehen. **preferably**
adv am besten. **preference** n Vorzug m.
preferential adj bevorzugt.

prefix [ˈpriːfiks] n Präfix neut, Vorsilbe f.

pregnant [ˈpregnənt] adj schwanger; (animals) trächtig; (fig) bedeutend, viel-
sagend. **pregnancy** n Schwangerschaft f.

prehistoric [ˌpriːhiˈstorik] adj vorgeschich-
tlich. **prehistory** n Vorgeschichte f.

prejudice [ˈpredʒədis] n Vorurteil neut. v
beeinträchtigen; (person) beeinflussen.
prejudiced adj voreingenommen. **prejudi-
cial** adj nachteilig, schädlich.

preliminary [priˈliminəri] adj vorläufig,
Vor-.

prelude [ˈpreljuːd] n Vorspiel neut,
Präludium neut.

premarital [priˈmaritl] adj vorehelich.

premature [ˈpreməˈtʃuə] adj frühzeitig.
premature birth Frühgeburt f. **prematuri-
ty** n Frühzeitigkeit f.

premeditate [priˈmediteit] v vorher
überlegen. **premeditated** adj (crime) vorsätzlich. **premeditation** n Vorbedacht m.

premier [ˈpremiə] adj erst. n
Premierminister m.

premiere [ˈpremiə] n Erstaufführung f,
Premiere f.

premise [ˈpremis] n Voraussetzung f,
Prämisse f.

premises [ˈpremisis] pl n Gelände neut
sing. **business premises** Büro neut, Ges-
chäftsräume pl. **on the premises** im
Hause.

premium [ˈpriːmiəm] n Prämie f.

premonition [ˌpreməˈniʃən] n Vorahnung
f.

prenatal [priˈneitl] adj prenatal, vor der
Geburt.

preoccupied [priˈokjupaid] adj vertieft
(in).

prepare [priˈpeə] v vorbereiten; (food)
zubereiten; (produce) herstellen. **prepare
for** sich vorbereiten auf. **preparation** n
Vorbereitung f; (med) Präparat neut;
(homework) Hausaufgaben pl. **preparato-
ry** adj vorbereitend. **prepared** adj bereit.

preposition [ˌprepəˈziʃən] n Präposition f.

preposterous [priˈpostərəs] adj absurd,
lächerlich.

prerogative [priˈrogativ] n Vorrecht neut.

prescribe [priˈskraib] v vorschreiben,
anordnen; (med) verordnen. **prescription**
n Verordnung f.

present[1] [ˈpreznt] adj (time) gegenwärtig;
(people) anwesend; (things) vorhanden. n
Gegenwart f. **at the present time** im
Moment, zur Zeit. **be present at**
Beiwohnen (+ dat). **presently** adv gleich.
presence n (people) Anwesenheit f,
Beisein neut; (things) Vorhandensein
neut. **presence of mind** Geistesgegenwart
f.

present[2] [ˈpreznt; v priˈzent] n Geschenk
neut. v vorlegen; (gift) schenken; (person)
vorstellen; (play) vorführen. **presentation**
n Vorlegung f; Schenkung f; Übergabe f;
Vorführung f.

preserve [priˈzəːv] v bewahren; (food)
einmachen. n Konserve f.

preside [priˈzaid] v den Vorsitz führen.
preside over (meeting) leiten.

president [ˈprezidənt] n Präsident m;
(comm) Generaldirektor m. **presidency** n
(pol) Präsidentschaft f; (meeting) Vorsitz
m. **presidential** adj Präsidenten-.

press [pres] v drücken; (iron) bügeln. n
Presse f. **press conference** Pressekonfer-
enz f. **press stud** Druckknopf m. **press-up**
n Liegestütz m. **pressing** adj dringend.

pressure ['preʃə] n Druck m. **pressure cooker** Schnellkochtopf m. **pressure gauge** Druckmesser m. **pressure group** Interessengruppe f. **pressurize** (aircraft) auf Normaldruck halten; (person) unter Druck setzen.

prestige [pre'stiːʒ] n Prestige neut. **prestigious** adj Prestige-.

presume [pri'zjuːm] v annehmen; (dare to) sich erlauben. **presumably** adv vermutlich. **presumption** n Vermutung f; (cheek) Unverschämtheit f. **presumptuous** adj unverschämt.

pretend [pri'tend] v vorgeben. **pretend to** so tun, als ob; (claim) Anspruch erheben (auf). **pretence** n Vorwand m, Anschein m. **under false pretences** unter Vorspiegelung falscher Tatsachen. **pretentious** adj anmaßend. **pretentiousness** n Anmaßung f.

pretext ['priːtekst] n Vorwand m, Ausrede f.

pretty ['priti] adj hübsch, niedlich. adv (coll) ziemlich. **prettify** v hübsch machen. **prettiness** n Schönheit f.

prevail [pri'veil] v (win) siegen (über); (be prevalent) vorwiegen, vorherrschen. **prevailing** adj vorherrschend; (opinion) allgemein. **prevalence** n Herrschen neut. **prevalent** adj (vor)herrschend.

prevent [pri'vent] v verhindern, verhüten. **prevention** n Verhütung f. **preventive** adj vorbeugend. **preventive measure** Vorsichtsmaßnahme f.

preview ['priːvjuː] n Vorschau f, Probeaufführung f.

previous ['priːviəs] adj vorhergehend, früher. **previously** adv vorher.

prey [prei] n Opfer neut. v **prey on** erbeuten.

price [prais] n Preis m, Kosten pl. v den Preis festsetzen für; (evaluate) bewerten. **priceless** adj unschätzbar. **price-tag** n Preiszettel m.

prick [prik] n Stich m. v stechen.

prickle ['prikl] n Stachel m, Dorn m. v prickeln, kribbeln. **prickly** adj stachelig; (person) reizbar, übellaunig.

pride [praid] n Stolz m; (arrogance) Hochmut m; (lions) Rudel neut. v **pride oneself on** stolz sein auf.

priest [priːst] n Priester m. **priestess** n Priesterin f. **priesthood** n Priesterschaft f. **priestly** adj priesterlich.

prim [prim] adj steif, affektiert. **primness** n Steifheit f.

primary ['praiməri] adj erst, ursprünglich; (main) primär, Haupt-; (basic) grundlegend. **primary school** Grundschule f. **primarily** adv hauptsächlich.

primate ['praimət] n (biol) Primat m.

prime [praim] adj erst; (main) Haupt-; (number) unteilbar; (best) erstklassig. **prime minister** Premierminister(in). n Blüte f. v (gun) laden; (paint) grundieren; (fig) vorbereiten. **primer** n (paint) Grundierfarbe f; (book) Elementarbuch neut. **priming** n Vorbereitung.

primeval [prai'miːvəl] adj urzeitlich.

primitive ['primitiv] adj (early) urzeitlich, Ur-; (crude, unrefined) primitiv. **primitiveness** n Primitivität f.

primrose ['primrouz] n Primel f.

prince [prins] n (ruler) Fürst m; (king's son) Prinz m. **princely** adj fürstlich. **princess** n Fürstin f, Prinzessin f. **principality** n Fürstentum neut.

principal ['prinsəpəl] adj erst, Haupt-. n Vorsteher(in); (comm) Kapital neut. **principally** adv hauptsächlich.

principle ['prinsəpl] n Prinzip neut, Grundsatz m; (basis) Grundlage f. **principled** adj mit hohen Grundsätzen.

print [print] v drucken. **printed matter** Drucksache f. **printer** n Drucker m. **printing** n Druck m. **printing press** Druckerei f. n Druck m; (of photograph) Abzug m, Kopie f.

prior ['praiə] adj früher. adv **prior to** vor. **priority** n Priorität f; (precedence) Vorrang m.

prise [praiz] v **prise open** aufbrechen.

prism ['prizm] n Prisma neut.

prison ['prizn] n Gefängnis neut. **prisoner** n Gefangene(r), Häftling m.

private ['praivət] adj privat; (personal) persönlich. n gemeiner Soldat m. **privacy** n Privatleben neut, Ruhe f.

privet ['privət] n Liguster m.

privilege ['privilidʒ] n Privilegium neut, Sonderrecht neut; (honour) Ehre f. **privileged** adj bevorrechtet. **be privileged to** die Ehre haben, zu.

privy ['privi] n Abort m. adj **be privy to** eingeweiht sein in. **privy council** Geheimer Rat m.

prize [praiz] n Preis m; (lottery) Los neut. adj Preis-. v hochschätzen.

probable ['prɔbəbl] *adj* wahrscheinlich. **probability** *n* Wahrscheinlichkeit *f*.

probation [prə'beiʃən] *n* Probezeit *f*; *(law)* bedingte Freilassung *f*. **probationary** *adj* Probe-.

probe [prəub] *n (tech)* Sonde *f*; *(enquiry)* Untersuchung *f*. *v* **probe into** eindringen in, erforschen.

problem ['prɔbləm] *n* Problem *neut*. **problematical** *adj* problematisch.

proceed [prə'siːd] *v* weitergehen; *(continue)* fortfahren; *(begin)* beginnen. **procedure** *n* Vorgehen *neut*. **proceedings** *pl n (law)* Verfahren *neut sing*. **proceeds** *pl n* Erlös *m sing*, Ertrag *m sing*.

process ['prəuses] *v* bearbeiten, verarbeiten. *n* Verfahren *neut*, Prozeß *m*. **processing** *n* Verarbeitung *f*.

procession [prə'seʃən] *n* Prozession *f*, Zug *m*.

proclaim [prə'kleim] *v* proklamieren, verkünden. **proclamation** *n* Proklamation *f*.

procreate ['prəukrieit] *v* erzeugen. **procreation** *n* Zeugung *f*.

procure [prə'kjuə] *v* beschaffen, besorgen.

prod [prɔd] *v* stechen, stoßen; *(coll: induce)* anspornen (zu). *n* Stich *m*, Stoß *m*.

prodigy ['prɔdidʒi] *n* Wunder *neut*; *(child)* Wunderkind *neut*. **prodigious** *adj* riesig, erstaunlich.

produce [prə'djuːs; *n* 'prɔdjuːs] *v (goods)* erzeugen, herstellen; *(submit)* vorlegen; *(cause, call forth)* hervorrufen; *(theatre)* aufführen; *(films)* herausbringen. *n* Erzeugnis *neut*, Produkte *pl*. **producer** *n* Hersteller; *(theatre, film)* Regisseur *m*. **product** *n* Produkt *neut*, Erzeugnis *neut*; *(result)* Ergebnis *neut*. **production** *n* Herstellung *f*, Produktion *f*; *(theatre)* Aufführung *f*; *(film)* Regie *f*. **production line** Fließband *neut*. **productive** *adj* fruchtbar, leistungsfähig. **productivity** *n* Leistungsfähigkeit *f*, Produktivität *f*.

profane [prə'fein] *adj* profan. **profanity** *n* Fluchen *neut*.

profess [prə'fes] *v* erklären. **profession** *n (occupation)* Beruf *m*; *(assertion)* Beteuerung *f*. **professional** *adj* Berufs-, beruflich; *(education)* fachlich, Fach-.

professor [prə'fesə] *n* Professor(in). **professorship** *n* Lehrstuhl *m*.

proficient [prə'fiʃənt] *adj* erfahren. **proficiency** *n* Erfahrenheit *f*.

profile ['prəufail] *n* Profil *neut*. *v* profilieren.

profit ['prɔfit] *n (comm)* Gewinn *m*, Profit *m*; *(advantage)* Vorteil *m*. *v* **profit from** Nutzen ziehen aus. **profitable** *adj* rentabel; *(advantageous)* vorteilhaft. **profiteer** *n* Profitmacher *m*; *v* sich bereichern.

program ['prəugram] *n (computer)* Programm *neut*. *v* programmieren. **programmer** *n* Programmierer(in).

programme ['prəugram] *n* Programm *neut*; *(TV, radio: broadcast)* Sendung *f*. *v* planen.

progress ['prəugres] *n* Fortschritt *m*; *(development)* Entwicklung *f*. *v* fortschreiten, sich entwickeln. **in progress** im Gange. **progression** *n* Fortbewegung *f*. **progressive** *adj* fortschrittlich.

prohibit [prə'hibit] *v* verbieten. **prohibition** *n* Verbot *neut*; *(of drinking)* Alkoholverbot *neut*. **prohibitive** *adj* verbietend; *(excessively high)* untragbar.

project ['prɔdʒekt; *v* prə'dʒekt] *n* Projekt *neut*, Plan *m*; *(school)* Planaufgabe *f*. *v (film, etc.)* projizieren; *(plan)* planen. **projection** *n* Projektion *f*. **projector** *n* Projektionsapparat *m*.

proletariat [prəulə'teəriət] *n* Proletariat *neut*. **proletarian** *adj* proletarisch. *n* Proletarier(in).

proliferate [prə'lifəreit] *v* sich vermehren, wuchern. **proliferation** *n* Wucherung *f*.

prolific [prə'lifik] *adj* fruchtbar.

prologue ['prəulɔg] *n* Prolog *m*.

prolong [prə'lɔŋ] *v* verlängern. **prolonged** *adj* anhaltend. **prolongation** *n* Verlängerung *f*.

promenade [prɔmə'naːd] *n* Promenade *f*; *(walk)* Spaziergang *m*. *v* promenieren, spazieren.

prominent ['prɔminənt] *adj (person)* prominent, maßgebend. **prominence** *n* Prominenz *f*, hervorragende Bedeutung *f*.

promiscuous [prə'miskjuəs] *adj* promiskuitiv. **promiscuity** *n* Promiskuität *f*.

promise ['prɔmis] *n* Versprechen *neut*. *v* versprechen. **promising** *adj* vielversprechend.

promontory ['prɔməntəri] *n* Landspitze *f*.

promote [prə'məut] *v (person)* befördern; *(encourage, support)* fördern, Vorschub leisten (+ *dat*); *(comm)* Reklame machen für. **promoter** *n (sport)* Promoter *m*. **pro-**

motion n Beförderung; (publicity) Werbung f, Reklame f.

prompt [prompt] adj sofortig, prompt. v (theatre) souffleren; (cause) hervorrufen. **promptness** n Pünktlichkeit f.

prone [proun] adj hingestreckt. **prone to** geneigt zu.

prong [proŋ] n Zinke f. **pronged** adj gezinkt.

pronoun ['prounaun] n Pronomen neut.

pronounce [prə'nauns] v aussprechen. **pronouncement** n Ausspruch m. **pronunciation** n Aussprache f.

proof [pruːf] n Beweis m, Nachweis m; (printing) Korrekturabzug m. adj undurchlässig, fest. **proof against** sicher vor. **proof-reader** n Korrektor(in).

prop¹ [prop] n Stütze f. v **prop up** stützen.

prop² [prop] n (theatre) Requisit neut.

propaganda [propə'gandə] n Propaganda f. **propagandist** n Propagandist(in).

propagate ['propageit] v fortpflanzen. **propagation** n Fortpflanzung f.

propel [prə'pel] v (an)treiben. **propellant** n Treibstoff m. **propeller** n Propeller m.

proper ['propə] adj (fitting) richtig, passend, geeignet; (thorough) ordentlich. **properly** adv richtig, wie es sich gehört.

property ['propəti] n Eigentum neut; (characteristic) Eigenschaft f; (real estate) Immobilien pl.

prophecy ['profəsi] n Weissagung f. **prophesy** v prophezeien. **prophet** n Prophet m. **prophetic** adj prophetisch.

proportion [prə'poːʃən] n Verhältnis neut; (part) Anteil m; (measurement) Ausmaß neut. **in proportion to** im Verhältnis zu. **be out of proportion to** in keinem Verhältnis stehen zu. **well-proportioned** adj wohlgestaltet. **proportional** adj verhältnismäßig, proportional.

propose [prə'pouz] v vorschlagen; (a motion) beantragen; (marriage) einen Heiratsantrag machen (+dat). **proposal** n Vorschlag m; (offer) Angebot neut; (marriage) Heiratsantrag m. **proposer** n Antragsteller m. **proposition** n Vorschlag m; (project) Projekt neut, Plan m.

proprietor [prə'praiətə] n Besitzer(in), Inhaber(in).

propriety [prə'praiəti] n Schicklichkeit f, Anstand m.

propulsion [prə'pʌlʃən] n Antrieb m.

prose [prouz] n Prosa f. adj Prosa-.

prosecute ['prosikjuːt] v (law) gerichtlich verfolgen. **prosecution** n Verfolgung f; (law) Anklage f.

prospect ['prospekt; v prə'spekt] n Aussicht f. v **prospect for** (gold, etc.) graben nach. **prospective** adj künftig, voraussichtlich.

prospectus [prə'spektəs] n (Werbe)-Prospekt m.

prosper ['prospə] v gedeihen. **prosperity** n Wohlstand m. **prosperous** adj erfolgreich, wohlhabend.

prostitute ['prostitjuːt] n Prostituierte f. v prostituieren. **prostitution** n Prostitution f.

prostrate ['prostreit; v pro'streit] adj hingestreckt. v zu Boden werfen. **prostrate oneself** sich demütigen (vor).

protagonist [prou'tagənist] n Hauptfigur f.

protect [prə'tekt] v (be)schützen. **protection** n Schutz m. **protectionism** n Schutzzollpolitik f. **protective** adj (be)schützend. **protector** n Beschützer m. **protectorate** n Schutzgebiet neut.

protégé ['protəʒei] n Schützling m.

protein ['proutiːn] n Protein neut, Eiweiß neut.

protest ['proutest; v prə'test] n Protest m, Einspruch m. v protestieren, Einspruch erheben (auf).

Protestant ['protistənt] n Protestant(in). adj protestantisch. **Protestantism** n Protestantismus m.

protocol ['proutəkol] n Protokoll neut.

prototype ['proutətaip] n Prototyp m.

protractor [prə'traktə] n Winkelmesser m.

protrude [prə'truːd] v herausstehen, hervorstehen.

proud [praud] adj stolz (auf); (arrogant) hochmütig.

prove [pruːv] v beweisen. **prove to be** sich erweisen als.

proverb ['provəːb] n Sprichwort neut. **proverbial** adj sprichwörtlich.

provide [prə'vaid] v versehen, versorgen. **provide for** sorgen für. **provided** conj vorausgesetzt.

provident ['providənt] adj fürsorglich. **providence** n Vorsehung f. **providential** adj glücklich.

province ['provins] n Provinz f. **provincial** adj Provinz-, provinzial; (limited, narrow) provinziell.

provision [prə'viʒən] *n* Vorrichtung *f*; (*regulation*) Vorschrift *f*. **provisions** *pl* Vorrat *m*. **provisional** *adj* vorläufig, provisorisch.

proviso [prə'vaizou] *n* Vorbehalt *m*, Klausel *f*.

provoke [prə'vouk] *v* (*cause*) veranlassen; (*person*) provozieren; (*annoy*) ärgern. **provocation** *n* Provokation *f*; (*challenge*) Herausforderung *f*.

prow [prau] *n* Bug *m*.

prowess ['prauis] *n* Tüchtigkeit *f*.

prowl [praul] *v* herumstreichen. **prowler** *n* Herumtreiber *m*.

proximity [prok'siməti] *n* Nähe *f*.

proxy ['proksi] *n* Vollmacht *f*; (*person*) Bevollmächtigte(r).

prude [pruid] *n* prüder Mensch *m*. **prudery** *n* Prüderie *f*. **prudish** *adj* prüde.

prudent ['pruidənt] *adj* vernünftig, umsichtig. **prudence** *n* Klugheit *f*.

prune[1] [pruin] *n* Backpflaume *f*.

prune[2] [pruin] *v* (*tree*) beschneiden.

pry [prai] *v* herumschnuffeln. **pry into** the Nase stecken in. **prying** *adj* neugierig.

psalm [saim] *n* Psalm *m*.

pseudonym ['sjuidənim] *n* Pseudonym *neut*, Deckname *m*.

psychedelic [ˌsaikə'delik] *adj* psychedelisch.

psychiatry [sai'kaiətri] *n* Psychiatrie *f*. **psychiatric** *adj* psychiatrisch. **psychiatrist** *m* Psychiater(in).

psychic ['saikik] *adj* psychisch.

psychoanalysis [ˌsaikouə'naləsis] *n* Psychoanalyse *f*. **psychoanalyst** *n* Psychoanalytiker(in).

psychology [sai'kolədʒi] *n* Psychologie *f*. **psychological** *adj* psychologisch. **psychologist** *n* Psycholog(in).

psychopath ['saikəpaθ] *n* Psychopath(in).

psychosomatic [ˌsaikəsə'matik] *adj* psychosomatisch.

pub [pʌb] *n* (*coll*) Kneipe *f*.

puberty ['pjubəti] *n* Pubertät *f*, Geschlechtsreife *f*.

pubic ['pjubik] *adj* Scham-.

public ['pʌblik] *adj* öffentlich; (*national*) Volks-, national. *n* Öffentlichkeit *f*, Publikum *neut*. **public house** *n* Wirtshaus *neut*. **public school** *n* Privatschule *f*. **public-spirited** *adj* gemeinsinnig. **publication** *n* Veröffentlichung *f*, Publikation *f*. **publicity** *n* Reklame *f*, Werbung *f*. **publicize** *v* veröffentlichen.

publish ['pʌbliʃ] *v* (*publicize*) veröffentlichen; (*book*) herausbringen. **publisher** *n* Verleger(in), Herausgeber(in); (*firm*) Verlag *m*. **publishing** *n* Verlagswesen *neut*.

pucker ['pʌkə] *v* runzeln; (*mouth*) spitzen.

pudding ['pudiŋ] *n* Pudding *m*. **black pudding** *n* Blutwurst *f*.

puddle ['pʌdl] *n* Pfütze *f*, Lache *f*.

puerile ['pjuərail] *adj* pueril.

puff [pʌf] *n* Hauch *m*; (*on cigar, etc.*) Zug *m*. *v* blasen, pusten. **powder puff** Puderquaste *f*. **puffed-up** *adj* (*coll*) aufgeblasen. **puff pastry** Blätterteig *m*. **puffy** *adj* angeschwollen.

pull [pul] *v* ziehen; (*tug*) zerren; (*rip*) reißen. *n* Zug *m*. **pull through** (*survive*) durchkommen.

pulley ['puli] *n* Rolle *f*.

pullover ['puˌlouvə] *n* Pullover *m*.

pulp [pʌlp] *n* Brei *m*; (*fruit*) Fruchtfleisch *neut*; (*paper*) Pulpe *f*. **pulpy** *adj* breiig, weich.

pulpit ['pulpit] *n* Kanzel *f*.

pulsate [pʌl'seit] *v* pulsieren. **pulsation** *n* Pulsieren *neut*.

pulse [pʌls] *n* Puls *m*, Pulsschlag *m*. *v* pulsieren.

pulverize ['pʌlvəraiz] *v* pulverisieren, zermahlen. **pulverization** *n* Pulverisierung *f*.

pump [pʌmp] *n* Pumpe *f*. *v* pumpen.

pumpkin ['pʌmpkin] *n* Kürbis *m*.

pun [pʌn] *n* Wortspiel *neut*.

punch[1] [pʌntʃ] *n* (*blow*) (Faust)Schlag *m*. *v* (mit der Faust) schlagen.

punch[2] [pʌntʃ] *n* (*drink*) Punsch *m*. **punchbowl** *n* Punschbowle *f*.

punch[3] [pʌntʃ] *n* (*tool*) Locher *m*, Lochzange *f*. *v* lochen; (*tickets*) knipsen. **punchcard** *n* Lochkarte *f*.

punctual ['pʌŋktʃuəl] *adj* pünktlich. **punctuality** *n* Pünktlichkeit *f*.

punctuate ['pʌŋktʃueit] *v* interpunktieren; (*fig*) unterbrechen. **punctuation** *n* Interpunktion *f*.

puncture ['pʌŋktʃə] *v* durchstechen, perforieren; (*tyre*) platzen. *n* Loch *neut*; (*tyre*) Reifenpanne *f*.

pungent ['pʌndʒənt] *adj* scharf.

punish ['pʌniʃ] *v* (be)strafen. **punishment** *n* Strafe *f*.

puny ['pjuini] *adj* schwächlich.

pupil¹ ['pjuːpl] *n* Schüler(in).

pupil² ['pjuːpl] *n* (*eye*) Pupille *f*.

puppet ['pʌpit] *n* Marionette *f*. **puppet show** Puppenspiel *neut*, Marionettentheater *neut*.

puppy ['pʌpi] *n* junger Hund *m*, Welpe *m*.

purchase ['pəːtʃəs] *n* Einkauf *m*. *v* (ein)kaufen. **purchaser** *n* Käufer(in).

pure ['pjuə] *adj* rein. **purebred** *adj* reinrassig. **purify** *v* reinigen, (*tech*) klären. **purification** *n* Reinigung *f*; Klärung *f*. **purity** *n* Reinheit *f*.

purée ['pjuərei] *n* Püree *neut*.

purgatory ['pəːgətəri] *n* Fegefeuer *neut*.

purge [pəːdʒ] *v* reinigen, säubern. *n* Reinigung *f*; (*pol*) Säuberung *f*.

puritan ['pjuəritən] *n* Puritaner(in). **puritanical** *adj* puritanisch. **puritanism** *n* Puritanismus *m*.

purl [pəːl] *n* Linksstricken *neut*. *v* linksstricken.

purple ['pəːpl] *adj* purpurn, purpurrot. *n* Purpur *m*.

purpose ['pəːpəs] *n* Zweck *m*, Ziel *neut*. **for the purpose of** zwecks (+*gen*). **on purpose** absichtlich. **purposeful** *adj* zielbewußt. **purposeless** *adj* zwecklos. **purposely** *adv* absichtlich.

purr [pəː] *v* schnurren, summen. *n* Schnurren *neut*.

purse [pəːs] *n* Portemonnaie *neut*, Geldbeutel *m*; Handtasche *f*; (*prize*) Börse *f*. *v* (*lips*) spitzen.

purser ['pəːsə] *n* Zahlmeister *m*.

pursue [pə'sjuː] *v* verfolgen; (*studies*) betreiben; (*continue*) fortfahren in. **pursuit** *n* Verfolgung *f*; (*activity*) Beschäftigung *f*; (*of happiness, etc.*) Jagd *f*, Suche *f*.

pus [pʌs] *n* Eiter *m*.

push [puʃ] *n* Stoß *m*, Schub *m*. **get the push** (*coll*) entlassen werden. *v* stoßen, schieben; (*button*) drücken; (*in crowd*) drängen. **be pushed for time** keine zeit haben. **push aside** beiseite schieben. **push open/to** (*door*) auf/zuschieben. **push off** (*coll*) abhauen. **push through** durchsetzen. **pushbike** *m* (*coll*) Rad *neut*. **pushbutton** *n* Druckknopf *m*. **pushchair** *n* Kinderwagen *m*. **pusher** *n* (*drugs*) Pusher *m*. **pushing** *adj* aufdringlich.

pussy ['pusi] *n* (*coll*) Mieze *f*.

*put [put] *v* stellen, setzen, legen; (*express*) ausdrücken; (*shot*) werfen. **put away** weglegen. **put back** (*clock*) nach-stellen; (*postpone*) aufschieben. **put by** aufsparen. **put down** hinlegen; (*revolt*) unterdrücken; (*animal*) töten. **put off** verschieben; (*discourage*) davon abraten (+*dat*). **put through** durchführen; (*phone*) verbinden. **put up** (*coll*) unterbringen. **put up with** dulden, ausstehen.

putrid ['pjuːtrid] *adj* verfault.

putt [pʌt] *v* putten.

putty ['pʌti] *n* Kitt *m*.

puzzle ['pʌzl] *n* Rätsel *neut*; (*jigsaw*) Puzzlespiel *neut*. *v* verwirren. **puzzlement** *n* Verwirrung *f*. **puzzling** *adj* rätselhaft.

pyjamas [pə'dʒaːməz] *n* Schlafanzug *m*.

pylon ['pailən] *n* (*elec*) Leitungsmast *m*.

pyramid ['pirəmid] *n* Pyramide *f*.

python ['paiθən] *n* Pythonschlange *f*.

Q

quack¹ [kwak] *n* (*duck*) Quaken *neut*. *v* quaken.

quack² [kwak] *n* (*doctor*) Quacksalber *m*. *adj* quacksalberisch.

quadrangle ['kwodraŋgl] *n* Viereck *neut*, Hof *m*. **quadrangular** *adj* viereckig.

quadrant ['kwodrənt] *n* Quadrant *m*.

quadrilateral [kwodrə'latərəl] *adj* vierseitig.

quadruped ['kwodruped] *n* Vierfüßer *m*.

quadruple [kwod'ruːpl] *adj* vierfach, vierfältig. *v* vervierfachen.

quagmire ['kwagmaiə] *n* Morast *m*.

quail¹ [kweil] *n* (*bird*) Wachtel *f*.

quail² [kweil] *v* verzagen, den Mut verlieren.

quaint [kweint] *adj* kurios, merkwürdig.

quake [kweik] *v* beben. *n* Erdbeben *neut*.

qualify ['kwolifai] *v* (sich) qualifizieren; (*limit*) einschränken. **qualification** *n* Qualifikation *f*; Einschränkung *f*. **qualified** *adj* qualifiziert, geeignet; eingeschränkt.

quality ['kwoləti] *n* Qualität *f*; (*property*) Eigenschaft *f*; (*type*) Sorte *f*. *adj* erstklassig, guter Qualität.

qualm [kwaːm] *n* Skrupel *m*.

quandary ['kwondəri] *n* Verlegenheit *f*.

quantify ['kwontifai] *v* messen, (quantitativ) bestimmen.

quantity ['kwɒntəti] n Quantität f, Menge f.

quarantine ['kwɒrəntin] n Quarantäne f. v unter Quarantäne stellen.

quarrel ['kwɒrəl] n Streit m, Zank m. v (sich) streiten, (sich) zanken. **quarrelsome** adj streitsüchtig, zänkig.

quarry[1] ['kwɒri] n (hunting) Jagdbeute f; (fig) Opfer neut.

quarry[2] ['kwɒri] n Steinbruch m. v brechen, hauen.

quart [kwɔtt] n Quart neut.

quarter ['kwɒttə] n (fourth, of town, etc.) Viertel neut; (of year) Quartal neut, Vierteljahr neut. v vierteln; (to house) unterbringen. **quarter of an hour** Viertelstunde f. **quarter to/past** Viertel vor/nach. **quarterdeck** n Achterdeck neut. **quarter-final** n Viertelfinale neut. **quarterly** adj vierteljährlich.

quartet [kwɔt'tet] n Quartett neut.

quartz [kwɔtts] n Quarz m.

quash [kwɒʃ] v annullieren; (resistance, etc.) unterdrücken.

quaver ['kweivə] v zittern. n (music) Achtelnote f.

quay [ki] n Kai m.

queasy ['kwizi] adj übel. I feel queasy mir ist übel.

queen [kwin] n Königin f; (cards, chess) Dame f. **queen bee** Bienenkönigin f. **queen mother** Königinmutter f.

queer [kwiə] adj seltsam, sonderbar; (odd) komisch; (coll: homosexual) schwul. n (coll) Homo m, Schwule(r).

quell [kwel] v unterdrücken.

quench [kwentʃ] v löschen.

query ['kwiəri] n Frage f, Erkundigung f. v in Frage stellen.

quest [kwest] n Suche f (nach).

question ['kwestʃən] n Frage f. v (be)fragen. **put** or **ask a question** eine Frage stellen. **out of the question** ausgeschlossen. **the question is** es handelt sich darum. **questionable** adj fragwürdig. **questioning** adj fragend. n Befragung f. **questionnaire** n Fragebogen m.

queue [kjut] n Schlange f. v Schlange stehen, sich anstellen.

quibble ['kwibl] v Haare spalten, spitzfindig sein.

quick [kwik] adj schnell; (nimble) flink; (temper) hitzig; (ear, eye) scharf. **quicken** v beschleunigen. **quickness** n Schnelligkeit f. **quicksand** n Treibsand m. **quicksilver** n Quecksilber neut. **quicktempered** adj hitzig, reizbar. **quickwitted** adj scharfsinnig.

quid [kwid] n (coll) Pfund neut.

quiet ['kwaiət] adj ruhig, still. **quieten** v beruhigen. **quietness** n Ruhe f, Stille f.

quill [kwil] n Feder f.

quilt [kwilt] n Steppdecke f.

quinine [kwi'nin] n Chinin neut.

quinsy ['kwinzi] n Mandelentzündung f.

quintet [kwin'tet] n Quintett neut.

quirk [kwətk] n Eigenart f.

*__quit__ [kwit] v (stop) aufhören; (leave) verlassen; (job) aufgeben. **notice to quit** Kündigung f. **quits** adj (coll) quitt.

quite [kwait] adv (fairly) ziemlich; (wholly) ganz, durchaus.

quiver[1] ['kwivə] v zittern.

quiver[2] ['kwivə] n (arrows) Köcher m.

quiz [kwiz] n Quiz neut. v (aus)fragen. **quizzical** ['kwizikl] adj spöttisch.

quota ['kwoutə] n Quote f, Anteil m.

quote [kwout] v zitieren. **quotation** n Zitat f; (comm) Preisangabe f. **quotation marks** Anführungszeichen pl.

R

rabbi ['rabai] n Rabbiner m.

rabbit ['rabit] n Kaninchen neut. **rabbit hutch** Kaninchenstall m.

rabble ['rabl] n Pöbel m.

rabies ['reibiz] n Tollwut f. **rabid** adj tollwütig; (coll: angry) wütend.

race[1] [reis] n Rennen neut, Wettlauf m. v um die Wette laufen (mit), rennen. **the races** Pferderennen pl. **racecourse** n Rennbahn f. **racehorse** n Rennpferd neut. **racing** n Pferderennen neut; adj Renn-. **racing driver** Rennfahrer m.

race[2] [reis] n (group) Rasse f. **racial** adj rassisch, Rassen-. **racialism** or **racism** n Rassismus m. **racialist** or **racist** n Rassist(in); adj rassistisch.

rack [rak] n Gestell neut; (luggage) Gepäcknetz neut. v **rack one's brains** sich den Kopf zerbrechen.

racket[1] ['rakit] n (sport) Rakett neut, Schläger m.

racket² ['rakit] n (noise) Krach m, Trubel m; (coll: swindle) Schwindel m. **racketeer** n Schwindler m, Gangster m.

radar ['reidaɪ] n Radar m or neut.

radial ['reidiəl] adj radial. n (tyre) Gürtelreifen m.

radiant ['reidiənt] adj strahlend. **radiance** n Strahlung f.

radiate ['reidieit] v ausstrahlen. **radiation** n Strahlung f. **radiator** n (house) Heizkörper m; (mot) Kühler m.

radical ['radikəl] adj radikal. n Radikale(r). **radicalism** n Radikalismus m.

radio ['reidiou] n (set) Radio neut; (network) Rundfunk m. v senden, durchgeben. **radio ham** (coll) Funkamateur m. **radio station** Sender m, Funkstation f. **radio wave** Radiowelle f.

radioactive [reidiou'aktiv] adj radioaktiv. **radioactivity** n Radioaktivität f.

radiology [reidi'olədʒi] n Radiologie f, Röntgenlehre f. **radiologist** n Radiologe m.

radiotherapy [reidiou'θerəpi] n Radiotherapie f, Strahlenbehandlung f.

radish ['radiʃ] n Radieschen neut.

radium ['reidiəm] n Radium neut.

radius ['reidiəs] n Radius m.

raffia ['rafiə] n Raffiabast m.

raffle ['rafl] n Tombola f. v verlosen.

raft [raːft] n Floß neut.

rafter ['raːftə] n Dachsparren m.

rag¹ [rag] n Fetzen m, Lumpen m; (coll: newspaper) Blatt neut. **rag doll** Stoffpuppe f. **ragged** adj zerfetzt.

rag² [rag] v (coll: tease) necken, piesacken.

rage [reidʒ] n Wut f. v wüten. **in a rage** wütend. **be all the rage** die große Mode sein.

raid [reid] n Angriff m, Überfall m; (police) Razzia f. v überfallen; eine Razzia machen auf.

rail [reil] n Riegel m, Schiene f. **by rail** mit der Bahn. **railing** n Geländer neut. **railway** or **railroad** n Eisenbahn f. **railway station** Bahnhof m.

rain [rein] n Regen m. v regnen. **rainbow** n Regenbogen m. **raincoat** n Regenmantel m. **rainfall** n Niederschlag m. **rainproof** adj wasserdicht. **rainstorm** n Regenguß m. **rainy** adj regnerisch.

raise [reiz] v erheben, aufrichten; (provoke) hervorrufen; (money) beschaffen. n (in pay) Erhöhung f. **raised** adj erhöht.

raisin ['reizən] n Rosine f.

rake [reik] n Rechen m. v rechen.

rally ['rali] n (meeting) (Massen)Versammlung f; (mot) Sternfahrt f, Rallye f. v (wieder) sammeln; (spirits) sich erholen. **rally round** sich scharen um.

ram [ram] n (zool) Widder m; (tech) Ramme f. v rammen.

ramble ['rambl] v wandern; (speech) drauflos reden. n Wanderung f, Bummel m. **rambler** n Wanderer m; (rose) Kletterrose f. **rambling** adj wandernd; (speech) unzusammenhängend, weitschweifig.

ramp [ramp] n Rampe f.

rampage [ram'peidʒ] v (herum)toben.

rampant ['rampənt] adj üppig, wuchernd.

rampart ['rampaːt] n Festungswall m.

ramshackle ['ramʃakl] adj wackelig.

ran [ran] V **run.**

ranch [raːntʃ] n Ranch f.

rancid ['ransid] adj ranzig.

rancour ['raŋkə] n Erbitterung f, Böswilligkeit f.

random ['randəm] adj zufällig. n **at random** wahllos, aufs Geratewohl.

randy ['randi] adj (coll) geil, wollüstig.

rang [raŋ] V **ring.**

range [reindʒ] n Reihe f; (mountains) Kette f; (reach) Tragweite f. v anordnen; (vary) variieren, schwanken; (rove) wandern.

rank¹ [raŋk] n (status) Rang m; (row) Reihe f. v rank with zählen zu. **the ranks** (mil) die Mannschaften pl.

rank² [raŋk] adj (plants) üppig; (offensive) widerlich; (coarse) grob.

rankle ['raŋkl] v nagen.

ransack ['ransak] v plündern, durchwühlen.

ransom ['ransəm] n Lösegeld neut. v loskaufen.

rap [rap] n Klopfen neut. v klopfen.

rape [reip] n Vergewaltigung f. v vergewaltigen. **rapist** n Vergewaltiger m.

rapid ['rapid] adj schnell, rasch. **rapidity** n Schnelligkeit f. **rapids** pl n Stromschnelle f.

rapier ['reipiə] n Rapier neut.

rapture ['raptʃə] n Verzückung f, Begeisterung f. **rapturous** adj hingerissen.

rare¹ ['reə] *adj* selten, rar; *(air)* dünn. **rarely** *adv* selten. **rarity** *n* Seltenheit *f.*

rare² ['reə] *adj* (cookery) nicht durchgebraten, englisch.

rascal ['rɑːskəl] *n* Schurke *m.* **rascally** *adj* schurkisch.

rash¹ [raʃ] *n (on skin)* Hautausschlag *m.*

rash² [raʃ] *adj* hastig, übereilt. **rashness** *n* Hast *f.*

rasher ['raʃə] *n* (Schinken)Schnitte *f.*

raspberry ['rɑːzbəri] *n* Himbeere *f.*

rat [rat] *n* Ratte *f.* **v rat on** *(coll)* verraten.

rate [reit] *n (comm)* Satz *m,* Kurs *m;* *(charge)* Gebühr *f;* *(speed)* Geschwindigkeit *f;* v schätzen. **rates** *pl* Gemeindesteuer *f.* **birth rate** Geburtenziffer *f.* **at any rate** auf jeden Fall. **first-rate** *adj* erstklassig. **second-rate, third-rate,** *etc. adj* minderwertig.

rather ['rɑːðə] *adv (quite)* ziemlich, etwas; *(preferably)* lieber, eher. *I would rather* ich möchte lieber.

ratify ['ratifai] *v* ratifizieren. **ratification** *n* Ratifizierung *f.*

ratio ['reiʃiou] *n* Verhältnis *neut.*

ration ['raʃən] *n* Ration *f.* v rationieren. **rations** *pl* Verpflegung *f sing.*

rational ['raʃənl] *adj* rational, vernünftig. **rationale** *n* Grundprinzip *neut.* **rationalization** *n* Rationalisierung *f.* **rationalize** *v* rationalisieren.

rattle ['ratl] *v* klappern, rasseln. *n* Gerassel *neut,* Klappern *neut.* **rattlesnake** *n* Klapperschlange *f.*

raucous ['rɔːkəs] *adj* rauh, heiser.

ravage ['ravidʒ] *v* verwüstern. *n* Verwüstung. **ravages of time** Zahn der Zeit *m.*

rave [reiv] *v* irre reden, toben. **rave about** *(coll)* schwärmen von. **raving** *adj* delirierend. **ravings** *pl n* Fieberwahn *m,* Delirien *pl.*

raven ['reivən] *n* Rabe *m.*

ravenous ['ravənəs] *adj* heißhungrig.

ravine [rə'viːn] *n* Schlucht *f.*

ravish ['raviʃ] *v (delight)* hinreißen; *(rape)* vergewaltigen. **ravishing** *adj* entzückend.

raw [rɔː] *adj* roh; *(voice)* rauh; *(sore)* wund. **rawhide** *n* Rohleder *neut.* **rawness** *n* Rohzustand *m.*

ray [rei] *n* Strahl *m.* **ray of light** Lichtstrahl *m.*

rayon ['reiɔn] *n* Kunstseide *f.*

razor ['reizə] *n* Rasiermesser *neut.* **electric razor** Elektrorasierer *m.* **razor blade** Rasierklinge *f.* **razor-sharp** *adj* messerscharf.

reach [riːtʃ] *v (arrive at)* erreichen; *(stretch to)* sich erstrecken (bis). *n* Reichweite *f.* **reach (out) for** reichen *or* greifen nach.

react [ri'akt] *v* reagieren. **reaction** *n* Reaktion *f.* **reactionary** *adj* reaktionär; *n* Reaktionär(in).

*read [riːd] *v* lesen; *(interpret)* auslegen, deuten. **read aloud** vorlesen. **read through** durchlesen. **readable** *adj* leserlich; *(worth reading)* lesenswert. **reader** *n* Leser(in); *(university)* Dozent *m.* **readership** *n* Leserkreis *m.* **reading** *n* Lesen *neut; (public)* Vorlesung *f.* **reading matter** Lektüre *f.*

readjust [riːə'dʒʌst] *v* wieder in Ordnung bringen; *(tech)* wieder einstellen; *(person)* (sich) wieder anpassen (an). **readjustment** *n* Wiederanpassung *f.*

ready ['redi] *adj* bereit, fertig; *(quick)* prompt. **get** *or* **make ready** sich vorbereiten; *(thing)* fertig machen. **readiness** *n* Bereitschaft *f.* **ready-made** *adj* Fertig-. **ready-reckoner** *n* Rechentabelle *f.* **readily** *adv* ohne weiteres.

real [riəl] *adj* wirklich, wahr; *(genuine)* echt. **real estate** Immobilien *pl.* **realism** *n* Realismus *m.* **realist** *n* Realist(in). **realistic** *adj* realistisch. **reality** *n* Wirklichkeit *f,* Realität *f.* **really** *adv* tatsächlich, in der Tat; *(very, actually)* wirklich.

realize ['riəlaiz] *v* begreifen, erkennen; *(bring about)* verwirklichen. **realizable** *adj* durchführbar. **realization** *n* Erkenntnis *f;* Verwirklichung *f.*

realm [relm] *n* Königreich *neut; (sphere)* Gebiet *neut.*

reap [riːp] *v* ernten, mähen. **reaper** *n* Mäher(in).

reappear [riːə'piə] *v* wieder erscheinen. **reappearance** *n* Wiedererscheinen *neut.*

rear¹ [riə] *adj* hinter, Hinter-. *n* Hinterseite *f,* Rückseite *f.* **rear lamp** Schlußlicht *neut.* **rear wheel** Hinterrad *neut.*

rear² [riə] *v (child)* erziehen; *(animals)* züchten.

rearrange [riːə'reindʒ] *v* neu ordnen, umordnen; *(date, etc.)* ändern. **rearrangement** *n* Neuordnung *f;* Änderung *f.*

reason ['riːzn] *n* Grund *m; (good sense)* Vernunft *f.* v folgern. **for this reason** aus diesem Grund. **by reason of** wegen (+gen). **reason with** zu überzeugen versuchen. **reasonable** *adj* vernünftig. **reasonableness** *n* Vernünftigkeit. **reasonably** *adv* vernünftigerweise; (*fairly*) ziemlich. **reasoning** *n* Schlußfolgerung *f*, Argument *neut*.

reassure [rɪəˈʃuə] *v* beruhigen. **reassurance** *n* Beruhigung *f*.

rebate [ˈriːbeit] *n* Rabatt *m*.

rebel [ˈrebl] *n* Rebell(in), Aufrührer(in). *adj* aufrührerisch. *v* rebellieren. **rebellion** *n* Aufstand *m*. **rebellious** *adj* aufrührerisch.

rebound [rɪˈbaund; *n* ˈriːbaund] *v* zurückprallen. *n* Rückprall *m*.

rebuff [rɪˈbʌf] *v* abweisen. *n* Abweisung *f*.

*rebuild [rɪˈbild] *v* wiederaufbauen.

rebuke [rɪˈbjuːk] *v* zurechtweisen, rüffeln. *n* Rüffel *m*.

recall [rɪˈkoːl] *v* (*call back*) zurückrufen; (*remember*) sich erinnern an. *n* Rückruf *m*; Erinnerung *f*.

recap [ˈriːkap] *v* kurz zusammenfassen. *n* Zusammenfassung *f*.

recede [rɪˈsiːd] *v* zurückgehen, zurückweichen.

receipt [rɪˈsiːt] *n* (*of letter*) Empfang *m*; (*of goods*) Annahme *f*; (*bill*) Quittung *f*; **receipts** *pl* Einnahmen *pl*. **acknowledge receipt** Empfang bestätigen.

receive [rɪˈsiːv] *v* empfangen, bekommen. **receiver** *n* (*phone*) Hörer *m*; (*comm*) Konkursverwalter *m*; (*radio*) Empfänger *m*. **receivership** *n* Konkursverwaltung *f*.

recent [ˈriːsnt] *adj* neu, modern, neulich entstanden. **recently** *adv* neulich, vor kurzem.

receptacle [rɪˈseptəkl] *n* Behälter *m*, Gefäß *neut*.

reception [rɪˈsepʃən] *n* Empfang *m*. **receptionist** *n* Empfangsdame *f*. **reception room** Empfangszimmer *neut*.

recess [rɪˈses] *n* Pause *f*, Unterbrechung *f*; (*holiday*) Ferien *pl*; (*niche*) Nische *f*. **recession** [rɪˈseʃən] *n* (*comm*) Rezession *f*.

recharge [rɪˈtʃɑːdʒ] *v* (*battery*) wieder aufladen.

recipe [ˈresəpi] *n* Rezept *neut*.

recipient [rɪˈsipiənt] *n* Empfänger(in).

reciprocate [rɪˈsiprəkeit] *v* erwidern. **reciprocal** *adj* gegenseitig. **reciprocation** *n* Erwiderung *f*.

recite [rɪˈsait] *v* vortragen, rezitieren. **piano/song recital** Klavier-/Liederabend *m*.

reckless [ˈrekləs] *adj* rücksichtslos. **recklessness** *n* Rücksichtslosigkeit *f*.

reckon [ˈrekən] *v* rechnen, zählen; (*believe*) meinen. **reckon on** sich verlassen auf. **reckon with** rechnen mit. **reckoning** *n* Abrechnung *f*.

reclaim [rɪˈkleim] *v* (*ask for back*) zurückfordern; (*land from sea*) gewinnen.

recline [rɪˈklain] *v* sich zurücklehnen (an).

recluse [rɪˈkluːs] *n* Einsiedler(in).

recognize [ˈrekəgnaiz] *v* (*wieder*) erkennen; (*acknowledge*) anerkennen; (*concede*) zugeben. **recognition**- *n* (Wieder)Erkennen *neut*; Anerkennung *f*. **recognizable** *adj* erkennbar.

recoil [rɪˈkoil; *n* ˈriːkoil] *v* zurückprallen; (*in fear*) zurückschrecken. *n* Rückprall *m*.

recollect [rekəˈlekt] *n* sich erinnern an. **recollection** *n* Erinnerung *f*.

recommence [riːkəˈmens] *v* wieder beginnen.

recommend [rekəˈmend] *v* empfehlen. **to be recommended** empfehlenswert. **recommendation** *n* Empfehlung *f*; (*suggestion*) Vorschlag *m*.

recompense [ˈrekəmpens] *n* Belohnung *f*. *v* belohnen.

reconcile [ˈrekənsail] *v* versöhnen. **reconcile oneself to** sich abfinden mit. **reconcilable** *adj* vereinbar (mit). **reconciliation** *n* Versöhnung *f*.

reconstruct [riːkənˈstrʌkt] *v* wiederaufbauen; (*events*) rekonstruieren. **reconstruction** *n* Wiederaufbau *m*; Rekonstruktion *f*.

record [rɪˈkoːd; *n* ˈrekoːd] *v* (*film, tape*) aufnehmen; (*write down*) aufschreiben, eintragen. *n* (*disc*) Schallplatte *f*; (*of proceedings, etc.*) Protokoll *neut*, Bericht *m*; (*sport*) Rekord *m*. **break the record** den Rekord brechen. **off the record** inoffiziell. **recorder** *n* (*music*) Blockflöte *f*. **recording** *n* Aufnahme *f*. **record-player** *n* Plattenspieler *m*.

recount [rɪˈkaunt] *v* (*narrate*) erzählen.

recoup [rɪˈkuːp] *v* (*loss*) wieder einholen.

recover [rɪˈkʌvə] *v* zurückgewinnen; (*get better*) sich erholen. **recovery** *n* Zurückgewinnung *f*; Erholung *f*.

recreation [rekrɪˈeiʃən] *n* Erholung *f*, Entspannung *f*. **recreation ground** *n* Spielplatz *neut*.

recrimination [ri͵krimi'neiʃən] n Gegenbeschuldigung f.

recruit [rə'kruːt] n Rekrut m. v rekrutieren. **recruitment** n Rekrutierung f.

rectangle ['rektaŋgl] n Rechteck neut. **rectangular** adj rechteckig.

rectify ['rektifai] v richtigstellen, korrigieren; (elec) gleichrichten. **rectification** n Richtigstellung f, Korrektur f.

rectum ['rektəm] n Mastdarm m. **rectal** adj rektal.

recuperate [rə'kjuːpəreit] v sich erholen. **recuperation** n Erholung f.

recur [ri'kəː] v wieder auftreten, sich wiederholen. **recurrence** n Wiederauftreten neut. **recurrent** adj wiederkehrend.

red [red] adj rot. n Rot neut. **red tape** Amtsschimmel m. **redden** v erröten, rot werden. **redness** n Röte f. **red-handed** adj auf frischer Tat.

redeem [ri'diːm] v (pledge) einlösen; (prisoner) loskaufen; (promise) einhalten. **redemption** n Ablösung f; Rückkauf m.

redevelop [͵riːdi'veləp] v neu entwickeln; (town) umbauen.

redress [rə'dres] n (legal) Rechtshilfe f; (compensation) Wiedergutmachung f. v wiedergutmachen. **redress the balance** das Gleichgewicht wiederherstellen.

reduce [rə'djuːs] v vermindern, verringern; (prices) herabsetzen; (tech) reduzieren; (slim) eine Abmagerungskur machen. **in reduced circumstances** verarmt. **reduction** n Verminderung f; Herabsetzung f; (tech) Reduktion f.

redundant [rə'dʌndənt] adj überflüssig; (jobless) arbeitslos. **be made redundant** entlassen werden. **redundancy** n Überflüssigkeit f; (worker) Entlassung f.

reed [riːd] n Rohr neut; (music) (Rohr)Blatt neut. **reedy** adj (voice) piepsig.

reef [riːf] n (Felsen)Riff neut.

reek [riːk] v stinken (nach). n Gestank m.

reel[1] [riːl] n Spule f; (cotton) Rolle f.

reel[2] [riːl] v taumeln, schwanken.

refectory [rə'fektəri] n Speisesaal m; (university) Mensa f.

refer [rə'fəː] v **refer to** hinweisen auf, sich beziehen auf; (mention) erwähnen; (a book) nachschlagen in. **reference** n Bezug m, Hinweis m; Erwähnung f; (in book) Verweis m. **with reference to** in Bezug auf, hinsichtlich (+gen). **reference book** Nachschlagewerk neut.

referee [refə'riː] n Schiedsrichter m.

referendum [refə'rendəm] n Volksentscheid m.

refill [ri'fil; n 'riːfil] v nachfüllen. n (for pen) Ersatzmine f.

refine [rə'fain] v (tech) raffinieren; (improve) verfeinern. **refined** adj raffiniert; (person, etc.) kultiviert **refinement** n Verfeinerung f; (good breeding) Kultiviertheit f. **refinery** n Raffinerie f.

reflation [rə'fleiʃn] n Wirtschaftsbelebung f.

reflect [rə'flekt] v widerspiegeln; (consider) nachdenken. **reflection** n Widerspiegelung f; (thought) Überlegung f; (remark) Bemerkung f. **reflective** adj zurückstrahlend; (thoughtful) nachdenklich. **reflector** n (mot) Rückstrahler m.

reflex ['riːfleks] n Reflex m.

reform [rə'foːm] n Reform f, Verbesserung f. v reformieren, (ver)bessern. **reformation** n Verbesserung f; (history) Reformation f. **reformatory** n Besserungsanstalt f. **reformed** adj verbessert. **reformer** n Reformer(in).

refract [rə'frakt] v brechen.

refrain[1] [rə'frein] v **refrain from** sich enthalten (+gen).

refrain[2] [rə'frein] n Refrain m.

refresh [rə'freʃ] v erfrischen; (memory) auffrischen. **refresher course** Wiederholungskurs m. **refreshing** adj erfrischend. **refreshment** n Erfrischung f. **refreshments** pl Imbiß m sing.

refrigerator [rə'fridʒəreitə] n Kühlschrank m. **refrigerate** v kühlen. **refrigeration** n Kühlung f.

refuel [ri'fjuːəl] v tanken.

refuge ['refjuːdʒ] n Zuflucht f, Schutz m. **refugee** n Flüchtling m.

refund ['riːfʌnd; v ri'fʌnd] n Rückvergütung f. v zurückzahlen.

refuse[1] [rə'fjuːz] v ablehnen, verweigern. **refusal** n Verweigerung f, Ablehnung f.

refuse[2] ['refjus] n Abfall m, Müll m. **refuse collection** Müllabfuhr f.

refute [ri'fjuːt] v widerlegen.

regain [ri'gein] v wiedergewinnen.

regal ['riːgəl] adj königlich.

regard [rə'gaːd] v ansehen, betrachten. n (esteem) (Hoch)Achtung f; (consideration) Rücksicht f, Hinblick m. **in this regard** in dieser Hinsicht. **with regard to** in bezug auf. **as regards** was ... betrifft. **regarding** prep hinsichtlich (+gen), bezüglich (+ *gen*). **regardless** *adj* ohne Rücksicht (auf).

regatta [rə'gatə] *n* Regatta *f*.

regent ['ri:dʒənt] *n* Regent(in).

regime [rei'ʒi:m] *n* Regime *f*.

regiment ['redʒimənt] *n* Regiment *neut*.

region ['ri:dʒən] *n* Gebiet *neut*, Gegend *f*. **in the region of** etwa, ungefähr. **regional** *adj* regional, örtlich.

register ['redʒistə] *v* registrieren; (*report*) sich eintragen lassen. *n* Register *neut*. **registered** *adj* eingetragen. **registered letter** Einschreibebrief *m*. **send by registered post** per Einschreiben schicken. **registrar** *n* (*births, etc.*) Standesbeamte(r); (*hospital, etc.*) Direktor *m*. **registration** *n* Registrierung *f*. **registration number** (*mot*) polizeiliches Kennzeichen *neut*. **registry office** Standesamt *neut*.

regress [ri'gres] *v* zurückgehen. **regression** *n* Regression *f*. **regressive** *adj* rückläufig.

regret [rə'gret] *v* bedauern. *n* Reue *f*, Bedauern *neut*. **regrettable** *adj* bedauerlich.

regular ['regjulə] *adj* regelmäßig; (*normal*) gewöhnlich; (*correct*) ordnungsgemäß. **regular** (*customer*) Stammgast *m*. **regularity** *n* Regelmäßigheit *f*.

regulate ['regjuleit] *v* regeln, ordnen. **regulation** *n* (*rule*) Vorschrift *f*; (*tech*) Regelung *f*. **regulator** *n* Regler *m*.

rehabilitate [riːhə'biliteit] *n* rehabilitieren. **rehabilitation** *n* Rehabilitation *f*.

rehearse [rə'həːs] *v* proben. **rehearsal** *n* Probe *f*.

reign [rein] *n* Regierung(szeit) *f*. *v* regieren, herrschen.

reimburse [riːim'bəːs] *v* (*person*) entschädigen. **reimbursement** *n* Entschädigung *f*.

rein [rein] *n* Zügel *m*.

reincarnation [riːinkɑː'neiʃən] *n* Reinkarnation *f*, Wiederverkörperung *f*.

reindeer ['reindiə] *n* Ren(tier) *neut*.

reinforce [riːin'foːs] *v* verstärken; (*concrete*) armieren. **reinforcement** *n* Verstärkung *f*.

reinstate [riːin'steit] *v* wiedereinsetzen. **reinstatement** *n* Wiedereinsetzung *f*.

reinvest [riːin'vest] *v* wiederinvestieren.

reissue [riː'iʃu] *v* neu herausgeben. *n* Neuausgabe *f*.

reject [rə'dʒekt] *n* 'riːdʒekt] *v* ablehnen,

verwerfen. **rejection** *n* Ablehnung *f*, Verwerfung *f*. *n* Ausschußartikel *m*.

rejoice [rə'dʒois] *v* sich freuen. **rejoicing** *adj* froh; *n* Freude *f*.

rejoin [rə'dʒoin] *v* sich wieder anschließen; (*reply*) erwidern. **rejoinder** *n* Erwiderung *f*.

rejuvenate [rə'dʒuːvəneit] *v* verjüngen. **rejuvenation** *n* Verjüngung *f*.

relapse [rə'laps] *v* zurückfallen; (*med*) einen Rückfall bekommen. *n* Rückfall *m*.

relate [rə'leit] *v* (*tell*) erzählen; (*link*) verbinden. **related** *adj* verwandt. **relating to** in bezug auf.

relation [rə'leiʃn] *n* Verhältnis *neut*; (*business*) Beziehung *f*; (*person*) Verwandte(r). **relationship** *n* Verhältnis *neut*; (*family*) Verwandtschaft *f*.

relative ['relətiv] *n* Verwandte(r). *adj* relativ, verhältnismäßig. **relatively** *adv* verhältnismäßig. **relativity** *n* Relativität *f*.

relax [rə'laks] *v* entspannen. **relaxation** *n* Entspannung *f*.

relay ['riːlei; *v* ri'lei] *n* (*race*) Staffellauf *m*; (*tech*) Relais *neut*. *v* weitergeben.

release [rə'liːs] *v* freilassen, entlassen; (*film, etc.*) freigeben; (*news*) bekanntgeben; (*let go*) loslassen. *n* Entlassung *f*; Freigabe *f*.

relent [rə'lent] *v* nachgiebig werden. **relentless** *adj* unbarmherzig.

relevant ['reləvənt] *adj* erheblich, relevant; (*appropriate*) entsprechend. **relevance** *n* Relevanz *f*.

reliable [ri'laiəbl] *adj* zuverlässig. **reliability** *n* Zuverlässigkeit *f*. **reliance** *n* Vertrauen *neut*.

relic ['relik] *n* Überbleibsel *neut*; (*rel*) Reliquie *f*.

relief [rə'liːf] *n* Erleichterung *f*; (*mil*) Ablösung *f*; (*help*) Hilfe *f*; (*geog*) Relief *neut*. **tax relief** Steuerbegünstigung *f*.

relieve [rə'liːv] *v* erleichtern; (*from burden*) entlasten; (*person*) ablösen; (*reassure*) beruhigen.

religion [rə'lidʒən] *n* Religion *f*. **religious** *adj* religiös.

relinquish [rə'liŋkwiʃ] *v* aufgeben, verzichten auf.

relish ['reliʃ] *v* sich erfreuen an. *n* (*fig*) Vergnügen *neut*; (*sauce*) Soße *f*.

reluctant [rə'lʌktənt] *adj* widerwillig. **be reluctant to do** ungern tun. **reluctance** *n* Widerstreben *neut*. **reluctantly** *adv* ungern.

rely [rə'lai] v sich verlassen (auf).

remain [rə'mein] v bleiben; (*be left over*) übrigbleiben. **remains** pl n Überreste pl; (*person*) die sterblichen Überreste pl. **remainder** n Rest m, Restbestand m. **remaining** adj übriggeblieben.

remand [rə'maind] v in Untersuchungshaft zurückschicken.

remark [rə'maːk] n Bemerkung f. v bemerken. **remarkable** adj bemerkenswert.

remarry [riː'mari] v wieder heiraten.

remedy ['remədi] n Gegenmittel neut; (*med*) Heilmittel neut. v berichtigen.

remember [ri'membə] v sich erinnern an. *remember me to your mother* grüße deine Mutter von mir. **remembrance** n Erinnerung f.

remind [ri'maind] v erinnern (an); (*someone to do something*) mahnen. **reminder** n Mahnung f.

reminiscence [remə'nisens] n Erinnerung f. **be reminiscent of** erinnern an.

remiss [ri'mis] adj nachlässig.

remit [rə'mit] v überweisen. **remittance** n Überweisung f.

remnant ['remnənt] n (Über)Rest m, Überbleibsel neut.

remorse [rə'mois] n Gewissensbisse pl, Reue f. **remorseful** adj reumütig. **remorseless** adj unbarmherzig.

remote [rə'mout] adj fern, entfernt. **remote control** Fernsteuerung f. **remoteness** n Ferne f.

remove [rə'muːv] v beseitigen, entfernen; (*move house*) umziehen. **removal** n Beseitigung f; Umzug m. **remover** n (Möbel)Spediteur m.

remunerate [rə'mjuunəreit] v belohnen. **remuneration** n Lohn m, Vergütung f.

renaissance [rə'neisəns] n Renaissance f.

rename [riː'neim] v umbenennen.

render ['rendə] v (*make*) machen; (*give back*) wiedergeben; (*service*) leisten.

rendezvous ['rondivuː] n Verabredung f, Stelldichein neut.

renegade ['renigeid] n Abtrünnige(r). adj abtrünnig.

renew [rə'njuː] v erneuern; (*contract*) verlängern. **renewal** n Erneuerung f.

renounce [ri'nauns] v verzichten auf; (*person*) verleugnen; (*beliefs*) abschwören.

renovate ['renəveit] v erneuern, renovier-

en. **renovation** n Renovierung f, Erneuerung f.

renown [rə'naun] n Ruhm m, Berühmtheit f. **renowned** adj berühmt.

rent [rent] n Miete f. v mieten; (*let*) vermieten. **rental** n Mietbetrag m.

renunciation [ri,nʌnsi'eiʃən] n (*rejection*) Ablehnung f.

reopen [riː'oupən] v wieder öffnen; (*shop, etc.*) wiedereröffnen.

reorganize [riː'oigənaiz] v reorganisieren, neugestalten. **reorganization** n Reorganisation f.

rep [rep] n (*coll: representative*) Vertreter(in).

repair [ri'peə] v reparieren, ausbessern; (*clothes*) flicken. n Reparatur f. **in good repair** in gutem Zustand. **in need of repair** reparaturbedürftig. **repair kit** Flickzeug neut. **reparation** n Wiedergutmachung f.

repartee [repaɪ'tiː] n Schlagabtausch m.

repatriate [riː'patrieit] v repatriieren. **repatriation** n Repatriierung f.

***repay** [ri'pei] v zurückzahlen; (*kindness*) erwidern. **repayable** adj rückzahlbar. **repayment** n Rückzahlung f.

repeal [rə'piːl] v aufheben, widerrufen. n Aufhebung f.

repeat [rə'piːt] v wiederholen. n Wiederholung f. **repeated** adj wiederholt.

repel [rə'pel] v abweisen. **repellent** adj abstoßend, widerlich.

repent [rə'pent] v bereuen. **repentance** n Reue f. **repentant** adj bußfertig.

repercussions [riːpə'kʌʃənz] pl n Rückwirkungen pl.

repertoire ['repətwaɪ] n Repertoire neut.

repetition [repə'tiʃn] n Wiederholung f. **repetitive** adj sich wiederholend.

replace [rə'pleis] v ersetzen. **replacement** n Ersatz m. **replacement part** Ersatzteil neut.

replay ['riːplei] n (*sport*) Wiederholungsspiel neut; (*tape*) Wiedergabe f.

replenish [ri'pleniʃ] v ergänzen.

replica ['replikə] n Kopie f.

reply [rə'plai] v antworten, erwidern. n Antwort f, Erwiderung f. **reply to** (*person*) antworten (+ dat); (*question, letter*) antworten auf. **in reply to** in Erwiderung auf.

report [rə'poɪt] n Bericht m; (*factual statement*) Meldung f. v berichten;

(*denounce*) melden; (*present oneself*) sich melden. **reporter** *n* Reporter *m*.

repose [rə'pouz] *n* Ruhe *f*. *v* ruhen.

represent [reprə'zent] *v* darstellen; (*act as representative*) vertreten. **representation** *n* Darstellung *f*; Vertretung *f*. **representative** *n* Vertreter(in). *adj* (*typical*) typisch.

repress [ri'pres] *v* unterdrücken; (*psychol*) verdrängen. **repression** *n* Unterdrückung *f*; Verdrängung *f*.

reprieve [rə'priːv] *v* begnadigen. *n* Strafaufschub *m*; (*fig*) Gnadenfrist *f*.

reprimand ['reprimaind] *v* rügen. *n* Rüge *f*, Verweis *m*.

reprint [riː'print; *n* 'riːprint] *v* neu drucken. *n* Neudruck *m*.

reprisal [rə'praizəl] *n* Repressalie *f*.

reproach [rə'proutʃ] *n* Vorwurf *m*, Tadel *m*. *v* Vorwürfe machen (*+dat*). **reproachful** *adj* vorwurfsvoll.

reproduce [riːprə'djuːs] *v* (sich) fortpflanzen; (*copy*) kopieren. **reproduction** *n* Fortpflanzung *f*; (*copy*) Reproduktion *f*.

reproof [rə'pruːf] *n* Verweis *m*, Rüge *f*. **reprove** *v* rügen.

reptile ['reptail] *n* Reptil *neut*, Kriechtier *neut*.

republic [rə'pʌblik] *n* Republik *f*. **republican** *adj* republikanisch; *n* Republikaner(in).

repudiate [rə'pjuːdieit] *v* zurückweisen, nicht anerkennen. *n* Nichtanerkennung *f*.

repugnant [rə'pʌgnənt] *adj* widerlich, widerwärtig.

repulsion [rə'pʌlʃn] *n* Abscheu *m*. **repulsive** *adj* widerwärtig, abscheulich.

repute [rə'pjuːt] *n* Ruf *m*. **reputation** *n* Ruf *m*. **reputed** *adj* angeblich. **be reputed** betrachtet sein (als).

request [ri'kwest] *n* Bitte *f*. *v* bitten (um). **on request** auf Wunsch.

requiem ['rekwiəm] *n* Requiem *neut*.

require [rə'kwaiə] *v* (*need*) brauchen; (*person*) verlangen (von); (*call for*) erfordern. **be required** erforderlich sein. **requirement** *n* Anforderung *f*; (*need*) Bedürfnis *neut*.

requisite ['rekwizit] *adj* erforderlich, notwendig.

re-route [ˌriː'ruːt] *v* umleiten.

resale [riː'seil] *n* Weiterverkauf *m*.

rescue ['reskjuː] *v* retten, befreien. *n* Rettung *f*. **come to the rescue of** zur Hilfe kommen (*+dat*). **rescuer** *n* Retter *m*.

research [ri'səːtʃ] *n* Forschung *f*. *v* forschen. **researcher** *n* Forscher *m*.

resemble [rə'zembl] *v* ähnlich sein (*+dat*). **resemblance** *n* Ähnlichkeit *f*.

resent [ri'zent] *v* übelnehmen. **resentful** *adj* ärgerlich (auf). **resentment** *n* Groll *m*, Unwille *m*.

reserve [rə'zəːv] *v* reservieren (lassen). *n* Reserve *f*; (*for animals*) Schutzgebiet *neut*; (*sport*) Ersatzmann *m*. **reserved** *adj* reserviert. **reservation** *n* Vorbehalt *m*; Reservierung *f*.

reservoir ['rezəvwaː] *n* Reservoir *neut*.

reside [rə'zaid] *v* wohnen. **residence** *n* Wohnung *f*; (*domicile*) Wohnsitz *m*. **resident** *adj* wohnhaft. **residential** *adj* Wohn-.

residue ['rezidjuː] *n* Rest *m*, Rückstand *m*. **residual** *adj* übrig, Rest-.

resign [rə'zain] *v* zurücktreten. **resign oneself to** sich abfinden mit. **resignation** *n* Rücktritt *m*; (*mood*) Resignation *f*. **hand in one's resignation** seinen Rücktritt einreichen. **resigned** *adj* resigniert, ergeben.

resilient [rə'ziliənt] *adj* elastisch; (*person*) unverwüstlich.

resin ['rezin] *n* Harz *neut*.

resist [rə'zist] *v* widerstehen. **resistance** *n* Widerstand *m*. **resistant** *adj* widerstehend, beständig.

*resit [riː'sit] *v* (*exam*) wiederholen.

resolute ['rezəluːt] *adj* entschlossen. **resolution** *n* (*determination*) Entschlossenheit *f*; (*decision*) Beschluß *m*.

resolve [rə'zolv] *v* (*problem*) lösen; (*tech*) auflösen; (*decide*) beschließen. *n* (*determination*) Entschlossenheit *f*. **resolved** *adj* entschlossen.

resonant ['rezənənt] *adj* widerhallend; (*voice*) volltönend. **resonance** *n* Resonanz *f*.

resort [rə'zoːt] *n* (*hope*) Ausweg *m*; (*place*) Ferienort *m*; (*use*) Anwendung *f*. **seaside resort** Seebad *neut*. *v* **resort to** zurückgreifen auf.

resound [rə'zaund] *v* widerhallen.

resource [rə'zoːs] *n* Mittel *neut*. **natural resources** Bodenschätze *pl*. **resourceful** *adj* findig.

respect [rə'spekt] *v* (hoch)achten; (*take account of*) berücksichtigen. *n* (*for person*) Hochachtung *f*, Respekt *m*; Rücksicht *f*. **in this respect** in dieser Hinsicht. **respectable** *adj* ansehnlich, respektabel.

respectful adj achtvoll. **respective** adj entsprechend. **respectively** adv beziehungsweise.

respiration [respə'reiʃn] n Atmung f.

respite ['respait] n **without respite** ohne Unterlaß.

respond [rə'spond] v **respond to** (question) antworten (auf); (react) reagieren (auf). **response** n Antwort f; Reaktion f.

responsible [rə'sponsəbl] adj verantwortlich. **responsibility** n Verantwortung f; (commitment) Verpflichtung f.

rest[1] [rest] n Ruhe f. **day of rest** Ruhetag m. **have a rest** sich ausruhen. **without rest** unaufhörlich. v ruhen. **rested** adj ausgeruht. **restful** adj ruhig. **restive** adj unruhig. **restless** adj ruhelos. **restlessness** n Unruhe f.

rest[2] [rest] n (remainder) Rest m.

restaurant ['restront] n Restaurant neut, Gaststätte f. **restaurant car** Speisewagen m.

restore [rə'stoɪ] v wiederherstellen. **restoration** n Wiederherstellung f; (of painting, etc.) Restauration f.

restrain [rə'strein] v zurückhalten. **restrained** adj zurückhaltend. **restraint** n Zurückhaltung f; (limitation) Einschränkung f.

restrict [rə'strikt] v einschränken, beschränken. **restricted** adj eingeschränkt, beschränkt. **restriction** n Einschränkung f, Beschränkung f. **restrictive** adj einschränkend.

result [rə'zʌlt] n Ergebnis neut, Resultat neut; (consequence) Folge f. v sich ergeben. **result in** enden mit. **resultant** adj daraus enstehend.

resume [rə'zjuːm] v wieder beginnen; (work) wieder aufnehmen. **resumption** n Wiederaufnahme f.

résumé ['reizumei] n Resümee neut.

resurgence [ri'səːdʒəns] n Wiederaufstieg m.

resurrect [rezə'rekt] v (thing) ausgraben, wieder einführen. **resurrection** n Auferstehung f.

resuscitate [rə'sʌsəteit] v wiederbeleben. **resuscitation** n Wiederbelebung f.

retail ['riːteil] n Einzelhandel m. adj Einzelhandels-. **retail price** Ladenpreis m. **retail shop** Einzelhandelsgeschäft neut. v im Einzelhandel verkaufen. **retailer** n Einzelhändler(in).

retain [rə'tein] v behalten. **retention** n Beibehaltung f.

retaliate [rə'talieit] v sich rächen. **retaliation** n Vergeltung f. **retaliatory** adj Vergeltungs-.

retard [rə'taɪd] v hindern. **retarded** adj zurückgeblieben.

reticent ['retisənt] adj schweigsam. **reticence** n Schweigsamkeit f, Zurückhaltung f.

retina ['retinə] n Netzhaut f.

retinue ['retinjuː] n Gefolge neut.

retire [rə'taiə] v sich zurückziehen; (from work) in den Ruhestand treten. **retired** adj pensioniert. **retirement** n Ruhestand m; (resignation) Rücktritt m. **retiring** adj zurückhaltend.

retort[1] [rə'toɪt] v (scharf) erwidern. n (schlagfertige) Antwort f.

retort[2] [rə'toɪt] n (vessel) Retorte f.

retrace [ri'treis] v zurückverfolgen.

retract [rə'trakt] v (draw in) einziehen; (take back) zurücknehmen, widerrufen. **retractable** adj einziehbar.

retreat [rə'triːt] v sich zurückziehen. n Rückzug m; (place) Zufluchtsort m.

retrieve [rə'triːv] v wiedererlangen, herausholen. **retriever** n Apporthund m.

retrograde ['retrəgreid] adj rückläufig.

retrospect ['retrəspekt] n Rückblick m. **in retrospect** rückschauend. **retrospective** adj rückwirkend.

return [rə'təɪn] v zurückkommen, wiederkehren; (give back) zurückgeben; (answer) erwidern. n Rückkehr f; (ticket) Rückfahrkarte f; (comm) Ertrag m. **tax return** Steuererklärung f. **many happy returns** herzlichen Glückwunsch.

reunite [riːju'nait] v wiedervereinigen. **reunion** n Wiedervereinigung f; (meeting) Treffen neut.

rev [rev] v (coll: mot) auf Touren bringen. **revs** pl n Drehzahl f sing.

reveal [rə'viːl] v enthüllen, offenbaren; (display) zeigen. **revealing** adj aufschlußreich. **revelation** n Enthüllung f, Offenbarung f.

revel ['revl] v feiern. **revel in** schwelgen in. **reveller** n Feiernde(r). **revelry** n Festlichkeit f.

revenge [rə'vendʒ] n Rache f. v rächen. **take revenge on** sich rächen ạn.

revenue ['revinjuː] n Einnahmen pl.

reverberate [rə'vəɪbəreit] v (sound)

widerhallen. **reverberation** n Widerhall m.

reverence ['revərəns] n Verehrung f. Ehrfurcht f. **revere** v (ver)ehren. **reverend** adj ehrwürdig. **reverent** adj ehrerbietig.

reverse [rə'vəːs] v umkehren. (mot) rückwarts fahren. n (opposite) Gegenteil neut; (of coin, etc.) Rückseite f; (mot) Rückwärtsgang m. **reverse-charge call** R-Gespräch neut. **reversible** adj (coat) wendbar; (law) umstoßbar.

revert [rə'vəːt] v zurückkehren.

review [rə'vjuː] n Nachprüfung f; (magazine) Rundschau f; (troops) Parade f. v nachprüfen. **reviewer** n Kritiker m.

revise [rə'vaiz] v revidieren; (book) überarbeiten. **revision** n Revision f; Überarbeitung f.

revive [rə'vaiv] v wiederbeleben. **revival** n Wiederbelebung f; (play) Wiederaufführung f.

revoke [rə'vouk] n widerrufen. **revocable** adj widerruflich. **revocation** n Widerruf m.

revolt [rə'voult] n Aufruhr m, Aufstand m. v revoltieren, sich empören; (disgust) abstoßen. **revolting** adj abstoßend.

revolution [revə'luːʃən] n (pol) Revolution f; (turning) Umdrehung f, Rotation f. **revolutions per minute** Drehzahl f. **revolutionary** adj revolutionär; n Revolutionär(in).

revolve [rə'volv] v (sich) drehen. **revolver** n Revolver m. **revolving** adj drehbar.

revue [rə'vjuː] n Revue f.

revulsion [rə'vʌlʃən] n Ekel m.

reward [rə'woːd] n Belohnung f; v belohnen. **rewarding** adj lohnend.

rhetoric ['retərik] n Rhetorik f; (empty) Redeschwall m. **rhetorical** adj rhetorisch.

rheumatism ['ruːmətizəm] n Rheumatismus m. **rheumatic** adj rheumatisch.

rhinoceros [rai'nosərəs] n Nashorn neut.

rhododendron [roudə'dendrən] n Rhododendron m or neut.

rhubarb ['ruːbɑːb] n Rhabarber m.

rhyme [raim] n Reim m. v reimen. **nursery rhyme** Kinderreim m.

rhythm ['riðəm] n Rhythmus m. **rhythmic** adj rhythmisch.

rib [rib] n Rippe f. **ribbed** adj (material) gerippt.

ribbon ['ribən] n Band neut; (typewriter) Farbband neut. **ribbons** pl (rags) Fetzen pl. **ribboned** adj gestreift.

rice [rais] n Reis m.

rich [ritʃ] adj reich, wohlhabend; (earth) fruchtbar; (food) schwer. **rich man/woman** Reiche(r). the **rich** die Reichen. **riches** pl n Reichtum m. **richness** n Reichtum m; (food) Schwere f; (finery) Pracht f.

rickety ['rikəti] adj (wobbly) wackelig.

***rid** [rid] v befreien, frei machen. **be rid of** los sein (+acc). **get rid of** loswerden (+acc). **good riddance to him!** Gott sei Dank ist man ihn los!

ridden ['ridn] V ride.

riddle ['ridl] n Rätsel neut.

riddled ['ridld] adj durchlöchert.

***ride** [raid] n reiten; (bicycle, motor cycle) fahren. **riding whip** Reitpeitsche f. n Ritt m; Fahrt f. **take for a ride** (coll) übers Ohr hauen. **rider** n Reiter(in); (cycle) Fahrer(in). **riding** n Reitsport m.

ridge [ridʒ] n Kamm m, Grat m; (roof) First m.

ridicule ['ridikjuːl] n Spott m. v verspotten, lächerlich machen. **ridiculous** adj lächerlich.

rife [raif] adj **be rife** vorherrschen, grassieren. **rife with** voll von.

rifle¹ ['raifl] n (gun) Gewehr neut. **rifle-range** n Schießstand m.

rifle² ['raifl] v ausplündern.

rift [rift] n Spalte f, Riß m.

rig [rig] n Takelung f; (coll) Vorrichtung f, Anlage f. v auftakeln. **rig out** (coll) ausstatten. **rigging** n Takelwerk neut.

right [rait] adj (correct) recht, richtig; (proper) angemessen; (right-hand) recht. **all right** in Ordnung. **be right** (thing) recht sein; (person) recht haben. **feel all right** sich wohl befinden. **right-handed** adj rechtshändig. **right-wing** adj Rechts-. adv (correctly) recht, richtig; (completely) ganz; (to the right) (nach) rechts. **right away** sofort. n Recht neut. **right of way** (mot) Vorfahrt f. v berichtigen. **rightly** adv mit Recht.

righteous ['raitʃəs] adj rechtschaffen, gerecht.

rigid ['ridʒid] adj starr, steif; (person) streng, unbeugsam. **rigidity** n Starrheit f.

rigmarole ['rigməroul] n (coll) Theater neut.

rigour ['rigə] n Strenge f, Härte f. **rigorous** adj streng.

rim [rim] n Rand m.

rind [raind] n (cheese) Rinde f; (bacon) Schwarte f.

ring[1] [riŋ] n Ring m; (comm) Kartell neut. **wedding ring** n Trauring m. **ringleader** n Rädelsführer m.

*****ring**[2] [riŋ] v (sound) läuten, klingeln; (echo) widerhallen. n (Glocken)Klang m, Klingeln neut. **there's a ring at the door** es klingelt. **ring (up)** (coll: phone) anrufen. **ringing** n Läuten neut.

rink [riŋk] n (ice) Eisbahn f.

rinse [rins] v ausspülen. n Spülung f.

riot ['raiət] n Aufruhr m, Tumult m. v randalieren. **rioter** n Aufführer(in). **riotous** adj aufrührerisch; (laughter) zügellos.

rip [rip] v reißen, zerreißen. n Riß m. **ripcord** n Reißleine f.

ripe [raip] adj reif. **ripen** v reifen, reif werden.

ripple ['ripl] n Kräuselung f; (noise) Platschern neut. v (sich) kräuseln.

*****rise** [raiz] v sich erheben; (get up) aufstehen; (meeting) vertagen; (prices) steigen. n Aufstieg m; (prices) Steigen neut; (increase) Zuwachs m; (pay) Erhöhung f. **give rise to** hervorrufen, veranlassen. **rising** adj steigend.

risen ['rizn] V rise.

risk [risk] n Risiko neut; (danger) Gefahr f. v riskieren. **take a risk** ein Risiko eingehen. **risky** adj riskant.

rissole ['risoul] n Boulette f, Frikadelle f.

rite [rait] n Ritus m, Zeremonie f.

ritual ['ritjuəl] n Ritual neut. adj rituell.

rival ['raivəl] n Rivale m, Rivalin f. adj rivalisierend. v rivalisieren or wetteifern mit. **rivalry** n Rivalität f.

river ['rivə] n Fluß m. **down river** stromabwärts. **up river** stromaufwärts. **riverside** n Flußufer neut; adj Ufer-.

rivet ['rivit] n Niet m. v vernieten; (captivate) fesseln.

road [roud] n Straße f; (esp. fig) Weg m. **main road** Landstraße f. **on the road to** auf dem Wege zu. **road accident** Verkehrsunfall m. **road block** Straßensperre f. **road sign** Straßenschild neut. **roadworks** pl n Straßenbauarbeiten pl.

roam [roum] v (umher)wandern.

roar [ro:] v brüllen; (person) laut schreien; (wind) toben. n Gebrüll neut. **roaring** adj (coll) enorm, famos.

roast [roust] v braten, rösten. n Braten m.

rob [rob] v rauben. **robber** n Räuber m. **robbery** n Raub m.

robe [roub] n Talar m. **bathrobe** Bademantel m. v kleiden.

robin ['robin] n Rotkehlchen neut.

robot ['roubot] n Roboter m.

robust [rə'bʌst] adj robust, kräftig. **robustness** n Robustheit f.

rock[1] [rok] n (stone) Fels m, Felsen m; (naut) Klippe f. **steady as a rock** felsenfest. **on the rocks** (fig) gescheitert; (drink) mit Eis. **rockery** n Steingarten m. **rocky** adj felsig.

rock[2] [rok] v schaukeln; (baby) wiegen. **rocking-horse** n Schaukelpferd neut. **rock 'n' roll** n Rock and Roll m.

rocket ['rokit] n Rakete f. v hochschießen.

rod [rod] n Rute f.

rode [roud] V ride.

rodent ['roudənt] n Nagetier neut.

roe [rou] n Rogen m.

rogue [roug] n Schurke m. **roguish** adj schurkisch.

role [roul] n Rolle f.

roll [roul] v rollen. **roll out** ausrollen. **roll over** sich herumdrehen. **roll up** aufwickeln, aufrollen. **roller** n Walze f. **roller blind** Rouleau neut. **roller-skate** n Rollschuh. **rolling-pin** n Nudelholz neut. **rollneck** n Rollkragen m. n Rolle f; (bread) Brötchen neut; (meat) Roulade f. **roll-call** n Namensaufruf m.

romance [rou'mans] n Romanze f. **romantic** romantisch; n Romantiker(in).

Rome [roum] n Rom neut. **Roman** adj römisch. n Römer(in). **Roman Catholic** römisch-katholisch.

romp [romp] v sich herumbalgen. **romp through** leicht hindurchkommen.

roof [ru:f] n (pl -s) Dach neut. v bedachen. **roofing** n Dachwerk neut.

rook[1] [ruk] n Saatkrähe f. v (coll) schwindeln, betrügen.

rook[2] [ruk] n (chess) Turm m.

room [ru:m] n (house) Zimmer neut; (space) Raum m, Platz m. v logieren (bei). **rooms** pl n Wohnung f. **room-mate** n Zimmergenosse m, -genossin f. **roomy** adj geräumig.

roost [ru:st] n Hühnerstall m. v (bird) auf der Stange sitzen, schlafen. **rooster** n Hahn m.

root¹ [ruːt] n Würzel f; (source) Quelle f. **take root** Wurzel schlagen. **rooted** adj eingewürzelt. **rootless** adj wurzellos.

root² [ruːt] v **root for** (pigs) wühlen nach. **root out** ausgraben.

rope [roup] n Seil neut; (naut) Tau neut. v festbinden. **know the ropes** sich auskennen. **ropeladder** n Strickleiter f. **ropy** adj (coll) kläglich, schäbig.

rosary ['rouzəri] n Rosenkranz m.

rose¹ [rouz] V rise.

rose² [rouz] n Rose f. **rosebush** n Rosenstrauch m. **rose-coloured** adj rosenrot. **through rose-coloured spectacles** durch eine rosarote Brille. **rosette** n Rosette f. **rosy** adj rosig.

rosemary ['rouzməri] n Rosmarin m.

rot [rot] v verfaulen. n Fäulnis f; (nonsense) Quatsch m. **rotten** adj faul, verfault; (corrupt) morsch, faul. **rottenness** n Fäule f. **rotter** n (coll) Schweinehund m.

rota ['routə] n Turnus m.

rotate [rou'teit] v sich drehen, rotieren; (crops) wechseln lassen. **rotary** adj rotierend, kreisend. **rotation** n Umdrehung f, Rotation f; (crops, etc.) Abwechselung f. **rotor** n Rotor m.

rouge [ruːʒ] n (make-up) Rouge neut.

rough [rʌf] adj rauh; (sea) stürmisch; (hair) struppig; (person) grob, roh; (approximate) ungefähr. **roughage** n Ballaststoffe pl. **roughen** v aufrauhen. **roughly** adv ungefähr. **roughness** n Rauhheit f.

roulette [ruːˈlet] n Roulette f.

round [raund] adj rund. adv rundherum. n Runde f. v runden; (corner) (herum)fahren um. **round off** abrunden. **round up** (cattle) zusammentreiben; (criminals) ausheben. **round trip** (Hinund) Rückfahrt f. **roundabout** n Karussell neut; (mot) Kreisverkehr m; (motor) weitschweifig. **roundly** adv gründlich. **roundness** n Rundheit f.

route [ruːt] n Weg m, Route f.

routine [ruːˈtiːn] n Routine f. adj üblich.

rove [rouv] v herumwandern. **rover** n Wanderer m.

row¹ [rou] n Reihe f. **in rows** reihenweise.

row² [rou] v (boat) rudern. **rowing** n Rudern neut; (sport) Rudersport m. **rowing boat** Ruderboot neut.

row³ [rau] n (quarrel) Streit m; (noise) Krach m. v sich streiten, zanken.

rowdy ['raudi] adj lärmend, flegelhaft. n Rowdy m.

royal ['roiəl] adj königlich. **royalist** n Royalist m. **royalty** n Königtum neut. **royalties** pl Tantieme f.

rub [rʌb] v reiben. **rub off** abreiben. **rub out** (erase) ausradieren. n Reiben neut.

rubber ['rʌbə] n Gummi m; (eraser) Radiergummi m. **rubber band** Gummiband neut. **rubber stamp** Gummistempel m.

rubbish ['rʌbiʃ] n Abfall m, Müll m; (nonsense) Quatsch m. **rubbishy** adj wertlos.

rubble ['rʌbl] n Trümmer pl, Schutt m.

ruby ['ruːbi] n Rubin m. adj (colour) rubinrot.

rucksack ['rʌksak] n Rucksack m.

rudder ['rʌdə] n Ruder neut.

rude [ruːd] adj grob, unverschämt; (rough) roh, wild. **rudeness** n Grobheit f; Roheit f.

rudiment ['ruːdimənt] n Rudiment neut. **rudiments** pl Grundlagen pl.

rueful ['ruːfəl] adj kläglich, traurig. **ruefulness** n Traurigkeit f.

ruff [rʌf] n Krause f; (bird's) Halskrause f.

ruffian ['rʌfiən] n Schurke m, Raufbold m.

ruffle ['rʌfl] v kräuseln. n Krause f.

rug [rʌg] n (floor) Vorleger m; (blanket) Wolldecke f.

rugby ['rʌgbi] n Rugby neut.

rugged ['rʌgid] adj wild, rauh; (face) runzelig. **ruggedness** n Rauheit f.

ruin [ruin] n Verfall m, Vernichtung f; (building) Ruine f. v vernichten, ruinieren. **ruins** pl Trümmer pl. **ruinous** adj ruinierend.

rule [ruːl] n Regel f; (pol) Regierung f; (drawing) Lineal neut. v regieren; (decide) entscheiden. **rule of thumb** Faustregel f. v (govern) regieren; (decide) entscheiden. **ruler** n (pol) Herrscher(in); (drawing) Lineal neut. **ruling** adj herrschend; n Entscheidung f.

rum [rʌm] n Rum m.

Rumania [ruːˈmainjə] n Rumänien neut. **Rumanian** n Rumäne m, Rumänin f; adj rumänisch.

rumble ['rʌmbl] v poltern, knurren. n Dröhnen neut, Gepolter neut.

rummage ['rʌmidʒ] v **rummage through** durchsuchen, herumwühlen in.

rumour ['ruːmə] n Gerücht neut.

rump [rʌmp] *n* Hinterteil *neut.* **rump steak** Rumpsteak *neut.*

*run [rʌn] *v* rennen, laufen; *(river)* fließen; *(machine)* laufen, in Gang sein; *(nose)* laufen. **run away** weglaufen. **run down** *(person)* heruntermachen. **run-down** *adj* erschöpft. **run out** zu Ende laufen. **run out of** knapp werden mit. **run over** *(fluchtig)* durchsehen. **runway** *n* Rollbahn *f.* n Lauf *m,* Rennen *neut.* **in the long run** auf die Dauer. **on the run** auf der Flucht. **runner** *n* Läufer(in). **running** *adj* laufend; *(water)* fließend.

rung[1] *V* **ring**[2].

rung[2] [rʌn] *n* Sprosse *f.*

rupture ['rʌptʃə] *n* Bruch *m.* *v* brechen, zerreißen.

rural ['ruərəl] *adj* ländlich, Land-.

rush[1] [rʌʃ] *v* stürzen, rasen. *n* Stürzen *neut.* **be in a rush** es eilig haben. **rush hour** Hauptverkehrszeit *f.*

rush[2] [rʌʃ] *n (bot)* Binse *f.*

rusk [rʌsk] *n* Zwieback *m.*

Russia ['rʌʃə] *n* Rußland *neut.* **Russian** *adj* russisch; *n* Russe *m,* Russin *f.*

rust [rʌst] *n* Rost *m.* *v* rosten, rostig werden. **rust-coloured** *adj* rostfarben. **rustproof** *adj* rostfrei. **rusty** *adj* rostig.

rustic ['rʌstik] *adj* ländlich, bäuerlich. *n* Bauer *m.*

rustle ['rʌsl] *v* rascheln, rauschen. *n* Rascheln *neut.*

rut [rʌt] *n* Furche *f.* **be stuck in a rut** beim alten Schlendrian verbleiben.

ruthless ['ruːθlis] *adj* unbarmherzig, rücksichtslos. **ruthlessness** *n* Unbarmherzigkeit *f.*

rye [rai] *n* Roggen *m.*

S

Sabbath ['sabəθ] *n* Sabbat *m.*

sabbatical [sə'batikəl] *adj* **sabbatical year** Urlaubsjahr *neut.*

sable ['seibl] *n* Zobel *m;* (fur) Zobelpelz *m. adj* Zobel-.

sabotage ['sabətaːʒ] *n* Sabotage *f.* *v* sabotieren. **saboteur** *n* Saboteur *m.*

sabre ['seibə] *n* Säbel *m.*

saccharin ['sakərin] *n* Saccharin *neut.*

sachet ['saʃei] *n* Kissen *neut,* Täschchen *neut.*

sack [sak] *n* Sack *m.* *v* entlassen. **get the sack** *(coll)* entlassen werden.

sacrament ['sakrəmənt] *n* Sakrament *neut.* **sacramental** *adj* sakramental.

sacred ['seikrid] *adj* heilig.

sacrifice ['sakrifais] *v* opfern. *n* Opfer *neut.* **sacrificial** *adj* Opfer-.

sacrilege ['sakrəlidʒ] *n* Sakrileg *neut.* **sacrilegious** *adj* gotteslästerlich.

sad [sad] *adj* traurig. **sadden** *v* traurig machen. **sadness** *n* Traurigkeit *f.*

saddle ['sadl] *n* Sattel *m,* (meat) Rücken *m.* *v* satteln; (with task) belasten. **saddlebag** *n* Satteltasche *f.* **saddler** *n* Sattler *m.*

sadism ['seidizəm] *n* Sadismus *m.* **sadist** *n* Sadist(in). **sadistic** *adj* sadistisch.

safe [seif] *adj* (secure) sicher; (not dangerous) ungefährlich; (careful) vorsichtig; (dependable) verläßlich. *n* Safe *m,* Geldschrank *m.* **safe and sound** gesund und munter. **safe conduct** Geleitbrief *m.* **safeguard** *n* Sicherung *f,* Vorsichtsmaßnahme *f.* **safety** *n* Sicherheit *f.* **safety belt** Sicherheitsgurt *m.* **safety pin** Sicherheitsnadel *f.*

saffron ['safrən] *n* Safran *m.* *adj* safrangelb.

sag [sag] *v* absacken, herabhängen.

saga ['saːgə] *n* Saga *f.*

sage[1] [seidʒ] *adj* weise. *n* Weise(r). **sagacious** *adj* scharfsinnig, klug. **sagacity** *n* Klugheit *f.*

sage[2] [seidʒ] *n* (bot) Salbei *f.*

Sagittarius [sadʒi'teəriəs] *n* Schütze *m.*

sago ['seigou] *n* Sago *m.*

said [sed] *V* **say**.

sail [seil] *n* Segel *neut.* *v* segeln; (depart) fahren. **sailing** *n* Segelsport *m.* **sailing boat** *n* Segelboot *neut.* **sailor** *n* Matrose *m.*

saint [seint] *n* Heilige(r). **saintliness** *n* Heiligkeit *f.* **saintly** *adj* fromm.

sake [seik] *n* **for the sake of** wegen (+ gen), um ... (+ gen) willen. **for heaven's sake** um Himmels willen. **for my sake** um meinetwillen.

salad ['saləd] *n* Salat *m.* **salad dressing** Salatsoße *f.*

salami [sə'laːmi] *n* Salami *f.*

salary ['saləri] *n* Gehalt *neut.* **salaried employee** Gehaltsempfänger(in). **salary increase** Gehaltserhöhung *f.*

sale [seil] n Verkauf m; (end of season) Schlußverkauf m. **on** or **for sale** zu verkaufen. **sales** pl Absatz m, Umsatz m. **sales department** Verkaufsabteilung f. **salesgirl** or **saleswoman** n Verkäuferin. **salesman** n Verkäufer m; (travelling) Geschäftsreisende(r).

saline ['seilain] adj salzig. **salinity** n Salzigkeit f.

saliva [sə'laivə] n Speichel m. **salivary** adj Speichel-.

sallow ['salou] adj bläßlich.

salmon ['samən] n Lachs m. adj (colour) lachsrot.

salon ['salon] n Salon m.

saloon [sə'luɪn] n Saal m, Salon m; (bar) Kneipe f, Ausschank m.

salt [soɪlt] n Salz neut. v salzen; (pickle) einsalzen. **salt beef** gepökeltes Rindfleisch neut. **salt cellar** Salzfäßchen neut. **salted** adj gesalzen. **saltiness** n Salzigkeit f. **salt water** Salzwasser neut. **salty** adj salzig.

salute [sə'luɪt] v grüßen. n Gruß m; (of guns) Salut m.

salvage [salvidʒ] n Bergung f, Rettung f. v bergen, retten.

salvation [sal'veifən] n Rettung f, Heil neut. **Salvation Army** Heilsarmee f.

same [seim] pron, adj derselbe, dieselbe, dasselbe; der/die/das gleiche. **all the same** trotzdem. **it's all the same to me** es ist mir gleich or egal. **the same old story** die alte Leier f. **sameness** n Gleichheit f; (monotony) Eintönigkeit f.

sample ['saimpl] n Muster neut, Probe f. v probieren.

sanatorium [sanə'toiriəm] n Sanatorium neut.

sanction ['sankfən] n Sanktion f. v billigen.

sanctity ['sanktəti] n Heiligkeit f.

sanctuary ['sanktfuəri] n Heiligtum neut; (place of safety) Asyl neut.

sand [sand] n Sand m. v **sand down** abschmirgeln. **sandbag** n Sandsack m. **sandbank** n Sandbank f. **sandpaper** n Sandpapier neut. **sand-pit** n Sandgrube f. **sandy** adj sandig.

sandal ['sandl] n Sandale f.

sandwich ['sanwidʒ] n Sandwich neut.

sane [sein] adj geistig gesund. **sanity** n geistige Gesundheit f.

sang [san] V sing.

sanitary ['sanitəri] adj hygienisch. **sanitary towel** Damenbinde f. **sanitation** n Sanierung f, sanitäre Einrichtungen pl.

sank [sank] V sink.

sap [sap] n Saft m. **sapling** n junger Baum m.

sapphire ['safaiə] n Saphir m.

sarcasm ['saɪkazəm] n Sarkasmus m. **sarcastic** adj sarkastisch, höhnisch.

sardine [sɑ'diɪn] n Sardine f.

sardonic [sɑ'donik] adj sardonisch, zynisch.

sash¹ [saf] n (garment) Schärpe f.

sash² [saf] n (window) Fensterrahmen m. **sash window** Fallfenster neut.

sat [sat] V sit.

satchel ['satfəl] n Schulmappe f.

satellite ['satəlait] n Satellit m; (pol) Satellitenstaat m.

satin ['satin] n Satin m. adj Satin-.

satire ['sataiə] n Satire f. **satirical** adj satirisch. **satirist** n Satiriker(in).

satisfy ['satisfai] v befriedigen. **satisfaction** n Befriedigung f; (contentment) Zufriedenheit f. **satisfactory** adj befriedigend. **satisfied** adj zufrieden.

saturate ['satfəreit] v sättigen. **saturation** n Sättigung f.

Saturday ['satədi] n Sonnabend m, Samstag m.

Saturn ['satən] n Saturn m. **saturnine** adj (person) stillschweigend, verdrießlich.

sauce [sois] n Soße f; (cheek) Frechheit f. **sauce-boat** n Soßenschüssel f.

saucepan ['soispən] n Kochtopf m, Kasserolle f.

saucer ['soisə] n Untertasse f. **flying saucer** fliegende Untertasse f.

saucy ['soisi] adj frech, keck.

sauna ['soinə] n Sauna f.

saunter [sointə] v schlendern.

sausage ['sosidʒ] n Wurst f.

savage ['savidʒ] adj (animal) wild; (tribe, etc.) primitiv, barbarisch; (behaviour) brutal, roh. n Wilde(r). **savageness** n Wildheit f. **savagery** n Unzivilisiertheit f.

save¹ [seiv] v (rescue) (er)retten; (money) sparen; (avoid) ersparen; (time) gewinnen; (protect) schützen. n (football) Abwehr f. **saving** n Ersparnis f. **savings** pl Ersparnisse pl. **savings account** Sparkonto neut. **savings bank** Sparkasse f. **savings book** Sparbuch neut.

save² [seiv] prep, conj außer (+dat), mit Ausnahme von (+dat).

saviour ['seivjə] *n* Retter *m*.

savoir-faire [savwa:'feə] *n* Gewandtheit *f*, Feingefühl *neut*.

savoury ['seivəri] *adj* wohlschmeckend, würzig. *n* (*piquant*) Vorspeise *f*.

saw[1] [sɔ:] *V* **see**[1].

*****saw**[2] [sɔ:] *n* Säge *f*. *v* sägen. **sawdust** *n* Sägemehl *neut*. **sawmill** *n* Sägewerk *neut*.

sawn [sɔ:n] *V* **saw**[2].

saxophone ['saksəfoun] *n* Saxophon *neut*. **saxophonist** *n* Saxophonist(in).

*****say** [sei] *v* sagen; (*maintain*) behaupten. **saying** *n* Sprichwort *neut*. **have one's say** seine Meinung äußern. **it goes without saying** selbstverständlich.

scab [skab] *n* Schorf *m*; (*strike-breaker*) Streikbrecher *m*.

scaffold ['skafəld] *n* (*execution*) Schafott *m*. **scaffolding** *n* Baugerüst *neut*, Gestell *neut*.

scald [skɔ:ld] *v* verbrühen. *n* Verbrühung *f*. **scalding** *adj* brühheiß.

scale[1] [skeil] *n* (*fish, etc.*) Schuppe *f*; (*kettle*) Kesselstein *m*. *v* schuppen. **scaly** *adj* schuppig.

scale[2] [skeil] *n also* **scales** *pl* Waage *f*.

scale[3] [skeil] *n* (*gradation*) Skala *f*; (*music*) Tonleiter *f*; (*proportion*) Maßstab *m*. *v* (*climb*) erklettern. **to scale** maßstabgetreu. **scale model** maßstabgetreues Modell *neut*.

scallop ['skaləp] *n* Kammuschel *f*.

scalp [skalp] *n* Kopfhaut *f*; (*as trophy*) Skalp *m*. *v* skalpieren.

scalpel ['skalpəl] *n* Skalpell *neut*.

scampi ['skampi] *pl n* Scampi *pl*.

scan [skan] *v* (*carefully*) prüfen, genau untersuchen; (*briefly*) (flüchtig) überblicken.

scandal ['skandl] *n* Skandal *m*. **scandalize** *v* schockieren. **scandalous** *adj* skandalös. **scandalmonger** *n* Lästermaul *neut*.

scant [skant] *adj* knapp, spärlich. **scanty** *adj* knapp; (*insufficient*) unzulänglich.

scapegoat ['skeipgout] *n* Sündenbock *m*.

scar [ska:] *n* Narbe *f*. *v* vernarben.

scarce [skeəs] *adj* knapp, selten. **scarcely** *adv* kaum. **scarcity** *n* Mangel *m*.

scare [skeə] *v* erschrecken, in Schrecken versetzen. *n* Schreck *m*. **scarecrow** *n* Vogelscheuche *f*. **scary** *adj* erschreckend.

scarf [ska:f] *n* Halstuch *neut*, Schal *m*.

scarlet ['ska:lit] *adj* scharlachrot. **scarlet fever** Scharlachfieber *neut*.

scathing ['skeiðiŋ] *adj* (*fig*) verletzend, beißend.

scatter ['skatə] *v* (ver)streuen; bestreuen (mit). **scatterbrain** *n* Wirrkopf *n*.

scavenge ['skavindʒ] *v* durchsuchen, herumwühlen (in). **scavenger** *n* (*zool*) Aasfresser *m*.

scene [si:n] *n* Szene *f*; (*situation*) Ort *m*. **scenery** *n* Landschaft *f*; (*theatre*) Bühnenbild *neut*. **scenic** *adj* malerisch.

scent [sent] *n* Duft *m*; (*perfume*) Parfüm *neut*. *v* (*smell*) riechen; (*perfume*) parfümieren. **scented** *adj* parfümiert.

sceptic ['skeptik] *n* Skeptiker(in). **sceptical** *adj* skeptisch. **scepticism** *n* Skeptizismus *m*.

sceptre ['septə] *n* Zepter *neut*.

schedule ['ʃedju:l] *n* Plan *m*; (*list*) Verzeichnis *neut*; (*trains*) Fahrplan *m*. *v* planen.

scheme [ski:m] *n* Schema *neut*; (*plan*) Plan *m*, Programm *neut*. *v* (*coll*) intrigieren. **schemer** *n* Ränkeschmied *m*.

schizophrenia [ˌskitsə'fri:niə] *n* Schizophrenie *f*. **schizophrenic** *adj* schizophren; *n* Schizophrene(r).

scholar ['skolə] *n* Gelehrte(r); (*pupil*) Schüler(in). **scholarly** *adj* gelehrt. **scholarship** *n* Gelehrsamkeit *f*; (*grant*) Stipendium *neut*.

scholastic [skə'lastik] *adj* akademisch.

school[1] [sku:l] *n* Schule *f*. *v* schulen. **schoolboy** *n* Schüler *m*. **schoolgirl** *n* Schülerin *f*. **schooling** *n* Unterricht *m*. **schoolteacher** *n* Lehrer(in).

school[2] [sku:l] *n* (*fish*) Zug *m*; (*whales*) Schar *f*.

schooner ['sku:nə] *n* Schoner *m*; (*glass*) Humpen *m*.

sciatica [sai'atikə] *n* Ischias *m* or *neut*.

science ['saiəns] *n* Wissenschaft *f*; (*natural science*) Naturwissenschaft *f*. **scientific** *adj* wissenschaftlich. **scientist** *n* Wissenschaftler(in).

scissors ['sizəz] *pl n* Schere *f sing*.

scoff[1] [skof] *v* spotten (über). *n* Spott *m*, Hohn *m*.

scoff[2] [skof] *v* (*coll*: *eat*) fressen, hinunterschlingen.

scold [skould] *v* schimpfen. **give a scolding** ausschelten (+*acc*).

scone [skon] *n* Teegebäck *neut*.

scoop [sku:p] *n* Schaufel *f*, Schöpfer *m*; (*newspaper*) (sensationelle) Erstmeldung *f*. *v* schöpfen.

scooter ['sku:tə] n Roller m.

scope [skəup] n Umfang m, Gebiet neut.

scorch [skɔ:tʃ] v verbrennen. **scorching** adj (weather) brennend.

score [skɔ:] n (score) Punktzahl f, Spielergebnis neut; (20) zwanzig (Stück); (music) Partitur f. v (points) zählen, machen. **know the score** (coll) Bescheid wissen. **scoreboard** n Anzeigetafel f.

scorn [skɔ:n] n Verachtung f, Spott m. v verachten. **scornful** adj verächtlich.

scorpion ['skɔ:piən] n Skorpion m.

Scotland ['skɔtlənd] n Schottland neut. **Scotch** n (schottischer) Whisky m. **Scotsman** n Schotte m. **Scotswoman** n Schottin f. **Scottish, Scots** adj schottisch.

scoundrel ['skaundrəl] n Schurke m, Schuft m.

scour[1] [skauə] v (clean) scheuern, schrubben. **scourer** n Scheuerlappen m.

scour[2] [skauə] v (search) durchsuchen.

scout [skaut] n (mil) Späher m; (boy scout) Pfadfinder m.

scowl [skaul] v finster (an)blicken. n finsterer Blick m.

scramble ['skrambl] v krabbeln, klettern; (eggs) rühren. **scramble for** balgen um. **scrambled egg(s)** Rührei neut.

scrap [skrap] n (piece) Stück neut, Fetzen m; (metal) Schrott m; (fight) Prügelei f. v (metal) verschrotten; (plan) verwerfen. **scrapbook** n Sammelalbum neut, Einklebebuch neut.

scrape [skreip] v schaben, kratzen. n Kratzen neut; (coll) Klemme f.

scratch [skratʃ] v (zer)kratzen. n Kratzstelle f, Riß m; (wound) Schramme f. **scratchy** adj kratzend.

scrawl [skrɔ:l] v kritzeln. n Gekritzel neut.

scream [skri:m] n Schrei m. v schreien. **it's a scream** es ist zum Schreien.

screech [skri:tʃ] n Gekreisch neut; (cry) (durchdringender) Schrei m. v kreischen.

screen [skri:n] n (Schutz)Schirm m, (Schutz)Wand f; (film) Leinwand f; (TV) Bildschirm m. v abschirmen. **screenplay** n Drehbuch neut.

screw [skru:] n Schraube f. v schrauben. **screwdriver** n Schraubenzieher m.

scribble ['skribl] n Gekritzel neut. v kritzeln. **scribbler** n Kritzler m.

script [skript] n Schrift f; (handwriting) Handschrift f; (film) Drehbuch neut.

scripture ['skriptʃə] n Heilige Schrift f.

scroll [skrəul] n Schriftrolle f; (decoration) Schnörkel m.

scrounge [skraundʒ] v (coll) schmarotzen, schnorren. **scrounger** n Schmarotzer m.

scrub[1] [skrʌb] v schrubben, scheuern. n Schrubben neut. **scrubbing brush** n Scheuerbürste f.

scrub[2] [skrʌb] n (bush) Gestrüpp neut, Busch m.

scruffy ['skrʌfi] adj schäbig.

scruple ['skru:pl] n Skrupel m. **scrupulous** adj peinlich, voller.

scrutiny ['skru:tini] n (genaue) Untersuchung f. **scrutinize** v genau untersuchen.

scuffle ['skʌfl] n Rauferei f. v sich raufen.

sculpt [skʌlpt] v formen, schnitzen. **sculptor** n Bildhauer m. **sculpture** n Skulptur f.

scum [skʌm] n Abschaum m.

scurf [skə:f] n Schorf m; (dandruff) Schuppen pl.

scurvy ['skə:vi] n Skorbut m.

scuttle ['skʌtl] n Kohleneimer m.

scythe [saið] n Sense f. v (ab)mähen.

sea [si:] n See f, Meer neut. **at sea** auf See. **all at sea** (coll) perplex, im Dunkeln. **on the high seas** auf hoher see. **go to sea** zur See gehen.

seabed ['si:bed] n Meeresgrund m.

sea front n Strandpromenade f.

seagoing ['si:gəuiŋ] adj Hochsee-.

seagull ['si:gʌl] n Möwe f.

seahorse ['si:hɔ:s] n Seepferdchen neut.

seal[1] [si:l] n Siegel neut. v besiegeln. **seal up** versiegeln. **sealing wax** Siegellack m.

seal[2] [si:l] n (zool) Robbe f, Seehund m. **sealskin** n Seehundsfell neut.

sea-level n Meeresspiegel m.

sea-lion n Seelöwe m.

seam [si:m] n Saum m, Naht f; (minerals) Flöz neut. v säumen.

seaman ['si:mən] n Seemann m, Matrose m. **seamanlike** adj seemännisch. **seamanship** n Seemannskunst f.

search [sə:tʃ] v suchen, forschen (nach); (for criminal) fahnden (nach); (person, place) durchsuchen (nach). **searchlight** n Scheinwerfer m. **search party** Suchtrupp m. **search warrant** Haussuchungsbefehl m. n Suche f; Untersuchung f. **searcher** n Sucher m, Forscher m. **searching** adj (enquiry) gründlich.

sea-shore n Seeküste f.

seasick ['siːsik] *adj* seekrank. **seasickness** *n* Seekrankheit *f*.

seaside ['siːsaid] *n* See *f*. **at the seaside** an der See. **to the seaside** an die See. **seaside town** Küstenstadt *f*.

season ['siːzn] *n* Jahreszeit *f*; (*comm*) Saison *f*. *v* (*cookery*) würzen; (*wood*) ablagern. **seasonal** *adj* saisonbedingt.

seasoning *n* Würze *f*. **season-ticket** *n* Zeitkarte *f*; (*theatre*) Abonnement *neut*.

seat [siːt] *n* Sitz *m*; (*train, theatre*) Platz *m*; (*residence*) Wohnsitz *m*. *v* setzen. *please be seated!* bitte setzen Sie sich! **seating** *n* Sitzgelegenheit *f*.

seaweed ['siːwiːd] *n* Tang *m*, Alge *f*.

seaworthy ['siːwəːði] *adj* seetüchtig.

secluded [si'kluːdid] *adj* abgelegen. **seclusion** *n* Zurückgezogenheit *f*.

second¹ ['sekənd] *n* (*time*) Sekunde *f*. *wait a second!* moment mal!

second² ['sekənd] *adj* zweit; (*next*) nächst, folgend. *adv* an zweiter Stelle. *n* Zweite(r). **for the second time** zum zweiten Mal. **on second thoughts** bei näherer Überlegung. **play second fiddle** die Nebenrolle spielen. **secondary** *adj* nebensächlich, sekundär. **secondary school** Sekundarschule *f*. **second-best** *adj* zweitbest. **second-class** *adj* zweitrangig. **second-hand** *adj* gebraucht, Gebraucht-. **secondly** *adv* zweitens. **second-rate** *adj* minderwertig.

secret ['siːkrit] *adj* geheim, heimlich. **keep secret** geheimhalten. *n* Geheimnis *neut*. **in secret** or **secretly** *adv* heimlich. **secrecy** *n* Verborgenheit *f*, Heimlichkeit *f*. **secretive** *adj* verschlossen. **secretiveness** *n* Verschlossenheit *f*.

secretary ['sekrətəri] *n* Sekretär(in). **secretarial** *adj* Sekretär-. **secretary general** Generalsekretär *m*.

secrete [si'kriːt] *v* absondern. **secretion** *n* Absonderung *f*.

sect [sekt] *n* Sekte *f*. **sectarian** *adj* sektiererisch.

section ['sekʃən] *n* (*part*) Teil *m*; (*of firm*) Abteilung *f*; (*of book, document*) Abschnitt *m*. *v* **section off** abteilen.

sector ['sektə] *n* Sektor *m*.

secular ['sekjulə] *adj* weltlich. **secularism** *n* Säkularismus *f*.

secure [si'kjuə] *adj* sicher. *v* sichern; (*affix*) festmachen (an); (*procure*) sich beschaffen. **security** *n* Sicherheit *f*; (*bond*)

Bürgschaft *f*. **securities** *pl* (*comm*) Wertpapiere *pl*.

sedate [si'deit] *adj* ruhig, gelassen. **sedateness** *n* Gelassenheit *f*. **sedative** *n* Beruhigungsmittel *neut*. **sedation** *n* (Nerven)Beruhigung *f*.

sediment ['sedimənt] *n* Sediment *neut*. **sedimentation** *n* Sedimentation *n*.

seduce [si'djuːs] *v* verführen. **seducer** *n* Verführer *m*. **seduction** *n* Verführung *f*. **seductive** *adj* verlockend.

***see¹** [siː] *v* sehen; (*understand*) einsehen, verstehen; (*consult*) konsultieren, besuchen. **see home** (*person*) nach Hause begleiten. **seeing that** da. **see through** (*understand*) durchschauen; (*finish*) zu Ende führen. **see to** sich kümmern um. **see to it that** darauf achten, daß. **wait and see** abwarten.

see² [siː] *n* Bistum *neut*.

seed [siːd] *n* Same *m*; (*pip*) Kern *m*. **seedy** *adj* schäbig.

***seek** [siːk] *v* suchen. **seeker** *n* Sucher(in).

seem [siːm] *v* scheinen. **seeming** *adj* scheinbar. **seemly** *adj* schicklich.

seen [siːn] *V* see¹.

seep [siːp] *v* (durch)sickern.

seesaw ['siːsɔː] *n* Wippe *f*. *v* schaukeln.

seethe [siːð] *v* sieden. **seething** *adj* (*coll*) wütend.

segment ['segmənt] *n* Abschnitt *m*, Segment *neut*.

segregate ['segrigeit] *v* trennen, absondern. **segregation** *n* Absonderung *f*; (*racial*) Rassentrennung *f*.

seize [siːz] *v* ergreifen. **seize up** festfahren. **seizure** *n* Ergreifung *f*; (*med*) Anfall *m*.

seldom ['seldəm] *adv* selten.

select [sə'lekt] *v* auswählen, auslesen. *adj* exklusiv. **selected** *adj* ausgewählt. **selection** *n* Auswahl *f*. **selective** *adj* auswählend.

self [self] *n* Selbst *neut*, Ich *neut*.

self-assured *adj* selbstsicher. **self-assurance** *n* Selbstsicherheit *f*.

self-centred *adj* ichbezogen.

self-confident *adj* selbstbewußt, selbstsicher. **self-confidence** *n* Selbstbewußtsein *neut*.

self-conscious *adj* gehemmt, befangen. **self-consciousness** *n* Befangenheit *f*.

self-contained *adj* (*flat*) separat; (*person*) zurückhaltend.

self-control n Selbstbeherrschung f.
self-defence n Selbstverteidigung f.
self-denial n Selbstverleugnung f.
self-discipline n Selbstdisziplin f.
self-employed adj selbständig.
self-esteem n Selbstachtung f.
self-evident adj selbstverständlich.
self-important adj wichtigtuerisch.
self-indulgent adj selbstgefällig.
self-interest n Eigennutz m. **self-interested** adj eigennützig.
selfish ['selfiʃ] adj selbstisch, selbstsüchtig. **selfishness** n Egoismus m.
selfless ['selfis] adj selbstlos.
self-made adj self-made man Emporkömmling m.
self-pity n Selbstmitleid neut.
self-portrait n Selbstporträt neut.
self-respect n Selbstachtung f.
self-righteous adj selbstgerecht.
self-sacrifice n Selbstaufopferung f. **self-sacrificing** adj aufopferungsvoll.
selfsame ['selfseim] adj ebenderselbe, ebendieselbe, ebendasselbe.
self-satisfied adj selbstzufrieden.
self-service n Selbstbedienung f. adj Selbstbedienungs-.
self-sufficient adj unabhängig; (person) selbstgenügsam.
self-will n Eigensinn m. **self-willed** adj eigensinnig.
*sell [sel] v verkaufen. **seller** n Verkäufer(in). **sell out** (betray) verraten. **sold out** ausverkauft.
Sellotape ® ['seləteip] n Tesa-Film m.
semantic [sə'mantik] adj semantisch. **semantics** n Semantik f.
semaphore ['seməfot] n Semaphor m.
semen ['siːmən] n Samen m, Sperma neut.
semicircle ['semisəːkl] n Halbkreis m. **semicircular** adj halbkreisförmig.
semicolon [semi'koulən] n Strichpunkt m.
semi-detached (house) adj halbfreistehend.
semifinal [semi'fainl] n Vorschlußrunde f; Halbfinale neut.
seminal ['seminl] adj Samen-; (influential) einflußreich, wichtig.
seminar ['seminaː] n Seminar neut.
semiprecious [semi'preʃəs] adj halbedel.
semolina [semə'liːnə] n Grieß m; (pudding) Grießbrei m.
senate ['senit] n Senat m. **senator** n Senator m. **senatorial** adj senatorisch.

*send [send] v schicken, senden. **send away** fortschicken. **send for** (person) schicken nach. **send off** (letter) absenden. **send-off** n Abschiedsfeier f. **sender** n Absender(in).
senile ['siːnail] adj senil. **senility** n Senilität f.
senior ['siːnjə] adj älter; (school) Ober-. n Ältere(r).
sensation [sen'seiʃən] n Gefühl neut, Empfindung f; (excitement) Sensation f. **sensational** adj sensationell. **sensationalism** n Effekthascherei f.
sense [sens] n Sinn m; (feeling) Gefühl neut. **common sense** Vernunft f. **make sense** sinnvoll sein. **sense of humour** Sinn für Humor m. v empfinden, spüren. **senseless** adj sinnlos.
sensible ['sensəbl] adj vernünftig. **sensibility** n Sensibilität f. **sensibleness** n Vernünftigkeit f.
sensitive ['sensitiv] adj empfindlich (gegen). **sensitivity** n Empfindlichkeit f; (appreciativeness) Sensibilität f. Feingefühl neut.
sensual ['sensjuəl] adj sinnlich. **sensuality** n Sinnlichkeit f.
sensuous ['sensjuəs] adj sinnlich. **sensuousness** n Sinnlichkeit f.
sent [sent] V send.
sentence ['sentəns] n Satz m; (punishment) Strafe f, Urteil neut. v verurteilen.
sentiment ['sentimənt] n Empfindsamkeit f; (feeling) Gefühl neut. **sentiments** pl Meinungen pl, Gesinnung f sing. **sentimental** adj sentimental. **sentimentality** n Sentimentalität f.
sentry ['sentri] n Wachposten m.
separate ['sepərət; v 'sepəreit] adj getrennt. v trennen; (couple) sich trennen. **separable** adj trennbar. **separateness** n Getrenntheit f. **separation** n Trennung f.
September [sep'tembə] n September m.
septic ['septik] adj septisch.
sequel ['siːkwəl] n (novel, etc.) Fortsetzung f; (consequence) Folge f.
sequence ['siːkwəns] n (Reihen)Folge f, Reihe f; (film) Szene f. **sequential** adj (aufeinander)folgend.
sequin ['siːkwin] n Paillette f.
serenade [serə'neid] n Serenade f.
serene [sə'riːn] adj heiter, gelassen. **serenity** n Heiterkeit f.

serf [sɜːf] n Leibeigene(r). **serfdom** n Leibeigenschaft f.

sergeant ['saɪdʒənt] n (mil) Feldwebel m; (police) Wachtmeister m.

serial ['sɪərɪəl] n (book) Fortsetzungsroman m; (TV, radio) Sendereihe f. adj Fortsetzungs-. **serial number** Seriennummer f.

series ['sɪərɪz] n Serie f.

serious ['sɪərɪəs] adj ernst(haft); (illness) gefährlich. **seriously** adv ernstlich, im Ernst; (injured) schwer. **seriousness** n Ernst m.

sermon ['sɜːmən] n Predigt f.

serpent ['sɜːpənt] n Schlange f.

servant ['sɜːvənt] n Diener(in). **domestic servant** Hausangestellte(r). **public servant** n Beamte(r), Beamtin f.

serve [sɜːv] v dienen (+ dat); (customer) bedienen; (food) servieren; (tennis) aufschlagen. **serve no purpose** nichts nützen. **it serves him right** es geschieht ihm recht.

service ['sɜːvɪs] n Dienst m; (shop, restaurant) Bedienung f; (after-sales) Kundendienst m; (mot) Inspektion; (favour) Gefallen m; (church) Gottesdienst m. **military service** Wehrdienst m. **service station** Tankstelle f. v (mot) warten, überholen. **serviceable** adj brauchbar.

serviette [ˌsɜːvɪ'et] n Serviette f.

servile ['sɜːvaɪl] adj servil. **servility** n Unterwürfigkeit f.

session ['seʃən] n Sitzung f; (university) Semester neut.

*set [set] v setzen, stellen; (date, etc.) festsetzen; (table) decken; (sun) untergehen; (become solid) gerinnen. set aside aufheben. setback n Rückschlag m. set fire to in Brand stecken. set off (on journey) sich auf den Weg machen, aufbrechen. set one's heart on sein Herz hängen an. set to darangehen. setting n Hintergrund m. n Satz m; (crockery) Service f; (radio) Apparat m; (clique) Kreis m, Clique f.

settee [se'tiː] n Sofa neut.

settle ['setl] v (arrange) festsetzen; (dispute) schlichten; (debt) bezahlen; (come to rest) sich niederlassen; (subside) sich senken; (in place) sich ansiedeln. **settle down** (calm down) sich beruhigen; (in place) sich niederlassen. **settle for** (coll)

annehmen. **settle in** sich einleben. **settle up** bezahlen. **settled** adj abgemacht, erledigt. **settlement** n (place) Siedlung f; (agreement) Übereinkommen neut. **settler** n Siedler(in).

seven ['sevn] adj sieben. n Sieben f. **seventh** adj siebt, siebent; n Siebtel neut.

seventeen [sevn'tiːn] adj siebzehn. n Siebzehn f. **seventeenth** adj siebzehnt.

seventy ['sevntɪ] adj siebzig. n Siebzig f.

sever ['sevə] v trennen. **severance** n Trennung f. **severance pay** Abfindungsentschädigung f.

several ['sevrəl] adj mehrere; (separate) getrennt. **severally** adv getrennt.

severe [sə'vɪə] adj streng, hart; (weather) rauh; (difficult) schwierig. **severity** n Strenge f. Härte f; (seriousness) Ernst m.

*sew [sou] v nähen. **sewing** n Näharbeit f. **sewing machine** Nähmaschine f.

sewage ['sjuːdʒ] n Abwasser neut. **sewer** n Abwasserkanal m. **sewerage** n Kanalisation f.

sewn [soun] V sew.

sex [seks] n Geschlecht neut, Sex m. adj Geschlechts-, sexual. **sexual** adj sexual. **sexual intercourse** Geschlechtsverkehr m. **sexuality** n Sexualität f. **sexy** adj sexy.

sextet [seks'tet] n Sextett neut.

shabby ['ʃabɪ] adj schäbig.

shack [ʃak] n Hütte f.

shackle ['ʃakl] v fesseln. **shackles** pl n Fesseln pl.

shade [ʃeɪd] n Schatten m. v beschatten; (protect) schützen; (drawing) schattieren. **shading** n Schattierung f. **shady** adj schattig; (dubious) fragwürdig.

shadow ['ʃadou] n Schatten m. **without a shadow of doubt** ohne den geringsten Zweifel. **shadow cabinet** Schattenkabinett neut. **shadowy** adj schattig.

shaft [ʃaːft] n (handle) Schaft m; (lift) Schacht m; (tech) Welle f.

shaggy ['ʃagɪ] adj zottig.

*shake [ʃeɪk] v schütteln; (shock) erschüttern; (tremble) zittern; (hand) drücken. **shake hands with** die Hand geben (+ dat). **shake off** (coll) loswerden. n Schütteln neut. **shaky** adj wackelig.

shall [ʃal] v (to form future) werden; (implying permission) sollen, dürfen. I **shall go** ich werde gehen. **shall I go?** soll ich gehen?

shallot [ʃə'lot] n Schalotte f.

shallow ['ʃalou] adj flach, seicht; (superficial) oberflächlich, seicht. **shallows** pl n Untiefe f. **shallowness** n Seichtheit f.

sham [ʃam] n Betrug m; (person) Schwindler m. adj falsch.

shambles ['ʃamblz] n Durcheinander neut.

shame [ʃeim] n Scham f, Schamgefühl neut; (scandal) Schande f. it's a shame that ... schade, daß ... shame-faced adj verschämt. **shamefacedness** n Verschämtheit f. what a shame! (wie) schade! v schämen. **shameful** adj schändlich. **shamefulness** n Schändlichkeit f. **shameless** adj schamlos. **shamelessness** n Schamlosigkeit f.

shampoo [ʃam'pu:] n Shampoo neut, Haarwaschmittel neut. v shampooieren.

shamrock ['ʃamrɔk] n Kleeblatt neut.

shanty[1] ['ʃanti] n (hut) Hütte f. **shanty town** Elendsviertel neut.

shanty[2] ['ʃanti] n (song) Matrosenlied neut.

shape [ʃeip] n Gestalt f, Form f. v gestalten, formen. **shaped** adj geformt. **shapeless** adj formlos. **shapelessness** n Formlosigkeit f. **shapely** adj wohlgeformt.

share [ʃeə] n (An)Teil m; (comm) Aktie f. v teilen. **shareholder** n Aktionär m.

shark [ʃɑːk] n Hai(fisch) m.

sharp [ʃɑːp] adj scharf; (pointed) spitz; (outline) deutlich. adv (coll) pünktlich. look sharp! mach schnell! **sharpen** v (knife) schleifen; (pencil) spitzen. **sharp-eyed** adj scharfsichtig. **sharpness** n Schärfe f. **sharpshooter** n Scharfschütze m. **sharp-witted** adj scharfsinnig.

shatter ['ʃatə] v zerschmettern; (glass) zersplittern. **shattered** adj (coll) erschüttert.

shave [ʃeiv] v (sich) rasieren. **clean-shaven** adj glattrasiert. **shaving brush** Rasierpinsel m. **shaving soap** Rasierseife f. **shaving foam** Rasierschaum m. n Rasur f. **shaver** n Rasierapparat m.

shawl [ʃɔːl] n Schal m.

she [ʃiː] pron sie.

sheaf [ʃiːf] n (pl **sheaves**) Garbe f.

*****shear** [ʃiə] v scheren. **shears** pl n Schere f sing. **shearer** n Scherer m. **shearing** n Schur f.

sheath [ʃiːθ] n Scheide f. **sheathe** v (sword) in die Scheide stecken. **sheathed** adj (tech) verkleidet.

*****shed**[1] [ʃed] v (tears, blood) vergießen; (leaves) abwerfen.

shed[2] [ʃed] n (hut) Schuppen m; (cows) Stall m.

sheen [ʃiːn] n Glanz m, Schimmer m.

sheep [ʃiːp] n (pl **sheep**) Schaf neut. **sheepdog** n Schäferhund. **sheepskin** n Schaffell neut. **sheepish** adj einfältig, verlegen.

sheer [ʃiə] adj (pure) bloß; (steep) steil.

sheet [ʃiːt] n (bed) Bettuch neut, (Bett)Laken neut; (paper, metal) Blatt neut.

shelf [ʃelf] n (pl **shelves**) Regal neut, Fach neut. on the shelf sitzengeblieben.

shell [ʃel] n Schale f; (snail) Schneckenhaus neut; (mil) Granate f. **shellfish** n Schaltier neut. **shell-shock** n Kriegsneurose f. v (egg) schälen; (nuts) enthülsen. **shelling** n (mil) Artilleriefeuer neut.

shelter ['ʃeltə] n Obdach neut; (little hut) Schutzhütte f. v beschützen; (take shelter) Schutz suchen.

shelve [ʃelv] v (plan) auf die lange Bank schieben, aufschieben.

shepherd ['ʃepəd] n Schäfer m, Hirt m. **shepherdess** n Schäferin f, Hirtin f.

sheriff ['ʃerif] n Sheriff m.

sherry ['ʃeri] n Sherry m.

shield [ʃiːld] n Schild m; (fig) Schutz m. v beschirmen.

shift [ʃift] v (sich) verschieben; (get rid of) beseitigen; (coll: move fast) schnell fahren; (gear) schalten. n Verschiebung f; (work) Schicht f. **shifty** adj schlau.

shimmer ['ʃimə] n Schimmer m. v schimmern.

shin [ʃin] n Schienbein neut. v **shin up** hinaufklettern.

*****shine** [ʃain] v scheinen, leuchten; (shoes) putzen. n Glanz m. **shiny** adj glänzend, strahlend.

shingle ['ʃingl] n (on beach) Strandkies m.

shingles ['ʃinglz] n (med) Gürtelrose f.

ship [ʃip] n Schiff neut. **shipowner** n Reeder m. **shipwreck** n Schiffbruch m. be shipwrecked Schiffbruch erleiden. **shipyard** n Werft f. v verschiffen, spedieren. **shipment** n Verladung f. **shipper** n Spediteur m.

shirk [ʃəːk] v sich drücken (vor). **shirker** n Drückeberger(in).

shirt [ʃəːt] n Hemd neut. **shirty** adj (coll) verdrießlich.

shit [ʃit] n (vulgar) Scheiße f. v scheißen. **shitty** adj beschissen.

shiver ['ʃivə] v zittern. n Zittern neut.

shoal [ʃoul] n Schwarm m, Zug m.

shock [ʃɔk] n (impact) Stoß m, Anprall m, (fright) Schreck m, Schock m; (med) Nervenschock m; (elec) Schlag m. v schockieren, entsetzen. **shocked** adj schockiert. **shocking** adj schockierend.

shod [ʃɔd] V shoe.

shoddy ['ʃɔdi] adj schäbig.

*****shoe** [ʃuː] n Schuh m; (horse) Hufeisen neut. shoe-horn n Schuhlöffel m. **shoelace** n Schnürsenkel m. v beschuhen. **shoemaker** n Schuhmacher m.

shone [ʃɔn] V shine.

shook [ʃuk] V shake.

*****shoot** [ʃuːt] v schießen; (hit) anschießen; (kill) erschießen; (film) drehen. **shoot down** (aeroplane) abschießen. **shooting** n (game, etc.) Jagd f. **shooting star** Sternschnuppe f.

shop [ʃɔp] n Laden m, Geschäft neut; (factory) Werkstatt f. **shop assistant** Verkäufer(in). **shopkeeper** n Ladenbesitzer m. **shop-lifting** n Ladendiebstahl m. **shop-steward** n Betriebsrat m. **shop-window** n Schaufenster neut. v (also go shopping) einkaufen gehen. **shopper** n Einkäufer(in). **shopping** n Einkäufe pl.

shore [ʃɔː] n Küste f, Strand m.

shorn [ʃɔːn] V shear.

short [ʃɔːt] adj kurz; (person) klein. adv plötzlich. **short of** knapp an.

shortage ['ʃɔːtidʒ] n Mangel m, Knappheit f.

shortbread ['ʃɔːtbred] n Mürbekuchen m.

short-circuit n Kurzschluß m. v kurzschließen.

shortcoming ['ʃɔːtkʌmiŋ] n Fehler m, Unzulänglichkeit f.

short cut n Abkürzung f.

shorthand ['ʃɔːthænd] n Kurzschrift f. **shorthand typist** Stenotypist(in).

short list v in die engere Wahl ziehen.

short-lived adj kurzlebig.

shortly ['ʃɔːtli] adv bald, in kurzer Zeit.

short-sighted adj kurzsichtig. **short-sightedness** n Kurzsichtigkeit f.

shorts [ʃɔːts] pl n kurze Hose f sing.

short-tempered adj reizbar.

short-term adj kurzfristig.

short-time adj **short-time work** Kurzarbeit f.

short-wave adj Kurzwellen-.

shot [ʃɔt] V shoot. n Schuß m; (pellets)

Schrot m; (sport) Kugel f; (films) Aufnahme f; (injection) Spritze f. adj (coll) erschüttert. **have a shot** (coll) versuchen. **shotgun** n Schrotflinte f. **shot put** Kugelstoß m

should [ʃud] v sollen. I should go ich sollte gehen. I should like (to) Ich möchte.

shoulder ['ʃouldə] n Schulter f, Achsel f. **shoulder-blade** n Schulterblatt neut.

shout [ʃaut] v rufen, schreien. n Schrei m, Ruf m. **shouting** n Geschrei neut.

shove [ʃʌv] v schieben, stoßen. n Stoß m, Schub m.

*****show** [ʃou] v zeigen; (goods, etc.) ausstellen. **showcase** n Schaukasten m. **showman** n Schausteller m. **show off** angeben, sich großtun. **show-off** n Angeber m, Großtuer m. **showpiece** n Paradestück neut. **showroom** n Ausstellungsraum m. **show** f; (theatre) Vorstellung f. **mere show** leerer Schein m.

shower ['ʃauə] n (rain) Schauer m; (bath) Dusche f. v sich duschen.

shown [ʃoun] V show.

shred [ʃred] n Fetzen m. v zerfetzen. **not a shred** of keine Spur m.

shrew [ʃruː] n Spitzmaus f; (woman) zankisches Weib neut.

shrewd [ʃruːd] adj scharfsinnig, schlau. **shrewdness** n Scharfsinn m.

shriek [ʃriːk] n Schrei m, Gekreisch neut. v schreien, kreischen.

shrill [ʃril] adj schrill, gellend.

shrimp [ʃrimp] n Garnele f.

shrine [ʃrain] n Schrein m.

*****shrink** [ʃriŋk] v einschrumpfen. **shrink from** zurückweichen von. **shrinkage** n Schrumpfung f.

shrivel ['ʃrivl] v runzelig werden, schrumpfen.

shroud [ʃraud] n Leichentuch neut. v (fig) umhüllen.

Shrove Tuesday [ʃrouv] n Fastnachtsdienstag m.

shrub [ʃrʌb] n Strauch m, Busch m. **shrubbery** n Gebüsch neut.

shrug [ʃrʌg] v zucken. n (Achsel)Zucken neut.

shrunk [ʃrʌŋk] V shrink.

shudder ['ʃʌdə] v schaudern. n Schauder m.

shuffle ['ʃʌfl] v (mit den Füßen) scharren, schlurfen; (cards) mischen. n Schlurfen neut; (cards) (Karten)Mischen neut.

shun [ʃʌn] v vermeiden.

shunt [ʃʌnt] v (rail) rangieren.

*****shut** [ʃʌt] v schließen, zumachen; (book) zuklappen. **shut down** stillegen. **shut off** abstellen. **shut out** aussperren. **shut up** (be silent) den Mund halten. adj geschlossen, zu.

shutter [ʃʌtə] n Fensterladen m; (phot) Verschluß m.

shuttle [ʃʌtl] n Pendelverkehr m.

shuttlecock [ʃʌtlkok] n Federball m.

shy [ʃai] adj schüchtern. v (horse) scheuen. **shy away from** zurückschrecken vor. **shyness** n Schüchternheit f.

sick [sik] adj krank. I feel sick mir ist übel. **sick humour** schwarzer Humor m. **sicken** v erkranken; (disgust) anekeln. **sickening** adj ekelhaft. **sick leave** Krankheitsurlaub m. **sickly** adj kränklich. **sickness** n Krankheit f; (vomiting) Erbrechen neut.

sickle [sikl] n Sichel f.

side [said] n Seite f; (edge) Rand m; (team) Mannschaft f. adj seitlich, Seiten-. **sideboard** n Buffet neut. **sideboards** or **sideburns** pl n Koteletten pl. **sidelight** n (mot) Standlicht neut. **sideline** n Nebenbeschäftigung f. **sidelong** adj seitlich. **sideshow** n Jahrmarktsbude f. **siding** n Nebengleis neut.

sidle [saidl] v sich schlängeln. **sidle up to** heranschleichen an.

siege [siːdʒ] n Belagerung f. **lay siege to** belagern.

sieve [siv] n Sieb neut. v (durch)sieben.

sift [sift] v (durch)sieben; (evidence, etc.) sorgfältig überprüfen.

sigh [sai] v seufzen. n Seufzer m.

sight [sait] n (power of) Sehvermögen neut; (instance of seeing) Anblick m; (range of vision) Sicht f; (of gun) Visier neut; (place of interest) Sehenswürdigkeit f. **at sight** (comm) bei Sicht. **at first sight** beim ersten Anblick. **sighted** adj sichtig. **sightless** adj blind. **go sightseeing** die Sehenswürdigkeiten besichtigen.

sign [sain] n Zeichen neut; (noticeboard, etc.) Schild neut. v unterschreiben. **signwriter** n Schriftmaler m. **signpost** n Wegweiser m.

signal [signəl] n Signal neut. v signalisieren.

signature [signətʃə] n Unterschrift f. **signature tune** Kennmelodie f. **signatory** n Unterzeichner m; (pol) Signatar m.

signify [signifai] v bedeuten. **significance** n Bedeutung f. **significant** adj wichtig.

silence [sailəns] n Ruhe f, Stille f; (absence of talking, etc.) Schweigen neut. v zum Schweigen bringen.

silent [sailənt] adj still, ruhig; stillschweigend. **be** or **fall silent** schweigen. **silent film** Stummfilm m.

silhouette [silu'et] n Silhouette f.

silk [silk] n Seide f. adj Seiden-.

sill [sil] n Fensterbrett neut; (door) Schwelle f.

silly [sili] adj dumm, albern. **silly season** Sauregurkenzeit f.

silt [silt] n Schlamm m. v **silt up** verschlammen.

silver [silvə] n Silber neut. adj silbern, Silber-. **silver plate** Tafelsilber neut. **silver-plated** adj versilbert.

similar [similə] adj ähnlich (+dat). **similarity** n Ähnlichkeit f. **similarly** adv gleichermaßen.

simile [simili] n Gleichnis neut.

simmer [simə] v leicht kochen (lassen).

simple [simpl] adj einfach. **simple-minded** adj einfältig. **simpleton** n Einfaltspinsel m. **simplicity** n Einfachheit f. **simplify** v vereinfachen. **simply** adv einfach.

simulate [simjuleit] v simulieren. **simulation** n Simulation f. **simulator** n Simulator m.

simultaneous [siməl'teinjəs] adj gleichzeitig.

sin [sin] n Sünde f. v sündigen. **sinful** adj sündig. **sinner** n Sünder(in).

since [sins] prep seit. I've been living here since 1960 ich wohne hier seit 1960. conj (time) seit(dem); (because) da. adv seitdem, seither; (in the meantime) inzwischen.

sincere [sin'siə] adj aufrichtig, ehrlich. **yours sincerely** mit freundlichen Grüßen. **sincerity** n Aufrichtigkeit f.

sinew [sinju] n Sehne f. **sinewy** adj sehnig.

*****sing** [siŋ] v singen. **singer** n Sänger(in). **singing** n Singen neut, Gesang m.

singe [sindʒ] v (ver)sengen.

single [siŋgl] adj einzig; (individual) einzeln; (room, bed, etc.) Einzel-; (unmarried) ledig. v **single out** auslesen. **single ticket** einfache Fahrkarte f. **single-handed** adj eigenhändig. **single-minded** adj zielstrebig. **singly** adv einzeln, allein.

singular ['siŋjulə] *adj* einzigartig; (*gramm*) im Singular. *n* (*gramm*) Singular *m*.

sinister ['sinistə] *adj* drohend, unheilvoll.

***sink** [siŋk] *v* sinken; (*cause to sink*) senken. *n* Spülbecken *neut*.

sinuous ['sinjuəs] *adj* gewunden, sich windend.

sinus ['sainəs] *n* (Nasen) Nebenhöhle *f*. **sinusitis** *n* Nebenhöhlenentzündung *f*.

sip [sip] *v* nippen an, schlürfen. *n* Schlückchen *neut*.

siphon ['saifən] *n* Heber *m*; (*soda*) Siphon *m*. *v* aushebern.

sir [sə:] *n* (mein) Herr. **Dear Sir** (*in letters*) sehr geehrter Herr!

siren ['saiərən] *n* Sirene *f*.

sirloin ['sə:loin] *n* Lendenstück *neut*.

sister ['sistə] *n* Schwester *f*; (*nurse*) Oberschwester *f*. **sister-in-law** *n* Schwägerin *f*. *adj* Schwester-. **sisterly** *adj* schwesterlich.

***sit** [sit] *v* sitzen; (*exam*) machen; (*hen*) brüten. **sit down** sich (hin)setzen. **sitting** *n* Sitzung *f*. **sitting duck** leichtes Opfer *neut*. **sitting-room** *n* Wohnzimmer *neut*.

site [sait] *n* Stelle *f*. **building site** Baustelle *f*. *v* placieren.

situation [sitju'eiʃən] *n* Lage *f*; (*state of affairs*) Situation *f*, (Sach)Lage *f*; (*job*) Stelle *f*, Posten *m*. **situated** *adj* gelegen.

six [siks] *adj* sechs. *n* Sechs *f*. **sixth** *adj* sechst; *n* Sechstel *neut*. **sixth form** Prima *f*.

sixteen [siks'ti:n] *adj* sechzehn. *n* Sechzehn *f*.

sixty ['siksti] *adj* sechzig. *n* Sechzig *f*.

size [saiz] *n* Größe *f*. *v* **size up** (*coll*) abschätzen.

sizzle ['sizl] *v* zischen.

skate[1] [skeit] *n* (*ice*) Schlittschuh *m*; (*roller*) Rollschuh *m*. *v* Schlittschuh/Rollschuh laufen. **skater** *n* Eisläufer(in); Rollschuhläufer(in).

skate[2] *n* (*fish*) Rochen *m*.

skeleton ['skelitn] *n* Skelett *neut*, Knochengerüst *neut*. **skeleton key** Dietrich *m*.

sketch [sketʃ] *n* Skizze *f*; (*theatre*) Sketch *m*. *v* skizzieren. **sketchy** *adj* oberflächlich.

skewer ['skjuə] *n* Fleischspieß *m*. *v* spießen.

ski [ski:] *n* Ski *m*. *v* Ski laufen. **skier** *n* Skiläufer(in). Skifahrer(in). **skiing** *n* Skilaufen *neut*, Skifahren *neut*.

skid [skid] *v* schleudern. *n* Schleudern *neut*.

skill [skil] *n* (*skilfulness*) Geschicklichkeit *f*, Gewandtheit *f*; (*expertise*) Fachkenntnis *f*. **skilled** *adj* geschickt. **skilled worker** Facharbeiter *m*. **skilful** *adj* geschickt.

skim [skim] *v* abschöpfen; (*milk*) entrahmen. **skim through** (*read*) überfliegen. **skim milk** Magermilch *f*.

skin [skin] *n* Haut *f*; (*animal*) Fell *neut*, Pelz *m*; (*fruit*) Schale *f*, Rinde *f*. **skin-deep** *adj* oberflächlich. **skin-diving** *n* Schwimmtauchen *neut*. **skinflint** *n* Geizhals *m*. **skin-tight** *adj* hauteng. *v* enthäuten. **skinny** *adj* mager.

skip [skip] *v* hüpfen; (*with rope*) seilspringen; (*miss*) auslassen. **skip through** (*read*) überfliegen. *n* Sprung *m*. **skipping-rope** *n* Hüpfseil *neut*.

skipper ['skipə] *n* (*coll: naut*) Kapitän *m*.

skirmish ['skə:miʃ] *n* Gefecht *neut*.

skirt [skə:t] *n* Rock *m*. *v* (*go around*) herumgehen um. **skirting board** Wandleiste *f*.

skittle ['skitl] *n* Kegel *m*. **play skittles** kegeln. **skittle alley** Kegelbahn *f*.

skull [skʌl] *n* Schädel *m*. **skull-cap** *n* Käppchen *neut*.

skunk [skʌŋk] *n* Skunk *m*, Stinktier *neut*.

sky [skai] *n* Himmel *m*. **sky-blue** *adj* himmelblau. **sky-high** *adj, adv* himmelhoch. **skylark** *n* Lerche *f*. **skylight** *n* Dachfenster *neut*. **skyscraper** *n* Hochhaus *neut*, Wolkenkratzer *m*.

slab [slab] *n* (*stone*) (Stein)Platte *f*; (*chocolate*) Tafel *f*.

slack [slak] *adj* schlaff, locker; (*person*) nachlässig; (*trade*) flau. **slacken** *v* lockern, entspannen; (*pace*, *etc.*) vermindern. **slackness** *n* Schlaffheit *f*.

slacks [slaks] *pl n* Hose *f sing*.

slag [slag] *n* Schlacke *f*. **slagheap** *n* Halde *f*.

slalom ['slɑ:ləm] *n* Slalom *m*.

slam [slam] *v* (*door*) zuknallen. *n* Knall *m*.

slander ['slɑ:ndə] *n* Verleumdung *f*. *v* verleumden. **slanderer** *n* Verleumder *m*. **slanderous** *adj* verleumderisch.

slang [slaŋ] *n* Jargon *m*. *v* beschimpfen.

slant [slɑ:nt] *n* Schräge *f*; (*attitude*) Einstellung *f*. *v* schräg liegen. **slant-eyed** *adj* mit schräggestellten Augen. **slanting** *adj* schräg.

slap [slap] *v* klapsen, schlagen. *n* Klaps *m*. Schlag *m*. **slapdash** *adj* schlampig.

slash [slaʃ] *v* schlitzen, zerfetzen. *n* Schnitt *m*, Schlitz *m*.

slat [slat] *n* Latte *f*. Leiste *f*.

slate [sleit] *n* Schiefer *m*; (*writing*) Schiefertafel *f*; (*on roof*) Dachschiefer *m*. *v* (*coll*) heftig tadeln, kritisieren.

slaughter [ˈslɔːtə] *v* schlachten. *n* Schlachten *neut*. **slaughterhouse** *n* Schlachthaus *neut*. **slaughterer** *n* Schlächter *m*.

slave [sleiv] *n* Sklave *m*, Sklavin *f*. **slave-driver** *n* Leuteschinder *m*. *v* **slave away** schuften. **slavery** *n* Sklaverei *f*. **slavish** *adj* sklavisch.

sledge [sledʒ] *n* Schlitten *m*.

sledgehammer [ˈsledʒˌhamə] *n* Schmiedehammer *m*, Schlägel *m*.

sleek [sliːk] *adj* glatt. **sleekness** *n* Glätte *f*.

*****sleep** [sliːp] *v* schlafen; (*spend the night*) übernachten. *n* Schlaf *m*. **go to sleep** einschlafen. **sleeper** *n* Schläfer(in); (*railway*) Schwelle *f*. **sleeping bag** Schlafsack *m*. **sleeping car** Schlafwagen *m*. **sleepless** *adj* schlaflos. **sleeplessness** *n* Schlaflosigkeit *f*. **sleepwalker** *n* Nachtwandler *m*. **sleepy** *adj* schläfrig, müde.

sleet [sliːt] *n* Schneeregen *m*.

sleeve [sliːv] *n* Ärmel *m*. **sleeved** *adj* mit Ärmeln. **sleeveless** *adj* ärmellos.

sleigh [slei] *n* Schlitten *m*.

slender [ˈslendə] *adj* schlank, schmal. **slenderness** *n* Schlankheit *f*.

slept [slept] *V* sleep.

slice [slais] *n* Scheibe *f*, Schnitte *f*. *v* aufschneiden. **sliced** *adj* geschnitten, in Scheiben. **slicer** *n* Schneidemaschine *f*.

slick [slik] *adj* glatt; (*person*) raffiniert. **slicker** *n* Gauner *m*.

slid [slid] *V* slide.

*****slide** [slaid] *v* gleiten, rutschen. **slide rule** Rechenschieber *m*. **sliding door** Schiebetür *f*. **sliding scale** gleitende Skala *f*. *n* (*phot*) Dia(positiv) *neut*; (*playground*) Schlitterbahn *f*.

slight [slait] *adj* gering, unbedeutend, klein; (*person*) schmächtig, dünn. **not in the slightest** nicht im geringsten. *v* (*person*) kränken. *n* Beleidigung *f*. **slightly** *adv* leicht, ein bißchen.

slim [slim] *adj* schlank, dünn; (*chance, etc.*) gering. *v* eine Schlankheitskur machen, abnehmen. **slimness** *n* Schlankheit *f*.

slime [slaim] *n* Schleim *m*. **slimy** *adj* schleimig.

*****sling** [sliŋ] *n* (*weapon*) Schleuder *m*; (*arm*) Schlinge *f*. *v* schleudern.

slink [sliŋk] *v* schleichen.

slip [slip] *n* Fehltritt *m*; (*underskirt*) Unterrock *m*. *v* gleiten, rutschen. **slip away** sich davonmachen. **slip off** (*clothes*) ausziehen. **slip on** (*clothes*) anziehen. **slip up** sich irren, sich vertun. **slipknot** *n* Laufknoten *m*. **slipshod** *adj* schlampig.

slipper [ˈslipə] *n* Pantoffel *m*.

slippery [ˈslipəri] *adj* schlüpfrig, glitschig; (*person*) aalglatt.

*****slit** [slit] *n* Schlitz *m*. *v* aufschlitzen. **slit-eyed** *adj* schlitzäugig.

slither [ˈsliðə] *v* rutschen, schlittern. **slithery** *adj* schlüpfrig.

slobber [ˈslobə] *v* sabbern, geifern. *n* Geifer *m*. **slobbery** *adj* sabbernd.

sloe [slou] *n* Schlehe *f*.

slog [slog] *v* hart schlagen; (*work hard*) schuften. *n* (harter) Schlag *m*.

slogan [ˈslougən] *n* Slogan *m*, Schlagwort *neut*.

slop [slop] *v* verschütten. *n* Pfütze *f*. **slops** *pl n* Abwasser *neut*.

slope [sloup] *n* Abhang *m*. *v* abfallen. **sloping** *adj* schräg.

sloppy [ˈslopi] *adj* matschig; (*slapdash*) schlampig. **sloppiness** *n* Matschigkeit *f*; Schlampigkeit *f*.

slot [slot] *n* Schlitz *m*; (*for coin*) Münzeinwurf *m*.

slouch [slautʃ] *v* latschen. **slouching** *adj* latschig.

slovenly [ˈslʌvnli] *adj* schlampig.

slow [slou] *adj* langsam; (*boring*) langweilig. *v* also **slow down** or **up** (sich) verlangsamen. **slow-down** *n* Verlangsamung *f*. **slow motion** Zeitlupentempo *neut*. **slowness** *n* Langsamkeit *f*; (*wits*) Schwerfälligkeit *f*.

sludge [slʌdʒ] *n* Schlamm *m*.

slug [slʌg] *n* Schnecke *f*.

sluggish [ˈslʌgiʃ] *adj* träge, schwerfällig; (*river*) langsam fließend. **sluggishness** *n* Schwerfälligkeit *f*.

sluice [sluːs] *n* Schleuse *f*. *v* ausspülen.

slums [slʌmz] pl n Elendsviertel neut.

slumber ['slʌmbə] v schlummern. n
Schlummer m.

slump [slʌmp] v hinplumpsen; (prices)
stürzen. n (comm) Geschäftsrückgang m,
Wirtschaftskrise f.

slung [slʌŋ] V sling.

slunk [slʌŋk] V slink.

slur [slɜː] v (words) verschlucken, undeutlich aussprechen. n Vorwurf m.

slush [slʌʃ] n Matsch m; (snow)
Schneematsch m; (sentimentality)
Schmalz m. slushy adj matschig;
schmalzig.

slut [slʌt] n Schlampe f. sluttish adj
schlampig.

sly [slai] adj schlau, hinterhältig. slyness
n Schlauheit f.

smack¹ [smak] n Klaps m, Klatsch m. v
schlagen, einen Klaps geben (+dat).

smack² [smak] n (flavour) Geschmack m.
v schmecken (nach).

small [smɔːl] adj klein; (number, extent)
gering. small change Kleingeld neut.
small talk Geplauder neut. smallness n
Kleinheit f.

smallpox ['smɔːlpɒks] n Pocken pl.

smart [smɑːt] adj schick, gepflegt; (coll:
clever) gescheit, raffiniert. smart aleck
(coll) Naseweis m. v (suffer) leiden.
smarten up zurechtmachen.

smash [smaʃ] v zerschmettern,
zerschlagen, (enemy, etc.) vernichten. n
(mot) Zusammenstoß m. smash hit
Bombenerfolg m. smashing adj (coll) toll,
sagenhaft.

smear [smiə] v (be)schmieren. n
(Schmutz) Fleck m; (med) Abstrich m.
smear campaign Verleumdung-
skampagne f.

*smell [smel] n Geruch m; (pleasant)
Duft m. v riechen. smell of riechen nach.
smelly adj übelriechend.

smelt [smelt] V smell.

smile [smail] v lächeln. n Lächeln neut.
smiling adj lächelnd.

smirk [smɜːk] v schmunzeln.

smock [smɒk] n Kittel m.

smog [smɒg] n Smog m, Rauchnebel m.

smoke [smouk] v rauchen; (meat, fish)
räuchern. n Rauch m. smokescreen n
Nebelvorhang m. smokestack n Schornstein m. smoker n Raucher(in); (train)
Raucherabteil m. smoking n Rauchen
neut. no smoking Rauchen verboten.

smooth [smuːð] adj glatt. smoothness n
Glätte f. smooth-tongued adj
schmeichlerisch. v glätten.

smother ['smʌðə] v ersticken; (with gifts,
etc.) überhäufen.

smoulder ['smouldə] v schwelen.

smudge [smʌdʒ] n Schmutzfleck n,
Klecks m. v beschmutzen.

smug [smʌg] adj selbstgefällig.

smuggle ['smʌgl] v schmuggeln. smuggler
n Schmuggler m. smuggling n Schmuggel
m.

snack [snak] n Imbiß m. snack bar
Imbißstube f.

snag [snag] n (difficulty) Haken m.

snail [sneil] n Schnecke f. at a snail's pace
im Schneckentempo.

snake [sneik] n Schlange f.

snap [snap] v (break) (zer)brechen; (dog)
schnappen; (noise) knacken; (phot) knipsen. snap at (person) anschnauzen. snap-
dragon n Löwenmaul neut. snap-fastener
n Druckknopf m. snapshot n Schnapp-
schuß m. snappy adj (coll) schnell,
lebhaft.

snare [sneə] n Schlinge f. v fangen.

snare drum n Schnarrtrommel f.

snarl [snɑːl] n Knurren neut. v knurren.

snatch [snatʃ] v schnell ergreifen. snatch
at greifen nach.

sneak [sniːk] v schleichen; (tell tales)
petzen. n Petzer m. sneakers pl n Turn-
schuhe pl. sneaking adj heimlich. sneaky
adj heimtückisch.

sneer [sniə] v spötteln (über). v höhnisch
lächeln. n Hohnlächeln neut.

sneeze [sniːz] v niesen. n Niesen neut.

sniff [snif] v schnüffeln. n Schnüffeln
neut.

snigger ['snigə] v kichern. n Kichern neut.

snip [snip] v schneiden. n. Schnitt m.

snipe [snaip] n Schnepfe f. v aus dem
Hinterhalt schießen. sniper n Hecken-
schütze m.

snivel ['snivl] v wimmern. snivelling adj
weinerlich.

snob [snɒb] n Snob m. snobbery n Snob-
ismus m. snobbish adj snobistisch.

snooker ['snuːkə] n Snooker neut.

snoop [snuːp] v herumschnüffeln. n
Schnüffler m.

snooty ['snuːti] adj hochnäsig.

snooze [snuːz] n Nickerchen neut. v ein
Nickerchen machen.

snore [snɔː] v schnarchen. n Schnarchen neut.

snorkel ['snɔːkəl] n Schnorchel m.

snort [snɔːt] n Schnauben neut. v schnauben.

snout [snaut] n Schnauze f.

snow [snou] n Schnee m. **snowball** n Schneeball m; v (develop) lawinenartig anwachsen. **snowdrift** n Schneewehe f. **snowdrop** n Schneeglöckchen neut. v schneien.

snub [snʌb] n Rüffel m, Verweis m. v rüffeln. adj stumpf.

snuff [snʌf] n Schnupftabak m. **take snuff** schnupfen.

snug [snʌg] adj gemütlich, bequem.

snuggle ['snʌgl] v sich schmiegen (an).

so [sou] adv so; (very) sehr. conj also, daher. **so that** damit. **so am/do I** ich auch. **so what?** na und? **I think so** ich glaube schon.

soak [souk] v durchtränken; (washing) einweichen. **soaking wet** triefend naß.

soap [soup] n Seife f. v (ein)seifen. **soapy** adj seifig. **soapy water** Seifenwasser neut.

soar [sɔː] v (fly up) hochfliegen; (rise) hoch aufsteigen.

sob [sob] v schluchzen. n Schluchzen neut.

sober ['soubə] adj nüchtern. v **sober up** nüchtern werden. **sobriety** n Nüchternheit f.

sociable ['souʃəbl] adj gesellig. **sociability** n Geselligkeit f.

social ['souʃəl] adj (animals) gesellig; (gathering) gesellschaftlich, gesellig; (of society) Gesellschafts-, Sozial-, gesellschaftlich. **social security** Sozialversicherung f. **social services** soziale Einrichtungen pl. **social worker** Sozialarbeiter(in). **socialism** n Sozialismus m. **socialist** n Sozialist(in).

society [sə'saiəti] n Gesellschaft f.

sociology [sousi'olədʒi] n Soziologie f. **sociological** adj soziologisch. **sociologist** n Soziologe m.

sock [sok] n Socke f.

socket ['sokit] n (elec) Steckdose f; (eye) Höhle f; (bone) Gelenkpfanne f.

soda ['soudə] n Soda; also **soda water** Soda(wasser) neut.

sodden ['sodn] adj durchnäßt.

sofa ['soufə] n Sofa neut.

soft [soft] adj weich; (voice, etc.) leise; (gentle) sanft, mild. **soften** v weich

machen or werden; (water) enthärten. **soft-hearted** adj weichherzig.

soggy ['sogi] adj feucht.

soil[1] [soil] n Boden m, Erde f.

soil[2] [soil] n (dirt) Schmutz m. v beschmutzen.

solar ['soulə] adj Sonnen-.

sold [sould] V sell.

solder ['sould] v löten. n Lot neut. **soldering iron** Lötkolben m.

soldier ['souldʒə] n Soldat m.

sole[1] [soul] adj (only) einzig, alleinig.

sole[2] [soul] n (of shoe) Sohle f. v besohlen.

sole[3] [soul] n (fish) Seezunge f.

solemn ['soləm] adj feierlich; (person) ernst. **solemnity** n Feierlichkeit f.

solicitor [sə'lisitə] n (law) Anwalt m.

solicitous [sə'lisitəs] adj fürsorglich; (eager) eifrig.

solid ['solid] adj (not liquid) fest; (pure) massiv. **solidarity** n Solidarität f. **solidify** v fest werden.

solitary ['solitəri] adj (person) einsam; (single) einzeln.

solitude ['solitjuːd] n Einsamkeit f.

solo ['soulou] n Solo neut. adj Solo-, Allein-. adv allein. **soloist** n Solist(in).

solstice ['solstis] n Sonnenwende f.

solve [solv] v lösen. **soluble** adj löslich; (problem) lösbar. **solution** n Lösung f. **solvent** ['solvənt] n Lösungsmittel neut; adj (comm) zahlungsfähig.

sombre ['sombə] adj düster.

some [sʌm] adj (several) einige; (a little) etwas; (some ... or other) (irgend)ein; (approx.) ungefähr. **somebody** or **someone** pron jemand. **some day** eines Tages. **something** pron etwas. **sometime** adv irgendwann. **sometimes** adv manchmal. **somewhat** adv ziemlich. **somewhere** adv irgendwo(hin).

somersault ['sʌməsɔːlt] n Purzelbaum m. v (person) einen Purzelbaum schlagen; (thing) sich überschlagen.

son [sʌn] n Sohn m. **son-in-law** n Schwiegersohn m.

sonata [sə'naːtə] n Sonate f.

song [son] n Lied neut, Gesang m. **songbird** n Singvogel m.

sonic ['sonik] adj Schall-. **sonic barrier** Schallgrenze f.

sonnet ['sonit] n Sonett neut.

soon [suːn] adv bald. **as soon as** sobald. **as soon as possible** so bald wie möglich. **sooner** adv früher.

soot [sut] n Ruß m. **sooty** adj rußig.

soothe [suːð] v beruhigen; (pain) lindern. **soothing** adj lindernd, besänftigend.

sophisticated [sə'fistikeitid] adj (person) kultiviert; (machinery, etc.) kompliziert, hochentwickelt. **sophistication** n Kultiviertheit f.

sopping ['sopiŋ] adj patschnaß.

soprano [sə'praːnou] n Sopranistin f; (voice) Sopran m. adj Sopran-.

sordid ['sordid] adj schmutzig, gemein.

sore [soː] adj wund; (inflamed) entzündet; (coll: annoyed) verärgert. n Wunde f. **sorely** adv äußerst. **soreness** n Empfindlichkeit f.

sorrow ['sorou] n Kummer m, Leid neut; (regret) Reue f. **sorrowful** adj betrübt, traurig.

sorry ['sori] adj traurig, betrübt; (sight, etc.) jämmerlich, traurig. interj Verzeihung! I am sorry es tut mir leid. I am/feel sorry for you Sie tun mir leid.

sort [sort] n Sorte f, Art f; (brand) Marke f. **all sorts of** allerlei. **a sort of** eine Art. **sort of** (coll) gewissermaßen. **that sort of thing** so etwas. v sortieren.

soufflé ['suːflei] n Auflauf m.

sought [sort] V seek. **sought-after** adj gesucht.

soul [soul] n Seele f. **not a soul** kein Mensch. **soul-destroying** adj seelentötend. **soulful** adj seelenvoll. **soulless** adj seelenlos.

sound¹ [saund] n Schall m; (noise) Geräusch neut, Klang m. **soundproof** adj schalldicht. **sound wave** Schallwelle f. v klingen. **sound the alarm** den Alarm schlagen. **sound the horn** hupen. **soundless** adj geräuschlos.

sound² [saund] adj (healthy) gesund; (safe) sicher; (reasoning) stichhaltig.

sound³ [saund] v loten, sondieren.

soup [suːp] n Suppe f, Brühe f.

sour [sauə] adj sauer.

source [sors] n Quelle f.

south [sauθ] n Süden m. adj also **southerly, southern** südlich, Süd-. adv also **southwards** nach Süden, südwärts. **South America** Südamerika neut. **south-east** n Südosten. **South Pole** Südpol m. **southwest** n Südwesten m.

souvenir [suːvə'niə] n Andenken neut.

sovereign ['sovrin] n Souverän m. adj souverän. **sovereignty** n Souveränität f.

Soviet Union ['souviət] n Sowjetunion f.

*sow¹ [sou] v säen; (field) besäen. **sower** n Säer m.

sow² [sau] n Sau f.

sown [soun] V **sow¹**.

soya ['soiə] n Sojabohne f.

spa [spaː] n Badekurort m.

space [speis] n Raum m; (gap) Zwischenraum m, Abstand m; (astron) Weltraum m. **space flight** Raumflug m. **spaceship** n Raumschiff neut. v (räumlich) einteilen. **spacious** adj geräumig.

spade¹ [speid] n Spaten m. **spadework** n (fig) Vorarbeit f.

spade² [speid] n (cards) Pik neut.

Spain [spein] n Spanien neut. **Spaniard** n Spanier(in). **Spanish** adj spanisch.

span [span] n (arch) Spannweite f; (time) Zeitspanne f.

spaniel ['spanjəl] n Spaniel m.

spank [spaŋk] v verhauen, prügeln.

spanner ['spanə] n Schraubenschlüssel m.

spare [speə] adj Ersatz-; (over) übrig; (thin) hager, dürr. **spare time** Freizeit f. **spare tyre** Ersatzreifen m. **spare rib** Rippenspeer m. v (pains, expense) scheuen; (give) übrig haben (für); (feelings, etc.) verschonen. **sparing** adj sparsam. n also **spare part** Ersatzteil m.

spark [spaːk] n Funke m. v funkeln. **spark or sparking plug** Zündkerze f.

sparkle ['spaːkl] v funkeln, glänzen. n Funkeln neut, Glanz m. **sparkler** n Wunderkerze f. **sparkling** adj funkelnd; (wine) schäumend.

sparrow ['sparou] n Spatz m, Sperling m.

sparse [spaːs] adj spärlich, dünn. **sparseness** n Spärlichkeit f.

spasm ['spazəm] n (med) Krampf m; (fig) Anfall m. **spasmodic** adj (fig) sprunghaft.

spastic ['spastik] adj spastisch. n Spastiker(in).

spat [spat] V **spit¹**.

spatial ['speiʃl] adj räumlich.

spatula ['spatjulə] n Spachtel m.

spawn [spoːn] n Laich m. v (eggs) ablegen; (fig) hervorbringen.

*speak [spiːk] v sprechen, reden. **speak out** frei herausreden. **speak to** reden mit. **speak up** laut sprechen. **speak up for** sich einsetzen für. **speaker** n Redner m.

spear [spiə] n Speer m. v aufspießen.

special ['speʃəl] adj besonder, speziell; (train, case) Sonder-. **specialist** n Fachmann m. **speciality** n Spezialität f. **specialization** n Spezialisierung f. **special-**

ize v spezialisieren. **specially** adv besonders.

species ['spiːʃiːz] n Art f; (biol) Spezies f.

specify ['spesifai] v spezifizieren, im einzeln angeben. **specific** adj spezifisch. **specifications** n pl. (tech) technische Daten pl.

specimen ['spesimin] n Muster neut, Probe f.

speck [spek] n Fleck m. **speckle** v flecken.

spectacle ['spektəkl] n Schauspiel neut. **spectacles** pl Brille f sing. **spectacular** adj sensationell.

spectator [spek'teitə] n Zuschauer(in).

spectrum ['spektrəm] n Spektrum neut.

speculate ['spekjuleit] v nachdenken; (comm) spekulieren. **speculation** n Mutmaßung f, Annahme f; (comm) Spekulation f. **speculative** adj spekulativ. **speculator** n Spekulant m.

sped [sped] V speed.

speech [spiːtʃ] n Sprache f; (a talk) Rede f. **make a speech** eine Rede halten.

*speed [spiːd] n Geschwindigkeit f, Tempo neut. v rasen, eilen; (exceed limit) (zu) schnell fahren. **speed up** beschleunigen. **speed limit** Geschwindigkeitsbegrenzung f. **speedboat** n Schnellboot neut. **speedometer** n Tachometer m. **speedy** adj schnell.

*spell[1] [spel] v (name the letters in) buchstabieren; (signify) bedeuten. how do you spell ... ? wie schreibt man ... ? **spell out** (fig) deutlich erklären. **spelling** n Rechtschreibung f.

spell[2] [spel] n (magic) Zauber m, Zauberspruch m. **cast a spell on** bezaubern. **spellbound** adj fasziniert.

spell[3] [spel] n (period) Periode f, Weile f. **spelt** [spelt] V spell[1].

*spend [spend] v (money) ausgeben; (time) verbringen. **spending money** Taschengeld neut. **spendthrift** n Verschwender(in); adj verschwenderisch.

spent [spent] V spend.

sperm [spəːm] n Sperma neut.

sperm whale n Pottwal m.

spew [spjuː] v (vulgar) sich erbrechen, kotzen. **spew out** ausspeien.

sphere [sfiə] n Kugel f; (fig) Bereich m. **spherical** adj kugelförmig.

spice [spais] n Gewürz neut. v würzen. **spiced** adj gewürzt. **spicy** adj pikant, scharf.

spider ['spaidə] n Spinne f. **spider's web** Spinngewebe neut. **spidery** adj spinnenartig.

spike [spaik] n Spitze f, Dorn m.

*spill [spil] v verschütten; (blood) vergießen. n (coll) Sturz, Fall m.

spilt [spilt] V spill.

*spin [spin] v (thread, web) spinnen; (turn) (herum)wirbeln, spinnen; (washing) schleudern. n (coll: in car, etc.) Spazierfahrt f. **spin-dryer** n Wäscheschleuder f. **spinning wheel** Spinnrad neut.

spinach ['spinidʒ] n Spinat m.

spindle ['spindl] n Spindel f. **spindly** adj spindeldürr.

spine [spain] n (thorn, etc.) Stachel m; (anat) Rückgrat neut, Wirbelsäule f. **spiny** adj stachelig.

spinster ['spinstə] n unverheiratete Frau f; (elderly) alte Jungfer f.

spiral ['spaiərəl] adj schraubenförmig, spiral. **spiral staircase** Wendeltreppe f. n Spirale f.

spire [spaiə] n Turmspitze f.

spirit ['spirit] n Geist m. **spirits** pl (drinks) Spirituosen pl, Alkohol m. **high spirits** Frohsinn m, gehobene Stimmung f. v **spirit away** hinwegzaubern. **spirited** adj lebhaft. **spiritual** adj geistig, geistlich.

*spit[1] [spit] n (saliva) Spucke f, Speichel m. v spucken.

spit[2] [spit] n (roasting) (Brat)Spieß m; (geog) Landzunge f.

spite [spait] n Boshaftigkeit f. **in spite of** trotz (+ gen). **spiteful** adj boshaft.

splash [splaʃ] v (be)spritzen. n Spritzen neut; (mark) Fleck m.

spleen [spliːn] n Milz f.

splendid ['splendid] adj prächtig, herrlich. **splendour** n Pracht f.

splice [splais] v (ropes) spleißen; (tapes, films) zusammenfügen.

splint [splint] n Schiene f. **splinter** n Splitter m. v zersplittern. **splinter group** Splittergruppe f.

*split [split] v (zer)spalten, sich spalten. **split up** sich trennen. **split hairs** Haarspalterei treiben. **splitting headache** rasende Kopfschmerzen pl. n Spalt m, Riß m. adj gespalten.

splutter ['splʌtə] v stottern.

*spoil [spoil] v verderben; (child) verwöhnen. **spoils** pl n Beute f. **spoilsport** n Spielverderber(in).

spoke[1] [spouk] *V* **speak**.

spoke[2] [spouk] *n* (*wheel*) Speiche *f*.

spoken ['spoukn] *V* **speak**.

spokesman ['spouksmən] *n* Sprecher *m*.

sponge [spʌndʒ] *n* Schwamm *m*. v **sponge down** (mit einem Schwamm) abwaschen. **sponge-cake** *n* Sandtorte *f*. **sponger** *n* (*coll*) Schmarotzer *m*. **spongy** *adj* schwammig.

sponsor ['sponsə] *n* Förderer *m*, Schirmherr *m*; (*radio*, *TV*) Sponsor *m*. v unterstützen, fördern. **sponsorship** *n* Schirmherrschaft *f*.

spontaneous [spon'teinjəs] *adj* spontan. **spontaneity** *n* Freiwilligkeit *f*, Spontaneität *f*.

spool [spuːl] *n* Spule *f*.

spoon [spuːn] *n* Löffel *m*. v **spoon out** auslöffeln. **spoon-feed** v verhätscheln. **spoonful** *n* Löffelvoll *m*.

sporadic [spə'radik] *adj* verstreut, sporadisch.

sport [spoːt] *n* Sport *m*; (*fun*) Spaß *m*. **play sports** Sport treiben. **sportscar** *n* Sportwagen *m*. **sportsman** *n* Sportler *m*. **sportswoman** *n* Sportlerin *f*. v scherzen; (*wear*) tragen. **sporting** *adj* sportlich.

spot [spot] *n* (*mark*) Fleck *m*; (*place*) Stelle *f*; (*pimple*) Pickel *m*. **spot check** Stichprobe *f*. **spotlight** *n* Scheinwerfer *m*. **spotless** *adj* fleckenlos. v beflecken; (*notice*) entdecken, erspähen. **spotted** *adj* fleckig. **spotty** *adj* pickelig.

spouse [spaus] *n* Gatte *m*. Gattin *f*, Gemahl(in).

spout [spaut] *n* Tülle *f*, Schnauze *f*. v (*coll*) deklamieren.

sprain [sprein] *n* Verrenkung *f*. v verrenken.

sprang [spraŋ] *V* **spring**.

sprawl [sproːl] *v* (*person*) sich rekeln; (*town*) sich ausbreiten.

spray[1] [sprei] v (be)sprühen. *n* (*aerosol*, *etc.*) Sprühdose *f*, Spray *m*; (*sea*) Schaum *m*.

spray[2] [sprei] *n* (*of flowers*) Blütenzweig *m*.

*spread [spred] *v* ausbreiten; (*butter*, *etc.*) streichen; (*rumour*) (sich) verbreiten. *n* Ausbreitung *f*; (*extent*) Umfang *m*, Spanne *f*; (*for bread*) Aufstrich *m*.

spree [spriː] *n* (*shopping*) Einkaufsbummel *m*.

sprig [sprig] *n* Schößling *m*.

sprightly ['spraitli] *adj* lebhaft, munter.

*spring [spriŋ] *n* (*season*) Frühling *m*; (*tech*) Feder *f*; (*water*) Brunnen *m*, Quelle *f*. **springboard** *n* Sprungbrett *neut*. v springen. **spring a leak** ein Leck bekommen. **springing** *n* Federung *f*. **springy** *adj* elastisch.

sprinkle ['spriŋkl] *v* sprenkeln. **sprinkler** *n* Brause *f*. **a sprinkling of** ein bißchen.

sprint [sprint] *n* Sprint *m*. v sprinten. **sprinter** *n* Sprinter *m*.

sprout [spraut] *v* sprießen. *n* Sprößling *m*. (**Brussels**) **sprouts** Rosenkohl *m sing*.

spruce [spruːs] *n* (*tree*) Fichte *f*.

sprung [sprʌŋ] *V* **spring**.

spur [spəː] *n* Sporn *m*; (*fig*) Ansporn *m*. v (*horse*) die Sporen geben (+*dat*); (*fig*) anspornen.

spurious ['spjuəriəs] *adj* falsch, unecht.

spurn [spəːn] *v* zurückweisen.

spurt [spəːt] *v* (*water*) hervorspritzen. *n* (*sport*) Spurt *m*.

spy [spai] *v* (*espy*) erspähen; (*pol*) spionieren. *n* Spion(in). **spy-glass** *n* Fernglas *neut*. **spying** *n* Spionage *f*.

squabble ['skwobl] *v* sich zanken. *n* Kabbelei *f*, Zank *m*.

squad [skwod] *n* Gruppe *f*; (*mil*) Zug *m*; (*police*) Kommando *neut*. **flying squad** Überfallkommando *neut*. **squad car** Streifenwagen *m*.

squadron ['skwodrən] *n* (*naut*) Geschwader *neut*; (*aero*) Staffel *f*. **squadron leader** Major *m*.

squalid ['skwolid] *adj* schmutzig. **squalor** *n* Schmutz *m*.

squall [skwoːl] *n* heftiger Windstoß *m*; (*storm*) Gewitter *neut*.

squander ['skwondə] *v* verschwenden, vergeuden.

square [skweə] *n* Quadrat *neut*, Viereck *neut*; (*in town*) Platz *m*. *adj* viereckig, quadratisch.

squash [skwoʃ] *n* (*people*) Gedränge *neut*; (*game*) Squash *neut*. v zerquetschen. **fruit squash** Fruchtsaft *m*.

squat [skwot] *v* hocken; (*ein Haus*) unberechtigt besetzen. *adj* gedrungen. **squatter** *n* Squatter *m*.

squawk [skwoːk] *n* Kreischen *neut*. v kreischen.

squeak [skwiːk] *v* (*wheel*, *etc.*) quietschen; (*mouse*, *etc.*) piepsen. *n* Quietschen *neut*; Piepsen *neut*. **squeaky** *adj* quietschend.

squeal [skwiːl] v schreien, quieken; (criminal) pfeifen. n Schrei m, Quieken neut.

squeamish ['skwiːmiʃ] adj überempfindlich. **squeamishness** n Überempfindlichkeit f.

squeeze [skwiːz] v drücken; (fruit) auspressen, ausquetschen. n Druck m. **credit squeeze** Kreditbeschränkung f. **squeezer** n Presse f.

squid [skwid] n Tintenfisch m.

squiggle ['skwigl] n Kritzelei f.

squint [skwint] n Schielen neut. v schielen. **squint-eyed** adj schielend.

squire ['skwaiə] n Junker m, Gutsherr m.

squirm [skwəːm] v sich winden.

squirrel ['skwirəl] n Eichhörnchen neut.

squirt [skwəːt] v spritzen. n Spritze f.

stab [stab] v (kill) erstechen. n Stich m. **stab wound** Stichwunde f. **make a stab at** versuchen.

stabilize ['steibilaiz] v stabilisieren. **stability** n Stabilität f. **stabilization** n Stabilisierung f.

stable[1] ['steibl] n Stall m. v einstallen. **stable-lad/man** n Stallknecht m.

stable[2] ['steibl] adj stabil.

staccato [stə'kaːtou] adj, adv staccato.

stack [stak] n Schober m; (wood, etc.) Stapel m. v aufschobern.

stadium ['steidiəm] n Stadion neut.

staff [staːf] n (stick) Stock m; (work force) Personal neut; (mil) Stab m. adj Personal-; stabs-.

stag [stag] n Rothirsch m. **stag party** Herrengesellschaft f.

stage [steidʒ] n (of development, etc.) Stufe f, Stadium neut; (theatre) Bühne. **stage fright** Lampenfieber neut. **stage-manager** n Inspizient m. v (play) aufführen; (fig) veranstalten.

stagger ['stagə] v schwanken, taumeln; (amaze) verblüffen. **staggering** adj taumelnd; phantastisch.

stagnant ['stagnənt] adj stillstehend, stagnierend. **stagnate** v stagnieren. **stagnation** n Stagnation f.

staid [steid] adj gesetzt, seriös.

stain [stein] n Fleck m; (for wood, etc.) Färbung f. v beflecken; färben. **stainless** adj (steel) rostfrei.

stair [steə] n Treppenstufe f. **(flight of) stairs** Treppe f. **stair-carpet** n Treppenläufer m.

stake[1] [steik] n (post) Pfahl m, Pfosten m.

---

stake a claim (to) Anspruch erheben (auf).

stake[2] [steik] n (betting) Einsatz m; (share) Anteil m. v (money) setzen. **put at stake** aufs Spiel setzen.

stale [steil] adj (bread) alt, altbacken; (beer, etc.) abgestanden; (thing) abgedroschen.

stalemate ['steilmeit] n (chess) Patt neut; (fig) Stillstand m. v pattsetzen.

stalk[1] [stoːk] n (bot) Stiel m.

stalk[2] [stoːk] v sich anpirschen an.

stall[1] [stoːl] n (stable) Stand m; (market) Bude f. **stalls** pl (theatre) Parkett neut sing. v (engine) aussetzen; (car) stehenbleiben.

stall[2] [stoːl] v (delay) ausweichen, Ausflüchte machen.

stallion ['staljən] n Hengst m.

stamina ['staminə] n Durchhaltevermögen neut, Ausdauer f.

stammer ['stamə] v stottern, stammeln. n Stottern neut, Gestammel neut. **stammerer** n Stotterer m. **stammering** adj stotternd.

stamp [stamp] v (with foot) stampfen; (rubber stamp) stempeln; (letters) frankieren. n Stempel m; (letter) Briefmarke f. **stamp album** Briefmarkenalbum neut. **stamp collector** Briefmarkensammler m.

stampede [stam'piːd] n wilde Flucht f.

***stand** [stand] n (sales, etc.) Bude f. Stand m; (attitude) Standpunkt m; (for spectators) (Zuschauer)Tribüne f; (resistance) Widerstand m. v stehen. **I can't stand him** ich kann ihn nicht ausstehen. **I can't stand it** ich kann es nicht aushalten. **as things stand** unter den Umständen. **my offer stands** mein Angebot gilt noch. **stand aside** beiseite treten. **stand back** zurücktreten. **stand by** (be loyal to) treu bleiben (+dat). **stand for** (mean) bedeuten, stehen für; (tolerate) sich gefallen lassen; (parliament) kandidieren. **stand in for** einspringen für. **stand up** aufstehen. **stand up to** sich verteidigen gegen. **standby** n Stütze f; (alert) Alarmbereitschaft f. **standing** n Stand m, Rang m. **standing order** (bank) Dauerauftrag m. **stand-offish** adj hochmütig.

standard ['standəd] n Standard m, Norm f. (flag) Standarte f. adj Normal-; (usual) gewöhnlich, normal. **standardize** v normen, standardisieren. **standardization** *n* Normung *f*.

stank [staŋk] *V* **stink**.

stanza ['stanzə] *n* Strophe *f*, Stanza *f*.

staple[1] [steɪpl] *n* Heftklammer *f* *v* heften. **stapler** *n* Heftmaschine *f*.

staple[2] [steɪpl] *adj* Haupt-.

star [staɪ] *n* Stern *m*; (*films, etc.*) Star *m*. **starlight** Sternenlicht *neut*. *v* die Hauptrolle spielen. **starring** *in* der Hauptrolle. **starry** *adj* (*sky*) Sternen-; (*night*) sternhell.

starboard ['stabəd] *n* Steuerbord *neut*. *adj* Steuerbord-.

starch [staɪtʃ] *n* (*Wäsche*)Stärke *f*. *v* stärken. **starched** *adj* gestärkt. **starchy** *adj* (*person*) steif, förmlich.

stare [steə] *n* starrer Blick *m*, Starrblick *m*. *v* starren. **stare at** anstarren.

stark [stak] *adj* kahl, öde. *adv* **stark naked** splitternackt. **stark-staring mad** total verrückt.

starling ['staliŋ] *n* Star *m*.

start [staɪt] *v* anfangen, beginnen; (*leave*) abfahren; (*arise*) entstehen; (*sport*) starten (lassen); (*engine*) anlassen; (*jump*) hochschrecken. *n* Anfang *m*, Beginn *m*; (*sport*) Start *m*; (*journey*) Abreise *f*. **from the start** vom Anfang an. **starter** *n* (*sport*) Starter *m*. **starter motor** Anlaßmotor *m*.

startle ['staɪtl] *v* erschrecken, überraschen. **startling** *adj* erschreckend.

starve [staɪv] *v* verhungern. **starvation** *n* Hungern *neut*, Verhungern *neut*.

state [steɪt] *n* (*pol*) Staat *m*; (*condition*) Zustand *m*; (*situation*) Lage *f*. *v* erklären, behaupten. *adj* Staats-, staatlich. **stated** *adj* angegeben. **stateless** *adj* staatenlos. **stately** *adj* stattlich. **statement** *n* Erklärung *f*. **statement of account** Kontoauszug *m*. **statesman** *n* Staatsmann *m*. **statesmanship** *n* Staatskunst *f*.

static ['statik] *adj* statisch. *n* statische Elektrizität *f*.

station ['steɪʃən] *n* Platz *m*, Posten *m*; (*rail*) Bahnhof *m*; (*standing*) Stand *m*. **station master** Bahnhofsvorsteher *m*. **station wagon** Kombi(wagen) *m*. *v* stationieren.

stationary ['steɪʃənəri] *adj* stillstehend, stationär.

stationer ['steɪʃənə] *n* Schreibwarenhändler *m*. **stationery** *n* Schreibwaren *pl*; (*office*) Büromaterial *neut*.

statistics [stə'tistiks] *n* Statistik *f*. **statistical** *adj* statistisch.

statue ['statjuː] *n* Standbild *neut*, Statue *f*.

stature ['statʃə] *n* Körpergröße *f*, Statur *f*; (*moral, etc.*) Kaliber *neut*.

status ['steɪtəs] *n* Status *m*; (*rank*) Stand *m*, Rang *m*. **status quo** Status Quo *m*. **status symbol** Statussymbol *neut*.

statute ['statjuːt] *n* Gesetz *neut*. **statutory** *adj* gesetzlich (vorgeschrieben).

staunch [stɔːntʃ] *adj* getreu, zuverlässig.

stay [steɪ] *v* bleiben; (*in hotel*) logieren, unterkommen; (*with friends, etc.*) zu Besuch sein (bei). **stay the night** übernachten. **stay behind** zurückbleiben. **stay in** zu Hause bleiben. *n* Aufenthalt *m*; Besuch *m*.

steadfast ['stedfaɪst] *adj* fest, treu.

steady ['stedi] *adj* sicher, fest, stabil; (*regular*) regelmäßig, gleichmäßig; (*cautious*) vorsichtig. *v* festigen. **steady on!** langsam!, vorsichtig! **steadiness** *n* Festigkeit *f*, Sicherheit *f*.

steak [steik] *n* Steak *neut*.

*****steal** [stiːl] *v* stehlen. **steal away** sich davonstehlen.

stealthy ['stelθi] *adj* heimlich. **stealth** *n* Heimlichkeit *f*.

steam [stiːm] *n* Dampf *m*. *v* dampfen; (*food*) dünsten. **steam-boiler** *n* Dampfkessel *m*. **steamer** *n* (*naut*) Dampfer *m*, Dampfschiff *neut*; (*cookery*) Dampfkochtopf *m*. **steam-roller** *n* Dampfwalze *f*; *v* (*opposition*) niederwalzen. **steamy** *adj* dampfig.

steel [stiːl] *n* Stahl *m*. *adj* stählern, Stahl-. **steelworks** *pl* *n* Stahlwerk *neut* *sing*. **steely** hart.

steep[1] [stiːp] *adj* steil, jäh; (*coll: improbable*) unwahrscheinlich; (*prices*) gepfeffert.

steep[2] [stiːp] *v* (*soak*) einweichen.

steeple ['stiːpl] *n* Kirchturm *m*, Spitzturm *m*.

steeplechase ['stiːpltʃeis] *n* Steeplechase *f*. **steeplejack** *n* Turmarbeiter *m*.

steer [stiə] *v* steuern, lenken. **steering column** Lenksäule *f*. **steering lock** Lenkradschloß *m*. **steering wheel** Lenkrad *neut*, Steuer *neut*.

stem[1] [stem] *n* (*stalk*) Stiel *m*; (*line of descent*) Stamm *m*. *v* **stem from** stammen von, zurückgehen auf.

stem[2] [stem] *v* eindämmen; (*blood*) stillen.

stench [stentʃ] n Gestank m.

stencil ['stensl] n Schablone f. v schablonieren.

step [step] v treten, schreiten. n Schritt m; (measure) Maßnahme f; (stage, gradation) Stufe f. step by step Schritt für Schritt. step on it (coll) Gas geben. step aside zur seite treten. step-ladder n Trittleiter f. stepping-stone n Trittstein m; (fig) Sprungbrett neut.

stepbrother ['stepbrʌðə] n Stiefbruder m.
stepdaughter ['stepdɔːtə] n Stieftochter f.
stepfather ['stepfaːðə] n Stiefvater m.
stepmother ['stepmʌðə] n Stiefmutter f.
stepsister ['stepsistə] n Stiefschwester f.
stepson ['stepsʌn] n Stiefsohn m.

stereo ['steriou] n Stereoanlage f. adj Stereo-. stereophonic adj stereophonisch.

stereotyped ['steriətaipt] adj stereotyp.

sterile ['sterail] adj steril. sterility n Sterilität f.

sterling ['stəːliŋ] n Sterling m.

stern[1] [stəːn] adj streng, hart. sternness n Strenge f. Härte f.

stern[2] [stəːn] n (naut) Heck neut.

stethoscope ['steθəskoup] n Stethoskop neut.

stew [stjuː] n Eintopfgericht neut. v schmoren. stewed adj geschmort.

steward ['stjuəd] n (ship, aeroplane) Steward m; (race, etc.) Ordner m. stewardess n Stewardeß f.

stick[1] [stik] n (wood) Stock m; (hockey) Schläger m.

*stick[2] [stik] v (with glue, etc.) kleben or heften (an); (pointed instrument) stecken; stick out (tongue) herausstrecken; (protrude) hervorstehen. stick to (remain with) bleiben bei. stick up for sich einsetzen für. be stuck steckenbleiben. stuck-up adj hochnäsig. sticking plaster Heftpflaster neut. sticky adj klebrig.

stiff [stif] adj steif, starr; (drink) stark; (difficult) schwierig. n (coll) Leiche f. stiffen v (ver)steifen, (ver)stärken. stiffnecked adj halsstarrig. stiffness n Steife f. Starrheit f.

stifle ['staifl] v ersticken. stifling adj zum Ersticken.

stigma ['stigmə] n Brandmal neut, Stigma neut.

stile [stail] n Zauntritt m.

still[1] [stil] adj still. adv (immer)noch. conj und doch, dennoch. v beruhigen. still

birth Totgeburt f. stillborn adj totgeboren. stillness n Stille f.

still[2] [stil] n (for spirits) Brennerei f.

stilt [stilt] n Stelze f. stilted adj gespreizt.

stimulus ['stimjuləs] n (pl -i) Stimulus m. stimulant n Reizmittel neut. stimulate v anregen. stimulating adj anregend. stimulation n Anreiz m.

*sting [stiŋ] v (insect) stechen; (be painful) brennen; (remark) kränken. n Stich m. stinging adj brennend; schmerzend. stinging nettle Brennessel f.

stingy ['stindʒi] adj geizig.

*stink [stiŋk] v stinken, übel riechen. n Gestank m; (coll: scandal) Skandal m.

stint [stint] v knausern mit. n (of work) Schicht f.

stipulate ['stipjuleit] v festsetzen; (insist on) bestehen auf. stipulation Bedingung f.

stir [stəː] v (liquids) (an)rühren; (move) sich rühren or bewegen; (excite) aufrühren, bewegen. n Rühren neut; (sensation) Sensation f. stirring adj aufregend.

stirrup ['stirəp] n Steigbügel m.

stitch [stitʃ] n Stich m; (knitting) Masche f; (pain) Stechen m. v nähen. stitch up vernähen. stitching n Näherei f.

stoat [stout] n Hermelin neut.

stock [stok] n (of goods) Vorrat m, Lager neut; (cookery) Brühe; (descent) Stamm m. stocks pl (comm) Aktien pl. stockbroker n Börsenmakler m. stock exchange Börse f. stockpile v aufstapeln. stock-still adj bewegungslos. stocktaking n Bestandaufnahme f. v (goods) führen, vorrätig haben.

stocking ['stokiŋ] n Strumpf m.

stocky ['stoki] adj stämmig, untersetzt.

stodge [stodʒ] n schwerverdauliches Zeug neut. stodgy adj schwer(verdaulich).

stoical ['stouikl] adj stoisch.

stoke [stouk] v schüren. stoker n Heizer m.

stole[1] [stoul] V steal.

stole[2] [stoul] n Stola f.

stolen ['stoulən] V steal.

stomach ['stʌmək] n Magen m; (coll: abdomen) Bauch m; (taste for) Appetit (zu) f. v ertragen. stomach-ache n Magenschmerzen pl.

stone [stoun] n Stein m; (fruit) Kern m. adj steinern, Stein-. v (fruit) entkernen; (to death) steinigen. stone age Steinzeit f.

stoned adj (coll) besoffen. **stone-deaf** adj stocktaub. **stonemason** n Steinmetz m. **stony** adj steinig.

stood [stud] V stand.

stool [stuːl] n Hocker m, Stuhl m; (med) Stuhlgang m.

stoop [stuːp] v sich bücken; (posture) gebeugt gehen. n Beugen neut, krumme Haltung f.

stop [stop] v (activity) aufhören; (motion) anhalten, stoppen; (clock) stehenbleiben; (put a stop to) einstellen; (bus, train) anhalten; (pipe, etc.) verstopfen. n Halt m, Stillstand m; (break) Pause f; (bus) Haltestelle f. **stoppage** n Stillstand m. **stopper** n Stöpsel m. **stop-watch** n Stoppuhr f.

store [stoː] v aufbewahren. n Vorrat m, Lager neut; (shop) Laden m. **storage** n Lagerung f. **storekeeper** n (shop) Ladenbesitzer m.

storey [ˈstoːri] n Stockwerk neut. **four-storied** adj vierstöckig.

stork [stoːk] n Storch m.

storm [stoːm] n Sturm m, Unwetter neut; (thunderstorm) Gewitter neut. **storm-tossed** adj sturmgepeitscht. v stürmen. **storm-troops** Sturmtruppen pl. **stormy** adj stürmisch.

story [ˈstoːri] n Geschichte f, Erzählung f. **to cut a long story short** um es ganz kurz zu sagen. **story-book** n Märchenbuch neut. **story-teller** n Erzähler(in).

stout [staut] adj dick, beleibt; (strong) kräftig. n dunkles Bier neut, Malzbier neut.

stove [stouv] n Ofen m; (cooking) Kochherd m. **stove-pipe** Ofenrohr neut.

stow [stou] v verstauen. **stowaway** blinder Passagier m.

straddle [ˈstradl] v (sitting) rittlings sitzen auf.

straggle [ˈstragl] v umherstreifen. **straggle behind** nachhinken. **straggler** n Nachzügler m.

straight [streit] adj gerade; (hair) glatt; (candid) offen, freimütig. adv gerade, direkt. **get straight** (clarify) klarstellen. **think straight** logisch denken. **straight on** or **ahead** gerade aus. **straightaway** adv sofort. **straighten** v geademachen. **straighten out** (put in order) in Ordnung bringen. **straightforward** adj (thing) einfach, schlicht; (person) offen, aufrichtig. n (sport) Gerade f.

strain[1] [strein] v spannen; (muscle) zerren; (tech) verzerren; (filter) sieben, filtern. **strain oneself** sich (über)anstrengen. n Überanstrengung f; (emotional) Streß m, Anspannung f; (med) Zerrung. **strained** adj (relations, etc.) gespannt.

strain[2] [strein] n (race) Abstammung f, Rasse f.

straits [streits] pl n Straße f, Meerenge f. **dire straits** Notlage f. **strait-jacket** n Zwangsjacke f.

strand[1] [strand] n (rope) Strang m; (hair) Strähne f; (thought) Faden m.

strand[2] [strand] n (shore) Strand m, Ufer neut. v stranden. **stranded** adj gestrandet.

strange [streindʒ] adj (odd) seltsam, sonderbar; (alien) fremd. **strangeness** n Seltsamkeit f; Fremdartigkeit f. **stranger** n Fremde(r). **be a stranger to** nicht verträut sein mit. **strangely** adv seltsamerweise.

strangle [ˈstraŋgl] v erwürgen, erdrosseln. **stranglehold** n Würgegriff m.

strap [strap] n Riemen m; (dress) Träger m. v festschnallen. **strapless** adj trägerlos. **strapping** adj stramm.

strategy [ˈstratədʒi] n Strategie f. **strategic** adj strategisch.

stratum [ˈstraɪtəm] n (pl -a) Schicht f.

straw [stroː] n Stroh neut; (single) Strohhalm m; (drinking) Trinkhalm m. adj Stroh-. **straw hat** Strohhut m.

strawberry [ˈstroːbəri] n Erdbeere f.

stray [strei] v sich verirren; (from path, etc.) abgehen (von); (attention) wandern. adj verirrt. n verirrtes Tier neut.

streak [striːk] n Streifen neut; (in character) Einschlag m. **streak of lightning** Blitzstrahl m. v streifen; (race, fly) rasen, sausen. **streaked** adj gestreift.

stream [striːm] n Bach m; (current) Strom m, Strömung f. v strömen. **streamer** n (party) Papierschlange f. **streamline** v (fig) rationalisieren. **streamlined** adj windschnittig.

street [striːt] n Straße f. **streetcar** n Straßenbahn f. **street lamp** Straßenlaterne f. **street-walker** n Straßendirne f.

strength [streŋθ] n Stärke f, Kraft f, Kräfte pl; (liquids) Stärke f; (mil) Macht f, Schlagkraft f. **strengthen** v (ver)stärken. **strengthening** n Verstärkung f.

strenuous ['strenjuəs] *adj* anstrengend.

stress [stres] *n* (*emphasis*) Nachdruck *m*; (*psychological*) Streß *m*; (*pronunciation*) Akzent *m*. *v* betonen. **stressful** *adj* belastend.

stretch [stretʃ] *v* (aus)strecken, ausdehnen; (*person*) sich strecken; (*e.g. land, town*) sich erstrecken. *n* (*time*) Zeitspanne *f*; (*place*) Strecke *f*. **stretcher** *n* Tragbahre *f*. **stretchy** *adj* dehnbar.

stricken ['strikən] *adj* (*sickness*) befallen (von); (*emotion*) ergriffen (von).

strict [strikt] *adj* streng. **strictness** *n* Strenge *f*.

stridden ['stridn] *V* stride.

***stride** [straid] *v* schreiten. *n* Schritt *m*. **make great strides** Fortschritte machen. **get into one's stride** in Schwung kommen.

strident ['straidənt] *adj* grell.

strife [straif] *n* Kampf *m*.

***strike** [straik] *v* schlagen; (*target*) treffen; (*workers*) streiken; (*match*) entzünden. **it strikes me** es fällt mir ein. **strike off** streichen von. *n* Schlag *m*, Stoß *m*; (*labour*) Streik *m*. **striking** *adj* auffallend.

***string** [striŋ] *n* Schnur *f*, Bindfaden *m*; (*instrument*) Saite *f*. **strings** *pl* (*mus*) Streicher *pl*. *v* (*instrument*) besaiten. **string together** verknüpfen. **stringed instrument** Streichinstrument *neut*.

stringent ['strindʒənt] *adj* streng. **stringency** *n* Strenge *f*.

strip¹ [strip] *v* abziehen; (*clothes*) ausziehen.

strip² [strip] *n* (*narrow piece*) (schmaler) Streifen *m*.

stripe [straip] *n* Streifen *m*, Strich *m*. *v* streifen. **striped** *adj* gestreift.

***strive** [straiv] *v* (*for*) streben (nach); (*to do*) sich anstrengen (zu).

striven ['strivn] *V* strive.

strode [stroud] *V* stride.

stroke¹ [strouk] *n* (*blow*) Schlag *m*; (*pen*) Strich *m*; (*med*) Schlaganfall *m*.

stroke² [strouk] *v* streicheln.

stroll [stroul] *v* schlendern. *n* Bummel *m*, Spaziergang *m*.

strong [strɔŋ] *adj* (*person, thing*) stark; (*person*) kräftig; (*flavour, etc.*) scharf. **be going strong** wohlauf sein. **strong-room** *n* Tresor *m*. **strong-willed** *adj* willensstark. **strongly** *adv* kräftig.

strove [strouv] *V* strive.

struck [strʌk] *V* strike.

structure ['strʌktʃə] *n* Struktur *f*. **structural** *adj* strukturell.

struggle ['strʌgl] *v* kämpfen, ringen. *n* Kampf *m*.

strum [strʌm] *v* klimpern (auf).

strung [strʌŋ] *V* string.

strut¹ [strʌt] *v* (herum)stolzieren. **strutting** *adj* prahlerisch.

strut² [strʌt] *n* Stütze *f*, Spreize *f*.

stub [stʌb] *n* Stumpf *m*; (*cheque*) Kontrollabschnitt *m*, Talon *m*; (*cigarette*) (Zigaretten)Stummel *m*. *v* **stub out** ausdrücken.

stubble ['stʌbl] *n* Stoppel *f*; (*beard*) Stoppeln *pl*. **stubbly** *adj* stoppelig.

stubborn ['stʌbən] *adj* hartnäckig, eigensinnig. **stubbornness** *n* Hartnäckigkeit *f*.

stuck [stʌk] *V* stick¹.

stud¹ [stʌd] *n* Beschlagnagel *m*; (*button*) Knopf *m*.

stud² [stʌd] *n* (*farm*) Gestüt *neut*; (*horse*) Zuchthengst *m*.

student ['stjudənt] *n* Student(in); (*at school, also fig*) Schüler(in).

studio ['stjudiou] *n* Studio *neut*.

study ['stʌdi] *n* Studium *neut*; (*piece of research, etc.*) Studie *f*, Untersuchung *f*; (*room*) Studierzimmer *neut*. *v* studieren.

stuff [stʌf] *n* Stoff *m*; (*coll*) Zeug *neut*, Kram *m*. *v* vollstopfen; (*taxidermy*) ausstopfen; (*cookery*) füllen. **stuffing** *n* Füllung *f*.

stuffy ['stʌfi] *adj* (*air*) dumpf, schwül; (*thing*) langweilig; (*person*) pedantisch; (*nose*) verstopft.

stumble ['stʌmbl] *v* stolpern. **stumbling-block** *n* Hindernis *neut*.

stump [stʌmp] *n* Stumpf *m*. *v* (*coll*) verblüffen. **stumpy** *adj* stumpfartig.

stun [stʌn] *v* betäuben; (*fig*) bestürzen. **stunning** *adj* (*coll*) phantastisch.

stung [stʌŋ] *V* sting.

stunk [stʌŋk] *V* stink.

stunt¹ [stʌnt] *v* (*growth*) hindern, hemmen. **stunted** *adj* verkümmert.

stunt² [stʌnt] *n* (*feat*) Kunststück *neut*.

stupid ['stjupid] *adj* dumm, blöd. **stupidity** *n* Dummheit *f*.

stupor ['stjupə] *n* Erstarrung *f*; (*dullness*) Stumpfsinn *m*.

sturdy ['stədi] *adj* robust, kräftig.

sturgeon ['stədʒən] *n* Stör *m*.

stutter ['stʌtə] n Stottern neut. v stottern. **stutterer** n Stotterer m.

sty [stai] n Schweinestall m.

style [stail] n Stil m. v (name) benennen; (shape) formen. **latest style** neueste Mode f. **hairstyle** n Frisur f. **stylish** adj elegant.

stylus ['stailəs] n Griffel m; (record-player) Nadel f.

suave [swaːv] adj weltmännisch, zuvorkommend.

subconscious [sʌb'konʃəs] adj unterbewußt. n das Unterbewußte neut.

subcontract [sʌbkən'trakt] n Nebenvertrag m. **subcontractor** n Unterkontrahent m.

subdue [səb'djuː] v unterwerfen. **subdued** adj (person) zurückhaltend; (lights) gedämpft.

subject ['sʌbdʒikt; v səb'dʒekt] n (school, etc.) Fach neut; (theme) Thema neut, Gegenstand m; (gramm) Subjekt neut; (citizen) Staatsangehörige(r). adj (to ruler) untertan (+dat); (liable) geneigt (zu); (exposed) ausgesetzt (+dat). v unterwerfen; (expose) aussetzen (+dat). **subjection** n Unterwerfung f. **subjective** adj subjektiv.

subjunctive [səb'dʒʌŋktiv] n Konjunktiv m.

*****sublet** [ˌsʌb'let] n untervermieten.

sublime [sə'blaim] adj sublim, erhaben.

submarine [ˈsʌbmərin] n Unterseeboot (U-Boot) neut. adj Untersee-.

submerge [səb'məːdʒ] v (ein)tauchen. **submerged** adj untergetaucht.

submit [səb'mit] v sich unterwerfen; (maintain) behaupten; (hand in) einreichen, vorlegen. **submission** n Unterwerfung f; (documents) Vorlage f. **submissive** adj gehorsam.

subnormal [sʌb'noːməl] adj (child, etc.) minderbegabt.

subordinate [sə'boːdinət] v unterordnen. adj untergeordnet. n Untergebene(r).

subscribe [səb'skraib] v (money) zeichnen. **subscribe to** (newspaper) abonnieren auf; (view, etc.) billigen. **subscriber** n Abonnent(in); (phone) Teilnehmer(in). **subscription** n Abonnement neut.

subsequent ['sʌbsikwənt] adj (nach)folgend. **subsequently** adv nachher, hinterher.

subservient [səb'səːviənt] adj unterwürfig. **subservience** n Unterwürfigkeit f.

subside [səb'said] v (noise, etc.) nachlassen, abnehmen; (sink) sich senken. **subsidence** n (Boden)Senkung f.

subsidiary [səb'sidiəri] adj Hilfs-, Neben-. n (company) Tochtergesellschaft.

subsidize ['sʌbsidaiz] v subventionieren.

subsidy n Subvention f.

subsist [səb'sist] v existieren. **subsist on** sich ernähren von. **subsistence** n Existenz f.

substance ['sʌbstəns] n Substanz f, Stoff m; (of argument, etc.) Gehalt neut, Kern m. **substantial** adj beträchtlich. **substantiate** v begründen.

substitute ['sʌbstitjuːt] n Ersatz m; (sport) Ersatzspieler(in). adj Ersatz-. v ersetzen. **substitution** n Einsetzung f.

subtitle ['sʌbtaitl] n Untertitel m.

subtle ['sʌtl] adj fein, subtil. **subtlety** n Feinheit f.

subtract [səb'trakt] v abziehen. **subtraction** n Abziehen neut; (thing subtracted) Abzug m.

suburb ['sʌbəːb] n Vorort m. **suburban** adj Vororts-; (coll: provincial) kleinstädtisch.

subvert [səb'vəːt] v (government) stürzen; (morals) untergraben. **subversion** n Sturz m; Untergrabung f. **subversive** adj umstürzlerisch.

subway ['sʌbwei] n (in UK) Fußgängerunterführung f; (in US) U-Bahn f.

succeed [sək'siːd] v (follow) folgen auf, nachfolgen (+dat); (be successful) Erfolg haben, erfolgreich sein; gelingen (impers). I succeeded in doing it es gelang mir, es zu tun. **success** n Erfolg m. **successful** adj erfolgreich. **succession** n Reihenfolge f, Folge f. **successive** adj (aufeinander)folgend. **successor** n Nachfolger(in).

succinct [sək'siŋkt] adj kurz(gefaßt).

succulent ['sʌkjulənt] adj saftig. n (bot) Sukkulente f. **succulence** n Saftigkeit f.

succumb [sə'kʌm] v nachgeben (+dat).

such [sʌtʃ] adj solch, derartig. **such a big house** ein so großes Haus. **no such thing** nichts dergleichen. **such as** wie zum Beispiel. **as such** an sich. **such is life** so ist das Leben.

suck [sʌk] v saugen; (sweet, thumb) lutschen. **sucker** n (coll) Gimpel m; (bot) Wurzelschößling m. **sucking pig** n Spanferkel neut. **suckle** v stillen. **suckling** n Säugling m.

suction ['sʌkʃən] v Saugwirkung f, Sog m.
sudden ['sʌdən] adj plötzlich. suddenness n Plötzlichkeit f.
suds [sʌdz] n Seifenlauge f.
sue [suː] v verklagen (auf).
suede [sweid] n Wildleder neut.
suet ['suit] n Nierenfett neut, Talg m.
suffer ['sʌfə] v leiden (an). sufferer n Leidende(r). suffering n Leiden neut; adj leidend (an).
sufficient [sə'fiʃənt] adj genügend, ausreichend.
suffocate ['sʌfəkeit] v ersticken. suffocating adj erstickend. suffocation n Ersticken neut.
sugar ['ʃugə] n Zucker m. v zuckern; süßen. sugar cane n Zuckerrohr neut. sugared adj gezuckert. sugary adj süßlich; (fig) zuckersüß.
suggest [sə'dʒest] v vorschlagen; (maintain) behaupten; (indicate) hindeuten auf. suggestion n Vorschlag m; (trace) Spur f. suggestive adj anzüglich, zweideutig. be suggestive of deuten auf.
suicide ['suisaid] n Selbstmord m. suicidal adj selbstmörderisch.
suit [suit] n (man's) Anzug m.; (woman's) Kostüm neut; (cards) Farbe f; (law) Klage f. follow suit dasselbe tun. suitcase n Handkoffer m. v (an)passen; (clothes) (gut) stehen (+dat); (food) bekommen (+dat). suitable adj geeignet, passend.
suite [switt] n (furniture) Garnitur f; (rooms) Zimmerflucht f.
sulk [sʌlk] v schmollen, trotzen. sulky adj mürrisch, schmollend.
sullen ['sʌlən] adj mürrisch.
sulphur ['sʌlfə] n Schwefel m. sulphurous adj schwefelig; (fig) hitzig.
sultan ['sʌltən] n Sultan m.
sultana [sʌl'tɑːnə] n (dried fruit) Sultanine f.
sultry ['sʌltri] adj schwül. sultriness n Schwüle f.
sum [sʌm] n Summe f; (money) Betrag m; (calculation) Rechenaufgabe f. v sum up zusammenfassen.
summarize ['sʌməraiz] v zusammenfassen. summary n Zusammenfassung f.
summer ['sʌmə] n Sommer m. adj sommerlich, Sommer-. summerhouse n Gartenhaus neut. summery adj sommerlich.
summit ['sʌmit] n Gipfel m. summit conference Gipfelkonferenz f.

summon ['sʌmən] v aufrufen, kommen lassen; (meeting) einberufen; (courage) fassen. summons n Berufung f; (law) (Vor)Ladung f. take out a summons against vorladen lassen.
sump [sʌmp] n Ölwanne f.
sumptuous ['sʌmptʃuəs] adj prächtig, kostspielig.
sun [sʌn] n Sonne f. v sun oneself sich sonnen.
sunbathe ['sʌnbeið] v ein Sonnenbad nehmen, sich sonnen.
sunbeam ['sʌnbiːm] n Sonnenstrahl m.
sunburn ['sʌnbəin] n Sonnenbrand m. sunburnt adj sonnenverbrannt.
sundae ['sʌndei] n Eisbecher m.
Sunday ['sʌndi] n Sonntag m. Sunday best Sonntagskleider pl.
sundial ['sʌndaiəl] n Sonnenuhr f.
sundry ['sʌndri] pl adj verschiedene, diverse. sundries pl n Verschiedenes neut sing.
sunflower ['sʌn,flauə] n Sonnenblume f.
sung [sʌŋ] V sing.
sun-glasses pl n Sonnenbrille f sing.
sunk [sʌŋk] V sink.
sunlight ['sʌnlait] n Sonnenlicht neut.
sunny ['sʌni] adj sonnig.
sunrise ['sʌnraiz] n Sonnenaufgang m.
sunset ['sʌnset] n Sonnenuntergang m.
sunshine ['sʌnʃain] n Sonnenschein m.
sunstroke ['sʌnstrouk] n Sonnenstich m.
sun-tan n (Sonnen)Bräune f.
super ['suːpə] adj (coll) prima.
superannuation [,suːpərənjuˈeiʃən] n (contribution) Altersversicherungsbeitrag m; (pension) Pension f. superannuated adj pensioniert.
superb [suːˈpəːb] adj herrlich, prächtig.
supercilious [,suːpəˈsiliəs] adj herablassend, hochmütig.
superficial [,suːpəˈfiʃəl] adj oberflächlich.
superfluous [suːˈpəːfluəs] adj überflüssig.
superhuman [,suːpəˈhjuːmən] adj übermenschlich.
superimpose [,suːpərimˈpouz] v legen (auf); (add) hinzufügen (zu). superimposed adj darübergelegt.
superintendent [,suːpərinˈtendənt] n Inspektor m, Vorsteher m.
superior [suːˈpiəriə] adj überlegen; (higher) höherliegend; (quality) hervorragend, erlesen. n Überlegene(r). mother superior Oberin f. superiority n Überlegenheit f.

superlative [suːˈpɜːlətiv] *adj* unübertrefflich, hervorragend. *n* Superlativ *m*.

supermarket [ˈsuːpəˌmaːkit] *n* Supermarkt *m*.

supernatural [ˌsuːpəˈnatʃərəl] *adj* übernatürlich. *n* das Übernatürliche *neut*.

supersede [ˌsuːpəˈsiːd] *v* ersetzen.

supersonic [ˌsuːpəˈsonik] *adj* Überschall-.

superstition [ˌsuːpəˈstiʃən] *n* Aberglaube *m*. **superstitious** *adj* abergläubig.

supervise [ˈsuːpəvaiz] *v* beaufsichtigen, kontrollieren. **supervision** *n* Beaufsichtigung *f*, Kontrolle *f*. **supervisor** *n* Aufseher *m*, Kontrolleur *m*. **supervisory** *adj* Aufsichts-.

supper [ˈsʌpə] *n* Abendessen *neut*.

supple [ˈsʌpl] *adj* geschmeidig, biegsam. **suppleness** *n* Geschmeidigkeit *f*.

supplement [ˈsʌpləmənt] *n* Ergänzung *f*; (*newspaper*) Beilage *f*. **supplementary** *adj* ergänzend, Zusatz-.

supply [səˈplai] *v* liefern, versorgen; (*a need*) decken. *n* Lieferung *f*. (*stock*) Vorrat *m*; (*water, electricity, etc.*) Versorgung *f*. **supply and demand** Angebot und Nachfrage. **supplies** *pl n* Zufuhren *pl*. **supplier** *n* Lieferant *m*.

support [səˈpoːt] *v* tragen, stützen; (*withstand*) ertragen; (*family*) unterhalten; (*cause*) befürworten. *n* (*tech*) Stütze *f*; Unterstützung *f*. **supporter** *n* Anhänger *m*.

suppose [səˈpouz] *v* annehmen, sich vorstellen; (*believe, think*) meinen. **supposed** *adj* angenommen. **be supposed to** sollen. **supposition** *n* Vermutung *f*, Annahme *f*.

suppository [səˈpozitri] *n* (Darm-) Zäpfchen *neut*.

suppress [səˈpres] *v* unterdrücken; (*truth*) verheimlichen. **suppression** *n* Unterdrückung *f*; Verheimlichung *f*.

supreme [suˈpriːm] *adj* oberst, höchst. **supremacy** *n* Obergewalt *neut*.

surcharge [ˈsɜːtʃaːdʒ] *n* Zuschlag *m*.

sure [ʃuə] *adj* sicher, gewiß. *adv* (*coll*) sicherlich. **for sure** gewiß. **make sure** sich vergewissern. **you can be sure** du kannst dich darauf verlassen. **sure-fire** *adj* todsicher. **surely** *adv* sicherlich. **sureness** *n* Sicherheit *f*. **surety** *n* Bürge *f*.

surf [sɜːf] *n* Brandung *f*. *v* wellenreiten. **surfboard** *n* Wellenreiterbrett *neut*. **surfer** *n* Wellenreiter(in).

surface [ˈsɜːfis] *n* Oberfläche *f*. *adj* oberflächlich. *v* auftauchen. **surface mail** gewöhnliche Post *f*.

surfeit [ˈsɜːfit] *n* Übermaß *neut*. *v* übersättigen.

surge [sɜːdʒ] *n* (*water*) Woge *f*; (*emotion*) Aufwallung *f*. *v* (*waves*) branden; (*crowd*) (vorwärts)drängen.

surgeon [ˈsɜːdʒən] *n* Chirurg *m*. **surgery** *n* Chirurgie *f*; (*consulting room*) Sprechzimmer *neut*. **surgical** *adj* chirurgisch.

surly [ˈsɜːli] *adj* verdrießlich, mürrisch. **surliness** *n* Verdrießlichkeit *f*.

surmount [səˈmaunt] *v* überwinden. **surmountable** *adj* überwindlich.

surname [ˈsɜːneim] *n* Familienname *m*, Zuname *m*.

surpass [səˈpaːs] *v* übertreffen. **surpass oneself** sich selbst übertreffen.

surplus [ˈsɜːpləs] *n* Überschuß *m*. *adj* überschüssig.

surprise [səˈpraiz] *v* überraschen. *n* Überraschung *f*. *adj* unerwartet. **surprised** *adj* überrascht. **surprising** *adj* erstaunlich.

surrealism [səˈriəlizəm] *n* Surrealismus *m*. **surrealist** *n* Surrealist(in). **surrealistic** *adj* surrealistisch.

surrender [səˈrendə] *v* sich ergeben, kapitulieren; (*office*) aufgeben; (*prisoner*) ausliefern. *n* Kapitulation *f*; Auslieferung *f*.

surreptitious [ˌsʌrəpˈtiʃəs] *adj* erschlichen; (*stealthy*) heimlich.

surround [səˈraund] *v* umgeben, umringen. *n* Einfassung *f*. **surrounding** *adj* umgebend. **surroundings** *pl n* Umgebung *f*.

survey [ˈsɜːvei; *v* səˈvei] *n* Überblick *m*; (*land, house, etc.*) Vermessung *f*; (*questionnaire*) Umfrage *f*. *v* überblicken; vermessen. **surveyor** *n* Landmesser *m*.

survive [səˈvaiv] *v* (*outlive*) überleben; (*continue to exist*) weiterleben, weiterbestehen. **survival** *n* Überleben *neut*. **survivor** *n* Überlebende(r).

susceptible [səˈseptəbl] *adj* anfällig, empfänglich (für). **susceptibility** *n* Anfälligkeit *f*, Empfänglichkeit *f*.

suspect [səˈspekt; *n* ˈsaspekt] *v* verdächtigen; (*believe*) vermuten. *n* Verdachtsperson *f*. *adj* verdächtig.

suspend [səˈspend] *v* aufhängen; (*person*) suspendieren; (*regulation*) (zeitweilig) aufheben. **suspended** *adj* ausgesetzt, verschoben. **suspender** *n* Strumpfhalter *m*. **suspenders** *pl* (*for trousers*) Hosenträger *pl.* **suspense** *n* Spannung *f.* **suspension** *n* (*mot*) Federung *f;* (*person*) Suspension *f.* **suspension bridge** Hängebrücke *f.* **suspension railway** Schwebebahn *f.*

suspicion [sə'spɪʃən] *n* Verdacht *m;* (*mistrust*) Mißtrauen *neut;* (*trace*) Spur *f.* **suspicious** *adj* mißtrauisch; (*behaviour*) verdächtig. **suspiciousness** *n* Mißtrauen *neut.*

sustain [sə'stein] *v* (*suffer*) erleiden; (*family*) ernähren. **sustained** *adj* anhaltend. **sustenance** *n* Ernährung *f.*

suture ['suːtʃə] *n* Naht *f. v* vernähen.

swab [swob] *n* (*med*) Abstrich *m.*

swagger ['swagə] *v* (herum)stolzieren. **swaggering** *adj* stolzierend.

swallow[1] ['swolou] *v* schlucken. *n* Schluck *m.*

swallow[2] ['swolou] *n* (*bird*) Schwalbe *f.*

swam [swam] *V* **swim.**

swamp [swomp] *n* Sumpf *m,* Moor *neut. v* überschwemmen. **swampy** *adj* sumpfig.

swan [swon] *n* Schwan *m.*

swank [swaŋk] *v* protzen, prahlen. **swanky** *adj* protzig.

swap [swop] *v* (aus)tauschen. *n* Tausch *m.*

swarm [swoːm] *n* Schwarm *m. v* schwärmen.

swarthy ['swoːði] *adj* dunkelhäutig, schwärzlich.

swat [swot] *v* zerquetschen.

sway [swei] *v* schwanken, schaukeln. *n* Schwanken *neut;* (*power*) Macht *f,* Einfluß *m.*

swear [sweə] *v* schwören; (*bad language*) fluchen. **swearword** *n* Fluch *m,* Fluchwort *neut.*

sweat [swet] *n* Schweiß *m. v* schwitzen. **sweater** *n* Pullover *m.* **sweaty** *adj* verschwitzt.

swede [swiːd] *n* Kohlrübe *f.*

Sweden ['swiːdn] *n* Schweden *neut.* **Swede** *n* Schwede *m,* Schwedin *f.* **Swedish** *adj* schwedisch.

sweep [swiːp] *v* kehren, fegen; (*mines*) suchen. **sweep aside** beiseite schieben, abtun. **sweepstake** *n* Toto *neut.* **sweep** *n* Schornsteinfeger *m.* **make a clean sweep** reinen Tisch machen. **sweeper** *n* Kehrer *m.* **sweeping** *adj* radikal, weitreichend. **sweepings** *pl* Kehricht *m sing.*

sweet [swiːt] *adj* süß; (*kind*) nett. **sweet corn** Mais *m.* **sweeten** *v* süßen. **sweetheart** *n* Schatz *m.* **sweet-tempered** *adj*

gutmütig. *n* Bonbon *m;* (*dessert*) Nachspeise *f.* **sweetshop** *n* Süßwarengeschäft *neut.* **sweetness** *n* Süßigkeit *f;* (*person*) Lieblichkeit *f.*

swell [swel] *v* (auf)schwellen. *n* (*sea*) Wellengang *m. adj* (*coll*) prima. **swelling** *n* (*med*) Schwellung *f.*

swelter ['sweltə] *v* vor Hitze kochen. **sweltering** *adj* schwül.

swept [swept] *V* **sweep.**

swerve [swəːv] *v* ausscheren.

swift [swift] *adj* (*zool*) Segler *m. adj* schnell, rasch. **swift-footed** *adj* schnellfüßig. **swiftness** *n* Schnelligkeit *f.*

swill [swil] *n* Schweinefutter *neut. v* spülen.

swim [swim] *v* schwimmen. **my head is swimming** mir ist schwindlig. *n* Schwimmen *neut,* Bad *neut.* **in the swim** auf dem laufenden. **swimmer** *n* Schwimmer(in). **swimming** *n* Schwimmen *neut.* **swimming pool** Schwimmbad *neut.*

swindle ['swindl] *v* betrügen. *n* Schwindel *m,* Betrug *m.* **swindler** *n* Schwindler(in).

swine [swain] *n* (*pl* **swine**) Schwein *neut.*

swing [swiŋ] *v* schwingen. *n* (*child's*) Schaukel *f.* **swing a door open/shut** eine Tür auf/zustoßen.

swipe [swaip] *v* hauen; (*coll: steal*) klauen. *n* Hieb *m.*

swirl [swəːl] *v* wirbeln. *n* Wirbel *m.*

swish [swiʃ] *v* rascheln. *n* Rascheln *neut.*

Swiss [swis] *n* Schweizer(in). *adj* schweizerisch. **Swiss German** Schweizerdeutsch *neut.*

switch [switʃ] *n* Schalter *m;* (*change*) Wechsel *m;* (*whip*) Rute *f.* **on/off-switch** *n* Ein/Ausschalter *m. v* (*change*) wechseln. **switchboard** *n* (*phone*) Vermittlung *f.* **switch on** einschalten. **switch off** ausschalten. **switch over to** übergehen zu.

Switzerland ['switsələnd] *n* die Schweiz *f.*

swivel ['swivl] *v* (sich) drehen.

swollen ['swoulən] *V* **swell.** *adj* geschwollen. **swollen-headed** *adj* eingebildet, aufgeblasen.

swoop [swuːp] *v* niederschießen, sich stürzen (auf).

swop [swop] *V* **swap.**

sword [soːd] *n* Schwert *neut.* **swordfish** *n* Schwertfisch *m.* **swordsman** *n* Fechter *m.*

swore [swoː] *V* **swear.**

sworn [swoːn] *V* **swear.** *adj* vereidigt; (*enemy*) geschworen.

swot [swɔt] v (coll) büffeln, pauken. n Büffler m.

swum [swʌm] V swim.

swung [swʌŋ] V swing.

sycamore ['sikəmɔ:] n Sykamore f.

syllable ['siləbl] n Silbe f.

syllabus ['siləbəs] n Lehrplan m.

symbol ['simbl] n Sinnbild neut, Symbol neut. **symbolic** adj sinnbildlich, symbolisch (für). **symbolism** n Symbolik f. **symbolize** v symbolisieren.

symmetry ['simitri] n Symmetrie f. **symmetrical** adj symmetrisch.

sympathy ['simpəθi] n Mitleid neut, Mitgefühl neut. **sympathetic** adj mitleidend.

symphony ['simfəni] n Sinfonie f. **symphonic** adj sinfonisch.

symposium [sim'pouziəm] n Symposion neut.

symptom ['simptəm] n Symptom neut. **symptomatic** adj symptomatisch.

synagogue ['sinəgog] n Synagoge f.

synchromesh ['siŋkroumeʃ] n Synchrongetriebe neut.

synchronize ['siŋkrənaiz] v synchronisieren.

syndicate ['sindikit] n Syndikat neut. **syndication** n Syndikatsbildung f.

syndrome ['sindroum] n (med) Syndrom neut.

synonym ['sinənim] n Synonym neut. **synonymous** adj synonym.

synopsis [si'nopsis] n (pl -ses) Synopse f, Zusammenfassung f. **synoptic** adj synoptisch.

syntax ['sintaks] n Syntax f. **syntactic** adj syntaktisch.

synthesis ['sinθisis] n (pl -ses) Synthese f. **synthetic** adj synthetisch, Kunst-.

syphilis ['sifilis] n Syphilis f.

syringe [si'rindʒ] n Spritze f.

syrup ['sirəp] n Sirup m, Zuckersaft m. **syrupy** adj sirupartig.

system ['sistəm] n System neut; (geol) Formation f. **systematic** adj systematisch.

T

tab [tab] n (in garment) Aufhänger m; (label) Etikett neut; (coll: bill) Rechnung f.

table ['teibl] n Tisch m; (math, etc.) Tabelle f. **table of contents** Inhaltsverzeichnis neut. **table-cloth** n Tischtuch neut. **table-spoon** n Eßlöffel m.

table d'hôte [ta:blə'dout] n Table d'hôte f.

tablet ['tablit] n Tablette f; (stone) Tafel f.

taboo [ta'bu:] adj tabu, n Tabu neut.

tacit ['tasit] adj stillschweigend. **taciturn** adj schweigsam.

tack [tak] n Reißnagel m; (naut) Lavieren neut; (sewing) Heftstich m. v lavieren; heften. **tacky** adj klebrig.

tackle ['takl] n (naut) Takel neut; (equipment, etc.) Zeug neut, Ausrüstung f. v (sport) angreifen; (person) angehen; (problem) anpacken.

tact [takt] n Takt m. **tactful** adj taktvoll. **tactless** adj taktlos.

tactics ['taktiks] pl n Taktik f. **tactical** adj taktisch.

tadpole ['tadpoul] n Kaulquappe f.

taffeta ['tafitə] n Taft m.

tag [tag] n (loop) Anhänger m, (label) Etikett neut. **price-tag** Preiszettel m.

tail [teil] n Schwanz m. v (coll: follow) beschatten. **tail end** Schluß m. **tailcoat** n Frack m. **tail-lamp** n Schlußlicht neut.

tailor ['teilə] n Schneider m. v schneidern. **tailor-made** adj nach Maß angefertigt.

taint [teint] n Fleck m, Makel m. v verderben.

*****take** [teik] v nehmen; (something somewhere) bringen; (prisoner) fassen; (photo, exam) machen. how long does it take? wie lange dauert es? wie lange braucht man? **take aback** verblüffen. **take along** mitnehmen. **take away** wegnehmen; (subtract) abziehen. **take back** (retract) zurücknehmen. **take down** (on paper) aufschreiben. **take off** (clothes) ausziehen; (mimic) nachäffen. **take over** übernehmen. **take up** aufnehmen.

taken ['teikn] V take.

talcum powder ['talkəm] n Talkumpuder m.

tale [teil] n Erzählung f. **old wives' tale** Ammenmärchen neut.

talent ['talənt] n Talent neut, Begabung f. **talented** adj begabt.

talk [tɔːk] n Rede neut; (conversation) Gespräch neut; (chat) Unterhaltung f. (lecture) Vortrag m. v reden, sprechen. **talk over** besprechen. **talkative** adj geschwätzig.

tall [tɔːl] adj groß, hoch. **tallness** n Größe, Höhe f. **tall story** unglaubliche Geschichte f.

tally ['tali] v (coll) übereinstimmen (mit), entsprechen (+dat).

talon ['talən] n Klaue f.

tambourine [tambə'riːn] n Tamburin neut.

tame [teim] adj zahm, gezähmt. v zähmen.

tamper ['tampə] v herumpfuschen (an), sich einmischen (in).

tampon ['tampon] n Tampon m.

tan [tan] v gerben; (skin) sich bräunen. n (colour) Gelbbraun neut; (skin) Sonnenbräunung f.

tandem ['tandəm] n Tandem neut.

tangent ['tandʒənt] n Tangente f.

tangerine [tandʒə'riːn] n Mandarine f.

tangible ['tandʒəbl] adj greifbar.

tangle ['taŋgl] n Gewirr neut. v verwickeln.

tank [taŋk] n Tank m, Behälter m; (mil) Panzer m. **tanker** n (ship) Tanker m.

tankard ['taŋkəd] n Krug m.

tantalize ['tantəlaiz] v quälen.

tantamount ['tantəmaunt] adj be **tantamount** to gleichkommen (+dat).

tantrum ['tantrəm] n Wutanfall m.

tap[1] [tap] v leicht schlagen, klopfen. n leichter Schlag m. **tap-dance** n Steptanz m.

tap[2] [tap] n Hahn m. v anzapfen. **taproom** n Schankstube f.

tape [teip] n Band neut, Streifen m; (recording) Tonband neut; (sport) Zielband m. v heften. **adhesive tape** Klebestreifen. **tape measure** n Metermaß m. **tape-recorder** n Tonbandgerät neut. **tape-recording** n Bandaufnahme f.

taper ['teipə] n (dünne) Wachskerze f. v spitz zulaufen. **tapered** adj spitz (zulaufend).

tapestry ['tapəstri] n Wandteppich m.

tapioca [tapi'oukə] n Tapioka f.

tar [taː] n Teer m.

tarantula [tə'rantjulə] n Tarantel f.

target ['taːgit] n (sport) Zielscheibe f; (ambition) Ziel neut.

tariff ['tarif] n (imports) Zolltarif m; (price list) Preisverzeichnis neut.

tarmac ® ['taːmak] n Asphalt m; (runway) Rollbahn f.

tarnish ['taːniʃ] v (metal) anlaufen; (reputation) beflecken.

tarpaulin [taː'pɔːlin] n Persenning f.

tarragon ['tarəgən] n Estragon m.

tart[1] [taːt] n Torte f; (prostitute) Dirne f.

tart[2] [taːt] adj sauer, herb.

tartan ['taːtan] n Tartan m, Schottenmuster neut.

tartar ['taːtə] n Weinstein m; (teeth) Zahnstein m.

task [taːsk] n Aufgabe f. **take to task** zur Rede stellen.

tassel ['tasəl] n Quaste f.

taste [teist] n Geschmack neut; (sample) Kostprobe f; (liking) Neigung f. v schmecken. **tasteful** adj geschmackvoll. **tasteless** adj geschmacklos. **tasty** adj schmackhaft.

tattered ['tatəd] adj zerrissen.

tattoo [tə'tuː] n Tätowierung f. v tätowieren.

taught [tɔːt] V teach.

taunt [tɔːnt] v sticheln, verspotten. n Stichelei f.

Taurus ['tɔːrəs] n Stier m.

taut [tɔːt] adj stramm, straff.

tavern ['tavən] n Taverne f, Kneipe f.

tax [taks] n Steuer f. **tax-free** adj steuerfrei. **taxpayer** n Steuerzahler(in). **tax return** n Steuererklärung f. v besteuern; (test) anstrengen. **taxable** adj steuerpflichtig.

taxi ['taksi] n Taxi neut. **taxi-driver** n Taxifahrer m.

tea [tiː] n Tee m; (meal) Abendbrot neut. **tea-cloth** n Geschirrtuch neut. **teacup** n Teetasse f. **teapot** n Teekanne f. **teaspoon** n Teelöffel m.

*****teach** [tiːtʃ] v lehren; (animals) dressieren. **teacher** n Lehrer(in). **teaching** n Unterricht m. **teachings** pl Lehre f sing.

teak [tiːk] n Teakholz neut.

team [tiːm] n (sport) Mannschaft f; (horses) Gespann neut. v **team up** sich zusammentun (mit). **teamwork** n Zusammenarbeit f.

*****tear**[1] [teə] v reißen, zerreißen. n Riß m. **tear away** wegreißen. **tear oneself away** sich losreißen.

tear[2] [tiə] n Träne f. **tear gas** n Tränengas neut. **tearful** adj weinerlich.

tease [tiːz] v necken.

teat [tiːt] n (bottle) Sauger m; (anat) Brustwarze f; (zool) Zitze f.

technical ['teknikəl] adj technisch. **technician** n Techniker m. **technique** n Technik f. **technological** adj technologisch. **technology** n Technologie f.

tedious ['tiːdiəs] adj langweilig. **tedium** n Langeweile f.

tee [tiː] n (golf) Abschlagstelle f.

teem [tiːm] v wimmeln (von).

teenage ['tiːneidʒ] adj Jugend-. **teenager** n Teenager m.

teeth [tiːθ] V tooth.

teethe [tiːð] v zahnen. **teething troubles** (fig) Kinderkrankheiten pl.

teetotal ['tiːtoutl] adj abstinent. **teetotaller** n Abstinenzler(in).

telecommunications [ˌtelikəmjuːni-ˈkeiʃənz] pl n Fernmeldewesen neut sing.

telegram ['teligram] n Telegramm neut. **by telegram** telegraphisch.

telegraph ['teligraːf] n Telegraph m. v telegraphieren. **telegraphic** adj telegraphisch.

telepathy [tə'lepəθi] n Telepathie f, Gedankenübertragung f. **telepathic** adj telepathisch.

telephone ['telifoun] n Fernsprecher m, Telefon neut. v anrufen, telefonieren. **by telephone** telefonisch. **telephone booth** Telefonzelle f. **telephone call** Telefongespräch neut, Anruf m. **telephone directory** Telefonbuch neut. **telephone exchange** (Telefon)Zentrale f. **telephonist** n Telefonist(in).

telescope ['teliskoup] n Fernrohr neut, Teleskop neut. **telescopic** adj teleskopisch.

television ['teliviʒən] n Fernsehen neut. **televize** v (im Fernsehen) übertragen. **on television** im Fernsehen.

telex ['teleks] n Fernschreiber m, Telex neut. v (durch Telex) übertragen.

***tell** [tel] v sagen; (story) erzählen; (recognize) erkennen. **telltale** n Klatschbase f. **tell the truth** die Wahrheit sagen. n Kassierer m. **telling** adj wirkungsvoll.

temper ['tempə] n Wut f, Zorn m; (mood) Laune f. **lose one's temper** in Wut geraten. v mildern; (steel) härten. **temperament** n Temperament neut. **temperamental** adj temperamentvoll. **temperance** n

Mäßigkeit f. **temperate** adj maßvoll; (climate) gemäßigt. **tempered** adj gehärtet.

temperature ['temprətʃə] n Temperatur f. **have a temperature** Fieber haben. **take (a person's) temperature** die Temperatur messen (+ dat).

tempestuous [tem'pestjuəs] adj stürmisch.

temple¹ ['templ] n (arch) Tempel m.

temple² ['templ] n (anat) Schläfe f.

tempo ['tempou] n Tempo neut.

temporary ['tempərəri] adj provisorisch, vorläufig.

tempt [tempt] v verlocken. **temptation** n Verlockung f. **tempting** adj verlockend; (food) appetitanregend.

ten [ten] adj zehn. n Zehn f. **tenth** adj zehnt; n Zehntel neut.

tenable ['tenəbl] adj haltbar.

tenacious [tə'neiʃəs] adj zäh. **tenacity** n Zähigkeit f.

tenant ['tenənt] n Mieter m. **tenancy** n Mietverhältnis neut.

tend¹ [tend] v (be inclined) neigen (zu), eine Tendenz haben (zu).

tend² [tend] v (care for) bedienen, sich kümmern um.

tendency ['tendənsi] n Tendenz f.

tender¹ ['tendə] adj zart; (affectionate) zärtlich. **tender-hearted** adj weichherzig. **tenderloin** n Filet neut. **tenderness** n Zartheit f; Zärtlichkeit f.

tender² ['tendə] v anbieten; (comm) ein Angebot machen. n Angebot neut.

tendon ['tendən] n Sehne f.

tendril ['tendril] n Ranke f.

tenement ['tenəmənt] n Mietshaus neut.

tennis ['tenis] n Tennis neut. **tennis ball** Tennisball m. **tennis court** Tennisplatz m. **tennis racket** (Tennis)Schläger m.

tenor ['tenə] n Tenor m. adj Tenor-.

tense¹ [tens] adj gespannt. v (sich) straffen. **tensile** adj dehnbar. **tension** n Spannung f.

tense² [tens] n (gramm) Zeitform f, Tempus neut.

tent [tent] n Zelt neut.

tentacle ['tentəkl] n Tentakel m, Fühler m; (octopus) Fangarm m.

tentative ['tentətiv] adj versuchend, Versuchs-; (temporary) vorläufig. **tentatively** adv versuchsweise.

tenterhooks ['tentəhuks] n **be on tenterhooks** wie auf heißen Kohlen sitzen.

tenuous ['tenjuəs] adj dünn; (argument) schwach.

tepid ['tepid] *adj* lauwarm. **tepidness** *n* Lauheit *f*.

term [tɜːm] *n* (*expression*) Ausdruck *m*; (*period of time*) Frist *f*; (*academic, two per year*) Semester *neut*; (*academic, three per year*) Trimester *neut*. **end of term** (*school*) Schulschluß *m*. **terms** *pl* Bedingungen *pl*. **be on good terms with** gut auskommen mit. **come to terms with** sich abfinden mit.

terminal ['tɜːminəl] *adj* End-, Schluß-; (*med*) unheilbar. *n* Terminal *neut*.

terminate ['tɜːmineit] *v* beendigen; (*contract*) kündigen. **termination** *n* Ende *neut*, Schluß *m*.

terminology [tɜːmi'nolədʒi] *n* Terminologie *f*.

terminus ['tɜːminəs] *n* Endstation *f*.

terrace ['terəs] *n* Terrasse *f*; (*houses*) Häuserreihe *f*.

terrain [tə'rein] *n* Terrain *neut*, Gelände *neut*.

terrestrial [tə'restriəl] *adj* irdisch.

terrible ['terəbl] *adj* schrecklich, furchtbar. **terribleness** *n* Schrecklichkeit *f*, Fürchterlichkeit *f*.

terrier ['teriə] *n* Terrier *m*.

terrify ['terifai] *v* erschrecken. **terrific** *adj* (*coll*) klasse, unwahrscheinlich. **terrified** *adj* erschrocken. **be terrified of** sich fürchten vor.

territory ['teritəri] *n* Gebiet *neut*, Territorium *neut*; (*pol*) Staatsgebiet *neut*. **territorial waters** Hoheitsgewässer *pl*.

terror ['terə] *n* Schrecken *m*, Entsetzen *neut*; (*pol*) Terror *m*. **terrorism** *n* Terrorismus *m*. **terrorist** *n* Terrorist(in); *adj* terroristisch.

test [test] *n* Versuch *m*, Probe *f*; (*examination*) Prüfung *f*. *v* prüfen, erproben. **test-case** *n* Präzedenzfall *m*.

testament ['testəmənt] *n* Testament *neut*.

testicle ['testikl] *n* Hoden *m*.

testify ['testifai] *v* bezeugen.

testimony ['testiməni] *n* Zeugnis *neut*. **testimonial** *n* Zeugnis *neut*, Empfehlungsschreiben *n*.

tetanus ['tetənəs] *n* Wundstarrkrampf *m*, Tetanus *m*.

tether ['teðə] *n* Haltestrick *m*. **be at the end of one's tether** mit seiner Geduld am Ende sein. *v* anbinden.

text [tekst] *n* Text *m*. **textbook** *n* Lehrbuch *neut*. **textual** *adj* textlich.

textile ['tekstail] *n* Gewebe *neut*, Faserstoff *m*. **textiles** *pl* Textilien *pl*.

texture ['tekstjuə] *n* Textur *f*.

than [ðən] *conj* als.

thank [θæŋk] *v* danken (+*dat*), sich bedanken bei. **thanks** *pl n* Dank *m* *sing*. *interj* danke! **thankful** *adj* dankbar. **thankless** *adj* undankbar. **thank you!** danke! **many thanks!** dankeschön! **thank goodness!** Gott sei Dank!

that [ðæt] *adj* der, die, das; jener, jene, jenes. *pron* das; (*who, which*) der, die, das, welch. **that is** (i.e.) das heißt (d.h.). **that's it!** so ist es! **like that** so. **that which** das, was. **the man that I saw** der Mann, den ich sah. **in order that** damit. *conj* daß. *adv* (*coll*) so, dermaßen.

thatch [θætʃ] *n* Dachstroh *neut*. **thatched roof** Strohdach *neut*.

thaw [θɔː] *v* tauen. *n* Tauwetter *neut*.

the [ðə] *art* der, die, das *sing*; die *pl*.

theatre ['θiətə] *n* Theater *neut*; (*operating*) Operationssaal *m*. **theatre-goer** *n* Theaterbesucher(in). **theatrical** *adj* theatralisch.

theft [θeft] *n* Diebstahl *m*.

their [ðeə] *poss adj* ihr, ihre, ihr. **theirs** *pron* der/die/das ihrige. **a friend of theirs** ein Freund von ihnen.

them [ðem] *pron* (*acc*) sie; (*dat*) ihnen.

theme [θiːm] *n* Thema *neut*.

then [ðen] *adv* (*at that time*) damals; (*next*) dann, darauf. *conj* also. *adj* damalig.

theology [θi'olədʒi] *n* Theologie *f*. **theologian** *n* Theologe *m*. **theological** *adj* theologisch.

theorem ['θiərəm] *n* Theorem *m*.

theory ['θiəri] *n* Theorie *f*. **theoretical** *adj* theoretisch. **theorist** *n* Theoretiker(in). **theorize** *v* theoretisieren.

therapy ['θerəpi] *n* Therapie *f*, Behandlung *f*. **therapeutic** *adj* therapeutisch. **therapist** *n* Therapeut(in).

there [ðeə] *adv* dort, da; (*to that place*) dahin, dorthin. **here and there** hier und da. **over there** da drüben. **thereabouts** *adv* so ungefähr. **thereafter** *adv* danach. **there and back** hin und zurück. **there are** es sind, es gibt. **there is** es ist, es gibt. **up there** da oben. *interj* na!

thermal ['θɜːml] *adj* thermal, Wärme-. *n* (*aero*) Thermik *f*.

thermodynamics [θɜːmoudai'næmiks] *n* Thermodynamik *f*.

thermometer [θə'mɔmitə] n Thermometer neut.

thermonuclear [θəːmouˈnjukliə] adj thermonukleär.

thermos ® ['θəːməs] n Thermosflasche f.

thermostat ['θəːməstat] n Thermostat m.

these [ðiːz] pl adj, pron diese. **one of these days** eines Tages. **these are** dies sind.

thesis ['θiːsis] n (pl -ses) These f, Satz m; (university) Dissertation f.

they [ðei] pl pron sie. **they say** man sagt.

thick [θik] adj dick; (hair, woods) dicht; (coll: stupid) dumm. **thicken** v dick machen or werden, (sich) verdicken; (cookery) legieren. **thickness** n Dicke f, Stärke f. **thick-skinned** adj (fig) dickfellig.

thief [θiːf] n (pl thieves) Dieb(in). **thieve** v stehlen. **thievish** adj diebisch.

thigh [θai] n (Ober)Schenkel m. **thighbone** n Schenkelknochen m.

thimble ['θimbl] n Fingerhut m.

thin [θin] adj dünn; (person) mager; (weak) schwach. v dünn machen or werden; (cookery) verdünnen. **thinner** n Verdünner m. **thinness** n Dünne f; Magerkeit f. **thin-skinned** adj empfindlich.

thing [θiŋ] n Ding neut. **things** pl Sachen pl, Zeug neut sing. **how are things?** wie geht es?

*think [θiŋk] v denken; (hold opinion) denken, meinen. **think about** denken an; (consider) überlegen, nachdenken über. **think of** (doing) daran denken, vorhaben. **what do you think of it?** was halten sie davon? **I think so** ich glaube schon. **thinker** n Denker(in). **thinking** n (opinion) Meinung f.

third [θəːd] adj dritt. n Drittel neut. **third party** Dritte(r). **third-party insurance** Haftpflichtversicherung f. **third-rate** adj (coll) minderwertig.

thirst [θəːst] n Durst (nach) m. **die of thirst** verdursten. v dursten. **thirsty** adj durstig. **be thirsty** Durst haben.

thirteen [θəːˈtiːn] adj dreizehn. n Dreizehn f. **thirteenth** adj dreizehnt.

thirty ['θəːti] adj dreißig. n Dreißig f. **thirtieth** adj dreißigst.

this [ðis] adj (pl these) dieser, diese, dieses. pron dies, das. **like this** so, folgendermaßen. **this morning** heute früh. **this year** dieses Jahr.

thistle ['θisl] n Distel f.

thorn [θɔːn] n Dorn m. **thorny** adj dornig.

thorough ['θʌrə] adj gründlich; (person) genau, sorgfältig. **thoroughbred** n Vollblut neut. adj Vollblut-. **thoroughfare** n Durchgangsstraße f. **thoroughness** n Gründlichkeit f.

those [ðouz] pl adj, pron jene.

though [ðou] conj obwohl, obgleich. adv aber, dennoch, jedoch. **as though** als ob. **even though** wenn ... auch.

thought [θɔːt] V think. **thought** n Gedanke m; (thinking) Denken neut; (reflection) Überlegung f. **thoughtful** adj gedankenvoll; (considerate) rücksichtsvoll. **thoughtless** adj gedankenlos; rücksichtslos.

thousand ['θauzənd] adj tausend. n Tausend neut. **thousandth** adj tausendst; n Tausendstel neut.

thrash [θraʃ] v verdreschen; (defeat) heftig schlagen. **thrash about** hin und her schlagen. **thrashing** n Prügel pl, Dresche f.

thread [θred] n Faden m; (screw) Gewinde neut. **threadbare** adj fadenscheinig. v (needle) einfädeln; (beads) einreihen. **thread one's way through** sich winden durch.

threat [θret] n Drohung f; (danger) Gefahr f, Bedrohung f. **threaten** v bedrohen; (endanger) gefährden. **threatening** adj drohend.

three [θriː] adj drei. n Drei f. **three-cornered** adj dreieckig. **three-dimensional** adj dreidimensional. **threefold** adv, adj dreifach. **three-ply** adj dreifach. **three-quarters of an hour** eine Dreiviertelstunde f.

thresh [θreʃ] v dreschen.

threshold ['θreʃould] n (Tür)Schwelle f.

threw [θruː] V throw.

thrift [θrift] n Sparsamkeit f. **thrifty** adj sparsam.

thrill [θril] v erregen, begeistern. n Zittern neut, Erregung f. **thriller** n Reißer m. **thrilling** adj sensationell.

thrive [θraiv] v gedeihen. **thriving** adj blühend.

throat [θrout] n Kehle f, Rachen m; (neck) Hals m. **throaty** adj rauh.

throb [θrob] v pulsieren, klopfen. n Pulsieren neut.

thrombosis [θromˈbousis] n Thrombose f.

throne [θroun] *n* Thron *m*.

throng [θrɒŋ] *n* Gedränge *neut*. *v* sich scharen.

throttle ['θrɒtl] *v* erwürgen. *n* (*tech*) Drosselklappe *f*. **open the throttle** (*mot*) Gas geben.

through [θruː] *prep, adv* durch. **fall through** (*coll*) ins Wasser fallen. **get through** fertig sein mit; (*exam*) bestehen. **go through with** zu Ende führen. **wet through** durchnäßt. **throughout** *adv* (*place*) überall in. **throughout the night** die ganze Nacht hindurch. *adj* (*ticket, train*) durchgehend.

*****throw** [θrou] *v* werfen. **throw away** wegwerfen; (*chance*) verpassen. **throwback** *n* Rückkehr *f*. **throw up** (*coll*) kotzen. **throw-in** (*sport*) Einwurf *m*. **throw** *m*.

thrush [θrʌʃ] *n* Drossel *f*.

*****thrust** [θrʌst] *v* stecken, schieben. *n* Stoß *m*, Hieb *m*; (*tech*) Schubkraft *f*.

thud [θʌd] *n* (dumpfer) Schlag *m*. *v* dumpf schlagen.

thumb [θʌm] *n* Daumen *m*. *v* **thumb through** durchblättern. **thumb a lift** per Anhalter fahren. **thumbtack** Reißnagel *m*.

thump [θʌmp] *n* Puff *m*, Schlag *m*. *v* puffen.

thunder ['θʌndə] *n* Donner *m*. *v* donnern. **thunderbolt** *n* Blitz *m*. **thunderclap** *n* Donnerschlag *m*. **thunderstorm** *n* Gewitter *neut*. **thunderstruck** *adj* wie vom Blitz getroffen.

Thursday ['θəːzdi] *n* Donnerstag *m*. **on Thursdays** donnerstags.

thus [ðʌs] *adv* so, folgendermaßen. **thus far** bis jetzt, soweit.

thwart [θwɔːt] *v* (*person*) entgegenarbeiten (+ *dat*); (*plan*) vereiteln.

thyme [taim] *n* Thymian *m*.

thyroid ['θairoid] *n* Schilddrüse *f*. *adj* Schilddrüsen-.

tiara [ti'ɑːrə] *n* Tiara *f*.

tick¹ [tik] *v* (*clock*) ticken; (*with pen*) abhaken. **tick over** (*mot*) im Leerlauf sein. *n* Ticken *neut*; Häkchen *neut*.

tick² [tik] *n* (*parasite*) Zecke *f*.

ticket ['tikit] *n* (*label*) Etikett *neut*, Zettel *m*; (*travel*) Fahrkarte *f*, Fahrschein *m*; (*theatre*) Karte *f*. **ticket-collector** *n* Schaffner *m*. **ticket-office** *n* Fahrkartenschalter *m*.

tickle ['tikl] *v* kitzeln; (*fig*) amüsieren. *n* Kitzel *m*, Juckreiz *m*. **ticklish** *adj* kitzlig.

tide [taid] *n* Gezeiten *pl*. Ebbe und Flut *f*. **high tide** Flut *f*, Hochwasser *neut*. **low tide** Ebbe *f*, Niedrigwasser *neut*. **tidal** *adj* Gezeiten-, Flut-.

tidy ['taidi] *adj* ordentlich, sauber. *v* in Ordnung bringen. **tidy up** aufräumen.

tie [tai] *v* (an)binden, festbinden; (*knot*) machen; (*necktie*) binden. **tie in with** übereinstimmen mit. **tie up** verbinden. **be tied up** nicht abkömmlich sein. *n* (*necktie*) Schlips *m*, Krawatte *f*; (*sport*) Unentschieden *neut*; (*obligation*) Verpflichtung *f*, Last *f*.

tier [tiə] *n* Reihe *f*, Rang *m*.

tiger ['taigə] *n* Tiger *m*. **tigress** *n* Tigerin *f*.

tight [tait] *v* fest, stramm; (*clothes*) eng, knapp; (*watertight, etc.*) dicht; (*in short supply*) knapp; (*coll: mean*) geizig. **tighten** *v* festziehen, straffen. **tight-fisted** *adj* geizig. **tights** *pl n* Strumpfhose *f sing*. *adv* **hold tight** festhalten. **sit tight** sitzenbleiben.

tile [tail] *n* (*roof*) (Dach)Ziegel *m*; (*wall*) Fliese *f*.

till¹ [til] *V* until.

till² [til] *n* (*in shop*) Kasse *f*.

till³ [til] *v* (*land*) bebauen, pflügen.

tiller ['tilə] *n* (*naut*) (Ruder)Pinne *f*.

tilt [tilt] *v* kippen, (sich) neigen. *n* Neigung *f*, Schräglage *f*. **tilt over** umkippen.

timber ['timbə] *n* (Bau)Holz *neut*. **timber forest** Hochwald *m*.

time [taim] *n* Zeit *f*; (*occasion*) Mal *neut*; (*era*) Zeitalter *neut*; (*music*) Takt *m*. **at all times** stets. **at this time** zu dieser Zeit. **behind the times** rückständig. **have a good time** sich gut unterhalten. **in good time** rechtzeitig. **time limit** *n* Frist *f*. **timepiece** *n* Uhr *f*. **timetable** *n* (*bus, train*) Fahrplan *m*; (*school*) Stundenplan *m*. **what time is it?** wieviel Uhr ist es? *or* wie spät ist es? *v* (*mit der Uhr*) messen, zeitlich abstimmen. **timeless** *adj* ewig. **timely** *adj* rechtzeitig.

timid ['timid] *adj* ängstlich, schüchtern. **timidity** *n* Ängstlichkeit *f*, Schüchternheit *f*.

tin [tin] *n* Zinn *neut*; (*can*) Dose *f*, Büchse *f*. *adj* zinnern, Zinn-. **tin can** Blechdose *f*. **tin foil** *n* Stanniol *neut*. **tin-opener** *n* Dosenöffner *m*.

tinge [tindʒ] v (leicht) färben. n Färbung f; (fig) Anstrich m.

tingle ['tiŋgl] v prickeln, kribbeln. n Prickeln neut.

tinker ['tiŋkə] n Kesselflicker m. v tinker with herumbasteln an.

tinkle ['tiŋkl] v klingeln. n Klingeln neut, Geklingel neut.

tinsel ['tinsəl] n Lametta neut.

tint [tint] n Farbton m. v tönen, leicht färben.

tiny ['taini] adj winzig.

tip¹ [tip] n (sharp end) Spitze f; (summit) Gipfel m. **tipped** adj (cigarette) Filter-. **on tiptoe** auf den Zehenspitzen.

tip² [tip] n (for rubbish) (Müll)Abladeplatz m. v kippen. **tip over** umkippen.

tip³ [tip] n (gratuity) Trinkgeld neut; (hint) Wink m, Tip m. v ein Trinkgeld geben (+dat); einen Tip geben (+dat). **tip off** n rechtzeitiger Wink m.

tipsy ['tipsi] adj (coll) beschwipst.

tire¹ ['taiə] v ermüden; (become tired) müde werden. **tire out** erschöpfen. **tired** adj müde. **tiredness** n Müdigkeit f. **tireless** adj unermüdlich. **tiresome** adj lästig.

tire² ['taiə] (US) V tyre.

tissue ['tiʃuː] n Gewebe neut; (paper handkerchief) Papiertaschentuch neut. **tissue paper** n Seidenpapier neut.

tit [tit] n (bird) Meise f.

title ['taitl] n Titel m; (right) Rechtstitel m. **titled** adj betitelt. **title-deed** Eigentumsurkunde f. **title-holder** n (sport) Titelverteidiger(in). **title-role** Titelrolle f.

to [tu] prep zu; (motion, travel) nach; (time of day) vor; (in order to) um zu. adv (shut) zu, geschlossen. **to and fro** auf und ab. **fix to the wall** an die Wand befestigen. **go to bed/the movies/school** ins Bett/ins Kino/in die Schule gehen. **go to Berlin** nach Berlin fahren. **I gave it to him** ich gab es ihm. **ten to one** (o'clock) zehn vor eins; (odds) zehn gegen eins. **to do** n Getue neut.

toad [toud] n Kröte f. **toadstool** n Pilz m.

toast [toust] n Toast m; (drink) Trinkspruch m, Toast m. v toasten. **toaster** n Toaster m. **toastmaster** n Toastmeister m.

tobacco [tə'bakou] n Tabak m. **tobacconist** n Tabakhändler m.

toboggan [tə'bogən] n Schlitten m, Rodel(schlitten) m. v rodeln.

today [tə'dei] n, adv heute. **today's** or of

today heutig, von heute; (of nowadays) der heutigen Zeit.

toddler ['todlə] n Kleinkind neut.

toe [tou] n Zehe f. **on one's toes** auf Draht. **toe-cap** n Kappe f. **toe-nail** n Zehennagel m.

toffee ['tofi] n Karamelle f.

together [tə'geðə] adv zusammen; (at the same time) gleichzeitig. **get together** (coll) sich treffen.

toil [toil] n Mühe f, schwere Arbeit f. v mühselig arbeiten, schuften (an).

toilet ['toilit] n (all senses) Toilette f; (WC) Klosett neut. **toilet-paper** Klosettpapier neut. **toilet soap** Toilettenseife f.

token ['toukən] n Zeichen neut, Beweis m; (voucher) Gutschein m, Bon m. adj nominell.

told [tould] V tell.

tolerate ['toləreit] v dulden, tolerieren. **tolerable** adj erträglich. **tolerance** n Toleranz f. **tolerant** adj duldsam, tolerant.

toll¹ [toul] n Zoll m.

toll² [toul] v (bell) läuten.

tomato [tə'maːtou] n (pl tomatoes) Tomate f.

tomb [tuːm] n Grabmal neut, Grab neut. **tombstone** n Grabstein m.

tomorrow [tə'morou] n, adv morgen. **tomorrow morning** morgen früh. **tomorrow's** or of tomorrow morgig, von morgen. **the day after tomorrow** übermorgen.

ton [tʌn] n Tonne f.

tone [toun] n Ton m; (muscle) Tonus m. **tone down** v mildern. **tonal** adj tonal.

tongs [toŋz] pl n Zange f sing.

tongue [tʌŋ] n Zunge f; (language) Sprache f. **tongue-tied** adj zungenlahm. **tongue-twister** n Zungenbrecher m.

tonic ['tonik] adj tonisch, Ton-. **tonic water** Tonic neut. **tonikum** neut.

tonight [tə'nait] adv heute abend, heute nacht.

tonsil ['tonsil] n Mandel f. **tonsillectomy** n Mandelentfernung f. **tonsillitis** n Mandelentzündung f.

too [tuː] adv (excessively) zu, allzu; (as well) auch, ebenfalls.

took [tuk] V take.

tool [tuːl] n Werkzeug neut. **toolbox** n Werkzeugkasten m. **tooling** n Bearbeitung f.

tooth [tuːθ] *n* (*pl* **teeth**) Zahn *m*. **tooth-ache** *n* Zahnweh *neut*. **toothbrush** *n* Zahnbürste *f*. **toothless** *adj* zahnlos. **toothpaste** *n* Zahnpasta *f*. **toothpick** *n* Zahnstocher *m*.

top¹ [top] *n* oberes Ende *neut*, obere Seite *f*; (*hill*) Gipfel *m*; (*lid*) Deckel *m*; (*page*) Kopf *m*. **on top of** oben auf; (*besides*) über. **top hat** Zylinder *m*. **top-heavy** *adj* kopflastig. **topsoil** *n* Ackerkrume *f*, Mutterboden *m*. **topmost** *adj* oberst, höchst; (*chief*) Haupt-. v krönen.

top² [top] *n* (*toy*) Kreisel *m*.

topaz ['toupæz] *n* Topas *m*.

topic ['topik] *n* Thema *neut*, Gegenstand *m*. **topical** *adj* aktuell.

topography [tə'pogrəfi] *n* Topographie *f*.

topple ['topl] v (um)kippen.

topsy-turvy [topsi'təːvi] *adv* durcheinander, in Unordnung.

torch [toːtʃ] *n* Fackel *f*; (*elec*) Taschenlampe *f*.

tore [toː] *V* **tear¹**.

torment [toː'ment; *n* 'toːment] v quälen. *n* Qual *f*. **tormentor** *n* Quälgeist *m*.

torn [toːn] *V* **tear¹**. *adj* zerrissen.

tornado [toː'neidou] *n* Tornado *m*, Wirbelsturm *m*.

torpedo [toː'piːdou] *n* Torpedo *m*.

torrent ['torənt] *n* Wildbach *m*; (*of abuse, etc.*) Strom *m*, Ausbruch *m*. **torrential** *adj* strömend. **torrential rain** Wolkenbruch *m*.

torso ['toːsou] *n* Torso *m*.

tortoise ['toːtəs] *n* Schildkröte *f*. **tortoise-shell** *n* Schildpatt *m*.

tortuous ['toːtʃuəs] *adj* gekrümmt.

torture ['toːtʃə] *n* Folter *f*, Folterung *f*; Tortur *f*. v foltern. **torturer** *n* Folterer *m*.

toss [tos] v (hoch)werfen; (*coin*) hochwerfen; *tossed about by the waves* von den Wellen hin und her geworfen.

tot¹ [tot] *n* (*whisky, etc.*) Schlückchen *neut*; (*child*) Knirps *m*.

tot² [tot] v **tot up** zusammenzählen.

total ['toutl] *adj* total, ganz, Gesamt-. *n* Summe *f*, Gesamtbetrag *m*. **in total** als Ganzes. **totalitarian** *adj* totalitär. **totalisator** *n* Totalisator *m*. v sich belaufen auf; (*person*) zusammenzählen. **totality** *n* Gesamtheit *f*. **totally** *adv* völlig, total.

totter ['totə] v taumeln, wanken. **tottering** *adj* wackelig.

touch [tʌtʃ] v berühren, anfassen; (*feel*) betasten; (*border on*) grenzen an; (*emotionally*) berühren. **touch down** landen.

touching *adj* rührend. **touchline** *n* Marklinie *f*. **touchstone** *n* Prüfstein *m*. *n* Berührung *f*, Anrühren *neut*; (*sense*) Tastsinn *m*, (*trace*) Spur *f*. **be/keep in touch with** in Verbindung stehen/bleiben mit. **touchy** *adj* empfindlich, reizbar.

tough [tʌf] *adj* zäh; (*person*) zäh, robust; (*difficult*) schwierig, sauer. **toughen** v zäher machen *or* werden. **toughness** *n* Zähigkeit *f*, Härte *f*.

toupee ['tuːpei] *n* Toupet *neut*.

tour [tuə] *n* Tour *f*, Rundreise *f*, (*of inspection*) Rundgang *m*; (*theatre*) Tournee *f*. v bereisen. **touring** *adj* Touren-. **tourism** *n* Tourismus *m*. **tourist** *n* Tourist(in).

tournament ['tuənəmənt] *n* Turnier *neut*.

tow [tou] v bugsieren, schleppen. *n* Schlepptau *neut*. **have in tow** im Schlepptau haben. **towline** *or* **towrope** *n* Schlepptau *neut*.

towards [tə'woːdz] *prep* (*place*) auf ... zu, nach ... hin; (*behaviour, attitude*) gegen(über). **towards midday** gegen Mittag.

towel ['tauəl] *n* Handtuch *neut*. **towelling** *n* Handtuchstoff *m*.

tower ['tauə] *n* Turm *m*. v (hoch)ragen.

town [taun] *n* Stadt *f*. *adj* Stadt-. **town council** Stadtrat *m*. **town hall** Rathaus *neut*. **town planning** Stadtplanung *f*.

toxic ['toksik] *adj* giftig, toxisch. **toxin** *n* Toxin *neut*.

toy [toi] *n* Spielzeug *neut*. **toys** *pl* Spielwaren *pl*. v **toy with** spielen mit.

trace [treis] *n* Spur *f*. v nachspüren, verfolgen; (*draw*) pausen, durchzeichnen. **tracing** *n* Pause *f*. **tracing paper** Pauspapier *neut*.

track [trak] *n* Spur *f*, Fährte *f*; (*rail*) Gleis *neut*; (*road*) Weg *m*, Pfad *m*; (*sport*) Bahn *f*. **track suit** Trainingsanzug *m*.

tract¹ [trakt] *n* (*land*) Strecke *f*. **digestive tract** Verdauungssystem *neut*.

tract² [trakt] *n* (*treatise*) Traktat *neut*.

tractor ['traktə] *n* Traktor *m*.

trade [treid] *n* Handel *m*; (*job, skill*) Gewerbe *neut*. **trade balance** *n* Handelsbilanz *f*. **trade fair** Messe *f*. **trademark** *n* Warenzeichen *neut*. **tradesman** *n* Lieferant *m*. **trade union** *n* Gewerkschaft *f*. **trade-unionist** *n* Gewerkschaftler(in). v handeln; (*exchange*) eintauschen. **trader** *n* Händler *m*.

tradition [trə'diʃən] n Tradition f. **traditional** adj traditionell.

traffic ['træfik] n Verkehr m. **traffic jam** Verkehrsstockung f. **trafficker** n Händler m. **traffic lights** Verkehrsampel f sing.

tragedy ['trædʒədi] n (theatre) Tragödie f; (fig) Unglück neut. **tragic** adj tragisch.

trail [treil] n Spur f. Fährte f. v schleifen, (nach)schleppen; (follow) verfolgen; (lag behind) nachhinken.

train [trein] n Zug m; (of dress) Schleppe f. v (person for job, etc.) ausbilden; (sport) trainieren; (child) schulen; (animal) dressieren. **trainee** n Lehrling m. **trainer** n (sport) Trainer m. **training** n Ausbildung f; (sport) Training neut.

trait [treit] n Zug m, Merkmal neut.

traitor ['treitə] n Verräter(in). **traitorous** adj verräterisch.

tram [træm] n Straßenbahn f.

tramp [træmp] n Landstreicher m. v stampfen.

trample ['træmpl] v trampeln.

trampoline ['træmpəliːn] n Trampoline f.

trance [trains] n Trance f.

tranquil ['træŋkwil] adj ruhig, friedlich. **tranquillity** n Ruhe f. **tranquillizer** n Beruhigungsmittel neut.

transact [tran'zakt] v durchführen. **transaction** n Geschäft neut, Transaktion f.

transcend [tran'send] v überschreiten. **transcendental** adj transzendental.

transcribe [tran'skraib] v abschreiben. **transcription** n Abschrift f.

transept ['transept] n Querschiff neut.

transfer [trans'fəː; n 'transfəː] v übertragen; (money) überweisen; (trains) umsteigen. n Übertragung f; Überweisung f; Umsteigen neut; (design) Abziehbild neut. **transferable** adj übertragbar. **transferred-charge call** R-Gespräch neut.

transform [trans'foːm] v umwandeln. **transformation** n Umwandlung f. **transformer** n (elec) Transformator m.

transfuse [trans'fjuːz] v (blood) übertragen. **transfusion** n (blood) Blutübertragung f.

transient ['tranziənt] adj vorübergehend.

transistor [tran'zistə] n Transistor m.

transit ['transit] n Durchfahrt f; (of goods) Transport m. adj Durchgangs-. **in transit** unterwegs.

transition [tran'ziʃən] n Übergang m. **transitional** adj Übergangs-.

transitive ['transitiv] adj transitiv.

translate [trans'leit] v übersetzen. **translation** n Übersetzung f. **translator** n Übersetzer(in).

translucent [trans'luːsnt] adj lichtdurchlässig.

transmit [tranz'mit] v übersenden; (radio, TV) senden. **transmitter** n (radio, TV) Sender m. **transmission** n (mot) Getriebe neut; (radio, TV) Sendung f.

transparent [trans'peərənt] adj durchsichtig, transparent; (fig) offensichtlich. **transparency** n Durchsichtigkeit f; (phot) (Dia)Positiv neut.

transplant [trans'plaint; n 'transplaint] v verpflanzen; (med) transplantieren. n (operation) Transplantation f; (actual organ) Transplantat neut. **transplantation** n Verpflanzung f.

transport [trans'poit; n 'transpoit] v befördern, transportieren. n Beförderung f. Transport m. **transportable** adj transportierbar. **transportation** n Transport m.

transpose [trans'pouz] v umstellen, versetzen.

transverse ['tranzvəːs] adj quer, Quer-.

trap [trap] n Falle f. **lay a trap** eine Falle stellen. **shut your trap!** (impol) halt die Klappe! **trapdoor** n Falltür f. v fangen. **trapper** n Trapper m.

trapeze [trə'piːz] n Trapez neut.

trash [traʃ] n Abfall m; (film, book, etc.) Kitsch m. **trash-can** n Abfalleimer m. **trashy** adj wertlos.

trauma ['troimə] n Trauma neut. **traumatic** adj traumatisch.

travel ['travl] v reisen. n Reisen neut. **travel agency** Reisebüro neut. **traveller** n Reisende(r). **travelling** adj Reise-. **travelling expenses** Reisespesen pl.

travesty ['travəsti] n Travestie f.

trawl [troil] n Grundschleppnetz neut, Trawl neut. v trawlen. **trawler** n Trawler m.

treachery ['tretʃəri] n Verrat m. **treacherous** adj verräterisch; (dangerous) gefährlich.

treacle ['triːkl] n Sirup m, Melasse f.

*****tread** [tred] n Tritt m, Schritt m; (tyre) Profil neut; (ladder) Sprosse f. v treten. **treadmill** n Tretmühle f.

treason ['triːzn] n Verrat m.

treasure ['treʒə] n Schatz m. v hochschätzen. **treasurer** n Schatzmeister(in); (club) Kassenwart m. **treasury** n

Schatzkammer f. **Treasury** n (pol) Finanzministerium neut.

treat [triːt] v behandeln. **treat someone to something** jemandem zu etwas einladen. n (coll) Genuß m, Vergnügen neut. **treatment** n Behandlung f.

treatise ['triːtiz] n Abhandlung f.

treaty ['triːti] n Vertrag m, Pakt m.

treble ['trebl] adj dreifach; (music) Diskant-. v (sich) verdreifachen.

tree [triː] n Baum m. **family tree** Stammbaum m.

trek [trek] n Treck m. v trecken.

trellis ['trelis] n Gitter neut, Gitterwerk neut.

tremble ['trembl] v zittern. n Zittern neut.

tremendous [trə'mendəs] adj enorm, kolossal; (coll: excellent) ausgezeichnet.

tremor ['tremə] n Beben neut.

trench [trentʃ] n Graben m; (mil) Schützengraben m. **trench coat** n Trenchcoat m.

trend [trend] n Tendenz f, Trend m. **trendy** adj (neu)modisch.

trespass ['trespəs] v unbefugt betreten. **trespasser** n Unbefugte(r). **trespassers will be prosecuted** Eintritt bei Strafe verboten.

trestle ['tresl] n Gestell n.

trial ['traiəl] n Probe f, Versuch m; (legal) Prozeß m. adj Probe-. **on trial** vor Gericht.

triangle ['traiaŋgl] n Dreieck neut; (music) Triangel m. **triangular** adj dreieckig.

tribe [traib] n Stamm m. **tribal** adj Stammes-. **tribesman** n Stammesangehörige(r).

tribunal [trai'bjuːnl] n Gerichtshof m, Tribunal neut.

tributary ['tribjutəri] n Nebenfluß m.

tribute ['tribjuːt] n Tribut m. **pay tribute** (fig) Anerkennung zollen.

trick [trik] n Trick m, Kniff m; (practical joke) Streich m; (cards) Stich m. adj Trick-. v betrügen. **trickery** n Betrügerei f. **trickster** n Schwindler(in). **tricky** adj knifflig.

trickle ['trikl] v tröpfeln, sickern. n Tröpfeln neut.

tricycle ['traisikl] n Dreirad neut.

tried [traid] adj erprobt, bewährt.

trifle ['traifl] n Kleinigkeit f; (cookery) Trifle m, (süßer) Auflauf m. **a trifle** ein bißchen. v spielen. **trifling** adj belanglos.

trigger ['trigə] n Abzug m. **pull the trigger** abdrücken. v **trigger off** auslösen.

trigonometry [trigə'nɔmətri] n Trigonometrie f.

trilby ['trilbi] n weicher Filzhut m.

trim [trim] adj gepflegt, nett; (slim) schlank. v zurechtmachen; (hair, etc.) ausputzen, beschneiden. **trimming** n Verzierung f.

trinket ['triŋkit] n Schmuckstück neut.

trio ['triːou] n Trio neut.

trip [trip] n Reise f, Ausflug m; (stumble) Fehltritt m, Stolpern neut. v stolpern; (dance) tänzeln, trippeln. **trip up** (someone else) ein Bein stellen (+ dat). **tripper** n Ausflügler(in).

tripe [traip] n Kaldaunen pl; (coll: nonsense) Quatsch m.

triple ['tripl] adj dreifach, Drei-. v verdreifachen. **triplet** n Drilling m. **triplex glass** Sicherheitsglas neut.

tripod ['traipod] n Dreifuß m; (phot) Stativ neut.

trite [trait] adj platt, banal.

triumph ['traiəmf] n Triumph m; Sieg m. v triumphieren. **triumphal** adj Triumph-, Sieger-. **triumphant** adj triumphierend, siegreich.

trivial ['triviəl] adj geringfügig, trivial. **triviality** n Trivialität f.

trod [trod] V tread.

trodden ['trodn] V tread.

trolley ['troli] n (supermarket) Einkaufswagen m; (tea) Serviertewagen m; (airport, etc.) Kofferkuli m; (tram) Straßenbahn f. **trolleybus** n O-Bus m.

trombone [trom'boun] n Posaune f. **trombonist** n Posaunist(in).

troop [truːp] n Trupp m. **troops** pl Truppen pl. **trooping the colour** Fahnenparade f.

trophy ['troufi] n (sport) Preis m; (mil, hunting) Trophäe f.

tropic ['tropik] n Wendekreis m. **tropics** pl Tropen pl. **tropical** adj tropisch.

trot [trot] n Trott m, Trab m. v trotten, traben.

trouble ['trʌbl] n Schwierigkeiten pl; (effort) Mühe f; (burden) Belästigung f; (tech) Störung f. v beunruhigen, stören. **troubles** pl (pol) Unruhe f, Aufruhr f. **be in trouble** Schwierigkeiten haben. **be troubled** bekümmert sein. **get into trouble** Ärger bringen (+ dat). **take (the) trouble** sich die Mühe ge'·nn. **trouble-maker** n Unruhestifter(in). **trou-**

ble shooter n Störungssucher(in). **troublesome** adj lästig

trough [trof] n Trog m.

trousers ['trauzəz] pl n Hose f sing.

trout [traut] n Forelle f.

trowel ['trauəl] n Kelle f; (gardening) Pflanzenheber m.

truant ['truːənt] n Schwänzer(in). **play truant** (die Schule) schwänzen. **truancy** n Schwänzerei f.

truce [truːs] n Waffenstillstand m.

truck [trʌk] n (road) Lastkraftwagen (Lkw) m; (rail) Güterwagen m. **truckdriver** n Lastwagenfahrer m.

trudge [trʌdʒ] v sich mühsam schleppen.

true [truː] adj wahr; (genuine) echt; (loyal) treu; (rightful) rechtmäßig. **truism** n Binsenwahrheit f. **truly** adv wirklich, in der Tat. **yours truly** hochachtungsvoll.

truffle [trʌfl] n Trüffel f.

trump [trʌmp] n Trumpf m. **trump card** Trumpfkarte f. v (über)trumpfen. **trumped up** falsch, erdichtet.

trumpet ['trʌmpit] n Trompete f. v trompeten. **trumpeter** n Trompeter m.

truncheon ['trʌntʃən] n Knüppel m.

trunk [trʌŋk] n (tree) Baumstamm m; (anat) Leib m; (case) Schrankkoffer m. (not) n Kofferraum m. **trunks** pl Badehose f sing. **trunk-call** Ferngespräch neut. **trunk-road** Fernstraße f.

truss [trʌs] n (med) Bruchband neut. v zusammenbinden; (cookery) dressieren.

trust [trʌst] v trauen (+dat); (hope) hoffen. n Vertrauen neut; (expectation) Erwartung f; (comm) Trust m. **hold in trust** als Treuhänder verwalten. **trustee** n Treuhänder m. **trusting** adj vertrauensvoll. **trustworthy** adj vertrauenswürdig. **trusty** adj treu.

truth [truːθ] n Wahrheit f. **truthful** adj wahr, wahrhaftig. **truthfulness** n Wahrhaftigkeit f.

try [trai] v (attempt) versuchen; (test, sample) probieren; (law) vor Gericht stellen, verhandeln gegen (wegen). **try on** (clothes) anprobieren. **try out** probieren. n Versuch m. **trying** adj peinlich, schwierig; (person) belästigend.

tsar [zaː] n Zar m.

T-shirt ['tiːʃəːt] n T-Shirt neut.

tub [tʌb] n (Bade)Wanne f; (barrel) Faß neut, Tonne f. **tubby** adj (coll) rundlich.

tuba ['tjuːbə] n Tuba f.

tube [tjuːb] n Rohr neut, Röhre f; (of

tyre) (Luft)Schlauch m; (coll: underground railway) U-Bahn f.

tuber ['tjuːbə] n Knolle f.

tuberculosis [tjubəːkju'ləusis] n Tuberkulose f.

tuck [tʌk] n Einschlag m. v **tuck in** (shirt) einstecken; (food) einhauen, zugreifen; (sheet) feststecken; (person) warm zudecken.

Tuesday ['tjuːzdi] n Dienstag m. **on Tuesdays** dienstags.

tuft [tʌft] n Büschel neut, Schopf m.

tug [tʌg] v ziehen, zerren; (boat) schleppen. n Zerren neut, Zug m; (boat) Schlepper m, Bugsierdampfer m.

tuition [tju'iʃən] n Unterricht m.

tulip ['tjuːlip] n Tulpe f.

tumble ['tʌmbl] v hinfallen, umstürzen. **tumbledown** adj baufällig. **tumble-dryer** (Wäsche)Trockner m. n Fall m, Sturz m. **tumbler** n Glas neut.

tummy ['tʌmi] n (coll) Bauch m, Bäuchlein neut. **tummy-ache** n Bauchweh neut.

tumour ['tjuːmə] n Geschwulst f, Tumor m.

tumult ['tjuːmʌlt] n Tumult m, Lärm m. **tumultuous** adj stürmisch.

tuna ['tjuːnə] n Thunfisch m.

tune [tjuːn] n Melodie f. **in/out of tune** gestimmt/verstimmt. **to the tune of** (coll) im Ausmaß von. v (ab)stimmen. **tune in** to einstellen auf. **tuneful** adj melodisch, wohlklingend. **tuner** n (pianos, etc.) Stimmer m.

tunic ['tjuːnik] n (school) Kittel m. (mil) Uniformrock m.

tunnel ['tʌnl] n Tunnel m, Unterführung f. v **tunnel through** einen Tunnel bauen durch.

tunny ['tʌni] V **tuna**.

turban ['təːbən] n Turban m.

turbine ['təːbain] n Turbine f.

turbot ['təːbət] n Steinbutt m.

turbulent ['təːbjulənt] adj unruhig, stürmisch. **turbulence** n Turbulenz f.

tureen [tə'riːn] n Terrine f.

turf [təːf] n Rasen m; (sport) Turf m, Rennbahn f. v **turf out** (coll) hinausschmeißen.

turkey ['təːki] n (cock) Truthahn m; (hen) Truthenne f.

Turkey ['təːki] n die Türkei f. **Turk** n Türke m, Türkin f. **Turkish** adj türkisch.

turmeric ['tɜːmərik] n Gelbwurz f.

turmoil ['tɜːmɔil] n Aufruhr m.

turn [tɜːn] v (sich) drehen; (become) werden. **turn around** or **round** (person) sich umdrehen; (thing) herumdrehen. **turn back** umkehren. **turn down** (offer) ablehnen; (radio) leiser stellen. **turning** n (mot) Abzweigung f. **turning point** Wendepunkt m. **turn left/right** links/rechts abbiegen. **turn loose** freilassen. **turn off** (light) ausschalten; (radio) abstellen; (mot) abbiegen. **turn on** einschalten. **turn out** (expel) ausweisen; (produce) herstellen. **turn-out** n (spectators) Teilnahme f. **turn over** (sich) umdrehen. **turnover** n (comm) Umsatz m. **turnstile** n Drehkreuz neut. **turntable** n (records) Plattenteller m. **turn up** (appear) auftauchen; (radio) lauter stellen. **turn-up** n (trousers) Umschlag m. n Umdrehung f; (change of direction) Wendung f. **it's my turn** ich bin an der Reihe. **do someone a good turn** jemandem einen Gefallen tun.

turnip ['tɜːnip] n (weiße) Rübe f.

turpentine ['tɜːpəntain] n Turpentin neut.

turquoise ['tɜːkwɔiz] n Türkis m. adj (colour) türkisblau.

turret ['tʌrit] n Türmchen neut; (gun) Geschützturm m, Panzerturm m.

turtle ['tɜːtl] n Schildkröte f. **turtle dove** Turteltaube f.

tusk [tʌsk] n Stoßzahn m.

tussle ['tʌsl] n Balgerei f, Ringen neut. v sich balgen, kämpfen.

tutor ['tjuːtə] n Privatlehrer m; (university) Tutor m.

tuxedo [tʌkˈsiːdou] n Smoking m.

tweed [twiːd] n Tweed m.

tweezers ['twiːzəz] pl n Pinzette f sing.

twelve [twelv] adj zwölf. n Zwölf f. **twelfth** adj zwölft.

twenty ['twenti] adj zwanzig. n Zwanzig f. **twentieth** adj zwanzigst.

twice [twais] adv zweimal. **twice as much** zweimal so viel. **think twice about** sich gründlich überlegen.

twiddle ['twidl] v herumdrehen, spielen mit.

twig [twig] n Zweig m.

twilight ['twailait] n (Abend)Dämmerung f, Zwielicht neut. adj Zwielicht-.

twin [twin] n Zwilling m. adj Zwillings-. **twin-cylinder engine** Zweizylindermotor m.

twine [twain] n Bindfaden m, Schnur f. v (threads) zusammendrehen. **twine around** winden um.

twinge [twindʒ] n Stich m, Stechen neut. **twinge of conscience** Gewissensbiß m. v zwicken, kneifen.

twinkle ['twiŋkl] v glitzern, funkeln; (eyes) blinzeln. n Glitzern neut; Blinzeln neut. **in a twinkle** im Nu.

twirl [twɜːl] v wirbeln. n Wirbel m.

twist [twist] v (sich) drehen, (sich) winden; (meaning) verdrehen; (features) verzerren. **twist one's ankle** sich den Fuß verrenken. **twisted** adj (person) verschroben. **twisting** adj sich windend. n Drehung f, Windung f; (in story) Wendung f.

twit [twit] n (coll) Dummkopf m.

twitch [twitʃ] v zucken. n Zucken neut.

twitter ['twitə] v zwitschern. n Gezwitscher neut, Zwitschern neut.

two [tuː] adj zwei. **two-faced** adj heuchlerisch. **twofold** adj zweifach. **two-stroke engine** Zweitaktmotor m. n Zwei f; (pair) Paar neut.

tycoon [taiˈkuːn] n Industriemagnat m.

type [taip] n Typ m, Sorte f, Klasse f; (person) Typ m; (print) Druck m, Druckschrift f. v (mit der Maschine) schreiben, tippen. **typed** adj maschinengeschrieben. **typewriter** n Schreibmaschine f. **typing error** Tippfehler m. **typist** n Typist(in).

typhoid ['taifoid] n Typhus m.

typhoon [taiˈfuːn] n Taifun m.

typical ['tipikəl] adj typisch. **typify** v verkörpern.

tyrant ['tairənt] n Tyrann(in). **tyrannical** adj tyrannisch. **tyrannize** v tyrannisieren. **tyranny** n Tyrannei f.

tyre ['taiə] or US **tire** n Reifen m.

U

ubiquitous [juˈbikwitəs] adj überall zu finden(d).

udder ['ʌdə] n Euter neut.

ugly ['ʌgli] adj häßlich. **ugliness** n Häßlichkeit f.

ulcer ['ʌlsə] n Geschwür neut.

ulterior [ʌl'tiəriə] *adj* **ulterior motives** Hintergedanken *pl.*

ultimate ['ʌltimət] *adj* allerletzt; (*conclusive*) endgültig, entscheidend. **ultimately** *adv* schließlich. **ultimatum** *n* Ultimatum *neut.*

ultraviolet [ʌltrə'vaiələt] *adj* ultraviolett.

umbilical [ʌm'bilikəl] *n* Nabelschnur *f.*

umbrella [ʌm'brelə] *n* Regenschirm *m.*

umlaut ['umlaut] *n* Umlaut *m.*

umpire ['ʌmpaiə] *n* Schiedsrichter *m.*

umpteen [ʌmp'tiin] *adj* zahllos. **umpteen times** x-mal.

unable [ʌn'eibl] *adj* unfähig. **be unable** nicht können.

unacceptable [ʌnək'septəbl] *adj* unannehmbar.

unaccompanied [ʌnə'kʌmpənid] *adj* unbegleitet; (*music*) ohne Begleitung.

unanimous [ju'nanimos] *adj* einstimmig. **unanimity** *n* Einstimmigkeit *f.*

unannounced [ʌnə'naunst] *adj* unangekündigt.

unarmed [ʌn'aimd] *adj* unbewaffnet.

unassuming [ʌnə'sjuimin] *adj* bescheiden.

unattractive [ʌnə'traktiv] *adj* reizlos, nicht anziehend.

unauthorized [ʌn'oiθəraizd] *adj* unbefugt.

unavoidable [ʌnə'voidəbl] *adj* unvermeidlich.

unaware [ʌnə'weə] *adj* **be unaware of** sich nicht bewußt sein (+ *gen*). **unawares** *adv* **take unawares** überraschen.

unbalanced [ʌn'balənst] *adj* unausgeglichen; (*mentally disturbed*) geistesgestört.

unbearable [ʌn'beərəbl] *adj* unerträglich.

unbelievable [ʌnbi'liivəbl] *adj* unglaublich. **unbeliever** *n* Ungläubige(r). **unbelieving** *adj* ungläubig.

*****unbend** [ʌn'bend] *v* (*person*) freundlicher werden. **unbending** *adj* unbeugsam.

unbounded [ʌn'baundid] *adj* unbegrenzt, grenzenlos.

unbreakable [ʌn'breikəbl] *adj* unzerbrechlich.

unbridled [ʌn'braidld] *adj* zügellos.

unbroken [ʌn'broukn] *adj* (*continuous*) ununterbrochen.

uncalled-for [ʌn'koildfoi] *adj* unangebracht.

uncanny [ʌn'kani] *adj* unheimlich.

uncertain [ʌn'səitn] *adj* unsicher, ungewiß. **uncertainty** *n* Unsicherheit *f,* Ungewißheit *f.*

uncle ['ʌnkl] *n* Onkel *m.*

unclean [ʌn'kliin] *adj* unrein.

uncomfortable [ʌn'kʌmfətəbl] *adj* unbequem; (*fact, etc.*) beunruhigend.

uncommon [ʌn'komən] *adj* ungewöhnlich, selten. **uncommonly** *adv* (*extremely*) außerordentlich.

unconditional [ʌnkən'difənl] *adj* bedingungslos, uneingeschränkt.

unconfirmed [ʌnkən'fəimd] *adj* unbestätigt.

unconscious [ʌn'konʃəs] *adj* (*unknowing*) unbewußt; (*med*) bewußtlos. **unconsciousness** *n* Bewußtlosigkeit *f.*

uncontrollable [ʌnkən'trouləbl] *adj* unbeherrscht, unkontrollierbar.

unconventional [ʌnkən'venʃənl] *adj* unkonventionell.

unconvinced [ʌnkən'vinst] *adj* nicht überzeugt. **unconvincing** *adj* nicht überzeugend.

uncooked [ʌn'kukt] *adj* roh, ungekocht.

uncork [ʌn'koik] *v* entkorken.

uncouth [ʌn'kuuθ] *adj* ungehobelt, unfein.

uncover [ʌn'kʌvə] *v* aufdecken.

uncut [ʌn'kʌt] *adj* (*gem*) ungeschliffen; (*grass*) ungemäht; (*book*) unbeschnitten.

undecided [ʌndi'saidid] *adj* (*thing*) unentschieden; (*person*) unentschlossen.

undeniable [ʌndi'naiəbl] *adj* unbestreitbar.

under ['ʌndə] *prep* unter; (*less than*) weniger als. **under age** minderjährig. **under construction** im Bau. **under cover of** im Schutz (+ *gen*). *adv* unten. **go under** zugrunde gehen. **under-** *pref* Unter-.

undercharge [ʌndə'tʃaidʒ] *v* zu wenig berechnen.

underclothes ['ʌndəklouðz] *pl n* Unterwäsche *f sing.*

undercoat ['ʌndəkout] *n* Grundierung *f,* Grundanstrich *m.*

undercover [ʌndə'kʌvə] *adj* Geheim-.

*****undercut** [ʌndə'kʌt] *v* (*comm*) unterbieten.

underdeveloped [ʌndədi'veləpt] *adj* unterentwickelt. **underdeveloped country** Entwicklungsland *neut.*

underdone [ʌndə'dʌn] *adj* (*meat*) nicht durchgebraten.

underestimate [ʌndə'estimeit] *adj* unterschätzen.

underexpose [ʌndərik'spouz] *v* unterbelichten. **underexposure** *n* Unterbelichtung *f.*

underfoot [ʌndə'fut] *adv* am Boden.

***undergo** [ʌndə'gou] *v* erleben; *(operation)* sich unterziehen (+ *dat*).

undergraduate [ʌndə'grædjuət] *n* Student(in).

underground ['ʌndəgraund; *adv* ʌndə'graund] *adj* unterirdisch, Untergrund-; *(pol)* geheim, Untergrund-. *n* *(rail)* Untergrundbahn *f*, *(coll)* U-Bahn *f*. *adv* unter die Erde. **go underground** *(hide)* untertauchen.

undergrowth ['ʌndəgrouθ] *n* Unterholz *neut*.

underhand [ʌndə'hand] *adj* heimlich, hinterlistig.

***underlie** [ʌndə'lai] *v* zugrunde liegen (+ *dat*).

underline [ʌndə'lain] *v* unterstreichen; *(stress)* betonen.

undermine [ʌndə'main] *v* unterminieren, untergraben.

underneath [ʌndə'niːθ] *prep* unter, unterhalb. *adv* unten, darunter.

underpants ['ʌndəpants] *pl n* Unterhose *f sing*.

underpass ['ʌndəpaɪs] *n* Unterführung *f*.

underprivileged [ʌndə'privilidʒd] *adj* benachteiligt.

underrate [ʌndə'reit] *v* unterschätzen.

***understand** [ʌndə'stand] *v* verstehen. **understandable** *adj* verständlich. **understanding** *n* Verständnis *neut*; *(agreement)* Verständigung *f*; *adj* verständnisvoll.

understate [ʌndə'steit] *v* untertreiben. **understatement** *n* Untertreibung *f*.

understudy ['ʌndəstʌdi] *n* Ersatzschauspieler(in).

***undertake** [ʌndə'teik] *v* übernehmen. **undertaker** *n* Leichenbestatter *m*. **undertaking** *n* Unternehmen *neut*; *(promise)* Versprechen *neut*.

undertone ['ʌndətoun] *n* Unterton *m*.

underwear ['ʌndəweə] *n* Unterwäsche *f*.

underweight [ʌndə'weit] *adj* untergewichtig.

underworld ['ʌndəwɔːld] *n* Unterwelt *f*.

***underwrite** [ʌndə'rait] *v* unterzeichnen, versichern. **underwriter** *n* Versicherer *m*.

undesirable [ʌndi'zaiərəbl] *adj* nicht wünschenswert, unerwünscht.

***undo** [ʌn'duɪ] *v* *(package)* öffnen, aufmachen; *(coat, knot)* aufknöpfen; *(work)* zunichte machen. **undoing** *n* Ruin *m*, Vernichtung *f*.

undoubted [ʌn'dautid] *adj* unbestritten. **undoubtedly** *adv* ohne Zweifel.

undress [ʌn'dres] *v* (sich) ausziehen. **undressed** *adj* unbekleidet.

undue [ʌn'djuː] *adj* übermäßig, übertrieben; *(improper)* unschicklich. **unduly** *adv* übertrieben.

undulate ['ʌndjuleit] *v* wogen, wallen. **undulation** *n* Wallen *neut*.

unearth [ʌn'ɔːθ] *v* ausgraben; *(fig)* ans Tageslicht bringen.

uneasy [ʌn'iːzi] *adj* *(person)* beunruhigt, ängstlich; *(feeling)* unbehaglich.

uneducated [ʌn'edjukeitid] *adj* ungebildet.

unemployed [ʌnem'ploid] *adj* arbeitslos. **unemployment** *n* Arbeitslosigkeit *f*.

unending [ʌn'endiŋ] *adj* endlos.

unequal [ʌn'iːkwəl] *adj* ungleich. **unequalled** *adj* unübertroffen.

uneven [ʌn'iːvn] *adj* uneben. **unevenness** *n* Unebenheit *f*.

uneventful [ʌni'ventfəl] *adj* ereignislos.

unexpected [ʌneks'pektid] *adj* unerwartet.

unfailing [ʌn'feiliŋ] *adj* unfehlbar.

unfair [ʌn'feə] *adj* ungerecht, unfair. **unfairness** *n* Unbilligkeit *f*.

unfaithful [ʌn'feiθfəl] *adj* untreu. **unfaithfulness** *n* Untreue *f*.

unfamiliar [ʌnfə'miljə] *adj* unbekannt.

unfasten [ʌn'faisn] *v* aufmachen, losbinden.

unfit [ʌn'fit] *adj* ungeeignet; *(sport)* nicht fit.

unfold [ʌn'fould] *v* (sich) entfalten.

unforeseen [ʌnfor'siːn] *adj* unvorhergesehen.

unforgettable [ʌnfə'getəbl] *adj* unvergeßlich.

unfortunate [ʌn'fortʃənət] *adj* unglücklich; *(regrettable)* bedauerlich. *n* Unglückliche(r). **unfortunately** *adv* unglücklicherweise, leider.

unfurnished [ʌn'fɔːnifd] *adj* unmöbliert.

ungrateful [ʌn'greitfəl] *adj* undankbar.

unhappy [ʌn'hapi] *adj* unglücklich; *(with something)* unzufrieden. **unhappily** *adv* leider. **unhappiness** *n* Unglück *neut*.

unhealthy [ʌn'helθi] *adj* *(person)* ungesund; *(damaging to health)* gesundheitsschädlich.

unhurt [ʌn'hɜːt] *adj* unverletzt.

unicorn ['juɪnikoɪn] *n* Einhorn *m*.

uniform ['juːnifɔːm] n Uniform f. Dienstkleidung f. adj einförmig, gleichförmig. **uniformity** n Gleichheit f.

unify ['juːnifai] v vereinigen. **unification** n Vereinigung f.

unilateral [juːni'lætərəl] adj einseitig.

uninhabited [ʌnin'habitid] adj unbewohnt. **uninhabitable** adj unbewohnbar.

unintelligible [ʌnin'telidʒəbl] adj unverständlich.

uninterested [ʌn'intristid] adj uninteressiert. **uninteresting** adj uninteressant.

union ['juːnjən] n Vereinigung f; (pol) Staatenbund m; (agreement) Eintracht f; (trade union) Gewerkschaft f. **unionize** v gewerkschaftlich organisieren.

unique [juː'niːk] adj einzigartig; (only) einzig.

unison ['juːnisn] n Einklang m.

unit ['juːnit] n Einheit f.

unite [juː'nait] v (sich) vereinigen. **united** adj vereint, vereinigt. **unity** n Einheit f; (accord) Einigkeit f.

United Kingdom n Vereinigtes Königreich.

United Nations pl n Vereinte Nationen.

United States of America n Vereinigte Staaten von Amerika.

universe ['juːnivəːs] n Weltall neut, Universum neut. **universal** adj universal.

university [juːni'vəːsəti] n Universität f, Hochschule f. adj Universitäts-, Hochschul-.

unjust [ʌn'dʒʌst] adj ungerecht.

unkempt [ʌn'kempt] adj ungepflegt.

unkind [ʌn'kaind] adj unfreundlich. **unkindness** n Unfreundlichkeit f.

unknown [ʌn'noun] adj unbekannt. n das Unbekannte.

unlawful [ʌn'lɔːfəl] adj rechtswidrig, unzulässig.

unless [ʌn'les] conj wenn ... nicht, es sei denn.

unlike [ʌn'laik] adj, prep unähnlich, (in contrast to) im Gegensatz zu. **unlikely** adv unwahrscheinlich.

unload [ʌn'loud] v (goods) abladen; (truck, etc.) entladen.

unlock [ʌn'lok] v aufschließen, öffnen. **unlocked** adj unverschlossen.

unlucky [ʌn'lʌki] adj unglücklich.

unmarried [ʌn'marid] adj ledig, unverheiratet.

unnatural [ʌn'natʃərəl] adj unnatürlich.

unnecessary [ʌn'nesəsəri] adj unnötig, nicht notwendig.

unobtainable [ʌnəb'teinəbl] adj unerhältlich.

unoccupied [ʌn'okjupaid] adj unbesetzt; (house) unbewohnt; (person) unbeschäftigt.

unofficial [ʌnə'fiʃəl] adj inoffiziell.

unorthodox [ʌn'ɔːθədoks] adj unorthodox.

unpack [ʌn'pak] v auspacken.

unpleasant [ʌn'pleznt] adj unangenehm. **unpleasantness** n Unannehmlichkeit f.

unpopular [ʌn'popjulə] adj unbeliebt.

unprecedented [ʌn'presidentid] adj unerhört.

unpretentious [ʌnpri'tenʃəs] adj anspruchslos.

unravel [ʌn'ravəl] v auftrennen; (fig) enträtseln.

unreal [ʌn'riəl] adj unwirklich. **unrealistic** adj unrealistisch.

unreasonable [ʌn'riːzənəbl] adj übertrieben, übermäßig; (person) unvernünftig.

unrelenting [ʌnri'lentiŋ] adj unerbittlich.

unreliable [ʌnri'laiəbl] adj unzuverlässig. **unreliability** n Unzuverlässigkeit f.

unrest [ʌn'rest] n Unruhe f.

unruly [ʌn'ruːli] adj unlenksam.

unsafe [ʌn'seif] adj unsicher, gefährlich.

unsatisfactory [ʌnsatis'faktəri] adj unbefriedigend. **unsatisfed** adj unzufrieden.

unscrew [ʌn'skruː] v aufschrauben.

unsettle [ʌn'setl] v beunruhigen. **unsettled** adj unruhig.

unsightly [ʌn'saitli] adj unansehnlich.

unskilled [ʌn'skild] adj ungelernt.

unsound [ʌn'saund] adj (advice, etc.) unzuverlässig. **of unsound mind** geistesgestört.

unspeakable [ʌn'spiːkəbl] adj unbeschreiblich; (horrible) scheußlich, entsetzlich.

unstable [ʌn'steibl] adj nicht fest, schwankend; (person) labil.

unsteady [ʌn'stedi] adj wackelig, unsicher.

unsuccessful [ʌnsək'sesfəl] adj erfolglos.

unsuitable [ʌn'suːtəbl] adj ungeeignet.

untangle [ʌn'taŋgl] v entwirren.

untidy [ʌn'taidi] adj unordentlich. **untidiness** n Unordentlichkeit f.

untie [ʌn'taɪ] v losbinden.
until [ən'tɪl] prep, conj bis. not until erst.
untoward [ʌntə'wɔːd] adj ungünstig.
untrue [ʌn'truː] adj unwahr, falsch; (friend) untreu. untruth n Unwahrheit f, Falschheit f. untruthful adj unwahr, unaufrichtig.
unusual [ʌn'juːʒuəl] adj ungewöhnlich, außergewöhnlich.
unwell [ʌn'wel] adj unwohl.
unwieldy [ʌn'wiːldɪ] adj unhandlich.
*unwind [ʌn'waɪnd] v loswickeln, abspulen; (rest) sich entspannen, (sich) ausruhen.
unworthy [ʌn'wəːðɪ] adj unwürdig.
unwrap [ʌn'ræp] v auswickeln.
up [ʌp] prep auf, hinauf. adv auf, hoch; hinauf, herauf; (out of bed) auf; (sun) aufgegangen. it's up to me es liegt an mir. up to now bis jetzt. up for trial vor Gericht. what's up? was ist los?
upbringing ['ʌpbrɪŋɪŋ] n Erziehung f.
update [ʌp'deɪt] v modernisieren; (book) neu bearbeiten.
upheaval [ʌp'hiːvl] n Umwälzung f.
uphill [ʌp'hɪl] adv bergauf. adj (fig) mühsam.
*uphold [ʌp'hould] v unterstützen, billigen.
upholster [ʌp'houlstə] v (auf)polstern. upholsterer n Polsterer m. upholstery n Polsterung f.
upkeep ['ʌpkiːp] n Instandhaltung f; (cost) Unterhaltskosten pl.
uplift [ʌp'lɪft] v erbauen.
upon [ə'pɒn] prep auf. once upon a time es war einmal.
upper [ʌp] adj ober, höher. uppermost adj oberst, höchst. (shoe) Oberleder neut.
upright ['ʌpraɪt] adj, adv gerade, aufrecht; (honest) aufrecht, aufrichtig.
uprising ['ʌpraɪzɪŋ] n Aufstand m.
uproar ['ʌprɔː] n Aufruhr m, Tumult m.
uproot [ʌp'ruːt] v ausreißen, entwurzeln.
*upset [ʌp'set] v; n 'ʌpset] v (person) bestürzen, beunruhigen; (plan) vereiteln; (tip over) umkippen. adj bestürzt, außer Fassung; (stomach) verstimmt. n (stomach) Verstimmung f.
upshot ['ʌpʃɒt] n Ergebnis neut.
upside down [ʌpsaɪ'daun] adv verkehrt herum, mit dem Kopf nach unten. turn upside down sich auf den Kopf stellen.
upstairs [ʌp'steəz] adv (go) nach oben, die

Treppe hinauf; (be) oben. adj (room) obere(r).
upstream [ʌp'striːm] adv stromaufwärts.
uptight ['ʌptaɪt] adj (coll) nervös, aufgeregt.
up-to-date [ʌptə'deɪt] adj modern, aktuell.
upward ['ʌpwəd] adj nach oben (gerichtet). upward glance Blick nach oben m. adv also upwards nach oben, nach oben.
uranium [ju'reɪnɪəm] n Uran neut.
Uranus ['juərəinəs] n Uranus m.
urban ['əːbən] adj städtisch, Stadt-. urbanization n Verstädterung f. urbanize v verstädtern.
urchin ['əːtʃɪn] n (boy) Bengel m.
urge [əːdʒ] v (implore) (dringend) bitten, raten (+dat); (insist on) betonen, bestehen auf. urge on antreiben. n Drang m, (An)Trieb m.
urgent ['əːdʒənt] adj dringend. urgency n Dringlichkeit f.
urine ['juːrɪn] n Urin m, Harn m. urinal n Urinbecken neut, Pissoir neut. urinary adj Urin-. urinate v urinieren.
urn [əːn] n Urne f.
us [ʌs] pron uns. both of us wir beide. all of us wir alle.
usage ['juːzɪdʒ] n Brauch m, Gebrauch m.
use [juːz; n juːs] v benutzen, gebrauchen; (apply) anwenden; (coll: exploit) ausbeuten. n Gebrauch m, Verwendung f. be of use von Nutzen sein, helfen. for the use of zum Nutzen von. it's no use es hilft nichts. make use of Gebrauch machen von. use up verbrauchen. I used to live here ich wohnte (früher) hier. she used to say sie hat immer gesagt, sie pflegte zu sagen. useful adj nützlich, brauchbar. usefulness n Nützlichkeit f. useless adj nutzlos, unnütz. user Benutzer(in). uselessness n Nutzlosigkeit f.

usher ['ʌʃə] n Platzanweiser(in). v usher in (fig) einleiten.
usual ['juːʒuəl] adj üblich, gewöhnlich. usually adv gewöhnlich, normalerweise.
usurp [ju'zəːp] v gewaltsam nehmen, usurpieren. usurpation n Usurpation f. usurper n Usurpator m.
utensil [ju'tensl] n Gerät neut, Werkzeug neut; (pl) Utensilien pl.
uterus ['juːtərəs] n Gebärmutter f, Uterus m. uterine adj Gebärmutter-.

utility [ju'tilǝti] *n* Nutzen *m.* **public utility** *n* öffentlicher Versorgungsbetrieb *m.*

utilize ['juttilatz] *v* verwenden. **utilization** *n* Verwendung *f.*

utmost ['ʌtmǝust] *adj* äußerst. **do one's utmost** sein möglichstes tun.

utter[1] ['ʌtǝ] *v* äußern, aussprechen. **utterance** *n* Äußerung *f.*

utter[2] ['ʌtǝ] *adj* rein, bloß, höchst.

U-turn ['ju:tǝn] *n* Wende *f;* (*pol*) Kehrtwendung *f.*

V

vacant ['veikǝnt] *adj* leer. **vacancy** *n* Leere *f;* (*job*) freie Stelle. **vacate** *v* verlassen; (*seat*) freimachen. **vacation** *n* Urlaub *m.*

vaccine ['vaksin] *n* Impfstoff *m.* **vaccinate** *v* impfen. **vaccination** *n* Impfung *f.*

vacillate ['vasileit] *v* schwanken. **vacillation** *n* Schwanken *neut.*

vacuum ['vakjum] *n* Vakuum *neut.* **vacuum-cleaner** *n* Staubsauger *m.* *v* (*coll*) mit dem Staubsauger reinigen. **vacuous** *adj* leer.

vagina [vǝ'dʒainǝ] *n* Scheide *f,* Vagina *f.*

vagrant ['veigrǝnt] *n* Vagabund *m,* Landstreicher *m.*

vague [veig] *adj* vage, undeutlich; (*person*) zerstreut. **vagueness** *n* Verschwommenheit *f.*

vain [vein] *adj* (*person*) eitel, eingebildet; (*thing*) eitel, leer; (*effort*) vergeblich. **in vain** umsonst, vergeblich.

valiant ['valiǝnt] *adj* tapfer, heroisch.

valid ['valid] *adj* gültig. **validate** *v* für gültig erklären. **validity** *n* Gültigkeit *f.*

valley ['vali] *n* Tal *neut.*

value ['valju:] *n* Wert *neut.* **value-added tax (VAT)** Mehrwertsteuer (Mwst) *f. v* (*establish value of*) einschätzen; (*treasure*) bewerten. **valuable** *adj* wertvoll, kostbar. **valuables** *pl n* Wertsachen *pl.* **valuation** *n* Schätzung *f.* **valued** *adj* hochgeschätzt. **valueless** *adj* wertlos.

valve [valv] *n* Ventil *neut;* (*anat*) Klappe *f;* (*elec*) Röhre *f.*

vampire ['vampaiǝ] *n* Vampir *m.*

van [van] *n* Lastwagen *m,* Lieferwagen *m.* **luggage van** Gepäckwagen *m.*

vandal ['vandl] *n* Vandale *m,* Vandalin *f.* **vandalism** *n* Vandalismus *m.*

vanilla [vǝ'nilǝ] *n* Vanille *f.*

vanish ['vanish] *v* verschwinden. **vanishing cream** Tagescreme *f.*

vanity ['vanǝti] *n* Eitelkeit *f.* **vanity bag** Kosmetiktasche *f.*

vapour ['veipǝ] *n* Dampf *m.* **vaporize** *v* verdampfen.

varicose veins ['varikous] *pl n* Krampfadern *pl.*

varnish ['varnish] *n* Lack *m,* Firnis *m. v* lackieren.

vary ['veǝri] *v* (*modify*) (ab)ändern, variieren; (*become changed*) sich ändern, variieren. **variable** *adj* veränderlich. **variation** *n* Veränderung; (*music, biology*) Variation *f.* **varied** *adj* verschiedenartig, abwechslungsvoll. **variety** *n* Verschiedenheit, Mannigfaltigkeit *f;* (*species*) Art *f.* Varietät *f.* **variety show** Varieté *neut.* **various** *adj* verschieden; (*several*) mehrere. **varying** *adj* wechselnd, unterschiedlich.

vase [va:z] *n* Vase *f.*

vasectomy [vǝ'sektǝmi] *n* Vasektomie *f.*

vast [va:st] *adj* ungeheuer, riesig; (*wide*) weit, ausgedehnt. **vast majority** überwiegende Mehrheit *f.* **vast numbers of** zahllos(e). **vastly** *adv* gewaltig. **vastness** *n* Weite *f.*

vat [vat] *n* großes Faß *neut.*

vault[1] [vo:lt] *n* (*ceiling*) Gewölbe *neut;* (*cellar*) Keller *m;* (*safe*) Stahlkammer *f.*

vault[2] [vo:lt] *v* (*jump*) springen (über). *n* Sprung *m.* **vaulting-horse** *n* Sprungpferd *neut.*

veal [vi:l] *n* Kalbfleisch *neut.*

veer [viǝ] *v* sich drehen; (*mot*) ausscheren.

vegetable ['vedʒtǝbl] *n* Gemüse *neut. adj* pflanzlich. **vegetarian** *n* Vegetarier(in); *adj* vegetarisch. **vegetation** *n* Pflanzenwuchs *m,* Vegetation *f.*

vehement ['viǝmǝnt] *adj* heftig, gewaltig.

vehicle ['viǝkl] *n* Fahrzeug *neut;* (*medium*) Mittel *neut,* Vehikel *neut.*

veil [veil] *n* Schleier *m. v* verschleiern. **veiled** *adj* verschleiert.

vein [vein] *n* Vene *f;* (*mood*) Stimmung *f;* (*in rock*) Ader *f.* **veined** *adj* geädert.

velocity [vǝ'losǝti] *n* Geschwindigkeit *f.*

velvet ['velvit] *n* Samt *m. adj* Samt-. **velvety** *adj* samtweich, samtartig.

vending machine ['vendɪŋ] *n* (Verkaufs)Automat *m*.

veneer [və'nɪə] *n* Furnier *neut*; (*fig*) Anstrich *m*. *v* furnieren.

venerate ['venəreit] *v* verehren, bewundern. **venerable** *adj* ehrwürdig. **veneration** *n* Verehrung *f*.

venereal disease [və'nɪəriəl] *n* Geschlechtskrankheit *f*.

Venetian blind [və'niːʃən] *n* Jalousie *f*.

vengeance ['vendʒəns] *n* Rache *f*. **take vengeance on** sich rächen an. **vengeful** *adj* rachsüchtig.

venison ['venisn] *n* Reh *neut*, Wildbret *neut*.

venom ['venəm] *n* (Tier)Gift *neut*. **venomous** *adj* giftig.

vent [vent] *n* Öffnung *f*, Luftloch *neut*; (*in jacket*) Schlitz *m*. *v* lüften; (*feelings*) freien Lauf lassen (+*dat*), äußern.

ventilate ['ventileit] *v* ventilieren, lüften. **ventilation** *n* Ventilation *f*, Lüftung *f*. **ventilator** *n* Ventilator *m*, Lüftungsanlage *f*.

venture ['ventʃə] *n* (*risk*) Risiko *neut*, Wagnis *neut*; (*undertaking*) Unternehmen *neut*. *v* wagen.

venue ['venjuː] *n* Schauplatz *m*; (*meeting place*) Treffpunkt *m*.

Venus ['viːnəs] *n* Venus *f*.

verb [vəːb] *n* Verbum *neut*, Zeitwort *neut*. **verbal** *adj* mündlich. **verbalize** *v* formulieren. **verbatim** *adv* wortwörtlich. **verbose** *adj* wortreich.

verdict ['vəːdikt] *n* Urteil *neut*.

verge [vəːdʒ] *n* Rand *m*, Grenze *f*; (*grass*) Grasstreifen *m*. **verge on** grenzen an.

verify ['verifai] *v* beweisen, bestätigen, beglaubigen. **verification** *n* Beglaubigung *f*.

vermin ['vəːmin] *pl n* Schädlinge *pl*.

vermouth ['vəːməθ] *n* Wermut *m*.

vernacular [və'nakjulə] *n* Volkssprache *f*.

versatile ['vəːsətail] *adj* (*person*) vielseitig. **versatility** *n* Vielseitigkeit *f*.

verse [vəːs] *n* (*stanza*) Strophe *f*; (*line*) Vers *m*; (*poetry*) Poesie *f*, Dichtung *f*. **versed** *adj* versiert.

version ['vəːʃən] *n* Fassung *f*, Version *f*; (*Bible, etc.*) Übersetzung *f*.

versus ['vəːsəs] *prep* gegen.

vertebra ['vəːtibrə] *n* (*pl* -ae) Wirbel *m*. **vertebral column** Wirbelsäule *f*. **vertebrate** *n* Wirbeltier *neut*.

vertical ['vəːtikl] *adj* senkrecht, lotrecht. *n* Senkrechte *f*.

vertigo ['vəːtigou] *n* Schwindelgefühl *neut*.

very ['veri] *adj* sehr. **very best** allerbest. *adj* that very day an ebendemselben Tag. **at the very beginning** gerade am Anfang.

vessel ['vesl] *n* Gefäß *neut*; (*ship*) Schiff *neut*.

vest [vest] *n* (*undershirt*) Unterhemd *neut*; (*waistcoat*) Weste *f*.

vestige ['vestidʒ] *n* Spur *f*.

vestments ['vestmənts] *pl n* (*rel*) Amtstracht *f*.

vestry ['vestri] *n* Sakristei *f*.

vet [vet] *n* (*animals*) Tierarzt *m*. *v* prüfen, überholen.

veteran ['vetərən] *n* Veteran *m*.

veterinary ['vetərinəri] *n* Tierarzt *m*.

veto ['viːtou] *n* Veto *neut*, Einspruch *m*. *v* Veto einlegen gegen.

vex [veks] *v* ärgern, belästigen. **vexation** *n* Ärger *m*. **vexed** *adj* ärgerlich; (*question*) strittig.

via [vaiə] *prep* über.

viable ['vaiəbl] *adj* lebensfähig; (*practicable*) durchführbar.

viaduct ['vaiədʌkt] *n* Viadukt *m*.

vibrate [vai'breit] *v* vibrieren. **vibration** *n* Vibrieren *neut*, Vibration *f*.

vicar ['vikə] *n* Pfarrer *m*. **vicarage** *n* Pfarrhaus *neut*.

vicarious [vi'keəriəs] *adj* aus zweiter Hand.

vice¹ [vais] *n* (*evil*) Laster *neut*, Untugend *f*.

vice² [vais] *n* (*tool*) Schraubstock *m*, Zwinge *f*.

vice-chancellor [vais'tʃɑːnsələ] *n* (*university*) Rektor *m*.

vice-president [vais'prezidənt] *n* Vizepräsident *m*.

vice versa [vaisi'vəːsə] *adv* umgekehrt.

vicinity [vi'siniti] *n* Nähe *f*, Nachbarschaft *f*.

vicious ['viʃəs] *adj* bösartig, gemein; (*blow, etc*) heftig, gewaltig. **vicious circle** Teufelskreis *m*. **viciousness** *n* Gemeinheit *f*.

victim ['viktim] *n* Opfer *neut*. **victimize** *v* ungerecht behandeln.

victor ['viktə] *n* Sieger(in). **victorious** *adj* siegreich. **victory** *n* Sieg *m*.

video-tape ['vidiouteip] *n* Magnetbildband *neut*.

view [vjuː] *n* Ausblick *m*, Aussicht *f*; (*picture, opinion*) Ansicht *f*. **in view** in Sicht. **viewfinder** *n* Sucher *m*. **viewpoint** *n* Gesichtspunkt *m*, Standpunkt *m*. **with a view to** mit der Absicht, zu. *v* ansehen, betrachten. **viewer** *n* (*TV*) Zuschauer(in).

vigil ['vidʒil] *n* Wachen *neut*. **keep vigil** wachen. **vigilance** *n* Wachsamkeit *f*. **vigilant** *adj* wachsam.

vigour ['vigə] *n* Kraft *f*, Vitalität *f*. **vigorous** *adj* kräftig, energisch.

vile [vail] *adj* gemein, ekelerregend, widerlich.

villa ['vilə] *n* Villa *f*.

village ['vilidʒ] *n* Dorf *neut*. *adj* dörflich, Dorf-. **villager** *n* Dorfbewohner(in).

villain ['vilən] *n* Schurke *m*; (*coll*) Schelm *m*. **villainous** *adj* schurkisch. **villainy** *n* Schurkerei *f*.

vindictive [vin'diktiv] *adj* rachsüchtig. **vindictiveness** *n* Rachsucht *f*.

vine [vain] *n* Rebe *f*, Weinstock *m*. **vineleaf** *n* Weinblatt *m*. **vineyard** *n* Weinberg *m*. **viniculture** *n* Weinbau *m*.

vinegar ['vinigə] *n* Essig *m*. **vinegary** *adj* sauer.

vintage ['vintidʒ] *n* Weinernte *f*; (*particular year*) Jahrgang *m*.

vinyl ['vainil] *n* Vinyl *neut*. *adj* Vinyl-.

viola [vi'oulə] *n* Viola *f*.

violate ['vaiəleit] *v* (*law*) übertreten; (*woman*) vergewaltigen. **violation** *n* Übertretung *f*.

violence ['vaiələns] *n* Gewalt *f*, Gewalttätigkeit *f*. **violent** *adj* (*blow*) heftig, gewaltig; (*person, action*) gewaltsam.

violet ['vaiəlit] *n* Veilchen *neut*. *adj* violett.

violin [vaiə'lin] *n* Geige *f*, Violine *f*. **violinist** *n* Geiger(in).

viper ['vaipə] *n* Viper *f*, Natter *f*.

virgin ['vəːdʒin] *n* Jungfrau *f*. *adj* jungfräulich; (*soil*) unbebaut. **virginity** *n* Jungfernschaft *f*.

Virgo ['vəːgou] *n* Jungfrau *f*.

virile ['virail] *adj* männlich, kräftig. **virility** *n* Männlichkeit *f*.

virtual ['vəːtʃuəl] *adj* eigentlich; (*coll*) praktisch. **virtually** *adv* praktisch.

virtue ['vəːtʃuː] *n* Tugend *f*. **by virtue of** wegen (+ *gen*). **virtuous** *adj* tugendhaft, rechtschaffen.

virtuoso [,vəːtju'ouzou] *n* Virtuose *m*, Virtuosin *f*. **virtuosity** *n* Virtuosität *f*.

virus ['vaiərəs] *n* Virus *neut*.

visa ['viːzə] *n* Visum *neut*.

viscount ['vaikaunt] *n* Vicomte *m*.

viscous ['viskəs] *adj* zähflüssig. **viscosity** *n* Viskosität *f*.

visible ['vizəbl] *adj* sichtbar. **visibility** *n* Sichtbarkeit *f*. **visibly** *adj* offenbar.

vision ['viʒən] *n* (*power of sight*) Sehvermögen *neut*; (*insight*) Einsicht *f*; (*mystical, etc.*) Vision *f*. **field of vision** Blickfeld *neut*. **visionary** *adj* phantastisch; *n* Hellseher(in).

visit ['vizit] *v* besuchen. *n* Besuch *m*. **visitation** *n* Besuchen *neut*. **visiting** *adj* Besuchs-. **visitor** *n* Besucher(in). **visitor's book** Gästebuch *neut*.

visor ['vaizə] *n* Visier *neut*; (*peak*) Schirm *m*.

visual ['viʒuəl] *adj* visuell. **visual aids** Anschauungsmaterial *neut*. **visualize** *v* vergegenwärtigen.

vital ['vaitl] *adj* lebenswichtig. **vitality** *n* Lebenskraft *f*.

vitamin ['vitəmin] *n* Vitamin *neut*.

vivacious [vi'veiʃəs] *adj* lebhaft, munter. **vivacity** *n* Lebhaftigkeit *f*.

vivid ['vivid] *adj* (*description*) lebendig; (*colour*) leuchtend; (*imagination*) lebhaft.

vixen ['viksn] *n* Füchsin *f*.

vocabulary [və'kabjuləri] *n* Wortschatz *m*; (*glossary*) Wörterverzeichnis *neut*.

vocal ['voukəl] *adj* stimmlich; (*music*) Vokal-. **vocal cords** *pl* Stimmbänder *pl*. **vocalist** *n* Sänger(in).

vocation [vou'keiʃən] *n* (*rel*) Berufung *f*; (*occupation*) Beruf *m*. **vocational** *adj* Berufs-.

vociferous [və'sifərəs] *adj* brüllend, lärmend.

vodka ['vodkə] *n* Wodka *m*.

voice [vois] *n* Stimme *f*. *v* ausdrücken, äußern.

void [void] *adj* leer; (*invalid*) nichtig, ungültig.

volatile ['volətail] *adj* flüchtig; (*person*) wankelmütig, sprunghaft.

volcano [vol'keinou] *n* Vulkan *m*. **volcanic** *adj* vulkanisch. **volcanic eruption** Vulkanausbruch *m*.

volley ['voli] *n* (*mil*) Salve *f*; (*tennis*) Flugschlag *m*.

volt [voult] *n* Volt *neut*. **voltage** *n* Spannung *f*.

volume ['voljum] *n* Volumen *neut*, Inhalt *m*; (*book*) Band *m*; (*noise level*) Lautstärke *f*.

voluntary ['vɒləntri] *adj* freiwillig.
volunteer [vɒlən'tiə] *n* Freiwillige(r). *adj* Freiwilligen-. *v* sich freiwillig melden.
voluptuous [və'lʌptʃuəs] *adj* wollüstig.
voluptuousness *n* Wollust *f*.
vomit ['vɒmit] *v* (sich) erbrechen.
voodoo ['vuːduː] *n* Wodu *m*.
voracious [və'reiʃəs] *adj* gierig.
vote [vout] *n* (*individual*) Stimme *f*; (*right to vote*) Stimmrecht *neut*; (*election*) Abstimmung *f*, Wahl *f*. **vote of no confidence** Mißtrauensvotum *neut*. *v* abstimmen. **vote for** stimmen für. **voter** *n* Wähler(in).
vouch [vautʃ] *v* (sich) bürgen für. **voucher** *n* Gutschein *m*. **vouchsafe** *v* gewähren.
vow [vau] *n* Gelübde *neut*. *v* schwören, geloben.
vowel ['vauəl] *n* Vokal *m*. *adj* vokalisch.
voyage ['vɒiidʒ] *n* Reise *f*. *v* reisen. **voyager** *n* Reisende(r).
vulgar ['vʌlgə] *adj* vulgär, ordinär. **vulgarity** *n* Ungezogenheit *f*.
vulnerable ['vʌlnərəbl] *adj* verwundbar.
vulture ['vʌltʃə] *n* Geier *m*.

W

wad [wɒd] *n* Bausch *m*; (*money*) Rolle *f*.
waddle ['wɒdl] *v* watscheln.
wade [weid] *v* waten.
wafer ['weifə] *n* Waffel *f*; (*rel*) Hostie *f*. **wafer-thin** *adj* hauchdünn.
waffle ['wɒfl] *n* Waffel *f*.
waft [wɒft] *v* wehen.
wag [wag] *v* wag one's head mit dem Kopf wackeln. **wag one's tail** wedeln.
wage [weidʒ] *n also* **wages** Lohn *m*. **wage agreement** Tarifvertrag *m*. **wage-earner** *n* Lohnempfänger(in). **wage freeze** *n* Lohnstopp *m*. **wage-packet** *n* Lohntüte *f*. *v* (*war*) führen.
waggle ['wagl] *v* wackeln (mit).
wagon ['wagən] *n* Wagen *m*; (*rail*) Waggon *m*.
waif [weif] *n* verwahrlostes Kind *neut*.
wail [weil] *v* jammern, wehklagen. **wailing** *n* Jammern *neut*.
waist [weist] *n* Taille *f*. **waistband** *n* Bund *m*. **waistcoat** *n* Weste *f*.
wait [weit] *v* warten. **no waiting** Parken

verboten. **wait and see** abwarten. **wait for** warten auf. **waiting-room** *n* Wartesaal *m*. **wait on** bedienen. *n* Wartezeit *f*. **waiter** *n* Kellner *m*. **waitress** *n* Kellnerin *f*.
waive [weiv] *v* verzichten auf.
*wake [weik] *v also* **waken** or **wake up** aufwachen, erwachen; (*awaken*) (auf)wecken, erwecken. **wakeful** *adj* wachsam. **waking** *adj* wach.
walk [wɔːk] *v* laufen, (zu Fuß) gehen. **walk out** streiken. **walk out on** im Stich lassen. **walk-over** *n* leichter Sieg *m*, Spaziergang *m*. *n* Spaziergang *m*; (*path*) Weg *m*. **go for a walk** einen Spaziergang machen, spazierengehen. **walk of life** Lebensstellung *f*.
wall [wɔːl] *n* Mauer *f*; (*internal*) Wand *f*. **wallpaper** *n* Tapete *f*. *v* tapezieren.
wallet ['wɒlit] *n* Brieftasche *f*, Geldtasche *f*.
wallop ['wɒləp] *v* prügeln. *n* (heftiger) Schlag *m*.
wallow ['wɒlou] *v* sich wälzen.
walnut ['wɔːlnʌt] *n* Walnuß *f*.
walrus ['wɔːlrəs] *n* Walroß *neut*.
waltz [wɔːlts] *n* Walzer *m*. *v* Walzer tanzen, walzen.
wand [wɒnd] *n* Rute *f*; (*magic*) Zauberstab *m*.
wander ['wɒndə] *v* wandern. **wander about** umherwandern. **wanderlust** *n* Wanderlust *f*. **wanderer** *n* Wanderer *m*. **wandering** *n* Wandern *neut*. *adj* wandernd.
wane [wein] *v* abnehmen.
wangle ['waŋgl] *v* organisieren, (hintenherum) beschaffen. **wangler** *n* Schieber *m*.
want [wɒnt] *v* wollen; (*need*) benötigen; (*wish*) wünschen. **wants** *pl n* Bedürfnisse *pl*. **wanted** *adj* gesucht. **be found wanting** den Erwartungen nicht entsprechen.
wanton ['wɒntən] *adj* lüstern; (*cruelty, etc*.) rücksichtslos.
war [wɔː] *n* Krieg *m*. **be at war with** Kriegführen mit. **prisoner-of-war** Kriegsgefangene(r). **war crime** *n* Kriegsverbrechen *neut*. **warfare** *n* Kriegführung *f*. **warlike** *adj* kriegerisch. **war memorial** Kriegerdenkmal *neut*.
warble ['wɔːbl] *v* trillern.
ward [wɔːd] *n* (*town*) Bezirk *n*; (*hospital*) Station *f*; (*of court*) Mündel *neut*. *v* **ward off** abwehren. **warden** *n* Vorsteher *m*. **warder** *n* Gefängniswärter *m*.

wardrobe ['woɪdroub] n Kleiderschrank m; (clothes) Garderobe f.

wares [weəz] pl n Waren pl.

warehouse ['weəhaus] n Lager(haus) neut.

warm [woɪm] adj warm. **warm-blooded** adj warmblütig. **warm-hearted** adj warmherzig. v (auf)wärmen. **warm up** v (become warm) warm werden; (engine) warmlaufen (lassen). **warmish** adj lauwarm. **warmth** n Wärme f.

warn [woɪn] v warnen. **warn off** verwarnen. **warning** n Warnung f. adj warnend. **warning light** Warnlicht neut.

warp [woɪp] v sich verziehen, krumm werden. **warped** adj verzogen.

warrant ['worənt] n Vollmacht f, Berechtigung f. warrant of arrest Haftbefehl m. **warren** ['worən] n Kaninchengehege neut.

warrior ['woriə] n Krieger m.

wart [woɪt] n Warze f.

wary ['weəri] adj vorsichtig, behutsam. **wary of** auf der Hut vor.

was [woz] V be.

wash [woʃ] v waschen; (oneself) sich waschen; (dishes) spülen. **washbasin** n Waschbecken neut. **wash down** abwaschen. **washed-out** adj verblaßt; (coll) ermüdet. **washed-up** adj (coll) ruiniert, fertig. **washing** n (laundry) Wäsche f. **washing machine** Waschmaschine f. **washing powder** Waschmittel neut. **wash up** v spülen, abwaschen. n Waschen neut, Wäsche f. **washable** adj waschecht. **washer** n (tech) Scheibe f, Dichtungsring m.

wasp [wosp] n Wespe f. **waspish** adj reizbar.

waste [weist] v verschwenden, vergeuden. **waste away** abnehmen, verfallen. n Verschwendung f; (rubbish) Abfall m. **waste of time** Zeitverschwendung f. adj (land) wüst; Abfall-. **lay waste** verwüsten. **waste-bin** n Abfalleimer m. **waste-paper basket** n Papierkorb neut. **wasteful** adj verschwenderisch.

watch [wotʃ] v (guard) bewachen; (observe) zusehen, beobachten; (pay attention to) achtgeben auf. **watch out!** paß auf! **watch out for** auf der Hut sein vor. **watch television** fernsehen. n Wache f; (wristwatch) Armbanduhr f. **keep watch** Wache halten. **watchdog** n Wachhund m. **watchman** n Wächter m. **watchful** adj wachsam.

water ['woɪtə] n Wasser neut. v wässern. **water down** verwässern.

water-closet n (Wasser)Klosett neut, WC neut.

water-colour n Aquarell neut. adj Aquarell-.

watercress ['woɪtəkres] n Brunnenkresse f.

waterfall ['woɪtəfoɪl] n Wasserfall m.

watering-can n Gießkanne f.

water-lily n Seerose f, Wasserlilie f.

waterlogged ['woɪtəlogd] adj vollgesogen.

watermark ['woɪtəmaɪk] n (in paper) Wasserzeichen neut.

water-melon n Wassermelone f.

water-mill n Wassermühle f.

waterproof ['woɪtəpruɪf] adj wasserdicht. n Regenmantel m. v imprägnieren.

watershed ['woɪtəʃed] n Wasserscheide f.

water-ski n Wasserski m. v Wasserski fahren.

watertight ['woɪtətait] adj wasserdicht; (argument) unanfechtbar.

water-way n Wasserstraße f.

waterworks ['woɪtəwəɪks] pl n Wasserwerk neut sing.

watery ['woɪtəri] adj wässerig; (eyes) tränend.

watt [wot] n Watt neut. **wattage** n Wattleistung f.

wave [weiv] n Welle f; (gesture) Wink m. **waveband** n Wellenband neut. **wavelength** n Wellenlänge f. v winken; (hair) in Wellen legen. **wavy** adj wellig; (hair) gewellt.

waver ['weivə] v schwanken.

wax[1] [waks] n Wachs neut. v (floor) bohnern. **waxen** adj wächsern. **waxwork** n Wachsfigur f.

wax[2] [waks] v (increase) wachsen; (become) werden.

way [wei] n Weg m; (direction) Richtung f; (method) Art f, Weise f; (respect) Hinsicht f, Beziehung f. **by the way** übrigens. **on the way** unterwegs. **out-of-the-way** adj abgelegen; (odd) ungewöhnlich.

*waylay ['weilei] v auflauern (+dat).

wayward ['weiwəd] adj eigensinnig. **waywardness** n Eigensinn m.

we [wiɪ] pl pron wir.

weak [wiɪk] adj schwach; (liquids) dünn. **weak-minded** adj charakterschwach. **weaken** v schwächen. n Schwächling m. **weakly** adj, adv schwächlich. **weakness** n Schwäche f; (disadvantage) Nachteil m; (liking) Vorliebe f.

wealth [welθ] *n* Reichtum *m*; *(fortune)* Vermögen *neut*. **wealthy** *adj* reich, wohlhabend.

wean [wiːn] *v* entwöhnen.

weapon [ˈwepən] *n* Waffe *f*.

*wear [weə] *v* tragen; *(wear out)* abnutzen; *(become worn)* abgenutzt werden; *n* Tragen *neut*; *(wear and tear)* Abnutzung *f*, Verschleiß *m*. **wear off** *(fig)* sich verlieren. **wear out** *(person)* ermüden.

weary [ˈwiəri] *adj* müde; *(task)* lästig. *v* ermüden; *(become tired of)* müde werden (+ *gen*). **weariness** *n* Müdigkeit *f*. **wearisome** *adj* ermüdend, langweilig.

weasel [ˈwiːzl] *n* Wiesel *neut*.

weather [ˈweðə] *n* Wetter *neut*. **weather-beaten** *adj* verwittert. **weathercock** *n* Wetterhahn *m*. **weather forecast** Wettervorhersage *f*. **weatherman** *n* *(coll)* Meteorologe *m*. **weather-proof** *adj* wetterfest.

*weave [wiːv] *v* weben. **weave into** einflechten. **weaving** *n* Weberei *f*; *(fig)* Web-.

web [web] *n* *(spider's)* Spinngewebe *neut*. **webbed foot** Schwimmfuß *m*. **webbing** *n* Gewebe *neut*. **web-footed** *adj* schwimmfüßig.

wedding [ˈwediŋ] *n* Hochzeit *f*. **wedding cake** Hochzeitskuchen *m*. **wedding day** Hochzeitstag *m*. **wedding ring** Trauring *m*.

wedge [wedʒ] *n* Keil *m*; *(of cheese)* Ecke *f*. **wedge-shaped** *adj* keilförmig. *v* einkeilen.

Wednesday [ˈwenzdi] *n* Mittwoch *m*. **on Wednesdays** mittwochs.

weed [wiːd] *n* Unkraut *neut*. *v* (Unkraut) jäten. **weedy** *adj* *(coll)* schmächtig.

week [wiːk] *n* Woche *f*. **weekday** *n* Wochentag *m*. **weekend** *n* Wochenende *neut*. **weekly** *adj* wöchentlich; *n* *(magazine)* Wochenzeitschrift *f*.

*weep [wiːp] *v* weinen. **weeping** *adj* weinend; *n* Weinen *neut*. **weeping willow** Trauerweide *f*.

weigh [wei] *v* wiegen. **weigh one's words** seine Worte abwägen. **weigh up** abschätzen. **weight** *n* Gewicht *neut*. **carry weight with** viel gelten bei. **lose weight** abnehmen. **put on weight** zunehmen. **weight-lifting** *n* Gewichtheben *neut*. **weighty** *adj* schwerwiegend.

weir [wiə] *n* Wehr *neut*.

weird [wiəd] *adj* unheimlich.

welcome [ˈwelkəm] *n* Willkommen *neut*. *adj, interj* willkommen. **you're welcome** *(coll)* bitte, nichts zu danken. *v* willkommen heißen; *(fig)* begrüßen.

weld [weld] *v* (ver)schweißen. *n* Schweißstelle *f*, Schweißnaht *f*. **welder** *n* Schweißer *m*. **welding** *n* Schweißen *neut*.

welfare [ˈwelfeə] *n* Wohlfahrt *f*, welfare state Wohlfahrtsstaat *m*.

well¹ [wel] *n* *(for water)* Brunnen *m*, Quelle *f*.

well² [wel] *adv* gut. **as well** auch. **as well as** sowohl ... als auch. **you may well ask** du kannst wohl fragen. *adj* *(healthy)* wohl, gesund. **feel well** sich wohl fühlen. **I'm not well** mir ist nicht wohl. *interj* na, schön.

well-being *n* Wohlergehen *neut*.

well-behaved *adj* artig.

well-bred *adj* wohlerzogen.

well-built *adj* gut gebaut; *(person)* kräftig gebaut.

well-done *adj* *(meat)* gut durchgebraten.

wellingtons [ˈweliŋtənz] *pl n* Gummistiefel *pl*.

well-known *adj* (wohl)bekannt.

well-meaning *adj* wohlmeinend.

well-off *adj* wohlhabend.

well-paid *adj* gut bezahlt.

well-spoken *adj* höflich.

well-to-do *adj* wohlhabend.

well-worn *adj* abgenutzt; *(phrase)* abgedroschen.

went [went] *V* go.

wept [wept] *V* weep.

west [west] *n* Westen *m*. *adj also* **westerly** westlich, West-. *adv also* **westwards** nach Westen; westwärts. **western** *adj* westlich; *n* Wildwestfilm *m*.

wet [wet] *adj* naß. **wet through** durchnäßt. **wet weather** Regenwetter *neut*. *n* Nässe *f*. *v* anfeuchten, naßmachen. **wetness** *n* Nässe *f*.

whack [wak] *v* schlagen, verhauen. *n* Schlag *m*.

whale [weil] *n* Wal *m*, Walfisch *m*. **whaler** *n* Walfänger *m*. **whaling** *n* Walfang *m*.

wharf [woːf] *n* Kai *m*.

what [wot] *pron* was. **so what?** na und? **what about ... ?** wie wäre es mit ... ? **whatever** *pron* was auch immer. **nothing whatever** überhaupt nichts. **what for?** wozu? **what's up?** was ist los? **what's your

name? wie heißt du? *or (polite)* wie ist Ihr Name? *adj* was für ein, welch.

wheat [wiit] *n* Weizen *m*.

wheel [wiil] *n* Rad *neut; (steering)* Lenkrad *neut.* **at the wheel** am Steuer. *v* rollen. **wheelbarrow** *n* Schubkarren *m.* **wheelchair** *n* Rollstuhl *m*.

wheeze [wiiz] *n* Keuchen *neut; (coll)* Plan *m. v* keuchen, schnaufen.

whelk [welk] *n* Wellhornschnecke *f*.

when [wen] *adv (question)* wann. *conj (with past tense)* als; *(with present tense)* wenn. **whenever** *conj* wann auch immer.

where [weə] *adv, conj* wo; *(motion)* wohin. **where from?** woher? **where to?** wohin? *where do you come from?* wo kommen Sie her? *where are you going?* wo gehen Sie hin? **whereabouts** *adv* wo; *n* Verbleib *m.* **whereas** *conj* wohingegen, während. **whereby** *adv* wodurch, womit. **whereupon** *adv* woraufhin. **wherever** *adv* wo auch immer.

whether [weðə] *conj* ob.

which [witʃ] *pron (question)* welch; *(the one that)* welch, der/die/das.

whiff [wif] *n* Hauch *m*.

while [wail] *conj* während; *(whereas)* wogegen. *n* Weile *f.* **a long while ago** schon lange her. **for a while** eine Zeitlang. **in a while** bald. *v* **while away the time** sich die Zeit vertreiben.

whim [wim] *n* Laune *f.* Einfall *m*.

whimper [wimpə] *n* Wimmer *neut. v* wimmern.

whimsical [wimzikl] *adj* launenhaft.

whine [wain] *n* Gewinsel *neut. v* winseln. **whining** *adj* weinerlich.

whip [wip] *n* Peitsche *f. v* peitschen; *(cream)* schlagen. **whipped cream** Schlagsahne *f.* **whipping** *n* Peitschen *neut.* **whipround** *n (coll)* Geldsammlung *f*.

whippet [wipit] *n* Whippet *m*.

whirl [wəːl] *n* Wirbel *m. v* wirbeln. **whirlwind** *n* Wirbelwind *m*.

whisk [wisk] *n* Schneebesen *m. v* schlagen. **whisk away/off** *v* wegzaubern.

whiskers [wiskəz] *pl n (animals)* Schnurrhaare *pl; (man's)* Barthaare *pl*.

whisky [wiski] *n* Whisky *m*.

whisper [wispə] *v* flüstern. *n* Flüstern *neut.*

whist [wist] *n* Whist *neut*.

whistle [wisl] *v* pfeifen. *n* Pfiff *m; (instrument)* Pfeife *f*.

white [wait] *adj* weiß; *(pale)* blaß. **white**

bread Weißbrot *neut.* **white lie** Notlüge *f.* **white man** Weiße(r) *m.* **whitewash** *v* tünchen. **white wine** Weißwein *m. v* Weiß *neut; (person)* Weiße(r). **whiten** *v* weiß machen; *(bleach)* bleichen. **whiteness** *n* Weiße *f*.

whiting [waitiŋ] *n* Weißfisch *m*.

Whitsun [witsn] *n* Pfingsten *neut sing*.

whiz [wiz] *v* zischen.

who [hu] *pron (question)* wer; *(the one which, that)* wer, welch, der/die/das. **whoever** *pron* wer auch immer.

whole [houl] *adj* ganz; *(undamaged)* heil, unverletzt. *n* das Ganze *neut; (collective)* Gesamtheit *f.* **on the whole** im großen und ganzen.

whole-hearted *adj* rückhaltlos.

wholemeal [houlmiil] *adj* Vollkorn-.

wholesale [houlseil] *adv* en gros; *(fig)* unterschiedslos. *adj* Großhandels-. *n* Großhandel *m.* **wholesaler** *n* Großhändler *m*.

wholesome [houlsəm] *adj* bekömmlich, gesund.

whom [huum] *pron (question) (acc)* wen; *(dat)* wem; *(that, the one whom)* den, dem.

whooping cough [huupiŋ] *n* Keuchhusten *m*.

whore [hot] *n* Hure *f. v* huren.

whose [huuz] *pron (question)* wessen; *(of whom)* dessen, deren. *whose is this?* wem gehört dies?

why [wai] *adv* warum. *interj* nun, ja. **that is why** deshalb. **the reason why** der Grund, weshalb.

wick [wik] *n* Docht *m*.

wicked [wikid] *adj* böse. **wickedness** *n* Bosheit *f*.

wicker [wikə] *adj* Weiden-, Korb-. **wickerwork** *n* Korbwaren *pl*.

wicket [wikit] *n (gate)* Pförtchen *neut*.

wide [waid] *adj* breit. *adv* weit. **far and wide** weit und breit. **wide awake** hellwach. **widespread** *adj* weitverbreitet. **widely** *adv* weit. **widely known** allgemein bekannt. **widen** *v* breiter machen *or* werden. **wideness** *n* Breite *f*.

widow [widou] *n* Witwe *f.* **widowed** *adj* verwitwet. **widower** *n* Witwer *m.* **widowhood** *n* Witwenstand *m*.

width [widθ] *n* Breite *f.* Weite *f*.

wield [wiild] *v (weapon)* handhaben; *(influence)* ausüben.

wife [waif] n (pl **wives**) Frau f.

wig [wig] n Perücke f.

wiggle [wigl] v wackeln. n Wackeln neut.

wild [waild] adj wild; (coll: angry) wütend. **be wild about** (coll) schwärmen für. **wildcat strike** wilder Streik m. **wild flower** Feldblume f. **Wildness** n Wildheit f.

wilderness ['wildənəs] n Wüste f.

wilful ['wilfəl] adj eigensinnig. **wilfulness** n Eigensinn m.

will[1] [wil] v (to form future) werden; (expressing wish or determination) wollen.

will[2] [wil] n Wille m; (testament) Testament neut. **will-power** n Willenskraft f.

willing ['wiliŋ] adj bereit. **willingly** adv bereitwillig. **willingness** n Bereitschaft f.

willow ['wilou] n Weide f.

wilt [wilt] v welken.

wily ['waili] adj schlau, listig.

*****win** [win] v gewinnen; (mil) siegen. n Sieg m.

wince [wins] v zusammenzucken. n (Zusammen)Zucken neut.

winch [wintʃ] n Winde f.

wind[1] [wind] n Wind m. **wind instrument** Blasinstrument neut.

*****wind**[2] [waind] v (sich) winden; (yarn) aufwickeln; (clock) aufziehen. **wind up** (come to a close) Schluß machen. (business) auflösen. **winder** n Winde f. **winding** adj sich windend, schlängelnd.

windlass ['windləs] n Winde f.

windmill ['wind,mil] n Windmühle f.

windpipe ['windpaip] n Luftröhre f.

window ['windou] n Fenster neut; (ticket office, etc.) Schalter m; (shop) Schaufenster neut. **window-box** n Blumenkasten m. **window-frame** n Fensterrahmen m. **window-pane** n Fensterscheibe f. **window-shopping** n Schaufensterbummel m. **window-sill** Fensterbrett neut.

windshield ['windʃild] n Windschutzscheibe f. **windshield-wiper** Scheibenwischer m.

windy ['windi] adj windig.

wine [wain] n Wein m. **wine bar** Weinstube f. **wineglass** n Weinglas neut.

wing [wiŋ] n Flügel m; (theatre) Kulisse f; (mot) Kotflügel m. **on the wing** im Fluge. **winged** adj geflügelt. **winger** n (sport) Außenstürmer m. **wing-nut** n Flügelmutter f.

wink [wiŋk] n Zwinkern neut. v wink at zuzwinkern (+dat).

winkle ['wiŋkl] n Strandschnecke f.

winner ['winə] n Sieger(in), Gewinner(in).

winnings pl n Gewinn m sing.

winter ['wintə] n Winter m. v überwintern. **wintry** adj winterlich.

wipe [waip] v wischen. **wipe out** (destroy) ausrotten. **wipe up** (dishes) abtrocknen. **wiper** n Wischer m.

wire [waiə] n Draht m; (telegram) Telegramm neut. **wire netting** Maschendraht m. v (house, etc.) Leitungen legen in. **wireless** n Radio neut. **wiring** n Leitungsnetz neut.

wiry ['waiəri] adj (person) sehnig, zäh, (hair) borstig.

wisdom ['wizdəm] n Weisheit f. **wisdom tooth** n Weisheitszahn m.

wise [waiz] adj weise, klug. **wise guy** (coll) Besserwisser m. **wise man/woman** Weise(r).

wish [wiʃ] v wünschen. **wish for** sich wünschen. I wish to know ich möchte wissen. **wished-for** adj erwünscht. n Wunsch m.

wisp [wisp] n (hair) Strähne f. **wispy** adj (hair) wuschelig.

wistful ['wistfəl] adj sehnsüchtig. **wistfulness** n Sehnsucht f.

wit [wit] n Witz m, Esprit m. **wits** pl n Verstand m.

witch [witʃ] n Hexe f. **witchcraft** n Hexerei f. **witch-doctor** n Medizinmann m.

with [wið] prep mit; (among people) bei. **weep with joy** vor Freude weinen. **stay with** bleiben bei.

*****withdraw** [wið'drɔː] v (sich) zurückziehen; (remark) zurücknehmen; (money) abheben. **withdrawal** n Zurückziehung f; Zurücknahme f; Abhebung f. **withdrawn** adj zurückgezogen.

wither ['wiðə] v verdorren, verwelken. **withered** adj welk.

*****withhold** [wið'hould] v zurückhalten.

within [wi'ðin] prep innerhalb (+gen). adv darin, innen. **within a short time** binnen kurzem.

without [wi'ðaut] prep ohne (+acc).

*****withstand** [wið'stænd] v widerstehen (+dat).

witness ['witnis] n Zeuge m, Zeugin f. **bear witness to** Zeuge ablegen von. **witness-box** n Zeugenstand m. v bezeugen; (be present at) erleben, sehen.

witty ['witi] *adj* witzig. **witticism** *n* Witz *m*.

wizard ['wizəd] *n* Zauberer *m*. **wizardry** *n* Zauberei *f*.

wobble ['wobl] *v* wackeln, schwanken. *n* Wackeln *neut*. **wobbly** *adj* wackelig.

woke [wouk] *V* wake.

woken ['woukn] *V* wake.

wolf [wulf] *n* (*pl* wolves) Wolf *m*. *v* (*gobble*) verschlingen. **she-wolf** *n* Wölfin *f*.

woman ['wumən] *n* (*pl* women) Frau *f*. **woman doctor** Ärztin *f*. **womanly** *adj* weiblich, fraulich.

womb [wu:m] *n* Gebärmutter *f*.

won [wʌn] *V* win.

wonder ['wʌndə] *n* (*marvel*) Wunder *neut*; (*astonishment*) Erstaunen *neut*, Verwunderung *f*. **no wonder** kein Wunder. *v* (*be surprised*) sich wundern; (*ask oneself, muse*) sich fragen, gespannt sein. **wonderful** *adj* wunderbar. **wondrous** *adj* erstaunlich.

wonky ['woŋki] *adj* wackelig.

wood [wud] *n* Holz *neut*; (*forest*) Wald *m*. **wooden** *adj* hölzern, Holz-.

woodcock ['wudkɔk] *n* Waldschnepfe *f*.

woodpecker ['wudpekə] *n*. Specht *m*.

wood-pigeon *n* Ringeltaube *f*.

woodwind ['wudwind] *n* Holzblasinstrument *neut*; Holzbläser *m*.

woodwork ['wudwə:k] *n* Holzarbeit *f*, Tischlerei *f*.

woodworm ['wudwə:m] *n* Holzwurm *m*.

woody ['wudi] *adj* Holz-, holzig; (*countryside*) Wald-, waldig.

wool [wul] *n* Wolle *f*. **woollen** *adj* wollen, Woll-. **woolly** *adj* wollig.

word [wə:d] *n* Wort *neut*. **break/keep one's word** sein Wort brechen/halten. **wording** *n* Fassung *f*. **wordy** *adj* wortreich, langatmig.

wore [wɔ:] *V* wear.

work [wə:k] *n* Arbeit *f*; (*piece of work, art, music, etc.*) Werk *neut*. **works** *pl* Werk *neut*. *v* arbeiten; (*of machine*) laufen, funktionieren; (*succeed*) klappen; (*land*) bebauen; (*metal*) schmieden; (*operate* (*machine*)) bedienen. **work off** (*debt*) abarbeiten; (*feelings*) abreagieren. **work out** ausrechnen. **out of work** arbeitslos. **worked-up** *adj* aufgeregt, aufgebracht. **worker** *n* Arbeiter(in).

working *adj* Arbeits-; (*person*) berufstätig. **working class** Arbeiterklasse *f*; *adj* Arbeiter-. **in working order** betriebsfähig.

working party Arbeitsgruppe *f*. **workman** *n* Handwerker *m*. **work-to-rule** *n* Bummelstreik *m*.

world [wə:ld] *n* Welt *f*. **not for all the world** nicht um alles in der Welt. **the world to come** das Jenseits *neut*. **world champion** Weltmeister(in). **world-famous** *adj* weltberühmt. **worldly-wise** *adj* weltklug. **world-wide** *adj* weitverbreitet. **worldly** *adj* irdisch.

worm [wə:m] *n* Wurm *m*.

worn [wɔ:n] *v* wear. *adj* (*worn out*) abgenutzt. **worn out** *adj* (*thing*) abgenutzt; (*person*) todmüde.

worry ['wʌri] *v* (*bother*) beunruhigen; (*be worried*) sich Sorgen machen, sich beunruhigen. *n* Sorge *f*, Besorgnis *f*. **worrying** *adj* beunruhigend. **worried** *adj* beunruhigt, besorgt.

worse [wə:s] *adj, adv* schlimmer, schlechter. **worse and worse** immer schlechter. **worsen** *v* (sich) verschlechtern or verschlimmern.

worship ['wə:ʃip] *n* Anbetung *f*, Verehrung *f*; (*in church*) Gottesdienst *m*. *v* anbeten, verehren. **worshipful** *adj* ehrwürdig. **worshipper** *n* Anbeter(in).

worst [wə:st] *adj* schlechtest, schlimmst. *adv* am schlechtesten or schlimmsten. **at the worst** im schlimmsten Falle.

worsted ['wustid] *n* Kammgarn *neut*.

worth [wə:θ] *n* Wert *m*. *adj* wert. **it's worth ten marks** es ist zehn Mark wert. **it's not worth it** es lohnt sich nicht. **worthless** *adj* wertlos. **worthwhile** *adj* der Mühe wert. **worthy** *adj* würdig, wert.

would [wud] *v* (*to form conditional*) würde, würdest, etc. (*used to*) pflegte, pflegtest, etc; (*expressing desire, volition*) wollte, wolltest, etc. **he would go** (*if*) er würde gehen(wenn). **I would like** ich möchte. **he would come in the summer** er pflegte im Sommer zu kommen. **he would not come** er wollte durchaus nicht kommen.

wound¹ [waund] *V* wind².

wound² [wu:nd] *n* Wunde *f*. *v* verwunden. **wounded** *adj* verletzt.

wove [wouv] *V* weave.

woven ['wouvn] *V* weave.

wrangle ['raŋgl] *v* zanken, streiten. *n* Zank *m*, Streit *m*.

wrap [rap] *v* wickeln. **wrap up** einwickeln. *n* Schal *m*. **wrapper** *n* Umschlag *m*. **wrap-**

ping n Verpackung f. **wrapping paper** Einwickelpapier neut.

wreath [ri:θ] n Kranz m.

wreck [rek] n wrack neut; (naut) Schiffbruch m. v zerstören. **wreckage** n Trümmer pl.

wren [ren] n Zaunkönig m.

wrench [rentʃ] v zerren, ziehen. n (tool) Schraubenschlüssel m.

wrestle ['resl] v ringen. **wrestler** n Ringer m. **wrestling** n Ringkampf m, Ringen neut.

wretch [retʃ] n Elende(r), armes Wesen neut. **wretched** adj unglücklich, elend.

wriggle ['rigl] v sich schlängeln. n Schlängeln neut.

*****wring** [riŋ] v (hands) ringen; (clothes) auswringen. **wringer** n Wringermaschine f. **wringing wet** triefend naß.

wrinkle ['riŋkl] n (face, brow) Runzel f, Falte f; (paper) Knitter m. **wrinkled** adj runzlig.

wrist [rist] n Handgelenk neut. **wristwatch** n Armbanduhr f.

writ [rit] n (law) (Vor)Ladung f. **Holy Writ** Heilige Schrift f.

*****write** [rait] v schreiben. **write down** aufschreiben. **write off** abschreiben. **write out** (cheque) ausstellen. **writer** n Schriftsteller(in). **writing** n Schreiben neut. **in writing** schriftlich. **writing-paper** n Schreibpapier neut.

written ['ritn] V write. adj schriftlich.

writhe [raið] v sich winden.

wrong [roŋ] adj (incorrect) falsch; (bad, immoral) unrecht. **be wrong** sich irren, unrecht haben. **what's wrong with ... ?** was ist los mit ... ? **that was wrong of you** das war unrecht von dir. **go wrong** (mech) kaputtgehen; (plan) schiefgehen. **get it wrong** es ganz falsch verstehen. **wrongdoer** n Missetäter(in). **wrongdoing** n Missetat f. **wrongly** adv mit Unrecht.

wrote [rout] V write.

wrought iron [,rott'aiən] n Schweißeisen neut.

wrung [rʌŋ] V wring.

wry [rai] adj verschroben.

X

xenophobia [zenə'foubiə] n Fremdenfeindlichkeit f.

Xerox ® ['ziəroks] n Fotokopiergerät neut. v fotokopieren.

X-ray [eks'rei] n Röntgenstrahl m; (picture) Röntgenbild neut. v röntgen. adj Röntgen-.

xylophone ['zailəfoun] n Xylophon neut.

Y

yacht [jot] n Jacht f. **yachting** n Segeln neut.

yank [jaŋk] v (coll) heftig ziehen (an). n Ruck m.

yap [jap] v kläffen; (coll) schwätzen. n Kläffen neut.

yard¹ [jaid] n (measure) Yard neut. **yardstick** n Maßstab m.

yard² [jaid] n Hof m.

yarn [jain] n Garn neut; (story) Geschichte f.

yawn [join] n Gähnen neut. v gähnen.

year [jiə] n Jahr neut. **5 years old** fünf Jahre alt. **for years** jahrelang. **yearbook** n Jahrbuch neut. **yearly** adj jährlich.

yearn [jəin] v sich sehnen (nach). **yearning** n Sehnsucht f.

yeast [jiist] n Hefe f.

yell [jel] v (gellend) aufschreien. n Schrei m.

yellow ['jelou] adj gelb. n Gelb neut.

yelp [jelp] v jaulen. n Jaulen neut.

yes [jes] adv ja, jawohl. **yes-man** n Jasager m.

yesterday ['jestədi] n, adv gestern. **yesterday morning** gestern früh. **yesterday's** or **of yesterday** gestrig, von gestern. **the day before yesterday** vorgestern.

yet [jət] adv noch, immer noch. conj aber.

yew [juɪ] n Eibe f.

yield [jiıld] n Ertrag m. **yielding** adj ergiebig.

yoga ['jougə] n Joga m.

yoghurt ['jogət] n Joghurt m.

yoke [jouk] n Joch m. v verbinden.

yolk [jouk] n Eidotter m, Eigelb neut.

yonder ['jondə] adv da, dort drüben. adj jene(r).

you [juː] *pron* (*fam sing*) du; (*fam pl*) ihr; (*polite sing or pl*) Sie; (*impers, one*) man. *acc*: dich; euch; Sie; einen. *dat*: dir; euch; Ihnen; einem.

young [jʌŋ] *adj* jung. *n* (Tier)Junge *pl*. **young children** kleine Kinder *pl*.

your [jɔː] *adj* (*fam sing*) dein; (*fam pl*) euer; (*polite sing or pl*) Ihr; (*impers, one's*) sein. **yours** (der/die/das) deine *or* eure *or* Ihre *or* seine. *a friend of yours* ein Freund von dir.

youth [juːθ] *n* Jugend *f*; (*lad*) Jüngling *m*. *adj* Jugend-. **youth hostel** Jugendherberge *f*. **youthful** *adj* jugendlich, jung.

Yugoslavia [juːgouˈslɑːvjə] *n* Jugoslawien *neut*. **Yugoslav** *n* Jugoslawe *m*, Jugoslawin *f*. *adj* jugoslawisch.

Z

zeal [ziːl] *n* Eifer *m*. **zealous** *adj* eifrig.

zebra [ˈzebrə] *n* Zebra *neut*. **zebra crossing** *n* Zebrastreifen *m*.

zero [ˈziərou] *n* Null *f*.

zest [zest] *n* Lust *f*, Begeisterung *f*.

zigzag [ˈzigzag] *adj* Zickzack-. *n* Zickzack *m*.

zinc [ziŋk] *n* Zink *neut*.

zip [zip] *n also* **zipper** Reißverschluß *m*. **zip code** Postleitzahl *f*.

zodiac [ˈzoudiak] *n* Tierkreis *m*. **signs of the zodiac** Tierkreiszeichen *pl*.

zone [zoun] *n* Zone *f*.

zoo [zuː] *n* Zoo *m*. **zoological** *adj* zoologisch. **zoologist** *n* Zoologe *m*. **zoology** *n* Zoologie *f*, Tierkunde *f*.

zoom [zuːm] *v* summen, brummen; (*coll: rush*) sausen; (*prices*) Hochschnellen. **zoom lens** *n* Zoom (objektiv) *neut*.

German—Englisch

A

Aal [aːl] m (pl -e) eel.

ab [ap] adv off; prep (abwärts, nach unten) from; (weg, fort) from. **ab und zu** now and again, from time to time. **auf und ab** up and down, to and fro.

abänderlich ['apɛndərlɪç] adj variable. **abändern** v change, modify. **Abänderung** f modification; (Pol) amendment.

abarbeiten ['aparbaitən] (Schuld) work off; (Werkzeug) wear out. **sich die Finger abarbeiten** work one's fingers to the bone.

Abbau ['apbau] m (unz.) demolition; (Personal) reduction of staff, staff-cut. **abbauen** v demolish; (Personal) cut.

abbestellen ['apbəʃtɛlən] v cancel.

****abbiegen** ['apbiːɡən] v deflect, turn aside; (Straße) bend; (Mot) turn off.

Abbild ['apbilt] neut image, likeness. **abbilden** v illustrate, depict. **Abbildung** f illustration, drawing.

abblenden ['apblɛndən] v (Mot) dip one's headlights.

****abbrechen** ['apbrɛçən] v break off; (Blumen, Obst) pick; (abbauen) demolish; (Lager) break.

****abbringen** ['apbriŋən] v dissuade, put off; (entfernen) remove.

Abbruch ['apbrux] m (unz.) (Haus) demolition; (Einstellung) stop, cessation.

abdanken ['apdaŋkən] v (König) abdicate; (Beamter) resign. **Abdankung** f (pl -en) abdication; resignation.

abdecken ['apdɛkən] v uncover; (Tisch)

clear; (schützen) shield, cover; (Verlust) make good.

abdichten ['apdɪçtən] v seal up; (wasserdicht machen) make watertight.

Abdomen [ap'doːmən] neut abdomen. **abdominal** adj abdominal.

abdrehen ['apdreːən] v unscrew, twist off; (Hals) wring.

Abdruck ['apdruk] m reprint, new impression; (Finger-) print. **abdrucken** v print.

abdrücken ['apdrʏkən] v (Pistole) fire.

Abend ['aːbənt] m (pl -e) evening. **gestern abend** yesterday evening, last night. **-brot** or **-essen** neut supper, dinner. **-land** neut West, Occident. **-mahl** neut Holy Communion. **abends** adv in the evening(s).

Abenteuer ['aːbəntɔyər] neut (pl -) adventure. **abenteuerlich** adj adventurous. **Abenteurer** m adventurer.

aber ['aːbər] conj but; (jedoch) however. **das ist aber schrecklich!** that's just awful! **Aberglaube** ['aːbərglaubə] m superstition. **abergläubisch** adj superstitious.

aberkennen ['aperkɛnən] v deprive, dispossess.

abermals ['aːbərmals] adv again, once more.

****abfahren** ['apfaːrən] v set off, depart; (Mot) drive off. **Abfahrt** f departure; (Ski) descent, downhill run.

Abfall ['apfal] 1 (unz.) falling off, decline; (Neigung) slope. 2 m waste, rubbish. **-eimer** m dustbin. **abfallen** v fall off, decline. **abfällig** adj disparaging.

abfassen ['apfasən] v compose, draw up, formulate. **Abfassung** f wording.

abfertigen ['apfɛrtɪɡən] v (Güter) (prepare for) dispatch; (Fahrzeug) check over, prepare (for departure); (Kundschaft) see to.

abfinden ['apfɪndən] v pay off. **sich abfinden mit** come to terms with (auch fig) **Abfindung** f (pl **-en**) settlement, agreement.

*****abfliegen** ['apfliːgən] v fly away; (Flugzeug) take off.

*****abfließen** ['apfliːsən] v flow away, drain off.

Abflug ['apfluːk] m (Flugzeug) take-off.

Abfluß ['apfluːs] m outflow, draining off. **–rohr** neut waste-pipe.

Abfuhr ['apfuːr] m removal. **abführen** v lead away. **Abführmittel** n laxative.

Abgabe ['apgaːbə] f delivery, handing over; (Steuer) tax, duty. **Abgaben** pl (Verkauf) sales. **abgabenfrei** adj tax-free, duty-free.

Abgang ['apgaŋ] m (Zug, usw.) departure; (Abtreten) retirement; (Verlust) loss, depreciation.

Abgas ['apgaːs] neut exhaust gas.

*****abgeben** ['apgeːbən] v give up, hand over; (Stimme) cast.

abgedroschen ['apgədrɔʃən] adj commonplace, hackneyed.

abgegriffen ['apgəgrɪfən] adj (Münze) worn; (Buch) dog-eared, well-thumbed.

*****abgehen** ['apgeːən] v go away, depart; (Straße) branch off; (Knopf, usw.) come off.

abgemacht ['apgəmaxt] adj agreed.

Abgeordnete(r) ['apgəɔrdnətə(r)] delegate; (Parlament) Member of Parliament; (US) congressman. **Abgeordnetenhaus** neut parliament; (GB) House of Commons.

Abgrund ['apgrʊnt] m abyss.

abhalten ['aphaltən] v keep away; (hindern) hinder, stop; (Versammlung, usw.) hold.

Abhandlung ['aphandluŋ] f essay, written report.

Abhang ['aphaŋ] m slope.

abhauen ['aphauən] v cut off; (umg.) go away, (umg.) buzz off.

abhelfen ['aphɛlfən] v remedy, correct.

abholen ['aphoːlən] v call for, pick up.

abhören ['aphœːrən] v (Platte) listen to; (Gespräch) eavesdrop on; (Telef) monitor, listen in, tap; (Zeugen) question. **Abhörgerät** neut (electronic) listening device, bug.

Abitur [abi'tuːr] neut school-leaving exam, 'A'-levels.

abkanzeln ['apkantsəln] v scold, reprimand.

abkehren ['apkeːrən] v sweep up. **sich abkehren** turn away.

abknöpfen ['apknœpfən] v unbutton.

Abkommen ['apkɔmən] neut (pl –) agreement, settlement.

abkühlen ['apkyːlən] v cool, cool off.

Abkunft ['apkʊnft] f descent, lineage.

abkürzen ['apkyrtsən] v shorten; (Wort) abbreviate. **Abkürzung** f abbreviation; (Weg) short cut.

*****abladen** ['aplaːdən] v unload.

Ablauf ['aplauf] m (Abfluß) outlet, drain; (Verlauf) sequence of events; (Ende) expiry, end. **ablaufen** v drain, flow off; (Zeit) elapse; (Schuhe) wear out.

ablegen ['apleːgən] v put down; (Kleider) take off; (Gewohnheiten) give up.

ablehnen ['apleːnən] v reject, refuse; (Einladung) decline. **Ablehnung** f (pl **-en**) refusal.

ableiten ['aplaɪtən] v divert, lead away; (Flüssigkeit) draw off. **Ableitung** f diversion.

ablenken ['aplɛŋkən] v turn away, divert.

abliefern ['apliːfərn] v deliver. **Ablieferung** f delivery.

ablösen ['aplœːzən] v (Person) relieve, replace; (Schuld) settle; (loslösen) loosen, free. **Ablösung** f relief; loosening.

abmachen ['apmaxən] v detach; (Geschäft) arrange, agree about. **Abmachung** f (pl **-en**) arrangement, agreement.

abmelden ['apmɛldən] v **sich abmelden** v give notice (of one's departure).

*****abmessen** ['apmɛsən] v measure off; (Grundstück) survey; (Worte) weigh. **Abmessung** f measurement, dimension.

Abnahme ['apnaːmə] f (pl **-n**) reduction, decrease; (Entfernung) removal.

*****abnehmen** ['apneːmən] v take off, take away; (sich vermindern) decrease; (schlanker werden) lose weight, grow slim. **Abnehmer** m (pl –) customer, consumer.

Abneigung ['apnaigun] f dislike, aversion.

abnorm [ap'nɔrm] adj abnormal. **Abnormität** f (pl -en) abnormality.

abnutzen ['apnutsən] v wear out. **Abnutzung** f wear (and tear).

Abonnement [abɔn'mã] neut (pl -s) subscription. **Abonnent** m (pl -en) subscriber. **abonnieren** v subscribe.

Abort [a'bɔrt] m (pl -e) lavatory.

abquälen ['apkvɛilən] v sich abquälen take great pains.

abraten ['apraitən] v advise against, dissuade from.

abräumen ['aprɔymən] v clear away.

abrechnen ['aprɛçnən] v settle; (abziehen) deduct. **abrechnen mit** settle up with.

Abrede ['apreidə] f agreement. In Abrede stellen deny. **abreden** v agree.

abreiben ['apraibən] v rub off; (trocknen) rub down.

Abreise ['apraizə] f departure. **abreisen** v depart, leave.

*abreißen ['apraisən] v tear off; (Haus) demolish, tear down; (sich ablösen) break off.

Abrieb ['aprip] m abrasion, wear.

*abrufen ['apruːfən] v cancel, call off; (Person) recall.

abrüsten ['aprystən] v disarm. **Abrüstung** f disarmament.

Absage ['apza:gə] f (pl -n) refusal. **absagen** v cancel, call off; (Einladung) decline, refuse.

Absatz ['apzats] 1 m (Pause) stop, break; (Schuh) heel; paragraph. 2 m (unz.) (Waren) sales (pl), turnover.

abschaffen ['apʃafən] v abolish, do away with. **Abschaffung** f abolition.

abschalten ['apʃaltən] v switch off.

abschätzen ['apʃɛtsən] v estimate, appraise. **Abschätzung** f estimate, assessment.

Abscheu ['apʃɔy] m or f horror, revulsion. **abscheulich** adj horrible, revolting.

abschicken ['apʃikən] v send off or away.

Abschied ['apʃiːt] m (pl -e) departure, leaving. **Abschied nehmen von** say goodbye to, take one's leave of.

*abschießen ['apʃiːsən] v (Gewehr) fire; (Flugzeug) shoot down.

Abschlag ['apʃlaːk] m reduction, rebate. **abschlagen** v strike off; (ablehnen) refuse.

*abschließen ['apʃliːsən] v lock up; (Geschäft, Vertrag) conclude, settle; end, close.

Abschluß ['apʃlus] m conclusion; (Geschäft, Vertrag) settlement. **–prüfung** f final exam(s), finals.

abschnallen ['apʃnalən] v unbuckle.

*abschneiden ['apʃnaidən] v cut off.

Abschnitt ['apʃnit] m section, part; (Kontroll-) counterfoil.

abschrauben ['apʃraubən] v unscrew.

abschrecken ['apʃrɛkən] v scare off, deter. **–d** adj deterrent. **Abschreckung** f deterrence. **–smittel** neut deterrent.

*abschreiben ['apʃraibən] v copy out, write out; (Verlust, usw.) abschreiben; (plagiieren) plagiarize.

Abschrift ['apʃrift] f copy.

Abschuß ['apʃus] m (Gewehr) firing; (Flugzeug) shooting down.

*absehen ['apze:ən] v see, perceive; (voraussehen) foresee. **absehbar** adj within sight; (Zeit) foreseeable.

abseits ['apzaits] adv aside.

*absenden ['apzɛndən] v send (off). **Absender** m sender.

absetzen ['apzɛtsən] v set down; (verkaufen) sell; (entlassen) dismiss; (aussteigen lassen) drop off.

Absicht ['apziçt] f (pl -en) intention, purpose. **absicht∥lich** adj deliberate; adv on purpose, deliberately. **–slos** adj unintentional.

absolut [apzo'luːt] adj absolute.

absondern ['apzɔndərn] v isolate, cut off, separate; (Med, Bot) secrete. **Absonderung** f (pl -en) isolation.

absorbieren [apzɔr'biːrən] v absorb. **Absorption** f absorption.

absperren ['apʃpɛrən] v block off; (Gas, Strom) cut off; (Straße) block, cordon off.

abspielen ['apʃpiːlən] v (Schallplatte, usw.) play; (Musik) sight-read; (Ball) pass.

*abspringen ['apʃpriŋən] v jump down (from), jump off; (Flugzeug) bale out; (Splitter) chip or break off; (Farbe) flake off.

abspülen ['apʃpyːlən] v wash, wash up. **Abspülwasser** neut dishwater.

abstammen ['apʃtamən] v be descended from. **Abstammung** f descent, lineage.

Abstand ['apʃtant] m distance. **Abstand halten** keep one's distance.

abstatten ['apʃtatən] v (Besuch) pay; (Dank) give.

*absteigen ['apʃtaigən] v climb down, descend; (vom Pferd) dismount.

abstellen ['apʃtɛlən] v (Gerät, Licht) turn off; (niederlegen) put down; (Mot) park.

Abstieg ['apʃtiːk] m (pl -e) descent.

abstimmen ['apʃtimən] v vote, (Instrument, Radio) tune. sich abstimmen agree. aufeinander abstimmen collate, coordinate. Abstimmung f vote, poll.

Abstinenz [apsti'nɛnts] f abstinence; (Alkohol) teetotalism. -ler m (pl -) abstainer; teetotaller.

abstoßend ['apʃtoːsənt] adj repulsive, repellent.

abstrakt [ap'strakt] adj abstract.

Absturz ['apʃturts] m (pl Abstürze) fall; (Flugzeug) crash; (Abgrund) precipice. abstürzen v fall, plummet; (Flugzeug) crash.

absurd [ap'zurt] adj absurd.

Abszeß [aps'tsɛs] m (pl Abszesse) abcess.

Abt [apt] m (pl Äbte) abbot. Abtei f (pl -en) abbey.

Abteil [ap'tail] neut (pl -e) compartment. abteilen v separate, divide off. Abteilung f (auch Mil) division; (einer Firma) department. -sleiter m head of department.

Äbtissin [ɛp'tisin] f (pl -nen) abbess.

*abtreiben ['aptraibən] v drive away; (Med) abort. Abtreibung f (pl -en) (induced) abortion.

Abtritt ['aptrit] m departure; (Theater) exit.

abtrocknen ['aptrɔknən] v wipe dry; (Geschirr) wipe up, dry.

abtrünnig ['aptrynic] adj disloyal, rebellious.

*abtun ['aptuːn] put aside; (Kleider) take off; (erledigen) close, settle; (Tier) put down.

abwandeln ['apvandəln] v vary. Abwandlung f variation.

abwarten ['apvartən] v wait for, expect; wait and see.

abwärts ['apvɛrts] adv downwards, down.

abwaschen ['apvaʃən] v wash off; (Geschirr) wash up.

Abwasser ['apvasər] neut waste water, effluent.

abwechseln ['apvɛksəln] v take turns; (wechseln) change, vary. -d adj alternating. adv alternately, in turns. Abwechslung f change.

Abwehr ['apveːr] f defence; (Widerstand)

resistance. abwehren v ward off; (Feind) repel.

*abweichen ['apvaiçən] v deviate. -d adj discrepant, anomalous; (Meinung) dissenting.

*abweisen ['apvaisən] v turn away, refuse; (Bewerber) turn down. -d adj unfriendly, dismissive.

*abwenden ['apvɛndən] v turn away or aside; (Gefahr) avert, prevent.

*abwerfen ['apvɛrfən] v throw off; (Bomben) drop; (Zinsen) yield.

abwerten ['apvɛrtən] v devalue. Abwertung f devaluation.

abwesend ['apveːzənt] adj absent; (zerstreut) absent-minded. Abwesenheit f absence.

abzahlen ['aptsaːlən] v pay off.

abzählen ['aptsɛːlən] v count; (Geld) count out.

abzäunen ['aptsɔynən] v fence off.

Abzeichen ['aptsaiçən] neut badge; (Kennzeichen) mark.

*abziehen ['aptsiːən] v draw off, remove; (Math) subtract; (fortgehen) go away, withdraw.

Abzug ['aptsuːk] m departure; (Geld) deduction; (Foto) print; (Abdruck) copy.

abzweigen ['aptsvaigən] v branch off. Abzweigung f (pl -en) branch; (Mot) turning.

ach! [ax] interj oh! ah!

Achse ['aksə] f (pl -n) (Rad) axle; (Math, Pol) axis.

Achsel ['aksəl] f (pl -n) shoulder. -bein neut shoulder-blade. -höhle f armpit. -zucken neut (pl -) shrug (of the shoulders).

acht [axt] adj eight. (heute) vor acht Tagen a week ago (today).

Acht [axt] f (unz.) attention. außer acht lassen ignore, disregard. sich in acht nehmen be careful, take care. acht||en v esteem. -en auf pay attention to, heed. -geben v pay attention. -los adj careless. -sam adj attentive. Achtung f attention; (Wertschätzung) esteem; interj watch out! look out!

achtzig ['axtsiç] adj eighty.

ächzen ['ɛçtsən] v groan.

Acker ['akər] m (pl Äcker) field. -bau m agriculture, farming.

addieren [a'diːrən] v add (up). Addiermaschine f adding machine.

Adel ['aɪdəl] m nobility, aristocracy. **ad(e)lig** adj noble, aristocratic. **Ad(e)lige(r)** noble(man), aristocrat.

Ader ['aɪdər] f (pl -n) blood vessel; vein, artery.

Adjektiv ['atjɛktiːf] neut (pl -e) adjective.

Adler ['aɪdlər] m (pl -) eagle.

Admiral [atmi'raɪl] m (pl -e) admiral. –**ität** f admiralty.

adoptieren [adɔp'tiɪrən] v adopt. **Adoptiv**-adopted, adoptive.

Adrenalin [adrena'liɪn] neut adrenaline.

Adresse [a'drɛsə] f (pl -n) address. **Adreßbuch** neut address book, directory. **adressieren** v address.

Advokat [atvo'kaɪt] m (pl -en) lawyer.

Affäre [a'fɛɪrə] f (pl -n) affair; (Liebes-) (love) affair.

Affe ['afə] m (pl -n) ape, monkey.

affektiert [afɛk'tiɪrt] adj affected, conceited.

äffen ['ɛfən] v ape, imitate.

Afrika ['afrika] neut Africa. **Afrikaner** m African. **afrikanisch** adj African.

After ['aftər] m (pl -) anus.

Agent [a'gɛnt] m (pl -en) agent. –**ur** f (pl -en) agency.

Agnostiker [a'gnɔstikər] m (pl -) agnostic. **agnostisch** adj agnostic.

Ägypten [ɛ'gyptən] neut Egypt. **Ägypter** m (pl -) Egyptian. **ägyptisch** adj Egyptian.

Ahn [aɪn] m (pl -en) ancestor.

ähneln ['ɛɪnəln] v look like, resemble.

ahnen ['aɪnən] v suspect, guess.

ähnlich ['ɛɪnliç] adj like, similar (to). **Ähnlichkeit** f (pl -en) likeness, similarity.

Ahorn ['aɪhɔrn] m (pl -e) maple.

Ähre ['ɛɪrə] f (pl -n) ear (of corn).

Akademie [akade'miɪ] f (pl -n) academy; (Hochschule, Fachschule) college. –**iker** m (pl -) university graduate. **akademisch** adj academic.

Akkord [a'kɔrt] m (pl -e) agreement; (Musik) chord. –**arbeit** f piece-work.

Akrobat [akro'baɪt] m (pl -en) acrobat. **akrobatisch** adj acrobatic.

Akt [akt] m (pl -e) act, action, deed; document; (Kunst) nude.

Akte ['aktə] f (pl -n) file, dossier. **zu den Akten legen** file (away). **Akten∥schrank** m filing cabinet. –**tasche** f briefcase.

Aktie ['aktsiə] f (pl -n) share. **Aktien∥gesellschaft** f joint-stock company. –**makler** m stockbroker.

Aktionär [aktsio'nɛɪr] m (pl -e) shareholder.

aktiv [ak'tiɪf] adj active. –**ieren** v activate.

aktuell [aktu'ɛl] adj current, contemporary, up-to-date.

Akzent [ak'tsɛnt] m (pl -e) accent.

akzeptieren [aktsɛp'tiɪrən] v accept.

Alarm [a'larm] m (pl -e) alarm. **alarm∥bereit** adj standing by, on the alert. –**ieren** v alarm.

albern ['albərn] adj silly, foolish.

Album ['album] neut (pl Alben) album.

Alge ['algə] f (pl -n) seaweed.

Algebra ['algebra] f algebra.

Alimente [ali'mɛntə] pl alimony sing.

Alkohol [alko'hoɪl] m (pl -e) alcohol. **alkoholfrei** adj non-alcoholic. **Alkoholiker** m alcoholic. **alkoholisch** adj alcoholic.

all [al] pron, adj all. **All** neut universe. **alle** pl all; everybody sing. **alle beide** both. **wir alle** we all, all of us. **die Milch ist alle** the milk is all gone. **alle zwei Tage** every other day. **alles** everything. **alledem** pron **trotz alledem** nevertheless.

Allee [a'leɪ] f (pl -n) avenue.

Allegorie [alego'riɪ] f (pl -n) allegory. **allegorisch** adj allegorical.

allein [a'lain] adj, adv alone; (ohne Hilfer) (by) oneself. conj but. **alleinstehend** adj (Haus) detached; (Person) single.

allemal ['aləmaɪl] adv always. **ein für allemal** once and for all.

allenfalls ['alənfals] adv if need be; (höchstens) at most.

aller∥best ['alərbɛst] adj very best, best of all. –**dings** adv certainly, surely, indeed. –**erst** adj first of all, very first. –**höchst** adj supreme, highest of all. –**lei** adj (undeklinierbar) various, all kinds of. –**liebst** adj (most) delightful, dearest. –**wenigst** adj very least.

allezeit ['aletsait] adv always, at any time.

allgemein ['algəmain] adj common, general. **im allgemeinen** in general.

Alliierte(r) [ali'iɪrtə(r)] m ally.

alljährlich [al'jɛɪrliç] adj annual.

allmächtig [al'mɛçtiç] adj all-powerful, almighty.

allmählich [al'mɛɪliç] adj gradual.

allseitig ['alzaitiç] adj universal, comprehensive.

alltäglich ['altɛɪkliç] adj everyday. adv every day.

allzu ['altsuː] *adv* much too, all too.

Almanach ['almanax] *m* (*pl* -e) almanac.

Alpen ['alpən] *pl* Alps *pl*.

Alphabet [alfa'beːt] *neut* (*pl* -e) alphabet. **alphabetisch** *adj* alphabetical.

Alptraum ['alptraum] *m* nightmare.

als [als] *conj* as; (*da, zu der Zeit*) when; (*nach Komparativen*) than. **als ob** as if. **nichts als** nothing but. *als dein Freund möchte ich sagen ...* as your friend, I would like to say ... *als ich noch ein Kind war* when I was a child.

also ['alzo] *conj* so, therefore.

alt [alt] *adj* old.

Alt [alt] *m* (*unz.*) alto (voice).

Altar [al'taːr] *m* (*pl* Altäre) altar.

Alter ['altər] *neut* (*unz.*) age; (*hohes Alter*) old age. **Alters‖fürsorge** *f* care of the aged. **-heim** *neut* old people's home. **altersschwach** *adj* (*Person*) senile, feeble. **Altertum** *neut* (*unz.*) antiquity. **altertümlich** *adj* ancient, archaic.

Aluminium [alu'miːnium] *neut* aluminium.

am [am] *prep* + *art* an dem.

Amboß [am'bos] *m* (*pl* Ambosse) anvil.

Ameise ['aimaizə] *f* (*pl* -n) ant.

Amerika [a'meɪrika] *neut* America. **Amerikaner** *m* American. **amerikanisch** *adj* American.

Ampel ['ampəl] *f* (*pl* -n) (*Verkehrs-*) traffic light; (*Hängelampe*) hanging lamp.

Amt [amt] *neut* (*pl* Ämter) office; (*Stellung*) official position, post; (*Telef*) exchange. **das Auswärtige Amt** the Foreign Office. **das Amt antreteten** take office. **amtieren** *v* officiate. **amtlich** *adj* official. **Amts‖geheimnis** *neut* official secret. **-gericht** *neut* district court. **-zeichen** *neut* dial tone.

amüsant [amy'zant] *adj* amusing. **amüsieren** *v* amuse. **sich amüsieren** amuse *or* enjoy oneself.

an [an] *prep* at; (*nahe*) near; (*auf*) on. *adv* on. *an diesem Tag* on this day. *an diesem Ort* at this place. *der Ort, an dem* the place where. *an der Wand* on the wall. *an die Tür klopfen* knock at *or* on the door. *von heute an* from today. *von jetzt an* from now on. *sie hat nichts an* she has nothing on.

analog [ana'loːk] *adj* analogous. **Analogie** *f* analogy. **analogisch** *adj* analogous.

Analphabet [analfa'beːt] *m* (*pl* -en) illiterate.

Analyse [ana'lyːzə] *f* (*pl* -n) analysis. **analysieren** *v* analyse. **Analytiker** *m* analyst. **analytisch** *adj* analytical.

Ananas ['ananas] *f* (*pl* -se) pineapple.

Anarchie [anar'çiː] *f* (*pl* -n) anarchy. **Anarchist** *m* (*pl* -en) anarchist.

Anatomie [anato'miː] *f* (*pl* -n) anatomy. **anatomisch** *adj* anatomical.

Anbau ['anbau] **1** *m* (*unz.*) cultivation, tillage. **2** *m* extension, annexe.

*anbeißen ['anbaisən] *v* bite into; (*Fisch*) bite, take the bait.

anbelangen ['anbəlaŋən] *v* concern, relate to. *was mich anbelangt* as to me, as far as I am concerned.

anbeten ['anbeːtən] *v* worship, adore.

*anbieten ['anbiːtən] *v* offer.

Anblick ['anblik] *m* sight, view; (*Aussehen*) appearance. **anblicken** *v* look at, gaze at.

*anbrechen ['anbreçən] *v* (*Essen, Vorrat*) break into, begin; (*Tag*) dawn, break; (*Nacht*) fall.

*anbrennen ['anbrenən] *v* (*Speisen*) burn; (*Zigarette, Lampe*) light.

*anbringen ['anbriŋən] *v* bring, place; (*befestigen*) attach; (*Klage*) lodge, bring.

Anbruch ['anbrux] *m* (*unz.*) beginning. *bei Anbruch der Nacht* at nightfall.

Andacht ['andaxt] *f* (*pl* -en) devotion.

Andenken ['andɛŋkən] *neut* (*pl* -) memory, remembrance; (*Erinnerungstück*) souvenir.

ander ['andər] *adj*, *pron* other, different. **ein andermal** *adv* another time.

ändern ['ɛndərn] *v* alter, change. **Änderung** *f* (*pl* -en) alteration, change. **ander‖thalb** ['andərthalp] *adj* one-and-a-half. **-nfalls** *adv* otherwise, else. **-s** *adv* differently. **-seits** *adv* on the other hand. **-swo** *adv* elsewhere.

andeuten ['andɔytən] *v* indicate, point to; (*anspielen*) imply, suggest, allude to. **Andeutung** *f* indication; suggestion, allusion.

andrehen ['andreːən] *v* turn on, switch on; (*Mot*) start up; (*umg.*) wangle, fix up.

andrer ['andrər] *pron* anderer. *V* ander.

aneignen ['anaignən] *v* **sich aneignen** appropriate; (*Kenntnisse*) acquire. **Aneignung** *f* (*pl* -en) appropriation; acquisition.

aneinander [anain'andər] *adv* to or against one another, together. **–liegend** *adj* neighbouring, adjacent. **–schließen** *v* join together.

***anerkennen** ['anɛrkɛnən] *v* recognize, acknowledge. **Anerkennung** *f* recognition, approval.

***anfahren** ['anfaːrən] *v* begin (to move); (*bringen*) convey, carry; (*ankommen*) arrive; (*zusammenstoßen*) drive into. **Anfahrt** *f* arrival; (*Zufahrtsstraße*) drive.

Anfall ['anfal] *m* attack.

Anfang ['anfaŋ] *m* beginning, start. **anfangen** *v* begin, start. **Anfänger** *m* (*pl* -) beginner. **anfangs** *adv* at first, initially. **Anfangsbuchstabe** *m* (*pl* -n) initial letter.

anfassen ['anfasən] *v* touch; (*ergreifen*) hold, grasp; (*Aufgabe*) set or go about.

anfecht||en ['anfɛçtən] *v* contest, dispute; (*beunruhigen*) trouble; (*Versuchung*) tempt. **–bar** *adj* questionable, contestable.

Anforderung ['anfɔrdərʊŋ] *f* demand, claim; (*Bedürfnis*) requirement.

Anfrage ['anfraːgə] *f* inquiry.

anfühlen ['anfyːlən] *v* touch, feel. **sich anfühlen** feel (to the touch).

anführen ['anfyːrən] *v* lead, command; (*Worte*) quote, state; (*täuschen*) trick, deceive. **Anführungszeichen** *pl* quotation marks.

anfüllen ['anfʏlən] *v* fill (up).

Angabe ['angaːbə] *f* declaration, statement. **–n** *pl* specifications, data. **nähere Angaben** details, particulars.

***angeben** ['angeːbən] *v* state, declare; (*anzeigen*) inform against; (*vorgeben*) pretend; (*prahlen*) brag, boast, show off. **Angeber** *m* (*pl* -) informer; (*Prahler*) show off, boaster. **angeblich** *adj* supposed, alleged.

angeboren ['angəboːrən] *adj* innate, inherent.

Angebot ['angəbɔt] *neut* (*pl* -e) offer. **Angebot und Nachfrage** supply and demand.

***angehen** ['angeːən] *v* begin; (*angreifen*) attack; (*betreffen*) concern. *das geht mich nichts an* that is none of my business.

angehören ['angəhœːrən] *v* belong (to). **Angehörige(r)** member.

Angeklagte(r) ['angəklaːktə(r)] (*Jur*) (the) accused, defendant.

Angelegenheit ['angəleːgənhait] *f* matter, concern, business.

angeln ['anəln] *v* fish, angle. **Angeln** *neut* angling, fishing. **Angelrute** *f* fishing rod.

Angelsachse ['anəlzaksə] *m* Anglo-Saxon. **angelsächsisch** *adj* Anglo-Saxon.

angemessen ['angəmɛsən] *adj* proper, suitable.

angenehm ['angəneːm] *adj* pleasant, agreeable.

angenommen ['angənɔmən] *adj* supposing, assuming.

angesehen ['angəzeːən] *adj* respected.

Angesicht ['angəziçt] *neut* face, countenance. **angesichts** *prep* considering, in view of.

Angestellte(r) ['angəʃtɛltə(r)] employee, office worker.

angewandt ['angəvant] *adj* applied, practical.

angewöhnen ['angəvœːnən] *v* accustom. **sich angewöhnen** get used to, make a habit of. **Angewohnheit** *f* habit, custom.

Angler ['aŋlər] *m* (*pl* -) angler, fisherman.

***angreifen** ['angraifən] *v* (*anfassen*) take hold of; (*feindlich*) attack; (*unternehmen*) set about. **Angreifer** *m* (*pl* -) aggressor, attacker.

angrenzen ['angrɛntsən] *v* border on, adjoin.

Angriff ['angrif] *m* attack. **angriffslustig** *adj* aggressive.

Angst [aŋst] *f* (*pl* Ängste) fear, anxiety. **Angst haben vor** be afraid of.

ängst||igen ['ɛŋstigən] *v* frighten. **–lich** *adj* fearful, timid; (*peinlich*) scrupulous, (over-)careful.

***anhaben** ['anhaːbən] *v* wear, have on.

Anhalt ['anhalt] *m* support, prop; (*fig*) clue. **anhalten** *v* stop; (*andauern*) continue, last. **Anhalter** *m* hitchhiker. **per Anhalter fahren** hitchhike.

Anhang ['anhaŋ] *m* appendix, supplement. **anhängen** *v* hang on, attach; (*hinzufügen*) add. **Anhänger** *m* follower; (*Fußball*) supporter; (*Mot*) trailer. **Anhängeschloß** *neut* padlock. **anhänglich** *adj* affectionate.

Anhöhe ['anhœːə] *f* (low) hill.

anhören ['anhøːrən] *v* listen (to).

Ankauf ['ankauf] *m* purchase. **ankaufen** *v* purchase, buy.

Anker ['aŋkər] *m* (*pl* -) anchor. **den Anker lichten/werfen** weigh/cast anchor. **ankern** *v* anchor.

Anklage ['anklaɪgə] f accusation, charge. **–bank** f dock. **anklagen** v accuse. **Ankläger** m plaintiff.

Anklang ['anklaŋ] m approval, recognition; (*Spur*) touch, echo.

anknüpfen ['anknʏpfən] v fasten (on), tie (on); (*fig*) take up, establish.

*ankommen ['ankɔmən] v arrive; (*abhängen*) depend (on). *es kommt darauf an* it depends.

ankündigen ['ankʏndigən] v announce, publicize. **Ankündigung** f announcement.

Ankunft ['ankunft] f (*pl Ankünfte*) arrival.

Anlage ['anlaɪgə] f installation; (*Entwurf*) plan, layout; park, gardens *pl*; (*Brief*) enclosure; (*Begabung*) talent; (*Neigung*) tendency, susceptibility; (*Komm*) investment; (*Fabrik*) plant, works.

anlangen ['anlaŋən] v (*ankommen*) arrive; (*betreffen*) concern.

Anlaß ['anlas] m (*pl Anlässe*) occasion, cause. **Anlaß geben** cause, give rise to.

anlassen v leave on; (*Mot*) start. **anläßlich** prep on the occasion of. **Anlasser** m (*pl -*) (*Mot*) starter-motor.

Anlauf ['anlauf] m start; (*kurzer Lauf*) run, dash. **anlaufen** v run at, rush at; (*Hafen*) put into; (*wachsen*) rise, increase.

anlegen ['anleɪgən] v put on or against; (*Gewehr*) aim at; (*gründen*) found; (*Geld*) invest; (*Schiff*) lie alongside.

Anleihe ['anlaɪə] f (*pl -n*) loan.

Anleitung ['anlaɪtuŋ] f instruction.

*anliegen ['anliːgən] v (*Schiff*) lie beside; (*Kleidung*) fit well. **Anliegen** neut (*pl -*) request. **anliegend** adj adjoining.

anlocken ['anlɔkən] v entice, attract.

anmachen ['anmaxən] v attach; (*Speisen*) prepare; (*Feuer*) kindle; (*Licht*) turn on.

Anmarsch ['anmarʃ] m advance, approach. **anmarschieren** v advance on, march on.

anmaßen ['anmaɪsən] v **sich anmaßen, zu** presume to, take it upon oneself to. **Anmaßung** f presumptuousness.

anmelden ['anmɛldən] v announce, report. **sich anmelden** v report; (*polizeilich*) register (with the police). **Anmeldung** f announcement; (*polizeilich*) registration.

anmerken ['anmɛrkən] v note, observe. **Anmerkung** f note, observation.

Anmut ['anmuːt] f grace, charm, elegance. **anmutig** adj graceful.

annähern ['annɛɪərn] v bring closer; (*ähnlich machen*) make similar. **sich annähern** approach. **annähernd** adj approaching. adv almost, close to.

Annahme ['annaɪmə] f (*pl -n*) acceptance; (*Vermutung*) assumption.

*annehm||en ['annɛɪmən] v accept, take; (*vermuten*) assume, suppose. **–bar** adj acceptable.

anonym [ano'nyːm] adj anonymous. **Anonymität** f anonymity.

anordnen ['anɔrdnən] v put in order, arrange; (*befehlen*) direct, command. **Anordnung** f arrangement; (*Befehl*) order, instruction.

anpacken ['anpakən] v grasp, seize.

anpassen ['anpasən] v fit, adapt. **sich anpassen** v adapt, adjust. **Anpassung** f adaptation, adjustment. **anpassungsfähig** adj adaptable. **Anpassungsfähigkeit** f adaptability.

anrechnen ['anrɛçnən] v charge; (*hochschätzen*) value, esteem highly.

Anrede ['anreɪdə] f speech, address. **anreden** v address, speak to.

anregen ['anreɪgən] v stimulate, incite; (*geistig*) excite, inspire. **–d** adj exciting. **Anregung** f excitement.

anrichten ['anrɪçtən] v (*Schaden*) cause, do; (*Essen*) prepare.

Anruf ['anruf] m call, shout; (*Telef*) call. **anrufen** v call, hail; (*Telef*) ring up, call. **anrühren** ['anryːrən] v touch, handle; (*Küche*) stir.

ans [ans] prep + art **an das**.

Ansage ['anzaɪgə] f announcement; (*Kartenspiel*) bidding. **ansagen** v announce, declare; bid. **Ansager** m (*pl -*) announcer.

ansammeln ['anzaməln] v collect. **sich ansammeln** gather. **Ansammlung** f collection, accumulation; (*Menge*) crowd, gathering.

Ansatz ['anzats] m (*Anfang*) start, beginning; (*Zusatzstück*) (added) piece, fitting. **–punkt** m starting point.

anschaffen ['anʃafən] v procure, obtain.

anschalten ['anʃaltən] v switch, turn on.

anschau||en ['anʃauən] v look at, view. **–lich** adj obvious, evident.

Anschein ['anʃain] m (*unz.*) (outer) appearance. **allem Anschein nach** to all appearances.

Anschlag ['anʃla:k] m (Med) stroke, attack; (Plakat) poster; (Kosten-) estimate; (Angriff) (criminal) attack, outrage.

*****anschließen** ['anʃli:tsən] v connect; (anketten) chain up. **–d** adj subsequent.

Anschluß ['anʃlus] m connection; (pol) annexation.

anschnallen ['anʃnalən] v fasten, buckle.

Anschove [an'ʃo:və] f (pl -n), **Anschovis** f (pl -) anchovy.

Anschrift ['anʃrift] f address.

anschuldigen ['anʃuldigən] v accuse (of), charge (with).

*****ansehen** ['anze:ən] v look at, consider. **Ansehen** neut appearance; (Hochachtung) respect, esteem. **ansehnlich** adj notable.

ansetzen ['anzɛtsən] v put on, attach; (Gewicht) put on; (anfangen) begin; (versuchen) try.

Ansicht ['anziçt] f view, sight; (Meinung) opinion.

Anspiel ['anʃpi:l] neut (Tennis) service; (Fußball) kick-off. **anspielen** v play first; (Tennis) serve; (Fußball) kick off. **anspielen auf** hint at, allude to. **Anspielung** f (pl -en) allusion.

ansprechen ['anʃprɛçən] v speak to, address; (auf der Straße, usw.) accost.

Anspruch ['anʃprux] m claim. **Anspruch haben auf** have a right to. **in Anspruch nehmen** lay claim to, claim; (Zeit) take up. **Ansprüche stellen** make demands. **anspruchsvoll** adj demanding.

Anstalt ['anʃtalt] f (pl -en) (Heim) institution; (Schule) institute; (Vorbereitung) arrangement.

Anstand ['anʃtant] m (unz.) decency. **anständig** adj decent, proper. **Anstandsdame** f chaperone.

anstatt ['anʃtat] prep instead of. **anstatt daß** rather than.

anstecken ['anʃtɛkən] v pin on (to); (Ring) put on; (Med) infect; (Feuer) light. **–d** adj infectious. **Ansteckung** f infection.

anstellen ['anʃtɛlən] v carry out, do; (Person) appoint, employ; (Mot) start; (Radio) switch on. **Anstellung** f appointment.

anstiften ['anʃtiftən] v cause, instigate.

Anstoß ['anʃto:s] m impulse; (Sport) kick-off. **Anstoß geben/nehmen** give/take offence (US offense). **anstoßen** v knock against; (Haus, usw.) adjoin.

anstrengen ['anʃtrɛŋən] v strain, exert; (Prozeß) bring in. **sich anstrengen** strain or exert oneself; make an effort.

Antarktika [an'tarktika] f Antarctica. **Antarktis** f Antarctic. **antarktisch** adj antarctic.

antasten ['antastən] v touch, handle; (Thema) touch on; (Recht, usw.) injure.

Anteil ['antail] m share, portion; (Mitgefühl) sympathy. **–nahme** f sympathy.

Antenne [an'tɛnə] f (pl -n) aerial.

Antibiotikum [antibi'o:tikum] neut (pl -biotika) antibiotic.

antik [an'ti:k] adj ancient, classical.

Antikörper ['antikœrpər] m antibody.

Antiquität [antikvi'tɛ:t] f (pl -en) antique. **–enhändler** m antique dealer.

antisemitisch [antize'mi:tiʃ] adj antisemitic.

Antiseptikum [anti'sɛptikum] m (pl -septika) antiseptic. **antiseptisch** adj antiseptic.

Antrag ['antra:k] m (pl Anträge) offer, proposal; (Pol) motion. **einen Antrag stellen** propose a motion. **Antragsteller** m applicant; (Pol) mover of (a motion).

*****antreffen** ['antrɛfən] v encounter.

*****antreiben** ['antraibən] v drive, propel; (Person) urge; (ans Ufer) drift ashore.

*****antreten** ['antre:tən] v (Amt) enter, take over; (Reise) set out on.

Antrieb ['antri:p] m drive, impulse; (Tech) drive. **aus eigenem Antrieb** of one's own free will.

Antritt ['antrit] m beginning; (Amt) entrance.

*****antun** ['antu:n] v (Kleidung) put on; (Verletzung) do, inflict.

Antwort ['antvort] f (pl -en) answer, reply. **antworten** v answer, reply (to).

anvertrauen ['anfɛrtrauən] v entrust.

Anwalt ['anvalt] m (pl Anwälte) (defending) lawyer, solicitor.

anwärmen ['anvɛrmən] v warm (up).

*****anweisen** ['anvaisən] v (zuweisen) assign; (anleiten) direct, show; (Geld) transfer. **Anweisung** f instruction, order; (Geld) remittance, transfer.

*****anwend||en** ['anvendən] v employ, use; (Gewalt, Methode, Wissenschaft, usw.) apply. **–bar** adj applicable. **Anwendung** f. application.

anwesend 214

anwesend ['anveɪzənt] *adj* present. **Anwesenheit** *f* presence.

Anzahl ['antsaːl] *f* number. **Anzahlung** *f* deposit, down payment.

Anzeichen ['antsaɪçən] *neut* mark, sign.

Anzeige ['antsaɪgə] *f* (*pl* -n) announcement; (*Inserat*) advertisement; (*bei der Polizei*) report. **-blatt** *neut* advertiser, advertising journal. **anzeigen** *v* announce; (*person*) inform against, report (to the police). **-pflichtig** *adj* notifiable.

***anziehen** ['antsiːən] *v* (*Kleider*) put on; (*Schraube*) tighten; (*Person*) dress; (*heranlocken*) attract. **sich anziehen** get dressed. **anziehend** *adj* attractive. **Anziehung** *f* attraction. **-skraft** *f* power of attraction; (*Person*) attractiveness.

Anzug ['antsuːk] **1** *m* (*unz.*) approach. **2** *m* suit.

anzünden [antsyndən] *v* light, ignite.

Apfel ['apfəl] *m* (*pl* Äpfel) apple. **-baum** *m* apple tree. **-garten** *m* apple orchard. **-kuchen** *m* apple cake. **-mus** *neut* apple sauce. **-saft** *m* apple juice. **-sine** *f* orange. **-wein** *m* cider.

Apostel ['apostəl] *m* (*pl* -) apostle. **-geschichte** *f* Acts of the Apostles.

Apostroph [apo'stroːf] *m* (*pl* -e) apostrophe.

Apotheke [apo'teːkə] *f* (*pl* -n) chemist's (shop), pharmacy. **-r** *m* (*pl* -) chemist, pharmacist. **-rkunst** *f* pharmacy, pharmaceutics.

Apparat [apa'raːt] *m* (*pl* -e) apparatus; (*Vorrichtung*) appliance, device; (*Foto*) camera; (*Telef*) telephone, handset. **am Apparat!** speaking! **am Apparat bleiben** hold the line.

appellieren [apɛ'liːrən] *v* appeal.

Appetit [ape'tiːt] *m* (*pl* -n) appetite.

Aprikose [apri'koːzə] *f* (*pl* -n) apricot.

April [a'prɪl] *m* (*pl* -e) April. **der erste April** April Fools' Day.

Aquarell [akva'rɛl] *neut* (*pl* -e) water-colour.

Aquarium [a'kvaːrium] *neut* (*pl* Aquarien) aquarium.

Äquator [ɛ'kvaːtor] *m* equator. **äquatorial** *adj* equatorial.

Arab||er [a'raːbər] *m* (*pl* -) Arab. **-ien** *neut* Arabia. **arabisch** *adj* Arab, Arabian.

Arbeit ['arbaɪt] *f* (*pl* -en) work; (*Beschäftigung*) job. **arbeiten** *v* work. **Arbeiter** *m* worker, workman. **-klasse** *f* working class. **Arbeitgeber** *m* employer. **Arbeits||amt** *neut* employment office. **-erlaubnis** *f* work permit. **arbeits||fähig** *adj* able to work. **-los** *adj* unemployed. **-losenunterstützung** *f* unemployment benefit. **-losigkeit** *f* unemployment.

Archäolog||ie [arçeolo'giː] *f* archaeology. **-e** *m* archaeologist. **archäologisch** *adj* archaeological.

Architekt [arçi'tɛkt] *m* (*pl* -en) architect. **-ur** *f* (*pl* -en) architecture.

Archiv [ar'çiːf] *neut* (*pl* -e) archives *pl*, records *pl*.

arg [ark] *adj* bad, evil; (*ernst*) serious.

Ärger ['ɛrgər] *m* (*unz.*) (*Verdruß*) annoyance, irritation; (*Zorn*) anger. **ärgerlich** *adj* (*Person*) angry, annoyed; (*Sache*) annoying. **ärgern** *v* annoy, irritate. **sich ärgern über** be angry about.

Argument [argu'mɛnt] *neut* (*pl* -e) argument, reasoning.

Argwohn ['arkvoːn] *m* (*unz.*) distrust, suspicion. **argwöhnisch** *adj* suspicious, mistrustful.

Aristokrat [aristo'kraːt] *m* (*pl* -en) aristocrat. **-ie** *f* aristocracy. **aristokratisch** *adj* aristocratic.

Arithmetik [arit'meːtik] *f* arithmetic. **arithmetisch** *adj* arithmetical.

Arktis ['arktis] *f* Arctic. **arktisch** *adj* arctic.

arm [arm] *adj* poor. **-arm** *adj* poor in . . . **nikotinarm** *adj* low-nicotine.

Arm [arm] *m* (*pl* -e) arm; (*Fluß*) branch, tributary.

Armaturenbrett [arma'tuːrənbrɛt] *neut* dashboard, instrument panel.

Armband ['armbant] *neut* bracelet. **-uhr** *f* (wrist)watch.

Armee [ar'meː] *f* (*pl* -n) army.

Ärmel ['ɛrməl] *m* (*pl* -) sleeve. **-kanal** *m* English Channel.

ärmlich ['ɛrmliç] *adj* poor, miserable.

armselig ['armzɛliç] *adj* wretched, miserable.

Arm||sessel *m* armchair. **-stuhl** *m* armchair.

Armut ['armuːt] *f* poverty.

Arrest [a'rɛst] *m* (*pl* -e) arrest, detention.

Arsch [arʃ] *m* (*pl* Ärsche) (*vulgär*) arse.

Art [art] *f* (*pl* -en) type, kind, sort; (*Weise*) way, method; (*Biol*) species; (*Brauch*) habit.

artig ['artiç] *adj* (*Kind*) good, well-behaved.

-artig [-artiç] *adj* – like.

Artikel [ar'tiːkəl] *m* (*pl* -) article.

Artillerie [artilə'riː] *f* (*pl* -n) artillery.

Artischocke [arti'ʃɔkə] *f* (*pl* -n) artichoke.

Artist [ar'tist] *m* (*pl* -en) artiste.

Arznei [arts'nai] *f* (*pl* -en) medicine, medicament, drug. **–mittel** *neut* medicine.

Arzt [artst] *m* (*pl* Ärzte) doctor, physician.

Ärztin ['ɛrtstin] *f* (*pl* -nen) (woman) doctor. **ärztlich** *adj* medical.

As [as] *neut* (*pl* -se) ace.

Asbest [as'bɛst] *m* asbestos.

Asche ['aʃə] *f* (*pl* -n) ash. **–nbecher** *m* ashtray.

Aspekt [as'pɛkt] *m* (*pl* -e) aspect.

Asphalt [as'falt] *m* asphalt, tarmac.

Assistent [asis'tɛnt] *m* (*pl* -en) assistant.

Ast [ast] *m* (*pl* Äste) bough, branch.

ästhetisch [ɛs'teːtiʃ] *adj* aesthetic.

Astronaut [astro'naut] *m* (*pl* -en) astronaut. **–ik** *f* astronautics. **astronautisch** *adj* astronautical.

Astronom [astro'noːm] *m* (*pl* -en) astronomer. **–ie** *f* astronomy. **astronomisch** *adj* astronomical.

Asyl [a'zyːl] *neut* (*pl* -e) asylum.

Atelier [atə'ljeː] *neut* (*pl* -s) studio.

Atem ['aːtəm] *m* (*pl* -) breath. **Atem holen** take breath.

Atheis∥mus [ate'ismus] *m* atheism. **–t** *m* (*pl* -en) atheist.

Äther ['ɛːtər] *m* ether. **ätherisch** *adj* ethereal.

Athlet [at'leːt] *m* (*pl* -en) athlete. **–ik** *f* athletics. **athletisch** *adj* athletic.

Atlantik [at'lantik] *m* Atlantic (Ocean).

Atlas¹ ['atlas] *m* (*pl* Atlanten) (*Buch*) atlas.

Atlas² *m* (*pl* -se) (*Stoff*) satin.

atmen ['aːtmən] *v* breathe.

Atmosphäre [atmos'fɛːrə] *f* (*pl* -n) atmosphere.

Atmung ['aːtmuŋ] *f* respiration, breathing. **–sapparat** *m* respirator.

Atom [a'toːm] *neut* (*pl* -e) atom. **–abfall** *m* atomic waste. **–antrieb** *m* nuclear propulsion. **–bombe** *f* atom bomb. **–kraft** *f* nuclear power. **–kraftwerk** *f* nuclear power station.

Attentat [atɛn'taːt] *neut* (*pl* -e) assassination (attempt). **Attentäter** *m* assassin, assailant.

ätzen ['ɛtsən] *v* corrode; (*Med*) cauterize; (*Kupferstich*) etch. **–d** *adj* corrosive, caustic.

Aubergine [ober'ʒiːnə] *f* (*pl* -n) aubergine.

auch [aux] *conj* also, too; (*sogar*) even; (*tatsächlich*) indeed, but. **nicht nur ... sondern auch ...** not only ... but also **... sowohl ... als auch ...** both ... and ... . **auch wenn** even if, (even) though. *ich auch!* me too! *ich auch nicht* nor me, me neither. *was er auch sagen mag* whatever he may say. *wer auch immer* whoever.

Audienz [audi'ɛnts] *f* (*pl* -en) audience, interview.

auf [auf] *prep* on. *adv* up; (*offenstehend*) open, **auf und ab** up and down. *auf den Tisch stellen* put on the table. *auf dem Tisch finden* find on the table. *auf die Schule gehen* go to school. *auf der Schule sein* be at school. *auf deutsch* in German. **auf einmal** at once.

Aufbau ['aufbau] *m* (*unz.*) building, construction; structure.

aufbessern ['aufbɛsərn] *v* improve; (*Gehalt*) increase. **Aufbesserung** *f* improvement; (*Gehalt*) increase, rise.

aufbewahren ['aufbəvaːrən] *v* store (up), keep. **Aufbewahrung** *f* storage, safe-keeping.

*aufblasen ['aufblaːzən] *v* blow up, inflate.

aufblicken ['aufblikən] *v* look up.

aufbrauchen ['aufbrauxən] *v* use up.

*aufbrechen ['aufbrɛçən] *v* break open; (*Knospen, Wunden*) open; (*abreisen*) set off.

*aufbringen ['aufbriŋən] *v* bring up, raise; (*ärgern*) imitate, provoke.

Aufbruch ['aufbrux] *m* departure, start.

aufdecken ['aufdɛkən] *v* uncover, reveal; (*Tisch*) spread. **Aufdeckung** *f* revealing, unveiling.

aufdrehen ['aufdreːən] *v* switch *or* turn on; (*Schraube*) unscrew.

aufdringlich ['aufdriŋliç] *adj* intrusive, importunate.

aufeinander [aufain'andər] *adv* (one) after another; (*gegeneinander*) one against the other. **–folgen** *v* follow (one after another). **–folgend** *adj* successive. **–stoßen** *v* (*Mot*) collide; (*Meinungen*) clash. **–treffen** *v* meet.

Aufenthalt ['aufənthalt] *m* (*pl* -e) (*kurze Wartezeit*) delay, stop; (*längerer Besuch usw.*) stay. **–serlaubnis** *f* residence permit.

auferlegen ['auferleigən] *v* impose.

*****auferstehen** ['aufɛrʃteiən] *v* rise from the dead. **Auferstehung** *f* resurrection.

*****auffahren** ['auffairən] *v* rise, go up; (*herauffahren*) draw up; (*aufspringen*) start, jump; (*zornig werden*) flare up; (*wagen*) collide. **Auffahrt** *f* (*in den Himmel*) Ascension; (*Zufahrtsweg*) drive.

*****auffallen** ['auffalən] *v* strike, come to one's attention. *es fiel mir ein* it struck me, I realized. **auffallend** *or* **auffällig** *adj* striking, remarkable.

auffassen ['auffasən] *v* pick up; (*begreifen*) understand; (*deuten*) interpret. **Auffassung** *f* comprehension; (*Auslegung*) interpretation; (*Meinung*) opinion.

*****auffliegen** ['auffliigən] *v* fly up; (*Flugzeug*) take off; (*Tür*) fly open; (*explodieren*) explode.

auffordern ['auffordərn] *v* challenge; (*einladen*) ask, invite. **Aufforderung** *f* challenge; (*Recht*) summons; (*Einladung*) invitation, request.

*****auffressen** ['auffrɛsən] *v* devour.

auffrischen ['auffriʃən] *v* freshen up; (*Kenntnisse*) refresh.

aufführen ['auffyːrən] *v* (*Theater*) put on, perform; (*Film*) show; (*Konzert*) give; (*zitieren*) cite; (*aufbauen*) erect. **Aufführung** *f* performance; (*Film*) showing; (*Benehmen*) behaviour.

Aufgabe ['aufgaibə] *f* task, duty; (*Übergabe*) handing in.

Aufgang ['aufgaŋ] *m* rise, ascent.

*****aufgeben** [aufgeibən] *v* give up; (*Gepäck*) check in.

aufgeblasen ['aufgəblaizən] *adj* arrogant, conceited.

aufgeklärt ['aufgəklɛirt] *adj* enlightened.

aufgelegt ['aufgəleikt] *adj* inclined, in the mood. **gut/schlecht aufgelegt** in a good/bad mood.

aufgeregt ['aufgərɛikt] *adj* excited.

aufgeschlossen ['aufgəʃlɔsən] *adj* enlightened, open-minded.

*****aufhalten** ['aufhaltən] *adj* keep open; (*anhalten*) stop; (*hinhalten*) delay. **sich aufhalten** stay.

*****aufhängen** ['aufhɛŋən] *v* hang up.

*****aufheben** ['aufheibən] *v* lift, raise; (*aufbewahren*) store, keep; (*abschaffen*) abolish, cancel. **Aufhebung** *f* raising, abolition.

aufheitern ['aufhaitərn] *v* cheer up. **sich aufheitern** (*Wetter*) brighten up.

aufhören ['aufhœirən] *v* stop, cease.

aufklären ['aufklɛirən] *v* (*Person*) enlighten; (*Sache*) clarify, explain. **Aufklärung** *f* clarification; (the) Enlightenment.

aufkleben ['aufkleibən] *v* stick on, paste on.

aufknöpfen ['aufknœpfən] *v* unbutton.

*****aufkommen** ['aufkɔmən] *v* arise. **aufkommen für** take responsibility for.

aufladen ['auflaidən] *v* load.

Auflage ['auflaigə] *f* (*Buch*) edition; (*Zeitung*) circulation.

*****auflassen** ['auflasən] *v* leave open.

Auflauf ['auflauf] *m* riot; (*Speise*) trifle, soufflé. **auflaufen** *v* run up; (*Schiff*) run aground; (*Geld*) increase.

auflegen ['aufleigən] *v* put on; (*Buch*) print, publish; (*Telef*) hang up.

auflösbar ['auflœizbair] *adj* soluble. **auflösen** *v* (*Knoten*) loosen; (*in Wasser, usw.*) dissolve; (*Rätsel*) solve; (*Vertrag*) cancel; (*Geschäft*) close down; (*Ehe*) break up. **Auflösung** *f* loosening; solution; cancellation; closure; break-up.

*****aufmachen** ['aufmaxən] *v* open; (*Knoten, Knöpfe*) undo. **sich aufmachen** set off. **Aufmachung** *f* outward appearance.

aufmerksam ['aufmɛrkzaːm] *adj* attentive. **jemanden auf etwas aufmerksam machen** draw something to someone's attention. **Aufmerksamkeit** *f* attentiveness, attention.

aufmuntern ['aufmuntərn] *v* encourage, cheer up.

Aufnahme ['aufnaimə] *f* (*pl* -n) taking up; (*Foto*) shot, picture; (*Tonband, usw.*) recording; (*Zulassung*) admission; (*Empfang*) reception. **aufnahmefähig** *adj* receptive. **Aufnahmeprüfung** *f* entrance exam.

*****aufnehmen** ['aufneimən] *v* take up; (*zulassen*) admit; (*empfangen*) receive; (*Radio*) pick up; (*Foto*) photograph; (*Protokoll, Tonband*) record.

aufopfern ['aufopfərn] *v* sacrifice.

aufpassen ['aufpasən] *v* pay attention; (*vorsichtig sein*) take care. **aufpassen auf** take care of, look after.

Aufprall ['aufpral] *m* (*pl* -e) impact, collision. **aufprallen** *v* strike, collide.

aufputzen ['aufputsən] *v* dress up, adorn; (*reinigen*) clean up.

aufräumen ['aufrɔymən] *v* tidy up, clean up; (*wegschaffen*) clear away. **Aufräumung** *f* cleaning up.

aufrecht ['aufrɛçt] *adj* upright, erect; (*fig*) upright, honest. **-erhalten** *v* maintain, keep up.

aufregen ['aufreːgən] *v* excite, upset. **sich aufregen** get excited *or* upset. **Aufregung** *f* excitement, agitation.

aufrichten ['aufrɪçtən] *v* erect, set up; (*trösten*) console.

aufrichtig ['aufrɪçtɪç] sincere, honest. **Aufrichtigkeit** *f* sincerity, honesty.

aufrücken ['aufrykən] *v* move up; (*Dienstgrad*) be promoted.

Aufruf ['aufruːf] *m* call, appeal. **aufrufen** *v* call out.

Aufruhr ['aufruːr] *m* (*pl* -e) tumult; (*Erhebung*) revolt. **aufrühren** *v* stir up; (*Erhebung*) incite to revolt. **Aufrührer** *m* (*pl* -) agitator, rebel. **aufrührerisch** *adj* rebellious, riotous.

aufrüsten ['aufrystən] *v* (re)arm. **Aufrüstung** *f* (re)armament.

aufs [aufs] *prep* + *art* auf das.

aufsagen ['aufzaːgən] *v* recite, repeat.

Aufsatz ['aufzats] *m* essay; (*Tech*) top (piece); (*Tafel-*) centre-piece.

*****aufsaugen** ['aufzaugən] *v* suck up. **-d** *adj* absorbent.

*****aufschieben** ['auffʃiːbən] *v* push open; (*fig*) put off, delay. **Aufschiebung** *f* postponement, delay.

Aufschlag ['auffʃlaːk] *m* surcharge, extra charge; (*Hose*) turn-up; (*Jacke*) lapel; (*Auftreffen*) impact; (*Tennis*) service. **aufschlagen** *v* (*Preis*) raise; (*Stoff*) turn up; (*auftreffen*) hit; (*Buch*) open, consult; (*Tennis*) serve.

*****aufschließen** ['auffʃliːsən] *v* open up, unlock; (*erklären*) explain.

Aufschluß ['auffʃlus] *m* unlocking; (*Erklärung*) explanation. **aufschlußreich** *adj* informative.

*****aufschneiden** ['auffʃnaidən] *v* cut open; (*Fleisch*) carve.

Aufschnitt ['auffʃnit] *m* (cold) sliced meat.

Aufschrei ['auffʃrai] *m* scream, shriek; (*fig*) outcry.

*****aufschreiben** ['auffʃraibən] *v* write down, note.

Aufschrift ['auffrit] *f* (*Briefumschlag*) address; (*Etikett*) labelling, information; (*Inschrift*) inscription.

Aufschub ['auffʃuːp] *m* delay, deferment.

Aufschwung ['auffʃvuŋ] *m* swinging up, rising up; (*Komm*) boom, upturn (in economy).

*****aufsehen** ['aufzeːən] *v* look up. **Aufsehen** *neut* (*unz.*) stir, sensation. **Aufseher** *m* (*pl* -) overseer, inspector.

aufsetzen ['aufzɛtsən] *v* put on; (*Schriftliches*) draft, draw up.

Aufsicht ['aufzɪçt] *f* supervision, control; (*Verantwortung*) charge, care. **-srat** *m* board of directors.

*****aufspringen** ['auffʃprɪŋən] *v* spring up; (*Tür*) fly open; (*Riß*) crack, open.

Aufstand ['auffʃtant] *m* revolt, rebellion.

aufstapeln ['auffʃtaːpəln] *v* stack up, pile up.

aufstauen ['auffʃtauən] *v* dam (up).

*****aufstehen** ['auffʃteːən] *v* stand up; (*morgens, usw.*) get up, rise; (*revoltieren*) revolt; (*offenstehen*) stand open.

*****aufsteigen** ['auffʃtaigən] *v* climb up, ascend, rise; (*Pferd*) mount.

aufstellen ['auffʃtɛlən] *v* set up; (*Kandidat*) nominate; (*Mil*) draw up; (*Theorie, usw.*) propose, advance.

Aufstieg ['auffʃtiːk] *m* ascent, rise.

aufsuchen ['aufzuːxən] *v* (*Arzt, Gasthaus*) visit; (*Person*) visit, look up.

auftanken ['auftaŋkən] *v* refuel.

*****auftauchen** ['auftauxən] *v* (*aus Wasser*) emerge; (*fig*) turn up, crop up.

auftauen ['auftauən] *v* thaw (out), melt.

aufteilen ['auftailən] *v* divide up; (*verteilen*) share out.

Auftrag ['auftraːk] *m* (*pl* Aufträge) (*Komm*) order; (*Aufgabe*) task. **auftragen** *v* (*Farbe*) apply; (*Essen*) serve. **Auftrag‖geber** *m* customer, purchaser. **-nehmer** *m* contractor, supplier.

*****auftreiben** ['auftraibən] *v* (*auffinden*) hunt out, find; (*Staub*) stir up; (*Geld*) raise.

*****auftreten** ['auftreːtən] *v* come forward, appear.

Auftritt ['auftrit] *m* (*Szene*) scene; (*Schauspieler*) appearance, entrance.

*****auftun** ['auftuːn] *v* open.

aufwachen ['aufvaxən] *v* wake up.

*****aufwachsen** ['aufvaksən] *v* grow up.

Aufwand ['aufvant] m (unz.) expenditure.

aufwärmen ['aufvɛrmən] v (Sport) warm up; (speisen) heat up.

aufwärts ['aufvɛrts] adv up(wards).

aufwecken ['aufvɛkən] v wake up.

*****aufwenden** ['augvɛndən] v (Geld) spend; (Zeit) devote; (Energie) expend. **-ig** adj expensive. **Aufwendung** f expenditure.

*****aufwerfen** ['aufvɛrfən] v throw up.

aufwerten ['aufvɛrtən] v raise the value of, revalue. **Aufwertung** f revaluation.

*****aufwinden** ['aufvindən] v wind up; (mit der Winde) winch up.

aufwirbeln ['aufvirbəln] v whirl up.

aufwischen ['aufviʃən] v wipe up.

aufwühlen ['aufvyːlən] v root up; (fig) stir up, agitate.

aufzählen ['auftsɛːlən] v count out.

aufzeichnen ['auftsaiçnən] v sketch; (niederschreiben) write down.

*****aufziehen** ['auftsiːən] v (Kind, Tier, Flagge) raise; (Vorhang) open; (Pflanze) grow; (necken) tease.

Aufzug ['auftsuːk] m lift, (US) elevator; (Festzug) procession, parade; (Theater) act.

Augapfel ['aukapfəl] m eyeball.

Auge ['augə] neut (pl -n) eye. **unter vier Augen** in private. **ins Auge fallen** be conspicuous, catch the eye. **Augen||arzt** m oculist, ophthalmologist. **-blick** m moment, instant. **-braue** f eyebrow. **-lid** neut eyelid. **-loch** neut eye socket.

August [au'gust] m (pl -e) August.

Aula ['aula] f (pl Aulen) (great) hall.

Au-pair-Mädchen [oˈpɛːrmɛitçən] neut au-pair girl.

aus [aus] prep from. adv out; (vorbei) over, finished. **aus London** from London. **aus dem Fenster** out of the window. **aus Liebe zu** for love of. **aus Holz** (made) of wood, wooden. **von mir aus** as far as I'm concerned. **es ist aus** it's over.

ausarbeiten ['ausarbaitən] v work out; (vervollkommnen) perfect, finish off. **Ausarbeitung** f working out; finishing off, completion.

ausarten ['ausartən] v degenerate.

ausatmen ['ausaːtmən] v exhale, breathe out.

ausbaggern ['ausbagərn] v dredge.

Ausbau ['ausbau] m (pl -ten) extension; (Fertigstellung) completion.

ausbauchen ['ausbauxən] v bulge. **Ausbauchung** f bulge.

ausbessern ['ausbɛsərn] v repair, mend.

Ausbeute ['ausbɔytə] f profit, gain; (Ernte) crop, yield. **ausbeuten** v exploit. **Ausbeut||er** m exploiter. **-ung** f exploitation.

ausbilden ['ausbildən] v educate; (Lehrling) train; (gestalten) develop, shape. **Ausbildung** f education; training; (Gestaltung) development, shaping.

*****ausbleiben** ['ausblaibən] v stay away; (aufhören) stop.

Ausblick ['ausblik] m view; (fig) prospect, outlook.

*****ausbrechen** ['ausbrɛçən] v break out.

ausbreiten ['ausbraitən] v spread (out), stretch (out), extend.

Ausbruch ['ausbrux] m outbreak; (vom Gefängnis) escape, break-out; (Zorn, Vulkan) eruption.

ausbrüten ['ausbryːtən] v hatch.

Ausdauer ['ausdauər] f endurance, perseverance. **ausdauern** v persevere, endure.

ausdehnen ['ausdeːnən] v extend; (Metall) expand. **Ausdehnung** f extension; expansion.

*****ausdenken** ['ausdɛŋkən] v invent, think out; (sich vorstellen) imagine.

ausdrehen ['ausdreːən] v turn off, switch off; (Gelenk) dislocate.

Ausdruck ['ausdruk] m expression, phrase. **ausdrück||en** v express; (auspressen) squeeze out. **-lich** adj express, explicit. **ausdrucks||los** adj expressionless, vacant. **-voll** adj expressive.

auseinander [ausainˈandər] adv apart. **-bauen** v take apart, dismantle. **-fallen** v fall to pieces. **-gehen** v break up; (sich trennen) part. **-nehmen** v take apart. **-setzen** v explain. **Auseinandersetzung** f (vigorous) discussion; (Streit) argument.

auserlesen ['ausɛrleːzən] adj selected.

ausersehen ['ausɛrzeːən] v choose, select.

auserwählen ['ausɛrvɛːlən] v choose, select.

*****ausfahren** ['ausfaːrən] v drive out; (Person) take for a drive or walk. **Ausfahrt** f exit; (Ausflug) excursion; (Ausfahren) departure.

Ausfall ['ausfal] m loss; (Fehlbetrag) deficiency, deficit; (Ergebnis) result; (Mil) attack, sally. **ausfallen** v fall out; (unterbleiben) fail, be wanting; attack.

ausfertigen ['ausfɛrtigən] v (Schriftliches) draw up; (ausstellen) issue.

ausfindig ['ausfindiç] adj **ausfindig machen** find out.

Ausflug ['ausfluːk] m excursion, outing.

ausfragen ['ausfraːgən] v question, interrogate.

Ausfuhr ['ausfuːr] f (pl -en) export.

ausführ‖en ['ausfyːrən] v carry out, perform; (Waren) export; (erklären) explain, set out (in detail). **–bar** adj feasible. **–lich** adj detailed, extensive; adv in full. **Ausführung** f execution, performance; (Darstellung) explanation.

ausfüllen ['ausfylən] v fill; (Formular) fill out.

Ausgabe ['ausgaːbə] f expenditure, expense; (Buch) edition.

Ausgang ['ausgaŋ] m going out; (Tür) way out, exit; (Ergebnis) result, issue; (freier Tag) day off.

*****ausgeben** ['ausgeːbən] v (Geld) spend; (herausgeben) distribute; (Karten) deal. **sich ausgeben für** pose as.

ausgeglichen ['ausgəgliçən] adj (well-)balanced.

*****ausgehen** ['ausgeːən] v go out; (enden) come to an end; (Vorrat) run out. **Ausgehverbot** neut curfew.

ausgelassen ['ausgəlasən] adj wild, unrestrained, boisterous.

ausgemacht ['ausgəmaxt] adj agreed, settled.

ausgenommen ['ausgənomən] prep except for.

ausgeprägt ['ausgəprɛːkt] adj marked, distinct.

ausgerechnet ['ausgəreçnət] adv precisely, just.

ausgeschlossen ['ausgəʃlosən] adj impossible, out of the question.

ausgesprochen ['ausgəʃproxən] adj pronounced, distinct. adv distinctly, very.

ausgewachsen ['ausgəvaksən] adj full-grown.

ausgezeichnet ['ausgətsaiçnət] adj excellent.

*****ausgießen** ['ausgiːsən] v pour out.

Ausgleich ['ausglaiç] m (pl -e) settlement; (Entschädigung) compensation; (Sport) equalizer. **ausgleichen** v equalize, make even; (Verlust) compensate; (Konto) balance.

Ausguß ['ausgus] m outlet; (Kanne) spout.

*****aushalten** ['aushaltən] v bear, endure; (durchhalten) persevere.

*****ausheben** ['ausheːbən] v pull out, lift out; (Truppen) enlist. **Aushebung** f enlistment; (Wehrdienst) conscription.

*****aushelfen** ['aushɛlfən] v help (out), assist.

Aushilfe ['aushilfə] f (temporary) help, assistance.

aushöhlen ['aushœːlən] v hollow out, excavate.

*****auskennen** ['auskɛnən] v **sich auskennen** (umg.) know what's what; (in einer Sache) know well.

auskleiden ['ausklaidən] v line. **sich auskleiden** undress.

*****auskommen** ['auskomən] v (mit etwas) manage or cope with; (mit einer Person) get on well with.

Auskunft ['auskunft] f (pl Auskünfte) information.

auslachen ['auslaxən] v laugh at.

*****ausladen** ['auslaːdən] v unload.

Auslage ['auslaːgə] f display; (Schaufenster) shop window. **–n** pl expenses pl.

Ausland ['auslant] neut foreign country or countries. **ins** or **im Ausland** abroad. **Ausländer** m (pl -), **Ausländerin** f (pl -nen) foreigner. **ausländisch** adj foreign.

*****auslassen** ['auslasən] v omit, leave out; (Butter) melt; (Kleider) let down. **Auslassung** f omission; (Äußerung) utterance. **–zeichen** neut apostrophe.

Auslauf ['auslauf] m outflow; (Schiff) sailing, departure; (Bewegungsfreiheit) room to move. **auslaufen** v run out; (Schiff) put to sea.

ausleeren ['ausleːrən] v empty. **Ausleerung** f emptying, draining.

auslegen ['ausleːgən] v lay out; (Geld) spend; (erklären) explain, interpret. **Auslegung** f display; (Erklärung) interpretation.

Auslese ['ausleːzə] f (pl -n) selection; (Wein) choice wine. **auslesen** v select; (Buch) read to the end.

ausliefern ['auslifərn] v deliver; (Verbrecher) extradite. **Auslieferung** f delivery; extradition.

auslösen ['auslœːzən] v loosen; (Gefangene) ransom; (veranlassen) cause, spark off.

ausmachen ['ausmaxən] v (Feuer, Licht) put out; (betragen) amount to; (ver-

abreden) agree, fix. **das macht nichts aus** that doesn't matter.

Ausmaß ['ausmaːs] *f (pl -n)* neut scale, extent.

Ausnahme ['ausnaːmə] *f (pl -n)* exception. **mit Ausnahme von** excepting, with the exception of. **-fall** *m* exception, special case. **-zustand** *m (Pol)* state of emergency. **ausnahms‖los** *adj* without exception. **-weise** *adv* by way of exception, just for once.

ausnehmen ['ausneːmən] *v* take out; (*ausschließen*) exclude, make an exception of.

ausnutzen ['ausnutsən] *v* take advantage of.

auspacken ['auspakən] *v* unpack.

ausprobieren ['ausprobiːrən] *v* try (out), test.

Auspuff ['auspuf] *m (pl -e)* exhaust. **-rohr** *neut* exhaust pipe. **-topf** *m* silencer.

ausradieren ['ausradiːrən] *v* erase, rub out.

ausräumen ['ausrɔymən] *v* clear out, clean out.

ausrechnen ['ausrɛçnən] *v* calculate, work out. **Ausrechnung** *f* calculation.

Ausrede ['ausreːdə] *f* excuse.

ausreichen ['ausraiçən] *v* be enough *or* sufficient. **-d** *adj* sufficient, enough.

Ausreise ['ausraizə] *f* outward journey; (*Grenzübertritt*) departure, exit. **ausreisen** *v* depart.

ausrichten ['ausriçtən] *v* adjust, align; (*durchsetzen*) accomplish, do; (*Botschaft*) convey.

ausrotten ['ausrotən] *v* stamp out, root out.

Ausruf ['ausruːf] *m* cry, exclamation; (*Bekanntmachung*) proclamation. **ausrufen** *v* cry out, exclaim; (*Namen*) call out. **Ausrufung** *f* exclamation. **-zeichen** *neut* exclamation mark.

ausruhen ['ausruːən] *v* rest.

ausrüsten ['ausrystən] *v* equip; (*Mil*) arm. **Ausrüstung** *f* equipment; (*Mil*) armament.

Aussage ['auszaːgə] *f (pl -n)* statement, declaration; (*Jur*) evidence, testimony. **aussagen** *v* declare, state; (*Jur*) give evidence, make a statement, testify.

ausschalten ['ausʃaltən] *v* switch off; (*fig*) exclude.

Ausschank ['ausʃaŋk] *m (Ausgabe)* service

(of alcoholic drinks); (*Kneipe*) bar, pub.
Ausschank über die Straße off-sales, off-licence.

ausscheiden ['ausʃaidən] *v* withdraw, retire; (*absondern*) separate. **Ausscheidung** *f* withdrawal; separation.

ausschicken ['ausʃikən] *v* send out.

ausschiffen ['ausʃifən] *v* disembark, land. **Ausschiffung** *f* disembarkation.

ausschimpfen ['ausʃimpfən] *v* scold, abuse.

ausschlafen ['ausʃlaːfən] *v* lie in, sleep until completely rested.

Ausschlag ['ausʃlaːk] *m (Med)* rash; (*Bot*) shoot; (*Zeiger*) deflection. **ausschlagen** *v* knock out; (*ablehnen*) refuse; (*Pferd*) kick out.

ausschließen ['ausʃliːsən] *v* shut out, lock out; (*fig*) exclude. **ausschließlich** *adj* exclusive; *prep* excluding, exclusive of. **Ausschließung** *f* exclusion; (*Arbeiter*) lock-out.

ausschneiden ['ausʃnaidən] *v* cut out.

Ausschnitt ['ausʃnit] *m (Teil)* section; (*Zeitung*) press cutting; (*Kleid*) low neck-line.

ausschöpfen ['ausʃœpfən] *v* (*Wasser*) scoop out; (*Boot*) bail out; (*Möglichkeiten*) exhaust.

ausschreiben ['ausʃraibən] *v* write out, copy out; (*Formular*) fill out; (*ankündigen*) announce.

Ausschreitung ['ausʃraituŋ] *f* excess, transgression.

Ausschuß ['ausʃus] **1** *m* committee, board. **2** *m (unz.) (Abfall)* refuse, rejects *pl*.

ausschweifen ['ausʃvaifən] *v (moralisch)* lead a dissolute life; (*von Thema*) digress. **Ausschweifung** *f* debauchery, immorality; digression.

aussehen ['auszeːən] *v* appear, look. *sie sieht hübsch aus* she looks pretty. *es sieht nach Regen aus* it looks like rain.

außen ['ausən] *adv* (to the) outside, outwards. **Außenbordmotor** *m* outboard motor.

aussenden ['auszendən] *v* send out; (*Strahlen*) emit; (*Radio*) transmit.

Außen‖handel *m* foreign trade. **-läufer** *m* wing-half. **-minister** *m* foreign minister. **-politik** *f* foreign policy; (*allgemein*) foreign affairs. **-seite** *f* outside. **-seiter** *m* outsider. **-stürmer** *m* wing (forward).

außer ['ausər] prep (räumlich) out of, outside; (ausgenommen) except. **außer Betrieb** out of order.

äußer ['oysər] adj external, exterior, outer.

außer||dem adv besides. **-halb** adv, prep outside.

äußerlich ['oysərliç] adj external.

äußern ['oysərn] v express, utter; (zeigen) manifest, reveal.

außerordentlich [ausər'ɔrdəntliç] adj extraordinary.

äußerst ['oysərst] adj the utmost.

aussetzen ['auszɛtsən] v (Pflanze) plant out; (Kind) abandon; (Tier) set free; (Geld) offer; (einer Gefahr, dem Spott, usw.) expose (to); (aufhören) stop; (Mot) stall.

Aussicht ['ausziçt] f outlook, prospect; (Blick) view. **aussichts||los** adj unpromising, hopeless. **-voll** adj promising.

aussondern ['auszɔndərn] v (auswählen) select; excrete. **Aussonderung** f separation; selection; excretion.

ausspeien ['ausʃpaiən] v spit out; (Rauch) belch out.

Aussprache ['ausʃpraːxə] f pronunciation.
*aussprechen ['ausʃprɛçən] v pronounce.

Ausspruch ['ausʃprux] m remark, saying; (Jur) verdict.

ausspülen ['ausʃpyːlən] v wash out, rinse.

Ausstand ['ausʃtant] m strike.

ausstatten ['ausʃtatən] v equip, furnish; (Tochter) provide with a dowry. **Ausstattung** f (pl -en) equipment, outfit; dowry.

*aussteigen ['ausʃtaigən] v get off, alight.

ausstellen ['ausʃtɛlən] v display, exhibit; (Paß, Urkunde) issue; (Quittung) write out. **Aussteller** m (pl -) exhibitor. **Ausstellung** f exhibition; issue; writing out.

*aussterben ['ausʃtɛrbən] v die out.

Ausstieg ['ausʃtiːg] m (pl -e) exit door.
*ausstoßen ['ausʃtoisən] v push out, thrust out; (Schrei) give.

ausstrahlen ['ausʃtraːlən] v radiate.

ausstrecken ['ausʃtrɛkən] v stretch out, extend.

*ausstreichen ['ausʃtraiçən] v (Wort) strike out, cross out; (Teig) roll out.

ausströmen ['ausʃtrøːmən] v (Flüssigkeit) pour out; (Gas) escape.

aussuchen ['auszuːxən] v search (out), select.

Austausch ['austauʃ] m exchange. **austauschen** v exchange.

austeilen ['austailən] v distribute, share out.

Auster ['austər] f (pl -n) oyster.

Austrag ['austraːg] m (pl Austräge) decision, end, result. **austragen** v carry out; (Kampf) decide; (Post) deliver.

Australi||en [au'straːliən] neut Australia. **-er** m (pl -), **-erin** f (pl -nen) Australian. **australisch** adj Australian.

*austreiben ['austraibən] v expel.

*austreten ['austreːtən] v leave, withdraw (from); (Schuhe, usw.) wear out.

*austrinken ['austriŋkən] v drain, drink off.

Austritt ['austrit] m leaving, departure.

ausüben ['ausyːbən] v practise; (Druck, Einfluß) exert; (Macht) wield. **-d** adj practising. **Ausübung** f practice, exercise.

Ausverkauf ['ausferkauf] m (clearance) sale. **ausverkauft** adj sold out.

Auswahl ['ausvaːl] f choice, selection.

Auswanderer ['ausvandərər] m emigrant. **auswandern** v emigrate. **Auswanderung** f emigration.

auswärtig ['ausvɛrtiç] adj foreign. **das Auswärtige Amt** the Foreign Office.

auswärts ['ausvɛrts] adv outwards; (nach draußen) outside.

auswechseln ['ausvɛksəln] v change (for).

Ausweg ['ausveːg] m way out.
*ausweichen ['ausvaiçən] v make way; (Frage) evade, dodge. **-d** adj evasive, elusive. **Ausweichung** f evasion.

Ausweis ['ausvais] m (pl -e) identity card or papers; (Paß) passport. **ausweisen** v expel, turn out. **Ausweisung** f expulsion. **auswendig** ['ausvɛndiç] adj external. **auswendig lernen** learn by heart.

*auswerfen ['ausverfən] v throw out; (Anker) cast.

auswirken ['ausvirkən] v obtain. **sich auswirken auf** have an effect on. **Auswirkung** f effect.

auswischen ['ausviʃən] v wipe out.

Auswuchs ['ausvuks] m growth; (Nebenerscheinung) (unwelcome) product, side-effect.

auszahlen ['austsaːlən] v pay out. **Auszahlung** f payment.

auszeichnen ['austsaiçnən] v (*Ware*) label; (*ehren*) honour; (*hervorheben*) distinguish, mark out. **sich auszeichnen** distinguish oneself. **Auszeichnung** f distinction, honour, award.

*ausziehen ['austsiːən] v pull out, extract; (*Person*) undress; (*aus einer Wohnung*) move out. **sich ausziehen** undress.

Auszug ['austsuːk] m removal; (*Abmarsch*) departure; (*Exzerpt*) excerpt.

authentisch [au'tɛntiʃ] adj authentic.

Auto ['auto] neut (pl -s) car, automobile. **-ausstellung** f motor show. **-bahn** f motorway. **-fahrer** m driver, motorist.

Autogramm [auto'gram] neut (pl -e) autograph.

Automat [auto'maːt] m (pl -en) vending machine. **automatisch** adj automatic. **automatisieren** v automate.

autonom [auto'noːm] adj autonomous.

Autor ['autɔr] m (pl -en) author.

autoritär [autori'tɛːr] adj authoritarian. **Autorität** f authority.

Auto||unfall m road accident. **-vermietung** f car hire.

avantgardistisch [avãgar'distiʃ] adj avant-garde.

Axt [akst] f (pl Äxte) axe.

B

Baby ['beːbi] neut (pl -s) baby.

Bach [bax] m (pl Bäche) stream, brook.

Backbord ['bakbɔrt] neut (naut) port (side).

Backe ['bakə] f (pl -n) cheek.

backen ['bakən] v bake.

Bäcker ['bɛkər] m (pl -) baker. **-ei** f (pl -en) bakery.

Back||ofen m oven. **-pulver** neut baking powder. **-stein** m brick.

Bad [baːt] neut (pl Bäder) bath; (*Badeort*) spa. **Bade||anstalt** f baths, swimming pool. **-anzug** m bathing costume. **-hose** f bathing trunks pl. **baden** v bathe. **Bade||wanne** f bath tub. **-zimmer** neut bathroom.

Bagger ['bagər] m (pl -) dredger, excavator. **baggern** v dredge, excavate.

Bahn [baːn] f (pl -en) railway; (*Weg*) path. **-brecher** m pioneer. **bahnen** v den Weg bahnen pave the way (for).

Bahn||hof m (railway) station. **-steig** m (railway) platform.

Bahre ['baːrə] f (pl -n) stretcher; (*Toten-*) bier.

Bai [bai] f (pl -en) (*Bucht*) bay.

Bajonett [bajo'nɛt] neut (pl -e) bayonet.

Bakterium [bak'teːrium] neut (pl Bakterien) bacterium (pl -a).

balancieren [balã'siːrən] v balance.

bald [balt] adv soon. **-ig** adj early, quick. **-möglichst** adv as soon as possible.

Balken ['balkən] m (pl -) beam.

Balkon [nal'kõː] m (pl -e) balcony.

Ball¹ [bal] m (pl Bälle) ball.

Ball² m (pl Bälle) (*Tanz*) dance, ball.

Ballade [ba'laːdə] f (pl -n) ballad.

ballen ['balən] v (*Faust*) clench. **sich ballen** cluster, clump together.

Ballen ['balən] m (pl -) bale, bundle; (*Anat*) palm. **-entzündung** f bunion.

Ballett [ba'lɛt] neut (pl -e) ballet. **Balletttänzer** m (pl -), **-tänzerin** f (pl -nen) ballet dancer. **Balletteuse** f (pl -n) ballerina.

Ballistik [ba'listik] f (unz.) ballistics. **ballistisch** adj ballistic.

Ballon [ba'lõː] m (pl -e) balloon.

Balsam ['balzaːm] m (pl -e) balsam; (*fig*) balm. **balsamieren** v embalm.

baltisch ['baltiʃ] adj Baltic.

Bambus ['bambus] m (pl -se) bamboo.

Banane [ba'naːnə] f (pl -n) banana.

Band¹ [bant] 1 neut (pl Bänder) tape; (*Haar*) ribbon; (*Anat*) ligament; (*Radio*) waveband. 2 neut (pl -e) bond, tie.

Band² m (pl Bände) (*Buch*) volume.

Band³ f (pl -s) (*Jazz*) band.

Bandage [ban'daːʒə] f (pl -n) bandage. **bandagieren** v bandage.

Bandaufnahme ['bantaufnaːmə] f tape recording.

Bande ['bandə] f (pl -n) gang, band.

bändigen ['bɛndigən] v tame, subdue; (*Wut*) control.

Bandit [ban'diːt] m (pl -en) bandit.

Bandscheibe ['bantʃaibə] f (*Anat*) disc. **-nverfall** m slipped disc.

bang(e) ['baŋ(ə)] adj afraid, anxious. **bangen** v be afraid or anxious.

Bank¹ [baŋk] f (pl Bänke) (*zum Sitzen*) bench, seat.

Bank² f (pl -en) (*Komm*) bank.

Bankett [baŋ'kɛt] neut (pl -e) banquet.

bankrott [baŋ'rɔt] adj bankrupt. **Bankrott** m (pl -e) bankruptcy. **Bankrott machen**

go bankrupt. **Bankrotteur** m (pl -e) bankrupt.

Bank‖**konto** neut bank account. – **note** f banknote.

Bann [ban] m (pl -e) ban; (Kirche) excommunication; (Zauber) spell.

bar [baɪr] adj bare; (Geld) ready, in cash. **für bare Münze nehmen** accept, take at face value.

Bar[baɪr] f (pl -s) bar, tavern.

Bär [bɛɪr] m (pl -en) bear.

Barbar [bar'baɪr] m (pl -en) barbarian. **Barbarei** f (pl -en) barbarism. **barbarisch** adj barbarian.

barfuß ['baɪrfuːs] adv barefoot. **barfüßig** adj barefoot.

Bargeld ['baɪrɡɛlt] neut cash.

Bariton ['bariton] m (pl -e) baritone.

Barmädchen ['baɪrmɛtçən] neut barmaid.

barmherzig [barm'hɛrtsiç] adj merciful, compassionate. **Barmherzigkeit** f mercifulness, mercy.

Barock [ba'rɔk] neut or m baroque. **barock** adj baroque.

Barometer [ba'rometər] neut barometer.

Baron [ba'roɪn] m (pl -e) baron. – **in** f (pl -nen) baroness.

Barre ['barə] f (pl -n) bar; (Gold) ingot.

Barriere [bari'eɪrə] f (pl -n) barrier, gate.

barsch [barʃ] adj rude, brusque.

Bart [baɪrt] m (pl **Bärte**) beard.

bärtig ['bɛɪrtiç] adj bearded.

Base[1] ['baɪzə] f (pl -n) (female) cousin.

Base[2] f (pl -n) alkali, base.

Basel ['baɪzəl] neut Basle, Bâle.

basieren [ba'ziɪrən] v be based (on). **Basis** f (pl **Basen**) basis (pl -ses), base.

Baß [bas] m (pl **Bässe**) bass. – **geige** f double-bass.

Bassist [ba'sist] m (pl -en) (Sänger) bass (singer); (Baßgeigenspieler) double-bass (player).

Bastard ['bastart] m (pl -e) bastard.

basteln ['bastəln] v put together, rig up; (umg.) do-it-yourself. **er bastelt gern** he loves to tinker around. **Bastler** m (pl -) handyman, tinkerer.

Bataillon [batai'ljoɪn] neut (pl -e) battalion.

Batterie [batə'riː] f (pl -n) battery.

Bau [bau] **1** m (unz.) building, construction; (Getreide, usw.) cultivation, growing. **2** m (pl -e) (Bergwerk) mine; (Tiere) burrow. **3** m (pl -ten) building. – **arbeiter** m construction worker.

Bauch [baux] m (pl **Bäuche**) belly, abdomen. **bauchig** adj bellied, bulging, convex. **Bauchweh** neut or **Bauchschmerzen** pl stomach-ache.

bauen ['bauən] build; (Bot) grow, cultivate.

Bauer ['bauər] m (pl -n) (small) farmer, peasant; (Schach) pawn.

Bäuerin ['bɔyərin] f (pl -nen) farmer's wife, peasant woman. **bäuerlich** adj rustic, rural.

Bauern‖**haus** neut farmhouse. – **hof** m farm(yard).

baufällig ['baufɛliç] adj dilapidated. **Bau**‖**genossenschaft** f building society. – **ingenieur** m structural or civil engineer. – **stelle** f building site.

Baum [baum] m (pl **Bäume**) tree; (Schiff) boom. – **garten** m orchard. – **wolle** f cotton.

Bayer ['baiər] m (pl -) Bavarian. – **n** neut Bavaria. **bay(e)risch** adj Bavarian.

beabsichtigen [bə'apziçtiɡən] v intend, propose.

beachten [bə'axtən] v pay attention to. **beachtungswert** adj noteworthy. **Beachtung** f attention, notice.

Beamte(r) [bə'amtə(r)] m, **Beamtin** f (Staats-) civil servant, official; (Privat-) officer, representative.

beängstigen [bə'ɛnstiɡən] v worry, frighten.

beanspruchen [bə'anʃpruxən] v claim, demand; (Person) make demands on. **Beanspruchung** f claim; (Belastung) strain, load.

*beantragen [bə'antraiɡən] v propose.

beantworten [bə'antvortən] v answer, reply to.

bearbeiten [bə'arbaitən] v work on; (Metall, Holz, Land) work; (Buch) edit, revise; (Musik) arrange; (Theaterstück) adapt. **Bearbeiter** m editor, reviser; arranger. **Bearbeitung** f working; (Verbesserung) revision, adaptation; (Musik) arrangement.

beaufsichtigen [bə'aufziçtiɡən] v supervise, control. **Beaufsichtigung** f supervision, control.

*beauftragen [bə'auftraiɡən] v commission, authorize. **Beauftragte(r)** m deputy, agent.

bebauen [bə'bauən] v (Gelände) build on; (Land) cultivate. **bebaute Fläche** f built-up area.

beben ['be:bən] v tremble, shake.
Becher ['bɛçər] m (pl -) tumbler, glass. – **glas** neut (laboratory) beaker.
Becken ['bɛkən] neut (pl -) basin; (Anat) pelvis; (Musik) cymbal.
bedacht [bə'daxt] adj thoughtful, mindful. **Bedacht** m consideration; (Überlegung) deliberation. **bedächtig** adj thoughtful, careful.
Bedarf [bə'darf] m (unz.) need; (Nachfrage) demand.
bedauerlich [bə'dauərliç] adj regrettable, unfortunate. **bedauern** v (Sache) regret, deplore; (Person) be or feel sorry for.
bedecken [bə'dɛkən] v cover. **bedeckt** adj (Himmel) overcast. **Bedeckung** f (pl -en) cover(ing).
*__bedenken__ [bə'dɛŋkən] v consider, think over. **sich bedenken** deliberate, weigh the consequences (of).
bedeuten [bə'dɔytən] v mean, signify. – **d** adj important. **Bedeutung** f meaning; (Wichtigkeit) significance, importance. **bedeutungs||los** adj meaningless. – **voll** adj significant.
bedienen [bə'di:nən] v serve, wait on; (Maschine) operate, work. **Bedienung** f service; (Maschine) operation; (Diener) staff, servants pl.
bedingt [bə'dɪŋkt] adj conditional, limited. **Bedingung** f (pl -en) condition.
Bedrängnis [bə'drɛŋnɪs] f (pl -se) distress, trouble.
bedrohen [bə'dro:ən] v threaten. **Bedrohung** f (pl -en) threat.
*__bedürfen__ [bə'dYrfən] v need, require. **Bedürfnis** neut (pl -se) need, requirement. **Bedürfnisanstalt** f public toilet.
beeilen [bə'ailən] v sich beeilen hurry.
beeindrucken [bə'aindrukən] v impress.
beeinflussen [bə'ainflusən] v influence, have an influence or effect on.
beeinträchtigen [bə'aintrɛçtigən] v reduce, inhibit, be detrimental to.
beenden [bə'ɛndigən] v end, finish. **Beendigung** f end, termination.
Beerdigung [bə'eːrdiguŋ] f burial, funeral.
Beere ['beːrə] f (pl -n) berry.
Beet [beːt] neut (pl -e) bed; (Blumen-) flowerbed; (Gemüse) vegetable patch.
befähigen [bə'fɛ:igən] v enable, make fit. **befähigt** adj able, qualified. **Befähigung** f (pl -en) capacity, fitness.

befahrbar [bə'faːrbaːr] adj passable, usable. **befahren** v travel or drive on.
*__befallen__ [bə'falən] v befall; (Krankheit) attack, strike.
befangen [bə'faŋən] adj shy, self-conscious; (parteiisch) biased.
befassen [bə'fasən] v sich befassen mit engage in, occupy oneself with.
*__befehlen__ [bə'fe:lən] v command, order. **Befehl** m (pl -e) command, order. **Befehlshaber** m (pl -) commander, commanding officer.
befestigen [bə'fɛstigən] v fasten; (stärken) strengthen; (Mil) fortify. **Befestigung** f (pl -en) fastening; strengthening; (Mil) fortification.
*__befinden__ [bə'findən] v find. **sich befinden** be, be situated; (Person) be, find oneself. **sich wohl befinden** feel well. **befindlich** adj present, to be found.
beflecken [bə'flɛkən] v stain, soil.
befolgen [bə'fɔlgən] v obey, follow.
befördern [bə'fœdərn] v convey, dispatch; (Rang) promote. **Beförderung** f (pl -en) transport, conveyance; promotion.
befragen [bə'fraːgən] v question. **sich befragen** enquire, inquire.
befreien [bə'fraiən] v liberate, free. **Befreier** m (pl -) liberator. **Befreiung** f (pl -en) liberation; (Entlassung) exemption.
befreunden [bə'frɔyndən] v sich befreunden mit make friends with. **befreundet** adj friendly (with); intimate. **eng befreundet sein mit** be a close friend of.
befriedigen [bə'fri:digən] v satisfy. – **d** adj satisfactory. **Befriedigung** f (pl -en) satisfaction.
befruchten [bə'fruxtən] v fertilize; (anregen) stimulate. **Befruchtung** f (pl -en) fertilization.
befugen [bə'fuːgən] v authorize, empower. **Befugnis** f (pl -se) authority, right.
befürchten [bə'fYrçtən] v fear; (vermuten) suspect. **Befürchtung** f (pl -en) fear, apprehension.
befürworten [bə'fYrvɔrtən] v recommend, advocate.
begabt [bə'gaːpt] adj talented, gifted. **Begabung** f talent, gift.
begatten [bə'gatən] v sich begatten mate, copulate. **Begattung** f (pl -en) mating, copulation.
*__begeben__ [bə'ge:bən] v sich begeben go, proceed; (verzichten) renounce, give up.

begegnen [bə'geignən] v meet, encounter. **Begegnung** f (pl -en) meeting, encounter.

*begehen [bə'geiən] (Unrecht) commit, do; (gehen auf) walk on.

begehren [bə'geirən] v desire, covet.

begeistern [bə'gaistərn] v inspire, fill with enthusiasm. **begeistert** adj inspired, enthusiastic. **Begeisterung** f enthusiasm.

Begier [bə'gir], f (unz.), also **Begierde** f (pl -n) desire, craving. **begierig** adj desirous, covetous.

begießen [bə'gi:sən] v water, sprinkle; (Braten) baste.

Beginn [bə'gin] m (unz.) beginning. **beginnen** v begin.

beglaubigen [bə'glaubigən] v certify, attest. **Beglaubigung** f (pl -en) certification.

begleiten [bə'glaitən] v accompany. **Begleit‖er** m (pl -) attendant; (Musik) accompanist. **-schreiben** neut covering letter. **-ung** f (pl -en) attendants pl, escort; (Musik) accompaniment.

beglücken [bə'glykən] v make happy. **beglückwünschen** v congratulate. **Beglückwünschung** f (pl -en) congratulations pl.

begnadigen [bə'gnaidigən] v pardon.

begnügen [bə'gnyigən] v **sich begnügen mit** content oneself with, be satisfied with.

*begraben [bə'graibən] v bury. **Begräbnis** neut (pl -se) burial, funeral.

*begreifen [bə'graifən] v understand, grasp, apprehend. **begreiflich** adj comprehensible.

begrenzt [bə'grɛntst] adj restricted, limited.

Begriff [bə'grif] m (pl -e) concept, idea. **Begriffsvermögen** neut comprehension.

begründen [bə'gryndən] v found, establish; (Behauptung) substantiate. **Begründer** m founder.

begrüßen [bə'gryisən] v greet, welcome.

begünstigen [bə'gynstigən] v (vorziehen) favour; (fördern) promote, further.

begütert [bə'gyitərt] adj wealthy, well-to-do.

begütigen [bə'gyitigən] v placate, appease.

behäbig [bə'hɛ:biç] adj (beleibt) portly, corpulent; (bequem, langsam) comfortable.

behagen [bə'haigən] v please, suit. **Behagen** neut (pl -) ease, comfort. **behaglich** adj comfortable, at ease.

*behalten [bə'haltən] v keep, retain; (im Gedächtnis) reimember. **Behälter** m (pl -) container; (Flüssigkeiten) tank.

behandeln [bə'handəln] v treat, handle. **Behandlung** f treatment, handling; (Med) treatment, therapy.

beharren [bə'harən] v persist. **beharrlich** adj persistent, pertinacious.

behaupten [bə'hauptən] v maintain, assert, state. **Behauptung** f (pl -eu) statement, assertion.

behend(e) [bə'hɛnt, bə'hɛndə] adj, also **behendig** nimble, agile. **Behendigkeit** f agility.

beherbergen [bə'hɛrbɛrgən] v rule, govern.

beherrschen [bə'hɛrʃən] v (Zorn, usw.) control; (meistern, können) master. **sich beherrschen** control oneself. **Beherrschung** f rule, control; mastery.

beherzigen [bə'hɛrtsigən] v take to heart.

behilflich [bə'hilfliç] adj helpful.

behindern [bə'hindərn] v hinder, obstruct. **Behinderung** f (pl -en) hindrance.

Behörde [bə'hoerdə] f (pl -n) authority, authorities pl.

behüten [bə'hyitən] v guard, protect. **Behüter** m (pl -) protector, guard.

bei [bai] prep at; (neben) near. bei mir at (my) home; (in der Tasche) on me. bei Herrn Schmidt at Herr Schmidt's (house). bei der Post arbeiten work for the Post Office. bei der Hand nehmen take by the hand. beim Aussteigen while or when getting out. bei Nacht at night. bei Tag during the day. bei der Arbeit at work. bei weitem by far. bei Shakespeare in Shakespeare.

*beibehalten ['baibəhaltən] v retain; keep.

*beibringen ['baibriŋən] v bring forward; (Verlust, Wunde) inflict; (lehren) teach.

Beichte ['baiçtə] f (pl -n) (Rel) confession. **beichten** v confess. **Beichtvater** m confessor.

beide ['baidə] adj, pron both. **alle beide** both. **einer von beiden** either of two. **in beiden Fällen** in either case. **wir beide** both of us. **zu beiden Seiten** on both sides. **beider‖lei** adj of both sorts. **-seitig** adj mutual, reciprocal. **-seits** adv mutually. **beidhändig** adj ambidextrous.

Beifahrer ['baifaɪrər] m (pl -) passenger.
Beifall ['baifal] m (unz.) applause; (Billigung) approval. **Beifall klatschen** applaud.
beifügen ['baify:gən] v enclose, attach.
*beigeben ['baɪgeːbən] v add. **klein beigeben** draw in one's horns, yield.
Beigeschmack ['baɪgəʃmak] m (after)taste; (fig) tinge.
Beihilfe ['baihilfə] f financial aid, subsidy; (Jur) aiding and abetting.
*beikommen ['baikɔmən] v get at, get near, reach.
Beil [bail] neut (pl -e) (Holz) hatchet; (Fleisch) cleaver.
Beilage ['bailaːgə] f enclosure, insert; (Zeitung) supplement.
beiläufig ['bailoyfiç] adj incidental. adv incidentally, by the way.
beilegen ['baileːgən] v add; (zuschreiben) attribute, ascribe; (schlichten) settle.
Beileid ['bailait] neut (unz.) condolence.
beiliegend ['bailiːgənt] adj enclosed.
beim [baim] prep + art bei dem.
*beimessen ['baimɛsən] v attribute, credit with.
Bein [bain] neut (pl -e) leg; (Knochen) bone.
beinah(e) ['bainaː(ə)] adv almost, nearly.
Beiname ['bainaːmə] m nickname. **mit dem Beinamen ...** known as ..., called ....
beirren [bəˈɪrən] v **sich nicht beirren lassen** stick to one's opinions, not be misled.
beisammen [baiˈzamən] adv together.
Beischlaf ['baiʃlaːf] m (sexual) intercourse.
beiseite [baiˈzaitə] adv to one side, aside. **-legen** v put aside or by.
Beispiel ['baiʃpiːl] neut (pl -e) example. **zum Beispiel** for example or instance. **beispielsweise** adv for instance, as an example.
*beißen [baisən] v bite. **beißend** adj biting; (Säure) caustic. **Beiß||zahn** m incisor. **-zange** f pincers.
Beistand ['baiʃtant] m help, assistance.
*beistehen ['baiʃteːən] v help, assist.
beistimmen ['baiʃtimən] v agree, consent. **Bestimmung** f agreement, consent.
Beitrag ['baitraːk] m (pl Beiträge) contribution; (Klub) subscription. **beitragen** v contribute. **Beiträger** m (pl -) contributor.

*beitreten ['baitreːtən] v join; (Meinung) agree to, accept.
Beiwagen ['baivaːgən] m sidecar.
beiwohnen ['baivoːnən] v be present at, attend; (beischlafen) have sex with.
beizeiten [baiˈtsaitən] adv early.
beizen [baitsən] v (Holz) stain; (Metall) etch; (Fleisch) salt, pickle.
bejahen [bəˈjaːən] v affirm, agree to.
bejahrt [bəˈjaːrt] adj aged.
bekämpfen [bəˈkɛmpfən] v fight (against), combat.
bekannt [bəˈkant] adj known. **bekannt werden mit** become acquainted with. **sich bekanntmachen mit** acquaint oneself with. **Bekannt||e(r)** acquaintance. **-gabe** f announcement, notification. **bekannt||geben** v make known, disclose. **-lich** adv as is well known. **Bekanntschaft** f acquaintance.
bekehren [bəˈkeːrən] v convert. **Bekehr||te(r)** convert. **-ung** f conversion.
*bekennen [bəˈkɛnən] v acknowledge, confess. **Bekenntnis** neut (pl -se) confession; (Glaube) faith, creed.
beklagen [bəˈklaːgən] v lament, deplore. **-swert** adj lamentable. **Beklagte(r)** m accused, defendant.
bekleiden [bəˈklaidən] v clothe; (beziehen) coat; (Amt) occupy. **Bekleidung** f clothing; (Material) coating.
*beklemmen [bəˈklɛmən] v oppress, frighten; (ersticken) stifle. **Angst beklemmt mich** I am seized by fear.
*bekommen [bəˈkɔmən] v obtain, get, receive; (Zug) catch; (Krankheit) catch, get. **bekömmlich** adj wholesome, beneficial.
bekräftigen [bəˈkrɛftigən] v confirm, strengthen.
bekreuzigen [bəˈkroytsigən] v **sich bekreuzigen** cross oneself.
bekümmern [bəˈkymərn] v trouble, distress. **bekümmert sein** be anxious or troubled.
bekunden [bəˈkundən] v state; (zeigen) show, manifest.
*beladen [bəˈlaːdən] v load.
Belag [bəˈlaːk] m (pl Beläge) covering, coating; (Aufstrich) spread. **Butterbrot mit Belag** sandwich.
belagern [bəˈlaːgərn] v besiege. **Belagerung** f siege.

belangen [bə'laŋən] v concern; (Jur) prosecute. **belanglos** adj unimportant.

belasten [bə'lastən] v burden; (Konto) debit, charge; (Jur) accuse.

belästigen [bə'lɛstɪgən] v pester, bother; (umg.) bug. **Belästigung** f bother, annoyance.

Belastung [bə'lastuŋ] f (pl -en) load; (Konto) debit, charge.

*belaufen [bə'laufən] v **sich belaufen auf** amount to, total.

belauschen [bə'lauʃən] v eavesdrop on, listen to (secretly).

beleben [bə'leɪbən] v animate; (Med) revive. **belebt** adj animated, lively; (Ort) crowded, bustling. **Beleb**‖**theit** f liveliness. **-ung** f animation; revival.

Beleg [bə'leɪk] m (pl -e) proof, evidence; (Urkunde) voucher. **belegen** v cover; (Platz) reserve; (Kursus) enrol for; (Brot) spread. **belegtes Brötchen** filled roll, sandwich. **Belegschaft** f personnel, staff.

belehren [bə'leɪrən] v instruct, teach.

beleibt [bə'laipt] adj portly, stout.

beleidigen [bə'laidɪgən] v insult. **beleidigend** adj insulting, offensive. **Beleidigung** f (pl -en) insult.

beleuchten [bə'lɔyçtən] v illuminate, light (up). **Beleuchtung** f lighting, illumination.

Belgien ['bɛlgiən] neut Belgium. **Belgier** m (pl -), **Belgierin** f (pl -nen) Belgian. **belgisch** adj Belgian.

belichten [bə'lɪçtən] v (Foto) expose. **Belichtung** f (pl -en) exposure. **Belichtungsmesser** m light meter.

belieben [bə'liːbən] v (gefallen) please; (wünschen) like, wish. **Belieben** neut pleasure, will. **nach Belieben** at will, as you like. **beliebig** adj any (you like), whatever. **beliebt** adj loved, popular.

bellen ['bɛlən] v bark.

belohnen [bə'loːnən] v reward, recompense. **Belohnung** f reward, recompense.

belüften [bə'lyftən] v ventilate. **Belüftung** f ventilation.

belustigen [bə'lustɪgən] v amuse. **Belustigung** f amusement.

bemächtigen [bə'mɛçtɪgən] v **sich bemächtigen** seize, take possession of.

bemerkbar [bə'mɛrkbaɪr] adj noticeable, observable. **bemerken** v notice; (sagen) remark. **-swert** adj remarkable, noteworthy. **Bemerkung** f (pl -en) remark.

*bemessen [bə'mɛsən] v measure. adj restricted.

bemitleiden [bə'mɪtlaidən] v pity, feel sorry for.

bemühen [bə'myːən] v trouble (oneself), take pains. **Bemühen** neut or **Bemühung** f (pl -en) effort, exertion.

benachbart [bə'naxbaɪrt] adj neighbouring.

benachrichtigen [bə'naxrɪçtɪgən] v inform. **Benachrichtigung** f report.

benannt [bə'nant] adj named.

*benehmen [bə'neːmən] v **sich benehmen** behave. **Benehmen** neut behaviour.

beneiden [bə'naidən] v envy.

*benennen [bə'nɛnən] v name, call. **Benennung** f (pl -en) name, title.

Bengel ['bɛŋəl] m (pl -) brat, little rascal.

benommen [bə'nɔmən] adj confused.

benötigen [bə'nøːtɪgən] v need, require.

benutzen [bə'nutsən] v use, make use of. **Benutzung** f use, employment.

Benzin [bɛn'tsiːn] neut petrol, (US) gasoline. **-uhr** f petrol or fuel gauge. **-verbrauch** m fuel consumption.

beobachten [bə'oɪbaxtən] v observe, watch; (bemerken) notice. **Beobach**‖**ter** m (pl -) observer, onlooker. **-tung** f (pl -en) observation.

bepflanzen [bə'pflantsən] v plant.

bequem [bə'kveɪm] adj comfortable; (mühelos) convenient. **bequemlich** adj lazy, comfort-loving.

*beraten [bə'raːtən] v advise. **sich beraten** confer. **beratend** adj advisory. **Berater** m adviser, counsellor. **Beratung** f consultation.

berauben [bə'raubən] v rob or deprive of.

berauschen [bə'rauʃən] v intoxicate.

berechenbar [bə'rɛçənbaɪr] adj calculable.

berechnen v calculate, evaluate. **berechnend** adj (Person) selfish, calculating. **Berechnung** f calculation, evaluation.

berechtigen [bə'rɛçtɪgən] v entitle, authorize. **berechtigt** adj entitled. **Berechtigung** f authorization, entitlement.

bereden [bə'reːdən] v persuade. **beredsam** adj eloquent.

Bereich [bə'raiç] m (pl -e) region, domain; (fig) field, sphere, realm.

bereichern [bə'raiçərn] v enrich. **sich bereichern** acquire wealth, get rich.

bereit [bə'rait] adj ready, prepared. **bereiten** v prepare, make ready. **bereit**‖**halten** v keep in readiness. **-machen**

v make ready. **Bereitschaft** *f* readiness.
bereit‖stehen *v* be ready. **–stellen** *v*
make ready, prepare. **Bereitung** *f (pl -en)*
preparation. **bereitwillig** *adj* ready.

bereuen [bəˈrɔyən] *v* regret, repent.

Berg [bɛrk] *m (pl -e)* mountain. **bergab**
adv downhill. **Bergarbeiter** *m* miner. **ber-**
gauf *adv* uphill. **Bergbau** *m* mining.

*bergen [ˈbɛrgən] *v* conceal; *(schützen)*
protect; *(Güter)* recover.

Bergführer [ˈbɛrkfyːrər] *m* mountain
guide.

bergig [ˈbɛrgiç] *adj* mountainous, hilly.
Berg‖leute *pl* miners. **–mann** *m* miner.
bergmännisch *adj* mining. **Berg‖rutsch** *m*
landslide. **–steigen** *neut* mountain
climbing. **–steiger** *m* (mountain) climber, mountaineer.

Bergung [ˈbɛrgun] *f (pl -en)* rescue;
(Schiff) salvage. **–sarbeiten** *f pl* salvage
or rescue operations.

Bergwerk [ˈbɛrkvɛrk] *neut* mine, pit.

Bericht [bəˈriçt] *m (pl -e)* report, account.
berichten *v* report, give an account. **Ber-**
ichterstatter *m (pl -)* reporter; *(Radio)*
commentator, correspondent.

berichtigen [bəˈriçtigən] *v* correct,
amend; *(Schulden)* pay. **Berichtigung** *f*
correction; *(Schulden)* settlement.

beritten [bəˈritən] *adj* mounted.

Bernstein [ˈbɛrnʃtain] *m* amber.

berüchtigt [bəˈryçtiçt] *adj* notorious, infamous.

berücksichtigen [bəˈrykziçtigən] *v* keep in
mind, consider, take account of. **Berück-**
sichtigung *f* consideration.

Beruf [bəˈruːf] *m (pl -e)* occupation, job,
profession; *(Gewerbe)* trade. **beruf‖en** *v*
appoint; *(kommen lassen)* summon, send
for. **–lich** *adj* professional, vocational.
Berufs‖ausbildung *f* vocational training.
–krankheit *f* occupational disease.
–schule *f* vocational school, technical
college. **berufstätig** *adj* employed. **Beruf-**
stätigkeit *f* employment, professional
activity. **Berufung** *f (pl -en)* appointment; *(Jur)* appeal.

beruhen [bəˈruːən] *v* rest (on), be founded
(on).

beruhigen [bəˈruːigən] *v* pacify, calm.
beruhigend *adj* calming. **Beruhigung** *f*
calming, pacification. **Beruhigungsmittel**
neut sedative.

berühmt [bəˈryːmt] *adj* famous, celebrat-

ed. **Berühmtheit** *f* fame; *(Person)* celebrity.

berühren [bəˈryːrən] *v* touch, handle;
(angrenzen) border; *(angehen)* concern;
(erwähnen) touch on.

besäen [bəˈzɛːən] *v* sow.

besänftigen [bəˈzɛnftigən] *v* soothe, calm
(down).

Besatzung [bəˈzatsun] *f (Mil)* garrison;
(Schiff, Flugzeug) crew; *(Pol)* occupation. **–szone** *f* occupied area (of a country).

beschädigen [bəˈʃɛːdigən] *v* damage.
Beschädigung *f* damage.

beschaffen [bəˈʃafən] *v* get, procure. *adj*
constituted.

beschäftigen [bəˈʃɛftigən] *v* employ; *(zu
tun geben)* occupy, keep busy. **beschäftigt**
adj employed; occupied, busy. **Beschäf-**
tigung *f (pl -en)* employment, occupation.

beschämen [bəˈʃɛːmən] *v* shame.

beschatten [bəˈʃatən] *v* shade; *(verfolgen)*
shadow.

beschauen [bəˈʃauən] *v* look at; *(prüfen)*
examine, look over. **Beschauer** *m (pl -)*
spectator, inspector. **beschaulich** *adj* con-
templative.

Bescheid [bəˈʃait] *m (pl -e)* information;
(Entscheidung) decision, ruling. **Bescheid**
geben/sagen give information, inform.
Bescheid wissen know the situation, be
well informed.

bescheinigen [bəˈʃainigən] *v* certify,
attest. **Bescheinigung** *f (pl -en)* certificate; *(Quittung)* receipt.

beschenken [bəˈʃɛnkən] *v* give a present
to, present (with).

bescheren [bəˈʃeːrən] *v* give presents.
Bescherung *f* giving (of presents). **eine**
schöne Bescherung a fine mess.

*beschießen [bəˈʃiːsən] *v* fire on, shell.
Beschießung *f* shelling, bombardment.

beschimpfen [bəˈʃimpfən] *v* insult.

Beschlag [bəˈʃlaːk] *m (pl Beschläge)*
clasp, catch; *(Jur)* seizure. **in Beschlag**
nehmen seize, confiscate. **beschlagen** *v*
cover, fit; *(Pferd)* shoe. **Beschlagnahme** *f*
(pl -n) confiscation, seizure.
beschlagnahmen *v* seize, confiscate.

beschleunigen [bəˈʃlɔynigən] *v* accelerate.
Beschleunigung *f* acceleration.

*beschließen [bəˈʃliːsən] *v* decide,
resolve; *(beendigen)* terminate, end.

Beschluß [bə'ʃlus] m (pl Beschlüsse) decision, resolution; (Ende) end, close.

beschmutzen [bə'ʃmutsən] v dirty, soil.

*beschneiden [bə'ʃnaidən] v cut, prune, clip; (Kind) circumcize. **Beschneidung** f circumcision.

beschränken [bə'ʃrɛnkən] v restrict, limit. **beschränkt** adj limited, confined. **Beschränkung** f limitation.

*beschreiben [bə'ʃraibən] v describe. **Beschreibung** f description.

beschuldigen [bə'ʃuldigən] v accuse. **Beschuldigte(r)** m accused, defendant. **Beschuldigung** f accusation.

beschützen [bə'ʃytsən] v protect.

Beschwerde [bə'ʃverdə] f (pl -n) complaint. **beschweren** v burden. **sich beschweren über** complain about. **beschwerlich** adj troublesome; (mühselig) tedious.

beschwichtigen [bə'ʃviçtigən] v appease, pacify. **Beschwichtigung** f allaying, appeasement.

beschwipst [bə'ʃvipst] adj (umg.) tipsy.

*beschwören [bə'ʃvœırən] v swear (on oath); (Person) implore, beg; (Erinnerungen, Geister) conjure up.

besehen [bə'zeːən] v look at, inspect.

beseitigen [bə'zaitigən] v remove, get rid of, eliminate; (Schwierigkeiten) overcome. **Beseitigung** f removal, elimination.

Besen ['beːzən] m (pl -) broom.

besessen [bə'zesən] adj possessed.

besetzen [bə'zetsən] v (Platz) occupy, take; (Mil) occupy; (Kleid) trim, decorate; (Posten) fill. **besetzt** adj (Theater) full; (Platz) taken; (WC) occupied, engaged; (Telef) engaged. **Besetzung** f occupation; (Theater) casting.

besichtigen [bə'ziçtigən] v inspect, view. **Besichtigung** f inspection; (Sehenswürdigkeiten) sightseeing.

besiedeln [bə'ziːdəln] v colonize.

besiegen [bə'ziːgən] v conquer.

*besinnen [bə'zinən] v **sich besinnen** remember, recollect. **Besinnen** neut reflection, consideration. **Besinnung** f contemplation; (Bewußtsein) consciousness. **besinnungslos** adj unconscious, senseless.

Besitz [bə'zits] m (pl -e) possession. **besitzen** v possess, own. **Besitzer** m (pl -) owner.

besoffen [bə'zɔfən] adj (vulgär) drunk.

Besoldung [bə'zɔlduŋ] f (pl -en) salary, wages pl.

besonder [bə'zɔndər] adj special, particular. **besonders** adv especially, particularly. **nichts Besonderes** nothing special, not up to much.

besonnen [bə'zɔnən] adj sensible, prudent. **Besonnenheit** f prudence.

besorgen [bə'zɔrgən] v take care of, see to; (beschaffen) obtain. **Besorgnis** f (pl -se) apprehension, anxiety. **besorgniserregend** adj giving cause for worry. **besorgt** adj anxious, worried. **Besorgung** f (pl -en) management; (Einkauf) purchase.

bespannen [bə'ʃpanən] v (verkleiden) cover; (Fahrzeug) harness; (Musik) string. **Bespannung** f (pl -en) covering; (Pferde) team (of horses).

*besprechen [bə'ʃprɛçən] v discuss; (Buch, Film) review. **Besprechung** f discussion; (Buch, Film) review.

besser ['besər] adj better. **desto besser** so much the better. **um so besser** all the better. **er ist besser dran** he is better off. **bessern** v improve, make better. **Besserung** f (pl -en) improvement.

best [best] adj best. **am besten** adv best. **aufs Beste** in the best possible way. **besten Dank!** many thanks!

Bestand [bə'ʃtant] m (pl Bestände) continuance, duration; (Vorrat) stock, supply.

beständig [bə'ʃtɛndiç] adj constant, lasting.

Bestandteil [bə'ʃtanttail] m component, part.

bestärken [bə'ʃterkən] v strengthen; (bestätigen) confirm. **Bestärkung** f strengthening; confirmation.

bestätigen [bə'ʃtɛtigən] v confirm, verify. **bestätigend** adj confirmatory. **Bestätigung** f (pl -en) confirmation.

bestatten [bə'ʃtatən] v bury. **Bestattung** f (pl -en) funeral, burial.

*bestechen [bə'ʃtɛçən] v bribe, corrupt. **bestechlich** adj corrupt, bribable. **Bestechung** f bribery, corruption.

Besteck [bə'ʃtɛk] neut (pl -e) cutlery; knife, fork, and spoon; (Med) (medical) instruments pl.

*bestehen [bə'ʃteːən] v exist, be; (überstehen) undergo; (Examen) pass; (fortdauern) endure, survive. **bestehen auf** insist on. **bestehen aus** consist of.

*besteigen [bə'ʃtaigən] v climb, ascend; (*Pferd*) mount. **Besteigung** f ascent; mounting.

bestellen [bə'ʃtɛlən] v (*Waren*) order; (*Zimmer*) reserve; (*Boden*) cultivate. **Bestellung** f order; reservation; cultivation.

bestenfalls ['bɛstənfals] adv at best. **bestens** adv in the best manner.

besteuern [bə'ʃtɔyərn] v tax. **Besteuerung** f taxation.

Bestie ['bɛstiə] f (pl -n) beast.

bestimmen [bə'ʃtimən] v determine, fix; (*ernennen*) appoint. **bestimmt** adj definite, certain. **Bestimmung** f determination; (*Vorschrift*) regulation; (*Ernennung*) appointment.

bestrafen [bə'ʃtraːfən] v punish. **Bestrafung** f punishment.

Bestrahlung [bə'ʃtraːluŋ] f radiation; (*Med*) radiotherapy.

bestreben [bə'ʃtreːbən] v **sich bestreben** strive, endeavour. **Bestreben** neut or **Bestrebung** f endeavour, exertion.

*bestreiten [bə'ʃtraitən] v dispute, contest.

bestürmen [bə'ʃtyrmən] v assault, storm.

bestürzen [bə'ʃtyrtsən] v startle, disconcert. **bestürzt** adj taken aback, dismayed.

Besuch [bə'zuːx] m (pl -e) visit, call. **Besuch haben** have visitors. **ich bin zu Besuch hier** I am visiting, I am a visitor. **besuchen** v visit, see; (*Schule*) go to, attend. **Besucher** m (pl -) visitor, caller; (*Gast*) guest.

betagt [bə'taːkt] adj aged, elderly.

betasten [bə'tastən] v finger, touch.

betätigen [bə'tɛːtigən] v put into action; (*Maschine*) operate; (*Bremse*) apply. **sich betätigen** occupy oneself, work; (*activ sein*) be active, participate. **Betätigung** f operation; (*Teilnahme*) participation.

betäuben [bə'tɔybən] v stun; (*narkotisieren*) anaesthetize. **Betäubung** f anaesthesia. **Betäubungsmittel** neut anaesthetic.

Bete ['beːtə] f beet, beetroot.

beteiligen [bə'tailigən] v give a share to. **sich beteiligen** participate in. **beteiligt sein an** be involved in. **Beteiligung** f (pl -en) participation; (*Anteil*) share.

beten ['beːtən] v pray.

beteuern [bə'tɔyərn] v affirm, declare; (*Unschuld*) protest. **Beteuerung** f (pl -en) affirmation, declaration.

Beton [be'tõ] m concrete.

betonen [bə'toːnən] v stress, emphasize. **Betonung** f stress, emphasis.

Betracht [bə'traxt] m (unz.) consideration. **außer Betracht lassen** leave aside, not consider. **in Betracht ziehen** take into consideration. **betrachten** v look at; (*ansehen als*) consider. **beträchtlich** adj considerable. **Betrachtung** f consideration.

Betrag [bə'traːk] m (pl Beträge) amount. **betragen** v amount to. **sich betragen** behave. **Betragen** neut behaviour.

betrauen [bə'trauən] v entrust.

Betreff [bə'trɛf] m (unz.) **in Betreff** with regard to, concerning. **betreff|en** v concern; (*befallen*) befall; (*erwischen*) surprise. **-end** adj in question. prep concerning. **-s** prep concerning.

*betreiben [bə'traibən] v carry on, follow; (*Studien*) pursue; (*Maschine*) operate.

*betreten [bə'treːtən] v tread on; (*eintreten*) enter. adj surprised, disconcerted.

Betrieb [bə'triːp] m (pl -e) firm, concern, business; (*Wirken*) running; (*Verkehr*) bustle, activity. **außer Betrieb** out of order. **in Betrieb** in operation, working, in use. **in Betrieb setzen** put into operation. **Betriebs‖anlage** f industrial plant, works. **-anweisung** f operating instructions pl. **-führer** m works manager. **-kosten** pl operating costs. **-rat** m works council. **-unfall** m industrial accident.

*betrinken [bə'triŋkən] v **sich betrinken** get drunk.

betroffen [bə'trɔfən] adj perplexed, disconcerted.

betrüben [bə'tryːbən] v grieve, depress. **betrübt** adj sad.

Betrug [bə'truːk] m (unz.) fraud, swindle, deception. **betrügen** v cheat, deceive. **Betrüger** m (pl -) cheat, swindler. **betrügerisch** adj deceitful.

betrunken [bə'truŋkən] adj drunk. **Betrunkenheit** f drunkenness.

Bett [bɛt] neut (pl -en) bed. **ins Bett gehen** go to bed. **-decke** f bedspread.

betteln ['bɛtəln] v beg.

bettlägerig ['bɛtlɛigəriç] adj bedridden.

Bettler ['bɛtlər] m (pl -) beggar.

Bett‖wäsche f bed linen. **-zeug** neut bedding.

beugen ['bɔygən] v bend; (*Gramm*) inflect. **sich beugen** bow; (*sich fügen*) submit. **Beugung** f bow, bend(ing).

Beule ['bɔylə] f (*pl* -n) swelling, lump; (*Metall*) dent.

beunruhigen [bə'unruːigən] v disturb, make anxious. **beunruhigt sein** be anxious *or* alarmed. **Beunruhigung** f agitation, uneasiness.

beurkunden [bə'uːrkundən] v certify, attest. **Beurkundung** f certification.

beurlauben [bə'uːrlaubən] v grant leave to, send on holiday.

beurteilen [bə'urtailən] v judge. **Beurteilung** f judgment.

Beute ['bɔytə] f (*unz.*) booty, loot.

Beutel ['bɔytəl] m (*pl* -) bag; (*Geld*) purse; (*Zool*) pouch. **beuteln** v be baggy, bulge. **Beuteltier** *neut* marsupial.

bevölkern [bə'fœlkərn] v populate. **dicht/spärlich bevölkert** densely/sparsely populated. **Bevölkerung** f population.

bevollmächtigen [bə'fɔlmɛçtigən] v authorize. **bevollmächtigt** *adj* authorized. **Bevollmächtigte(r)** m authorized agent *or* representative; (*Jur*) attorney.

bevor [bə'foːr] *conj* before.

*bevorstehen [bə'foːrʃteːən] v be imminent, be at hand.

bevorzugen [bə'foːrtsuːgən] v favour, prefer.

bewachen [bə'vaxən] v guard.

bewaffnen [bə'vafnən] v arm. **bewaffnet** *adj* armed. **Bewaffnung** f armament.

bewahren [bə'vaːrən] v keep, preserve.

bewähren [bə'vɛːrən] v **sich bewähren** prove true. **bewährt** *adj* tried, proved. **Bewahrung** f (*pl* -en) preservation.

Bewährung [bə'vɛːruŋ] f trial, test; (*Jur*) probation. **-sfrist** f probation (period).

bewältigen [bə'vɛltigən] v overpower; (*Schwierigkeit*) master, overcome.

bewässern [bə'vɛsərn] v irrigate. **Bewässerung** f irrigation.

*bewegen [bə'veːgən] v move; (*rühren*) move, touch; (*überreden*) persuade. **sich bewegen** move. **Beweggrund** m motive. **beweglich** *adj* movable, mobile. **bewegt** *adj* excited; (*gerührt*) touched, moved. **Bewegung** f (*pl* -en) motion, movement; (*Rührung*) emotion. **in Bewegung setzen** set in motion.

Beweis [bə'vais] m (*pl* -e) proof, evidence.

beweisen v prove, demonstrate.

Beweis‖führung f reasoning, demonstration. **-stück** *neut* (piece of) evidence, exhibit.

bewerben [bə'vɛrbən] v **sich bewerben um** apply for. **Bewerber** m applicant, candidate. **Bewerbung** f application, candidacy.

bewerkstelligen [bə'vɛrkʃtɛligən] v accomplish, achieve.

bewerten [bə'veːrtən] v value, rate.

bewilligen [bə'viligən] v allow, grant. **Bewilligung** f (*pl* -en) grant, permission.

bewirken [bə'virkən] v bring about, cause.

bewirten [bə'virtən] v entertain. **bewirtschaften** v manage, administer. **Bewirtung** f hospitality.

bewohnbar [bə'voːnbaːr] *adj* inhabitable. **bewohnen** v live in, inhabit. **Bewohner** m (*pl* -) inhabitant, resident.

bewölken [bə'vœlkən] v **sich bewölken** (*Himmel*) become cloudy. **bewölkt** *adj* overcast, cloudy.

Bewunderer [bə'vundərər] m (*pl* -) admirer. **bewundern** v admire. **bewundernswert** *adj* admirable. **Bewunderung** f admiration.

bewußt [bə'vust] *adj* conscious, deliberate; (*klar*) aware, conscious. **ich bin mir meines Fehlers bewußt** I am aware of my mistake. **Bewußtheit** f awareness. **bewußtlos** *adj* unconscious. **Bewußt‖losigkeit** f unconsciousness. **-sein** *neut* consciousness. **zu Bewußtsein kommen** regain consciousness.

bezahlen [bə'tsaːlən] v pay for; (*Rechnung*) pay. **Bezahlung** f payment, settlement.

bezaubern [bə'tsaubərn] v enchant, charm, bewitch. **Bezauberung** f spell.

bezeichnen [bə'tsaiçnən] v designate; (*Zeichen*) mark. **Bezeichnung** f (*Beschreibung*) description; (*Name*) designation; (*Zeichen*) mark.

bezeugen [bə'tsɔygən] v testify (to), provide evidence of.

*beziehen [bə'tsiːən] v cover; (*Geige*) string; (*Wohnung*) move into; (*Posten*) take up; (*Gehalt*) draw; (*erhalten, kaufen*) procure. **das Bett frisch beziehen** change the sheets. **sich beziehen auf** refer to, relate to. **Beziehung** f relation(ship). **in Beziehung auf** with regard *or* respect to. **beziehungsweise** *adv* respectively, or.

Bezirk [bə'tsirk] m (pl -e) district, area.
Bezug [bə'tsuːk] m (pl Bezüge) covering; (Kopfkissen) pillow-case; (Waren) supply, purchase. **bezüglich** prep concerning, relating to.
bezweifeln [bə'tsvaifəln] v doubt.
*bezwingen** [bə'tsviŋən] v conquer, overcome. **sich bezwingen** control or restrain oneself.
Bibel ['biːbəl] f (pl -n) Bible. **–stelle** f (biblical) text or passage.
Biber ['biːbər] m (pl -) beaver.
Bibliographie [bibliogra'fiː] f (pl -n) bibliography. **bibliographisch** adj bibliographic.
Bibliothek [biblio'teːk] f (pl -en) library. **–ar** m (pl -e) librarian.
biblisch ['biːbliʃ] adj biblical.
bieder ['biːdər] adj honest, upright, respectable. **Biedermann** m honest man or fellow.
*biegen** ['biːgən] v bend; (beim Fahren, usw.) turn. **biegsam** adj supple; (f –ügsam) yielding. **Biegung** f (pl -en) bend; curve.
Biene ['biːnə] f (pl -n) bee. **Bienen||stich** m bee sting; (Kuchen) almond pastry. **–stock** m beehive. **–wabe** f honeycomb. **–zucht** f beekeeping. **–züchter** m beekeeper.
Bier [biːr] neut (pl -e) beer. **–faß** neut beer barrel, cask. **–garten** m beer garden.
Biest [biːst] neut (pl -er) beast; (fig) brute.
*bieten** ['biːtən] v offer; (Versteigerung) bid.
Bigamie [biga'miː] f bigamy. **bigamisch** adj bigamous.
bigott [bi'gɔt] adj bigoted.
Bikini [bi'kiːni] m (pl -s) bikini.
Bilanz [bi'lants] f (pl -en) balance (sheet), annual accounts.
Bild [bilt] neut (pl -er) picture; (Buch) illustration; (Vorstellung) idea.
bilden ['bildən] v form, shape; (erziehen) educate; (darstellen) constitute.
Bilder||buch neut picture book. **–galerie** f (picture) gallery. **Bild||feld** neut field of vision. **–hauer** m sculptor. **bildhübsch** adj very pretty, lovely. **Bildnis** neut (pl –se) image, likeness. **bildsam** adj plastic, flexible; (fig) docile. **Bildsäule** f statue.
Bildung ['bilduŋ] f (pl -en) formation; (Erziehung) education.

Billard ['biljart] neut (pl -e) billiards; (Tisch) billiard table. **–stock** m cue.
Billett [bil'jet] neut (pl -s or -e) ticket; (Zettel) note.
billig ['biliç] adj cheap, inexpensive; (gerecht) fair. **–en** v approve. **Billig||keit** f cheapness, fairness. **–ung** f approval.
Billion [bil'joːn] f (pl -en) billion, (US) trillion.
Bimsstein ['bimsʃtain] m pumice stone.
binär [bi'neːr] adj binary.
Binde ['bində] f (pl -n) bandage; (Arm) sling. **–haut** f conjunctiva.
*binden** ['bindən] v bind, tie. **Bind||estrich** m hyphen. **–faden** m string. **–ung** f binding; (Verpflichtung) obligation.
binnen ['binən] prep within. **Binnenhandel** m internal trade.
Biograph [bio'graf] m (pl -en) biographer. **–ie** f biography. **biographisch** adj biographical.
Biologe [bio'loːgə] m (pl -n) biologist. **Biologie** f biology. **biologisch** adj biological.
Birke ['birkə] f (pl -n) birch.
Birne ['birnə] f (pl -n) pear; (Glühbirne) light-bulb.
bis [bis] prep (räumlich) as far as, (up) to; (zeitlich) until, till, to. conj until, till. **bis an, bis nach,** or **bis zu** up to, as far as. **bis jetzt** until now. **bis morgen** by tomorrow; (Gruß) see you tomorrow.
Bischof ['biʃɔf] m (pl Bischöfe) bishop. **bischöflich** adj episcopal.
bisher [bis'heːr] adv until now, hitherto. **–ig** adj until now, previous.
Biß [bis] m (pl Bisse) bite. **ein bißchen** a bit, a little.
bisweilen [bis'vailən] adv occasionally, sometimes.
bitte ['bitə] interj please. **Bitte** f request. **bitten** v request, ask; (anflehen) beg, implore.
bitter ['bitər] adj bitter. **Bitter||keit** f bitterness. **–salz** neut Epsom salts. **bittersüß** adj bittersweet.
Bizeps ['bitseps] m (pl -e) biceps.
Blamage [bla'maːʒə] f (pl -n) disgrace. **blamieren** v disgrace, compromise.
blank [blaŋk] adj bright, polished; (rein) clean; (bloß) bare.
blanko ['blaŋko] adj blank. **Blankoscheck** m blank cheque.

Blase ['blaɪzə] f (pl -n) bubble; (Haut) blister; (Harn) bladder. **blasen** v blow.
blasiert [bla'ziːrt] adj blasé, conceited.
Blasinstrument ['blaɪzɪnstrumɛnt] neut wind instrument.
blaß [blas] adj pale. **Blässe** f paleness, pallor. **bläßlich** adj pale, palish.
Blatt [blat] neut (pl Blätter) leaf; (Papier) sheet; (Zeitung) newspaper; (Klinge) blade. **blätterabwerfend** adj deciduous. **blättern** v (Buch) leaf through. **Blätterteig** m puff pastry. **Blatt‖grün** neut chlorophyll. **-laus** f greenfly, aphid.
blau [blau] adj blue; (umg.) drunk. **blaues Auge** black eye. **Blau** neut blue.
Blech [blɛç] neut (pl -e) sheet metal, tin. **-bläser** f (Musik) brass (section). **-dose** f tin-can.
blecken ['blɛkən] show, bare (teeth).
Blei [blai] neut (pl -e) lead.
*****bleiben** ['blaibən] v remain, stay. **bleiben bei** keep or stick to.
bleich [blaiç] adj pale, faded. **Bleiche** f paleness. **bleichen** v black; (farblos werden) grow pale, fade. **Bleich‖mittel** neut bleach(ing agent). **-sucht** f anaemia. **bleichsüchtig** adj anaemic.
Bleistift ['blaiʃtɪft] m (pl -e) pencil.
Blende ['blɛndə] f (pl -n) blind, shutter; (Foto) shutter. **blenden** v blind, dazzle. **-d** adj dazzling, brilliant.
Blick [blik] m (pl -e) glance, look; (Aussicht) view. **blicken** v look.
blind [blint] adj blind. **Blind‖darm** m (Anat) appendix. **-darmentzündung** f appendicitis. **-e(r)** m blind man. **-enhund** m guide dog. **-enschrift** f braille. **-gänger** m dud (bomb or shell). **-heit** f blindness. **blindlings** adv blindly.
blinken ['blɪŋkən] v sparkle, twinkle, glitter. **Blinker** m (Mot) indicator. **Blinklicht** neut flashing light.
blinzeln ['blɪntsəln] v blink, wink.
Blitz [blits] m (pl -e) lightning. **blitzen** v flash, emit flashes. **Blitzlicht** neut (Foto) flash, flashlight. **blitz‖sauber** adj spruce, very clean. **-schnell** adj quick as lightning. **Blitzschlag** m flash of lightning.
Block [blɔk] m (pl Blöcke) block; (Papier) pad. **-ade** f blockade. **-flöte** f (Musik) recorder. **blockieren** v blockade, block. **Blockschrift** f block letters.
blöd(e) [blœt, 'blœːdə] adj silly, daft. **Blöd‖heit** f stupidity, silliness. **-sinn** m idiocy. **blödsinnig** adj idiotic, silly.

blöken ['blœkən] v bleat.
blond [blɔnt] adj blond, fair-haired. **Blondine** f blonde.
bloß [bloːs] adj bare, simple. adv only, merely.
Blöße ['blœːsə] f nakedness; (fig) weakness.
bloßlegen ['bloːsleːgən] v reveal, expose.
blühen ['blyːən] v bloom, flower. **blühend** adj blooming; (fig) flourishing.
Blume ['bluːmə] f (pl -n) flower; (Wein) bouquet. **Blumen‖beet** neut flowerbed. **-blatt** neut petal. **-kohl** m cauliflower. **-muster** neut floral pattern. **-strauß** m bunch of flowers, bouquet. **-topf** m flowerpot. **-zwiebel** f bulb.
Bluse ['bluːzə] f (pl -n) blouse.
Blut [bluːt] neut blood. **-druck** m blood pressure. **blutdurstig** adj bloodthirsty.
Blüte ['blyːtə] f (pl -n) blossom, bloom.
bluten ['bluːtən] v bleed. **Blut‖gefäß** neut blood vessel. **-gerinnsel** neut blood clot. **-gruppe** f blood group. **blutig** adj bloody. **Blut‖übertragung** f blood transfusion. **-untersuchung** f blood test.
Bö [bœː] f (pl -en) squall, gust of wind.
Bock [bɔk] m (pl Böcke) (Schaf-) ram; (Ziegen-, Reh-) buck; (Sport) horse. **bockig** adj obstinate. **Bockwurst** f saveloy, large Frankfurter.
Boden ['boːdən] m (pl Böden) (Erde) ground; (Fuß-) floor; (Dach-) loft; (Fluß-, Meeres-) bottom, bed. **bodenlos** adj bottomless.
Bogen ['boːgən] m (pl -) curve, arch; (Waffe, auch für Geige) bow. **-schießen** neut archery. **-schütze** m archer.
Bohne ['boːnə] f (pl -n) bean.
bohren ['boːrən] v bore, drill. **Bohrer** m (pl -) borer, drill. **Bohrmaschine** f drill.
Boje ['boːjə] f (pl -n) buoy.
Bollwerk ['bɔlvɛrk] neut (pl -e) bulwark.
Bolzen ['bɔltsən] m (pl -) peg; (Tech) bolt; (Pfeil) arrow, bolt.
bombardieren [bɔmbar'diːrən] v bombard.
Bombe ['bɔmbə] f (pl -n) bomb. **Bomben‖angriff** m bombing raid. **-anschlag** m (terrorist) bombing. **-flugzeug** neut bomber.
Bonbon [bõ'bõ] neut (pl -s) sweet, (US) candy.
Boot [boːt] neut (pl -e) boat.

Bord[1] [bɔrt] *neut* (*pl* -e) board.

Bord[2] *m* (*pl* -e) edge, rim. **an Bord gehen** go aboard, board.

Bordell [bɔr'dɛl] *neut* (*pl* -e) brothel.

borgen ['bɔrgən] *v* (*entleihen*) borrow; (*verleihen*) lend. **Borger** *m* (*pl* -) (*Entleiher*) borrower; (*Verleiher*) lender.

Borke ['bɔrkə] *f* (*pl* -n) bark.

Börse ['bœrzə] *f* (*pl* -n) stock exchange; (*Beutel*) purse. **-nmakler** *m* stockbroker.

Borste ['bɔrstə] *f* (*pl* -n) bristle.

bös(e) ['bœz(ə)] *adj* bad; (*Mensch*) wicked; (*Geist*) evil; (*Kind*) naughty; (*wütend*) cross. **bösartig** *adj* malicious; (*Med*) malignant. **Böse** *neut* mischief; *m* evil person, devil.

boshaft ['bɔshaft] *adj* malicious, spiteful. **Boß** [bɔs] *m* (*pl* Bosse) boss.

böswillig ['bœːzvɪlɪç] *adj* malicious, malevolent. **Böswilligkeit** *f* malice.

Botanik [bo'taːnɪk] *f* botany. **-er** *m* (*pl* -) botanist. **botanisch** *adj* botanical.

Bote ['boːtə] *m* (*pl* -n) messenger. **Bot||engang** *m* errand. **-schaft** *f* message; (*Gesandtschaft*) embassy. **-schafter** *m* ambassador.

Bottich ['bɔtɪç] *m* (*pl* -e) tub, vat.

Bowle ['boːlə] *f* (*pl* -n) (*Getränk*) punch, fruit cup; (*Gefäß*) punchbowl.

boxen ['bɔksən] *v* box. **Boxer** *m* (*pl* -) boxer. **Boxkampf** *m* boxing match.

brach [braːx] *adj* fallow, untilled.

Branche ['brãːʃə] *f* (*pl* -n) (*Geschäftszweig*) line of business, trade; (*Abteilung*) department.

Brand [brant] *m* (*pl* Brände) fire, blaze; (*Med*) gangrene; (*Bot*) mildew. **-bombe** *f* incendiary bomb. **brandmarken** *v* brand, stigmatize. **Brand||stifter** *m* arsonist, fire-raiser. **-stiftung** *f* arson.

Brandung ['brandʊŋ] *f* (*pl* -en) surf, breakers *pl*.

Branntwein ['brantvain] *m* brandy.

braten ['braːtən] *v* roast; (*in der Pfanne*) fry; (*auf dem Rost*) grill. **Braten** *m* roast (meat), joint. **Brat||fisch** *m* fried fish. **-hähnchen** *neut* roast chicken. **-kartoffeln** *pl* fried potatoes. **-pfanne** *f* frying pan. **-wurst** *f* fried sausage.

Bräu [brɔy] *neut* brew; (*Brauerei*) brewery.

Brauch [braux] *m* (*pl* Bräuche) custom, usage. **brauchbar** *adj* serviceable; usable; (*nützlich*) useful. **brauchen** *v* need, require; (*gebrauchen*) use.

brauen ['brauən] *v* brew. **Brauerei** *f* brewery.

braun [braun] *adj* brown. **Braun** *neut* brown.

Braunschweig ['braunʃvaik] *neut* Brunswick.

Brause ['brauzə] *f* (*pl* -n) (*Dusche*) shower; (*Gießkanne*) rose; (*Limonade*) lemonade, pop. **-bad** *neut* shower.

Braut [braut] *f* (*pl* Bräute) (*am Hochzeitstag*) bride; (*Verlobte*) fiancée.

Bräutigam ['brɔytɪgam] *m* bridegroom.

Braut||jungfer *f* bridesmaid. **-kleid** *neut* wedding dress.

bräutlich ['brɔytlɪç] *adj* bridal.

brav [braːf] *adj* honest, worthy; (*tapfer*) brave; (*artig*) good, well-behaved.

brechen ['brɛçən] *v* break; (*Marmor*) quarry. **Bahn brechen** (*fig*) blaze a trail. **Brech||bohne** *f* French bean. **-mittel** *neut* emetic.

Brei [brai] *m* (*pl* -e) paste, pulp.

breit [brait] *adj* broad, wide. **Breite** *f* breadth, width; (*Geog*) latitude.

Bremse[1] ['brɛmzə] *f* (*pl* -n) brake. **bremsen** *v* brake. **Brems||licht** *neut* brake light, stop light. **-pedal** *neut* brake pedal.

Bremse[2] *f* (*pl* -n) horse-fly.

brennbar ['brɛnbaːr] *adj* combustible, inflammable. **brennen** *v* burn; (*Branntwein*) distill. **Brenn||erei** *f* distillery. **-nessel** *f* stinging nettle. **-punkt** *m* focus. **-stoff** *m* fuel.

Brett [brɛt] *neut* (*pl* -er) board; (*Regal*) shelf.

Brezel ['breːtsəl] *f* (*pl* -n) pretzel.

Brief [briːf] *m* (*pl* -e) letter. **-kasten** *m* letterbox. **-kopf** *m* letterhead. **brieflich** *adj* written. **Brief||marke** *f* (postage) stamp. **-tasche** *f* wallet, pocket book. **-träger** *m* postman.

Brigade [bri'gaːdə] *f* (*pl* -n) brigade.

brillant [bril'jant] *adj* brilliant.

Brille ['brilə] *f* (*pl* -n) spectacles, glasses; (*Schutz*) goggles.

bringen ['brɪŋən] *v* bring; (*mitnehmen, begleiten*) take; (*Zeitung*) print, publish; (*Theater*) present, put on. **es weit bringen** do well, go far. **ans Licht bringen** bring to light.

Brite ['britə] *m* (*pl* -n), **Britin** *f* (*pl* -nen) Briton.

bröckelig ['brœkəlɪç] *adj* crumbly. **bröckeln** *v* crumble.

Brocken ['brɔkən] m (pl -) crumb; (pl) scraps, bits and pieces.

Brombeere ['brɔmbeɪrə] f blackberry. **Brombeerstrauch** m blackberry bush, bramble.

Bronze ['brɔ̃sə] f (pl -n) bronze. **bronzefarben** adj bronze(-coloured).

Brosche ['brɔʃə] f (pl -n) brooch.

Broschüre [brɔ'ʃyɪrə] f (pl -n) brochure.

Brot [broɪt] neut (pl -e) bread; (Laib) loaf.

Brötchen ['brœɪtçən] neut bread roll.

Brot∥schnitte f slice (of bread). **–verdiener** m bread-winner.

Bruch [brux] m (pl Brüche) break; (Knochen) fracture; (Math) fraction; (Versprechen, Vertrag) breech; (Gesetz) violation, breech. **bruchfest** adj unbreakable.

brüchig [bryçiç] adj brittle.

Bruch∥landung f crash landing. **–stück** neut fragment. **–teil** m fraction.

Brücke ['brykə] f (pl -n) bridge.

Bruder ['bruɪdər] m (pl Brüder) brother.

brüderlich ['bryɪdaarliç] adj brotherly. **Brüderschaft** f brotherhood.

Brühe ['bryɪə] f (pl -n) broth; (Suppengrundlage) stock. **brühen** v scald. **brühheiß** adj boiling hot.

brüllen ['brylən] v bellow; (Sturm, Raubtier) roar. **Brüllfrosch** m bullfrog.

brummen ['brumən] growl; (Insekten) buzz, hum; (mürrisch sein) grumble; (umg.) go to prison, do time.

brünett [bry'nɛt] adj brunette, dark brown. **Brünette** f brunette.

Brunnen ['brunən] m (pl -) well; (Quelle) spring.

Brunst [brunst] f (pl Brünste) lust, ardour; (Tier) heat. **brünstig** adj lusty; (Tier) in heat.

Brüssel ['brysəl] neut Brussels.

Brust [brust] f (pl Brüste) breast, chest; (Frauen) breast. **–kasten** m chest. **–krebs** m breast cancer. **–schwimmen** neut breaststroke. **–warze** f nipple.

brutal [bru'taɪl] adj brutal.

brüten ['bryɪtən] v brood.

brutto ['bruto] adj gross. **Bruttogewicht** neut gross weight. **Bruttosozialprodukt** neut gross national product.

Bube ['buɪbə] m (pl -n) boy, lad; (Karten) jack, knave.

Buch [buɪx] neut (pl Bücher) book.

Buche ['buɪxə] f (pl -n) beech (tree).

buchen ['buɪçən] v record, enter (in a book).

Bücherei ['byçəraɪ] f (pl -en) library. **Bücherschrank** m bookcase.

Buchfink ['buɪçfiŋk] m chaffinch.

Buch∥halter m book-keeper. **–haltung** f book-keeping; accounts department. **–händler** m bookseller. **–handlung** f bookshop. **–macher** m bookmaker.

Büchse ['byksə] f (pl -n) box; (Blechdose) tin, can; (Gewehr) rifle.

Buchstabe ['buɪxʃtaɪbə] f (pl -n) letter (of the alphabet). **buchstabieren** v spell. **Buchstabierung** f spelling. **buchstäblich** adj literal.

Bucht [buxt] f (pl -en) bay.

Buckel ['bukəl] m (pl -n) hump, mound; (am Rücken) humpback. **buckelig** adj hunchbacked.

bücken ['bykən] v sich bücken stoop, bow.

Bude ['buɪdə] f (pl -n) booth; (Markt) stall; (umg.) lodgings, digs, room(s).

Budget [by'dʒeɪ] neut (pl -s) budget.

Büfett [by'fɛt] neut (pl -s) sideboard, dresser. **kaltes Büfett** cold buffet.

Büffel ['byfəl] m (pl -) buffalo.

Bug [buɪk] m (pl -e) (Schiff) bow; (Flugzeug) nose; (Pferd) shoulder.

Bügel ['byɪgəl] m (pl -) hoop, handle; (Kleider-) hanger; (Steig-) stirrup. **–brett** neut ironing board. **–eisen** neut iron. **bügelt** adj permanent press, non-iron. **bügeln** v iron.

bugsieren [bug'ziɪrən] v tow. **Bugsierer** m tugboat.

Bühne ['byɪnə] f (pl -n) stage. **Bühnen∥bild** neut set, scenery. **–dichter** m playwright. **–deutsch** neut high German, standard German.

Bulgare [bul'gaɪrə] m (pl -n), **Bulgarin** f (pl -nen) Bulgarian. **Bulgarien** neut Bulgaria. **bulgarisch** adj Bulgarian.

Bulle ['bulə] m (pl -n) bull; (umg.) cop.

Bummel ['buməl] m (pl -) stroll. **bummeln** v stroll; (nichts tun) loaf, loiter. **Bummel∥streik** m work-to-rule, go-slow. **–zug** m slow train, local (train).

Bund[1] [bunt] neut (pl -e) bundle; (Schlüssel, Radieschen, usw.) bunch.

Bund[2] m (pl Bünde) band; (Verein) association, league; (Staat) federation.

Bündel ['byndəl] neut (pl -) bundle, bunch. **bündeln** bundle (up).

Bundes‖bahn f federal railway, West German railway. **–haus** parliament buildings. **–präsident** m federal (West German) president. **–rat** m (BRD, Österreich) upper house (of parliament); (Schweiz) (Swiss) government. **–republik Deutschland (BRD)** f Federal Republic of Germany, West Germany. **–tag** m West German parliament, federal parliament. **–staat** m federal state.

Bündnis ['byntnɪs] neut (pl -se) alliance.

Bunker ['buŋkər] m (pl -) bunker.

bunt [bunt] adj brightly coloured, gay.

Bürde ['byrdə] f (pl -n) burden.

Burg [burk] f (pl -en) castle; (Festung) fort.

Bürge ['byrgə] m (pl -n) surety, guarantor. **bürgen** v guarantee, vouch for; (Jur) stand bail for.

Bürger ['byrgər] m (pl -) citizen; (Stadt) townsman; bourgeois. **–krieg** m civil war. **bürgerlich** adj bourgeois, middle-class; (Küche) simple, plain; (zivil) civilian. **Bürger‖meister** m mayor. **–recht** neut civil rights. **–schaft** f citizenry, citizens. **–stand** m middle class(es). **–steig** m pavement, (US) sidewalk.

Bürgschaft ['byrkʃaft] f (pl -en) surety, bond.

Büro [by'roː] neut (pl -s) office. **–klammer** f paperclip. **–krat** m (pl -en) bureaucrat. **–kratie** f bureaucracy. **bürokratisch** adj bureaucratic.

Bursche ['burʃə] m (pl -n) lad, fellow.

Bürste ['byrstə] f (pl -n) brush. **bürsten** v brush.

Busch [buʃ] m (pl Büsche) bush, shrub.

Büschel ['byʃəl] neut (pl -) bunch; (Haare) tuft.

buschig ['buʃiç] adj bushy.

Busen ['buːzən] m (pl -) breast. **–freund** m bosom friend.

Buße ['buːsə] f (pl -n) penance; (Geld) fine.

büßen ['byːsən] v do penance (for).

Büste ['byːstə] f (pl -n) bust. **–nhälter** m brassière.

Butter ['butər] f (unz.) butter. **–blume** f buttercup. **–brot** neut (slice of) bread and butter. **–brotpapier** neut greaseproof paper.

C

Café [ka'feː] neut (pl -s) café, coffee house.

campen ['kɛmpən] v camp. **Camper** m camper. **Camping** neut camping. **–platz** m camp(ing) site.

Caravan ['karavan] m (pl -s) caravan; (Kombiwagen) estate car.

Cellist [tʃe'lɪst] m (pl -en), **Cellistin** f (pl -nen) cellist. **Cello** neut cello.

Cembalo ['tʃɛmbalo] neut (pl -s) harpsichord.

Champagner [ʃam'panjər] m (pl -) champagne.

Champignon ['ʃampinjɔ] m (pl -s) mushroom.

Chance ['ʃãːsə] f (pl -n) chance. **Chancengleichheit** f equality of opportunity.

Chaos ['kaːɔs] neut (unz.) chaos. **chaotisch** adj chaotic.

Charakter ['karaktər] m (pl -e) character. **charakterisieren** v characterize. **charakteristisch** adj characteristic.

Chauffeur [ʃɔ'fœːr] m (pl -e) driver, chauffeur.

Chaussee [ʃo'seː] f (pl -n) highway, main road.

Chef [ʃɛf] m (pl -s) boss, head; (Arbeitgeber) employer.

Chemie [çe'miː] f (unz.) chemistry. **Chemikalien** f pl chemicals. **Chemiker** m (pl -) (industrial or research) chemist. **chemisch** adj chemical. **–e Reinigung** f dry cleaning.

China ['çiːna] neut China. **Chinese** m (pl -n), **Chinesin** f (pl -nen) Chinese (person). **chinesisch** adj Chinese.

Chirurg [çi'rurk] m (pl -en) surgeon. **–ie** f surgery. **chirurgisch** adj surgical.

Chlor [kloːr] neut (unz.) chlorine. **Chloroform** neut chloroform. **Chlorophyll** neut chlorophyll. **Chlorwasser** neut chlorinated water.

Cholera ['kolera] f (unz.) cholera.

Chor [koːr] m (pl Chöre) choir; (Gesang) chorus. **–direktor** m choirmaster.

Christ [krɪst] m (pl -en) Christian. **christlich** adj Christian. **Christ‖nacht** f Christmas Eve. **–us** m Christ.

Chrom [kroːm] neut (unz.) chromium; (Verchromung) chrome, chrome-plating. **chromiert** adj chrome-plated.

Chronik ['kroːnɪk] f (pl -en) chronicle. **chronisch** adj chronic.

Computer [kɔm'pjuːtər] *m* (*pl* -) computer.

Coupé [ku'peɪ] *neut* (*pl* -s) railway carriage.

Cousin [ku'zɛ̃] *m* (*pl* -s) (male) cousin. **-e** *f* (female) cousin.

Creme [kreɪm] *f* (*pl* -s) cream; (*Süßspeise*) cream pudding; (*Hautsalbe*) handcream, skincream.

D

da [da] *adv* (*örtlich*) there; (*zeitlich*) then. *conj* because, since. **da draußen/drinnen** out/in there. **da sein** be present. **da bin ich** here I am. **da siehst Du!** see! **da hingegen** whereas.

dabei [da'baɪ] *adv* close (by), near; (*bei diesem*) thereby; (*außerdem*) moreover. **dabei sein** be present. **es bleibt dabei** that is *or* remains settled. **was ist dabei?** what does it matter? **dabei sein, es zu tun** be on the point of doing it. **dabei bleiben** stick to one's opinion.

Dach [dax] *neut* (*pl* **Dächer**) roof. **-boden** *m* attic. **-fenster** *neut* skylight. **-gesellschaft** *f* holding company. **-kammer** *f* attic, garret. **-rinne** *f* gutter.

Dachs [daks] *m* (*pl* -e) badger. **-hund** *m* dachshund.

Dachziegel [daxtsiːgəl] *m* roof tile.

dadurch [da'durç] *adv* for this reason, in this way. **dadurch daß** because, since.

dafür [da'fyːr] *adv* for that; (*Gegenleistung*) in return. **dafür sein** be in favour (of it). **er kann nichts dafür** he can't help it.

dagegen [da'geɪgən] *adv* against it; (*Vergleich*) in comparison. *conj* on the contrary, however. **ich habe nichts dagegen** I have no objections. **er stimmt dagegen** he is voting against it.

daher [da'heːr] *adv* from there. *conj* hence, accordingly. **daher kommt es** hence it follows. **daher, daß** since, because.

dahin [da'hin] *adv* there, to that place.

dahinten [da'hintən] *adv* back there.

dahinter [da'hintər] *adv* behind it or that. **-kommen** *v* find out (about it), get to the bottom of it. **-stecken** *v* lie behind, be the cause.

damals [da'maɪls] *adv* then, at that time.

Dame ['daɪmə] *f* (*pl* -n) lady; (*Karten*) queen. **-brett** *neut* draughtboard, (*US*) checker-board. **Damen||binde** *f* sanitary towel. **-toilette** *f* ladies' lavatory. **-wäsche** *f* lingerie. **Dame||spiel** *neut* draughts. **-stein** *m* draughtsman, (*US*) checker.

Damm [dam] *m* (*pl* **Dämme**) dam; dike; (*Bahn-, Straßen-*) embankment.

dämmen ['dɛmən] *v* dam (up).

dämmern ['dɛmərn] *v* (*morgens*) dawn, grow light; (*abends*) grow dark. **es dämmert** dawn is breaking. **Dämmerung** *f* (*pl* -en) (*morgens*) dawn; (*abends*) twilight, dusk.

Dampf [dampf] *m* (*pl* **Dämpfe**) steam, vapour. **dampfen** *v* steam; (*Rauch*) smoke, fume.

dämpfen ['dɛmpfən] *v* (*Ofen*) damp down; (*Schall*) muffle; (*Licht*) soften; (*Küche*) steam.

Dampf||er ['dampfər] *m* (*pl* -) steamer, steamship. **-kessel** *m* boiler. **-kochtopf** *m* pressure cooker. **-maschine** *f* steam engine. **-schiff** *neut* steamship, steamer.

Däne ['dɛɪnə] *m* (*pl* -n), **Dänin** (*-nen*) Dane. **Dänemark** *neut* Denmark. **dänisch** *adj* Danish.

daneben [da'neɪbən] *adv* beside (it); (*außerdem*) besides.

Dank [daŋk] *m* (*unz.*) thanks. **dankbar** *adj* grateful, thankful. **Dankbarkeit** *f* gratitude. **danken** *v* thank.

dann [dan] *adv* then.

daran [da'ran] *adv* on *or* at *or* by it. **nahe daran sein zu** be on the point of. **nahe daran** close by. **gut daran sein** be well off.

darauf [da'rauf] *adv* on it; (*nachher*) afterwards. **es kommt darauf an (ob)** it depends (whether). **wie kommt er darauf?** why does he think so?

daraus [da'raus] *adv* out of it, from it. **es ist nichts daraus geworden** nothing has come of that.

*∗**darbieten** ['daːrbiːtən] *v* offer, present.

darein [da'rain] *adv* in(to) it; (*hierin*) therein.

darin [da'rin] *adv* in it, within; (*hierin*) therein.

darlegen ['daːrleɪgən] *v* explain, expound. **Darlegung** *f* explanation.

Darlehen ['daːrleːən] *neut* (*pl* -) loan.

Darm [darm] *m* (*pl* **Därme**) intestines *pl.* **-verstopfung** *f* constipation.

darstellen ['daːrʃtɛlən] *v* represent. **Darsteller** *m* (*Theater*) actor, performer. **Darstellung** *f* exhibition.

darüber [da'ryːbər] *adv* over it; (*davon*) about it; (*hinüber*) across. **darüber hinaus** over and above that, furthermore.

darum [da'rum] *adv* around *or* about it, for it. *conj* therefore.

darunter [da'runtər] *adv* under *or* beneath it; (*dazwischen*) among them; (*weniger*) less.

das [das] *art* the. *pron* which, that.

Dasein ['daːzain] *neut* (*unz.*) existence, being; (*Vorhandensein*) presence. **Daseinskampf** *m* struggle for existence.

daß [das] *conj* that.

Daten ['daːtən] *neut pl* data *pl.* **-verarbeitung** *f* data processing.

datieren [da'tiːrən] *v* date.

Datum ['daːtum] *neut* (*pl* **Daten**) date; (*Tatsache*) fact.

Dauer ['dauər] *f* (*unz.*) period (of time), duration. **-auftrag** *m* (*Bank*) standing order. **dauerhaft** *adj* lasting, durable. **Dauerkarte** *f* season ticket. **dauern** *v* last, continue. **-d** *adj* lasting, permanent. **Dauerwelle** *f* perm, permanent wave.

Daumen ['daumən] *m* (*pl* -) thumb.

Daunendecke ['daunəndɛkə] *f* eiderdown, continental quilt.

davon [da'fon] *adv* of *or* from it; (*weg*) away; (*darüber*) about it. **-kommen** *v* escape. **sich davonmachen** *v* (*umg.*) make one's escape, slide off.

davor [da'foːr] *adv* (*örtlich*) before it, in front of it; (*zeitlich*) before that *or* then. **Angst haben davor** be afraid of it. **eine Stunde davor** an hour earlier.

dawider [da'viːdər] *adv* against it.

dazu [da'tsuː] *adv* to it; (*Zweck*) for this (purpose), to that end; (*überdies*) in addition.

dazwischen [da'tsviʃən] *adv* between *or* among them. **-treten** *v* intervene.

Debatte [de'batə] *f* (*pl* -n) debate. **debattieren** *v* debate.

Debet ['deːbɛt] *neut* (*pl* -s) debit.

Debüt [de'byː] *neut* (*pl* -s) début.

Deck [dɛk] *neut* (*pl* -e) deck.

Decke ['dɛkə] *f* (*pl* -n) cover(ing); (*Bett*) blanket; (*Zimmer*) ceiling. **-l** *m* lid. **decken** *v* cover; set (the table).

Deck||mantel *m* pretext. **-name** *m* pseudonym. **-ung** *f* cover(ing); (*Verteidigung*) protection.

definieren [defi'niːrən] *v* define. **definitiv** *adj* definite.

Defizit ['deːfitsit] *neut* (*pl* -e) deficit.

degenerieren [degene'riːrən] *v* degenerate.

dehnbar ['deːnbaːr] *adj* elastic, malleable; (*Begriff*) loose, vague. **Dehnbarkeit** *f* elasticity, malleability. **dehnen** *v* stretch. **Dehnung** *f* stretching, expansion.

Deich [daiç] *m* (*pl* -e) dike.

Deichsel ['daiksəl] *f* (*pl* -n) shaft, pole. **deichseln** *v* (*umg.*) wangle.

dein [dain] *adj* your. *pron* yours. **deinerseits** *adv* on *or* for your part. **deinesgleichen** *pron* your likes, people like you. **deinethalben, deinetwegen,** *or* **deinetwillen** *adv* for your sake. **deinige** *pron* **der, die, das deinige** yours.

dekadent [deka'dɛnt] *adj* decadent. **Dekadenz** *f* decadence.

Dekan [de'kaːn] *m* (*pl* -e) dean.

deklamieren [dekla'miːrən] *v* declaim.

deklarieren [dekla'riːrən] *v* declare.

Deklination [deklinatsi'oːn] *f* (*pl* -en) declension. **deklinieren** *v* decline.

Dekor [de'koːr] *m* (*pl* -s) decoration(s). **dekorieren** *v* decorate.

Dekret [de'kreːt] *neut* (*pl* -e) decree.

delegieren [dele'giːrən] *v* delegate. **Delegierte(r)** *m* delegate.

delikat [deli'kaːt] *adj* (*Person, Angelegenheit*) delicate; (*Speise*) delicious. **Delikatesse** *f* (*pl* -n) delicacy.

Delikt [de'likt] *neut* (*pl* -e) crime.

Delphin [dɛl'fiːn] *m* (*pl* -e) dolphin.

dem [deːm] *art* to the. *pron* to this *or* that (one); (*wem*) to whom, to which.

Dementi [de'mɛnti] *neut* (*pl* -s) (official) denial. **dementieren** *v* deny.

demgemäß [deːmgəmɛɪs] *adv* accordingly.

Demission [demisi'oːn] *f* (*pl* -en) resignation. **demissionieren** *v* resign.

demnach [deːmnaːx] *adv* accordingly.

demnächst [deːmnɛːçst] *adv* shortly, soon.

Demokrat [demo'kraːt] *m* (*pl* -en) democrat. **-ie** *f* democracy. **demokratisch** *adj* democratic.

demolieren [demo'liːrən] *v* demolish.

Demonstrant [demon'ʃtrant] *m* (*pl* -en) demonstrator. **Demonstration** *f* (*pl* -en) demonstration. **demonstrieren** v demonstrate. **demonstrativ** adj demonstrative.

Demut ['demuːt] f (unz.) humility. **demütig** adj humble. **-en** v humiliate, humble. **Demütigung** f (pl **-en**) humiliation.

demzufolge [demtsufɔlgə] adv accordingly. pron according to which.

den [deɪn] art the. pl to the. pron whom, which. pl to these. **denen** pron to whom or which.

Denkart ['deŋkaɪrt] f way of thinking. **denk‖bar** adj conceivable, thinkable. **-en** v think. **Denk‖en** neut thinking, thought. **-er** m (pl **-**) thinker. **-freiheit** f freedom of thought. **-mal** neut monument. **denkwürdig** adj memorable. **Denkzettel** m lesson, punishment.

dennoch ['dennɔx] conj nevertheless.

Denunziant [denuntsiˈant] m (pl **-en**) informer. **denunzieren** v denounce, inform against.

Depesche [deˈpɛʃə] f (pl **-n**) telegram, dispatch.

deponieren [depoˈniːrən] v deposit.

Depot [deˈpoː] neut (pl **-s**) warehouse, storehouse, depot.

Depression [depresiˈoːn] f (pl **-en**) depression. **depressiv** adj depressed.

deprimieren [depriˈmiːrən] v depress. **-d** adj depressing.

der [deɪr] art the; (to) the. pron who, which; (to) whom or which.

derart ['deɪraɪrt] adv in such a way, so. **-ig** adj of such a type, such, of that kind.

derb [dɛrp] adj crude, coarse; (Person) rough, tough. **Derbheit** f crudeness; (Person) roughness.

deren ['deɪrən] pron whose, or which. **derenthalben, derentwegen,** or **derentwillen** adv on whose account, for whose sake.

dergleichen [deɪrˈglaiçən] adv suchlike, of the kind.

derjenige ['deɪrjeɪnigə] **diejenige, dasjenige** pron he who, she who, that which. **dermaßen** ['deɪrmaisən] adv to such a degree, in such a way.

derselbe [deɪrˈzɛlbə] pron **dieselbe, dasselbe** the same.

derzeitig ['deɪrtsaitiç] adj present; (damalig) of that time.

des [des] art of the.

desgleichen [desˈglaiçən] adv likewise.

deshalb ['deshalp] adv therefore.

Desillusion [dezɪluziˈoːn] f disillusionment.

Desinfektion [dezɪnfɛktsiˈoːn] f disinfection. **-smittel** neut disinfectant. **desinfizieren** v disinfect.

dessen ['desən] pron whose, of which.

destillieren [destiˈliːrən] v distil.

desto ['desto] adv the, all the, so much. **je ... desto ...** the ... the ... .

deswegen ['desveɪgən], **deswillen** adv therefore.

Detail [deˈtai] neut (pl **-s**) detail, item. **-geschäft** neut retail firm or business. **-handel** m retail trade. **detaillieren** v detail, particularize.

deuten ['dɔytən] v explain, interpret. **deuten auf** point to, indicate, suggest. **deutlich** adj clear, plain. **Deutlichkeit** f clearness, distinctness.

deutsch [dɔytʃ] adj German. **Deutsch** neut German (language). **Deutsche(r)** German. **Deutschland** neut Germany.

Devise [deˈviːzə] f (pl **-n**) motto; (pl foreign currency or exchange. **Devisenkurs** m rate of exchange.

Dezember [deˈtsɛmbər] m (pl **-**) December.

dezimal [detsiˈmaːl] adj decimal.

Dia ['diːa] neut (pl **-s**), also **Diapositiv** slide, transparency.

Dialekt [diaˈlɛkt] m (pl **-e**) dialect.

Dialog [diaˈloːk] m (pl **-e**) dialogue.

Diamant [diaˈmant] m (pl **-en**) diamond. **diamanten** adj diamond.

Diät [diˈɛːt] f (pl **-en**) diet.

dich [diç] pron sing you.

dicht [diçt] adj dense; (Wald, Nebel, Stoff) thick; (nahe) close (by); (wasserdicht) watertight.

dichten¹ ['diçtən] v seal, make watertight or airtight.

dichten² v write (poetry); (erträumen) invent. **Dichter** m (pl **-**). **Dichterin** f (pl **-nen**) poet. **dichterisch** adj poetic. **Dichtheit** ['diçthait] or **Dichtigkeit** f density.

Dichtung ['diçtuŋ] f poetry, literature.

dick [dik] adj thick; (Person) fat. **Dick‖darm** m large intestine. **-e** f fatness, thickness. **-icht** neut thicket.

die [diː] art the; pron who, which.

Dieb [diːp] m (pl **-e**) thief. **diebisch** adj thieving. **Diebstahl** m theft.

Diele ['diːlə] f (pl **-n**) board, plank; (Vor-

raum) hall, vestibule; (*Eis-*) ice-cream parlour. **Dielenbrett** *neut* floorboard.

dienen ['diːnən] *v* serve. **Diener** *m* (*pl* -). **Dienerin** *f* (*pl* -nen) servant. **Dienerschaft** *f* servants *pl*, domestics *pl*. **Dienst** *f* (*pl* -e) service; (*Amt*) duty.

Dienstag ['diːnstaːk] *m* Tuesday.

Dienst‖entlassung *f* dismissal. **-grad** *m* rank. **-leistung** *f* service. **dienstlich** *adj*, *adv* official(ly). **Dienst‖mädchen** *neut* (serving) maid. **-pflicht** *f* conscription. **-stunden** *f pl* working hours. **-wohnung** *f* official residence.

dieser ['diːzər] **diese, dieses** *pron*, *adj* this.

dies‖jährig *adj* this year's. **-mal** *adv* this time. **-seits** *adv* on this side.

Dietrich ['diːtriç] *m* (*pl* -e) skeleton key.

diffizil [difiˈtsiːl] *adj* difficult, awkward.

Diktat [dikˈtaːt] *neut* (*pl* -e) dictation. **Diktator** *m* (*pl* -en) dictator. **diktatorisch** *adj* dictatorial. **Diktatur** *f* (*pl* -en) dictatorship. **diktieren** *v* dictate. **Diktiergerät** *neut* dictaphone, dictating machine.

Diner [diˈneː] *neut* (*pl* -s) dinner, dinnerparty.

Ding [diŋ] *neut* (*pl* -e) thing. **vor allen Dingen** above all. **Dingelchen** *neut* (pretty) little thing. **Dingsbums** *neut* (*umg.*) what's-it's-name, what's-his-name.

Diplom [diˈploːm] *neut* (*pl* -e) diploma. **-at** *m* (*pl* -e) diplomat. **-atie** *f* diplomacy. **diplomatisch** *adj* diplomatic. **Diplomingenieur** *m* graduate engineer.

dir [diːr] *pron sing* to you.

Dirigent [diriˈgɛnt] *m* (*pl* -en) (*Musik*) conductor. **dirigieren** *v* conduct.

Dirne ['dirnə] *f* (*pl* -n) prostitute, whore; wench.

diskontieren [diskɔnˈtiːrən] *v* discount. **Diskontsatz** *m* bank-rate.

Diskothek [diskoˈteːk] *f* (*pl* -en) disco(theque).

diskriminieren [diskrimiˈniːrən] *v* discriminate (against). **Diskriminierung** *f* discrimination.

Diskussion [diskusˈioːn] *f* (*pl* -en) discussion. **diskutieren** *v* discuss.

disponieren [dispoˈniːrən] *v* arrange, dispose (of). **disponieren über** have at one's disposal.

Dissident [disiˈdɛnt] *m* (*pl* -en) dissident, dissenter.

Distel ['distəl] *f* (*pl* -n) thistle.

Disziplin [distsiˈpliːn] *f* (*pl* -en) discipline.

disziplinarisch *adj* disciplinary. **Disziplinarverfahren** *neut* disciplinary action.

D-Mark ['deːmark] *f* (*pl* -) (West) German mark.

doch [dɔx] *conj* nevertheless, yet, but; *adv* indeed, oh yes.

Docht [dɔxt] *m* (*pl* -e) wick.

Dock [dɔk] *neut* (*pl* -e) dock. **-arbeiter** *m* docker, (*US*) longshoreman.

Dogge ['dɔgə] *f* (*pl* -n) Great Dane; bulldog.

Dogma ['dɔgma] *f* (*pl* **Dogmen**) Dogma. **dogmatisch** *adj* dogmatic.

Doktor ['dɔktɔr] *m* (*pl* -en) doctor. **-arbeit** *f* doctoral or PhD thesis. **-at** *neut* doctorate, PhD.

Dolch [dɔlç] *m* (*pl* -e) dagger.

dolmetschen ['dɔlmɛtʃən] *v* interpret. **Dolmetscher** *m* interpreter.

Dom [doːm] *m* (*pl* -e) cathedral. **-herr** *m* canon. **-pfaff** (*Zool*) *m* bullfinch.

Domino ['dɔmino] *neut* (*pl* -s) dominoes. **-stein** *m* domino.

Donau ['dɔnau] *f* Danube.

Donner ['dɔnər] *m* (*pl* -) thunder. **donnern** *v* thunder.

Donnerstag ['dɔnərstaːk] *m* Thursday.

Donnerwetter ['dɔnərvɛtər] *neut* thunderstorm. *interj* damn!

doof [doːf] *adj* (*umg.*) daft, dumb, stupid.

Doppel ['dɔpəl] *neut* (*pl* -) duplicate. **Doppel-** *adj* double-. **Doppel‖bett** *neut* double bed. **-ehe** *f* bigamy. **-gänger** *m* ghostly double; doppelgänger doppeln *v* double. **Doppel‖punkt** *m* colon. **-sinn** *m* ambiguity. **doppelt** *adj* double(d).

Dorf [dɔrf] *neut* (*pl* **Dörfer**) village. **-bewohner** *m* villager.

Dorn [dɔrn] *m* (*pl* -en) thorn. **-röschen** *neut* Sleeping Beauty.

Dorsch [dɔrʃ] *m* (*pl* -e) cod.

dort [dɔrt] *adv* there. **-her** *adv* (from) there. **-herum** *adv* around there. **-hin** (to) there. **-ig** *adj* of that place.

Dose ['doːzə] *f* (*pl* -n) tin, box; (*Konserven-*) tin, can. **Dosenöffner** *m* tinopener, can-opener.

dosieren [doˈziːrən] *v* measure out (a dose of). **Dosis** *f* (*pl* **Dosen**) dose.

Dotter ['dɔtə] *m* (*pl* -) (egg) yolk.

Dozent [doˈtsɛnt] *m* (*pl* -en) university or college lecturer.

Drache ['draxə] *m* (*pl* -n) dragon.

Drachen ['draxən] m (pl -) kite.

Draht [draɪt] m (pl Drähte) wire, (Kabel) cable. **–anschrift** f telegraphic address. **–seil** neut cable. **–seilbahn** f cable car, funicular.

Drama ['draɪma] neut (pl Dramen) drama. **–tiker** m (pl -) dramatist. **dramatisch** adj dramatic.

dran [dran] V **daran**.

Drang [draŋ] m (pl Dränge) drive, urge; (Druck) pressure.

drängeln ['drɛŋəln] v jostle, shove.

drängen ['drɛŋən] v press, urge.

drapieren [dra'piːrən] v drape.

drastisch ['drastiʃ] adj drastic.

drauf [drauf] V **darauf**.

draußen ['drausən] adv outside, out of doors.

Dreck [drɛk] m (unz.) filth, dirt; (Kot) excrement; (Kleinigkeit) trifle. **dreckig** adj filthy, dirty.

Dreh [dreɪ] m (pl -e) turn. **den Dreh heraushaben** get the hang or knack of it. **–bank** f lathe. **–buch** neut film-script, scenario. **drehen** v turn, rotate. **Dreh‖punkt** m pivot. **–ung** f (pl -en) turn, rotation, revolution. **–zahl** f revolutions per minute, rpm.

drei [drai] adj three. **Dreieck** neut triangle. **dreieckig** adj triangular. **dreifach** adj triple, treble. **Dreifuß** m tripod. **dreimal** adv three times. **Dreirad** neut tricycle.

dreißig ['draisiç] adj thirty.

dreist [draist] adj cheeky, impudent.

dreiviertel ['draifirtəl] adj three-quarter. adv three-quarters. **Dreiviertelstunde** f three-quarters of an hour.

dreizehn ['draitseɪn] adj thirteen.

*dreschen ['drɛʃən] v thresh.

dressieren [drɛ'siːrən] v train.

Drillich ['driliç] m (pl -e) (Stoff) drill, canvas.

Drilling ['driliŋ] m (pl -e) triplet.

drin [drin] V **darin**.

*dringen ['driŋən] v penetrate. **dringen auf** insist on. **dringen in** implore, urge.

dritte ['dritə] adj third. **Drittel** neut (pl -) third.

Droge ['droɪgə] f (pl -n) drug. **Drogerie** f (pl -n) chemist's (shop), pharmacy. **Drogist** m (pl -en) pharmacist, chemist.

drohen ['droɪən] v threaten. **–d** adj threatening; (Gefahr, usw.) impending, imminent.

Drohne ['droɪnə] f (pl -n) drone.

dröhnen ['drœɪnən] v roar; (Kanone) boom; (Donner) rumble.

Drohung ['droɪuŋ] f (pl -en) threat.

Droschke ['drɔʃkə] f (pl -n) taxi; (Pferde-) cab.

Drossel ['drɔsəl] f (pl -n) (Vogel) thrush; (Mot) throttle. **–ader** f jugular vein. **drosseln** v throttle.

drüben ['dryɪbən] adv over there.

Druck¹ [druk] m (pl Drücke) pressure.

Druck² m (pl -e) print; (Auflage) impression. **drucken** v print.

drücken ['drykən] v press, push; (Hand) shake; (bedrücken) oppress. **sich drücken** get out of, avoid.

Druck‖er ['drukər] m (pl -) printer. **–erei** f (pl -en) printing plant, press. **–fehler** m misprint. **–knopf** m push button; (Kleidung) snap fastener. **–luft** f compressed air. **–messer** m pressure gauge. **–sache** f printed matter. **–schrift** f publication; (Buchstaben) block letter.

drum [drum] V **darum**.

drunter ['druntər] V **darunter**.

Drüse ['dryɪzə] f (pl -n) gland.

Dschungel ['dʒuŋəl] m (pl -) jungle.

du [duɪ] pron you.

Dübel ['dyɪbəl] m (pl -) dowel, wall-plug.

ducken ['dukən] v humble, humiliate. **sich ducken** duck; (fig) cower.

Dudelsack ['duɪdəlzak] m bagpipes pl.

Duell [du'ɛl] neut (pl -e) duel. **–ant** m duellist.

Duett [du'ɛt] neut (pl -e) duet.

Duft [duft] m (pl Düfte) fragrance, aroma; (Blumen) scent. **dufte** adj (umg.) splendid, fine. **duften** v smell (sweet), be fragrant. **–d** adj fragrant, aromatic.

dulden ['duldən] v endure; (erlauben) tolerate, allow. **duldsam** adj tolerant, patient.

dumm [dum] adj stupid. **–heit** f stupidity; (Tat) foolish action, blunder. **–kopf** m idiot, fool.

dumpf [dumpf] adj (Klang) dull, hollow, muffled; (schwül) close, sultry; (muffig) musty.

Düne ['dyɪnə] f (pl -n) dune.

Düngemittel ['dyŋəmitəl] neut fertilizer. **düngen** v fertilize, manure. **Dünger** m manure.

dunkel ['duŋkəl] adj dark; (düster) gloomy, dim; (ungewiß) obscure. **Dunkel‖heit** f darkness, obscurity.

–kammer f (*Foto*) darkroom. **dunkeln** v es dunkelt it is growing dark.

Dünkel ['dyŋkəl] m arrogance.

dünn [dyn] adj thin. **Dünn||darm** m small intestine.

Dunst [dunst] m (pl **Dünste**) haze, mist. **dunsten** v steam.

dünsten ['dynstən] v steam; (*Küche*) stew.

Dur [duːr] neut (*Musik*) major (key).

durch [durç] prep through; (*mittels*) by, through; (*Zeit*) during. adv through(out). **durch Zufall** by chance. **durch und durch** thoroughly.

durchaus [durç'aus] adv completely, thoroughly.

durchblättern [durç'blɛtərn] v leaf through, skim through.

durchbohren ['durçboːrən] v pierce, bore through.

*****durchbrechen** ['durçbreçən] v break through. **Durchbruch** m break-through; (*Öffnung*) breach.

*****durchdringen** ['durçdriŋən] v penetrate; ['driŋən] (*durchsickern*) permeate.

durcheinander [durçain'andər] adv in confusion, in disorder, in a mess. **Durcheinander** neut muddle. **durcheinanderbringen** v muddle up; (*aufregen*) upset, excite.

Durchfahrt ['durçfaːrt] f passage; (*Tor*) gate. **keine Durchfahrt** no thoroughfare.

Durchfall ['durçfal] m failure; (*Med*) diarrhoea. **durchfallen** v fall through; (*Prüfung*) fail.

durchführen ['durçfyːrən] v carry out, perform; (*begleiten*) lead through. **Durchführung** f implementation, execution.

Durchgabe ['durçgaːbə] f transmission.

Durchgang ['durçgaŋ] m passage.

durchgeben ['durçgeːbən] v transmit, pass on.

durchgehen ['durçgeːən] v walk or go through, (*fliehen*) run away; (*durchdringen*) penetrate. **–d** adj continuous; (*Zug*) through.

*****durchkommen** ['durçkɔmən] v come or pass through.

durchlaufen ['durçlaufən] v run through.

durchleuchten [durç'lɔyçtən] v (*Med*) x-ray.

durchmachen ['durçmaxən] v endure, live through.

durchmesser ['durçmɛsər] m diameter.

Durchreise ['durçraizə] f journey through, passage, transit.

durchs [durçs] prep+art durch das.

Durchsage ['durçzaːgə] f announcement. **durchsagen** v announce.

Durchschlag ['durçʃlaːk] m carbon (copy); (*Sieb*) strainer, sieve. **–papier** neut carbon paper.

Durchschnitt ['durçʃnit] m cutting through; (*Querschnitt*) cross-section; (*Mittelwert*) mean, average. **durchschnittlich** adj average. **Durchschnittsmensch** m average person, man in the street.

Durchschrift ['durçʃrift] f (carbon) copy.

*****durchsehen** ['durçzeːən] v look or see through; (*prüfen*) look through or over.

Durchsicht ['durçziçt] f (pl **-en**) perusal, inspection. **durchsichtig** adj transparent.

durchsuchen ['durçzuːxən] v search.

durchtrieben [durç'triːbən] adj cunning, sly.

*****durchwinden** ['durçvindən] v sich durchwinden struggle through.

*****durchziehen** ['durçtsiːən] v pass through; (*etwas durch etwas*) pull or draw through; [-'tsiːən] traverse; (*durchdringen*) fill, permeate.

*****dürfen** ['dyrfən] v be allowed or permitted to, may. **darf ich?** may I? **wenn ich bitten darf** if you please. **du darfst nicht** you may or must not.

dürftig ['dyrftiç] adj needy, poor. **Dürftigkeit** f poverty.

dürr [dyr] adj arid, dry; (*hager*) lean. **Dürre** f drought; (*Magerkeit*) leanness.

Durst [durst] m thirst. **dursten** v be thirsty. **–ig** adj thirsty. **–stillend** adj thirst-quenching.

Dusche ['duʃə] f (pl **-n**) shower. **duschen** v shower, have or take a shower.

Düse ['dyːzə] f (pl **-n**) jet, nozzle. **Düsen||antrieb** m jet propulsion. **–flugzeug** neut jet (plane).

düster ['dyːstər] adj dark; (*fig*) gloomy.

Dutzend ['dutsənt] neut (pl **-e**) dozen.

duzen ['duːtsən] v address familiarly (using du), be on first-name terms with.

Dynamik [dy'naːmik] f dynamics. **dynamisch** adj dynamic.

Dynamit [dyna'miːt] neut (*unz.*) dynamite.

Dynamo [dy'naːmo] m (pl **-s**) dynamo.

Dynastie [dynas'tiː] f (pl **-n**) dynasty.

D-Zug ['deːtsuːk] m (pl **D-Züge**) express train.

E

Ebbe ['ɛbə] f (pl -n) ebb; (Niedrigwasser) low tide. **ebben** v ebb.

eben ['eːbən] adj level, even. adv just. ich war eben abgereist I had just left. eben deswegen for that very reason. **Ebenbild** neut image. **ebenbürtig** adj equal (in rank). **Ebene** f (pl -n) plain; (Math) plane. **ebenfalls** adv likewise. **Eben||heit** f evenness, smoothness. **-holz** neut ebony. **ebenso** adv just so. **-gut** adv just as well. **-viel** adv just as much.

Eber ['eːbər] m (pl -) boar.

ebnen ['eːbnən] v level, smooth.

Echo ['ɛço] neut (pl -s) echo.

echt [ɛçt] adj genuine, real. **Echtheit** f genuineness, authenticity.

Eck [ɛk] neut (pl -e) corner. **-ball** m corner (kick). **-e** f corner, angle. **eckig** adj angular. **Eckzahn** m eyetooth.

edel ['eːdəl] adj noble. **Edel||mann** m nobleman. **-metall** neut precious metal. **-stein** m precious stone, gemstone.

Edikt [e'dikt] neut (pl -e) edict.

Efeu ['eːfɔy] m ivy.

Effekten [ɛ'fɛktən] pl effects, personal belongings; (Komm) bonds, shares. **Effekthascherei** f sensationalism. **effekt||iv** adj effective, actual. **-voll** adj effective.

egal [e'gaːl] adj equal, (all) the same. das ist mir ganz egal it's all the same to me.

Egoismus [ego'ismus] m (pl Egoismen) selfishness, egotism. **Egoist** m egotist. **egoistisch** adj egotistic, selfish.

ehe ['eːə] conj, adv before. **-malig** adj former.

Ehe ['eːə] f (pl -n) marriage. **-brecher** m adulterer. **-brecherin** f adulteress. **ehebrecherisch** adj adulterous. **Ehe||bruch** m adultery. **-frau** f wife, married woman. **ehe||lich** adj matrimonial, conjugal. **-los** adj unmarried, single. **Ehe||mann** m husband. **-paar** neut married couple.

eher ['eːər] adv sooner; (lieber) rather.

Ehre ['eːrə] f (pl -n) honour. **ehren** v honour. **-haft** adj honourable. **Ehrenmal** neut war memorial. **ehrenvoll** adj honourable.

Ehrfurcht ['eːrfurçt] f awe. **ehrfürchtig** adj full of awe or reverence.

Ehr||gefühl neut sense of honour, self-respect. **-geiz** m ambition. **ehrgeizig** adj ambitious.

ehrlich ['eːrliç] adj honest, sincere. **Ehrlichkeit** f honesty. **ehrlos** adj dishonourable. **Ehrung** f (pl -en) honour, award. **ehrwürdig** adj venerable.

Ei [ai] neut (pl -er) egg. **-abstoßung** f ovulation. **-dotter** m yolk.

Eiche ['aiçə] f (pl -n) oak. **Eich||el** f acorn. **-hörnchen** neut squirrel.

Eid [ait] m (pl -e) oath. einen Eid ablegen swear an oath.

Eidechse ['aidɛksə] f lizard.

Eidgenosse m confederate. **-nschaft** f confederacy; (Schweiz) Switzerland. **eidgenössisch** adj confederate; (schweizerisch) Swiss.

Eier||becher ['aiərbɛçər] m eggcup. **-kuchen** m omelette. **-schale** f eggshell. **-stock** m ovary.

Eifer ['aifər] m (unz) fervour, zeal. **-sucht** f jealousy. **eifersüchtig** adj jealous. **eifrig** adj eager, zealous. **Eifrigkeit** f zeal.

Eigelb ['aigɛlp] neut (pl -e) (egg) yolk.

eigen ['aigən] adj own; (eigentümlich) particular; (eigenartig) peculiar. sich etwas zu eigen machen get or acquire something. etwas auf eigene Faust unternehmen do something of one's own accord.

Eigenart f (pl -en) peculiarity. **eigenartig** adj peculiar.

eigen||händig adj by oneself. **-mächtig** adj arbitrary. **Eigen||name** m proper name. **-nutz** m self-interest.

Eigenschaft f (pl -en) quality, attribute, trait. **-swort** neut adjective.

Eigensinn m obstinacy. **eigensinnig** adj obstinate, headstrong.

eigen||ständig adj independent. **-süchtig** adj egoistic.

eigentlich ['aigəntliç] adv actually, really. adj real, actual.

Eigentum ['aigəntuːm] neut (pl Eigentümer) property. **Eigentümer** m owner. **eigentümlich** adj peculiar.

eignen ['aignən] v sich eignen für or zu be suited for.

Eil||bote ['ailbotə] m (pl -n) courier, express messenger. **-brief** m express letter.

Eile ['ailə] f haste, hurry. **eilen** v hurry, hasten. **eilig** adj hasty, fast. **Eil||sendung** f

(*Post*) special delivery. **–zug** *m* fast train, limited-stop train.

Eimer ['aimər] *m* (*pl* -) bucket, pail.

ein [ain], **eine, ein** *art* a, an. *pron, adj* one.

einander [ain'andər] *pron* each other, one another.

einatmen ['ainatmən] *v* inhale, breathe in. **Einatmung** *f* inhalation.

Einbahnstraße ['ainba:nʃtraisə] *f* one-way street.

einbalsamieren [ainbalza'mi:rən] *v* embalm.

Einband ['ainbant] *m* binding, cover (of book).

Einbau ['ainbau] *m* installation. **einbauen** *v* install, build in; (*fig*) incorporate (into).

*****einbegreifen** ['ainbəgraifən] *v* include, comprise. **mit einbegriffen** included.

*****einbiegen** ['ainbi:gən] *v* bend in; (*Straße*) turn into.

einbilden ['ainbildən] *v* **sich einbilden** imagine. **Einbildung** *f* imagination; (*Dünkel*) conceit. **–svermögen** *neut* (power of) imagination.

Einblick ['ainblik] *m* insight.

*****einbrechen** ['ainbreçən] *v* break open; (*Haus*) break into, burgle. **Einbrecher** *m* burglar. **Einbruch** *m* break-in, burglary; (*Mil*) invasion. **–diebstahl** *m* burglary.

einbürgern ['ainbyrgərn] *v* naturalize. **sich einbürgern** become naturalized; (*Wort, usw.*) come into use, gain acceptance. **Einbürgerung** *f* naturalization.

eindeutig ['aindɔytiç] *adj* unequivocal, clear.

*****eindringen** ['aindriŋən] *v* enter by force; (*Mil*) invade. **eindringlich** *adj* urgent.

Eindruck ['aindruk] *m* impression. **eindrücken** *v* press in. **sich eindrücken** leave an impression. **eindrucksvoll** *adj* impressive.

einerlei ['ainərlai] *adj* of one kind. **est ist einerlei** it makes no difference.

einerseits ['ainərzaits] *adv* on (the) one hand.

einfach ['ainfax] *adj* simple; (*nicht doppelt*) single. **Einfachheit** *f* simplicity.

*****einfahren** ['ainfarən] *v* drive in; (*Mot*) run in; (*einbringen*) bring in. **Einfahrt** *f* entrance, way in; (*Hineinfahren*) arrival, entrance.

Einfall ['ainfal] *m* idea, inspiration; (*Mil*) invasion, assault. **einfallen** *v* fall in;

(*idee*) occur (to). **es fällt mir ein** it strikes me.

einfältig ['ainfɛltiç] *adj* naive, artless. **Einfältigkeit** *f* naivety, artlessness.

einfetten ['ainfɛtən] *v* grease, lubricate.

*****einfinden** ['ainfindən] *v* **sich einfinden** appear, turn up.

*****einflechten** ['ainfleçtən] *v* interweave; (*Wort*) put in.

Einflug ['ainflu:k] *m* incursion; (*Aero*) approach.

Einfluß ['ainflus] *m* influence. **einflußreich** *adj* influential.

einförmig ['ainfœrmiç] *adj* monotonous, uniform.

einfügen ['ainfy:gən] *v* fit in.

einfühlen ['ainfy:lən] *v* **sich einfühlen in** sympathize with, get into the spirit of. **Einfühlung** *f* sympathizing, sympathy.

Einfuhr ['ainfur] *f* (*pl* -en) import. **einführen** *v* bring in; (*Waren*) import; (*Gebrauch*) introduce. **Einfuhrhandel** *m* import trade. **Einführung** *f* introduction. **Einfuhrverbot** *neut* import ban.

Eingang ['aingaŋ] *m* way in; (*Ankunft*) arrival; (*Einleitung*) introduction.

*****eingehen** ['ainge:ən] *v* go *or* enter into; (*aufhören*) stop; (*welken*) decay; (*Risiko*) run; (*zustimmen*) agree. **–d** *adj* thorough, detailed.

eingebildet ['aingəbildət] *adj* conceited; (*erfunden*) imaginary.

eingeboren ['aingəborən] *adj* native; (*angeboren*) innate. **Eingeborene(r)** *m* native.

Eingebung ['aingeibuŋ] *f* (*pl* -en) inspiration.

*****eingehen** see above

eingemacht ['aingəmaxt] *adj* bottled; canned; (*Fleisch*) potted.

eingenommen ['aingənomən] *adj* biased (in favour of).

Eingeweide ['aingəvaidə] *neut* (*pl* -) intestines *pl*, entrails *pl*.

Eingeweihte(r) ['aingəvaitə(r)] *m* (*pl* -) initiate.

eingewöhnen ['aingəvœinən] *v* accustom. **sich eingewöhnen** become accustomed (to).

eingießen ['aingi:sən] *v* pour in *or* out.

eingliedern ['aingli:dərn] *v* incorporate; (*einordnen*) classify. **Eingliederung** *f* incorporation; classification.

*****eingreifen** ['aingraifən] *v* catch (hold of); (*einmischen*) interfere. **Eingriff** *m*

catch; interference; (*Übergriff*) encroachment.

*einhalten ['ainhaltən] v restrain, check;
observe; stop.

einhändig ['ainhɛndiç] adj with one hand.
  −en v hand in.

einheimisch ['ainhaimiʃ] adj native, indigenous.

Einheit ['ainhait] f (pl -en) unit; (*Pol*)
unity. einheitlich adj uniform.

einholen ['ainholən] v collect; (*einkaufen*)
shop, buy; (*erreichen*) catch up with.

einig ['ainiç] adj united, at one. einig sein
be in agreement. −en v unite. sich
einigen agree.

einiger ['ainigər], einige, einiges pron
some, any. einigermaßen adv to some
extent.

Einigkeit f (*unz.*) unity; (*Eintracht*)
agreement. Einigung f unification; agreement.

einjährig ['ainjɛːriç] adj one-year-old;
(*Bot*) annual.

einkassieren ['ainkasiːrən] v cash (in).

Einkauf ['ainkauf] m (pl Einkäufe)
purchase. einkaufen v buy, purchase.
einkaufen gehen go shopping.

einkehren ['ainkeːrən] v call in (at).

Einklang ['ainklaŋ] m (pl Einklänge) harmony.

*einkommen ['ainkɔmən] v come in,
arrive. Einkommen neut income.

einkreisen ['ainkraisən] v encircle.

Einkünfte ['ainkynftə] pl revenue, income
sing.

*einladen ['ainlaːdən] v invite. Einladung
f (pl -en) invitation.

Einlage ['ainlaːgə] f (pl -n) lining, filler;
(*Brief*) enclosure; (*Geld*) deposit.

Einlaß ['ainlas] m (pl Einlässe) admission; (*Öffnung*) inlet. einlassen v let in,
admit.

*einlaufen ['ainlaufən] v arrive; (*Wasser*)
run in.

einleben ['ainleːbən] v sich einleben in
accustom oneself to.

einlegen ['ainleːgən] v enclose, insert;
(*Beschwerde*) file; (*Fleisch*) salt, pickle.

einleiten ['ainlaitən] v introduce, initiate;
(*beginnen*) start. Einleitung f introduction.

einlösen ['ainlœːzən] v redeem. Einlösung
f payment, redemption.

einmachen ['ainmaxən] v (*Obst*) preserve,
bottle.

einmal ['ainmal] adv once. auf einmal all
at once. noch einmal (once) again. nicht
einmal not even. −ig adj unique.

Einmarsch ['ainmarʃ] m (pl Einmärsche)
marching in, entry. einmarschieren v
enter, march in (to).

einmischen ['ainmiʃən] v sich einmischen
in interfere or meddle in.

einmünden ['ainmyndən] v run or flow
(into), join.

Einnahme ['ainnaːmə] f (pl -n) receipts pl,
revenue.

*einnehmen ['ainneːmən] v take (in);
(*Geld*) receive.

Einöde ['ainøːdə] f (pl -n) desert, wasteland.

einölen ['ainøːlən] v oil.

einordnen ['ainɔrdnən] v order, arrange;
(*Mot*) get in lane.

einpacken ['ainpakən] v pack, wrap up.

einpökeln ['ainpøːkəln] v pickle.

einprägen ['ainpreːgən] v imprint.
jemandem etwas einprägen impress
something on somebody.

einrahmen ['ainraːmən] v frame.

einräumen ['ainrɔymən] v tidy up, put
away; (*zugeben*) concede; (*einrichten*)
furnish; (*Platz*) vacate, give up.

Einrede ['ainreːdə] f (pl -n) objection.
einreden v persuade; (*widersprechen*)
contradict.

einreichen ['ainraiçən] v hand over or in.

Einreise ['ainraizə] f (pl -n) entry.

einrichten ['ainriçtən] v arrange, set up;
(*gründen*) establish; (*Zimmer*) furnish.
Einrichtung f establishment; arrangement; (*Anstalt*) institution; (*Zimmer*)
fittings pl, furnishings pl.

einrücken ['ainrykən] v enter.

eins [ains] pron one.

einsam ['ainzaːm] adj lonely, solitary.
Einsamkeit f loneliness.

Einsatz ['ainzats] m (pl Einsätze) insertion; insert, filling; (*Spiel*) stake; (*Mil*)
mission, operation.

einschalten ['ainʃaltən] v switch on;
(*einfügen*) insert, put in. Einschaltung f
switching on; insertion.

einschiffen ['ainʃifən] v bring on board,
load (into a ship). sich einschiffen go on
board, embark.

*einschlafen ['ainʃlaːfən] v go to sleep,
fall asleep.

Einschlag ['ainʃlaik] m (pl **Einschläge**) impact; (*Umschlag*) wrapper. **einschlagen** v drive in, break; (*einwickeln*) wrap; (*Weg*) take, follow; (*Hände*) shake hands; (*zustimmen*) agree.

*****einschließen** ['ainʃliːsən] v lock up or in; (*umfassen*) comprise, include; (*umzingeln*) encircle. **einschließlich** adj inclusive; prep including, inclusive of. **Einschluß** m (pl **Einschlüsse**) inclusion.

einschmeicheln ['ainʃmaiçəln] v **sich einschmeicheln bei** ingratiate oneself with.

einschränken ['ainʃrɛnkən] v restrict, limit. **Einschränkung** f restriction, limitation.

Einschreibebrief ['ainʃraibəbriːf] m registered letter. **einschreiben** v register; (*eintragen*) inscribe, write in. **per Einschreiben** adv (by) registered mail. **Einschreibung** f registration.

einschüchtern ['ainʃyçtərn] v intimidate.

*****einsehen** ['ainzeːən] v inspect, look over; (*prüfen*) examine; (*begreifen*) realize.

einseitig ['ainzaitiç] adj one-sided; (*Pol*) unilateral.

einsenden ['ainzɛndən] v send in.

einsetzen ['ainzɛtsən] v set in, put in; (*Amt*) install; begin; (*Geld*) deposit. **Einsicht** ['ainziçt] f (pl **-en**) insight; (*Verständnis*) understanding. **einsichtsvoll** adj judicious, sensible.

Einsiedler ['ainziːdlər] m (pl **-**) hermit.

einspannen ['ainʃpanən] v (*Pferd*) harness; (*mit Rahmen*) stretch.

einsperren ['ainʃpɛrən] v lock in or up; (*Gefängnis*) imprison, jail.

einspritzen ['ainʃpritsən] v inject.

Einspruch ['ainʃprux] m (pl **Einsprüche**) objection, protest. **Einspruch erheben gegen** raise an objection against.

einst [ainst] adv (*Vergangenheit*) once, at one time; (*Zukunft*) some day, one day.

einstecken ['ainʃtɛkən] v put in; (*in die Tasche*) pocket.

*****einsteigen** ['ainʃtaigən] v (*Auto, Schiff, usw.*) get in, get on, board.

einstellen ['ainʃtɛlən] v cease, stop; (*tech*) adjust; (*phot*) focus; (*radio, usw.*) tune. **– bar** adj adjustable. **Einstellung** f stop, suspension; adjustment; (*Ansicht*) attitude.

einstig ['ainstiç] adj former.

einstimmen ['ainʃtimən] v agree; join (in). **einstimmig** adj unanimous.

einstmalig ['ainstmaːliç] adj former.

einstöckig ['ainʃtœkiç] adj one-storeyed.

*****einstoßen** ['ainʃtoːsən] v push or drive in(to); (*Tür*) knock or break down.

einströmen ['ainʃtrœmən] v flow or stream in(to).

einstufen ['ainʃtuːfən] v classify, grade.

einstürmen ['ainʃtyrmən] v rush in; (*angreifen*) attack.

Einsturz ['ainʃturts] m (pl **Einstürze**) downfall, collapse. **einstürzen** v collapse; (*niederreißen*) knock down, demolish.

einstweilen ['ainstvailən] adv meanwhile, for the time being. **einstweilig** adj temporary, provisional.

eintägig ['aintɛːgiç] adj one-day.

Eintausch ['aintauʃ] m exchange. **eintauschen** v exchange, trade.

einteilen ['aintailən] v divide up, classify; (*Skala*) graduate; (*Arbeit*) plan out.

eintönig ['aintøːniç] adj monotonous.

Eintopf ['aintɔpf] m stew, casserole.

Eintracht ['aintraxt] f (*unz.*) harmony, unity.

Eintrag ['aintraːk] m (pl **Einträge**) (*Komm*) entry; (*Schaden*) damage. **eintragen** v carry in; (*einschreiben*) enter; (*einbringen*) yield. **einträglich** adj profitable. **Eintragung** f entry.

*****eintreten** ['aintreːtən] v come in; (*eindrücken*) kick in; (*beitreten*) join; (*geschehen*) occur.

Eintritt ['aintrit] m entrance; (*Anfang*) beginning. **–skarte** f admission ticket.

einverleiben ['ainfɛrlaibən] v incorporate.

einverstanden ['ainfɛrʃtandən] adj in agreement. **einverstanden sein mit** agree with, approve of.

Einwand ['ainvant] m (pl **Einwände**) objection. **einwandfrei** adj perfect, faultless.

Einwanderer ['ainvandərər] m (pl **-**) immigrant. **einwandern** v immigrate. **Einwanderung** f immigration.

einwärts ['ainvɛrts] adv inwards.

einwechseln ['ainvɛksəln] v change; exchange.

Einwegflasche ['ainveːkflaʃə] f non-returnable bottle.

einweichen ['ainvaiçən] v soak, steep.

einweihen ['ainvaiən] v inaugurate; (*Person*) initiate; (*Kirche*) consecrate. **Einweihung** f inauguration; initiation; consecration.

Einwendung ['ainvɛnduŋ] f (pl -en) objection.

einwickeln ['ainvikəln] v wrap (up).

einwilligen ['ainviligən] v consent, agree. **Einwilligung** f consent.

einwirken ['ainvirkən] v einwirken auf influence, affect. **Einwirkung** f influence.

Einwohner ['ainvoːnər] m (pl -) inhabitant.

Einzahl ['aintsaːl] f (unz.) (Gramm) singular.

einzahlen ['aintsaːlən] v pay in, deposit.

Einzel||erscheinung ['aintsəlɛrʃainuŋ] f (isolated) phenomenon. **-fall** m individual case. **-handel** m retail trade. **-handelsgeschäft** neut retail shop. **-händler** m retailer. **-haus** neut detached house. **-heit** f detail. **-kind** neut only child. einzeln adj single; (getrennt) isolated; (alleinstehend) detached. einzelnstehend adj detached. **Einzelzimmer** neut single room.

einziehen ['aintsiːən] v pull or draw in; (einkassieren) collect; (beschlagnahmen) confiscate; (Rekruten) draft; (Wohnung) move in.

einzig ['aintsiç] adj only, single.

Einzug ['aintsuːk] m entry, entrance; (Wohnung) moving in.

Eis [ais] neut (unz.) ice; (Speise) ice-cream. **-bahn** f ice/skating rink. **-bär** m polar bear. **-bein** neut knuckle of pork. **-berg** m iceberg.

Eischale ['aiʃaːlə] f eggshell.

Eisen ['aizən] neut (pl -) iron. **-bahn** f railway. **-händler** m ironmonger. **-waren** f pl ironmongery.

eisern ['aizərn] adj iron.

eisig ['aiziç] adj icy. **eiskalt** adj ice-cold. **Eis||lauf** m skating. **-läufer** m (pl -) skater. **-laufbahn** f skating rink. **-meer** neut polar sea. **-regen** m freezing rain. **-tüte** f ice-cream cone/cornet. **-vogel** m kingfisher. **-würfel** m ice cube. **-zapfen** m icicle.

eitel ['aitəl] adj vain. **Eitelkeit** f vanity.

Eiter ['aitər] m (unz.) pus. **eitern** v fester, suppurate.

Eiweiß ['aivais] neut (unz.) egg-white; protein; albumen. **-stoff** m protein.

Ekel ['eːkəl] m (unz.) disgust, repugnance. **ekelhaft** adj loathsome, disgusting. **sich ekeln** be disgusted by.

Ekzem [ɛkˈtseːm] neut (pl -e) eczema.

elastisch [eˈlastiʃ] adj elastic.

Elefant [eleˈfant] m (pl -en) elephant.

elegant [eleˈgant] adj elegant. **Eleganz** f elegance.

elektrifizieren [elɛktrifiˈtsiːrən] v also **elektrisieren** electrify. **Elektriker** m electrician. **elektrisch** adj electric(al). **Elektrizität** f electricity.

Elektro||gerät [eˈlɛktrogɛrɛːt] neut electric appliance. **-installateur** m electrician. **-motor** m electric motor.

Elektronik [elɛkˈtroːnik] f electronics. **elektronisch** adj electronic.

Elektrotechnik [eˈlɛktroˈtɛçnik] f electrical engineering.

Element [eleˈmɛnt] neut (pl -e) element; (Zelle) battery. **elementar** adj elementary.

elend ['eːlɛnt] adj miserable. **Elend** neut misery. **-sviertel** neut slums pl.

elf [ɛlf] pron, adj eleven.

Elf [ɛlf] m (pl -en) elf, fairy.

Elfenbein ['ɛlfənbain] neut (unz.) ivory.

elfte [ɛlftə] adj eleventh.

Elite [eˈliːtə] f (pl -n) elite.

Ellbogen ['ɛlboːgən] m (pl -) elbow.

Ellipse [ɛˈlipsə] f (pl -n) ellipse. **elliptisch** adj elliptical.

Elsaß ['ɛlsas] neut Alsace. **Elsässer** m (pl -), **Elsässerin** f (pl -nen) Alsatian. **elsässisch** adj Alsatian.

Elster ['ɛlstər] f (pl -n) magpie.

Eltern ['ɛltərn] pl parents. **elterlich** adj parental.

Email [eˈmai̯] neut (pl -s) enamel.

emanzipieren [emantsiˈpiːrən] v emancipate. **Emanzipation** f emancipation.

Empfang [ɛmˈpfaŋ] m (pl Empfänge) welcome, reception. **empfangen** v welcome, receive; (Kind) conceive. **Empfänger** m receiver. **empfänglich** adj susceptible. **Empfängnis** f conception. **-verhütung** f contraception.

***empfehlen** [ɛmˈpfeːlən] v recommend. **-swert** adj to be recommended. **Empfehlung** f recommendation. **-sschreiben** neut letter of recommendation.

empfinden [ɛmˈpfindən] v feel. **empfindlich** adj sensitive; (reizbar) touchy. **Empfindung** f feeling; (Wahrnehmung) perception.

empor [ɛmˈpoːr] adv up(wards). **-ragen** v tower (up/over). **-streben** v struggle up(wards).

empören [ɛm'pœːrən] v shock, revolt; (erregen) stir up. **sich empören** rebel.

emsig ['ɛmziç] adj diligent, industrious.

Ende ['ɛndə] neut (pl -n) end.

endemisch [ɛn'deːmiʃ] adj endemic.

enden ['ɛndən] v finish, end. **end**||**gültig** adj final. **−lich** adv finally, at last; adj final; (beschränkt) finite. **−los** adj endless, infinite.

End||**punkt** m end (point). **−spiel** neut (Sport) final. **−station** f terminus. **−zweck** m (ultimate) goal or purpose.

Energie [enɛr'giː] f (pl -n) energy. **−krise** energy crisis. **energisch** adj energetic.

eng [ɛŋ] adj narrow; (dicht) tight, close; (Freund) close. **Enge** f narrowness; tightness; (Klemme) difficulty.

Engel ['ɛŋəl] m (pl -) angel. **engelhaft** adj angelic.

England ['ɛŋlant] neut England. **Engländer** m (pl -) Englishman. **Engländerin** f (pl -nen) Englishwoman. *ich bin Engländer(in)* I am English. **englisch** adj English.

Engpaß ['ɛŋpas] m narrow pass; (Verkehr) bottleneck; (Klemme) difficulty, tight spot.

engros [ã'groː] adv wholesale.

engstirnig ['ɛnʃtirniç] adj narrow-minded.

Enkel ['ɛŋkəl] m (pl -) grandson. **−in** f granddaughter. **−kind** neut grandchild.

enorm [e'nɔrm] adj enormous.

entarten [ɛnt'artən] v degenerate. **Entartung** f degeneracy, degeneration.

entbehrlich [ɛnt'beːrliç] adj dispensable, (to) spare.

*entbinden [ɛnt'bindən] v release, set free; (eine Frau) deliver. **Entbindung** f release, setting free; (Geburt) delivery.

entblößen [ɛnt'bløːsən] v uncover; (berauben) deprive, rob.

entdecken [ɛnt'dɛkən] v discover. **Entdecker** m discoverer. **Entdeckung** f discovery.

Ente ['ɛntə] f (pl -n) duck; (Falschmeldung, Lüge) hoax, canard.

entehren [ɛnt'eːrən] v dishonour, disgrace.

enteignen [ɛnt'aignən] v expropriate, dispossess. **Enteignung** f expropriation; seizure.

enterben [ɛnt'ɛrbən] v disinherit.

*entfallen [ɛnt'falən] v fall or slip from; (Gedächtnis) slip, escape.

entfalten [ɛnt'faltən] v unfold; (zeigen) display, (Mil) deploy; **Entfaltung** f unfolding; display; deployment; development.

entfernen [ɛnt'fɛrnən] v remove. **sich entfernen** go away, withdraw. **Entfernung** f distance; (Wegbringen) removal.

entflammen [ɛnt'flamən] v inflame, kindle.

*entfliehen [ɛnt'fliːən] v flee from.

entfremden [ɛnt'frɛmdən] v alienate, estrange. **Entfremdung** f alienation, estrangement.

entführen [ɛnt'fyːrən] v abduct; (Flugzeug) hijack. **Entführer** m abductor, kidnapper; hijacker. **Entführung** f abduction, kidnapping; hijacking.

entgegen [ɛnt'geːgən] prep against, contrary to; (hinzu) towards. adv towards. **−kommen** v meet; (Kompromiß) make concessions. **−sehen** v look forward to. **−treten** v move towards; (widerstehen) oppose. **−wirken** v work against.

entgegnen [ɛnt'geːgnən] v retort, answer back.

*entgehen [ɛnt'geːən] v escape from.

Entgelt [ɛnt'gɛlt] neut (unz.) compensation.

entgiften [ɛnt'giftən] v decontaminate.

entgleisen [ɛnt'glaizən] v be or become derailed. **Entgleisung** f derailment.

entgräten [ɛnt'grɛːtən] v bone; fillet (fish).

enthaaren [ɛnt'haːrən] v remove hair from, depilate.

*enthalten [ɛnt'haltən] v hold, contain. **sich enthalten** refrain (from). **enthaltsam** adj abstemious. **Enthaltung** f abstention.

enthaupten [ɛnt'hauptən] v behead, decapitate.

enthüllen [ɛnt'hylən] v uncover, reveal.

Enthusiasmus [ɛntuzi'asmus] m (unz.) enthusiasm. **enthusiastisch** adj enthusiastic.

entkernen [ɛnt'kɛrnən] v (Obst) stone.

entkleiden [ɛnt'klaidən] v (Person) undress, strip; (wegnehmen) divest. **sich entkleiden** undress.

*entkommen [ɛnt'kɔmən] v escape.

entkuppeln [ɛnt'kupəln] v disconnect; (Mot) declutch.

entladen [ɛnt'laidən] v unload; (Gewehr, Batterie) discharge.

entlang [ɛnt'laŋ] prep, adv along. **−fahren** v travel along. **−gehen** walk along.

*entlassen [ɛnt'lasən] v dismiss, discharge, (umg.) fire, sack; (Gefangene) release. **entlassen werden** be dismissed, (*coll*) get the sack. **Entlassung** *f* dismissal, discharge; release.

entlasten [ɛnt'lastən] *v* unburden; (*erleichtern*) relieve; (*Bank*) credit; (*Verdachtsperson*) clear, exonerate.

entleeren [ɛnt'leɪrən] *v* empty. **sich entleeren** relieve oneself.

entlegen [ɛnt'leɪgən] *adj* remote.

entmilitarisieren [ɛntmilitari'ziɪrən] *v* demilitarize.

entmutigen [ɛnt'muːtɪgən] *v* discourage. **Entmutigung** *f* discouragement.

Entnahme [ɛnt'naɪmə] *f* (*unz.*) taking *or* drawing out; (*Geld*) withdrawal; (*Strom*) use.

entnazifizieren [ɛntnatsifi'tsiɪrən] *v* denazify.

****entnehmen** [ɛnt'neɪmən] *v* take away *or* out; (*folgern*) conclude, infer; (*Geld*) withdraw; (*Strom*) use. **Entnehmer** *m* (*Komm*) drawer (of bills); (*Strom*) user.

entrahmen [ɛnt'raɪmən] *v* skim (milk).

entrüsten [ɛnt'rystən] *v* irritate, anger. **Entrüstung** *f* indignation, anger.

entsagen [ɛnt'zaɪgən] *v* renounce, give up.

entschädigen [ɛnt'ʃɛːdɪgən] *v* compensate. **Entschädigung** *f* compensation.

Entscheid [ɛnt'ʃait] *m* (*pl* -e) decision. **entscheiden** *v* decide. **sich entscheiden** decide, resolve, make up one's mind. **entscheidend** *adj* decisive. **Entscheidung** *f* decision; (*Urteil*) sentence.

entschieden [ɛnt'ʃiɪdən] *adj* determined, resolute. *adv* decidedly. **Entschiedenheit** *f* determination.

****entschließen** [ɛnt'ʃliɪsən] *v* **sich entschließen** decide, determine.

entschlossen [ɛnt'ʃlɔsən] *adj* determined, resolute.

Entschluß [ɛnt'ʃlus] *m* (*pl* **Entschlüsse**) decision. **-kraft** *f* power of decision, decisiveness.

entschuldigen [ɛnt'ʃuldɪgən] *v* excuse, pardon. **sich entschuldigen** apologize, excuse oneself. **entschuldigen Sie!** excuse me! **Entschuldigung** *f* apology; *interj* I'm sorry! pardon me!

entsetzen [ɛnt'zɛtsən] *v* horrify, appal; (*von einem Posten*) dismiss; (*Mil*) relieve. **Entsetzen** *neut* horror. **entsetzlich** *adj* dreadful, horrible. **entsetzt** *adj* horrified, shocked.

entspannen [ɛnt'ʃpanən] *v* relax, release. **sich entspannen** relax, calm down. **Entspannung** *f* relaxation; (*Pol*) détente.

****entsprechen** [ɛnt'ʃprɛçən] *v* correspond (to); (*Anforderung*) comply with. **entsprechend** *adj* corresponding, appropriate.

****entspringen** [ɛnt'ʃprɪŋən] *v* escape from, run away from.

entstammen [ɛnt'ʃtamən] *v* descend (from).

****entstehen** [ɛnt'ʃteɪən] *v* arise, originate. **Entstehung** *f* origin.

enttäuschen [ɛnt'tɔyʃən] *v* disappoint. **enttäuscht** *adj* disappointed. **Enttäuschung** *f* disappointment.

entvölkern [ɛnt'fœlkərn] *v* depopulate.

entwachsen [ɛnt'vaksən] *v* grow out of.

entwaffnen [ɛnt'vafnən] *v* disarm.

entwässern [ɛnt'vɛsərn] *v* drain; (*austrocknen*) dehydrate. **Entwässerung** *f* drainage; dehydration.

entweder [ɛnt'veɪdər] *conj* either.

****entweichen** [ɛnt'vaiçən] *v* escape.

entweihen [ɛnt'vaiən] *v* desecrate, profane.

****entwerfen** [ɛnt'vɛrfən] *v* design, plan, (*skizzieren*) sketch; (*Fassung*) draft, draw up.

entwerten [ɛnt'vɛrtən] *v* devalue; (*Briefmarke*) cancel. **Entwertung** *f* devaluation; cancellation.

entwickeln [ɛnt'vikəln] *v* develop. **sich entwickeln** develop. **Entwicklung** *f* development. **Entwicklungs‖land** *neut* developing country. **-lehre** *f* theory of evolution.

entwirren [ɛnt'virən] *v* disentangle.

entwischen [ɛnt'viʃən] *v* slip *or* steal away from.

entwürdigen [ɛnt'vyrdɪgən] *v* degrade, debase.

Entwurf [ɛnt'vurf] *m* (*pl* **Entwürfe**) design, plan; (*Skizze*) sketch; (*Fassung*) draft.

entwurzeln [ɛnt'vurtsəln] *v* uproot; (*vernichten*) eradicate.

****entziehen** [ɛnt'tsiɪən] *v* take away, withdraw; (*rauben*) deprive.

entziffern [ɛnt'tsifərn] *v* decipher, make out.

entzücken [ɛnt'tsykən] *v* delight, enchant. **Entzücken** *neut* delight, enchantment. **entzückt** *adj* delighted, enchanted. **entzückend** *adj* delightful, enchanting.

entzündbar [ɛnt'tsyntbar] *adj* inflammable. **entzünden** *adj* kindle, light. **sich entzünden** catch fire. **Entzündung** *f* ignition; (*med*) inflammation.

entzwei [ɛnt'tsvai] *adv* in two, asunder.
-brechen *v* break in two.

Enzyklopädie [ɛntsyklope'diː] *f* (*pl* -n) encyclopedia.

Epidemie [epide'miː] *f* (*pl* -n) epidemic.
epidemisch *adj* epidemic.

Epilepsie [epilɛp'siː] *f* (*unz.*) epilepsy.
Epileptiker *m* epileptic. **epileptisch** *adj* epileptic.

Episode [epi'zoːdə] *f* (*pl* -n) episode.

er [ɛr] *pron* he.

erachten [ɛr'axtən] *v* think, consider.
Erachten *neut* opinion, judgment. **meines Erachtens** in my opinion.

Erbarmen [ɛr'barmən] *neut* (*unz.*) pity, compassion. **erbärmlich** *adj* pitiful, pitiable. **erbarmungs||los** *adj* merciless, pitiless. **-voll** *adj* compassionate, merciful.

erbauen [ɛr'bauən] *v* build, erect.

Erbe ['ɛrbə] *m* (*pl* -n) heir; *neut* (*unz.*) inheritance. **Erbeinheit** *f* gene. **erben** *v* inherit. **Erb||fehler** *m* hereditary defect.
-feind *m* traditional enemy. **-gut** *neut* inheritance; (*Erbhof*) ancestral estate.
erblich *adj* hereditary.

erbittern [ɛr'bitərn] *v* embitter. **erbittert** *adj* embittered, bitter.

erblassen [ɛr'blasən] *v* grow pale.

erblicken [ɛr'blikən] *v* glimpse, catch sight of.

erblinden [ɛr'blindən] *v* blind.

***erbrechen** [ɛr'brɛçən] *v* **sich erbrechen** vomit.

Erbschaft ['ɛrpʃaft] *v* (*pl* -en) legacy, inheritance.

Erbse ['ɛrpsə] *f* (*pl* -n) pea.

Erd||beben ['ɛrtbeːbən] *neut* (*pl* -) earthquake. **-beere** *f* strawberry. **-boden** *m* earth, soil.

Erde ['ɛrdə] *v* (*pl* -n) earth. **erden** *v* (*Strom*) earth.

***erdenken** [ɛr'dɛnkən] *v* think of, think out; (*erfinden*) invent.

Erdgas *neut* natural gas.

erdichten [ɛr'diçtən] *v* fabricate, invent.
Erdichtung *f* fabrication, invention.

Erd||kreis *m* globe, earth. **-kunde** *f* geography. **erdkundlich** *adj* geographic(al). **Erd||nuß** *f* peanut. **-öl** *neut* oil, petroleum.

erdrosseln [ɛr'drɔsəln] *v* strangle.

erdulden [ɛr'duldən] *v* endure.

ereignen [ɛr'aignən] *v* **sich ereignen** happen. **Ereignis** *neut* event, occurrence.

***erfahren** [ɛr'faːrən] *v* experience; (*hören, lernen*) learn, hear of. *adj* experienced, proficient. **Erfahrung** *f* experience.

erfassen [ɛr'fasən] *v* seize; (*einschließen*) include; (*begreifen*) understand, grasp.

***erfinden** [ɛr'findən] *v* invent. **Erfinder** *m* inventor. **erfinderisch** *adj* inventive.
Erfindung *f* invention.

Erfolg [ɛr'fɔlk] *m* (*pl* -e) success; (*Ergebnis*) result, outcome. **Erfolg haben** achieve success, succeed. **erfolgen** *v* result, follow. **erfolg||los** *adj* unsuccessful. **-reich** *adj* successful.

erforderlich [ɛr'fordərliç] *adj* necessary.
erfordern *v* require, need; (*verlangen*) demand. **Erfordernis** *neut* necessity; (*Voraussetzung*) requirement.

erforschen [ɛr'forʃən] *v* investigate.
Erforsch||er *m* investigator. **-ung** *f* investigation.

erfreuen [ɛr'frɔyən] *v* delight, gladden. **sich erfreuen an** enjoy, take delight in. **erfreulich** *adj* gratifying. **erfreut** *adj* gratified.

***erfrieren** [ɛr'friːrən] *v* freeze to death.
Erfrierung *f* frostbite.

erfrischen [ɛr'friʃən] *v* refresh. **-d** *adj* refreshing. **Erfrischung** *f* refreshment.

erfüllen [ɛr'fylən] *v* fill; (*Aufgabe*) carry out; (*Bitte, Forderung*) comply with, fulfil. **Erfüllung** *f* accomplishment, fulfilment.

ergänzen [ɛr'gɛntsən] *v* supplement, add to; (*vervollständigen*) complete.
Ergänzung *f* supplement; completion.

***ergeben** [ɛr'geːbən] *v* yield. **sich ergeben** surrender; (*folgen*) result. **Ergebenheit** *f* devotion; (*Fügsamkeit*) submissiveness.
Ergebnis *neut* result.

***ergehen** [ɛr'geːən] *v* (*Gesetz*) be promulgated, come out.

ergiebig [ɛr'giːbiç] *adj* productive, profitable.

***ergreifen** [ɛr'graifən] *v* grasp, seize; (*rühren*) touch, move (deeply). **-d** *adj* touching, affecting. **Ergreifung** *f* seizure.

erhaben [ɛr'haːbən] *adj* exalted, sublime.

***erhalten** [ɛr'haltən] *v* receive, obtain; (*bewahren*) preserve, maintain. **erhältlich** *adj* available, obtainable. **Erhaltung** *f* preservation, maintenance.

***erheben** [ɛr'heːbən] *v* lift up; (*Einspruch*) raise. **sich erheben** rise (up). **Anspruch erheben auf** lay claim to. **erheblich** *adj* considerable. **Erhebung** *f* uprising.

erheitern [er'haitərn] v cheer up; (unterhalten) amuse. **sich erheitern** (Himmel) brighten, clear up.

erhitzen [er'hitsən] v heat (up); (Person) inflame.

erhöhen [er'hø:ən] v raise, heighten. **Erhöhung** f raising, heightening.

erholen [er'ho:lən] v **sich erholen** recover, get better; (sich ausruhen) rest. **Erholung** f recovery; rest; (Unterhaltung) recreation.

erinnern [er'inərn] v remind. **sich erinnern an** remember. **Erinnerung** f (pl -en) memory, remembrance.

erkälten [er'kɛltən] v cool. **sich erkälten** catch (a) cold. **Erkältung** f (pl -en) (Med) cold.

erkennbar [er'kɛnbaɪr] adj recognizable. **erkennen** v recognize; (Fehler) acknowledge; (merken) perceive.

Erkenntnis¹ [er'kɛntnis] neut (pl -se) judgment, sentence.

Erkenntnis² f (pl -se) recognition; (Einsicht) understanding.

Erkennung [er'kɛnuŋ] f (pl -en) recognition. **-swort** neut password. **-szeichen** neut distinguishing mark.

Erkerfenster ['ɛrkərfɛnstər] neut bay window.

erklären [er'klɛɪrən] v explain; (aussprechen) declare. **sich erklären** declare oneself. **Erklärung** f explanation; declaration.

erkranken [er'kraŋkən] v fall ill, become sick.

erkundigen [er'kundigən] v **sich erkundigen** (nach) inquire (about). **Erkundigung** f inquiry.

erlangen [er'laŋən] v obtain, acquire; (erreichen) get to, reach.

Erlaß [er'las] m (pl Erlässe) decree, edict. *****erlassen** [er'lasən] v issue; (befreien) release, absolve.

erlauben [er'laubən] v permit. **Erlaubnis** f permission.

erläutern [er'lɔytərn] v explain, elucidate. **Erläuterung** f explanation; pl commentary, notes.

erleben [er'le:bən] v live through, experience. **Erlebnis** neut (pl -se) experience.

erledigen [er'le:digən] v take care of, deal with; (beenden) finish (off). **erledigt** adj settled; (erschöpft) exhausted. **Erledigung** f (pl -en) carrying out, execution.

erlegen [er'le:gən] v kill.

erleichtern [er'laiçtərn] v ease, aid, lighten. **Erleichterung** f (pl -en) relief.

*****erleiden** [er'laidən] v suffer, undergo.

erlernen [er'lɛrnən] v learn, acquire.

Erlös [er'lø:s] m (pl -e) proceeds pl.

*****erlöschen** [er'lœʃən] v go or die out.

ermächtigen [er'mɛçtigən] v authorize, empower.

ermahnen [er'ma:nən] v admonish.

Ermangelung [er'maŋəluŋ] f (pl -) **in Ermangelung** in the absence or default (of).

ermäßigen [er'mɛɪsigən] v reduce, lower. **Ermäßigung** f reduction.

ermitteln [er'mitəln] v ascertain, find out.

ermöglichen [er'mø:kliçən] v enable, render possible.

ermorden [er'mordən] v murder, assassinate.

ermüden [er'my:dən] v tire out; grow tired.

ermuntern [er'muntərn] v encourage, cheer up.

ermutigen [er'mu:tigən] v encourage. **Ermutigung** f encouragement.

ernähren [er'nɛɪrən] v feed, nourish. **sich ernähren** support oneself. **Ernährer** m breadwinner. **Ernährung** f nourishment.

*****ernennen** [er'nɛnən] v appoint, designate. **Ernennung** f appointment.

erneuern [er'nɔyərn] v renew; renovate, restore. **Erneuerung** f renewal; renovation. **erneut** adj repeated; adv again.

erniedrigen [er'ni:drigən] v lower; (degradieren) degrade, humble.

ernst [ɛrnst] adj serious, grave. **Ernst** m seriousness, gravity. **im Ernst** in earnest. **ernsthaft** adj earnest, serious. **-lich** adj serious.

Ernte ['ɛrntə] f (pl -n) harvest; (Wein) vintage. **ernten** v harvest, reap.

ernüchtern [er'nyçtərn] v disillusion, disenchant; (vom Rausch) sober (up). **sich ernüchtern** sober up. **Ernüchterung** f disillusionment; sobering up.

Eroberer [er'o:bərər] m (pl -) conqueror. **erobern** v conquer. **Eroberung** f conquest.

eröffnen [er'œfnən] v open; (anfangen) open, begin. **Eröffnung** f opening, beginning.

erörtern [er'œrtərn] v discuss. **Erörterung** f discussion.

Erotik [e'rɔitik] f (unz.) eroticism. **erotisch** adj erotic.

erpressen [ɛr'prɛsən] v (Sache) extort; (Person) blackmail. **Erpresser** m blackmailer. **erpresserisch** adj extortionate. **Erpressung** f blackmail, extortion.

erproben [ɛr'proːbən] v try (out), test. **Erprobung** f trial, test.

*erraten [ɛr'raːtən] v guess.

errechnen [ɛr'rɛçnən] v calculate.

erregen [ɛr'reːgən] v excite; (hervorrufen) create, produce. **erregbar** adj excitable. **erregend** adj exciting. **erregt** adj excited. **Erregung** f excitement.

erreichen [ɛr'raiçən] v attain, reach. **erreichbar** adj attainable. **Erreichung** f attainment.

errichten [ɛr'riçtən] v erect, build; (gründen) set up, establish.

erröten [ɛr'røːtən] v blush.

Errungenschaft [ɛr'rʊŋənʃaft] f (pl -en) achievement.

Ersatz [ɛr'zats] m (unz.) substitute; (Wiedergutmachung) compensation; (Nachschub) reinforcements pl. **-kaffee** m coffee substitute. **-rad** neut spare wheel. **-spieler** m (Sport) substitute. **-teil** neut spare part.

*erschaffen [ɛr'ʃafən] v create. **Erschaffer** m creator. **Erschaffung** f creation.

*erscheinen [ɛr'ʃainən] v appear. **Erscheinung** f phenomenon; (Aussehen) appearance.

*erschießen [ɛr'ʃiːsən] v shoot (dead). **Erschießungskommando** neut firing squad.

*erschließen [ɛr'ʃliːsən] v open up; (folgern) infer, deduce.

erschöpfen [ɛr'ʃœpfən] v exhaust, use up; (Person) exhaust, tire out. **erschöpft** adj exhausted. **Erschöpfung** f exhaustion.

*erschrecken [ɛr'ʃrɛkən] v scare, frighten; be frightened or scared. **Erschrecken** neut fright. **erschreckend** adj frightening. **erschrocken** [ɛr'ʃrɔkən] adj frightened, terrified. **Erschrockenheit** f fright, terror.

erschüttern [ɛr'ʃytərn] v shake; (Person) shake, disturb, shock. **Erschütterung** f shock.

erschweren [ɛr'ʃveːrən] v make (more) difficult, aggravate.

*ersehen [ɛr'zeːən] v perceive, see.

ersetzen [ɛr'zɛtsən] v replace; (Schaden) make good. **ersetzlich** adj replaceable, renewable.

ersichtlich [ɛr'ziçtliç] adj evident.

*ersinnen [ɛr'zinən] v contrive, devise.

ersparen [ɛr'ʃpaːrən] v save.

erst [eirst] adj first. adv at first; (nur) only, just.

erstarren [ɛr'ʃtarən] v stiffen, become rigid; (Flüssigkeit) congeal, solidify. **Erstarrung** f stiffness.

erstatten [ɛr'ʃtatən] v restore; (ersetzen) replace. **Bericht erstatten** report, make a report. **Erstattung** f restitution.

Erstaufführung ['eirstauffyːrʊŋ] f (pl -en) première, first performance.

erstaunen [ɛr'ʃtaunən] v astonish; be astonished. **Erstaunen** neut astonishment, amazement. **erstaunlich** adj astonishing.

erste(r) ['eirstə(r)], **erste**, **erste(s)** adj first.

erstens ['eirstəns] adv first(ly).

ersticken [ɛr'ʃtikən] v suffocate; (fig) stifle. **erstickend** adj suffocating. **Erstickung** f suffocation, stifling.

erst‖klassig adj first-class. **-malig** adj for the first time, first-time.

erstrecken [ɛr'ʃtrɛkən] v **sich erstrecken** stretch, extend.

ertappen [ɛr'tapən] v catch, surprise. **auf frischer Tat ertappen** catch red-handed.

Ertrag [ɛr'traik] m (pl Erträge) profit; (Boden) yield. **ertragen** v bear, stand. **erträglich** adj bearable, tolerable.

ertränken [ɛr'trɛŋkən] v (cause to) drown.

*ertrinken [ɛr'triŋkən] v drown, be drowned.

erwachen [ɛr'vaxən] v awake, wake up.

*erwachsen [ɛr'vaksən] v grow up. **Erwachsene(r)** m adult.

erwägen [ɛr'vɛigən] v consider, weigh. **Erwägung** f consideration.

erwähnen [ɛr'vɛinən] v mention. **Erwähnung** f mention.

erwärmen [ɛr'vɛrmən] v warm, heat.

erwarten [ɛr'vartən] v expect. **über Erwarten** better than expectation. **wider Erwarten** contrary to expectation. **Erwartung** f (pl -en) expectation.

erwecken [ɛr'vɛkən] v awaken; (erregen) arouse, rouse.

*erweisen [ɛr'vaizən] v prove; (Dienst) render, do; (Ehrung) pay. **sich erweisen als** prove to be.

erweitern [ɛr'vaitərn] v enlarge, widen, extend. **Erweiterung** f (pl -en) extension, enlargement.

Erwerb [ɛr'vɛrp] m (pl -e) acquisition; (*Lohn*) earnings. **erwerben** v acquire; (*Verdienen*) earn. **erwerbstätig** adj (gainfully) employed. **Erwerbung** f acquisition.

erwidern [ɛr'viːdərn] v reply; (*vergelten*) retaliate. **Erwiderung** f reply.

erwischen [ɛr'viʃən] v (*Person*) catch.

erwünscht [ɛr'vynʃt] adj desired, wished-for.

erwürgen [ɛr'vyrgən] v strangle.

Erz [ɛrts] neut (pl -e) ore.

erzählen [ɛr'tsɛːlən] v tell, relate. **Erzähler** m narrator; story-teller. **erzählerisch** adj narrative. **Erzählung** f story.

Erz∥bischof n archbishop. –**engel** m archangel.

erzeugen [ɛr'tsɔʏgən] v (*herstellen*) produce; (*Strom*) generate; (*Kinder*) procreate. **Erzeuger** m producer; father, procreator. **Erzeugnis** neut product(ion); (*Boden*) produce.

Erz∥feind m arch-enemy. –**herzog** m archduke. –**herzogin** f archduchess.

*****erziehen** [ɛr'tsiːən] v (*Tiere, Menschen*) bring up; (*Bildung*) educate. **Erzieher** m educator. **erzieherisch** adj educational. **Erziehung** f upbringing; (*Bildung*) education.

erzogen [ɛr'tsoːgən] adj **gut/schlecht erzogen** well/badly brought up.

es [ɛs] pron it.

Esche ['ɛʃə] f (pl -n) ash (tree).

Esel ['eːzəl] m (pl -) donkey, ass. **eselhaft** adj asinine. **Eselsohr** neut dog's-ear (on page).

esoterisch [ezo'teːriʃ] adj esoteric.

Essay ['ɛsɛ] m, neut (pl -s) essay.

eßbar ['ɛsbar] adj edible.

essen ['ɛsən] v eat. **zu Mittag essen** lunch, have lunch. **zu Abend essen** dine, have supper. **Essen** neut food; (*Mahlzeit*) meal.

Essig ['ɛsiç] m (pl -e) vinegar. –**gurke** f pickled cucumber, gherkin.

Eß∥kastanie f sweet chestnut. –**löffel** m tablespoon. –**tisch** m dinner table. –**zimmer** neut dining room.

etablieren [eta'bliːrən] v establish.

Etage [e'taːʒə] f (pl -n) storey, floor. –**nwohnung** f flat, (*US*) apartment.

Etat [e'ta] m (pl -s) budget; (*Komm*) balance-sheet.

Ethik ['eːtik] f (*unz.*) ethics. **ethisch** adj ethical.

ethnisch ['ɛtniʃ] adj ethnic.

Etikett [eti'kɛt] neut (pl -e) tag, label.

Etikette [eti'kɛtə] f (pl -n) etiquette.

etliche ['ɛtliçə] pron pl some, several.

Etui [e'tviː] neut (pl -s) (small) case; (*Zigaretten*) cigarette-case; (*Brillen*) spectacles-case.

etwa ['ɛtva] adv about, around; (*vielleicht*) perhaps.

etwas ['ɛtvas] pron something, anything. adj some, any, a little.

Etymologie [etymolo'giː] f (pl -n) etymology.

euch [ɔʏç] pron you; (to) you.

euer ['ɔʏər] pl adj your. pron yours.

Eule ['ɔʏlə] f (pl -n) owl.

Eunuch [ɔʏ'nuːx] m (pl -en) eunuch.

Europa [ɔʏ'roːpa] neut Europe. **Europäer** m European. **europäisch** adj European. **Europäische Gemeinschaften (EG)** European Community. **Europäische Wirtschaftsgemeinschaft (EWG)** European Economic Community (EEC).

evakuieren [evaku'iːrən] v evacuate.

evangelisch [evan'geːliʃ] adj Protestant. **Evangelium** neut gospel.

eventuell [eventu'ɛl] adj possible. adv possibly, if necessary.

ewig ['eːviç] adj eternal, everlasting. **auf ewig** for ever. **Ewigkeit** f eternity.

exakt [ɛ'ksakt] adj exact, accurate.

Examen [ɛ'ksaːmən] neut (pl -, or **Examina**) exam(ination).

Exempel [ɛ'ksɛmpəl] neut (pl -) example.

Exemplar [ɛksɛm'plaɪr] neut (pl -e) specimen; (*Buch*) copy.

Exil [ɛ'ksiːl] neut (pl -e) exile.

Existenz [ɛksis'tɛnts] f (pl -en) existence; (*Unterhalt*) livelihood. **existieren** v exist.

exklusiv [ɛksklu'ziːf] adj exclusive.

exkommunizieren [ɛkskomuni'tsiːrən] v excommunicate.

exotisch [ɛ'ksoːtiʃ] adj exotic.

Expedition [ɛkspediʦi'oːn] f (pl -en) expedition; (*Versendung*) dispatching.

Experiment [ɛksperi'mɛnt] neut (pl -e) experiment. **experimentell** adj experimental. **experimentieren** v experiment.

explodieren [ɛksplo'diːrən] v explode. **Explosion** f explosion. **explosiv** adj explosive.

Export [ɛks'pɔrt] m (pl -e) export. –**eur** m exporter. –**handel** m export trade. **exportieren** v export.

extrem [eks'treɪm] *adj* extreme. **Extrem‖ismus** *m* extremism. **–ist(in)** extremist.

Exzentriker [ek'tsentrikər] *m* (*pl* -) eccentric. **exzentrisch** *adj* eccentric.

F

Fabel ['faɪbəl] *f* (*pl* -n) fable; (*Handlungsablauf*) plot. **fabelhaft** *adj* fabulous, marvellous.

Fabrik [fa'briːk] *f* (*pl* -en) factory. **–ant** *m* (*pl* -en) manufacturer. **–arbeiter(in)** factory worker. **–at** *neut* (*pl* -e) manufacture. **fabrizieren** *v* manufacture.

Fach [fax] *neut* (*pl* **Fächer**) (*Abteil*) compartment, pigeonhole; (*Wissensgebiet*) subject; speciality. **–arbeiter** *m* skilled worker. **–arzt** *m* medical specialist.

fächeln ['feçəln] *v* fan. **Fächer** *m* (*pl* -) fan.

Fach‖mann *m* specialist. **–schule** *f* technical college or school. **–sprache** *f* technical language, jargon. **–wort** *neut* technical term. **–zeitschrift** *f* technical journal.

Fackel ['fakəl] *f* (*pl* -n) torch.

fade ['faɪdə] *adj* insipid, boring; (*Essen*) tasteless.

Faden ['faɪdən] *m* (*pl* **Fäden**) thread.

Fagott [fa'ɡɔt] *neut* (*pl* -e) bassoon.

fähig ['fɛɪç] *adj* capable, able. **Fähigkeit** *f* (*pl* -en) ability.

fahl [faɪl] *adj* pale, sallow.

Fahne ['faɪnə] *f* (*pl* -n) flag, standard; (*mil*) colours. **Fahnen‖flucht** *f* desertion. **–flüchtige(r)** *m* deserter. **–stock** *m* flagstaff.

Fahrbahn ['faɪrbaɪn] *f* (*Mot*) lane. **fahrbar** *adj* passable; (*Wasser*) navigable; (*beweglich*) mobile.

Fähre ['fɛɪrə] *f* (*pl* -n) ferry.

*fahren ['faɪrən] *v* go, travel; (*Mot, Zug*) drive; (*Rad, Motorrad*) ride. **Fahrer** *m* driver.

Fahr‖gast *m* passenger. **–geld** *neut* fare. **–gestell** *neut* (*Mot*) chassis; (*Flugzeug*) undercarriage. **–karte** *f* ticket. **–kartenschalter** *m* ticket office.

fahrlässig ['faɪrlɛsɪç] *adj* careless, negligent.

Fahr‖plan *m* timetable. **–preis** *m* fare.

–prüfung *f* driving test. **–rad** *neut* bicycle. **–schein** *m* ticket. **–schule** *f* driving school. **–stuhl** *m* lift, (*US*) elevator.

Fahrt [faɪrt] *f* (*pl* en) drive, journey.

Fährte ['fɛɪrtə] *f* (*pl* -n) track, trail.

Fahrzeug ['faɪrtsɔyk] *neut* vehicle.

Faktur [fak'tuːr] *f* (*pl* -en) *also* **Faktura** invoice. **fakturieren** *v* invoice.

Fakultät [fakul'tɛɪt] *f* (*pl* -en) faculty.

Falke ['falkə] *m* (*pl* -n) hawk, falcon.

Fall [fal] *m* (*pl* **Fälle**) (*Sturz*) fall; (*Angelegenheit*) case. **–beil** *neut* guillotine. **–brücke** *f* drawbridge.

Falle ['falə] *f* (*pl* -n) trap, snare; (*umg.*) bed. **in die Falle gehen** go to bed.

*fallen ['falən] *v* fall. **Fallen** *neut* fall, decline.

fällen ['fɛlən] *v* cut down; (*Urteil*) pass; (*Chem*) precipitate.

fällig ['fɛlɪç] *adj* due.

falls [fals] *conj* if, in case.

Fall‖schirm *m* (*pl* -e) parachute. **–schirmjäger** *m* paratrooper. **–sucht** *f* epilepsy. **–tür** *f* trapdoor.

falsch [falʃ] *adj* false.

fälschen ['fɛlʃən] *v* falsify, fake; (*Geld*) counterfeit. **Fälscher** *m* (*pl* -) counterfeiter, forger.

Falschheit ['falʃhaɪt] *f* (*pl* -en) falsehood.

Fälschung ['fɛlʃuŋ] *f* (*pl* -en) falsification; (*Geld*) forgery, counterfeiting.

Falte ['faltə] *f* (*pl* -n) crease, fold. **falten** *v* crease; (*zusammenlegen*) fold.

familiär [famil'jɛɪr] *adj* familiar.

Familie [fa'miːliə] *f* (*pl* -n) family. **–stand** *m* personal *or* marital status. **–zulage** *f* family allowance. **Familien‖name** *m* surname.

famos [fa'moːs] *adj* splendid, excellent.

Fanatiker [fa'naːtikər] *m* (*pl* -) fanatic. **fanatisch** *adj* fanatical.

Fanfare [fan'faɪrə] *f* (*pl* -n) fanfare.

Fang [faŋ] *m* (*pl* **Fänge**) catch. **fangen** *v* catch.

Farbe ['farbə] *f* (*pl* -n) colour. **Farbe bekennen** show one's colours; (*Karten*) follow suit.

färben ['fɛrbən] *v* colour, tint; (*Stoff*) dye. **farbenblind** ['farbanblint] *adj* colour blind. **Farb‖fernsehen** *neut* colour television. **–film** *m* colour film. **–stoff** *m* dye. **farbig** *adj* coloured. **Farbiger(r)** *m* coloured (man). **farblos** *adj* colourless.

Fasan [fa'zaɪn] *m* (*pl* -e) pheasant.

Fasching ['faʃiŋ] *m* (*pl* -e) carnival.
Faschismus [fa'ʃismus] *m* (*unz.*) fascism. **Faschist** *m* (*pl* -en) fascist. **faschistisch** *adj* fascist.
Faser ['faizər] *f* (*pl* -n) fibre; (*fein*) filament. **-stoff** *m* synthetic fibre, man-made material.
Faß [fas] *neut* (*pl* **Fässer**) barrel, cask, vat. **-bier** *neut* draught beer.
Fassade [fa'saidə] *f* (*pl* -n) façade.
fassen ['fasən] *v* grasp, seize; (*begreifen*) understand. **sich fassen** pull oneself together; (*ausdrücken*) express oneself. **Fassung** *f* (*Kleinod*) mounting; (*Gemütsruhe*) composure; (*Wortlaut*) wording; (*Verständnis*) comprehension. **-skraft** *f* (power of) comprehension.
fast [fast] *adv* almost, nearly.
fasten ['fastən] *v* fast. **Fasten** *neut* fasting. **-zeit** *f* Lent. **Fastnacht** *f* Shrove Tuesday.
fatal [fa'tail] *adj* disastrous; (*peinlich*) awkward.
faul [faul] *adj* rotten; (*person*) lazy. **-en** *v* rot. **-enzen** *v* idle, be lazy. **Faul|enzer** *m* loafer. **-heit** *f* laziness, sloth.
Fäulnis ['foylnis] *f* rottenness, putrefaction.
Faust [faust] *f* (*pl* **Fäuste**) fist. **-handschuh** *m* mitten.
Februar ['feb
ruair] *m* (*pl* -e) February.
***fechten** ['fɛçtən] *v* fence, fight (with swords).
Feder ['feidər] *f* (*pl* -n) feather; (*tech*) spring; (*schreiben*) pen. **-bett** *neut* feather-bed. **-gewicht** *neut* featherweight. **federleicht** *adj* light as a feather. **Federung** *f* suspension, springs *pl*.
Fee [fei] *f* (*pl* -n) fairy.
fegen ['feigən] *v* sweep.
Fehde ['feidə] *f* (*pl* -n) feud.
fehlbar ['feilbair] *adj* fallible. **Fehl|betrag** *m* deficit. **-druck** *m* misprint; (*Briefmarken*) error. **fehlen** *v* (*mangeln*) be missing or lacking; (*abwesend*) be absent; (*irren*) make a mistake. **-d** *adj* missing, absent. **Fehler** ['feilər] *m* (*pl* -) mistake; (*Schwäche*) weakness; (*Mangel*) defect. **fehler|frei** *adj* flawless. **-haft** *adj* faulty, defective.
Fehlgeburt ['feilgəburt] *f* miscarriage. **fehlschlagen** *v* fail, not succeed. **Fehl|tritt** *m* false move or step, slip. **-zündung** *f* (*Mot*) misfire.

Feier ['faiər] *f* (*pl* -n) festival. **Feierabend** *m* evening leisure time, free time. **Feierabend machen** finish work (for the day). **feierlich** *adj* solemn, ceremonial. **feiern** *v* celebrate. **Feiertag** *m* holiday; (*Festtag*) festival.
feige ['faigə] *adj* cowardly.
Feige ['faigə] *f* (*pl* -n) fig.
Feig|heit *f* (*unz.*) cowardice. **-ling** *m* coward.
feil [fail] *adj* for sale; (*bestechlich*) venal, corrupt.
Feile ['failə] *f* (*pl* -n) file. **feilen** *v* file.
feilschen ['failʃən] *v* haggle.
fein [fain] *adj* fine.
Feind [faint] *m* (*pl* -e) enemy. **feindlich** *adj* hostile. **Feindschaft** *f* enmity, hostility. **feind/schaftlich** *adj* inimical. **-selig** *adj* hostile.
Fein|gehaltsstempel *m* hallmark (stamp). **-heit** *f* fineness. **-schmecker** *m* gourmet.
Feld [fɛlt] *neut* (*pl* -er) field; (*Schach*) square. **-bau** *m* agriculture. **-blume** *f* wild flower. **-früchte** *f pl* crops. **-herr** *m* commander(-in-chief). **-messer** *m* surveyor. **-zug** *m* campaign.
Fell [fɛl] *neut* (*pl* -e) skin, hide.
Fels [fɛls] *m* (*pl* -en) rock, boulder. **-enklippe** *f* cliff. **-sturz** *m* rockfall.
Femininum [femi'niːnum] *neut* (*pl* **Feminina**) (*Gramm*) feminine (gender).
Fenster ['fɛnstər] *neut* (*pl* -) window.
Ferien ['feirjən] *neut pl* holiday. **in die Ferien gehen** go on holiday. **-kolonie** *f* holiday-camp. **-ort** *m* holiday resort.
Ferkel ['fɛrkəl] *neut* (*pl* -) piglet.
Ferment [fɛr'mɛnt] *neut* (*pl* -e) enzyme, ferment.
fern [fɛrn] *adj* far(away), distant. **-bleiben** *v* stay away. **Ferne** *f* distance. **ferner** *adj* farther; *adv* further; *conj* in addition. **-hin** *adv* in future.
Fern|gespräch *neut* (*phone*) long-distance call. **-glas** *neut* telescope. **-laster** *m* long-distance lorry. **-lenkung** *f* remote control. **-meldedienst** *m* telecommunications. **-rohr** *neut* telescope. **-schreiber** *m* teletype machine; Telex. **-sehapparat** *m* television (set). **-sehen** *neut* television. *v* watch television. **-sprecher** *m* telephone. **-straße** *f* trunkroad. **-zug** *m* long-distance train.
Ferse ['fɛrzə] *f* (*pl* -n) heel.

fertig ['fɛrtiç] adj (bereit) ready; (beendet) finished. **–en** v produce. **Fertigkeit** f (pl -en) skill, proficiency. **fertigmachen** v finish; (umg.) beat (into submission).

Fessel ['fɛsəl] f (pl -n) fetter, chain. **fesseln** v fetter, chain. **–d** adj fascinating; (bezaubernd) enchanting.

fest [fɛst] adj firm, secure; (dicht) solid.

Fest [fɛst] neut (pl -e) festival. **–essen** neut banquet.

*festhalten ['fɛsthaltən] v hold (tight); (Bild, Buch) portray; (anpacken) seize. **festigen** v make firm or secure. **Festland** neut continent. **festlegen** v lay down, fix. **sich festlegen** commit oneself.

festlich ['fɛstliç] adj festive. **Festlichkeit** f festivity.

fest‖machen v fasten; (vereinbaren) agree, arrange. **–nehmen** v arrest, capture. **–setzen** v settle, fix. **Festsetzung** f settling, establishment. **fest‖stehen** v stand fast. **–stellen** v settle; (herausfinden) establish, ascertain. **Feststellung** f establishment, ascertaining.

Festtag ['fɛsttak] m holiday.

Festung ['fɛstuŋ] f (pl -en) fortress.

Festzug ['fɛsttsuːk] m procession.

fett [fɛt] adj fat; (schmierig) greasy. **Fett** neut (pl -e) fat; grease. **fettig** adj fatty; greasy.

Fetzen ['fɛtsən] m (pl -) rag, shred.

feucht [fɔyçt] adj damp, moist. **–en** v dampen, moisten. **Feuchtigkeit** f dampness, moisture.

Feuer ['fɔyər] neut (pl -) fire. **–alarm** m fire alarm. **feuer‖beständig** or **–fest** adj fireproof. **–gefährlich** adj inflammable. **Feuerlöscher** m fire extinguisher. **feuern** v fire. **Feuer‖schaden** m fire damage. **–spritze** f fire engine. **–stein** m flint. **–waffe** f gun. **–wehr** f fire brigade, (US) fire department. **–wehrmann** m fireman. **–zeug** neut (cigarette) lighter.

Feuilleton ['fœjətɔ̃] neut (pl -s) newspaper supplement, review section.

feurig ['fɔyriç] adj fiery.

Fiber ['fiːbər] f (pl -n) fibre.

Fichte ['fiçtə] f (pl -n) fir, spruce (tree).

Fieber ['fiːbər] neut (pl -) fever. **fieberartig** adj feverish. **fieberhaft** adj feverish.

Fiedel ['fiːdəl] f (pl -n) fiddle, violin. **fiedeln** v (play the) fiddle.

Figur [fi'guːr] f (pl -en) figure; (Schach) piece, chessman.

fiktiv [fik'tiːf] adj fictitious.

Filiale [fili'aːlə] f (pl -n) (Komm) branch.

Film [film] m (pl -e) film.

Filter ['filtər] m (pl -) filter. **filtrieren** v filter.

Filz [filts] m (pl -e) felt; (Geizhals) miser.

Finanz [fi'nants] f (pl -en) finance. **–amt** neut tax office, Inland Revenue. **finanziell** adj financial. **Finanzier** m (pl -s) financier. **finanzieren** v finance. **Finanz‖jahr** m financial year. **–minister** m finance minister.

*finden ['findən] v find; (glauben) think, believe. **Finder** m (pl -) finder. **findig** adj clever, resourceful.

Finger ['fiŋər] m (pl -) finger. **–abdruck** m fingerprint. **–hut** m thimble; (Bot) foxglove. **–nagel** m fingernail. **–spitze** f fingertip.

Fink [fiŋk] m (pl -en) finch.

Finne ['finə] m (pl -), **Finnin** f (pl -nen) Finn. **finnisch** adj Finnish. **Finnland** neut Finland. **Finnländer(in)** f Finn.

finster ['finstər] adj dark; (düster) gloomy; (drohend) foreboding. **Finsternis** f darkness; gloom.

Firma ['firma] f (pl **Firmen**) firm, business.

Firnis ['firnis] m (pl -se) varnish.

Fisch [fiʃ] m (pl -e) fish. **Fische** pl (Astrol) Pisces. **fischen** v fish. **Fischer** m (pl -) fisherman. **–boot** neut fishing boat. **–ei** f fishing. **–korb** m creel. **–otter** m or f otter. **–reiher** m heron. **–zeug** neut (fishing) tackle.

fix [fiks] adj firm; (fig) quick.

flach [flax] adj flat, even; (nicht tief) shallow; (uninteressant) dull.

Fläche ['flɛçə] f (pl -n) flatness; (Gebiet) area; (Oberfläche) surface. **–ninhalt** m surface area.

Flachs [flaks] m (unz.) flax.

flackerig ['flakəriç] adj flickering. **flackern** v flicker, flare.

Flagge ['flagə] f (pl -n) flag.

Flamme ['flamə] f (pl -n) flame. **flammen** v flame, blaze.

Flanell [fla'nɛl] m (pl -e) flannel.

Flanke ['flaŋkə] f (pl -n) flank. **flankieren** v (out)flank.

Flasche ['flaʃə] f (pl -n) bottle. **Flaschen–** adj cylindrical. **Flaschenöffner** m bottle-opener.

flattern ['flatərn] v flutter.

flau [flau] *adj* weak; (*Getränke*) flat; (*Komm*) slack, dull.

Flaum [flaum] *m* (*unz.*) down. **flaumig** *adj* downy.

Flaute ['flautə] *f* (*pl* -n) lull, calm; (*Wirtschaft*) recession.

Flechte ['flɛçtə] *f* (*pl* -n) braid; (*Bot*) lichen; (*Med*) ringworm, herpes. **flechten** *v* braid, interweave; (*Korb*) weave. **Flechtkorb** *m* wicker basket.

Fleck [flɛk] *m* (*pl* -e) stain, spot; (*Makel*) blemish, flaw. **flecken** *v* stain.

Fledermaus ['fleɪdərmaus] *f* bat.

flehen ['fleɪən] *v* implore, entreat (for). **–tlich** *adj* imploring.

Fleisch [flaiʃ] *neut* (*unz.*) meat. **–brühe** *f* (meat) stock. **Fleischer** *m* (*pl* -) butcher. **–ei** *f* (*pl* -en) butcher's (shop). **fleisch‖farbig** *adj* flesh-coloured. **–fressend** *adj* carnivorous. **–ig** *adj* fleshy. **–lich** *adj* carnal. **Fleisch‖topf** *m* meat saucepan; (*fig*) fleshpot. **–werdung** *f* (*Rel*) Incarnation. **–wolf** *m* mincer.

Fleiß [flais] *m* (*unz.*) diligence, industry. **fleißig** *adj* industrious, hard-working.

Flick [flik] *m* (*pl* -en) patch. **–arbeit** *f* patching; (*Pfuscherei*) botch. **flicken** *v* mend, patch.

Fliege ['fliːgə] *f* (*pl* -n) fly. **fliegen** *v* fly. **Flieger** *m* (*pl* -) aviator, flier. **–abwehr** *f* anti-aircraft defence.

*****fliehen** ['fliːən] *v* flee.

Fließband ['fliːsbant] *neut* conveyor belt, assembly line. **fließen** *v* flow. **fließend** *adj* flowing, running.

flimmern ['flimərn] *v* glimmer, twinkle.

flink [fliŋk] *adj* nimble, agile.

Flinte ['flintə] *f* (*pl* -n) musket; (*Schrot*) shotgun.

flirten ['flirtən] *v* flirt.

Flitterwochen ['flitərvɔxən] *f pl* honeymoon *sing*.

Flocke ['flɔkə] *f* (*pl* -n) flake; (*Wolle, Haar*) flock, tuft. **flocken** *v* fall in flakes. **flockig** *adj* flaky; (*Haar, usw.*) fluffy.

Floh [floː] *m* (*pl* Flöhe) flea. **–stich** *m* fleabite.

Floskel ['flɔskəl] *f* (*pl* -n) flowery *or* fine phrase.

Floß [floːs] *neut* (*pl* Flöße) raft.

Flosse ['flɔsə] *f* (*pl* -n) fin.

Flöte ['fløːtə] *f* (*pl* -n) flute. **flöten** *v* play the flute. **Flötist(in)** flautist.

flott [flɔt] *adj* brisk; (*Schnell*) fast;

(*schick*) smart; (*schwimmend*) afloat. **Flotte** *f* fleet, navy.

Flöz [fløːts] *neut* (*pl* -e) (*Mineralien*) seam.

Fluch [fluːx] *m* (*pl* Flüche) curse; (*Fluchwort*) swear-word. **fluchen** *v* swear, curse.

Flucht [fluxt] *f* (*pl* -en) flight, escape; (*Reihe*) row.

flüchtig ['flyçtiç] *adj* fleeting, cursory. **Flüchtling** *m* (*pl* -e) refugee.

Flug [fluːk] *m* (*pl* Flüge) flight, flying; (*Vögel*) flock. **–bahn** *f* trajectory. **–blatt** *neut* handbill, pamphlet.

Flügel ['flyːgəl] *m* (*pl* -) wing; (*Klavier*) grand piano. **–fenster** *neut* French window.

Flug‖gast *m* air passenger. **–hafen** *m* airport. **–post** *f* air-mail. **–schiff** *m* flying-boat. **–schrift** *f* pamphlet. **–wesen** *neut* aviation, flying. **–zeug** *neut* aeroplane. **–zeug-halle** *f* hangar. **–zeug-träger** *m* aircraft-carrier.

flunkern ['fluŋkərn] *v* fib, lie; (*übertreiben*) exaggerate, brag.

Flur [fluːr] *m* (*pl* -e) floor; (entrance) hall.

Fluß [flus] *m* (*pl* Flüsse) river. **fluß‖abwärts** *adv* downstream. **–aufwärts** *adv* upstream. **Flussfisch** *m* fresh-water fish.

flüssig ['flysiç] *adj* liquid. **Flüssigkeit** *f* liquid.

flüstern ['flystərn] *v* whisper.

Flut [fluːt] *f* (*pl* -en) flood; (*Hochwasser*) (high) tide. **Ebbe und Flut** ebb and flow. **fluten** *v* flood.

Fohlen ['foːlən] *neut* (*pl* -) foal.

Föhn [føːn] *m* (*pl* -e) (warm) south wind.

Folge ['fɔlgə] *f* (*pl* -n) succession; (*Wirkung*) consequence. **folgen** *v* follow; (*gehorchen*) obey. **folgend** *adj* (the) following. **–ermaßen** *adv* as follows. **folger‖ichtig** *adj* consistent, logical. **folgern** *v* conclude, infer. **Folgerung** *f* (*pl* -en) conclusion, inference. **folgewidrig** *adj* inconsistent, illogical. **folglich** *adv* consequently.

Folter ['fɔltər] *f* (*pl* -n) torture; (*Gerät*) rack. **foltern** *v* torture. **Folterung** *f* torture, torturing.

Fön [føːn] *m* (*pl* -e) hairdrier.

Fonds [fɔ̃ː] *m* (*pl* -) fund.

Förderer ['fœrdərər] *m* (*pl* -) promoter, sponsor. **förderlich** *adj* useful, beneficial.

fordern ['fɔrdərn] v demand; (*beanspruchen*) claim.

fördern ['fœrdərn] v further, promote.

Forderung ['fɔrdəruŋ] f (pl -en) demand.

Förderung ['fœrdəruŋ] f (pl -en) furtherance, advancement; (*Komm*) promotion; (*Kohle*) mining.

Forelle [fo'rɛlə] f (pl -n) trout.

Form [fɔrm] f (pl -en) form; (*tech*, *Kuchen*) mould. **in Form** (*sport*) fit, on form. **Formel** f (pl -n) formula. **form‖ell** adj formal. **-en** v form, shape. **-los** adj shapeless, formless. **Formular** neut (pl -e) (question) form; (*US*) blank. **formulieren** v formulate.

forschen ['fɔrʃən] v investigate; (*fragen*) inquire; (*Wissenschaft*) do research. **forschend** adj searching. **Forscher** m (pl -) investigator, enquirer; researcher. **Forschung** f (pl -en) investigation; research.

Forst [fɔrst] m (pl -e) forest.

Förster ['fœrstər] m (pl -) forester.

Forstwirtschaft ['fɔrstvirtʃaft] f forestry.

fort [fɔrt] adv away; (*vorwärts*) forward(s); (*weiter*) on.

fortan [fɔrt'an] adv from now on.

fortbestehen ['fɔrtbəʃteːən] v continue (to exist), live on, survive.

Fortbildung ['fɔrtbilduŋ] f further education.

fortbleiben ['fɔrtblaibən] v remain away.

fortdauern ['fɔrtdauərn] v last, continue. **-d** adj continual, incessant.

fortfahren ['fɔrtfarən] v drive away, depart; (*weitermachen*) proceed, continue.

fortgehen ['fɔrtgeːən] v go away.

fortgeschritten ['fɔrtgəʃritən] adj advanced.

fortkommen ['fɔrtkɔmən] v escape; (*fig*) prosper, make progress.

fortlaufen ['fɔrtlaufən] v run away; (*fortkommen*) escape; (*weiterlaufen*) continue. **-d** adj continuous.

fortleben ['fɔrtleːbən] v survive. **Fortleben** neut survival; (*nach dem Tode*) afterlife.

fortpflanzen ['fɔrtpflantsən] v **sich fortpflanzen** reproduce, multiply; (*Krankheit*) spread.

fortschreiten ['fɔrtʃraitən] v go forward, proceed.

Fortschritt ['fɔrtʃrit] m (pl -e) progress. **fortschrittlich** adj progressive.

fortsetzen ['fɔrtzɛtsən] v continue. **Fortsetzung** f continuation.

fortwährend ['fɔrtvɛːrənt] adj continuous, incessant.

Fossil [fɔ'siːl] neut (pl -ien) fossil.

Foto ['foto] neut (pl -s) (*umg.*) photo.

Fötus ['fœtus] m (pl -se) foetus.

Fracht [fraxt] f (pl -en) freight. **-brief** m consignment or dispatch note. **-gut** neut cargo, goods. **-schiff** neut merchantman.

Frack [frak] m (pl **Fräcke**) dresscoat, tails. **-hemd** neut dress shirt. **-zwang** m obligatory evening dress, formal dress.

Frage ['fraːgə] f (pl -n) question. **-bogen** m questionnaire. **fragen** v ask. **Fragezeichen** neut question mark. **frag‖lich** adj in question, doubtful. **-los** adj unquestionable.

Fragment [fra'gment] neut (pl -e) fragment.

fragwürdig ['fraːkvurdiç] adj questionable.

Fraktion [fraktsi'oːn] f (pl -en) (*Pol*) parliamentary party, faction.

Fraktur [frak'tuːr] f (pl -en) fracture; (*Druck*) Gothic type or script.

frankieren [fraŋ'kiːrən] v (*Brief*) stamp; (*Päckchen*) pre-pay. **franko** adv post paid.

Frankreich ['fraŋkraiç] neut France.

Franse ['franzə] f (pl -n) fringe. **fransig** adj fringed; (*ausgefasert*) frayed.

Franzose [fran'tsoːzə] m (pl -n) Frenchman. **Französin** f (pl -nen) Frenchwoman. **französisch** adj French.

Fratze ['fratsə] f (pl -n) grimace. **Fratzen schneiden** make or pull faces.

Frau [frau] f (pl -en) woman; (*Ehefrau*) wife; (*Titel*) Mrs. **Frauen‖arzt** m gynaecologist. **-befreiung** f women's liberation. **frauenhaft** adj womanly. **Frauen‖rechtlerin** f (pl -nen) feminist. **-welt** f womankind, women pl.

Fräulein ['frɔylain] neut (pl -) young lady; (*Titel*) Miss.

frech [frɛç] adj cheeky, insolent. **Frechheit** f cheek, insolence.

frei [frai] adj free; (*nicht besetzt*) vacant, unoccupied; (*offen*) candid. **Freibad** ['fraibat] neut outdoor swimming pool.

freiberuflich ['fraibəruːfliç] adj freelance, self-employed, professional.

Freibrief ['fraibriːf] m charter.

Freie ['fraiə] neut (*unz.*) outdoors, open air. **im Freien** in the open air.

Freigabe ['fraigaːbə] f release.

***freigeben** ['fraigeːbən] v set free; (Straße, usw.) open; (Waren, Arznei) pass, approve, decontrol. **freigebig** adj generous.

Freihandel ['fraihandəl] m free-trade.

Freiheit f ['fraihait] f (pl -en) freedom, liberty. **freiheitlich** adj liberal.

Freiherr ['fraiher] m (pl -) baron. **-in** f (pl -nen) baroness.

Freikarte ['fraikaːrtə] f complimentary ticket.

***freilassen** ['frailasən] v set free.

freilich ['frailiç] adv certainly, indeed, of course.

freimachen ['fraimaxən] v deliver (from captivity), release.

Freimaurer ['fraimaurər] m (pl -) freemason.

Freimut ['fraimuːt] m (unz.) candour, frankness. **freimütig** adj candid, frank.

***freisprechen** ['fraiʃprɛçən] v acquit, discharge.

Freitag ['fraitaːk] m Friday.

freiwillig ['fraiviliç] adj voluntary.

Freizeit ['fraitsait] f leisure time, spare time.

fremd [frɛmt] adj strange; (ausländisch) foreign. **Fremde(r)** stranger; foreigner. **Fremd‖zimmer** neut guest room. **-heit** f strangeness. **-körper** m foreign body. **-sprache** f foreign language. **-wort** neut foreign word, loan word.

Frequenz [fre'kvɛnts] f (pl -en) frequency.

***fressen** ['frɛsən] v eat, devour.

Freude ['frɔydə] f (pl -en) joy; (Vergnügen) delight. **-ntag** m red-letter day. **freudig** adj joyful, joyous.

freuen ['frɔyən] v give pleasure to. **es freut mich I am glad or pleased. sich freuen** be glad, rejoice. **sich freuen auf** look forward to.

Freund [frɔynt] m (pl -e) friend; (Liebhaber) boyfriend. **-in** f (pl -nen) (girl) friend. **freundlich** adj friendly; (liebenswürdig) kind. **Freund‖lichkeit** f friendliness. **-schaft** f friendship. **freundschaftlich** adj friendly.

Frevel ['freːfəl] m (pl -) sacrilege. **frevelhaft** adj sacrilegious.

Friede(n) ['friːdə(n)] m (pl -) peace. **Friedens‖bruch** m breach of the peace. **-stifter** m peacemaker. **-vertrag** m peace (treaty). **Friedhof** m cemetery. **friedlich** adj peaceful.

***frieren** ['friːrən] v freeze.

Frikadelle [frika'dɛlə] f (pl -n) rissole.

frisch [friʃ] adj fresh; (lebhaft) lively. **Frische** f freshness; liveliness.

Friseur [fri'zœːr] m, (pl -e) **Friseuse** f (pl -n) hairdresser; (nur für Herren) barber. **frisieren** v cut or style hair; (Bücher) cook, falsify; (Mot) soup up. **Frisiersalon** m hairdressing salon.

Frist [frist] f (pl -en) period, time; (Termin) time limit, deadline.

Frisur [fri'zuːr] f (pl en) hairstyle; (umg.) hairdo.

froh [froː] adj glad, cheerful, happy.

fröhlich ['frøːliç] adj cheerful, joyous. **Fröhlichkeit** f cheerfulness.

frohlocken [froː'lɔkən] v rejoice. **Frohsinn** m gaiety.

fromm [frɔm] adj pious, religious. **frömmeln** ['frœməln] adj religiose, hypocritical. **Frömmler** m hypocritic.

Fronleichnam [froːn'laiçnaːm] m Corpus Christi Day.

Front [frɔnt] f (pl -en) front, face; (Pol) front. **-antrieb** m front-wheel drive.

Frosch [frɔʃ] m (pl Frösche) frog; (Feuerwerk) squib, banger.

Frost [frɔst] m (pl Fröste) frost; (Kälte) coldness, chill. **-beule** f chilblain. **frostig** adj chilly, frosty. **Frostschutzmittel** neut antifreeze.

Frucht [fruxt] f (pl Früchte) fruit. **fruchtbar** adj fertile. **Fruchtbarkeit** f fertility. **fruchtlos** adj fruitless. **Fruchtsaft** m fruit juice.

früh [fryː] adj early. **Frühe** f early hour, early morning. **früher** adj earlier; (ehemalig) former. **frühestens** adv earliest.

Früh‖geburt f premature birth. **-jahr** neut spring. **-ling** m spring. **-reife** f precocity. **-stück** neut breakfast. **früh‖stücken** v breakfast. **-zeitig** adj premature, untimely; (rechtzeitig) early, in good time.

Fuchs [fuks] m (pl Füchse) fox. **Füchsin** f ['fyçsin] f (pl -nen) vixen.

Fuge [fuːgə] f (pl -n) joint; (Musik) fugue.

fügen ['fyːgən] v join together; (ordnen) dispose. **sich fügen** submit. **fügsam** adj submissive, obedient.

fühlen ['fyːlən] v touch, feel. **sich fühlen** feel. **sich glücklich fühlen** feel or be happy. **Fühlen** neut feeling. **Fühler** m feeler. **Fühlung** f touch.

führen ['fyːrən] v lead, direct; (Waren) stock, carry; (Bücher) keep. **-d** adj prominent, leading. **Führer** m leader, guide. **-haus** neut (Zug) driver's cab. **-schaft** f leadership. **-schein** m driving licence, (US) driver's license. **-sitz** m driver's or pilot's seat. **Führung** f command, management.

Fülle ['fylə] f (pl -n) abundance, plenty. **Hülle und Fülle** plentiful, in plenty. **füllen** v fill (up). **Füllfeder** f fountain-pen. **-ung** f (pl -en) filling.

Fundament [funda'mɛnt] neut (pl -e) foundation, base.

fünf [fynf] adj five. **fünft** adj fifth. **Fünftel** neut fifth. **fünf||zehn** pron. adj fifteen.

fungieren [fuŋ'giːrən] v function (as), act (as).

Funk [funk] m (unz.) radio, wireless. **-e** m (pl -n) spark. **funkeln** v sparkle. **Funksendung** f (Radio) programme transmission.

Funktion [funktsi'oːn] f (pl -en) function. **-är** m (pl -e) functionary. **funktionieren** v function.

für [fyːr] prep for.

Furche ['furçə] f (pl -n) furrow; (Runzel) wrinkle. **furchen** v furrow.

Furcht [furçt] f (unz.) fear. **furchtbar** adj frightful.

fürchten ['fyrçtən] v fear. **sich fürchten vor** be afraid of. **fürchterlich** adj terrible, dreadful.

Furnier [fur'niːr] neut (pl -e) veneer.

Fürsorge ['fyːrzɔrgə] f care; (Hilfstätigkeit) welfare work; (Geld) social security. **-arbeit** f social work.

Fürsprecher ['fyːrʃprɛçər] m advocate. **fürsprechen** v intercede.

Fürst [fyrst] m (pl -en) prince. **-in** f (pl -nen) princess. **fürstlich** adj princely.

Furz [furts] m (pl Fürze) (vulgär) fart. **furzen** v fart.

Fuß [fuːs] m (pl Füße) foot. **-ball** m football. **-boden** m floor. **-bremse** f footbrake. **-gänger** m pedestrian. **-pflege** f chiropody. **-steig** m pavement, (US) sidewalk. **-tritt** m kick; (Gang) step. **-volk** neut infantry. **-weg** m footpath.

Futter ['futər] neut (pl -) feed, fodder; (Kleider) lining.

füttern ['fytərn] v feed; line. **Fütterung** f feeding, fodder; lining.

G

Gabe ['gaːbə] f (pl -n) gift.

Gabel ['gaːbəl] f (pl -n) fork. **gabeln** v fork. **Gabelung** f fork, branching.

gackern ['gakərn] v cackle.

gähnen ['gɛːnən] v yawn.

galant [ga'lant] adj polite, gallant.

Galeere [ga'leːrə] f (pl -n) galley.

Galerie [galə'riː] f (pl -n) gallery.

Galgen ['galgən] m (pl -) gallows pl.

Galle ['galə] f (pl -n) gall, bile; (fig) rancour.

Gallen||blase ['galənblaːzə] f gallbladder. **-stein** m gallstone.

Galopp [ga'lɔp] m (pl -e) gallop. **galoppieren** v gallop.

galvanisieren [galvani'ziːrən] v galvanize.

Gang [gaŋ] m (pl Gänge) walk; (Gangart) gait; (Flur) corridor; (Essen) course; (Mot) gear. **im Gang** in motion. **Gang||art** f gait. **-schalter** m gear lever.

Gans [gans] f (pl Gänse) goose.

Gänse||blume ['gɛnzəbluːmə] f daisy. **-braten** m roast goose. **-füßchen** pl quotation marks. **-rich** m gander.

ganz [gants] adj whole, all; (vollständig) complete. adv quite; (vollends) fully. **Ganze** neut whole.

gar [gaːr] adj (Kochen) done, cooked. adv very. **gar nicht** not at all. **gar keiner** none whatever.

Garantie [garan'tiː] f (pl -n) guarantee.

Garde ['gardə] f (pl -n) guard.

Garderobe [gardə'roːbə] f (pl -n) cloakroom; (Kleider) wardrobe.

Gardine [gar'diːnə] f (pl -n) curtain.

***gären** ['gɛːrən] v ferment.

garnieren [gar'niːrən] v garnish; (Kleidung) trim.

Garnison [garni'zoːn] f (pl -en) garrison.

Garnitur [garni'tuːr] f (pl -en) (Verzierung) trimming; (Satz) set; (Ausrüstung) equipment.

Garten ['gartən] m (pl Gärten) garden. **-bau** m horticulture. **-haus** neut summer house. **-laube** f arbour.

Gärtner ['gɛrtnər] m (pl -) gardener. **-ei** f (pl -en) nursery.

Gärung ['gɛːrʊŋ] f (pl -en) fermentation.

Gas [gaːs] neut (pl -e) gas. -flasche f gas cylinder or bottle. -hebel m accelerator. -hahn m gas cock. -herd m gas cooker.

Gasse ['gasə] f (pl -n) alley, lane.

Gast [gast] m (pl Gäste) guest. gastfreundlich adj hospitable. Gast‖freundschaft f hospitality. -geber m (pl -) host. -geberin f (pl -nen) hostess. -hof m hotel, inn. -mahl neut banquet. -stätte f restaurant, café. -wirt m landlord, innkeeper.

Gatte ['gatə] m (pl -n) spouse, husband. gatten v match. Gattin f (pl -nen) spouse, wife.

Gattung ['gatʊŋ] f (pl -en) sort, kind; (Biol) species.

gaukeln ['gaʊkəln] v perform tricks, juggle.

Gaul [gaʊl] m (pl Gäule) nag.

Gaumen ['gaʊmən] m (pl -) palate.

Gauner ['gaʊnər] m (pl -) swindler, trickster.

Gaze ['gaːzə] f (pl -n) gauze.

Gazelle [ga'tsɛlə] f (pl -n) gazelle.

geartet [gə'aːrtət] adj constituted, composed.

Gebäck [gə'bɛk] neut (pl -e) pastry, cakes; (Keks) biscuit.

Gebärde [gə'bɛːrdə] f (pl -n) gesture.

***gebären** [gə'bɛːrən] v give birth to, bear. Gebärmutter f womb.

Gebäude [gə'bɔydə] neut (pl -) building.

***geben** ['geːbən] v give. sich geben relent, abate. es gibt there is/are. was gibt es? what is the matter? sich zufrieden geben be content. das gibt's nicht! that's impossible! Geben neut giving. Geber m (pl -), Geberin f (pl -nen) giver, donor.

Gebet [gə'beːt] neut (pl -e) prayer. -buch neut prayerbook.

Gebiet [gə'biːt] neut (pl -e) (Staats-) territory; (Gegend) area, district; (fig) field, sphere.

Gebilde [gə'bildə] neut (pl -) (Erzeugnis) product; (Form) structure, shape. gebildet [gə'bildət] adj educated, cultured.

Gebirge [gə'birgə] neut (pl -) mountain range, mountains pl.

Gebiß [gə'bis] neut (pl Gebisse) (set of) teeth; (Zaum) bit; (künstlich) denture.

Gebläse [gə'blɛːzə] neut (pl -) blower, bellows pl; (Mot) supercharger.

geboren [gə'boːrən] adj born. geborener

Hamburger native of Hamburg. Frau Maria Müller, geborene (geb.) Schmidt Mrs. Maria Müller, née Schmidt.

Gebot [gə'boːt] neut (pl -e) order. die zehn Gebote the Ten Commandments.

Gebrauch [gə'braʊx] neut (pl Gebräuche) custom; (Benutzen) use. gebrauchen v use. gebräuchlich adj customary. Gebrauchs‖anweisung f or -anleitung f instructions (for use). Gebrauchtwagen m second-hand car.

gebrechlich [gə'brɛçliç] adj (Gegenstand) fragile; (Person) frail.

Gebrüder [gə'brydər] m pl brothers. Gebrüder Schmidt Schmidt Bros.

Gebrüll [gə'bryl] neut (unz.) roar, roaring.

Gebühr [gə'byːr] f (pl -en) fee, charge. Gebühr f (unz.) decency, propriety. nach Gebühr duly. gebühren v be due. sich gebühren be fitting or decent. gebührend adj seemly, proper.

gebunden [gə'bʊndən] adj bound.

Geburt [gə'buːrt] f (pl -en) birth. Geburten‖beschränkung f or -regelung f birth control. gebürtig adj born (in). Geburts‖fehler m congenital defect. -helfer m obstetrician. -helferin f midwife; (Ärztin) obstetrician. -hilfe f obstetrics. -mal neut mole. -ort m birthplace. -schein m birth certificate. -tag m birthday.

Gebüsch [gə'byʃ] neut (pl -e) (clump of) bushes.

Gedächtnis [gə'dɛçtnis] neut (pl -se) memory. -feier f commemoration. -schwund m loss of memory, amnesia.

Gedanke [gə'daŋkə] m (pl -n) thought. sich Gedanken machen über worry about. gedankenlos adj thoughtless. gedanklich adj mental.

Gedeck [gə'dɛk] neut (pl -e) cover, place-setting; menu.

***gedeihen** [gə'daɪən] v flourish, thrive.

***gedenken** [gə'dɛŋkən] v think (of); (vorhaben) intend. Gendenkfeier f commemoration.

Gedicht [gə'diçt] neut (pl -e) poem. -sammlung f anthology (of verse).

gediegen [gə'diːgən] adj (echt) genuine; (rein) pure; (solide) solid; (sorgfältig) thorough.

Gedränge [gə'drɛŋə] neut (unz.) crowd, press; (Notlage) difficulty. gedrängt adj narrow, close; (Stil) terse, concise.

gedruckt [gə'drukt] *adj* printed.

gedrückt [gə'drykt] *adj* depressed.

Geduld [gə'dult] *f* patience. **geduldig** *adj* patient. **Geduldspiel** *neut* puzzle.

geehrt [gə'eɪrt] *adj* honoured. **sehr geehrter Herr (Smith)** Dear Sir (Dear Mr Smith).

geeignet [gə'aignət] *adj* suitable, adapted (to).

Gefahr [gə'fair] *f* (*pl* **-en**) danger. **gefährden** *v* endanger, jeopardize. **gefährlich** *adj* dangerous. **gefahr∥los** *adj* safe, without risk. **-voll** *adj* dangerous.

Gefährte [gə'fɛirtə] *m* (*pl* **-n**), **Gefährtin** *f* (*pl* **-nen**) companion.

*****gefallen** [gə'falən] *v* please. **es gefällt mir** I like it. **sich nicht gefallen lassen** not put up with.

Gefallen¹ [gə'falən] *neut* (*unz.*) pleasure.

Gefallen² *m* (*pl* **-**) favour. **tun Sie mir den Gefallen und . . .** Do me the favour of . . . .

gefällig [gə'fɛliç] *adj* pleasing; obliging.

gefangen [gə'faŋən] *adj* captive. **Gefangene(r)** *m* prisoner, captive. **Gefangenschaft** *f* captivity.

Gefängnis [gə'fɛŋnis] *neut* (*pl* **-se**) prison. **-wärter** *m* warder, prison officer.

Gefäß [gə'fɛis] *neut* (*pl* **-e**) container, vessel.

gefaßt [gə'fast] *adj* collected, calm, (*bereit*) ready.

Gefecht [gə'fɛçt] *neut* (*pl* **-e**) fight, combat.

Gefieder [gə'fiidər] *neut* (*unz.*) feathers *pl*; plumage.

Geflügel [gə'flyigəl] *neut* (*unz.*) poultry.

Gefolge [gə'fɔlgə] *neut* (*pl* **-**) followers *pl*, entourage.

gefräßig [gə'frɛisiç] *adj* voracious, gluttonous.

Gefrier∥punkt [gə'friirpuŋkt] *m* freezing point. **-schutzmittel** *neut* antifreeze.

gefügig [gə'fyigiç] *adj* pliant, submissive.

Gefühl [gə'fyil] *neut* (*pl* **-e**) feeling. **gefühl-los** *adj* unfeeling. **Gefühlsinn** *m* sense of touch. **gefühlvoll** *adj* full of feeling, emotional.

gegebenenfalls [gə'geibənənfals] *adv* if need be, should the need arise. **Gegebenheit** *f* (*pl* **-en**) reality.

gegen [ˈgeigən] *prep* against; (*in Richtung*) towards; (*ungefähr*) about; compared with; (*Tausch*) in exchange for.

Gegen∥angriff *m* counterattack. **-besuch** *m* return visit. **-bild** *neut* counterpart.

Gegend [ˈgeigənt] *f* (*pl* **-en**) district, area.

gegeneinander [ˈgeigənainandər] *adv* against one another.

Gegen∥gift *neut* antidote. **-leistung** *f* return (service). **-mittel** *neut* remedy. **-satz** *m* opposite, contrary. **gegen∥sätzlich** *adj* opposite, contrary. **-seitig** *adj* reciprocal, mutual. **Gegen∥stand** *m* object; (*Thema*) subject. **-stück** *neut* counterpart. **-teil** *neut* opposite, contrary. **im Gegenteil zu** contrary to, in contrast to.

gegenüber [ˈgeigənybər] *adv*, *prep* opposite. **-liegend** *adj* opposite. **-stehen** *v* stand opposite. **Gegenüberstellung** *f* confrontation; antithesis.

Gegenwart [ˈgeigənvairt] *f* (*unz.*) present; (*Anwesenheit*) presence. **gegenwärtig** *adj* present, current.

Gegner [ˈgeignər] *m* (*pl* **-**) opponent, enemy. **gegnerisch** *adj* antagonistic, hostile.

Gehalt¹ [gə'halt] *m* (*unz.*) contents *pl*; (*Wert*) worth, value.

Gehalt² *neut* (*pl* **Gehälter**) salary, pay. **Gehalts∥empfänger** *m* salaried employee. **-erhöhung** *f* rise (in salary).

gehässig [gə'hɛsiç] *adj* spiteful, malicious.

Gehäuse [gə'hoyzə] *neut* (*pl* **-**) case, box; (*Tech*) casing.

geheim [gə'haim] *adj* secret. **Geheim∥agent** *m* secret agent. **-dienst** *m* secret or intelligence service. **geheimhalten** *v* keep secret. **Geheimnis** *neut* (*pl* **-se**) secret; (*unerklärbar*) mystery. **geheimnisvoll** *adj* mysterious. **Geheim∥polizei** *f* secret police. **-schrift** *f* code, cipher. **geheimtuerisch** *adj* secretive.

*****gehen** [ˈgeiən] *v* walk, go (*on foot*); (*Maschine*) go, work. **wie geht es Ihnen?** how are you? **es geht** it's all right. **es geht nicht** it can't be done, that's no good. **sie geht mit ihm** she is going out with him. **an die Arbeit gehen** set to work.

Gehilfe [gə'hilfə] *m* (*pl* **-n**) assistant, help.

Gehirn [gə'hirn] *neut* (*pl* **-e**) brain. **-erschütterung** *f* concussion. **-schlag** *m* cerebral apoplexy. **-wäsche** *f* brainwashing.

gehoben [gə'hoibən] *adj* high, elevated.

Gehör [gə'hœir] *neut* (*unz.*) hearing; (*Musik*) ear.

gehorchen [gə'hɔrçən] v obey.

gehören [gə'hœːrən] v belong (to). **es gehört sich** it is proper or fitting. **gehörig** adj fit, proper.

gehorsam [gə'hoːrzaɪm] adj obedient. **Gehorsam** m obedience. **–verweigerung** f insubordination.

Geh||steig [ˈgeɪʃtaik] m (pl -e) pavement. **–werk** neut movement, works.

Geier ['gaɪər] m (pl -) vulture.

Geifer ['gaɪfər] m (unz.) spittle, slaver; (fig) venom. **geifern** v slaver; (fig) rave, foam with rage.

Geige [gaɪgə] f (pl -n) violin, fiddle. **–r** m violinist.

Geisel ['gaɪzəl] m (pl -) hostage.

Geist [gaɪst] **1** m (unz.) mind; (Witzigkeit) wit; (nichtmaterielle Eigenschaften) spirit. **2** m (pl -er) (Genius) genius; (Gespenst) ghost, spirit. **geistesabwesend** adj absent-minded. **Geistes||blitz** m brainwave. **–freiheit** f freedom of thought. **geisteskrank** adj mentally ill, insane. **Geisteskranke(r)** m mental patient. **geist||ig** adj intellectual; (nicht körperlich) spiritual; (Getränke) alcoholic. **–lich** adj spiritual, religious; (kirchlich) clerical. **Geistliche(r)** m cleric, clergyman. **geistreich** adj clever, ingenious.

Geiz [gaits] m (unz.) avarice, miserliness. **geizig** adj miserly, avaricious.

Gekicher [gə'kiçər] neut (unz.) giggling.

Geklapper [gə'klapər] neut (unz.) clatter(ing).

Geklimper [gə'klimpər] neut (unz.) jingling, chinking; (Instrument) strumming.

Geklingel [gə'klinəl] neut (unz.) tinkling, ringing.

gekünstelt [gə'kynstəlt] adj artificial, affected.

Gelächter [gə'lɛçtər] neut (pl -) laughter.

geladen [gə'laɪdən] adj loaded; (Batterie) charged.

Gelände [gə'lɛndə] neut (pl -) tract of land, area; (Bau-) site; (Sport-) grounds pl. **–lauf** m cross-country (running).

Geländer [gə'lɛndər] neut (pl -) railing, banister.

gelangen [gə'laŋən] v reach, arrive at; (Ziel) attain.

gelassen [gə'lasən] adj calm, composed.

geläufig [gə'lɔyfiç] adj familiar; (Sprache) fluent.

gelaunt [gə'laʊnt] adj disposed. **gut**

gelaunt sweet-tempered. **schlecht** or **übel gelaunt** bad-tempered.

gelb [gɛlp] adj yellow. **Gelb** neut yellow. **–sucht** f jaundice. **gelbsüchtig** adj (Med) jaundiced.

Geld [gɛlt] neut (pl -er) money. **–ausgabe** f expenditure. **–beutel** m purse. **–geber** m financial backer. **geldlich** adj pecuniary. **Geld||nehmer** m borrower. **–strafe** f fine. **–stück** neut coin. **–sucht** f avarice.

Gelee [ʒe'leː] neut (pl -s) jelly.

gelegen [gə'leɪgən] adj situated; (günstig) convenient, opportune. **Gelegenheit** f (pl -en) opportunity, occasion. **Gelegenheits||arbeit** f casual work. **–kauf** m bargain. **gelegentlich** adj occasional.

gelehrig [gə'leːriç] adj eager to learn; (klug) intelligent. **gelehrt** adj learned. **Gelehrte(r)** m scholar.

Geleit [gə'laɪt] neut (pl -) escort, entourage. **–brief** m (letter of) safe conduct. **geleiten** v escort, accompany.

Gelenk [gə'lɛŋk] neut (pl -e) joint. **–entzündung** f arthritis.

gelernt [gə'lɛrnt] adj skilled, trained.

Geliebte(r) [gə'liːptə] m beloved, sweetheart.

gelinde [gə'lində] adj gentle, mild.

gelingen [gə'liŋən] v succeed, be successful. **es gelingt mir, zu ...** I am able to ...

geloben [gə'loːbən] v vow, promise solemnly.

*gelten** [gɛltən] v be worth, cost; (gültig sein) be valid; (betreffen) concern. **–d** adj valid. **geltend machen** urge, insist (on).

Gelübde [gə'lypdə] neut (pl -) vow.

Gemach [gə'max] neut (pl Gemächer) room, chamber.

Gemahl [gə'maɪl] m (pl -e) husband. **–in** f (pl -nen) wife.

Gemälde [gə'mɛldə] neut (pl -) painting, picture. **–galerie** f picture gallery.

gemäß [gə'mɛis] prep in accordance with. adj suitable.

gemein [gə'main] adj common; (öffentlich) public; vulgar, low; (böse) nasty, mean.

Gemeinde [gə'maində] f (pl -n) community; (Kommune) municipality, town; (Kirche) congregation. **–rat** m local council; (Person) councillor. **–schule** f village school. **–steuer** f rates pl.

Gemeine(r) [gə'mainə(r)] m (Mil) private.
Gemeinheit f meanness, nastiness; (Tat) mean trick, piece of spite. **gemein‖nützig** adj charitable. **–sam** adj joint, common. **Gemeinschaft** f community; (Komm) partnership. **–serziehung** f coeducation. **–sschule** f coeducational school.
Gemenge [gə'mɛŋə] neut (pl -n) mixture; (Gewühl) scuffle.
gemessen [gə'mɛsən] adj measured, sedate.
Gemisch [gə'miʃ] neut (pl -e) mixture. **gemischt** adj mixed.
Gemurmel [gə'murməl] neut (unz.) murmuring.
Gemüse [gə'myːzə] neut (pl -) vegetable(s). **–gärtner** m market gardener. **–händler** m greengrocer.
Gemüt [gə'myːt] neut (pl -er) disposition, temperament, heart. **gemütlich** adj comfortable, cosy; (leutselig) good-natured. **Gemütlichkeit** f cosiness, comfortableness; good-nature.
Gen [gɛn] neut (pl -e) gene.
genannt [gə'nant] adj named, called.
genau [gə'nau] adj precise, exact. **Genauigkeit** f precision, exactness.
genehmigen [gə'neːmigən] v authorize, permit. **Genehmigung** f (pl -en) authorization, permission.
geneigt [gə'naikt] adj disposed, inclined.
General [gene'raːl] m (pl -e) general. **–police** f comprehensive insurance policy. **–probe** f dress rehearsal. **–sekretär** m secretary-general. **–versammlung** f general meeting.
Generation [generatsi'oːn] f (pl -en) generation.
*genesen [gə'neːzən] v recover, convalesce, get better. **Genesung** f recovery. **–sheim** neut convalescent home.
Genetik [ge'neːtik] f genetics. **genetisch** adj genetic.
Genf [gɛnf] neut Geneva.
genial [geni'aːl] adj (Person) brilliant, gifted; (Sache) ingenious, inspired.
Genick [gə'nik] neut (pl -e) (nape of the) neck.
Genie [ʒe'niː] neut (pl -s) genius.
genieren [ʒe'niːrən] v bother, trouble. **sich genieren** to be embarrassed.
genießbar [gə'niːsbaːr] adj enjoyable; (Essen, Trinken) palatable. **genießen** v enjoy; eat; drink. **Genießer** m (pl -) epicure, gourmet.

Genitalien [geni'taːliən] pl genitals.
Genosse [gə'nɔsə] m (pl -n), **Genossin** f (pl -nen) comrade; (Kollege) colleague. **Genossenschaft** f cooperative (society). **genossenschaftlich** adj cooperative.
genug [gə'nuːk] adv, adj enough, sufficient(ly). **genügen** v be enough, suffice. **–d** adj sufficient, enough. **genügsam** adj easily satisfied. **Genugtuung** f satisfaction.
Genuß [gə'nus] m (pl Genüsse) pleasure, enjoyment.
Geograph [geo'graːf] m (pl -en) geographer. **–ie** f geography. **geographisch** adj geographical.
Geologe [geo'loːgə] m (pl -n) geologist. **Geologie** f geology. **geologisch** adj geological.
Geometrie [geome'triː] f (pl -n) geometry. **geometrish** adj geometrical.
Gepäck [gə'pɛk] neut (unz.) baggage, luggage. **–aufbewahrung** f left-luggage office. **–netz** neut luggage rack. **–träger** m porter.
gepflegt [gə'pfleːkt] adj well-tended; (Person) well-groomed, well-dressed.
gepanzert [gə'pantsərt] adj armoured.
Gepflogenheit [gə'pfloːgənhait] f (pl -en) habit, custom.
Geplapper [gə'plapər] neut (unz.) chatter.
Geplauder [gə'plaudər] neut (unz.) chat, small talk.
Gepräge [gə'prɛːgə] neut (pl -) stamp; (Münze) coinage; (Eigenart) character.
Geprassel [gə'prasəl] neut (unz.) clatter.
gerade [gə'raːdə] adj straight; (direkt) direct; (Haltung) erect; (Zahl) even. adv just; (genau) exactly, precisely; (direkt) straight, directly. **–aus** adv straight on or ahead. **–so** adv just so, just the same. **–stehen** v stand erect, stand up straight. **–swegs** adv immediately; (ohne Umwege) directly. **–zu** adv directly; (freimütig) plainly, flatly; (durchaus) sheer, downright. **Geradheit** f straightness; (Ehrlichkeit) honesty. **gerad‖läufig** adj straight. **–zahlig** adj even(-numbered).
Geranie [ge'raːniə] f (pl -n) geranium.
Gerassel [gə'rasəl] neut (unz.) clatter, rattle.
Gerät [gə'rɛːt] neut (pl -e) tool, implement; (kompliziert) instrument; (Maschine) device, appliance; (Radio, TV) set; (Ausrüstung) equipment.

*geraten [gə'raɪtən] v come upon; (gelingen) turn out well; (gedeihen) thrive. **in Schwierigkeiten geraten** get into difficulties. **in Zorn geraten** fly into a rage. **über etwas geraten** come across, stumble upon something.

Geratewohl [gə'raɪtəvoɪl] neut **aufs Geratewohl** at random.

geräumig [gə'rɔymɪç] adj roomy, spacious.

Geräusch [gə'rɔyʃ] neut (pl -e) noise.

gerben [ˈgɛrbən] v tan. **Gerber** m (pl -) tanner. **Gerberei** f (pl -en) tannery.

gerecht [gə'rɛçt] adj just, fair; (geeignet) suitable. **-fertigt** adj justified; (legitim) legitimate. **Gerechtigkeit** f justice; (Rechtschaffenheit) righteousness.

Gerede [gə'reɪdə] neut (unz.) gossip.

Gericht[1] [gə'rɪçt] neut (pl -e) (Essen) dish; (Gang) course.

Gericht[2] neut (pl -e) law-court; (fig) justice, judgment. **gerichtlich** adj judicial, legal. **Gerichts||hof** m (law) court. **-kosten** pl (legal) costs. **-medizin** f forensic medicine. **-saal** m courtroom. **-schreiber** m clerk (of the court). **-verfahren** neut legal proceedings pl. **-vollzieher** m bailiff.

gerieben [gə'riːbən] adj grated.

gering [gə'rɪŋ] adj small; (Vorrat) short; (Preis) low; (unbedeutend) unimportant, insignificant. **-fügig** adj trivial, insignificant. **-schätzen** v think little of, despise. **-schätzig** adj disdainful.

gerinnen [gə'rɪnən] v congeal; (Blut) clot. **Gerinnsel** neut clot.

Gerippe [gə'rɪpə] neut (pl -) skeleton.

Germane [gɛr'maːnə] m (pl -n), **Germanin** f (pl -nen) German; f Germanic (tribes or peoples). **germanisch** adj Germanic.

gern(e) [ˈgɛrn(ə)] adv willingly, gladly, readily. **gern haben** or **mögen** be fond of, like. **gern tun** like to do. *ich möchte gern ...* I would like ... . **gut und gern** easily.

Gerste [ˈgɛrstə] f barley.

Geruch [gə'rʊx] m (pl Gerüche) smell, odour. **-ssinn** m (sense of) smell.

Gerücht [gə'rʏçt] neut (pl -e) rumour.

Gerümpel [gə'rʏmpəl] neut junk, trash.

Gerüst [gə'rʏst] neut (pl -e) scaffolding.

gesamt [gə'zamt] adj whole, entire. **Gesamt||betrag** m total (amount). **-heit** f whole, totality. **-schule** comprehensive

school. **-übersicht** f overall view. **-versicherung** f comprehensive insurance. **-zahl** f total (number).

Gesandte(r) [gə'zantə] m (pl -n) ambassador. **Gesandtschaft** f embassy.

Gesang [gə'zaŋ] m (pl Gesänge) song; (Singen) singing. **-buch** neut songbook; (Kirche) hymnbook.

Gesäß [gə'zɛːs] neut (pl -e) seat, bottom.

Geschäft [gə'ʃɛft] neut (pl -e) business; (Laden) shop; (Handel) deal. **das Geschäft blüht** business is booming. **ein unsauberes Geschäft** a dirty business. **ein gutes Geschäft machen** get a bargain. **geschäftlich** adj commercial, business. **Geschäfts||freund** m business associate, customer. **-führer** m manager; (Verein) secretary. **-haus** neut firm. **-jahr** neut business year. **-mann** m businessman. **-raum** m or **-räume** pl office(s). **geschäftsmäßig** adj businesslike. **Geschäfts||reisende(r)** m commercial traveller, representative. **-schluß** m closing time. **-stunden** pl office hours.

*geschehen [gə'ʃeːən] v happen.

gescheit [gə'ʃaɪt] adj clever, smart.

Geschenk [gə'ʃɛŋk] neut (pl -e) present, gift.

Geschichte [gə'ʃɪçtə] f (pl -n) (Erzählung) story; (Vergangenheit) history; (Angelegenheit) affair. **Geschichtenbuch** neut story book. **geschichtlich** adj historical. **Geschichts||buch** neut history book. **-forscher** m (research) historian. **-schreiber** m historian.

Geschick [gə'ʃɪk] neut (pl -e) aptitude; (Schicksal) fate. **-lichkeit** f skill. **geschickt** adj able, skilful.

geschieden [gə'ʃiːdən] adj divorced.

Geschirr [gə'ʃɪr] neut (pl -e) crockery, dishes; (Pferde) harness. **-tuch** neut dishcloth. **-spülmaschine** f dishwasher.

Geschlecht [gə'ʃlɛçt] neut (pl -er) sex; (Art) kind, sort; (Familie) family, house; (Gramm) gender. **geschlechtlich** adj sexual. **Geschlechts||krankheit** f venereal disease. **-reife** f puberty. **-teile** pl genitals. **-verkehr** m sexual intercourse.

geschlossen [gə'ʃlɔsən] adj closed.

Geschmack [gə'ʃmak] m (pl Geschmäcke) taste. **geschmacklos** adj tasteless. **Geschmacks||sache** f matter of taste. **-sinn** m sense of taste. **geschmackvoll** adj tasteful.

Geschnatter [gə'ʃnatər] neut (unz.) cackling.

Geschöpf [gə'ʃœpf] neut (pl -e) creature.

Geschoß [gə'ʃɔs] neut (pl Geschosse) projectile, missile; (Kanone) shell; (Stockwerk) floor, storey.

Geschrei [gə'ʃrai] neut (pl -e) cry, shouting, crying; (fig) fuss, noise.

Geschütz [gə'ʃyts] neut (pl -e) gun, cannon.

Geschwätz [gə'ʃvɛts] neut idle talk, prattle. geschwätzig adj talkative.

geschweige [gə'ʃvaigə] conj geschweige denn let alone, to say nothing of.

geschwind [gə'ʃvint] adj quick, fast. Geschwindigkeit f speed, velocity. Geschwindigkeits‖grenze f speed limit. –messer m speedometer.

Geschwister [gə'ʃvistər] pl brother(s) and sister(s); siblings. haben Sie Geschwister? have you any brothers and sisters?

Geschworene(r) [gə'ʃvoirənə] m (pl -n) juror. Geschworenengericht neut (trial by) jury.

Geschwür [gə'ʃvyr] neut (pl -e) ulcer, sore.

Geselle [gə'zɛlə] m (pl -n) comrade, companion; (Bursche) lad, fellow; (gelehrter Handwerker) journeyman. gesellig adj sociable. Gesellschaft f society; (Firma) company; (Verein) society, association; (Abend-, usw.) party, social gathering; (Begleitung) company. gesellschaftlich adj social. Gesellschaftsanzug m evening dress. gesellschaftsfeindlich adj antisocial. Gesellschafts‖kleid neut party dress. –steuer f corporation tax. –tanz m society dance, ball.

Gesetz [gə'zɛts] neut (pl -e) law. –buch neut statute book, law code. –entwurf m bill. gesetzgebend adj legislative. Gesetzgebung f legislation. gesetz‖lich adj legal, lawful. –los adj lawless. –mäßig adj legal, lawful.

gesetzt [gə'zɛtst] adj sedate, quiet.

gesetzwidrig [gə'zɛtsviidriç] adj illegal, unlawful.

Gesicht [gə'ziçt] neut (pl -er) face; (Miene) expression. Gesichts‖ausdruck m (facial) expression. –farbe f complexion. –feld neut field of vision. –punkt m viewpoint.

gesinnt [gə'zint] adj disposed, minded. Gesinnung f opinion, mind, conviction. gesinnungslos adj unprincipled.

Gespann [gə'ʃpan] neut (pl -e) (Pferden) (team of) horses.

gespannt [gə'ʃpant] adj tense; (Verhältnis) strained. gespannt sein be eager or anxious.

Gespenst [gə'ʃpɛnst] neut (pl -er) ghost. gespenstig adj ghostly.

Gespräch [gə'ʃprɛiç] neut (pl -e) conversation, talk. Gespräche pl talks, discussion sing. gesprächig adj talkative.

Gestalt [gə'ʃtalt] f (pl -en) form, shape; (Körper-) figure, build; (Literatur) character. gestalt‖en v form, shape. –et adj formed, shaped. –los adj shapeless. Gestaltung f (unz.) shaping, formation.

Geständnis [gə'ʃtɛntnis] neut (pl -se) confession.

Gestank [gə'ʃtaŋk] m stink, stench.

gestatten [gə'ʃtatən] v permit, allow.

Geste ['gɛstə] f (pl -n) gesture.

*gestehen [gə'ʃteiən] v confess.

Gestell [gə'ʃtɛl] neut (pl -e) (Rahmen) frame, stand; (Bock) trestle; (Regal) shelf; (Bett-) bedstead.

gestern ['gɛstərn] adv yesterday.

Gesträuch [gə'ʃtrɔyç] neut (unz.) shrubbery, bushes pl.

gestrichen [gə'ʃtriçən] adj painted. frisch gestrichen newly painted; wet paint.

gestrig ['gɛstriç] adj yesterday's.

Gestrüpp [gə'ʃtryp] neut undergrowth, scrub.

Gesuch [gə'zuix] neut (pl -e) petition. gesucht adj in demand; (Person) wanted.

gesund [gə'zunt] adj healthy, well. Gesundheit f health. interj bless you! gesundheitlich adj sanitary. gesundheits‖förderlich adj wholesome, healthy. Gesundheitslehre f hygiene. gesundheitsschädlich adj insanitary, unhealthy.

Getränk [gə'trɛŋk] neut (pl -e) drink.

Getreide [gə'traidə] neut (pl -) grain, cereals pl.

getreu [gə'trɔy] adj loyal, faithful.

Getriebe [gə'triibə] neut (pl -) commotion, bustle; (Tech) transmission, gears pl. –gehäuse neut gearbox.

getrost [gə'troist] adj confident. adv without hesitation.

Getto ['gɛtot] neut (pl -s) ghetto.

geübt [gə'ypt] adj practised, skilful.

Gewächs [gə'vɛks] neut (pl -e) plant; (Med) growth.

gewachsen [gə'vaksən] *adj* grown. **gewachsen sein** be equal (to), be up (to).

gewagt [gə'vaːkt] *adj* bold, daring.

gewählt [gə'vɛːlt] *adj* select(ed), choice.

Gewähr [gə'vɛːr] *f* (*unz.*) guarantee, surety. **gewähren** *v* allow, grant. **gewährleisten** *v* guarantee, vouch for.

Gewalt [gə'valt] *f* (*pl* -en) force; (*Macht*) power; (*Obrigkeit*) authority; (*Gewalttätigkeit*) violence. **–herrscher** *m* tyrant. **gewalt‖ig** *adj* forceful, powerful; enormous; (*gewalttätig*) violent. **–los** *adj* powerless. **–sam** *adj* violent; *adv* by force. **tätig** *adj* violent.

Gewand [gə'vant] *neut* (*pl* Gewänder) garment, robe.

gewandt [gə'vant] *adj* skilled, skilful. **Gewandtheit** *f* dexterity, skill.

Gewässer [gə'vɛsər] *neut* (*pl* -) water(s).

Gewebe [gə'veːbə] *neut* (*pl* -) material, textile; (*Biol*) tissue; (*Lügen, usw.*) web, network.

geweckt [gə'vɛkt] *adj* bright, lively.

Gewehr [gə'veːr] *neut* (*pl* -e) rifle, gun. **–kugel** *f* (rifle) bullet.

Geweih [gə'vai] *neut* (*pl* -e) antlers *pl*.

Gewerbe [gə'vɛrbə] *neut* (*pl* -) trade. **–schule** *f* technical school. **gewerb‖lich** *adj* industrial. **–smäßig** *adj* professional.

Gewerkschaft [gə'vɛrkʃaft] *f* (*pl* -en) (trade) union. **–ler** *m* (trade) unionist. **gewerkschaftlich** *adj* trade-union.

Gewicht [gə'viçt] *neut* (*pl* -e) weight; (*fig*) importance. **–heben** *neut* weight-lifting. **gewichtig** *adj* heavy; (*fig*) important.

Gewimmel [gə'viməl] *neut* (*pl* -) crowd, swarm.

Gewinde [gə'vində] *neut* (*pl* -) (*Schraube*) thread.

Gewinn [gə'vin] *m* (*pl* -e) profit; (*Ertrag*) yield, returns; (*Preis*) prize; (*Erwerben*) gaining. **–beteiligung** *f* profit-sharing. **gewinn‖bringend** *adj* profitable. **–en** *v* (*Preis*) win; (*erwerben*) gain, acquire; (*siegen*) win. **–süchtig** *adj* acquisitive.

Gewirr [gə'vir] *neut* (*pl* -e) confusion, tangle.

gewiß [gə'vis] *adj* certain, sure. *adv* certainly. *ein gewisser Herr Schmidt* a certain Mr Schmidt. *ein gewisses Etwas* a certain something.

Gewissen [gə'visən] *neut* (*unz.*) conscience. **gewissen‖haft** *adj* conscientious. **–los** *adj* unscrupulous. **Gewissens‖bisse** *pl* pangs of conscience. **–konflikt** *m* conflict of conscience.

gewissermaßen [gə'visərmaːsən] *adv* to some extent.

Gewißheit [gə'vishait] *f* (*unz.*) certainty.

Gewitter [gə'vitər] *neut* (*pl* -) thunderstorm. **gewitterhaft** *adj* stormy.

gewogen [gə'voːgən] *adj* well disposed, favourably inclined.

gewöhnen [gə'vøːnən] *v* accustom. **sich gewöhnen an** become accustomed to, get used to. **Gewohnheit** *f* (*pl* -en) habit; (*Brauch*) custom. **gewohnheitsmäßig** *adj* customary. **gewöhnlich** *adj* usual, ordinary; (*unfein*) vulgar. *adv* usually. **gewohnt** *adj* used (to).

Gewölbe [gə'vœlbə] *neut* (*pl* -) vault. **gewölbt** *adj* arched, vaulted.

Gewühl [gə'vyːl] *neut* (*unz.*) crowd, tumult.

Gewürz [gə'vyrts] *neut* (*pl* -e) spice, seasoning. **gewürzig** *adj* spicy. **gewürzt** *adj* spiced, seasoned.

gezackt [gə'tsakt] *adj* serrated; (*Fels*) jagged.

geziemend [gə'tsiːmənt] *or* **geziemlich** *adj* seemly.

geziert [gə'tsiːrt] *adj* affected.

gezwungen [gə'tsvuŋən] *adj* forced; (*steif*) formal, stiff.

Gicht [giçt] *f* (*unz.*) gout.

Giebel ['giːbəl] *m* (*pl* -) gable. **–dach** *neut* gabled roof.

Gier [giːr] *f* greed; (*nach etwas*) craving, burning desire (for). **gierig** *adj* greedy.

*gießen ['giːsən] *v* pour; (*Pflanzen*) water; (*schmelzen*) cast. **Gieß‖erei** *f* (*pl* -en) foundry. **–kanne** *f* watering can.

Gift [gift] *neut* (*pl* -e) poison. **–gas** *neut* poison gas. **giftig** *adj* poisonous. **Giftschlange** *f* poisonous snake.

Ginster ['ginstər] *m* (*pl* -) (*Bot*) broom.

Gipfel ['gipfəl] *m* (*pl* -) peak, summit. **–gespräche** *pl* summit talks. **–leistung** *f* record.

Gips [gips] *m* (*pl* -e) gypsum; (*erhitzt*) plaster (of Paris). **–verband** *m* plaster cast.

Giraffe [gi'rafə] *f* (*pl* -n) giraffe.

Giro ['dʒiːro] *neut* (*pl* -s) giro. **–konto** *neut* current account.

Gitarre [gi'tarə] *f* (*pl* -n) guitar.

Gitter ['gitər] *neut* (*pl* -) grille, grating; (*Fenster*) bars; (*Spalier*) trellis.

Glanz [glants] m (unz.) shine, brilliance, brightness; (fig) splendour.

glänzen ['glɛntsən] v gleam, shine; (fig) excel, shine. **–d** adj brilliant.

Glas [glaːs] neut (pl **Gläser**) glass. **–haus** neut greenhouse, hothouse. **–perle** f bead. **–scheibe** f (window) pane. **glasieren** v glaze; (Kuchen) ice. **Glasur** f glaze; (Kuchen) icing.

glatt [glat] adj smooth; (glitschig) slippery. **Glatteis** neut (Mot) black ice. **glattrasiert** adj clean-shaven.

Glaube ['glaubə] m (unz.) belief; (Rel) faith. **glauben** v believe; (vermuten) think, suppose; (vertrauen) trust. **glaubhaft** adj credible.

gläubig ['glɔybiç] adj believing; (fromm) pious. **Gläubige(r)** m believer; (Komm) creditor.

glaublich ['glaupliç] adj credible. **glaubwürdig** adj (Person) trustworthy; (Sache) credible.

gleich [glaiç] adj (the) same, equal; (eben) level. adv equally; (sofort) at once; (schon) just. **von gleichem Alter** of the same age. **das ist mir gleich** it makes no difference to me. **das gleiche gilt für Dich** the same goes for you. **Ich komme gleich** I'm just coming. **gleich viel** just as much. **gleich||artig** adj similar. **–bedeutend** adj synonymous. **–berechtigt** adj having equal rights.

*****gleichen** ['glaiçən] v equal; (ähnlich sein) resemble.

gleichermaßen ['glaiçərmaːsən] or **gleicherweise** adv likewise.

gleich||falls adv also, likewise. **–gesinnt** adj like-minded.

Gleichgewicht ['glaiçgəviçt] neut equilibrium, balance.

gleichgültig ['glaiçgyltiç] adj unconcerned, indifferent. **Gleichgültigkeit** f indifference.

Gleich||heit f equality. **–maß** neut proportion, symmetry. **–mut** m equanimity. **–nis** neut (pl **-se**) simile; (Erzählung) parable.

gleichschalten ['glaiçʃaltən] v coordinate; (Tech) synchronize.

Gleichschritt ['glaiçʃrit] m **Gleichschritt halten** keep step.

Gleich||strom m direct current. **–ung** f (pl **-en**) equation.

gleich||viel adv no matter. **–wertig** adj equivalent, of the same value. **–wohl** adv nonetheless. **–zeitig** adj simultaneous.

Gleis [glais] neut (pl **-e**) track, platform.

*****gleiten** ['glaitən] v slide, slip. **Gleitflugzeug** neut glider, sailplane.

Gletscher ['glɛtʃər] m (pl **-**) glacier. **Gletscherspalte** f crevasse.

Glied [gliːt] neut (pl **-er**) limb; (Kette) link. **gliedern** v organize, arrange; divide into. **Gliederung** f (pl **-en**) organization, arrangement.

Glocke ['glokə] f (pl **-n**) bell. **Glocken||blume** f bluebell. **–turm** m belltower.

glorreich ['glɔrraiç] adj glorious.

Glossar [glɔ'saːr] neut (pl **-e**, **-ien**) glossary. **Glosse** f (pl **-n**) comment.

glotzen ['glɔtsən] v stare.

Glück [glyk] neut luck; (Geschick) fortune; (Freude) happiness. **glück||lich** adj happy, fortunate. **–licherweise** adv fortunately, luckily. **–selig** adj blissful. **Glücks||fall** m lucky chance. **–spiel** neut game of chance.

glühen ['glyːən] v glow. **Glüh||hitze** f white heat. **–wein** m mulled wine.

Glut [gluːt] f (pl **-en**) glow. **–asche** f embers pl.

Gnade ['gnaːdə] f (pl **-n**) grace, mercy. **Gnaden||frist** f reprieve, period of grace. **–stoß** m coup de grâce.

gnädig ['gnɛːdiç] adj gracious; kind. **gnädige Frau** Madam.

Gold [gɔlt] neut (unz.) gold. **–barren** m gold bar or ingot. **gold||en** adj golden. **–ig** adj sweet, lovely.

Golf[1] [gɔlf] m (pl **-e**) gulf.

Golf[2] neut (unz.) (Sport) golf.

gönnen ['gœnən] v not begrudge; grant, allow.

Gönner m (pl **-**) patron, sponsor. **gönnerhaft** adj patronizing; condescending.

Gosse ['gɔsə] f (pl **-n**) gutter.

Gott [gɔt] m God; (pl **Götter**) god. **grüß Gott!** greetings! God be with you! **Gott sei dank!** thank God! **um Gottes willen!** for God's sake! **Gottes||dienst** m (church) service. **–lästerung** f blasphemy. **Gottheit** f godhead, divinity.

Göttin ['gœtin] f (pl **-nen**) goddess. **göttlich** adj divine.

Götze ['gœtsə] m (pl **-n**) idol, false god.

Grab [graːp] neut (pl **Gräber**) grave. **graben** v dig. **Graben** m ditch, trench. **Grab||schrift** f epitaph. **–stätte** f grave. **–stein** m tombstone.

Grad [graːt] m (pl -e) degree; (Rang) rank, grade. **–messer** m (fig) indication, sign.

graduieren [gradu'iːrən] v graduate. **Graduierte(r)** m graduate.

Graf [graːf] m (pl -en) count.

Gräfin ['grɛːfin] f (pl -en) countess.

Grafschaft ['graːfʃaft] f (pl -en) county.

Gram [graːm] m (unz.) grief.

Gramm [gram] neut (pl -e) gram(me).

Grammatik [gra'matik] f (pl -en) grammar.

Granatapfel [gra'naːtapfəl] m (pl Granatäpfel) pomegranate.

Granate [gra'naːtə] f (pl -n) shell, grenade.

Granit [gra'niːt] m (pl -e) granite.

Graphik ['graːfik] f (unz.) graphics. **-er** m (pl -) designer, commercial artist. **graphisch** adj graphic. **graphische Darstellung** graph.

Gras [graːs] neut (pl Gräser) grass. **grasen** v graze.

gräßlich ['grɛːsliç] adj horrible, ghastly.

Grat [graːt] m (pl -e) ridge, edge.

Gräte ['grɛːtə] f (pl -n) fishbone. **–nmuster** neut herringbone pattern.

gratulieren [gratu'liːrən] v congratulate.

grau [grau] adj grey. **Graubrot** neut ryebread.

grauen ['grauən] v be horrible. **es graut mir vor** I have a horror of. **–haft** adj dreadful, horrible.

Graupe ['graupə] f (pl -n) groats pl, pearl barley.

graupeln ['graupəln] pl sleet sing.

grausam ['grauzaːm] adj cruel. **Grausamkeit** f cruelty. **grausig** adj fearful, dreadful.

gravieren [gra'viːrən] v engrave.

greif||en ['graifən] v seize, grasp. **–bar** adj (Waren) available, at hand; (fig) tangible. **greifen an** touch. **greifen in** dip into.

Greis [grais] m (pl -e) old man.

grell [grɛl] adj (Ton) shrill, harsh; (Farbe) glaring.

Grenze ['grɛntsə] f (pl -n) (eines Staates) border, frontier; (einer Stadt, Zone) boundary; (fig) limit. **grenzen** border (on). **Grenz||fall** m borderline case. **–übergang** m crossing (of a frontier).

Greuel ['grɔyəl] m (pl -) (Abscheu) horror; (Scheußlichkeit) atrocity, abomination.

Grieche ['griːçə] m (pl -n) Greek (man). **Griechenland** neut Greece. **Griechin** f (pl -nen) Greek (woman). **griechisch** adj Greek.

Grieß [griːs] m (unz.) (Essen) semolina; (Kies) gravel. **–pudding** m semolina pudding.

Griff [grif] m (pl -e) (Henkel, Knopf, usw.) handle; (Greifen) hold, grip.

Grille ['grilə] f (pl -n) (Insekt) cricket; (Laune) whim.

Grimasse [gri'masə] f (pl -n) grimace.

grimmig ['grimiç] adj furious.

grinsen ['grinzən] v grin.

Grippe ['gripə] f (pl -n) influenza.

grob [groːp] adj coarse; (Benehmen) coarse, rude; (Scherz) crude, coarse; (Fehler) gross, serious. **Grobheit** f coarseness, rudeness.

Groll [grɔl] m animosity, rancour. **grollen** v be resentful, be angry.

gros [groː] en **gros** wholesale.

Gros¹ [groː] neut (pl -) (Armee) main body.

Gros² [grɔs] neut (pl -e) gross, twelve dozen.

Groschen ['grɔʃən] m (pl -) (Österreich) Groschen; (BRD) ten-pfennig piece; (fig) penny.

groß [groːs] adj big, large; (wichtig) great, grand; (hoch) tall. **im großen und ganzen** on the whole. **–artig** adj splendid, grand.

Großbritannien [groːsbri'taniən] neut Great Britain.

Großbuchstabe ['groːsbuːxʃtaːbə] m capital (letter).

Großeltern ['groːseltərn] pl grandparents. **großenteils** ['groːsentails] adv mostly, for the most part.

Groß||handel m wholesale trade. **–händler** m wholesaler.

großherzig ['groːshɛrtsiç] adj magnanimous.

Groß||industrie f large-scale industry. **–macht** f great power. **–maul** neut braggart, big-mouth. **–mutter** f grandmother. **–stadt** f large town, city.

größtenteils ['grœːstəntails] adv mostly, largely.

Groß||teil m bulk. **–tuer** m show-off, big-head. **–vater** m grandfather.

großzügig ['groːtstsyːgiç] adj generous; (weittragend) large-scale. **Großzügigkeit** f generosity; largeness.

grotesk [gro'tɛsk] *adj* grotesque.

Grübchen ['gry:pçən] *neut* (*pl* -) dimple.

Grube ['gru:bə] *f* (*pl* -n) pit, hole; (*Bergbau*) mine, pit; (*Höhle*, *Bau*) hole, burrow; (*Falle*) snare.

grübeln ['gry:bəln] *v* brood, ponder.

grün [gry:n] *adj* green. **Grün** *neut* green. **–anlage** *f* public park, open space.

Grund [grunt] *m* (*pl* Gründe) (*Erdboden*) ground, soil; (*Veranlassung*) reason, grounds *pl*; (*Grundlage*) basis, base; (*Grundbesitz*) land; (*eines Meeres*) bottom. **–bau** *m* foundation. **–besitz** *m* landed property, real estate. **im Grunde** (**genommen**) basically.

gründen ['gryndən] *v* found, establish. **sich gründen auf** be based on. **Gründer** *m* (*pl* -) founder.

Grund‖gesetz *neut* basic law; (*Verfassung*) constitution. **–lage** *f* basis, foundation.

gründlich ['gryntliç] *adj* thorough.

grundlos ['gruntlo:s] *adj* unfounded, baseless.

Grund‖maß *neut* standard of measurement. **–riß** *m* outline, design. **–satz** *m* principle, axiom. **grundsätzlich** *adj* fundamental.

Grund‖schule *f* primary school. **–stoff** *m* raw material; (*Chem*) element. **–stück** *neut* lot of land.

Gründung ['gryndun] *f* (*pl* -en) establishment, foundation.

Grund‖unterschied *m* basic difference. **–zahl** *f* cardinal number. **–zug** *m* characteristic, feature.

Grünkohl ['gry:nko:l] *m* kale.

grunzen ['gruntsən] *v* grunt.

Grünzeug ['gryntsɔyk] *neut* greens *pl*, green vegetables *pl*.

Gruppe ['grupə] *f* (*pl* -n) group. **–nführer** *m* section leader. **gruppieren** *v* group.

gruselig ['gru:zəliç] *adj* gruesome; (*umg.*) creepy.

Gruß [gru:s] *m* (*pl* Grüße) greeting; (*Mil*) salute. **herzliche Grüße** kind regards, best wishes.

grüßen ['gry:sən] *v* greet; (*Mil*) salute.

gucken ['gukən] *v* (take a) look, peep.

Gulasch ['gu:laʃ] *neut*, *m* (*pl* -e) goulash.

gültig ['gyltiç] *adj* valid; (*Gesetz*) in force. **Gültigkeit** *f* validity, currency. **–sdauer** *f* (period of) validity.

Gummi ['gumi] *neut* (*pl* -s) rubber; (*Kleb-*

stoff) gum; (*Kau-*) (chewing) gum. **–band** *neut* rubber band. **gummiert** *adj* (*Briefmarke*, *usw.*) gummed.

Gunst [gunst] *f* (*unz.*) favour.

günstig ['gynstiç] *adj* favourable, advantageous.

gurgeln ['gurgəln] *v* gargle. **Gurgelwasser** *neut* gargle.

Gurke ['gurkə] *f* (*pl* -n) cucumber; (*saure*) gherkin.

Gurt [gurt] *m* (*pl* -e) belt; (*Pferd*) girth.

Gürtel ['gyrtəl] *m* (*pl* -) belt; (*Geog*) zone. **–reifen** *m* radial-ply tyre, (*umg.*) radial.

Guß [gus] *m* (*pl* Güsse) (*Regen*) downpour, gush; (*Metall*) casting, founding.

gut [gu:t] *adj* good. *adv* well. **gut sein mit** be on good terms with. *es wird schon alles gut werden* everything will be all right. *das tut mir gut* that does me good. *schon gut!* that's all right. **gut aussehen** look good; (*gesund*) look well. **Gut** *neut* (*pl* Güter) possession; (*Land*) landed estate; (*Ware*) commodity. **gutartig** *adj* good-natured. **Gutdünken** *neut* discretion. **nach (Ihrem) Gutdünken** at your discretion.

Güte ['gy:tə] *f* (*unz.*) kindness, goodness; (*Qualität*) quality.

Güter‖flugzeug *neut* cargo plane. **–zug** *m* freight train.

gut‖gelaun *adj* good-humoured. **–gesinnt** *adj* friendly, well-disposed. **–gläubig** *adj* acting in good faith, bona-fide; *adv* in good faith.

Guthaben ['gu:tha:bən] *neut* credit (balance).

*gut‖heißen *v* approve. **–herzig** *adj* kind-hearted.

gütig ['gy:tiç] *adj* kind.

gutmachen ['gu:tmaxən] *v* **wieder gutmachen** make amends for, make good.

gutmütig ['gu:tmy:tiç] *adj* good-natured.

Gutschein ['gu:tʃain] *m* (*pl* -e) voucher, credit-note.

Gymnasium [gym'na:zium] *neut* (*pl* Gymnasien) grammar school.

Gymnastik [gym'nastik] *f* gymnastics. **gymnastisch** *adj* gymnastic.

H

Haag, Den [deɪn'haɪk] m The Hague.

Haar [haːr] neut (pl -e) hair. **sich die Haare schneiden lassen** have a haircut. **haarig** adj hairy. **Haar‖nadelkurve** f hairpin bend. **–schnitt** m haircut. **haarsträubend** adj hair-raising.

Habe [ˈhaːbə] f (unz.) property, possessions pl. **haben** v have. **habsüchtig** adj greedy, (umg.) grasping.

Hackbrett [ˈhakbrɛt] neut chopping board. **hacken** v chop, hack; (Fleisch) mince. **Hackfleisch** neut mince, minced meat.

Hafen [ˈhaːfən] m (pl Häfen) port, harbour. **–arbeiter** m docker. **–damm** m pier, mole. **–sperre** f embargo. **–stadt** f port.

Hafer [ˈhaːfər] m (pl -) oats pl. **–flocken** f pl rolled oats, oat-flakes.

Haft [haft] f arrest, detention, custody. **haften** v adhere, cling. **haften für** be liable for, answer for. **Haftpflichtversicherung** f (compulsory) third-party insurance.

Hagel [ˈhaːgəl] m (pl -) hail. **–korn** neut hailstone. **hageln** v es **hagelt** it is hailing.

hager [ˈhaːgər] adj lean, haggard.

Hahn [haɪn] m (pl Hähne) cock; (Wasser-, usw.) tap. **Hahnenkamm** m cockscomb.

Hähnchen [ˈhɛɪnçən] neut (pl -) cock; (Wasser-, usw.) tap.

Hai [haɪ] m (pl -e) or **Haifisch** m shark.

Hain [haɪn] m (pl -e) grove.

Häkelarbeit [ˈhɛːkəlaɪrbaɪt] f crochet work. **häkeln** v crochet.

haken [ˈhaːkən] v hook. **sich haken an** catch on, get caught on. **Haken** m (pl -) hook; (fig) snag. **–kreuz** neut swastika.

halb [halp] adj half. **um halb drei** at half past two. **eine halbe Stunde** half an hour. **–jährlich** adj half-yearly. **Halb‖kreis** m semicircle. **–kugel** f hemisphere. **–messer** m radius. **–starke(r)** m hooligan. **halbwegs** adv halfway. **Halbzeit** f half-time.

Hälfte [ˈhɛlftə] f (pl -n) half.

Halfter [ˈhalftər] f or neut (pl -n) halter.

Hall [hal] m (pl -e) sound, peal.

Halle [ˈhalə] f (pl -n) hall; (Hotel) lobby; (Flugzeug-) hangar.

hallen [ˈhalən] v sound, resound.

Hallenbad [ˈhalənbaːt] neut indoor swimming-pool or baths.

Halm [halm] m (pl -e) stalk; (Gras) blade.

Hals [hals] m (pl Hälse) neck; (innerer Hals, Kehle) throat. **–band** neut (Hund) collar; (Frauen) necklace, choker. **–binde** f tie. **–kette** f necklace. **–weh** neut sore throat.

Halt [halt] m (pl -e) (Anhalten) stop, halt; (Stütze) hold, support; (Standhaftigkeit) steadiness, firmness. **haltbar** adj durable, lasting. **haltbar bis ...** (Speisen) use by .... **halten** v hold; (bewahren) keep; (dauern) last, keep; (Gebot, usw.) observe; (anhalten) stop. **viel halten von** think highly of. **halten für** consider (to be), think of as. **Halte‖stelle** f (Bus) bus-stop. **–tau** neut guy-rope. **haltmachen** v stop. **Haltung** f (pl -en) attitude; (Körper-) bearing, posture.

hämisch [ˈhɛːmɪʃ] adj spiteful, sardonic.

Hammelfleisch [ˈhaməlflaɪʃ] neut mutton.

Hammer [ˈhamər] m (pl Hämmer) hammer.

hämmern [ˈhɛmərn] v hammer.

Hämorrhoiden [hɛmoroˈiːdən] pl piles, haemorrhoids pl.

Hamster [ˈhamstər] m (pl -) hamster. **hamstern** v hoard.

Hand [hant] f (pl Hände) hand. **an Hand von** with the aid of. **bei der Hand** ready, at hand. **mit der Hand** by hand. **von Hand gemacht** hand-made. **zur linken/rechten Hand** on the left/right hand side. **Hand‖arbeit** f handiwork; (Nadelarbeit) needlework. **–becken** neut hand basin. **–bremse** f handbrake. **–buch** neut manual, handbook.

Händedruck [ˈhɛndədruk] m handshake.

Handel [ˈhandəl] m trade, commerce; (Geschäft) transaction, deal. **handeln** v act. **handeln mit** (Person) trade or deal with; (Waren) trade or deal in. **handeln von** treat, deal with. **Handels‖beziehungen** pl trade relations. **–bilanz** f balance of trade. **–schule** f business or commercial school. **–sperre** f (trade) embargo.

handfest [ˈhantfɛst] adj sturdy, strong.

Hand‖fläche f palm. **–gebrauch** m everyday use. **–gelenk** neut wrist. **–gepäck** neut hand luggage.

handhaben [ˈhanthaɪbən] v (gebrauchen) use, employ; (fig) handle.

Händler [ˈhɛntlər] m (pl -) trader, dealer.

handlich [hantlɪç] adj handy.

Handlung ['hantluŋ] *f* (*pl* -en) deed, act; (*Roman*, *usw*.) plot; (*Geschäft*) business, firm; (*Laden*) shop.

Hand‖schellen *pl* handcuffs *pl*. **–schuh** *m* glove. **–tasche** *f* handbag. **–tuch** *neut* towel. **–werk** *neut* craft, trade. **–werker** *m* craftsman, workman.

Hang [haŋ] *m* (*pl* Hänge) slope; (*Neigung*) tendency.

Hängematte ['hɛŋəmatə] *f* hammock.

*****hängen**[1] ['hɛŋən] *v* be suspended, hang; (*sich neigen*) slope; (*unentschieden*) be pending, remain undecided; (*abhängen*) depend.

hängen[2] *v* hang, suspend; (*hinrichten*) hang.

Hannover [ha'noıfər] *neut* Hanover.

hantieren [han'tiırən] *v* busy oneself, potter around.

Happen ['hapən] *m* (*pl* -) mouthful, bite.

Harfe ['harfə] *f* (*pl* -n) harp.

harmlos ['harmloıs] *adj* harmless.

Harmonie [harmo'niı] *f* (*pl* -n) harmony. **harmonisch** *adj* harmonic. **harmonisieren** *v* harmonize.

Harn [harn] *m* urine. **–blase** *f* (*Anat*) bladder.

Harnisch ['harnıʃ] *m* (*pl* -e) armour; harness.

Harpune [har'puınə] *f* (*pl* -n) harpoon.

harren ['harən] *v* wait for, await.

hart [hart] *adj* hard; (*fig*) harsh, rough.

Härte ['hɛırtə] *f* (*pl* -n) hardness; (*Strenge*) severity; (*Grausamkeit*) cruelty. **härten** *v* harden; (*Metall*) temper.

hart‖gekocht *adj* hard-boiled. **–näckig** *adj* stubborn.

Harz [harts] *neut* (*pl* -e) resin.

Haschisch ['haʃıʃ] *neut* hashish.

Hase ['haızə] *m* (*pl* -n) hare.

Haselnuß ['haızəlnus] *f* hazelnut.

Haspe ['haspə] *f* (*pl* -n) hinge.

Haß [has] *m* hate.

hassen ['hasən] *v* hate. **–swert** *adj* hateful, odious.

häßlich ['hɛslıç] *adj* ugly; (*fig*) wicked, nasty. **Häßlichkeit** *f* ugliness; (*fig*) wickedness.

Hast [hast] *f* haste. **hasten** *v* hasten. **hastig** *adj* hasty.

hätscheln ['hɛıtʃəln] *v* (*liebkosen*) caress, fondle; (*verwöhnen*) pamper.

Haube ['haubə] *f* (*pl* -n) bonnet, cap; (*Mot*) bonnet, (*US*) hood.

Hauch [haux] *m* (*pl* -e) breath; (*fig*) touch, trace.

Haue ['hauə] *f* (*pl* -n) pick; (*umg.*) beating, spanking. **hauen** *v* hew; (*zerhacken*) chop up; (*umg.*) beat, belt.

Haufen ['haufən] *m* (*pl* -) heap, pile; (*umg.*) heaps of, lots of.

häufen ['hɔyfən] *v* heap (up), accumulate.

häufig ['hɔyfıç] *adj* frequent, numerous. *adv* frequently.

Haupt [haupt] *neut* (*pl* Häupter) head; (*Führer*) leader, chief. **–bahnhof** *m* main railway station, central station. **–buch** *neut* ledger. **–film** *m* feature film, main film. **–leitung** *f* (*Gas*, *Strom*) mains *pl*. **–mann** *m* (*Mil*) captain. **–rolle** *f* (*Theater*) leading part or role.

Hauptsache ['hauptzaxə] *f* main thing *or* point. **hauptsächlich** *adj* essential. *adv* principally, mainly.

Haupt‖sitz *m* head office. **–stadt** *f* capital (city). **–straße** *f* main street. **–wort** *neut* noun.

Haus [haus] *neut* (*pl* Häuser) house; (*Heim*) home. **zu Hause** at home. **–arbeit** *f* housework; (*Schule*) homework. **–aufgaben** *pl* (*Schule*) homework *sing*.

Häuschen ['hɔsçən] *neut* (*pl* -) cottage, small house.

Haus‖frau *f* housewife. **–halt** *m* household; (*Budget*) budget. **–hälterin** *f* housekeeper. **–haltsplan** *m* budget.

hausieren [hau'ziırən] *v* peddle, hawk.

häuslich ['hɔyslıç] *adj* domestic.

Haus‖mädchen *neut* housemaid. **–meister** *m* caretaker. **–tür** *f* front door. **–wart** *m* caretaker. **–wirt** *m* landlord. **–wirtin** *f* landlady. **–wirtschaft** *f* housekeeping.

Haut [haut] *f* (*pl* Häute) skin; (*Tier*) hide, pelt. **–auschlag** *m* rash. **–krem** *m* skin cream.

Hebamme ['heıpamə] *f* (*pl* -n) midwife.

Hebel ['heıbəl] *m* (*pl* -) lever.

*****heben** ['heıbən] *v* lift, raise; (*Steuer*) raise, levy. **sich heben** rise. **Hebung** *f* raising; (*Beseitigung*) removal.

Hecht [hɛçt] *m* (*pl* -e) pike.

Heck [hɛk] *neut* (*pl* -e) stern; (*eines Autos*) rear. **–klappe** *f* (*Mot*) hatchback, tailgate.

Hecke ['hɛkə] *f* (*pl* -n) hedge; (*Brut*) brood, hatch. **–nschütze** *m* sniper.

Heer [heːr] *neut* (*pl* -e) army.

Hefe [ˈheːfə] *f* yeast.

Heft [hɛft] *neut* (*pl* -e) notebook, exercise book; (*Zeitschrift*) issue; (*Griff*) handle, haft.

heftig [ˈhɛftiç] *adj* violent; (*leidenschaftlich*) passionate, vehement.

hegen [ˈheːgən] *v* (*hätscheln*) cherish; (*schützen*) protect; (*Gedanken*) nurture.

Heide[1] [ˈhaidə] *m* (*pl* -n) heathen, pagan.

Heide[2] *f* (*pl* -n) heath, moor. **-kraut** *neut* heather.

Heidelbeere [ˈhaidəlbeːrə] *f* bilberry.

heidnisch [ˈhaidniʃ] *adj* heathen, pagan.

heikel [ˈhaikəl] *adj* delicate, awkward.

heil [hail] *adj* safe, uninjured; (*geheilt*) healed; (*ganz*) whole. **Heil** *neut* welfare; (*Kirche*) salvation. **-and** *m* saviour. **heil‖bringend** *adj* salutary. **-en** *v* heal, cure.

heilig [ˈhailiç] *adj* holy, sacred. **Heiliger Abend** Christmas Eve. **Heilige(r)** *m* saint. **Heiligenschein** *m* halo.

Heil‖kunde *f* medicine, medical science. **-mittel** *neut* remedy, cure.

heim [haim] *adv* home(ward). **Heim** *neut* (*pl* -e) home.

Heimat [ˈhaimaːt] *f* (*unz.*) home(land), native place. **-land** *neut* homeland. **heimatlos** *adj* homeless. **Heimatstadt** *f* home town.

Heimfahrt [ˈhaimfaːrt] *f* return journey. **heimisch** *adj* domestic; (*heimatlich*) native. **Heimkehr** *f* return (home).

heim‖lich *adj* secret. **-suchen** *v* plague, afflict. **-tückisch** *adj* malicious, insidious.

Heimweh [ˈhaimveː] *neut* homesickness. **Heimweh haben** be homesick.

Heirat [ˈhairaːt] *f* (*pl* -en) marriage. **heiraten** *v* marry.

heiser [ˈhaizər] *adj* hoarse.

heiß [hais] *adj* hot.

*****heißen** [ˈhaisən] *v* be called *or* named; (*bedeuten*) mean. **wie heißt Du?** what's your name? **das heißt (d.h.)** that is (i.e.).

heiter [ˈhaitər] *adj* (*Person*) serene; (*Erzählung*) bright; (*Wetter*) bright, clear. **Heiterkeit** *f* serenity.

Heiz‖apparat [ˈhaitsaparaːt] *m* (*pl* -e) heater. **-decke** *f* electric blanket. **heizen** *v* heat. **Heiz‖ung** *f* heating. **-material** *neut* fuel.

Hektar [hɛkˈtaːr] *neut* (*pl* -e) hectare.

Held [hɛlt] *m* (*pl* -en) hero. **Helden‖mut** *m* heroism. **-tat** *f* heroic deed, exploit. **Heldin** *f* (*pl* -nen) heroine.

helfen [ˈhɛlfən] *v* help, assist; (*nützen*) help, do good. **Helfer** *m* (*pl* -), **Helferin** *f* (*pl* -nen) helper, assistant.

hell [hɛl] *adj* (*Licht*) bright; (*Farbe*) light, (*Klang*) clear. **hellblau** *adj* light blue. **Hellseher** *m* (*pl* -), **Hellseherin** *f* (*pl* -nen) clairvoyant.

Helm [hɛlm] *m* (*pl* -e) helmet; (*Naut*) rudder; (*Kuppel*) dome.

Hemd [hɛmt] *neut* (*pl* -en) shirt. **-särmel** *m* shirtsleeve.

hemmen [ˈhɛmən] *v* restrain, hinder, inhibit; (*Psychol*) inhibit. **Hemmung** *f* (*pl* -en) hindrance, stoppage; (*Psychol*) inhibition. **hemmungslos** *adj* unrestrained.

Hengst [hɛŋst] *m* (*pl* -e) stallion.

Henkel [ˈhɛŋkəl] *m* (*pl* -) handle.

Henker [ˈhɛŋkər] *m* (*pl*-) hangman.

her [heːr] *adv* (to) here; (*zeitlich*) ago, since; (*von*) from. **hin und her** to and fro, back and forth. **komm her!** come here! **wo kommen Sie her?** where do you come from? **schon lange her** a long time ago. **von weit her** from afar.

herab [hɛˈrap] *adv* down(wards). **-hängen** *v* hang down. **-lassen** *v* lower. **sich herablassen** condescend. **herab‖lassend** *adj* patronizing. **-setzen** *v* reduce; (*Person*) degrade. **-setzend** *adj* contemptuous. **-würdigen** *v* debase, degrade.

heran [hɛˈran] *adv* near, up to; (*hierher*) (to) here. **-gehen** *v* go up to, approach. **-kommen** *v* approach, draw near.

herauf [hɛˈrauf] *adv* (up) here; (*hinauf*) upwards. **-beschwören** *v* conjure up. **-ziehen** *v* pull up.

heraus [hɛˈraus] *adv* out; (*draußen, aus dem Hause*) outside. **-fordern** *v* challenge. **Herausforderung** *f* challenge. **herausgeben** *v* give out; (*Buch, usw.*) publish. **Herausgeber** *m* publisher. **herauswachsen aus** *v* grow out of.

herb [hɛrp] *adj* sharp, tart; (*Wein*) dry; (*fig*) harsh.

herbei [hɛrˈbai] *adv* (to) here, this way. **-führen** *v* cause.

Herberge [ˈhɛrbɛrgə] *f* (*pl* -n) hostel.

Herbst [hɛrpst] *m* (*pl* -e) autumn, (*US*) fall. **herbstlich** *adj* autumnal.

Herd [hɛrt] *m* (*pl* -e) cooker, stove.

Herde [ˈheːrdə] *f* (*pl* -n) herd.

herein [hε'raɪn] *adv* in, inside, in here. **–führen** *v* usher in. **–treten** *v* enter.

*****hergeben** ['hεrgeɪbən] *v* hand over.

hergebracht ['hεrgəbraxt] *adj* traditional, customary.

Hering ['heɪrɪŋ] *m* (*pl* -e) herring.

*****herkommen** ['hεrkɔmən] *v* come here; (*abstammen*) come from. **herkommen von** be caused by, be due to. **herkömmlich** *adj* customary, traditional.

Herkunft ['hεrkunft] *f* (*unz*) origin; (*Person*) birth, descent.

herleiten ['hεrlaɪtən] *v* lead here; (*fig*) derive, deduce. **Herleitung** *f* derivation.

Hermelin [hεrmə'liɪn] *neut* (*pl* -e) ermine.

hernach [hεr'naɪx] *adv* afterwards, after this.

Heroin [hero'iɪn] *neut* heroin.

Herr [hεr] *m* (*pl* -en) (*Anrede*) Mr; (*Herrscher*) master, lord. **der Herr Gott** Lord God. **dieser Herr** this gentleman. **Herren‖artikel** *pl* men's clothing. **–haus** *neut* manor house. **–toilette** *f* men's lavatory.

herrichten ['hεrɪçtən] *v* prepare, arrange.

Herrin ['hεrɪn] *f* (*pl* -nen) lady, mistress.

herr‖isch *adj* overbearing, domineering. **–lich** *adj* splendid, magnificent. **Herr‖lichkeit** *f* splendour, magnificence. **–schaft** *f* power, rule; (*fig*) mastery. **herrschen** *v* rule, govern; (*vorhanden sein*) prevail. **Herrscher** *m* (*pl* -) ruler.

her‖rühren ['hεrryɪbər] *v* originate (from). **–stammen** *v* descend (from). **–stellen** *v* manufacture, make; (*reparieren*) repair. **Hersteller** *m* manufacturer, maker. **Herstellung** *f* manufacture.

herüber [hε'ryɪbər] *adv* across, over here.

herum [hε'rum] *adv* (a)round, about. **–fahren** *v* drive around. **–pfuschen** *v* tinker, mess around (with). **–streichen** *v* roam about, wander around.

herunter [hε'runtər] *adv* downwards, down (here). **–kommen** *v* come down; (*sinken*) decline.

hervor [hεr'foɪr] *adv* forth, out. **–bringen** *v* produce, (*Worte*) utter. **–heben** *v* make prominent, bring out. **–ragen** *v* stand out, jut out. **–ragend** *adj* outstanding. **–rufen** *v* arouse; (*verursachen*) cause. **–treten** *v* come forward.

Herz [hεrts] *neut* (*pl* -en) heart. **–anfall** *m* heart attack. **herz‖erfreuend** *adj* heartening, cheering. **–erschütternd** *adj* appalling. **–haft** *adj* stout-hearted. **–ig** *adj* lovely. **–lich** *adj* hearty. **–los** *adj* heartless.

Herzog ['hεrtsoɪk] *m* (*pl* Herzöge) duke. **–in** *f* (*pl* -nen) duchess. **Herzogtum** *neut* duchy, dukedom.

herzu [hεr'tsuɪ] *adv* (to) here, towards.

Hessen ['hεsən] *neut* Hesse.

Hetze ['hεtsə] *f* (*pl* -n) hounding, baiting; (*Eile*) mad rush, dash; (*Jagd*) hunt. **hetzen** *v* hound; rush, dash; hunt.

Heu [hɔy] *neut* hay. **Heu‖fieber** *neut* hay fever. **–gabel** *f* pitchfork. **–schober** *m* haystack. **–schrecke** *f* grasshopper, locust.

Heuchelei [hɔyçə'laɪ] *f* (*pl* -en) hypocrisy. **heucheln** *v* be hypocritical. **Heuchler** *m* (*pl* -), **Heuchlerin** *f* (*pl* -nen) hypocrite. **heuchlerisch** *adj* hypocritical.

heulen ['hɔylən] *v* cry, howl.

heute ['hɔytə] *adv* today. **heutig** *adj* today's; (*gegenwärtig*) present, current. **heutzutage** *adv* nowadays, these days.

Hexe ['hεksə] *f* (*pl* -n) witch.

Hieb [hiɪp] *m* (*pl* -e) blow, stroke; (*Schnitt*) cut, slash.

hier [hiɪr] *adv* here. **hier und da** now and then. **hier und dort** here and there. **hier‖auf** *adv* then, upon this. **–aus** *adv* from this. **–bei** *adv* hereby, herewith; (*Brief*) enclosed. **–für** *adv* for this.

hi-fi ['haɪfaɪ] *adj* hi-fi.

Hilfe ['hɪlfə] *f* (*pl* -n) help, assistance. **–ruf** *m* cry for help. **hilf‖los** *adj* helpless. **–reich** *adj* helpful. **–sbereit** *adj* eager to help. **Hilfs‖lehrer** *m* assistant teacher. **–mittel** *neut* remedy, aid.

Himbeere ['hɪmbeɪrə] *f* raspberry.

Himmel ['hɪməl] *m* (*pl* -) sky; (*Paradies*) heaven. **–fahrt** *f* Ascension. **–reich** *neut* heaven. **–skörper** *m* celestial body. **himmlisch** ['hɪmlɪʃ] *adj* celestial, heavenly.

hin [hɪn] *adv* (to) there, from here, towards. **hin und her** to and fro, back and forth. **hin und wieder** now and again. **hin und zurück** there and back. **vor sich hin** to oneself. **es ist noch lange hin** there's a long time to go.

hinab [hɪ'nap] *adv* down(wards). **–lassen** *v* lower, let down. **–steigen** *v* descend.

hinan [hɪ'nan] *adv* up, upwards.

hinauf [hɪ'nauf] *adv* up (there), upwards. **die Treppe hinauf** up the stairs. **–setzen** *v* put up. **–ziehen** *v* pull up, (*umziehen*) move up.

hinaus [hi'naus] *adv* out, forth. **–gehen** *v* go out. **hinausgehen über** surpass, exceed **hinaus‖kommen** *v* come out. **–werfen** *v* throw out.

Hinblick ['hinblik] *m* **im Hinblick auf** with regard to.

hinderlich ['hindərliç] *adj* restrictive, hindering. **hindern** *v* hinder; (*verhindern*) prevent. **Hindernis** *neut* (*pl* **-se**) obstacle, hindrance.

hindeuten ['hindɔytən] *v* point (at); (*fig*) hint (at).

hindurch [hin'durç] *adv* through, across; (*zeitlich*) throughout.

hinein [hi'nain] *adv* in(to). **sich hineindrängen** *v* force one's way in. **hineinziehen** *v* draw in; (*fig: verwickeln*) involve; (*umziehen*) move to.

hinfahren ['hinfaːrən] *v* drive there; (*hinbringen*) take there. **Hinfahrt** *f* outward journey, way there.

hinfallen ['hinfalən] *v* fall down. **hinfällig** *adj* feeble, frail; (*Meinung*) untenable, invalid.

Hingabe ['hingaːbə] *f* devotion.

*****hingeben** ['hingeːbən] *v* give up. **sich hingeben** devote oneself (to).

hingegen ['hingeːgən] *conj* on the other hand, whereas.

*****hingehen** ['hingeːən] *v* go there; (*Zeit*) pass, elapse. **etwas hingehen lassen** let something pass.

hinken ['hiŋkən] *v* limp.

hin‖kommen *v* arrive, get there; (*umg.*) manage. **–langen** *v* reach. **–länglich** *adj* sufficient. **–legen** *v* put down. **sich hinlegen** lie down. **hin‖nehmen** *v* put up with, bear. **–reichend** *adj* sufficient.

Hinreise ['hinraizə] *f* outward journey, way there.

hinreißen ['hinraisən] *v* carry along; (*entzücken*) charm, transport. **–d** *adj* charming, enchanting.

hinrichten ['hinriçtən] *v* (*Person*) execute. **Hinrichtung** *f* execution.

*****hinschreiben** ['hinʃraibən] *v* write down.

Hinsicht ['hinziçt] *f* **in Hinsicht auf** with regard to. **in dieser Hinsicht** in this regard. **hinsichtlich** *adv* with regard to.

hinten ['hintən] *adv* behind, at the back. **nach hinten** to the back, backwards. **von hinten** from behind.

hinter ['hintər] *prep* behind, after. *adj* rear, back. **Hinter‖achse** *f* rear axle. **–bein** *neut* hind leg. **Hintere(r)** *m* back

part; (*Körper*) bottom, backside. **hintergehen** *v* deceive, fool.

Hinter‖grund *m* background. **–halt** *m* ambush. **aus dem Hinterhalt überfallen** ambush. **Hinterhof** *m* rear court, back yard.

hinter‖lassen *v* leave (behind). **–legen** *v* deposit.

Hintern ['hintərn] *m* (*pl* **-**) bottom, backside.

Hinter‖schiff *neut* stern. **–teil** *m* back part. **–tür** *f* back door.

hinterziehen [hintər'tsiːən] *v* (*Steuern*) evade. **Hinterziehung** *f* (tax) evasion.

hinüber [hi'nyːbər] *adv* over, across, to the other side. **–gehen** *v* cross (over).

hinunter [hi'nuntər] *adv* downwards, down (there). **die Treppe hinunter** downstairs.

hinweg [hin'vɛk] *adv* away (from here), off. **Hinweg** *m* outward journey. **hinwegkommen über** get over.

Hinweis ['hinvais] *m* (*pl* **-e**) indication, hint. **hinweisen** *v* point out, show; (*Person*) direct; (*anspielen*) refer, allude.

*****hinziehen** ['hintsiːən] *v* draw, attract; (*verzögern*) drag out.

hinzu [hin'tsuː] *adv* in addition, as well. **–fügen** *v* add. **–kommen** *v* be added. **–kommend** *adj* additional. **–ziehen** *v* draw or bring in; (*Fachmann*) consult.

Hirn [hirn] *neut* (*pl* **-e**) brain.

Hirsch [hirʃ] *m* (*pl* **-e**) stag. **–fleisch** *neut* venison. **–kalb** *neut* fawn. **–kuh** *f* doe, hind.

Hirt [hirt] *m* (*pl* **-en**) shepherd, herdsman. **–in** *f* (*pl* **-nen**) shepherdess.

hissen ['hisən] *v* hoist.

Historiker [hi'stoːrikər] *m* (*pl* **-**) historian. **historisch** *adj* historical; (*bedeutend*) historic.

Hitze ['hitsə] *f* (*unz.*) heat; (*Leidenschaft*) passion. **hitzebeständig** *adj* heat-resistant. **hitzig** *adj* hot; (*fig*) fiery, passionate. **Hitz‖kopf** *m* hothead. **–schlag** *m* heat-stroke.

hoch [hoːx] (**hoher, hohe, hohes, höher, höchst**) *adj* high; (*Baum*) tall; (*Alter*) old, advanced. *adv* highly, greatly. **hohe Blüte** full bloom. **hohe See** See high *or* open sea. **10 hoch 4** 10 to the power of 4. **Hoch** *neut* (*pl* **-s**) cheer; (*Hochdruckgebiet*) high-pressure area. **Dreimal hoch** three cheers.

Hochachtung [ˈhoːxaxtuŋ] f respect, esteem. **hochachtungsvoll** respectfully, yours faithfully.

hochdeutsch [ˈhoːxdɔytʃ] adj high German, standard German.

Hoch‖druck m high pressure. –**ebene** f plateau. –**flut** f high tide. –**frequenz** f high frequency.

***hochhalten** [ˈhoːxhaltən] v think highly of, esteem.

Hoch‖haus neut tall building, high-rise block. –**konjunktur** f boom. –**land** neut highland(s). –**leistung-** adj heavy-duty. –**mut** m pride, arrogance. **hochmütig** adj proud, arrogant.

Hoch‖ruf m cheer. –**schätzung** f (high) esteem. –**schule** f college, university; (technische) polytechnic. –**spannung** f high tension, high voltage. –**sprung** m high jump. –**verrat** m high treason. –**wasser** neut high tide, high water; (Überschwemmung) flooding. **Hochzeit** f wedding. **hochzeitlich** adj nuptial, bridal. **Hochzeitskleid** neut wedding dress.

höchst [hœːxst] adj highest, greatest. adv very (much), greatly, highly.

hochstehend [ˈhoːxʃteːənt] adj high-ranking, eminent.

höchstens [ˈhœːxstəns] adv at most, at best.

Höchst‖geschwindigkeit f maximum speed. –**preis** m maximum price.

hocken [ˈhokən] v squat, crouch. **Hocker** m (pl -) stool.

Hode [ˈhoːdə] f (pl -n) or **Hoden** m (pl -) testicle.

Hof [hoːf] m (pl Höfe) (court)yard; (Landwirtschaft) farm; (fürstlich) court.

hoffen [ˈhofən] v hope. **hoffentlich** adv I hope (so); let us hope (that). **Hoffnung** f (pl -en) hope. **hoffnungslos** adj hopeless. –**voll** adj hopeful.

höflich [ˈhøːflɪç] adj polite, courteous. **Höflichkeit** f courtesy, politeness.

hohe(r) [ˈhoːə(r)] V hoch.

Höhe [ˈhøːə] f (pl -n) height; (Gipfel) top; (Geog) latitude; (Hügel) hill.

Hoheit [ˈhoːhait] f (unz.) grandeur, greatness; (Titel) Highness. –**sgewässer** pl territorial waters.

Höhepunkt [ˈhøːəpuŋkt] m climax.

höher [ˈhøːər] V hoch.

hohl [hoːl] adj hollow, (Linse) concave.

Höhle [ˈhøːlə] f (pl -n) cave; (Loch) hole;

(eines Tiers) burrow, hole. **höhlen** v hollow (out).

höhnen [ˈhøːnən] v mock, taunt. **höhnisch** adj mocking, scornful.

hold [holt] adj charming, gracious. –**selig** adj most charming, most gracious.

holen [ˈhoːlən] v fetch. **Atem holen** draw breath. **sich Rat holen bei** ask for advice.

Holländer [ˈhoːlɛndər] m (pl -) Dutchman. –**in** f (pl -nen) Dutchwoman. **holländisch** adj Dutch.

Hölle [ˈhœlə] f (pl -n) hell.

Holunder [hoˈlundər] m (pl -) elder (tree). –**beere** f elderberry.

Holz [holts] neut (pl Hölzer) wood. –**blasinstrument** neut woodwind instrument. **hölzern** [ˈhœltsərn] adj wooden; (fig) stiff, awkward, clumsy. **holzig** [ˈholtsɪç] adj woody. **Holz‖klotz** m wooden block. –**kohle** f charcoal. –**schnitt** m woodcut. –**weg** m **auf dem Holzwege sein** be on the wrong track. **Holzwurm** m woodworm.

Homosexualität [homozɛksualiˈtɛːt] f homosexuality. **homosexuell** adj homosexual. **Homosexuelle(r)** m homosexual.

Honig [ˈhoːnɪç] m honey. –**biene** f honeybee.

Honorar [honoˈraːr] neut (pl -e) fee, honorarium; (eines Autors) royalties pl.

Hopfen [ˈhopfən] m (pl -) hops pl.

hörbar [ˈhøːrbaːr] adj audible.

horchen [ˈhorçən] v listen (to); (heimlich) eavesdrop.

Horde [ˈhordə] f (pl -n) horde.

hören [ˈhøːrən] v hear; (Radio) listen to. **Hören** neut (sense of) hearing. –**sagen** neut hearsay. **Hörer** m hearer; (Radio) listener; (Telef) receiver; (pl) audience. –**schaft** f audience. **Hörgerät** neut hearing aid.

Horizont [horiˈtsont] m (pl -e) horizon. **horizontal** adj horizontal.

Hormon [horˈmoːn] neut (pl -e) hormone.

Horn [horn] neut (pl Hörner) horn. –**brille** f horn-rimmed spectacles. –**haut** f (Anat) cornea.

Horoskop [horoˈskoːp] neut (pl -e) horoscope.

Hör‖probe f audition. –**saal** m lecture hall. –**spiel** neut radio play.

Hose [ˈhoːzə] f (pl -n) trousers. **Hosen‖schlitz** m flies, (US) fly. –**träger** pl braces, (US) suspenders.

Höschen ['hœsçən] *neut* (*pl* -) knickers *pl*; panties *pl*.

Hotel [ho'tel] *neut* (*pl* -s) hotel.

Hub [hup] *m* (*pl* Hübe) lift; (*Mot*) stroke. **-raum** *m* cylinder capacity.

hübsch [hypʃ] *adj* pretty, nice; (*Mann*) good-looking.

Hubschrauber ['hupʃraubər] *m* (*pl* -) helicopter.

Huf [hutf] *m* (*pl* -e) hoof. **-eisen** *neut* horseshoe.

Hüftbein ['hyftbain] *neut* hipbone. **Hüfte** *f* hip.

Hügel ['hyːgəl] *m* (*pl* -) hill. **hügelig** *adj* hilly.

Huhn [huːn] *neut* (*pl* Hühner) hen; (*Küche*) chicken.

Hühner‖auge *neut* (*Med*) corn. **-braten** *m* roast chicken. **-brühe** *f* chicken broth. **-ei** *neut* hen's egg. **-stall** *m* henhouse

huldigen ['huldigən] *v* pay homage to; (*Ansicht*) hold, subscribe to. **Huldigung** *f* homage.

Hülle ['hylə] *f* covering, wrapping; (*Umschlag*) envelope; (*Buch*) jacket, cover. **in Hülle und Fülle** in abundance. **hüllen** *v* wrap, cover.

Hülse ['hylzə] *f* (*pl* -n) husk, shell; (*Erbse*) pod; (*aus Papier, usw.*) case, casing.

human [hu'maːn] *adj* humane. **Humanist** *m* (*pl* -en) humanist. **humanitär** *adj* humanitarian.

Hummel ['huməl] *f* (*pl* -n) bumblebee.

Hummer ['humər] *m* (*pl* -) lobster.

Humor [hu'moːr] *m* (sense of) humour. **humorvoll** *adj* humorous.

humpeln ['humpəln] *v* hobble, limp.

Hund [hunt] *m* (*pl* -e) dog. **Hunde‖hütte** *f* kennel. **-leine** *f* leash.

hundert ['hundərt] *adj, pron* hundred. **Hundert‖füßler** *m* centipede. **-jahrfeier** *f* centenary. **hundert‖mal** *adv* a hundred times. **-prozentig** *adj* one-hundred-per-cent, complete.

Hündin ['hyndin] *f* (*pl* -nen) bitch.

Hunger ['huŋər] *m* hunger. **Hunger haben** be hungry. **-lohn** *m* starvation wages *pl*; pittance. **hungern** *v* starve; be hungry. **Hungersnot** *f* famine. **Hungerstreik** *m* hungerstrike. **hungrig** *adj* hungry.

Hupe ['huːpə] *f* (*pl* -n) (*Mot*) horn. **hupen** *v* sound the horn, beep.

hüpfen ['hypfən] *v* hop, skip.

Hürde ['hyrdə] *f* (*pl* -n) hurdle; (*Schafe*) fold, pen.

Hure ['huːrə] *f* (*pl* -n) whore.

hurra [hu'raː] *interj* hurrah!

husten ['huːstən] *v* cough. **Husten** *m* (*pl* -) cough.

Hut¹ [huːt] *m* (*pl* Hüte) hat.

Hut² *f* (*unz.*) (*Schutz*) protection; (*Vorsicht*) care; (*Aufsicht*) guard. **auf der Hut sein** (**vor**) be on one's guard (against).

hüten ['hyːtən] *v* guard. **sich hüten** (**vor**) be careful *or* wary (of).

Hütte ['hytə] *f* (*pl* -n) hut, cabin; (*Metall*) foundry, ironworks. **-nkäse** *m* cottage cheese.

Hyäne [hy'ɛːnə] *f* (*pl* -n) hyena.

Hydraulik [hy'draulik] *f* hydraulics. **hydraulisch** *adj* hydraulic.

Hygiene [hygi'eːnə] *f* hygiene. **hygienisch** *adj* hygienic.

Hymne ['hymnə] *f* (*pl* -n) hymn.

Hypnose [hyp'noːzə] *f* (*pl* -n) hypnosis. **hypno‖tisch** *adj* hypnotic. **-tisieren** *v* hypnotize.

Hypothek [hypo'teːk] *f* (*pl* -en) mortgage.

Hypothese [hypo'teːzə] *f* (*pl* -n) hypothesis. **hypothetisch** *adj* hypothetical.

Hysterie [hyste'riː] *f* hysteria. **hysterisch** *adj* hysterical. **hysterische Anfälle** *pl* hysterics.

I

ich [iç] *pron* I. **Ich** *neut* self, ego. **ichbezogen** *adj* egocentric.

ideal [ide'aːl] *adj* ideal. **Ideal** *neut* (*pl* -e) ideal. **Idealismus** *m* idealism.

Idee [i'deː] *f* (*pl* -n) idea.

identifizieren [identifi'tsiːrən] *v* identify. **identisch** *adj* identical. **Identität** *f* identity.

Idiot [idi'oːt] *m* (*pl* -en) idiot. **idiotisch** *adj* idiotic.

Igel ['iːgəl] *m* (*pl* -) hedgehog.

ignorieren [igno'riːrən] *v* ignore.

ihm [iːm] *pron* (*Person*) (to) him; (*Sache*) (to) it.

ihn [iːn] *pron* (*Person*) him; (*Sache*) it.

ihnen ['iːnən] *pron* (to) them. **Ihnen** *pron* (to) you.

ihr [iːr] *pron* you; (*Dat*) (to) her. *pron, adj* (*Person*) her; its; their. **Ihr** *pron, adj* your. **ihrer, ihre, ihres** *pron* hers; its; theirs. **Ihrer, Ihre, Ihres** yours. **ihrerseits** *adv* for your part. **ihr‖esgleichen** *adv* like her (it, them). **-etwegen** or **-etwillen** on her (its, their) account. **der, die, das ihrige** pron hers; its; theirs.

Illusion [iluzi'o:n] f (pl -en) illusion. **illusorisch** adj illusory.

illustrieren [ilu'stri:rən] v illustrate. **Illustrierte** f (illustrated) magazine.

im [im] prep + art **in dem**.

Imbiß ['imbis] m (pl **Imbisse**) snack. **-stube** f snack bar.

Immatrikulation [imatrikulatsi'o:n] f (pl -en) matriculation, registration.

immer ['imər] adv always. **immer mehr** more and more. **immer noch** still. **immer wieder** again and again. **wenn auch immer** although. **auf immer** forever. **-fort** adv constantly. **-grün** adj evergreen. **-hin** adv nevertheless. **-zu** adv all the time.

Immigrant [imi'grant] m (pl -en) immigrant.

Immobilien [imo'bi:liən] pl real estate sing.

Imperialismus [imperia'lismus] m imperialism. **Imperialist** m (pl -en) imperialist.

impfen ['impfən] v inoculate, vaccinate. **Impfung** f (pl -en) inoculation, vaccination.

imponieren [impo'ni:rən] v impress. **-d** adj impressive.

Import [im'port] m (pl -e) import(ation); (Ware) import. **-eur** m (pl -e) importer. **-handel** m import trade. **importieren** v import.

impotent ['impotent] adj impotent.

imprägnieren [impreg'ni:rən] v impregnate, saturate.

improvisieren [improvi'zi:rən] v improvise. **improvisiert** adj improvized, ad-lib.

imstande [im'ʃtandə] adv **imstande sein** be able or capable.

in [in] prep (+ Dat) in; (+ Acc) into, in; (Zeit) (with)in.

Inanspruchnahme [in'anʃpruxna:mə] f demands pl.

Inbegriff ['inbəgrif] m essence, epitome. **mit Inbegriff von** inclusive of. **inbegriffen** adj, adv (included, inclusive(ly).

Inbrunst ['inbrunst] f ardour, fervour.

indem [in'de:m] conj (dadurch daß) in that, by; (während) while.

Inder ['indər] m (pl -) (Asian) Indian.

indessen [in'desən] conj (inzwischen) meanwhile, in the meantime; (immerhin) however, nevertheless.

Indianer [indi'a:nər] m (pl -) (American) Indian. **indianisch** adj (American) Indian.

Indien ['indiən] neut India.

indirekt ['indirekt] adj indirect.

indisch ['indiʃ] adj (Asian) Indian.

indiskret ['indiskre:t] adj indiscreet, tactless.

Individualist [individua'list] m (pl -en) individualist. **individualistisch** adj individualist(ic). **individuell** adj individual. **Individuum** neut (pl -duen) individual.

industrialisieren [industriali'zi:rən] v industrialize. **Industrie** f (pl -n) industry. **-gebiet** neut industrial region. **industriell** adj industrial. **Industrielle(r)** m industrualist.

ineinander [inain'andər] adv in(to) each other. **-greifen** v (Tech) engage; (fig) overlap.

Infanterie [infantə'ri:] f infantry. **Infanterist** m (pl -en) infantryman.

infiltrieren [infil'tri:rən] v infiltrate.

infizieren [infi'tsi:rən] v infect. **sich infizieren** become infected, catch a disease.

Inflation [inflatsi'o:n] f (Komm) inflation. **inflationär, inflationistisch** adj inflationary.

infolge [in'fɔlgə] prep on account of, owing to. **-dessen** adv consequently.

Information [informatsi'o:n] f (pl -en) information. **eine Information** a piece of information.

informell ['informel] adj informal.

informieren [infor'mi:rən] v inform, instruct. **sich informieren über** find out about, gather information about.

Ingenieur [inʒe'njœ:r] m (pl -e) engineer. **-schule** f engineering college. **-wesen** neut engineering.

Ingwer ['iŋve:r] m ginger.

Inhaber ['inha:bər] m (pl -) owner; (Titel, Paß, Patent) holder.

inhalieren [inha'li:rən] v inhale.

Inhalt ['inhalt] m (pl -e) contents pl; (Bedeutung) meaning, content. **-sverzeichnis** neut table of contents.

Initiative [initsia'ti:və] f (unz.) initiative. **die Initiative ergreifen** take the initiative.

inklusive [inklu'zi:və] prep including, inclusive of.

inkonsequent ['inkɔnzekvent] adj inconsistent.

Inkontinenz ['inkɔntinɛns] f incontinence.

inkorporieren [inkɔrpo'riːrən] v incorporate.

Inkrafttreten [in'kraftreːtən] neut coming into effect.

Inland ['inlant] neut inland, interior.

inmitten [in'mitən] prep in the midst of, among.

inne ['inə] adv within.

innen ['inən] adv within, inside. **nach innen** inwards. **Innen∥ausstattung** f interior decoration, decor. –**minister** m Home Secretary, Minister of the Interior. –**politik** f domestic policy. **innenpolitisch** adj (relating to) internal affairs **Innenraum** m interior.

inner ['inər] adj internal, inner. **Innereien** pl offal. **Innere(s)** neut (pl -(e)n) interior. **inner∥halb** prep within. –**lich** adj inward, internal. **innerst** adj innermost.

innewohnen ['inəvoːnən] v be inherent (in).

innig ['iniç] adj (Gefühle) sincere; (Freunde) intimate.

ins [ins] prep + art in das.

Insasse [in'zasə] m (pl -n) inmate.

insbesondere [insbə'zɔndərə] adv particularly.

Inschrift ['inʃrift] f inscription.

Insekt [in'zɛkt] neut (pl -en) insect. –**enpulver** neut insect powder. –**izid** neut insecticide.

Insel ['inzəl] f (pl -n) island.

Inserat [inzə'raːt] neut (pl -e) (newspaper) advertisement.

insgesamt [insgə'zamt] adv altogether.

insofern [inzo'fɛrn] conj so far as; [in'zofɛrn] (bis zu diesem Punkt) to that extent. **insofern als** inasmuch as.

insoweit [inzo'vait] adv to that extent.

Inspektor [in'spɛktor] m (pl -en) inspector.

instand halten [in'ʃtant haltən] v maintain (in good order). **instand setzen** v repair, overhaul; (Person) enable. **Instandhaltung** f upkeep, maintenance.

Instanz [in'stants] f (pl -en) authority. **durch die Instanzen** through official channels.

instinktiv [instiŋk'tiːf] adj instinctive.

Institut [insti'tuːt] neut (pl -e) institute.

Instrument [instru'mɛnt] neut (pl -e) instrument.

inszenieren [instse'niːrən] v (Film,

Schauspiel) produce; (fig) create, engineer.

integrieren [inte'griːrən] v integrate. **Integration** f integration.

intellektuell [intelɛktu'ɛl] adj intellectual.

intelligent [inteli'gɛnt] adj intelligent, clever.

interessant [intərɛ'sant] adj interesting. **Interesse** neut interest. **interessieren** v interest. **sich interessieren für** take an interest in, be interested in.

intern [in'tɛrn] adj internal.

Internat [intər'naːt] neut (pl -e) boarding school.

international [intərnatsio'naːl] adj international.

Interview [intər'vjuː] neut (pl -s) interview. **interviewen** v interview. **Interviewer** m interviewer. **Interviewte(r)** interviewee.

intim [in'tiːm] adj intimate.

Intrige [in'triːgə] f (pl -n) intrigue. **intrigieren** v plot, scheme.

Invalide(r) [inva'liːdə(r)] m invalid. **Invaliden∥heim** neut home for the disabled. –**rente** f disability pension. **invalid** adj invalid.

Inventar [invɛn'taːr] neut (pl -e) inventory.

Inventur [invɛn'tuːr] f (pl -en) stock-taking.

inwendig ['invɛndiç] adj inner.

inwiefern [invi'fɛrn] conj to what extent, how far.

inzwischen [in'tsviʃən] adv meanwhile.

irdisch ['irdiʃ] adj earthly, worldly.

Ire ['iːrə] m (pl -n) Irishman. **Irin** f (pl -nen) Irishwoman.

irgend ['irgənt] adv perhaps, ever. pron some, any. **irgend etwas** something, anything. **irgend jemand** someone, anyone. **irgend∥ein** adj some, any. –**wann** adv (at) sometime (or other). –**was** pron something, anything. –**wie** adv somehow, anyhow. –**wo** adv somewhere, anywhere.

Iris ['iːris] f (–) (Anat) iris.

irisch ['iːriʃ] adj Irish.

Irland ['irlant] neut Ireland. **Irländer** m (pl -) Irishman. **Irländerin** f (pl -nen) Irishwoman. **irländisch** adj Irish.

Ironie [iro'niː] f (pl -n) irony. **ironisch** adj ironic; (spöttisch) ironical.

irre ['irə] adj (geistesgestört) insane, mad; (verwirrt) confused. adv (von Ziel weg) astray. **irr werden** go insane. **irren** v err.

Irre(r) madman/woman). **irreführen** v lead astray; (täuschen) mislead. **Irrenanstalt** f mental home. **Irrglaube** m heresy. **irrig** adj erroneous. **Irrsinn** m insanity, madness. **irrsinnig** adj insane. **Irrtum** m (pl **Irrtümer**) error. **irrtümlich** adj erroneous, wrong.

Isolierband [izo'li:rbant] neut insulating tape; **isolieren** v isolate; (Elek) insulate. **Isolierung** f isolation; insulation.

Italien [i'tali:ən] neut Italy. **Italiener** m (pl -). **Italienerin** f (pl -**nen**) Italian. **italienisch** adj Italian.

J

ja [ja] adv yes. **ja doch** to be sure, but yes. **ja freilich** yes indeed. **wenn ja** if so.
Jacht [jaxt] f (pl -**en**) yacht.
Jacke [jakə] f (pl -**n**) jacket.
Jagd [ja:kt] f (pl -**en**) hunt; (Jagen) hunting. **-flugzeug** neut fighter plane. **-hund** m hound. **-schloß** neut hunting lodge.
jagen [ja:gən] v hunt; (treiben) drive (away); (verfolgen) pursue; (eilen) rush, race.
Jäger [jɛ:gər] m (pl -) hunter; (Flugzeug) fighter.
jäh [jɛ:] adj steep; (plötzlich) sudden.
Jahr [ja:r] neut (pl -**e**) year. **-buch** neut yearbook. **jahrelang** adv for years. **Jahres‖einkommen** neut annual income. **-ende** neut end of the year. **-tag** m anniversary. **-viertel** neut quarter. **-wende** f New Year, turn of the year. **-zeit** f season. **jahreszeitlich** adj seasonal. **Jahrhundert** neut century.
jährig [jɛ:riç] adj lasting a year. **dreijährig** adj three-year-old.
jährlich [jɛ:rliç] adj yearly, annual.
Jahr‖markt m fair. **-zehnt** neut decade.
Jalousie [ʒalu'zi:] f (pl -**n**) venetian blind.
Jammer [jamər] m (unz.) wailing; (Elend) misery; (Verzweiflung) despair.
jämmerlich [jɛmərliç] adj pitiable.
jammern [jamərn] v wail; (klagen) complain.
Januar [januar] m (pl -**e**) January.
Japan [ja:pan] neut Japan. **-er** m (pl -). **Japanerin** f (pl -**nen**) Japanese. **japanisch** adj Japanese.
jauchzen [jauxtsən] v shout joyfully, rejoice.

jawohl [ja'vo:l] adv, interj yes indeed, certainly.
Jazz [dʒɛs] m jazz.
je [je:] adv ever. **je und je** always. **je zwei** two each. conj je mehr, desto besser the more, the better. **je nachdem** that depends.
jedenfalls [je:dənfals] adv in any case.
jeder [je:dər], **jede, jedes** pron, adj each, every. **jedermann** pron everybody.
jederzeit adv always, (at) any time.
jedesmal [je:dəsma:l] adv each time.
jedoch [je'dɔx] adv however, yet.
jemals [je:ma:ls] adv ever, at any time.
jemand [je:mant] pron someone; (Fragen) anyone.
jener [je:nər], **jene, jenes** pron, adj that, pl those; (zuerst erwähnt) the former. **jenseits** adv on the other side. prep on the other side of, across.
jetzig [jɛtsiç] adj current, present. **jetzt** adv now, at present.
jeweilig [jervailiç] adj at the time; (Vergangenheit) at that time, then. **jeweils** adv at a(ny) given time.
Jiddisch [jidiʃ] neut Yiddish (language).
Joch [jɔx] neut (pl -**e**) yoke.
Jockei [dʒɔki] m (pl -**s**) jockey.
Jod [jo:t] neut iodine.
jodeln [jo:dəln] v yodel.
Joghurt [jo:gurt] neut (pl -**s**) yoghurt.
Johannisbeere [jo'hanisbe:rə] f redcurrant. **schwarze Johannisbeere** blackcurrant.
Journalismus [ʒurna'lismus] m journalism. **Journalist** m (pl -**en**) journalist. **journalistisch** adj journalistic.
Jubel [ju:bəl] m rejoicing, jubilation. **jubeln** v rejoice. **Jubiläum** neut (pl -**äen**) anniversary, jubilee.
jucken [jukən] v itch. **Jucken** neut itch.
Jude [ju:də] m (pl -**n**), **Jüdin** f (pl -**nen**) Jew. **jüdisch** adj Jewish.
Judo [ju:do] neut judo.
Jugend [ju:gənt] f (unz.) youth. **-gericht** neut juvenile court. **-herberge** f youth hostel. **-kriminalität** f juvenile delinquency. **jugendlich** adj youthful, young, juvenile. **jugendlicher Verbrecher** m juvenile delinquent. **Jugendliche(r)** m youth, juvenile.
Jugoslawe [jugo'sla:və] m, **Jugoslawin** f Yugoslav. **Jugoslawien** neut Yugoslavia. **jugoslawisch** adj Yugoslav.

Juli ['juːli] *m* (*pl* -s) July.

jung [juŋ] *adj* young. **Junge** *m* (*pl* -n) boy; (*Lehrling*) apprentice; (*Karten*) jack. **jungenhaft** *adj* boyish.

jünger ['jyŋər] *adj* younger, junior. **Jünger** *m* (*pl* -) disciple.

Junges ['juŋəs] *neut* (*pl* **Jungen**) young (animal), offspring.

Jung‖fer *f* (*pl* -n) virgin; (*Mädchen*) girl. **alte Jungfer** old maid, spinster. **–frau** *f* virgin. **jungfräulich** *adj* maidenly, chaste. **Junggeselle** *m* bachelor.

Jüngling ['jyŋliŋ] *m* (*pl* -e) youth, young man. **–salter** *neut* youth, adolescence.

jüngst [jyŋst] *adj* youngest; (*letzt*) latest. **das jüngste Gericht** the Last Judgment.

Juni ['juːni] *m* (*pl* -s) June.

Junker ['juŋkər] *m* (*pl* -) squire; (*jung*) young aristocrat.

Jura[1] ['juːra] *f* law *sing*. **Jura studieren** study law.

Jura[2] *m* (*pl* -s) the Jura, Jura Mountains.

Jurist [ju'rist] *m* (*pl* -en) lawyer.

just [just] *adv* just, exactly.

Justiz [jus'tiːts] *f* (*unz.*) justice, administration of the law. **–irrtum** *m* miscarriage of justice. **–wesen** *neut* legal affairs, the law.

Juwel [ju'veːl] *neut* (*pl* -en) jewel. **–ier** *m* (*pl* -e) jeweller.

Jux [juks] *m* (*pl* -e) joke, prank. **aus Jux** as a joke, for fun.

K

Kabarett [kaba'rɛt] *neut* (*pl* -e) cabaret.

Kabel ['kaːbəl] *neut* (*pl* -) cable.

Kabeljau ['kaːbəljau] *m* (*pl* -e) cod.

kabeln ['kaːbəln] *v* cable, wire.

Kabine [ka'biːnə] *f* (*pl* -n) (*Schiff*) cabin; (*Umkleide-*) cubicle; (*Seilbahn*) cable-car.

Kabinett [kabi'nɛt] *neut* (*pl* -e) (*Pol*) cabinet; (*Zimmer*) closet.

Kadaver [ka'daːvər] *m* (*pl* -) carcass.

Kadett [ka'dɛt] *m* (*pl* -en) cadet.

Käfer ['kɛːfər] *m* (*pl* -) beetle.

Kaffee [ka'feː] *m* (*pl* -s) coffee. **–bohne** *f* coffee bean. **–kanne** *f* coffee-pot. **–mühle** *f* coffee-grinder. **–satz** *m* coffee grounds *pl*.

Käfig ['kɛːfiç] *m* (*pl* -e) cage.

kahl [kaːl] *adj* bald; (*Landschaft*) bare,

barren. **Kahlheit** *f* baldness. **kahlköpfig** *adj* bald-headed.

Kahn [kaːn] *m* (*pl* **Kähne**) small boat, punt; (*Last-*) barge.

Kai [kai] *m* (*pl* -e) quay, wharf.

Kaiser ['kaizər] *m* (*pl* -) emperor. **–in** *f* empress. **kaiserlich** *adj* imperial. **Kaiserreich** *neut* empire.

Kakao [ka'kao] *m* cocoa.

Kaktee [kak'teː] *f*, **Kaktus** *m* (*pl* **Kakteen**) cactus.

Kalb [kalp] *neut* (*pl* **Kälber**) calf. **–fleisch** *neut* veal. **–sbraten** *m* roast veal.

Kalender [ka'lɛndər] *m* (*pl* -) calendar.

Kaliber [ka'liːbər] *neut* (*pl* -) calibre.

Kalk [kalk] *m* (*pl* -e) lime. **–stein** *m* limestone.

Kalorie [kalo'riː] *f* (*pl* -n) calorie.

kalt [kalt] *adj* cold. **–blütig** *adj* cold-blooded.

Kälte ['kɛltə] *f* (*unz.*) cold(ness).

Kamel [ka'meːl] *neut* (*pl* -e) camel.

Kamera ['kamera] *f* (*pl* -s) camera. **–mann** *m* cameraman.

Kamerad [kame'raːt] *m* (*pl* -en) companion, comrade. **–schaft** *f* companionship, comradeship.

Kamin [ka'miːn] *m* (*pl* -e) (*Feuerstelle*) hearth, fireplace; (*Schornstein*) chimney. **–feger** *m* chimneysweep. **–gesims** *neut* mantelpiece. **–vorsatz** *m* fireguard, fender.

Kamm [kam] *m* (*pl* **Kämme**) comb; (*Vogel*) crest; (*Berg*) ridge, crest.

kämmen ['kɛmən] *v* comb. **sich kämmen** comb one's hair.

Kammer ['kamər] *f* (*pl* -n) small room, chamber; (*Mil, Pol*) chamber. **–frau** *f* chambermaid. **–herr** *m* chamberlain. **–musik** *f* chamber music.

Kampf [kampf] *m* (*pl* **Kämpfe**) fight, struggle; (*Schlacht*) battle.

kämpfen ['kɛmpfən] *v* fight, struggle. **Kämpfer** *m* (*pl* -) fighter. **Kampf‖handlung** *f* (*Mil*) engagement; action. **–platz** *m* battlefield. **–wagen** *m* (*Mil*) tank.

Kanada ['kanada] *neut* Canada. **Kanadier** *m* (*pl* -), **Kanadierin** *f* (*pl* -nen) Canadian. **kanadisch** *adj* Canadian.

Kanal [ka'naːl] *m* (*pl* **Kanäle**) canal; (*natürlicher, auch Radio, fig*) channel; (*Abwasser*) drain, sewer. **–inseln** *pl* Channel Islands.

Kanarienvogel [ka'nɑːriənfoːɡəl] m canary.

Kandidat [kandi'daːt] m (pl -en) candidate. **kandidieren** v (Wahl) stand (for election); (Posten) apply (for).

Känguruh [kɛŋɡu'ruː] neut (pl -s) kangaroo.

Kaninchen [ka'niːnçən] neut (pl -) rabbit. – **stall** m rabbit hutch.

Kanne [ˈkanə] n (pl -n) can; (Kaffee, Tee) pot; (Krug) jug, pitcher.

Kannibale [kani'baːlə] m (pl -n) cannibal. **kannibalisch** adj cannibal.

Kanon ['kanɔn] m (pl -s) canon.

Kanone [ka'noːnə] f (pl -n) cannon, gun. **Kanonen||feuer** neut bombardment. – **kugel** f cannonball.

Kante ['kantə] f (pl -n) edge.

Kantine [kan'tiːnə] f (pl -n) canteen.

Kanton [kan'tɔn] m (pl -e) canton.

Kanzel ['kantsəl] f (pl -n) pulpit. – **rede** f sermon.

Kanzlei [kants'lai] f (pl -en) (Büro) office; (Behörde) chancellery. – **papier** neut foolscap.

Kanzler ['kantslər] m (pl -) chancellor.

Kap [kap] neut (pl -s) cape, headland.

Kapazität [kapatsi'tɛːt] 1 f (unz.) capacity. 2 f (pl -en) (Könner) authority, expert.

Kapelle [ka'pɛlə] f (pl -n) chapel; (Musik) band.

Kaper ['kaːpər] f (pl -n) (Gewürz) caper.

kapieren [ka'piːrən] v (umg.) understand, catch on, (umg.) get.

Kapital [kapi'taːl] neut (Komm) capital. – **ismus** m capitalism. – **ist** m capitalist. **kapitalistisch** adj capitalist.

Kapitän [kapi'tɛːn] m (pl -e) (ship's) captain.

Kapitel [ka'piːtəl] neut (pl -) chapter.

kapitulieren [kapitu'liːrən] v capitulate, surrender. **Kapitulation** f (pl -en) capitulation, surrender.

Kaplan [ka'plaːn] m (pl Kapläne) chaplain.

Kappe ['kapə] f (pl -n) cap; (Deckel) top; (Arch) dome; (Schuh) toecap.

Kapriole [kapri'oːlə] f (pl -n) caper, cartwheel.

kaputt [ka'put] adj broken, (umg.) bust; (erschöpft) exhausted, (umg.) shattered. – **machen** v break, ruin.

Kapuze [ka'puːtsə] f (pl -n) hood.

Karaffe [ka'rafə] f (pl -n) carafe.

Karamelle [kara'mɛlə] f (pl -n) toffee.

Karat [ka'raːt] neut (pl -e) carat.

Karate [ka'raːtə] neut karate.

Karawane [kara'vaːnə] f (pl -n) caravan.

Kardinal [kardi'naːl] m (pl Kardinäle) cardinal.

Karfreitag [kaɪr'fraitak] m Good Friday.

karg [kark] adj meagre, poor; (geizig) miserly.

kärglich ['kɛrkliç] adj scanty, poor.

kariert [ka'riərt] adj chequered, checked.

Karies ['kaːriɛs] f (Med) caries.

Karikatur [karika'tuːr] f (pl -en) caricature.

karmesin [karmɛ'ziːn] adj crimson.

Karneval ['karnɛval] m (pl -s) (Shrovetide) carnival.

Karo ['kaːro] neut (pl -s) square; (Karten) diamonds.

Karosserie [karɔsə'riː] f (pl -n) body, coachwork.

Karotte [ka'rɔtə] f (pl -n) carrot.

Karpfen ['karpfən] m (pl -) carp.

Karre ['karə] f (pl -n), **Karren** m (pl -) cart.

Karriere [kari'ɛːrə] f (pl -n) rise, (successful) career; (Pferd) full gallop.

Karte ['kartə] f (pl -n) (Blatt) card; (Land-) map; (Eintritt, Reise) ticket.

Kartei [kar'tai] f (pl -en) card file, card index.

Kartell [kar'tɛl] neut (pl -e) cartel, combine.

Karten||ausgabe f ticket office. – **spiel** neut card game.

Kartoffel [kar'tɔfəl] f (pl -n) potato. – **chips** pl potato crisps (US chips). – **püree** neut mashed potatoes pl. – **puffer** m potato pancake. – **salat** m potato salad.

Karton [kar'tɔ̃] m (pl -s) cardboard; (Schachtel) cardboard box, carton; (Skizze) cartoon.

Kartusche [kar'tuʃə] f (pl -n) cartridge.

Karussell [karu'sɛl] neut (pl -s) roundabout, merry-go-round.

Kaschmir [kaʃ'miːr] neut cashmere.

Käse ['kɛːzə] m (pl -) cheese.

Kaserne [ka'zɛrnə] f (pl -n) barracks pl.

Kasino [ka'ziːno] neut (pl -s) casino; (Mil) (officers') mess; (Gesellschaftshaus) club.

Kasse ['kasə] f (pl -n) cash box, till; (Laden, Supermarkt) cash-desk; (Kino, Theater) box office; (Bank) cashier's window, counter. **gut/schlecht bei Kasse sein** be flush/hard up. **Kassen||buch** neut cash book. – **wart** m treasurer.

Kassette [ka'sɛtə] f (pl -n) small box, casket, (Geld) strong-box; (Tonband) cassette. **–nrecorder** m cassette recorder.

kassieren [ka'siːrən] v (Geld) receive (Scheck) cash; (Urteil) annul, reverse; (Mil) cashier, dismiss. **Kassierer** m cashier.

Kastanie [ka'stanjə] f (pl -n) chestnut. **kastanienbraun** adj chestnut, auburn.

Kasten [kastən] m (pl Kästen) box, chest; (Schrank) cupboard.

kastrieren [ka'striːrən] castrate.

Kasus ['kaːzus] m (pl -) (Gramm) case.

Katalog [kata'loːg] m (pl -e) catalogue.

Katarakt[1] [kata'rakt] m (pl -e) rapids, waterfall.

Katarakt[2] f (pl -e) (Med) cataract.

Katarrh [ka'tar] m (pl -e) catarrh.

katastrophal [katastro'faːl] adj catastrophic. **Katastrophe** f (pl -n) catastrophe.

Kategorie [katego'riː] f (pl -n) category. **kategorisch** adj categorical.

Kater ['kaːtər] m (pl -) tom cat; (Katzenjammer) hangover.

Kathedrale [kate'draːlə] f (pl -n) cathedral.

Katholik(in) [kato'liːk(in)] Catholic. **katholisch** adj Catholic. **Katholizismus** m Catholicism.

Kätzchen ['kɛtsçən] neut kitten.

Katze ['katsə] f (pl -n) cat. **katzenartig** adj feline, cat-like. **Katzen‖auge** neut (Rückstrahler) rear reflector. **–jammer** m hangover.

Kauderwelsch ['kaudərvɛlʃ] neut gibberish.

kauen ['kauən] v chew.

kauern ['kauərn] v cower.

Kauf [kauf] m (pl Käufe) purchase. **einen guten Kauf machen** make a good buy, get a bargain. **kaufen** v buy, purchase. **Käufer** ['kɔyfər] m (pl -) buyer. **Kauf‖haus** neut department store. **–kraft** f purchasing power.

käuflich ['kɔyflɪç] adj saleable, purchasable; (bestechlich) corrupt, venal. **Kaufmann** m businessman; (Kleinhandel) shopkeeper; (Großhandel) merchant. **kaufmännisch** adj commercial, mercantile. **Kaufpreis** m purchase price.

kaum [kaum] adv hardly, scarcely.

Kaution [kau'tsioːn] f (pl -en) security, deposit. **gegen Kaution freilassen** release on bail.

Kauz [kauts] m (pl Käuze) screech owl; (fig) odd fellow.

Kavaller‖ie [kavalə'riː] f (pl -n) cavalry. **–ist** m cavalryman.

Kaviar ['kaːfviar] m (pl -e) caviar.

keck [kɛk] adj pert, cheeky.

Kegel ['keːgəl] m (pl -) cone; (Spiel) skittle. **–bahn** f bowling alley. **kegel‖förmig** adj conical. **–n** v play skittles, go bowling. **Kegelspiel** neut skittles, bowling.

Kehle ['keːlə] f (pl -n) throat. **Kehlkopf** m larynx. **–entzündung** f laryngitis.

kehren[1] ['keːrən] v sweep, brush.

kehren[2] v turn. **sich kehren** turn (round). **sich kehren an** pay attention to.

Kehricht ['keːrɪçt] m (unz.) sweepings pl.

Kehr‖reim m refrain. **–seite** f reverse, other side.

Keil [kail] m (pl -e) wedge; (Arch) keystone. **keilen** v wedge; (werben) win over. **sich keilen** scuffle.

Keiler ['kailər] m (pl -) (wild) boar.

Keilriemen ['kailriːmən] m (Mot) fanbelt.

Keim [kaim] m (pl -e) germ; (Bot) bud; embryo; (Anfang) origin. **keimen** v germinate; bud. **Keim‖träger** m carrier. **–ung** f germination.

kein [kain] keine, kein pron, m, f no one, nobody; neut nothing, none. adj no, not any. **kein anderer als** none other than. **keine Ahnung!** (I've) no idea! **keiner von beiden** neither (of the two). **keinerlei** adj of no sort. **keines‖falls** adv on no account. **–wegs** adv not at all.

Keks [keːks] m (pl -e) biscuit.

Keller ['kɛlər] m (pl -) cellar. **–ei** f wine cellar. **–geschoß** neut basement.

Kellner ['kɛlnər] m (pl -) waiter. **–in** f waitress.

*kennen ['kɛnən] v know. **–lernen** v get to know, become acquainted with. **Kenner** m (Wein, Kunst) connoisseur; (Fachmann) expert. **kenntlich** adj distinguishable, distinct. **Kenntnis** f knowledge. **kenntnisreich** adj experienced. **Kennwort** neut password. **kennzeichnen** v (fig) characterize, distinguish. **–d** adj characteristic. **Kennziffer** f reference or code number; (Math) index.

kentern ['kɛntərn] v capsize.

Kerbe ['kɛrbə] f (pl -n) notch.

Kerker ['kɛrkər] m (pl -) dungeon.

Kerl [kɛrl] m (pl -e) fellow.

Kern [kɛrn] m (pl -e) kernel; (Obst) stone, pit; (Atom) nucleus; (fig) core, essence. **kerngesund** adj thoroughly healthy. **Kern‖haus** neut core. **–reaktion** f nuclear reaction. **–waffe** f nuclear weapon. **–kraftwerk** neut nuclear power station.

Kerze ['kɛrtsə] f (pl -n) candle. **Kerzen‖leuchter** neut candlestick. **–licht** neut candlelight.

Kessel ['kɛsəl] m (pl -) kettle; (Tech) boiler; (Geog) depression, hollow.

Kette ['kɛtə] f (pl -n) chain, link. **ketten** v chain, link. **Ketten‖gebirge** neut mountain range. **–geschäft** neut chain store. **–raucher** m chain smoker. **–reaktion** f chain reaction.

Ketzer ['kɛtsər] m (pl -) heretic. **–ei** f (pl -en) heresy. **ketzerisch** adj heretical.

keuchen ['kɔyçən] v gasp, pant. **Keuchhusten** m whooping cough.

Keule ['kɔylə] f (pl -n) club, bludgeon; (Fleisch) leg.

keusch [kɔyʃ] adj chaste, modest. **Keuschheit** f chastity.

kichern ['kiçərn] v giggle.

Kiefer[1] ['kiːfər] m (pl -) (Anat) jaw.

Kiefer[2] f (pl -n) (Bot) pine.

Kieferknochen ['kiːfərknɔxən] m jawbone.

Kiefern‖holz neut pinewood. **–wald** m pine forest.

Kiel [kiːl] m (pl -e) keel.

Kieme [kiːmə] f (pl -n) gill.

Kies [kiːs] m (pl -e) gravel. **Kiesel** m (pl -) pebble, flint. **–stein** m pebble. **Kiesgrube** f gravelpit.

Kilo ['kiːlo] neut (pl -) kilo, kilogram(me). **–gramm** neut (pl -) kilogram(me). **Kilometer** neut (pl -) kilometre. **–zähler** m milometer, odometer.

Kind [kint] neut (pl -er) child. **ein Kind bekommen/erwarten** have/expect a baby.

Kinder‖arzt m paediatrician. **–bett** neut cot, crib. **–buch** neut children's book. **–heilkunde** f paediatrics. **–jahre** pl childhood sing. **–lähmung** f polio. **–spiel** neut children's game; (fig) child's play. **–wagen** m pram, (US) baby carriage.

Kindheit f childhood. **kindisch** adj childish. **kindlich** adj childlike.

Kinn [kin] neut (pl -e) chin.

Kino ['kiːno] neut (pl -s) cinema.

Kiosk ['kiːɔsk] m (pl -e) kiosk.

kippen ['kipən] v tip, tilt. **Kippwagen** m tipper, tip cart.

Kirche ['kirçə] f (pl -n) church. **Kirchen‖gemeinde** f parish. **–lied** neut hymn. **–schändung** f desecration, profanation. **Kirch‖gänger** m church-goer. **–hof** m churchyard. **kirchlich** adj ecclesiastical, church.

Kirsch [kirʃ] m kirsch, cherry brandy. **–e** f (pl -n) cherry.

Kissen ['kisən] neut (pl -) cushion; (Kopf-) pillow; (pl) bedding.

Kiste ['kistə] f (pl -n) chest, case, box.

Kitsch [kitʃ] m (tasteless) trash, kitsch. **kitschig** adj trashy.

Kittel ['kitəl] m (pl -) smock.

Kitzel ['kitsəl] m (pl -) tickle. **kitzeln** v tickle. **kitzlig** adj ticklish.

klaffen ['klafən] v gape, yawn. **–d** adj gaping.

Klage ['klaːgə] f (pl -n) complaint, grievance; (Jur) action, lawsuit. **klagen** v complain, (Jur) bring an action. **Klagende(r)** plaintiff.

kläglich ['klɛːkliç] adj miserable, pitiful.

Klammer ['klamər] f (pl -n) clamp; (kleine) clip; (Wäsche) peg. **klammern** v clamp; (befestigen) fasten. **sich klammern an** cling to.

Klamotten [kla'mɔtən] pl (umg.) gear sing, clothes pl.

Klang [klaŋ] m (pl Klänge) sound.

klapp‖en ['klapən] flap, clap; (umg.) work out, be all right. **–bar** adj collapsible, folding. **Klappe** f flap; (umg.) mouth, trap. **halt die Klappe!** (vulgär) shut up!

Klapper ['klapər] f (pl -n) rattle. **klapperig** adj clattering, rattling. **klappern** v rattle, clatter.

Klapp‖messer neut jack-knife. **–stuhl** m folding chair. **–tür** f trapdoor.

klar [klaːr] adj clear.

klären ['klɛːrən] v clarify.

Klarheit f ['klaːrhait] f clarity, clearness.

Klarinette [klari'nɛtə] f (pl -n) clarinet. **Klarinettist** m clarinettist.

klarlegen ['klaːrleːgən] v clear up.

Klärung ['klɛːruŋ] f clarification.

klarwerden ['klaːrveːrdən] v become clear.

klasse ['klasə] adj (umg.) marvellous, splendid. **Klasse** f class. **ein Musiker von Klasse** an excellent musician. **ein Restaurant erster Klasse** a first-class restaurant.

klassenbewußt adj class-conscious. **Klassenzimmer** neut classroom.

Klassik ['klasik] f classical era; (Literatur, Musik) classicism. – **er** m classicist. **klassisch** adj classical.

Klatsch [klatʃ] m (pl -e) slap, smack; (Gerede) gossip, chatter. – **base** f gossip, chatterbox. **klatschen** v clap; (reden) gossip, chatter.

Klaue ['klauə] f (pl -n) claw; (Raubvogel) talon. **klauen** v (umg.) steal, pinch.

Klausel ['klauzəl] f (pl -n) clause.

Klavier [kla'viːr] neut (pl -e) piano. – **spieler(in)** pianist.

Klebeband ['kleːbəbant] neut (adhesive) tape. **kleben** v glue, paste; (anhaften) stick. **klebrig** adj sticky. **Klebstoff** m glue.

Klecks [klɛks] m (pl -e) blot, spot.

Klee [kleː] m clover. – **blatt** neut cloverleaf.

Kleid [klait] neut (pl -er) garment; (Frau) dress; (pl) clothes. **kleiden** v clothe. **Kleider‖bügel** m coat-hanger. – **bürste** f clothes brush. – **schrank** m wardrobe. **Kleidung** f clothing, clothes. – **sstück** neut article of clothing, garment.

klein [klain] adj small, little. **der kleine Mann** the ordinary man. **klein stellen** turn down, put on low. **im kleinen** (Komm) retail.

Klein‖anzeige f classified advertisement. – **asien** neut Asia Minor. – **bürger** m petty bourgeois. – **geld** neut (small) change. – **handel** m retail trade. **Kleinigkeit** f (pl -en) trifle, trivial matter. **Klein‖kind** neut infant. – **lebewesen** neut microorganism. **klein‖lich** adj petty. – **mütig** adj fainthearted, cowardly.

Kleinod ['klainoːt] neut (pl -ien) jewel, gem.

Kleister ['klaistər] m (pl -) paste, gum.

Klemme ['klɛmə] f (pl -n) clamp; (Haar) grip; (Klammer) clip. **in der Klemme sitzen** be in a dilemma or tight corner. **klemmen** v squeeze, pinch.

Klempner ['klɛmpnər] m (pl -) plumber; (Metall) metalworker. – **ei** f plumbing. **klempnern** v do plumbing.

Kleriker ['kleːrikər] m (pl -) cleric, clergyman. **Klerus** m (unz.) clergy.

Kletterer ['klɛtərər] m (pl -) climber. **klettern** v climb. **Kletterpflanze** f climbing plant, creeper.

Klima ['kliːma] neut (pl -te) climate. – **anlage** f air-conditioning (equipment). **klimatisch** adj climatic.

Klinge ['klɪŋə] f (pl -n) blade.

Klingel ['klɪŋəl] f (pl -n) (door)bell. **klingeln** v ring the bell, ring.

klingen ['klɪŋən] v sound; ring.

Klinik ['kliːnik] f (pl -en) clinic, hospital. **klinisch** adj clinical.

Klinke ['klɪŋkə] f (pl -n) doorhandle, latch.

Klippe ['klɪpə] f (pl -n) cliff; (im Meer) rocks pl, reef.

klirren ['klɪrən] v tinkle, jangle.

Klischee [kli'ʃeː] neut (pl -s) (fig) cliché.

Klo [kloː] neut (pl -s) (umg.) toilet, loo.

Kloake [klo'aːkə] f (pl -n) sewer.

klopfen ['klɔpfən] v (Tür) knock; (Herz) beat; (Schulter) tap, pat. **Klopfen** neut knocking; beating.

Klosett [klo'zɛt] neut (pl -s) toilet. – **papier** neut toilet paper.

Kloß [kloːs] m (pl Klöße) dumpling; (Fleisch) meatball.

Kloster ['kloːstər] neut (pl Klöster) monastery, abbey, convent. – **gang** m cloister.

Klotz [klɔts] m (pl Klötze) block, log.

Klub [klup] m (pl -s) club, association.

Kluft [kluft] m (pl Klüfte) cleft; (Abgrund) chasm, abyss; (fig) rift.

klug [kluːk] adj clever; (Ansicht, Rat) sensible, prudent. **Klugheit** f cleverness, intelligence.

Klumpen ['klumpən] m (pl -) lump; (Gold) nugget.

knabbern ['knabərn] v nibble.

Knabe ['knaːbə] m (pl -n) boy. – **nalter** neut boyhood, youth. **knabenhaft** adj boyish.

Knäckebrot ['knɛkəbrɔt] neut crispbread.

knacken ['knakən] v crack.

Knall [knal] m (pl -e) bang; explosion. – **bonbon** m cracker. **knallen** v crack, bang; explode. **Knallfrosch** m banger, jumping jack.

knapp [knap] adj scant, insufficient; (Kleidung) tight. **knapp sein** be in short supply. **knapp werden** be running short or out. **knapp bei Kasse sein** be hard up. **knapp drei Meter** just under (or barely) three metres.

knarren ['knarən] v creak.

knattern ['knatərn] v crackle, rattle.

Knebel ['kneːbəl] m (pl -) gag. **knebeln** v gag.

Knecht [knɛçt] *m* (*pl* -e) (farm) worker; (*Diener*) servant.

***kneifen** ['knaifən] *v* pinch, nip. **Kneifzange** *f* pincers.

Kneipe ['knaipə] *f* (*pl* -n) pub, bar. **kneipen** *v* go boozing.

kneten ['kneitən] *v* knead; (*Körper*) massage.

Knick [knik] *m* (*pl* -e) crack; (*Kniff*) crease; (*Kurve*) sharp bend. **knicken** *v* break, crack; fold, crease.

Knicks [kniks] *m* (*pl* -e) curtsey.

Knie [kniː] *neut* (*pl* -e) knee. **knien** *v* kneel. **-d** *adj* kneeling, on one's knees. **Kniescheibe** *f* kneecap.

Kniff [knif] *m* (*pl* -e) pinch; (*Falte*) crease; trick. **den Kniff heraushaben** get the hang of it.

knipsen ['knipsən] *v* punch, clip; (*Foto*) snap.

knirschen ['knirʃən] *v* gnash.

Knitter ['knitər] *m* (*pl* -) crease. **knitter||frei** *adj* crease-resistant. **-n** *v* crease.

Knoblauch ['knoplaux] *m* garlic.

Knöchel ['knœçəl] *m* (*pl* -) (*Finger*) knuckle; (*Bein*) ankle.

Knochen ['knɔxən] *m* (*pl* -) bone. **-bruch** *m* fracture. **-gerüst** *neut* skeleton. **-mark** *neut* (bone) marrow. **knochig** *adj* bony.

Knödel ['knœidəl] *m* (*pl* -) dumpling.

Knolle ['knɔlə] *f* (*pl* -n) tuber; (*Zwiebel, Tulpe*) bulb.

Knopf [knɔpf] *m* (*pl* **Knöpfe**) button. **knöpfen** ['knœpfən] *v* button.

Knorpel ['knɔrpəl] *m* (*pl* -) cartilage; (*bei gekochtem Fleisch*) gristle.

Knospe ['knɔspə] *f* (*pl* -n) bud. **knospen** *v* bud.

Knoten ['knoːtən] *m* (*pl* -) knot; (*Tech*) node. **knoten** *v* knot. **Knotenpunkt** *m* junction.

knüpfen ['knypfən] *v* join, tie.

knusprig ['knuspriç] *adj* crisp.

Koalition [koali'tsioːn] *f* (*pl* -en) coalition.

Kobold ['koːbɔlt] *m* (*pl* -e) goblin.

Koch [kɔx] *m* (*pl* **Köche**) cook. **-buch** *neut* cookery book. **kochen** *v* cook; (*sieden*) boil. **-d** boiling. **Kocher** *m* cooker. **Kochherd** *m* kitchen range.

Köchin ['kœçin] *f* (*pl* -nen) (female) cook.

Koch||platte *f* hotplate, ring. **-topf** *m* saucepan, pot.

Köder ['kœidər] *m* (*pl* -) bait. **ködern** *v* lure, entice.

Koexistenz [koːɛksi'stɛnts] *f* coexistence. **koexistieren** *v* coexist.

Koffer ['kɔfər] *m* (*pl* -) suitcase; (*Schrankkoffer*) trunk. **-kuli** *m* (luggage) trolley. **-raum** *m* (*Mot*) trunk.

Kohl [koːl] *m* (*pl* -e) cabbage.

Kohle ['koːlə] *f* (*pl* -n) coal; (*Holzkohle*) charcoal. **Kohle||bergwerk** *neut* coal mine, pit. **-säure** *f* carbonic acid; (*in Getränken*) carbon dioxide. **-hydrat** *neut* carbohydrate. **-stoff** *m* carbon. **Kohle||papier** *neut* carbon paper. **-stift** *m* charcoal crayon.

Kohl||rabi [koːl'rabi] *m* (*pl* -s) kohlrabi. **-rübe** *f* swede.

Koje ['koːjə] *f* (*pl* -n) bunk, berth; (*Zimmer*) cabin.

kokett [ko'kɛt] *adj* coquettish. **-ieren** *v* flirt.

Kokosnuß ['koːkɔsnus] *f* coconut.

Koks [koːks] *m* (*pl* -e) coke.

Kolben ['kɔlbən] *m* (*pl* -n) club; (*Gewehr*) butt; (*Zylinder*) piston.

Kollege [kɔ'leːgə] *m* (*pl* -n) **Kollegin** *f* (*pl* -nen) colleague.

kollektiv [kɔlɛk'tiːf] *adj* collective.

Köln [kœln] *neut* Cologne. **-ischwasser** *neut* eau de Cologne.

Kolon ['koːlɔn] *neut* (*pl* -s) colon.

kolonial [kolo'niaːl] *adj* colonial. **Kolonialwaren** *pl* groceries. **-händler** *m* grocer.

Kolonne [ko'lɔnə] *f* (*pl* -n) column.

Kombi ['kɔmbi] *m* (*pl* -s) estate car. **Kombination** [kɔmbina'tsioːn] *f* (*pl* -en) combination; (*Sport*) teamwork; (*Unterkleidung*) combinations *pl*; (*Schützkleidung*) one-piece suit; (*Ideen*) conjecture. **kombinieren** *v* combine.

Komet [ko'meːt] *m* (*pl* -en) comet.

Komfort [kɔm'foːr] *m* (*unz.*) comfort. **komfortabel** *adj* comfortable.

Komiker ['koːmikər] *m* (*pl* -) comedian, comic. **komisch** *adj* funny; (*seltsam*) strange.

Komitee [komi'teː] *neut* (*pl* -s) committee.

Komma ['kɔma] *neut* (*pl* -s) comma.

Kommandant [kɔman'dant] *m* (*pl* -en) commander. **kommandieren** *v* command. **Kommanditgesellschaft** (**KG**) [kɔman'ditgəzɛlʃaft (ka'geːɪ)] *f* limited-liability company.

Kommando [kɔ'mandoː] *neut* (*pl* -s) order, command; (*Abteilung*) squad, detachment, detail. **-truppe** *f* commando (unit).

*kommen ['kɔmən] v come. **kommen lassen** send for. **um etwas kommen** lose something. **hinter etwas kommen** get to the bottom of something. **Kommen** neut arrival, coming. **kommend** adj coming.

Kommentar [kɔmɛn'taɪr] m (pl -e) commentary. **kommentieren** v comment on.

Kommerz [kɔ'mɛrts] m commerce. **kommerziell** adj commercial.

Kommissar [kɔmi'saɪr] m (pl -e) commissioner; (Polizei) inspector. **Kommission** f commission.

kommun [kɔ'muɪn] adj common. **-al** adj municipal. **Kommune** f (pl -n) commune; (Gemeinde) municipality.

Kommunikation [komunika'tsioɪn] f (pl -en) communication.

Kommuniqué [kɔmyni'keɪ] neut (pl -s) communiqué.

Kommunismus [kɔmu'nizmus] m communism. **Kommunist(in)** communist. **kommunistisch** adj communist.

Komödie [kɔ'mœɪdiə] f (pl -n) comedy; (Ereignis) farce.

Kompaß ['kɔmpas] m (pl Kompasse) compass. **-strich** m point of the compass.

kompetent [kɔmpe'tɛnt] adj competent.

Komplex [kɔm'plɛks] m (pl -e) complex.

Kompliment [kɔmpli'mɛnt] neut (pl -e) compliment.

komplizieren [kɔmpli'tsiɪrən] v complicate. **kompliziert** adj complicated, complex.

Komplott [kɔm'plɔt] neut (pl -e) plot, conspiracy.

komponieren [kɔmpo'niɪrən] v compose. **Komponist** m (pl -en) composer.

Kompott [kɔm'pɔt] neut (pl -e) stewed fruit, compote.

Kompresse [kɔm'prɛsə] f (pl -n) compress.

Kompromiß [kɔmpro'mis] m (pl Kompromisse) compromise. **kompromittieren** v compromise.

kondensieren [kɔndɛn'siɪrən] v condense. **Kondensmilch** f condensed milk.

Konditorei [kɔndito'raɪ] (pl -en) patisserie, cake shop. **-waren** pl pastries, cakes.

Kondom [kɔn'dɔɪm] m (pl -e) condom.

Konferenz [kɔnfe'rɛnts] f (pl -en) conference.

Konfession [kɔnfe'sioɪn] f (pl -en) confession, creed, faith.

Konflikt [kɔn'flikt] m (pl -e) conflict.

konform [kɔn'fɔrm] adj in agreement, in accordance.

Konfrontation [kɔnfrɔnta'tsioɪn] f (pl -en) confrontation. **konfrontieren** v confront.

konfus [kɔn'fuɪs] adj confused, muddled. **Konfusion** f confusion.

Kongreß [kɔn'grɛs] m (pl Kongresse) congress.

König ['kœɪniç] m (pl -e) king. **-in** f (pl -nen) queen. **-inmutter** m queen mother. **königlich** adj royal, regal. **Königreich** neut kingdom, realm.

Konjunktur [kɔnjuŋk'tuɪr] f (pl -en) (state of the) economy, economic trends pl; (Aufschwung) boom.

Konkurrent [kɔnku'rɛnt] m (pl -en) competitor. **Konkurrenz** f (unz.) competition. **konkurrenzfähig** adj competitive. **konkurrieren** v compete.

Konkurs [kɔn'kurs] m (pl -e) bankruptcy, insolvency. **in Konkurs gehen** become bankrupt.

*können ['kœnən] v can, be able (to); (dürfen) may, be allowed (to); (gelernt haben) know. **tun können** know how to do. **eine Sprache können** speak a language. Ich kann nicht mehr! I can't go on. **das kann sein** it may be so. er kann nichts dafür it's not his fault, he can't help it. **Können** neut ability.

konsequent [kɔnze'kvɛnt] adj consistent. **Konsequenz** f consistency; (Folge) consequence. **die Konsequenzen tragen** bear the consequences. **Konsequenzen ziehen** draw conclusions.

konservativ [kɔnzɛrva'tiɪf] adj conservative. **Konservative(r)** conservative.

Konserve [kɔn'zɛrvə] f (pl -n) preserve, tinned or bottled food. **Konservenbüchse** f tin (of preserves). **konservieren** v preserve.

konsolidieren [kɔnzɔli'diɪrən] v consolidate.

Konsonant [kɔnzo'nant] m (pl -en) consonant.

konstant [kɔn'stant] adj constant.

konstruieren [kɔnstru'iɪrən] v construct. **Konstruktion** f (pl -en) construction; (Entwurf) design.

Konsul [kɔn'zuɪl] m (pl -n) consul. **-at** neut (pl -e) consulate.

Konsum [kɔn'zuɪm] m consumption. **-gesellschaft** f consumer society. **konsumieren** v consume. **Konsumverein** m co-operative society.

Kontakt [kɔn'takt] *m* (*pl* -e) contact.

Kontinent [kɔnti'nɛnt] *m* (*pl* -e) continent.

Konto ['kɔnto] *neut* (*pl* **Konten**) account. **–auszug** *m* (bank) statement. **–buch** *neut* passbook. **–inhaber** *m* accountholder.

Kontrabaß ['kɔntrabas] *m* double bass.

konträr [kɔn'trɛr] *adj* adverse.

Kontrast [kɔn'trast] *m* (*pl* -e) contrast. **kontrastieren** *v* contrast.

Kontrolle [kɔn'trɔlə] *f* (*pl* -n) control, supervision. **–abschnitt** *m* counterfoil. **–eur** *m* controller. **kontrollieren** *v* control, supervise. **Kontrollpunkt** *m* checkpoint. **unter Kontrolle** under control.

konventionell [kɔnvɛntsio'nɛl] *adj* conventional.

Konversation [kɔnvɛrza'tsiɔn] *f* (*pl* -en) conversation. **–slexikon** *neut* encyclopedia.

konvertieren [kɔnvɛr'tiːrən] *v* convert.

konvex [kɔn'vɛks] *adj* convex.

Konzentrat [kɔntsən'traːt] *neut* (*pl* -e) concentrate. **–ion** *f* (*pl* -en) concentration. **–ionslager** *neut* concentration camp. **konzentrieren** *v* concentrate.

Konzept [kɔn'tsɛpt] *neut* (*pl* -e) rough draft.

Konzert [kɔn'tsɛrt] *neut* (*pl* -e) concert; (*Stück*) concerto.

Kopf [kɔpf] *m* (*pl* **Köpfe**) head. **auf den Kopf stellen** turn upside down. **pro Kopf** per capita, each. **im Kopf haben** be preoccupied with. **–ball** *m* (*Sport*) header. **köpfen** ['kœpfən] *v* behead, decapitate. **Kopf‖haut** *f* scalp. **–hörer** *m* headphone. **–kissen** *neut* pillow. **–putz** *m* headdress. **–salat** *m* lettuce. **–schmerzen** *pl* headache *sing.* **–sprung** *m* header. **–stand** *m* headstand. **kopfüber** *adv* headlong, head first.

Kopie [ko'piː] *f* (*pl* -n) copy. **kopieren** *v* copy.

Kopulation [kɔpula'tsiɔn] *f* (*pl* -en) copulation. **kopulieren** *v* copulate; (*Bäume*) graft.

Koralle [ko'ralə] *f* (*pl* -n) coral. **–nriff** *neut* coral reef.

Korb [kɔrp] *m* (*pl* **Körbe**) basket. **–ball** *m* basketball. **–geflecht** *neut* basketwork.

Kord [kɔrt] *or* **Kordsamt** *m* cord(uroy). **Kordhose** *f* corduroy trousers; (*umg.*) cords.

Korinthe [ko'rintə] *f* (*pl* -n) currant.

Kork [kɔrk] *m* (*pl* -e) cork. **–enzieher** *m* corkscrew.

Korn [kɔrn] *neut* (*pl* **Körner**) grain, corn.

Körnchen ['kœrnçən] *neut* (*pl* -) granule.

Koronarthrombose [koro'naːrtrɔmboːzə] *f* (*pl* -n) coronary thrombosis.

Körper [kœrpər] *m* (*pl* -) body. **–bau** *m* physique, build. **körperbehindert** *adj* physically handicapped. **Körper‖bildung** *f* body-building. **–geruch** *m* body odour. **–gewicht** *neut* weight. **–haltung** *f* posture.

körperlich ['kœrpərliç] *adj* bodily, physical; (*Strafe*) corporal.

Körper‖maß *neut* cubic measure. **–pflege** *f* hygiene. **–schaft** *f* (*pl* -en) corporation.

Korporal [kɔrpo'raːl] *m* (*pl* -e) corporal.

korrekt [kɔ'rɛkt] *adj* correct. **Korrektur** *f* (*pl* -en) correction; (*Druck*) proof.

Korrespondent [kɔrɛspɔn'dɛnt] *m* (*pl* -en) correspondent. **Korrespondenz** *f* correspondence.

korrigieren [kɔri'giːrən] *v* correct; (*gedrucktes*) proofread.

Kosename ['koːzənaːmə] *m* pet name.

Kosmetik [kɔz'meːtik] *f* (*unz.*) cosmetics *pl.* **kosmetisch** *adj* cosmetic.

Kosmos ['kɔsmɔs] *m* (*pl* **Kosmen**) cosmos, universe. **kosmisch** *adj* cosmic.

Kost [kɔst] *f* (*unz.*) food, fare. **Kost und Wohnung** board and lodging. **kräftige Kost** rich diet.

kostbar ['kɔstbaːr] *adj* expensive; (*sehr wertvoll*) precious.

kosten¹ ['kɔstən] *v* (*probieren*) taste, try, sample.

kosten² *v* cost. **Kosten** *pl* costs. **auf meine Kosten** at my expense. **kostenlos** *adj* free (of charge).

köstlich ['kœstliç] *adj* delicious; (*reizend*) charming; (*wertvoll*) precious.

kostspielig ['kɔstʃpiːliç] *adj* expensive.

Kostüm [kɔs'tyːm] *neut* (*pl* -e) costume; (*Damen-*) suit. **–ball** *m* fancy-dress ball. **–probe** *f* dress rehearsal.

Kot [koːt] *m* dung, droppings *pl*; (*Schmutz*) dirt, mud.

Kotelett [kɔtə'lɛt] *neut* (*pl* -e) chop, cutlet. **–en** *pl* sideburns, mutton-chop whiskers.

Kotflügel ['koːtflyːgəl] *m* mudguard; fender.

kotzen ['kɔtsən] v (*vulgär*) puke, be sick. **zum Kotzen** enough to make you sick.

Krabbe ['krabə] f (*pl* -n) shrimp.

krabbeln ['krabəln] v scuttle, scurry.

Krach [krax] m (*pl* -e) noise; (*Streit*) quarrel, row; (*Knall*) crash.

krächzen ['krɛçtsən] v croak.

kraft [kraft] *prep* on the strength of, by virtue of. **Kraft** f (*pl* Kräfte) strength; (*Macht*) power. **-fahrer** m driver. **-fahrzeug** *neut* motor vehicle.

kräftig ['krɛftiç] *adj* strong; (*mächtig*) powerful; (*Essen*) substantial. **-en** v strengthen. **-end** *adj* invigorating.

kraftlos *adj* powerless. **Kraft||probe** f trial of strength. **-rad** *neut* motorcycle. **-stoff** m fuel. **-wagen** m motor vehicle. **-werk** *neut* power station.

Kragen ['kraigən] m (*pl* -) collar.

Krähe ['krɛə] f (*pl* -n) crow. **krähen** v crow.

Kralle ['kralə] f (*pl* -n) claw. **krallen** v claw. **sich krallen an** clutch.

Kram [kraim] m stuff, trash; (*umg.*) things, stuff.

Krampf [krampf] m (*pl* Krämpfe) cramp, spasm. **krampfhaft** *adj* convulsive; (*heftig*) frenzied, frantic.

Kran [krain] m (*pl* Kräne) (*Mech*) crane.

Kranich ['krainiç] m (*pl* -e) (*Zool*) crane.

krank [krank] *adj* sick, ill, unwell. **Kranke(r)** patient.

kränken ['krɛnkən] v vex, annoy.

Kranken||haus *neut* hospital. **-kasse** f health insurance (company). **-schein** m medical certificate. **-schwester** f nurse. **-versicherung** f health insurance. **-wagen** m ambulance. **krankhaft** *adj* diseased, unhealthy. **Krankheit** f (*pl* -en) disease, illness.

Kranz [krants] m (*pl* Kränze) wreath, garland.

Krapfen ['krapfən] m (*pl* -) fritter; doughnut.

kraß [kras] *adj* crass, gross.

kratzen ['kratsən] v scratch. **Kratzwunde** f scratch.

kraulen ['kraulən] *or* **kraulschwimmen** v swim the crawl. **Kraulstil** m crawl.

kraus [kraus] *adj* curly, crinkled.

Kraut [kraut] *neut* (*pl* Kräuter) herb; (*Kohl*) cabbage; (*grüne Pflanzen*) vegetation.

Kräuter||buch ['krɔytərbuːx] *neut* herbal. **-tee** m herb tea.

Krawall [kra'val] m (*pl* -e) brawl.

Krawatte [kra'vatə] f (*pl* -n) (neck)tie.

Krebs [kreːps] m (*pl* -e) crab; (*Med*) cancer; (*Astrol*) Cancer.

Kredit [kre'diːt] m (*pl* -e) (*Komm*) credit. **-brief** m letter of credit. **kreditieren** v credit.

Kreide ['kraidə] f (*pl* -n) chalk. **-fels** m chalk cliff.

Kreis ['krais] m (*pl* -e) circle; (*Gebiet*) district, area. **-bahn** f orbit. **-bewegung** f rotation, revolution. **-bogen** m arc (of a circle).

kreischen ['kraiʃən] v screech, shriek.

Kreisel ['kraizəl] m (*pl* -) (spinning) top. **kreiseln** v spin (like a top).

kreis||en v revolve, rotate. **-förmig** *adj* circular. **Kreis||lauf** m circulation. **-säge** f circular saw. **-umfang** m circumference.

Krem [kreim] f (*pl* -s) cream.

Krematorium [krema'toːrium] *neut* (*pl* Krematorien) crematorium.

Kreml ['krəməl] m Kremlin.

Krempel ['krɛmpəl] m junk, rubbish.

krepieren [kre'piːrən] v burst; (*umg.*) die.

Kresse ['krɛsə] f (*pl* -n) cress.

Kreuz [krɔyts] *neut* (*pl* -e) cross; (*Karten*) club(s); (*Anat*) small of the back. **kreuz und quer** in all directions. **kreuzen** v cross; (*Schiff*) cruise. **sich kreuzen** intersect. **Kreuzer** m (*pl* -) cruiser. **Kreuz||fahrer** m crusader. **-fahrt** f (*Schiff*) cruise; (*Kreuzzug*) crusade.

kreuzigen ['krɔytsigən] v crucify. **Kreuzigung** f (*pl* -en) crucifixion.

Kreuzung f (*pl* -en) crossing.

Kreuz||verhör *neut* cross-examination. **-verweis** m cross-reference. **-weg** m crossroads. **-worträtsel** *neut* crossword puzzle. **-zug** m crusade.

***kriechen** ['kriːçən] v creep, crawl; (*fig*) cringe, grovel. **kriecherisch** *adj* cringing, servile.

Krieg [kriːk] m (*pl* -e) war. **den Krieg erklären/führen** declare/wage war. **Krieger** m (*pl* -) warrior. **kriegführend** *adj* belligerent. **Kriegs||dienstverweigerer** m conscientious objector. **-gefangene(r)** prisoner of war. **-gericht** *neut* court-martial. **-hetzer** m warmonger. **-verbrecher** m war criminal. **-zeit** f wartime.

Krimi ['krimi] *neut* (*pl* -s) detective novel, thriller.

kriminal [krimi'naıl] *adj* criminal.
Kriminal‖polizei *f* detective force, CID.
–roman *m* detective novel, thriller.

Krippe ['krɪpə] *f* (*pl* -n) crib; (*Kinder-*) crèche.

Krise ['kriːzə] *f* (*pl* -n) crisis.

Kristall [kri'stal] *m* (*pl* -e) crystal. **kristallisieren** *v* crystallize.

Kritik [kri'tiːk] *f* (*pl* -en) criticism. **–er** *m* critic. **kritisch** *adj* critical. **kritisieren** *v* criticize; (*Buch, Film*) review.

Krokodil [kroko'diːl] *neut* (*pl* -e) crocodile.

Krone ['kroːnə] *f* (*pl* -n) crown.

krönen ['krœːnən] *v* crown. **Krönung** *f* coronation.

Kröte ['krœːtə] *f* (*pl* -n) toad.

Krücke ['krykə] *f* (*pl* -n) crutch.

Krug [kruːk] *m* (*pl* **Krüge**) jug; (*Becher*) mug.

Krume ['kruːmə] *f* (*pl* -n) crumb.

Krümel ['kryməl] *m* (*pl* -) crumb. **krümelig** ['kryməlıç] *adj* crumbly.

krumm [krum] *adj* crooked. **–beinig** *adj* bow-legged.

Krumme ['krumə] *f* (*pl* -n) sickle.

Krümmung ['krymuŋ] *f* curve, bend.

Krüppel ['krypəl] *m* (*pl* -) cripple.

Kruste ['krustə] *f* (*pl* -n) crust. **–ntier** *neut* crustacean.

Kruzifix [kruttsi'fiks] *neut* (*pl* -e) crucifix.

Kubikinhalt [ku'biːkinhalt] *m* volume.

Küche ['kyçə] *f* (*pl* -n) kitchen; cookery, cuisine.

Kuchen ['kuːxən] *m* (*pl* -) cake.

Küchen‖schabe *f* cockroach. **–schrank** *m* kitchen cupboard.

Kuckuck ['kukuk] *m* (*pl* -e) cuckoo.

Kugel ['kuːgəl] *f* (*pl* -n) ball; (*Gewehr*) bullet; (*Math*) sphere. **kugel‖fest** *adj* bullet-proof. **–förmig** *adj* spherical. **Kugel‖lager** *neut* ball-bearing. **–schreiber** *m* ball(point) pen.

Kuh [kuː] *f* (*pl* **Kühe**) cow.

kühl [kyːl] *adj* cool. **Kühle** *f* coolness. **kühlen** *v* cool. **Kühl‖schrank** *m* refrigerator. **–ung** *f* cooling.

kühn [kyːn] *adj* daring, bold, audacious. **Kühnheit** *f* daring, boldness, audacity.

Kuhstall ['kuːʃtal] *m* (*pl* -) cowshed.

Kulisse [ku'lısə] *f* (*pl* -) (*Theater*) scenery *sing*. **hinter den Kulissen** (*fig*) behind the scenes.

Kult [kult] *m* (*pl* -e) cult; (*Verehrung*) worship.

kultivieren [kulti'viːrən] *v* cultivate.

Kultur [kul'tuːr] *f* (*pl* -en) culture; (*Boden*) cultivation; (*Bakterien*) culture. **kulturell** *adj* cultural.

Kümmel ['kyməl] *m* caraway (seed).

Kummer ['kumər] *m* (*unz.*) sorrow, distress.

kümmerlich ['kymərlıç] *adj* miserable, poor. **kümmern** *v* grieve; (*angehen*) concern. **sich kümmern um** take care of, look after.

Kumpel ['kumpəl] *m* (*pl* -s) (*umg.*) mate, buddy; (*Bergmann*) miner.

kund [kunt] *adj* (generally) known.

Kunde[1] ['kundə] *f* information, (*Nachrichten*) news.

Kunde[2] *m*, **Kundin** *f* customer, client.

Kundendienst ['kundəndiːnst] *m* after-sales service.

***kundgeben** ['kuntgeːbən] *v* make known, declare. **Kundgebung** *f* demonstration; (*Kundgeben*) declaration.

kündigen ['kyndigən] *v* give notice. **Kündigung** *f* notice.

Kundschaft ['kuntʃaft] *f* (*unz.*) customers *pl*, clientele.

künftig ['kynftıç] *adj* future.

Kunst [kunst] *f* (*pl* **Künste**) art; (*Fertigkeit*) skill. **–akademie** *f* art college. **kunstfertig** *adj* skilled. **Kunst‖gegenstand** *m* objet d'art. **–griff** *m* trick, dodge. **–handwerker** *m* craftsman.

Künstler ['kynstlər] *m*, **Künstlerin** *f* artist. **künstlerisch** *adj* artistic.

künstlich ['kynstlıç] *adj* artificial. **künstliche Atmung** *f* artificial respiration.

Kunst‖stück [*neut* stunt, trick. **–werk** *neut* work of art.

Kupfer ['kupfər] *neut* (*pl* -) copper. **kupfer‖farben** *adj* copper(-coloured). **–n** *adj* copper.

Kuppel ['kupəl] *f* (*pl* -n) dome, cupola.

Kuppelei [kupə'laı] *f* (*unz.*) procuring, pimping. **kuppeln** *v* unite, couple; (*Mot*) declutch. **Kuppler** *m* procurer. **Kupplerin** *f* procuress. **Kupplung** *f* coupling; (*Mot*) clutch.

Kur [kuːr] *f* (*pl* -en) (course of) treatment. **–anstalt** *f* sanatorium.

Kurbel ['kurbəl] *f* (*pl* -n) crank, handle. **–welle** *f* crankshaft.

Kürbis ['kyrbis] *m* (*pl* -se) pumpkin.

Kurfürst ['kuːrfyrst] *m* elector, electoral prince.

Kurort m spa.

Kurs [kurs] m (pl -e) course; (Komm) rate. **-buch** neut railway timetable.

kursiv [kur'ziːf] adv in italics.

Kurve ['kurvə] f (pl -n) curve; (Straße) bend.

kurz [kurts] adj short. **kurze Hose** shorts pl. **kurz und gut** in a word, in short. **sich kurz fassen** be brief, make it short. **Kurz||arbeit** f short time (work). **-ausgabe** f abridged edition.

Kürze ['kyrtsə] f (pl -n) shortness; (Zeit) brevity. **kürzen** v shorten. **kürzlich** adv recently, lately.

Kurz||meldung f news flash. **-schluß** m short circuit. **-schrift** f shorthand. **kurzsichtig** adj nearsighted, shortsighted. **Kürzung** f (pl -en) shortening, reduction.

Kurz||waren f pl haberdashery. **-welle** f shortwave.

Kusine [ku'ziːnə] f (pl -n) (female) cousin.

Kuß [kus] m (pl Küsse) kiss.

küssen ['kysən] v kiss.

Küste ['kystə] f (pl -n) coast, shore. **-nwache** f coastguard.

Kutsche ['kutʃə] f (pl -n) carriage, coach. **-r** m (pl -) coachman.

L

labil [la'biːl] adj unstable; (oft krank) delicate, sickly.

Labor [la'boːr] neut (pl -s) (umg.) lab.

Laboratorium [labora'toːrium] neut (pl Laboratorien) laboratory, (umg.) lab.

lächeln ['lɛçəln] v smile. **Lächeln** neut smile.

lachen ['laxən] v laugh. **Lachen** neut laughter, laugh. **zum Lachen bringen** make laugh. **das ist zum Lachen** that's ridiculous.

lächerlich ['lɛçərliç] adj ridiculous.

Lachs [laks] m (pl -e) salmon.

Lack [lak] m (pl -e) lacquer; (mit Farbstoff) (enamel) paint. **-farbe** f (enamel) paint. **-leder** neut patent leather.

***laden¹** ['laːdən] v load.

***laden²** v invite; (Jur) summon.

Laden ['laːdən] m (pl Läden) shop; (Fenster) shutter. **-diebstahl** m shoplifting. **-schluß** m closing time. **-tisch** m counter.

Lade||platz m loading place; (Schiff) wharf. **-raum** m hold. **Ladung** (pl -en) f load; (Schiffe) cargo.

Lage ['laːgə] f (pl -n) situation, position. **in der Lage sein** be in a position to.

Lager ['laːgər] neut (pl -) camp; (Speicher) store(s); (Tier) lair; (Geol) stratum, layer; (Tech) bearing. **-feuer** neut campfire. **-haus** neut warehouse. **lagern** v (im Freien rasten) camp; (aufbewahren) store; (einlegen) lay down, place; (aufbewahrt werden) be stored.

Lagune [la'guːnə] f (pl -n) lagoon.

lahm [laːm] adj crippled; (müde) exhausted; (schwach) lame, feeble. **lähmen** ['lɛːmən] v cripple, paralyze; (fig) obstruct. **Lähmung** f (pl -en) paralysis.

Laib [laip] m (pl -e) loaf.

Laie ['laiə] m (pl -n) layman. **Laien||priester** m lay preacher. **-stand** m laity.

Lakritze [la'kritsə] f (pl -n) liquorice.

Lamm [lam] neut (pl Lämmer) lamb. **-fleisch** neut lamb. **-wolle** f lambswool.

Lampe ['lampə] f (pl -n) lamp.

Land [lant] 1 neut (unz.) (Erdboden, Grundstück, Festland) land; (Landschaft) country(side). 2 neut (pl Länder) land, country; (Provinz) state, province. **an Land gehen** go ashore, disembark. **Hügeliges Land** hilly country or terrain. **auf dem Lande** in the country. **Land||arbeiter** m farmworker. **-besitz** m land, property. **landen** v land; (umg.) land up, end up. **Landenge** f isthmus.

Landes||bank f national bank; regional bank. **-flagge** f national flag. **-verrat** m high treason.

Land||gut neut (landed) estate. **-haus** neut country house. **-karte** f map. **-leute** pl country folk.

ländlich ['lentliç] adj rural.

Land||mann m countryman; (Bauer) farmer. **-messer** m surveyor. **-mine** f landmine. **-schaft** f countryside; (Malerei) landscape; (Gebiet) area, region. **-schule** f village school. **-smann** m fellow countryman. **-spitze** f cape, headland. **-straße** f highway, main road. **-streicher** m tramp, vagrant.

Landung ['landuŋ] f (pl -en) landing. **-ssteg** m gangway, landing ramp.

Landweg ['lantveːk] m land route. **auf dem Landwege** by land.

Landwirt ['lantvırt] *m* farmer. **landwirtschaftlich** *adj* agricultural.

lang [laŋ] *adj* long; (*Mensch*) tall. **viele Jahre lang** for many years. **lange** *adv* (for) a long time.

Länge ['lɛŋə] *f* (*pl* -n) length; (*Mensch*) height; (*Größe*) size; (*Geog*) longitude.

langen ['laŋən] *v* suffice. **langen nach** reach for.

länger ['lɛŋər] *adj* longer; taller. **länger machen** lengthen, extend. **auf längere Zeit** for a considerable period.

Langeweile ['laŋəvailə] *f* boredom.

lang∥jährig *adj* of long standing. **-lebig** *adj* long-lived.

länglich ['lɛŋliç] *adj* oblong, longish. **-rund** *adj* oval, elliptical.

längs [lɛŋs] *prep* along.

langsam ['laŋzaim] *adj* slow. **Langsamkeit** *f* slowness.

Langspielplatte ['laŋʃpiilplatə] *f* long-playing record, LP.

längst [lɛŋst] *adj* longest. *adv* long ago. **-ens** *adv* (*höchstens*) at the most; (*spätestens*) at the latest.

langweilen ['laŋvailən] *v* bore. **sich langweilen** be bored. **langweilig** *adj* boring, tedious.

Lanze ['lantsə] *f* (*pl* -n) lance.

Lappen ['lapən] *m* (*pl* -) rag, (cleaning) cloth; (*Anat*, *Bot*) lobe. **lappig** (*umg.*) flabby; (*Anat*, *Bot*) lobed.

Lärche ['lɛrçə] *f* (*pl* -n) larch.

Lärm [lɛrm] *m* (*unz.*) noise, din. **lärmen** *v* make a noise. **-d** *adj* noisy.

Laser ['leizər] *m* (*pl* -) laser.

*lassen ['lasən] *v* (*erlauben*) let, allow; (*unterlassen*) leave, stop; (*überlassen*) leave. **außer Acht lassen** disregard. **bleiben lassen** leave alone. **fallen lassen** (let) drop. **kommen lassen** send for. **sich machen lassen** have done *or* made. **lassen von** renounce. **sich nicht beschreiben lassen** be indescribable *or* beyond words. **laß mich gehen!** let me go! **laß mich in Ruhe!** leave me alone. **es läßt sich nicht machen** it can't be done.

lässig ['lɛsiç] *adj* careless, negligent.

Last [last] *f* (*pl* -en) load; (*Bürde*) burden; (*Gewicht*) weight; (*Fracht*) cargo.

Laster[1] ['lastər] *m* (*pl* -) (*umg.*) lorry, truck.

Laster[2] *neut* (*pl* -) vice. **lasterhaft** *adj* immoral.

lästern ['lɛstərn] slander. **Lästerung** *f* slander.

lästig ['lɛstiç] *adj* irksome, bothersome.

Last∥kahn *m* barge, lighter. **-kraftwagen** (Lkw) *m* lorry, truck. **-pferd** *neut* packhorse.

Latein [la'tain] *neut* Latin (language). **-amerika** *neut* Latin America. **lateinisch** *adj* Latin.

Laterne [la'tɛrnə] *f* (*pl* -n) lantern. **-npfahl** *m* lamppost.

Latte ['latə] *f* (*pl* -n) lath.

lau [lau] *adj* lukewarm, tepid; (*Wetter*) mild.

Laub [laup] *neut* (*pl* -e) foliage. **-baum** *m* deciduous tree. **-säge** *f* fretsaw. **-wald** *m* deciduous forest. **-werk** *neut* foliage.

Lauch [laux] *m* (*pl* -e) leek.

lauern ['lauərn] *v* lurk, lie in ambush; (*umg.*) hang around, wait impatiently.

Lauf [lauf] *m* (*pl* Läufe) run; (*Sport*) race; (*Fluß*) course; (*Gewehr*) barrel; (*Maschine*) running, operation. **-bahn** *f* career. **laufen** *v* (*Maschine, Wasser, Weg, usw.*) run; (*zu Fuß gehen*) walk. **laufend** *adj* current, running; (*Zahl*) consecutive. **auf dem laufenden** up to date.

Läufer ['lɔyfər] *m* (*pl* -) (*Sport*) runner; (*Schach*) bishop.

läufig ['lɔyfiç] *adj* (*Hündin*) in heat.

Lauf∥planke *f* gangway. **-werk** *neut* mechanism, drive.

Lauge ['laugə] *f* (*pl* -n) lye; (*Seifen*-) suds. **laugenartig** *adj* alkaline, (*Chem*) basic.

Laune ['launə] *f* (*pl* -n) mood, temper; (*Grille*) whim. **launenhaft** *adj* capricious, whimsical. **launig** *adj* humorous, funny. **launisch** *adj* moody, capricious.

Laus [laus] *f* (*pl* Läuse) louse.

lauschen ['lauʃən] *v* listen (to); (*heimlich*) listen in, eavesdrop.

lausig ['lauziç] *adj* lousy.

laut[1] [laut] *adj* loud. *adv* aloud.

laut[2] *prep* according to.

Laut [laut] *m* (*pl* -e) sound.

Laute ['lautə] *f* (*pl* -n) lute.

lauten ['lautən] *v* read, say; (*klingen*) sound.

läuten ['lɔytən] *v* ring, sound.

lauter ['lautər] *adj* pure; (*echt*) genuine; (*nichts als*) nothing but, sheer.

Laut∥sprecher *m* loudspeaker. **-stärke** *f* volume, loudness.

lauwarm ['lauvarm] *adj* lukewarm.

Lawine [la'viːnə] f (pl -n) avalanche.
lax [laks] adj lax.

leben ['leːbən] v live. **von ... leben** live on .... **Es lebe die Königin!** Long live the Queen! **Leben** neut (pl -) life; (Geschäftigkeit) activity, bustle. **am Leben** alive. **ums Leben kommen** lose one's life, die. **lebend** adj living, alive. **-ig** adj alive, living; (munter) lively.

Lebens|art f lifestyle. **-freude** f joy of life. **-funktion** f vital function. **-gefahr** f danger to life. **-haltungskosten** pl cost of living sing. **-jahr** neut year of one's life. **im 16. Lebensjahr** during the sixteenth year of his/her life.

lebenslänglich ['leːbənslɛŋlɪç] adj lifelong; (Jur) for life.

Lebens|lauf m curriculum vitae, c.v. **-mittel** pl food sing. **-standard** m standard of living. **-stil** m lifestyle. **-unterhalt** m livelihood. **-versicherung** f life insurance. **-weise** f way of life.

Leber ['leːbər] f (pl -n) liver. **-fleck** m birthmark. **-wurst** f liver sausage.

Lebe|wesen neut living creature, organism. **-wohl** neut farewell.

lebhaft ['leːphaft] adj lively. **Lebhaftigkeit** f liveliness.

leblos ['leːploːs] adj lifeless.

leck [lɛk] adj leaky. **Leck** neut (pl -e) leak.

lecken ['lɛkən] v lick.

lecker ['lɛkər] adj delicious. **-bissen** m delicacy, titbit.

Leder ['leːdər] neut (pl -) leather. **-hose** f leather shorts pl. **ledern** adj leather; (fig) dry, boring. **Leder|riemen** m leather strap. **-waren** pl leather goods.

ledig ['leːdɪç] adj single, unmarried; (frei) free (of). **lediger Stand** m celibacy. **lediglich** adv solely.

Lee [leː] f lee.

leer [leːr] adj empty; (unbesetzt) unoccupied; (Stellung) open; (Seite) blank. **Leere** f emptiness; (Physik) vacuum. **leeren** v empty. **Leer|lauf** m (Mot) idling, tick-over. **-ung** f (pl -en) emptying; (Post) collection.

legal [le'gaːl] adj legal.

legen ['leːgən] v lay, place, put (down); (Eier) lay; (installieren) install, fit. **sich legen** lie down; (Wind) abate.

Legende [le'gɛndə] f (pl -n) legend.

legieren [le'giːrən] v (Metalle) alloy; (Suppe) thicken.

legitim [legi'tiːm] adj legitimate.

Lehm [leːm] m (pl -e) loam.

Lehne ['leːnə] f (pl -n) support, prop; (Stuhl) back. **lehnen** v lean, rest. **sich lehnen** lean, rest. **Lehn|sessel** or **-stuhl** m armchair, easy chair.

Lehrbuch ['leːrbuːx] neut textbook. **Lehre** f (pl -n) teaching; (Lehrzeit) training. **lehren** v teach. **Lehrer** m (pl -) teacher, schoolmaster. **-in** f (pl -nen) teacher, schoolmistress. **Lehr|film** m educational film. **-gang** m curriculum, course of instruction. **-ling** m (pl -e) apprentice. **lehrreich** adj instructive. **Lehr|satz** m rule, proposition. **-zeit** f training, apprenticeship.

Leib [laip] m (pl -er) body. **Leibes|frucht** f foetus. **-übung** f physical exercise.

Leiche ['laiçə] f (pl -n) corpse. **Leichen|halle** neut mortuary. **-schau** f postmortem, autopsy. **Leichnam** m (pl -e) corpse.

leicht [laiçt] adj light; (einfach) easy. **leicht zugänglich** easily accessible. **es sich leicht machen** take it easy. **Leichtathletik** f athletics. **leichtfertig** adj superficial; (Antwort) glib. **Leichtgewichtler** m lightweight. **leichtgläubig** adj credulous. **Leichtigkeit** f lightness; (Mühelosigkeit) ease. **leichtlebig** adj easy-going. **-sinnig** adj thoughtless.

leid [lait] adj disagreeable, painful. **es ist** (or **es tut**) **mir leid** I am sorry. **Leid** neut (unz.) sorrow, grief; (Schaden) harm. **leiden** v suffer; (erlauben) tolerate, allow. **leiden an** suffer from. **ich kann ihn nicht leiden** I can't stand him. **leidend** adj suffering; (kränklich) sickly.

Leidenschaft ['laidənʃaft] f (pl -en) passion. **leidenschaft||lich** adj passionate. **-slos** adj dispassionate.

leider ['laidər] adv unfortunately. **leider muß ich ...** I am afraid I have to ....

leidig ['laidɪç] adj tiresome, disagreeable.

leidlich ['laitlɪç] adj tolerable.

Leier ['laiər] f (pl -n) lyre. **die alte Leier** the same old story. **leiern** v (sprechen) drawl.

leihen ['laiən] v lend; (borgen) borrow. **Leihbibliothek** f lending library.

Leim [laim] m (pl -e) glue.

Lein [lain] m (pl -e) flax.

Leine ['lainə] f (pl -n) line, cord; (Hund) leash.

leinen ['lainən] adj linen. **Leinen** neut linen.

leise ['laizə] adj quiet; (sanft) gentle, soft.

Leiste ['laistə] f (pl -n) (Anat) groin.

leisten ['laistən] v do; (schaffen) accomplish, achieve; (ausführen) carry out. **Hilfe leisten** help, assist. **sich leisten** allow oneself. **ich kann mir einen neuen Wagen nicht leisten** I cannot afford a new car. **Leistung** f (pl -en) achievement, accomplishment; (Tat) deed; (Arbeit) output. **leistungsfähig** adj capable; productive. **Leistungsfähigkeit** f ability (to work); productivity.

leiten ['laitən] v (führen) (Elek, Musik) conduct. **-d** adj guiding, leading; (Person) prominent, senior.

Leiter[^1] ['laitər] m (pl -) leader; manager.

Leiter[^2] f (pl -n) ladder.

Leit||faden m clue; (Lehrbuch) guide, textbook. **-satz** m guiding principle. **-ung** f (pl -en) (Führung) leadership; (Verwaltung) management; (Elek) circuit; (Draht) wire; (Wasser) pipes pl, mains pl.

Lektüre lɛk'tyːrə] f (pl -n) reading; (Lesestoff) reading material, literature.

Lende ['lɛndə] f (pl -n) (Anat) lumbar region; (Fleisch) loin.

lenken ['lɛŋkən] v steer; (führen) direct. **Lenk||er** m guide; (Flugzeug) pilot; (Leiter) manager. **-rad** m steering wheel. **-ung** f (pl -en) (Mot) steering; (Leitung) direction.

Leopard [leo'part] m (pl -en) leopard.

lepra ['leːpra] f leprosy. **-kranke(r)** leper.

Lerche ['lɛrçə] f (pl -n) lark.

lernen ['lɛrnən] v learn. **Lernen** neut (unz.) learning.

lesbar ['leːsbaːr] adj readable. **Lese** f (pl -n) vintage. **Lesebuch** neut reading book.

lesen v read; lecture; (sammeln, ernten) gather, harvest. **Leser** m (pl -), **Leserin** f (pl -en) reader. **leserlich** adj legible. **Leserschaft** f readership, readers. **Lesesaal** m reading room.

letzt [lɛtst] adj last; (spätest) latest, final. **letzte Nummer** current issue. **letztens** adv lately; (zum Schluß) lastly.

Leuchte ['lɔyçtə] f (pl -n) light, lamp. **leuchten** v emit light, shine. **-d** adj shining, luminous. **Leuchter** m (pl -) candlestick. **Leuchtturm** m lighthouse.

leugnen ['lɔygnən] v deny.

Leukämie [lɔykɛ'miː] f leukaemia.

Leute ['lɔytə] pl people.

Leutnant ['lɔytnant] m (pl -e) lieutenant.

leutselig ['lɔytzeːliç] adj affable, sociable.

Lexikon ['lɛksikɔn] neut (pl Lexika) dictionary.

Libelle [li'bɛlə] f (pl -n) (Insekt) dragonfly; (Tech) (spirit) level.

liberal [libe'raːl] adj liberal.

licht [liçt] adj bright; (Farbe) light; (Wald) sparse, thin. **Licht** neut (pl -er) light; (Kerze) candle. **-bild** neut photograph. **lichtdurchlässig** adj translucent.

lichten ['liçtən] v (Wald) clear; (Anker) weigh.

Licht||jahr neut lightyear. **-pause** f blueprint. **-signal** neut light signal. **lichtundurchlässig** adj opaque.

Lichtung ['liçtuŋ] f (pl -en) glade, clearing.

Lid [liːt] neut (pl -er) eyelid.

lieb [liːp] adj dear; (nett) nice; (angenehm) agreeable. **ein liebes Kind** a good child. **es wäre ihm lieb** he would appreciate it. **das ist lieb von Ihnen** that is most kind of you.

Liebchen ['liːpçən] neut (pl -) darling.

Liebe ['liːbə] f (pl -n) love. **Liebelei** f (pl -en) flirtation. **lieben** v love. **liebens||wert** adj lovable. **-würdig** adj amiable, helpful, kind.

lieber ['liːbər] adj dearer. adv rather; (besser) better. **lieber haben** prefer. **lieber als** rather than. **Ich gehe lieber zu Fuß** I prefer to walk. **das hättest Du lieber nicht sagen sollen** you had better not say that.

Liebes||affäre f (love) affair. **-brief** m love letter. **-paar** neut lovers pl, couple.

liebevoll ['liːbəfɔl] adj affectionate, loving.

°liebhaben ['liːphaːbən] v love, like.

Liebhaber m (pl -), **Liebhaberin** f (pl -nen) lover.

lieb||kosen v caress, fondle. **-lich** adj lovely. **Lieb||ling** m darling; (Günstling) favourite. **-reiz** m charm, attraction.

liebst [liːpst] adj favourite, best-loved. adv **am liebsten haben** like best of all. **am liebsten machen** like doing best.

Lied [liːt] neut (pl -er) song. **-erbuch** neut songbook; (Rel) hymnbook.

liederlich adj slovenly; (sittenlos) debauched, dissipated.

Lieferant [liːfə'rant] m (pl -en) supplier. **liefern** v deliver, supply; (Ertrag) yield. **Lieferung** f (pl -en) delivery, supply.

[^1]: Leiter
[^2]: Leiter

Liege ['liːgə] f (pl -n) couch. **liegen** v lie. **-bleiben** v remain; (Waren) be unsold; (Arbeit) remain unfinished; (Panne haben) break down. **-lassen** v leave (behind). **Liege‖platz** m berth. **-stuhl** m deckchair.

Liga ['liːga] f (pl Ligen) league.

Likör m (pl -e) liqueur.

lila ['liːla] adj lilac, purple. **Lila** neut lilac, purple.

Lilie ['liːliə] f (pl -n) lily.

Limonade [limo'naːdə] f (pl -n) lemonade, soda-pop.

Linde ['lɪndə] f (pl -n) lime tree.

lindern ['lɪndərn] v alleviate, mitigate.

Lineal [line'aːl] neut (pl -e) ruler, rule.

Linie ['liːniə] f (pl -n) line.

Linke ['lɪŋkə] f (pl -n) left, left(-hand) side; (Pol) the Left. **linkisch** adj clumsy. **links** adv (on or to the) left. **Linkshänder** m left-hander. **linkshändig** adj left-handed. **Links‖radikale(r)** m (radical) left-winger. **-steuerung** f left-hand drive.

Linse ['lɪnzə] f (pl -n) (Foto, Anat) lens; (Küche) lentil.

Lippe ['lɪpə] f (pl -n) lip. **-nstift** m lipstick.

lispeln ['lɪspəln] v lisp.

Lissabon ['lɪsabɔn] neut Lisbon.

List [lɪst] f (pl -en) (Schlauheit) cunning; trick, ruse.

Liste ['lɪstə] f (pl -n) list.

listig ['lɪstiç] adj cunning.

Litanei [lita'naɪ] f (pl -en) litany.

Liter ['liːtər] neut or m (pl -) litre.

literarisch [lite'raːriʃ] adj literary. **Literatur** f literature.

Live-Sendung ['laɪfzɛnduŋ] f live or direct broadcast.

Lizenz [li'tsɛnts] f (pl -en) licence. **-inhaber** m licensee.

Lob [loːp] neut (pl -e) praise. **loben** v praise. **Lob‖gesang** m song of praise. **-hudelei** f adulation.

Loch [lɔx] neut (pl Löcher) hole; (Reifen) puncture. **lochen** v pierce, punch; (perforieren) perforate.

löcherig ['lœçəriç] adj full of holes.

Lochung ['lɔxuŋ] f (pl -en) perforation.

Locke ['lɔkə] f (pl -n) curl, lock.

locken ['lɔkən] v lure, entice.

locker ['lɔkər] adj loose; (Lebensart) lax, slack. **lockern** v loosen (up). **sich lockern** v become loose; (entspannen) relax.

lockig ['lɔkiç] adj curly.

Lock‖speise f bait. **-vogel** m decoy.

lodern ['loːdərn] v blaze (up); (fig) glow, smoulder.

Löffel ['lœfəl] m (pl -) spoon.

Loge ['loːʒə] f (pl -n) (Theater) box; (Freimaurer) lodge.

logieren [lo'ʒiːrən] v lodge.

Logik ['loːgik] f logic. **logisch** adj logical.

Lohn [loːn] m (pl Löhne) (Gehalt, Bezahlung) wages pl, pay; (Belohnung) reward; (verdiente Strafe) deserts pl. **-arbeiter** m wage-earner, (weekly-paid) worker. **lohnen** v reward. **es lohnt sich (nicht)** it's (not) worth it. **Lohn‖forderung** f wage claim. **-schreiber** m hack (writer). **-stopp** m wage freeze. **-tag** m payday.

lokal [lo'kaːl] adj local. **Lokal** neut (pl -e) pub, tavern.

Lokomotive [lokomo'tiːvə] f (pl -n) locomotive.

Lorbeer ['lɔrbeːr] m (pl -en) laurel. **-blatt** neut bay leaf. **-kranz** m laurel wreath.

los [loːs] adj free; (nicht fest) loose. adv away, off. **los!** go on! off you go! **was ist los?** what's going on? **was ist mit dir los?** what's the matter (with you)? **etwas/jemanden los sein/werden** be/get rid of something/someone.

Los neut (pl -e) (Schicksal) fate, lot; (Lotterie) lottery ticket. **das Los ziehen** draw lots.

lösbar ['løːsbaːr] adj soluble.

*los‖binden v untie. **-brechen** v break loose.

löschen ['lœʃən] v (Feuer) put out, extinguish; (Licht) turn off, switch off; (Schuld) cancel, write off; (Tinte) blot; (Firma) liquidate; (Durst) quench. **Löscher** m (Feuer) extinguisher; (Tinte) blotter.

lose ['loːzə] adj loose.

Lösegeld ['løːzəgɛlt] neut ransom.

lösen ['løːzən] v loosen; (Knoten) unravel (a plot); (Verschluß) unfasten; (Rätsel, Problem) solve; (abtrennen) detach; (Chem) dissolve.

*los‖fahren v drive off. **-gehen** v set out, get going. **-knüpfen** v untie. **-kommen** v get away or free. **-lassen** v let go.

löslich ['løːsliç] adj soluble.

los‖lösen v free, detach. **-machen** v unfasten, release. **-reißen** v tear away. **-sagen** v **sich lossagen von** renounce.

los‖schießen v fire away/off. –schrauben v unscrew. –sprechen v acquit, release.

Losung ['loːzʊŋ] f (pl -en) password.

Lösung ['løːzʊŋ] f (pl -en) solution; (Lösen) loosening. –smittel neut solvent.

los‖werden v get rid of. –ziehen v set out.

Lot [loːt] neut (pl -e) plumbline; (zum Löten) solder. loten v take soundings. löten v solder.

lotrecht ['loːtrɛçt] adj perpendicular, vertical.

Lotse ['loːtsə] f (pl -n) (Schiff) pilot.

Lotterie [lotə'riː] f (pl -n) lottery.

Löwe ['løːvə] m (pl -n) lion. –nzahn m dandelion. Löwin f lioness.

Luchs [luks] m (pl -e) lynx.

Lücke ['lʏkə] f (pl -n) gap; (Auslassung) omission; (eines Gesetzes) loophole. –nbüßer m stopgap. luckenhaft adj defective; (fig) patchy, full of gaps.

Luft [luft] f (pl Lüfte) air. –ansicht f aerial view. –bild neut aerial photograph. –bremse f air brake.

–brücke f airlift. luftdicht adj airtight. lüften ['lʏftən] v ventilate, air.

Luftfahrt ['luftfaːrt] f aviation. luftgekühlt adj air-cooled. Lufthafen m airport. luftig adj airy, breezy. Luft‖krankheit f airsickness. –krieg m aerial warfare. –post f airmail. –reifen m pneumatic tyre, (US tire). –röhre f windpipe. –schiff neut airship.

Lüftung ['lʏftʊŋ] f (pl -en) ventilation.

Luftverkehr ['luftvɛrkeːr] m air traffic. –sgesellschaft f airline.

Lüge ['lyːgə] f (pl -n) lie. lügen v (tell a) lie. –haft adj lying. Lügner m liar.

Lump [lump] m (pl -) rag. –händler m rag-and-bone man.

Lunge ['luŋə] f (pl -n) lung. Lungen‖entzündung f pneumonia. –krebs m lung cancer.

Lupe ['luːpə] f (pl -n) magnifying glass. unter die Lupe nehmen scrutinize, examine closely.

Lust [lust] f (pl Lüste) delight, pleasure; (Verlangen) desire; (Wollust) lust. Lust haben an take pleasure in. Lust haben (zu tun) feel like (doing). keine Lust haben (zu tun) not be in the mood (to do), not feel like doing.

lüstern ['lʏstərn] adj (geil) lascivious, lecherous.

Lustfahrt ['lustfaːrt] f pleasure trip. lustig adj merry, joyful; (unterhaltend) amusing, funny. sich lustig machen über make fun of. Lustigkeit f gaiety, merriment. lustlos adj dull, inactive. Lust‖mord m sex murder. –spiel neut comedy.

lutschen ['lutʃən] v suck. Lutscher m (baby's) dummy, (US) pacifier.

Luxus ['luksus] m luxury. –artikel m luxury item; f luxuries.

Luzern ['lutsɛrn] neut Lucerne.

lyrisch ['lyːriʃ] adj lyrical.

M

Maat [maːt] m (pl -e) mate; (Kriegsmarine) petty officer.

machen ['maxən] v make; do; (Rechnung) come to. eine Prüfung machen sit an exam fertig machen get ready. Licht machen switch on a light. (das) macht nichts, it doesn't matter, never mind. mach's gut! good luck! all the best!

Macht [maxt] f (pl Mächte) power.

mächtig ['mɛçtiç] adj powerful; mighty; (riesig) immense.

Machtkampf m power struggle. machtlos adj powerless. Machtprobe f trial of strength.

Mädchen ['mɛːtçən] neut (pl -) girl. mädchenhaft adj girlish. Mädchenname m maiden name.

Made ['maːdə] f (pl -n) maggot.

Mädel ['mɛːdəl] neut (pl -) girl.

Magazin [maga'tsiːn] neut (pl -e) store(house); (Zeitschrift, auch Gewehr-) magazine.

Magd [maːkt] f (pl Mägde) maid(servant).

Magen ['maːgən] m (pl -Mägen) stomach. –brennen neut heartburn. –schmerzen pl stomach-ache sing.

mager ['maːgər] adj thin, lean.

Magie [ma'giː] f magic. magisch adj magic(al).

Magnet [mag'neːt] m (pl -en) magnet. magnetisch adj magnetic.

Mahagoni [maha'goːni] neut (pl -s) mahogany.

Mähdrescher ['mɛːdrɛʃər] m combine harvester. mähen v mow.

Mahl [maːl] neut (pl -e) meal.

*mahlen ['maːlən] v mill, grind.

Mahl‖zahn m molar. **–zeit** f meal; *interj* good appetite!

Mähne ['mɛːnə] f (pl **-n**) mane.

mahnen ['maːnən] v remind, admonish; warn. **Mahnung** f reminder, warning.

Mai [mai] m (pl **-e**) May. **–blume** f lily of the valley.

Mais [mais] m maize, (US) corn. **–kolben** m cob of corn. **–mehl** neut cornflour.

Majestät [majɛsˈtɛːt] f (pl **-en**) majesty. **majestätisch** adj majestic.

Majoran [majoˈraːn] m marjoram.

Makel ['maːkəl] m (pl **-**) stain, spot; (Fehler) defect, fault. **makellos** adj spotless; faultless.

Makler ['maiklər] m (pl **-**) broker.

Makrele [maˈkreːlə] f (pl **-n**) mackerel.

mal [maːl] adv (Math) times; (einmal) once, just. **drei mal fünf** three times five. **hör' mal!** just listen!

Mal¹ [maːl] neut (pl **-e**) time. **zum ersten Mal** for the first time.

Mal² [maːl] neut (pl **-e** or **Mäler**) mark, sign; (Denkmal) monument; (Grenzstein) boundary stone.

Malaria [maˈlaːria] f malaria.

malen ['maːlən] v paint; (zeichnen) draw. **Maler** m (pl **-**) painter. **Malerei** f (pl **-en**) painting. **malerisch** adj picturesque.

Malz [malts] neut (pl **-e**) malt. **–bier** neut malt beer, stout.

Mama [maˈma] f (pl **-s**) mamma.

man [man] pron one, you; (die Leute) people. **man sagt** people say, it is said. **man tut das nicht** that is not done, you shouldn't do that.

Manager ['mɛnidʒər] m (pl **-**) manager.

manch [manç] pron, adj many a, some. **manche** pl several, many. **–mal** adv sometimes.

Mandat [manˈdaːt] neut (pl **-e**) mandate.

Mandel ['mandəl] f (pl **-n**) almond; (Anat) tonsil. **–entfernung** f tonsillectomy. **–entzündung** f tonsillitis.

Mangel¹ ['maŋəl] f (pl **Mängel**) mangle.

Mangel² [m (pl **Mängel**) lack, want; (Knappheit) shortage; (Fehler) fault.

mangeln ['maŋəln] v lack, want. **es mangelt mir an** I lack.

Manie [maˈniː] f (pl **-n**) mania.

Manier [maˈniːr] f (pl **-en**) manner, way; (Stil) style. **Manieren** pl manners. **manieriert** adj affected, mannered. **manierlich** adj well-mannered, civil.

Manifest [maniˈfɛst] neut (pl **-e**) manifesto.

manisch ['maːniʃ] adj manic.

Mann [man] m (pl **Männer**) man; (Ehemann) husband.

Männchen ['mɛnçən] neut (pl **-**) little man; (Tier) male.

Mannesalter ['manəsaltər] neut (age of) manhood. **mannhaft** adj manly.

Mannequin [manəˈkɛ] neut (pl **-s**) mannequin, fashion model.

mannigfaltig ['maniçfaltiç] adj varied, manifold.

männlich ['mɛnliç] adj male; (fig, Gramm) masculine. **Männlichkeit** f manhood; masculinity.

Mannschaft ['manʃaft] f (pl **-en**) crew; (Sport) team; (Belegschaft) personnel. **–führer** m (Sport) captain.

Manöver [maˈnøːvər] neut (pl **-**) manoeuvre. **manövrieren** v manoeuvre.

Manschette [manˈʃɛtə] f (pl **-n**) cuff.

Mantel ['mantəl] m (pl **-Mäntel**) coat; (Umhang) cloak.

Manuskript [manuˈskript] neut (pl **-e**) manuscript.

Mappe ['mapə] f (pl **-n**) briefcase; (Aktenmappe) folder, portfolio.

Märchen ['mɛːrçən] neut (pl **-**) fairytale. **märchenhaft** adj fairytale, magical.

Margarine [margaˈriːnə] f (pl **-n**) margarine.

Marien‖bild neut (picture of the) Madonna. **–käfer** m ladybird.

Marine [maˈriːnə] f (pl **-n**) (Kriegsmarine) navy; (Handelsmarine) merchant navy. **–soldat** m marine.

marinieren [mariˈniːrən] v marinate.

Marionette [marioˈnɛtə] f (pl **-n**) marionette.

Mark¹ [mark] neut (unz.) (bone) marrow. **bis ins Mark** (fig) to the core.

Mark² f (pl **-**) (Geld) mark.

Mark³ f (pl **-en**) boundary; (Grenzgebiet) marches pl, border-country.

Marke ['markə] f (pl **-n**) (Zeichen) mark, stamp; (Fabrikat, Sorte) brand; (Handelszeichen) trademark; (Briefmarke) (postage) stamp; (Wertschein) token. **–nname** m tradename, brand-name.

Markt [markt] m (pl **Märkte**) market. **–halle** f covered market, market hall. **–platz** m marketplace. **–tag** m market day. **–wirtschaft** f (free) market economy.

Marmelade [marmə'laɪdə] f (pl -n) jam.

Marmor ['marmɔr] m (pl -e) marble.

Mars [maɪrs] m Mars. **-bewohner** m Martian.

Marsch¹ [marʃ] m (pl Märsche) march.

Marsch² [marʃ] f (pl -en) marsh.

Marschall ['marʃal] m (pl Marschälle) marshal.

marschieren [marˈʃiːrən] v march.

Märtyrer ['mɛrtyrər] m (pl -) martyr. **-tum** neut martyrdom.

Märtyrin [mɔrˈtyrɪn] f (pl -nen) martyr.

Marxismus [marˈksɪsmus] m (unz.) Marxism.

März [mɛrts] m (pl -e) March.

Masche ['maʃə] f (pl -n) mesh; (Stricken) stitch; (Trick) trick.

Maschine [maˈʃiːnə] f (pl -en) machine; (Mot) engine. **Maschinen‖bau** m mechanical engineering. **-fabrik** f engineering works. **-gewehr** neut machine-gun. **-schreiben** neut typewriting, typing. **-schreiber(in)** m typist.

Maske ['maskə] f (pl -n) mask. **Masken‖ball** m fancy-dress ball. **-kostüm** neut fancy dress (costume).

Maß [maɪs] neut (pl -e) measure; (Mäßigung) moderation; (Grenze) limit; (Umfang) extent. **in hohem Maße** to a great extent. **Maß halten** be moderate.

Masse ['masə] f (pl -n) mass; (Jur) estate, assets. **die Massen** the masses. **Massen‖erzeugung** f mass production. **-karambolage** f multiple collision, (umg.) pile-up. **-versammlung** f mass meeting. **massenweise** adv wholesale, in large numbers.

Maßgabe ['maɪsgaɪbə] f standard. **maßgeblich** adj authoritative.

mäßig ['mɛːsɪç] adj moderate. **mäßigen** v moderate. **Mäßigung** f modulation.

massiv [maˈsiːf] adj massive.

maßlos ['maɪsloːs] adj immoderate. **Maßnahme** f (pl -n) measure, step. **Maßnahmen treffen** take steps. **Maßstab** m measure; (Tech) scale; (fig) yardstick.

Mast [mast] m (pl -e or -en) mast.

mästen ['mɛstən] v fatten.

Material [materiˈaɪl] neut (pl -ien) material. **-ismus** m materialism. **materialistisch** adj materialist(ic).

Materie [maˈteɪriə] f (pl -n) matter, stuff, substance.

Mathematik [matemaˈtiːk] f (unz.) mathe-

matics. **-er** m (pl -) mathematician. **mathematisch** adj mathematical.

Matratze [maˈtratsə] f (pl -n) mattress.

Mätresse [mɛˈtrɛsə] f (pl -n) mistress.

Matrize [maˈtriːtsə] f (pl -n) (Druck) stencil; (Math) matrix.

Matrose [maˈtroːzə] m (pl -n) sailor.

Matsch [matʃ] m mud; (Schnee-) slush. **matschig** adj muddy; (breiig) squashy.

matt [mat] adj faint, weary; (glanzlos) dull, matt; (Licht) dim; (Schach) mate.

Matte ['matə] f (pl -n) mat.

Mattheit ['mathait] f weariness; dullness. **mattherzig** adj fainthearted.

Mauer ['mauər] f (pl -n) wall. **mauern** v build (a wall). **Mauerwerk** neut masonry.

Maul [maul] neut (pl Mäuler) (animals) mouth, snout, muzzle; (vulgär) (person's) mouth.

Maurer ['maurər] m (pl -) bricklayer, building worker.

Maus [maus] f (pl Mäuse) mouse. **Mause‖falle** f mousetrap. **-loch** neut mousehole.

maximal [maksiˈmaɪl] adj maximum. **Maximum** neut maximum.

Mechanik [meˈçanɪk] **1** f (unz.) mechanics. **2** (pl -en) (Mechanismus) mechanism. **-er** m mechanic. **mechanisch** adj mechanical.

meckern ['mɛkərn] v bleat; (nörgeln) grumble, moan.

Medaille [meˈdaijə] f (pl -n) medal.

Medikament [medikaˈmɛnt] neut (pl -e) medicine.

Medizin [mediˈtsiɪn] f (pl -en) medicine. **-er** m doctor, physician; (student) medical student. **medizinisch** adj medical.

Meer [meɪr] neut (pl -e) sea. **-enge** f straits pl. **Meeres‖boden** m sea bed. **-spiegel** m sea level.

Mehl [meɪl] neut (pl -e) flour. **mehlig** adj floury, mealy.

mehr [meɪr] adv, adj more. **mehr als** more than. **nicht mehr** no longer. **immer mehr** more and more. **noch mehr** still more. **Mehrbetrag** m surplus. **mehrdeutig** adj ambiguous.

mehrere ['meɪrərə] pl pron, adj several. **mehrfach** adj multiple.

Mehr‖gepäck neut excess baggage. **-gewicht** neut excess weight. **-heit** f majority.

mehr‖mals adv repeatedly, several times. **-seitig** adj many-sided; (Math) polygo-

nal. **—sprachig** adj multilingual. **—stöckig**
adj multistoreyed.

Mehr‖wertsteuer (MwSt) f value added
tax (VAT). **—zahl** f majority; (Gramm)
plural.

*meiden ['maidən] v avoid.

Meierei ['maiərai] f (pl **-en**) farm;
(Milchwirtschaft) dairy farm.

Meile ['mailə] f (pl **-n**) mile.

mein [main] adj, pron my; mine. **meinerseits** adv for my part. **meinesgleichen**
pron people like me, the likes of me.
meinethalben, meinetwegen, meinetwillen
adv for my sake. **meinige** pron (der, die,
das meinige) mine.

Meineid ['mainait] m (pl **-e**) perjury.

meinen ['mainən] v mean; (denken)
think; (äußern) say; (beabsichtigen)
intend. **Meinung** f opinion. **Ich bin der
Meinung, daß** I am of the opinion that.
meiner Meinung nach in my opinion.
Meinungs‖forschung f opinion research.
—umfrage, f opinion poll. **—verschiedenheit** f difference of opinion.

Meißel ['maisəl] m (pl **-**) chisel. **meißeln** v
chisel.

meist [maist] adj most. **die meis-
ten(Leute)** most people. **am meisten** for
the most part. **Meistbietende(r)** m highest bidder. **meistens** adv mostly.

Meister ['maistər] m (pl **-**) master; (Sport)
champion. **meisterhaft** adj masterly.
Meisterin f (Sport) champion. **meistern** v
master. **Meister‖schaft** f mastery; (Sport)
championship. **—schaftsspiel** neut championship match. **—stück** or **—werk** neut
masterpiece.

meistgekauft ['maistgəkauft] adj best-sell-
ing.

Meldeamt ['mɛldəamt] neut registration
office. **melden** v inform; (ankündigen)
announce. **sich melden** report, present
oneself; (Stelle) apply. **Meldung** f report;
(ankündigung) announcement; (bei der
Polizei, usw.) registration.

*melken ['mɛlkən] v milk. **Melkmaschine**
f milking machine.

Melodie [melo'di:] f (pl **-n**) melody.
melodisch adj melodious.

Melone [me'lo:nə] f (pl **-n**) melon.

Membran(e) [mɛm'bra:n] f (pl **Mem-
branen**) membrane.

Menge ['mɛŋə] f (pl **-n**) quantity; (Menschen) crowd. **eine (ganze) Menge** a lot

(of), lots (of). **mengen** v mix. **sich
mengen in** meddle.

Mensa ['mɛnsa] f (pl **Mensen**) student
refectory.

Mensch [mɛnʃ] m (pl **-en**) human (being),
man, person. **Menschenfeind** m misan-
thrope. **menschenfeindlich** adj misanthropic. **Menschenfreund** m philanthropist. **menschenfreundlich** adj philanthropic; (gütig) affable. **Menschen‖kunde**
f anthropology. **—leben** neut human life;
(Lebenszeit) lifetime. **—liebe** f human
kindness. **—rechte** pl human rights.
—würde f human dignity.

Menschheit ['mɛnʃhait] f mankind,
human race. **menschlich** adj human;
(human) humane. **Menschlichkeit** f
humanity.

menstrual [mɛnstru'a:l] adj menstrual.
Menstruation f (pl **-nen**) menstruation.
menstruieren v menstruate.

Mentalität [mɛntali'tɛt] f (pl **-en**) mentality.

merkbar ['mɛrkba:r] adj noticeable.
merken v notice, note. **sich etwas merken**
make a mental note of something. **mer-
klich** adj evident. **Merkmal** (pl **-e**) neut
characteristic, attribute. **merkwürdig** adj
remarkable, peculiar.

Meßband ['mɛsbant] neut tape measure.
meßbar adj measurable.

Messe ['mɛsə] f (pl **-n**) (Rel) mass; (Ausstellung) (trade) fair.

*messen ['mɛsən] v measure. **sich messen
mit** compete with.

Messer¹ ['mɛsər] m (pl **-**) (Gerät) gauge,
meter.

Messer² neut (pl **-**) knife.

Messing ['mɛsiŋ] neut (pl **-**) brass.

Messung ['mɛsuŋ] f (pl **-en**) measurement; (Messen) measuring.

Metall [me'tal] neut (pl **-e**) metal. **metallisch** adj metallic.

Meteor [mete'o:r] neut (pl **-e**) meteor.
—ologe m meteorologist. **—ologie** f meteorology. **meteorologisch** adj meteorologist.

Meter ['me:tər] neut (pl **-**) metre.

Methode [me'to:də] f (pl **-n**) method.
methodisch adj methodical.

metrisch ['mɛtriʃ] adj metric.

Mettwurst ['mɛtvurst] f a type of German sausage.

metzen ['mɛtsən] v massacre, slaughter.

Metzger m (pl -) butcher. –ei f (pl -en) butcher's shop.

Meuchelmord ['mɔyçəlmɔrt] m assassination.

Meuterei [mɔytəˈrai] f (pl -en) mutiny. meutern v mutiny.

mich [miç] pron me.

Mieder ['miːdər] neut (pl -) bodice.

Miene ['miːnə] f (pl -n) expression, look.

mies [miːs] adj (umg.) nasty, wretched.

Miete ['miːtə] f (pl -n) hire; (für Wohnung) rent. mieten v (Haus, Wohnung) rent; (Wagen, usw.) hire. Mieter m (pl -), Mieterin f (pl -nen) tenant, lessee. Miet||haus neut block of flats, tenement. –wagen m hired car. –wohnung f rented apartment.

Mikrophon [mikroˈfoːn] neut (pl -e) microphone.

Mikroskop [mikroˈskɔp] neut microscope. mikroskopisch adj microscopic.

Milbe ['milbə] f (pl -n) mite.

Milch [milç] f milk. milchig adj milky. Milchstraße f Milky Way.

mild [milt] adj mild; (sanft) soft, gentle. Milde f mildness; gentleness. mildern v alleviate, moderate. Milderung f (pl -en) alleviation. mildtätig adj charitable.

Militär [miliˈtɛːr] 1 neut (unz.) army, military. 2 m (pl -s) military man, soldier.

Milliarde [milˈjardə] f (pl -n) thousand million, (US) billion.

Million [milˈjoːn] f (pl -en) million. –är m (pl -e) millionaire.

Mimik ['mimik] f (pl -en) mimicry, miming. –er m (pl -) mimic.

minder ['mindər] adj lesser, smaller. adv less.

Minderheit f minority. Minderjährige(r) minor. minderjährig adj under age. minderwertig adj inferior. Minderwertigkeit f inferiority.

mindest ['mindəst] adj least; (kleinst) smallest. –ens adv at least. Mindestzahl f minimum number; (Pol) quorum.

Mine ['miːnə] f (pl -n) mine.

Mineral [mineˈraːl] neut (pl -ien) mineral. –wasser neut mineral water.

Miniatur [miniaˈtuːr] f (pl -en) miniature.

minimal [miniˈmaːl] adj minimum. Minimum neut minimum.

Minister [miˈnistər] m (pl -) minister. –ium neut ministry. –präsident m prime minister.

minus ['miːnus] adv minus, less.

Minute [miˈnuːtə] f (pl -n) minute.

mir [miːr] pron (to) me.

mischen ['miʃən] v mix, blend. sich mischen in meddle or interfere in. Misch||ling m (Pflanze) hybrid; (Tier) mongrel; (Mensch) half-breed. –sprache f pidgin. –ung f (pl -en) mixture.

mißach||ten [misˈaxtən] v disregard. Mißachtung f disregard.

Mißbildung ['misbilduŋ] f deformity.

mißbilligen ['misbiligən] v disapprove (of), object (to). Mißbilligung f disapproval.

Mißbrauch ['misbraux] m misuse, abuse. mißbrauchen v misuse, abuse.

mißdeuten [misˈdɔytən] v misinterpret, misunderstand. Mißdeutung f misinterpretation.

Mißerfolg ['misɛrfɔlk] m failure.

Missetat ['misətaːt] f misdeed. Missetäter m wrong-doer; (Verbrecher) criminal.

*mißfallen [misˈfalən] v displease. Mißfallen neut displeasure.

Mißgeschick ['misgəʃik] neut misfortune.

mißgestaltet ['misgəʃtaltət] adj misshapen.

mißhandeln [misˈhandəln] v maltreat. Mißhandlung f maltreatment.

Mission [misiˈoːn] f (pl -en) mission. –ar m (pl -e) missionary.

Mißklang ['misklaŋ] m discord.

mißlich ['misliç] adj awkward, embarrassing.

*mißlingen v fail. mißlungen adj failed, unsuccessful.

mißtrauen [misˈtrauən] v distrust. Mißtrauen neut distrust. –svotum neut vote of no confidence.

Mißverständnis ['misfɛrʃtɛntnis] neut misunderstanding. mißverstehen v misunderstand.

Mist [mist] m (pl -e) dung, manure.

Mistel ['mistəl] f (pl -n) mistletoe.

mit [mit] prep with; (mittels) by; (Zeit) at. adv along with; (außerdem) also, as well. kommst du mit? are you coming (with us)? mit 10 Jahren at the age of ten. mit einemmal suddenly. mit dabei sein be concerned or involved.

Mitarbeiter ['mitarbaitər] m colleague, fellow worker; (Zeitschrift) contributor.

Mitbestimmung ['mitbəʃtimuŋ] f worker participation, co-determination.

mitbeteiligt ['mitbətailiçt] *adj* participating, taking part.

*****mitbringen** ['mitbriŋən] *v* bring along.

miteinander [mitain'andər] *adv* together, with each other.

miteinbegriffen [mit'ainbəgrifən] *adj* included.

Mitgefühl ['mitgəfyːl] *neut* sympathy.

Mitglied ['mitgliːt] *neut* member. **–schaft** *f* membership.

mithin [mit'hin] *adv* consequently, therefore.

*****mitkommen** ['mitkɔmən] *v* come along (with); keep up.

Mitlaut ['mitlaut] *m* consonant.

Mitleid ['mitlait] *neut* pity, sympathy. **mitleid haben mit** have pity on, be sorry for.

mitmachen ['mitmaxən] *v* take part in, join in; (*erleben*) go *or* live through.

Mitmensch ['mitmɛnʃ] *m* fellow man.

*****mitnehmen** ['mitneːmən] *v* take (along); (*im Auto*) give a lift to; (*erschöpfen*) exhaust. **Essen zum Mitnehmen** food to take away.

mitnichten [mit'niçtən] *adv* by no means.

*****mitreißen** ['mitraisən] *v* drag along; (*fig*) sweep along, transport.

Mittag ['mitaːk] *m* noon, midday. **–essen** *neut* lunch, midday meal. **mittags** *adv* at noon. **Mittagspause** *f* lunch hour.

Mitte ['mitə] *f* (*pl* **-n**) middle, centre; (*Math*) mean.

mitteilen ['mittailən] *v* communicate, inform of, tell. **jemandem etwas mitteilen** inform *or* notify someone of something. **Mitteilung** *f* communication, report.

Mittel ['mitəl] *neut* (*pl* **-**) means, way; (*Ausweg*) remedy; (*Durchschnitt*) average, mean. **–alter** *neut* Middle Ages. **mittelalterlich** *adj* medieval.

Mittel‖amerika *f* Central America. **–gewichtler** *m* middleweight.

mittelgroß ['mitəlgroːs] *adj* of medium size.

Mittelläufer ['mitəlɔyfər] *m* (*Fußball*) centre-half.

mittel‖los *adj* destitute. **–mäßig** *adj* mediocre.

Mittel‖meer *neut* Mediterranean (Sea). **–punkt** *m* centre.

mittels ['mitəls] *prep* by (means of).

Mittel‖stand *m* middle classes *pl*. **–stürmer** *m* (*Fußball*) centre-forward.

mitten ['mitən] *adv* in the middle, midway. **mitten in/auf/unter** in the middle of. **mitten drin** in the middle.

Mitternacht ['mitərnaxt] *f* midnight.

mittler ['mitlər] *adj* **in mittlerem Alter** middle aged. **mittlerweile** *adv* in the meantime.

Mittwoch ['mitvɔx] *m* (*pl* **-e**) Wednesday.

mitwirken ['mitvirkən] *v* cooperate, take part, participate. **–d** *adj* participating, contributing.

Möbel ['møːbəl] *neut* (*pl* **-**) piece of furniture; (*pl*) furniture *sing*.

mobil [mo'biːl] *adj* movable, mobile; (*flink*) active, lively.

möblieren [mø'bliːrən] *v* furnish. **möbliert** *adj* furnished.

Mode ['moːdə] *f* (*pl* **-n**) fashion, vogue. **in Mode sein** be in fashion. **aus der Mode kommen** become unfashionable. **Modeartikel** *pl* fancy goods, fashions.

Modell [mo'dɛl] *neut* (*pl* **-e**) model; (*Muster*) pattern. **Modellierbogen** *m* cutting-out pattern. **modellieren** *v* model.

Modenschau ['moːdənʃau] *f* fashion show. **Modezeichner** *m* dress *or* fashion designer.

Moder ['moːdər] *m* decay, mould. **moderig** *adj* mouldy, putrid. **modern** *v* rot, decay.

modern [mo'dɛrn] *adj* modern. **modernisieren** *v* modernize.

modifizieren [modifi'tsiːrən] *v* modify.

modisch ['moːdiʃ] *adj* fashionable.

mogeln ['moːgəln] *v* cheat.

*****mögen** ['møːgən] *v* like; (*wünschen*) wish; (*können*) may, might. **nicht mögen** dislike. **Ich mag ihn** I like him. **das mag sein** that may be so. **Wer mag das sein?** who might that be? **Ich möchte** I would like. **Ich möchte lieber** I would prefer. **Er mag ruhig warten!** let him wait!

möglich ['møːgliç] *adj* possible. **–erweise** *adv* possibly. **Möglichkeit** *f* possibility. **möglichst** *adv* as ... as possible.

Mohammedaner [mohame'daːnər] *m* (*pl* **-**) Muslim, Mohammedan. **mohammedanisch** *adj* Muslim, Mohammedan.

Mohn [moːn] *m* (*pl* **-e**) poppy; (*Samen*) poppyseed.

Mohr [moːr] *m* (*pl* **-en**) moor, black(man).

Möhre ['møːrə] *f* (*pl* **-n**) carrot.

Mohrrübe ['moːrybə] *f* (*pl* **-n**) carrot.

Molekül [mole'kyːl] *neut* (*pl* -e) molecule. **molekular** *adj* molecular.

Molkerei [mɔlkə'raɪ] *f* (*pl* -en) dairy.

Moll [mɔl] *neut* (*unz.*) (*Musik*) minor.

Moment¹ [mo'mɛnt] *m* (*pl* -e) moment, instant. **Moment mal!** Just a moment!

Moment² *neut* (*unz.*) (*Physik*) moment; (*Anlaß*) motive; (*Umstand*) factor.

Monarch [mo'narç] *m* (*pl* -en) monarch. **-ie** *f* (*pl* -n) monarchy. **-ist** *m* (*pl* -en) monarchist.

Monat ['moːnat] *m* (*pl* -e) month. **monatelang** *adv* for months. **monatlich** *adj* monthly. **Monats||blutung** *f* menstruation. **-karte** *f* (monthly) season ticket.

Mönch [mœnç] *m* (*pl* -e) monk.

Mond [moːnt] *m* (*pl* -e) moon. **-finsternis** *f* lunar eclipse. **-schein** *m* moonlight. **-strahl** *m* moonbeam.

Monogramm [mono'gram] *neut* (*pl* -e) monogram, initials.

Monopol [mono'poːl] *neut* (*pl* -e) monopoly. **monopolisieren** *v* monopolize.

Montag ['moːntaɪk] *m* Monday. **montags** *adv* (on) Mondays.

Montage [mɔn'taːʒə] *f* (*pl* -n) assembly; installation. **-band** *neut* assembly line.

Monteur ['mɔntœːr] *m* (*pl* -e) mechanic, fitter. **montieren** *v* install, assemble.

Moor [moːr] *neut* (*pl* -e) marsh, moor.

Moos [moːs] *neut* (*pl* -e) moss.

Moped ['mopet] *neut* (*pl* -s) moped.

Moral [mo'raːl] *f* (*pl*-en) moral; (*Sittlichkeit*) morality; (*Zuversicht*) morale. **moralisieren** *v* moralize.

Mord [mɔrt] *m* (*pl* -e) murder.

Mörder ['mœrdər] *m* (*pl* -) murderer. **mörderisch** *adj* murderous.

morgen ['mɔrgən] *adv* tomorrow. **morgen früh** tomorrow morning. **Morgen** *m* (*pl* -) morning. **-dämmerung** *f* dawn. **-land** *neut* Orient. **-stern** *m* morning star, Venus.

Morphium ['mɔrfiʊm] *neut* morphine.

morsch [mɔrʃ] *adj* rotten.

Morseschrift ['mɔrzəʃrift] *f* Morse code.

Mörtel ['mœrtəl] *m* (*pl* -) mortar, cement.

Mosaik [moza'iɪk] *neut* (*pl* -e) mosaic.

Moschee [mɔ'ʃeɪ] *f* (*pl* -n) mosque.

Mosel ['moːzəl] *f* Moselle.

Moskau ['mɔskau] *neut* Moscow.

Most [mɔst] *m* (*pl* -e) new wine, must.

Motiv [mo'tiːf] *neut* (*pl* -e) (*Antrieb*)

motive; (*Kunst, Dichtung*) theme, motif. **motivieren** *v* motivate.

Motor ['moːtor] *m* (*pl* -en) motor, engine. **-ausfall** *m* engine failure. **-boot** *neut* motorboat. **-haube** *f* bonnet, (*US*) hood. **-rad** *neut* motorcycle. **-roller** *m* (motor) scooter.

Motte ['mɔtə] *f* (*pl* -n) moth.

Möwe ['mœːvə] *f* (*pl* -n) seagull.

Mücke ['mykə] *f* (*pl* -n) midge, gnat. **Mücken||netz** *neut* mosquito net. **-stich** *m* midge or gnat bite.

müde ['myːdə] *adj* tired. **Müdigkeit** *f* tiredness, fatigue.

Muff¹ [muf] *m* (*unz.*) musty smell.

Muff² *m* (*pl* -e) (*Pelz*) muff.

Muffel ['mufəl] *m* (*pl* -) grumpy person. **muffelig** *adj* grumpy, sullen.

muffig ['mufiç] *adj* (*moderig*) musty.

Mühe ['myːə] *f* (*pl* -n) trouble, pains *pl*. **sich Mühe geben** take pains. **nicht der Mühe wert** not worth the trouble. **mühelos** *adj* effortless. **sich mühen** trouble oneself, take pains. **mühevoll** *adj* laborious, troublesome.

Mühle ['myːlə] *f* (*pl* -n) mill.

mühsam ['myːzaːm] *adj* also **mühselig** troublesome; (*schwierig*) difficult.

Mulde ['muldə] *f* (*pl* -n) trough; (*Landschaft*) depression, hollow.

Mull [mul] *m* (*pl* -e) muslin.

Müll [myl] *m* refuse, rubbish, (*US*) garbage. **-abfuhr** *f* refuse disposal. **-eimer** *m* dustbin.

Müller ['mylər] *m* (*pl* -) miller.

Multiplikation [multiplikatsi'oɪn] *f* (*pl* -en) multiplication. **multiplizieren** *v* multiply.

Mumie ['mumiə] *f* (*pl* -n) mummy.

Mummenschanz ['mumənʃants] *m* (*pl* -e) masquerade.

München ['mynçən] *neut* Munich. **Münchner** *adj* (of) Munich.

Mund [munt] *m* (*pl* **Münder**) mouth. **-art** *f* dialect.

münden ['myndən] *v* **münden in** (*Fluß*) flow into; (*Straße*) run into, join.

mund||faul *adj* taciturn. **-fertig** *adj* glib. **-gerecht** *adj* appetizing. **Mund||geruch** *m* bad breath, halitosis. **-harmonika** *f* mouth organ, harmonica.

mündig ['myndiç] *adj* of age. **mündig werden** come of age. **Mündigkeit** *f* majority, full legal age.

mündlich ['myntlɪç] adj oral.
Mundstück ['muntʃtyk] neut mouthpiece.
Mündung ['myndʊŋ] f (pl -en) (Fluß) estuary.
Munition [munitsi'oːn] f (pl -en) ammunition.
munter ['muntər] adj lively, cheerful, merry. **Munterkeit** f liveliness, cheer.
Münze ['myntsə] f (pl -n) coin; (Anstalt) mint. **für bare Münze nehmen** take at face value. **Münze||einwurf** m coin-slot. **–fernsprecher** m pay phone, call box.
mürbe ['myrbə] adj (Fleisch) tender; (morsch) rotten, soft; (brüchig) brittle; (Gebäck) crumbly. **Mürbeteig** m short pastry.
murmeln ['murməln] v murmur.
murren ['murən] v grumble.
mürrisch ['myrɪʃ] adj morose, grumpy.
Mus [muːs] neut purée.
Muschel ['muʃəl] f (pl -n) mussel; (Telef) (telephone) receiver. **–tier** neut mollusc.
Museum [mu'zeːʊm] neut (pl Museen) museum.
Musical ['mjuːzikəl] neut (pl -s) musical.
Musik [mu'ziːk] f music; (Kapelle) band. **musikalisch** adj musical. **Musik||antenknochen** m (umg.) funnybone. **–er** m (pl -) musician. **–freund** m music-lover. **–instrument** m musical instrument.
Muskat [mus'kaːt] m (pl -e) nutmeg. **–blüte** f mace. **–nuß** f nutmeg.
Muskel ['muskəl] m (pl -n) muscle. **–kraft** f muscular strength. **–krampf** m muscle spasm. **–zerrung** f pulled muscle.
Muße ['muːsə] f leisure. **müßig** adj idle.
***müssen** ['mysən] v must, have to. **ich mußgehen** I must go. **ich muß nicht gehen** I don't have to go. **ich muß fort** I must leave. **ich müßte** I ought to.
Muster ['mustər] net (pl -) model, pattern; (Stoffverzierung) pattern, design; (warenprobe) sample. **–stück** neut sample, specimen. **–zeichnung** f design.
Mut [muːt] m courage. **mutig** adj brave, courageous. **mutlos** adj discouraged, despondent.
mutmaßen ['mutmaːsən] v suppose, surmise. **Mutmaßung** f (pl -en) conjecture.
Mutter[1] ['mutər] net f (pl Mütter) mother.
Mutter[2] f (pl -n) (Tech) nut.
mütterlich ['mytərlɪç] adj motherly.

–erseits adv on one's mother's side, maternal.
Mutter||liebe f mother-love. **–mal** neut **birthmark**. **–schaft** f motherhood. **–sprache** f mother tongue, native language.
Mütze ['mytsə] f (pl -n) cap.
mysteriös [mysteri'øːs] adj mysterious.
Mystik ['mystik] f (unz.) mysticism. **–er** m mystic. **mystisch** adj mystical.
Mythe ['myːtə] f myth. **mythisch** adj mythical.

N

na [na] interj well! (come) now!
Nabe ['naːbə] f (pl -n) hub.
Nabel ['naːbəl] m (pl -) navel. **–schnur** f umbilical cord.
nach [naːx] prep after; (örtlich) to, towards; (gemäß) according to, by. adv after. **nach und nach** gradually. **der Größe nach** by size. **nach außen** externally.
nachahmen ['naːxaːmən] v imitate. **Nachahmung** f imitation.
Nachbar ['naːxbaːr] m (pl -n) neighbour. **–land** neut neighbouring country. **–schaft** f neighbourhood.
Nachbildung ['naːxbɪldʊŋ] f copy, replica.
nachdem [naːx'deːm] adv afterwards. conj after. **je nachdem** according as.
***nachdenken** ['naːxdɛŋkən] v think (over), reflect. **Nachdenken** neut reflection, thinking over. **nachdenklich** adj reflective, thoughtful.
Nachdruck ['naːxdruk] m (Betonung) emphasis, stress; (Festigkeit) vigour. **nachdrücklich** adj emphatic; forceful.
nacheifern ['naːxaifərn] v emulate.
nacheinander ['naːxainandər] adv one after another.
Nachfolge ['naːxfɔlgə] f succession. **nachfolgen** v succeed, follow. **Nachfolger** m successor.
Nachfrage ['naːxfraːgə] f (Erkundigung) inquiry; (Komm) demand.
***nachgeben** ['naːxgeːbən] v give way or in.
Nachgeburt ['naːxgəbuːrt] f afterbirth.
***nachgehen** ['naːxgeːən] v follow; (untersuchen) investigate; (Uhr) be slow.

nachgemacht ['naːxgəmaxt] *adj* imitated, false.

Nachgeschmack ['naːxgəʃmak] *m* aftertaste.

nachgiebig ['naːxgiːbiç] *adj* pliable, flexible; (*Person*) compliant, yielding.

nachher [naːx'heːr] *adv* afterwards.

Nachhilfe ['naːxhilfə] *f* help, assistance. **-stunden** *pl* coaching *sing*, private tuition *sing*.

nachholen ['naːxhoːlən] *v* fetch later; (*fig*) make up for, catch up on.

Nach||hut ['naːxhuːt] *f* rearguard. **-klang** *m* echo, resonance.

Nachkomme ['naːxkɔmə] *m* (*pl* **-n**) descendant. **nachkommen** *v* follow, come after; (*Verpflichtung*) fulfil. **Nachkommenschaft** *f* posterity, descendants *pl*.

Nachkriegszeit ['naːxkriːkstsait] *f* postwar era.

Nachlaß ['naːxlas] *m* (*pl* **Nachlässe**) (*Preis*) reduction, discount; (*Erbschaft*) inheritance, estate. **nachlassen** *v* slacken, abate; (*aufhören*) cease; (*Strafe*) remit; (*Preis*) reduce. **nachlässig** *adj* careless, negligent.

nachmachen ['naːxmaxən] *v* copy, imitate.

Nachmittag ['naːxmitak] *m* afternoon. **nachmittags** *adv* in the afternoon(s).

Nachnahme ['naːxnaːmə] *f* **gegen** *or* **per Nachnahme** cash on delivery (COD).

Nachname ['naːxnaːmə] *m* (*pl* **-n**) surname.

nachprüfen ['naːxpryːfən] *v* verify, check again.

Nachricht ['naːxriçt] *f* (*pl* **-en**) report, (item of) news. **Nachrichten** *pl* news *sing*. **Nachrichten||büro** *neut* news agency. **-dienst** *m* (*Radio*) news service; (*Mil*) intelligence service.

Nachruf ['naːxruːf] *m* (*Zeitung*) obituary; (*Rede*) memorial address.

*****nachschlagen** ['naːxʃlaːgən] *v* (*Buch*) look up, consult. **Nachschlagebuch** *neut* reference book.

Nach||schrift ['naːxʃrift] *f* (*Brief*) postscript; (*eines Vortrages*) transcript. **-schub** *m* (*Mil*) reinforcement(s); (*Material*) supplies *pl*.

*****nach||sehen** ['naːxzeːən] *v* (*nachblicken*) watch, follow with one's eyes; (*prüfen*) examine, check; (*nachschlagen*) consult; (*verzeihen*) overlook. **-senden** *v* send on; (*Post*) forward.

Nach||sicht ['naːxziçt] *f* leniency. **-sorge** *f* (*medical*) aftercare. **-spiel** *neut* epilogue, sequel. **-speise** *f* dessert.

nächst [nɛːçst] *adj* next; (*Entfernung*) nearest; (*Verwandte*) close, closest; (*umg*: *kürzest*) shortest. *adv* next. *prep* next to. **am nächsten** next. **nächste Woche** next week. *das nächste Dorf liegt 10 km von hier entfernt* the nearest village is 10 km away. **Nächste(r)** fellowman, neighbour.

*****nach||stehen** ['naːxʃteːən] *v* be inferior to. **-stellen** re-adjust; (*Uhr*) put back; (*Frau*) molest, bother.

Nächstenliebe ['nɛːçstənliːbə] *f* charity, love of one's fellow men. **nächstens** *adv* shortly.

Nacht [naxt] *f* (*pl* **Nächte**) night. **heute Nacht** tonight. **über Nacht** overnight.

Nachteil ['naːxtail] *m* disadvantage; (*Schaden*) damage, detriment. **nachteilig** *adj* disadvantageous, unfavourable.

Nachthemd ['naxthemt] *neut* nightshirt, nightgown.

Nachtigall ['naxtigal] *f* (*pl* **-en**) nightingale.

Nach||tisch ['naːxtiʃ] *m* dessert. **-trag** *m* supplement. **nachträglich** *adj* subsequent, later.

nachts [naxts] *adv* at *or* by night. **Nachtwächter** *m* nightwatchman. **nachtwandeln** *v* sleepwalk.

Nach||untersuchung ['naːxuntərzuːxuŋ] *f* check-up. **-wahl** *f* by-election. **-weis** *m* proof, evidence. **nachweisen** *v* prove, demonstrate.

Nach||wirkung ['naːxvirkuŋ] *f* after-effect. **-wort** *neut* epilogue. **-wuchs** *m* new *or* young generation.

*****nachziehen** ['naːxtsiːən] *v* drag, draw along; (*nachzeichnen*) trace; (*folgen*) follow.

Nachzügler ['naːxtsyːklər] *m* (*pl* **-**) straggler, late-comer.

Nacken ['nakən] *m* (*pl* **-**) (nape of the) neck.

nackt [nakt] *adj* naked, bare. **Nacktheit** *f* nakedness.

Nadel ['naːdəl] *f* (*pl* **-n**) needle; (*Stecknadel*) pin. **-baum** *m* conifer. **-öhr** *neut* eye (of a needle). **-wald** *m* coniferous forest.

Nagel ['naːgəl] *m* (*pl* **Nägel**) nail. **-feile** *f* nail-file. **-haut** *f* cuticle. **-lack** *m* nail varnish. **nageln** *v* nail. **nagelneu** *adj* brand-new. **Nagelschere** f nail scissors pl.

nagen ['naːgən] v gnaw.

Nagetier ['naːgətiːr] neut rodent.

nah(e) ['naː(ə)] adj, adv near, close. prep near to. **einer Person zu nahe treten** offend a person. **nahe dabei** or **gelegen** nearby. **nahe Freundschaft** close friendship.

Nahaufnahme ['naːaufnaːmə] f (Foto) close-up.

Nähe ['nɛːə] f nearness; (Sicht-, Hörweite) vicinity. **in der Nähe** close by, in the vicinity.

*nahe||kommen v approach. –liegend adj obvious; (örtlich) close, nearby.

nähen ['nɛːən] v sew, stitch.

näher ['nɛːər] adj nearer, closer; (ausführlicher) more detailed. **nähere Angaben** further details. **nähere Umstände** exact circumstances. **Nähere(s)** neut particulars pl, details pl. **nähern** v bring near. **sich nähern** approach, draw near.

nahe||stehend adj close, friendly. **–zu** adv nearly, almost.

Näh||kasten m sewing box. **–machine** f sewing machine. **–nadel** f sewing needle.

nähren ['nɛːrən] v nourish; (unterhalten) support. **sich nähren von** live on.

nahrhaft ['naːrhaft] adj nutritious.

Nähr||mittel ['nɛːrmitəl] pl foodstuffs, food sing.

Nahrung ['naːruŋ] f (unz.) food; (Unterhalt) support. **–smittel** pl foodstuffs.

Naht [naːt] f (pl Nähte) seam; (Med) suture.

naiv [na'iːf] adj naive.

Name ['naːmə] or **Namen** m (pl Namen) name. **namens** adv named, by the name of.

nämlich ['nɛːmliç] adv that is (to say), namely.

Napf [napf] m (pl Näpfe) basin, bowl.

Narbe ['narbə] f (pl -n) scar.

Narkose [nar'koːzə] f (pl -n) (Betäubung) anaesthesia. **Narkotikum** neut (pl Narkotika) narcotic. **narkotisch** adj narcotic.

Narr [nar] m (pl -en) fool. **zum Narren haben** make a fool of. **Narrheit** f folly, foolishness.

närrisch ['nɛriʃ] adj foolish, crazy, silly.

Nase ['naːzə] f (pl -n) nose. **die Nase voll haben von** be fed up with. **Nasen||loch**

neut nostril. **–höhle** f (anat) sinus. **–spitze** f tip of the nose. **naseweis** adj cheeky.

naß [nas] adj wet; (feucht) moist, damp.

Nässe ['nɛsə] f wet, wetness.

Nation [natsi'oːn] f (pl -en) nation. **national** adj national. **National||flagge** f national flag. **–hymne** f national anthem.

nationalisieren [natsionali'ziːrən] v nationalize. **Nationalisierung** f nationalization. **Nationalismus** m nationalism. **nationalistisch** adj nationalist(ic).

National||mannschaft f national team. **–sozialismus** m national socialism, Nazism. **–tracht** f national costume.

Natter ['natər] f (pl -n) adder.

Natur [na'tuːr] f (pl -en) nature. **–anlage** f temperament, disposition. **–forscher** m scientist, naturalist. **–kunde** f natural history. **natürlich** adj natural. **Natur||schutz** m preservation (of nature). **–trieb** m instinct. **–wissenschaft** f natural science.

Nazi ['naːtsi] m (pl -s) Nazi.

Nebel ['neːbəl] m (pl -en) fog; (dünner) mist. **–horn** neut foghorn. **nebelig** adj foggy; misty.

neben ['neːbən] prep near (to), beside; (im Vergleich zu) compared with, next to. **–an** adv next door. **–bei** adv by the way; (außerdem) besides. **Neben||beschäftigung** f second job, sideline. **–buhler** m rival.

nebeneinander ['neːbənaınandər] adv side by side. **–stellen** v juxtapose.

Neben||fach neut subsidiary subject. **–fluß** m tributary. **–gebäude** neut annexe. **–kosten** pl extras, additional expenses.

nebensächlich ['neːbənzɛçliç] adj incidental.

necken ['nɛkən] v tease.

Neffe ['nɛfə] m (pl -n) nephew.

negativ ['neːgatiːf] adj negative.

Neger ['neːgər] m (pl -) Negro, Black. **–in** f (pl -nen) Black (woman).

*nehmen ['neːmən] v take.

Neid [nait] m envy, jealousy. **neid||en** v envy. **–isch** adj envious, jealous.

Neige ['naıgə] f (pl -en) slope, incline. **neigen** v incline. **neigen zu** tend (to), be inclined (to). **sich neigen** incline, slope. **Neigung** f slope; (fig) inclination.

nein [nain] *adv* no.

Nelke ['nɛlkə] *f* (*pl* -n) carnation; (*Gewürz*) clove.

***nennen** ['nɛnən] *v* call, name. **Nenn‖er** *m* denominator. **-ung** *f* naming; (*Sport*) entry. **-wert** *m* nominal value.

Nerv [nɛrf] *m* (*pl* -en) nerve. **Nerven‖kitzel** *m* thrill. **-krankheit** *f* nervous disease. **nervös** *adj* nervous.

Nessel ['nɛsəl] *f* (*pl* -n) nettle.

Nest [nɛst] *neut* (*pl* -er) nest.

nett [nɛt] *adj* nice; (*gepflegt*) neat.

netto ['nɛto] *adv* net. **Netto‖gewinn** *m* net profit. **-preis** *m* net price.

Netz [nɛts] *neut* (*pl* -e) net; (*System*) grid, network. **-haut** *f* retina. **-werk** *neut* network.

neu [nɔy] *adj* new; (*modern*) modern. **-artig** *adj* novel.

Neu‖ausgabe *f* new edition. **-bau** *n* new building.

neuerdings ['nɔyərdiŋs] *adv* recently, lately.

Neuerer ['nɔyərər] *m* (*pl* -) innovator.

Neuerscheinung ['nɔyɛrʃainuŋ] *f* (*pl* -en) new book.

Neu‖erung f ['nɔyərun] *f* (*pl* -en) innovation.

neuestens ['nɔyəstəns] *adv* of late.

neu‖geboren *adj* new-born. **-gestalten** *v* reorganize.

Neugier(de) ['nɔygiːr(də)] *f* (*unz.*) curiosity. **neugierig** *adj* curious.

Neu‖heit *f* (*pl* -en) novelty. **-igkeit** *f* (*pl* -en) (item of) news. **-jahr** *neut* New Year. **-jahrstag** *m* New Year's Day.

neulich ['nɔyliç] *adv* recently, lately.

neun [nɔyn] *pron, adj* nine. **neunte** *adj* ninth. **neunzehn** *pron, adj* nineteen. **neunzig** *pron, adj* ninety.

Neu‖ordnung *f* reorganization. **-reiche(r)** nouveau riche, wealthy parvenu.

Neurologe [nɔyro'loːgə] *m* (*pl* -n) neurologist. **Neurologie** *f* neurology. **neurologisch** *adj* neurological.

Neurose [nɔy'roːzə] *f* (*pl* -n) neurosis. **neurotisch** *adj* neurotic.

Neuseeland [nɔy'zeːlant] *neut* New Zealand.

neutral [nɔy'traːl] *adj* neutral. **neutralisieren** *v* neutralize. **Neutralität** *f* neutrality.

neuzeitlich ['nɔytsaitliç] *adj* modern.

nicht [niçt] *adv* not. **durchaus nicht** not at all. **nicht einmal** not even. **bitte nicht** please don't. **nicht mehr** no longer. **nicht wahr?** isn't it? don't you agree?

Nicht‖achtung *f* disregard. **-annahme** *f* nonacceptance. **-beachtung** *f* nonobservance.

Nichte ['niçtə] *f* (*pl* -n) niece.

Nicht‖einmischung *f* nonintervention. **-erscheinen** *neut* nonappearance.

nichtig ['niçtiç] *adj* futile, empty; (*ungültig*) null, void. **Nichtigkeit** *f* futility; invalidity.

Nicht‖mitglied *neut* non-member. **-raucher** *m* non-smoker. **-raucherabteil** *neut* no-smoking compartment.

nichts [niçts] *pron* nothing. **nichts daraus machen** not take seriously. **(es) macht nichts** it doesn't matter. **nichts dergleichen** nothing of the kind. **Nichts** *neut* nothing(ness).

nichts‖sagend *adj* meaningless. **-würdig** *adj* worthless, base.

Nicht‖vorhandensein *neut* lack, absence. **-zutreffende(s)** *neut* (that which is) nonapplicable.

Nickel ['nikəl] *neut* nickel.

nicken ['nikən] *v* nod, bow; doze, nod off. **Nickerchen** *neut* nap.

nie [niː] *adv* never.

nieder ['niːdər] *adj* low; (*fig*) inferior. *adv* down.

***nieder‖brennen** *v* burn down. **-drücken** *v* depress. **-fallen** *v* fall down.

Nieder‖frequenz *f* low frequency. **-gang** *m* decline, downfall; (*Sonne*) setting.

***nieder‖gehen** *v* go down; (*Aero*) land. **-geschlagen** *adj* depressed.

Niederlage ['niːdərlaːgə] *f* defeat.

Niederlande ['niːdərlandə] *pl* Netherlands. **Niederländer** *m* Dutchman. **-in** *f* Dutchwoman. **niederländisch** *adj* Dutch.

***niederlassen** ['niːdərlasən] *v* lower. **sich niederlassen** settle down; (*Vogel*) land, settle. **Niederlassung** *f* (*pl* -en) settlement; (*Komm*) branch.

niederlegen ['niːdərleːgən] *v* lay down.

Niedersachsen ['niːdəzaksən] *neut* Lower Saxony.

Niederschlag ['niːdərʃlaːk] *m* (*Regen, usw.*) precipitation; (*auf Fensterscheiben*) condensation; (*Chem*) sediment, precipitation; (*Boxen*) knock-down.

***niederschlagen** *v* knock down; (*Augen*) lower; (*Aufstand*) suppress.

nieder‖schmettern v strike down. **–schreiben** v write down. **–setzen** v put down. **–werfen** v throw down. **sich niederwerfen** prostrate oneself.

niedlich ['niːtlɪç] adj nice, (umg.) cute, dainty.

niedrig ['niːdrɪç] adj low. **Niedrigkeit** f lowness. **Niedrigwasser** neut low water, low tide.

niemals ['niːmals] adv never.

niemand ['niːmant] pron no one, nobody. **Niemandsland** neut no-man's-land.

Niere ['niːrə] f (pl -n) kidney.

nieseln ['niːzəln] v drizzle.

niesen ['niːzən] v sneeze. **Niesen** neut sneeze.

Niet [niːt] neut (pl -e) rivet.

Niete ['niːtə] f (pl -n) (Lotterie) blank (ticket); (Person) nonentity, failure; (Theater) flop.

Nikotin [niko'tiːn] neut nicotine.

Nilpferd ['niːlpfeːrt] neut hippopotamus.

nimmer ['nɪmər] adv never. **–mehr** adv never again.

nippen ['nɪpən] v sip.

nirgends ['nɪrgənts] or **nirgendwo** adv nowhere.

Nische ['niːʃə] f (pl -n) niche, alcove.

nisten ['nɪstən] v (build a) nest.

Niveau [ni'voː] neut (pl -s) level; (fig) standard; (geistig) culture, good education. **Niveau haben** be cultured or sophisticated.

noch [nox] adv (außerdem) in addition. conj nor. **noch nicht** not yet. **noch einmal** once again. **noch etwas?** anything else? **noch dazu** in addition. **weder ... noch ...** neither ... nor .... **nochmals** adv once again.

Nockenwelle ['nɔkənvɛlə] f camshaft.

Nomade [no'maːdə] m (pl -n) nomad.

Nominativ ['noːminatiːf] m (pl -e) nominative.

nominell [nomi'nɛl] adj nominal.

Nonne ['nɔnə] f (pl -n) nun. **–kloster** neut convent, nunnery.

Nord [nɔrt] m north. **–amerika** f North America. **–en** m north. **nordisch** adj northern; (Skandinavisch) nordic. **Nordländer** 1 m (pl -) Northerner. 2 pl northern countries.

nördlich ['nœrtlɪç] adj northern. adv northwards. **prep** to the north of. **Nordost(en)** ['nɔrtɔst(ən)] m northeast. **nordöstlich** adj northeast(ern).

Nord‖pol m North Pole. **–rhein-Westfalen** neut North Rhine-Westphalia. **–see** f North Sea. **nordwärts** adv northwards.

Nordwest(en) ['nɔrtvɛst(ən)] m northwest. **nordwestlich** adj northwest(ern).

nörgeln ['nœrgəln] v grumble, grouse.

Norm [nɔrm] f (pl -en) standard, norm. **normal** adj normal. **–erweise** adv normally. **normalisieren** v normalize. **–maß** neut standard measure. **normgerecht** adj conforming to a standard.

Norwegen ['nɔrveːgən] neut Norway. **Norweger** m (pl -), **Norwegerin** f (pl -nen) Norwegian. **norwegisch** adj Norwegian.

Not [noːt] f (pl Nöte) (Armut) need, want; (Gefahr) danger; (Bedrängnis) distress; (Knappheit) lack, shortage.

Notar [no'taːr] m (pl -e) notary.

Not‖ausgang m emergency exit. **–bremse** f emergency brake. **–durft** f call of nature. **–dürftig** adj scanty; hard up.

Note ['noːtə] f (pl -n) note; (Schul-) mark, grade; banknote, (US) bill; (Musik) note. **–nständer** m music stand.

Not‖fall m emergency. **–hilfe** f emergency service.

notieren [no'tiːrən] v note.

nötig ['nœːtɪç] adj necessary. **–en** v compel, force.

Notiz [no'tiːts] f (pl -en) notice; (Vermerk) note. **–buch** neut notebook.

Not‖lage f distress, predicament. **–landung** f emergency landing. **–lüge** f white lie. **notleidend** adj distressed; (arm) needy, destitute.

notorisch [no'toːrɪʃ] adj notorious.

Not‖ruf m distress call; (Telef) emergency call. **–stand** m emergency.

notwendig [nɔttvɛndɪç] adj necessary. **Notwendigkeit** f necessity.

Notzucht ['nɔttsuxt] f rape.

Novelle [no'vɛlə] f (pl -n) short story, short novel.

November [no'vɛmbər] m (pl -) November.

Novize [no'viːtsə] m (pl -n) novice.

Nuance [ny'ãsə] f (pl -n) nuance.

Nüchternheit ['nyçtərnhait] f sobriety; (fig) realism, clear-headedness.

Nudeln ['nuːdəln] pl noodles.

null [nul] adj nil, zero; (ungültig) null. **null und nichtig** null and void. **Null** f (pl -en) nought, zero.

numerieren [numeˈriːrən] v number. **numerisch** adj numerical.

Nummer [ˈnumər] f (pl -n) number. **Nummern‖scheibe** f (telephone) dial. **–schild** neut number plate.

nun [nuːn] adv now. interj well! **was nun?** what now? **nun also** why then. **–mehr** adv (by) now.

nur [nuːr] adv only, merely; (eben) just. conj nevertheless, but. **nur noch** only, still. **nicht nur ... sondern auch ...** not only ... but also ...

Nürnberg [ˈnyrnbɛrk] neut Nuremberg.

Nuß [nus] f (pl Nüsse) nut. **–baum** m walnut tree. **Nuß‖knacker** m nutcracker. **–schale** f nutshell.

nutz [nuts] adj useful. **–bar** adj useful. **–bringend** adj profitable.

nutzen [ˈnutsən] or **nützen** v be of use, be useful; (gebrauchen) make use of, use. **Nutzen** m (pl -) use; (Vorteil) profit, advantage. **Nutzen ziehen aus** derive advantage from, benefit from. **zum Nutzen von** for the benefit of. **Nutzfahrzeug** neut commercial vehicle.

nützlich [ˈnytsliç] adj useful. **Nützlichkeit** f usefulness.

nutzlos [ˈnutsloːs] adj useless. **Nutz‖losigkeit** f uselessness. **–nießer** m beneficiary. **–ung** f use, utilization.

Nylon [ˈnailon] neut (pl -s) nylon.

O

Oase [oˈaːzə] f (pl -n) oasis.

ob [ɔp] conj whether. **als ob** as if, as though.

Obdach [ˈɔpdax] neut (unz.) shelter. **obdachlos** adj homeless.

oben [ˈoːbən] adv above, at the top; (Haus) upstairs. **oben auf** on top of. **von oben** from above.

ober [ˈoːbər] adj upper, higher; (fig) superior; (Dienstgrad) senior, principal. **Ober** m (pl -) (head) waiter. **die Oberen** those in authority.

Ober‖arm m upper arm. **–befehlshaber** m commander-in-chief. **–bürgermeister** m (lord) mayor. **–fläche** f surface (area). **oberflächlich** adj superficial.

oberhalb [ˈoːbərhalp] adv, prep above.

Ober‖hand f upper hand, ascendancy. **–haupt** m chief, head. **–hemd** neut shirt.

–in f (pl -nen) (Rel) mother superior; (Krankenschwester) matron.

oberirdisch [ˈoːbərˈirdiʃ] adj above ground; (Leitung) overhead.

Ober‖kellner m head waiter. **–klasse** f upper class. **–schicht** f ruling class, upper classes pl. **–schule** f secondary school. **–schwester** f (Med) sister. **–seite** f upper side.

oberst [ˈoːbərst] adj highest, uppermost; (fig) supreme. **Oberst** m (pl -en) colonel.

obgleich [ɔpˈglaiç] conj although.

Obhut [ˈɔphuːt] f (unz.) care, protection. **in seine Obhut nehmen** take care of, take under one's wing.

obig [ˈoːbiç] adj above-mentioned, foregoing.

Objekt [ɔpˈjɛkt] neut (pl -e) object. **objektiv** adj objective.

*****obliegen** [ˈɔpliːgən] v (einer Aufgabe) perform, carry out. **es liegt ihm ob, zu** it is his job or duty to. **Obliegenheit** f duty.

obligatorisch [ɔbligaˈtoːriʃ] adj obligatory, compulsory.

Obmann [ˈɔpman] m foreman; (Vorsitzender) chairman; (Sprecher) spokesman.

Oboe [oˈboːə] f (pl -n) oboe. **Oboist** m oboist.

Obrigkeit [ˈoːbriçkait] f (pl -en) authorities pl, government.

obschon [ɔpˈʃoːn] conj although.

Observatorium [ɔpzɛrvaˈtoːrium] neut (pl Observatorien) observatory.

obskur [ɔpsˈkuːr] adj obscure.

Obst [oːpst] neut (unz.) fruit. **–baum** m fruit tree. **–garten** m orchard. **–händler** m fruiterer.

obszön [ɔpsˈtsøːn] adj obscene.

obwohl [ɔpˈvoːl] conj although.

Ochse [ˈɔksə] m (pl -n) ox. **Ochsen‖fleisch** neut beef. **–schwanz** m oxtail.

Ode [ˈoːdə] f (pl -n) ode.

öde [ˈøːdə] adj desolate, bleak; (fig) dull, bleak. **Öde** f (unz.) desert, wasteland; (fig) dullness, tedium.

oder [ˈoːdər] conj or.

Ofen [ˈoːfən] m (pl Öfen) stove; (Back-, Tech) oven.

offen [ˈɔfən] adj open; (freimütig) open, frank; (Stellung) vacant. **–bar** adj obvious. **–baren** v reveal, disclose. **Offenheit** f openness, frankness. **offen‖herzig** adj open-hearted. **–kundig** adj evident. **–sichtlich** adj obvious, evident.

offensiv [ɔfɛn'ziːf] *adj* offensive. **Offensive** *f* (*pl* -n) offensive.

offenstehend ['ɔfənʃteːənt] *adj* open; (*Schuld*) outstanding.

öffentlich ['œfəntlɪç] *adj* public. **Öffentlichkeit** *f* publicity; (*das Volk*) public.

offiziell [ɔfi'tsjɛl] *adj* official.

Offizier [ɔfi'tsiːr] *m* (*pl* -e) officer. **Offiziers‖messe** *f* officers' mess. –**patent** *neut* (officer's) commission.

offiziös [ɔfi'tsjøːs] *adj* semi-official.

öffnen ['œfnən] *v* open. **Öffnung** *f* opening. –**zeiten** *pl* opening hours.

oft [ɔft] *adv* often; frequently. **wie oft?** how many times?

öfter ['œftər] *adj* frequent. *adv* more often or frequently. **öfters** *adv* often.

Oheim ['oːhaim] *m* (*pl* -e) uncle.

ohne ['oːnə] *prep, conj* without. **ohne daß ich es wußte** without my knowledge. **ohne‖dies** or –**hin** *adv* all the same, besides.

Ohnmacht ['oːnmaxt] *f* unconsciousness, faint. **ohnmächtig** *adj* unconscious. **ohnmächtig werden** *v* faint.

Ohr [oːr] *neut* (*pl* -en) ear. **die Ohren spitzen** prick up one's ears. **ganz Ohr sein** be all ears.

Öhr [œːr] *neut* (*pl* -e) eye (of a needle).

Ohren‖schmalz *neut* ear wax. –**schmerz** *m* earache. **Ohrfeige** *f* slap across the face. **ohrfeigen** *v* slap (across the face). **Ohr‖läppchen** *neut* ear lobe. –**muschel** *f* (external) ear. –**ring** *m* earring.

Ökonom [œko'noːm] *m* (*pl* -en) (*Hausverwalter*) caretaker, steward; (*Wirtschaftswissenschaftler*) economist. –**ie** *f* housekeeping; economics. **ökonomisch** *adj* economic; (*sparsam*) economical.

Oktave [ɔk'taːvə] *f* (*pl* -n) octave.

Oktober [ɔk'toːbər] *m* (*pl* -) October.

Okzident ['ɔktsidɛnt] *m* occident.

Öl [øːl] *neut* (*pl* -e) oil. –**baum** *m* olive tree. **ölen** *v* oil, lubricate. **Ölfarbe** *f* oil paint.

Olive [o'liːvə] *f* (*pl* -n) olive. **olivengrün** *adj* olive-green. **olivenöl** *neut* olive oil.

Öl‖leitung *f* (oil) pipeline. –**meßstab** *m* dipstick.

Olympiade [olympi'aidə] *f* (*pl* -n) Olympiad, Olympic games. **olympisch** *adj* Olympic.

Ölzweig ['œːltsvaik] *m* olive branch.

Oma ['oːma] *f* (*pl* -s) granny, grandma.

Omelett [ɔmə'lɛt] *neut* (*pl* -e) or **Omelette** *f* (*pl* -n) omelette.

Ondulieren [ɔndu'liːrən] *v* wave.

Onkel ['ɔŋkəl] *m* (*pl* -) uncle.

Opa ['oːpa] *m* (*pl* -s) grandad, grandpa.

Opal [o'paːl] *m* (*pl* -e) opal.

Oper ['oːpər] *f* (*pl* -n) opera; (*Opernhaus*) opera house.

Operation [operatsi'oːn] *f* (*pl* -en) operation. –**ssaal** *m* operating theatre. **operieren** *v* operate.

Opfer ['ɔpfər] *neut* (*pl* -) (*Verzicht, Gabe*) sacrifice; (*Geopfertes*) victim. **opfern** *v* sacrifice, offer. **Opferung** *f* sacrifice.

Opium ['oːpium] *neut* opium.

opportun [ɔpɔr'tuːn] *adj* opportune.

Opposition [ɔpozitsi'oːn] *f* (*pl* -n) opposition. –**sführer** *m* leader of the opposition.

Optik ['ɔptik] *f* optics. –**er** *m* optician.

optimal [ɔpti'maːl] *adj* optimum. **Optimismus** *m* optimism. **Optimist** *m* optimist. **optimistisch** *adj* optimistic.

optisch ['ɔptiʃ] *adj* optic(al).

Orange [o'rãːʒə] *f* (*pl* -n) orange. **orange** *adj* orange. **Orangensaft** *m* orange juice.

Orchester [ɔr'kɛstər] *neut* (*pl* -) orchestra.

Orchidee [ɔrçi'deːə] *f* (*pl* -n) orchid.

Orden ['ɔrdən] *m* (*pl* -) (*Gesellschaft*) order; (*Ehrenzeichen*) decoration, order. **Ordens‖bruder** *m* member of an order; (*Rel*) monk, friar. –**schwester** *f* nun.

ordentlich ['ɔrdəntlɪç] *adj* (*ordnungsgemäß*) orderly; (*ordnungsliebend, geordnet*) tidy; (*anständig, auch umg.*) proper, decent. **Ordentlichkeit** *f* orderliness; decency, respectability.

ordinär [ɔrdi'nɛːr] *adj* common, vulgar.

Ordinarius [ɔrdi'naːriʊs] *m* (*pl* **Ordinarien**) professor.

Ordination [ɔrdina'tsioːn] *f* (*pl* -en) ordination. **ordinieren** *v* ordain.

ordnen ['ɔrdnən] *v* put in order, arrange, classify. **Ordner** *m* (*pl* -) organizer; (*Versammlungen*) steward; (*Mappe*) file. **Ordnung** *f* (*pl* -en) (*Regel*) regulation. **ordnungs‖gemäß** or –**mäßig** *adj* orderly, lawful. *adv* properly, duly. –**widrig** *adj* irregular, illegal.

Organ [ɔr'gaːn] *neut* (*pl* -e) organ. –**isation** *f* organization. **organ‖isch** *adj* organic. –**isieren** *v* organize. **Organismus** *m* (*pl* **Organismen**) organism.

Orgasmus [ɔr'gazmus] m (pl **Orgasmen**) orgasm.

Orgel ['ɔrgəl] f (pl -n) organ. **-spieler** m (pl -), **-spielerin** f (pl -nen) organist.

Orgie ['ɔrgiə] f (pl -n) orgy.

Orient ['ɔriɛnt] m Orient. **Orientale** m (pl -n), **Orientalin** (pl -nen) Oriental. **orientalisch** adj oriental.

orientieren [ɔriɛn'tiːrən] v locate. **sich orientieren** orientate oneself. **Orientierung** f orientation. **Orientierungs‖punkt** m reference point. **-vermögen** neut sense of direction.

original [ɔrigi'naːl] adj original. **Original** neut (pl -e) original.

originell [ɔrigi'nɛl] adj original, novel; (eigenartig) peculiar.

Orkan [ɔr'kaːn] m (pl -e) hurricane.

Ornat [ɔr'naːt] m (pl -e) (official) robes.

Ort [ɔrt] m (pl -e) place; (Ortschaft) town; (Dorf) village; (Punkt) point.

orthodox [ɔrto'dɔks] adj orthodox.

Orthopädie [ɔrtopɛ'diː] f orthopaedics.

örtlich ['œrtliç] adj local.

Orts‖gespräch neut local call. **-verkehr** m local traffic. **-zeit** f local time.

Öse ['œːzə] f (pl -n) eye(let). **Haken** und **Ösen** hooks and eyes.

Ost(en) ['ɔst(ən)] m east. **der Nahe/Ferne Osten** the Middle/Far East. **Ostblock** m Eastern bloc, Eastern Europe.

Oster‖ei neut Easter egg. **-hase** m Easter bunny.

Ostern ['ɔːstərn] neut pl Easter.

Österreich ['œːstəraiç] neut Austria. **Österreicher** m (pl -), f **Österreicherin** (pl -nen) Austrian. **österreichisch** adj Austrian.

Osteuropa ['ɔstɔyropa] f Eastern Europe.

östlich ['œstliç] adj east(ern).

Ost‖politik f East policy, policy towards the Eastern bloc. **-see** f Baltic Sea.

Otter ['ɔtər] m (pl -) or f (pl -n) otter.

Ouvertüre [uvɛr'tyːrə] f (pl -n) overture.

Ovarium [o'vaːrium] neut (pl **Ovarien**) ovary.

oval [o'vaːl] adj oval.

Oxyd [ɔ'ksyːt] neut (pl -e) oxide. **oxydieren** v oxidize.

Ozean ['ɔːtseaːn] m (pl -e) ocean. **ozeanisch** adj oceanic.

P

paar [paːr] adj **ein paar** a few. **Paar** neut (pl -e) pair, couple. **paaren** v (Tiere) pair, couple; (vereinigen) join. **sich paaren** couple, mate. **Paarung** f (pl -en) mating. **paarweise** adv in couples.

Pacht [paxt] f (pl -en) lease; (Entgelt) rent. **-brief** m lease. **pachten** v lease.

Pächter ['pɛçtər] m (pl -) leaseholder; (Bauer) tenant farmer.

Pack [pak] m (pl **Päcke**) pack; packet; bundle.

Päckchen ['pɛkçən] neut (pl -) packet, small parcel.

packen ['pakən] v grasp, seize; (einpacken) pack. **-d** adj thrilling, fascinating. **Pack‖kasten** m packing case. **-pferd** neut pack-horse. **-esel** m (fig) drudge. **-stoff** m packing (material). **Packung** f (pl -en) package.

Pädagogik [pɛda'goːgik] f pedagogy, education. **pädagogisch** adj pedagogic. **pädagogische Hochschule** teacher-training college.

Paddel ['padəl] neut (pl -) paddle. **paddeln** v paddle.

Page ['paːʒə] m (pl -n) page(boy).

Paket [pa'keːt] neut (pl -e) packet, parcel.

Pakt [pakt] m (pl -e) pact, agreement.

Palast [pa'last] m (pl **Paläste**) palace.

Palästina [palɛs'tiːna] neut Palestine.

Palette [pa'lɛtə] f (pl -n) palette.

Palme ['palmə] f (pl -n) palm. **Palmsonntag** m Palm Sunday.

Pampelmuse ['pampəlmuːzə] f (pl -n) grapefruit.

Panda ['panda] m (pl -) panda.

Paneel [pa'neːl] neut (pl -e) panel, panelling.

paniert [pa'niːrt] adj coated with breadcrumbs.

Panik ['paːnik] f (pl -en) panic. **panisch** adj panic-stricken, panicky.

Panne ['panə] f (pl -n) breakdown.

Pantoffel [pan'tɔfəl] m (pl -n) slipper.

Pantomime [panto'miːmə] f (pl -n) pantomime.

Panzer ['pantsər] m (pl -) armour; (Panzerwagen) tank; (Tiere) shell. **-hemd** neut coat of mail. **panzern** v armour. **Panzer‖ung** f (pl -en) armourplating. **-wagen** m tank, armoured car. **-weste** f bullet-proof vest.

Papa [pa'pai, 'papa] m (pl -s) daddy, papa.

Papagei [papa'gai] m (pl -en) parrot.

Papier [pa'piir] neut (pl -e) paper. **-bogen** m sheet of paper. **-korb** m wastepaper basket. **-tüte** f paper hag. **-waren** pl stationery sing.

Pappe ['papə] f (pl -n) cardboard.

Pappel ['papəl] f (pl -n) poplar.

pappen [papən] v paste (together).

Pappschachtel ['papʃaxtəl] f cardboard box.

Paprika ['paprika] m (pl -s) paprika. **-schote** f green or red pepper, capsicum.

Papst [paipst] m (pl Päpste) pope.

päpstlich ['peipstlıç] adj papal.

Parabel [pa'raibəl] f (pl -n) parable; (Math) parabola.

Parade [pa'raidə] f (pl -n) parade. **paradieren** v parade; (fig) make a show, show off.

Paradies [para'diis] neut (pl -e) paradise.

paradox [para'doks] adj paradoxical. **Paradoxie** f paradox.

Paragraph [para'graif] m (pl -en) paragraph, section.

parallel [para'leil] adj parallel. **Parallele** f parallel.

Paralyse [para'lyizə] f (pl -n) paralysis. **paralysieren** v paralyse. **Paralytiker** m paralytic. **paralytisch** adj paralytic.

Paranuß ['paranus] f Brazil nut.

Parasit [para'ziit] m (pl -en) parasite.

Pärchen ['peirçən] neut (pl -) couple, lovers.

Parenthese [parɛn'teizə] f (pl -n) parenthesis.

Parfüm [par'fyim] neut (pl -e) perfume. **parfümieren** v perfume, scent.

parieren [pa'riirən] v (Angriff) parry; (Pferd) rein (in); (gehorchen) obey, toe the line.

Parität [pari'teit] f (pl -en) parity.

Park [park] m (pl -s) park. **-anlagen** f pl park, public gardens. **parken** v park.

Parkett [par'ket] neut (pl -e) (Fußboden) parquet; (Theater) stalls.

Park||platz m car park, (US) parking lot. **-uhr** f parking meter.

Parlament [parla'mɛnt] neut (pl -e) parliament. **-arier** m (pl -) parliamentarian. **parlamentarisch** adj parliamentary.

Parodie [paro'diï] f (pl -n) parody. **parodieren** v parody.

Partei [par'tai] f (pl -en) (Pol, Jur) party. **-führer** m party leader. **parteiⅡisch** or **-lich** adj biased, partial. **-los** adj impartial. **ParteiⅡpolitik** f party politics. **-tag** m party conference.

Parterre [par'ter] neut (pl -s) ground floor; (Theater) pit. **-wohnung** f ground-floor flat.

Partie [par'tiï] f (pl -n) (Teil, Musik) part; (Spiel, Heirat) match; (Jagd-) party.

Partikel [par'tiikəl] f (pl -n) particle.

Partisan [parti'zain] m (pl -en) partisan.

Partitur [parti'tuir] f (pl -en) (Musik) score.

Partizip [parti'tsiïp] neut (pl -ien) participle.

Partizipation [parrtisipa'tsioin] f participation. **partizipieren** v participate.

Partner ['pairtnər] m (pl -) partner. **Partnerschaft** f partnership.

Party ['parti] f (pl -s) party.

Parzelle [par'tsɛlə] f (pl -n) plot (of land).

Paß [pas] m (pl Pässe) (Reisepaß) passport; (Durchgang) pass.

passabel [pa'saibəl] adj tolerable, passable.

Passage [pa'sarʒə] f (pl -n) passage. **Passagier** m (pl -e) passenger.

Passant [pa'sant] m (pl -en) passer-by.

Paßbild ['pasbilt] neut passport photograph.

passen ['pasən] v fit, suit; (Kartenspiel) pass. **gut zueinander passen** go well together. **das paßt mir nicht** that doesn't suit me. **passend** adj fitting, suitable.

passieren [pa'siirən] v (geschehen) happen; (vorübergehen) pass; (überqueren) cross. **Passierschein** m permit, pass.

Passion [pasi'oin] f (pl -en) passion. **sich passionieren für** be enthusiastic about. **passioniert** enthusiastic, dedicated. **PassionsⅡspiel** neut Passion Play. **-woche** f Holy Week.

passiv ['pasif] adj passive. **Passiv** neut passive.

Paßkontrolle ['paskontroiə] f passport inspection.

Pastellfarbe [pa'stɛlfaɪrbə] f pastel colour.

Pastete [pa'steitə] f (pl -n) (savoury) pie, pasty.

pasteurisieren [pastœri'ziïrən] v pasteurize.

Pastille [pa'stiïlə] f (pl -n) lozenge.

Pastor ['pastɔr] m (pl -en) pastor, priest.

Pate ['paːtə] m (pl -n) godfather. **–nkind** neut godchild.

Patent [pa'tɛnt] neut (pl -e) patent; (Erlaubnis) licence; (Mil) commission. **patentieren** v patent. **Patentinhaber** m patentee.

pathetisch [pa'teːtiʃ] adj (feierlich) solemn, lofty; (übertrieben) rhetorical, flowery.

Pathologe [pato'loːgə] m (pl -n) pathologist. **Pathologie** f pathology. **pathologisch** adj pathological.

Patient [pa'tsjɛnt] m (pl -en) patient.

Patin ['paːtin] f (pl -nen) godmother.

Patriot [patri'oːt] m (pl -en) patriot. **patriotisch** adj patriotic. **Patriotismus** m patriotism.

Patron [pa'troːn] m (pl -e) patron; (umg.) fellow, customer.

Patrone [pa'troːnə] f (pl -n) cartridge.

Patrouille [pa'truljə] f (pl -n) patrol.

Patt [pat] neut (pl -s) stalemate.

Pauke ['paukə] f (pl -n) kettledrum. **pauken** v (umg.) cram, swot. **Pauker** m drummer; (umg.) crammer.

pausbackig ['pausbakiç] adj chubby(-faced).

pauschal [pau'ʃaːl] adj all-inclusive. **Pauschalsumme** f lump sum.

Pause ['pauzə] f (pl -n) pause, break; (Theater) interval. **Pause machen** take a break. **pausenlos** adj uninterrupted, continuous.

Pavian ['paːviaːn] m (pl -e) baboon.

Pazifik [pa'tsiːfik] m Pacific Ocean. **pazifisch** adj Pacific.

Pazifismus [patsi'fismus] m pacifism. **Pazifist** m (pl -en) pacifist.

Pech [pɛç] neut (pl -e) pitch; (fig) bad luck. **Pech haben** be unlucky. **pechdunkel** adj pitch dark.

Pedal [pe'daːl] neut (pl -e) pedal.

Pedant [pe'dant] m (pl -en) pedant. **pedantisch** adj pedantic.

peilen ['pailən] v take (one's) bearings; (loten) sound; (umg.) sound out.

Pein [pain] f (unz.) pain, torment, agony. **pein‖igen** v torment. **–lich** adj awkward, embarrassing; (genau) (over-)careful, fussy.

Peitsche ['paitʃə] f (pl -n) whip, lash.

Pelikan ['peːlikaːn] m (pl -e) pelican.

Pelle ['pɛlə] f (pl -n) peel, skin.

Pellkartoffel pl potatoes (boiled) in their jackets.

Pelz [pɛlts] m (pl -e) fur, pelt. **pelzig** adj furry. **Pelzmantel** m fur coat.

Pendel ['pɛndəl] neut (pl -) pendulum. **pendeln** v swing, oscillate; (fig) commute. **Pendler** m commuter.

penibel [pe'niːbəl] adj meticulous.

pennen ['pɛnən] v (umg.) doss, kip down. **Penne** f (umg.) school. **Penner** m dosser.

Pension [pã'sjoːn] f (pl -en) guest house, boarding house; (Ruhegehalt) pension. **pensionieren** v pension off. **Pensionierte(r)** m pensioner.

per [pɛr] prep by, per. **per Adresse** care of, c/o.

perfekt [pɛr'fɛkt] adj perfect. **einen Vertrag perfekt machen** clinch a deal.

perforieren [pɛrfo'riːrən] v perforate. **Perforation** f perforation.

Pergament [pɛrga'mɛnt] neut (pl -e) parchment. **–papier** neut greaseproof paper.

Periode [peri'oːdə] f (pl -n) period. **periodisch** adj periodic.

Perle ['pɛrlə] f (pl -n) pearl; (Glas-) bead. **perlen** v sparkle. **Perl‖enkette** f string of pearls. **–mutter** f mother-of-pearl.

permanent [pɛrma'nɛnt] adj permanent.

perplex [pɛr'plɛks] adj perplexed, confused.

Person [pɛr'zoːn] f (pl -en) person.

Personal [pɛrzo'naːl] neut staff, personnel. **–abteilung** f personnel department. **–ausweis** m pass, ID card. **–chef** m personnel manager.

Personen‖kraftwagen (Pkw) m (passenger) car. **–verzeichnis** neut (Theater) dramatis personae. **–zug** m (local) passenger train.

persönlich [pɛr'zœːnliç] adj personal. **Persönlichkeit** f personality.

Perspektive [pɛrspɛk'tiːvə] f (pl -n) perspective.

Perücke [pe'rykə] f (pl -n) wig.

pervers [pɛr'vɛrs] adj perverse. **Perversion** f perversion.

Pessimismus [pɛsi'mismus] m pessimism. **Pessimist** m (pl -en) pessimist. **pessimistisch** adj pessimistic.

Pest [pɛst] f (pl -en) plague.

Petersilie [petər'ziːliə] f (pl -n) parsley.

Petroleum [pe'troːleum] neut petroleum; (Kerosin) paraffin, (US) kerosene.

petzen ['pɛtsən] v (umg.) tell tales, sneak.
Pfad [pfaːt] m (pl -e) path. **-finder** m Boy Scout.
Pfahl [pfaːl] m (pl **Pfähle**) post, stake; (Stange) pole. **-werk** neut paling, palisade.
Pfalz [pfalts] f Palatinate.
Pfand [pfant] neut (pl **Pfänder**) pledge, security; (Flaschen, usw.) deposit. **-brief** m mortgage (deed). **-leiher** m pawnbroker.
Pfanne ['pfanə] f (pl **-n**) pan.
Pfannkuchen m pancake.
Pfarrbezirk ['pfarrbətsirk] m parish. **Pfarrer** m parson. **Pfarrhaus** neut parsonage.
Pfau [pfau] m (pl **-en**) peacock.
Pfeffer ['pfɛfər] m (pl -) pepper. **-kuchen** m gingerbread. **-minz** neut (pl -e) peppermint (sweet). **-minze** f (Bot) peppermint.
Pfeife ['pfaifə] f (pl **-n**) pipe. **pfeifen** v whistle. **Pfeifer** m whistler; (Pfeife) piper.
Pfeil [pfail] m (pl -e) arrow.
Pfeiler ['pfailər] m (pl -) pillar.
pfeilschnell ['pfailʃnɛl] adj swift as an arrow. **Pfeilschütze** m archer.
Pfennig ['pfɛniç] m (pl -e) pfennig; (fig) penny.
Pferch [pfɛrç] m (pl -e) fold, pen. **pferchen** v pen.
Pferd [pfeːrt] neut (pl -e) horse. **Pferde||bremse** f horsefly. **-knecht** m groom. **-rennbahn** f race course. **-rennen** neut horseracing. **-stall** m stable. **-stärke** (Ps) f horsepower (hp).
Pfiff [pfif] m (pl -e) (Ton) whistle; (Kniff) trick.
Pfifferling ['pfifərliŋ] m (pl -e) (Bot) chanterelle (edible mushroom). **das ist keinen Pfifferling wert** that's (worth) nothing.
Pfingsten ['pfiŋstən] neut (pl -) Whitsun(tide).
Pfirsich ['pfirziç] m (pl -e) peach.
Pflanze ['pflantsə] f (pl **-n**) plant. **pflanzen** v plant. **-fressend** adj herbivorous. **Pflanzen||fresser** m herbivore. **-öl** neut vegetable oil. **-reich** neut vegetable kingdom.
Pflaster ['pflastər] neut (pl -) (Straße) pavement; (Wunden) plaster. **-stein** m paving stone.
Pflaume ['pflaumə] f (pl **-n**) plum.

Pflege ['pfleːgə] f (pl **-n**) care. **-dienst** m service. **-eltern** pl foster parents. **-kind** neut foster child. **-mutter** f foster mother. **pflegeleicht** adj easy-care.
pflegen ['pfleːgən] v care for; (Kranken) nurse; (Pflanzen) cultivate; (gewohnt sein) be accustomed to. **er pflegte zu sagen** he used to say. **Pfleger** m male nurse; (Vormund) guardian. **Pflegerin** f nurse, sister.
Pflege||sohn m foster son. **-mutter** f foster mother. **-tochter** f foster daughter. **-vater** m foster father.
pfleglich ['pfleːkliç] adj careful. **pfleglich behandeln** handle with care.
Pflicht [pfliçt] f (pl **-en**) duty. **pflicht||bewußt** adj conscientious. **-gemäß** adj dutiful, in accordance with duty. **-getreu** adj dutiful, conscientious.
Pflock [pflɔk] m (pl **Pflöcke**) peg, pin.
pflücken ['pflʏkən] v pluck, gather.
Pflug [pfluːk] m (pl **Pflüge**) plough.
pflügen ['pflyːgən] v plough.
Pflüger ['pflyːgər] m ploughman.
Pforte ['pfɔrtə] f (pl -n) door, gate.
Pförtner ['pfœrtnər] m (pl -) doorkeeper, porter.
Pfosten ['pfɔstən] m (pl -) post, stake.
Pfote ['pfoːtə] f (pl **-n**) paw.
Pfropf [pfrɔpf] m (pl -e **oder Pfröpfe**) (Blutgerinsel) blood clot; (Watte) wad (of cotton wool). **pfropfen** v (Flasche) cork, stopper; (Bäume) graft; (stopfen) pack, stuff. **Pfropf||en** m (pl -) cork, stopper. **-reis** neut graft.
pfui [pfui] interj pooh, ugh.
Pfund [pfunt] neut (pl -e) pound.
pfuschen ['pfuʃən] v botch, bungle, make a mess. **Pfuscher** m botcher, bungler. **-ei** f bungling; (Arbeit) botch-job, botch-up.
Pfütze ['pfʏtsə] f (pl **-n**) puddle.
Phänomen [fɛnoˈmeːn] neut (pl -e) phenomenon.
Phantasie [fantaˈziː] f (pl **-n**) (Einbildungskraft) imagination; (Trugbild) fantasy. **phantasie||los** adj unimaginative. **-reich** adj imaginative. **-ren** v fantasize, daydream; (Med) be delirious. **phantastisch** adj fantastic.
Phantom [fanˈtɔm] neut (pl -e) phantom.
Phase ['faːzə] f (pl -n) phase.
Philister [fiˈlistər] m (pl -) philistine. **philisterhaft** adj philistine, narrow-minded.

Philosoph [filo'zɔtf] *m* (*pl* **-en**) philosopher. **-ie** *f* philosophy. **philosophisch** *adj* philosophical.

Phonetik [fo'neːtik] *f* (*unz.*) phonetics. **phonetisch** *adj* phonetic.

Phosphor [ˈfɔsfɔr] *m* (*unz.*) phosphorus.

Photo [ˈfoːto] *neut* (*pl* **-s**) photo, photograph. **-album** *neut* photograph album. **-apparat** *m* camera. **photogen** *adj* photogenic. **Photograph** *m* (*pl* **-en**) photographer. **-ie** *f* photography. **photograph|ieren** *v* photograph. **-isch** *adj* photographic.

Phrase [ˈfraːzə] *f* (*pl* **-n**) phrase; (*fig*) empty talk, fine phrases.

Physik [fyˈziːk] *f* physics. **-er** *m* physicist.

Physiologie [fyziolo'giː] *f* physiology. **physiologisch** *adj* physiological.

physisch [ˈfyːzɪʃ] *adj* physical.

Pianist [pia'nist] *m* (*pl* **-en**), **Pianistin** *f* (*pl* **-nen**) pianist.

Pickel¹ [ˈpikəl] *m* (*pl* **-**), **Picke** *f* (*pl* **-n**) pickaxe.

Pickel² [ˈpikəl] *m* (*pl* **-**) (*Med*) pimple, spot.

piep [piːp] *interj* cheep. **nicht piep sagen** not say a word. **Piep** *m* (*pl* **-se**) peep, chirp. **piep||en** *v* chirp. **-sen** *v* (*Maus*) squeak.

Pietät [pie'tɛːt] *f* piety; (*Ehrfurcht*) reverence.

Pik [piːk] *neut* (*pl* **-s**) spades *pl*.

pikant [pi'kant] *adj* spicy; (*fig*) suggestive, racy.

Pikkoloflöte [ˈpikoloˌfløːtə] *f* piccolo.

Pilger [ˈpilgər] *m* (*pl* **-**), **Pilgerin** *f* (*pl* **-nen**) pilgrim. **Pilgerfahrt** *f* pilgrimage.

Pille [ˈpilə] *f* (*pl* **-n**) pill. **die Pille** (*umg.*) the (contraceptive) pill.

Pilot [pi'loːt] *m* (*pl* **-en**) pilot.

Pilz [pilts] *m* (*pl* **-e**) mushroom.

Pinguin [ˈpiŋguˈiːn] *m* (*pl* **-e**) penguin.

Pinie [ˈpiːniə] *f* (*pl* **-n**) stone pine. **-nnuß** *f* pine kernel.

Pinne [ˈpinə] *f* (*pl* **-n**) pin, peg; (*Ruder-*) tiller.

Pinsel [ˈpinzəl] *m* (*pl* **-**) brush; (*Farbe*) paintbrush. **pinseln** *v* paint, daub.

Pionier [pio'niːr] *m* (*pl* **-e**) pioneer.

Pirat [pi'raːt] *m* (*pl* **-en**) pirate.

Piste [ˈpistə] *f* (*pl* **-n**) track; (*Ski*) ski-run; (*Flugzeug*) runway.

Pistole [pi'stoːlə] *f* (*pl* **-n**) pistol.

pissen [ˈpisən] *v* (*vulgär*) piss.

Plackerei [plakəˈrai] *f* (*pl* **-en**) drudgery, toil.

plädieren [plɛˈdiːrən] *v* plead. **Plädoyer** *neut* (*pl* **-s**) (*Jur*) plea.

Plage [ˈplaːgə] *f* (*pl* **-n**) nuisance, bother, vexation, **plagen** *v* torment, annoy.

Plagiat [plagi'aːt] *neut* (*pl* **-e**) plagiarism. **plagieren** *v* plagiarize.

Plakat [pla'kaːt] *neut* (*pl* **-e**) poster, placard.

Plan [plaːn] *m* (*pl* **Pläne**) (*Absicht*) plan, intention; (*Zeichnung*) plan, diagram; (*Stadt*) map; (*Skizze*) design, scheme.

Plane [ˈplaːnə] *f* (*pl* **-n**) awning.

planen [ˈplaːnən] *v* plan.

Planet [pla'neːt] *m* (*pl* **-en**) planet. **-arium** *neut* (*pl* **-arien**) planetarium.

planieren [pla'niːrən] *v* plane, level, smooth. **Planierraupe** *f* grader, bulldozer.

Planke [ˈplaŋkə] *f* (*pl* **-n**) plank.

Plänkelei [plɛŋkəˈlai] *f* (*pl* **-en**) (*Gefecht*) skirmish; (*Wortstreit*) bantering.

planmäßig [ˈplaːnˌmɛːsiç] *adj* systematic; (*nach einem Plan*) according to plan. **der Zug fährt planmäßig um drei Uhr ab** the train is scheduled to leave at 3 o'clock.

Plantage [plan'taːʒə] *f* (*pl* **-n**) plantation.

Planung [ˈplaːnuŋ] *f* planning. **Planwirtschaft** *f* planned economy.

plappern [ˈplapərn] *v* chatter.

plärren [ˈplɛrən] *v* blubber, cry, sob.

Plastik [ˈplastik] *f* (*pl* **-en**) (*Kunst*) sculpture; (*Med*) plastic surgery; (*Kunststoff*) plastic. **plastisch** *adj* plastic.

Platin [pla'tiːn] *neut* platinum.

plätschern [ˈplɛtʃərn] *v* (*Bach*) babble; (*Regen*) splash, patter; (*planschen*) paddle.

platt [plat] *adj* flat, level; (*Redensart*) silly, trite; (*erstaunt*) tongue-tied, flabbergasted. **Plattdeutsch** *neut* Low German.

Platte [ˈplatə] *f* (*pl* **-n**) plate, dish; (*Stein*) flag; (*Metall, Holz*) sheet, slab; (*Tisch*) leaf; (*Schallplatte*) record, disc. **-nspieler** *m* record-player.

Platz [plats] *m* (*pl* **Plätze**) place; (*Sitz*) seat; (*Raum*) space, room; (*Stadt*) square. **-anweiser** *m* usher. **-anweiserin** *f* usherette.

platzen [ˈplatsən] *v* burst, split; (*explodieren*) explode; (*Scheck*) bounce.

Platz||karte *f* seat-reservation ticket. **-patrone** *f* blank cartridge. **-regen** *m* downpour, heavy shower.

plaudern ['plaudərn] v chat.

plausibel [plau'ziːbəl] adj plausible.

Plazenta [pla'sɛnta] f (pl -s or Plazenten) placenta.

pleite ['plaitə] adj bankrupt; (umg.) broke. **Pleite** f bankruptcy, (fig) flop, wash-out.

plombieren [plɔm'biːrən] v seal; (Zahn) fill.

plötzlich ['plœtslɪç] adj sudden.

plump [plump] adj (grob) coarse; (ungeschickt) clumsy. **plumps** Interj bump, thud. **plumpsen** v fall down (with a thud), plump down.

plündern ['plyndərn] v plunder.

Plural ['pluːraːl] m (pl -e) plural.

pneumatisch [pnɔy'maːtɪʃ] adj pneumatic.

Pöbel ['pøːbəl] m mob, rabble.

pochen ['pɔxən] v knock, tap; (Herz) beat.

Pocken ['pɔkən] pl smallpox sing.

Pokal [po'kaːl] m (pl -e) (Sport) cup. **-endspiel** neut (Sport) cup final. **-spiel** neut cup tie.

Pökel ['pøːkəl] m (pl -) brine (for pickling). **pökeln** v pickle, salt.

Pol [poːl] m (pl -e) pole. **polar** adj polar. **Polarmeer** neut Arctic Ocean. **südliches Polarmeer** Antarctic Ocean.

Polemik [po'leːmɪk] f (pl -en) polemic, controversy. **polemisch** adj polemic(al).

Polen ['poːlən] neut Poland. **Pole** m (pl -n), **Polin** f (pl -nen) Pole. **polnisch** adj Polish.

Police [po'liːs, po'liːsə] f (pl -n) (insurance) policy.

polieren [po'liːrən] v polish. **Poliermittel** neut polish.

Politik [poli'tiːk] f (unz.) (Staatskunst) politics; (Verfahren, Programm) policy. **-er** m (pl -) politician. **politisch** adj political.

Politur [poli'tuːr] f (pl -en) polish.

Polizei [poli'tsai] f (pl -en) police. **-hund** m police dog. **-kommissar** or **-kommissär** m police inspector. **polizeilich** adj police. **Polizei‖präsident** m chief constable, commissioner. **-stunde** f closing time. **-wache** f police station. **Polizist** m (pl -en) policeman. **-in** f (pl -nen) policewoman.

Polster ['pɔlstər] neut (pl -) cushion; (Polsterung) upholstery. **polstern** v upholster. **Polsterung** f upholstery.

Poltergeist ['pɔltərgaist] m poltergeist, hobgoblin.

Polyp [po'lyːp] m (pl -en) (umg.) copper.

Polytechnikum [poly'tɛçnikum] neut (pl Polytechniken) technical college.

Pommern ['pɔmərn] neut (unz.) Pomerania.

Pommes frites [pɔm'friːt] pl (potato) chips, (US) French fries.

Pomp [pɔmp] m pomp. **pomphaft** adj stately, with pomp.

Pony ['pɔni] neut (pl -s) pony; (Frisur) fringe.

Pop-Musik ['pɔp mu'ziːk] f pop (music).

populär [popu'lɛːr] adj popular. **popularisieren** v popularize.

Pore ['poːrə] f (pl -n) pore.

Pornographie [pɔrnogra'fiː] f pornography. **pornographisch** adj pornographic. **porös** [po'røːs] adj porous.

Porree ['pɔre] m (pl -s) leek.

Portion [pɔrtsi'oːn] f (pl -en) portion, helping.

Porto ['pɔrto] neut (pl -s) postage. **portofrei** adv post-free.

Porträt [pɔr'trɛː, pɔr'trɛːt] neut (pl -s) portrait.

Portugal ['pɔrtugal] neut Portugal. **Portugiese** m (pl -n), **Portugiesin** f (pl -nen) Portuguese. **portugiesisch** adj Portuguese.

Porzellan [pɔrtsɛ'laːn] neut (pl -e) porcelain, china.

Posaune [po'zaunə] f (pl -n) trombone.

Pose ['poːzə] f (pl -n) pose, attitude. **Poseur** m poseur. **posieren** v (strike a) pose.

Position [pozitsi'oːn] f (pl -en) position.

positiv ['poːzitiːf] adj positive.

Posse ['pɔsə] f (pl -n) (Theater) farce. **Possen** m (pl -) prank, practical joke, trick. **possenhaft** adj farcical.

possessiv ['pɔsesiːf] adj possessive.

Post [pɔst] f (pl -en) post (office), postal service; (Briefe) post, mail. **-amt** neut post office. **-anweisung** f postal order. **-beamte(r)** m post office official. **-bote** m postman.

Posten ['pɔstən] m (pl -) place, post; (Stellung) position, post; (Mil) sentry; (Ware) item; (Streik-) picket.

Post‖fach ['pɔstfaks] neut post-office box, PO box. **-gebühr** f postage. **-karte** f postcard.

postlagernd ['pɔstlaːgərnt] adj poste restante, (US) general delivery.

post||leitzahl f postal code. **–sparkasse** f post-office savings bank. **–stempel** m postmark.

Postulat [postu'laːt] neut (pl **-e**) postulate. **postulieren** v postulate.

postwendend ['postvɛndənt] adj by return (of) post. **Postwertzeichen** neut postage stamp.

potent [po'tɛnt] adj capable; (Med) potent.

potential [potɛntsi'aːl] adj potential. **Potential** neut potential. **potentiell** adj potential, possible.

Potenz [po'tɛnts] f (pl **-en**) power.

Pottasche ['pɔtaʃə] f potash.

Pracht [praxt] f splendour, magnificence. **prächtig** ['prɛçtiç] adj splendid, magnificent.

Prag [praːk] neut Prague.

Präge ['prɛɡə] f (pl **-n**) mint. **prägen** v stamp; (Münze) mint, coin.

pragmatisch [prag'maːtiʃ] adj pragmatic. **Pragmatiker** m (pl **-**) pragmatist.

prägnant [prɛg'nant] adj precise, terse.

prahlen ['praːlən] v brag, boast. **Prahler** m (pl **-**)braggart. **prahlerisch** adj boastful.

Praktikant [prakti'kant] m (pl **-en**), **Praktikantin** f (pl **-nen**) trainee, probationer. **Praktik||er** m experienced person, expert. **–um** neut (pl **-a**) training course, field course. **praktisch** adj practical; (zweckmäßig) useful; (Person) handy.

prall [pral] adj (rund) plump, chubby; (straff) tight; (sonne) blazing. **Prall** m (pl **-e**) collision, impact. **prallen** v (Ball) bounce, rebound. **prallen gegen** collide with, bump into.

Prämie ['prɛmiə] f (pl **-n**) bonus; (Versicherungs-) premium.

Prämisse [prɛ'misə] f (pl **-n**) premise.

Präparat [prɛpa'raːt] neut (pl **-e**) preparation; (Med) medicament.

präsentieren [prɛzɛn'tiːrən] v present. **Präsenz** f (pl **-en**) presence.

Präsident [prɛzi'dɛnt] m (pl **-en**) president. **–enwahl** f presidential election. **–schaft** f presidency. **präsidieren** v preside, act as chairman.

prasseln ['prasəln] v clatter; (Regen) patter, drum; (Feuer) crackle.

präventiv [prɛvɛn'tiːf] adj preventive. **Präventiv||maßnahme** f preventive measure. **–mittel** neut contraceptive.

Praxis ['praksis] f (pl **Praxen**) practice.

Präzedenzfall [prɛtse'dɛntsfal] m precedent.

präzis [prɛ'tsiːs] adj precise.

predigen ['preːdiɡən] v preach. **Prediger** m (pl **-**) preacher. **Predigt** f (pl **-en**) sermon.

Preis [prais] m (pl **-e**) price; (Belohnung) prize; (Lob) praise.

Preißelbeere ['praisəlbeːrə] f cranberry.

preisgeben ['praisɡeːbən] v give up, abandon; (opfern) sacrifice. **Preisgebung** f surrender; sacrifice.

Preis||liste f price list. **–senkung** f price reduction. **–steigerung** f price rise. **–stopp** m price freeze. **–sturz** m slump or fall in prices. **preiswert** adj cheap. **Preiszettel** m price tag.

prellen ['prɛlən] v (betrügen) swindle, cheat; (Ball) bounce.

Premiere [prem'jɛːrə] f (pl **-n**) première, first night.

Premierminister [prem'jeːrministər] prime minister, premier.

Presse ['prɛsə] f (pl **-n**) (Zeitungen) the press; (Druckmaschine) press; (Saft) squeezer. **–agentur** f press agency. **–freiheit** f freedom of the press. **pressen** v press.

Preß||holz neut chipboard. **–kohle** f briquette. **–luftbohrer** m pneumatic drill.

Preuße ['prɔysə] m (pl **-n**), **Preußin** f (pl **-nen**) Prussian. **Preußen** neut Prussia. **preußisch** adj Prussian.

prickeln ['prikəln] v prickle, tingle. **–d** adj tingling.

Priester ['priːstər] m (pl **-**) priest. **–in** f priestess. **priesterlich** adj priestly.

prima ['priːma] adj (umg.) first-rate, excellent. **Prima** f sixth form.

primär [pri'mɛːr] adj primary.

Primarschule [pri'maːrʃuːlə] f primary school (in Switzerland).

Primel ['priːməl] f (pl **-n**) primrose.

primitiv [primi'tiːf] adj primitive.

Prinz [prints] m (pl **-en**) prince. **-essin** f (pl **-nen**) princess.

Prinzip [prin'tsiːp] f (pl **-ien**) principle. **aus Prinzip** on principle. **im Prinzip** in principle, theoretically. **Prinzipal** m principal.

Priorität [priori'tɛːt] f (pl **-en**) priority.

Prise ['priːzə] f (pl **-n**) pinch.

Prisma ['prisma] neut (pl **Prismen**) prism.

privat [pri'vaːt] adj private. **Privat||adresse**

f home address. **–angelegenheit** *f* personal matter.

Privileg [privi'leːk] *neut* (*pl* **-ien**) privilege. **privilegiert** *adj* privileged.

Probe ['proːbə] *f* (*pl* **-n**) (*Versuch*) test, trial; (*Theater*) rehearsal; (*Muster*) sample, specimen. **auf Probe** on approval. **auf die Probe stellen** put to the test. **Probe||abzug** *m* (*Druck*) proof. **–zeit** *f* probationary period. **probieren** *v* (*versuchen*) try, attempt; (*Speise*) taste, sample.

Problem [pro'bleːm] *neut* (*pl* **-e**) problem. **problematisch** *adj* problematic.

Produkt [pro'dukt] *neut* (*pl* **-e**) product; (*Landwirtschaft*) produce. **–ion** *f* production. **produktiv** *adj* productive. **Produzent** *m* producer; (*Landwirtschaft*) grower. **produzieren** *v* produce.

Professor [pro'fɛsɔr] *m* (*pl* **-en**) professor. **professorisch** *adj* professorial. **Professur** *f* (*pl* **-en**) professorship.

Profil [pro'fiːl] *f* (*pl* **-e**) profile; (*Reifen*) tread. **profilieren** *v* outline, sketch.

Profit [pro'fiːt] *m* (*pl* **-e**) profit. **profit||abel** *adj* profitable. **–ieren** *v* profit, gain. **Profitmacher** *m* profiteer.

Prognose [pro'gnoːzə] *f* (*pl* **-n**) (*Med*) prognosis; (*Wetter*) outlook, forecast.

Programm [pro'gram] *neut* (*pl* **-e**) programme. **programmgemäß** *adj* according to plan. **programmieren** *v* (*Computer*) program. **Programm||ierer** *m* (*pl* **-**), **–iererin** *f* (*pl* **-nen**) programmer. **–ierung** *f* programming.

Projekt [pro'jɛkt] *neut* (*pl* **-e**) (*Plan*) plan; (*Entwurf*) scheme. **projektieren** *v* plan; scheme. **Projektionsapparat** *m* projector. **projizieren** [proji'tsiːrən] *v* project.

proklamieren [prokla'miːrən] *v* proclaim.

Proletariat [proletari'aːt] *neut* (*pl* **-e**) proletariat. **Proletarier** *m* proletarian. **proletarisch** *adj* proletarian.

Prolog [pro'loːk] *m* (*pl* **-e**) prologue.

Promenade [promə'naːdə] *f* (*pl* **-n**) promenade.

Promotion [promotsi'oːn] *f* (*pl* **-en**) (awarding of a) doctorate; (*Komm*) (sales) promotion. **promovieren** *v* be awarded a doctorate.

prompt [prɔmpt] *adj* prompt.

Propaganda [propa'ganda] *f* propaganda. **Propagandist** *m* (*pl* **-en**) propagandist.

Propeller [pro'pɛlər] *m* (*pl* **-**) propeller.

Prophet [pro'feːt] *m* (*pl* **-en**) prophet. **–ie**

f prophecy. **prophe||tisch** *adj* prophetic. **–zeien** *v* prophesy. **Prophezeiung** *f* (*pl* **-en**) prophecy.

Proportion [proportsi'oːn] *f* (*pl* **-en**) proportion. **proportional** *adj* proportional.

Prosa ['proːza] *f* prose.

prosit ['proːzit] *interj* cheers! your health! **prosit Neujahr!** a Happy New Year!

Prospekt [pro'spɛkt] *m* (*pl* **-e**) prospectus, leaflet; (*Ansicht*) prospect.

prostituieren [prostitu'iːrən] *v* prostitute. **Prostituierte** *f* (*pl* **-n**) prostitute. **Prostitution** *f* prostitution.

Protest [pro'tɛst] *m* (*pl* **-e**) protest. **Protestant** [prote'stant] *m* (*pl* **-en**) Protestant. **protest||antisch** *adj* protestant. **–ieren** *v* protest.

Prothese [pro'teːzə] *f* (*pl* **-n**) prosthesis; (*Arm-, Bein-*) artificial limb; (*Zahn-*) denture.

Protokoll [proto'kɔl] *neut* (*pl* **-e**) (*Jur*) record; (*einer Versammlung*) minutes *pl*; (*Diplomatie*) protocol.

Protz [prɔts] *m* (*pl* **-en**) snob. **protzen** *v* put on airs, swagger. **–haft** *adj* snobbish.

Proviant [provi'ant] *m* provisions *pl*, victuals *pl*.

Provinz [pro'vints] *f* (*pl* **-en**) province. **provinzial** *adj* provincial, regional. **provinziell** *adj* provincial, narrow-minded.

Provision [provizi'oːn] *f* (*pl* **-en**) (*Komm*) commission.

provisorisch [provi'zoːriʃ] *adj* provisional. **provozieren** [provo'tsiːrən] *v* provoke.

Prozedur [protse'duːr] *f* (*pl* **-en**) procedure.

Prozent [pro'tsɛnt] *neut* (*pl* **-e**) percent. **–satz** *m* percentage.

Prozeß [pro'tsɛs] *m* (*pl* **Prozesse**) (*Jur*) lawsuit, trial; (*Vorgang*) process.

Prozession [protsɛsi'oːn] *f* (*pl* **-en**) procession.

prüde ['pryːdə] *adj* prudish.

prüfen ['pryːfən] *v* (*Kenntnisse*) examine, test; (*erproben*) try, test; (*untersuchen*) inspect, check. **Prüf||ling** *m* (*pl* **-e**) (examination) candidate. **–stein** *m* touchstone. **–ung** *f* (*pl* **-en**) examination, test.

Prügel ['pryːgəl] *m* (*pl* **-**) cudgel, club; *pl* beating. **prügeln** *v* beat, thrash. **Prügelstrafe** *f* corporal punishment.

Prunk [pruŋk] *m* pomp, show, splendour. **prunken** *v* show off. **Prunkstück** *neut* showpiece. **prunk**||**süchtig** *adj* ostentatious. –**voll** *adj* magnificent, gorgeous.

Psalm [psalm] *m* (*pl* -en) psalm.

Pseudonym [psoydo'nyːm] *neut* (*pl* -e) pseudonym.

Psychiater [psyki'aːtər] *m* (*pl* -) psychiatrist. **Psychiatrie** *f* psychiatry. **psychiatrisch** *adj* psychiatric. **psychisch** *adj* psychic.

Psycho||**analyse** [psyçoana'lyːzə] *f* psychoanalysis. –**loge** *m* (*pl* -n) psychologist. **psychologisch** *adj* psychological.

Psycho||**path** *m* (*pl* -en) psychopath. –**therapeut** *m* (*pl* -en) psychotherapist. –**therapie** *f* psychotherapy.

Pubertät [pubɛr'tɛːt] *f* puberty.

Publikum ['puːblikum] *neut* public; (*Zuhörer*) audience.

publizieren [publi'tsiːrən] *v* publish. **Publizist** *m* journalist.

Pudding ['pudɪŋ] *m* (*pl* -s) pudding.

Pudel ['puːdəl] *m* (*pl* -) poodle.

Puder ['puːdər] *m* (*pl* -) powder.

Puff[1] [puf] 1. *m* (*pl* Püffe) push, thump. 2. *m* (*pl* -e) pouffe.

Puff[2] *neut* (*Spiel*) backgammon.

puffen ['pufən] *v* shove, thump; (*knallen*) pop. **Puffer** *m* buffer; (*Kartoffel-*) pancake, fritter. **Puff**||**mais** *m* popcorn. –**spiel** *neut* backgammon.

Pulli ['puli] *m* (*pl* -s) pullover. **Pullover** (*pl* -) pullover.

Puls [puls] *m* (*pl* -e) pulse. **pulsieren** *v* pulsate, throb. **Puls**||**schlag** *m* pulse. –**zahl** *f* pulse rate.

Pult [pult] *neut* (*pl* -e) desk. –**dach** *neut* lean-to roof.

Pulver ['pulvər] *neut* (*pl* -) powder. **pulver**||**artig** *adj* powdery. –**isieren** *v* pulverize.

Pumpe ['pumpə] *f* (*pl* -n) pump. **pumpen** *v* pump.

Pumpernickel ['pumpərnikəl] *m* black (rye) bread.

Punkt [puŋkt] *m* (*pl* -e) point; (*Ort*) place, spot; (*Gramm*) full stop. **punktieren** *v* punctuate; (*Med*) puncture; (*tüpfeln*) dot. **punktiert** *adj* dotted.

pünktlich ['pyŋktliç] *adj* punctual, on time. **Pünktlichkeit** *f* punctuality.

Pupille [pu'pilə] *f* (*pl* -n) (*Anat*) pupil.

Puppe ['pupə] *f* (*pl* -n) doll; (*Theater*) puppet; (*Insekten*) pupa, chrysalis. **Puppen**||**haus** *neut* doll's house. –**theater** *neut* puppet show.

pur [puːr] *adj* pure, unadulterated; (*Getränk*) neat.

Puritaner [puri'taːnər] *m* (*pl* -) Puritan. **puritanisch** *adj* puritan.

Purpur ['purpur] *m* purple. **purpurn** *adj* purple.

Purzelbaum *m* somersault. **purzeln** *v* somersault.

Pustel ['pustəl] *f* (*pl* -n) pustule.

Pute ['puːtə] *f* (*pl* -n) turkey (hen). **Puter** *m* (*pl* -) turkey (cock).

Putsch [putʃ] *m* (*pl* -e) putsch, uprising. **putschen** *v* revolt, rise.

Putz ['puts] *m* (*pl* -e) (*Kleidung*) finery, fine dress; (*Zierat*) ornaments pl, trimmings pl; (*Bewurf*) plaster. **putzen** *v* clean; (*Schuhe*) polish. **sich putzen** dress up. **sich die Nase putzen** wipe one's nose. **Putzer** *m* (*pl* -), **Putzerin** *f* (*pl* -nen) cleaner. **Putz**||**frau** *f* charwoman, cleaner. –**tuch** *f* polishing cloth.

Pyjama [pi'dʒaːma] *m* (*pl* -s) pyjamas pl.

Pyramide [pyra'miːdə] *f* (*pl* -n) pyramid.

Q

quabbelig ['kvabəliç] *adj* flabby, wobbly. **quabbeln** *v* wobble, quiver.

Quacksalber ['kvakzalbər] *m* (*pl* -) quack, charlatan.

Quadrat [kva'draːt] *neut* (*pl* -e) square. –**meter** *neut* square metre. –**wurzel** *f* square root. –**zahl** *f* (*Math*) square. **quadrieren** *v* (*Math*) square.

quäken ['kvɛːkən] *v* squeak.

Qual [kvaːl] *f* (*pl* -en) torment, pain. **quälen** ['kvɛːlən] *v* torment; (*foltern*) torture. **sich quälen** toil. **quälerisch** *adj* tormenting.

Qualifikation [kvalifikatsi'oːn] *f* (*pl* -en) qualification; (*Fähigkeit*) ability, fitness. **qualifizieren** *v* qualify. **sich qualifizieren** be fit (for).

Qualität [kvali'tɛːt] *f* (*pl* -en) quality.

Qualle ['kvalə] *f* (*pl* -n) jellyfish.

Qualm [kvalm] *m* dense smoke; (*Wasser*) vapour, steam. **qualmen** *v* smoke; (*Wasser*) steam.

qualvoll ['kvaːlfɔl] *adj* painful; agonizing.

Quantität [kvanti'tɛːt] *f* (*pl* -en) quantity.

Quarantäne [karan'tɛːnə] *f* (*pl* -n) quarantine.

Quark [kvark] *m* curds *pl*, curd cheese; (*fig*) tripe, rubbish. **-käse** *m* curd cheese.

Quartal [kvar'taːl] *neut* (*pl* -e) quarter (of a year).

Quartett [kvar'tɛt] *neut* (*pl* -e) quartet.

Quartier [kvar'tiːr] *neut* (*pl* -e) accommodation; (*Mil*) quarters *pl*; (*Stadt*) quarter, district.

Quarz [kvarts] *m* (*pl* -e) quartz.

quasi ['kvaːzi] *adv* as it were, in a way.

Quatsch [kvatʃ] *m* (*umg.*) rubbish, nonsense. **quatschen** *v* babble, talk nonsense. **Quecksilber** ['kvɛkzilbər] *neut* quicksilver, mercury.

Quelle ['kvɛlə] *f* (*pl* -n) (*Wasser*) spring; (*Herkunft*) source, origin; (*Öl*) well. **aus guter Quelle** on good authority. **quellen** *v* spring, gush; arise.

quer [kveːr] *adj* cross, transverse; (*seitlich*) lateral. *adv* across, crosswise. **kreuz und quer** hither and thither. **Quer‖balken** *m* crossbeam. **-baum** *m* crossbar. **querdurch** *adv* (right) across.

quetschen ['kvɛtʃən] *v* squeeze, squash. **Quetschung** *f* (*pl* -en) bruise.

quietschen ['kviːtʃən] *v* (*Person, Bremsen*) squeal; (*Tür*) squeak.

Quintett [kvin'tɛt] *neut* (*pl* -e) quintet.

Quirl [kvirl] *m* (*pl* -e) whisk, beater. **quirlen** *v* whisk, beat.

quitt [kvit] *adj* quits, even.

Quitte [kvitə] *f* (*pl* -n) quince.

quittieren [kvi'tiːrən] *v* (*aufgeben*) abandon; (*Rechnung*) give a receipt for. **Quittung** *f* (*pl* -en) receipt.

R

Rabatt [ra'bat] *m* (*pl* -e) discount, rebate.

Rabbiner [ra'biːnər] *m* (*pl* -) rabbi.

Rabe ['raːbə] *m* (*pl* -n) raven. **rabenschwarz** *adj* jet-black.

rabiat [rabi'aːt] *adj* furious, raging.

Rache ['raxə] *f* revenge, vengeance. **Rache nehmen an** revenge oneself on.

Rachen ['raxən] *m* (*pl* -) throat; (*Maul*) jaws *pl*, mouth.

rächen ['rɛçən] *v* avenge. **sich rächen an** take revenge on.

Rad [raːt] *neut* (*pl* Räder) wheel.

Radar ['raːdaːr] *neut* or *m* radar.

Rädchen ['rɛːtçən] *neut* (*pl* -) caster.

Rädelsführer ['rɛːdəlsfyːrər] *m* ringleader.

*****radfahren** ['raːtfaːrən] *v* cycle. **Radfahrer** *m* (*pl* -), **Radfahrerin** *f* (*pl* -nen) cyclist.

radieren [ra'diːrən] *v* erase, rub out; (*Kupfer*) etch. **Radiergummi** *m* rubber, eraser.

Radieschen [ra'diːsçən] *neut* (*pl* -) radish.

radikal [radi'kaːl] *adj* radical. **Radikal‖(e)r** radical. **-ismus** *m* radicalism.

Radio ['raːdio] *neut* (*pl* -s) radio. **radioaktiv** *adj* radioactive. **Radioaktivität** *f* radioactivity.

Radium ['raːdium] *neut* radium. **-therapie** *f* radiotherapy.

raffen ['rafən] *v* snatch (up); (*Stoff*) gather; (*langes Kleid*) take up.

raffinier‖en [rafi'niːrən] *v* refine. **-t** *adj* refined; (*fig*) clever, crafty.

ragen ['raːgən] *v* project, tower up.

Rahm [raːm] *m* cream.

rahmen ['raːmən] *v* frame. **Rahmen** *m* (*pl* -) frame; (*fig*) framework, limit; (*Umgebung*) surroundings *pl*, setting. **im Rahmen von** in the context of.

Rakete [ra'keːtə] *f* (*pl* -n) rocket.

Rakett [ra'ket] *neut* (*pl* -e) (*Sport*) racket.

Ramme ['ramə] *f* (*pl* -n) pile-driver.

Rampe ['rampə] *f* (*pl* -n) ramp; (*Bühne*) apron. **-nlicht** *neut* footlight.

*****ran** [ran] *V* heran.

Rand [rant] *m* (*pl* Ränder) edge; (*Seite*) margin; (*Gefäß, Hut*) brim; (*Grenze*) border, boundary. **-bemerkung** *f* marginal note.

Rang [raŋ] *m* (*pl* Ränge) rank, class; (*Theater*) circle.

rangieren [rã'ʒiːrən] *v* rank; (*Eisenbahnwagen*) shunt.

Ranke ['raŋkə] *f* (*pl* -n) tendril, shoot.

Ränke ['rɛŋkə] *pl* intrigues *pl*, machinations *pl*.

Ranzen ['rantsən] *m* (*pl* -) knapsack; (*Schule*) satchel.

ranzig ['rantsiç] *adj* rancid.

rar [raːr] *adj* rare, scarce. **Rarität** *f* (*pl* -en) rarity.

rasch [raʃ] *adj* rapid, swift.

rascheln ['raʃəln] *v* rustle.

Raschheit ['raʃhait] *f* swiftness.

rasen ['raːzən] *v* rage, storm; (*eilen*) race.

Rasen ['raːzən] *m* (*pl* -) lawn, grass.

rasend ['raːzənt] *adj* furious, raving. **rasend werden** go mad, (*umg.*) blow one's top.

rasieren [ra'ziːrən] v shave. **Rasierapparat** f safety razor. **elektrischer Rasierapparat** electric razor. **sich rasieren** shave (oneself). **Rasier‖klinge** f razor blade. – **krem** f shaving cream. – **messer** neut razor. – **pinsel** m shaving brush.

Raspel ['raspəl] f (pl -n) rasp; (Küche) grater.

Rasse ['rasə] f (pl -n) race; (Tiere) breed. **Rassehund** m pedigree dog.

Rassel ['rasəl] f (pl -n) rattle. **rasseln** v rattle, clatter.

Rassen‖diskriminierung f racial discrimination. – **haß** m racial hatred. – **integration** f racial integration. – **kreuzung** f cross-breeding. – **trennung** f racial segregation.

rassig ['rasiç] adj purebred; (schwungvoll) racy.

rassisch ['rasiʃ] adj racial. **Rassismus** m racialism, (US) racism. **rassistisch** adj racialist, (US) racist.

Rast [rast] f (pl -en) rest; (Pause) halt, break. **rasten** v rest. **rastlos** adj restless; (unermüdlich) unwearying. **Raststätte** f (motorway) service area.

Rasur [ra'zuːr] f (pl -en) (Radieren) erasure; (Rasieren) shave.

Rat [raːt] m (unz.) advice. **2** (pl **Räte**) (Versammlung) council; (Beamter) councillor. **um Rat fragen** ask for advice. **sich Rat holen bei** consult. **Rat wissen** know what has to be done.

Rate [raːtə] f (pl -n) instalment, payment. *raten* ['raːtən] v advise; (mutmaßen) guess.

Ratenkauf ['raːtənkauf] m hire purchase. **ratenweise** adv by instalments.

Rat‖geber(in) adviser, counsellor. – **haus** neut town hall.

ratifizieren [ratifi'tsiːrən] v ratify. **Ratifizierung** f ratification.

Ration [ra'tsioːn] f (pl -en) ration.

rationalisieren [ratsionali'ziːrən] v rationalize. **Rationalisierung** f rationalization. **rationell** adj rational.

rationieren [ratsio'niːrən] v ration.

rat‖los ['raːtloːs] adj helpless, perplexed. – **sam** adj advisable; (nützlich) useful; (förderlich) expedient. **Ratschlag** m (piece of) advice. **ratschlagen** v deliberate, consult together.

Rätsel ['rɛːtsəl] neut (pl -) puzzle, riddle; (Geheimnis) mystery. **rätselhaft** adj puzzling; mysterious.

Rats‖herr ['raːtshɛːr] m (town) councillor. – **keller** m town-hall restaurant. – **versammlung** f council meeting.

Ratte ['ratə] f (pl -n) rat.

Raub [raup] m robbery; (Beute) loot. – **anfall** m (armed) raid. **rauben** v rob; (Person) abduct; (plündern) plunder.

Räuber ['rɔybər] m (pl -) robber.

raubgierig ['raupgiːriç] adj rapacious. **Raub‖tier** m beast of prey. – **vogel** m bird of prey.

Rauch [raux] m smoke. – **rauchen** v smoke. **Rauchen** neut smoking. **Raucher** m (pl -) smoker.

räuchern ['rɔyçərn] v cure, smoke.

Rauch‖fang m chimney. – **fleisch** neut smoked meat. **rauch‖frei** adj smokeless. – **ig** adj smokey.

rauf [rauf] V **herauf**.

Raufbold ['raufbolt] f (pl -e) ruffian, rowdy. **raufen** v (Haare) tear out. **sich raufen mit** brawl with. **Rauferei** f (pl -en) fight, brawl. **rauflustig** adj quarrelsome.

rauh [rau] adj rough; (grob) coarse; (Klima) inclement. **Rauheit** f roughness; coarseness; harshness.

Raum [raum] **1** m (unz.) room, space. **2** m (pl **Räume**) room; (Gebiet) area.

räumen ['rɔymən] v evacuate, remove; (Zimmer) vacate.

Raum‖fahrt f space travel. – **inhalt** m volume, capacity.

räumlich ['rɔymliç] adj spatial, of space. **Raumschiff** ['raumʃif] neut space ship.

Räumung ['rɔymuŋ] f (pl -en) evacuation, removal; (Gebiet) cleaning.

Raupe ['raupə] f (pl -n) caterpillar. – **nkette** f caterpillar track.

raus [raus] V **heraus**.

Rausch [rauʃ] m (pl **Räusche**) intoxication.

rauschen ['rauʃən] v (Blätter) rustle; (Bach) babble, murmur.

Rauschgift ['rauʃgift] neut drug, narcotic. – **sucht** f drug addiction. – **süchtige(r)** (drug) addict.

Reagenzglas [rea'gɛntsglaːs] neut test tube.

reagieren [rea'giːrən] v react.

Reaktion [reaktsi'oːn] f (pl -en) reaction. **reaktionär** adj reactionary.

real [re'aːl] adj real. – **isieren** v realize. **Real‖ismus** m realism. – **ist** m (pl -en) realist. **realistisch** adj realistic.

Rebe ['reːbə] f (pl -n) vine.

Rebell [re'bɛl] m (pl -en) rebel. **rebellieren** v rebel. **Rebellion** f (pl -en) rebellion. **rebellisch** adj rebellious.

Rebhuhn ['rɛphuːn] neut partridge.

Rebstock ['reːpʃtɔk] m vine.

rechen ['rɛçən] v rake. **Rechen** m (pl -) rake.

Rechen||fehler m miscalculation. **-kunst** f arithmetic. **-maschine** f calculating machine. **-schaft** f (unz.) account.

rechnen ['rɛçnən] v calculate. **rechnen auf** count on. **rechnen mit** reckon with. **Rechnen** neut arithmetic. **Rechner** m calculator. **Rechnung** f calculation; (Waren) invoice; (Gaststätte) bill. **Rechnungs||abschluß** m balancing of accounts. **-führer** m accountant, book-keeper. **-prüfer** m auditor. **-wesen** neut accountancy, accounting.

recht [rɛçt] adj right. adv (sehr) quite, very. *mir ist das recht* that suits me. **recht haben** be (in the) right. **ganz recht!** just so! **Recht** neut (pl -e) right; (Gesetze) law. **-e** f right (side), right-hand side; (Pol) the Right. **-eck** neut rectangle. **Rechtfertigung** f justification. **recht||fertigen** v justify. **-gläubig** adj orthodox. **Rechthaber** m (pl -) dogmatic person, (umg.) know-all. **recht||haberisch** adj dogmatic, obstinate. **-lich** adj legal, of law; (ehrlich) honest, just. **-mäßig** adj legal, lawful.

rechts [rɛçts] adv on or to(wards) the right.

Rechtsanwalt m lawyer.

Rechtschreibung f spelling.

Rechts||fall m law suit, case. **-gleichheit** f equality before the law. **-händer** m right-handed person, right-hander. **rechts||händig** adj right-handed. **-kräftig** adj legally binding, legal.

Rechtsprechung f (pl -en) judicial decision, verdict; (Gerichtsbarkeit) jurisdiction.

rechtsradikal adj extreme right-wing. **Rechts||radikale(r)** m right-wing radical. **-spruch** m (Urteil) verdict, judgment; (Strafe) sentence. **-steuerung** f right-hand drive. **-streit** m law suit. **rechtswidrig** adj illegal.

recht||winklig adj right-angled. **-zeitig** adj timely, opportune; adv in (good) time.

recken ['rɛkən] v stretch.

Redakt||eur [redak'tœːr] m (pl -) editor. **-ion** f editing; (Arbeitskräfte) editorial staff.

Rede ['reːdə] f (pl -n) speech, talk, address. **redefertig** adj fluent, eloquent. **Rede||freiheit** f freedom of speech. **-kunst** f rhetoric.

reden ['reːdən] v speak, talk. **offen reden** speak out. **mit sich reden lassen** be open to persuasion, listen to reason. **Reden** neut speech, talking. **-sart** f expression, idiom. **Redewendung** f turn of speech, idiom.

redigieren [redi'giːrən] v edit.

redlich ['reːtliç] adj honest, upright, just. **Redlichkeit** f honesty.

Redner ['reːdnər] m (pl -) speaker, orator.

reduzieren [redu'tsiːrən] v reduce, decrease. **sich reduzieren** diminish, be reduced.

Reeder ['reːdər] m (pl -) shipowner.

reell [re'ɛl] adj respectable, honest, reliable.

Referat [refe'raːt] neut (pl -e) lecture, talk; (Gutachten) report, review. **Referent** m lecturer, speaker; (Fachmann) expert adviser, reviewer.

reflektieren [reflɛk'tiːrən] v reflect.

Reflex [re'flɛks] m (pl -e) reflex. **-bewegung** f reflex action.

Reform [re'fɔrm] f (pl -en) reform. **-ation** f reformation. **-er** m (pl -) reformer. **-haus** neut health-food shop. **reformieren** v reform.

Regal [re'gaːl] neut (pl -e) (book)shelf.

rege ['reːgə] adj active, lively.

Regel ['reːgəl] f (pl -n) rule. **regel||los** adj irregular (unordentlich) chaotic. **-mäßig** adj regular. **regelmäßigkeit** f regularity. **regeln** v regulate, arrange. **Regelung** f regulation, arrangement. **regelwidrig** adj against the rule(s). **Regelwidrigkeit** f irregularity; (Sport) foul.

Regen ['reːgən] m rain. **-bogen** m rainbow. **-fall** m rainfall. **-mantel** m raincoat. **-tropfen** m raindrop. **-wetter** neut rainy weather. **-wurm** m earthworm. **-zeit** f rainy season, rains pl.

Regie [re'ʒiː] f (pl -n) (Theater, Film) direction; (Verwaltung) administration, management.

regieren [re'giːrən] v rule, govern. **Regierung** f government.

Regiment [regɪ'mɛnt] *neut* (*pl* -er) regiment.

Regisseur [reʒɪ'sœr] *m* (*pl* -e) (theatre or film) director.

Register [re'gɪstər] *neut* (*pl* -) register; (*Buch*) index. **registrieren** *v* register. **Registrierkasse** *f* cash register.

Regler [re'glər] *m* (*pl* -) regulator.

regnen ['re:gnən] *v* rain. **regnerisch** *adj* rainy.

regulieren [regu'li:rən] *v* regulate.

Regung ['re:guŋ] *f* (*pl* -en) motion; (*Gefühle*) stirring, emotion; (*Antrieb*) impulse.

Reh [re:] *neut* (*pl* -e) roe deer. **–bock** *m* roebuck. **rehfarben** *adj* fawn. **Reh||fleisch** *neut* venison. **–kalb** *neut* fawn. **–ziege** *f* doe.

*****reiben** ['raɪbən] *v* rub; (*Käse, usw.*) grate. **Reibung** *f* rubbing; (*fig, Tech*) friction; (*Käse*) grating.

reich [raɪç] *adj* rich.

Reich [raɪç] *neut* (*pl* -e) empire; (*fig*) realm; (*Tier-, Pflanzen*) kingdom.

reichen ['raɪçən] *v* reach; (*überreichen*) pass, hand; (*anbieten*) offer; (*genügen*) be enough.

reich||haltig *adj* copious; (*Programm*) full. **–lich** *adj* plentiful, ample.

Reichs||adler *m* (German) imperial eagle. **–tag** *m* (German) Imperial Parliament (1871–1934).

Reichtum ['raɪçtu:m] *m* (*pl* Reichtümer) wealth, riches *pl*; (*Fülle*) abundance.

Reichweite ['raɪçvaɪtə] *f* range.

reif [raɪf] *adj* (*Frucht*) ripe; (*Person*) mature.

Reif [raɪf] *m* hoarfrost.

Reife ['raɪfə] *f* (*Frucht*) ripeness; (*Person*) maturity. **reifen** *v* mature.

Reifen ['raɪfən] *m* (*pl* -) ring, hoop; (*Mot*) tyre. **–druck** *m* tyre pressure.

Reihe ['raɪə] *f* (*pl* -n) row; (*Satz*) series, set. *ich bin an der Reihe* it is my turn. *eine ganze Reihe (von)* a lot (of), a whole series (of). **reihen** *v* line up, put in a row; (*Perlen*) string; (*Stoff*) gather; (*heften*) tack. **Reihenfolge** *f* order, sequence.

Reiher ['raɪər] *m* (*pl* -) heron.

Reim [raɪm] *m* (*pl* -e) rhyme. **reimen** *v* rhyme. *sich reimen* make sense.

rein [raɪn] *adj* pure; (*sauber*) clean; (*vollkommen*) perfect; (*Komm*) net. *ins Reine bringen* clear up, settle. *adv* completely. *die reine Wahrheit* the plain truth.

***'rein** [raɪn] *V* **herein**.

Reinemachen ['raɪnəmaxən] *neut* cleaning. **Reinheit** *f* purity; cleanness, cleanliness. **reinigen** *v* clean; (*fig*) purify, cleanse. **Reinigung** *f* cleaning; purification. **chemische Reinigung** *f* dry cleaning. **rein||lich** *adj* clean, neat, tidy. **–rassig** *adj* purebred; (*Pferd*) thoroughbred.

Reis [raɪs] *m* rice.

Reise ['raɪzə] *f* (*pl* -n) trip, journey; (*See*) voyage. **–büro** *neut* travel agency. **–leiter(in)** courier. **reisen** *v* travel. **–d** *adj* itinerant, travelling. **Reisende(r)** traveller. **Reise||paß** *m* passport. **–tasche** *f* travelling bag. **–scheck** *m* traveller's cheque.

Reißbrett ['raɪsbrɛt] *neut* drawing board. **reißen** *v* tear, rip; (*zerren*) pull. *sich reißen um* fight for. **reißend** *adj* rapid; (*Schmerz*) sharp, shooting. **Reiß||kohle** *f* charcoal. **–verschluß** *m* zip, zipper.

*****reiten** ['raɪtən] *v* ride. **Reit||en** *neut* riding. **–er** *m* rider, horseman. **–erin** *f* rider, horsewoman. **–kunst** *f* horsemanship, equitation.

Reiz [raɪts] *m* (*pl* -e) charm, attractiveness; (*Erregung*) stimulation. **reiz||bar** *adj* irritable. **–en** *v* excite, stimulate; (*anziehen*) attract, charm; (*zornig machen*) irritate. **–end** *adj* charming, enchanting.

Reklame [re'kla:mə] *f* (*pl* -n) advertising, publicity; (*einzelne*) advertisement. **Reklame machen für** promote, advertise.

Rekord [re'kɔrt] *m* (*pl* -e) record.

Rekrut [re'kru:t] *m* (*pl* -en) recruit. **rekrutieren** *v* recruit.

Rektor ['rɛktor] *m* (*pl* -en) (*Universität*) vice-chancellor; (*andere Schulen*) principal, head.

relativ [rela'ti:f] *adj* relative. **Relativität** *f* relativity.

Relief [rə'ljɛf] *neut* (*pl* -s) (*Kunst*) relief.

Religion [religi'o:n] *f* (*pl* -en) religion. **–sbekenntnis** *neut* confession of faith. **religiös** *adj* religious.

Ren [rɛn] *neut* (*pl* -e) reindeer.

Rennbahn ['rɛnba:n] *f* racecourse. **rennen** *v* run; (*Sport*) race. **Renn||en** *neut* running; race. **–pferd** *neut* racehorse. **–wagen** *m* racing car.

renovieren [reno'vi:rən] *v* renovate.

rentabel [rɛn'taːbəl] *adj* profitable. **Rentabilität** *f* profitability. **Rente** *f* (*Alters-*) pension; (*Versicherung*) annuity. **rentieren** *v* sich rentieren be profitable. **Rentner** *m* (*pl* -) **Rentnerin** *f* (*pl* -nen) pensioner.

Reparatur [repara'tuːr] *f* (*pl* -en) repair. **-werkstatt** *f* repair shop. **reparieren** *v* repair.

Report [re'pɔrt] *m* (*pl* -e) report. **-age** *f* (*pl* -n) (eye-witness) report. **-er** *m* (*pl* -) reporter.

Repressalien [reprɛ'saːliən] *pl* reprisals.

Reproduktion [reproduk'tsioːn] *f* (*pl* -en) reproduction. **reproduzieren** *v* reproduce.

Reptil [rɛp'tiːl] *neut* (*pl* -ien) reptile.

Republik [repu'bliːk] *f* (*pl* -en) republic. **-aner** *m* (*pl* -) republican. **republikanisch** *adj* republican.

Reserve [re'zɛrvə] *f* (*pl* -n) reserve. **-rad** *neut* spare wheel. **reservier||en** *v* reserve, book. **-t** *adj* reserved.

Residenz [rezi'dɛnts] *f* (*pl* -en) residence.

Resonanz [rezo'nants] *f* (*pl* -en) resonance.

Respekt [re'spɛkt] *m* respect. **respekt||abel** *adj* respectable. **-ieren** *v* respect. **-los** *adj* disrespectful. **-voll** *adj* respectful.

Rest [rɛst] *m* (*pl* -e) remainder, rest. **Restbetrag** *m* balance, remainder. **restlich** *adj* remaining.

Restaurant [resto'rã] *neut* (*pl* -s) restaurant.

Resultat [rezul'taːt] *neut* (*pl* -e) result.

retablieren [reta'bliːrən] *v* re-establish.

Retorte [re'tɔrtə] *f* (*pl* -n) retort.

retten ['rɛtən] *v* save. **Retter** *m* (*pl* -) rescuer; (*Rel*) Saviour. **Rettung** *f* (*pl* -en) rescue, deliverance. **Rettungs||boot** *neut* lifeboat. **-gürtel** *m* lifebelt.

Reue ['rɔyə] *f* remorse, regret. **reuen** *v* regret. *es reut mich, daß ich es getan habe* I regret doing that, I am sorry I did that.

Revanche [re'vãːʃə] *f* (*pl* -n) revenge, vengeance. **sich revanchieren** *v* take one's revenge.

Revers[1] [re'vɛrs] *m* (*pl* -e) (*Rückseite*) reverse, back.

Revers[2] [re'vɛːr] *m* or *neut* (*pl* -) (*Jacke*) lapel.

Revers[3] [re'vɛrs] *m* (*pl* -e) written undertaking, bond.

reversibel [revɛr'siːbəl] *adj* (*Med*, *Chem*) reversible.

revidieren [revi'diːrən] *v* revise.

Revier [re'viːər] *neut* (*pl* -e) district; (*Polizei*) beat; (*Wache*) station.

Revis||ion [revi'zioːn] *f* (*pl* -en) revision; (*Jur*) appeal; (*Komm*) auditing. **-or** *m* auditor.

Revolte [re'vɔltə] *f* (*pl* -n) revolt, insurrection.

Revolution [revolutsi'oːn] *f* (*pl* -en) revolution. **revolutionär** *adj* revolutionary. **Revolutionär** *m* (*pl* -e) revolutionary. **revolutionieren** *v* revolutionize.

Revolver [re'vɔlvər] *m* (*pl* -) revolver.

rezensieren [retsɛn'ziːrən] *v* review.

Rezept [re'tsɛpt] *neut* (*pl* -e) recipe; (*Med*) prescription.

Rhabarber [ra'barbər] *m* rhubarb.

Rhapsodie [rapso'diː] *f* (*pl* -n) rhapsody.

Rhein [rain] *m* Rhine. **-hessen** *neut* Rhenish Hesse. **rheinisch** *adj* Rhine, Rhenish **Rheinland** *neut* Rhineland. **--Pfalz** *f* Rhineland-Palatinate. **Rheinwein** *m* hock, Rhine wine.

rhetorisch [re'toːriʃ] *adj* rhetorical.

Rheumatismus [rɔyma'tizmus] *m* (*pl* **Rheumatismen**) rheumatism.

Rhinozeros [ri'noːtserɔs] *neut* (*pl* -se) rhinoceros.

rhythmisch ['rytmiʃ] *adj* rhythmic(al). **Rhythmus** *m* (*pl* **Rhythmen**) rhythm.

richten ['riçtən] *v* (*zurechtmachen*) arrange, prepare; (*einstellen*) adjust, set; (*reparieren*) repair; (*Frage, Brief*) address; (*Gewehr*) aim; (*Jur*) judge. **sich richten an** address oneself to. **sich richten nach** follow. **Richter** *m* (*pl* -) judge.

richtig ['riçtiç] *adj* correct, right. *ein richtiger Berliner* a real Berliner. **Richtigkeit** *f* correctness, rightness. **richtigstellen** *v* correct, set right.

Richt||linie *f* guideline. **-preis** *m* recommended price.

Richtung ['riçtuŋ] *f* (*pl* -en) direction; (*Neigung*) trend, tendency.

Richtweg ['riçtvɛk] *m* short cut.

***riechen** ['riçən] *v* smell. **riechen nach** smell of. **gut/übel riechen** smell good/bad.

Riegel ['riːgəl] *m* (*pl* -) bolt, bar; (*Seife, Schokolade*) bar. **riegeln** *v* bolt, bar.

Riemen ['riːmən] *m* (*pl* -) strap, belt; (*Gürtel*) belt.

Riese ['riːzə] *m* (*pl* -n) giant. **Riesen-** *adj* colossal, huge. **Riesenerfolg haben** be a great success, (*umg.*) be a smash hit.

riesengroß or **riesig** adj gigantic, huge. **Riesin** f (pl **-nen**) giantess.

Riff [rif] neut (pl **-e**) reef.

Rille ['rilə] f (pl **-n**) groove; (Furche) furrow.

Rind [rint] neut (pl **-er**) (Ochse) ox; (Kuh) cow.

Rinde ['rində] f (pl **-n**) (Baum) bark; (Käse) rind; (Brot) crust.

Rind‖erbraten m roast beef. **–fleisch** neut beef. **–vieh** neut cattle.

Ring [riŋ] m (pl **-e**) ring; (Straße) ring road; (Komm) combine, cartel; (Kettenglied) link. **–elchen** neut (pl **-**) ringlet.

***ringen** ['riŋən] v wrestle; (Hände) wring. **ringen um** struggle for. **Ringen** neut struggle, battle.

Ringfinger m ring finger. **ringförmig** adj ring-shaped.

Ringkampf m wrestling (match).

rings [riŋs] adv around. **–herum** adv all around.

Ringstraße f ring road.

Rinne ['rinə] f (pl **-n**) channel, groove; (Dach-) gutter.

Rippchen ['ripçən] neut (pl **-**) cutlet, chop. **Rippe** f (pl **-n**) rib.

Risiko ['riːziko] neut (pl **-s** or **Risiken**) risk. **risk‖ant** adj risky. **–ieren** v risk.

Riß [ris] m (pl **Risse**) (Stoff, Haut) tear; (Mauer) crack; (fig) breach, rift; (Zeichnung) technical drawing, plan.

rissig ['risiç] adj cracked; (Haut) chapped.

Ritt [rit] m (pl **-e**) ride.

Ritter ['ritər] m (pl **-**) knight. **ritterlich** adj chivalrous. **Ritterlichkeit** f chivalry.

rittlings ['ritliŋs] adv astride.

rituell [ritu'ɛl] adj ritual. **Ritus** m (pl **Riten**) rite.

Ritz [rits] m (pl **-e**) or **Ritze** f (pl **-n**) crack; (Schramme) scratch.

Robbe ['robə] f (pl **-n**) seal.

Roboter ['robɔtər] m (pl **-**) robot.

Rock [rɔk] m (pl **Röcke**) (Frauen) skirt; (Obergewand) cloak; (Jacke) jacket, coat.

Rodel ['roːdəl] m (pl **-**) toboggan. **rodeln** v toboggan.

roden ['roːdən] v clear (land). **Rodung** f (pl **-en**) cleared land.

Rogen ['roːgən] m (pl **-**) (fish) roe.

Roggen ['rɔgən] m rye. **–brot** neut ryebread.

roh [roː] adj raw; (grausam) cruel, brutal; (Stein, Person) rough. **rohe Gewalt** brute force. **Rohheit** f rawness; brutality; rough-

ness. **Roh‖gewicht** neut gross weight. **–öl** neut crude oil.

Rohr [roːr] neut (pl **-e**) tube, pipe; (Gewehr) barrel; (Bot) seed.

Röhre ['røːrə] f (pl **-n**) tube, pipe; (Radio) valve; (Leitung) conduit, duct.

Rohr‖leitung f pipeline. **–leitungen** pl pipes, plumbing sing. **–stock** m cane, bamboo. **–stuhl** m cane chair. **–zucker** m cane sugar.

Rohstoff m raw material.

Rolladen ['rollaidən] m (pl **-** or **Rolläden**) rolling shutter.

Rollbahn f runway.

Rolle ['rolə] f (pl **-n**) roll; (Theater, Film) role; (Tech) pulley. **eine Rolle spielen** play a part. **keine Rolle spielen** make no difference, not matter.

rollen ['rolən] v roll; (Flugzeug) taxi.

Roll‖mops m pickled herring. **–schuh** m roller skate. **–schuhlaufen** neut rollerskating. **–stuhl** m wheelchair. **–treppe** f escalator. **–tür** f sliding door.

Rom [roːm] neut Rome.

Roman [ro'maːn] m (pl **-e**) novel.

Romantik [ro'mantik] f Romanticism. **–er** m (pl **-**) romantic. **romantisch** adj romantic.

Römer ['rœmər] m (pl **-**) Roman. **römisch** adj Roman. **römisch-katholisch** adj Roman Catholic.

röntgen [rœntgən] v x-ray. **Röntgen‖behandlung** f radiation therapy. **–bild** neut x-ray (photograph) **–strahlen** pl x-rays.

rosa ['roːza] adj pink, rose.

Rose ['roːzə] f (pl **-n**) rose. **Rosen‖busch** m rose bush. **–kohl** m Brussels sprouts pl. **–kranz** m rose garland; (Rel) rosary.

Rosine [ro'ziːnə] f (pl **-n**) raisin.

Rosmarin [rozma'riːn] m rosemary.

Roß [rɔs] neut (pl **Rosse**) steed, horse. **–kastanie** f horse chestnut.

Rost¹ [rɔst] m (pl **-e**) grate; (Kochen) grill.

Rost² m rust.

rost‖beständig adj rustproof. **–braun** adj rust(-brown).

Röstbrot ['rœstbroːt] neut toast.

rosten ['rɔstən] v rust.

rösten ['rœstən] v roast; (Brot) toast.

rot [roːt] adj red. **Rot** neut red.

Röte ['rœːtə] f red(ness).

Röteln ['rœːtəln] pl German measles, rubella.

rot‖glühend adj red-hot. **–haarig** adj red-haired. **Rot‖käppchen** neut Little Red Riding Hood. **–kehlchen** neut robin.

rötlich ['rœtlɪç] adj reddish.

Rotte ['rɔtə] f (pl -n) gang, band; (Tiere) pack. **sich rotten** v band together, gang up.

Roulade [ru'laːdə] f (pl -n) rolled meat; (Musik) trill.

Rübe [ru'biːn] f (pl -n) (Bot) rape. **weiße/gelbe/rote Rübe** turnip/carrot/beetroot.

Rubin [ru'biːn] m (pl -e) ruby.

Rubrik ['ruːbrik] f (pl -en) (Titel) title, heading; (Spalte) column; (fig) category.

ruchbar ['ruːxbaːr] adj notorious.

Ruck [ruk] m (pl -e) jolt, jerk, start.

Rück‖ansicht f rear view. **–blende** f flashback. **–blick** m glance back; (fig) retrospect.

rücken ['rykən] v move, shift; (Platz machen) move up, shift up.

Rücken ['rykən] m (pl -) back. **–lehne** f back (of a chair). **–mark** neut spinal cord. **–schmerzen** pl backache sing. **–schwimmen** neut backstroke.

Rück‖erstattung f return; (Geld) repayment. **–fahrkarte** f return ticket. **–fahrt** f return journey. **–gabe** f return, restoration. **–gang** m decline, retrogression. **rückgängig** adj retrograde. **rückgängig machen** cancel, annul. **Rück‖grat** neut backbone. **–griff** m recourse. **–halt** m support. **–handschlag** m (Tennis) backhand (stroke). **–kehr** f return. **–licht** neut rear light.

Rucksack ['rukzak] m rucksack, pack.

Rück‖schlag m set-back, reverse. **–schritt** m retrogression, relapse. **–seite** f reverse (side), back.

Rücksicht f consideration, regard. **Rücksicht nehmen auf** take into consideration; (Person) show consideration to. **mit Rücksicht auf** with respect to. **Rücksichtnahme** f consideration, regard. **rücksichtslos** adj inconsiderate, (hart) ruthless. **Rücksichtslosigkeit** f lack of consideration; ruthlessness.

Rück‖sitz m back seat. **–spiegel** m rearview mirror. **–spiel** neut return match.

Rückstand m rest, remainder. **im Rückstand** in arrears. **rückständig** adj in arrears; (altmodisch) old-fashioned, backward.

Rücktritt m resignation; (in den Ruhestand) retirement.

rückwärts adv back(wards). **–gehen** v decline, retrogress.

Rück‖wirkung f reaction, repercussion, **–zug** m retreat. **–zahlung** f repayment, reimbursement.

Rudel ['ruːdəl] neut (pl -) (Schar) troop; (Hunde) pack; (Rehe, Schafe) herd.

Ruder ['ruːdər] neut (pl -) oar; (Steuer) rudder. **–boot** neut rowing boat. **rudern** v row. **Rudersport** m rowing.

Ruf [ruːf] m (pl -e) call, shout; (Tier) cry; (Vogel) call; (Ruhm) reputation, good name; (Aufforderung) summons. **rufen** v call, shout, cry. **Rufnummer** f telephone number.

Rüge ['ryːgə] f (pl -n) rebuke, reprimand. **rügen** v rebuke, reprimand.

Ruhe ['ruːə] f quiet, stillness; (Erholung) rest; (Gefaßtheit) composure, calm. **in Ruhe lassen** leave alone. **zur Ruhe gehen** go to bed. **ruhelos** adj restless. **Ruhelosigkeit** f restlessness. **ruhen** v rest; (schlafen) sleep; (begründet sein) be based. **–d** adj resting; (Tech) latent.

Ruhe‖pause f break, rest period. **–platz** m resting place. **–stand** m retirement. **–stätte** f resting place. **–störung** f breach of the peace. **–tag** m day of rest.

ruhig ['ruːɪç] adj still, quiet; (gefaßt) calm, composed.

Ruhm [ruːm] m fame, glory.

rühmen ['ryːmən] v praise. **sich rühmen** boast. **rühmlich** adj glorious.

Ruhr [ruːr] f dysentery.

Rührei ['ryːrai] neut scrambled egg(s). **rühren** v (bewegen) move; (vermischen) stir; (innerlich) move, affect. **sich rühren** stir, move. **rühr‖end** adj (fig) touching, moving. **–selig** adj sentimental. **Rührung** f (unz.) feeling, emotion.

Ruine [ru'iːnə] f (pl -n) ruin. **ruinieren** v ruin.

Rülps [rylps] m (pl -e) belch. **rülpsen** v belch.

Rum [rum] m (pl -s) rum.

Rumäne [ru'mɛːnə] m (pl -n) Rumanian. **Rumänien** n Rumania. **Rumänin** f (pl -nen) Rumanian (woman). **rumänisch** adj Rumanian.

Rummel ['ruməl] m (unz.) (umg.) bustle, activity; (Lärm) hubbub, racket. **–platz** m fairground.

Rumpf [rumpf] m (pl **Rümpfe**) trunk, torso; (Tier) carcass; (Schiff) hull; (Flugzeug) fuselage.

rümpfen [rympfən] v turn up (one's nose).

rund [runt] adj round. adv about. **Rundblick** m panorama. **Runde** f (pl -n) circle; (Boxen) round; (Rennen) lap; (Sport) heat; (Polizist) beat. **runden** v round (off).

Rund||**fahrt** f (circular) tour. **-frage** f questionnaire. **-funk** m radio; (Übertragung) broadcasting. **-funksendung** f radio programme. **-gang** m tour (of inspection); (Spaziergang) stroll. **-heit** f roundness.

rund||**heraus** adv frankly, flatly. **-lich** adj rotund, plump.

Rund||**schau** f panorama; (Zeitschrift) review. **-schreiben** neut circular. **-ung** f curve.

'runter ['runtər] V herunter.

Runzel ['runtsəl] f (pl -n) wrinkle. **runzelig** adj wrinkled. **runzeln** v wrinkle. **die Stirn runzeln** frown.

rupfen ['rupfən] v pluck.

Ruß [rus] m soot.

Russe ['rusə] m (pl -n) Russian.

rußig ['rusiç] adj sooty.

Russin ['rusin] f (pl -nen) Russian (woman). **russisch** adj Russian.

Rußland ['ruslant] neut Russia.

rüsten ['rystən] v prepare; (Mil) arm, prepare for war. **sich rüsten (auf)** get ready (for). **Rüstung** f armament; (Kriegsvorbereitung) arming; **Rüstungs**||**fabrik** f armaments factory. **-wettbewerb** m arms race.

Rute ['rutə] f (pl -n) rod; (Gerte) switch; (Anat) penis.

Rutsch [rutʃ] m (pl -e) slide; (Erde) landslip. **rutschen** v slip; (gleiten) slide. **-ig** adj slippery.

rütteln ['rytəln] v shake (up); (beim Fahren) jolt.

S

Saal [zail] m (pl **Säle**) hall, large room.

Saat [zait] f (pl -en) (Samen) seed; (Säen) sowing; (grün) green corn. **-korn** neut seed corn.

Sabbat ['zabat] m (pl -e) Sabbath.

Säbel ['zɛibəl] m (pl -) sabre.

Sabotage [zabo'taːʒə] f sabotage. **sabotieren** v sabotage.

Saccharin [zaxa'riːn] neut saccharine.

Sachbearbeiter ['zaxbaarbaitar] m executive, official in charge. **Sache** f thing; (Angelegenheit) affair, matter; (Tat) fact. **Sachen** pl things, belongings; (Kleider) things, clothes. **Sach**||**kundige(r)** expert. **-lage** f situation, state of affairs. **sachlich** adj businesslike, matter-of-fact; (objektiv) objective.

Sachse ['zaksə] m (pl -n) Saxon. **Sachsen** neut Saxony.

Sächsin ['zɛksin] f (pl -nen) Saxon (woman). **sächsisch** adj Saxon.

sacht(e) ['zaxt(ə)] adv softly, gently.

Sack [zak] m (pl **Säcke**) sack, bag. **-gasse** f cul-de-sac, (US) dead end.

Sadismus [za'dizmus] m sadism. **Sadist** m (pl -en) sadist. **sadistisch** adj sadistic.

säen ['zɛiən] v sow.

Safari [za'faːri] f (pl -s) safari.

Safe [seːf] m (pl -s) safe.

Saft [zaft] m (pl **Säfte**) juice; (Baum) sap; (umg.: Strom, Benzin) juice. **saftig** adj juicy; (Witz) spicy.

Sage ['zaːgə] f (pl -n) legend, fable.

Säge ['zɛigə] f (pl -n) saw. **-maschine** f mechanical saw. **-mehl** neut sawdust.

*sagen ['zaːgən] v say; (mitteilen) tell. **was Sie nicht sagen!** you don't say! **sagen wir** let's say, suppose. **wie gesagt** as I said. **das sagt mir etwas** that means something to me.

sägen ['zɛigən] v saw.

sagenhaft ['zaːgənhaft] adj legendary; (umg.) splendid, great.

Sahne ['zaːnə] f cream. **-kuchen** m cream cake. **sahnig** adj creamy.

Saison [zɛ'zõ] f (pl -s) season. **stille Saison** off-season.

Saite ['zaitə] f (pl -n) string. **-ninstrument** neut stringed instrument.

Sakrament [zakra'mɛnt] neut (pl -e) sacrament.

Salat [za'laːt] m (pl -e) salad; (Kopfsalat) lettuce. **-kopf** m head of lettuce.

Salbe ['zalbə] f (pl -n) ointment, salve.

Salbei ['zalbai] f or m (Bot) sage.

salben ['zalbən] v anoint.

Saldo ['zaldo] m (pl **Salden**) (Komm) balance.

Salon [za'lõ] *m* (*pl* -e) drawing room. **salonfähig** *adj* presentable (in society).

Salut [za'lu:t] *m* (*pl* -e) salute. **salutieren** *v* salute.

Salve ['zalvə] *f* (*pl* -n) volley.

Salz [zalts] *neut* (*pl* -e) salt. **salzen** *v* salt. **Salzfaß** *neut* salt cellar. **salzig** *adj* salty. **Salz**‖**kartoffeln** *pl* boiled potatoes. **–wasser** *neut* salt water.

Samen ['za:mən] *m* (*pl* -) seed; (*Tiere*) sperm. **–erguß** *m* ejaculation. **–händler** *m* seed merchant. **–pflanze** *f* seedling. **–staub** *m* pollen.

Sämischleder ['zɛːmɪʃleːdər] *neut* chamois (leather).

sammeln ['zaməln] *v* gather; (*Hobby*) collect. **Sammel**‖**platz** *m* assembly point. **–ler** *m* collector. **–lung** *f* collection.

Samstag ['zamstaːk] *m* Saturday. **samstags** *adv* on Saturdays.

samt [zamt] *prep* (together) with, including.

Samt [zamt] *m* (*pl* -e) velvet.

sämtlich ['zɛmtlɪç] *adj* complete, entire; (*alle*) all; (*Werke*) complete.

Sand [zant] *m* (*pl* -e) sand.

Sandale [zan'daːlə] *f* (*pl* -n) sandal.

Sandbank *f* sandbank. **sandfarben** *adj* sandy(-coloured). **Sand**‖**papier** *neut* sandpaper. **–stein** *m* sandstone.

sanft [zanft] *adj* gentle, soft. **Sanftheit** *f* gentleness, softness. **sanftmütig** *adj* gentle, mild.

Sänger ['zɛŋər] *m* (*pl* -), **Sängerin** *f* (*pl* -nen) singer.

sanieren [za'niːrən] *v* heal; (*Betrieb*) rationalize, make viable; (*Stadt, Viertel*) redevelop. **Sanierung** *f* (*Komm*) reorganization; (*Gebäude*) renovation.

sanitär [zani'tɛːr] *adj* sanitary, hygienic. **sanitäre Anlagen** *pl* sanitation *sing*.

Sankt [zaŋkt] *adj* Saint.

Sanktion [zaŋk'tsioːn] *f* (*pl* -en) sanction. **sanktionieren** *v* sanction.

Saphir [zafiːr] *m* (*pl* -e) sapphire.

Sardelle [zar'dɛlə] *f* (*pl* -n) anchovy.

Sardine [zar'diːnə] *f* (*pl* -n) sardine.

Sarg [zark] *m* (*pl* Särge) coffin.

sarkastisch [zar'kastɪʃ] *adj* sarcastic.

Satan ['zaːtan] *m* (*pl* -e) Satan; (*böser Mensch*) devil, demon. **satanisch** *adj* satanic.

Satellit [zate'liːt] *m* (*pl* -en) satellite.

Satin [za'tɛ̃] *m* (*pl* -s) satin.

Satire [za'tiːrə] *f* (*pl* -n) satire. **Satiriker** *m* (*pl* -) satirist. **satirisch** *adj* satirical.

satt [zat] *adj* satisfied, satiated; (*Farbe*) deep, rich. **satt sein** have had enough; (*nach dem Essen*) be full. **satt haben** have had enough of, be tired of.

Sattel ['zatəl] *m* (*pl* **Sättel**) saddle. **satteln** *v* saddle. **Sattel**‖**schlepper** *m* (tractor for an) articulated truck. **–tasche** *f* saddlebag.

Satz [zats] *m* (*pl* **Sätze**) (*Sprung*) leap, jump; (*Gramm*) sentence; (*Sammlung, Math*) set; (*Musik*) movement; (*Bodensatz*) sediment; (*Wein*) dregs *pl*; (*Grundsatz*) principle; (*Geld*) price, rate; (*Druck*) composition, setting. **–lehre** *f* syntax.

Satzung ['zatsuŋ] *f* (*pl* -en) statute; (*Vorschrift*) rule. **satzungs**‖**gemäß** *or* **–mäßig** *adj* statutory.

Sau [zau] *f* (*pl* **Säue**) sow.

sauber ['zaubər] *adj* clean; (*hübsch*) pretty, nice; (*ordentlich*) tidy. **Sauberkeit** *f* cleanliness; niceness; tidiness.

säuberlich ['zɔybərlɪç] *adj* clean; (*ordentlich*) tidy; (*anständig*) proper.

saubermachen *v* clean (up).

sauer ['zauər] *adj* (*Geschmack*) sour; (*säurehältig*) acid. **Sauerbraten** *m* roast marinated beef.

Sauerei *f* (*pl* -en) (*Unanständigkeit*) smuttiness; (*Pfuscherei*) mess.

Sauerkraut ['zauərkraut] *neut* pickled cabbage, sauerkraut.

Sauerstoff *m* oxygen. **sauersüß** *adj* bittersweet; (*Speise*) sweet-and-sour.

*****saufen** ['zaufən] *v* drink; (*umg.*) drink, booze.

Säufer ['zɔyfər] *m* (*pl* -) heavy drinker, boozer.

*****saugen** ['zaugən] *v* suck; (*einziehen*) absorb. **Saugen** *neut* suction, sucking.

säugen ['zɔygən] *v* suckle, nurse. **Säug**‖**en** *neut* suckling, nursing. **–etier** *neut* mammal. **–ling** *m* baby.

Säule ['zɔylə] *f* (*pl* -n) column, pillar.

Saum [zaum] *m* (*pl* **Säume**) seam, hem; (*Rand*) border, margin.

säumen[1] ['zɔymən] *v* (*Kleid*) hem; (*allgemein*) edge; (*fig*) skirt, fringe.

säumen[2] *v* (*zögern*) delay, hesitate.

Säumnis ['zɔymnɪs] *f* (*pl* -se) *or* *neut* (*pl* -e) delay.

Saumpferd ['zaumpfeːrt] *neut* packhorse.

Sauna ['zauna] *f* (*pl* -s) sauna.

Säure ['zɔyrə] *f* (*pl* -n) acid; sourness.

Sauregurkenzeit [zaurə'gurkəntsait] *f* silly season.

sausen ['zauzən] *v* (*eilen*) rush, dash, zoom; (*Wind*) howl, whistle.

Saxophon [zakso'foːn] *neut* (*pl* -e) saxophone.

schaben ['ʃaːbən] *v* scrape; (*Fleisch*) cut into strips.

schäbig ['ʃɛːbiç] *adj* shabby.

Schablone [ʃa'bloːnə] *f* (*pl* -n) stencil, pattern, model.

Schach [ʃax] *neut* (*Spiel*) chess; (*Warnruf*) check. **in Schach halten** keep in check. **Schachbrett** *neut* chessboard.

Schacherei [ʃaxə'rai] *f* haggling, bargaining.

Schachfigur *f* chessman.

Schacht [ʃaxt] *m* (*pl* -e) shaft.

Schachtel ['ʃaxtəl] *f* (*pl* -n) box.

schade ['ʃaːdə] *adv* a pity. *es ist schade* it's a pity, it's a shame. *schade, daß Sie ...* what a pity that you ... . *wie schade!* what a pity!

Schädel ['ʃɛːdəl] *m* (*pl* -) skull.

schaden ['ʃaːdən] *v* harm, injure, hurt. **Schaden** *m* damage; (*Verlust*) loss; (*körperlich*) injury, harm. **–ersatz** *m* compensation. **–freude** *f* malicious joy, gloating. **schadenfroh** *adj* malicious, gloating. **schadhaft** *adj* damaged.

schädigen ['ʃɛːdigən] *v* harm, damage; (*körperlich*) injure. **Schädigung** *f* damage; injury. **schädlich** *adj* dangerous, injurious.

Schaf [ʃaːf] *neut* (*pl* -e) sheep.

Schäfer ['ʃɛːfər] *m* (*pl* -) shepherd. **–hund** *m* sheepdog; (*deutscher*) Alsatian (dog). **–in** *f* (*pl* -nen) shepherdess.

Schaffell *neut* sheepskin, fleece.

*schaffen[1] ['ʃafən] *v* (*hervorbringen, gestalten*) create.

schaffen[2] *v* (*bringen*) bring, convey; (*fertigbringen*) manage, accomplish; (*arbeiten*) work.

Schaffner ['ʃafnər] *m* (*pl* -) (*Zug*) guard; (*Bus*) conductor. **–in** *f* (*pl* -nen) guard; conductress.

Schaf‖pelz *m* sheepskin. **–stall** *m* sheepfold.

Schaft [ʃaft] *m* (*pl* **Schäfte**) shaft; (*Griff*) handle; (*Gewehr*) stock; (*Baum*) trunk.

Schale ['ʃaːlə] *f* (*pl* -n) (*Schüssel*) bowl, basin; (*Ei, Nuß*) shell; (*Frucht, Gemüse*) peel, skin; (*fig*) cover(ing).

schälen ['ʃɛːlən] *v* shell; peel.

Schalk [ʃalk] *m* (*pl* -e) rogue, knave. **schalkhaft** *adj* roguish.

Schall [ʃal] *m* (*pl* -e) sound. **–dämpfer** *m* silencer. **schallen** *v* sound, resound; (*Glocke*) ring, peal. **Schall‖platte** *f* (gramophone) record. **–welle** *f* soundwave.

schalten ['ʃaltən] *v* switch; (*Mot*) change (gear). **Schalt‖er** *m* (*Bank, usw.*) counter, window; (*Elek*) switch. **–hebel** *m* control lever, switch; (*Mot*) gear lever. **–jahr** *neut* leap year. **–plan** *m* circuit diagram. **–ung** *f* wiring; (*Mot*) gear-change.

Scham [ʃaːm] *f* shame; (*Scheu*) modesty.

schämen ['ʃɛːmən] *v* **sich schämen** *v* be ashamed.

scham‖haft *adj* bashful, modest. **–los** *adj* shameless, immodest.

Schampoo [ʃam'puː] *neut* shampoo. **schampoonieren** *v* shampoo.

Schande ['ʃandə] *f* (*pl* -n) disgrace, shame.

schänden ['ʃɛndən] *v* disgrace; (*verderben*) spoil; (*entheiligen*) desecrate; (*Frau*) rape, violate.

Schandfleck ['ʃantflɛk] *m* blemish, stain. **schändlich** ['ʃɛntliç] *adj* shameful, disgraceful.

Schandtat ['ʃanttaːt] *f* misdeed, crime.

Schank ['ʃaŋk] *m* (*pl* **Schänke**) bar.

Schanze ['ʃantsə] *f* (*pl* -n) fortification; (*Erdwall*) earthworks *pl*; (*Skilauf*) skijump.

Schar [ʃaːr] *f* (*pl* -en) troop, band; (*Gänse*) flock; (*Hunde*) pack. **sich scharen** *v* gather, congregate.

scharf [ʃarf] *adj* sharp; (*Gewürze*) spicy, hot.

Schärfe ['ʃɛrfə] *f* (*pl* -n) sharpness, edge; (*Ätzkraft*) acidity; (*Klarheit*) clarity. **schärfen** *v* sharpen.

Scharfschütze *m* marksman, sharpshooter. **scharfsichtig** *adj* sharpsighted. **Scharfsinn** *m* shrewdness. **scharfsinnig** *adj* shrewd.

Scharlachfieber ['ʃarlaxfiːbər] *neut* scarlet fever. **scharlachrot** *adj* scarlet.

Scharm [ʃarm] *m* charm. **scharmant** *adj* charming, delightful.

Scharnier ʃar'niːr] *neut* (*pl* -e) hinge.

scharren ['ʃarən] *v* scrape, scratch.

Schatten ['ʃatən] m (pl -) shadow; (Dunkel) shade. **in den Schatten stellen** overshadow. **Schattenbild** neut silhouette. **schatten||haft** adj shadowy. **-ig** adj shaded.

Schatz [ʃats] m (pl Schätze) treasure; (fig) darling. **-amt** neut treasury.

schätzen ['ʃɛtsən] v value; (ungefähr) estimate. **-swert** adj valuable, estimable.

Schatz||kammer f treasury. **-meister** m treasurer.

Schätzung ['ʃɛtsuŋ] f (pl -en) estimate; (Hochschätzung) esteem. **schätzungsweise** adv approximately; at a guess.

Schau [ʃau] f (pl -en) show; (Ausstellung) exhibition; (Überblick) survey, review. **zur Schau stellen** exhibit.

schaudern ['ʃaudərn] v shudder, shiver. **-haft** adj horrible.

schauen ['ʃauən] v look (at), observe.

Schauer ['ʃauər] m (pl -) (Regen) shower; (Schrecken) horror; (Zittern) thrill.

Schaufel ['ʃaufəl] f (pl -n) shovel; (Tech) blade.

Schaufenster neut shop window.

Schaukel ['ʃaukəl] f (pl -n) (child's) swing. **-pferd** neut rocking horse. **-stuhl** m rocking-chair.

Schaum [ʃaum] m (pl Schäume) foam; (Seife) lather.

schäumen ['ʃɔymən] v foam; (Wein) sparkle.

schaumig ['ʃaumiç] adj foamy.

Schauspiel neut play; drama; (fig) spectacle. **-er** m (pl -) actor. **-erin** f (pl -nen) actress. **-haus** neut theatre.

Scheck [ʃɛk] m (pl -s) check. **-buch** neut check book.

Scheibe ['ʃaibə] f (pl -n) disc; (Brot, Wurst) slice; (Glas) pane. **Scheiben||bremse** f disc brake. **-wischer** m windshield wiper.

Scheide ['ʃaidə] f (pl -n) sheath; (Anat) vagina; (Grenze) limit. **scheiden** v separate; (Ehepartner) divorce. **sich scheiden** part, separate. **sich scheiden lassen** get a divorce. **Scheideweg** m crossroads. **Scheidung** f separation; (Ehe) divorce.

Schein [ʃain] m (pl -e) (Aussehen) appearance; (Licht) light; (Glanz) shine; (Geld) bill (US); banknote; (Bescheinigung) certificate. **schein||bar** adj apparent, ostensible. **-en** v (aussehen) appear, seem; (leuchten) shine. **-heilig** adj sanctimonious. **Schein||heilige(r)** hypocrite. **-krankheit** f feigned sickness. **-werfer** m (pl -) searchlight; (Reflektor) reflector; (Theater) spotlight; (Mot) headlight.

Scheiße ['ʃaisə] f (vulgär) shit. **scheißen** v shit.

Scheitel ['ʃaitəl] m (pl -) top; (Kopf) crown, top of the head; (Haar) parting.

scheitern ['ʃaitərn] v fail, come to nought; (Schiff) be wrecked.

Schelle ['ʃɛlə] f (pl -n) small bell; (Hand-) handcuff.

Schellfisch ['ʃɛlfiʃ] m haddock.

Schelm [ʃɛlm] m (pl -e) rogue.

Schema ['ʃema] neut (pl -ta or Schemen) scheme; (Muster) pattern; (Darstellung) diagram.

Schenkel ['ʃɛŋkəl] m (pl -) thigh. **-knochen** m thigh-bone, femur.

schenken ['ʃɛŋkən] v give, present; (Getränk) pour (out). **Schenk||er** m (pl -) donor, giver. **-ung** f donation.

Scherbe ['ʃɛrbə] f (pl -n) fragment.

Schere ['ʃeirə] f (pl -n) scissors pl; (große) shears pl; (Krebs) claw. **scheren** v (Wolle) shear; (Haare) cut; (Hecke) cut, trim; (Rasen) mow.

Scherz [ʃɛrts] m (pl -e) joke; (Unterhaltung) fun. **scherz||en** v joke, have fun. **-haft** adj joking.

scheu [ʃɔy] adj shy.

Scheuche ['ʃɔyçə] f (pl -n) scarecrow.

scheuen ['ʃɔyən] v shy away from, avoid; (Pferd) shy; (Mühe, usw.) spare. **sich scheuen vor** be afraid of.

Scheuerbürste ['ʃɔyərbyrstə] f scrubbing brush. **scheuern** v scrub, scour.

Scheune ['ʃɔynə] f (pl -n) barn.

Scheusal ['ʃɔyzal] neut (pl -e) monster.

scheußlich ['ʃɔysliç] adj horrible, hideous. **Scheußlichkeit** f hideousness.

Schicht [ʃiçt] f (pl -en) layer; (Arbeit) shift; (Gesellschaft) class. **-arbeit** f shift work. **-holz** neut plywood. **-ung** f stratification; (fig) classification.

schick [ʃik] adj elegant, chic, smart.

schicken ['ʃikən] v send. **sich schicken** (sich gehören) suit, be becoming; (sich entwickeln) happen.

schicklich ['ʃikliç] adj becoming, fit, proper. **Schicklichkeit** f fitness, propriety.

Schicksal ['ʃikzal] neut (pl -e) fate, destiny. **-sschlag** m stroke of fate, blow.

Schiebedach ['ʃiːbədax] *neut* sliding roof; (*Mot*) sun-roof. **schieben** *v* push; (*Schuld*) pass on; (*Arbeit*) put off. **Schiebetür** *f* sliding door.

Schieds||**gericht** ['ʃiːtsgəriçt] *neut* arbitration court, tribunal. **-richter** *m* arbitrator. (*Sport*) referee, umpire. **-spruch** *m* arbitration, award.

schief [ʃiːf] *adj* slanting, sloping; (*fig*) wrong, amiss.

Schiefer ['ʃiːfər] *m* (*pl* -) slate.

*****schiefgehen** *v* go wrong *or* amiss.

schielen ['ʃiːlən] *v* squint. **Schielen** *neut* (*Med*) strabismus, squint.

Schienbein ['ʃiːnbain] *neut* shin(bone).

Schiene ['ʃiːnə] *f* (*pl* -n) rail; (*Med*) splint.

*****schießen** ['ʃiːsən] *v* shoot. **Schieß**||**en** *neut* shooting. **-erei** *f* gunfight.

Schiff [ʃif] *neut* (*pl* -e) ship; (*Kirche*) nave. **-ahrt** *f* navigation; (*Verkehr*) shipping. **-bau** *m* shipbuilding. **-bruch** *m* shipwreck. **-brüchig** *adj* shipwrecked. **Schiffs**||**küche** *f* galley. **-raum** *m* hold; (*Inhalt*) tonnage. **-verkehr** *m* shipping. **-werft** *f* shipyard.

Schikane [ʃiˈkaːnə] *f* (*pl* -n) chicanery. **schikanieren** *v* make trouble for.

Schild[1] [ʃilt] *m* (*pl* -e) shield.

Schild[2] *neut* (*pl* -er) sign; (*Namen-*) name-plate; (*Flasche*) label; (*Mütze*) peak.

schildern ['ʃildərn] *v* depict, describe. **Schilderung** *f* depiction, description. **Schildkröte** *f* turtle; (*Land*) tortoise.

Schilf [ʃilf] *neut* (*pl* -e) reed.

Schilling ['ʃiliŋ] *m* (*pl* -e) (Austrian) Schilling.

Schimmel ['ʃiməl] *m* (*pl* -) mildew, mould. **schimmel**||**ig** *adj* mouldy. **-n** *v* become mouldy.

Schimmer ['ʃimər] *m* (*pl* -) glimmer, gleam. **schimmern** *v* gleam, shine.

Schimpanse [ʃimˈpanzə] *m* (*pl* -n) chimpanzee.

Schimpf [ʃimpf] *m* (*pl* -e) abuse, insult. **schimpfen** *v* swear, curse; (*umg.: tadeln*) curse, scold. **Schimpfwort** *neut* swearword.

*****schinden** ['ʃindən] *v* (*ausnützen*) exploit. **sich schinden** work hard, slave.

Schinken ['ʃiŋkən] *m* (*pl* -) ham.

Schippe ['ʃipə] *f* (*pl* -n) shovel; (*Karten*) spade(s).

Schirm [ʃirm] *m* (*pl* -e) (*Regen-*) umbrella; (*Lampen-*) shade; (*Bild-*) screen; (*Mütze*) peak; (*fig: Schutz*) protection. **schirmen** *v* protect, screen.

schizophren [ʃitsoˈfreːn] *adj* schizophrenic. **Schizophrenie** *f* schizophrenia.

Schlacht [ʃlaxt] *f* (*pl* -en) battle. **schlachten** *v* slaughter.

Schlächter ['ʃleçtər] *m* (*pl* -) butcher. **Schlacht**||**feld** *neut* battlefield. **-hof** *m* slaughterhouse. **-schiff** *neut* battleship.

Schlaf [ʃlaːf] *m* sleep. **-anzug** *m* pyjamas *pl*. **schlafen** *v* sleep. **-d** *adj* sleeping; (*fig*) dormant. **Schlafenszeit** *f* bedtime.

Schläfer ['ʃleːfər] *m* (*pl* -) sleeper.

schlaff [ʃlaf] *adj* slack; (*fig*) lax; (*welk*) limp.

Schlaf||**losigkeit** *f* sleeplessness, insomnia. **-mittel** *neut* sleeping pill.

schläfrig ['ʃleːfriç] *adj* sleepy.

Schlaf||**wagen** *m* sleeping car. **-zimmer** *neut* bedroom.

Schlag [ʃlaːk] *m* (*pl* Schläge) blow, stroke; (*Elek*) shock; (*Med*) stroke; (*Art*) sort, kind. **schlagen** *v* hit, strike; (*besiegen*) beat, defeat; (*mit der Faust*) punch; (*Vögel*) warble, sing; (*Wurzel*) take root. **kurz und klein schlagen** smash to pieces. **Alarm schlagen** sound the alarm. **nach jemandem schlagen** take after someone. **Schlagen** *neut* striking, hitting. **schlagend** *adj* striking; (*fig*) impressive; (*entscheidend*) decisive. **Schlager** *m* (*pl* -) (great) success, hit; (*Musik*) hit (song).

Schläger ['ʃleːgər] *m* (*pl* -) (*Tennis*) racket; (*Golf*) club; (*Kochen*) beater; (*Raufbold*) rowdy.

schlagfertig ['ʃlaːkfertiç] *adj* quick-witted. **Schlag**||**instrument** *neut* percussion instrument. **-sahne** *f* whipped cream. **-wort** *neut* slogan. **-zeile** *f* headline. **-zeug** *neut* percussion (instrument).

Schlamm [ʃlam] *m* (*pl* -e) mud. **schlammig** *adj* muddy.

Schlampe ['ʃlampə] *f* (*pl* -n) slut. **schlampig** *adj* slovenly.

Schlange ['ʃlaŋə] *f* (*pl* -n) snake; (*Reihe Menschen*) queue, (*US*) line. **Schlange stehen** *v* queue, (*US*) line up. **Schlangen**||**gift** *neut* snake venom. **-leder** *neut* snakeskin.

schlank [ʃlaŋk] *adj* slender, slim. **Schlank**||**heit** *f* slenderness, slimness. **-skur** *f* (reducing) diet.

schlapp [ʃlap] *adj* slack, limp.
schlau [ʃlau] *adj* cunning, sly, clever. **Schlauheit** *f* cunning, slyness.
Schlauch [ʃlaux] *m* (*pl* **Schläuche**) hose; (*Reifen*) inner tube.
schlecht [ʃlɛçt] *adj* bad; (*unwohl*) ill; (*Qualität*) poor, inferior; (*Luft*) stale, foul. **mir ist schlecht** I feel ill. **–gelaunt** *adj* bad-tempered. **Schlechtigkeit** *f* wickedness. **Schlechtheit** *f* badness. **schlechthin** *adv* simply, plainly.
Schlegel [ʃleːgəl] *m* (*pl* -) (wooden) mallet; (*Trommel*) drumstick.
*****schleichen** [ʃlaiçən] *v* creep; (*heimlich*) slink, sneak.
Schleier [ʃlaiər] *m* (*pl* -) veil.
Schleife [ʃlaifə] *f* (*pl* -n) loop, slip-knot; (*Band*) bow.
*****schleifen**[1] [ʃlaifən] *v* slide, glide, slip.
schleifen[2] *v* (*schleppen*) drag; (*Messer*) sharpen, grind; (*Edelstein*) cut.
Schleim [ʃlaim] *m* (*pl* -e) slime; (*Med*) mucus. **schleimig** *adj* slimy; mucous.
*****schließen** [ʃliːsən] *v* slit; (*spalten*) split; (*reißen*) rip, tear.
schlendern [ʃlɛndərn] *v* saunter. **Schlendrian** *m* (*pl* -) (*umg.*) old routine.
Schleppboot [ʃlɛpboːt] *neut* tug(boat). **schleppen** *v* drag, pull; (*tragen*) carry, lug. **sich schleppen** *v* drag oneself along.
Schlesien [ʃleːziən] *neut* Silesia.
Schleuder [ʃlɔydər] *f* (*pl* -n) sling, catapult; (*Wäsche*) spin-drier, spinner; (*Zentrifuge*) centrifuge. **–preis** *m* cut-price, give-away price. **schleudern** *v* sling, hurl; (*Mot*) skid; (*Wäsche*) spin-dry; (*Komm*) dump, sell off cheap.
schleunig [ʃlɔyniç] *adj* prompt, speedy.
Schleuse [ʃlɔyzə] *f* (*pl* -n) sluice; (*Kanal*) lock.
schlicht [ʃliçt] *adj* simple, plain; (*bescheiden*) modest. **–en** *v* (*glätten*) smooth; (*ebnen*) level; (*Streit*) settle. **Schlichtung** *f* (*pl* -en) settlement.
*****schließen** [ʃliːsən] *v* close, shut; (*mit dem Schlüssel*) lock; (*zum Schluß bringen*) close, end, conclude; (*folgern*) conclude, infer. **Schließfach** *neut* (*Bank*) safe-deposit box. **schließlich** *adv* finally, (at) last.
schlimm [ʃlim] *adj* bad. **schlimmstenfalls** *adv* at worst.
Schlinge [ʃliŋə] *f* (*pl* -n) noose, loop; (*Jagd, fig*) snare, trap.

*****schlingen**[1] [ʃliŋən] *v* wind; (*flechten*) twist; (*verknüpfen*) tie, knot.
*****schlingen**[2] *v* (*schlucken*) swallow; (*gierig essen*) devour, wolf.
Schlitten [ʃlitən] *m* (*pl* -) sledge. **Schlittschuh** *m* skate. **Schlittschuh laufen** skate.
Schlitz [ʃlits] *m* (*pl* -e) slit; (*Münzeinwurf*) slot; (*Hosen-*) fly.
Schloß [ʃlɔs] *neut* (*pl* **Schlösser**) lock; (*Burg*) castle.
Schlosser [ʃlɔsər] *m* (*pl* -) fitter, mechanic, locksmith.
Schlot [ʃloːt] *m* (*pl* -e) chimney.
schlott(e)rig [ʃlɔt(ə)riç] *adj* (*wackelig*) wobbly, shaky; (*schlaff*) loose; (*kleider*) baggy.
Schluck [ʃluk] *m* (*pl* -e) sip, gulp, mouthful. **–auf** *m* hiccup. **schlucken** *v* swallow.
Schlund [ʃlunt] *m* (*pl* **Schlünde**) throat; (*geog*) abyss, gorge; (*fig*) gulf.
schlüpfen [ʃlypfən] *v* slip, slide. **Schlüpfer** *m* knickers *pl*. **schlüpfrig** *adj* slippery; (*fig*) lewd.
Schlupfwinkel [ʃlupfviŋkəl] *m* hiding place.
Schluß [ʃlus] *m* (*pl* **Schlüsse**) end, close; (*Folgerung*) inference, conclusion. **zum Schluß** finally. **Schluß machen** stop, finish.
Schlüssel [ʃlysəl] *m* (*pl* -) key; (*Musik*) clef; (*Tech*) spanner, (*US*) wrench. **–bein** *neut* collarbone. **–bund** *m* bunch of keys. **–loch** *neut* keyhole. **–ring** *m* keyring.
Schluß]prüfung *f* final examination, finals *pl*. **–runde** *f* (*Sport*) final. **–verkauf** *m* end-of-season sale.
Schmach [ʃmax] *f* disgrace, dishonour.
schmächtig [ʃmɛçtiç] *adj* slim, slender.
schmackhaft [ʃmakhaft] *adj* appetizing, delicious.
schmal [ʃmaːl] *adj* narrow, thin, slender; (*fig*) scanty, poor.
Schmalz [ʃmalts] *neut* (*pl* -e) fat, grease, dripping; (*fig*) sentimentality.
schmarotzen [ʃmaˈrɔtsən] *v* (*umg.*) sponge, scrounge. **Schmarotzer** *m* (*Tier, Pflanze*) parasite; (*Person*) scrounger, parasite.
schmatzen [ʃmatsən] *v* smack one's lips, eat noisily; (*küssen*) give a smacking kiss.
schmecken [ˈʃmɛkən] *v* taste; (*gut*) taste good. **schmecken nach** taste of. (*wie*)

schmeckt es? do you like it? **es schmeckt (mir)** I like it, it's good.

Schmeichelei [ʃmaɪçə'laɪ] f (pl -en) flattery. **schmeicheln** v flatter. **Schmeichler** m (pl -) flatterer. **schmeichlerisch** adj flattering.

*****schmeißen** ['ʃmaɪsən] v throw, cast; (umg.) chuck; (Schlagen) strike, smash.

Schmelz [ʃmɛlts] m (pl -e) (Email) enamel; (Glasur) glaze; (Stimme, Töne) mellowness, sweetness. **schmelzen** v melt; (Erz) smelt.

Schmerz [ʃmɛrts] m (pl -en) pain; (seelisch) grief, pain. **Schmerzen haben** be in pain. **schmerzen** v hurt; (seelisch) grieve, pain. **schmerz‖haft** adj painful. **-lich** adj painful, hurtful. **-los** adj painless.

Schmetterling ['ʃmɛtərlɪŋ] m (pl -e) butterfly. **-sschwimmen** neut butterfly (stroke).

Schmied [ʃmiːt] m (pl -e) (black)smith. **Schmiede** f (pl -n) forge, smithy. **-eisen** neut wrought iron. **schmieden** v forge; (Pläne) devise.

Schmiere ['ʃmiːrə] f (pl -n) grease; (Theater, umg.) small (touring) company. **schmieren** v grease; (ölen) oil, lubricate; (streichen) spread. **Schmierung** f (pl -en) lubrication.

Schminke ['ʃmɪŋkə] f (pl -n) make-up. **schminken** v make up. **sich schminken** put on make-up; make oneself up.

Schmorbraten ['ʃmɔːrbraːtən] m stewed steak, pot roast. **schmoren** v stew, braise.

Schmuck [ʃmʊk] m (pl -e) ornament, decoration; (Juwelen) jewellery. **schmücken** ['ʃmʏkən] v adorn, decorate; (Kleider) trim.

schmuggeln ['ʃmʊgəln] v smuggle. **Schmuggelware** f contraband. **Schmuggler** m (pl -) smuggler.

Schmus [ʃmuːs] m (umg.) (empty) chatter, soft-soap; **schmusen** v chatter, soft-soap.

Schmutz [ʃmʊts] m dirt, filth. **schmutzig** adj dirty, filthy. **Schmutzpresse** f gutter press.

Schnabel ['ʃnaːbəl] m (pl Schnäbel) bill, beak.

Schnalle ['ʃnalə] f (pl -n) clasp; (Schuh, Gürtel) buckle; (Tür) latch. **schnallen** v buckle.

schnappen ['ʃnapən] v snap; (erwischen) grab, catch. **nach Luft schnappen** gasp for air.

schnarchen ['ʃnarçən] v snore.

schnattern ['ʃnatərn] v (Geflügel) cackle; (Menschen) prattle.

schnaufen ['ʃnaʊfən] v pant, puff.

Schnauze ['ʃnaʊtsə] f (pl -n) snout, muzzle; (Kanne) spout. **halt die Schnauze!** (vulgär) shut up! belt up!

Schnecke ['ʃnɛkə] f (pl -n) snail; (nackte) slug.

Schnee [ʃneː] m snow. **-glöckchen** neut snowdrop. **-lawine** f avalanche. **-mann** m snowman. **-schläger** m egg whisk. **-schuh** m ski. **-sturm** m blizzard. **-wehe** f snowdrift.

schneien ['ʃnaɪən] v snow.

schnell [ʃnɛl] adj fast, quick. **mach schnell!** hurry up! get a move on! **Schnellboot** neut speedboat. **schnellen** v jerk, spring. **Schnell‖gaststätte** f fastfood restaurant, cafeteria. **-igkeit** f speed. **-imbiß** m snack. **-zug** m express train.

Schneide ['ʃnaɪdə] f (pl -n) (cutting) edge. **schneiden** v cut; (Braten) carve. **Schneider** m (pl -e) tailor. **-ei** f (pl -en) tailor's shop. **-in** f (pl -nen) dressmaker, seamstress.

schnippisch ['ʃnɪpɪʃ] adj pert, saucy.

Schnitt [ʃnɪt] m (pl -e) cut; (Scheibe) slice; (Art) style; (Math) intersection; (Zeichnung) (cross-)section. **-lauch** m chive(s). **-ling** m (Bot) cutting.

Schnitzel ['ʃnɪtsəl] neut (pl -) chip, shaving; (Fleisch) cutlet, escalope.

schnitzen ['ʃnɪtsən] v carve (wood). **Schnitzer** m carver; (Fehler) blunder, bloomer.

Schnörkel ['ʃnœrkəl] m (pl -) flourish, (Kunst, Architektur) scroll.

schnüffeln ['ʃnʏfəln] v snuffle, sniff; (fig) snoop, nose around.

Schnuller ['ʃnʊlər] m (pl -) (baby's) dummy, (US) pacifier.

schnupfen ['ʃnʊpfən] v take snuff. **Schnupfen** m (pl -) catarrh, (head) cold. **einen Schnupfen bekommen/haben** catch/have a cold. **Schnupftabak** m snuff.

Schnur [ʃnuːr] f (pl Schnüre) string, cord; (Elek) flex, wire.

schnüren ['ʃnyːrən] v tie (up), fasten.

schnurgerade ['ʃnurgəraɪdə] *adj, adv* (as) straight (as a die).

Schnurrbart ['ʃnurbaɪrt] *m* moustache.

schnurren ['ʃnurən] *v* hum, buzz; (*Katze*) purr.

Schock [ʃɔk] *m (pl -s or -e)* shock. **schokieren** *v* shock, scandalize.

Schokolade [ʃoko'laːdə] *f (pl -n)* chocolate.

Scholle ['ʃɔlə] *f (pl -n)* (*Erde*) clod, clump; (*Eis*) floe; (*Fisch*) plaice; (*fig*) native soil, home.

schon [ʃoːn] *adv* already; (*bestimmt*) certainly; (*zwar*) indeed. **schon lange** for a long time. **schon lange her** a long time ago. **ich komme schon!** I'm coming! **schon wieder** yet again. **schon der Name** the mere name, the name alone.

schön [ʃøːn] *adj* beautiful, pretty; (*Wetter*) fine, fair. **danke schön** thank you. **bitte schön** (if you) please. **schön machen** beautify.

schonen ['ʃoːnən] *v* spare; treat carefully, go carefully with. **-d** *adj* considerate, careful.

Schönheit ['ʃøːnhaɪt] *f (pl -en)* beauty. **Schönheits‖fehler** *m* blemish, flaw. **-königin** *f* beauty queen. **-pflege** *f* beauty treatment.

Schonkost ['ʃoːnkɔst] *f* (bland) diet.

Schopf [ʃɔpf] *m (pl Schöpfe)* shock, tuft.

schöpfen ['ʃœpfən] *v* scoop, ladle; (*Atem*) take, draw; (*Mut*) take.

Schöpfer¹ ['ʃœpfər] *m (pl -)* creator.

Schöpfer² *m (pl -)* (*zum Schöpfen*) scoop.

schöpferisch ['ʃœpfərɪʃ] *adj* creative.

Schöpflöffel ['ʃœpflœfəl] *m* ladle.

Schöpfung ['ʃœpfuŋ] *f* creation.

Schornstein ['ʃɔrnstaɪn] *m* chimney. **-feger** *m* chimney-sweep. **-kappe** *f* chimney-pot.

Schoß¹ [ʃoːs] *m (pl Schöße)* lap; (*fig*) bosom. **-hund** *m* lap-dog.

Schoß² [ʃɔs] *m (pl Schosse)* (*Bot*) shoot, sprout.

Schote ['ʃoːtə] *f (pl -n)* pod. **Schoten** *pl* (green) peas.

Schotte ['ʃɔtə] *m (pl -n)* Scot, Scotsman. **Schottin** *f (pl -nen)* Scot, Scotswoman. **schottisch** *adj* Scottish, Scots. **Schottland** *neut* Scotland.

schräg [ʃrɛːk] *adj* sloping, slanting, oblique.

Schrank [ʃraŋk] *m (pl Schränke)* cupboard; (*Kleider*) wardrobe.

Schranke ['ʃraŋkə] *f (pl -n)* barrier, bar. **schrankenlos** *adj* limitless, boundless.

Schraube ['ʃraʊbə] *f (pl -n)* screw. **Schraubdeckel** *m* screw-cap. **Schrauben‖schlüssel** *m* spanner, (*US*) wrench. **-zieher** *m* screwdriver.

Schrebergarten ['ʃreːbərɡartən] *m* allotment (garden).

Schreck [ʃrɛk] *m (pl -e)* or **Schrecken** *m (pl -)* fright, terror. **einen Schreck bekommen/kriegen** receive/get a fright. **schrecken** *v* terrify, frighten. **schrecklich** *adj* terrible, frightful.

Schrei [ʃraɪ] *m (pl -e)* cry, shout, scream. **schreien** *v* cry, shout; (*kreischen*) shriek, screech; (*weinen*) cry, weep.

*schreiben ['ʃraɪbən] *v* write; (*buchstabieren*) spell. **schreibfaul** *adj* lazy about writing (letters). **Schreib‖fehler** *m* spelling error. **-krampf** *m* writer's cramp. **-maschine** *f* typewriter. **-tisch** *m* desk. **-ung** *f (pl -en)* spelling. **-waren** *pl* stationery *sing*.

Schrein [ʃraɪn] *m (pl -e)* (*Kasten*) chest, box; (*Reliquien*) shrine. **-er** *m (pl -)* joiner, carpenter.

*schreiten ['ʃraɪtən] *v* stride, step.

Schrift [ʃrɪft] *f (pl -en)* writing; (*Handschrift*) handwriting; (*Geschriebenes*) pamphlet, paper; (*Art*) script, type. **schriftlich** *adj* in writing, written. **Schrift‖steller** *m (pl -)*, **Schriftstellerin** *f (pl -nen)* writer, author. **-stück** *neut* document, paper.

Schritt [ʃrɪt] *m (pl -e)* step, stride; (*Gangart*) gait; (*Tempo*) pace. **Schritt halten mit** keep pace with. **Schrittmacher** *m (fig, Med)* pacemaker. **schrittweise** *adv* step-by-step.

schroff [ʃrɔf] *adj* steep, precipitous; (*fig*) gruff, surly.

Schrot [ʃroːt] *m or neut (pl -e)* (*Getreide*) groats *pl*; (*Bleikügelchen*) (buck)shot. **-brot** *neut* wholemeal bread.

Schrott [ʃrɔt] *m (pl -e)* scrap (metal).

schrubben ['ʃrubən] *v* scrub.

schrumpfen ['ʃrumpfən] *v* shrink. **Schrumpfung** *f* shrinking, contraction.

Schub [ʃuːp] *m (pl Schübe)* shove, push; (*Tech*) thrust. **-fach** *neut* drawer. **-karren** *m* wheelbarrow. **-lade** *f* drawer.

schüchtern ['ʃʏçtərn] *adj* shy. **Schüchternheit** *f* shyness.

Schuft [ʃuft] m (pl -e) rascal, rogue. **schuften** v (umg.) toil, sweat, graft.

Schuh [ʃuː] m (pl -e) shoe. –**krem** f shoe polish. –**macher** m shoemaker. –**werk** neut footwear.

Schul‖arbeit f homework, task. –**buch** neut school book.

schuld [ʃult] adj guilty. **schuld haben** be guilty. **Schuld** f (pl -en) (Geld, fig) debt; (Rel, Jur) guilt. **schuld sein an** be to blame for. **Schulden haben** be in debt. **die Schuld schieben auf** push the blame onto. **schulden** v owe. **Schuldgefühl** neut sense of guilt. **schuldig** adj guilty; (Geld) indebted. **Schuldig‖e(r)** guilty person, culprit. –**keit** f (unz.) obligation; (Pflicht) duty. –**sprechung** f conviction, verdict of guilty.

Schuldirektor m headmaster. –**in** f headmistress.

schuldlos ['ʃultlɔɪs] adj innocent. **Schuld‖ner** m (pl -), –**nerin** f (pl -nen) debtor. –**schein** m promissory note, IOU.

Schule ['ʃuːlə] f (pl -n) school. **schulen** v school, train.

Schüler ['ʃyːlə] m (pl -) schoolboy; (bei einem Meister) pupil; (Rel) disciple. –**in** f (pl -nen) schoolgirl; pupil; disciple.

Schul‖fach neut (school) subject. –**ferien** pl school holidays. **schulfrei haben** have a holiday. **Schul‖freund** m school friend. –**geld** neut school fees. –**hof** m (school) playground. –**junge** m schoolboy. –**lehrer** m (pl -), –**lehrerin** f (pl -nen) schoolteacher. –**mädchen** neut schoolgirl. –**schluß** m end of term, breaking-up.

Schulter ['ʃultə] f (pl -en) shoulder. –**blatt** neut shoulder blade.

Schulung ['ʃuːluŋ] f (pl -en) schooling, training. **Schul‖wesen** neut educational system. –**zimmer** neut classroom, schoolroom.

Schund [ʃunt] m trash, rubbish.

Schuppe ['ʃupə] f (pl -n) scale. **Schuppen** pl dandruff. **schuppig** adj scaly.

schüren ['ʃyːrən] v stir up, incite; (Feuer) poke, stoke.

schürfen ['ʃyrfən] v (Haut) scratch, graze; (Metall) prospect. **Schürfung** f (pl -en) graze, abrasion; prospecting.

Schurke ['ʃurkə] m (pl -n) villain, scoundrel.

Schürze ['ʃyrtsə] f (pl -n) apron.

Schuß [ʃus] m (pl Schüsse) shot. –**loch** neut bullet-hole. –**waffe** f firearm. –**weite** f range. –**wunde** f gunshot wound.

Schüssel ['ʃysəl] f (pl -n) bowl, dish.

Schuster ['ʃuːstər] m (pl -) cobbler, shoemaker.

Schutt [ʃut] m (Trümmer) debris; (Abfall) refuse.

schütteln ['ʃytəln] v shake.

schütten ['ʃytən] v pour (out). **es schüttet** it's pouring (with rain).

schüttern ['ʃytərn] v tremble, shake.

Schutz [ʃuts] m (pl -e) protection; (Obdach) shelter; (Schirm) screen. –**anzug** m protective clothing. –**brille** f goggles pl.

Schütze ['ʃytsə] m (pl -n) marksman, sharpshooter; (Bogen) archer. **schützen** v protect, defend; (behüten) guard.

Schutz‖farbe f camouflage. –**heilige(r)** m patron saint.

Schützling ['ʃytslɪŋ] m (pl -e) protégé(e), charge.

schutzlos ['ʃutslɔːs] adj defenceless. **Schutz‖mann** m policeman. –**maßnahme** f precaution, preventive measure. –**mittel** neut preservative. –**umschlag** m (Book) jacket, dust cover.

Schwabe ['ʃvaːbə] m (pl -n) Swabian (man). –**n** neut Swabia.

Schwäbin ['ʃvɛːbɪn] f (pl -nen) Swabian woman. **schwäbisch** adj Swabian.

schwach [ʃvax] adj weak; (kränklich) delicate, sickly; (klein) small; (gering) scanty, poor.

Schwäche ['ʃvɛçə] f (pl -n) weakness. **schwächen** v weaken.

Schwachheit ['ʃvaxhait] f (pl -en) weakness.

schwächlich ['ʃvɛçlɪç] adj feeble, sickly, delicate.

Schwachsinn ['ʃvaxzɪn] m feeblemindedness. **schwachsinnig** adj feebleminded.

Schwager ['ʃvaːgər] m (pl Schwäger) brother-in-law.

Schwägerin ['ʃvɛːgərɪn] f (pl -nen) sister-in-law.

Schwalbe ['ʃvalbə] f (pl -n) (Vogel) swallow.

Schwall [ʃval] m (pl -e) flood, torrent.

Schwamm [ʃvam] m (pl Schwämme) sponge.

Schwan [ʃvaɪn] m (pl Schwäne) swan.

schwanger ['ʃvaŋər] *adj* pregnant. **Schwangere** *f* (*pl* -n) pregnant woman. **Schwangerschaft** *f* pregnancy. –**vorsorge** *f* ante-natal care.

schwanken ['ʃvaŋkən] *v* sway, swing; (*taumeln*) stagger, reel; (*zögern*) waver; (*Preise*) fluctuate. –**d** *adj* (*Person*) wavering. **Schwankung** *f* (*pl* en) swaying, wavering, fluctuation.

Schwanz [ʃvants] *m* (*pl* **Schwänze**) tail.

Schwarm [ʃvarm] *m* (*pl* **Schwärme**) swarm; (*Vogel*) flock; (*Fische*) shoal; (*Rind, Schaf*) herd; (*Menschen*) crowd; (*fig*) craze.

schwärmen ['ʃvermən] *v* swarm; (*fig*) deploy. **schwärmen für** rave about, gush over. **schwärmerisch** *adj* wildly enthusiastic.

schwarz [ʃvarts] *adj* black. **Schwarz** *neut* black (colour). –**brot** *neut* black bread. –**e**(r) *Black*, Negro.

Schwärze ['ʃvɛrtsə] *f* (*pl* -n) blackness; (*Druck*) printer's ink. **schwärz‖en** *v* blacken. –**lich** *adj* blackish, darkish.

Schwarz‖markt *m* black market. –**wald** *m* Black Forest. **schwarzweiß** *adj* black-and-white.

schwatzen ['ʃvatsən] *v* also **schwätzen** chatter, prattle; (*Geheimnisse*) gossip.

Schwebe ['ʃveːbə] *f* suspense. **in der Schwebe** *adj* undecided, pending. **schweben** *v* float, hover; (*hängen*) hang, be suspended; (*fig*) remain undecided.

Schwede ['ʃveːdə] *m* (*pl* -n), **Schwedin** *f* (*pl* -nen) Swede. **Schweden** *neut* Sweden. **schwedisch** *adj* Swedish.

Schwefel ['ʃveːfəl] *m* sulphur.

schweifen ['ʃvaifən] *v* roam, wander.

*****schweigen** ['ʃvaigən] *v* be silent. **ganz zu schweigen von** to say nothing of. **Schweigen** *neut* silence. **schweigsam** *adj* silent; (*fig*) secretive.

Schwein [ʃvain] *neut* (*pl* -e) pig; (*fig*) (good) luck. **Schweine‖braten** *m* roast pork. –**fett** *neut* lard. –**fleisch** *neut* pork. –**hund** *m* (*vulgär*) bastard, swine. –**rei** *f* filthy mess; (*fig*) dirty trick. –**stall** *m* pigsty. **Schweinsrippchen** *neut* pork chop.

Schweiß [ʃvais] *m* (*pl* -e) sweat, perspiration. **schweißen** *v* weld; (*Wild*) bleed.

Schweiz [ʃvaits] *f* **die Schweiz** Switzerland. **Schweizer** *m* (*pl* -), **Schweizerin** *f* (*pl* -nen) Swiss. **schweizerisch** *adj* Swiss.

Schwelle ['ʃvɛlə] *f* (*pl* -n) threshold; (*Eisenbahn*) sleeper.

*****schwellen** ['ʃvɛlən] *v* swell.

schwemmen ['ʃvɛmən] *v* wash down; (*Vieh*) water.

Schwengel ['ʃvɛŋəl] *m* (*pl* -) (*Glocke*) clapper; (*Pumpe*) pump handle.

schwenken ['ʃvɛŋkən] *v* turn; (*Fahne, Hut*) wave, flourish.

schwer [ʃveːr] *adj* heavy; (*schwierig*) difficult; (*ernst*) serious. **es ist 2 Kilo schwer** it weighs two kilos. **schwere Arbeit** hard work. –**beschädigt** *adj* seriously disabled. **Schwere** *f* weight. **schwerfällig** *adj* clumsy, awkward. **Schwergewichtler** *m* heavyweight. **schwerhörig** *adj* hard of hearing. **Schwer‖industrie** *f* heavy industry. –**kraft** *f* gravity. **schwer‖lich** *adj* with difficulty, hardly. –**mütig** *adj* melancholy, sad.

Schwert [ʃveːrt] *neut* (*pl* -er) sword.

Schwester ['ʃvestər] *f* (*pl* -n) sister. **schwesterlich** *adj* sisterly. **Schwesternschaft** *f* sisterhood.

Schwieger‖eltern *pl* parents-in-law; (*umg.*) in-laws. –**mutter** *m* mother-in-law. –**sohn** *m* son-in-law. –**tochter** *f* daughter-in-law. –**vater** *m* father-in-law.

schwierig ['ʃviːriç] *adj* difficult, hard. **Schwierigkeit** *f* (*pl* -en) difficulty.

Schwimmbad ['ʃvimbat] *neut* swimming pool. **Schwimmbecken** *neut* swimming pool. **schwimmen** *v* swim; (*Gegenstand*) float. **Schwimmen** *neut* swimming. **schwimmend** *adj* swimming; floating. **Schwimmer** *m* (*pl* -) swimmer; float.

Schwindel ['ʃvindəl] *m* (*pl* -) giddiness; (*Täuschung*) swindle, fraud. **schwindel‖haft** *adj* giddy; fraudulent. –**ig** *adj* giddy, dizzy. **schwindeln** *v* cheat, swindle. **mir schwindelt** I feel giddy. **Schwindler** *m* (*pl* -) swindler, cheat.

*****schwingen** ['ʃviŋən] *v* swing; (*Fahne, Waffe*) wave, flourish. **Schwingung** *f* (*pl* -en) oscillation, vibration.

schwitzen ['ʃvitsən] *v* sweat.

*****schwören** ['ʃvøːrən] *v* swear.

schwul [ʃvuːl] *adj* (*vulgär*) queer, homosexual.

schwül [ʃvyːl] *adj* sultry, hot and humid.

Schwulst [ʃvulst] *m* (*pl* **Schwülste**) bombast, pomposity. **schwülstig** *adj* bombastic, pompous.

Schwund [ʃvunt] *m* contraction, shrinkage; (*Med*) atrophy.

Schwung [ʃvuŋ] m (pl **Schwünge**) impetus, momentum; (fig) drive, vitality, verve. **–kraft** f centrifugal force; (fig) verve. **–rad** neut flywheel.

Schwur [ʃvuːr] m (pl **Schwüre**) oath. **–gericht** neut court with jury.

sechs [zɛks] pron, adj six. **sechst** adj sixth. **Sechstel** neut sixth (part).

sechzehn [ˈzɛçtseːn] pron, adj sixteen. **sechzehnte** adj sixteenth.

sechzig [ˈzɛçtsɪç] pron, adj sixty. **die sechziger Jahre** the '60s. **sechzigst** adj sixtieth.

See [zeː] **1** m (pl **-n**) lake. **2** f (pl **-n**) sea. **–fahrt** f voyage. **–jungfer** f mermaid. **seekrank** adj seasick.

Seele [ˈzeːlə] f (pl **-n**) soul, spirit. **seelisch** adj spiritual.

See‖löwe m sealion. **–räuber** m pirate. **–wasser** neut sea water.

Segel [ˈzeːgəl] neut (pl **-**) sail. **–boot** neut sailing boat. **–flugzeug** neut glider, sailplane. **segeln** v sail. **Segeltuch** neut canvas.

Segen [ˈzeːgən] m (pl **-**) blessing; (Tischgebet) grace. **segnen** v bless. **Segnung** f (pl **-en**) blessing.

***sehen** [ˈzeːən] v see; (anblicken) look; (beobachten) watch, observe. **sehen lassen** display, show. **Sehen** neut (eye)sight, vision. **–swürdigkeit** f (tourist) sight. **Seh‖feld** neut field of vision. **–kraft** f eyesight, vision.

Sehne [ˈzeːnə] f (pl **-n**) sinew, tendon; (Bogen) string.

sehnen [ˈzeːnən] v **sich sehnen nach** long for.

sehr [zeːr] adv very.

Sehweite [ˈzeːvaɪtə] f range of vision.

seicht [zaɪçt] adj shallow.

Seide [ˈzaɪdə] f (pl **-n**) silk.

Seife [ˈzaɪfə] f (pl **-n**) soap. **Seifen‖schaum** m lather. **–wasser** neut suds pl, soapy water.

Seil [zaɪl] neut (pl **-e**) rope; (Kabel) cable. **–bahn** f funicular.

sein¹ [zaɪn] adj, pron his, its. **seinerseits** adv on or for his part. **seinesgleichen** pron the likes of him pl, people like him pl. **seinethalben, seinetwegen,** or **seinetwillen** for his sake. **seinige** pron **der, die, das seinige** his.

***sein²** v be. **es sei denn, daß** unless, kann **sein** perhaps. **sein lassen** leave alone. **mir ist kalt/warm** I feel cold/warm.

seit [zaɪt] prep since. **–dem** conj since; adv since then. **seit damals** since then. **seit wann?** since when? **seit zwei Jahren** for two years.

Seite [ˈzaɪtə] f (pl **-n**) side; (Buch) page. **auf die Seite bringen** put aside. **von seiten** on the part (of). **Seiten‖lampe** f side lamp. **–schiff** neut aisle. **–straße** f side street. **–wagen** m sidecar.

seither [zaɪtˈheːr] adv since then.

seitlich [ˈzaɪtlɪç] adj lateral, side. **seitwärts** adv sideways.

Sekretär [zekreˈtɛːr] m (pl **-e**) secretary; (Schreibschrank) bureau, locking desk. **–in** f (pl **-nen**) secretary.

Sekt [zɛkt] m (pl **-e**) sparkling wine.

Sekte [ˈzɛktə] f (pl **-n**) sect. **sektiererisch** adj sectarian.

sekundär [zekʊnˈdɛːr] adj secondary.

Sekunde [zeˈkʊndə] f (pl **-n**) second.

selber [ˈzɛlbər] V **selbst**.

selbst [zɛlpst] pron self. adv even. **ich selbst** I myself. **von selbst** on one's own accord; (Sache) by itself. **sie kann es selbst machen** she can do it by herself. **selbst wenn** even though. **Selbst** neut self. **–achtung** f self-respect.

selbständig [ˈzɛlpstɛndɪç] adj independent. **Selbständigkeit** f independence.

Selbst‖bedienung f self-service. **–beherrschung** f self-control. **–mitleid** f self-pity. **–bestimmung** f self-determination.

selbstbewußt adj self-confident; (eingebildet) conceited. **Selbstbewußtsein** neut self-confidence; conceit.

Selbsterkenntnis f self-knowledge.

selbst‖gebacken adj home-made. **–gefällig** adj self-satisfied. **–gerecht** adj self-righteous.

Selbsthilfe f self-help; (Jur) self-defence.

selbst‖klebend adj adhesive, gummed. **–los** adj selfless.

Selbst‖mord m suicide. **–mörder** m suicide. **–schutz** m self-defence.

selbstsicher adj self-confident. **Selbstsicherheit** f self-confidence.

Selbstsucht f selfishness. **selbstsüchtig** adj selfish.

Selbst‖täuschung f self-deception. **–versorgung** f self-sufficiency.

selbstverständlich adj self-evident. adv obviously, naturally.

Selbstvertrauen neut self-confidence.

siedeln

selig ['zeɪlɪç] *adj* blessed; (*verstorben*) late, deceased; (*überglücklich*) blissful, delighted.

Sellerie ['zɛlərɪ] *f* (*pl* -n) *or m* (*pl* -s) celeriac. – **stangen** *pl* celery sing.

selten ['zɛltən] *adj* rare. *adv* rarely, seldom.

seltsam ['zɛltzaɪm] *adj* strange, odd, curious.

Semester [ze'mɛstər] *neut* (*pl* -) semester, (half-yearly) session.

Seminar [zemi'naɪr] *neut* (*pl* -e) training college; tutorial group.

Semit [ze'miɪt] *m* (*pl* -en) Semite. **semitisch** *adj* Semitic.

Semmel ['zɛməl] *f* (*pl* -n) bread roll.

Senat [ze'naɪt] *m* (*pl* -e) senate. – **or** *m* (*pl* -en) senator.

*senden ['zɛndən] *v* send; (*Funk*) transmit, broadcast. **Sender** *m* (*pl* -) (*Gerät*) transmitter; (*Anstalt*) station. **Sendung** *f* (*pl* -en) package; (*Waren*) consignment; (*Funk*) broadcast.

Senf [zɛnf] *m* (*pl* -e) mustard.

sengen ['zɛŋən] *V* singe.

Senkblei ['zɛŋkblaɪ] *neut* plumb-line.

Senkel ['zɛŋkəl] *m* (*pl* -) (shoe)lace.

senken ['zɛŋkən] *v* lower; (*Kopf*) bow; (*Preise*) reduce. **sich senken** sink. **senkrecht** *adj* vertical, perpendicular. **Senkung** *f* (*pl* -en) sinking; (*Preise*) reduction; (*Vertiefung*) depression.

Sensation [zɛnzatsi'oɪn] *f* (*pl* -en) sensation. **sensationell** *adj* sensational.

Sense ['zɛnzə] *f* (*pl* -n) scythe.

sensibel [zɛn'ziːbəl] *adj* sensitive.

sentimental [zɛntimɛn'taɪl] *adj* sentimental.

separieren [zɛpa'riɪrən] *v* separate.

September [zɛp'tɛmbər] *m* (*pl* -) September.

septisch ['zɛptɪʃ] *adj* septic.

Serie ['zeɪriə] *f* (*pl* -n) series. – **nherstellung** *f* mass production.

seriös [zeri'øɪs] *adj* serious, earnest; (*Firma*) reliable, honourable.

Service[1] [zɛr'viɪs] *neut* (*pl* -) (dinner) service.

Service[2] *neut or m* (*pl* -s) (customer) service.

servieren [zɛr'viɪrən] *v* serve. **Servierwagen** *m* trolley. **Serviette** *f* (*pl* -n) (table) napkin.

Sesam ['zɛzaɪm] *m* sesame.

Sessel ['zɛsəl] *m* (*pl* -) armchair. – **lift** *m* chairlift.

seßhaft ['zɛshaft] *adj* settled, established; (*ansässig*) resident.

setzen ['zɛtsən] *v* set, put, place; (*einpflanzen*) plant; (*Druck*) compose, set; (*Spiel*) wager, bet. **in Bewegung setzen** set in motion. **außer Kraft setzen** invalidate. **in die Welt setzen** give birth to. **sich setzen** sit down. **sich in Verbindung setzen mit** get in contact with.

Seuche ['zɔʏçə] *f* (*pl* -n) epidemic.

seufzen ['zɔʏftsən] *v* sigh. **Seufzer** *m* (*pl* -) sigh.

Sex [zɛks] *m* (*pl* -) sex. **Sexualität** *f* sexuality. – **aufklärung** *f* sex education. **sexuell** *adj* sexual. **sexy** *adj* sexy.

sezieren [ze'tsiɪrən] *v* dissect.

sich [zɪç] *pron* himself, herself, itself, yourself, oneself, yourselves; themselves; (*miteinander*) (with) one another, each other. **an (und für) sich** in itself. **bei sich haben** have with one. **sich die Hände waschen** wash one's hands. **sie lieben sich** they love each other.

Sichel ['zɪçəl] *f* (*pl* -n) sickle; (*Mond*-) crescent.

sicher ['zɪçər] *adj* safe, secure; (*gewiß*) sure, certain. *adv* surely, certainly. **Sicherheit** *f* safety; certainty; trustworthiness; (*Pol, Psychol*) security. **Sicherheits**‖**bestimmungen** *pl* safety regulations. – **gurt** *m* safety belt. – **nadel** *f* safety pin. **sicherlich** *adv* surely, certainly. – **n** *v* secure; (*schützen*) protect. – **stellen** *v* secure, guarantee. **Sicherung** *f* (*pl* -en) protection; (*Elek*) fuse; (*Tech*) safety device.

Sicht [zɪçt] *f* (*unz.*) sight; (*Aussicht*) view; (*Sichtbarkeit*) visibility. **sichtbar** *adj* visible. **Sichtbarkeit** *f* visibility.

sickern ['zɪkərn] *v* trickle, seep.

sie [ziɪ] *pron* she, it; her; they; them. **Sie** *pron* you.

Sieb [ziɪp] *neut* (*pl* -e) sieve; (*Tee*) strainer.

sieben[1] ['ziɪbən] *v* sift, sieve.

sieben[2] *pron, adj* seven. **siebent or siebt** *adj* seventh.

siebzehn ['ziɪptsein] *pron, adj* seventeen. **siebzehnt** *adj* seventeenth.

siebzig ['ziɪptsɪç] *pron, adj* seventy. **siebzigt** *adj* seventieth.

siedeln ['ziɪdəln] *v* settle, colonize.

*sieden ['ziːdən] v boil. **Siedepunkt** m boiling point.

Siedler ['ziːdlər] m (pl -) settler. **Siedlung** f (pl -en) settlement (place); (am Stadtrand) housing estate.

Sieg [ziːk] m (pl -e) victory.

Siegel ['ziːgəl] neut (pl -) seal, signet.

siegen ['ziːgən] v win, triumph, be victorious. **Sieger** m (Mil) conqueror, victor; (Sport) winner. **siegreich** adj victorious.

Signal [zig'naːl] neut (pl -e) signal. **–feuer** neut beacon. **–rakete** f rocket-flare.

Signatur [zigna'tuːr] f (pl -en) mark, symbol; (Unterschrift) signature.

Silbe ['zilbə] f (pl -n) syllable.

Silber ['zilbər] neut silver. **silbern** adj silver.

Silvesterabend [zil'vestəraːbənt] m New Year's Eve.

simpel ['zimpəl] adj simple.

Sims [zims] neut (pl -e) (Fenster) window-sill.

simulieren [zimu'liːrən] v pretend; (Krankheit) malinger; (Tech) simulate.

Sinfonie [zinfo'niː] f (pl -n) symphony.

*singen ['ziŋən] v sing. **Singvogel** m songbird.

*sinken ['ziŋkən] v sink; (fig) diminish; (Preise) fall. **Sinken** neut fall, drop; (Werte) depreciation; (fig) decline.

Sinn [zin] m (pl -e) sense; (Gedanken) mind, thoughts pl. **es hat keinen Sinn** it makes no sense. **es kam mir in den Sinn, daß** ... it crossed my mind that .... **Sinn für Humor** sense of humour. **Sinn für Literatur** interest in literature. **Sinnbild** neut symbol. **sinn‖bildlich** adj symbolic. **–en** v reflect, think (over). **–lich** adj sensual. **–los** adj senseless. **Sinnspruch** m epigram, maxim.

Sippe ['zipə] f (pl -n) tribe; (Verwandte) kin.

Sirup ['ziːrup] m (pl -e) syrup.

Sitte ['zitə] f (pl -n) custom; (Gewohnheit) habit. **Sitten** pl morals. **Sittenlehre** f ethics. **sittenlos** adj immoral. **sittlich** adj moral. **Sittlichkeit** f morality. **–sverbrechen** neut indecent assault.

Situation [zituatsi'oːn] f (pl -en) situation.

Sitz [zits] m (pl -e) seat; (Kleidung) fit. **–bank** f bench. **sitzen** v sit; (Kleidung) fit. **–bleiben** v remain seated. **Sitzung** f (pl -en) sitting; (Versammlung) session.

Skala ['skaːla] f (pl Skalen) scale. **Skalenscheibe** f dial.

Skandal [skan'daːl] m (pl -e) scandal. **skandalös** adj scandalous.

Skandinavien [skandi'naːviən] neut Scandinavia. **Skandinavier** m (pl -), **Skandinavierin** f (pl -nen) Scandinavian. **skandinavisch** adj Scandinavian.

Skelett [ske'lɛt] neut (pl -e) skeleton.

Skeptiker ['skɛptikər] m (pl -) sceptic. **skeptisch** adj sceptical.

Ski [ʃiː] m (pl -er) ski. **–fahrer(in)** skier.

Skizze ['skitsə] f (pl -n) sketch. **skizzieren** v sketch.

Sklave ['sklaːvə] m (pl -n) slave. **Sklaverei** f slavery. **Sklavin** f (pl -nen) (female) slave, slave girl.

Skorpion ['skɔrpioːn] m (pl -e) (Tier) scorpion; (Astrol) Scorpio.

Skrupel ['skruːpəl] m (pl -) scruple. **skrupellos** adj unscrupulous. **skrupulös** adj scrupulous.

Skulptur [skulp'tuːr] f (pl -en) sculpture.

Smaragd [sma'rakt] m (pl -e) emerald. **smaragdgrün** adj emerald(-green).

Smoking ['smoːkiŋ] m (pl -s) dinner jacket, (US) tuxedo.

so [zoː] adv thus, so, in this way. conj consequently, therefore. **so daß** so that. **so ein** such a. **so sehr** so much. **so ... wie ... as ... as ...** um so besser all the better. **–bald** conj as soon as.

Socke ['zɔkə] f (pl -n) sock.

Sockel ['zɔkəl] m (pl -) pedestal, base.

sodann [zo'dan] adv, conj then, in that case.

Sodawasser ['zoːdavasər] neut soda water.

Sodbrennen ['zoːtbrenən] neut heartburn.

soeben [zo'eːbən] adv just (now).

Sofa ['zoːfa] neut (pl -s) sofa.

sofern [zo'fɛrn] conj as or so far as.

sofort [zo'fɔrt] adv at once, immediately. **–ig** adj immediate.

Sog [zoːk] m (pl -e) suction; (Boot) wake.

sogar [zo'gaːr] adv even.

sogenannt ['zoːgənant] adj so-called.

Sohle ['zoːlə] f (pl -n) (Fuß, usw.) sole. **sohlen** v sole.

Sohn [zoːn] m (pl Söhne) son.

solang(e) [zo'laŋ(ə)] conj as long as; (während) while.

solch [zɔlç] pron, adj such. **solcher‖art** adv of this sort, along these lines. **–lei** adj of such a kind. **–weise** adv in such a way.

Soldat [zɔl'daɪt] *m* (*pl* -en) soldier. **Soldat werden** enlist, join up.

Söldner ['zœldnər] *m* (*pl* -) mercenary.

solid [zo'liːt] *adj also* **solide** (*Person*) reliable, decent; (*Leben*) decent, respectable; (*Gegenstand*) solid, robust. **–arisch** *adj* united, unanimous. **Solidarität** *f* solidarity.

Solist [zo'list] *m* (*pl* -en), **Solistin** *f* (*pl* -nen) soloist.

Soll [zɔl] *neut* (*pl* -s) (*Komm*) debit; (*Produktion*) target. **sollen** *v* ought to, have to, should; (*angeblich*) be supposed to be. *ich sollte* I should. *was soll das?* what is this supposed to be *or* mean? *sie soll reich sein* she is said to be rich. *Kinder sollen gehorchen* children should be obedient. *du sollst nicht töten* thou shalt not kill.

Solo ['zoːlo] *neut* (*pl* -s *or* **Soli**) solo. **–sänger** *m* soloist, solo singer.

Sommer ['zɔmər] *m* (*pl* -) summer. **–ferien** *pl* summer holidays. **–sprosse** *f* freckle.

Sonate [zo'naːtə] *f* (*pl* -n) sonata.

Sonde ['zɔndə] *f* (*pl* -n) (*Tech*) probe.

Sonder||angebot *neut* special offer. **–ausgabe** *f* special edition. **sonder||bar** *adj* strange, peculiar. **–lich** *adj* remarkable, special.

sondern¹ [zɔndərn] *v* separate.

sondern² *conj* but. **nicht nur ... sondern auch ...** not only ... but also ... .

Sonder||preis *m* special price. **–ung** *f* (*pl* -en) separation.

Sonnabend ['zɔnaːbənt] *m* Saturday. **sonnabends** *adv* on Saturdays.

Sonne ['zɔnə] *f* (*pl* -n) sun. **sonnen** *v* air, put out in the sun. **sich sonnen** sun oneself, lie in the sun.

Sonnen||aufgang *m* sunrise. **–blume** *f* sunflower. **–brand** *m* sunburn. **–bräune** *f* suntan. **–finsternis** *f* solar eclipse. **–schein** *m* sunshine. **–stich** *m* sunstroke. **–system** *neut* solar system. **–untergang** *m* sunset.

sonnig ['zɔniç] *adj* sunny.

Sonntag ['zɔntaːk] *m* Sunday. **sonntags** *adv* on Sundays.

sonst [zɔnst] *adv* otherwise, else. **sonst etwas?** anything else? **sonst nichts** nothing else. **wer sonst?** who else? **wie sonst** as usual. **–ig** *adj* other, miscellaneous. **–wie** *adv* some other way. **–wo** *adv* elsewhere.

Sopran [zo'praːn] *m* (*pl* -e) soprano. **–istin** *f* (*pl* -nen) soprano (singer).

Sorge ['zɔrgə] *f* (*pl* -n) (*Kummer*) care, worry; (*Pflege*) care. **sich Sorgen machen (um)** worry (about). **sorgen für** take care of. **dafür sorgen, daß** make sure that, see to it that. **sich sorgen** be anxious, worry. **sorgen||frei** *or* **–los** *adj* carefree. **–voll** *adj* careworn. **sorg||lich** *adj* careful, caring. **–los** *adj* careless. **–sam** *adj* careful, cautious.

Sorte ['zɔrtə] *f* (*pl* -n) sort, kind; (*Ware*) brand. **sortieren** *v* sort (out). **Sortiment** *neut* (*pl* -e) assortment.

Soße ['zoːsə] *f* (*pl* -n) sauce; (*für Fleisch*) gravy.

Souveränität [suvərɛni'tɛɪt] *f* sovereignty.

soviel ['zofiːl] *conj* as far as. *adv* as or so much. **soviel wie** as much as. **soweit** *conj* as or so far as; *adv* so far. **sowenig(wie)** *conj* as little (as). **sowie** *conj* as soon as; (*außerdem*) as well as, and also. **sowieso** *adv* in any case.

Sowjet [zɔ'vjɛt] *m* (*pl* -e) Soviet. **sowjetisch** *adj* Soviet. **Sowjetunion** *f* Soviet Union.

sowohl [zo'voːl] *conj* as well as. **sowohl ... als auch ...** both ... and ... .

sozial [zoʦi'aːl] *adj* social. **Sozial||abgaben** *pl* national insurance contributions. **–demokrat** *m* social democrat. **–einrichtungen** *pl* social services. **–fürsorge** *f* (social) welfare.

Sozialismus [zoʦia'lizmus] *m* socialism. **Sozialist** *m* socialist. **sozialistisch** *adj* socialist.

Sozial||politik *f* social policies *pl*. **–produkt** *neut* (gross) national product. **–unterstützung** *f* social security.

Soziologe [zoʦio'loːgə] *m* (*pl* -n) sociologist. **Soziologie** *f* sociology. **soziologisch** *adj* sociological.

sozusagen [zoʦu'zaːgən] *adv* so to speak.

spähen ['ʃpɛːən] *v* look out, watch; (*Mil*) scout.

Spalt [ʃpalt] *m* (*pl* -e) crack, slit. **–e** *f* (*Druck*) column; crack, crevice. **spalten** *v* split.

Span [ʃpaːn] *m* (*pl* Späne) chip, shaving; (*Splitter*) splinter.

Spange ['ʃpaŋə] *f* (*pl* -n) clasp; (*Schnalle*) buckle.

Spanien ['ʃpaːniən] *neut* Spain. **Spanier** *m* (*pl* -). **Spanierin** *f* (*pl* -nen) Spaniard. **spanisch** *adj* Spanish.

Spann [ʃpan] *m* (*pl* -e) instep.

Spanne [ʃpanə] *f* (*pl* -n) span.

spannen [ʃpanən] *v* stretch; (*straff ziehen*) tighten. **-d** *adj* thrilling, exciting. **Spann‖seil** *neut* guy(-rope). **-ung** *f* (*pl* -en) tension.

sparen [ʃparən] *v* save; (*sparsam sein*) economize. **Sparer** *m* (*pl* -) saver.

Spargel [ʃpargəl] *m* (*pl* -) asparagus. **-kohl** *m* broccoli.

Sparkasse [ʃparkasə] *f* savings bank. **-nbuch** *neut* deposit book.

spärlich [ʃpɛːrliç] *adj* scanty, meagre. **Spärlichkeit** *f* scarcity.

Sparmaßnahme [ʃparmaːsnaːmə] *f* economy measure.

Spaß [ʃpaːs] *m* (*pl* Späße) fun; (*Scherz*) joke. Spaß haben an enjoy. es macht uns Spaß it amuses us, it is fun. **spaß‖en** *v* make fun, joke. **-haft** or **-ig** *adj* comical. **Spaßvogel** *m* joker, clown.

spät [ʃpɛːt] *adj* late. wie spät ist es? what is the time?

Spaten [ʃpaːtən] *m* (*pl* -) spade.

später [ʃpɛːtər] *adj* later. spätestens *adv* at the latest.

Spatz [ʃpats] *m* (*pl* -en) sparrow.

spazieren [ʃpaˈtsiːrən] *v* go for a walk, stroll. **-fahren** *v* go for a drive. **-gehen** *v* go for a walk, walk. **Spazier‖fahrt** *f* drive. **-gang** *m* walk, stroll.

Specht [ʃpɛçt] *m* (*pl* -e) woodpecker.

Speck [ʃpɛk] *m* (*pl* -e) bacon; (*Schmalz*) lard, fat. **speckig** *adj* greasy.

spedieren [ʃpeˈdiːrən] *v* forward, transport, ship. **Spediteur** *m* (*pl* -e) shipping agent, haulier, carrier. **Spedition** *f* (*pl* -en) shipping (agency).

Speer [ʃpeːr] *m* (*pl* -e) spear.

Speichel [ʃpaiçəl] *m* spittle, saliva.

Speicher [ʃpaiçər] *m* (*pl* -) warehouse, storehouse; (*Getreide*) granary; (*Computer*) memory. **speichern** *v* store.

Speise [ʃpaizə] *f* (*pl* -n) food; (*Gericht*) dish. **-eis** *neut* ice cream. **-karte** *f* menu. **speisen** *v* dine, eat. **Speise‖röhre** *f* gullet. **-saal** *m* dining room. **-wagen** *m* dining car.

Spektakel [ʃpɛkˈtaːkəl] *m* (*pl* -) spectacle; (*Aufregung*) uproar.

Spekulation [ʃpekulatsiˈoːn] *f* (*pl* -en) speculation. **spekulieren** *v* speculate.

Spende [ʃpɛndə] *f* (*pl* -n) donation. **spenden** *v* contribute, donate. **Spender** *m* (*pl* -), **Spenderin** *f* (*pl* -nen) donor.

Sperre [ʃpɛrə] *f* (*pl* -n) barrier; (*Verbot*) ban. **sperren** *v* close, bar; (*untersagen*) ban; (*Strom*) cut off. **Sperr‖riegel** *m* (door) bolt. **-kette** *f* door chain. **-klinke** *f* safety catch. **-ung** *f* blocking, barring. **-zeit** *f* closing time.

Spesen [ʃpeːzən] *pl* expenses.

Spezialfach [ʃpetsiˈaːlfax] *neut* speciality. **spezialisieren** *v* specialize. **Spezialist** *m* (*pl* -en) specialist. **speziell** *adj* special.

spezifisch [ʃpeˈtsiːfiʃ] *adj* specific.

Sphäre [sfɛːrə] *f* (*pl* -n) sphere.

Spiegel [ʃpiːgəl] *m* (*pl* -) mirror; (*Schiff*) stern. **-ei** *neut* fried egg. **-glas** *neut* plate glass. **spiegeln** *v* reflect; (*glänzen*) shine. **Spiegelung** *f* (*pl* -en) reflection.

Spiel [ʃpiːl] *neut* (*pl* -e) game; (*Theater*) play; (*Glücksspiel*) gambling. aufs Spiel setzen put at stake. auf dem Spiel stehen be at stake. **-automat** *m* slot machine. **-bank** *f* casino. **-brett** *neut* board.

spielen [ʃpiːlən] *v* play; (*Geld*) gamble. **Spieler** *m* (*pl* -), **Spielerin** *f* (*pl* -nen) player; (*Schauspiel*) actor *m*, actress *f*; (*Geld*) gambler. **Spielergebnis** *neut* result, (final) score. **spielerisch** *adj* playful. **Spiel‖feld** *neut* playing field. **-karte** *f* playing card. **-platz** *m* playground. **-zeug** *neut* toy.

Spieß [ʃpiːs] *m* (*pl* -e) spear; (*Bratspieß*) spit. **-bürger** *m* philistine.

Spinat [ʃpiˈnaːt] *m* (*pl* -e) spinach.

Spindel [ʃpindəl] *f* (*pl* -n) spindle, axle.

Spinne [ʃpinə] *f* (*pl* -n) spider. **spinnen** *v* spin; (*umg.*) talk nonsense. du spinnst ja! you're crazy!

Spion [ʃpiˈoːn] *m* (*pl* -e) spy. **-age** *f* espionage. **spionieren** *v* spy.

Spirale [ʃpiˈraːlə] *f* (*pl* -n) spiral.

Spirituosen [ʃpirituˈoːzən] *pl* spirits, liquor *sing*.

spitz [ʃpits] *adj* sharp, pointed. **Spitze** *f* (*pl* -n) point, tip. **Spitzen** *pl* (*Gewebe*) lace *sing*. **spitzen** *v* sharpen. **Spitzen‖geschwindigkeit** *f* top speed. **-leistung** *f* maximum performance, record. **Spitzer** *m* (*pl* -) pencil-sharpener. **spitzfindig** *adj* shrewd, ingenious; (*haarspalterisch*) over-critical, hair-splitting. **Spitzname** *m* nickname.

Splitter [ʃplitər] *m* (*pl* -) splinter. **-gruppe** *f* splinter group.

spontan [ʃponˈtaːn] *adj* spontaneous.

Stand

Spore ['ʃpoːrə] f (pl -n) spore.
Sporn [ʃpɔrn] m (pl **Sporen**) spur. **spornen** v spur.
Sport [ʃpɔrt] m (pl -e) sport. Sport **treiben** go in for sport(s). **Sport‖feld** neut sports ground. **-ler** m (pl -) sportsman. **-lerin** f (pl -nen) sportswoman. **sportlich** adj sporting.
Spott [ʃpɔt] m ridicule. **spottbillig** adj dirt cheap. **spotten über** ridicule, deride.
spöttisch ['ʃpœtiʃ] adj mocking, scornful.
Sprache ['ʃpraːxə] f (pl -n) language, speech. **Sprachfehler** m speech defect; (Gramm) grammatical error. **sprach‖lich** adj linguistic. **-los** adj speechless.
*__sprechen__ ['ʃprɛçən] v speak. **sprechen mit** talk to, speak with. **Sprecher** m (pl -). **Sprecherin** f (pl -nen) speaker; (offiziell) spokesman.
sprengen ['ʃprɛŋən] v explode, blow up; (aufbrechen) burst open; (bespritzen) sprinkle. **Spreng‖kopf** m warhead. **-stoff** m explosive.
Sprichwort ['ʃpriçvɔrt] neut (pl **Sprichwörter**) proverb.
*__sprießen__ ['ʃpriːsən] v sprout.
Spring [ʃpriŋ] m (pl -e) spring. **-brunnen** m fountain. **springen** v jump, spring; (Ball) bounce; (platzen) burst, break; (Schwimmen) dive. **Springen** neut jumping; (Schwimmen) diving. **Springer** m (pl -) jumper; (Schach) knight. **Spring‖feder** f spring. **-seil** neut skipping rope.
Sprit [ʃprit] m (pl -e) (umg.) gas, juice.
Spritze ['ʃpritsə] f (pl -n) syringe; (Einspritzung) injection; (Tech) spray. **spritzen** v squirt; (besprengen) sprinkle; (Med) inject.
spröde ['ʃprøːdə] adj brittle; (Person) reserved, cool.
Sproß [ʃprɔs] m (pl **Sprosse**) shoot, sprout.
Spruch [ʃprux] m (pl **Sprüche**) saying, aphorism; (Jur) sentence.
Sprudel ['ʃpruːdəl] m (pl -) spring, source (of water); mineral water. **sprudeln** v bubble up; (Mineralwasser, usw.) sparkle. **-d** adj bubbling; sparkling. **Sprudelwasser** neut mineral water.
Sprühdose ['ʃpryːdoːtsə] f spray can, aerosol pack. **sprühen** v spray; (Regen) drizzle. **Sprühregen** m drizzle.
Sprung [ʃpruŋ] m (pl **Sprünge**) leap, jump; (Schwimmen) dive; (Riß) crack, split. **-brett** neut diving board.

spucken ['ʃpukən] v spit.
Spuk [ʃpuːk] m (pl -e) ghost.
Spülbecken ['ʃpyːlbɛkən] neut sink.
Spule ['ʃpuːlə] f (pl -n) spool; (Elek) coil. **spulen** v wind.
spülen ['ʃpyːlən] v rinse, wash; (Geschirr) wash up, (WC) flush. **Spül‖ung** f rinsing, washing; flushing. **-wasser** neut dishwater.
Spur [ʃpuːr] f (pl -en) track, trail; (fig) trace.
spürbar ['ʃpyːrbaːr] adj perceptible, noticeable. **spüren** v trace; (folgen) track; (fühlen) feel. **Spürsinn** m shrewdness.
Staat [ʃtaːt] m (pl -e) state. **staatlich** adj state. **Staats‖angehörige(r)** m citizen, national. **-angehörigkeit** f nationality. **-anwalt** m public prosecutor. **-bürger** m citizen. **-mann** m statesman. **-streich** m coup d'état.
Stab [ʃtaːp] m (pl **Stäbe**) staff; (Metall) bar; (Holz) stick, pole.
stabil [ʃtaˈbiːl] adj stable. **-isieren** v stabilize. **Stabilität** f stability.
Stachel ['ʃtaxəl] m (pl -n) spike, prickle; (Biene) sting. **-beere** f gooseberry. **-draht** m barbed wire. **stachel‖ig** adj prickly; stinging. **-n** v prick; sting. **Stachelschwein** neut porcupine.
Stadion ['ʃtaːdiɔn] neut (pl **Stadien**) stadium.
Stadt [ʃtat] f (pl **Städte**) town, city.
städtisch ['ʃtɛtiʃ] adj urban; (Verwaltung) municipal.
Stadt‖mitte f town centre. **-plan** m town map. **-rat** m town council; (Person) councillor.
Staffel ['ʃtafəl] f (pl -n) rung, step; (Mil) detachment; (Lauf) relay. **-ei** f (pl -en) easel.
Stahl [ʃtaːl] m (pl -e) steel.
Stall [ʃtal] m (pl **Ställe**) (Pferde) stable; (Hunde) kennel; (Schweine) sty; (Kuhe) cowshed.
Stamm [ʃtam] m (pl **Stämme**) (Volk) tribe; (Baum) trunk; (Stengel) stalk, stem. **-baum** m family tree, genealogy; (Hund) pedigree. **stammen (von)** v (Ort) come (from); (Familie) be descended (from); (fig, Gramm) be derived (from).
stampfen ['ʃtampfən] v stamp; (zerstampfen) mash, crush.
Stand [ʃtant] m (pl **Stände**) stand; (Markt) stall; (Höhe) level, height; (Stellung) position, situation.

Standard ['ʃtandart] m (pl -s) standard.
Standbild ['ʃtantbilt] neut statue.
Ständer ['ʃtɛndər] m (pl -) stand.
Standesamt ['ʃtandəsamt] neut registry office.
standhaft ['ʃtanthaft] adj steadfast. **Standhaftigkeit** f steadfastness. **standhalten** v stand firm.
ständig ['ʃtɛndiç] adj permanent; (laufend) constant.
Stand∥ort m position, station. –**punkt** m standpoint.
Stange ['ʃtaŋə] f (pl -n) pole, bar.
Stanniol [ʃtani'oːl] neut (pl -e) tinfoil.
Stapel ['ʃtaːpəl] m (pl -) pile, heap, stack. **stapeln** v pile up.
Star¹ [ʃtaːr] m (pl -e) (Vogel) starling.
Star² m (pl -s) (Film) star.
Star³ m (pl -e) (Med) cataract.
stark [ʃtark] adj strong; (Zahl) numerous; (dick) thick(set). **starke Erkältung** severe cold. **stark gesucht** in great demand.
Stärke ['ʃtɛrkə] f (pl -n) strength; (Dicke) stoutness; (Gewalt) violence; (Wäsche-, Chem) starch. **stärken** v strengthen.
starr [ʃtar] adj rigid; (Blick) fixed, staring. **starren** v stare. **Starrheit** f rigidity; (Charakter) obstinacy.
Start [ʃtart] m (pl -e) start; (Flugzeug) take-off. **starten** v start; take off. **Starter** m (pl -) (Mot, Sport) starter. –**klappe** f (Mot) choke.
Station [ʃtatsi'oːn] f (pl -en) station; (Krankenhaus) ward.
Statistik [ʃta'tistik] f (pl -en) statistics. **statistisch** adj statistical.
statt [ʃtat] prep instead of. **Statt** f place, stead.
Stätte ['ʃtɛtə] f (pl -n) place, spot.
*stattfinden v take place. –haft adj allowed, permissible. –lich adj stately; (Summe) considerable.
Statut [ʃta'tuːt] neut (pl -en) statute.
Staub [ʃtaup] m dust. **staubig** adj dusty. **Staubtuch** neut duster.
stauen ['ʃtauən] v dam (up); (Ladung) stow (away). **sich stauen** accumulate, pile up.
staunen ['ʃtaunən] v be astonished. **Staunen** neut (unz.) astonishment.
Steak [steːk] neut (pl -s) steak.
*stechen ['ʃtɛçən] v (Insekt) sting; (Dorn) prick; (mit einer Waffe) stab, jab. –d adj stinging; (fig) piercing. **Stechpalme** f holly.

Steck∥brief m warrant (for arrest). –**dose** f (Elek) socket.
stecken ['ʃtɛkən] v put, place, insert; (sich befinden) be, lie. **etwas in die Tasche stecken** put something in one's pocket. **in Brand stecken** set fire to. **da steckt er!** there he is! that's where he's hiding! **es steckt etwas dahinter** there's more to it than meets the eye. **steckenbleiben** v be or get stuck. **Steck∥enpferd** neut hobbyhorse; (fig) hobby. –**er** m (pl -) (Elek) plug. –**nadel** f pin.
Steg [ʃteːk] m (pl -e) (foot)path; (Brücke) (foot)bridge; (Geige) bridge.
*stehen ['ʃteːən] v stand; (sein) be (situated). **in Verdacht stehen** be suspected. **offen stehen** be open. **das Kleid steht dir (gut)** the dress suits you. **stehenbleiben** v (nicht weitergehen) come to a standstill, stop; (nicht umfallen) remain standing. –**d** adj standing; (ständig) permanent.
*stehlen ['ʃteːlən] v steal. **Stehlen** neut (unz.) stealing, theft.
steif [ʃtaif] adj stiff. **Steifheit** f stiffness.
Steig [ʃtaik] m (pl -e) path. –**bügel** m stirrup. **steigen** v rise; (klettern) climb. –**d** adj rising; (wachsend) growing.
steigern ['ʃtaiɡərn] v raise, increase. **Steigerung** f (pl -en) rise, increase.
Steigung ['ʃtaiɡuŋ] f (pl -en) rise, incline.
steil [ʃtail] adj steep.
Stein [ʃtain] m (pl -e) stone. –**bock** m (Tier) ibex; (Astrol) Capricorn. –**bruch** m quarry. **steinern** adj stone. **Steingut** neut stoneware, pottery. **steinigen** v stone (to death). **Steinzeit** f Stone Age.
Stelle ['ʃtɛlə] f (pl -n) place; (Arbeit) job, position; (in einem Buch) passage. **an Ort und Stelle** on the spot. **an Stelle von** in place of. **eine Stelle bekleiden** hold a position.
stellen ['ʃtɛlən] v put, place; (Frage) ask; (Forderung) make. **zufriedenstellen** satisfy. **eine Falle stellen** set a trap. **sich stellen** present oneself; (vortäuschen) pretend, feign.
Stellen∥angebot neut vacancy, vacant position. –**nachweis** m employment agency.
Stellung ['ʃtɛluŋ] f (pl -en) position; (Arbeit) post, position; (Ansicht) attitude, opinion; (Körperhaltung) posture. –**nahme** f comment, opinion.

stellvertretend adj deputy, delegated. **Stellvertret||er** m deputy, representative. **–ung** f representation.

Stelze [ˈʃtɛltsə] f (pl –n) stilt.

Stempel [ˈʃtɛmpəl] m (pl –) stamp. **–geld** neut (umg.) dole money. **stempeln** v stamp. **stempeln gehen** (umg.) go on the dole.

Stengel [ˈʃtɛŋəl] m (pl –) stalk.

Stenograph [ʃtenoˈɡraːf] m (pl –en) stenographer. **–ie** f shorthand. **Stenotypist(in)** shorthand typist.

Steppe [ˈʃtɛpə] f (pl –n) steppe, prairie.

Sterbe||bett neut deathbed. **–fall** m a death.

*sterben [ˈʃtɛrbən] v die. **Sterben** neut death. **sterblich** adj mortal. **Sterblichkeit** f mortality.

Stereoanlage [ˈʃtereoanlaːgə] f stereo (system).

steril [ʃteˈriːl] adj sterile. **–isieren** v sterilize.

Stern [ʃtɛrn] m (pl –e) star. **–bild** neut constellation. **–chen** neut asterisk. **–kunde** f astronomy.

stet [ʃtɛt] or **stetig** adj constant, continual. **stets** adv always, constantly.

Steuer [ˈʃtɔyər] f (pl –n) tax.

Steuer||behörde f inland revenue, (US) internal revenue. **–berater** m tax consultant. **–erklärung** f tax return. **–hinterziehung** f tax evasion.

steuern [ˈʃtɔyərn] v steer.

steuerpflichtig [ˈʃtɔyərpfliçtiç] adj taxable, subject to taxation.

Steuer||rad neut steering wheel. **–säule** f steering column.

Steuerung [ˈʃtɔyərʊŋ] f (pl –en) steering.

Steuerzahler [ˈʃtɔyərtsaːlər] m tax-payer.

Stich [ʃtiç] m (pl –e) prick; (Insekt) sting; (Messer) stab; (Nähen) stitch; (Kartenspiel) trick. **im Stich lassen** abandon, leave in the lurch.

sticken [ˈʃtikən] v embroider. **Stickerei** f embroidery.

Stickstoff [ˈʃtikʃtɔf] m nitrogen.

Stiefbruder [ˈʃtiːfbruːdər] m stepbrother.

Stiefel [ˈʃtiːfəl] m (pl –) boot.

Stief||eltern pl step-parents. **–kind** neut stepchild. **–mutter** f stepmother. **–mütterchen** neut pansy. **–schwester** f stepsister. **–sohn** m stepson. **–tochter** f stepdaughter. **–vater** m stepfather.

Stiel [ʃtiːl] m (pl –e) handle; (Bot) stalk.

Stier [ʃtiːr] m (pl –e) bull. **–kampf** m bullfight.

Stift[1] [ʃtift] m (pl –e) peg; (Bleistift) pencil; (Pflocke) pin.

Stift[2] neut (pl –e or –er) (charitable) foundation; (Kloster) monastery.

stiften [ˈʃtiftən] v donate, (gründen) found, establish; (Frieden) make. **Stifter** m founder. **Stiftung** f (pl –en) (charitable) foundation, institution; (geschenktes Vermögen) endowment, bequest.

Stil [ʃtiːl] m (pl –e) style.

still [ʃtil] adj quiet, still; (schweigend) silent. **Stille** f quiet, stillness, silence. **stillen** v allay, stop; (Schmerz) soothe; (Durst) quench; (Säugling) nurse. **stillschweigen** v be silent. **–d** adj silent; (fig) implicit, tacit. **Stillstand** m standstill. **stillstehen** v stand still; (aufhören) stop.

Stimme [ˈʃtimə] f (pl –n) voice; (Wahl) vote; (Musik) part. **seine Stimme abgeben** cast one's vote. **sich der Stimme enthalten** abstain (from voting). **stimmen** v (richtig sein) be right or true, tally; (Wahl) vote; (Instrument) tune. **hier stimmt etwas nicht** something's wrong here! **stimmt schon!** that's all right. **Stimm||enthaltung** f abstention. **–recht** neut franchise. **–ung** f (pl –en) mood, atmosphere; (Musik) tuning.

*stinken [ˈʃtiŋkən] v stink.

Stipendium [ʃtiˈpɛndiʊm] neut (pl Stipendien) scholarship, (student) grant.

Stirn [ʃtirn] f (pl –en) forehead. **die Stirn runzeln** frown.

stöbern [ˈʃtøːbərn] v rummage (about).

Stock [ʃtɔk] m (pl Stöcke) stick, rod; (Musik) baton; (Etage) storey. **stockdunkel** adj pitch dark.

stocken [ˈʃtɔkən] v stoop, come to a standstill; (Milch) curdle. **Stockung** f (pl –en) standstill, stop; (Verkehr) congestion, jam.

Stockwerk [ˈʃtɔkvɛrk] neut floor, storey.

Stoff [ʃtɔf] m (pl –e) matter; (Gewebe, fig) material.

stöhnen [ˈʃtøːnən] v groan.

Stolle [ˈʃtɔlə] f (pl –n) or **Stollen** m (pl –) (German) Christmas cake.

stolpern [ˈʃtɔlpərn] v stumble.

stolz [ʃtɔlts] adj proud. **Stolz** m pride.

stopfen [ˈʃtɔpfən] v stuff, fill; (Strümpfe) darn; (sättigen) fill up; (Med) constipate.

Stopp [ʃtɔp] m (unz.) hitchhiking.
Stoppel [ʃtɔpəl] f (pl -n) stubble.
stoppen [ʃtɔpən] v stop. **Stopplicht** neut brake light.
Stöpsel [ʃtœpsəl] m (pl -) stopper; (Elek) plug.
Storch [ʃtɔrç] m (pl **Störche**) stork.
stören [ʃtøːrən] v disturb; (belästigen) bother, trouble; (Radio) interfere. **Störend** adj disturbing, troublesome. **Störenfried** m troublemaker. **Störung** f (pl -en) disturbance; trouble; (Radio) interference.
Stoß [ʃtoːs] m (pl **Stöße**) push, shove; (Schlag) blow; (Tritt) kick; (Haufen) heap. **–dämpfer** m shock-absorber. **stoßen** v push, shove; knock; (fig) take offence. **stoßen an** run across. **sich stoßen an** bump into or against; (fig) take offence at. **Stoß||stange** f bumper. **–zahn** m tusk.
stottern [ʃtɔtərn] v stutter, stammer.
Straf||anstalt f prison, penal institution. **–arbeit** f (Schule) punishment, lines pl. **strafbar** adj punishable.
Strafe [ʃtraːfə] f (pl -n) punishment; (fig) penalty; (Jur) sentence. **strafen** v punish. **Straferlaß** m pardon; (allgemeiner) amnesty.
straff [ʃtraf] adj tight, taught; (fig) strict, stern.
Straf||geld neut fine. **–gericht** neut criminal court.
sträflich [ʃtrɛːfliç] adj punishable. **Sträfling** m prisoner.
Straf||recht neut criminal law. **–tat** f offence.
Strahl [ʃtraːl] m (pl -en) ray, beam; (Blitz) flash; (Wasser) jet. **strahlen** v radiate; (fig) beam. **–d** adj beaming. **Strahlmotor** m jet engine. **Strahlung** f radiation.
Strand [ʃtrant] m (pl -e) beach, shore. **stranden** v run aground; (fig) founder.
strapazieren [ʃtrapaˈtsiːrən] v fatigue, tire; (abnutzen) wear out.
Straße [ʃtraːsə] f (pl -n) street. **Straßen||bahn** f tram, (US) street car. **–kreuzung** f crossing. **–laterne** f street lamp. **–sperre** f roadblock. **–überführung** f overpass. **–unterführung** f underpass.
sträuben [ʃtrɔybən] v ruffle (up). **sich sträuben** (Haare) stand up on end; (fig) struggle (against), resist.
Strauch [ʃtraux] m (pl **Sträucher**) bush.

Strauß¹ [ʃtraus] m (pl -e) (Vogel) ostrich.
Strauß² m (pl **Sträuße**) bouquet, bunch (of flowers).
streben [ʃtreːbən] v strive.
Strecke [ʃtrɛkə] f (pl -n) stretch, distance; (Math, Sport) distance; (Teilschnitt) section. **strecken** v stretch (out), extend.
Streich [ʃtraiç] m (pl -e) stroke, blow; (Peitsche) lash; (Possen) trick, prank.
streicheln [ʃtraiçəln] v stroke, pet.
***streichen** [ʃtraiçən] v stroke, rub; (Farbe) paint; (gehen) wander, ramble. **Streich||instrument** neut string instrument. **–musik** f string music. **–quartett** neut string quartet.
Streife [ʃtraifə] f (pl -n) patrol; (Streifzug) stroll, look around.
Streifen [ʃtraifən] m (pl -) stripe; (Land) strip.
streifen [ʃtraifən] v streak, stripe; (berühren) brush (against), touch; (wandern) wander, roam.
Streik [ʃtraik] m (pl -s) strike. **–brecher** m strike-breaker; (umg.) scab. **streiken** v (go on) strike.
Streit [ʃtrait] m (pl -e) dispute, quarrel; (Kampf) conflict; (Schlägerei) fight, brawl. **streiten** v dispute, quarrel. **sich streiten um** quarrel about, fight over. **Streitfrage** f matter in dispute. **streit||ig** adj contested; (fraglich) controversial. **–lustig** adj quarrelsome, aggressive.
streng [ʃtrɛŋ] adj stern, severe, strict. **Strenge** f severity, strictness.
streuen [ʃtrɔyən] v scatter, spread.
Strich [ʃtriç] m (pl -e) stroke, line; (Vogel) flight; (Gebiet) district; (Kompaß) compass point. **–punkt** m semicolon.
Strick [ʃtrik] m (pl -e) cord, string, (thin) rope; (Kind) rascal. **–arbeit** f knitting; (Artikel) knitwear. **stricken** v knit. **Strick||maschine** f knitting machine. **–nadel** f knitting needle. **–zeug** neut knitting.
strittig [ʃtritiç] adj questionable, debatable; (Angelegenheit) disputed.
Stroh [ʃtroː] neut straw. **–dach** neut thatched roof.
Strolch [ʃtrɔlç] m (pl -e) tramp, vagabond. **strolchen** v roam, stroll about.
Strom [ʃtroːm] m (pl **Ströme**) (Fluß) (large) river; (Strömung, Elek) current;

(fig) stream. **strom∥abwärts** adv downstream. **-aufwärts** adv upstream.

strömen ['ʃtrœɪmən] v stream, flow; (Regen) pour.

Strom∥erzeuger m generator. **-sperre** f power cut.

Strömung ['ʃtuˈdiːrən] f (pl -en) current.

Struktur [ʃrukˈtuːr] f (pl -en) structure.

Strumpf [ʃrumpf] m (pl Strümpfe) stocking; (Socke) sock.

Stube ['ʃtuːbə] f (pl -n) room, chamber. **stubenrein** adj house-trained.

Stück [ʃtyk] neut (pl -e) piece; (Theater) play; (Vieh) head. **in Stücke gehen** fall to pieces. **Stückchen** neut bit, little piece; (Papier) scrap. **stückeln** v cut or chop into pieces.

Student [ʃtuˈdɛnt] m (pl -en) student. **-enheim** neut hall of residence, (US) dorm(itory). **Studentin** f (pl -nen) (woman) student.

Studien∥direktor m headmaster, (US) principal. **-plan** m syllabus.

studieren [ʃtuˈdiːrən] v study. **Studio** neut studio. **Studium** neut studies pl; (Untersuchung) study.

Stufe ['ʃtuːfə] f (pl -n) step; (Leiter) rung; (fig) stage. **stufen∥los** adj infinitely variable. **-weise** adv gradually.

Stuhl [ʃtuːl] m (pl Stühle) chair; (ohne Lehne) stool. **-gang** m bowel movement.

stumm [ʃtum] adj mute, dumb; (schweigend) silent. **Stumme(r)** m mute, dumb person.

Stummel ['ʃtuməl] m (pl -) stump. **Stumm∥film** m silent film. **-heit** f dumbness.

stumpf [ʃtumpf] adj blunt; (Mensch) dull. **Stumpf∥heit** f bluntness; dullness. **-sinn** m stupidity. **stumpfsinnig** adj stupid, dull-witted.

Stunde ['ʃtundə] f (pl -n) hour; (Unterricht) lesson. **Stunden∥plan** m timetable. **-satz** m hourly rate.

stupid [ʃtuˈpiːt] adj half-witted, idiotic.

stur [ʃtuːr] adj stubborn.

Sturm [ʃturm] m (pl Stürme) storm; (Angriff) attack.

stürmen ['ʃtyrmən] v storm; (Wind) blow. **Stürmer** m (pl -) assailant; (Fußball) forward. **stürmisch** adj stormy.

Sturz [ʃturts] m (pl Stürze) fall; (Zusammenbruch) collapse.

stürzen ['ʃtyrtsən] v (fallen) fall (down); (umkippen) overturn; (Regierung) over-

throw; (eilen) dash, rush. **sich stürzen auf** rush at.

Sturzhelm ['ʃturtshɛlm] m crash-helmet.

Stute ['ʃtuːtə] f (pl -n) mare. **-nfüllen** neut foal, filly.

Stütze ['ʃtytsə] f (pl -n) prop, support.

stutzen¹ ['ʃtutsən] v stop short, be startled.

stutzen² v (schneiden) clip, trim; (Schwanz) dock.

stützen ['ʃtytsən] v prop, support. **Stützpunkt** m fulcrum; (Mil) stronghold.

subjektiv [subjɛkˈtiːf] adj subjective.

subtil [zupˈtiːl] adj subtle.

Subvention [zupvɛntsiˈoːn] f (pl -en) subsidy.

Suche ['zuːxə] f (pl -n) search. **suchen** v look for, search for. **Sucher** m (pl -) searcher. **Sucht** f (pl Süchte) addiction; (fig) craving, passion.

süchtig ['zyçtiç] adj addicted. **Süchtige(r)** m addict.

Süd(en) [zyt ('zyːdən)] m south. **Süd∥afrika** neut South Africa. **-amerika** neut South America. **-länder(in)** southerner.

südlich ['zyːtliç] adj southern.

Südost(en) [zyːtˈɔst(ən)] m southeast. **südöstlich** adj southeast(ern); (Wind, Richtung) southeasterly.

Südpol ['zyːtpoːl] m South Pole.

südwärts ['zyːtvɛrts] adv southwards.

Südwest(en) [zyːtˈvɛst(ən)] m southwest. **südwestlich** adj southwest(ern); (Wind, Richtung) southwesterly.

Sühne [zyːnə] f (pl -n) atonement. **sühnen** v atone for.

Sultanine [zultaˈniːnə] f (pl -n) sultana.

Sülze ['zyltsə] f (pl -n) brawn.

Summe ['zumə] f (pl -n) sum total; (Geld) sum, amount.

summen ['zumən] v buzz, hum.

summieren [zuˈmiːrən] v add up. **Summierung** f summation.

Sumpf [zumpf] m (pl Sümpfe) swamp, marsh.

Sund [zunt] m (pl -e) sound, channel.

Sünde ['zyndə] f (pl -n) sin. **-nbock** m scapegoat. **Sünder(in)** sinner. **sündhaft** adj sinful.

Suppe ['zupə] f (pl -n) soup.

süß [zyːs] adj sweet. **Süße** f sweetness. **süßen** v sweeten. **Süßigkeit** f sweetness. **Süßigkeiten** pl sweets, (US) candy sing. **süßlich** adj sweetish; (fig) slushy, sentimental. **Süß‖waren** pl sweets, (US) candy sing. **–wasser** neut fresh water.

Symbol [zym'bo:tl] neut (pl -e) symbol. **symbol‖isch** adj symbolic. **–isieren** v symbolize.

sympathisch [zym'pa:tiʃ] adj likeable, congenial.

Symptom [zymp'to:m] neut (pl -e) symptom.

Synagoge [zyna'go:gə] f (pl -n) synagogue.

synchron ['zynkron] adj synchronous. **–isieren** v synchronize.

Synthese [zyn'te:zə] f (pl -n) synthesis.

Syphilis ['zy:filis] f syphilis.

System [zys'te:m] neut (pl -e) system. **systematisch** adj systematic.

Szene ['stse:nə] f (pl -n) scene.

T

Tabak ['ta:bak] m (pl -e) tobacco.

Tabelle [ta'bɛlə] f (pl -n) table, list. **tabellenförmig** adj tabular.

Tablette [ta'blɛtə] f (pl -n) pill, tablet.

Tadel ['ta:dəl] m blame; reproach, reprimand; (Schule) bad mark. **tadellos** adj faultless. **tadeln** v reproach, scold, criticize.

Tafel ['ta:fəl] f (pl -n) board; (Schule) blackboard; (Schokolade) bar; (Tabelle) table, chart. **die Tafel decken** lay the table.

Tag [ta:k] m (pl -e) day. **am Tag** by day. **Tages‖anbruch** m dawn, daybreak. **–licht** neut daylight. **–zeitung** f daily (newspaper). **täglich** adj daily.

Taille ['taljə] f waist.

Takelwerk ['ta:kəlvɛrk] neut rigging.

Takt [takt] m (Musik) time, beat; (Tech) stroke; (Höflichkeit) tact. **Zweitaktmotor** m two-stroke engine.

Taktik ['taktik] f (pl -en) tactics pl. **taktisch** adj tactical.

taktlos ['taktlo:s] adj tactless.

Tal [ta:l] neut (pl Täler) valley, vale.

Talent [ta'lɛnt] neut (pl -e) talent, gift. **talentiert** adj talented, gifted.

Talk [talk] m talcum.

Tampon [tã'põ] m (pl -s) (Med) swab; (für Frauen) tampon.

tändeln ['tɛndəln] v flirt; (langsam gehen,

usw.) dawdle, dally. **Tändelei** f (pl -en) flirtation.

Tang [taŋ] m (pl -e) seaweed.

Tank [taŋk] m (pl -e) tank. **tanken** v (Mot) refuel, fill up. **Tank‖schiff** neut tanker. **–stelle** f petrol station.

Tanne ['tanə] f fir. **Tannen‖baum** m fir-tree. **–zapfen** m fir-cone.

Tante ['tantə] f (pl -n) aunt.

Tanz [tants] m (pl Tänze) dance; (Tanzen) dancing. **tanzen** v dance. **Tänzer** m (pl -), **Tänzerin** f (pl -nen) dancer. **Tanz‖lokal** neut dancehall. **–platz** m dance-floor.

Tapete [ta'pe:tə] f (pl -n) wallpaper. **tapezieren** v paper, decorate.

tapfer ['tapfər] adj brave, courageous. **Tapferkeit** f bravery, courage.

tappen ['tapən] v grope, fumble about.

Tarif [ta'ri:f] m (pl -e) price list. **–verhandlungen** pl collective bargaining sing.

tarnen ['tarnən] v camouflage. **Tarnung** f camouflage.

Tasche ['taʃə] f (pl -n) pocket; suitcase; handbag; (Schule) satchel; (Aktentasche) briefcase. **Taschen‖dieb** m pickpocket. **–geld** neut pocket money. **–lampe** f torch. **–messer** neut penknife.

Tasse ['tasə] f (pl -n) cup. **eine Tasse Kaffee** a cup of coffee.

Taste ['tastə] f (pl -n) (Klavier, Schreibmaschine) key; (push)button. **tasten** v feel, touch. **Tastenbrett** (Musik) neut also **Tastatur** keyboard.

Tat [ta:t] f (pl -en) deed, act. **in der Tat** in reality, really.

tätig ['tɛ:tiç] adj active, busy, employed. **tätig sein als** be employed as, practise. **tätig sein bei** work for. **Tätigkeit** f (pl -en) activity; (Beruf) work, occupation.

tätowieren [tɛto'vi:rən] v tattoo. **Tätowierung** f (pl -en) tattoo.

Tatsache ['ta:tzaxə] f (pl -n) fact. **tatsächlich** adj real, actual. **adv** really, actually. **interj** really? is that so?

Tatze ['tatsə] f (pl -n) paw.

Tau¹ [tau] neut (pl -e) (Seil) rope, cable.

Tau² m (unz.) dew. **Tauwetter** neut thaw.

taub [taup] adj deaf.

Taube ['taubə] f (pl -n) pigeon, dove.

taubstumm ['taupʃtum] adj deaf and dumb. **Taubstumme(r)** deaf mute.

tauchen ['tauxən] v dive, plunge; immerse, dip. **Tauchen** neut diving. **Taucher** m (pl -) diver.

tauen ['tauən] v thaw, melt.

Taufe ['taufə] f (pl -n) baptism, christening. **taufen** v baptize, christen. **Taufname** m Christian name.

taugen ['taugən] v taugen zu be good or fit for. zu nichts taugen be useless or worthless. **Taugenichts** m (pl -e) good-for-nothing.

taumeln ['tauməln] v stagger, reel.

Tausch [tauʃ] m (pl -e) exchange. **tausch||bar** adj exchangeable. **-en** v exchange, swap.

täuschen ['tɔyʃən] v deceive, delude. **-d** adj deceptive.

Tauschhandel ['tauʃhandəl] m barter.

Täuschung ['tɔyʃuŋ] f (pl -en) delusion, illusion; (Schwindel) deception, fraud.

tausend ['tauzənt] adj thousand.

Taxe ['taksə] f (pl -n) charge, fee; (Schätzung) valuation. **taxieren** v value, assess.

Taxi ['taksi] neut or m (pl -s) taxi. **-fahrer** m taxi-driver.

Technik ['tɛçnik] f (pl -en) technique; engineering, technology. **-er** m (pl -) technician. **Technologie** f technology. **technologisch** technological.

Tee [te] m tea. **-kanne** f teapot. **-löffel** m teaspoon. **-service** neut tea-set.

Teer [ter] m (pl -e) tar, pitch.

Teich [taiç] m (pl -e) pond.

Teig [taik] m (pl -e) dough; (flüssig) batter. **-waren** pl noodles pl.

Teil [tail] m or neut (pl -e) part; share, portion. **teilbar** adj divisible. **Teil||beschäftigung** f part-time work. **-chen** neut particle. **teil||en** v divide; share out. **-haben** take part (in). **Teilnahme** f participation; interest; (Mitleid) sympathy. **teil||nehmen** v take part in. **-s** adv partly. **Teilung** f (pl -en) division, partition; sharing out, distribution. **teilweise** adj partial. adv partly.

Telegramm [tele'gram] neut (pl -e) telegram.

Telephon [tele'fo:n] neut (pl -e) telephone. **-buch** neut telephone directory. **telephonieren** v telephone, ring up. **Telephon||zelle** f call box. **-zentrale** f telephone exchange.

Teleskop [tele'sko:p] neut (pl -e) telescope.

Teller ['tɛlər] m (pl -) plate; (Tech) disc.

Tempel ['tɛmpəl] m (pl -) temple.

Temperament [tempera'mɛnt] neut (pl -e) temperament, disposition. **temperamentvoll** adj high-spirited, lively.

Temperatur [tempera'tu:r] f temperature.

Tempo ['tempo] neut (pl -s or -pi) pace, tempo.

temporär [tempo'rɛːr] adj temporary.

Tendenz [tɛn'dɛnts] f (pl -en) tendency, propensity.

Tennis ['tɛnis] neut tennis. **-platz** m tennis court. **-schläger** m tennis racket.

Tenor [tɛ'no:r] m (pl -e) tenor.

Teppich ['tɛpiç] m (pl -e) carpet, rug; (Wand) tapestry.

Termin [tɛr'mi:n] m (pl -e) fixed date; closing date, deadline. **-geschäft** neut (Komm) futures pl.

Terpentinöl [tɛrpɛn'ti:nœːl] neut turpentine.

Terrasse [tɛ'rasə] f (pl -n) terrace.

Terror ['tɛrɔr] m terror. **-ismus** m terrorism. **-ist(in)** terrorist. **terroristisch** adj terrorist.

Testament [testa'mɛnt] neut (pl -e) will; (Bibel) testament. **Testaments||bestätigung** f probate. **-vollstrecker** m executor.

testieren [tɛs'ti:rən] v make one's will; bequeath.

teuer ['tɔyər] adj expensive, dear; (lieb) dear, cherished. adv dearly. **Teuerung** f (pl -en) rising prices pl, increase in the cost of living. **Teuerungszulage** f cost-of-living bonus.

Teufel ['tɔyfəl] m devil. Satan. **Teufels||beschwörung** f exorcism. **-skreis** m vicious circle. **teuflisch** adj devilish, diabolical.

Text [tɛkst] m (pl -e) text; (Lied) lyrics pl; (Oper) libretto. **-buch** neut libretto.

Textilien [tɛks'ti:liən] or **Textilwaren** pl textiles.

Theater [te'a:tər] neut (pl -) theatre; (umg.) fuss, to-do. **theatralisch** adj theatrical.

Thema ['te:ma] neut (pl Themen) theme, subject.

Theologe [teo'lo:gə] m (pl -n) theologian. **Theologie** f theology. **theologisch** adj theological.

Theoretiker [teo're:tikər] m (pl -) theorist. **theoretisch** adj theoretical. **Theorie** f (pl -n) theory.

Therapie [tera'pi:] f (pl -n) therapy.

thermisch ['tɛrmiʃ] *adj* thermal.
Thermometer [tɛrmo'meːtər] *neut* (*pl* -) thermometer.
Thermosflasche ['tɛrmɔsflaʃə] *f* vacuum flask, thermos.
Thermostat [tɛrmo'ʃtaːt] *m* (*pl* -en) thermostat.
These [teːzə] *f* (*pl* -n) thesis.
Thrombose [trɔm'boːzə] *f* (*pl* -n) thrombosis.
Thron [troːn] *m* (*pl* -e) throne. **-erbe** *m* heir to the throne.
Thunfisch ['tuːnfiʃ] *m* tuna.
Thüringen ['tyːrɪŋən] *neut* Thuringia.
Thymian ['tyːmiaːn] *m* thyme.
ticken ['tɪkən] *v* tick.
tief [tiːf] *adj* deep; (*Musik*) low(-pitched), bass; (*Stimme*) deep; (*Sinn*) profound; extreme. *adv* deep; (*Atmen*) deeply. **aus tiefstem Herzen** from the bottom of one's heart. **tief in der Nacht** at dead of night. **tiefbewegt** *adj* deeply moved. **Tief||druckgebiet** *neut* low-pressure area. **-e** *f* depth. **-ebene** *f* lowlands *pl*. **tief||gekühlt** *adj* deep-frozen. **-greifend** *adj* far-reaching. **Tief||kühltruhe** *f* freezer, deep freeze. **-punkt** *m* low(est) point.
Tiegel ['tiːɡəl] *m* (*pl* -) saucepan.
Tier [tiːr] *neut* (*pl* -e) animal, beast. **hohes Tier** (*umg.*) big shot. **Tier||arzt** *m* veterinary surgeon, (*umg.*) vet. **-garten** *m* zoological gardens *pl*. **tierisch** *adj* animal; (*brutal*) bestial, brutal. **Tier||kreis** *m* zodiac. **-welt** *f* animal kingdom, fauna. **-zucht** *f* livestock breeding.
Tiger ['tiːɡər] *m* (*pl* -) tiger.
tilgen ['tɪlɡən] *v* (*streichen*) delete, erase; (*ausrotten*) exterminate; (*Schuld*) pay off. **Tilgung** *f* (*pl* -en) deletion; extermination; discharge, repayment.
Tinte ['tɪntə] *f* ink. **-nklecks** *m* ink-stain.
Tip [tɪp] *m* (*pl* -s) hint; (*Sport*) tip.
tippen ['tɪpən] *v* tap; (*mit der Schreibmaschine*) type. **Tippfehler** *m* typing error.
Tisch [tɪʃ] *m* (*pl* -e) table. **den Tisch decken/abdecken** lay/clear the table. **Tisch||gast** *m* diner, guest (at table). **-gesellschaft** *f* dinner party.
Tischler ['tɪʃlər] *m* carpenter, cabinetmaker. **-arbeit** *f* carpentry.
Titel ['tiːtəl] *m* (*pl* -) title. **-bild** *neut* frontispiece. **-kopf** *m* heading.
Toast [toːst] *m* (*pl* -e) toast. **toasten** *v* toast. **Toaster** *m* (*pl* -) toaster.

toben ['toːbən] *v* rage, rave. **tobsüchtig** *adj* raving, frantic.
Tochter ['tɔxtər] *f* (*pl* Töchter) daughter.
Tod [toːt] *m* (*pl* -e) death. **Todes||anzeige** *f* obituary. **-fall** *m* (a case of) death. **-kampf** *m* death throes *pl*. **-strafe** *f* death penalty. **-wunde** *f* mortal wound. **Todfeind** *m* deadly enemy. **tödlich** *adj* deadly, fatal, lethal. **todmüde** *adj* dead tired.
Toilette [toa'lɛtə] *f* (*pl* -n) toilet, lavatory; toilette; dressing-table. **-papier** *neut* toilet paper.
tolerant [tole'rant] *adj* tolerant. **Toleranz** *f* toleration. **tolerieren** *v* tolerate.
toll [tɔl] *adj* raving mad, crazy, wild; (*umg.*) fantastic. **Toll||heit** *f* (*pl* -en) madness; fury. **-wut** *f* rabies.
Tölpel ['tœlpəl] *m* (*pl* -e) awkward person; oaf, boor.
Tomate [to'maːtə] *f* (*pl* -n) tomato.
Ton¹ [toːn] *m* (*pl* -e) clay.
Ton² *m* (*pl* Töne) sound; (*Musik*) tone, note; accent, stress; tone, fashion. **-art** *f* (*Musik*) key, pitch. **-band** *neut* magnetic tape. **-bandgerät** *neut* tape-recorder. **-blende** *f* tone control.
tönen ['tøːnən] *v* ring, resound; (*Foto*) shade, tint.
Ton||fall *m* intonation; (*Musik*) cadence. **-fülle** *f* volume (of sound). **-leiter** *f* (*musical*) scale. **-spur** *f* soundtrack.
Tonne ['tɔnə] *f* (*pl* -n) ton; cask, barrel.
Topf [tɔpf] *m* (*pl* Töpfe) pot.
Töpfchen ['tœpfçən] *neut* (*pl* -) (child's) potty. **Töpfer** *m* (*pl* -) potter. **-waren** *pl* pottery *sing*.
Tor¹ [toːr] *m* (*pl* -en) fool.
Tor² *neut* (*pl* -e) gate; (*Sport*) goal. **-schütze** *m* (football) scorer.
Torf [tɔrf] *m* peat.
Torheit ['toːrhait] *f* (*pl* -en) folly.
töricht ['tœːrɪçt] *adj* foolish. **Törin** *f* (*pl* -nen) fool, foolish woman.
torkeln ['tɔrkəln] *v* stagger, reel.
Torpedo [tɔr'peːdo] *m* (*pl* -s) torpedo. **-boot** *neut* torpedo boat.
Torte ['tɔrtə] *f* (*pl* -n) (fruit) flan, tart, gâteau.
Tor||wächter *m* (*pl* -) gatekeeper. **-wart** *m* goalkeeper.
tot [toːt] *adj* dead.
total [to'taːl] *adj* total, complete.
Tote(r) ['toːtə(r)] dead person.

töten ['tœtən] v kill.

Toten‖bett neut deathbed. **–gräber** m gravedigger. **–hemd** neut shroud. **–wagen** m hearse.

totgeboren ['toːtgəbøːrən] adj stillborn. **sich totlachen** v split one's sides laughing. **totschießen** v shoot dead.

Totschlag ['tɔtʃlaːk] m manslaughter. **tot‖schlagen** v slay, kill; (Zeit) waste (time). **–schweigen** v hush up. **–sicher** adj absolutely or dead certain.

Tötung ['tøːtʊŋ] f (pl -en) killing.

Tour [tuːr] f (pl -en) tour, trip. **–ismus** m tourism. **–ist** m (pl -en) tourist.

Trab [traːp] m trot. **traben** v trot.

Tracht [traxt] f (pl -en) costume, dress.

Tradition [traditsi'oːn] f (pl -en) tradition. **traditionell** adj traditional.

träge ['trɛːgə] adj (faul) lazy; (langsam) ponderous, slow; (schläfrig) sleepy.

*tragen ['traːgən] v carry; (Kleider) wear; (stützen) support; (ertragen) endure, bear.

Träger ['trɛːgər] m (pl -) carrier; (Mensch) porter; (Balken) girder.

Trägheit ['trɛːkhait] f laziness; (Langsamkeit) slowness.

tragisch ['traːgiʃ] adj tragic. **Tragödie** f (pl -n) tragedy.

Trainer ['trɛːnər] m (pl -) (Sport) coach, trainer. **trainieren** v train. **Training** neut training. **–anzug** m track suit.

Traktor ['traktɔr] m (pl -en) tractor.

trampeln ['trampəln] v trample, stamp.

trampen ['trɛmpən] v hitchhike.

Tran [traːn] m (pl -e) whale oil.

tranchieren [trãˈʃiːrən] v carve. **Tranchiermesser** neut carving knife.

Träne ['trɛːnə] f (pl -n) tear.

Trank [traŋk] m (pl Tränke) drink.

tränken ['trɛŋkən] v water; (durchtränken) soak.

transatlantisch [transatˈlantiʃ] adj transatlantic.

Transmission [transmisi'oːn] f (pl -en) transmission.

Transport [transˈpɔrt] m (pl -e) transportation. **transportieren** v transport. **Transportunternehmen** neut haulage or shipping company.

Tratte ['tratə] f (pl -n) bill of exchange, draft.

Traube ['traubə] f (pl -n) grape; bunch of grapes. **Trauben‖lese** f vintage. **–saft** m grape juice. **–zucker** m glucose.

trauen ['trauən] v trust; (Ehepaar) marry, join in wedlock. **sich trauen** dare.

Trauer ['trauər] f sorrow, grief; (für Tote) mourning. **–anzeige** f death notice. **–gottesdienst** m funeral service. **trauern** v grieve, mourn. **Trauer‖spiel** neut tragedy. **–weide** f weeping willow. **traurig** adj sad.

Traufe ['traufə] f (pl -n) eaves pl. **aus dem Regen in die Traufe** out of the frying pan into the fire. **Traufrinne** f gutter.

traulich ['trauliç] adj snug, cosy, comfortable.

Traum [traum] m (pl Träume) dream. **–bild** neut vision.

träumen ['trɔymən] v dream. **Träumer** m (pl -) dreamer. **–ei** f (pl -en) daydream, reverie. **träumerisch** adj dreamy.

Trau‖ring m wedding ring.

*treffen ['trɛfən] v (begegnen) meet; (erreichen) hit; (betreffen) concern; (Vorkehrungen) make; (Maßnahmen) take. **sich treffen** meet; (zufällig geschehen) happen. **Treffen** neut meeting. **treffend** adj striking; (Antwort) pertinent. **Treffpunkt** m meeting place.

*treiben ['traibən] v drive, move; (drängen) urge, impel; (Metall) work; (Pflanzen) force; (tun) do, occupy oneself with; (Blüte) blossom; (im Wasser) float. **treibend** adj driving; (im Wasser) floating. **Treib‖er** m driver; (Vieh) drover. **–haus** neut hothouse. **–kraft** f moving force. **–stoff** m fuel.

trennbar ['trɛnbar] adj separable. **trennen** v separate; (abtrennen) sever, cut; (Telef) cut off. **sich trennen** part, separate. **Trennung** f (pl -en) separation.

Treppe ['trɛpə] f (pl -n) staircase, stairs pl. **–ngeländer** neut handrail, banister.

*treten ['treːtən] v tread, step; (betreten) step on; (stoßen) kick. **Trethebel** m treadle.

treu [trɔy] adj loyal, faithful, true; (redlich) honest, sincere. **Treubruch** m disloyalty, breach of faith. **Treue** f loyalty, faithfulness. **treu‖lich** adj loyal, faithful. **–los** adj disloyal, faithless.

Tribüne [triˈbyːnə] f (pl -n) platform; (für Zuschauer) gallery.

Trichter ['triçtər] m (pl -) funnel; (Bombe) crater.

Trick [trik] m (pl -s) trick. **–film** m animated cartoon.

Trieb [triːp] *m* (*pl* -e) force, drive; (*Antrieb*) impulse; (*Bot*) shoot; (*Instinkt*) instinct.

*****triefen** ['triːfən] *v* trickle, drip. **triefnaß** *adj* dripping wet.

triftig ['triftiç] *adj* convincing, plausible.

Triller ['trilər] *m* (*pl* -) trill. **trillern** *v* trill.

trinkbar ['triŋkbaːr] *adj* drinkable, potable. **trinken** *v* drink. **Trink**||**er** *m* (*pl* -) drinker. **-geld** *neut* tip. **-halm** *m* (drinking) straw. **-spruch** *m* toast.

Tripper ['tripər] *m* (*pl* -) gonorrhoea.

Tritt [trit] *m* (*pl* -e) step, tread; (*Stoß*) kick; (*Fußspur*) footprint. **-leiter** *f* stepladder.

Triumph [tri'umf] *m* (*pl* -e) triumph.

trocken ['trɔkən] *adj* dry. **Trockenheit** *f* dryness. **trocknen** *v* dry. **Trockner** *m* (*pl* -) drier.

Trödel ['trøːdəl] *m* junk, rubbish. **trödeln** *v* dawdle; (*handeln*) trade in old junk.

Trommel ['trɔməl] *f* (*pl* -n) drum. **-fell** *neut* drumskin; (*Anat*) eardrum. **trommeln** *v* drum. **Trommler** *m* (*pl* -) drummer.

Trompete [trɔm'peːtə] *f* (*pl* -n) trumpet.

Tropen ['troːpən] *pl* tropics.

tröpfeln ['trœpfəln] *v* trickle, drip.

Tropfen ['trɔpfən] *m* (*pl* -) drop.

tropisch ['troːpiʃ] *adj* tropical.

Trost [troːst] *m* consolation, solace, comfort.

trösten ['trøːstən] *v* console, solace, comfort. **sich trösten mit** take comfort in.

trostlos ['troːstloːs] *adj* disconsolate.

Tröstung ['trøːstuŋ] *f* (*pl* -en) consolation, comfort.

Trott [trɔt] *m* (*pl* -e) trot.

Trottel ['trɔtəl] *m* (*pl* -) idiot, fool.

trotz [trɔts] *prep* despite, in spite of. **Trotz** *m* defiance; (*Eigensinn*) obstinacy. **trotzdem** *conj, adv* nevertheless. **trotzen** *v* defy; (*widersetzlich sein*) be obstinate. **trotzig** *adj* defiant, obstinate.

trüb(e) ['tryːb(ə)] *adj* cloudy, opaque; (*glanzlos*) dull; (*fig*) gloomy. **trüben** *v* cloud, dim, darken. **Trübsinn** *m* gloom, depression. **trübsinnig** *adj* gloomy, miserable.

Trug [truːk] *m* (*Täuschung*) fraud, deceit; (*Sinnes-*) delusion.

*****trügen** ['tryːgən] *v* be deceptive; (*betrügen*) deceive. **trügerisch** *adj* treacherous, deceitful.

Truhe ['truːə] *f* (*pl* -n) chest, trunk.

Trümmer *pl* ruins, debris *sing*.

Trumpf [trumpf] *m* (*pl* **Trümpfe**) trump. **-karte** *f* trump (card).

Trunk [truŋk] *m* (*pl* **Trünke**) drink. **-enheit** *f* drunkenness, intoxication. **-sucht** *f* alcoholism.

Trupp [trup] *m* (*pl* -s) troop, gang, band. **Truppe** *f* (*pl* -n) (*Theater*) company; (*Mil*) (combat) troops *pl*. **Truppen** *pl* troops.

Truthahn ['truːthaːn] *m* turkey-cock.

Tscheche ['tʃɛçə] *m* (*pl* -n), **Tschechin** *f* (*pl* -nen) Czech. **tschechisch** *adj* Czech. **Tschechoslowakei** *f* Czechoslovakia.

Tuberkulose [tubɛrku'loːzə] *f* tuberculosis, TB.

Tuch [tuːx] **1** *neut* (*pl* -e) cloth, fabric. **2** *neut* (*pl* **Tücher**) (piece of) cloth; (*zum Trocknen*) towel. **-händler** *m* draper.

tüchtig ['tyçtiç] *adj* capable, able; (*leistungsfähig*) efficient; (*fleißig*) hard-working; (*klug*) clever. **Tüchtigkeit** *f* ability; efficiency; cleverness.

Tücke ['tykə] *f* (*pl* -n) spite, malice. **tückisch** *adj* spiteful.

Tugend ['tuːgənt] *f* (*pl* -en) virtue. **tugendhaft** *adj* virtuous.

Tulpe ['tulpə] *f* (*pl* -n) tulip.

*****tun** [tuːn] *v* do; (*machen*) make. **tun als ob** pretend to. **nur so tun** pretend. **zu tun haben** be busy, have things to do. **groß tun** boast. **etwas in etwas tun** put something into something.

Tünche ['tynçə] *f* (*pl* -n) whitewash, distemper.

Tunke ['tuŋkə] *f* (*pl* -n) sauce. **tunken** *v* dip, dunk.

Tunnel ['tunəl] *m* (*pl* -) tunnel.

Tupfen ['tupfən] *m* (*pl* -) dot, spot. **tupfen** *v* dot.

Tür [tyːr] *f* (*pl* -en) door.

Türkis [tyr'kiːs] *m* (*pl* -e) turquoise. **Türklinke** ['tyːrkliŋkə] *f* doorhandle.

Turm [turm] *m* (*pl* **Türme**) tower; (*Schach*) rook, castle; (*Elek*) pylon. **-spitze** *f* spire, steeple.

turnen ['turnən] *v* do gymnastics. **Turnen** *neut* gymnastics. **Turnhalle** *f* gymnasium.

Turnier [tur'niːr] *neut* (*pl* -e) tournament.

Türschwelle ['tyːrʃvɛlə] *f* threshold.

Tusche ['tuʃə] *f* (*pl* -n) Indian ink, drawing ink.

tuscheln ['tuʃəln] *v* whisper.

Tüte ['tytə] f (pl -n) paperbag.
tuten ['tuːtən] v hoot, honk.
Typ [tyːp] m (pl -en) type. -e f (Druck) type.
Typhus ['tyːfus] m typhoid (fever).
typisch ['tyːpɪʃ] adj typical.
Tyrann [ty'ran] m (pl -en) tyrant. -ei f tyranny. tyrannisch adj tyrannical. -isieren v tyrannize.

U

U-Bahn ['uːbaːn] f underground (railway), (US) subway.
übel ['yːbəl] adj evil, wicked; (schlecht) bad; (unwohl) sick, ill. mir wird übel I feel sick. übel daran sein be in a bad way. Übel neut (pl -) evil; (Mißgeschick) misfortune; (Krankheit) sickness. übelgelaunt adj bad-tempered. -gesinnt adj evil-minded. -nehmen v be offended by, take amiss. -riechen v smell bad.
üben ['yːbən] v practise.
über ['yːbər] prep over, above; (quer über) across; (während) during. (betreffend) about; (mehrals) over; (weg) via.
überall ['yːbər'al] adv everywhere.
überanstrengen [yːbər'anʃtrɛŋən] v overwork. sich überanstrengen overexert oneself. Überanstrengung f overexertion.
überarbeiten [yːbər'aɪrbaɪtən] v revise. sich überarbeiten v overwork, work too hard.
überbelichten ['yːbərbəlɪçtən] v (Foto) overexpose.
*überbieten [yːbər'biːtən] v outbid; (fig) surpass, beat.
Überbleibsel ['yːbərblaɪpsəl] neut (pl -) remainder.
Überblick ['yːbərblɪk] m survey, overall view.
*überbringen [yːbər'brɪŋən] v deliver.
überbrücken [yːbər'brykən] v bridge.
überdies [yːbər'diːs] adv besides.
überdrüssig [yːbər'drysɪç] adj sick (of), disgusted (with).
übereifrig [yːbər'aɪfrɪç] adj too eager, over-zealous.
übereilen [yːbər'aɪlən] v rush, hurry too much. übereilt adj hasty; (Benehmen) inconsiderate.
übereinander [yːbər'ain'andər] adv one

upon another. -greifen v overlap. -legen v lay one upon another.
*übereinkommen [yːbər'aɪnkɔmən] v agree. Übereinkommen neut (pl -) or -kunft f agreement.
übereinstimmen [yːbər'aɪnʃtɪmən] v concur, agree; (zueinander passen) correspond, tally. Übereinstimmung f agreement, concord.
überempfindlich ['yːbərɛmpfɪntlɪç] adj hypersensitive.
*überfahren [yːbər'faːrən] take or drive across. (Mot) run over. Überfahrt f crossing.
Überfall ['yːbərfal] m (sudden) attack, assault. überfallen v attack (suddenly). Überfallkommando neut flying squad.
Überfluß ['yːbərflus] m excess, overabundance. überflüssig adj superfluous.
überführen ['yːbərfyːrən] v transport, convey. [-'ryːrən] (Jur) convict. Überführung f transport; (Brücke) viaduct, overpass.
Übergabe ['yːbərgaːbə] f surrender, handing-over.
Übergang ['yːbərgaŋ] m crossing, passage; (fig) transition.
*übergeben ['yːbərgeːbən] v deliver, hand over; (Mil) surrender. sich übergeben vomit.
übergehen ['yːbərgeːən] v cross (over); (werden) pass into, become. [-'geːən] omit, overlook.
Übergewicht ['yːbərgəvɪçt] neut overweight.
*übergreifen ['yːbərgraɪfən] v overlap. übergreifen auf encroach on.
*überhandnehmen [yːbər'hantneːmən] v increase (rapidly).
überhaupt [yːbər'haupt] adv in general. wenn überhaupt if at all. überhaupt nicht not at all. überhaupt kein ... no ... whatever.
*überheben [yːbər'heːbən] v exempt, spare. einer Mühe überheben spare the trouble. überheblich adj presumptuous, arrogant.
überholen [yːbər'hoːlən] v overtake; (Tech) overhaul. überholt adj outmoded.
überhören [yːbər'hœːrən] v not hear; (ignorieren) ignore, let pass.
überirdisch ['yːbərirdɪʃ] adj celestial; (übernatürlich) supernatural.
überkochen ['yːbərkɔxən] v boil over.

*überlassen [yɪbər'lasən] v leave.
überlaufen ['yɪbərlaufən] v overflow; (Mil) defect.
überleben [yɪbər'leɪbən] v survive.
überlegen [yɪbər'leɪgən] v consider, reflect. adj superior. Überlegenheit f superiority. überlegt adj considered, deliberate. Überlegung f consideration, reflection.
überleiten ['yɪbərlaɪtən] v lead on to; (fig) convert.
überliefern [yɪbər'liːfərn] v deliver; (der Nachwelt) pass on, hand down.
Übermacht ['yɪbərmaxt] f superiority. übermächtig adj overwhelming, too powerful.
Übermaß ['yɪbərmaɪs] neut excess. übermäßig adj excessive.
Übermensch ['yɪbərmɛnʃ] m superman. übermenschlich adj superhuman.
übermitteln [yɪbər'mɪtəln] v convey.
übermorgen ['yɪbərmɔrgən] adv the day after tomorrow.
übermüdet [yɪbər'myɪdət] adj overtired.
Übermut ['yɪbərmuɪt] m arrogance; (Ausgelassenheit) high spirits pl. übermütig adj arrogant; high-spirited.
übernächst ['yɪbərneɪçst] adj the next but one, the one after.
übernachten [yɪbər'naxtən] v spend the night, stay overnight.
übernatürlich ['yɪbərnatuɪrlɪç] adj supernatural.
*übernehmen [yɪbər'neɪmən] v take over; (Pflicht) undertake.
überprüfen [yɪbər'pryɪfən] v verify, check, examine. Überprüfung f verification, check.
überqueren [yɪbər'kveɪrən] v cross.
überragen [yɪbər'raɪgən] v rise above, tower above; (fig) surpass, outdo. –d adj excellent.
übersinnlich ['yɪbərzɪnlɪç] adj spiritual, transcendental.
überspannen [yɪbər'ʃpanən] v overstretch, overtighten; (fig) go too far, exaggerate; (bedecken) stretch over. überspannt adj eccentric.
*überspringen [yɪbər'ʃprɪŋən] v jump over; (auslassen) omit, skip.
*überstehen [yɪbər'ʃteɪən] v survive.
*übersteigen [yɪbər'ʃtaɪgən] v climb over, surmount; (fig) exceed.
Überstunden ['yɪbərʃtundən] pl overtime

sing. Überstunden machen v work overtime. überstürzen [yɪbər'ʃtyrtsən] v rush, hurry. sich überstürzen rush, act too hastily. überstürzt adj hasty.
Übertrag ['yɪbərtraɪk] m (pl Überträge) balance brought forward. übertragen v carry over; (Komm) bring forward; (befördern) transport; (übersetzen) translate; (Radio, Med) transmit. Übertragung f transfer; (Radio, Med) transmission; (Übersetzung) translation.
*übertreffen [yɪbər'trɛfən] v excel, surpass.
*übertreiben [yɪbər'traɪbən] v exaggerate. Übertreibung f exaggeration.
*übertreten [yɪbər'treɪtən] v overstep. ['yɪbər-] (Fluß) overflow; (Sport) step over.
übertrieben [yɪbər'triːbən] adj exaggerated.
Übervölkerung [yɪbər'fœlkəruŋ] f overpopulation.
überwachen [yɪbər'vaxən] v supervise. Überwachung f supervision.
überwältigen [yɪbər'vɛltɪgən] v overpower, overwhelm. –d adj overwhelming. Überwältigung f overpowering, conquest.
*überweisen [yɪbər'vaɪzən] v transfer. Überweisung f transfer; (Post-) money order.
überwiegend [yɪbər'viːgənt] adj preponderant. adv primarily, mainly.
*überwinden [yɪbər'vɪndən] v overcome. sich überwinden (zu) bring oneself (to). Überwindung f overcoming, conquest.
überwuchern [yɪbər'vuxərn] v overrun, overgrow.
überzeugen [yɪbər'tsɔygən] v convince. –d adj convincing. überzeugt adj convinced, sure. Überzeugung f conviction.
*überziehen ['yɪbərtsiːən] v pull over, put on. [-'tsiːən] cover; (Konto) overdraw; (Bett) change (the sheets of). Überziehung f overdraft.
Überzug ['yɪbərtsuɪk] m cover(ing).
üblich ['yɪplɪç] adj usual.
U-Boot ['uːboɪt] neut submarine.
übrig ['yɪbrɪç] adj remaining, left(-over). die Übrigen the rest, the others. übrig haben have left (over). –bleiben v remain, be left (over). –ens adv by the way, incidentally.
Übung ['yɪbuŋ] f (pl -en) exercise; (Üben) practice.

Ufer ['uːfər] neut (pl -) bank, shore.
–**damm** m embankment.

Uhr [uːr] f (pl -en) clock; (Armbanduhr) watch; (Gas, usw.) meter; (Kraftstoff) gauge. –**armband** neut watch strap. –**werk** neut clockwork. –**zeiger** m (clock) hand. –**zeigersinn** m clockwise direction. **im Uhrzeigersinn** adv clockwise. **entgegen dem Uhrzeigersinn** adv anticlockwise. **entgegen dem Uhrzeigersinn** (US) counterclockwise.

Ulk [ulk] m (pl -e) fun, lark. **ulkig** adj funny.

Ulme ['ulmə] f (pl -n) elm.

um [um] prep (zeitlich, örtlich) around, about; (wegen) for; (Maßangaben) by; (ungefähr) about. adv about. conj in order to. **um zu** (in order) to. **um diese Zeit** around this time. **um so besser** so much the better. **bitten um** ask for. **um 2 cm länger** longer by 2 cm.

umändern ['umɛndərn] v change, alter. **Umänderung** f change, alteration.

umarmen [um'armən] v embrace. **Umarmung** f embrace.

Umbau ['umbau] m alteration, rebuilding, conversion. **umbauen** v rebuild, alter, convert.

umbilden ['umbildən] v transform, remodel. **Umbildung** f transformation.

*umbinden ['umbindən] v tie (up), tie around (oneself), put on.

Umblick ['umblik] m panorama, survey. **umblicken** v (sich umblicken) look around.

*umbringen ['umbriŋən] v kill. (sich umbringen) commit suicide.

umdrehen ['umdreːən] v turn over or around. **sich umdrehen** rotate, spin; (Person) turn around. **Umdrehung** f turn, rotation.

*umfahren ['umfaːrən] v run over, knock down; [-'faːrən] drive around.

*umfallen ['umfalən] v fall over.

Umfang ['umfaŋ] m (pl Umfänge) (Kreis) circumference; (Ausdehnung) extent; (Größe) size. **umfangreich** adj extensive.

Umfrage ['umfraːgə] f poll, inquiry.

Umgang ['umgaŋ] m circuit, turn; (Verkehr) intercourse, (social) contact. **umgänglich** adj sociable.

*umgeben [um'geːbən] v surround.

Umgebung f surroundings pl, environment.

*umgehen v ['umgeːən] go around; (behandeln) handle, deal with; (mit Menschen) associate (with). [-'geːən] go around; (vermeiden) avoid.

umgekehrt ['umgekeːrt] adv the other way round. adj inverted, reverse(d).

umgestalten ['umgəʃtaltən] v alter, transform; (umorganisieren) reorganize. **Umgestaltung** f alteration, transformation; reorganization.

Umhang ['umhaŋ] m wrap, cape.

umher [um'heːr] adv about, (a)round. –**blicken** v look around. –**laufen** run around.

umhüllen [um'hylən] v wrap up.

Umkehr ['umkeːr] f turning back, return; (fig) change, conversion. **umkehren** v turn back, return; (umdrehen) turn over; (fig) reform.

umkippen ['umkipən] v tip over.

umklammern [um'klamərn] v clasp.

umkleiden ['umklaidən] v sich umkleiden change (one's clothes). **Umkleideraum** m changing room.

*umkommen ['umkomən] v die, perish, be killed; (verderben) go bad.

Umkreis ['umkrais] m neighbourhood, vicinity. **umkreisen** v (en)circle.

Umlauf ['umlauf] m circulation. **im Umlauf** in circulation.

Umlaut ['umlaut] m vowel modification.

umleiten ['umlaitən] v divert. **Umleitung** f diversion.

umlernen ['umlɛrnən] v learn anew, relearn.

umliegend ['umliːgənt] adj surrounding.

umordnen ['umordnən] v rearrange.

umpflanzen ['umpflantsən] v transplant.

umrahmen [um'raːmən] v frame.

umrechnen ['umrɛçnən] v convert, (ex)change. **Umrechnung** f conversion. –**skurs** m rate of exchange.

*umreißen ['umraisən] v pull down, demolish. [-'raisən] sketch, outline.

umringen [um'riŋən] v surround.

Umriß ['umris] m sketch, outline. **umrissen** adj defined.

umrühren ['umryːrən] v stir.

ums [ums] prep + art um das.

Umsatz ['umzats] m turnover, sales.

umsäumen ['umzɔymən] v hem. [-'zɔymən] enclose, surround.

umschalten ['umʃaltən] v (fig) switch or change over. **Umschaltung** f (fig) change-over, switch.

umschauen ['umʃauən] v sich umschauen look around.

umschiffen [um'ʃifən] v circumnavigate; trans-ship. **Umschiffung** f circumnavigation.

Umschlag ['umʃlaik] m cover; (Brief) envelope; (Buch) wrapper, jacket; (Hose) turn-up; (Kleid) hem; (Veränderung) change; (Komm) turnover. **umschlagen** v change (Boot) capsize; (Wind) veer; (umwenden) turn over; (umwerfen) knock down.

***umschließen** [um'ʃliːsən] v surround, enclose.

***umschreiben** ['umʃraibən] v rewrite; transcribe. [-'ʃraibən] paraphrase.

umschulen ['umʃuːlən] v retrain; (neue Schule) send to a new school. **Umschulung** f retraining.

Umschwung ['umʃvuŋ] m turn; (fig) sudden change, reversal.

***umsehen** ['umzeːən] v sich umsehen look around; (rückwärts) look round.

umsetzen ['umzetsən] v transpose; (Pflanze) transplant; (verkaufen) sell.

Umsicht ['umziçt] f prudence, circumspection. **umsichtig** adj prudent, circumspect.

umsiedeln ['umziːdəln] v resettle. **Umsiedlung** f resettlement.

umsonst [um'zɔnst] adv free (of charge); (vergebens) in vain.

Umstand ['umʃtant] m circumstance. in anderen Umständen (umg.) expecting, in the family way. ohne Umstände without fuss. nähere Umstände further particulars. unter diesen Umständen in these circumstances.

***umsteigen** ['umʃtaigən] v change (trains, buses, etc.). **Umsteiger** m through-ticket.

***umstoßen** ['umʃtoːsən] v overturn, knock over; (ungültig machen) revoke; (Pläne) upset.

Umsturz ['umʃturts] m overthrow; (Pol) revolution. **umstürzen** v overturn; (Regierung) overthrow; (umfallen) fall over.

Umtausch ['umtauʃ] m exchange. **umtauschen** v exchange, (umg.) swap.

umwälzen ['umvɛltsən] v roll over; (gründlich ändern) revolutionize.

umwandeln ['umvandəln] v change, transform; (Elek) transform, (Komm) convert.

Umweg ['umveik] m detour, long way round.

Umwelt ['umvelt] f environment. **umweltfreundlich** adj non-polluting, conservationist. **Umweltverschmutzung** f (environmental) pollution.

***umwenden** ['umvendən] v turn over; (Wagen) turn round.

***umwerben** [um'verbən] v court.

***umwerfen** ['umverfən] v upset, overturn; (Kleider) wrap round oneself.

umwickeln [um'vikəln] v wrap round.

umzäunen [um'tsɔynən] v fence in.

***umziehen** ['umtsiːən] v move (house); (Kind) change (clothes). sich umziehen change (clothes).

Umzug ['umtsuik] m move, removal; procession.

unabänderlich [unap'ɛndərliç] adj unalterable.

unabhängig ['unapheŋiç] adj independent. **Unabhängig‖e(r)** (Pol) independent. **–keit** f independence.

unabkömmlich ['unapkœmliç] adj indispensable.

unablässig ['unaplesiç] adj incessant.

unabsichtlich ['unapziçtliç] adj unintentional.

unachtsam ['unaxtzaim] adj careless.

unähnlich ['unɛinliç] adj unlike, dissimilar (to).

unangemessen ['unangəmesən] adj unsuitable; (Forderung) unreasonable.

unangenehm ['unangəneim] adj unpleasant; (peinlich) awkward.

Unannehmlichkeit ['unannemliçkait] f unpleasantness; (lästige Mühe) inconvenience.

unansehnlich ['unanzeinliç] adj unsightly.

unanständig ['unanʃtendiç] adj indecent, improper. **Unanständigkeit** f indecency.

unartig ['unairtiç] adj badly-behaved, rude.

unauffällig ['unauffeliç] adj inconspicuous.

unaufgefordert ['unaufgəfordət] adj unbidden, unasked.

unaufhörlich ['unaufhœrliç] adj incessant.

unaufmerksam ['unaufmerkzaim] adj inattentive.

unaufrichtig ['unaufrɪçtɪç] adj insincere.

unausgeglichen ['unausgəglɪçən] adj uneven, unbalanced.

unbändig [unbɛndɪç] adj tremendous.

unbeabsichtigt ['unbəapzɪçtɪçt] adj unintentional.

unbeachtet ['unbəaxtət] adj unnoticed, unheeded.

unbedacht ['unbədaxt] adj inconsiderate, thoughtless, rash.

unbedeutend ['unbədɔytənt] adj unimportant, insignificant.

unbedingt ['unbədɪŋt] adj absolute, unconditional. adv by all means.

unbefahrbar ['unbəfairbair] adj impassable.

unbefriedigend ['unbəfriːdɪgənt] adj unsatisfactory.

unbefugt ['unbəfukt] adj unauthorized.

unbegreiflich ['unbəgraiflɪç] adj incomprehensible, inconceivable.

Unbehagen ['unbəhaːgən] neut uneasiness, discomfort. **unbehaglich** adj uneasy, uncomfortable.

unbeholfen ['unbəhɔlfən] adj clumsy, awkward.

unbekannt ['unbəkant] adj unknown.

unbekümmert ['unbəkymərt] adj unconcerned.

unbemerkt ['unbəmɛrkt] adj unnoticed, unobserved.

unbemittelt ['unbəmɪtəlt] adj poor, without means.

unbequem ['unbəkveːm] adj uncomfortable.

umberechenbar ['unbəreːçənbair] adj incalculable.

unberechtigt ['unbəreçtɪçt] adj (ungerechtfertigt) unjustified; (unbefugt) unauthorized. adv without authority.

unberührt ['unbəryːrt] adj untouched, intact.

unbeschränkt ['unbəʃrɛnkt] adj unlimited, unrestricted.

unbeschreiblich ['unbəʃraiplɪç] adj indescribable.

unbesonnen ['unbəzɔnən] adj imprudent; (unüberlegt) rash, hasty.

unbeständig ['unbəʃtɛndɪç] adj unsettled, unstable; (nicht dauernd) inconstant.

unbestimmt ['unbəʃtɪmt] adj indefinite.

unbestreitbar ['unbəʃtraitbair] adj indisputable.

unbestritten ['unbəʃtritən] adj undisputed, uncontested.

unbeteiligt ['unbətailɪçt] adj unconcerned; (nicht beteiligt) uninvolved.

unbeweglich ['unbəveːklɪç] adj immovable; (bewegungslos) motionless.

unbewußt ['unbəvust] adj unconscious.

unbiegsam ['unbiːkzaːm] adj unbending.

unbrauchbar ['unbrauxbair] adj useless.

und [unt] conj and.

undankbar ['undankbair] adj ungrateful; (Arbeit) thankless. **Undankbarkeit f** ingratitude.

undenkbar [un'dɛnkbair] adj unthinkable.

undeutlich ['undɔytlɪç] adj unclear, indistinct.

undurchdringlich ['undurçdrɪŋlɪç] adj impenetrable.

undurchlässig ['undurçlɛsɪç] adj impermeable; (Wasser-) water-proof.

undurchsichtig ['undurçzɪçtɪç] adj opaque; (Person) inscrutable.

uneben ['uneːbən] adj uneven, rough.

unecht ['unɛçt] adj not genuine, false; (künstlich) artificial.

unehelich ['uneːəlɪç] adj illegitimate.

unehrlich ['uneːrlɪç] adj dishonest. **Unehrlichkeit f** dishonesty.

unendlich [un'ɛntlɪç] adj endless, infinite.

unentbehrlich [unɛnt'beːrlɪç] adj indispensable.

unentschieden ['unɛntʃiːdən] adj undecided; (Fußball) drawn. **Unentschiedenheit f** indecision.

unentschlossen ['unɛntʃlɔsən] adj undecided, irresolute. **Unentschlossenheit f** indecision, irresolution.

unentwickelt ['unɛntvikəlt] adj undeveloped.

unentzündbar ['unɛntzyntbair] adj non-flammable.

unerbittlich [unɛr'bitlɪç] adj relentless.

unerfahren ['unɛrfairən] adj inexperienced.

unerhört [unɛr'høːrt] adj unheard-of, outrageous.

unerklärbar ['unɛrklɛirbair] adj inexplicable.

unerläßlich [unɛr'lɛslɪç] adj indispensable.

unerlaubt ['unɛrlaupt] adj not permitted; (ungesetzlich) forbidden, illegal.

unermeßlich [unɛr'mɛslɪç] adj immense, immeasurable.

unermüdlich [unɛr'myːtlɪç] adj indefatigable, untiring.

unerreichbar ['unεraiçbaɪr] *adj* unattainable. **unerreicht** *adj* unequalled, unrivalled.

unersättlich ['unεrzεtlıç] *adj* insatiable.

unerschrocken ['unεrʃrɔkən] *adj* fearless, undaunted.

unerschütterlich ['unεrʃytərlıç] *adj* imperturbable, unshakeable.

unersetzlich ['unεrzεtslıç] *adj* irreplaceable.

unerträglich ['unεrtrεklıç] *adj* unbearable, intolerable.

unerwartet ['unεrvaɪrtət] *adj* unexpected.

unfähig ['unfεıç] *adj* incapable; *(nicht instande)* unable. **Unfähigkeit** *f* incapacity; inability.

unfair ['unfεɪr] *adj* unfair.

Unfall ['unfal] *m* accident. **–station** *f* first-aid post. **–verhütung** *f* accident prevention.

unfaßbar ['unfasbaɪr] *adj* inconceivable.

unfehlbar [un'feɪlbaɪr] *adj* infallible.

unflätig ['unflεtıç] *adj* filthy, coarse.

unfreundlich ['unfrɔyntlıç] *adj* unfriendly; *(barsch)* rude; *(Wetter)* disagreeable, inclement. **Unfreundlichkeit** *f* unfriendliness, unkindness.

Unfug ['unfuk] *m* misconduct; *(Dummheiten)* mischief.

unfühlbar ['unfyɪlbaɪr] *adj* intangible, impalpable.

Ungar ['ungar] *m* *(pl* **-n)**, **Ungarin** *f* *(pl* **-nen)** Hungarian. **ungarisch** *adj* Hungarian. **Ungarn** *neut* Hungary.

ungastlich ['ungastlıç] *adj* inhospitable.

ungeachtet ['ungəaxtət] *adj* overlooked, disregarded. *prep* notwithstanding.

ungebeten ['ungəbeɪtən] *adj* uninvited.

ungebildet ['ungəbıldət] *adj* uneducated; *(Benehmen)* ill-mannered.

ungebührend ['ungəbyɪrənt] *or* **ungebührlich** *adj* improper, unbecoming.

ungebunden ['ungəbundən] *adj* unbound; *(fig)* unrestrained, free.

Ungeduld ['ungədult] *f* impatience. **ungeduldig** *adj* impatient.

ungeeignet ['ungəaiknət] *adj* unsuitable.

ungefähr ['ungəfεɪr] *adv* approximately, about, roughly. *adj* approximate.

ungefährlich ['ungəfεɪrlıç] *adj* not dangerous.

ungeheuer ['ungəhɔyər] *adj* enormous. **Ungeheuer** *neut* *(pl* **-)** monster.

ungehorsam ['ungəhɔrzaɪm] *adj* disobedient. **Ungehorsam** *m* disobedience.

ungekünstelt ['ungəkynstəlt] *adj* unaffected, natural.

ungelegen ['ungəleɪgən] *adj* inconvenient.

ungelernt ['ungəlεrnt] *adj* unskilled.

ungemächlich ['ungəmεçlıç] *adj* uncomfortable, unpleasant.

ungemein ['ungəmain] *adj* uncommon, extraordinary.

ungemütlich ['ungəmyɪtlıç] *adj* uncomfortable; *(grob)* unpleasant, nasty.

ungenannt ['ungənant] *adj* unnamed.

ungeniert ['unʒəniɪrt] *adj* free and easy, relaxed and informal.

ungenießbar ['ungəniɪsbaɪr] *adj* inedible, unenjoyable.

ungenügend ['ungənyɪgənt] *adj* insufficient; *(Qualität)* inadequate.

ungeraten ['ungəraɪtən] *adj* *(Kind)* spoiled.

ungerecht ['ungərεçt] *adj* unjust.

ungereimt ['ungəraimt] *adj* *(fig)* nonsensical, absurd.

ungern ['ungεrn] *adv* unwillingly, reluctantly.

Ungeschick ['ungəʃik] *neut* ineptitude, clumsiness. **ungeschickt** *adj* clumsy, awkward.

ungesellig ['ungəzεlıç] *adj* unsociable.

ungesetzlich ['ungəzεtslıç] *adj* illegal, unlawful.

ungestüm ['ungəʃtyɪm] *adj* impetuous.

ungesund ['ungəzunt] *adj* unhealthy, unwell.

ungewiß ['ungəvis] *adj* uncertain. **Ungewißheit** *f* uncertainty.

ungewöhnlich ['ungəvœɪnlıç] *adj* unusual, uncommon. **ungewohnt** *adj* unaccustomed.

Ungeziefer ['ungətsiɪfər] *neut* vermin.

ungezogen ['ungətsoɪgən] *adj* rude; *(Kind)* naughty.

ungezwungen ['ungətsvuɪŋən] *adj* free, natural, uninhibited.

ungläubig ['unglɔybıç] *adj* incredulous, disbelieving; *(Rel)* unbelieving. **Ungläubige(r)** *m* sceptic; *(Rel)* unbeliever.

unglaublich ['unglauplıç] *adj* incredible, unbelievable. **unglaubwürdig** *adj* *(Person)* untrustworthy, unreliable; *(Sache)* incredible.

ungleich ['unglaiç] *adj* unequal, uneven; *(verschieden)* different; *(unähnlich)* unlike; *(Zahl)* odd. **Ungleichheit** *f* inequality; difference.

Unglück ['unglyk] *neut* misfortune; (*Katastrophe*) disaster, catastrophe; (*Pech*) bad luck. **unglücklich** *adj* unlucky; (*traurig*) unhappy. **—erweise** *adv* unfortunately, **Unglücksfall** *m* accident.

Ungnade ['ungnaɪdə] *f* disgrace, displeasure. **ungnädig** *adj* ungracious, churlish.

ungünstig ['ungynstiç] *adj* unfavourable.

unhaltbar ['unhaltbaɪr] *adj* untenable.

Unheil ['unhail] *neut* mischief, harm. **unheil||bar** *adj* incurable. **—bringend** *adj* unlucky, fateful.

unheimlich ['unhaimliç] *adj* weird, sinister, uncanny. *adv* (*umg.*) tremendously.

unhöflich ['unhœfliç] *adj* impolite, rude. **Unhöflichkeit** *f* rudeness, incivility.

unhörbar ['unhœɪrbaɪr] *adj* inaudible.

uniform [uni'form] *adj* uniform. **Uniform** *f* (*pl* -en) uniform.

uninteressant ['unintərəsant] *adj* uninteresting. **uninteressiert** *adj* disinterested.

universal [univer'saɪl] *or* **universell** *adj* universal.

Universität [univerzi'tɛɪt] *f* (*pl* -en) university.

Universum [uni'verzum] *neut* universe.

unkenntlich ['unkentliç] *adj* unrecognizable. **Unkenntnis** *f* ignorance.

unklar ['unklaɪr] *adj* unclear, obscure; (*trübe*) muddy, cloudy.

unklug ['unkluk] *adj* unwise, unintelligent.

Unkosten ['unkostən] *pl* expenses, costs; (*Komm*) overheads.

Unkraut ['unkraut] *neut* weed.

unlängst ['unlɛŋst] *adv* recently, lately.

unlauter ['unlautər] *adj* impure; (*nicht ehrlich*) unfair, dishonest. **unlauterer Wettbewerb** unfair competition.

unlesbar ['unleɪzbaɪr] *adj* illegible, unreadable.

unlogisch ['unloɪgiʃ] *adj* illogical.

unlösbar ['unlœɪsbaɪr] *adj* insoluble.

unmäßig ['unmeɪsiç] *adj* immoderate.

Unmenge ['unmɛŋə] *f* huge quantity.

Unmensch ['unmɛnʃ] *m* brute, monster, barbarian. **unmenschlich** *adj* inhuman, brutal. **Unmenschlichkeit** *f* inhumanity.

unmittelbar ['unmitəlbaɪr] *adj* immediate, direct.

unmodisch ['unmoɪdiʃ] *adj* unfashionable.

unmöglich ['unmœɪkliç] *adj* impossible. **Unmöglichkeit** *f* impossibility.

unmoralisch ['unmoɪrailiʃ] *adj* immoral.

unmündig ['unmyndiç] *adj* under age.

unnachgiebig ['innaxgiɪbiç] *adj* unyielding, uncompromising.

unnatürlich ['unnatyrliç] *adj* unnatural.

unnötig ['unnœɪtiç] *adj* unnecessary.

unnütz ['unnyts] *adj* useless, unprofitable.

unordentlich ['unordəntliç] *adj* disorderly, untidy. **Unordentlichkeit** *f* untidiness, disorderliness. **—nung** *f* disorder.

unorganisch ['unorgainiʃ] *adj* inorganic.

unpaar ['unpaɪr] *adj* odd.

unparteiisch ['unpartaiiʃ] *or* **unparteilich** *adj* impartial, unbiased. **Unparteilichkeit** *f* impartiality.

unpassend ['unpasənt] *adj* unsuitable, inappropriate; (*unschicklich*) improper.

unpersönlich ['unperzœɪnliç] *adj* impersonal.

unpolitisch ['unpolitiʃ] *adj* nonpolitical.

Unrat ['unrait] *m* refuse, dirt.

unratsam ['unraitzam] *adj* inadvisable.

unrecht ['unrɛçt] *adj* wrong; (*ungerecht*) unjust. **Unrecht** *neut* wrong; (*Ungerechtigkeit*) injustice. **unrechtmäßig** *adj* illegal, unlawful, illegitimate.

unregelmäßig ['unregalmeɪsiç] *adj* irregular. **Unregelmäßigkeit** *f* irregularity.

unreif ['unraif] *adj* unripe; (*Mensch*) immature.

unrein ['unrain] *adj* dirty, unclean; (*fig*) impure.

unrentabel ['unrentaɪbəl] *adj* unprofitable.

unrichtig ['unriçtiç] *adj* incorrect.

Unruhe ['unruːə] *f* restlessness; (*Aufruhr*) unrest. (*Uhr*) balance(-wheel). **unruhig** *adj* restless.

uns [uns] *pron* (to) us; (*Reflexiv*) (to) ourselves.

unsauber ['unzaubər] *adj* unclean, dirty; (*unfair*) unfair.

unschätzbar ['unʃetsbaɪr] *adj* inestimable.

unscheinbar ['unʃainbaɪr] *adj* inconspicuous.

unschicklich ['unʃikliç] *adj* improper, unseemly.

unschlüssig ['unʃlysiç] *adj* irresolute.

unschön ['unʃœɪn] *adj* unlovely, unpleasant.

Unschuld ['unʃult] *f* innocence. **unschuldig** *adj* innocent.

unselbständig ['unzelpʃtendiç] *adj* dependent.

unselig ['unzeːliç] adj unfortunate, fatal.

unser ['unzər] adj our. pron ours. **unser(er) seits** adv for our part, as for us. **unser(es)gleichen** pron people like us. pron der, die, das uns(e)rige ours. **unserthalben, unsertwegen, unsertwillen** for our sakes.

unsicher ['unziçər] adj unsafe, insecure; (zweifelhaft) uncertain. **Unsicherheit** f insecurity, uncertainty.

unsichtbar ['unziçtbaːr] adj invisible.

Unsinn ['unzin] m nonsense. **unsinnig** adj nonsensical.

unsittlich ['unzitliç] adj indecent, immoral. **Unsittlichkeit** f immorality.

unsre ['unzrə] V unser.

unsrige ['unzrigə] V unser.

unsterblich ['unʃterpliç] adj immortal. **Unsterblichkeit** f immortality.

unstet ['unʃtet] adj unsteady, inconstant.

Unstimmigkeit ['unʃtimiçkait] f (pl -en) inconsistency; (Meinungsverschiedenheit) disagreement.

unsympathisch ['unzympatiʃ] adj disagreeable, unpleasant.

Untat ['untaːt] f outrage, crime.

untätig ['untɛːtiç] adj inactive, idle. **Untätigkeit** f inactivity, idleness.

untauglich ['untaukliç] adj unfit; (Sache) unusable.

unten ['untən] adv below, at the bottom; (im Hause) downstairs. **nach unten** downwards. **von oben bis unten** from top to bottom. **von unten an** from the bottom (up).

unter ['untər] prep below, under; (zwischen) between, among. adj lower. **unter allen Umständen** under any circumstances. **unter uns** between you and me. **unter vier Augen** in private. **unter der Hand** secretly.

Unterarm ['untərarm] m forearm.

Unterbau ['untərbau] m foundations pl.

unterbelichten ['untərbəliçtən] v (Foto) underexpose.

unterbevölkert ['untərbəfœlkərt] adj underpopulated.

unterbewußt ['untərbəvust] adj subconscious. **Unterbewusstsein** neut subconsciousness.

*unterbleiben [untər'blaibən] v not occur.

*unterbrechen [untər'breçən] v interrupt; (Telef) cut off, disconnect. **Unterbrechung** f interruption.

*unterbringen ['untərbriŋən] v accommodate, lodge, shelter; (lagern) store.

unterdrücken [untər'drykən] v suppress. **Unterdrückung** f suppression.

untereinander [untərain'andər] adv with each other, with one another.

unterentwickelt ['untərentvikəlt] adj underdeveloped.

Unterführung [untər'fyːruŋ] f underpass.

Untergang ['untərgaŋ] m (Sonne) setting; (Schiff) sinking, wreck; (fig) decline, fall.

Untergebene(r) [untər'geːbənə(r)] m subordinate.

*untergehen ['untərgeːən] v sink; (Sonne) set; (fig) perish, be lost.

untergeordnet ['untərgəordnət] adj subordinate.

Untergestell ['untərgəʃtɛl] neut undercarriage.

Untergewicht ['untərgəviçt] neut short weight. **Untergewicht haben** be underweight.

*untergraben [untər'graːbən] v undermine.

Untergrund ['untərgrunt] m subsoil. **–bahn** f underground (railway), (US) subway.

unterhalb ['untərhalp] prep below, under(neath).

Unterhalt ['untərhalt] m support, keep; (Instandhaltung) maintenance. **unterhalten** v (Person) keep, support; (Instand halten) maintain; (zerstreuen) entertain. **sich unterhalten** enjoy oneself; (reden mit) converse (with), talk (to). **unterhaltsam** adj entertaining, amusing. **Unterhaltung** f entertainment, amusement; (Instandhaltung) maintenance. **–skosten** pl maintenance costs.

unterhandeln [untər'handəln] v negotiate.

Unterhaus ['untərhaus] neut lower chamber (of parliament).

Unterhemd ['untərhɛmt] neut vest, (US) undershirt.

Unterholz ['untərholts] neut undergrowth.

Unterhose ['untərhoːzə] f underpants pl.

unterirdisch ['untərirdiʃ] adj underground.

*unterkommen ['untərkɔmən] v find accommodation or shelter; (Arbeit) find work.

Unterkunft ['untərkunft] f accommodation, lodgings pl.

Unterlage ['ʊntərlaːgə] f base, basis, foundation; (*Beweisstück*) (documentary) evidence.

Unterlaß ['ʊntərlas] m **ohne Unterlaß** incessantly, unceasingly.

*__unterlassen__ [ʊntər'lasən] v neglect, fail (to do), omit. **Unterlassung** f omission.

unterlegen [ʊntər'leːgən] adj inferior.

Unterleib ['ʊntərlaip] m abdomen.

*__unterliegen__ [ʊntər'liːgən] v be defeated. **es unterliegt keinem Zweifel** it is not open to doubt.

Untermieter ['ʊntərmiːtər] m lodger.

*__unternehmen__ [ʊntər'neːmən] v undertake, attempt. **Unternehmen** neut undertaking, enterprise; (*Firma*) firm. **Unternehmer** m entrepreneur, contractor. **unternehmungslustig** adj enterprising.

Unteroffizier ['ʊntərɔfitsiːr] m noncommissioned officer, NCO.

Unterredung [ʊntər'reːduŋ] f (pl **-en**) conversation, discussion.

Unterricht ['ʊntərrɪçt] m (pl **-e**) instruction, lessons pl, teaching. **Unterricht geben** teach, give lessons. **unterrichten** v teach, give lessons. **unterrichten** v instruct, teach; (*benachrichtigen*) inform.

Unterrock ['ʊntərrɔk] m slip, petticoat.

unters ['ʊntərs] prep + art **unter das**.

untersagen [ʊntər'zaːgən] v forbid, prohibit.

*__unterscheiden__ [ʊntər'ʃaidən] v distinguish. **sich unterscheiden** differ.

*__unterschieben__ [ʊntər'ʃiːbən] v attribute (to); substitute.

Unterschied ['ʊntərʃiːt] m (pl **-e**) difference. **unterschiedlich** adj different.

*__unterschlagen__ [ʊntər'ʃlaːgən] v (*Geld*) embezzle; (*Nachricht*) suppress. **Unterschlagung** f embezzlement; suppression.

Unterschlupf ['ʊntərʃlʊpf] m (pl **Unterschlüpfe**) refuge, hiding place.

*__unterschreiben__ [ʊntər'ʃraibən] v sign. **Unterschrift** ['ʊntərʃrɪft] f signature.

Unterseeboot ['ʊntərzeːboːt] neut submarine. **unterseeisch** adj submarine.

unterst ['ʊntərst] adj lowest, bottom, undermost.

*__unterstehen__ [ʊntər'ʃteːən] v be subordinate (to). **sich unterstehen** dare.

*__unterstreichen__ [ʊntər'ʃtraiçən] v underline.

unterstützen [ʊntər'ʃtʏtsən] v support, assist. **Unterstützung** f (pl **-en**) support, assistance.

untersuchen [ʊntər'zuːxən] v examine. **Untersuchung** f examination. **-shaft** f imprisonment on remand.

Untertan ['ʊntərtaːn] m (pl **-en**) subject.

Untertasse ['ʊntərtasə] f saucer.

untertauchen ['ʊntərtauxən] v dive; (*verschwinden*) disappear.

Unterteil ['ʊntərtail] m bottom (part).

Untertitel ['ʊntərtiːtəl] m (Film) subtitle.

unterwärts ['ʊntərvɛrts] adv downwards.

Unterwäsche ['ʊntərvɛʃə] f underwear.

unterwegs [ʊntər'veːks] adv on the way, en route.

*__unterweisen__ [ʊntər'vaizən] v instruct, teach. **Unterweisung** f instructions pl.

Unterwelt ['ʊntərvɛlt] f underworld.

*__unterwerfen__ [ʊntər'vɛrfən] v subject (to); (*besiegen*) subjugate. **sich unterwerfen** submit, surrender. **unterworfen** adj subject (to).

unterwürfig [ʊntər'vʏrfɪç] adj obsequious.

unterzeichnen [ʊntər'tsaiçnən] v sign. **Unterzeichnung** f signature.

*__unterziehen__ [ʊntər'tsiːən] v subject. **sich unterziehen** undergo, submit (to).

untief ['ʊntiːf] adj shallow.

untreu ['ʊntrɔy] adj unfaithful.

untrüglich [ʊn'tryːklɪç] adj infallible, certain.

untüchtig ['ʊntʏçtɪç] adj incompetent, incapable.

Untugend ['ʊntuːgənt] f vice.

unüberlegt ['ʊnyːbərleːkt] adj ill-considered, hasty.

unüberwindlich ['ʊnyːbərvɪntlɪç] adj impregnable; insurmountable, insuperable.

ununterbrochen ['ʊnʊntərbrɔxən] adj uninterrupted.

unveränderlich ['ʊnfɛrɛndərlɪç] adj unchangeable.

unverantwortlich [ʊnfɛr'antvɔrtlɪç] adj irresponsible. **Unverantwortlichkeit** f irresponsibility.

unverbesserlich [ʊnfɛr'bɛsərlɪç] adj incorrigible.

unverbindlich ['ʊnfɛrbɪntlɪç] adj not binding; (*Komm*) without obligation.

unverdaulich ['ʊnfɛrdaulɪç] adj indigestible.

unverderblich ['ʊnfɛrdɛrplɪç] adj incorruptible.

unverdient ['unferdiːmt] *adj* unearned, undeserved.

unvereinbar [unfer'ainbaır] *adj* incompatible.

unverfroren ['unferfroːrən] *adj* impudent, brazen. **Unverfrorenheit** *f* impudence.

unvergänglich ['unfergeːsliç] *adj* imperishable; immortal.

unvergeßlich [unfer'geːsliç] *adj* unforgettable.

unverhältnismäßig ['unferheltnismeːsiç] *adj* disproportionate.

unverheiratet ['unferhairaːtət] *adj* unmarried.

unvermeidlich [unfer'maitliç] *adj* unavoidable.

unvermittelt ['unfermitəlt] *adj* sudden, unexpected.

Unvermögen ['unfermœːgən] *neut* inability, powerlessness.

unvermutet ['unfermuːtət] *adj* unexpected.

unvernünftig ['unfernynftiç] *adj* unreasonable.

unverschämt ['unferʃeːmt] *adj* impudent, impertinent. **Unverschämtheit** *f* impudence, impertinence.

unversehens ['unferzeːəns] *adv* suddenly, unexpectedly.

unversöhnlich ['unferzœːnliç] *adj* irreconcilable.

unverständlich ['unferʃtɛntliç] *adj* unintelligible.

unverträglich ['unfertreːkliç] *adj* incompatible; unsociable.

unverzagt ['unfertsaːkt] *adj* undaunted, fearless.

unverzüglich ['unfertsyːkliç] *adj* immediate, instant.

unvollkommen ['unfɔlkɔmən] *adj* imperfect.

unvoreingenommen ['unfɔraingənɔmən] *adj* unprejudiced.

unvorsichtig ['unfɔrziçtiç] *adj* careless, incautious; (*unklug*) imprudent.

unvorstellbar ['unfɔrʃtɛlbaır] *adj* unimaginable.

unvorteilhaft ['unfɔrtailhaft] *adj* unfavourable.

unwahr ['unvaır] *adj* untrue. **-haftig** *adj* untruthful. **Unwahrheit** *f* untruth, falsehood. **unwahrscheinlich** *adj* unlikely, improbably; (*umg.*) fantastic, incredible. *adv* (*umg.*) incredibly.

unweit ['unvait] *prep, adv* near, not far (from).

Unwetter ['unvetər] *neut* storm.

unwichtig ['unviçtiç] *adj* unimportant. **Unwichtigkeit** *f* unimportance; (*Sache*) trifle.

unwiderruflich [unviːdər'ruːfliç] *adj* irrevocable.

unwiderstehlich [unviːdər'ʃteːliç] *adj* irresistible.

unwillig ['unviliç] *adj* indignant; (*widerwillig*) unwilling, reluctant.

unwillkürlich ['unvilkyːrliç] *adj* involuntary; instinctive.

unwirksam ['unvirkzaːm] *adj* ineffective.

unwissend ['unvisənt] *adj* ignorant. **Unwissenheit** *f* ignorance. **unwissentlich** *adv* unconsciously, unwittingly.

unwürdig ['unvyrdiç] *adj* unworthy.

Unzahl ['untsaːl] *f* endless number.

unzählbar ['untseːlbaır] *or* **unzählig** *adj* innumerable.

unzeitgemäß ['untsaitgəmeːs] *adj* inopportune; (*unmodisch*) outdated. **unzeitig** *adj* premature; (*Obst*) unripe.

unzerbrechlich [untser'breçliç] *adj* unbreakable.

unzertrennlich [untser'trɛnliç] *adj* inseparable.

unziemlich ['untsiːmliç] *adj* unseemly.

Unzucht ['untsuxt] *f* lechery, fornication; (*Jur*) sexual offence. **unzüchtig** *adj* lewd, lecherous.

unzufrieden ['untsufriːdən] *adj* dissatisfied.

unzugänglich ['untsuːgɛnliç] *adj* inaccessible.

unzulänglich ['untsuːlɛnliç] *adj* inadequate, insufficient.

unzulässig ['untsuːlɛsiç] *adj* inadmissible.

unzureichend ['untsuraiçənt] *adj* insufficient, inadequate.

unzuverlässig ['untsuferlɛsiç] *adj* unreliable.

unzweifelhaft ['untsfaifəlhaft] *adj* undoubted.

üppig ['ypiç] *adj* abundant, luxuriant; (*blühend*) exuberant; (*wollüstig*) voluptuous.

uralt ['uralt] *adj* very old, ancient.

Uran [u'raːn] *neut* uranium.

uranfänglich ['uranfeŋliç] *adj* original, premordial.

Uraufführung ['urauffyːruŋ] *f* first performance, première.

urban ['ur'bain] *adj* urbane.

urbar ['uirbair] *adj* arable.

Ureinwohner ['uirainvoinər] *m* aboriginal.

Ureltern ['uireltərn] *pl* ancestors.

Urenkel ['uireŋkəl] *m* (*Kind*) great-grandchild, (*Junge*) great-grandson. **–in** *f* great-granddaughter.

Urgeschichte ['uirgəʃiçtə] *f* prehistory.

Urgroß‖eltern ['uirgroiseltərn] *pl* great-grandparents. **–mutter** *f* great-grandmother. **–vater** *m* great-grandfather.

Urheber ['uirheibər] *m* (*pl* -) author, creator. **–recht** *neut* copyright.

Urin [u'riin] *m* urine. **urinieren** *v* urinate.

Urkunde ['uirkundə] *f* document, deed; (*Zeugnis*) certificate. **urkundlich** *adj* documentary.

Urlaub ['uirlaup] *m* (*pl* -e) leave (of absence); (*Ferien*) holiday, vacation. **im** or **auf Urlaub** on holiday, on vacation.

Urmensch ['uirmenʃ] *m* primitive man.

Urne ['uirnə] *f* (*pl* -n) urn.

Ursache ['uirzaxə] *f* cause. **keine Ursache!** don't mention it!

Ursprung ['uirʃpruŋ] *m* source, origin. **ursprünglich** *adj* original. **Ursprungsland** *neut* country of origin.

Urteil ['urtail] *neut* judgment, verdict; (*Strafmaß*) sentence; (*Urteilskraft*) judgment. **urteilen** *v* judge. **Urteils‖kraft** *f* (power of) judgment, discernment. **–spruch** *m* verdict, sentence.

Urvater ['uirfaitər] *m* forefather.

Urwelt ['uirvelt] *f* primeval world.

Urzeit ['uirtsait] *f* prehistory, earliest times *pl.* **urzeitlich** *adj* primordial, primeval.

Utopie [uto'pii] *f* (*pl* -n) Utopia. **utopisch** *adj* utopian.

V

vag [vaik] *adj* vague.

Vagabund [vaga'bunt] *m* (*pl* -en) vagabond, tramp.

vakant [va'kant] *adj* vacant.

Vakuum ['vaikuum] *neut* (*pl* Vakua) vacuum.

validieren [vali'diirən] *v* make valid, validate.

Valuta [va'luitə] *f* (*pl* Valuten) (*Wert*) value; (*Währung*) currency.

Vampir ['vampir] *m* (*pl* -e) vampire.

Vandale [van'dailə] *m* (*pl* -n) vandal. **Vandalismus** *m* vandalism.

Vanille [va'niljə] *f* vanilla.

Varietät [varie'teit] *f* (*pl* -en) variety.

Variation [variatsi'oin] *f* (*pl* -en) variation.

Vase ['vaizə] *f* (*pl* -en) vase.

Vater ['faitər] *m* (*pl* Väter) father. **–land** *neut* native land, fatherland. **vaterländisch** *adj* national; patriotic. **väterlich** ['feitərliç] *adj* paternal, fatherly. **väterlicherseits** *adv* on the father's side. **Vaterschaft** ['faitərʃaft] *f* (*pl* -en) paternity.

Vegetarier [vege'tairiər] *m* (*pl* -) vegetarian. **vegetarisch** *adj* vegetarian.

Veilchen ['failçən] *neut* (*pl* -) violet. **veilchenblau** *adj* violet.

Vene ['veinə] *f* (*pl* -n) vein. **Venenentzündung** (*Med*) phlebitis.

Venedig [ve'neidiç] *neut* Venice. **venezianer** *m* (*pl* -), **Venezianerin** *f* (*pl* -nen) Venetian. **venezianisch** *adj* Venetian.

Ventil [ven'tiil] *neut* (*pl* -e) valve. **–ator** *m* (*pl* -en) ventilator. (*Mot*) fan; (*Elek*) electric fan.

verabreden [fer'apreidən] *v* agree (upon); (*Ort, Zeitpunkt*) fix, appoint. **Verabredung** *f* agreement; appointment.

verabscheuen [fer'apʃoyən] *v* abhor, detest.

verabschieden [fer'apʃiidən] *v* dismiss; (*Gesetze*) pass. **sich verabschieden von** take one's leave of, say goodbye to.

verachten [fer'axtən] *v* despise. **verächtlich** *adj* contemptible. **Verachtung** *f* contempt.

verallgemeinern [feralgə'mainərn] *v* generalize. **Verallgemeinerung** *f* generalization.

veralten [fer'altən] *v* become outmoded, go out of use. **veraltet** *adj* out-of-date.

veränderlich [fer'endərliç] *adj* changeable. **verändern** *v* change, alter. **sich verändern** change, alter. **Veränderung** *f* change, alteration.

Verankern [fer'aŋkərn] *v* moor, anchor.

veranlagt [fer'anlaikt] *adj* talented, gifted.

veranlassen [fer'anlasən] *v* cause, bring about. **Veranlassung** *f* cause; (*Beweggrund*) motive.

veranschaulichen [fer'anʃauliçən] *v* make clear.

veranstalten [fɛrˈanʃtaltən] v organize, arrange. **Veranstalt‖er** m (pl -) organizer. **-ung** f (pl -en) event, function; (Veranstalten) organization.

verantworten [fɛrˈantvɔrtən] v take responsibility for, answer for. **verantwortlich** adj responsible. **Verantwort‖lichkeit** f responsibility. **-ung** f (pl -en) responsibility; (Rechtfertigung) justification.

verarbeiten [fɛrˈaɪbaɪtən] v manufacture, make; (bearbeiten) work, process; (durchdenken) assimilate. **Verarbeitung** f manufacture; working; assimilation.

verargen [fɛrˈarɡən] v blame.

verärgern [fɛrˈɛrɡərn] v annoy, vex.

verarmen [fɛrˈaɪmən] v become poor. **verarmt** adj impoverished.

Verb [vɛrp] neut (pl -en) verb.

Verband [fɛrˈbant] m (pl Verbände) (Med) bandage, dressing; (Verein) association, society.

verbannen [fɛrˈbanən] v banish. **Verbann‖te(r)** m exile. **-ung** f banishment, exile.

***verbergen** [fɛrˈbɛrɡən] v hide.

verbessern [fɛrˈbɛsərn] v improve; (berichtigen) correct. **Verbesserung** f (pl -en) improvement; correction.

verbeugen v **sich verbeugen** bow.

***verbieten** [fɛrˈbiːtən] v forbid, prohibit.

***verbinden** [fɛrˈbɪndən] v connect, join; (Med) bandage, dress; (Telef) connect, put through. **sich verbinden mit** join up with, combine with. **verbindlich** adj binding, obligatory; (zuvorkommend) obliging. **Verbindung** f connection; (Med) bandage, dressing; (Telef) connection. **in Verbindung mit** in association with. **in Verbindung treten mit** get in touch with. **in Verbindung stehen mit** be in contact with. **in Verbindung setzen mit** put in contact with.

verbissen [fɛrˈbɪsən] adj grim, dogged.

verbittern [fɛrˈbɪtərn] v embitter. **Verbitterung** f bitterness.

verblassen [fɛrˈblasən] v turn or grow pale; (Farbe, Erinnerung) fade.

Verbleib [fɛrˈblaip] m whereabouts. **verbleiben** v remain.

verblenden [fɛrˈblɛndən] v blind, dazzle, delude; (Mauerwerk) face. **Verblendung** f blindness, delusion.

verblüffen [fɛrˈblyfən] v dumbfound, nonplus. **verblüfft** adj dumbfounded, nonplussed. **Verblüffung** f amazement, stupefaction.

verbluten [fɛrˈbluːtən] v bleed to death.

verbohrt [fɛrˈboːrt] adj stubborn.

verborgen [fɛrˈbɔrɡən] adj hidden. **Verborgenheit** f concealment, secrecy.

Verbot [fɛrˈboːt] neut (pl -e) prohibition, ban. **verboten** adj prohibited, forbidden.

Verbrauch [fɛrˈbraux] m consumption, use. **verbrauchen** v consume, use up. **Verbraucher** m (pl -) consumer. **Verbrauchsgüter** pl consumer goods pl.

Verbrechen [fɛrˈbrɛçən] neut crime. **-er** m criminal. **verbrechen** v commit a crime. **verbrecherisch** adj criminal.

verbreiten [fɛrˈbraitən] v spread. **weit verbreitet** adj widespread.

***verbrennen** [fɛrˈbrɛnən] v burn; (Leichen) cremate. **Verbrennung** f burning; cremation. **-smotor** m internal combustion engine.

***verbringen** [fɛrˈbrɪŋən] v spend (time).

verbrühen [fɛrˈbryːən] v scald.

Verbum [ˈvɛrbum] neut (pl Verben) verb.

verbünden [fɛrˈbyndən] v **sich verbünden mit** ally oneself with. **Verbündete(r)** m ally.

verchromt [fɛrˈkroːmt] adj chromium-plated. **Verchromung** f chromium plating.

Verdacht [fɛrˈdaxt] m (pl -e) suspicion. **in Verdacht kommen** arouse suspicion, be suspected. **verdächtig** adj suspicious. **-en** v suspect.

verdammen [fɛrˈdamən] v condemn, damn. **verdammt** adj damned. interj damn! **Verdammung** f damnation.

verdampfen [fɛrˈdampfən] v evaporate, vaporize. **Verdampfung** f evaporation, vaporization.

verdanken [fɛrˈdaŋkən] v owe.

verdauen [fɛrˈdauən] v digest. **verdaulich** adj digestible. **Verdauung** f digestion.

Verdeck [fɛrˈdɛk] neut (pl -e) canopy, covering; (Mot) roof; (Schiff) deck. **verdecken** v cover, conceal. **verdeckt** adj masked, concealed.

Verderb [fɛrˈdɛrp] m ruin, destruction. **verderben** v spoil, ruin; (verführen) corrupt; (Speisen) spoil, go bad; (Menschen) come to grief, perish. **Verderben** neut ruin, destruction. **verderblich** adj destructive, pernicious; (Waren) perishable. **verderbt** adj corrupt(ed).

verdeutlichen [fɛrˈdɔytliçən] v make clear, elucidate.

verdichten [fɛrˈdiçtən] v compress. **Verdichtung** f compression.

verdicken [fɛrˈdikən] v thicken.

verdienen [fɛrˈdiːnən] v (Geld) earn, (Beachtung, Lob) deserve. er hat es verdient he deserves it; (negativ) it serves him right. **Verdienst** 1 m (pl -e) earnings pl, gains pl. 2 neut (pl -e) deserts pl. –spanne f margin (of profit).

verdingen [fɛrˈdiŋən] v hire out.

verdoppeln [fɛrˈdɔpəln] v double. **Verdoppelung** f doubling.

verdorben [fɛrˈdɔrbən] adj spoilt; (fig) corrupted.

verdrängen [fɛrˈdrɛŋən] v displace, push out; (vertreiben) drive away; (Psychol) repress.

verdrehen [fɛrˈdreːən] v distort, twist.

*verdrießen [fɛrˈdriːsən] v vex, annoy. **verdrießlich** adj sullen, disgruntled; tiresome irksome.

verdrossen [fɛrˈdrɔsən] adj sullen. **Verdruß** [fɛrˈdrus] m annoyance.

verdummen [fɛrˈdumən] v stupefy; (dumm werden) grow stupid.

verdunkeln [fɛrˈduŋkəln] v darken.

verdünnen [fɛrˈdynən] v dilute, thin.

veredeln [fɛrˈeːdəln] v ennoble; (fig) improve, refine.

verehren [fɛrˈeːrən] v (Rel) worship; (lieben) adore; (hochschätzen) venerate, respect. **Verehr∥er** m worshipper; adorer; admirer. **–ung** f worship; adoration; veneration.

Verein [fɛrˈain] m (pl -e) society, association; (Klub) club. **vereinbar** adj reconcilable, compatible. **vereinbar∥en** v agree upon. **–t** adj agreed (upon). **Vereinbarung** f (pl -en) agreement.

vereinfachen [fɛrˈainfaxən] v simplify.

vereinheitlichen [fɛrˈainhaitliçən] v unify, standardize.

vereinigen [fɛrˈainigən] v unite, join. sich **vereinigen** unite. **vereinigt** adj united. die **Vereinigten Staaten** pl the United States. **Vereinigung** f (pl -en) union; association, society; (Zusammenschluß) combination. –spunkt m meeting point.

vereint [fɛrˈaint] adj united.

vereiteln [fɛrˈaitəln] v frustrate. **Vereitelung** f frustration.

vererben [fɛrˈɛrbən] v leave, bequeath;

(Krankheit, Eigenschaft) transmit. **vererblich** adj hereditary. **Vererbung** f heredity.

verewigen [fɛrˈeːvigən] v immortalize.

verfahren [fɛrˈfaːrən] v act, proceed. sich **verfahren** lose one's way. **Verfahren** neut procedure; (Methode) method; (Tech) process.

Verfall [fɛrˈfal] m ruin; (allmählich) decline, decay. **verfallen** v decline, decay.

verfälschen [fɛrˈfɛlʃən] v falsify. **Verfälschung** f falsification.

verfassen [fɛrˈfasən] v compose, write; (Urkunde) draw up. **Verfasser** m (pl -). **Verfasserin** f (pl -nen) author, writer.

*verfechten [fɛrˈfɛçtən] v fight for, defend.

verfehlen [fɛrˈfeːlən] v miss, not reach; (versäumen) fail. **Verfehlung** f mistake, lapse.

verfeinern [fɛrˈfainərn] v refine.

verflechten [fɛrˈflɛçtən] v interweave; (fig) involve.

verfluchen [fɛrˈfluːxən] v curse. **verflucht** adj cursed, damned. interj damn (it)!

verfolgen [fɛrˈfɔlgən] v pursue; (beobachten) follow; (gerichtlich) prosecute; (plagen) persecute. **Verfolger** m pursuer; persecutor. **Verfolgung** f pursuit; prosecution; persecution.

Verformung [fɛrˈfɔrmuŋ] f distortion, warping.

verfügbar [fɛrˈfyːkbair] adj available. **verfügen** v order, decree. **verfügen über** have at one's disposal, dispose of. **Verfügung** f disposal; (Anordnung) order. **zur Verfügung stehen/stellen** be/put at the disposal (of).

verführen [fɛrˈfyːrən] v seduce; (verleiten) lead astray. **Verführ∥er** m seducer; tempter. **–ung** f seduction; temptation.

vergangen [fɛrˈgaŋən] adj past. **Vergangenheit** f past. **vergänglich** adj transitory, impermanent.

Vergaser [fɛrˈgaːzər] m (pl -) carburettor.

*vergeben [fɛrˈgeːbən] v (verzeihen) forgive; (verschenken) give away; (verteilen) distribute. **vergeb∥ens** adv in vain. **–lich** adj vain. adv in vain. **Vergebung** f forgiveness. interj pardon me!

vergegenwärtigen [fɛrgeːgənˈvɛrtigən] v represent.

*vergehen [fɛrˈgeːən] v pass. **vergehen vor** die of. sich **vergehen** v commit an offence, err. **Vergehen** neut misdeed.

*vergelten [fɛr'gɛltən] v pay back. Vergeltung f reward; retaliation.

*vergessen [fɛr'gɛsən] v forget. Vergessenheit f oblivion. vergeßlich adj forgetful.

vergeuden [fɛr'gɔydən] v waste, squander. Vergeudung f waste, dissipation.

vergewaltigen [fɛrgə'valtigən] v rape. Vergewaltiger m rapist. Vergewaltigung f rape.

*vergießen [fɛr'giːsən] v shed, spill.

vergiften [fɛr'giftən] v poison. Vergiftung f poisoning.

Vergißmeinnicht [fɛr'gismainniçt] neut (pl -e) forget-me-not.

verglasen [fɛr'glaːzən] v glaze.

Vergleich [fɛr'glaiç] m (pl -e) comparison; (Redewendung) simile; (Abkommen) agreement, settlement. einen Vergleich schließen come to an agreement. im Vergleich mit/zu in comparison with/to. vergleichbar adj comparable. vergleichen v compare; settle, agree.

Vergnügen [fɛr'gnyːgən] neut enjoyment. vergnügen v amuse. sich vergnügen amuse oneself. vergnügt adj merry, happy. Vergnügung f pleasure, enjoyment. -spark m amusement park.

vergoldet [fɛr'gɔldət] adj (Metall) gold-plated; (Holz) gilt.

vergöttern [fɛr'gœtərn] v deify; (fig) idolize.

vergraben [fɛr'graːbən] v bury.

vergriffen [fɛr'grifən] adj sold out; (Buch) out of print.

vergrößern [fɛr'grœsərn] v enlarge, magnify. Vergrößerung f (pl -en) enlargement.

Vergünstigung [fɛr'gynstiguŋ] f (pl -en) privilege; (Rabatt) discount.

vergüten [fɛr'gyːtən] v compensate (for); (Unkosten) reimburse. Vergütung f (pl -en) compensation; reimbursement.

verhaften [fɛr'haftən] v arrest. verhaftet adj arrested; (fig) bound, connected. Verhaftung f (pl -en) arrest.

*verhalten [fɛr'haltən] v hold back. sich verhalten behave, act; (Sache) be. Verhalten neut behaviour.

Verhältnis [fɛr'hɛltnis] neut (pl -se) relation, proportion; (Beziehungen) relation; (Liebesaffäre) relationship; liaison. im Verhältnis zu in comparison with. Verhältnisse pl circumstances. Verhältnismäßig adj proportional. adv relatively, comparatively.

verhandeln [fɛr'handəln] v negotiate. Verhandlung f negotiation.

Verhängnis [fɛr'hɛŋnis] neut (pl -se) fate, destiny. verhängnisvoll adj fateful.

verhaßt [fɛr'hast] adj odious, hated.

verheeren [fɛr'heːrən] v devastate, lay waste.

verheimlichen [fɛr'haimliçən] v conceal, keep secret.

verheiraten [fɛr'hairatən] v marry. sich verheiraten get married, marry.

*verheißen [fɛr'haisən] v promise.

*verhelfen [fɛr'hɛlfən] v assist, help.

verherrlichen [fɛr'hɛrliçən] v glorify. Verherrlichung f glorification.

verhindern [fɛr'hindərn] v prevent. Verhinderung f prevention.

verhöhnen [gɛr'hœːnən] v ridicule, mock.

Verhör [fɛr'hœːr] neut (pl -e) interrogation, examination. verhören v interrogate, examine. sich verhören hear wrongly, misunderstand.

verhungern [fɛr'huŋərn] v starve (to death).

verhüten [fɛr'hyːtən] v prevent, ward off. -d adj preventive. Verhütung f prevention. -smittel neut contraceptive.

verirren [fɛr'irən] v sich verirren go astray, get lost.

verjüngen [fɛr'jyŋən] v rejuvenate; (erneuern) renew. Verjüngung f rejuvenation; renewal.

Verkauf [fɛr'kauf] m sale. verkaufen v sell. Verkäufer m seller; (Angestellter) salesman; (im Laden) sales assistant. -in f saleswoman, sales assistant. verkäuflich adj for sale. Verkaufs||abteilung f sales department. -automat m vending machine. -bedingungen (pl) terms of sale. -förderung f sales promotion. -preis m selling price.

Verkehr [fɛr'keːr] m traffic; (Umgang) intercourse; (Handel) trade. verkehren v (Bus) run; (verdrehen) distort; (besuchen) frequent; (Menschen) associate (with). Verkehrs||ampeln f pl traffic lights. -ordnung f traffic regulation. -spitze f rush hour. -stockung f traffic jam. -unfall m road accident. verkehrt adj inverted, wrong way round; (falsch) wrong.

*verkennen [fɛr'kɛnən] v mistake, misjudge; (Person) not recognize.

verklagen [fɛr'klaːgən] v (*Jur*) sue (for); (*umg.*) inform against.

verklären [fɛr'klɛːrən] v transfigure; (*fig*) illumine. **Verklärung** f transfiguration; illumination.

verkleiden [fɛr'klaidən] v cover, mask; (*Wand*) face. **sich verkleiden** disguise oneself. **Verkleidung** f (*pl* -en) disguise; facing, lining.

verkleinern [fɛr'klainərn] v reduce, diminish. **Verkleinerung** f (*pl* -en) reduction, diminution.

verknüpfen [fɛr'knypfən] v knot (together), join; (*fig*) connect. **verknüpft** adj connected.

***verkommen** [fɛr'kɔmən] v (*Person*) degenerate, (*umg.*) go to the dogs; (*speisen*) go bad; (*Gebäude*) decay, be neglected.

verkörpern [fɛr'kœrpərn] v embody. **Verkörperung** f embodiment, incarnation.

verkrümmen [fɛr'krymən] v bend, make crooked. **Verkrümmung** f (*pl* -en) crookedness, distortion; (*Rückgrat*) curvature.

verkrüppeln [fɛr'krypəln] v cripple.

verkünden [fɛr'kyndən] v announce, proclaim; (*Urteil*) pronounce. **verkündigen** v proclaim. **Mariä Verkündigung** Annunciation, Lady Day.

verkürzen [fɛr'kyrtsən] v shorten, abbreviate; (*Buch*) abridge. **sich verkürzen** shrink, diminish. **Verkürzung** f shortening; (*Buch*) abridgment.

***verladen** [fɛr'laːdən] v load; (*verschicken*) dispatch. **Verladung** f loading.

Verlag [fɛr'laːk] m (*pl* -e) publishing house, publisher.

verlangen [fɛr'laŋən] v demand; (*benötigen*) require. **verlangen nach** long for. **Verlangen** neut demand; (*Wunsch*) desire. **auf Verlangen** on demand.

verlängern [fɛr'lɛŋərn] v extend, lengthen; (*Gültigkeit, usw.*) extend. **Verlängerung** f (*pl* -en) extension.

verlangsamen [fɛr'laŋzaɪmən] v · slow down.

Verlaß [fɛr'las] m trustworthiness, reliability. **verlassen** v leave; (*im Stich lassen*) desert, abandon. adj abandoned, forsaken. **sich verlassen auf** rely on. **verläßlich** adj reliable.

Verlauf [fɛr'lauf] m course. **verlaufen** v (*Zeit*) pass; (*Angelegenheit*) go, turn out; (*Weg*) run, to. *es ist alles gut verlaufen*

everything went very well. **sich verlaufen** lose one's way.

verlautbaren [fɛr'lautbaːrən] v notify.

verlegen [fɛr'leːgən] v misplace; (*Platz ändern*) transfer, remove; (*Buch*) publish; (*Termin*) postpone. adj embarrassed. **Verleg‖enheit** f embarrassment; (*Schwierigkeit*) difficulty. **-er** m (*pl* -) publisher.

***verleihen** [fɛr'laiən] v lend; (*Preise*) confer, bestow.

verleiten [fɛr'laitən] v lead astray, mislead.

verlernen [fɛr'lɛrnən] v forget.

***verlesen** [fɛr'leːzən] v read out; (*auslesen*) pick. **sich verlesen** misread.

verletzen [fɛr'lɛtsən] v injure, wound; (*kränken*) hurt, offend; (*Gesetze*) infringe. **verletzlich** adj vulnerable; (*fig*) sensitive, touchy. **Verletzung** f (*pl* -en) injury; (*Vergehen*) offence.

verleugnen [fɛr'lɔygnən] v deny; (*Kind, Freunde*) disown.

verleumden [fɛr'lɔymdən] v slander. **Verleumder** m (*pl* -) slanderer. **verleumderisch** adj slanderous. **Verleumdung** f (*pl* -en) slander.

verlieben [fɛr'liːbən] v **sich verlieben in** fall in love with.

***verlieren** [fɛr'liːrən] v lose. **sich verlieren** get lost.

verloben [fɛr'loːbən] v **sich verloben mit** get engaged to. **Verlobte** f (*pl* -n) fiancée. **Verlobter** m (*pl* -en) fiancé. **Verlobung** f (*pl* -en) engagement.

verlocken [fɛr'lɔkən] v tempt, entice. **-d** adj tempting. **Verlockung** f (*pl* -en) enticement, temptation.

verlogen [fɛr'loːgən] adj untruthful, lying.

verloren [fɛr'loːrən] adj lost. **-gehen** v be lost.

Verlust [fɛr'lust] m (*pl* -e) loss. **verlustbringend** adj detrimental.

vermachen [fɛr'maxən] v bequeath, leave. **Vermächtnis** neut (*pl* -se) (*Testament*) will; (*Vermachtes*) legacy, bequest.

vermehren [fɛr'meːrən] v also **sich vermehren** increase. **Vermehrung** f (*pl* -en) increase.

***vermeiden** [fɛr'maidən] v avoid. **vermeidlich** adj avoidable. **Vermeidung** f avoidance.

vermeintlich [fɛr'maintliç] adj supposed, presumed.

Vermerk [fɛr'mɛrk] m (pl -e) note, remark. **vermerken** v note, remark.

*****vermessen** [fɛr'mɛsən] v measure; (Land) survey. adj presumptuous. **Vermess||er** m surveyor. **-ung** f measurement; (Land) survey.

vermieten [fɛr'miːtən] v let, rent (out). **Vermiet||er** m landlord. **-ung** f letting.

vermindern [fɛr'mɪndərn] v reduce, decrease. **Verminderung** f reduction, decrease.

vermischen [fɛr'mɪʃən] v mix, blend.

vermissen [fɛr'mɪsən] v miss. **vermißt** adj missing.

vermitteln [fɛr'mɪtəln] v mediate, negotiate; (verschaffen) procure, obtain. **Vermittl||er** m mediator, go-between; (Komm) agent. **-ung** f (pl -en) mediation, negotiation; (Telef) exchange.

*****vermögen** [fɛr'mœːgən] v be able (to). **-d** adj well-to-do. **Vermögen** neut fortune, wealth, property; (Fähigkeit) ability. **-sverwalter** m trustee (of an estate).

vermuten [fɛr'muːtən] v suppose, suspect. **vermutlich** adj supposed. adv probably, presumably. **Vermutung** f (pl -en) supposition, suspicion.

vernachlässigen [fɛr'naxlɛsɪgən] v neglect.

vernarren [fɛr'narən] v **sich vernarren in** become infatuated with; (Kind) dote on.

*****vernehmen** [fɛr'neːmən] v perceive; (Gefangene) interrogate. **vernehmlich** adj perceptible.

verneinen [fɛr'nainən] v deny; (Frage) say no, answer in the negative. **Verneinung** f denial; negation.

vernichten [fɛr'nɪçtən] v destroy, annihilate. **-d** adj annihilating, crushing. **Vernichtung** f destruction, annihilation.

vernieten [fɛr'niːtən] v rivet.

Vernunft [fɛr'nʊnft] f reason; (Besonnenheit) sense, commonsense. **zur Vernunft kommen** come to one's senses. **vernünftig** adj sensible, reasonable.

veröden [fɛr'œːdən] v become desolate.

veröffentlichen [fɛr'œfəntliçən] v publish. **Veröffentlichung** f publication.

verordnen [fɛr'ɔrdnən] v order; (Med) prescribe. **Verordnung** f order; prescription.

verpachten [fɛr'paxtən] v lease, let.

verpacken [fɛr'pakən] v pack.

verpassen [fɛr'pasən] v miss.

verpfänden [fɛr'pfɛndən] v pawn, pledge.

verpflegen [fɛr'pfleːgən] v feed. cater for. **Verpflegung** f food, board.

verpflichten [fɛr'pflɪçtən] v oblige, commit. **sich verpflichten** bind or commit oneself. **Verpflichtung** f obligation, commitment, duty.

verpfuschen [fɛr'pfuːʃən] v bungle, botch, make a mess of.

verprügeln [fɛr'pryːgəln] v thrash, beat.

verputzen [fɛr'pʊtsən] v plaster; (umg.) scoff, put away.

Verrat [fɛr'raːt] m (unz.) treachery; (Pol) treason; (eines Geheimnisses) betrayal. **verraten** v betray. **Verräter** m (pl -) traitor. **verräterisch** adj treacherous.

verrechnen [fɛr'rɛçnən] v reckon up. **sich verrechnen** miscalculate. **Verrechnung** f miscalculation.

verreisen [fɛr'raizən] v go away (on a journey).

verrenken [fɛr'rɛŋkən] v dislocate, sprain. **Verrenkung** f (pl -en) dislocation, sprain.

verrichten [fɛr'rɪçtən] v perform, do, execute.

verriegeln [fɛr'riːgəln] v bolt, bar.

verringern [fɛr'rɪŋərn] v reduce, lessen.

verrotten [fɛr'rɔtən] v rot. **verrottet** adj rotten.

verrücken [fɛr'rykən] v shift, displace. **verrückt** adj crazy.

Verruf [fɛr'ruːf] m ill repute, disrepute. **in Verruf bringen/kommen** bring/fall into disrepute.

Vers [fɛrs] m (pl -e) line; (Strophe) verse.

versagen [fɛr'zaːgən] v fail; (verweigern) refuse. **Versager** m (pl -) failure.

versammeln [fɛr'zaməln] v assemble, gather. **sich versammeln** meet. **Versammlung** f (pl -en) meeting, assembly, convention.

Versand [fɛr'zant] m dispatch, shipment, forwarding. **-handel** m mail-order (trading).

versäumen [fɛr'zɔymən] v neglect, fail; (verpassen) miss. **Versäumnis** f neglect, omission.

verschaffen [fɛr'ʃafən] v obtain, procure.

verschämt [fɛr'ʃɛːmt] adj bashful, ashamed.

Verschanzung [fɛr'ʃantsʊŋ] f (pl -en) fortification, entrenchment.

verschärfen [fɛr'ʃɛrfən] v sharpen, intensify.

*****verscheiden** v die. **verschieden** adj dead.

verschicken [fɛrˈʃɪkən] v send off, dispatch.

*****verschieben** [fɛrˈʃiːbən] v move, shift; (*Termin*) postpone. **Verschiebung** f displacement; postponement.

verschieden [fɛrˈʃiːdən] adj different. **–artig** adj various. **Verschiedenheit** f difference.

verschiffen [fɛrˈʃɪfən] v ship.

verschimmeln [fɛrˈʃɪməln] v moulder, grow mouldy.

*****verschlafen** [fɛrˈʃlaːfən] v oversleep; (*Sorgen*) sleep off. adj sleepy.

Verschlag [fɛrˈʃlaːk] m shed.

verschlechtern [fɛrˈʃlɛçtərn] v make worse, aggravate. **sich verschlechtern** deteriorate, get worse. **Verschlechterung** f deterioration.

verschleiern [fɛrˈʃlaiərn] v veil; (*fig*) camouflage, conceal.

Verschleiß [fɛrˈʃlais] m (*pl* -e) wear and tear. **verschleißen** v wear out.

verschleudern [fɛrˈʃlɔydərn] v waste, squander.

verschließbar [fɛrˈʃliːsbaːr] adj lockable. **verschließen** v lock; (*Sachen*) lock up or away.

verschlimmern [fɛrˈʃlɪmərn] v make worse, aggravate. **sich verschlimmern** become worse, deteriorate. **Verschlimmerung** f deterioration.

*****verschlingen** [fɛrˈʃliŋən] v devour, gorge; (*verflechten*) twist, intertwine.

verschlossen [fɛrˈʃlɔsən] adj locked; (*Person*) reserved, withdrawn.

verschlucken [fɛrˈʃlukən] v swallow.

Verschluß [fɛrˈʃlus] m fastening; (*Propfen*) stopper, plug; (*Phot*) shutter.

verschmähen [fɛrˈʃmɛːən] v despise, scorn.

*****verschmelzen** [fɛrˈʃmɛltsən] v melt, fuse; (*ineinander*) merge.

*****verschneiden** [fɛrˈʃnaidən] v trim, prune; (*Wein*) mix, adulterate; (*kastrieren*) castrate.

verschollen [fɛrˈʃɔlən] adj missing.

verschonen [fɛrˈʃoːnən] v spare.

verschönern [fɛrˈʃøːnərn] v beautify.

verschränken [fɛrˈʃrɛŋkən] v fold, cross.

verschulden [fɛrˈʃuldən] v fall into or be in debt; (*Übel*) be to blame for. **Verschulden** neut guilt, fault. **verschuldet** adj in debt.

*****verschweigen** [fɛrˈʃvaigən] v keep secret, hide. **Verschweigung** f concealment.

verschwenden [fɛrˈʃvɛndən] v waste, squander. **verschwenderisch** adj wasteful. **Verschwendung** f waste.

verschwiegen [fɛrˈʃviːgən] adj discreet; (*Platz*) secluded, quiet. **Verschwiegenheit** f discretion.

*****verschwinden** [fɛrˈʃvɪndən] v disappear.

verschwommen [fɛrˈʃvɔmən] adj blurred, hazy.

verschwören [fɛrˈʃvœːrən] v renounce, abjure. **sich verschwören** conspire, plot. **Verschwör||er** m conspirator, plotter. **–ung** f conspiracy.

*****versehen** [fɛrˈzeːən] v (*versorgan*) provide, supply; (*Dienst*) discharge; (*Haus, usw.*) look after. **sich versehen** make a mistake. **Versehen** neut mistake; (*Übersehen*) oversight. **versehentlich** adv by mistake.

*****versenden** [fɛrˈzɛndən] v send, dispatch.

versengen [fɛrˈzɛŋən] v singe, scorch.

versenken [fɛrˈzɛŋkən] v lower; (*unter Wasser*) submerge; (*Schiff*) sink. **sich versenken in** become absorbed in.

versessen [fɛrˈzɛsən] adj **versessen auf** mad about or on.

versetzen [fɛrˈzɛtsən] v move, transfer; (*verpfänden*) pawn; (*umg.*) leave in the lurch, jilt. **Versetzung** f removal, transfer.

verseuchen [fɛrˈzɔyçən] v contaminate.

versichern [fɛrˈzɪçərn] v insure; (*überzeugen*) assure. **sich versichern** make certain. **Seien Sie versichert, daß** you may rest assured that. **Versicherung** f insurance. **–spolice** f insurance policy.

versiegeln [fɛrˈziːgəln] v seal.

versöhnen [fɛrˈzøːnən] v reconcile. **sich versöhnen mit** become reconciled with. **versöhnlich** adj conciliatory. **Versöhnung** f reconciliation.

versorgen [fɛrˈzɔrgən] v (*Kind, usw.*) provide for. **versorgen mit** provide or supply with. **Versorgung** f care, provision; (*staatlich*) maintenance, (public) assistance.

verspäten [fɛrˈʃpɛːtən] v delay. **verspätet** adj late, delayed. **Verspätung** f (*pl* -en) delay. **10 Minuten Verspätung haben** be running 10 minutes late.

versperren [fɛrˈʃpɛrən] v bar; obstruct.

verspielen [fɛrˈʃpiːlən] v gamble away, lose.

verspotten [fɛr'ʃpɔtən] *v* scoff at, ridicule. **Verspottung** *f* ridicule.

*****versprechen** [fɛr'ʃprɛçən] *v* promise. **sich versprechen** make a (verbal) mistake. **Versprechen** *neut* (*pl* -) promise.

versprengen [fɛr'ʃprɛŋən] *v* (*Mil*) scatter, disperse.

versprochen [fɛr'ʃprɔxən] *adj* promised.

verstaatlichen [fɛr'ʃtaːtliçən] *v* nationalize. **Verstaatlichung** *f* nationalization.

Verstand [fɛr'ʃtant] *m* understanding; (*Geist*) mind, intelligence. **den Verstand verlieren** lose one's reason, go out of one's mind. **verständig** *adj* intelligent; sensible. **verständigen** *v* inform. **sich verständigen mit** (**über**) come to an understanding with (about). **Verständigung** *f* understanding, arrangement. **verständlich** *adj* intelligible. **Verständnis** *neut* understanding, comprehension. **verständnis∥los** *adj* uncomprehending, unappreciative. **-voll** *adj* understanding, sympathetic.

verstärken [fɛr'ʃtɛrkən] *v* strengthen; (*Ton*) amplify; (*Farbe, Spannung*) intensify. **Verstärk∥er** *m* amplifier. **-ung** *f* strengthening; (*Ton*) amplification; (*Mil*) reinforcements *pl*.

Versteck [fɛr'ʃtɛk] *neut* (*pl* -e) hiding place. **verstecken** *v* hide. **sich verstecken** hide. **versteckt** *adj* hidden; (*Anspielung*) veiled, implied.

*****verstehen** [fɛr'ʃteːən] *v* understand. **zu verstehen geben** give to understand. **sich verstehen mit** come to an understanding with.

Versteigerer [fɛr'ʃtaigərər] *m* (*pl* -) auctioneer. **versteigern** *v* (sell by) auction. **Versteigerung** *f* (*pl* -en) auction.

versteinern [fɛr'ʃtainərn] *v* petrify. **versteinert** *adj* petrified.

verstellbar [fɛr'ʃtɛlbaːr] *adj* adjustable, movable. **verstellen** *v* adjust; (*versperren*) block, bar; (*unkenntlich machen*) disguise. **sich verstellen** feign, dissemble. **Verstellung** *f* (*pl* -en) adjustment; (*fig*) pretence.

verstimmt [fɛr'ʃtimt] *adj* (*Musik*) out of tune; (*Person*) bad-tempered; (*Magen*) upset.

verstockt [fɛr'ʃtɔkt] *adj* stubborn.

verstohlen [fɛr'ʃtoːlən] *adj* furtive, stealthy.

verstopfen [fɛr'ʃtɔpfən] *v* plug, stop up; (*Med*) constipate. **Verstopfung** *f* obstruction; (*Med*) constipation.

verstorben [fɛr'ʃtɔrbən] *adj* deceased, late. **Verstorbene(r)** the deceased.

Verstoß [fɛr'ʃtoːs] *m* offence. **verstoßen** *v* offend; (*von sich stoßen*) reject.

verstricken [fɛr'ʃtrikən] *v* entangle, ensnare.

verstümmeln [fɛr'ʃtyməln] *v* mutilate, maim.

Versuch [fɛr'zuːx] *m* (*pl* -e) attempt; (*Probe*) test, trial; (*Experiment*) experiment. **versuchen** *v* attempt, try; (*kosten*) taste, try. **Versuchs∥fahrt** *f* trial run. **-kaninchen** *neut* (*pl* -) guinea pig.

vertagen [fɛr'taːgən] *v* adjourn.

vertauschen [fɛr'tauʃən] *v* exchange.

verteidigen [fɛr'taidigən] *v* defend. **Verteidig∥er** *m* (*pl* -) defender; (*Jur*) defence counsel. **-ung** *f* (*pl* -en) defence.

verteilen [fɛr'tailən] *v* distribute; (*zerteilen*) divide. **Verteil∥er** *m* (*pl* -) distributor. **-ung** *f* (*pl* -en) distribution.

vertiefen [fɛr'tiːfən] *v* deepen. **sich vertiefen in** be absorbed in. **vertieft** *adj* sunk; (*fig*) absorbed. **Vertiefung** *f* depression, hollow; (*fig*) absorption.

vertikal [vɛrti'kaːl] *adj* vertical.

vertilgen [fɛr'tilgən] *v* exterminate; (*vernichten*) destroy. **Vertilgung** *f* extermination; destruction.

Vertrag [fɛr'traːk] *m* (*pl* **Verträge**) contract; (*Pol*) treaty. **vertragen** *v* bear, endure. **sich vertragen mit** get on well with. **vertraglich** *adj* stipulated, agreed.

verträglich [fɛr'trɛːkliç] *adj* (*Person*) good-natured, obliging; (*Speise*) light, digestible.

Vertrags∥bruch *m* breach of contract. **-nehmer** *m* contractor.

vertrauen [fɛr'trauən] *v* trust. **vertrauen auf** trust in, have confidence in. **Vertrauen** *neut* trust, confidence. **Vertrauens∥sache** *f* confidential affair. **-votum** *neut* vote˙of confidence. **vertrauens∥voll** *adj* trustful, trusting. **-würdig** *adj* trustworthy. **vertraulich** *adj* confidential. **vertraut** *adj* familiar.

*****vertreiben** [fɛr'traibən] *v* expel, drive away; (*verkaufen*) sell. **Vertreibung** *f* (*pl* -en) expulsion.

*****vertreten** [fɛr'treːtən] *v* represent; (*vorübergehend*) replace, stand in for; (*eintreten für*) advocate. **Vertret∥er** *m* (*pl*

-) representative; (*Komm*) sales representative; **-ung** *f* (*pl* **-en**) representation.

Vertrieb [fer'triːp] *m* (retail) sale.

°**vertun** [fer'tuːn] *v* squander, spend.

vertuschen [fer'tuʃən] *v* hush up.

verunglimpfen [fer'unglimpfən] *v* defame, revile.

verunglücken [fer'unglykən] *v* be involved in an accident; (*Angelegenheit*) fail.

verunreinigen [fer'untainigən] *v* pollute, soil.

verunstalten [fer'unʃtaltən] *v* disfigure.

veruntreuen [fer'untrɔyən] *v* embezzle.

verursachen [fer'uːrzaxən] *v* cause, bring about.

verurteilen [fer'urtailən] *v* condemn; (*Jur*) sentence. **Verurteilung** *f* condemnation; conviction.

vervielfältigen [fer'fiːlfeltigən] *v* duplicate, copy. **Vervielfältigung** *f* reproduction, duplication.

vervollkommnen [fer'folkɔmnən] *v* perfect.

vervollständigen [fer'folʃtendigən] *v* complete.

°**verwachsen** [fer'vaksən] *v* grow together; (*Wunde*) heal up; (*bucklig werden*) become deformed; (**sich verbinden**) be tied to. *adj* deformed.

verwahren [fer'vairən] *v* keep; (*schützen*) protect, preserve.

verwahrlosen [fer'vailozən] *v* neglect. **verwahrlost** *adj* neglected; (*Kind*) scruffy, unkempt.

verwalten [fer'valtən] *v* administer, manage. **Verwalter** *m* administrator; (*Fabrik, Büro*) manager; (*Gut, Haus*) steward. **Verwaltung** *f* administration; management.

verwandeln [fer'vandəln] *v* transform; (*ändern*) change. **Verwandlung** *f* transformation; change.

verwandt [fer'vant] *adj* related. **Verwandt‖e(r)** relative, relation. **-schaft** *f* relationship; (*Verwandte*) relatives *pl*.

verwechseln [fer'veksəln] *v* confuse. **verwechseln mit** mistake for, confuse with. **Verwechslung** *f* confusion.

verwegen [fer'veigən] *adj* bold, audacious.

verweichlicht [fer'vaiçliçt] *adj* effeminate.

verweigern [fer'vaigərn] *v* refuse. **Verweigerung** *f* refusal.

verweilen [fer'vailən] *v* linger, stay.

Verweis [fer'vais] *m* (*pl* **-e**) reprimand,

rebuke; (*Hinweis*) reference. **verweisen** *v* reprimand, rebuke; (*verbannen*) exile, banish. **verweisen auf** refer to.

°**verwenden** [fer'vendən] *v* use, employ; apply; (*Zeit*) spend. **Verwendung** *f* use; application.

°**verwerfen** [fer'verfən] *v* throw away; (*zurückweisen*) reject.

verwesen[1] [fer'veisən] *v* (*verwalten*) administer.

verwesen[2] *v* (*verfaulen*) decay.

verwickeln [fer'vikəln] *n* entangle. **sich verwickeln in** become involved in. **verwickelt** *adj* complicated. **Verwicklung** *f* (*pl* **-en**) entanglement, complication.

verwirken [fer'virkən] *v* forfeit.

verwirklichen [fer'virkliçən] *v* realize. **sich verwirklichen** come true, materialize. **Verwirklichung** *f* realization.

°**verwirren** [fer'virən] *v* confuse, bewilder. **verwirrt** *adj* confused. **Verwirrung** *f* confusion.

verwischen [fer'viʃən] *v* blur, smear; (*fig*) cover up, wipe out.

verwitwet [fer'vitvət] *adj* widowed.

verwöhnen [fer'vœmən] *v* spoil. **verwöhnt** *adj* pampered, spoiled.

verworfen [fer'vorfən] *adj* depraved.

verworren [fer'vorən] *adj* confused.

verwundbar [fer'vuntbair] *adj* vulnerable. **verwunden** *v* wound, hurt. **verwundet** *adj* wounded. **Verwundete(r)** injured person; (*Mil*) casualty. **Verwundung** *f* wound, injury.

verwunderlich [fer'vundəarliç] *adj* surprising. **verwundern** *v* surprise, astonish. **sich verwundern über** be astonished by, wonder about. **Verwunderung** *f* astonishment.

verwünschen [fer'vynʃən] *v* curse. **verwünscht** *adj* cursed, bewitched.

verwüsten [fer'vyistən] *v* devastate. **Verwüstung** *f* devastation.

verzagt [fer'tsaikt] *adj* downcast, despondent.

verzaubern [fer'tsaubərn] *v* enchant, charm. **verzaubert** *adj* enchanted, magic.

Verzehr [fer'tseir] *m* consumption (of food and drink). **verzehren** *v* consume, take, eat.

verzeichnen [fer'tsaiçnən] *v* note, enter, write down. **Verzeichnis** *neut* (*pl* **-se**) list, catalogue; (*Buch*) index; (*Register*) register.

*verzeihen [fɛr'tsaiən] v pardon, forgive. **verzeihen Sie!** pardon (me)! I'm sorry! **Verzeihung** f pardon, forgiveness. *interj* I beg your pardon! excuse me!

verzerren [fɛr'tsɛrən] v distort.

Verzicht [fɛr'tsiçt] m (pl -e) renunciation. **verzichten auf** renounce, do without.

verziehen [fɛr'tsiːən] v distort; (Kinder) spoil.

verzieren [fɛr'tsiːrən] v decorate, adorn.

verzögern [fɛr'tsœːɡərn] v delay. **Verzögerung** f (pl -en) delay.

verzollen [fɛr'tsɔlən] v pay duty on.

verzücken [fɛr'tsykən] v enrapture. **verzückt** adj enraptured, ecstatic. **Verzückung** f (pl -en) rapture, ecstasy.

verzuckern [fɛr'tsukərn] v sugar.

Verzug [fɛr'tsuːk] m (unz.) delay.

verzweifeln [fɛr'tsvaifəln] v despair. **verzweifelt** adj desperate. **Verzweiflung** f despair.

verzwickt [fɛr'tsvikt] adj complicated, difficult.

veterinär [veteri'nɛːr] adj veterinary. **Veterinär** m (pl -e) veterinary surgeon.

Vetter ['fɛtər] m (pl -n) (male) cousin.

Vibration [vibratsi'oːn] f (pl -en) vibration. **vibrieren** v vibrate.

Vieh [fiː] 1 neut (unz.) cattle pl. 2 neut (pl Viecher) beast. **viehisch** adj bestial, brutal. **Vieh∥stall** m cowshed. **–treiber** m drover. **–zucht** f cattle-breeding.

viel [fiːl] adj much. **viele** pl adj many. **so viel** so much. **viel besser** much better. **viel mehr als** far more than. **recht viel** a great deal. **viel halten von** think much or highly of. **viel∥fach** adj multiple. *adv* frequently, many times. **–fältig** adj various, manifold.

vielleicht [fi'laiçt] adv perhaps.

viel∥mal(s) adv often, many times. **–mehr** adv, conj rather. **–seitig** adj many-sided. **–versprechend** adj (very) promising.

vier [fiːr] pron, adj four. **Viereck** neut square, rectangle. **viereckig** adj square, rectangular. **viermal(s)** adv four times. **viert** adj fourth. **Viertaktmotor** m four-stroke engine. **Viertel** neut quarter. **–stunde** f quarter (of an) hour. **viertens** adv fourthly.

vierzehn ['fiːrtseːn] pron, adj fourteen. **vierzehn Tage** fortnight. **vierzehnt** adj fourteenth.

vierzig ['fiːrtsiç] pron, adj forty. **vierzigst** adj fortieth.

Villa ['vila] f (pl Villen) villa.

Viola [vi'oːla] f (pl Violen) viola. **Viol∥ine** f violin. **–inist** m (pl -), **–inistin** f (pl -nen) violinist. **–oncello** neut violoncello, cello.

Virtuose [virtu'oːzə] m (pl -n) virtuoso.

Visite [vi'ziːtə] f (pl -n) visit. **–nkarte** f visiting card.

Visum ['viːzum] neut (pl Visa) visa.

Vitamin [vita'miːn] neut (pl -e) vitamin.

Vlies [fliːs] neut (pl -e) fleece.

Vogel ['foːɡəl] m (pl Vögel) bird. **–gesang** m bird-song. **–haus** neut aviary. **–kunde** f ornithology. **–perspektive** f or **–schau** f bird's-eye view.

vokal [vo'kaːl] adj vocal. **Vokal** m vowel.

Volk [fɔlk] neut (pl Völker) people, folk; nation.

Völker∥kunde f ethnology. **–schaft** people, tribe. **völkisch** adj national.

Volks∥eigentum neut public property. **–entscheid** m plebiscite, referendum. **–gruppe** f ethnic group. **–lied** neut (traditional) folksong. **–menge** f crowd. **–schule** f primary school. **–staat** m republic. **–tanz** m folk dance. **–tracht** f national costume.

volkstümlich ['fɔlkstyːmliç] adj popular. **Volkswirt** ['fɔlksvirt] m economist. **–schaft** f (political) economy. **volkswirtschaftlich** adj economic.

voll [fɔl] adj full. adv fully. der Topf ist voll Wasser the pot is full of water. ein Glas voll Milch a glassful of milk. in voller Blüte in full bloom. volles Gesicht round face. **voll∥auf** adv in abundance. **–automatisch** adj fully automatic. **–berechtigt** adj fully authorized. **–beschäftigt** adj fully employed. **–blütig** adj full-blooded.

*vollbringen [fɔ'briŋən] v accomplish. **Vollbringung** f accomplishment.

vollenden [fɔl'ɛndən] v finish, end, complete. **vollendet** adj completed; (vervollkomnet) perfect. **Vollendung** f completion; perfection.

voller ['fɔlər] adj or **voll von** full (of).

völlig ['fœliç] adj complete, entire, whole.

vollkommen ['fɔlkɔmən] adj perfect, finished. **Vollkommenheit** f perfection.

Voll∥kornbrot neut wholemeal bread. **–macht** f power of attorney, authority. **–milch** f whole milk.

voll‖ständig adj complete. **-stopfen** v stuff.

vollstrecken [fɔl'ʃtrekən] v execute, carry out. **Vollstreck‖er** m (pl -). **-erin** f (pl -nen) executor. **-ung** f (pl -en) execution.

*vollziehen [fɔl'tsi:ən] v carry out, execute.

Volontär [volɔn'tɛːr] m (pl -e) volunteer (worker), unpaid helper.

vom [fɔm] prep + art von dem.

von [fɔn] prep from; (einer Person gehörig) of; (einer Person stammend) by. das Buch von Peter Peter's book. ein Buch von Greene a book by Greene. ein Freund von ihm a friend of his. **von ...** an starting, from. **von nun an** from now on. von mir aus as far as I am concerned. **von selbst** by itself, automatically.

vor [foːr] prep in front of; (zeitlich) before. vor acht Tagen a week ago. vor allem above all. nach wie vor as ever. nicht vor not until. **Viertel vor 12** (a) quarter to twelve. vor Zeiten formerly. **Vorabend** ['foːraːbənt] m eve.

Vorahnung ['foːraːnuŋ] f presentiment.

voran [fo'ran] adv at the head, in front, first. **-gehen** v go ahead, precede. **-kommen** v make progress.

Voranschlag ['foːranʃlaːk] m rough estimate.

Vorarbeiter ['foːrarbaitər] m foreman, supervisor.

voraus [fo'raus] adv ahead, in front. im voraus in advance. **vorausbestimmen** v predetermine. **vorausgesetzt daß** provided that. **Voraussage** f prediction. **voraus‖sagen** v predict, forecast. **-sehen** v foresee. **Voraus‖setzung** f assumption; (Vorbedingung) prerequisite. **-sicht** f foresight. **voraussichtlich** adv probably. **Vorauszahlung** f advance payment.

vorbedacht ['foːrbədaxt] adj premeditated. **Vorbedacht** m forethought. **mit Vorbedacht** on purpose, advisedly.

Vorbedingung ['foːrbədiŋuŋ] f precondition, prerequisite.

Vorbehalt ['foːrbəhalt] m (pl -e) reservation, proviso. **vorbehalten** v hold in reserve, withhold.

vorbei [for'bai] adv (örtlich) past, by; (zeitlich) past, over. **vorbei sein** be all over. **vorbei‖gehen** v go past, pass. **-kommen** v pass by. **-marschieren** v march past.

vorbereiten ['foːrbəraitən] v prepare. **Vorbereitungen** pl preparations.

vorbestellen ['foːrbəʃtɛlən] v book in advance.

Vorbestrafte(r) ['foːrbəʃtraːftə(r)] m person with previous conviction.

vorbeugen ['foːrbɔygən] v prevent. **Vorbeugung** f prevention.

Vorbild ['foːrbilt] neut model, example. **vorbildlich** adj model, exemplary.

*vorbringen ['foːrbriŋən] v bring up, put forward.

vorder ['fɔrdər] adj fore(most) front. **Vorder‖bein** neut foreleg. **-grund** m foreground. **-radantrieb** m front-wheel drive. **-seite** f façade; obverse; face (of coin). **-teil** m front (part). **-tür** f front door.

*vordringen ['foːrdriŋən] v advance, press forward. **vordringlich** adj urgent, pressing.

voreilig ['foːrailiç] adj premature, hasty, precipitate.

voreingenommen ['foːraingənɔmən] adj prejudiced. **voreingenommen gegen** prejudiced against. **voreingenommen für** biased in favour of. **Voreingenommenheit** f prejudice.

*vorenthalten ['foːrɛnthaltən] v hold back, withhold.

vorerst ['foːrɛrst] adv for the time being.

vorerwähnt ['foːrɛrvɛːnt] adj above-mentioned, already mentioned, aforesaid.

Vorfahr ['foːrfaːr] m (pl -en) ancestor.

Vorfahrt ['foːrfaːrt] f right-of-way.

Vorfall ['foːrfal] m incident.

vorführen ['foːrfyːrən] v bring forward, present; (zeigen) show; (Film) project. **Vorführung** f presentation, demonstration; (Film) showing.

Vorgang ['foːrgaŋ] m event, incident; (Tech) process; (Komm) file, record. **Vorgänger** m predecessor.

*vorgeben ['foːrgeːbən] v pretend.

Vorgebirge ['foːrgəbirgə] neut foothills pl; (Kap) promontory.

vorgeblich ['foːrgeːpliç] adj alleged, ostensible.

vorgefaßt ['foːrgəfast] adj preconceived.

Vorgefühl ['foːrgəfyːl] neut presentiment.

*vorgehen ['foːrgeːən] v go forward; (handeln) act, proceed; (geschehen) occur; (Uhr) be fast; (wichtiger sein) take precedence; (führen) lead (on). **Vorgehen** neut advance; proceedings pl.

vorgenannt ['foɪrgənant] *adj* above-mentioned.

Vorgeschichte ['foɪrgəʃiçtə] *f* previous history; (*Urgeschichte*) prehistory.

Vorgeschmack ['foɪrgəʃmak] *m* foretaste.

Vorgesetzte(r) ['foɪrgəzɛtstə] superior.

vorgestern ['foɪrgɛstərn] *adv* the day before yesterday.

*vorhaben ['foɪrhaɪbən] *v* intend, plan. *haben Sie heute etwas vor?* have you anything arranged for today?

Vorhalle ['foɪrhalə] *f* vestibule, entrance (hall).

vorhanden ['foɪrhandən] *adj* existing, available. **Vorhandensein** *neut* existence, availability.

Vorhang ['foɪrhaŋ] *m* (*pl* **Vorhänge**) curtain.

vorher [foɪr'heɪr] *adv* before(hand), previously. **Vorhersage** *f* prediction. **vorher‖sagen** *v* predict. **–sehen** *v* foresee.

vorherrschend ['foɪrhɛrʃənt] *adj* predominant.

vorhin ['foɪrhin] *adv* a short while ago, just now.

Vorhut ['foɪrhuːt] *f* (*pl* **-en**) vanguard.

vorig ['foɪriç] *adj* previous.

Vorjahr ['foɪrjaɪr] *neut* last year. **vorjährig** *adj* last year's.

vorjammern ['foɪrjamərn] *v* lament, complain.

Vorkämpfer ['foɪrkɛmpfər] *m* (*pl* **-**) advocate, champion.

Vorkehrung ['foɪrkeɪruŋ] *f* (*pl* **-en**) precaution.

Vorkenntnis ['foɪrkɛntnis] *f* previous knowledge. **Vorkenntnisse** *pl* rudiments, basic knowledge *sing*.

*vorkommen ['foɪrkɔmən] *v* (*geschehen*) happen, take place; (*sich finden*) occur, be found; (*nach vorn kommen*) come forward; (*scheinen*) seem, appear.

*vorladen ['foɪrlaɪdən] *v* summon. **Vorladung** *f* summons.

Vorlage ['foɪrlaɪgə] *f* submission, presentation; (*Muster*) model; (*Gesetz*) bill.

Vorläufer ['foɪrlɔyfər] *m* forerunner. **vorläufig** *adv* provisional, temporary.

vorlaut ['foɪrlaut] *adj* forward, nosy.

vorlegen ['foɪrleɪgən] *v* present; (*Essen*) serve.

*vorlesen ['foɪrleɪzən] *v* read out, read aloud. **Vorlesung** *f* (*pl* **-en**) lecture.

vorletzt ['foɪrlɛtst] *adj* last but one, penultimate.

Vorliebe ['foɪrliːbə] *f* preference, liking.

*vorliegen ['foɪrliɪgən] *v* be, exist; (*Arbeit*) be in hand. **der vorliegende Fall** the case in point, the case in question.

Vormachtstellung ['foɪrmaxtʃtɛluŋ] *f* hegemony.

vormals ['foɪrmaɪls] *adv* formerly.

Vormittag ['foɪrmitaɪk] *m* morning. **vormittags** *adv* in the morning.

Vormund ['foɪrmunt] *m* guardian.

vorn [fɔrn] *adv* in front, ahead. **nach vorn** forward. **von vorn** from the start.

Vorname ['foɪrnaɪmə] *m* first name, Christian name.

vornehm ['foɪrneɪm] *adj* (*von höherem Stand*) distinguished; (*edel*) noble; elegant, (*umg.*) posh.

vornherein ['fɔrnherain] *adv* **von vornherein** from the start.

Vorort ['foɪrɔrt] *m* outpost.

Vorrang ['foɪraŋ] *m* precedence, priority.

Vorrat ['foɪraɪt] *m* supply, stock. **vorrätig** *adj* in stock.

Vorrecht ['foɪrɛçt] *neut* privilege.

Vorrede ['foɪreɪdə] *f* introduction; (*Buch*) preface.

Vorrichtung ['foɪriçtuŋ] *f* (*pl* **-en**) device.

vorrücken ['foɪrykən] *v* move forward, advance.

Vorsatz ['foɪrzats] *m* intention, purpose. **vorsätzlich** *adj* intentional.

Vorschau ['foɪrʃau] *f* preview; (*Film*) trailer.

*vorschieben ['foɪrʃiːbən] *v* push forward; (*Entschuldigung*) plead (as an excuse).

vorschiessen ['foɪrʃiːsən] *v* advance (money).

Vorschlag ['foɪrʃlaɪk] *m* suggestion, proposal. **vorschlagen** *v* suggest, propose.

Vorschlußrunde ['foɪrʃlusrundə] *f* semifinal.

vorschneiden ['foɪrʃnaidən] *v* carve.

vorschreiben ['foɪrʃraibən] *v* prescribe, order.

Vorschrift ['foɪrʃrift] *f* rule, regulation; (*Befehl*) order; (*Med*) prescription. **vorschrifts‖gemäß** *adj*, *adv* in accordance with regulations. **–widrig** *adj*, *adv* contrary to regulations.

Vorschub ['foɪrʃuːp] *m* assistance, support. **Vorschub leisten** assist, support.

Vorschule ['foɪrʃuːlə] *f* prep school.

Vorschuß ['foɪrʃus] *m* (cash) advance.

vorschützen ['fo:rʃytsən] v pretend. **Unwissenheit vorschützen** plead ignorance.

vorsehen ['fo:rze:ən] v assign, earmark. **sich vorsehen** take care, mind. **Vorsehung** f providence.

vorsetzen ['fo:rzɛtsən] v put (forward); (anbieten) offer, put before.

Vorsicht ['fo:rzɪçt] f caution, care. interj be careful! take care! **vorsichtig** adj careful, cautious. **Vorsichtsmaßnahme** f precaution.

Vorsitz ['fo:rzɪts] m chair(manship). **den Vorsitz führen** be in the chair, preside. **Vorsitzende(r)** chairman.

Vorsorge ['fo:rzɔrgə] f (unz.) provision, precaution, advance measure. **versorglich** adj provident. adv as a precaution.

Vorspeise ['fo:rʃpaizə] f hors d'oeuvre, starter.

vorspiegeln ['fo:rʃpi:gəln] v **jemandem etwas vorspiegeln** delude someone with something. **Vorspiegelung** f misrepresentation.

Vorspiel ['fo:rʃpi:l] neut prelude.

*****vorspringen** ['fo:rʃprɪŋən] v leap forward; (hervorragen) project.

Vorsprung ['fo:rʃprʊŋ] m (Vorteil) lead, advantage; (Arch) projection.

Vorstadt ['fo:rʃtat] f suburb.

Vorstand ['fo:rʃtant] m board of directors, management.

*****vorstehen** ['fo:rʃte:ən] v protrude; (leiten) manage, be head of. **-d** adj protruding; (vorangehend) preceding. **Vorsteher** m chief, superintendant, manager. **-in** f manageress.

vorstellbar ['fo:rʃtɛlbaɪr] adj imaginable. **vorstellen** v put forward; (Person) introduce; (bedeuten) mean. **sich vorstellen** introduce oneself. **sich etwas vorstellen** imagine something. **Vorstellung** f introduction; (Begriff) idea; (Theater) performance. **-skraft** f (power of) imagination.

vorstrecken ['fo:rʃtrɛkən] v stretch out.

Vorstufe ['fo:rʃtu:fə] f first stage.

Vorteil ['fo:rtail] m advantage. **vorteilhaft** adj advantageous, favourable.

Vortrag ['fo:rtraɪk] m (pl **Vorträge**) (Vorlesung) talk, lecture; (Komm) balance carried forward. **vortragen** v lecture; (Gedicht) recite; (Meinung) express;

(Rede) deliver. **Vortragssaal** m lecture hall.

vortrefflich ['fo:rtrɛfliç] adj excellent.

*****vortreten** ['fo:rtre:tən] v step forward; (hervorragen) protrude.

Vortritt ['fo:rtrɪt] m precedence.

vorüber [fo'ry:bər] adv past; (Zeit) over, past. **-gehen** v pass. **-gehend** adj passing, temporary.

Vorurteil ['fo:rurtail] neut prejudice. **vorurteilsfrei** adj unprejudiced.

Vorverkauf ['fo:rfɛrkauf] m advance sale; (Theater) advance booking.

Vorwahl ['fo:rva:l] f preliminary election, (US) primary. **Vorwahlnummer** f (Telef) area code.

Vorwand ['fo:rvant] f pretence, pretext, excuse.

vorwärts ['fo:rvɛrts] adv forward(s), onward(s). **-bringen** v promote, further. **-gehen** v go ahead. **-kommen** v make progress.

vorweg [for'vɛk] adv in advance. **-nehmen** v anticipate, forestall.

vorwerfen ['fo:rvɛrfən] v reproach with.

vorwiegend ['fo:rvi:sən] adj preponderant. adv chiefly, mostly.

Vorwissen ['fo:rvɪsən] neut foreknowledge, prescience.

Vorwort ['fo:rvɔrt] neut (pl **-e**) preface, foreword.

Vorwurf ['fo:rvurf] m reproach.

Vorzeichen ['fo:rtsaiçən] neut omen; (Math) sign.

*****vorzeigen** ['fo:rtsaigən] v produce, display.

Vorzeit ['fo:rtsait] f antiquity. **vorzeitig** adj premature, too early.

*****vorziehen** ['fo:rtsi:ən] v (bevorzugen) prefer; (hervorziehen) pull forward.

Vorzug ['fo:rtsuːk] m preference; (Vorteil) advantage; (Eigenschaft) merit, good quality. **vorzüglich** adj excellent, superb. **Vorzugsrecht** neut priority.

vulgär [vul'gɛːr] adj vulgar.

Vulkan [vul'ka:n] m (pl **-e**) volcano. **vulkanisch** adj volcanic.

W

Waage ['vaːgə] f (pl -n) scales pl. **waage-recht** adj horizontal.

wabbelig ['vabəliç] adj wobbly, flabby.

Wabe ['vaːbə] f (pl -n) honeycomb.

wach [vax] adj awake. **Wache** f (pl -n) watch, guard; (Polizei) station. **wachen** v be awake; (Wache halten) keep watch. **wachen über** watch over.

Wachs [vaks] neut (pl -e) wax.

wachsam ['vaxzaːm] adj watchful, alert. **Wachsamkeit** f watchfulness, vigilance.

*****wachsen** ['vaksən] v grow. **-d** adj increasing, growing. **Wachstum** neut growth.

Wacht [vaxt] f (pl -en) watch, guard.

Wachtel ['vaxtəl] f (pl -n) quail.

Wächter ['vɛçtər] m (pl -) watchman, guard. **Wacht**||**hund** neut watchdog. **-meister** m sergeant-major; (Polizist) constable. **-turm** m watchtower.

wackelig ['vakəliç] adj wobbly, shaky. **wackeln** v wobble, shake.

wacker ['vakər] adj brave, stout; (anständig) worthy.

Wade ['vaːdə] f (pl -n) (Anat) calf.

Waffe ['vafə] f (pl -n) weapon.

Waffel ['vafəl] f (pl -n) waffle; (Eis) wafer.

waffenlos ['vafənloːs] adj unarmed. **waffnen** v arm. **Waffenstillstand** m armistice.

wagehalsig ['vaːgəhalziç] adj reckless, daring. **Wagemut** m daring. **wagen** v dare, risk, venture. **sich wagen** venture.

Wagen ['vaːgən] m (pl -) (Mot) car; (Kutsche) coach; (Karren) wagon, cart; (Eisenbahn) carriage.

*****wägen** ['vɛːgən] v weigh.

Wagen||**führer** m driver. **-heber** m (Mot) jack.

Waggon [va'gɔ̃] m (pl -s) (railway) wagon.

Wagnis ['vaːknis] neut (pl -se) (Mut) daring; (Unternehmen) venture; (Risiko) risk.

wahl [vaːl] f (pl -en) choice; (Pol) election. **wahlberechtigt** adj enfranchised, entitled to vote. **Wahl**||**bezirk** m constituency, electoral district. **-bude** f polling booth.

wählen ['vɛːlən] v choose; (Pol) elect; (Telef) dial.

wählerisch ['vɛːləriʃ] adj particular, fussy, choosy. **Wählerschaft** f electorate, voters pl.

Wahl||**feldzug** m (election) campaign.

-gang m ballot. **wahllos** adj indiscriminate. **Wahlrecht** neut franchise, suffrage.

Wählscheibe ['vɛːlʃaibə] f (telephone) dial.

Wahl||**tag** m election day. **-zettel** m ballot (paper).

Wahn [vaːn] m (unz.) delusion; madness. **-sinn** m insanity, madness. **wahnsinnig** adj insane, mad. **Wahnsinnige(r)** madman, madwoman.

wahr [vaːr] adj true; (wirklich) real; (echt) genuine.

wahren ['vaːrən] v take care of; (schützen) protect; (erhalten) maintain.

währen ['vɛːrən] v last.

während ['vɛːrənt] prep during. conj while.

wahrhaft ['vaːrhaft] adj true, genuine. adv really, truly. **-ig** adj sincere, truthful. adv really, indeed. **Wahr**||**haftigkeit** f truthfulness. **-heit** f (pl -en) truth. **wahr**||**nehmen** v perceive; (Interessen) protect; (Gelegenheit) seize, take. **-sagen** v foretell (the future). **-scheinlich** adj likely, probable. **Wahrscheinlichkeit** f probability.

Wahrung ['vaːruŋ] f preservation, maintenance.

Währung ['vɛːruŋ] f (pl -en) currency.

Waise ['vaizə] f (pl -n) orphan. **-nknabe** m orphan boy.

Wal [vaːl] m (pl -e) whale.

Wald [valt] m (pl Wälder) wood, forest. **-beere** f cranberry. **-brand** m forest fire. **waldig** adj wooded. **Wald**||**ung** f (pl -en) woodland. **-wirtschaft** f forestry.

Walfang ['vaːlfaŋ] m whaling.

Wall [val] m (pl Wälle) earthworks pl, embankment.

wallen ['valən] v boil.

*****wallfahren** ['valfaːrən] v go on a pilgrimage. **Wall**||**fahrer** m pilgrim. **-fahrt** f pilgrimage.

Walnuß ['valnus] f walnut.

Wal||**öl** neut whale-oil. **-roß** neut walrus.

Walze ['valtsə] f (pl -n) roller. **walzen** v roll; (tanzen) waltz.

wälzen ['vɛltsən] v roll.

Walzer ['valtsər] m (pl -) waltz.

Wand [vant] f (pl Wände) wall.

Wandel ['vandəl] m change. **wandelbar** adj variable; (Person) changeable, fickle. **wandeln** v change. **sich wandeln in** change or turn into.

Wanderer ['vandərər] *m* (*pl* -) wanderer; (*auf dem Lande*) hiker, rambler. **Wanderlust** *f* wanderlust. **wandern** *v* wander; ramble, hike. **-d** *adj* wandering; (*Volk, Tiere*) migratory. **Wanderung** *f* (*pl* -en) (*zu Fuß*) walking-tour, hike; (*Volk, Tiere*) migration.

Wandgemälde ['vantgəmɛldə] *neut* mural.

Wandlung ['vandluŋ] *f* (*pl* -en) change; (*total*) transformation; (*Rel*) transubstantiation.

Wange ['vaŋə] *f* (*pl* -n) cheek.

Wankelmut ['vaŋkəlmuːt] *m* fickleness, inconstancy. **wankelmütig** *adj* fickle, inconstant.

wanken ['vaŋkən] *v* rock, sway; (*Person*) totter, reel; (*fig*) waver, vacillate. **-d** *adj* wavering.

wann [van] *adv* when.

Wanne ['vanə] *f* (*pl* -n) tub; (*Badewanne*) bath(tub). **-nbad** *neut* bath.

Wanze ['vantsə] *f* (*pl* -n) bug.

Wappen ['vapən] *neut* (*pl* -) (coat of) arms. **-kunde** *f* heraldry.

Ware ['vaːrə] *f* (*pl* -n) article, commodity. **Waren** *pl* goods, wares, merchandise *sing*. **Waren‖haus** *neut* department store. **-markt** *m* commodity market.

warm [varm] *adj* warm; (*Getränk, Essen*) hot. **warmer Bruder** (*umg.*) homosexual. **Wärme** ['vɛrmə] *f* warmth; temperature; (*Physik*) heat. **wärmen** *v* warm (up), heat. **Wärmflasche** *f* hot-water bottle.

warnen ['varnən] *v* warn. **Warnung** *f* (*pl* -en) warning.

Warschau ['varʃau] *neut* Warsaw.

warten ['vartən] *v* wait; (*pflegen*) care for; (*Maschine*) service, maintain. **warten auf** wait for.

Wärter ['vɛrtər] *m* (*pl* -), **Wärterin** *f* (*pl* -nen) attendant; (*Kranken*) nurse; (*Gefängnis*) warder.

Warte‖saal *m* waiting room. **-zimmer** *neut* waiting room. **Wartung** *f* maintenance, upkeep.

warum [va'rum] *adv* why.

Warze ['vartsə] *f* (*pl* -n) wart; (*Brust*) nipple.

was [vas] *pron* what; (*umg.*) something. **ach was!** nonsense! **was ist mit ...** how about .... **was für ...** what sort of .... **alles was ich sehe** everything that I see.

Waschbecken ['vaʃbɛkən] *neut* wash basin.

Wäsche ['vɛʃə] *f* (*pl* -n) washing, laundry.

waschecht [vaʃɛçt] *adj* (*Farbe*) (colour-) fast; (*fig*) thorough, dyed-in-the-wool.

Wäsche‖klammer *f* clothes-peg, (*US*) clothes-pin. **-korb** *m* laundry basket. **-leine** *f* clothes-line.

***waschen** ['vaʃən] *v* wash.

Wäscherei ['vɛʃəˌrai] *f* (*pl* -en) laundry.

Wasch‖lappen *m* facecloth. **-maschine** *f* washing machine. **-mittel** *neut* detergent, washing powder. **-tag** *m* wash(ing) day.

Wasser ['vasər] *neut* (*pl* -) water. **-abfluß** *m* drain. **-abfuhr** *f* drainage. **-behälter** *m* tank, reservoir. **-dampf** *m* steam, water vapour.

wasser‖dicht *adj* waterproof; (*Gefäß*) watertight. **-fest** *adj* waterproof.

wässerig ['vɛsəriç] *adj* watery.

Wasser‖kraftwerk *neut* hydroelectric plant. **-leitung** *f* water mains *pl*. **-mann** *m* (*Astrol*) Aquarius.

wässern ['vɛsərn] *v* water; (*bewässern*) irrigate; (*Erbsen, usw.*) soak.

Wasser‖pflanze *f* aquatic plant. **-rad** *neut* water wheel. **-stoff** *m* hydrogen. **-tier** *neut* aquatic animal.

Wässerung ['vɛsəruŋ] *f* watering; (*Bewässern*) irrigation.

Wasser‖versorgung *f* water supply. **-weg** *m* waterway. **-werk** *neut* waterworks *pl*.

Watte ['vatə] *f* (*pl* -n) wadding, cotton wool. **-bausch** *m* swab.

weben ['veːbən] *v* weave. **Web‖er** *m* (*pl* -), **Weberin** *f* (*pl* -nen) weaver. **-stoff** *m* textile. **-stuhl** *m* loom.

Wechsel ['vɛksəl] *m* (*pl* -) change; (*Austausch*) exchange; (*Komm*) bill (of exchange). **-folge** *f* alternation. **-geld** *neut* change. **-jahre** *pl* menopause *sing*, change of life *sing*. **wechseln** *v* (ex)change; (*variieren*) vary. **wechselseitig** *adj* alternating; (*gegenseitig*) mutual, reciprocal. **Wechsel‖strom** *m* alternating current. **-zahn** *m* milk tooth.

wecken ['vɛkən] *v* awaken, wake up. **Wecker** *m* (*pl* -) alarm clock.

wedeln ['veːdəln] *v* (*Schwanz*) wag.

weder ['veːdər] *conj* neither. **weder ... noch ...** neither ... nor ....

weg [vɛk] *adv* away, off, gone. **Hände weg!** hands off! **er ist schon weg** he has already left. **meine Uhr ist weg** my watch has gone. **weit weg** far off. **Weg** *m* (*pl* -e) way; (*Straße*) road; (*Pfad*) path.

weg‖bleiben v stay away. **–blicken** v look away. **–bringen** v take away, remove.

wegen ['veːgən] prep because of, on account of.

weg‖fahren v drive away; (abfahren) leave. **–fallen** v fall away; (aufhören) stop; (ausgelassen werden) be omitted. **–führen** v lead away. **–gehen** v go away. **–kommen** v get away. **–lassen** v omit. **–müssen** v must go, have to leave.

Wegnahme ['veːknaːmə] f (pl -n) confiscation, seizure. **wegnehmen** v take away; (beschlagnahmen) confiscate, seize; (Zeit, Raum) occupy.

weg‖räumen v clear away. **–schaffen** v get rid of. **–schicken** v send away. **–schließen** v lock away. **–treiben** v drive off.

Wegweiser ['veːkvaizər] m (pl -) signpost; (Buch, Mensch) guide.

weg‖wenden v turn aside. **–werfen** v throw away, discard. **–werfend** adj disdainful. **–ziehen** v pull aside; (Wohnsitz wechseln) move away.

weh [veː] adj sore, painful; (seelisch) sad. interj alas. **mein Hals tut mir weh** my throat hurts. **sich weh tun** hurt oneself. **jemandem weh tun** hurt someone, cause someone pain. **Weh** neut (pl -e) pain; sorrow.

Wehe ['veːə] f (pl -n) drift (of snow or sand). **wehen** v blow; (Fahne) flutter.

Wehr[1] [veːr] f (pl -en) (Waffe) weapon; (Schutz) defence; (Rüstung) armament; (Widerstand) resistance.

Wehr[2] neut (pl -e) weir, dam.

Wehrdienst ['veːrdiːnst] m military service. **–verweigerer** m conscientious objector. **wehren** v restrain. **sich wehren gegen** defend oneself against. **wehrlos** adj (waffenlos) unarmed; (schutzlos) defenceless. **Wehr‖macht** f armed forces pl. **–pflicht** f compulsory military service. **–pflichtige(r)** person liable for military service.

Weib [vaip] neut (pl -er) woman; (Gattin) wife. **–chen** neut (Tier) female. **weiblich** adj female; (Gramm) feminine.

weich [vaiç] adj soft; (sanft) gentle.

Weiche ['vaiçə] f (pl -n) (Anat) side, flank.

weichen[1] ['vaiçən] v soften; (einweichen) soak.

weichen[2] v give way; (nachgeben) yield; (Preise) fall.

Weichheit ['vaiçhait] f softness. **weichherzig** adj tender-hearted, gentle. **Weichkäse** m soft cheese. **weichlich** adj soft, weak, effeminate.

Weide[1] ['vaidə] f (pl -n) (Baum) willow.

Weide[2] f (pl -n) (Wiese) pasture.

***weiden** ['vaidən] v graze. **sich weiden an** feast one's eyes on.

weigern ['vaigərn] v **sich weigern** refuse. **Weigerung** f (pl -en) refusal.

Weihe ['vaiə] f (pl -n) consecration; (Einweihung) initiation. **weihen** v consecrate.

Weihnachten ['vainaxtən] neut (pl -) Christmas. **Weihnachts‖abend** m Christmas Eve. **–baum** m Christmas tree. **–geschenk** neut Christmas present. **–lied** neut Christmas carol. **–mann** m Father Christmas, (US) Santa Claus.

weil [vail] conj because, since.

Weile ['vailə] f while, short time.

Wein [vain] m (pl -e) wine; (Pflanze) vine. **–berg** m vineyard. **–brand** m brandy.

weinen ['vainən] v cry, weep. **Weinen** neut crying, weeping, tears pl.

Wein‖lese f (pl -n) vintage. **–stock** m vine. **–stube** f wine bar. **–traube** f bunch of grapes.

weise ['vaizə] adj wise.

Weise ['vaizə] f (pl -n) manner, way; (Melodie) melody. **Art und Weise** manner, way. **auf diese/jede/kleine Weise** in this way/in any case/by no means.

weisen ['vaizən] v show; (Finger, Zeiger) point. **weisen auf** point to. **weisen nach** direct to.

Weisheit ['vaishait] f (pl -en) wisdom. **–zahn** m wisdom tooth.

weiß [vais] adj white. **Weißbrot** neut white bread. **Weiße** f whiteness. **Weiße(r)** White (man/woman). **weiß‖en** v whitewash. **–glühend** adj white-hot. **Weiß‖kohl** m (white) cabbage. **–waren** pl linens. **–wein** m white wine.

weit [vait] adj wide; (breit) broad; (geräumig) vast, spacious; (lang) long; (entfernt) far (off). **bei weitem** by far. **von weitem** from a distance. **weit entfernt** (von) far away (from). **weit‖ab** adv far away. **–aus** adv by far. **Weite** f (pl -n) width; (Ausdehnung) extent; (Größe) size. **weiten** v widen; (vergrößern) enlarge.

rivalry. **wetteifern mit** vie with, compete with. **wetten** v bet.

Wetter ['vɛtər] neut (pl -) weather. **−bericht** m weather report. **−kunde** f meteorology. **−vorhersage** f weather forecast.

Wett‖kampf m contest, match. **−kämpfer** m contestant. **−lauf** m race. **−streit** m contest.

wichtig ['viçtiç] adj important. **Wichtigkeit** f importance. **−tuer** m busybody; pompous person.

Widder ['vidər] m (pl -) ram; (Astrol) Aries.

wider ['viːdər] prep against, contrary to. **−fahren** v happen to, befall.

Wider‖haken m barbed hook. **−hall** m response; (Echo) echo. **widerhallen** v echo.

wider‖legen v refute. **−lich** adj re███████, (ekelhaft) disgusting ██████rlich adj unnatural ███████ch adj unlawful, ille-███████

Widerruf ['viːdərruf] m (Befehl) revocation, countermand; (Nachricht) denial. **widerrufen** v revoke, countermand; deny.

widersetzen [viːdər'zɛtsən] v **sich widersetzen** oppose. **widersetzlich** adj obstructive.

wider‖spenstig adj contrary, difficult, stubborn. **−spiegeln** v reflect. **−sprechen** v contradict. **Widerspruch** m contradiction.

Widerstand ['viːdərʃtant] m resistance, opposition.

widerstehen [viːdər'ʃteːən] v resist.

Widerstreit ['viːdərʃtrait] m (Kampf) conflict; (Widersprüche) opposition.

widerwärtig ['viːdərvɛrtiç] adj disgusting, repulsive.

Widerwille ['viːdərvilə] m aversion, intense dislike. **widerwillig** adj reluctant, unwilling.

widmen ['vitmən] v devote, dedicate; (Buch) dedicate. **Widmung** f (pl -en) dedication.

widrig ['viːdriç] adj adverse, unfavourable.

wie [viː] adv how. conj as.

wieder ['viːdər] adv again; (zurück) back. **immer wieder** again and again.

Wiederaufbau ['viːdəraufbau] m reconstruction, rebuilding. **wiederaufbauen** v reconstruct, rebuild. **Wiederauf‖erstehung** f resurrection. **−nahme** f resumption. **wiederauf‖nehmen** v resume.

−tauchen v come to light again, resurface.

wieder‖bringen v bring back, return. **−erkennen** v recognize.

Wiedergabe ['viːdərgaːbə] f reproduction. **wiedergeben** v give back, return; (darbieten) render.

wiedergeboren ['viːdərgəbɔirən] adj reborn, regenerated. **Wiedergeburt** f rebirth, regeneration.

wieder‖gewinnen v recover, retrieve. **−gutmachen** v make up for, compensate for.

wiederholen [viːdər'hoːlən] v repeat. **wiederholt** adj repeated. **Wiederholung** f (pl -en) repetition.

Wiederhören ['viːdərhœirən] n **auf Wiederhören!** (Telef) goodbye!

wieder‖kehren v return. **−kommen** v come back, return.

wiedersehen ['viːdərzeiən] v see or meet again. **Wiedersehen** neut reunion. **auf Wiedersehen!** goodbye!

wiederum ['viːdərum] adv (nochmals) again, afresh; (andererseits) on the other hand.

wieder‖vereinigen v reunite; (versöhnen) reconcile. **−verheiraten** v remarry.

Wiege ['viːgə] f (pl -n) cradle.

wiegen[1] ['viːgən] v (Gewicht) weigh.

wiegen[2] v (sanft schaukeln) rock.

Wiegenlied ['viːgənliːt] neut lullaby.

wiehern ['viːərn] v neigh; (Mensch) guffaw.

Wien [viːn] neut Vienna.

Wiese ['viːzə] f (pl -n) meadow.

Wiesel ['viːzəl] neut (pl -) weasel.

wieso [viː'zoː] adv why.

wieviel [viː'fiːl] adj, adv how much. **wieviele** pl how many.

wild [vilt] adj wild; (unzivilisiert, ungestüm) savage. **Wild** neut game. **−dieb** m poacher. **−heit** f wildness; savageness. **−leder** neut deerskin. **−nis** f wilderness.

Wille ['vilə] m (pl -n) or **Willen** m (pl -) will. **um ... willen** for the sake of. **willens‖schwach** adj weak-willed. **−stark** adj strong-willed. **willig** adj willing.

willkommen ['vilkɔmən] adj welcome. **willkommen heißen** v welcome, greet. **Willkommen** neut welcome.

Willkür ['vilkyːr] f arbitrariness, whim. **willkürlich** adj arbitrary.

wimmeln ['viməln] v **wimmeln von** swarm or teem with.

Wimper ['vimpər] f (pl -n) eyelash. **ohne mit der Wimper zu zucken** without batting an eyelid.

Wind [vint] m (pl -e) wind.

Winde ['vində] f (pl -n) windlass; (Bot) bindweed.

Windel ['vindəl] f (pl -n) nappy, (US) diaper.

*****winden** ['vindən] v wind, twist. **sich winden** wind.

Wind||hund m greyhound. **-mühle** f windmill. **-pocken** pl chickenpox sing. **-schutzscheibe** f windscreen, (US) windshield. **-stoß** m gust, blast of wind.

Windung ['vindun] f (pl -en) winding, turn.

Wink [vink] m (pl -e) sign; (Hand) wave; (Kopf) nod; (Augen) wink; (fig) hint.

Winkel ['vinkəl] m (pl -) (Ecke) corner; (Math) angle. **winkelig** adj angular. **winkelrecht** adj rectangular.

Winter ['vintər] m (pl -) winter. **winterlich** adj wintry. **Winter||schlaf** m hibernation. **-sport** m winter sports pl.

winzig ['vintsiç] adj tiny.

Wipfel ['vipfəl] m (pl -) treetop.

Wippe ['vipə] f (pl -n) seesaw, balance.

wir [vir] pron we.

Wirbel ['virbəl] m (pl -) whirl; (Wasser) whirlpool; (Luft) whirlwind; (Trommeln) roll; (Rücken) vertebra; (Scheitel) crown (of head). **wirbel||los** adj spineless; (Tiere) invertebrate. **-n** v whirl, swirl; (Trommeln) roll. **Wirbel||säule** f spine. **-tier** neut vertebrate. **-wind** m whirlwind.

wirken ['virkən] v work (on), act (on). **-d** adj active; (erfolgreich) effective. **wirklich** adj real, actual; (echt) genuine. **Wirklichkeit** f reality. **wirksam** adj effective. **Wirkung** f (pl -en) effect.

wirr [vir] adj tangled, disorderly; (Haare) dishevelled. **Wirrwarr** m chaos, jumble, disorder.

Wirt [virt] m (pl -e) innkeeper, landlord; (Gastgeber) host; (Zimmervermieter) landlord. **-in** f (pl -nen) innkeeper, landlady; hostess; landlady. **wirtlich** adj hospitable.

Wirtschaft ['virtʃaft] f (pl -en) economy; (Haushaltung) housekeeping; (Gaststätte) inn, public house. **wirtschaft||en** v manage; (Haushalt) keep house. **-lich** adj economic; (sparsam) economical. **Wirtschafts||krise** f economic crisis. **-politik** f

economic policy. **-wunder** neut economic miracle.

Wirtshaus ['virtshaus] neut inn, public house.

wischen ['viʃən] v wipe. **Wischlappen** m cloth, duster.

wispeln ['vispəln] or **wispern** v whisper.

Wißbegier(de) ['visbəgir(də)] f intellectual curiosity, thirst for learning. **wißbegierig** adj inquisitive, eager to learn.

*****wissen** ['visən] v know. **etwas tun wissen** know how to do something. **Wissen** neut knowledge.

Wissenschaft ['visənʃaft] f (pl -en) science, knowledge. **-ler** m (pl -), **-lerin** f (pl -nen) scientist. **wissenschaftlich** adj scientific.

wissentlich ['visəntliç] adj conscious, deliberate. adv knowingly, wittingly.

Witterung ['vitərun] f (pl -en) weather (conditions).

Witwe ['vitvə] f (pl -n) widow. **Witwer** m (pl -) widower.

Witz [vits] m (pl -e) (Gabe) wit; (Spaß) joke. **-bold** m witty fellow, clown. **-blatt** neut comic (paper). **witzig** adj witty; (spaßhaft) humorous, funny. **witzeln über** joke about.

wo [vo] adv where. conj when. **ach wo!** what nonsense! **wo||anders** adv elsewhere. **-bei** adv whereby, by which.

Woche ['voxə] f (pl -n) week. **Wochen||blatt** neut weekly (paper). **-ende** neut weekend.

wöchentlich ['vœçtliç] adj weekly.

Wodka ['vodkə] m (pl -s) vodka.

wo||durch adv whereby, by which; (Frage) how? by what means? **-für** adv for which; (Frage) for what? what ... for? **-gegen** adv against which. conj whereas. **-her** adv from where, whence. **-hin** adv (to) where, whither.

wohl [voil] adv well; (vermutend) probably, I suppose. **Wohl** neut well-being, welfare.

wohlauf [voil'auf] adv well. interj come on! cheer up!

Wohl||befinden neut well-being, (good) health. **-behagen** neut comfort.

wohl||bekannt adj well-known. **-erzogen** adj well brought up.

Wohlfahrt ['voilfart] f welfare. **-staat** m welfare state.

wohl‖gemeint adj well-intentioned. **–geraten** adj well done; (Kind) well-behaved.

Wohl‖geruch m perfume, fragrance. **–geschmack** m pleasant or agreeable taste.

wohlhabend ['voːlhaːbənt] adj well-to-do, well-off.

Wohlklang ['voːlklaŋ] m harmony.

Wohlstand ['voːlʃtant] m prosperity, affluence. **–gesellschaft** f affluent society.

Wohl‖tat f kindness, kind deed; (Annehmlichkeit) boon, benefit. **–täter** m benefactor. **–täterin** f benefactress. **wohltätig** adj charitable. **Wohltätigkeit** f charity. **–verein** m charitable association.

*wohltun ['voːltuːn] v do good.

Wohlwollen ['voːlvɔlən] neut good will, benevolence. **wohlwollend** adj benevolent.

wohnen ['voːnən] v live, dwell, reside. **wohnhaft** adj resident. **Wohn‖ort** m place of residence. **–Schlafzimmer** neut bedsitting room, (umg.) bedsit. **–ung** f (pl -en) flat, (US) apartment. **–wagen** m caravan, (US) trailer. **–zimmer** neut living-room, sitting-room.

Wölbung ['vœlbuŋ] f (pl -en) vault, arch, dome.

Wolf [vɔlf] m (pl Wölfe) wolf.

Wölfin ['vœlfin] f (pl -nen) she-wolf.

Wolke ['vɔlkə] f (pl -n) cloud. **–nkratzer** m skyscraper.

Wolle ['vɔlə] f (pl -n) wool.

*wollen[1] ['vɔlən] v want, wish. ich will gehen I want to go, I intend to go. ich will nicht gehen I don't want to go, I will not go. wollen Sie bitte . . . would you please . . . . tun Sie, was Sie wollen do as you please.

wollen[2] adj woollen, (US) woolen.

wollig ['vɔliç] adj woolly.

Wollust ['vɔlust] f lust, voluptuousness. **wollüstig** adj lustful, voluptuous, sensual.

wo‖mit adv with which; (Frage) with what? **–nach** adv after which, whereupon.

Wonne ['vɔnə] f (pl -n) bliss; (Freude) joy; (Entzücken) rapture.

woran [vo'ran] adv on which. **woran denkst du?** what are you thinking about? **woran liegt es, daß . . . ?** how is it that . . . ? **wo‖rauf** adv upon which, whereup-

on. **–raus** adv from which, whence. **–rin** adv in(to) which.

Wort [vɔrt] **1** neut (pl Wörter) word. **2** neut (pl Worte) (spoken) word.

Wörterbuch ['vœrtərbuːx] neut dictionary. **wörtlich** adj literal.

Wort‖schatz m vocabulary. **–spiel** neut pun.

wovon [vo'fɔn] of or from which; (Frage) from what? **wovon lebt er?** what does he live on? **wovon spricht er?** what is he talking about? **wozu** adv to which; (warum) what . . . for, why.

*Wrack [vrak] neut (pl -s) wreck.

*wringen ['vriŋən] v wring.

Wucher ['vuːxər] m profiteering. **wuchern** v profiteer; (Pflanze) proliferate, be rampant. **Wucherpreis** m exorbitant price.

Wuchs [m (pl Wüchse) growth; (Körperbau) physique, build.

Wucht [vuxt] f (pl -en) weight, impetus, force. **wuchtig** adj heavy, weighty.

wühlen ['vyːlən] v root, dig; (durchstöbern) rummage; (Gefühle) well up. **sich wühlen in** burrow into. **wühlerisch** adj subversive.

Wulst [vulst] m (pl Wülste) swelling, bulge. **wulstig** adj swollen.

wund [vunt] adj sore. **Wunde** f (pl -n) wound.

Wunder ['vundər] neut (pl -) miracle, wonder. **wunderbar** adj wonderful, marvellous. **Wunder‖kind** neut child prodigy. **–land** neut fairy-land. **wunder‖lich** adj odd, strange, peculiar. **–n** v surprise, astonish. **sich wundern über** be astonished by, wonder at. **wunderschön** adj (very) beautiful. **Wundertat** f miracle, miraculous feat.

Wunsch [vunʃ] m (pl Wünsche) wish, desire.

wünschen ['vynʃən] v wish, desire. **–swert** adj desirable.

Würde ['vyrdə] f (pl -n) dignity; (Ehre) honour. **würde‖los** adj undignified. **–voll** adj dignified. **würdig** adj worthy. **–en** v appreciate. **Würdigung** f (pl -en) appreciation.

Wurf [vurf] m (pl Würfe) throw, cast; (Tiere) litter, brood.

Würfel ['vyrfəl] m (pl -) cube; (Spielstein) die.

würgen ['vyrgən] v choke; (erwürgen) strangle, throttle.

Wurm [vurm] *m* (*pl* **Würmer**) worm. **wurmig** *adj* worm-eaten.

Wurst [vurst] *f* (*pl* **Würste**) sausage.

Würstchen ['vyrstçən] *neut* (*pl* -) (small) sausage; (*Mensch*) little man, insignificant person.

Würze ['vyrtsə] *f* (*pl* -n) seasoning, spice.

Wurzel ['vyrtsəl] *f* (*pl* -n) root. **wurzeln** *v* take root; (*fig*) be rooted in.

würzen ['vyrtsən] *v* season, spice. **würzig** *adj* seasoned, spiced.

wüst [vyst] *adj* desert, desolate; (*wirr*) disorderly; (*Person*) coarse, vile. **Wüste** *f* (*pl* -n) desert, waste.

wut [vut] *f* rage, fury.

wüten ['vytən] *v* rage, be furious. **-d** *adj* furious.

X

X-Beine ['iksbainə] *pl* knock-knees. **X-beinig** *adj* knock-kneed.

x-mal ['iksmail] *adj* (*umg.*) many times, *n* times.

X-Strahlen ['iksʃtrailən] *pl* x-rays.

Z

Zacke ['tsakə] *f* (*pl* -n) or **Zacken** *m* (*pl* -) point, jag; (*Gabel*) prong; (*Kamm*) tooth. **zackig** *adj* pointed, jagged; pronged; toothed.

zaghaft ['tsaikhaft] *adj* timid.

zäh [tsei] *adj* tough; (*Flüssigkeit*) thick; (*Person*) stubborn.

Zahl [tsail] *f* (*pl* -en) number; (*Ziffer*) figure, numeral. **zahlbar** *adj* payable. **zahlen** *v* pay.

zählbar ['tseilbair] *adj* countable. **zählen** *v* count; (*Sport*) keep the score. **zählen auf** count or rely on.

Zahler ['tsailər] *m* (*pl* -) payer.

Zähler ['tseilər] *m* (*pl* -) counter; (*Bank*) teller; (*Gerät*) meter, recorder.

zahl||los [tsail] *adj* countless. **-reich** *adj* numerous. **Zahl||tag** *m* payday. **-ung** *f* (*pl* -en) payment.

Zählung ['tseilun] *f* (*pl* -en) counting; (*Volkszählung*) census.

zahlungs||fähig [*adj* (*Komm*) solvent. **-unfähig** *adj* insolvent.

zahm [tsaim] *adj* tame.

zähmen ['tseimən] *v* tame.

Zahn [tsain] *m* (*pl* **Zähne**) tooth. **-a** dentist. **-bürste** *f* toothbrush. **-fle** *neut* gum, gums *pl*. **-paste** *f* toothpas. **-rad** *neut* cogwheel, gearwheel **-schmerz** *m* toothache.

Zange ['tsaŋə] *f* (*pl* -n) pliers *pl*, tongs *pl*; (*Pinzette*) tweezers *pl*.

Zank [tsaŋk] *m* (*pl* **Zänke**) quarrel. **zanken** *v* scold. **sich zanken** quarrel.

Zapfen ['tsapfən] *m* (*pl* -) plug, bung; (*Bot*) cone.

zappelig ['tsapəliç] *adj* fidgety. **zappeln** *v* fidget.

Zar [tsair] *m* (*pl* -en) tsar, czar. **-in** *f* (*pl* -nen) tsarina.

zart [tsairt] *adj* (*Fleisch, Gemüt*) tender; (*sanft*) gentle, soft; (*zerbrechlich*) delicate. **-heit** *f* tenderness; gentleness.

zärtlich ['tseirtliç] *adj* tender, loving, affectionate. **Zärtlichkeit** *f* tenderness, affection.

Zauber ['tsaubər] *m* (*pl* -) magic. **-bann** *m* spell, charm. **-ei** *f* magic, sorcery. **-er** *m* (*pl* -) magician, sorcerer. **-erin** *f* (*pl* -nen) magician, sorceress. **zauberhaft** *adj* magical. **Zauber||kunst** *f* sorcery; (*Sinnestäuschung*) conjuring. **-künstler** *m* conjurer. **-kunststück** *neut* conjuring tricks *pl*. **zaubern** *v* practise magic; (*Zauberkunst*) conjure. **Zauberspruch** *m* magic spell.

zaudern ['tsaudərn] *v* hesitate, waver.

Zaum [tsaum] *m* (*pl* **Zäume**) rein, bridle. **zäumen** ['tsoymən] *v* (*Pferd*) bridle; (*fig*) curb, restrain.

Zaun [tsaun] *m* (*pl* **Zäune**) fence; (*Hecke*) hedge.

Zebra ['tseibra] *neut* (*pl* -s) zebra.

Zeche ['tseçə] *f* (*pl* -n) (*Gasthaus*) bill; (*Bergwerk*) mine, pit.

Zehe ['tseiə] *f* (*pl* -n) toe. **-nspitze** *f* tip of the toe.

zehn [tsein] *pron, adj* ten. **zehnte** *adj* tenth. **Zehntel** *neut* tenth (part).

zehren ['tseirən] *v* **zehren an** (*fig*) gnaw at. **zehren von** live or feed on.

Zeichen ['tsaiçən] *neut* (*pl* -) sign; (*Merkmal*) mark; (*Signal*) signal; (*Hinweis*) indication. **-brett** *neut* drawing board. **-(trick)film** *m* animated cartoon. **zeichnen** *v* draw; (*kennzeichnen*) mark; (*unterschreiben*) sign; (*Muster*) *design.* **Zeichnung** *f* drawing; marking; (*Muster*) design.

Zeigefinger ['tsaigəfiŋər] *m* forefinger, index finger. **zeigen** *v* point out, show; (*zur Schau stellen*) show, display; (*beweisen*) demonstrate, show. **Zeiger** *m* pointer, indicator; (*Uhr*) hand.

Zeile ['tsailə] *f* (*pl* -n) line.

Zeit ['tsait] *f* (*pl* -en) time. **auf Zeit** on credit. **freie Zeit** spare *or* free time. **für alle Zeiten** for all time. **in kurzer Zeit** shortly, soon. Zeit||**alter** *neut* age, era. –**folge** *f* chronological order. –**geist** *m* spirit of the age.

Zeitgenosse ['tsaitgənɔsə] *m* (*pl* -n), **Zeitgenossin** *f* (*pl* -nen) contemporary. **zeitgenössisch** *adj* contemporary.

zeitig ['tsaitiç] *adj* early.

Zeit||**karte** *f* season ticket. –**lang** *f* while. **ein Zeitlang** for some time, for a while. **Zeitlauf** *m* course of time.

zeitlich ['tsaitliç] *adj* temporal.

Zeit||**punkt** *m* (point in) time, moment. –**raum** *m* period. –**schrift** *f* magazine, periodical.

Zeitung ['tsaituŋ] *f* (*pl* -en) newspaper. **Zeitungs**||**anzeige** *f* newspaper advertisement. –**ausschnitt** *m* press cutting. –**händler** *m* newsagent. –**stand** *m* newsstand, kiosk. –**wesen** *neut* the press, journalism.

Zeit||**verschwendung** *f* waste of time. –**vertreib** *m* pastime, diversion. **zeitweilig** *adj* temporary.

Zeitwort ['tsaitvɔrt] *neut* verb.

Zelle ['tsɛlə] *f* (*pl* -n) cell.

Zelt [tsɛlt] *neut* (*pl* -e) tent. –**decke** *f* awning, canopy. **zelten** *v* camp. **Zeltplatz** *m* camp.

Zement [tse'mɛnt] *m* (*pl* -e) cement.

Zensur [tsɛn'zuːr] *f* (*pl* -en) censorship; (*Schule*) mark.

Zentimeter [tsɛnti'meːtər] *m or neut* centimetre.

Zentner ['tsɛntnər] *m* (*pl* -) hundredweight, 50 kilos.

zentral [tsɛn'traːl] *adj* central. **Zentrale** *f* (*pl* -n) central office; (*Telef*) telephone exchange. **Zentral**||**heizung** *f* central heating. –**isierung** *f* centralization. **Zentrum** *neut* (*pl* **Zentren**) centre.

zerbrechen [tsɛr'brɛçən] *v* break (in pieces), shatter. **zerbrechlich** *adj* fragile, breakable.

zerdrücken [tsɛr'drykən] *v* crush; (*Kleider*) crumple, crease.

Zeremonie [tseremo'niː] *f* (*pl* -n) ceremony. **zeremoniell** *adj* ceremonial.

Zerfall [tsɛr'fal] *m* decay, disintegration; (*Chem*) decomposition. **zerfallen** *v* disintegrate, fall to pieces; (*auflösen*) dissolve. **zer fallen mit** fall out with.

zerfetzen [tsɛr'fɛtsən] *v* shred, tear up.

*****zerfressen** [tsɛr'frɛsən] *v* gnaw; (*Chem*) corrode.

*****zergehen** [tsɛr'geːən] *v* melt.

zergliedern [tsɛr'gliːdərn] *v* dismember; (*fig*) analyse.

zerhacken [tsɛr'hakən] *v* chop up, chop into pieces.

zerkleinern [tsɛr'klainərn] *v* cut up, chop up.

zerlegen [tsɛr'leːgən] *v* take apart, separate; (*Fleisch*) carve; (*fig*) analyse. **Zerlegung** *f* (*pl* -en) taking apart; carving; analysis.

zerlumpt [tsɛr'lumpt] *adj* ragged.

zermahlen [tsɛr'maːlən] *v* grind.

zermürben [tsɛr'myrbən] *v* wear down. **Zermürbung** *f* attrition. –**skrieg** *m* war of attrition.

zerplatzen [tsɛr'platsən] *v* explode, burst.

zerquetschen [tsɛr'kvɛtʃən] *v* squash, crush.

Zerrbild ['tsɛrbilt] *neut* distortion, caricature.

*****zerreißen** [tsɛr'raisən] *v* tear up/to pieces; (*entzweigehen*) rip, tear, break.

zerren ['tsɛrən] *v* tug, pull; (*Med*) strain, pull. **Zerrung** *f* (*pl* -en) (*Med*) strain.

zerschellen [tsɛr'ʃɛlən] *v* be dashed to pieces.

*****zerschlagen** [tsɛr'ʃlaːgən] *v* knock *or* smash to pieces.

zerschlissen [tsɛr'ʃlisən] *adj* tattered, shredded.

*****zerschneiden** [tsɛr'ʃnaidən] *v* cut up.

zersetzen [tsɛr'zɛtsən] *v* disintegrate; (*untergraben*) undermine, demoralize. **sich zersetzen** disintegrate; (*Chem*) decompose. **Zersetzung** *f* disintegration.

zersplittern [tsɛr'ʃplitərn] *v* splinter, shatter; (*fig*) split up. **Zersplitterung** *f* splintering; splitting-up.

zersprengen [tsɛr'ʃprɛŋən] *v* blow up, burst (open).

zerstäuben *v* pulverize; (*Flüssigkeit*) spray, atomize. **Zerstäuber** *m* spray atomizer.

zerstören [tser'ʃtœːrən] v destroy. –d adj destructive. Zerstör||er m destroyer. –ung f destruction.

zerstreuen [tser'ʃtrɔyən] v disperse, scatter; (unterhalten) amuse, entertain. zerstreut adj scattered; (geistig) distracted, absent-minded. Zerstreuung f dispersion; distraction; (Unterhaltung) amusement.

zerteilen [tser'tailən] v divide, separate; (zerstückeln) cut up.

*zertreten [tser'treːtən] v tread on, trample on.

zertrümmern [tser'trymərn] v smash, wreck; (vernichten) destroy.

zerzausen [tser'tsauzən] v rumple, tousle. zerzaust adj tousled, dishevelled.

zetern ['tseːtərn] v cry out, shout (for help).

Zettel ['tsetəl] m (pl -) slip (of paper); (Merkzettel) note; (Preis) ticket.

Zeug [tsɔyk] neut (pl -e) material, stuff; (Arbeitsgeräte) tools pl; (allerlei Dinge) stuff, things pl.

Zeuge ['tsɔygə] m (pl -n) witness.

zeugen[1] ['tsɔygən] v testify, give evidence. von etwas zeugen be evidence of something.

zeugen[2] v (Kind) procreate, beget; (fig) generate, produce.

Zeugen||bank f witness box. –beweis m evidence. Zeugin (pl -nen) f (female) witness. Zeugnis neut evidence, testimony; (Bescheinigung) certificate; (Schule) report.

Zeugung ['tsɔyguŋ] f (pl -en) generation, procreation.

Zickzack ['tsiktsak] m (pl -e) zigzag.

Ziege ['tsiːgə] f (pl -n) goat.

Ziegel ['tsiːgəl] m (pl -) (Backstein) brick; (Dachziegel) (roof-)tile. –stein m brick.

Ziegen||bock m billy goat. –leder neut kid (leather), goatskin. –milch f goat's milk.

*ziehen ['tsiːən] v pull, draw; (Zeichnen) draw; (strecken) stretch; (wandern) wander; (marschieren) march; (Tee) infuse; (Zigarre) draw or pull (on); (umziehen) move. es zieht (Luft) there is a draught. sich in die Länge ziehen drag on.

Ziel [tsiːl] neut (pl -e) aim, goal; (Geschoß) target; (Wettlauf) finish. ziel||en v aim (at). –los adj aimless. Zielscheibe f target.

ziemlich ['tsiːmliç] adj considerable. adv rather, moderately.

Zier [tsiːr] f (pl -en) decoration. zier||en v decorate. sich zieren be affected, behave with affectation. –lich adj dainty; (elegant) elegant.

Ziffer ['tsifər] f (pl -n) cipher, numeral. –blatt neut clock-face.

Zigarette [tsiga'retə] f (pl -n) cigarette. Zigaretten||etui neut cigarette case. –stummel m cigarette end. Zigarre f (pl -n) cigar.

Zigeuner [tsi'gɔynər] m (pl -), Zigeunerin f (pl -nen) Gipsy.

Zimmer ['tsimər] neut (pl -) room. –arbeit f carpentry. –mann m carpenter. –spiel neut (parlour) game.

zimperlich ['tsimpərliç] adj prim.

Zimt [tsimt] m (pl -e) cinnamon.

Zink [tsiŋk] neut zinc.

Zinke ['tsiŋkə] f (pl -n) prong; (Kamm) tooth.

Zinn [tsin] neut tin. zinnern adj tin. Zinnfolie f tinfoil.

Zins [tsins] m (pl -en) (Miete) rent; (Abgabe) tax, duty. Zinsen pl interest. Zinsfuß m rate of interest.

Zipfel ['tsipfəl] m (pl -) tip; (Ecke) corner.

Zirkel ['tsirkəl] m (pl -) (Kreis) circle; (Gerät) (pair of) compasses pl.

Zirkus ['tsirkus] m (pl -se) circus.

zirpen ['tsirpən] v chirp.

zischen ['tsiʃən] v kiss.

Zitat [tsi'taːt] neut (pl -e) quotation, quote. zitieren v quote, cite; (vorladen) summon.

Zitrone [tsi'troːnə] f (pl -n) lemon.

zittern ['tsitərn] v tremble, shake.

Zitze ['tsitsə] f (pl -n) nipple, teat.

zivil [tsi'viːl] adj civil. Zivilisation f (unz.) civilization. zivil||isieren v civilize. –isiert adj civilized, cultured. Zivil||ist m (pl -en) civilian. –kleidung f civilian clothes pl.

zögern ['tsœːgərn] v hesitate.

Zoll[1] [tsɔl] m (pl -e) (Längenmaß) inch.

Zoll[2] m (pl Zölle) (customs) duty; (umg.: Zollabfertigungsstelle) customs pl.

Zoll||abfertigung f customs clearance. –beamte(r) m customs official.

Zone ['tsoːnə] f (pl -n) zone.

Zoo [tsoː] m (pl -s) zoo. –loge m (pl -n) zoologist. –logie f zoology. zoologisch adj zoological.

Zopf [tsɔpf] m (pl Zöpfe) plait, pigtail.

Zorn [tsɔrn] m anger. **zornig** adj angry.

zu [tsuː] prep (Richtung) to, toward(s); (Ziel, Ort) at, in; (neben) beside. **zu** too; (geschlossen) closed, shut. **zu Hause** at home. **zu verkaufen** for sale. **zu Mittag** at noon. **zu Fuß** on foot. **ab und zu** now and then. **um zu** in order to.

Zubehör ['tsuːbəhœːr] neut (pl -e) fittings pl; (Tech) accessories pl. **–teil** neut attachment, accessory.

zubereiten ['tsuːbəraitən] v prepare.

*****zubringen** ['tsuːbriŋən] v bring or take (to); (Zeit) spend.

Zucht [tsuxt] f 1 (unz.) discipline; (Pflanzen) cultivation, breeding; (Vieh) rearing, breeding. **2** f (pl -en) breed.

züchten ['tsyçtən] v breed. **Züchter** m breeder; (Bienen) beekeeper; (Pflanzen) grower.

züchtigen ['tsyçtigən] v punish, discipline. **Züchtigung** f (pl -en) punishment.

zuchtlos ['tsuxtloːs] adj undisciplined.

Zuck [tsuk] m (pl -e) jerk. **zucken** v start, jerk.

Zucker ['tsukər] m sugar. **zuckerkrank** adj diabetic. **Zucker‖kranke(r)** m diabetic. **–krankheit** f diabetes. **–rohr** m sugarcane.

zudecken ['tsuːdekən] v cover (up).

zudem [tsuːdeːm] adv moreover, besides.

zudrehen ['tsuːdreːən] v turn off.

zudringlich ['tsuːdriŋliç] adj importunate, pushing.

zueinander [tsuain'andər] adv to each other.

zuerst [tsuʔeːrst] adv (at) first.

Zufahrt ['tsuːfaːrt] f approach, driving in. **–straße** f access road; (Haus) driveway.

Zufall ['tsuːfal] m chance, accident. **glücklicher Zufall** happy coincidence. **zufällig** adj accidental, chance; adv by chance, accidentally.

Zuflucht ['tsuːfluxt] f refuge, shelter.

Zufluß ['tsuːflus] m (pl Zuflüsse) influx; (Fluß) tributary; (Waren) supply.

zufolge [tsuːˈfɔlɡə] prep owing to, in consequence of.

zufrieden [tsuːˈfriːdən] adj contented. **Zufriedenheit** f content(ment). **zufriedenstellen** v satisfy.

zufügen ['tsuːfyːɡən] v add (to); (Böses) inflict (on).

Zufuhr ['tsuːfuːr] f (pl -en) supply. **zuführen** v supply; (zuleiten) lead to.

Zug [tsuːk] m (pl Züge) pull; (Eisenbahn) train; (Charakter) trait; (Gesicht) feature; (Luft) draught; (Schub) thrust; (Brettspiel) move; (Einatmen) inhalation; (Rauchen) puff, pull; (Festzug) procession; (Zeichnen) stroke, dash; (Umriß) outline; (Vögel) migration.

Zugabe ['tsuːɡaːbə] f addition; (Zuschlag) extra.

Zugang ['tsuːɡaŋ] m entry, access; (Eingang) entrance; accession. **zugänglich** adj accessible; (Mensch) approachable.

Zugbrücke ['tsuːkbrykə] f drawbridge.

*****zugeben** ['tsuːɡeːbən] v add; (einräumen) admit; (gestatten) permit.

zugegen [tsuːˈɡeːɡən] adj present.

*****zugehen** ['tsuːɡeːən] v close, be closed; (weitergehen) go on; (geschehen) happen. **zugehören** ['tsuːɡəhœːrən] v belong (to).

Zügel ['tsyːɡəl] m (pl -) rein(s); (fig) curb. **zügel‖los** adj unrestrained, unbridled. **–n** v rein; (beherrschen) control, curb.

Zugeständnis ['tsuːɡəʃtɛntnis] neut concession.

*****zugestehen** ['tsuːɡəʃteːən] v admit, concede.

Zugführer ['tsuːkfyːrər] m (Eisenbahn) guard, (US) conductor.

*****zugießen** ['tsuːɡiːsən] v pour (in).

zugig ['tsuːɡiç] adj draughty.

Zugluft ['tsuːkluft] f draught.

*****zugreifen** ['tsuːɡraifən] v grasp, grab; (helfen) lend a hand; (bei Tisch) help oneself.

zugrunde [tsuːˈɡrundə] adv **zugrunde gehen** v perish, be ruined.

zugunsten [tsuːˈɡunstən] prep in favour of.

zugute [tsuːˈɡuːtə] adv to one's advantage. **zugute halten** v take into consideration, allow for.

*****zuhalten** ['tsuːhaltən] v keep shut. **zuhalten auf** head for. **Zuhälter** m pimp.

zuhanden [tsuːˈhandən] adj (ready) at hand, ready.

Zuhause [tsuːˈhauzə] f (unz.) home.

zuhören ['tsuːhœːrən] v listen. **Zuhörer** m (pl -), **Zuhörerin** f (pl -nen) listener. **Zuhörer** pl audience sing; (Radio) listeners.

zuklappen ['tsuːklapən] v slam, clap shut.

zuknöpfen ['tsuːknœpfən] v button up.

*****zukommen** ['tsuːkɔmən] v (gebühren) befit. **zukommen lassen** send, supply. **zukommen auf** come up to.

zerstören [tsɛrˈʃtœːrən] v destroy. **-d** adj destructive. **Zerstör‖er** m destroyer. **-ung** f destruction.

zerstreuen [tsɛrˈʃtrɔyən] v disperse, scatter; (*unterhalten*) amuse, entertain. **zerstreut** adj scattered; (*geistig*) distracted, absent-minded. **Zerstreuung** f dispersion; distraction; (*Unterhaltung*) amusement.

zerteilen [tsɛrˈtailən] v divide, separate; (*zerstückeln*) cut up.

*zertreten [tsɛrˈtreːtən] v tread on, trample on.

zertrümmern [tsɛrˈtrymərn] v smash, wreck; (*vernichten*) destroy.

zerzausen [tsɛrˈtsauzən] v rumple, tousle. **zerzaust** adj tousled, dishevelled.

zetern [ˈtseːtərn] v cry out, shout (for help).

Zettel [ˈtsɛtəl] m (pl -) slip (of paper); (*Merkzettel*) note; (*Preis*) ticket.

Zeug [tsɔyk] neut (pl -e) material, stuff; (*Arbeitsgeräte*) tools pl; (*allerlei Dinge*) stuff, things pl.

Zeuge [ˈtsɔygə] m (pl -n) witness.

zeugen¹ [ˈtsɔygən] v testify, give evidence. **von etwas zeugen** be evidence of something.

zeugen² v (*Kind*) procreate, beget; (*fig*) generate, produce.

Zeugen‖bank f witness box. **-beweis** m evidence. **Zeugin** (pl -nen) f (female) witness. **Zeugnis** neut evidence, testimony; (*Bescheinigung*) certificate; (*Schule*) report.

Zeugung [ˈtsɔyguŋ] f (pl -en) generation, procreation.

Zickzack [ˈtsiktsak] m (pl -e) zigzag.

Ziege [ˈtsiːgə] f (pl -n) goat.

Ziegel [ˈtsiːgəl] m (pl -) (*Backstein*) brick; (*Dachziegel*) (roof-)tile. **-stein** m brick.

Ziegen‖bock m billy goat. **-leder** neut kid (leather), goatskin. **-milch** f goat's milk.

*ziehen [ˈtsiːən] v pull, draw; (*Zeichnen*) draw; (*strecken*) stretch; (*wandern*) wander; (*marschieren*) march; (*Tee*) infuse; (*Zigarre*) draw or pull (on); (*umziehen*) move. **es zieht** (*Luft*) there is a draught. **sich in die Länge ziehen** drag on.

Ziel [tsiːl] neut (pl -e) aim, goal; (*Geschoß*) target; (*Wettlauf*) finish. **-los** v aim (at). **-los** adj aimless. **Zielscheibe** f target.

ziemlich [ˈtsiːmlɪç] adj considerable. adv rather, moderately.

Zier [tsiːr] f (pl -en) decoration. **zier‖en** v decorate. **sich zieren** be affected, behave with affectation. **-lich** adj dainty; (*elegant*) elegant.

Ziffer [ˈtsɪfər] f (pl -n) cipher, numeral. **-blatt** neut clock-face.

Zigarette [tsigaˈrɛtə] f (pl -n) cigarette. **Zigaretten‖etui** neut cigarette case. **-stümmel** m cigarette end. **Zigarre** f (pl -n) cigar.

Zigeuner [tsiˈgɔynər] m (pl -), **Zigeunerin** f (pl -nen) Gipsy.

Zimmer [ˈtsɪmər] neut (pl -) room. **-arbeit** f carpentry. **-mann** m carpenter. **-spiel** neut (parlour) game.

zimperlich [ˈtsɪmpərlɪç] adj prim.

Zimt [tsɪmt] m (pl -e) cinnamon.

Zink [tsɪŋk] neut zinc.

Zinke [ˈtsɪŋkə] f (pl -n) prong; (*Kamm*) tooth.

Zinn [tsɪn] neut tin. **zinnern** adj tin.

Zinnfolie f tinfoil.

Zins [tsɪns] m (pl -en) (*Miete*) rent; (*Abgabe*) tax, duty. **Zinsen** pl interest. **Zinsfuß** m rate of interest.

Zipfel [ˈtsɪpfəl] m (pl -) tip; (*Ecke*) corner.

Zirkel [ˈtsɪrkəl] m (pl -) (*Kreis*) circle; (*Gerät*) (pair of) compasses pl.

Zirkus [ˈtsɪrkus] m (pl -se) circus.

zirpen [ˈtsɪrpən] v chirp.

zischen [ˈtsɪʃən] v kiss.

Zitat [tsiˈtaːt] neut (pl -e) quotation, quote. **zitieren** v quote, cite; (*vorladen*) summon.

Zitrone [tsiˈtroːnə] f (pl -n) lemon.

zittern [ˈtsɪtərn] v tremble, shake.

Zitze [ˈtsɪtsə] f (pl -n) nipple, teat.

zivil [tsiˈviːl] adj civil. **Zivilisation** f (unz.) civilization. **zivil‖isieren** v civilize. **-isiert** adj civilized, cultured. **Zivil‖ist** m (pl -en) civilian. **-kleidung** f civilian clothes pl.

zögern [ˈtsøːgərn] v hesitate.

Zoll¹ [tsɔl] m (pl -e) (*Längenmaß*) inch.

Zoll² m (pl **Zölle**) (customs) duty; (*umg.: Zollabfertigungsstelle*) customs pl. **Zoll‖abfertigung** f customs clearance. **-beamte(r)** m customs official.

Zone [ˈtsoːnə] f (pl -n) zone.

Zoo [tsoː] m (pl -s) zoo. **-loge** m (pl -n) zoologist. **-logie** f zoology. **zoologisch** adj zoological.

Zopf [tsɔpf] m (pl Zöpfe) plait, pigtail.
Zorn [tsɔrn] m anger. **zornig** adj angry.
zu [tsuː] prep (Richtung) to, toward(s); (Ziel, Ort) at, in; (neben) beside. adv too; (geschlossen) closed, shut. **zu Hause** at home. **zu verkaufen** for sale. **zu Mittag** at noon. **zu Fuß** on foot. **ab und zu** now and then. **um zu** in order to.
Zubehör ['tsuːbəhœːr] neut (pl -e) fittings pl; (Tech) accessories pl. **-teil** neut attachment, accessory.
zubereiten ['tsuːbəraitən] v prepare.
*****zubringen** ['tsuːbrɪŋən] v bring or take (to); (Zeit) spend.
Zucht [tsuxt] **1** f (unz.) discipline; (Pflanzen) cultivation, breeding; (Vieh) rearing, breeding. **2** f (pl -en) breed.
züchten ['tsʏçtən] v breed. **Züchter** m breeder; (Bienen) beekeeper; (Pflanzen) grower.
züchtigen ['tsʏçtɪgən] v punish, discipline. **Züchtigung** f (pl -en) punishment.
zuchtlos ['tsuxtloːs] adj undisciplined.
Zuck [tsuk] m (pl -e) jerk. **zucken** v start, jerk.
Zucker ['tsukər] m sugar. **zuckerkrank** adj diabetic. **Zucker‖kranke(r)** m diabetic. **-krankheit** f diabetes. **-rohr** m sugarcane.
zudem [tsuˈdeːm] adv moreover, besides.
zudecken ['tsuːdɛkən] v cover (up).
zudrehen ['tsuːdreːən] v turn off.
zudringlich ['tsuːdrɪŋlɪç] adj importunate, pushing.
zueinander [tsuainˈandər] adv to each other.
zuerst [tsuˈeːrst] adv (at) first.
Zufahrt ['tsuːfaːrt] f approach, driving in. **-straße** f access road; (Haus) driveway.
Zufall ['tsuːfal] m chance, accident. **glücklicher Zufall** happy coincidence. **zufällig** adj accidental, chance; adv by chance, accidentally.
Zuflucht ['tsuːfluxt] f refuge, shelter.
Zufluß ['tsuːfluːs] m influx; (Fluß) tributary; (Waren) supply.
zufolge [tsuˈfɔlgə] prep owing to, in consequence of.
zufrieden [tsuˈfriːdən] adj contented. **Zufriedenheit** f content(ment). **zufriedenstellen** v satisfy.
zufügen ['tsuːfyːgən] v add (to); (Böses) inflict (on).
Zufuhr ['tsuːfuːr] f (pl -en) supply.
zuführen v supply; (zuleiten) lead to.

Zug [tsuːk] m (pl Züge) pull; (Eisenbahn) train; (Charakter) trait; (Gesicht) feature; (Luft) draught; (Schub) thrust; (Brettspiel) move; (Einatmen) inhalation; (Rauchen) puff, pull; (Festzug) procession; (Zeichnen) stroke, dash; (Umriß) outline; (Vögel) migration.
Zugabe ['tsuːgaːbə] f addition; (Zuschlag) extra.
Zugang ['tsuːgaŋ] m entry, access; (Eingang) entrance; accession. **zugänglich** adj accessible; (Mensch) approachable.
Zugbrücke ['tsuːgbrʏkə] f drawbridge.
*****zugeben** ['tsuːgeːbən] v add; (einräumen) admit; (gestatten) permit.
zugegen [tsuˈgeːgən] adj present.
*****zugehen** ['tsuːgeːən] v close, be closed; (weitergehen) go on; (geschehen) happen.
zugehören ['tsuːgəhœːrən] v belong (to).
Zügel ['tsyːgəl] m (pl -) rein(s); (fig) curb. **zügel‖los** adj unrestrained, unbridled. **-n** v rein; (beherrschen) control, curb.
Zugeständnis ['tsuːgəʃtɛntnis] neut concession.
*****zugestehen** ['tsuːgəʃteːən] v admit, concede.
Zugführer ['tsuːkfyːrər] m (Eisenbahn) guard, (US) conductor.
*****zugießen** ['tsuːgiːsən] v pour (in).
zugig ['tsuːgɪç] adj draughty.
Zugluft ['tsuːgluft] f draught.
*****zugreifen** ['tsuːgraifən] v grasp, grab; (helfen) lend a hand; (bei Tisch) help oneself.
zugrunde [tsuˈgrundə] adv **zugrunde gehen** v perish, be ruined.
zugunsten [tsuˈgunstən] prep in favour of.
zugute [tsuˈguːtə] adv to one's advantage. **zugute halten** v take into consideration, allow for.
*****zuhalten** ['tsuːhaltən] v keep shut. **zuhalten auf** head for. **Zuhälter** m pimp.
zuhanden [tsuˈhandən] adj (ready) at hand, ready.
Zuhause [tsuˈhauzə] f (unz.) home.
zuhören ['tsuːhœːrən] v listen. **Zuhörer** m (pl -), **Zuhörerin** f (pl -nen) listener. **Zuhörer** pl audience sing; (Radio) listeners.
zuklappen ['tsuːklapən] v slam, clap shut.
zuknöpfen ['tsuːknœpfən] v button up.
*****zukommen** ['tsuːkɔmən] v (gebühren) befit. **zukommen lassen** send, supply. **zukommen auf** come up to.

Zukunft ['tsuːkunft] *f* future. **zukünftig** *adj* future; *adv* in (the) future.

Zulage ['tsuːlaːɡə] *f* extra pay, bonus.

zulänglich ['tsuːlɛŋlɪç] *adj* sufficient.

*****zulassen** ['tsuːlasən] *v* permit. admit; (*hereinlassen*) let in, admit. **zulässig** *adj* permissible. **Zulassung** *f* permission; admission; (*Mot*) registration. **–schein** *m* permit, licence.

zuleiten ['tsuːlaɪtən] *v* lead to.

zuletzt [tsuˈlɛtst] *adv* finally, last.

zuliebe [tsuˈliːbə] *adv* jemandem zuliebe to please someone.

Zulieferer ['tsuːliːfərər] *m* (*pl* -) subcontractor.

zum [tsum] *prep + art* zu dem.

zumachen ['tsuːmaxən] *v* shut, close.

zumeist [tsuˈmaɪst] *adv* mostly.

zumindest [tsuˈmɪndəst] *adv* at least.

zumute [tsuˈmuːtə] *adv* gut/schlecht zumute sein to be in high/low spirits.

zumuten ['tsuːmuːtən] *v* expect, demand. **Zumutung** *f* presumption, unreasonable expectation.

zunächst [tsuˈnɛːçst] *adv* first (of all). *prep* near, close to.

Zunahme ['tsuːnaːmə] *f* (*pl* -n) increase.

Zuname ['tsuːnaːmə] *m* surname.

zünden ['tsyndən] *v* catch fire, light; (*Mot, Tech*) ignite.

Zunder ['tsundər] *m* (*pl* -) tinder.

Zünder ['tsyndər] *m* (*pl* -) fuse, detonator. **Zünd‖kerze** *f* sparking plug. **–schlüssel** *m* ignition key. **–ung** *f* ignition; (*Sprengladung*) detonation.

*****zunehmen** ['tsuːneːmən] *v* increase; (*wachsen*) grow; (*dicker werden*) put on weight. **–d** *adj* increasing, accelerating.

zuneigen ['tsuːnaɪɡən] *v* incline, lean; (*fig*) incline, tend. **Zuneigung** *f* inclination; (*Sympathie*) affection.

Zunft [tsunft] *f* (*pl* Zünfte) guild.

Zunge ['tsuŋə] *f* (*pl* -n) tongue. **zungenfertig** *adj* glib, fluent.

zunichte [tsuˈnɪçtə] *adv* zunichte machen (*Hoffnungen*) destroy, shatter; (*Pläne*) frustrate.

zunicken ['tsuːnɪkən] *v* nod to.

zunutze [tsuˈnutsə] *adv* sich etwas zunutze machen utilize something, put something to use.

zuoberst [tsuˈoːbərst] *adv* at the top.

zupfen ['tsupfən] *v* pluck; (*Fasern*) pick.

zur [tsuːr] *prep + art* zu der.

zurechnen ['tsuːrɛçnən] *v* (*zuschreiben*) ascribe, attribute. **Zurechnung** *f* attribution.

zurecht [tsuˈrɛçt] *adv* right, correctly, in order. **sich zurechtfinden** *v* find one's way. **zurechtkommen** *v* arrive in time. **zurechtkommen mit** get along with. **zurecht‖machen** *v* prepare. **–weisen** *v* reprimand.

zureden ['tsuːreːdən] *v* urge, coax.

zureichen ['tsuːraɪçən] *v* (*ausreichen*) do, be enough; (*hinreichen*) hand, pass. **–d** *adj* sufficient.

zurichten ['tsuːrɪçtən] *v* prepare, get ready; (*umg.*) mess up, make a mess of.

zürnen ['tsyrnən] *v* be angry.

zurück [tsuˈryk] *adv* back(wards); (*hinten*) behind. **–behalten** *v* keep back, detain. **–bekommen** *v* get back, recover. **–bezahlen** *v* refund, pay back. **–bleiben** *v* remain behind. **–blicken** *v* look back. **–bringen** *v* bring back. **–datieren** *v* backdate; (*stammen aus*) date back. **–erstatten** *v* return, restore; (*ausgelegtes Geld*) reimburse. **–fahren** *v* drive back; (*vor Schreck*) recoil, start.

Zurückgabe [tsuˈrykɡaːbə] *f* restitution, restoration. **zurückgeben** *v* give back, restore.

zurück‖gehen *v* go back, return; (*nachlassen*) decrease, fall off. **zurückgehen auf** originate in, go back to. **–gezogen** *adj* retiring, withdrawn.

zurückhalten [tsuˈrykhaltən] *v* (*Person*) keep, detain; (*Sache*) retain, withhold. **–d** *adj* reserved; (*vorsichtig*) cautious. **Zurückhaltung** *f* reserve.

zurück‖kehren *v* return. **–kommen** *v* come back; (*wieder aufgreifen*) revert (to). **–legen** *v* put aside; (*Geld*) put by. **–melden** *v* report back.

Zurücknahme [tsuˈryknaːmə] *f* (*pl* -n) withdrawal, taking back. **zurücknehmen** *v* take back; (*Worte*) withdraw; (*Anordnung, Auftrag*) cancel.

zurück‖scheuen *v* shrink back (from), shy (at). **–schicken** *v* send back. **–setzen** *v* put *or* place back; (*herabsetzen*) reduce; (*Person*) neglect, slight. **–strahlen** *v* reflect. **–reten** *v* step back; (*vom Posten*) resign, retire. **–weisen** *v* refuse, reject. **–zahlen** *v* pay back, repay. **–ziehen** *v* draw back, withdraw. **sich zurückziehen** withdraw, retire.

Zuruf ['tsuːruf] *m* shout. **zurufen** *v* shout, call.

Zusage ['tsuːzaːgə] *f* promise; (*Bejahung*) assent, consent. **zusagen** *v* (*versprechen*) promise; (*Einladung*) accept, agree to come; (*gefallen*) suit, please.

zusammen [tsuˈzamən] *adv* together; (*insgesamt*) all told, all together.

Zusammenarbeit *f* cooperation. **zusammenarbeiten** *v* cooperate.

zusammenballen *v* roll up; (*Faust*) clench. **sich zusammenballen** gather.

*zusammenbrechen *v* collapse, break down. **Zusammenbruch** *m* collapse.

zusammendrängen *v* **sich zusammendrängen** crowd together.

*zusammen‖fahren *v* travel together; (*aufeinanderstoßen*) collide; (*zusammenschrecken*) wince, start. **–fallen** *v* fall down, collapse; coincide.

zusammenfassen *v* summarize. **–d** *adj* comprehensive. **Zusammenfassung** *f* summary.

zusammengesetzt *adj* composed, compounded.

Zusammenhang *m* (*Verbindung*) connection; (*Text*) context. **zusammenhängen** *v* (*verbunden sein*) be connected. **–d** *adj* coherent.

zusammenklappen *v* fold up.

Zusammenkunft *f* (*pl* **Zusammenkünfte**) meeting.

zusammen‖legen *v* put together; (*falten*) fold (up); (*vereinigen*) combine; (*Geld*) pool. **–passen** *v* go (well) together, match; (*Menschen*) get on well.

Zusammenprall *m* collision. **zusammenprallen** *v* collide.

*zusammenschließen *v* join together. **sich zusammenschließen** unite. **Zusammenschluß** *m* union, merger.

zusammensetzen *v* put together, construct. **sich zusammensetzen** sit down with one another; (*bestehen*) consist (of). **Zusammensetz‖spiel** *neut* jigsaw puzzle. **–ung** *f* composition.

zusammenstellen *v* (*vereinigen*) join; (*vergleichen*) compare.

Zusammenstoß *m* collision; (*Streit*) clash, conflict. **zusammenstoßen** *v* collide; clash, conflict.

Zusammentreffen *neut* coincidence; (*Begegnung*) encounter, meeting.

*zusammenziehen *v* close, draw together; (*verkürzen*) shorten, contract;

(*verbinden*) join together; (*sammeln*) gather. **sich zusammenziehen** (*Stoff*) shrink. **Zusammenziehung** *f* shrinking; contraction.

Zusatz ['tsuːzats] *m* addition; (*Ergänzung*) supplement; (*Anhang*) appendix. **zusätzlich** *adj* additional, extra.

zuschauen ['tsuːʃauən] *v* watch, look on, observe. **Zuschauer** *m* (*pl* -), **Zuschauerin** *f* (*pl* -nen) spectator, onlooker.

Zuschlag ['tsuːʃlaːk] *m* surcharge, extra charge. **zuschlagen** *v* hit (out); (*Tür*) slam (shut).

*zuschließen ['tsuːʃliːsən] *v* lock (up).

*zuschneiden ['tsuːʃnaidən] *v* cut out. **Zuschnitt** *m* cut, style.

*zuschreiben ['tsuːʃraibən] *v* attribute, ascribe; (*übertragen*) transfer to. *das hast du dir selbst zuzuschreiben* you have yourself to blame for that.

Zuschuß ['tsuːʃus] *m* subsidy, allowance.

*zusehen ['tsuːzeːən] *v* look on, watch. **zusehen, daß** see to it that.

zusenden ['tsuːzendən] *v* send on, forward.

zusetzen ['tsuːzetsən] *v* (*hinzufügen*) add; (*verlieren*) lose; (*bedrängen*) press, importune.

Zuspruch ['tsuːʃprux] *m* encouragement, approval.

Zustand ['tsuːʃtant] *m* condition, state.

zustande [tsuˈʃtandə] *adv* **zustande bringen** achieve, bring about. **zustande kommen** come about, materialize.

zuständig ['tsuːʃtendiç] *adj* appropriate; competent; responsible.

zustellen ['tsuːʃtelən] *v* deliver; (*Klage*) serve on. **Zustellung** *f* (*pl* -en) delivery.

zustimmen ['tsuːʃtimən] *v* consent, agree. **Zustimmung** *f* consent, agreement.

zustopfen ['tsuːʃtɔpfən] *v* plug (up), stop (up); (*flicken*) darn.

*zustoßen ['tsuːʃtoːsən] *v* (*Tür*) push to; (*geschehen*) happen (to), befall.

zutage [tsuˈtaːgə] *adv* **zutage bringen** bring to light.

Zutaten ['tsuːtaːtən] *f pl* ingredients; (*Beiwerk*) trimmings.

zuteilen ['tsuːtailən] *v* assign, allocate, issue. **Zuteilung** *f* allocation.

zutiefst [tsuːtiːfst] *adv* deeply.

*zutragen ['tsuːtraːgən] *v* carry to. **sich zutragen** happen, take place. **zuträglich** *adj* beneficial.

zutrauen ['tsuːtrauən] v credit (with), believe (of). **Zutrauen** neut confidence, trust, faith.

*****zutreffen** ['tsuːtrɛfən] v be right, be or hold true. −d adj right, accurate.

Zutritt ['tsuːtrit] m access. **Zutritt verboten!** keep out! no admission!

*****zutun** ['tsuːtuːn] v (hinzutun) add; (schließen) shut.

zuverlässig ['tsuːfɛrlɛsiç] adj reliable. **Zuverlässigkeit** f reliability.

Zuversicht ['tsuːfɛrziçt] f confidence, trust. **zuversichtlich** adj confident.

zuviel [tsuˈfiːl] adv too much.

zuvor [tsuˈfoːr] adv before, previously. −**kommen** v anticipate.

Zuwachs ['tsuːvaks] m growth; (Vermehrung) increase.

zuwege [tsuˈveːgə] adv **zuwege bringen** bring about, cause.

zuweilen [tsuˈvailən] adv sometimes, at times.

*****zuweisen** ['tsuːvaizən] v assign, allot.

*****zuwenden** ['tsuːvɛndən] v turn (towards); (geben) present, let have. **sich zuwenden** apply oneself (to).

zuwider [tsuˈviːdər] prep (entgegen) contrary to. adj (widerwärtig) repugnant.

zuwinken ['tsuːviŋkən] v wave (to).

*****zuziehen** ['tsuːtsiːən] v draw together; (Vorhänge) draw; (Wohnung) move in. **sich zuziehen** incur; (Med) contract, catch.

Zwang [tsvaŋ] m (pl Zwänge) compulsion; (Gewalt) force; (Hemmung) restraint.

zwängen ['tsvɛŋən] v force, press.

zwanglos ['tsvaŋloːs] adj unconstrained; (ohne Förmlichkeit) informal. **Zwangs‖arbeit** f hard labour. −**kauf** m compulsory purchase. **zwangsläufig** adj inevitable.

zwanzig ['tsvantsiç] pron, adj twenty. **zwanzigst** adj twentieth.

zwar [tsvaːr] adv indeed, certainly. **und zwar** namely, in fact.

Zweck [tsvɛk] m (pl -e) purpose, object; (Ziel) goal. **es hat keinen Zweck** it's pointless, it is of no use.

Zwecke ['tsvɛkə] f (pl -n) tack; (Reißnagel) drawing pin, (US) thumbtack.

zweck‖los adj pointless. −**mäßig** adj expedient, appropriate. −**s** prep for the purpose of.

zwei [tsvai] pron, adj two. **zwei‖deutig** adj ambiguous. −**erlei** adj of two kinds or sorts.

Zweifel ['tsvaifəl] m (pl -) doubt. **zweifel‖haft** adj doubtful. −**los** adj doubtless. −**n** v doubt.

Zweig [tsvaik] m (pl -e) branch, twig; (fig) branch. −**stelle** f branch (office).

zwei‖jährig adj two-year-old; (Bot) biennial. −**jährlich** adj biennial. −**mal** adv twice. −**seitig** adj two-sided; (fig) bilateral. −**sprachig** adj bilingual.

zweit [tsvait] adj second. −**ens** adv secondly. −**klassig** adj second-rate.

zweiwöchentlich ['tsvaivœçəntliç] adj fortnightly.

Zwerchfell ['tsvɛrçfɛl] neut diaphragm.

Zwerg [tsvɛrk] m (pl -e) dwarf. **zwergenhaft** adj dwarf.

Zwetsche ['tsvɛtʃə] or **Zwetschge** f (pl -n) plum.

Zwick [tsvik] m (pl -e) pinch. **zwicken** v pinch; (Fahrschein) punch, clip.

Zwieback ['tsviːbak] m (pl -e) rusk, biscuit.

Zwiebel ['tsviːbəl] f (pl -n) onion; (Blumen) bulb.

Zwiegespräch ['tsviːgəʃprɛç] neut dialogue.

Zwielicht ['tsviːliçt] neut twilight.

Zwiespalt ['tsviːʃpalt] m (inner) conflict; (Uneinigkeit) dissension, discord.

Zwietracht ['tsviːtraxt] f conflict, dissension.

Zwilling ['tsviliŋ] m (pl -e) twin. **Zwillinge** pl (Astrol) Gemini. **Zwillings‖bruder** m twin brother. −**schwester** f twin sister.

Zwinge ['tsviŋə] f (pl -n) vice.

*****zwingen** ['tsviŋən] force, compel; (leisten können) manage, cope with.

zwischen ['tsviʃən] prep between; (mitten unter) among. **Zwischen‖bemerkung** f remark, aside. −**händler** m middleman. −**raum** m (intervening) space, interval. −**satz** m insertion. −**stunde** f free period, break, interval. −**zeit** f interim, interval. **in der Zwischenzeit** (in the) meantime.

zwitschern ['tsvitʃərn] v chirp, twitter.

zwo [tsvoː] V **zwei.**

zwölf [tsvœlf] pron, adj twelve. **zwölft** adj twelfth.

zyklisch ['tsyːkliʃ] adj cyclic.

Zyklone [tsyˈkloːnə] f (pl -n) low-pressure area, depression.

Zyklus ['tsɪklus] *m* (*pl* **Zyklen**) cycle.

Zylinder [tsi'lindər] *m* (*pl* -) cylinder; (*Hut*) top hat. **–kopf** *m* cylinder head.

Zyniker ['tsyːnikər] *m* (*pl* -) cynic. **zynisch** *adj* cynical.

Zypern ['tsyːpərn] *neut* Cyprus. **Zyprer** *m* (*pl* -), **Zyprerin** *f* (*pl* **-nen**) Cypriot. **zyprisch** *adj* Cypriot.